D1789609

תלמוד בבלי

עם פירוש רש״י ותוספות

ובצירוף תרגום ופירוש והערות באנגלית

מסכת

פאה

על ידי

ישעיה מאיר לערמן ז״ל

מסכת

דמאי

על ידי

משה צבי סגל ז״ל

מסכת

כלאים

על ידי

יעקב איזריעלסטאם ז״ל

בעריכת

יחזקאל (איזידור) אפשטין ז״ל

דפוס שונצין

שנת להחזיר העטרה ליושנה לפ״ק

לונדון

HEBREW-ENGLISH EDITION OF
THE BABYLONIAN TALMUD

PE'AH

TRANSLATED INTO ENGLISH
WITH NOTES, GLOSSARY AND INDICES BY
RABBI DR. S.M. LEHRMAN, M.A., PH.D.

DEMAI

TRANSLATED INTO ENGLISH
WITH NOTES, GLOSSARY AND INDICES BY
RABBI M.H. SEGAL, M.A.

KIL'AYIM

TRANSLATED INTO ENGLISH
WITH NOTES, GLOSSARY AND INDICES BY
REV. J. ISRAELSTAM, B.A.

UNDER THE EDITORSHIP OF
RABBI DR. I. EPSTEIN, B.A., PH.D. LITT.D.

LONDON
THE SONCINO PRESS
1989

COPYRIGHT © THE SONCINO LTD. 1989
ALL RIGHTS RESERVED INCLUDING THE RIGHT TO
REPRODUCE THIS BOOK OR PARTS THEREOF IN ANY FORM

1-871055059

PUBLISHERS' NOTE

This HEBREW-ENGLISH EDITION of THE SONCINO TALMUD is being published to facilitate the easier reference to the original text by scholars and students.

The Publishers wish to express their sincere thanks to Rabbi Dr. A. Melinek, B.A., Ph.D., for his painstaking care in examining the texts and making the necessary corrections for the preparation of these Tractates.

It has been necessary to duplicate some of the original Hebrew-Aramaic pages in this Tractate where the text has been of such length as to require more than one page of English translation.

נדפס בדפוס האחים גרויס
Printed in U.S.A. GROSS BROS. Printing Co. Inc.
3125 SUMMIT AVENUE, UNION CITY, NJ 07087
Tel. (201) 865-4606 • (212) 594-7757

INTRODUCTION

PE'AH

The texts of the eight chapters that comprise this Tractate, Pe'ah ('corner' *sc.* of the field), are to be found in Lev. XIX, 9–10, XXIII, 22 and Deut. XIV, 28–29 which, with characteristic brevity, command that a portion of the harvest is to be given to the poor. It was, accordingly, only natural that when Israel planned its national life on the constitution of the Torah, the exigencies of experience demanded a further and more comprehensive elucidation of these humane laws.

In common with the other volumes that comprise Zera'im, with the sole exception of Berakoth, Pe'ah, the second in the Order, is unaccompanied in the Babylonian Talmud by a Gemara. In the Palestinian Talmud it is furnished with a Gemara which further elucidates several Mishnaic passages and contains many an *Haggadic* homily (v. *J. E.* IX, s. v. *Pe'ah*). Yet even in our small treatise, other laws are discussed besides those indicated by the name *Pe'ah*, the opening key word of the first Mishnah. It is of passing interest to note that the Tanna of our Mishnah somewhat reverses the strict Biblical order of *Pe'ah*, *Leket* ('Gleanings') and *Shikhah* ('Forgotten Sheaf') and always quotes *Leket*, *Shikhah* and *Pe'ah*, an order describing perhaps more the process of reaping.

The contents of the Tractate are soon told. The first four chapters deal almost exclusively with the laws of the 'Corner of the field', and because these constitute the bulk of the book, *Pe'ah* has been chosen as the title to the whole treatise.

Chapter I enumerates in the first Mishnah the good deeds for which man is rewarded in this life, though this recompense is but an earnest of the real reward in the world to come. Making peace among men is one of such good deeds. This Mishnah has been made famous by its recension in the daily liturgy. A discussion then ensues as to the kind of produce, the amounts and the prescribed period within which this duty had to be discharged. The following chapters discuss the types of field and orchard that are exempt from this law (II), the size of the holding and the case of a field partially harvested (III). An important rule is that all *hefker* ('ownerless property') is exempt from all dues.

Chapters IV–V discuss whether *Pe'ah* may be retained for certain individuals and the case of a harvest 'dedicated' to the Sanctuary and redeemed later. Interesting is the note regarding grain found in ant-hills. The case is also cited of one away from home. The next two Chapters VI–VII describe all the laws appertaining to *Leket* and to the 'Forgotten Sheaf'.

The last Chapter deals with the supervisors of the poor, who are instructed as to the amount to be given to the applicants after due investigation as to their *bona fides*. The Tractate concludes on an *Haggadic* note, warning that he who feigns poverty or affliction in order to receive aid, will in time actually suffer from such afflictions; but giving also assurance that he who tries to subsist without aid, though he needs assistance, will in time become so prosperous that he will assist others.

Thus the two most salient characteristics of the Jewish people receive prominence in this work. The inherent Jewish love for the soil of Eretz Israel, and the reminder of the command of supporting our poor. For the Jewish God is best hallowed through charity and righteousness.

S. M. LEHRMAN

INTRODUCTION

DEMAI

NAME

a *Demai* (דמאי[1] דמי[2]) is the name given to produce about which there is a suspicion that it has not been tithed. It is opposed on the one hand to ודאי (ודי[2], 'certainty', *infra* III, 3; IV, 4; V, 11), produce which is known to be certainly untithed; and on the other hand to מתקן (מתוקן, 'set right', III, 1; VII, 7), produce which is known to have been properly tithed. The exact meaning, the derivation, and even the correct pronunciation of the term דמאי are alike doubtful. Already the Palestinian *Amoraim* of the second generation after the redaction of the Mishnah felt the need of explaining the term, which is a testimony to its great antiquity. The explanation they give is, unfortunately, itself obscure. They seem to have derived the term from an Aramaic interrogative particle meaning 'whether?' i.e., 'Is this tithed or not?'[3] Other old popular explanations, cited by the author of the Talmudic lexicon, the '*Aruch*[4] (11th century C.E.) are also based on an Aramaic derivation, such as דין מאי, דא מאי 'what is this?'; דמאי 'of a hundredth', an allusion to the *Terumah* of Tithes contained in *demai* produce (cf. below). Mussafia, the annotator of the '*Aruch* (17th century) derived it from the Greek δῆμος, people, viz., produce of the '*am ha-arez*, the people of the land (cf. below), a derivation which was much in favour with Jewish scholars of the last century. But the term is undoubtedly of pure Hebrew origin. Judging by its grammatical form, it seems to be derived from the Hebrew root דמה, to be like, resemble; and in the intensive stem, to imagine, fancy, though it is hard to see the semantic connection of the term with this verb.

It is traditionally pronounced דְּמַאי, *demai*, as a noun formed from the simple stem דָּמָה.[5] But some scholars pronounce it דַּמַּאי,[6] *dammai* (cf. וַדַּאי), as if formed from the intensive stem דִּמָּה. In this work I have followed the traditional pronunciation which is supported by the old popular explanations, cited above, identifying the first letter with the Aramaic relative pronoun ד

TERUMAH AND TITHES

The Tractate deals with the various problems which arise for the scrupulous Jew from the laxity of other Jews in respect of tithing their produce. To make these problems clearer to the reader, it may be desirable to summarize here some of the laws which, according to Biblical law as interpreted by the Rabbis, regulate the treatment of produce before it can be used for food.

(1) As soon as the produce is gathered, *terumah* (תרומה, heave-offering, also called תרומה גדולה) has to be given to the priest (Num. XVIII, 8, 11–12; Tractate Terumoth). The exact quantity of *terumah* is not fixed in the Bible, but in practice it varied from $^1/_{60}$ to $^1/_{40}$ (or $^1/_{30}$) of the produce, according to the generosity of the owner. The average quantity was $^1/_{50}$ (Ter. IV, 3). Produce from which *terumah* has not been taken is known as *tebel* (טבל *infra* V, 8, n. 3; VII, 5). The consumption of *terumah*, and thus also of *tebel*, by a non-priest is an act of sacrilege (Lev. XXII, 10, 14–16).

a (1) The Babylonian spelling. (2) The Palestinian spelling. (3) V. J. Ma'as. Sh. end; Soṭ. IX, 11, end. (4) Cf. Kohut, *Aruch Completum*, III, p. 22, 80.

(5) Cf. M. H. Segal, *A Grammar of Mishnaic Hebrew* (Oxford 1927), § 223. (6) I have so pointed it, op. cit. p. 107 bottom.

(2) After *terumah*, one tenth of the residue of the produce is to be given to the Levite (Tithe, מעשר; or First Tithe, מעשר ראשון; Num. XVIII, 21–24; Tractate Ma'aseroth). Of this tithe the Levite has to give to the priest one tenth as *Terumah* of the Tithe (תרומת מעשר, also known as תרומה קטנה; Num. XVIII, 25–28) The consumption of *Terumah* of the Tithe by a non-priest is also an act of sacrilege.

(3) From the residue of the produce after *terumah* and the First Tithe have been taken, one tenth has to be set aside in the first, second, fourth and fifth years of the Sabbatical cycle as a Second Tithe, which itself or its equivalent in money must be taken up to Jerusalem and consumed there. In the third and sixth year of the Sabbatical cycle the tithe thus set aside is designated מעשר עני (Poorman's Tithe) and is given to the poor; Deut. XIV, 22–29; XXVI, 12–15; Ma'as. Sh.

All Jews were known to be scrupulous in the separation from their produce of *terumah*, because the sanctity of this tax was so great and its quantity comparatively small. But some Jews, especially the uninstructed rustics (the *'am ha-areẓ*,), were suspected of neglecting to give tithes. The produce of an *'am ha-areẓ* and, generally, of a person not definitely known as scrupulous ('trustworthy', נאמן II, 2; III, 1, 5, 6) was suspected of not having been tithed, *demai*. The buyer of such produce had to tithe it for the First (Levitical) Tithe and for the Second Tithe, or, in the third and sixth year, for the Poorman's Tithe. But actually he had to separate from the produce only *Terumah* of the Tithe, because its consumption was a heinous sin. First Tithe and Poorman's Tithe, which were permitted to be eaten by any one and anywhere, he needed only to 'designate', i.e., to declare that these tithes were to be found in such and such a part of the produce (cf. *infra* IV, 3, n. 7), but he was not bound to give these tithes to the Levite and the poor respectively, unless they could bring evidence to prove that the *demai* produce had certainly not been tithed by its previous owner (cf. IV, 3, n. 7). As for Second Tithe, it could be eaten anywhere by exchanging it for money, and reserving the money for being spent at some future date in Jerusalem (cf. II, 2; V, 1ff; Deut. XIV, 25).

CONTENTS

Chapter I. The Tractate opens with a list of products which are exempt from the rules of *demai* (1, 3, 4, end), giving incidentally a list of rules wherein *demai* produce is like, or is unlike, ordinary produce (2, 4).

Chapter II. List of products liable to the rules of *demai* outside the Land of Israel (1); duties of the 'trustworthy' and of the 'associate' (2, 3); merchants and the duty of tithing *demai* (4, 5).

Chapter III. Rules applying to giving *demai* produce, or leaving it, as food for other persons.

Chapter IV. Rules applying to eating *demai* produce with persons who are not trustworthy, or buying it from them.

Chapter V. Rules about tithing *demai* produce bought from various persons, and about tithing produce of one kind for produce of another kind.

Chapter VI. Rules of tithing produce of land or trees rented or leased (1, 6); of tithing the produce of partners and heirs (7, 10); of produce sold in Syria (11); of produce bought for an *'am ha-areẓ* (12).

Chapter VII. Tithing of food consumed with an *'am ha-areẓ* (1, 2); rules of tithing by 'designation' (4–6, 8); of mixtures (7).

DATE AND HISTORICAL VALUE

The institution of *demai* is traditionally ascribed to the Hasmonean High Priest, Joḥanan Hyrcanus (135–104 B.C.E.; cf. Ma'as. Sh. V, 15; Soṭ. IX, 10; Soṭ. 78*a*). But the contents of our Tractate reflect chiefly conditions which prevailed in Judea and in Galilee during the second century C.E.; in particular the conditions of Galilee after the War of Bar Cochba in the latter half of the second century. To this age belong also most of the Tannaim whose opinions are recorded in our Tractate. Cf. A. Büchler, *Der galilaeische 'Am-ha-'Areṣ*, p. 5ff.

The Tractate contains valuable data concerning the social life and institutions of the time. It affords interesting glimpses of the social and commercial relations between the various classes of the population, the 'associate', the *'am ha-areẓ*, the Samaritan, the Gentile usurper, the employer and his workmen, the innkeeper and her guests, and the like.

M. H. SEGAL

INTRODUCTION

KIL'AYIM

The Tractate Kil'ayim ('Diverse Kinds') deals with the Scriptural precepts prohibiting the mingling of heterogeneous 'seeds', the crossing and yoking together of diverse animals, and against covering oneself with material composite of wool and linen (Lev. XIX, 19; Deut. XXII, 9–11).

'Seeds' is deemed as including five species of grain (viz., wheat, barley, oats, rye and spelt), legumes, and greens whose roots or stalks are used for human consumption. The term *'field'* in Lev. XIX, 19 is held to imply a prohibition against grafting as between heterogeneous fruit-trees. Since *'vineyard'* is particularly specified, in the Deuteronomy passage, it is subject to special rules in respect of *kil'ayim*. The law with regard to animals affects beasts, both wild and tame, birds and fishes. The two latter are not mentioned in our Tractate but in the Mishnah Baba Ḳamma V, 7.[1]

Chapter I enumerates pairs of 'seeds', fruit-trees and animals which are not regarded as mutually heterogeneous, and such as, despite appearances to the contrary; are nevertheless heterogeneous; and deals with grafting as between greens and trees or vines.

Chapter II discusses the remedy in the event of an area already sown in prohibited fashion; the procedure in the event of one's desiring to substitute one crop for another heterogeneous therewith, and in the event of one's desiring to sow heterogeneous species in one field, viz., by sowing them apart.

Chapter III defines such intervening spaces, and discusses various ways of planning a field thus to be sown.

Chapter IV determines the intervening spaces as between a vineyard and 'seeds'.

Chapter V answers the questions: what constitutes a vineyard, and what condemns a vineyard as *kil'ayim?*

Chapter VI. More about vineyards. The law when vine-shoots trail over a hedge or a tree.

Chapter VII. 'Seeds' sown over or close to vine-shoots conducted underground (and emerging above ground some distance away). The responsibility of a person the proximity of whose vines compromises another person's 'seeds'.

Chapter VIII defines what actions are prohibited with regard

a (1) V. B.Ḳ. 54*b* and 55*a*.

to species of flora and fauna which are *kil'ayim*.

CHAPTER IX deals with *kil'ayim* of fibrous materials *(sha'aṭnez)*.

The nature of the anonymous material in this Tractate, as well as the names of the Tannaim cited—none later than of the fourth generation (Frankel's classification)—show the Tractate to be one of early compilation.

The Tractate is valuable as a source of information on agriculture, horticulture, and especially viticulture in ancient Palestine.

J. ISRAELSTAM

PREFATORY NOTE BY THE EDITOR

The Editor desires to state that the translation of the several Tractates, and the notes thereon, are the work of the individual contributors and that he has not attempted to secure general uniformity in style or mode of rendering. He has, nevertheless, revised and supplemented, at his own discretion, their interpretation and elucidation of the original text, and has himself added the footnotes in square brackets containing alternative explanations and matter of historical and geographical interest.

ISIDORE EPSTEIN

תלמוד בבלי

מסכת

פאה

תלמוד בבלי

מסכת

דמאי

תלמוד בבלי

מסכת

כלאים

CHAPTER I

MISHNAH 1. THE FOLLOWING ARE THE THINGS FOR
a WHICH NO DEFINITE QUANTITY IS PRESCRIBED:[1] THE CORNERS [OF THE FIELD],[2] FIRST-FRUITS,[3] [THE OFFERINGS BROUGHT] ON APPEARING [BEFORE THE LORD AT THE THREE PILGRIM FESTIVALS],[4] THE PRACTICE OF LOVINGKINDNESS,[5] AND THE STUDY OF THE TORAH.[6] THE FOLLOWING ARE THE THINGS FOR WHICH A MAN ENJOYS THE FRUITS IN THIS WORLD WHILE THE PRINCIPAL REMAINS FOR HIM IN THE WORLD TO COME: THE HONOURING OF FATHER AND MOTHER,[7] THE PRACTICE OF CHARITY, AND THE MAKING OF PEACE BETWEEN A MAN AND HIS FRIEND; BUT THE STUDY OF THE TORAH IS EQUAL TO THEM ALL.[8]

a (1) In the Torah; but v. the next Mishnah where Rabbinic tradition fixes the minimum at one-sixtieth. (2) Lev. XIX, 9 and XXIII, 22 enjoin the owner to leave unreaped the former for the poor and the stranger to gather. (3) *Bikkurim*; v. Ex. XXIII, 19; Deut. XXVI, 1–11. These were presented to the priests in the Temple. (4) *Re'ayon*; v. Ex. XXIII, 17; Deut. XVI, 16. Biblically, '*every man according to the gift of his hand*' (Deut. XVI, 17), but Rabbinic *halachah* prescribes a *ma'ah* (a silver coin) as the minimum value of the burnt-offering and two silver coins that of the festival offering, v. Ḥag. 1a. According to Bertinoro, *Re'ayon* denoted 'appearing' in the Temple, i.e., there is no limit as to the number of times the Israelite may enter the Temple during the three festivals. (5) *Gemilluth ḥasadim*, a term implying more than mere charity and denoting personal service to all men of all classes. (6) Josh. I, 8. (7) Fifth Commandment; Ex. XX, 12, Deut. V, 16. (8) The fuller version given in our Prayer Books (v. *P.B.* p. 5) is based on a Baraitha quoted in Shab. 127a.

ב א) *אין פוחתין לפאה מששים ואע"פ שאמרו אין לפאה שיעור הכל לפי גודל השדה ולפי רוב העניים ולפי רוב הענוה: ג ב) נותנים פאה מתחלת השדה ומאמצעה ר' שמעון אומר ב ובלבד שיתן בסוף כשיעור רבי יהודה אומר אם שייר קלח אחד סומך לו משום פאה ואם לאו אינו נותן אלא משום הפקר: ד ג) כלל אמרו בפאה ג כל שהוא אוכל ונשמר וגדולו מן הארץ ולקיטתו כאחת ומכניסו לקיום חייב בפאה ד והתבואה והקטניות

העולם כולו אינו שוה אפי' לדבר אחד מה"ת וחד אמר אפי' כל מצותיה של תורה אינן שוות לדבר א' מה"ת ר' תנחומא א"ר אליעזר ור' יוסי בן זמרא חד אמר כהדין וחד אמר כהדין ר' אבא אבוי דר' אבא בר מרי בשם ר' אחא כתוב א' אומר וכל חפציך לא ישוו בה (משלי ג) וכתוב א' אומר כל חפצים לא ישוו בה (שם ח) חפצים אלו אבנים טובות ומרגליות חפציך אלו [א] דברי תורה דכתיב כי באלה חפצתי נאום ה' (ירמיה ט): ב משׂשים · מדרבנן אע"פ דמדאורייתא אין לפאה שיעור כדאמרי' בחולין (דף קלז:): לפי גודל השדה ולפי רוב העניים דאם שדה גדולה ועניים מועטין נותן לפי השדה ואם שדה קטנה ועניים מרובים נותן לפי רוב העניים יותר מששים ועל זה קאי ולפי הענוה שבזה לא נתנו חכמים שיעור ולפי ענוותו יוסיף וירבה לעניים מלשון וענותך תרבני (תהלים יח) ועוד יש לפרש ענוה בוי"ו כמו ענבה בבי"ת דגרגרים של תבואה אשכחן דקרי להו ענבה בירושל' בהלכ' בפ' כ"ג (הלכ' ה') דאמר עדשים היו אלא שהיתה ענבה יפה כשל שעורין ותנן לקמן בפ"ו (מ"ז) רואין כאילו היא ענבה של שעורים והשתא הכי פירושו ולפי הענוה לפי שיש שדה שחטיה יפות בצד אחד ורעות בצד אחר כנומות דקות שדופות קדים וכדאמרי' בריש השוכר את האומנין (דף עז:) מעידית שבה ומזיבורית שבה שהשדה עצמה מגדלת תבואה במקום אחד יותר מבצדה האחר לכך קאמר לפי הענוה שלא יתן מן הרע שבה ששים בכל אלא ישער נרע וליפה: ירושלמי (הלכה ב') · תני אין אומרים לו הבא גמלים וטעון מתני' ביותר מכשיעור אבל בכשיעור אומרים לו הבא גמלים וטעון שדהו מרובה ועניים מועטין נותן לפי השדה שדהו מעוטה ועניים מרובים נותן לפי העניים ר"ש דריש שני דברים לקולו של בעל הבית שדהו מרובה ועניים מועטים נותן לפי עניים שדהו מעוטה ועניים מרובים נותן לפי שדהו מתני' לא אמרה כן אלא הכל לפי גודל השדה ולפי העניים ולפי הענוה · פי' אין אומרים לעני הבא גמלים וטעון אם יתעשר העני בפאה אין להרבות הפאה שלא יפקיע את המעשר וכי קאמר מתני' ביותר מכשיעור דהיינו בשדה מעוטה ועניים מרובים שנותן יותר מששים התם הוא דקתני דאין אומרים לו הבא גמלים דאין להרבות כל כך שיתעשרו בה אבל בכשיעור דהיינו בששים אומרים לעני הבא וטעון דכיון שהוא עני עתה יכול ליטול הרבה כאחת כדתנן בסוף מכילתין היו לו מאתים חסר דינר אפילו אלף נותנין לו כאחת: ג מתחלת השדה ומאמצעה · לפי שאמרה תורה פאה בסוף שדהו כדמשמע לשון פאה איצטריך לאשמעינן דבתחלה ובאמצע נמי קדשה ופטורה מן המעשר ובירושלמי שם (הלכה ג') מרבי לה מדכתיב לקצור (יתירה) אפילו יש לו קמה לקצור: רבי שמעון אומר ובלבד שיתן בסוף כשיעור · כשיעור המשתייר נותן כדמוכח בירושלמי ואיצטריך לאשמעינן דלא תימא כיון שנתן בתחלה או באמצע כבר נפטר כל השדה מן הפאה אע"פ שאין בו אחד מששים ואם יתן בסוף להשלים יתחייב במעשר קמ"ל דאדרבה גם בסוף נמי חייב בפאה ולפרושי מלתא דתנא קמא קאתי ולא פליג וכן רבי יהודה נמי לא לפלוגי אדר' שמעון קאתי דבמלתא אחריתי איירי ר"י ומיהו לשון התוספתא (פ"א) משמע דר"ש פליג את"ק ולתנא קמא יכול ליתן פאה בכל ענין שירצה בין בתחלה בין באמצע בין בסוף ומיפטר שדהו מפאה ור"ש סבר דאע"ג דרבי קרא בתחלה ובאמצע שיש תורת פאה למה שנותן מ"מ לא מיפטר אא"כ נותן בסוף והא דמסיק בירושלמי דנותן לר' שמעון כשיעור המשתייר יש לפרש בשני עניינים כגון שהשלים בסוף עד ששים עם מה שהוא נותן בתחלה ובאמצע כדפרשינן אי נמי האי משתייר על התבואה הנשארת קאמר דנותן ממנה שלא תאמר ששים בכל השדה שהיתה מקודם שנתן בכלל נותן עתה בסוף: אם שייר קלח אחד סומך לו משום פאה · כשנתן שיעור פאה ומבקש להוסיף איירי דיכול להוסיף על המחובר ויש לתוספת תורת פאה לפטור מן המעשר ואם לאו כלומר שכבר תלשו אין נותן אלא משום הפקר דכל מה שמוסיף מן התלוש אין לו תורת פאה ואין נפטר מן המעשר אא"כ הפקיר אף לעשירים כשמיטה כבית הלל דלקמן פרק ו' (מ"א) אבל היכא דלא נתן כלל מן המחובר מודה ר' יהודה דנותן מן התלוש כדמוכח בתוספתא: הבקר · כמו הפקר: ירושלמי (שם) · ראשונה מהו מן מה דתני הרי זו פאה וצריך ליתן בסוף כשיעור הדה אמרה קדשה משום פאה מה כשיעור כל שדהו או כשיעור המשתייר אפשר לומר קדשה משום פאה ותימר כשיעור כל שדהו אלא כשיעור המשתייר רבי חייא בשם רבי יוחנן במחובר ר' יסא בשם ר' יוחנן בתלוש מה במתכוין לפטור את שדהו או לא נשמעינה מן הדא דא"ר יסא בשם ר' יוחנן לעולם הוא מוסיף והולך מה אנן קיימין אם במתכוין לפטור את שדהו כבר נפטרה אלא כי אנן קיימין בשאין מתכוין לפטור את שדהו פי' ראשונה מהו בעיא היא בתחלה או באמצע אם היא פאה לר' שמעון אי לא ופשיט לה דקדשה מדתני ר"ש בתוספתא הרי זו פאה וצריך שיתן בסוף כשיעור והדר מבעיא ליה אם כשיעור כל שדהו או כשיעור המשתייר וקא מתמה היך אפשר לומר דקדשה משום פאה א"ת דצריך ליתן כשיעור כל שדהו מה בעיא היא הא דקאמר ר' יוסי דבתלוש הויא פאה במתכוין לפטור שדהו שלא נתן במחובר את דינו או אפי' בנתן במחובר כל דינו ופשיט לה מאידך מלתא דר' יוסי דקתני דלעולם מוסיף דמשמע לעולם אפי' בתלוש ומשמע מוסיף אע"פ שכבר נפטר שדהו והשתא דר' יוסי דלא כר' יהודה וצריך נומר לר' יוסי דר"ש פליג עליה בהא ולא כמו שפירשתי במתני' דלא פליגי (ד) והא דפירשנו בריש פירקין דהיכא דכבר נפטר וחזר והוסיף חייב במעשרות היינו היכא דנתן פאה כדינו בסוף שדה אבל הכא איירינן בנתן בתחלת שדה או באמצעה; תניא בתוספתא · נותן אדם פאה בתחלת השדה באמצע ובסוף ואם נתן בין בתחלה בין באמצע בין בסוף יצא ר"ש אומר אם נתן בין בתחלה בין באמצע בין בסוף הרי זו פאה וצריך שיתן בסוף כשיעור ר' יהודה אומר אם שייר קלח אחד סומך לו נותן משום פאה ואם לאו אינו נותן אלא משום הפקר אמר רבי יהודה בד"א בזמן שנתן את הפאה ומבקש להוסיף לא נתן מן הקמה נותן מן העמרים לא נתן מן העמרים נותן מן הגדיש לא נתן מן הגדיש נותן מן הכרי עד שלא מירחו מירחו מעשר ונותן לו אר"ש מפני ארבעה דברים לא יתן אדם פאה אלא בסוף מפני גזל עניים ומפני ביטול עניים מפני מראית העין ומפני הרמאים מפני גזל עניים כיצד שלא יראה שעה שאין אדם ויאמר לקרובו עני בא וטול לך פאה זו מפני בטול עניים כיצד שלא יהו עניים יושבים ומשמרים כל היום ויאמרו עכשיו נותן פאה עכשיו נותן פאה אלא מתוך שנותנה בסוף הולך ועושה מלאכתו ובא ונוטלה באחרונה מפני מראית העין כיצד שלא יהיו עוברים ושבים אומרים ראו פלוני שקצר את שדהו ולא נתן פאה [ב] שהרי אמרה תורה לא תכלה פאת שדך מפני הרמאים כיצד שלא יאמרו כבר נתננו דבר אחר שלא יניח את היפה ויתן מן הרע פירוש אם נתן רישא קתני נותן לכתחלה והכא קתני אם נתן דיעבד אלא חדא מינייהו בנתן בשנים ושלשה מקומות אחד מששים בכל השדה: סומך לו נותן משום פאה במתני' קתני סומך משום פאה מירחו מעשר ונותן לו אבל מן העיסה לא דקסבר שינוי קונה כדאמרי' בריש הגוזל קמא (דף לד.) ור' ישמעאל פליג התם ואמר אף מפריש מן העיסה ונותן לו משום דשינוי אינו קונה א"כ משום תעזוב יתירא והאי דמעשר ונותן לו ואפי' מיפסר מדאורייתא מיחייב מדרבנן כיון דמירחו כדאשכחן בפרק כילד מברכין (דף מ:) דא"ר יצחק א"ר יוחנן משום ר' אליעזר בן יעקב הלקט והשכחה והפאה שעשאן לגורן הוקבעו: מפני הרמאים בפרק במה מדליקין (דף כג.) מייתי לה וקתני משום לא תכלה ולא קתני מפני הרמאים ופריך עלה אטו כולהו לאו משום לא תכלה נינהו אמר רבא מפני הרמאים ועל פי מסקנא דהתם כתבו כאן כן: ד כלל אמרו בפאה · בפרק כלל גדול (סח.) ובפרק מקום שנהגו (נו:) ובפרק בא סימן (כ·) מייתי לה. בריש כלל גדול אמרי' אוכל למעוטי ספיחי סטים וקוצה ונשמר למעוטי הפקר וגידולו מן הארץ למעוטי כמהין ופטריות ולקיטתו כאחת למעוטי תאנה ומכניסו לקיום למעוטי ירק והא דנקט למעוטי כל דבר שאינו אוכל דהכי איצטריך ליה משום דלחזו קלא לאכילה וקמ"ל דלא חשיבא אכילה דידהו ומהאי טעמא נמי נקט ספיחי ולא נקט סטים וקוצה עצמן דהנהו פשיטא דלא חזו כלל ומיהו בכל דוכתא נמי נקט בלשון ספיחים במס' שביעית (פ"ז מ"א) דקתני ממין הצבעין ספיחי סטים וקוצה ויש מפרשים משום דאין דרך ללקטן בשנה שנזרעים אלא לסוף ארבע וחמש שנים משהשרשים מתפשטין בארץ ומצמיחין לשורש שלהן עיקר הוא · סטים ויסר"א קוצה וודל"ה · כמהין ופטריות אין להן שורש בארץ ויונקין משמנונית הקרקע ומאוירא קא רבו . למעוטי תאנה לאו דוקא דרוב אילנות אין לקיטתם כאחת דליכא שלקיטתן כאחת אלא הני דחשיב במתני' (ה) ומיהו על כרחין לאו כולהו חשיב דהא איכא בנות שוח שלקיטתן כאחת כדמוכח בפ"ק דר"ה (דף טו:) גבי הא דאמר ר' יוחנן נהגו העם בחרובין כר' נחמיה וצריך לומר דהא תנא ושייר: למעוטי ירק רוב ירק קאמר דיש ירק חייב בפאה כגון שומין ובצלים כדתנן לקמן (פ"ו מ"ט) דהנהו מכניסן לקיום ובמכניסו לקיום כגון ע"י דבר אחר פליגי אנשי יריחו וחכמים בפרק מקום שנהגו (דף נו:) ובתורת כהנים ממעט כל הני מקרא דדריש התם יכול הירק והקישואים והאבטיחים והדלועים והמלפפונות הכל בכלל תלמוד לומר קציר מה קציר מיוחד שהוא אוכל ונשמר ועוד שדך כתיב: ולקיטתו כאחת · דשתם קציר מתבשל ביחד ושתם קציר מכניסו לקיום ילאו ירקות שאע"פ שלקיטתן כאחת אין מכניסן לקיום אין לקיטתן כאחת: והתבואה והקטניות בכלל הזה. בירושלמי (הלכה ד') דרשינן ובקצרכם אין לי אלא תבואה קטניות מנין תלמוד לומר ארצכם אילנות מנין תלמוד לומר שדך והיכא דיליף מכרם וזית ובפרק הזרוע (דף קלא.) דרשינן בהן שכחה ופאה ומסתברא דדרשה דתורת כהנים אסמכתא בעלמא מדאיצטריך קרא בפרק הזרוע לכרם וזית ומדאורייתא לא מיחייב בפאה אלא דגן תירוש ויצהר דלא שייך קצירה אלא בתבואה ותירוש ויצהר דהוא כרם וזית דריש בפרק הזרוע מדכתיב אחריך וצריך טעם מאי שנא מעשר דתיקון בכל דבר אף בתאנה וירק כדדייקינן בפרק כלל גדול ובפרק בא סימן ממתניתין דמסכת מעשרות דלא תני בכלל דידיה לקיטתו כאחת ומכניסו לקיום ומאי שנא פאה דלא תיקון בה תרווייהו לא נהגו מדאורייתא אלא בדגן תירוש ויצהר ויש ליתן טעם דבדבר שאין לקיטתו כאחת לא תיקון פאה משום בטול עניים כדאמרי' בפרק

מביא לידי מעשה: ב יש מי שיקרא ענוה בוי"ו ופירושו מה שתענה הארץ אם זרע רב או מעט ויש מי שיקרא ענבה בבי"ת ופירושו גודל הגרגרים או דקותם ורוע פריהם ושני העניינים קרובים זה לזה והסברא היולא משלש אלה הדרכים אינו אלא לתת לעניים מתנה יתירה ואם תהיה השדה גדולה והעניים מועטים יתנו לפי גודל השדה ואם הארץ מעוטה והעניים רבים יתנו לפי רוב העניים וכן אם תוליא הארץ זרע רב והעניים מועטין יתנו הרבה ומאשר זכרנו יתבאר לך שאר עניני ההקש בג' עניינים אלו: ג דעת ת"ק שיעזוב הפאה מאיזה צד שירצה. ור"ש אומר שהיא פאה מכ"מ שיניחנה אך לא תעלה לו מצות פאה עד שיעזוב בקצה שדה על כל פנים כשיעור פאה הראויה לשדה ההיא מפני הרמאים שהם קוצרים פאת השדה וכשיש אל אותם אומרים במקום אחר הניחנה וכן יאמרו לכל מי שיראם והם קוצרים בכ"מ עד שיקצרו כל השדה ור"י אומר שהמניח באיזה מקום שירצה או בקצה (כ"א בתחלת השדה או באמצעה אינו פאה בשום פנים אבל הוא הפקר ולא נקרא פאה משיניח בתחלת השדה או באמצעיתו אא"כ הניח בקצה ואפי' שורש א' לפאה ויעזוב כל מה שיעזוב בזולת המקום ההוא נסמך אל השרש ההוא והוא מה שיאמרו סומך לו משום פאה. ופי' שייר השאיר והותיר. ופי' הפקר הדבר המשולח לכל ב"א לקחתו כמו שיתבאר בזו המסכת' ודע כי הפאה היא לעניים בלבד ופי' משום מלך כך וכך ומי שאומר שהפאה שהניח בתחלת השדה או באמצע השדה הפקר ר"ל הוא מותר לכל בני אדם ור' שמעון אומר שהוא פאה ואף ע"פ שלא עלתה לו מצות פאה עד שיניחנה בסוף השדה לא יתירוהו אלא לעניים בלבד והלכה כר"ש: ד נאמר א] בכאן אוכל להוליא הכופר ופירושו אלחנ"א והלינוגא והאלפיר והם למחים שילבעו בהם מיני הלבעונים והדומה להם שאינם חייבים בפאה לפי שאמר הכתוב (ויקרא יט) ובקצרכם ומלת קציר נופלת על קצירת כל דבר הנאכל . ופירוש נשמר שיהיה במשמרת שכל דבר המופקר ואינו בשימור אינו חייב בפאה לפי שאמר הכתוב בענין פאה תעזוב אותם (שם) וזה מלשון משולח ונעזב ר"ל הפקר : וגדולו מן הארץ. ר"ל שיהיו לשרשיו שריגים משתרגים תחת הארץ ובהם יפרה להוליא מכללם הכמהי' והפטריו' שאינם חייבי' בפאה מפני שאמר הכתוב קציר ארלכ'(שם): ולקיטתו כאחת. ר"ל שיאספהו כולו בפעם אחת ואז יהיה חייב בפאה להוליא התאנים והדומה להם שלא יאספו בפעם אחת עד שנתבשל זה אחר זה שאין לנו לחייב בפאה אלא כל שיקצרוהו בפעם אחת כי הוא לשון קציר : ופירוש מכניסו לקיום ר"ל אפשר בו להיות אוצר וכמוס באסמים להוליא מכללו הירקות כולם שאין לנו לחייב בפאה אלא כל דבר הנאגר כגון החטה והשעורה כמ"ש הכתוב פאת שדך לקצור ולא יפול על שדה ירק שם קצירה : ושם תבואה נופל על חמשת המינים והוא חטה והוא שני מינים והשעורה והוא שלשה מינים

מסורת הש"ס

א) חולין פי"א קלז: ב) תורת כהנים פ' קדושים: ג) שבת פ"ז סח. פסחים פ"ד נו: נדה פ"ו דף נ.

פירוש ר"י בן מלכי צדק

כל העולם כולו אינו שוה לדבר אחד מן התורה והרינא אמר פי' כל מצותיה של תור' אינן שוות לדבר אחד מן התורה והוי פירוש כנגד כולן: ר' מנא שמע כולהון מן הדין קרא כי לא דבר ריק הוא מכם זה תלמוד תורה כי הוא חייכם זה כבוד אב ואם ובדבר הזה תאריכו ימים זו גמילות חסדים על האדמה זה הבאת שלום בין אדם לחבירו . ואיתקש כולהו להדדי:

ב אין פוחתין לפאה וכו'. אוקימנא בחולין [דף קל"ז] הא מתני' מדרבנן ובארץ: הכל לפי גודל השדה ולפי רוב העניים והכל תלוי בענוה שאפילו שדהו אלף כורין טוען אחד מששים הוא נותן כדין פאה ויש מפרשין הענוה לפי השבלים כדתנן לקמן בפ"ו משנה ז' רואין אותה כאלו היא ענוה [ס"א ענבה] של שעורין והיינו שאם היו לו י' אמות שדופות וי' אמות מלאות לא יתן כל שיעור הפאה מן השדופות אלא יתן כשיעור הראוי להגיע מן המליאות ועיין בפירושין: ג נותנין פאה מתחלת השד' ומאמציעתה. פי' מאמצע השדה והוא הדין בסוף [דתניא בתוספתא פ"א] נותן אדם פאה מתחלת השדה מאמצע ובסוף מנא ה"מ ר' יוסי בשם ר' שמעון בן לקיש אמר ובקצרכם את קציר ארצכם לא תכלה פאת שדך מה ת"ל לקצור אלא אפי' יש לו כמה לקצור ווו הפאה שנותן בתחלת השד' או באמצעית' או בסוף קדשה משום פאה ואין צריך ליתן פאה אחרת: רבי שמעון אומר וכו'. כלומר ודאי מה שנתן בתחלה או באמצע קדשה משום פאה כמו דתנינן בתוספ' ר' שמעון אומר אם נתן בין בתחלה בין באמצע הרי זו פאה. ומאחר דהויא פאה מ"ט שנינו ר"ש אומ' ובלבד שיתן בסוף כשיעור לא מכל השדה שכבר נתן אלא מאותו שנשתייר יתן בסוף פאה ממנו אחד מס' משום דר"ש בעי סוף עיקר לא שנא במחובר לא שנא בתלוש וכן תנינן בתוספתא פירקא קמא ר' שמעון אומר מפני ד' דברים לא יתן אדם פאה אלא בסוף וכו': ר' יהודה אומר וכו'. הכין מתרץ בגמ' דאם נתן פאה כשיעור ורוצה עוד להוסיף א"ר יהודה אם שייר קלח אחד בשדהו שלא כילה עדיין שדהו על כל שמוסיף לשם הבקר כלומר סומך לו משום פאה ואינה חייבת במעשר כמו הפאה אבל אם כילה כל שדהו שוב אינו יכול להוסיף ואי מוסיף לענין פאה חייבת במעשר אלא אם נותן להבקיר וכו' אבל לענין פאה שוב אינו יכול ליתן ונמצא חולק עם רבי שמעון דרבי שמעון סבר אע"פ שכילה שדהו מוסיף לשם פאה מן התלוש: ד כלל אמרו בפאה וכו' פי' זה הכלל אמרו חכמים

ח א מיי' פ"א מהל' מתנות עניים הל' יו סמג לאוין רפד:
ט ב מיי' שם פ"ב הל' יב סמג שם:
י ג מיי' פ"ב מהל' מתנות עניים הל"א:
יא ד שם הל' ג:

פי' הרא"ש

(ד) ול"נ דאף ר"ש מודה שחייב במעשר כי לא הפקיר מה שהוסיף בתלוש אלא לשם פאה הוסיף ואין עליו תורת פאה והוי פאה בטעות וחייב במעשר אבל אם לא נתן פאה כלל מן המחובר מודה רבי יהודה דנותן מן התלוש והכי איתא בתוספתא א"ר יהודה בד"א בזמן שנותן את הפאה וכו' לא נתן מן הקמה נותן מן העמרים וכו' עד מירחו מעשר ונותן לו: (ה) והא דנקט למעוטי תאנה לפי שפירותיה מפוזרים ביותר בבישולם כדאי' בריש חזקת הבתים (כח:) אכל תלתא פירי בתלתא יומי כגון תאנה ליכוי חזקה:

הגהות הגר"א

[א] שם דברי תורה: נמחק דברי. וכ"ב מצות של: [ב] שם מ"ג שהרי. נמחק וכ"ב ומפני מה:

הגהות הרי"ו לנדא

פ"א משנה ד בר"מ א] נאמר בכאן אוכל. ועי' שביעית פ"ז מ"ו:

MISHNAH 2. ONE SHOULD NOT MAKE THE AMOUNT OF PE'AH LESS THAN ONE-SIXTIETH[9] [OF THE ENTIRE CROP]. BUT ALTHOUGH NO DEFINITE AMOUNT IS GIVEN FOR PE'AH,[10] YET EVERYTHING DEPENDS UPON THE SIZE OF THE FIELD,
a THE NUMBER OF POOR MEN,[1] AND THE EXTENT OF THE STANDING CROP.[2]

MISHNAH 3. PE'AH MAY BE GIVEN EITHER AT THE BEGINNING OF THE [REAPING OF THE] FIELD OR AT THE MIDDLE THEREOF.[3] R. SIMEON SAYS: [THIS IS SO] PROVIDED HE GIVES AT THE END ACCORDING TO THE AMOUNT FIXED.[4] R. JUDAH SAYS: SHOULD HE EVEN LEAVE [FOR THE CONCLUSION OF THE REAPING] ONE STALK, HE CAN RELY ON THIS[5] AS [FULFILLING THE LAW OF] PE'AH; AND IF HE DID NOT DO SO, [THEN EVEN THOSE STALKS LEFT AT THE BEGINNING OR AT THE MIDDLE] ARE TO BE REGARDED AS OWNERLESS PROPERTY.[6]

MISHNAH 4. A GENERAL PRINCIPLE HAS BEEN ENJOINED CONCERNING PE'AH: WHATSOEVER IS USED FOR FOOD,[7]
b AND IS LOOKED AFTER,[1] AND GROWS FROM THE SOIL,[2] AND IS HARVESTED ALTOGETHER,[3] AND IS BROUGHT IN FOR STORAGE,[4] IS SUBJECT TO THE LAW OF PE'AH. GRAIN[5] AND

(9) But he can, of course, give more. (10) V. *supra* I, 1.
a (1) If the field is large and the poor few, the amount of *Pe'ah* is determined by the size of the field, and he has to give the minimum of one-sixtieth; if, on the other hand, the field is small and the poor many, it is determined by the number of the poor and is to be increased beyond the barest minimum. (2) *Pe'ah* may not be chosen only of the inferior crop, but from the whole field. ענוה usually identified with ענבה whence the adopted translation. V. *infra* VI, 7. Others render: 'according to the piety (of the landowner)'. (3) *Pe'ah* need not necessarily be given at the very end of the reaping. (4) Opinion varies as to the precise meaning of this proviso. Maim. maintains that one-sixtieth must be left at the end, irrespective of what he has left before; others interpret R. Simeon's statement to mean that what he leaves at the end must supplement towards the minimum quantity prescribed. The object of the proviso is to counteract a deceitful plea that *Pe'ah* had been set aside already before. Tosephta and Yerushalmi cite other reasons. (5) I.e., the last stalk and that which he gave at the beginning or middle together constitute the *Pe'ah*. (6) If nothing is set aside for *Pe'ah* at the end, then even that left hitherto is *hefker* (v. Glos.), and even the rich can acquire possession thereof no less than the poor. In this R. Judah differs from R. Simeon, whereas according to R. Simeon *all* that he left counts as *Pe'ah* and is reserved for the poor; but according to R. Judah, if nothing is left as *Pe'ah* at the end, then the stalks left before are treated as *hefker*. (7) To exclude aftergrowths not fit for human food. *And when ye harvest*, Lev. XIX, 9 rules out crop not normally cut.
b (1) To exclude *hefker*, which is already the property of the poor; hence Lev. XIX, 10 can no longer apply to it. (2) Mushrooms, which according to the Rabbis, receive their nurture not from the soil, are thus excluded. Lev. XIX, 9 stresses *the harvest of your land* (soil). (3) Not singly as they ripen, as in the case of figs. (4) Hence greens and herbs that will not keep are excluded. (5) Of this, five species are included: wheat, barley, rye, oats and spelt.

PULSE[6] FALL INTO THIS GENERAL PRINCIPLE.[7]

MISHNAH 5. AMONG TREES: THE SUMMACH, THE CAROB,[8] THE NUT, THE ALMOND, THE VINE, THE POMEGRANATE, THE OLIVE AND THE PALM[9] ARE SUBJECT TO PE'AH.

MISHNAH 6. ONE CAN ALWAYS GIVE PE'AH,[10] AND BE EXEMPT FROM GIVING TITHES[11] [FROM IT] UNTIL IT IS FINALLY STACKED.[12] OR ONE MAY PRONOUNCE [HIS FIELD] OWNERLESS AND BE EXEMPT FROM GIVING TITHE THEREOF UNTIL IT IS

a FINALLY STACKED.[1] ONE MAY FEED CATTLE, WILD ANIMALS AND BIRDS [OF THE CROP] BEFORE IT IS FINALLY STACKED AND BE EXEMPT FROM TITHES.[2] HE MAY TAKE FROM THE THRESHING FLOOR AND USE AS SEED AND BE EXEMPT FROM TITHES UNTIL IT IS STACKED.[3] SO R. AKIBA. IF A PRIEST OR LEVITE PURCHASE [THE GRAIN OF] A THRESHING FLOOR THE TITHES ARE THEIRS UNLESS THE STACKING HAS TAKEN PLACE.[4] ONE WHO DEDICATED [HIS CROP][5] AND REDEEMS IT [AFTERWARDS] IS BOUND TO GIVE TITHES SO LONG AS THE TREASURER HAD NOT YET FINALLY STACKED IT.

(6) Such as lentils and peas. (7) Because they fulfil the conditions concerning which the general principle was laid down, they are subject to the law of *Pe'ah*. (8) Or St. John's bread; cf. Ma'as. I, 3. The 'Aruch (s.v. חרב) says it takes seventy years for this tree to bear fruit from its planting. (9) The eight trees here mentioned in no wise exclude others that fulfil the given conditions, but only those most common in Palestine are enumerated. (10) If omitted from the standing corn, the stipulated amount (I, 2) must be given from the corn already cut. (11) Tithes are of three kinds: (*a*) that given to the Levite, who in turn gives a tenth thereof to the priest (Num. XVIII, 26), is called First Tithe (cf. Num. XVIII, 21); (*b*) that which the owner himself must eat in Jerusalem (Deut. XIV, 23) is known as Second Tithe. The produce could be converted into money for which, plus one quarter of its original value, food was bought and eaten in Jerusalem (Deut. XIV, 26); (*c*) in the third and sixth year of the seven-year cycle a tithe was taken from the produce and given to the poor. This was known as Poor Man's Tithe, Deut. XIV, 29; XXVI, 12. Tithes are not given from *Pe'ah*. (12) שימרח, 'to smoothe, to make level'. The custom was to stack the produce, after the winnowing, in upright piles, broad at the base and thinning towards the top. The 'smoothing' was the final act of making the pile even prior to its being stored. If, however, the giving of the *Pe'ah* was delayed until after the stacking, the tithes had to be given from it.

a (1) The exemption of *hefker* from tithes is based on Deut. XIV, 28. A declaration of *hefker* after the process of stacking, when the duty of tithes had already become incumbent, does not exempt the 'ownerless' produce from tithes. The fear was lest an *'am ha-arez* eat thereof under the impression that it had been tithed as soon as it had been finally stacked. Cf. Dem. III, 2. (2) He could even snatch an improvised meal for himself since the law of tithe does not become binding prior to the final stacking. His cattle, however, could partake of regular meals therefrom. This is based on a statement in Ma'as. I, 1: 'Whatsoever is not used for food at first but only in its later stage, is not liable to tithes until it has become fit for human food'. (3) In Deut. XIV, 23, *and thou shalt eat* is used in reference to tithes; that used for seed is therefore excluded. Rabbinic tradition, however, compels also the tithe to be given from seeds. R. Akiba maintains that all seed before stacking is exempt. (4) Had they purchased the store after the stacking, the tithes would not have been theirs as a penalty for snatching away the 'gifts' which might have been given to other priests and Levites. The custom indulged by some Levites of buying the grain prior to the winnowing in order to make sure of the tithes was condemned by the Rabbis. (5) *Hekdesh* (v. Glos.) like *hefker* was not liable to tithes. Should this redemption take place before the Temple Treasurer had stacked it, the duty falls on the redeemer. Only if the stacking was done when it was still in the possession of the Sanctuary does it become exempt. The point stressed throughout the Mishnah is that the law of tithes comes into force with the stacking.

במה מדליקין (דף כג.) גבי פאה בסוף שדה שלא יהו עניים משמרין והכא נמי כשרואין אותו לוקט כסבורים לוקט את הכל ומשמרין וירק נמי היינו טעמא פירות מועט לעניים כיון דאין מכניסו לקיום ומפסידין במקום אחר ויש מפרשים טעם משום דפאה נוהגת בכל דבר מדאורייתא כדדרים בתורת כהנים ומשום תאנה וירק לחודייהו לא רצו לעשות תקנה אבל מעשר דמדאורייתא דגן תירוש ויצהר דוקא כשהתחילו לתקן תקון בכל דבר ולא יתכן כלל כדפרישית דפאה נמי מדאורייתא דגן תירוש ויצהר דוקא ועוד אמו תאנה. לחודה קא ממעט מפאה הא רוב פירות אין לקיטתן כאחת חוץ מהכך שמונה דקא חשיב במתני':

והקטניות בכלל הזה: **ה** ובאילן [א]האוג והחרובין והאגוזין והשקדים והגפנים והרמונים והזיתים והתמרים חייבים בפאה: **ו** (ו) [ב]לעולם הוא נותן משום פאה ופטור מן המעשרות עד שימרח [ג]ונותן משום הפקר ופטור מן המעשרות עד שימרח [ד]ומאכיל לבהמה לחיה ולעופות ופטור מן המעשרות עד שימרח ונוטל מן הגורן וזורע ופטור מן המעשרות [ה]עד שימרח דברי ר"ע [ו]כהן ולוי שלקחו את הגורן המעשרות שלהן עד שימרחו [ז]המקדיש ופודה חייב במעשרות עד שימרח הגזבר:

מינים א] ואלו הם חמשת מינים הנזכרים בכל מקום: וקטניו'. הם כמו פולים ואפונים והלוביא והשומשמין וזולתם מן הדומה להם: ופירוש בכלל הזה כשנשלמו בהם אלו התנאים הראוים בחיוב פאה ולפיכך יתחייבו בפאה: **ה** אוג. הוא הסומאק אשר בארץ הצבי והוא צמח ג] שיעבדו בו העורות ויש לו אשכלות כאשכלות הגפן ויאכלו: חרובין. ידוע: ואגוזים ושקדים. כמו כן ידועים ואלה האילנות כולם נמצאים בהם התנאים הנזכרים בכל מה שיתחייב פאה ולפיכך הם מחויבים בפאה: **ו** דע שהפאה לא תתחייב להוציא ממנה מעשרות ושמור זה העיקר שכל מי שלא הניח פאה וקצר כל השדה כולה יוציא הפאה ממה שקצר וכן אם לא הוציא מן השבלים הקצורים יוציא מן החטה אחר שידושו אותה וימרחוה ויבררוה ואפילו טחנה יוציא הפאה מן הקמח וזה העיקר מבואר בגמרא מכות (דף טז:) וממה שיש לך לזכור תמיד שההפקר והוא הדבר הנעזב והמשולח אינו חייב במעשרות ופירוש מריחה מריקה וזאת המלה מושאלת בדרך המליצה בענין ברירת החטה מן התבן והשלמת צרכי הזרע עד שלא ישאר לעשות בו אלא להוליכו אל האוצר והוא דומה כמו הממרק לכלים שאין עושין אותו המרוק אלא כשנשלם הכלי וכשיקצר הזרע הנזרע כולו וידוש ונברר מן התבן אז יפריש מן הזרע ההוא תרומה ומעשרות המחויבות לו ואח"כ יוציא הפאה שנתחייב בה בזרע ויתנה לעניים אבל קודם הברירה צריך להפריש הפאה תחלה ואחר כן המעשרות ויתן הפאה לעניים והפאה עצמו אינה מחויבת במעשרות. וכן יש לו להפקיר מן הזרע מה שירצה קודם ברירתו אבל אחר הברירה לא יפקיר ממנו כלום עד שיפריש המעשרות: ור"ע אומר. שמותר לו לקחת החטה הגדושה בטרם שיבררו אותה ויזרענה: והעיקר בידינו שהכהן והלוי כשיקנו החטה אחר הקצירה והדישה והברירה יש להם להוציא התרומה והמעשר המחויבות באותו הזרע מרשותם ולתת אותם לכהנים ולוים אחרים ואת קנס להם וכןאמרו קנס קנסו בהם שלא יהו קופצין לגרנות ולגיתות ועל כן אמר בכאן שהמעשרות שלהן כל זמן שלא נכנס לגורן בענין שיתחייב מעשר והוא כשימרחו אותו. וההקדש אינו מחויב מתנה מכל המתנות לא מעשרות ולא זולתם ונזכר שם הפקיד האומר נכסי ההקדש ואמר שכל מי שהקדיש גרנו ואח"כ פדאו מיד הגזבר ועודנו בקמה או קציר בטרם הברירה יתחייב להוציא המעשרות ואם ימרחהו הגזבר נפדאוהו בעליו אחר כן לא יתחייב במעשרות שבעת שנכנס בחזקת חיוב המעשרות היה ברשות ההקדש שאינו מחויב במעשר ואין הלכה כרבי עקיבא:

אלו

ה האוג. אילן שפריו אדום כדתנן בריש מעשרות (פרק א מ"ב) האוג והתותים משיאדימו וי"א שזהו אילן שקורין קורנליי"ר בלע"ז ולא יתכן דאין מכניסו לקיום: **ו** נותן משום פאה ופטור. (עי' באגרת) כדתניא לעיל מירחו מעשר ונותן לו [א] וכן הפקירה קודם מירוח פטור לאחר מירוח חייב וכן כולם וטעמא דמירוח משום דאין מתחייב במעשר [עד שימרח] כדתנן במס' מעשרות (פ"א משנה ו') דכתיב דגנך ודרשינן דיגונך דגורן תלינהו רחמנא כדאמרי' בב"מ בפ' השוכר את הפועלים (דף פ"ח:) ולמאן דבעי התם ראיית פני הבית מיירי מתני' עד שימרח בבית וכגון דלא הכניס התבואה במוץ שלה אלא לאחר שנסהרה מן המוץ הכניסה בבית ומירחה שם ומאחר שחל עליה חיוב מעשר תו לא מיפטרא אפי' הפקיר ויתכן דאפי' מירחה בשדה ואח"כ הפקיר דמחייבת מדרבנן אם חזר והכניסה בבית אותו שזוכה בה ובפ"ג דמעשר שני (הלכה ג') משמע בירושלמי דלבית הלל הפקר פטור אפי' בדבר שנגמר מלאכתו ושם פירשנו ומירוח קורא לאחר שמסהרין את התבואה מן המוץ שלה וצוברין אותה במקום א' ומייפים פני הצבור ומחליקין אותו והוא המירוח ובירושלמי (הל' ה') אמרי' מתני' דב"ש היא דב"ש אמרי הפקר לעניים הפקר משמע שרוצה לומר דאיירי משנתן פאה שכבר נפטר מן הפאה ואחרי כן בא להוסיף עליה לכל מה שמוסיף עד שלא נתמרח פטור מן המעשר לבית שמאי מטעם הפקר אע"פ שאין מפקיר אלא לעניים דהא משום פאה נותן אף התוספת: (ע"כ שייך מה שבאגרת). ולב"ה לא מיפטרה התוספת עד שיופקר לעניים ולעשירים כשמטה כדתנן לקמן פרק ו' (משנה א') אבל בעיקר הפאה אפילו לא הפרישה מן המחובר אלא מן התלוש עד שלא מירחו מודים בית הלל דפטור מן המעשר כדמשמע בפרק מקום שנהגו (דף נד') מעובדא דבן בוסין וטעמא דהפקר פטור מןהמעשר מפרש לקמן בירוש' (מעשרות פ"א ה"א) מדכתיב (דברים יד) ובא הלוי כי אין לו חלק ונחלה עמך יצא הפקר שידך וידו שוים אם הוא לוי עני אבל הפקר לעניים לא מצינן למיפטר מטעם זה דאינו הפקר לב"ה כלל ואפי' זכה בו עני חייב להחזיר כדמוכח בשילהי אלו מציאות (דף ל:) ודבר תימה הוא למה לי האי קרא תיפוק ליה דהזוכה מן ההפקר מיפטר מידי דהוה אלוקח דדרשינן בפרק השוכר את הפועלים (דף פח:) עשר תעשר ואכלת ולא מוכר תבואת זרעך ולא לוקח ומיהו איכא למימר דאיצטריך היכא דחזר וזכה איהו גופיה כמו הפקיר כרמו ולשחר השכים ובצרו דקרינא ביה תבואת זרעך ואפ"ה מיפטר מדכתיב ובא הלוי ופאה נמי דפטרינן בספרי מהאי קרא דובא הלוי אי לאו האי קרא הוה מחייבינןלהו לעניים דכיון דזכי להו רחמנא בהאי שדה תבואת זרעך קרינא ביה ועוד ניחא לפי מה שאומר ר"ת דלא מיפטר לוקח אלא כשלקח אחר מירוח משום דקשה ליה ההיא דסוף פ"ק דבכורות (דף יא:) גבי לוקח טבלים ממורחין מן הנכרי מעשרן והן שלו דמשמע דמעשרן מדאורייתא מדקאמר מעשרן דאין קנין ואי מדרבנן אפי' יש קנין חייב כדמוכח בפ' הקומץ רבה (דף לא') גבי עובדא דר"ש שזורי ועוד דמדכתיב ואל הלוים תדבר דריש התם טבלים שאתה לוקח מישראל אתה מפריש מהן תרומת מעשר ונותנן לכהן טבלים שאתה לוקח מן הנכרי אי אתה מפריש ומתרץ רבינו תם דלוקח קודם מירוח חייב דקרינא ביה תבואת זרעך כיון דמרחינהו לוקח אבל לקחן ממורחים פטור והיא דלוקח טבלים ממורחין מן הנכרי מוקי לה התם דמרחינהו ישראל ברשות נכרי שקיבל ישראל את השדה באריסות והיא דהקומץ רבה דמשמע דאי אין קנין לא מצי למימר ליה לך קח מן הנכרי וכן אם אין רוב עמי הארץ מעשרין לא מצי למימר ליה לך קח מן השוק דהוי מן החיוב על הפטור אע"ג דאם היה לוקח ממורחים פטור מדאורייתא מ"מ היה נראה כמו מחיוב על הפטור והא דאיצטריך לן מירוח הנכרי פטור נפקא מינה לנכרי התורם וכותי שתרמו תרומתן תרומה א"נ לישראל שמכר לנכרי קודם מירוח ולאחר מירוח חזר ולקחה דאי משום תבואת זרעך לא מיפטר ומשום מירוח נכרי מיפטר וכן יש קנין איצטריך משום תרומת נכרי א"נ משום לוקח גופיה דאפי' תימא' לומר דלוקח קודם מירוח פטור איצטריך משום הביא שלים ביד נכרי ולקחה ישראל ממנו דחשיב תבואת זרעך כיון דלוקח במחובר ומשום יש קנין פטור א"כ נמירחינהו ברשות נכרי דהיינו אריס של נכרי וקשה לפי' ר"ת דבפ' השוכר את הפועלים (שם) דריש כנפשך כן נפשו של פועל מה נפשך אתה אוכל ופטור הא לוקח חייב ומוקי לה בתאנה העומדת בגגה ונופה נוטה לחצר או לבית דבעה"ב עיניו בתאנתו ולוקח עיניו במקחו ופריך ולוקח מדאורייתא מי מחייב והתניא כו' ומאי קושיא הא קודם מירוח מיירי דקא קני לה בעודה מחוברת בתאנה ועוד דעל כרחין קודם מירוח איירי דהא אין פועל אוכל בדבר שנגמרה מלאכתו למעשר כדתנן התם (ד' פז:) ועוד מדפריך בבכורות גבי לוקח טבלים ממורחים מן הנכרי אילימא דמרחינהו נכרי דיגונך אמר רחמנא ולא דיגון נכרי דהוה ליה לאקשויי הא לוקח ממורחים פטור מדאורייתא אפי' לוקח מישראל ועוד דסתם לוקח דמאי היינו לאחר מירוח ואם איתא דליכא חששא דאיסורא דאורייתא לא היו גוזרים על הדמאי אחר שרוב ע"ה מעשרין ועוד גבי הפקר והקדש הוי איפכא דמחייבינן לאחר מירוח ספי מקודם מירוח לפיכך היה נראה לפרש איפכא מרבינו תם דלוקח קודם מירוח פטור אבל אם נתמרח ביד מוכר דחל עליו חיוב מעשר תו לא מיפטר לוקח והיא דבכורות דטבלים ד] שאתה לוקח מן הנכרי מיירי בנכרי המעשר פירותיו ונותן ללוי דלא מיחייב הלוי ליתן תרומת מעשר לכהן ומעשר שלו דאורייתא אי אין קנין ואין מירוח הנכרי פוטר ואפי' למאן דאמר מירוח הנכרי פוטר אפשר שהקדימו בשבלים ואפשר דעכשיו קיים טעמא דקאמר התם לעיל קאתינא מכח גברא כלומר כמו שמעשר שהנכרי מפריש ונותן ללוי אין הלוי חייב ליתן ממנו תרומת מעשר לכהן כמו כן כשקונה הלוי טבלים מן הנכרי והפריש מעשר אינו חייב ליתן ממנו תרומת מעשר אלא מפרישו והוא שלו משום דאמר ליה קאתינא מכח גברא דאי לאו הכי אע"ג דלוקח פטור מדאורייתא מ"מ היה חייב ליתן לכהן מדרבנן ויש ברייתא בתוספתא (פאה פ"ב) שאין אדם יכול לישבה והכי תניא גר שמת ובזבזו ישראל את נכסיו המחזיק במחובר לקרקע חייב בכל בתלוש מן הקרקע פטור מן הכל החזיק בקמה פטור מן הלקט שכחה ופאה וחייב במעשרות והשתא נכסי הגר הרי הן הפקר והך סיפא היא איפכא מהא דתניא בפ' המניח את הכד (דף כח.) ובפ' אין בין המודר (דף עד:) המפקיר את כרמו ולשחר עמד ובצרו חייב בפרט ובעוללות ובשכחה ופטור מן המעשר והא דמחייב ספי בשכחה ובפאה משום דכתיב תעזוב יתירא כלמפרש בפ"ק דתמורה (דף ו.) ובפ"ק דקדושין כתובה ביותר בירושלמי (פ"א הל' ה') והכי איתא התם רב חסדא אמר נכסי הגר החזיק בצפונן על מנת לקנות בדרומן בדרומן על מנת לקנות בצפונן ולא נתכוין לקנות באמצעיתן לא קנה עד שיתכוין לקנות באמצעיתן מתני' פליגא על דרב חסדא גר שמת ובזבזו ישראל את נכסיו המחזיק בקרקע חייב בכל המחזיק בקמה חייב בשכחה ופאה ופטור מן המעשרות ואין אויר מפסיק בין שבולת לשבולת בתמיה וגירסא זו ניחא דהחזיק בקרקע לא דמי למפקיר כרמו דפטור מן המעשר דבההיא לא זכה בקרקע מן ההפקר ודמי למחזיק בקמה א"כ במחזיק בקמה קודם הבאת שליש: מאכיל לבהמה ולחיה ולעופות כו'. ה"ה אפי' הוא עצמו מותר באכילת עראי קודם מירוח אלא דבהמה שריא אפי' אכילת קבע כי ההיא דא"ר אושעיא בכמה דוכתי מערים אדם על תבואתו ומכניסה במוץ שלה כדי שתהא בהמתו אוכלת ופטורה מן המעשר ועוד נקט כאן בהמה לאשמעינן דלאחר מירוח אפי' בהמה אסורה: נוטל מן הגורן וזורע ופטור מן המעשרות עד שימרח דברי ר"ע. אמרי' בירוש' (הל' ה') אתיא דר"ע כחנויות בני חנון דתניא (ב"מ דף פח.) למה חרבו חנויות בני חנון ג' שנים עד שלא חרב הבית שהיו מוציאין פירותיהן מכלל המעשרות דהוו דרשין עשר תעשר את כל תבואת זרעך (דברים יד) פרט ללוקח ואכלת פרט למוכר והשתא אין ר"ל דר"ע סבר כוותייהו לפוטרן אפי' מדרבנן דהם ושלום שהרי מזכיר אותם לגנאי התם וגמ' שלנו בפ' השוכר את הפועלים (דף פח:) אלא ה"ק אתיא דר"ע לאפוקינהו מדידהו דמשמירח אסור לזרוע עד שיעשר מדרבנן אע"ג דלא קרינן ביה ואכלת וכי היכי דממעטינן מיניה לוקח איכא למעוטי נמי זורע: כהן ולוי מן הדין אפי' לקחו לאחר מירוח המעשרות שלהן אלא מפרש בירושלמי (הל' ה') א"ר יוחנן קנס קנסו להן שלא יהו קופצין לגיתות ולגרנות עוד קאמר התם טבח כהן חבריא בשם ריב"ל פסר לו טבח אחת ר' יודן מדמי לה להדא דר' יוחנן משום קנס קנסו בהן ובפ' הזרוע (דף קלב:) דרש רבא מאת זובחי הזבח אפי' כהן טבח במשמע: עד שימרח הגזבר. כשמירח וחזר וקנאו אפי' מדרבנן לא מחייב ולא דמי למירוח נכרי דבפרק רבי ישמעאל במנחות (דף סז') דלא שייך גבי הקדש לגזור משום בעלי כיסן:

אלו

פי' מהר"י בן מלכי צדק

חכמים בחיוב פאה כל שהוא אוכל פי' אוכל למעוטי ספיחי סטים וקוצה. ונשמר פי' שיושב שם שומר לאפוקי הבקר. וגידוליו מן הארץ לאפוקי כמהין ופטריות דמאוירא קא רבו. ולקיטתו כאחת פי' שנלקטין הפירו' ביחד לאפוקי תאנין. ותניא [בתוספת'] התאנין אע"פ שנכנסין לקיום אין לקיטתן כאחת. ומכניסו לקיום פי' אם הוא מקשםכנים אדם ממנו לאוצר ואינו מרקיב מהרה ואינו יבש לאפוקי ירק ותניא [שם בתוספתא] הירק אף על פי שלקיטתו כאחת אין מכניסו לקיום והתבואה. פי' חמשת מינין. והקטניות. פי' פוליןואפוניןוכןאורז ודוחן טולן בכלל הזה וחייבין בפאה. מנהני מילי [ת"כ בפרשת קדושים וירושלמי כאן] דכתב ובקצרכם אין לי אלא קצר תולש מנין ת"ל לקצור אין לי אלא תבואה קטניות מנין ת"ל ארצכם. אילנות מנין ת"ל שדך. ת"ר בסיפרא [שם] יכול הירק והקשואין והדלועיןוהאבטיחין והמלפפונות הכל בכלל ת"ל קציר מה קציר מיוחד שהוא אוכל ונשמר וכו' עד יצאו ירקות שאע"פ שלקיטתן כאחת אבל אין מכניסן לקיום. יצאו תאנין שאף על פי שמכניסן לקיום אין לקיטתן כאחת והתבואה והקטניות בכלל הזה: ה ובאילן. פי' חיוב פאה באילן האוג וכו' שכל אלו מכניסן לקיום והוא אדום וכן שנינו [בריש מעשרות] האוג והתותים משיאדימו והרב היה מלמדנו האוג בלע"ז קורנולי ולשון יווני נקראין אקרניא היאיתו ונראין דברי הגאון שמין צביעה הוא דגרסי' בירושלמי בשביעית בפ' כלל גדול צבעים לבהמה מהו שיהא עליהן קדושת שביעית ושמעינן מן הדא עיקר הוורד ועיקר התאנה ועיקר האוג אין בהן משום קדושת שביעית: חרובים בוינילי וזרעם כן נקראין כרובי. תנא דידן תני דתמרים חייבין בפאה ר' יוסי בר' יהודה תני דפטורין מן הפאה ואומר מעם מפני שאין הראשון שבהן ממתין לאחרון שבהן. רבנן מאי טעמא אמר רבי זעירא מפני שכולן מטילין שאור בבת אחת. נמצאת אומר כל האילנות פטורין מן הפאה חוץ מח' אילנות הללו ששנינו: ו לעולם הוא נותןמשום פאה וכו'. פי' ואפי' בתלוש ואפי' ר' יהודה דעד כאן לא קאמר ר"י אינו נותן אלא משום הבקר אלא בשנתן פאה ומבקש להוסיף אבל אם לא הניח פאה מן הקמה נותן מן העמרים והכי מפרש בתוספ'. וכן [נותן משום] הבקר ומאכיל לבהמה [עד שימרח] הא אם מרח חייב במעשרות ואינו יכול ליתן משום פאה ולא משום הבקר ולא להאכיל לבהמה לחיה ולעופות תנם לא ליטול מן הגורן לזרוע עד שיעשר. ודלא כבית הלל דאי כבית הלל אפי' אםנתמרח הכרי יכול להפקירו ולפוטרו מן המעשר. ועיקרו בירושלמי דמעשר שני פרק ג' הלכה ג': כהן ולוי שלקחו את הגורן המעשרות שלהן עד שימרחו. הא אם קנין לאחר מירוח אינן שלהן מאי טעמא א"ר יוחנן קנס קנסו בהן שלא יהו קופצין לגיתות ולגרנות. אבל בשלקחו גדיש שלא נתמרח ממרחין ומעשרין והמעשרות שלהן מאי טעמא משום דמלתא דלא שכיחא הוא ולא גזרו רבנן: המקדיש ופודה חייב במעשרות עד שימרח הגזבר (פירש רבינו וימרוח על השחין*) כי כל המשלים נותנו לוקח לוח ומרשה בו כל הגורן ולשון מיכה היא פר"ש ימהר כרי התבואה מן חקש והתבן ערב"י) פי' שכיון שנתמרח ברשות הגזבר איפטר ליה מן המעשר וכשקנה מן הגזבר כקונה דבר גמור דמי. ותנינן בחלה פ"ג הקדישן עד שלא נגמרו ונמרן הגזבר ואח"כ פדאן פטורה שבשעת חובתן וכו' ויש דבר שמחייב התבואה בלא מירוח משיעמיד ערימה:

*) אולי צ"ל מירוח לשון משיחה ומדידה הוא כו' א"נ לשון סיכה היא ור"ש פי' שמעשר ככרי מן הקש כו'

ואלו

עין משפט נר מצוה

יא א שם הל' ב:

יב ב מיי' פ"ב מהל' מתנות עניים הלכה יא:

יג ג מיי' פ"ג מהלכות מעשר הלכה ב:

יד ד מיי' פ"ו מהל' מעשר הלכה ג: (ע"ש ברמב"ם ובכ"מ שם וצ"ע):

טו ה מיי' שם הל' טו סמג עשין קלה טוש"ע י"ד סי' שלא סעיף קכב:

טז ו ז מיי' פ"ג מהל' מעשר הל' כה:

פי' הרא"ש

(ו) לעולם הוא נותן וכו' עד שימרח. ופטור העני מלעשר דפאה פטורה מן המעשר כדדרשינן בספרי ובא הלוי כי אין לו חלק ונחלה עמך יצא זה שיש לו חלק ונחלה עמך אם הלוי עני יש לו חלק עמך בפאה. הלכך קודם מירוח א"צ הבעל הבית לעשר כשנותן פאה אבל אם המתין מליתן פאה עד אחר המירות אם היה מפריש קמה קודם שיעשר הכרי הוה עני צריך להפריש מעשר מן הפאה כיון שכבר נגמר ספרי נמצא העני מפסיד אחד מעשרה ולכך חייבו את הבעה"ב שיפריש פאה:

הגהות הרי"ב לנדא

משנה ד בר"מ א] ואלו הם חמשת המינין. עיין מנחות ע. כוסמין מין חטין שבולת שועל ושיפון מין שעורים: שם ב] והוא צמח. צמח דהכא הוא ג"כ אילן עיין תוי"ע ד"ס האוג: מ"ו בר"ש ג] ברשות נכרי. צריך להיות ישראל: שם ד] שאתה לוקח מן הנכרי. עיין תוס' בכורות:

הגהות הגאון בצלאל רנשבורג

[א] משנה ו בר"ש וכן הפקירה קודם מירוח פטור. נ"ב עיין שער המלך פ"ח מהל' לולב הל' ב' ד"ס ושל דמאי וכו':

א אלו מפסיקין לפאה· בפ' הכונס(סא.)ובפ' חזקת הבתים (נ"ה.) משמע דאם הפריש פאה משדה לחברתה לא קידשה כדאי' בירושל' ואין לה תורת פאה להפטר מן המעשר ובת"כ בפ' קדושים נפקא לן מדכתיב שדך לחייב על כל שדה ושדה מכאן אמרו אלו מפסיקין לפאה: הנחל· מלשון נחלי מים ולא יתכן לומר מל' נחל איתן דהיינו בור (א) ואע"ג דתנא נחל תנא שלולית דאמרי' בפ' הכונס (שם) אמת המים שמחלקת שלל לאגפיה וזו אף זו קתני הנחל היינו נהר : דרך היחיד. ד' אמות : דרך הרבים ט"ז אמה. כך מפרש בשילהי המוכר פירות (דף לט:) : שביל. זוטר טובא (ב) כדאשכחן בשילהי המוכר פירות (ק') כי היכי דשקיל כרעא ומנח כרעא: ירושלמי (הל' א') מכיון דתנינן דרך היחיד דרך הרבים מאי צריכא אתא למימר לך אפי' דרך הרבים אין מפסיק לאילנות אלא גדר מכיון דתנינן שביל היחיד שביל הרבים מה צריכא להוציא את הקבוע בימות החמה ואינו קבוע בימות הגשמים פי' אינו מפסיק לאילן בסיפא דמתני' תנן דכל הני אין מפסיקין לאילן להוציא את הקבוע בימות החמה דרגל בני אדם מצויין בהן לאחר שנקצרו התבואות ובימות הגשמים שהשדות זרועים אינם מצויין ואשמעינן דאפי' שביל רבים אינו מפסיק אא"כ קבוע והשתא כולהו צריכי דמאי אמרת ליתני דרך הרבים למימר דאפי' לאילן אינו מפסיק ושביל היחיד דאפי' לזרעים מפסיק ולישתוק מכולהו אחריני א"כ הוה אמינא א]דרך הרבים דלא קביע גרע משביל היחיד דקביע ושביל הרבים דקביע עדיף להפסיק לאילן מדרך הרבים דלא קביע והאי טעמא הוה מצי למימר בירושלמי : הבור. שדה בור שאינה זרועה כדכתיב (בראשית מז) והאדמה לא תשם תרגום וארעא לא תבור : הניר. חרישה כדכתיב (ירמיה ד) נירו לכם ניר: ירושלמי (הל' א') רב אמר בור וניר בית רובע וזרע אחר אפי' כ"ש רבי יוחנן אמר בור וניר וזרע אחר כשלשה תלמים של פתיח (ג) : והקוצר לשחת מפסיק. קא סבר דכל לשחת לאו קצירה היא דלא חשיבא לה אתחלתא דקצירה ובפרק רבי ישמעאל במנחות (דף עא:) מפרש אי איירי בשהביאה שליש או בשלא הביאה שליש : ב אמת המים. היינו שלולית דקאמר ת"ק דבכל ענין מפסיק ואתא ר' יהודה למימר דוקא באינה יכולה ליקצר כאחת שאם עומד באמצע אינו יכול לקצור מכאן ומכאן כדמשמע בתוספתא ומיהו בתוספתא משמע דתרי מילי נינהו דקא חשיב לשחת ושלשה תלמים של פתיח ואמת המים שאינה אומר אם עומד באמצע וקוצר מכאן ומכאן מפסיק מפסיק אע"פ שעומד מצד אחד וקוצר מצד השני: ... ההר ובקעה נחשבים כשדה אחת כיון דנעדרים ... זקוף ואין בקר וכליו יכולים לעלות:ג הכל מפסיק לאתויי הא דאמר ריש לקיש בירושל' (הל' ב')היה שם סלע על פני כל שדהו אם עוקר הוא את המחרישה מצד זה ונותנה מצד זה מפסיק ...

פרק שני

אלו [א] מפסיקין לפאה [א]הנחל [א] ושלולי' דרך [ב]היחיד ודרך הרבים ושביל הרבים ושביל היחיד הקבוע בימות החמה ובימות הגשמים [ג]הבור והניר וזרע אחר והקוצר לשחת מפסיק דברי ר"מ וחכ"א אינו מפסיק [ד]אלא א"כ חרש : **ב** [ה]אמת המים שאינה יכולה להקצר כאחת רבי יהודה אומר מפסקת וכל [ו]ההרים אשר במעדר יעדרון אע"פ שאין הבקר יכול לעבור בכליו הוא נותן פאה לכל : **ג** הכל מפסיק לזרעים [ז]ואינו מפסיק לאילן אלא גדר ואם היה שער כותש אינו מפסיק אלא נותן פאה לכל : **ד** [ח]ולחרובין כל הרואין זא"ז אמר ר"ג נוהגין היו בית אבא שהיו נותנין פאה אחת לזיתים [ט]שהיו להם בכל רוח ולחרובין כל הרואין זא"ז ר"א ברבי צדוק אומר משמו אף לחרובין שהיו להן בכל העיר : **ה** [י]הזורע את שדהו מין אחד אע"פ שהוא עושהו שתי גרנות נותן פאה אחת זרעה שני מינין אע"פ שעשאן גורן אחת נותן שתי פאות [כ]הזורע את שדהו שני מיני חטים עשאן גורן אחת נותן פאה אחת שתי גרנות נותן שתי פאות : **ו** מעשה שזרע ר' שמעון איש המצפה *לפני רבן גמליאל ועלו ללשכת הגזית ושאלו [ג] אמר נחום הלבלר מקובל אני מרבי מיאשה שקבל *מאבא שקבל מן הזוגות שקבלו מן הנביאים הלכה למשה מסיני בזורע שדהו שני מיני חטים אם עשאן גורן אחת נותן פאה אחת שתי גרנות נותן שתי פאות : **ז** [ל]שדה שקצרוה נכרים לסטים קרסמוה נמלים ...

א אלו מפסיקין לפאה · לחלק השדה ולעשותה שתי שדות ויתחייב להניח פאה בכל אחת מהם כפי מה שנתחייב כמו שאמר הכתוב פאת שדך (ויקרא יט) ואמרו ובלבד שלא יוציא משדה לחברתה : ושלולית · היא תעלה או גולת מים שנמשכים ממנה אמת המים להשקות בהם מקומות אחרים וכן אמרו(ב"ק דף ס"א·) בפירוש זאת המלה אמת המים המחלקת שלל לחברותיה:ודרך היחיד·ד' אמות ודרך הרבים ט"ז אמה : ושביל הרבים ושביל היחיד. הוא שיהיה דרך בין שתי השדות אם לאיש אחד שעובר משם לגנו או לשדהו או שיהיה השביל לרבים אפילו שיהיה אותו השביל צר מאד ובלבד שתהיה הדרך ההיא סלולה ותמידה בימי החום ובימי הקור אבל אם לא היתה תמידה רק תהיה נפסקת בימות הגשמים לא הפריש בין ב' השדות אלא אם תהיה רחבה כפי המדה אשר זכרנו ר"ל ארבע אמות ליחיד וט"ז אמה לרבים והודיענו דרך היחיד ודרך הרבים לפי שילמדנו שניהם עכ"פ שאלו היה אומר ...

א) ב"ק פ"ו סא. ב"ב פ"ג נה. מנחות פ"ו עא: תורת כהנים פ' קדושים: ב) נזיר פרק ו ט:

פירוש ר"י בן מלכי צדק

CHAPTER II

MISHNAH 1. THE FOLLOWING SERVE AS DIVIDING-LINES
a FOR PE'AH:[1] A STREAM, A POOL,[2] A PRIVATE ROAD,[3] A PUBLIC ROAD,[4] A PUBLIC PATH,[5] OR A PRIVATE PATH IN CONSTANT USE IN SUMMER AND THE RAINY SEASON, FALLOW LAND, NEWLY-CULTIVATED LAND AND A DIFFERENT SEED.[6] IF ONE CUT [YOUNG CORN] FOR FODDER, [THE PLOT SO REAPED] SERVES AS A DIVIDING-LINE.[7] THUS R. MEIR. BUT THE SAGES SAY: IT DOES NOT SERVE AS A BOUND FOR PE'AH UNLESS [THIS PLOT USED FOR FODDER] IS RE-PLOUGHED.[8]

MISHNAH 2. IF A WATER CHANNEL MAKES THE CUTTING OF THE CORN [ON EITHER SIDE] IMPOSSIBLE [FROM ITS MIDST],[9] R. JUDAH SAYS: IT SERVES AS A DIVISION.[10] ANY HILL-TOP THAT CAN BE DUG WITH A HOE,[11] ALTHOUGH THE HERD[12] CANNOT PASS OVER IT IN THEIR OUTFIT,[13] [IS REGARDED AS PART OF THE FIELD] FROM WHICH ONLY ONE PE'AH IS
b GRANTED.[1]

MISHNAH 3. ALL [THESE ABOVE ENUMERATED] SERVE AS DIVISIONS IN THE CASE OF SOWN CROPS,[2] BUT IN THE CASE OF TREES NOTHING SAVE A FENCE SERVES AS A DIVISION.[3] SHOULD THE BRANCHES INTERTWINE,[4] THEN [EVEN A FENCE] DOES NOT DIVIDE AND ONE PE'AH IS GRANTED FOR THE WHOLE FIELD.

MISHNAH 4. AS FOR CAROB TREES, THE GENERAL PRINCIPLE IS THAT THEY MUST BE IN SIGHT OF ONE ANOTHER.[5] RABBAN GAMALIEL SAID: THE CUSTOM PREVAILING IN THE HOUSE OF MY FATHER WAS TO GIVE SEPARATE PE'AH FROM THE OLIVE TREES IN EACH DIRECTION[6] AND [ONE PE'AH] FOR ALL THE CAROB TREES WITHIN SIGHT OF EACH OTHER. R. ELEAZAR SON OF R. ZADOK SAID IN HIS NAME, THAT ALSO FOR THE CAROB TREES THEY HAD IN THE WHOLE CITY[7] [ONE PE'AH ONLY WAS GIVEN].

MISHNAH 5. HE WHO SOWS HIS FIELD WITH ONE KIND OF SEED, THOUGH HE MAKES UP OF IT TWO THRESHING-FLOORS, NEED GIVE ONLY ONE PE'AH [FOR THE LOT]. IF HE SOWS IT OF TWO KINDS, THEN EVEN, IF ONLY HE MAKES UP OF IT ONE THRESHING-FLOOR, HE MUST GIVE TWO PE'AHS.[8] HE WHO
c SOWS HIS FIELD WITH TWO SPECIES OF WHEAT[1] AND HE MAKES UP OF IT ONE THRESHING-FLOOR, HE GIVES ONLY ONE PE'AH; BUT IF TWO THRESHING-FLOORS, HE GIVES TWO PE'AHS.

MISHNAH 6. THE STORY IS TOLD OF R. SIMEON OF MIẒPAH[2] THAT HE SOWED ONCE HIS FIELD [WITH TWO DIFFERENT KINDS] AND CAME BEFORE RABBAN GAMALIEL. THEY BOTH WENT UP TO THE CHAMBER OF HEWN STONE[3] AND ENQUIRED [THE LAW]. NAHUM THE SCRIBE[4] SAID: I HAVE A TRADITION FROM R. ME'ASHA,[5] WHO RECEIVED IT FROM ABBA,[6] WHO RECEIVED IT FROM THE ZUGOTH,[7] WHO RECEIVED IT FROM THE PROPHETS AS AN HALACHAH OF MOSES FROM SINAI,[8] THAT A MAN WHO SOWS HIS FIELD WITH TWO KINDS OF WHEAT AND MAKES IT UP INTO ONE THRESHING-FLOOR MUST GIVE ONE PE'AH, IF TWO THRESHING-FLOORS, [HE GIVES] TWO PE'AHS.[9]

MISHNAH 7. A FIELD REAPED BY GENTILES,[10] OR ROBBERS, OR WHICH ANTS HAVE BITTEN [THE GRAINS THEREOF

a (1) From a field divided by these into sections, *Pe'ah* is given separately from each. (2) A 'wady', smaller than a stream. (3) Only four cubits in breadth. (4) Sixteen cubits. (5) Much smaller than a road. If used constantly, it is a division. (6) E.g. a plot growing spelt 'twixt two growing wheat. The length of the last three divisions mentioned must be three turns of the plough at least. (7) Corn not quite a third of its full growth used to serve as fodder for cattle; hence is not to be regarded as crop from which *Pe'ah* is due. V. *supra* I, 4. (8) The Sages hold that the cutting of fodder is to be regarded as the beginning of the reaping and consequently one *Pe'ah* for the whole field is to be given. Only when the plot cut for fodder is broken afresh does it indicate its separateness from the rest of the field. (9) The reaper, standing in mid-stream, is unable to reap the field on either side. (10) R. Judah opposes the view of the preceding Mishnah where a שלולית (the same as אמת המים) is held always to serve as a division, regardless of the stipulation here given. (11) Isa. VII, 25. The criterion is the hoeing; the fact that its height precludes the oxen from passing over it does not serve as a division. (12) Var. lec.: הבקר 'the herdsman'. (13) Pack-saddle and cushions.
b (1) It will not be regarded on this account as fallow ground which serves as a division. People will interpret this inability of the oxen or herdsmen to pass over it as a disinclination on their part to dig to-day. (2) Should even a rock interrupt the even tenure of the plough across the field, it is regarded as a division (*J.*). (3) The fence must be at least ten handbreadths in height. Not all trees come under this category, for the following Mishnah prescribes a different rule for the carob and olive trees. *Pe'ah* was given also from trees. (4) שער 'hair'; here, the ramifications of a tree; כותש from כתש 'to crush'; here, 'to twine'. This intertwining renders the fence no division as to *Pe'ah*. (5) Not even a fence divides as long as, standing near one tree, the other can be seen. (6) East, west, north and south. (7) Even when not in sight of one another. (8) The point stressed is that *Pe'ah* is given from every kind and not according to quantity.
c (1) Even of the same kind but of two different colours, like dark and white. Wheat is in a different category from seed, for here quantity rather than different species decides. (2) With the def. article: Josh. XV, 38 (in Judah); XVIII, 26 (in Benjamin); II Kings XXV, 23. In Hos. V, 1 Mizpah appears without the def. article. (3) V. Mid. V, 4; Sanh. XI, 2. One of the five chambers in the Temple Court, north of the Court of the Israelites. Named גזית either because of its hewn stone, or because it was 'cut off' (separate) from the other chambers, or on account of it being the seat of the Sanhedrin. (4) לבלר from the Latin '*libellarius*'. (5) The only reference to this Palestinian Tanna who lived in the time of Hillel's descendants. (6) Or '(his) father'. As a praenomen the reference here is probably to Abba, a contemporary of R. Joḥanan b. Zakkai (v. *J.E.* I, s.v.). (7) For a century and a half—from the time of Jose b. Joezer (c. 160 B.C.E.) to the time of Hillel and Shammai, there were two chiefs of the Sanhedrin, a President (נשיא) and a Vice-President (אב ב״ד). V. Aboth I, 4—10; Ḥag. II, 2. (8) A formula denoting an ancient established tradition not derived from the Written Law. (9) This tradition makes quantity the decisive factor in the giving of *Pe'ah* and contradicts the view of the preceding Mishnah which made the different species of wheat the criterion. (10) Some versions instead of 'gentiles' read 'Cutheans', a sect of Samaritans. This is due to censorial influence. The Mishnah refers to non-Jews who reaped their own field; for had they been in the employ of Jews, *Pe'ah* would have been due.

AT THE ROOTS], OR WHICH WIND AND CATTLE HAVE BROKEN
a DOWN, IS EXEMPT FROM PE'AH.[1] IF [THE OWNER] REAPED HALF THEREOF AND ROBBERS THE REMAINING HALF, IT IS EXEMPT FROM PE'AH; FOR THE OBLIGATION OF PE'AH IS IN THE STANDING CORN.[2]

MISHNAH 8. IF ROBBERS REAPED HALF AND THE OWNER THE OTHER HALF, HE GIVES PE'AH FROM WHAT HE HAS REAPED. IF HE REAPED HALF AND SOLD THE OTHER HALF, THEN THE PURCHASER MUST GIVE PE'AH FOR THE WHOLE.[3] IF HE REAPED HALF AND DEDICATED THE OTHER HALF, THEN HE WHO REDEEMS IT FROM THE TREASURER MUST GIVE PE'AH FOR THE WHOLE.[4]

CHAPTER III

b MISHNAH 1. IN THE CASE OF PLOTS OF CORN[1] BETWEEN OLIVE TREES, BETH SHAMMAI SAY ONE MUST GIVE PE'AH FROM EACH PLOT;[2] BUT BETH HILLEL MAINTAIN THAT FOR ALL [THE PLOTS] ONE PE'AH IS GIVEN. BETH SHAMMAI AGREE, HOWEVER, THAT IF THE ENDS OF THE ROWS BORDER ON ONE ANOTHER, ONE PE'AH IS GRANTED FROM ONE PLOT FOR THE WHOLE.[3]

MISHNAH 2. IF ONE GIVES A STRIPED APPEARANCE[4] TO HIS FIELD AND LEAVES BEHIND SOME MOIST STALKS,[5] R. AKIBA SAID, HE GIVES PE'AH FROM EVERY PATCH.[6] BUT THE SAGES SAY: FROM ONE PATCH ONLY FOR ALL. THE SAGES, HOWEVER, AGREE WITH R. AKIBA THAT ONE WHO SOWS DILL[7] OR MUSTARD SEED IN THREE PLACES MUST GIVE PE'AH FROM EACH PLACE.[8]

c MISHNAH 3. HE WHO PLUCKS[1] FRESH ONIONS FOR THE MARKET AND LEAVES THE DRY ONES [IN THE GROUND] FOR LATER STORAGE, MUST GIVE PE'AH FROM EACH SEPARATELY.[2] THE SAME APPLIES TO BEANS[3] AND TO A VINEYARD. IF HE, HOWEVER, ONLY THINS THEM OUT,[4] THEN HE GIVES [PE'AH] FROM THE REMAINDER ACCORDING TO THE QUANTITY OF THAT WHICH HE LEFT. HE THAT PLUCKS UP FROM ONE PLACE,[5] GIVES FROM THE REMAINDER FOR THE WHOLE.

MISHNAH 4. SEED ONIONS[6] ARE LIABLE TO PE'AH, BUT R. JOSE EXEMPTS THEM.[7] IN THE CASE OF PLOTS OF ONIONS [GROWING] BETWEEN VEGETABLES, R. JOSE SAYS: PE'AH MUST BE GIVEN FROM EACH [PLOT],[8] BUT THE SAGES SAY: FROM ONE [PLOT] FOR ALL.

MISHNAH 5. [TWO] BROTHERS WHO HAVE DIVIDED [AN INHERITANCE] MUST GIVE [TWO] PE'AHS.[9] IF THEY AFTERWARDS AGAIN BECOME PARTNERS [IN THE WHOLE POSSESSION], THEY NEED ONLY GIVE ONE PE'AH.[10] TWO WHO PURCHASE A TREE[11] GIVE ONE PE'AH. IF ONE BUYS THE NORTHERN SECTION THEREOF AND THE OTHER ITS SOUTHERN PART, EACH MUST GIVE PE'AH SEPARATELY. HE WHO SELLS THE
d TREE-STALKS IN HIS FIELD[1] MUST GIVE PE'AH FROM EACH STALK. R. JUDAH SAID: THIS IS ONLY WHEN THE OWNER OF THE FIELD LEFT NOTHING [FOR HIMSELF],[2] BUT IF HE DID LEAVE AUGHT FOR HIMSELF, HE GIVES ONE PE'AH FOR THE WHOLE.[3]

a (1) Even if the produce reaped had been returned (v. *supra* I, 6). The principle to bear in mind is that ובקצרכם (Lev. XXIII, 22) excludes *Pe'ah* from any reaping not done *by* or *for* the owner. (2) Since the Law of *Pe'ah* comes into force with the cutting of the standing corn, it does not apply when reaped by someone other than the owner. (3) For the *Pe'ah* due from the first reaping is included in that part of the field subsequently bought by the purchaser. (4) Likewise the dedication cannot declare 'holy' the *Pe'ah* already due from the moment of the first reaping; accordingly the redeemer must return to the poor their due. In *supra* I, 6 the 'dedication' took place before *Pe'ah* was due, i.e., prior to any reaping whatsoever.

b (1) Garden beds ploughed and sown with seed between the trees and arranged in square shapes in the form of bricks. Olive trees are specifically mentioned to teach that though liable to *Pe'ah* (II, 4) they do not, according to Beth Hillel, act as divisions between the grain plots. Others take מלבנות to refer to the light (white) colour of the grain. (2) Since the corn of each row does not touch that of the other, each plot acts as a separate unit for *Pe'ah*. (3) Since the entire field is then regarded as one, regardless of the intervening plots. (Cf. *supra* II, 4 in reference to the carob trees whose branches intertwined.) (4) Each patch is reaped separately as soon as its corn is ready for cutting, a process the effect of which is to give a speckled appearance to the field. The more manured parts would, of course, ripen first. (5) Those still unripe and not ready for cutting. (6) When he later proceeds to cut the remaining stalks; for each patch must be regarded as a distinct unit. (7) Dill is an 'umbelliferous, annual, yellow-flowered herb' (*Concise Oxford Dictionary*). (8) Each patch is rendered a separate unit for *Pe'ah*, since the normal practice is not to have more than one plot of these in one field. Dill and mustard seed are subject to *Pe'ah*, though the general rule is to exempt vegetables (v. *supra* I, 4), since they are kept for seed.

c (1) מחליק, the act of removing at least three trees growing side by side. Another explanation is to divide the field's products into portions, some for storing and others for the market. (2) Different objects in view convert the onions, as it were, into two kinds. *Supra* II, 5. (3) Cf. Kel. III, 2. (4) מדל is explained as the act of removing one or two olive tree seeds to allow the others crowded together more 'breathing-space'. Those seeds removed to make room for the others are not subject to *Pe'ah*, since their removal cannot be regarded as the beginning of reaping. (5) יד, 'place'. Maim. explains it to mean that he reserved special parts of the field respectively for storage purposes and for the market. The Bertinoro explains מאחת יד, 'If he uprooted some of the onions for the same purpose for which he leaves the rest (i.e., either for storage or for sale)'. (6) Lit., 'the roots of onions'. (7) Onions left in the ground too long become unfit to eat and therefore not subject to *Pe'ah*. (8) Since this is not the usual practice, each plot must be regarded as a different unit, cf. *supra* II, 5. (9) Each from his own portion. (10) Since each has a right in the whole field, the number of owners makes no difference. (11) Of those trees mentioned in I, 5.

d (1) Stalks or tree-trunks from which *Pe'ah* is due. Cf. Kil. I, 8. Since he does not sell with the stalks the soil on which they grow, there is no connecting link to make them all of one 'kind'. (2) Also provided that the owner did not begin to reap the field prior to selling it, for in that case his would have been the duty of giving one *Pe'ah* for the whole (cf. II, 8). (3) R. Judah elucidates the opinion of the first authority quoted anonymously in the Mishnah, without in any way differing from him.

שברתה הרוח או בהמה פטורה [א]קצר חציה וקצרו לסטים חציה פטורה [ה]שחובת הפא׳ בקמה:
ח [ב]קצרוה לסטים חציה וקצר הוא חציה נותן פאה*ממה שקצר קצר חציה ומכר חציה[ו]הלוקח נותן פאה לכל קצר חציה והקדיש חציה הפודה מיד הגזבר הוא נותן פאה לכל:

פרק שלישי

א מלבנות [ג]התבואה שבין הזיתים בש״א פאה מכל א׳ וא׳ וב״ה אומרים מאחת על הכל ומודים שאם היו ראשי שורות מעורבים שהוא נותן פאה מאחת על הכל:

ב [ה]המנמר את שדהו ושייר קלחים לחים ר״ע אומר נותן פאה מכל א׳ וא׳ וחכ״א [ד]מא׳ על הכל [ג] [ה]ומודים חכמים לר״ע בזורע שבת או חרדל *בשלשה מקומות שהוא נותן פאה לכל א׳ וא׳:

ג [ו]המחליק בצלים לחים לשוק ומקיים יבשים לגורן נותן פאה לאלו לעצמן ולאלו לעצמן וכן באפונין וכן בכרם [ז]המדל נותן מן המשואר על מה ששייר המחליק מאחת יד נותן מן המשואר על הכל:

ד [ח]האמהות של בצלים חייבות בפאה ור׳ יוסי פוטר [ג] מלבנות הבצלים שבין הירק רבי יוסי אומר פאה מכל אחת ואחת וחכ״א [ט]מאחת על הכל:

ה [י]האחין שחלקו נותנין שתי פאות חזרו ונשתתפו נותנין פאה אחת [כ]שנים שלקחו את האילן נותנין פאה אחת לקח זה צפונו וזה דרומו [ד] זה נותן פאה לעצמו וזה נותן פאה לעצמו [ד] [ל]המוכר [ה] קלחי אילן בתוך שדהו נותן פאה מכל א׳ וא׳ אמר ר׳ יהודה אימתי בזמן שלא שייר בעל השדה אבל אם שייר בעל השדה הוא נותן פאה לכל:

לוקח חייב [א]:ך בית רובע · מפרש בתוספתא א] דכלאים (פ"ב) י' אמות על י' אמות ומחצה ואינו מכוון ממש לפי חשבון סאתים בחצר המשכן דהוי ק' על נ' (ו):העושה סאתים · רבי יהושע לא אזיל בתר זריעה אלא קרקע המוציא סאתים : כדי לקצור ולשנות · דרך הקוצרים אוחז מלא כפו מן הקמה וקוצר בידו השניה ואם יש בקמה כדי למלאות את כפו ב' פעמים חייב בפאה: ירושלמי (הל' ו'). מ"ט דר"א נאמר כאן שדך ונאמר בכלאים שדך מה שדך האמור להלן בית רובע אף כאן בית רובע מ"ט דר"י נאמר כאן שדך ונאמר להלן ושכחת עומר בשדה מה שדה שנאמר להלן סאתים אף כאן סאתים מ"ט דר"ט ו' על ו' מערוגה ריב"ב אומר כדי לקצור ולשנות מה קצירה כדרך הקוצרין או ... כל שהוא מן מה דכתיב שלא מלא כפו ... הדא אמרת קצירה כדרך הקוצרין פי' ... מר להלן רובע (דתניא) [דתנן] פ"ב ... אים(מ"י) ובתבואה ג] בית רובע ותנן(שם ...) כל סאה שיש בה רובע ממין אחר ימעט : ... תים כדתנן (לקמן פ"ו מ"ו) עומר שיש בו ... תים ושכחו אינו שכחה. ור"ט יליף מערוגה ... תנן(כלאים פ"ג מ"א)ערוגה שהיא ו' על ו' ... ין לתוכה ה' זרעונין :מה קצירה בעיא היא ... פשים כדרך הקוצרים: קרקע כ"ש חייבת ... ה· דסדך כל דהו משמע ול"ל גזירה שוה ... ך:ירושלמי (הל' ז')·נגע עצמך שהיה ... שבולת אחת עד שלא קצר אין כאן היוב ... קצר אין כאן שיור ר"ח בשם ר' פנחס ... תר שהיה שם שבולת אח' [כ"א קלח] וכו ... שבולים : ובבכורים· כתב בהו אדמתך ... לוהי פ' לא יחפור (כז:) מוקי לה בחמה ... אילן בעי י"ו אמה סביב ואע"ג דמטה ... יניקתה ג' טפחים מדמרחקינן הזרעים ... הכותל ג' טפחים כדתנן ב"ב (דף יז) ... מוכחא היא דערוגה ו' על ו' (כלאים ... מ"א) הא נמי כל שהוא קרינא לה אבל לפירוש זה ...

ך ר"א אומר קרקע בית רובע חייבת בפאה רבי יהושע אומר העושה סאתים ר"ט אומר ששה על ששה טפחים ר' יהודה בן בתירא אומר כדי לקצור ולשנות והלכה כדבריו א) ר"ע אומר קרקע כל שהוא חייבת בפאה ובבכורים ולכתוב עליו פרוזבול ב) ולקנות עמו נכסים שאין להם אחריות בכסף ובשטר ובחזקה:ך ג) הכותב נכסיו שכיב מרע שייר קרקע כל שהוא מתנתו מתנה לא שייר קרקע כל שהוא אין מתנתו מתנה הכותב נכסיו לבניו (יד) וכתב לאשתו קרקע כל שהוא אבדה כתובתה ד) ר' יוסי אומר אם קבלה עליה אף על פי שלא כתב לה איבדה כתובתה:ח ה) הכותב ג] נכסיו לעבדו יצא בן חורין שייר קרקע כל שהוא לא יצא בן חורין ר' שמעון אומר לעולם הוא בן חורין עד שיאמר הרי כל נכסי נתונין לאיש פלוני עבדי חוץ מאחד מריבוא שבהן :

ך בית רובע. מקום שיזרע בו רובע קב ועוד נבאר אלו המדות והסאין בסוף מסכת זו (פ"ח מ"ה):ולקצור ולשנות. הוא שיקצור מן השבולים כפי שתי אגודות שלא יכול לקבץ אותם בידו באגודה אחת: ובבכורים. רוצה לומר הבאת בכורים ועוד יתבאר לך בסוף זה הסדר שהבכורים לא יתחייב להביאם אלא מי שיש לו שדה: ופרוזבול. שטר שלא יכתבוהו אלא על הקרקעות ועוד נבאר ענין זה השטר במס' שביעית מן הסדר הזה ומן העקרים שיש בידינו שכל הנכסים חוץ מן הקרקע כגון מיני סחורות וזהב וכסף ואבנים יקרות נקראים שאין להם אחריות ופירוש שאין להם אחריות שאין להם חזרת תביעה וזה שכל מי שיש עליו חוב ומכר סחורות שהיו. אללו אחר שלקח החוב ואחר כך טען שאין לו מה שיפרע אין לבעל חוב לחזור באחריות על הקונה הסחורות ושיוציאם מיד הקונה אבל אם ימכור מי שיש לו עליו החוב קרקע אחר שלקח החוב טען שאין לו מה שיפרע יחזור בעל חוב על קונה הקרקע ויוציאנו מידו ובשביל זה נקרא קרקע נכסים שיש להם אחריות ומן העקרים שיש בידינו גם כן שהנכסים שאין להם אחריות והם הנקראים מטלטלין אין נקנין בכסף ולא בשטר ...

MISHNAH 6. R. ELIEZER SAYS: A PIECE OF GROUND, ONE FOURTH OF A KAB[4] IN SIZE IS SUBJECT TO PE'AH. R. JOSHUA SAYS: IT MUST [BE LARGE ENOUGH] TO PRODUCE TWO SE'AHS.[5] R. TARFON MAINTAINS THAT IT MUST BE SIX HANDBREADTHS BY SIX.[6] R. JUDAH B. BATHYRA[7] SAYS: [IT MUST BE LARGE ENOUGH] FOR THE SICKLE TO CUT AT LEAST TWO HANDFULS.[8] THE HALACHAH IS ACCORDING TO HIS WORDS. R. AKIBA SAYS: EVEN THE TINIEST PLOT IS LIABLE TO PE'AH AND THE FIRST-FRUITS,[9] AND [IS SUFFICIENT] FOR THE WRITING OF THE PROZBUL,[10] AND ALSO
a TO ACQUIRE THROUGH IT MOVABLE PROPERTY[1] BY MONEY, BY DEED OF SALE, OR BY A CLAIM BASED ON UNDISTURBED POSSESSION.[2]

MISHNAH 7. IF A MAN ON THE POINT OF DYING[3] ASSIGNED HIS PROPERTY IN WRITING [TO ANOTHER], AND HE RETAINED ANY LAND, HOWEVER SMALL,[4] HE RENDERS HIS GIFT VALID; BUT IF HE RETAINS NO LAND WHATSOEVER, HIS GIFT IS NOT VALID.[5] HE WHO ASSIGNED IN WRITING HIS PROPERTY TO HIS CHILDREN, AND HE ASSIGNED TO HIS WIFE IN WRITING ANY PLOT OF LAND, HOWEVER SMALL, SHE THEREBY FORFEITS[6] HER KETHUBAH. R. JOSE SAYS: IF SHE ACCEPTED [SUCH AN ASSIGNMENT] EVEN THOUGH HE DID NOT ASSIGN IT TO HER IN WRITING, SHE FORFEITS HER KETHUBAH.[7]

MISHNAH 8. IF A MAN ASSIGNED IN WRITING HIS POSSESSIONS TO HIS SLAVE, HE THEREBY BECOMES A FREED-
b MAN.[1] IF HE, HOWEVER, RESERVED FOR HIMSELF ANY IMMOVABLE PROPERTY, HOWEVER SMALL, HE DOES NOT BECOME A FREEDMAN.[2] R. SIMEON SAYS: HE BECOMES A FREEDMAN UNDER ALL CONDITIONS,[3] UNLESS [THE MASTER] SAYS: 'BEHOLD, ALL MY GOODS ARE GIVEN TO SO-AND-SO MY SLAVE, WITH THE EXCEPTION OF ONE TEN-THOUSANDTH PART OF THEM.'[4]

(4) Approximately $10^1/_2 \times 10$ cubits (Bert.). (5) Twelve *kabs'* space or forty-eight times the size required by R. Eleazar; R. Joshua stresses the produce rather than size of soil. (6) One handbreadth equals four fingerbreadths (*circa.* $9^1/_3$ centimetres). R. Tarfon measures by distance instead of by dry measure. His measure equals one cubit or six handbreadths. (7) A Tanna of the First Generation (c. 10–80 C.E.). (8) Lit., 'to cut and repeat'. Reapers usually cut a handful at a time, cf. Ps. CXXIX, 7. If there is sufficient for two cuttings, the law of *Pe'ah* is binding. (9) Ex. XXIII, 19. The word ארמתך is there mentioned and refers to wheat and barley. The stipulation regarding first-fruits, that there should be sixteen cubits soil round the tree—the space required for its proper nurture, applies only to fruits of the tree (Bert.). (10) Explained as an abbreviation of πρὸς βουλῇ (before the council). A declaration made in court by the creditor to the effect that the operation of the law of the Sabbatical year (Deut. XV, 2) shall not apply to the loan transacted. V. Sheb. X, 3 and Giṭ. (Sonc. ed.) 36a n. b 4. The *'Prozbul'* could only be drawn up when the debtor possessed immovable property. Of this, even the smallest amount sufficed in regarding the debt as mortgaged in a Court of Law, the principle being that the law of defrauding does not apply to immovable property, v. Sheb. X, 6.

a (1) Lit., 'property that has no security'. Movable goods cannot be resorted to by the creditor in the case of non-payment. (2) Usucaption. The legally fixed period is three years and with it there must be a plea of purchase or any other mode of legal acquisition, v. B.B. 28a. Movable property is generally acquired by the purchaser 'drawing' it to himself (*Meshikah*, v. Glos.). But the tiniest piece of immovable property acquired by means of money, writ, or usucaption effects title to any movable property brought together along with it. (3) Lit., 'one that lies sick'. (4) Thus indicating that the assignment was not prompted by thoughts of death, with the result that he cannot retract from the gift on his recovery. Bertinoro calls attention to the fact that קרקע (land, immovable property) mentioned in this and the following Mishnah, does not refer specifically to immovable property; for even the minimum amount of movable goods is included in this term. The word קרקע is used here since it is the *sine qua non* of *Pe'ah*, *Bikkurim* and *Prozbul* mentioned in the Mishnah preceding. (5) Had he not anticipated death, he would not have left himself penniless; his recovery, therefore, revokes the validity of his gift. (6) The implication is that she prefers to be regarded among the heirs of her husband rather than demand her rights under her marriage settlement, the *kethubah* (v. Glos.). (7) She cannot afterwards retract and claim it.

b (1) Since the slave is part of the master's possessions, he becomes owner of himself, too. A more correct reading, which not all versions have, is 'all his possessions'. (2) Perhaps the slave is included in the part reserved for himself; if so, then the entire gift is nullified, since a slave has no legal right of possession. It is only when the master explicitly says: 'I give thee thyself and my property', that the slave becomes free, even if the owner still reserves aught for himself. (3) Whether the master possessed naught else beside the slave and the portion reserved for himself, in which case the assignment of his possessions must refer to the slave; or whether he had other goods besides the portion reserved for himself, the slave becomes free. R. Simeon wishes to stress that the modification made in the assignment afterwards by no means invalidates the emancipation of the slave. (4) Since this fraction is not specified, it may easily refer to the slave, though he be worth ever so much more.

CHAPTER IV

MISHNAH 1. PE'AH IS GIVEN FROM [THE CROP] STILL
a DIRECTLY CONNECTED WITH THE SOIL,[1] BUT IN THE CASE OF HANGING VINE-BRANCHES[2] AND THE DATE-PALM, THE OWNER BRINGS DOWN [THE FRUIT] AND DISTRIBUTES IT AMONG THE POOR.[3] R. SIMEON SAYS: THE SAME APPLIES TO SMOOTH NUT TREES.[4] EVEN IF NINETY-NINE [OF THE POOR][5] URGE DISTRIBUTION [BY THE OWNER] AND ONE ONLY IS [IN FAVOUR] OF INDIVIDUAL SNATCHING, THIS LATTER IS LISTENED TO,[6] SINCE HE SPOKE IN ACCORDANCE WITH THE HALACHAH.

MISHNAH 2. BUT IT IS OTHERWISE WITH HANGING VINE-BRANCHES AND PALM TREES;[7] FOR EVEN IF NINETY-NINE URGE INDIVIDUAL SNATCHING AND ONE POOR MAN PRESSES FOR DISTRIBUTION,[8] THE LATTER IS LISTENED TO, SINCE HE SPOKE ACCORDING TO THE HALACHAH.

MISHNAH 3. IF [A POOR MAN] TOOK SOME OF THE PE'AH [ALREADY COLLECTED] AND CAST IT OVER THE REMAINDER
b [NOT YET COLLECTED],[1] HE THEREBY FORFEITS THE WHOLE.[2] IF HE FELL DOWN UPON IT,[3] OR SPREAD HIS CLOAK OVER IT,[4] IT IS TAKEN AWAY FROM HIM.[5] THE SAME APPLIES TO GLEANINGS,[6] AND THE FORGOTTEN SHEAF.[7]

MISHNAH 4. [THE POOR] MAY NOT REAP PE'AH WITH SCYTHES OR TEAR IT UP WITH SPADES, SO THAT THEY MIGHT NOT STRIKE AT ONE ANOTHER [WITH THESE IMPLEMENTS].[8]

MISHNAH 5. THRICE A DAY [THE POOR] MAKE A SEARCH:[9] MORNING,[10] NOON,[11] AND SUNSET.[12] RABBAN GAMALIEL SAYS, THESE [TIMES] WERE SET LEST THE POOR SEARCH LESS
c OFTEN.[1] ACCORDING TO R. AKIBA: THESE WERE SET LEST

a (1) The Law: '*Thou shalt leave it to the poor and the stranger*' (Lev. XIX, 10) implies that the *Pe'ah* must be left to the poor to seize for themselves while it is still joined to the ground. (2) Branches of the vine twined to an espalier. (3) Every caution must be taken to obviate any risk to the poor during their gathering. 'Distribution' is stressed, because the owner is precluded from giving the *Pe'ah* to a poor relative or to the first poor man who chances to pass by the field. (4) Smooth nut trees, being free from joints or protuberances are all the more difficult to climb. (5) This refers to the first clause of the Mishnah. (6) Though his claim might be weakened by the fact that he is stronger or more voracious than the other poor and likely to obtain more of the *Pe'ah*. (7) In whose case the *Pe'ah* is given after the fruit has been plucked by the owner, as stated in the preceding Mishnah. (8) Though he may be weakest of the poor and his claim construed as due to the fear lest he receive little *Pe'ah*, his view must be upheld.

b (1) Under the impression that he has in this wise gained possession of the rest; though legally, this act by no means effects a title, v. B.M. 10*b*. (2) Even the *Pe'ah* he had gathered; this is a punishment for his greed. (3) The law which enables a man to claim possession of things found within his four cubits, applies only to alleys adjoining open places or short cuts to public roads; not to fields owned by others. Moreover, by falling across the *Pe'ah*, his intention seems to have been to acquire possession by the act of falling and not by the law of ד״א אמות (B.M. 10aff.). (4) Either as an assertion of possession or to hide the *Pe'ah* from the view of the other poor. (5) From our text it would seem, that with the exception of the first instance, only the *Pe'ah* over which he fell or spread his cloak is taken away from him, but that he is allowed to retain that gathered in the ordinary way. According to Maim., however, it would seem that in all cases is the fine imposed on him by taking away even the *Pe'ah* he had already gathered. (So Tosaf. Y.T.). (6) V. *infra* 10. (7) V. *infra* V, 8. (8) So great might the throng of poor be, that in their eagerness to gather they might accidentally strike one another with their sickles and spades; or some quarrels might easily break out between them and these implements be improvised as weapons. (9) אבעיות, 'searchings'. Another rendering is 'appearings'. The translation, accordingly, would be: 'Thrice a day does the owner appear in his field to attract the poor to come'. The word has also been connected with הכבעה (B.K.I., 1) and the following translation effected: 'Thrice daily is the crop of *Pe'ah* removed from the field'. Cf. T.J. IV, 3. (10) To enable poor nursing mothers to come, whilst the children are still asleep. (11) So that young children, awake by now, assist their poor parents in the search. (12) To enable the old and the infirm, whose pace is of necessity slow, to obtain their share before the day passes.

c **(1) In order to afford an equal opportunity for all poor to come.**

◁ *For the continuation of the English translation of this page see overleaf.*

א ב במחובר לקרקע · דגבי קציר כתיב תעזוב דמשמע שיניח לפניהם תבואה בקשיה : דלית. גפן גדולה המודלה ע"ג עצים או על גבי אילנות אחרים : מוריד ומחלק · דהכי שיש סכנה בעלייתם מצות פאה בתלוש ובירושלמי דריש לה מקרא וכן בת"כ בפ' קדושים : חליקי אגוזים · אילן של אגוזים ופי' בערוך דקרי ליה חליקי לפי שהוא חלק שאין לו לא קשרים ולא ענפים : אפילו צ"ט · ארישא קאי דבמחובר ואם יש כאן ק' עניים וצ"ט מהם אומרים לבעל הבית שיקצור הכל ויחלק להם הפאה ויש אחד שאינו רוצה אין שומעין להם אלא ירצו ויבוזו ובדלית שמצותה בתלוש איפכא דשומעין ליחיד הרוצה ליחלק :

מסורת הש"ס

א) תורת כהנים פ' קדושים: ב) ב"מ פ"א דף י. ג) חלה פ"ג מ"ד: ד) גיטין פ"א יא: ב"מ דף ט:

פרק רביעי

א הפאה ניתנת במחובר לקרקע א) בדלית ובדקל בעה"ב מוריד ומחלק לעניים רבי שמעון אומר אף בחליקי אגוזים אפי' תשעים ותשעה אומרים לחלק ואחד אומר לבוז לזה שומעין שאמר כהלכה: **ב** בדלית ובדקל אינו כן אפילו תשעים ותשעה אומרים לבוז ואחד אומר לחלק לזה שומעין שאמר כהלכה: **ג** נטל ב) מקצת פאה וזרק על השאר אין לו בה כלום נפל לו עליה ופירש טליתו עליה מעבירין אותו הימנה וכן בלקט וכן בעומר השכחה: **ד** פאה אין קוצרין אותה במגלות (ב) ואין עוקרין אותה בקרדומות כדי שלא יכו איש את רעהו : **ה** שלש אבעיות ביום בשחר בחצות ובמנחה רבן גמליאל אומר לא אמרו אלא כדי שלא יפחתו ר"ע אומר לא אמרו אלא כדי שלא יוסיפו של בית נמר היו מלקטין על החבל ונותנים פאה מכל אומן ואומן : **ו** נכרי שקצר את שדהו ואחר כך נתגייר פטור מן הלקט ומן השכחה ומן הפאה ר' יהודה מחייב בשכחה שאין השכחה אלא בשעת העמור : **ז** הקדיש קמה ופדה קמה חייב עומרין ופדה עומרין חייב קמה ופדה עומרין פטורה שבשעת חובתה היתה פטורה: **ח** ג) כיוצא בו המקדיש פירותיו עד שלא באו לעונת המעשרות ופדאן חייבין משבאו לעונת המעשרות ופדאן חייבין הקדישן עד שלא נגמרו וגמרן הגזבר ואח"כ פדאן פטורין שבשעת חובתן היו פטורין : **ט** ד) מי שלקט את הפאה ואמר הרי זו * לאיש פלוני

ס"א לפלוני

א ב אמר הכתוב לא תכלה פאת שדך בקצרך (ויקרא כג) בא ללמדו שיניחם פאה מחוברת לקרקע וזה בקציר ומה שדומה לזה מן הדברים שאפשר לקטן ולגדול לקחתה: ודלית. הם לגפן כמו דליותיו (יחזקאל יז) : ובדקל התמר. וחליקי האגוזים אגוזי פרך והם מין אגוזים והוא מאד גבוה : ופירוש לבוז שיקח כל אחד מה שיוכל ואין הלכה כרבי שמעון : ג כשיקח מקלתו ויכסה מקלתו לוקחין מידו הכל בין מה שלקח ובא לידו ובין מה שכסה וזה קנס וכן אמרו קונסין אותו ומעבירין ממנו את הכל את התלוש ואת המחובר ועומר השכחה יתבאר אחר זה : ד מגלות. הם חרמשים וקרדומות הם ממיני הפטישים והדבר כולו מבואר : ה שלש אבעיות. שלש בקשות מלשון אם תבעיון בעיו (ישעיה כא) ואמרו נותנין הפאה בשחר בשביל המניקות שהם מוטרדות לאכול בבקר ובחצות בשביל הנערים הקטנים שהם ישנים בבקר ויתהלכו ללקוט עד חצות היום במנחה בשביל הזקנים שלא יגיעו לשדה* אלא עד אותה השעה: ובית נמר . שם מקום : וענין על החבל הוא על קו מישור מתחלת השדה עד סופה : מכל אומן ואומן · ר"ל מכל שורה ושורה שכן היו קוצרים שורה אחר שורה וכל שורה נקראת אומן ואין הלכה כרבן גמליאל ולא כר' עקיבא אלא בג' שעות אלו בלבד תנתן הפאה כדי שיהיו שעות ידועות להתקבץ בהם העניים : ו שכחה. הוא מה שאמר הכתוב (דברים כד) ושכחת עומר בשדה וזה יהיה כשמוליכין העומרים ממקום למקום כמו שיתבאר ודעת החכמים שכל זרע שלא נתחייב בחיובי קמה והם לקט ופאה לא יתחייב ג"כ בחובת העומר והיא השכחה ואין הלכה כר' יהודה : ז כשיקדיש קמה ופדה קמה נתחייב בפאה ובלקט . וכשיקדיש עומרים ופדה עומרים חייב בשכחה : ואם הקדיש קמה וקצר הגזבר ועשאם עומרין ואחר כן פדאם לא יתחייב בהם ואפי' בשכחה וזה דעת החכמים כפי מה שהקדמנו מן העקרים שיש אצלנו : ח עונת המעשרות . היא שעה שיתחייב במעשרות וזמנם משתנה כפי שנוי הזרעים ועוד אבאר אותו במס' מעשרות ומה שאמר וגמרן הגזבר ר"ל ונגמרו הן ביד הגזבר : ט זה אשר לקט את הפאה ואמר הרי זה לפלוני אם יהיה זה הלוקט עני ותהיה ראויה לו אותה הפאה אין מחלוקת שזכה לו וזכה בה האיש האחר אע"פ שאינו כאן שאנו אומרים אחרי שיש לו רשות לקחתם יש לו רשות להקנותם לאיש אחר אבל מחלוקת ר' אליעזר וחכמים אם היה הלוקט עשיר שר' אליעזר אומר אחר שיש לו רשות להפקיר נכסיו ויאכל הפאה ההיא יש לו רשות להקנותה לאיש אחר וחכ"א לא אמרי' תרי מיגו שנאמר אחרי שיש לו רשות להפקיר נכסיו יהיה כאילו הפקירם ונאמר אחר כן אחר שאם הפקיר נכסיו והם ראוים לו יוכל להקנותם לאחרים . והעיקר אצל רבי מאיר שאין קנין לנכרי בארץ ישראל להפקיע מן המעשרות ולפיכך לקט והשכחה ופאה שלו חייבין במעשרות לדעתו ואין הלכה .

ירושלמי (הל' א') · כתיב לא תכלה פאת שדך בקצרך מכאן שהפאה ניתנת במחובר לקרקע יכול אפילו בדלית ובדקל ת"ל קציר מה קציר מיוחד שהקטן מושל בהם כגדול יצאו הדלית והדקל שאין הקטן מושל בהן כגדול ואית דבעיא משמעיה מן הדא תעזוב הנח לפניהם תבואה בקשיה תלתן בעמיר תמרים במכבדות יכול בדלית ובדקל כן ת"ל אותם מה ראית לרבות את אלו ולהוציא את אלו אחר שריבה הכתוב ומיעט מרבה אני את אלו שאינם של סכנה ומוציא אני את אלו שהם של סכנה פירוש תמרים במכבדות אין סכנה בלקיטתן שאינן בראשו של דקל ומבעיא ליה בירושלמי בדלית ובדקל היכא קורא שם פאה אם למעלה או למטה בתלוש והוצאה משל מי ור"ל דאם קורא שם פאה למעלה הוצאה משל עניים ואם קורא שם למטה הוצאה משל בעל הבית ומסיק שאפי' תאמר קורא שם פאה למעלה הטריחו על בעל הבית שתהא הוצאה שלו מפני הסכנה תניא בת"כ בפרשת קדושים תעזוב הנח לפניהם והם יבוזו אפילו צ"ט אומרים לחלק ואחד לבזבז אפילו בריא אפילו ידיו יפות לזה שומעין שאומר כהלכה יכול בדלית ובדקל כן ת"ל אותם אפי' צ"ט אומרים לבזבז ואחד אומר לחלק אפי' זקן אפי' חולה לזה שומעין שאומר כהלכה: ירושלמי (שם) · בעל הבית שקרא שם פאה וכילה קורא אני עליו לא תכלה פאת שדך בקצרך [לא קרא שם פאה וכילה קורא אני עליו לא תכלה פאת שדך בקצרך] התנו ביניהן אפילו כן אין שומעין לו בעל הבית מחלק בידו שלא יראה לעני מודעתו וישליך לפניו ר' שמואל בר אבודימא בעי כילה שדהו אתמר חזרה פאה לעמרים אפי' כן בעל הבית מחלק בידו שלא יראה לעני מודעתו וישליך לפניו פי' שקרא שם וכילה שלא כדין עשה שהיה לו להניח לעניים לבזבז במחובר ואף על פי שעבר בלאו [לא] נשתנה דינו וקורא אני עליו לא תכלה דכתיב בסיפא דקרא תעזוב דמוכח שדינס לבזבז ולא לחלק כמו שדרשנו למעלה לנתינה במחובר ולא מיבעיא כשקרא שם במחובר וכילה אלא אפי' לא קרא שם נמי כך דינו דבינקך ובין כך קורא אני עליו לא תכלה ותעזוב אלא שהעניים התנו ביניהן ושמא ע"פ ב"ד עשו תנאי זה דאי בעל הבית אין שומעין לו לעוות עני האומר לבוז אלא בעל הבית מחלק בידו לכולם בשוה · שלא יראה לעני מודעתו מלשון הלא בועז מודעתנו כלומר הידוע וניכר לו וישליך לפניו רבי שמואל בר אבודימא בעי כלומר מילתא דפשיטא לן מיבעיא ליה לר"ש בר אבודימא כילה את שדהו אתמר חזרה פאה לעמרים כי הכיא דתניא בריש הגוזל קמא (דף צד·) מצות פאה להפריש מן הקמה לא הפריש מן הקמה מפריש מן העמרים אפי' כן בעל הבית מחלק כלומר אע"פ שחזרה פאה לעמרים להיות דינה לבזבז כמו הקמה אמרי' דאפ"ה מחלק שלא יראה לעני מודעתו וישליך לפניו : ג נטל אחד מן העניים מקצת הפאה · שליקט כבר וזרק לו על השאר כדי לקנות אין לו בה כלום אבל מה שליקט לא הפסיד ובתוספתא ובירושלמי (הל' ב') תנו בשם ר"מ קונסין אותו ומוציאין ממנו את התלוש ואת המחובר: נפל לו עליה· בפרק שנים אוחזין (דף י'·) פריך מהכא לר"ל דאמר ארבע אמות של אדם קונות לו בכל מקום ומשני בשדה דבעל הבית לא תקינו לו רבנן ועוד משני כיון דנפל גלי אדעתיה דבנפילה ניחא ליה דליקני (א): בירושלמי (שם) מייתי הא דתני רבי חייא שנים שהיו מתכסין [א] על העומר ובא עני אחר וחטפו זכה בו ושמא היינו נמי נפילה והתם משני כולהו בשלא אמר יזכו לי ארבע אמות ובגמרא שלנו לא קאי דפריך אי תקינו להו רבנן כי לא אמר מאי הוי : ד ה אבעיות. בירושלמי (שם) מפרש מלשון נבעו מצפוניו תרגום איתגליין מטמרוהי (עובדי' א) שהבעל הבית מתגלה ונראה לתוך שדהו כדי שיקחו העניים פאה (ג) : בשחר · מפרש בירושלמי (שם) מפני המניקות שבניהן ישנים בשחר ופנויות ללקט פאה: בחצות · מפני התינוקות שדרכן לצאת בחצות והולכין ללקט פאה ובשחרית ומנחה ישנים : ובמנחה · מפני הנמושות בריש אלו מציאות (דף כא:) אמרי' מאי נמושות סבי דאזלי אתיגרא מלשון מחזיק בפלך תרגום בתגרין (שמואל ב ג) : שלא יפחתו · משלש עתים הללו (ד) : של בית נמר· דכתיב את בית נמרה (במדבר לב) : על החבל · קושרין חבל בצד הקמה וקוצרין והולכין עד שיכלה החבל וחוזרין וקושרין ומניחין פאה לכל החבל והיינו מכל אומן ואומן כלומר מכל שורה ושורה ואמרי' בירושלמי (שם) שעל זה מזכירין אותן לשבח אבל מזכירין אותן לגנאי שלא היו נותנין אלא א' ממאה דהא תנן לא יפחות מששים : ו ואחר כך נתגייר פטור [וכו'] ומן הפאה. כדתניא בתורת כהנים בפרשת קדושים ובקצרכם פרט לשקצרוה נכרים מכאן אמרו נכרי שקצר שדהו ואח"כ נתגייר פטור והאי קרא גבי פאה ולקט כתיב ודרשינן נמי בספרי מקרא דכתיב גבי שכחה בסוף פרשת כי תצא כי תקצור קצירך בשדך ושכחת עומר פרט לשקצרוהו נכרים מכאן אמרו נכרי שקצר שדהו ואח"כ נתגייר פטור · ובירושלמי (הל' ג) דריש מקרא אחרינא : ירושלמי (שם) יאות א"ר יודה מאי טעמא דרבנן · ר' יוסי בשם רב* רבי חזקיה רב יהודה בשם שמואל כתיב ושכחת עומר בשדה זו שכחת קמה · את שיש לו שכחת קמה יש לו שכחת עמרים את שאין לו שכחת קמה אין לו שכחת עמרים פי' דדרשינן בספרי בס"פ כי תצא בשדה לרבות שכחת קמה הלכך זה שהיה נכרי בשעת קצירה פטור בשעת עימור אף על פי שנתגייר : ז הקדיש קמה ופדה עומרים פטורה · דמקרא דממעטינן קציר נכרי ממעטינן נמי קציר הקדש דלאו קצירך הוא ולענין שכחה הוו פליגי ר' יהודה ורבנן כי היכי דפליגי בגר : ח עד שלא באו לעונת המעשרות ופדאן· שפדאן קודם מירוח : וגמרן הגזבר · שמירחן בכרי דמירוח הקדש פוטר :

רבי

[תיבת רב ליתא בס"א]

פי' מהר"י בן מלכי צדק

פרק ד א הפאה ניתנת במחובר לקרקע . בדלית ובדקל לא כן אלא בעה"ב מחלק : ר' שמעון אומר אף בחליקי אגוזים בעל הבית מוריד ומחלק. פי' דלית גפן גדולה המודלה על גבי עצים או על גבי אילנות אחרות מנא הני מילי דכתיב לא תכלה פאת שדך בקצרך מיכן שהפאה ניתנת במחובר לקרקע יכול אף בדלית ובדקל כן ת"ל קציר מה קציר מיוחד שהקטן מושל בהן כגדול יצאו הדלית והדקל שאין הקטן מושל בהן כגדול וכו' . ותו מנהני מילי דהפאה ניתנת במחובר לקרקע דכתי' תעזוב. הנח לפניהם תבואה בקשיה תלתן בעמיר תמרין במכבדות יכול בדלית ובדקל כן ת"ל אותם ומה ראית לרבות את אילו ולהוציא את אילו אחר שריבה הכתוב ומיעט מרבה אני את אילו שאינן של סכנה ומוציא אני את אילו שהן של סכנה : מוריד ומחלק לעניים. קתני מחלק כלומר עליה דידיה רמי לפלוגי בידיה שלא יראה לעני מדעתו וישלך לפניו ובעיין בירו' שהפאה בדלית ובדקל היכן קורא במחובר או בשאינו מחובר פי' למעלה או למטה אין תימר מצות פאה במחובר קורא שם פאה למעלה אין תימר בשאינו מחובר קורא שם פאה למטה . אין תימר למעלן הוצאה של עניים להוריד הפירות לממן . אין תימר לממן הוצאה של בעל הבית . הדר אמרי אפי' למעלה הטריחו על בעה"ב שתהא הוצאה שלו מפני סכנה : ר"ש אומר אף בחליקי אגוזין. פי' לאילנות של אגוזין קורא חליקי מפני שאין להן לא ענפים ולא קשרים. פי' בעה"ב מוריד ומחלק לעניי' דאלו דסכנה הן דא"ר חנינה בשם ריש לקיש מעשה שמתו ד' אחין בה' חליקי אגוזין: אפי' תשעי' ותשעה וכו'. פירוש הדר לרישא דקאמר תנא קמא הפאה ניתנת במחובר לקרקע והלכה ברורה היא ולא תזוח מינה שאפי' צ"ט אומרין לחלק וא' אומר לבוז פי' לבוזו כל אחד וא' כפי יכולתו. ת"ר בספר' (פ' קדושים) תעזוב הנח לפניהן והם יבוזון ואפי' צ"ט אומרין לחלק ואחד אומר לבוז לזה שומעין שאמר כהלכה ואפילו בריא ואפילו ידיו יפות : ב בדלית ובדקל וכו'. ופשוטה היא . תניא בספרא שם יכול בדלית ובדקל וכו' עד וקבע את קובעיהם נפש : ג נטל מקצת הפאה וכו'. זה העני וזרק לו על השאר אין לו בה כלום . תניא ר"מ אומר קונסין אתו ונוטלין הימנו הכל . נמצא מה שביקש לא נתנו לו ושלו נוטלין מידו . וכן מצינו בנחש הקדמוני שנתן עיניו וכו' (סוטה דף ט:): נפל לו עליה . פי' על הפאה וכו' גרסינן בשלא אמר יזכו לי ד' אמות שלי אסו הכי לא קנה : וכן בלקט לקמן בעי לפרושי אי זהו לקט וכו' : ד פאה אין קוצרין אותה במגלות. פליצי ותנן בחולין השוחט במגל קציר : ואין עוקרין אותה בקרדומות . וטעמא מפרש במשנה כדי שלא יכו איש את רעהו והיא לה מצוה הבאה בעבירה : ה שלש אבעיות ביום. פי' עתות. גרסי' בירוש' מהו אבעיות אמר ר' אבין כמה דתימר איך נחפשו עשו נבעו מצפוניו ומתרגמינן אתגליין מטמרוהי כלומר ג' פעמים נגלה בעל השדה בשדהו כדי שיראוהו עניים ויבואו . בשחר. בחצות היום. במנחה . באילו ג' עתות נכנס בעל הבית בשדהו והעניים באים ונוטלין פאה ולקט ושכחה. גרסינן בירושלמי בשחר מפני המניקות כלומר בשעה שישינין תלדותיהן הן פנויות ובאות ונוטלות פאה ובחצות מפני התינוקות שדרכן לילך בחצי היום שבשחר ובמנחה ישנין. ובמנחה מפני הגמושות. ואמרינן מאי גמושות סבי דאזלי אתיגרא פי' מטה מתרגם הירושלמי תיגרא : לא אמרו ג' עתות אלו אלא שלא יפחיתו הא אם רוצה להוסיף מוסיף : ר' עקיבא אומר לא אמרו אלא שלא יוסיפו כלומר חשו לטורח בעל הבית אבל אם רוצה לפחות פוחת : של בית נמר. בית פלוני כדתנן תמן בית אבטינס היו מלקטין על החבל פי' היו מודדין חבל של ק' אמה וכן אחרת וכן אחרת והיו קושרין ראש החבל בצד הקמה עד שכלה החבל היו קוצרין ומניחין פאה אחת לכל חבל וזהו פי' מכל אומן ואומן מכל שורה ושורה . וכן גרסינן לקמן בסוף פרק ז' כל רגליות ורגליות אומן בפני עצמו הוא : תני אבא שאול אומר מזכירין אותן לגנאי ומזכירין אותן לשבח מזכירין אותן לגנאי שהיו נותנין פאה אחד מק' פי' ואנן תנינן אין פוחתין וכו' ומזכירין אותן לשבח שהיו מלקטין עם חבל וכו' כלומר בדקדוק נותנין פאה מכל שורה ושורה . בתוספתא . בין תני' יא ר' שמעון אומר כדי הקפת הר הבית משלו משל למה הדבר דומה לחבל של ק' אמה כיצד ראה בתחלת ק' ובסוף נ' ובסוף ק' (אתינן להאי חבל לרווחי פי' דחבל דהכא) : ו נכרי שקצר את שדהו וכו'. קתני קצר קצר אין עימר לא . ואחר כן נתגייר ומשנתגייר עימר פטור מן הלקט ומן הפאה ומן (ההבקר) [השכחה] מאי טעמא שבשעת חובתה היתה פטורה. [תניא] בסיפרא ובקצרכם פרט לשקצרוה גוים מיכן אמרו נכרי שקצר שדהו ואח"כ נתגייר וכו' ומן השכחה מ"ט א"ר יוסי א"ר חזקיה אמר רב יהודא אמר שמואל אמר קרא ושכחת עומר בשדה זו שכחת קמה את שיש לו שכחת קמה יש לו שכחת עומרין את שאין לו שכחת קמה אין לו שכחת עומרין ור' יהודה מחייב בשכחה שאין השכחה אלא בשעת עימור ועימור משנתגייר. עמר. ושכחת עומר. ושכחת קמה לא דריש : ומן ההבקר שאינו נותן לעניים כמו ישראל דמבקרי מדידהו לעניים דתנן אין פוחתין לעני וכו' : ז הקדיש קמה . פשוטה היא · ח כיוצא בו המקדיש פירותיו עד שלא באו לעונת המעשרות . פי' שלא הביאה התבואה שליש כדתנן מאימתי הפירות חייבין במעשר וכו' התבואה והזיתין משיכנסו שליש ופדאן מיד חייבין הקדישן עד שלא נגמרו הפירות פירוש עד שלא הביאו שליש ביד הגזבר ואחר כך פדאן וקצרן מיד פטורין . ומתניתין דתנינן בפרק קמא דחלה המקדיש וכו' פירוש בירושלמי דצריכא הא והא : ט מי שליקט וכו' ואמר הרי זה לאיש פלוני עני זכה לו וכו'. פי' בעל הבית ליקט פאה. גרסינן א"ר יהושע בן לוי לא נחלקו אלא בבעל הבית עשיר דר' אליעזר סבר אמרינן תרי מיגו מיגו דאי מפקר להו לנכסיה והוי עני חזי ליה ומיגו (דחזי) [דזכי] ליה לנפשיה (חזי) [זכי] נמי לחבריה ורבנן סברי לא אמרינן תרי מיגו אבל בבעל הבית עני דברי הכל זכה לו מאי טעמא מתוך שהוא ראוי ליטלה שהוא עני וזוכה נמי לחבירו

עין משפט נר מצוה

א א מיי' פ"ב מהל' מתנ' עניים הט"ו:
ב ב שם הלכה טז (ופ"א הלכה ב):
ג ג שם פ"ב הט"ו :
ד ד שם הלכה טז:
ה ה שם הלכה יח:
ו ו שם הל' טו (יט):
ז ז ח שם הלכה יז :
ח ט מיי' פ"ב מהל' מתנות עניים הל' (ט) [יז] :
ט י שם הלכה ח :
י כ מיי' פ"ב מהל' מעשר הלכה ח :
יא ל מיי' פ"ג שם הלכה כה :

פי' הרא"ש

פ"ד (א) ורשע לא מיקרי הנוטלה ממנו דדוקא בחררה דמכר או שכירות הנמצא במקום אחר נקרא רשע אבל במקו' הפקר לא: (ב) פי' מגלות קוצרים בהם חטים ושעורים . קרדומות גדולות קוצצים בהם שבולת שועל ושיפון : (ג) אבל לא בשחר אבעיות היום לפי שאין כל העניים בשדה ושמא יקבע בעה"ב לעניים מיודעיו זמן שיבואו אליו או ויטלו הפאה: (ד) אבעיות פירשתי באחד מג' הזמנים משום דהוה קשה לי לפרושי בכל אלו הג' זמנים משום דבפעם א' מניח אדם פאה בתוך שדהו ומיד העניים נוטלים הכל ולהכי פירושא אפשר לפרש דפלוגתא דר"ג ור"ע משום לקט הם דכל זמן שאין בעה"ב בשדה אין העניים רשאין ליכנוס וליטול הלקט בשביל עמרי השדה ולכך הוא צריך להראות ג"פ ביום בתוך שדהו כדי שיכנסו העניים ויטלו להלקט והולכי' ובאי' העניים כמה פעמים זה אח"ז ומה שמציירים אלו מוצאים אלו :

הגהות הגר"א

מי שאין לו קרקע פטור מן הודוי דכתיב ואת האדמה אשר נתתה לנו רבי יוסי כו' :
פ"ד [א] מ"ג בר"ש שנים שהיו מתכסין. נמחק תיבת מתכסין וכ"כ מתכתשין :

Continuation of translation from previous page as indicated by ◁

[THEY SEARCH] MORE OFTEN.[2] [THE MEN] OF BETH NAMER[3] USED TO REAP [THEIR CROPS] WITH THE AID OF A ROPE,[4] AND LEFT PE'AH AT THE END OF EACH FURROW.

MISHNAH 6. IF A GENTILE REAPED HIS FIELD AND BECAME AFTERWARDS A PROSELYTE, HE IS EXEMPT FROM [LEAVING] GLEANINGS, THE FORGOTTEN SHEAF AND PE'AH.[5] R. JUDAH DECLARES HIM LIABLE TO LEAVE THE FORGOTTEN SHEAF SINCE THAT BECOMES DUE AT THE TIME OF THE SHEAF-BINDING.[6]

MISHNAH 7. IF A MAN DEDICATED STANDING CORN [TO THE TEMPLE], AND REDEEMED IT WHILE IT WAS YET STANDING CORN, HE IS LIABLE [TO GIVE THE POOR MAN'S GIFTS].[7] [IF HE DEDICATED] SHEAVES AND REDEEMED THEM WHILST THEY WERE YET SHEAVES, HE IS ALSO LIABLE [TO RENDER THE GIFTS].[8] [IF HE DEDICATED] STANDING CORN AND REDEEMED IT [WHEN IT WAS ALREADY IN] SHEAVES, HE IS
d
EXEMPT,[1] SINCE AT THE TIME WHEN IT BECAME LIABLE [AS STANDING CORN], IT WAS EXEMPT [BY BEING DEDICATED].

MISHNAH 8. SIMILARLY IF ONE DEDICATED HIS HARVESTED PRODUCTS PRIOR TO THE STAGE WHEN THEY ARE SUBJECT TO TITHES[2] AND REDEEMED THEM AFTERWARDS, THEY ARE LIABLE[3] [TO THE GIFTS]. IF [HE DEDICATED THEM] WHEN THEY HAD ALREADY BECOME SUBJECT TO TITHES AND REDEEMED THEM, THEY ARE ALSO LIABLE [TO THE GIFTS].[4] IF HE DEDICATED THEM BEFORE THEY HAD RIPENED, AND THEY BECAME RIPE WHILE IN THE POSSESSION OF THE [TEMPLE] TREASURER, AND HE AFTERWARDS REDEEMED THEM, THEY ARE EXEMPT, SINCE AT THE TIME WHEN THEY WOULD HAVE BEEN LIABLE, THEY WERE EXEMPT.[5]

MISHNAH 9. IF ONE COLLECTED PE'AH AND SAID: 'THIS IS FOR SUCH-AND-SUCH A POOR MAN',[6] THEN R. ELIEZER

(2) Probably so as not to take up the time of the owner unduly. (3) Either the town mentioned in Num. XXXII, 3, or the name of a family. It has been identified by some with the modern Nimrin in Transjordania. Others explain it as a field cultivated in irregular strips and patches (cf. *supra* III, 2). (4) A rope was tied around the standing corn in a straight line and the reaping went on till the end of the measuring line. This generous practice is here held up for commendation for it enabled the poor to gather at the end of each furrow, instead of waiting patiently for the very end of the reaping. Other explanations have also been offered. The people of Beth Namer used to divide the field into three portions with a rope, a portion being reaped at each of the three searches, (v. n. 1 *supra*); the idea being that the three kinds of poor for whom provision was made do not encroach upon one another. Var lec.: מלקיטים, 'they *made* the poor to gather'. (5) The phrase *'and when ye reap'* (Lev. XXIII, 22) in reference to Gleanings and *Pe'ah* rules out non-Jews. In speaking of the Forgotten Sheaf, the word is also *'thy reaping'* (Deut. XXIV, 19); hence a proselyte is exempt from giving the 'poor man's gifts' if the reaping took place before his conversion. (6) When he has already become a Jew, upon whom all obligations are due. (7) The law being binding as long as the corn is rooted in the soil, regardless of the change of ownership that took place in the interval. (8) Even the Forgotten Sheaf (*supra* IV, 6); for Gleanings and *Pe'ah* automatically become due with the first reaping.
d
(1) The same word *'thy reaping'* (Deut. XXIV, 19) that excludes non-Jews also excludes all Temple property from gifts to the poor and tithes. R. Judah would no doubt disagree with the Sages here, too, as he does in the case of the non-Jew who becomes a proselyte after the reaping. (2) At the time when they were finally stacked (*supra* I, 6). Had they been finally stacked by the Treasurer they would be exempt from tithes. (V. Ma'as. I, 2 for the times when the various fruits became subject to tithes). By 'Tithes' is understood the Heave-offering, the First (or Levitic) Tithe and the Second Tithe, and the Poor Man's Tithe in the third and sixth years of the seven years' cycle. (3) Since they ripen in his possession. (4) One cannot dedicate the property of another, and the tithes were already virtually the property of the poor prior to the dedication. (5) Temple property was exempt from tithes and gifts and by becoming ripe when still in the possession of the Temple, the law does not apply to them at all. (6) A man not poor himself, i.e., a man possessing more than two hundred *zuz*, who wishes to acquire the *Pe'ah* for a poor friend.

א) תורת כהנים פ' קדושים: ב) ב"מ פ"א דף י. ג) חלה פ"ג מ"ד: ד) גיטין פ"א יא: ב"מ דף ט:

א ב במחובר לקרקע · דגבי קציר כתיב תעזוב דמשמע שיניח לפניהם תבואה בקשיה : דלית. גפן גדולה המודלית ע"ג עצים או על גבי אילנות אחרים : מוריד ומחלק · דהכי שיש סכנה בעלייתם מצות פאה בתלוש ובירושלמי דריש לה מקרא וכן בת"כ בפ' קדושים : חליקי אגוזים · אילן של אגוזים ופי' בערוך דקרי ליה חליקי לפי שהוא חלק שאין לו לא קשרים ולא ענפים : אפילו צ"ט · ארישא קאי דבמחובר ואם יש כאן ק' עניים וצ"ט מהם אומרים לבעל הבית שיקצור הכל ויחלק להם הפאה ויש אחד שאינו רוצה אין שומעין להם אלא ירוצו ויבוזו ובדלית שמצותה בתלוש איפכא דשומעין ליחיד הרוצה ליחלק :

פרק רביעי

א הפאה ניתנת במחובר לקרקע א) בדלית ובדקל בעה"ב מוריד ומחלק לעניים רבי שמעון אומר אף בחליקי אגוזים אפי' תשעים ותשעה אומרים לחלק ואחד אומר לבוז לזה שומעין שאמר כהלכה: **ב** בדלית ובדקל אינו כן אפילו תשעים ותשעה אומרים לבוז ואחד אומר לחלק לזה שומעין שאמר כהלכה: **ג** נטל ב) מקצת פאה וזרק על השאר אין לו בה כלום נפל לו עליה ופירש טליתו עליה מעבירין אותו הימנה וכן בלקט וכן בעומר השכחה: **ד** פאה אין קוצרין אותה במגלות (ב) ואין עוקרין אותה בקרדומות כדי שלא יכו איש את רעהו: **ה** שלש אבעיות ביום בשחר בחצות ובמנחה רבן גמליאל אומר לא אמרו אלא כדי שלא יפחתו ר"ע אומר לא אמרו אלא כדי שלא יוסיפו של בית נמר היו מלקטין על החבל ונותנים פאה מכל אומן ואומן: **ו** נכרי שקצר את שדהו ואחר כך נתגייר פטור מן הלקט ומן השכחה ומן הפאה ר' יהודה מחייב בשכחה שאין השכחה אלא בשעת העמור: **ז** הקדיש קמה ופדה קמה חייב עומרין ופדה עומרין חייב קמה ופדה עומרין פטורה שבשעת חובתה היתה פטורה: **ח** ג) כיוצא בו המקדיש פירותיו עד שלא באו לעונת המעשרות ופדאן חייבין משבאו לעונת המעשרות ופדאן חייבין הקדישן עד שלא נגמרו וגמרן הגזבר ואח"כ פדאן פטורין שבשעת חובתן היו פטורין: **ט** ד) מי שלקט את הפאה ואמר הרי זו * לאיש פלוני

[ס"א לפלוני]

ירושלמי (הל' א') · כתיב לא תכלה פאת שדך בקצרך מכאן שהפאה ניתנת במחובר לקרקע יכול אפילו בדלית ובדקל ת"ל קציר מה קציר מיוחד שהקטן מושל בהם כגדול יצאו הדלית והדקל שאין הקטן מושל בהן כגדול ואית דבעיא משמעיניה מן הדא תעזוב הנח לפניהם תבואה בקשיה תלתן בעמיר תמרים במכבדות יכול בדלית ובדקל כן ת"ל אותם מה ראית לרבות את אלו ולהוציא את אלו אחר שריבה הכתוב ומיעט מרבה אני את אלו שאינם של סכנה ומוציא אני את אלו שהם של סכנה פירוש תמרים במכבדות אין סכנה בלקיטתן שאינן בראשו של דקל ומבעיא ליה בירושלמי בדלית ובדקל היכא קורא שם פאה אם למעלה או למטה בתלוש והוצאה משל מי ור"ל דאם קורא שם פאה למעלה הוצאה משל עניים ואם קורא שם למטה הוצאה משל בעל הבית ומסיק שאפי' תאמר קורא שם פאה למעלה הטריחו על בעל הבית שתהא הוצאה שלו מפני הסכנה תניא בת"כ בפרשת קדושים תעזוב הנח לפניהם והם יבוזו אפילו צ"ט אומרים לחלק ואחד לבזבז אפילו בריא אפילו ידיו יפות לזה שומעין שאומר כהלכה יכול בדלית ובדקל כן ת"ל אותם אפי' צ"ט אומרים לבזבז ואחד אומר לחלק אפי' זקן אפי' חולה לזה שומעין שאומר כהלכה: ירושלמי (שם) · בעל הבית שקרא שם פאה וכילה קורא אני עליו לא תכלה פאת שדך בקצרך [לא קרא שם פאה וכילה קורא אני עליו לא תכלה פאת שדך בקצרך] התנו ביניהן אפילו כן אין שומעין לו בעל הבית מחלק בידו שלא יראה לעני מודעתו וישליך לפניו ר' שמואל בר אבודימא בעי כילה שדהו אתמר חזרה פאה לעמרים אפי' כן בעל הבית מחלק בידו שלא יראה לעני מודעתו וישליך לפניו פי' שקרא שם וכילה שלא כדין עשה שהיה לו להניח לעניים לבזבז במחובר ואף על פי שעבר בלאו [לא] נשתנה דינו וקורא אני עליו לא תכלה דכתיב בסיפא דקרא תעזוב דמוכח שדינם לבזבז ולא לחלק כמו שדרשנו למעלה לנתינה במחובר ולא מיבעיא כשקרא שם במחובר וכילה אלא אפי' לא קרא שם נמי כך דינו דבינוכך ובין כך קורא אני עליו לא תכלה ותעזוב אלא שהעניים התנו ביניהן ושמא ע"פ ב"ד עשו תנאי זה דאי בעל הבית אין שומעין לו לעוות עני האומר לבוז אלא בעל הבית מחלק בידו לכולם בשוה · שלא יראה לעני מודעתו מלשון הלא בועז מודעתנו כלומר הידוע וניכר לו וישליך לפניו רבי שמואל בר אבודימא בעי כלומר מילתא דפשיטא לן מיבעיא ליה לר"ש בר אבודימא כילה את שדהו אתמר חזרה פאה לעמרים כי ההיא דתניא בריש הגוזל קמא (דף לד·) מצות פאה להפריש מן הקמה לא הפריש מן הקמה מפריש מן העמרים אפי' כן בעל הבית מחלק כלומר אע"פ שחזרה פאה לעמרים להיות דינה לבזבז כמו הקמה אמרי' דאפ"ה מחלק שלא יראה לעני מודעתו וישליך לפניו : ג נטל אחד מן העניים מקצת הפאה · שליקט כבר וזרק לו על השאר כדי לקנות אין לו בה כלום אבל מה שליקט לא הפסיד ובתוספתא ובירושלמי (הל' ב') תנו בשם ר"מ קונסין אותו ומוציאין ממנו את התלוש ואת המחובר:נפל לו עליה· בפרק שנים אוחזין (דף י·) פריך מהכא לר"ל דאמר ארבע אמות של אדם קונות לו בכל מקום ומשני בשדה דבעל הבית לא תקינו לו רבנן ועוד משני כיון דנפל גלי אדעתיה דבנפילה ניחא ליה דליקני (א): בירושלמי (שם) מייתי הא דתני רבי חייא שנים שהיו מתכסין [א] על העומר ובא עני אחר וחטפו זכה בו ושמא היינו נמי נפילה והתם משני כולהו בשלא אמר יזכו לי ארבע אמות ובגמרא שלנו לא קאי דפריך אי תקינו להו רבנן כי לא אמר מאי הוי : ד ה אבעיות. בירושלמי (שם) מפרש מלשון נבעו מצפוניו תרגום איתגליין מטמרוהי (עובדי' א) שהבעל הבית מתגלה ונראה לתוך שדהו כדי שיקחו העניים פאה (ג) : בשחר · מפרש בירושלמי (שם) מפני המניקות שבניהן ישנים בשחר ופנויות ללקט פאה : בחצות · מפני התינוקות שדרכן לצאת בחצות והולכין ללקט פאה ובשחרית ומנחה ישנים : ובמנחה · מפני הנמושות בריש אלו מציאות (דף כא:) אמרי' מאי נמושות סבי דאזלי אתיגרא מלשון מחזיק בפלך תרגום בתגרין (שמואל ב ג) : שלא יפחתו · משלש עתים הללו (ד) : של בית נמר · דכתיב את בית נמרה (במדבר לב) : על החבל · קושרין חבל בצד הקמה וקוצרין והולכין עד שיכלה החבל ומניחין פאה לכל החבל וחוזרין וקושרין ומניחין פאה והיינו מכל אומן ואומן כלומר מכל שורה ושורה ואמרי' בירושלמי (שם) שעל זה מזכירין אותן לשבח אבל מזכירין אותן לגנאי שלא היו נותנין אלא א' ממאה דהא תנן לא יפחות מששים : ו ואחר כך נתגייר פטור [וכו'] ומן הפאה. כדתניא בתורת כהנים בפרשת קדושים ובקצרכם פרט לשקצרוהו נכרים מכאן אמרו נכרי שקצר שדהו ואח"כ נתגייר פטור והאי קרא גבי פאה ולקט כתיב ודרשינן נמי בספרי מקרא דכתיב גבי שכחה בסוף פרשת כי תצא כי תקצור קצירך בשדך ושכחת עומר פרט לשקצרוהו נכרים מכאן אמרו נכרי שקצר שדהו ואח"כ נתגייר פטור · ובירושלמי (הל' ג) דריש מקרא אחרינא : ירושלמי (שם) יאות א"ר יודה מאי טעמא דרבנן · ר' יוסי בשם רב* רבי חזקיה רב יהודה בשם שמואל כתיב ושכחת עומר בשדה זו שכחת קמה · את שיש לו שכחת קמה יש לו שכחת עמרים את שאין לו שכחת קמה אין לו שכחת עמרים פי' דדרשינן בספרי בס"פ כי תצא בשדה לרבות שכחת קמה הלכך זה שהיה נכרי בשעת קצירה פטור בשעת עימור אף על פי שנתגייר : ז הקדיש קמה ופדה עומרים פטורה · דמקרא דממעטינן קציר נכרי ממעטינן נמי קציר הקדש דלאו קצירך הוא ולענין שכחה הוו פליגי ר' יהודה ורבנן כי היכי דפליגי בגר : ח עד שלא באו לעונת המעשרות ופדאן · שפדאן קודם מירוח : וגמרן הגזבר · שמירחן בכרי דמירוח הקדש פוטר : רבי

[תיבת רב ליתא בס"א]

א ב אמר הכתוב לא תכלה פאת שדך בקצרך (ויקרא כג) בא ללמדנו שיניחו פאה מחוברת לקרקע וזה בקציר ומה שדומה לזה מן הדברים שאפשר לקטן ולגדול לקחתה: ודלית. שם לגפן כמו דליותיו (יחזקאל יז) : ובדקל התמר. וחליקי האגוזים אגוזי פרך והם מין אגוזים והוא מאד גבוה : ופירוש לבוז שיקח כל אחד מה שיוכל ואין הלכה כרבי שמעון : ג כשיקח מקצתו ויכסה מקצתו לוקחין מידו הכל בין מה שלקח ובא לידו ובין מה שכסה וזה קנס וכן אמרו קונסין אותו ומעבירין ממנו את הכל את התלוש ואת המחובר ועומר השכחה יתבאר אחר זה : ד מגלות . הם חרמשים וקרדומות הם ממיני הפטישים והדבר כולו מבואר : ה שלש אבעיות . שלש בקשות מלשון אם תבעיון בעיו (ישעיה כא) ואמרו נותנין הפאה בשחר בשביל המניקות שהם מלטרכות לאכול בבקר ובחצות בשביל הנערים הקטנים שהם ישנים בבקר ויתהלכו לאטם עד חצות היום במנחה בשביל הזקנים שלא יגיעו לשדה* אלא עד אותה השעה: ובית נמר . שם מקום : וענין על החבל הוא על קו מישור מתחלת השדה עד סופה : מכל אומן ואומן · ר"ל מכל שורה ושורה שכן היו קוצרים שורה אחר שורה וכל שורה נקראת אומן ואין הלכה כרבן גמליאל ולא כר' עקיבא אלא בג' שעות אלו בלבד תנתן הפאה כדי שיהיו שעות ידועות להתקבץ בהם העניים : ו שכחה . הוא מה שאמר הכתוב (דברים כד) ושכחת עומר בשדה וזה יהיה כשמוליכין העומרים ממקום למקום כמו שיתבאר ודעת החכמים שכל זרע שלא נתחייב בחיובי קמה והם לקט ופאה לא יתחייב ג"כ בחובת העומר והיא השכחה ואין הלכה כר' יהודה : ז כשיקדיש קמה ופדה קמה נתחייב בפאה ובלקט . וכשיקדיש עומרים ופדה עומרים חייב בשכחה : ואם הקדיש קמה וקצר הגזבר ועשאם עומרין ואחר כן פדאם לא יתחייב בהם ואפי' בשכחה וזה דעת החכמים כפי מה שהקדמנו מן העקרים שיש אצלנו : ח עונת המעשרות . היא שעה שיתחייב במעשרות וזמנם משתנה כפי שנוי הזרעים ועוד אבאר אותו במס' מעשרות ומה שאמר וגמרן הגזבר ר"ל ונגמרו הן ביד הגזבר : ט זה אשר לקט את הפאה ואמר הרי זה לפלוני אם יהיה זה הלוקט עני ותהיה ראויה לו אותה הפאה אין מחלוקת שזכה לו וזכה בה האיש האחר אע"פ שאינו כאן שאנו אומרים אחרי שיש לו רשות לקחתם יש לו רשות להקנותם לאיש אחר אבל מחלוקת ר' אליעזר וחכמים אם היה הלוקט עשיר שר' אליעזר אומר אחר שיש לו רשות להפקיר נכסיו ויאכל הפאה ההיא יש לו רשות להקנותה לאיש אחר וחכ"א לא אמרי' תרי מיגו שנאמר אחרי שיש לו רשות להפקיר נכסיו יהיה כאילו הפקירם ונאמר אחר כן אחר שאם הפקיר נכסיו והם ראוים לו יוכל להקנותם לאחרים . והעיקר אצל רבי מאיר שאין קנין לנכרי בארץ ישראל להפקיע מן המעשרות ולפיכך לקט והשכחה ופאה שלו חייבין במעשרות לדעתו ואין הלכה .

[ר"א לנוי]

פי' מהר"י בן מלכי צדק

פרק ד א הפאה נתנית במחובר לקרקע. בדלית ובדקל: לא כן אלא בעה"ב מחלק: ר' שמעון אומר אף בחליקי אגוזים בעל הבית מוריד ומחלק. פי' דלית גפן גדולה המודלה על גבי עצים או על גבי אילנות אחרות מנא הני מילי דכתיב לא תכלה פאת שדך בקצרך מיכן שהפאה ניתנת במחובר לקרקע יכול אף בדלית ובדקל כן ת"ל קציר מה קציר מיוחד שהקטן מושל בהן כגדול יצאו הדלית והדקל שאין הקטן מושל בהן כגדול וכו'. ותו מנהני מילי דהפאה נתנית במחובר לקרקע דכתי' תעזב. הנח לפניהם תבואה בקשיה תלתן בעמיר תמרים במכבדות יכול בדלית ובדקל כן ת"ל אותם ומה ראית לרבות את אילו ולהוציא את אילו אחר שריבה הכתוב ומיעט מרבה אני את אילו שאינן של סכנה ומוציא אני את אילו שהן של סכנה. מוריד ומחלק לעניים. קתני מחלק כלומר עליה דידיה רמי לפלוני בידיה שלא יראה לעני מודעתו וישליך לפניו ובעיון בירו' שהפאה בדלית ובדקל היכן קורא במחובר או בשאינו מחובר פי' למעלה או למטה אין תימר מצות פאה במחובר קורא שם פאה למעלה אין תימר בשאינו מחובר קורא שם פאה למטה. אין תימר למעלן הוצאה של עניים להוריד הפירות למטן. אין תימר למטן הוצאה של בעל הבית. הדר אמרי אפי' למעלה הטריחו על בעה"ב שתהא הוצאה שלו מפני סכנה: ר"ש אומר אף בחליקי אגוזין. פי' לאילנות של אגוזין קורא חליקי מפני שאין להן לא ענפים ולא קשרים. פי' בעה"ב מוריד ומחלק לעניי' דאלו דסכנה הן דא"ר חנינה בשם ריש לקיש מעשה שמתו ד' אחין בה' חליקי אגוזין: אפי' תשעי' ותשעה וכו'. פירוש הדר לרישא דקאמר תנא קמא הפאה ניתנת במחובר לקרקע והלכה ברורה היא ולא תזוז מינה שאפי' צ"ט אומרין לחלק וא' אומר לבוז פי' לבזבז כל אחד וא' כפי יכולתו.ת"ר בספר' (פ' קדושים) תעזוב הנח לפניהן והם יבוזון ואפי' צ"ט אומרין לחלק ואחד אומר לבוז לזה שומעין שאמר כהלכה ואפילו בריא ואפילו ידיו יפות : ב בדלית ובדקל וכו'. ופשוטה היא . תניא בספרא שם יכול בדלית ובדקל וכו' עד וקבע את קובעיהם נפש : ג נטל מקצת הפאה וכו'.זה העני וזרק לו על השאר אין לו בה כלום . תניא ר"מ אומר קונסין אותו ונוטלין הימנו הכל . נמצא מה שביקש לא נתנו לו ושלו נוטלין מידו . וכן מצינו בנחש הקדמוני שנתן עיניו וכו' (סוטה דף ט:):נפל לו עליה . פי' על הפאה וכו' גרסינן בשלא אמר יזכו לי ד' אמות שלי אתו הכי לא קנה : וכן בלקט לקמן בעי לפרושי אי זהו לקט וכו' : ד פאה אין קוצרין אותה במגלות.פליגי ותנן בחולין השוחט במגל קציר : ואין עוקרין אותה בקרדומות . וטעמא מפרש במשנה כדי שלא יכו איש את רעהו והויא לה מצוה הבאה בעבירה : ה שלש אבעיות ביום. פי' עתות. גרסי' בירוש' מהו אבעיות אמר ר' אבין כמה דתימר איך נחפשו עשו נבעו מצפוניו ומתרגמינן אתגליין מטמרוהי כלומר ג' פעמים נגלה בעל השדה בשדהו כדי שיראוהו עניים ויבואו . בשחר. בחצות היום. במנחה . באילו ג' עתות נכנס בעל הבית בשדהו והעניים באים ונוטלין פאה ולקט ושכחה.גרסינן בירושלמי בשחר מפני המניקות כלומר בשעה שישנין ולדותיהן הן פנויות ובאות ונוטלות פאה ובחצות מפני התינוקות כלומר ילקטו התינוקות שדרכן לילך בחצי היום שבשחר ובמנחה ישנין. ובמנחה מפני הנמושות.ואמרינן מאי נמושות סבי דאזלי אתיגרא פי' מטה מתרגם הירושלמי תיגרא : לא אמרו ג' עתות אלו אלא שלא יפחתו הא אם רוצה להוסיף מוסיף : ר' עקיבא אומר לא אמרו אלא שלא יוסיפו כלומר חשו לטורח בעל הבית אבל אם רוצה לפחות פוחת : של בית נמר. בית פלוני כדתנן תמן בית אבטינס היו מלקטין על החבל פי' היו מודדין חבל של ק' אמה וכן אחרת וכן אחרת והיו קושרין ראש החבל בצד הקמה עד שכלה החבל היו קוצרין ומניחין פאה אחת לכל חבל וזהו פי' מכל אומן ואומן מכל שורה ושורה. וכן גרסינן לקמן בסוף פרק ז' כל רגליות ורגליות אומן בפני עצמו הוא : תני אבא שאול אומר מזכירין אותן לגנאי ומזכירין אותן לשבח מזכירין אותן לגנאי שהיו נותנין פאה אחד מק' פי' ואנן תנינן אין פוחתין וכו' ומזכירין אותן לשבח שהיו מלקטין עם חבל וכו' כלומר בדקדוק נותנין פאה מכל שורה ושורה . בתוספתא .בין תנ"א ר' שמעון אומר כדי הקפת הר הבית משלו משל למה הדבר דומה לחבל של ק' אמה כיצד ראה בתחלת ק' ובסוף ג' ובסוף ק' (אתינן להאי חבל לרווחי פי' דחבל דהכא) : ו נכרי שקצר את שדהו וכו'. קתני קצר קצר אין עימר לא . ואחר כן נתגייר ומשנתגייר עימר פטור מן הלקט ומן הפאה ומן (ההבקר) [השכחה] מאי טעמא שבשעת חובתה היתה פטורה. [תניא] בסיפרא ובקצרכם פרט לשקצרוה גוים מיכן אמרו נכרי שקצר שדהו ואח"כ נתגייר וכו' ומן השכחה מ"מ א"ר יוסי א"ר חזקיה אמר רב יהודא אמר שמואל אמר קרא ושכחת עומר בשדה זו שכחת קמה את שיש לו שכחת קמה יש לו שכחת עומרין את שאין לו שכחת קמה אין לו שכחת עומרין ור' יהודה מחייב בשכחה שאין השכחה אלא בשעת עימור ועימור משנתגייר. עמר. ושכחת עומר. ושכחת קמה לא דריש : ומן ההבקר שאינו נותן לעניים כמו ישראל דמבקרי מדידהו לעניים דתנן אין פוחתין לעני וכו' : ז הקדיש קמה . פשוטה היא · ח כיוצא בו המקדיש פירותיו עד שלא באו לעונת המעשרות . פי' שלא הביאה התבואה שליש כדתנן מאימתי הפירות חייבין במעשר וכו' התבואה והזיתין משיכנסו שליש ופדאן מיד חייבין הקדישן עד שלא נגמרו הפירות פירוש עד שלא הביאו שליש והביאו שליש ביד הגזבר ואחר כך פדאן וקצרן מיד פטורין . ומתניתין דתנינן בפרק קמא דחלה המקדיש וכו' פירוש בירושלמי דצריכא הא והא : ט מי שליקט וכו' ואמר הרי זה לאיש פלוני עני זכה לו וכו'. פי' בעל הבית ליקט פאה. גרסינן א"ר יהושע בן לוי לא נחלקו אלא בבעל הבית עשיר דר' אליעזר סבר אמרינן תרי מיגו מיגו דאי מפקר להו לנכסיה והוי עני חזי ליה ומיגו (דחזי) [זכי] נמי לחבריה ורבנן סברי לא אמרינן תרי מיגו אבל בבעל הבית עני דברי הכל זכה לו מאי טעמא מתוך שהוא ראוי ליטלה שהוא עני זוכה נמי לחבירו

עין משפט נר מצוה

א א מיי' פ"ב מהל' מתנו' עניים הט"ו:
ב ב שם הלכה טז (ופ"א הלכה ב):
ג ג שם פ"ב הט"ו :
ד ד שם הלכה טז:
ה ה שם הלכה יח :
ו ו שם הל' טו (יט):
ז ז ח שם הלכה יז :
ח ט מיי' פ"ב מהל' מתנות עניים הל' (ט) [יז] :
ט י שם הלכה ח :
י כ מיי' פ"ב מהל' מעשר הלכה ח :
יא ל מיי' פ"ב שם הלכה כה :

פי' הרא"ש

פ"ד (א) ורשע לא מיקרי הנוטלה ממנו דדוקא בתרומה דמכר או שכירות הנמצא במקום אחר נקרא רשע כל מקום הפקר לא: (ב) פי' מגלות קוצרים בהם חטים ושעורים. קרדומות גדולות קוצצים בהם שבולת שועל וכוסמין: (ג) אבל לא באלו אבעיות היום לפי שאין כל העניים בשדה ואם יקבע בעה"ב לעניים מיודעים זמן שיבואו אליו או יטלו הפאה: (ד) אבעיות פירשתי באחד מג' הזמנים משום דהוה קשה לי אמאי לא אלו ג' זמנים משום דבפשט א' מנית אדם פאה בתוך שדהו ומיד העניים נוטלים הכל ולהך פירושו אפשר לפרש דפלוגתא דר"ג ור"ע אם שאין כאן שכ"ל דכל זמן שאין העניים בשדה אין העניים ראשין ליכנס ולילקט הלקט בשביל עומרי השדה ולכן הוא צריך להראות ג"פ ביום בתוך שדהו כדי שיכנסו העניים ויטלו הלקט והשכחה ובאי' העניים כמה פעמים זה ואת"ח ומה שמשיירים אלו מוגלים אלו:

הגהות הגר"א

מי שאין לו קרקע פטור מן הודוי דכתיב ואת האדמה אשר נתתה לנו רבי יוסי כו' :
פ"ד [א] מ"ג בר"ש שנים שהיו מתכסין .נמחק תיבת מתכסין וצ"ב מתכתשין :

יב א מיי' פ"ב מה' מתנות עניים ה"ח:
יג ב מיי' פ"ב מהל' תרומות הלכה י:
יד ג מיי' פ"ד מה' מתנות עניים ה"א:
טו ד שם הלכה ב:
טז ה שם הלכה א:
יז ו מיי' פ"ד מהל' מתנות עניים ה"ו:
א ח מיי' פ"ד מהל' מתנות עניים ה"ו:
ב ט שם הלכה ה:
ג י שם הלכה ב:
ד כ שם הלכה י:

א) גיטין פ"ד ד' מז. ב) ביצה פ"ה דף לה: ג) חולין פ"י ד' קלד: ד) שקלים פ"א דף ג. ה) ב"מ פ"ט דף קה: ו) עדיות פ"ב משנה ד:

מן רבי אליעזר אומר זכה לו. בפרק שנים אוחזין (ד' ט':) אמרינן אמר עולא מחלוקת מעשיר לעני דר' אליעזר סבר אמרי' תרי מיגו מיגו דאי בעי מפקיר להו לנכסיה והוי עני וחזי ליה ומיגו דאי בעי זכי לנפשיה זכי נמי לחבריה. ורבנן סברי חד מיגו אמרי' תרי מיגו לא אמרינן. אבל מעני לעני דברי הכל זכה. ורב נחמן אמר מעני לעני מחלוקת. ובפ"ק דגיטין (יא:) מפרש טעמא דרבנן משום לא תלקט לעני ור"א מוקי ליה להזהיר עני על שלו. ובפרק שנים אוחזין (שם) פי' בקונטרס דמי שליקט את הפאה באדם בעלמא איירי שאינו בעל השדה דאי בעל השדה לא אמר ר' אליעזר זכה לו דליכא למימר מיגו דזכי לנפשיה דאפי' הוא עני מוזהר הוא שלא ללקט פאה משדהו כדאמרי' לא תלקט לעני להזהיר עני על שלו וקשה לפירושו מהא דתנן לקמן בפרק ה' (משנה ב) שבולת של לקט שנתערבה בגדיש מעשר שבולת אחת ונותן לו. אמר ר' אליעזר וכי היאך העני הזה מחליף דבר שלא בא לרשותו. ואמרינן עלה בירושלמי (הל' ב) ר' אבהו בשם ר' יוחנן מחלפא שיטתיה דר' אליעזר תמן הוא אומר זכה לו וכאן הוא אומר כן. ומסיק דלדבריהם קאמר להו משמע בהדיא דבעל השדה גופיה יכול לזכות בשביל עני (ה): אלא אם כן הפקיר. למאן דאמר אין קנין לנכרי בארץ ישראל להפקיע מיד מעשר מוקי לה בסוף השולח גט (ד' מז.) דלקטינהו ישראל וטעמא דהפקיר הא לא הפקיר לא. ולמאן דאמר יש קנין מוקי לה בשדה דישראל ולקטינהו נכרי. וכי תימא הא מפקרי וקיימי. כי אפקרינהו אדעתא דישראל מפקרי אדעתא דנכרי לא מפקרי. ובירושל' יש שיטה אחרת: ירושלמי (הל' ה) ר' חזקיה ר' ירמיה בשם רבי יוחנן כמאן דאמר יש לנכרי קנין בארץ ישראל לפוטרו מן המעשר. ברם כמאן דאמר אין לנכרי קנין בארץ ישראל לפוטרו מן המעשר אפי' הפקירו חייב. ר' יוסי בשם ר' יוחנן כמאן דאמר אין לנכרי קנין בארץ ישראל לפוטרו מן המעשר. ברם כמאן דאמר יש לנכרי קנין בארץ ישראל לפוטרו מן המעשר קל הקלו חכמים בליקוטים. ר' אליעזר שאל ואין לו קנין נכסים. ומסיק [ב]בירוש' דר' אליעזר אכולהו שאל בין לר' ירמיה בשם ר' יוחנן בין לר' יוסי בשם ר' יוחנן: י הנושר (ו). כלומר שבלים הנופלים: תלש מלא קומצו. דרך התולש לקמץ את ידו: הכהו קוץ ונפל מידו. כל היכא דנושר מחמת אונס ממעט ליה בתורת כהנים בפ' קדושים דתניא ולקט קצירך לא תלקט ולא לקט קיטוף לקט קצירך אין לקט אלא מחמת הקציר מכאן אמרו היה קוצר וקצר מלא ידו תלש מלא קמצו הכהו קוץ עקצו עקרב ונבעת ונפל מידו על הארץ הרי של בעה"ב: תוך היד. אגשר קאי כלומר תוך היד ונשר דהנושר מתוך היד ומתוך המגל לעניים. אבל הנושר מאחר היד ומאחר המגל לבעל הבית דאינו בדרך קצירה: ראש היד. כשידו מלאה ויש שבלים בין ראשי אצבעותיו לפס ידו הנושר משם וכן הנושר מראש המגל: ר' ישמעאל אומר לעניים. דמדמי ליה לתוך היד ולתוך המגל: ר' עקיבא אומר לבעל הבית. דמדמי ליה לאחר היד ולאחר המגל: יא חורי נמלים. בסוף הזרוע (קנג.) מייתי לה דרך הנמלים להכנים תבואה בחוריהן כדכתיב (משלי ו) אגרה בקציר מאכלה: שבתוך הקמה. חורים שבתוך הקמה עד שלא התחילו לקצור: של אחר הקוצרים. כלומר לאחר שהתחילו לקצור שמא הביאו שם הנמלים מן הלקט הלכך העליונים כלומר חטים העליונים שבחורים או שבולים העליונים לעניים דיש שם לקט אבל חטים התחתונים לבעל הבית דמן הקמה היה. ויש לברר הדבר כדמפרש בירושלמי (הל' ה') רב יהודה בשם שמואל העליונים לעניים בלבנים. והתחתונים לבעל הבית בירוקים. שכשהתבואה יבשה ומתלבנת קוצרים אותה: שספק לקט לקט. מפרש בירושלמי (שם) טעמא דר' מאיר משום דאי אפשר לגורן בלא ירוקים בתורת כהנים בפ' קדושים תניא מנין שספק לקט לקט ספק שכחה שכחה ספק פאה פאה ת"ל לגר ליתום ולאלמנה יהיה וכל חד וחד נפיק לן ומזכיר התנא שלשתם אע"ג דלא נפקי מחד קרא שכך דרכו של תנא כדאשכחן נמי התם גבי פרט לשקצרוהו נכרים: ירושלמי (שם) ומנין שספק לקט לקט ר' ישמעאל בר נחמני בשם ר' יהונתן עני ורש הצדיקו (תהלים פב) הצדיקו במתנותיו. ריש לקיש אמר בשם בר קפרא לא תטה משפט אביונך בריבו (שמות כג) בריבו אין אתה מטהו אבל אתה מטהו במתנותיו. א"ר יוחנן ומה היא מה ששנה לנו רבי תעזוב (ויקרא יט) הנח לפניהם משלך א"ר לא כתיב לגר ליתום ולאלמנה יהיה (דברים כד) בין דידך בין דידיה הב ליה. פי' ר' יוחנן מייתי קרא דתורת כהנים ורבי מייתי קרא דסיפרי:

פלוני עני ר' אליעזר אומר זכה לו וחכמים אומרים יתננה לעני שנמצא ראשון א) הלקט והשכחה והפאה של נכרי חייב במעשרות אלא א"כ הפקיר: י ב) איזהו לקט הנושר בשעת הקצירה [היה * קוצר] מלא ידו תלש מלא קומצו הכהו קוץ ונפל מידו לארץ הרי הוא של בעל הבית תוך היד ותוך המגל לעניים אחר היד ואחר המגל לבעל הבית ראש היד וראש המגל ר' ישמעאל אומר לעניים ר' עקיבא אומר לבעל הבית: יא ג) חורי הנמלים שבתוך הקמה הרי הן של בעל הבית של אחר הקוצרים העליונים לעניים והתחתונים של בעל הבית ר' מאיר אומר הכל לעניים שספק לקט לקט:

פרק חמישי

א גדיש ד) שלא לוקט תחתיו כל *הנוגעות בארץ הרי הוא של עניים ה) הרוח שפזרה את העמרים אומדין אותה כמה לקט היא ראויה לעשות ונותן לעניים רבן שמעון בן גמליאל אומר נותן לעניים בכדי נפילה: ב ו) שבולת שבקציר וראשה מגיע לקמה אם *נקצרה עם הקמה הרי היא של בעה"ב ואם לאו הרי היא של עניי' שבולת של לקט שנתערבה בגדיש מעשר שבולת אחת ונותן לו אמר ר' אליעזר וכי היאך העני הזה מחליף דבר שלא בא ברשותו אלא מזכה את העני בכל הגדיש ומעשר שבולת אחת

וכשיפקיר לא יתחייב כל הדבר ההוא מעשר כפי מה שהקדמנו שההפקר אינו חייב במעשר ואין הלכה כר' אליעזר: י פי' הנושר נופל. פי' תלש שלף מעל הארץ: תוך היד ותוך המגל. ר"ל מה שיפול ממה שיהיה בתוך היד או המגל הוא לקט ומה שיפול מאחורי היד ומאחורי המגל הוא לבעל הזרע ומה שיפול מקלה היד ומקלה המגל והוא מה שיפול בין הקצוות ולא יפול עליו לא לשון תוך ולא לשון אחור הוא מחלוקת ר' ישמעאל ור' עקיבא והל' כר"ע: יא חורי הנמלים הם חורי הנמלים שהם עושין בארץ לאגור שם הזרע כשיהיו בקמה הם בחזקת בעה"ב כי אין לעניים בקמה כלום וכשימלאו מאחרי הקוצרים שהרי יש שם זכות לעניים במה שנפל אמר שהזרע העליון והוא הלבן לעניים לפי שנאמר שהם מן הזרע החדש והזרע התחתון והוא השחור לבע"ה לפי שנאמר שהוא קדמון ומזרע השנה שעברה הוא ור"מ אומר כי אפשר להיות השחור ההוא מזה החדש כי אי אפשר שלא יהיה בזרע טוב ורע ואחרי שהדבר ספק נאמר ספק לקט לקט והלכה כרבי מאיר: גדיש שלא לוקט תחתיו. הוא שיקבץ ערימות חטים על מקום שלא נלקט ממנו לקט של עניים אבל קבלוהו והושם על הלקט וקנסו קנס שיתן מן הערימה ההיא כל הנוגע ממנו בפני הארץ מחובר אל מה שיהיה שם מן הלקט. ופי' אומדין הוא השיעור על דרך קירוב. פי' נפילה שיעור מה שזרע בה בשעת הזריעה ואין הלכה כרבן שמעון בן גמליאל: ב שבולת שבקציר. פי' כשיקצור השבלים אפשר שתשאר שבולת אחת בארץ נמלטה מן המגל ונקצר כל מה שסביב ואמר שאם הגיע לקמה עומדת יהיה דינה כדין הקמה והיא של בעל הבית ואם לא יגיע ראשה לקמה עומדת היא כמו לקט ויקחוה העניים: ומה שאמר מעשר שבולת אחת. כבר באר טעמו [ג] והוא שיקח שתי שבלים מן הגדיש ההוא ויקח אחת מהן ויאמר אם תהיה זאת שבולת לקט טוב ואם אינה שבולת הלקט יהיו המעשרות המחוייבות לה בזאת השבולת האחרת ויתן הראשונה לעני והשניה לכהן ואמר ר"א כי העני לא זכה בשבולת ההיא עד יקח תמורתה אחרת אא"כ נתן לו הזרע כלו על מנת שיחזירהו לו וזה הדין נוהג אצלנו מתנה על מנת להחזיר שמה מתנה והיה אז אותה השבולת שהוא לקט באה ליד העני. ואז יוכל שיקח אחרת על הענין הנקדם ואין הלכה כר"א:

א גדיש שלא לוקט תחתיו. אסף העמרים למקום אחד בתוך השדה ועדיין לא ליקטו שם העניים את הלקט: כל הנוגעות בארץ לעניים. הא דלא אמר הכא כמו בסיפא מפרש בירוש' (הל' א) דקנסוהו רבנן משום שהגדיש על הלקט. ואפי' הגדיש חטים על גבי לקט של שעורים פטור מן המעשרות: שפזרה את העמרים. על גבי הלקט: בכדי נפילה. מפרש בפרק המקבל (קה:) ארבעה קבין נפילה לכור זרע ואין כדי נפילה דר' יהודה דמתני' דהתם גבי מקבל שדה מחבירו ולא עשתה כמו כדי נפילה דהתם כדי זריעה מלשון עד שיזרע חטה ושעורה במפולת יד וכדי נפילה דהכא שיעור לקט שרגיל להיות כלומר שיעור שרגיל ליפול בשעת קצירה דהיינו ארבעת קבין לכור זרע. ולא בא רשב"ג לחדש א] דברי ת"ק אלא כלומר אין הדבר צריך אומד שכבר קצוב נפילה ועומד: ירושלמי (שם) הכא את אמר אומדין אותה כמה לקט ראויה היא לעשות ונותן לעניים וכה את אמר כל הנוגעות בארץ הרי הם של עניים. ר' אבהו בשם רבי יוחנן קנס קנסו בו שגדש ע"ג ליקטן של עניים. עד כדון מזיד אפילו שוגג אפי' כריכות אפילו חטים על גבי שעורים אפי' גדשו אחרים חוץ מדעתו אפי' קרא לעניים ולא באו רבי אמי בשם ריש לקיש דב"ש היא דאמרי הבקר לעניים הבקר [א]. א"ר יוסי שמענו שהוא פטור ממעשרות [ב] שהבקר בית דין הבקר דכתיב (עזרא י) כל אשר לא יבא לשלשת הימים בעצת השרים והזקנים יחרם כל רכושו והוא יבדל מקהל הגולה מנין שהוא פטור מן המעשרות. ר' יוחנן בר ילחק בר אחא שמע לה מן הדא אין מעברין את השנה לא בשביעית ולא במוצאי שביעית ואם עיברוה הרי זה מעוברת בחדש אחד שהוא מוסיף לא פטור מן המעשרות הוא. פירוש דבית שמאי היא כלוגתא לקמן בפרק ו' (מ"א) אבל לבית הלל לא הוה קנסינן ליה משום דמדאורייתא חייב במעשר והעני נוהג בו דין לקט רבי יוסי סבר דאפי' לב"ה פטור משום הפקר ב"ד כדדריש מקרא דיחרם כל רכושו ור' יוחנן מייתי ראיה מב"ד שעיברו את השנה שלא כדין: ב שבולת שבקציר. בקצירתו שייר שבולת אחת שלא קצר וראש אותה שבולת מגיע לקמה ושכחה ולא קצרה אם אותה שבולת נקצרת עם הקמה הרי היא של בעל הבית שהקמה מצילתה כדתנן לקמן בפ"ו (מ"ח) שהקמה מצלת את הקמה דאמרי' בירושלמי (הל' ב) אי זו היא קמה שמצלת את הקמה אמר רבי יוחנן כהדה דתנינן שבולת שבקציר וראשה מגיע עד הקמה אמר ר' יוסי שיהא הקציר סובבה ובסיפרי נפקא לן מקרא דתניא בסיפרי בפרשת כי תצא לא תשוב לקחתו מכאן אמר ר' ישמעאל שבולת של קציר וראשה מגיע לקמה כו': מעשר שבולת אחת ונותן לו. לפי שחייב ליתן לו דבר מתוקן כמו שהיתה שבולת של לקט דפטורה מן המעשרות ואע"פ שעדיין לא נתמרחה חל שם מעשר עליו כי ההיא דאשכחן בפ' כל שעה (דף לה:) ובכמה דוכתין למעשר ראשון שהקדימו בשבלים. ומה שאין מזכיר כאן תרומה גדולה לאו משום דמיפטר מחמת שהקדימו בשבלים דהא דאמרי' התם פטור מתרומה גדולה היינו המעשר כדדריש התם מעשר מן המעשר אמרתי לך ולא תרומה גדולה ותרומת מעשר מן המעשר אבל החולין [שלא] נתרמה שהופרש מהן המעשר חייבין בת"ג ועוד דוקא נקט הקדימו דהיינו שעבר והקדים מעשר לתרומה אבל במצותו מפריש ת"ג ואח"כ מעשר בין קודם מירוח בין לאחר מירוח (א): ירושלמי (שם) כילד הוא עושה מביא שתי שבלים ואומר אם לקט הוא זה הרי יפה ואם לאו הרי המעשרות קבועין בזו ונותן לו את הראשונה ותני לומר שמא אותה שקבע בה מעשרות שמא לקט הוא א"ר יונה

ידו ושבראש מגלו משום הכי מה שנושר לקט. ר"ע מדמי ליה לאחר יד. ר"ש פי' ראש היד וראש המגל פלוגתא דר' ישמעאל ור' עקיבא ר' ישמעאל סבר הרי זה ספק כלומר ספק לתוך ידו או ספק לאחר ידו הלכך מספיקא ספק לקט לקט. ור' עקיבא וכו' לא פי' והעיקר מה שפירשנו אנחנו דאם איתה ליתני הכל לעניים שספק לקט לקט כאשר שנה ר' מאיר ותו לא מידי: יא חורי. פי' מלשון חורי הבית ותנן חור שחררוהו מים. פי' החטים שיש בחורים של נמלים שבתוך הקמה שעדיין לא התחילו לקצור שם של בעל הבית: ושל אחר הקוצרין. פי' חורין העומדין במקום הקציר: העליונים לעניים. פי' דאמרינן ממה שנשר מן הקוצרין בעת הקצירה דהוה לקט מיניה גררו והכניסו בחוריהן. מי מוכיח אמרינן בירושלמי אמר רב יהודה אמר שמואל העליונים לעניים בלבנים והתחתונים לבעל הבית בירוקין: ר"מ אומר הכל לעניים. ור' מאיר שפיר קאמרי רבנן ור' מאיר אמר לך אי אפשר לגורן בלא ירוקין והוי ספק וספק לקט לקט. בספרא מנין שספק לקט לקט ספק שכחה שכחה ספק פאה פאה ת"ל לגר ליתום ולאלמנה יהיה. א"ר אילא כתיב לגר ליתום ולאלמנה יהיה בין מן דידך בין מן דידיה הב ליה:

פרק ה א גדיש שלא לוקט תחתיו וכו'. פי' מי שהגדיש בקרקע שהיה בו מקצת לקט ולא לקטוהו עניים. גרסינן בירושלמי אפי' אם היה הלקט שעורין והגדיש חטין או אפילו גידשו אחרים חוץ מדעתו ואפילו קרא לעניים ולא באו: כל הנוגעות בארץ הרי הן של עניים. מאי טעמא א"ר אבהו א"ר יוחנן קנס קנסו בו שהגדיש על ליקטן של עניים קתני כל הנוגעות בארץ הרי הן של עניים פי' אע"ג דלא הוה לקט מבקירין דידיה לעניים דהבקר בית דין הבקר ופטור מן המעשרות: הרוח שפזרה את העומרין וכו'. פי' דרך בני אדם קוצרין ואח"כ מעמרין כדתנן בפירקין דלעיל נכרי שקצר את שדהו ותנן איזהו לקט הנושר בשעת הקצירה ולא נלקט עד שימר תבואתו ובאה הרוח ופיזרתו על השדה אומדין אותה כמה לקט היא ראויה לעשות אותה השדה ונותן לעניים. ע"מדין פי' אומדין כדתנינן התם כיצד מעברין רב ושמואל חד תני מעברין וחד תני מאברין אלמא עיי"ן עם אלף משתמשין במקום אחד: נותן לעניים בכדי נפילה גרסינן בירושלמי א"ר אבהו ד' קבין לבית שדה כור ועוד מקשה בירושלמי סיפא לרישא דאילו רישא כל הנוגעות בארץ לעניים בלא אמידה. ובסיפא תני אמידה. ופריק ר' אבהו בשם ר' יוחנן קנס קנסו בו וכו': ב שבולת שבקציר וראשו מגיע לקמה וכו'. פי' התחיל לקצור ושכח שבולת אחת שלא קצר וראש השבולת ההיא מגיע לקמה אם נקצרת אותה שבולת עם הקמה הרי של בעל הבית שקמה מצלת את השבולת שהיא קמה. ת"ר בסיפרי לא תשוב לקחתו מיכן אמר ר' ישמעאל שבולת שבקציר וראשה מגיע לקמה וכו'. גרסי' א"ר יוסי שיהא הקציר סובבה. והוא שיהא ראשה מגיע לקמה והוא שיהא יכולה להיקצר עם הקמה: שבולת של לקט שנתערבה בגדיש ואינו מכירה מעשר שבולת אחת ונותן לו כיצד עושה א"ר יונה מביא ב' שבולין ואומר אם זו לקט יפה ואם לאו הרי מעשרותיה קבועין בזו ונותן לו אותה שאם לקט היא שפיר ואם לאו כבר נתעשרה מיהא שמעינן שהעני מחליף לקט לישראל: א"ר אליעזר וכי היאך העני הזה מחליף וכו'. גרסינן מחלפא שטתיה

פי' מהר"י בן מלכי צדק

לחבירו: הלקט והשכחה והפאה של נכרי. אם נותן לעני חייב העני לעשרן. פי' בפירות ארץ ישראל היא. ותניא אא"כ הבקיר העני אז פטור מלעשר

הגהות הגר"א

[ב] ומסיק בירושל'.

[ג] מ"ש בר"ש בכר. כ"ב ברש"ב עניים מעשרים והולכים.

SAYS HE HAS THUS ACQUIRED IT FOR HIM.[7] THE SAGES SAY:
a HE MUST GIVE IT TO THE POOR MAN HE FIRST COMES ACROSS.[1] GLEANINGS, THE FORGOTTEN SHEAF AND THE PE'AH OF GENTILES ARE SUBJECT TO TITHES,[2] UNLESS HE [THE GENTILE] HAD DECLARED THEM OWNERLESS.[3]

MISHNAH 10. WHAT CONSTITUTES GLEANINGS?[4] THAT WHICH FALLS DOWN DURING THE REAPING. IF WHILE HE WAS REAPING, HE GRASPED A HANDFUL OR PLUCKED A FISTFUL, AND THEN A THORN PRICKED HIM, AND WHAT HE HAD IN HIS HAND FELL TO THE GROUND, IT STILL BELONGS TO THE OWNER.[5] [THAT WHICH DROPS FROM] INSIDE THE HAND OR THE SICKLE [BELONGS] TO THE POOR,[6] BUT [THAT WHICH FALLS FROM] THE BACK OF THE HAND OR THE SICKLE [BELONGS] TO THE OWNER.[7] [ANYTHING FALLING OUT OF] THE TOP OF THE HAND OR SICKLE,[8] R. ISHMAEL SAYS, BELONGS TO THE POOR;[9] BUT R. AKIBA SAYS, IT BELONGS TO THE OWNER.[10]

MISHNAH 11. [GRAIN FOUND IN] ANT-HOLES[11] WHILE THE CORN IS STILL STANDING[12] BELONGS TO THE OWNER;[13] AFTER THE REAPERS [HAD PASSED OVER THEM][14] THOSE
b [FOUND LYING] UPPERMOST[1] [IN THE ANT-HOLES BELONG] TO THE POOR, BUT [THOSE FOUND] BENEATH[2] [BELONG] TO THE OWNER. R. MEIR SAYS: EVERYTHING BELONGS TO THE POOR;[3] FOR GLEANINGS ABOUT WHICH THERE IS ANY DOUBT ARE REGARDED AS GLEANINGS.

CHAPTER V

MISHNAH 1. IF A HEAP OF CORN WAS PLACED [ON PART OF A FIELD] FROM WHICH GLEANINGS HAD NOT YET BEEN
c COLLECTED,[1] WHATEVER TOUCHES THE GROUND BELONGS TO THE POOR.[2] IF THE WIND SCATTERED THE SHEAVES,[3] ONE ESTIMATES THE AMOUNT OF GLEANINGS THE FIELD WOULD HAVE YIELDED AND GIVES THAT TO THE POOR.[4] R. SIMEON B. GAMALIEL SAYS: ONE MUST GIVE TO THE POOR THE USUAL AMOUNT THAT FALLS [AT THE TIME OF REAPING].[5]

MISHNAH 2. IF THE TOP OF A SINGLE EAR OF CORN [THAT ESCAPED THE SICKLE] AFTER THE REAPING[6] TOUCHES THE STANDING CORN, IF IT CAN BE CUT WITH THE STANDING CORN, IT BELONGS TO THE OWNER;[7] BUT IF NOT, IT IS THE PROPERTY OF THE POOR. IF AN EAR OF CORN OF GLEANINGS BECAME MIXED UP WITH THE STACKED CORN, [THE OWNER] MUST TITHE ONE EAR OF CORN AND GIVE THAT TO HIM [THE POOR].[8] R. ELIEZER SAID: HOW CAN THIS POOR MAN GIVE IN EXCHANGE SOMETHING THAT HAD NOT YET BECOME
d HIS?[1] NO; [THE OWNER] MUST TRANSFER TO THE POOR MAN THE OWNERSHIP OF THE WHOLE STACK[2] AND THEN TITHE

(7) Because he could easily have declared all his possession 'ownerless' and thus rendered himself qualified to get the *Pe'ah* for himself; and consequently he can acquire it for another.

a (1) The Sages do not admit the argument advanced by R. Eliezer (v. B.M. 9*b*). But if the poor man for whom he had collected passes by first, it is given to him. (2) The law of tithes does not apply to the gifts of the poor; but since a non-Jew is exempt from tithes, the gifts of the poor obtained from his field are not treated as such and any Jew who acquires them must set aside tithes. (3) Ownerless property is exempt from dues. (4) Lev. XIX, 9. (5) That which drops accidentally out of his hand is not subject to 'Gleanings'. The Bible stresses '*the gleaning of thy reaping*' (Lev. XXIII, 22), thus precluding any accidental falling, such as the pricking of a thorn. (6) After being within the hand, its falling out is not considered as accidental. (7) This is evidently a pure accident. (8) His fist is full to capacity and the grains that fall are those between his fingers. (9) R. Ishmael regards the tops of his fingers as part of the hand (v. *supra* n. 6). (10) R. Akiba regards the tops of the fingers as the back of the hand, hence the falling is accidental. (11) Ants usually bring the grain into their holes. (12) Prior to the reaping. (13) While the corn is yet uncut, the poor have no claim. (14) The ants had probably gathered the grains from the gleanings.

b (1) I.e., grain still fresh and whitish in appearance (Bert.). (2) The grain showing signs of staleness in appearance—an even better proof that the grains had been stored in these ant-holes for some considerable time before the reaping. (3) Even the grain found below, for some rotten grains are found even among corn freshly cut. What assurance is there that these have not been brought even after the reaping had commenced or finished?

c (1) A fine is imposed lest his intention was to hide the 'Gleanings' due to the poor. (2) Even if he heaps up wheat upon 'Gleanings' of barley, the wheat which touches the ground also belongs to the poor. (3) With the result that the sheaves of the owner got confused with those of 'Gleanings' belonging to the poor. (4) In accordance with R. Meir's principle, *infra* V, 3. (5) So Bertinoro and Tiferes Yisrael; roughly, the prescribed fortyfifth part. Maim., however, in B.M. IX, 5 explains as the amount of seed required for the field. (6) Cf. 'Ed.' II, 4. (7) If it is so near that it can be cut together with the standing corn in one fistful, the standing corn saves it from being regarded as 'Gleanings' since the words '*thou shalt not go back to fetch it*' (Deut. XXIV, 19) do not apply to it. (8) Upon each ear of corn there is the doubt whether it is 'Gleanings' and so exempt from all tithes, or whether it belongs to the owner and is subject to tithes. To solve this doubt, the owner must take another 'ear of corn' and give that to the poor, for the poor must be given that which is free from dues. Tithes, unlike *Pe'ah* (which falls due with the reaping), become liable with the final stacking. (V. *supra* I, 6). The 'tithing' here referred to is thus performed: Two ears of corn are brought from the stack which contains the 'ear' that became mixed up. The owner then says over one of the 'ears': 'Should this one be the "Gleanings", well and good; but if not, then let the tithe due from it be fixed in the other ear and the first be given to the poor'.

d (1) R. Eliezer is surprised at the view of the Sages seeing that they maintained (*supra* IV, 9) that the owner has no proprietary right to transfer gifts to any particular poor. How can they now allow the owner to exchange, in the name of a poor man, an ear of corn which had so far not become his? (It will be remembered that R. Eliezer in IV, 9 was of the opinion that a man could transfer ownership of *Pe'ah* to another). (2) Holding the view that a gift given on condition of returning it later is valid. This makes the exchange possible here.

AN EAR OF CORN AND GIVE IT TO HIM.[3]

MISHNAH 3. ONE SHOULD NOT [IN SOWING] MIX INFERIOR SEEDS [WITH THE REST OF THE GRAIN],[4] THUS R. MEIR. THE SAGES PERMIT IT, BECAUSE IT IS STILL POSSIBLE [FOR THE POOR TO GET THEIR PROPER DUE].[5]

MISHNAH 4. IF A MAN OF PROPERTY[6] WAS TRAVELLING ABOUT FROM PLACE TO PLACE AND HAPPENED TO BE IN NEED OF TAKING GLEANINGS, THE FORGOTTEN SHEAF, PE'AH OR THE POOR MAN'S TITHE,[7] HE MAY TAKE THEM; AND ON HIS RETURN HOME, HE MUST PAY [FOR THE AMOUNT GATHERED]. SO R. ELIEZER. THE SAGES, HOWEVER, SAY: HE WAS A POOR MAN AT THAT TIME [AND SO HE NEED MAKE NO RESTITUTION].

MISHNAH 5. HE THAT MAKES AN EXCHANGE WITH THE
a POOR,[1] [WHAT THEY GIVE IN EXCHANGE] FOR HIS IS EXEMPT [FROM TITHES],[2] BUT WHAT [HE GIVES IN EXCHANGE] FOR THAT OF THE POOR IS SUBJECT [TO TITHES].[3] TWO[4] WHO LEASE A FIELD ON A TENANCY[5] MUST GIVE, EACH TO THE OTHER, HIS DUE OF THE POOR MAN'S TITHE.[6] ONE[7] WHO UNDERTAKES TO REAP A FIELD MUST NOT TAKE GLEANINGS, THE FORGOTTEN SHEAF, PE'AH OR THE POOR MAN'S TITHE.[8] R. JUDAH SAID: WHEN IS THIS SO? WHEN HE RENTS FROM THE OWNER ON THE TERMS OF [PAYING] A HALF, THIRD OR QUARTER[9] [OF THE CROP]; BUT [IF THE OWNER] HAD STIPULATED WITH HIM THAT: 'A THIRD OF WHAT THOU REAPEST IS THINE',[10] THEN HE IS PERMITTED TO TAKE GLEANINGS, THE FORGOTTEN SHEAF AND PE'AH, BUT NOT THE POOR MAN'S TITHE.[11]

MISHNAH 6. IF ONE SELLS A FIELD THE VENDOR IS
b PERMITTED[1] [TO GATHER THE DUES OF THE POOR], BUT NOT THE PURCHASER. A MAN MAY NOT HIRE A LABOURER ON THE CONDITION THAT THE SON [OF THE LABOURER] SHOULD GATHER THE GLEANINGS AFTER HIM.[2] ONE WHO PREVENTS THE POOR TO GATHER, OR ALLOWS ONE BUT NOT ANOTHER, OR HELPS ONE OF THEM [TO GATHER], IS DEEMED TO BE A ROBBER OF THE POOR. CONCERNING SUCH A ONE HATH IT BEEN SAID: REMOVE NOT THE LANDMARK OF THOSE THAT COME UP.[3]

MISHNAH 7. A SHEAF WHICH THE LABOURERS HAD FORGOTTEN BUT NOT THE LANDLORD, OR WHICH THE LANDLORD FORGOT BUT NOT THE LABOURERS;[4] OR A SHEAF IN FRONT OF WHICH THE POOR STOOD, OR COVERED UP WITH STUBBLE, IS NOT TO BE REGARDED AS A FORGOTTEN SHEAF.

MISHNAH 8. IF ONE BINDS SHEAVES TO COVER THE TOP OF THE HEAP[5] OR TO PLACE AT THE BOTTOM OF THE STACK,[6] OR FOR A TEMPORARY PILE,[7] OR INTO [SMALL BUNDLES OF]
c SHEAVES,[1] HE IS NOT SUBJECT TO THE LAW OF THE FORGOTTEN SHEAF;[2] IF THEY ARE AFTERWARDS TAKEN THENCE TO THE THRESHING-FLOOR, THE LAW OF THE FORGOTTEN

(3) The Sages, without agreeing with R. Eliezer, would reply that in this case the ear of corn was regarded as the poor man's property, in order to make the exchange possible. (4) So Bert. and Maim. who take מופח to be an inferior type of barley seed or beans; for this mixing would be to the detriment of the poor (for the 'Gleanings' might fall from the inferior grain). *Aliter:* One should not irrigate the field (before Gleanings have been taken) with a pitcher (מיפח) of water (an irrigation); since this would make it all the more difficult for the poor to glean. (5) Is it not equally possible for the 'Gleanings' to fall from the superior kinds of grain? According to the second explanation: 'Is it not possible for the owner of the field to compensate the poor for their loss?' (6) Lit., 'a householder'; one who possesses more than two hundred *zuz* is disqualified from receiving these poor man's dues (v. *infra* VIII, 8). (7) In the third and sixth years of the Sabbatical cycle, the Second Tithe was given to the poor (Deut. XIV, 29).
a (1) Giving them some other produce in exchange for the 'Gleanings'. (2) All the dues of the poor are exempt from tithes. (3) The produce of the owner must be tithed prior to the exchange. (4) Poor men. (5) An אריס is a labourer who accepts as his payment a stipulated portion of the field's harvest. The labourer thus becomes virtually the owner of the field and, though poor otherwise, is disqualified from taking the dues. (6) In Lev. XIX, 10 the words לא תלקט לעני are taken to refer as a warning to the poor not to gather their own 'Gleanings'. From this verse is also derived the law that one cannot gather 'dues' for another poor man (v. Giṭ. 12*a*). Hence here, each one being the owner of his part of the field, can only accept the tithe due to the other (cf. Ḥul. 131*b*). (7) A poor man. (8) He is no longer regarded as poor. (9) The produce then becomes the property of the labourer already before the reaping, when still attached to the soil. (10) Since in this case, the poor man has only a share in the corn after its reaping, the duty falls upon the owner. Even from the Forgotten Sheaf is the poor man exempt, although its law comes into force at the time of the stacking of the sheaves (after reaping), since the word '*thy reaping*' cannot here be applied; for it becomes the poor man's only after it had been cut. (11) Since the tithe becomes due after the reaping (I, 6) when the poor man is already owner of his share in the produce.
b (1) If compelled by poverty to do so. This only applies if he sold the field together with the standing corn thereon. For should he dispose of the latter and reserve the field for himself, both the vendor and buyer would be debarred; the former because '*thy field*' (Lev. XIX, 9) still applies to him, and the latter because of the application in his case of '*thy reaping*' (ibid.). (2) On account of this concession, the labourer reduces his fees and the employer is thus found settling part of his debts with money due to the poor. (3) Prov. XXII, 28; the word עולם 'of old' is read by the Mishnah as עולים 'those who go up', a euphemistic name for the poor, who 'have come down in the world' (יורדים); cf. *infra* VII, 3. Bert. also gives the following rendering: 'Do not change the warnings (fences round the law) that were given to those who went up from Egypt'. (4) The principle is that before being regarded as (Forgotten Sheaf), it must have been forgotten by both. (5) In the shape of a hat. Or perhaps the hat improvised from a few sheaves and worn by the labourers as a protection from the sun (Bert.). (6) As a foundation for the pile above. Others explain the reference to the holes dug in the field in which the sheaves were stacked temporarily. (7) Often used with which to bake an improvised cake (חררה) or two on live coals. Bert. appends this illuminating note: 'Some cut corn and heap it up into one place, afterwards carrying it to the threshing-floor. The names in the Mishnah are those given to the shapes of the piles prior to their removal to the threshing-floor. Accordingly, this temporary stacking does not constitute the end of the process'. In view of this explanation, חררה is a cake-shaped temporary pile.
c (1) To be arranged afterwards into bigger piles, from which the threshing will be done. (2) Those sheaves dropped during the process of carrying from place to place; for just as the law of *Pe'ah* in Deut. XXIV, 19 refers to the end of reaping, so the law of the Forgotten Sheaf applies only to the very end of the process of threshing.

מסורת הש"ם

א) חולין פ"י ד' קל:

מביא שתי שבלים ואומר אם לקט זה הרי יפה ואם לאו הרי מעשרותיה קבועין בזו ונותן לו אחת מהן (א) פי' הראשונה שאמר עליה אם לקט היא ופריך ושמא אותה שקבע בה מעשרות דהיינו אותה שעיכב לקט היא ואין המעשרו' קבועין בה ומאל (ג) העני אוכל טבלים ומשני רבי יונה דמביא שתי שבלים מלבד אותה שנותן לעני וקובע המעשרות על אחת מהן ואומר על הראשונה אם לקט היא יפה ואם לאו הרי מעשרותיה קבועין על השניה ואח"כ אומר על השניה דאם היא של לקט הרי מעשרות הראשונה קבועין על השלישית והשתא יש כאן שתי שבלים ולא ידעינן בהי מינייהו המעשרות קבועין ואין יכול ליתן לעני אלא הראשונה והא דנקט ונותן לו אחת מהן לא חש לומר ונותן לו הראשונה הואיל וכבר פירש מעיקרא והכי קאמר ונותן לו אחת מהן כלומר אחת מהן יקח עליה ויתן לעני · וכשבא לעשות תקנה לגדיש אי אפשר לעשר מיניה וביה דשמא שבולת של לקט מעורב בו ונמצא מפריש מן הפטור על החיוב או מן החיוב על הפטור למ"ד אין בילה בפ"ק דר"ה (דף י"ג:) וצריך לבקש פרנסה ממקום אחר לעשר על הגדיש חוץ מעל שבולת אחת משום ספק שבולת של לקט דלא ידעינן אם היא באותן שבולים שלקט או בגדיש · ואח"כ עומד ומתנה אם השבולת של לקט בגדיש הרי יפה ואם אינה בגדיש אותה שבולת שלא עישר עליה ממקום אחר מעשרותיה יהו קבועים באחת מאלו השתים · ונמצא השתא על אלו השתים מספק שלש מעשרות בכל אחת ואחת ושלש תרומות שני מעשרות ושתי תרומות של שני שבלים ותרומה ומעשר של עצמה בין ממעשר ראשון בין ממעשר שני או ממעשר עני דנמצאו בכל אחת ואחת שלש תרומות וששה מעשרות לפי מה שפירשנו לעיל דמפרים בשבלין לא מיפסר מת"ג אלא המעשר לבדו אם הקדימו לתרומה דהא יש בה מספק מעשרות של שבולת שנתן לעני ומעשרות כל אחת בחברתה ג] ומעשרות של עצמה דשמא שלשתן אינן של לקט שנשאר הלקט בגדיש · וקלא תימה כל טורח זה למה שצריך להביא שתי שבלים מלבד שבולת שנותן לעני ולהתנות כמה תנאים והלא כיון דלבסוף יהא זקוק לבקש לו פרנסה ממקום אחר בענין שאפשר לעשות תקנה לגדיש כדפרישית א"כ מתחלתו יעשה כן ויעשר ממקום אחר על כל הגדיש חוץ מעל שבולת אחת של לקט שנתערבה עמו · וי"ל דבשעת הקציר אין כל כך פרנסה מזומנת ועוד שהיה צריך להביא כאן כדי לעשר ולתרום מן המוקף וגם אי אפשר לכוין מעשרותיו בשבלים שלא ירבה במעשרות ואי אפשר לעשר מאומד והעניים באים כל שעה ושעה בשדה ליקח הלקט ואין יכולין להמתין על זה לפיכך נוקח לאלתר שלשה שבלים ומתנה עליהן ונותן לעני את האחד מיד · ואם היתה מזומנת לו שבולת אחת של ודאי טבל לא היה צריך להביא שלש אלא מביא אחת מן הגדיש ואומר אם של לקט היא הרי יפה ואם לאו מעשרותיה קבועים בשל ודאי טבל וכן כשיבוא לתקן כל הגדיש ומעשר עליה ממקום אחר חוץ משבולת אחת שבה מתנה דאם יש שם שבולת של לקט הרי יפה ואם לאו מעשרות השבולת יהו קבועין בשבולת של ודאי טבל ונמצא דליכא שום ספק על אותה שבולת ושמא הכי נמי קאמר ר' יונה שתי שבלים שתהא אחת מהן של ודאי טבל כן צריך ליישב דברי ר' יונה : שלא בא לרשותו · מפרש בירושלמי (שם) ר' אליעזר לדבריהם דרבנן קאמר להו דלדידיה הא אמר ר' אליעזר בפירקין דלעיל זכה לו ובפ"ק דגיטין (דף יא:) ובפרק שנים אוחזין (דף ט:) מייתי לה וטעמייהו דרבנן כדאמרינן בירושלמי רבי אבהו בשם ריש לקיש דרבי יוסי היא דתנן שרבי יוסי אומר כל שחליפיו ביד כהן פטור מן המתנות ורבי מאיר מחייב משנה היא בבכורות פרק שני ואמרי' התם (דף יח:) טעמא דר' יוסי דעשו את שאינו זוכה כזוכה : ירושלמי (שם) ר' אבהו בשם ר' יוחנן מחלפה שיטתיה דר"א תמן הוא אומר זכה לו וכאן הוא אומר כן כשיטתן השיבם כשיטתכם שאתם אומרים דלא זכה לו ע"י חליפין איך העני זה מחליף דבר שלא בא לרשותו : ג בטופח ג] · מלשון משקה טופח אל ירבץ שדהו כל כך שיהא משקה טופח בה משום דמזיק לעניים הבאים בשביל הלקט וחכמים מתירין ושמין הפסד העניים ובעה"ב משלם לעניי אותה העיר ולר"מ דאמר אין מגלגלין שמין לבעה"ב בהפסדו כמו שפירשו מוכיח בירושלמי : ד עני היה · ופטור מלשלם : ה שלו פטור · מן המעשר דהיינו מה שנתן לו העני דהוא של לקט שכחה ופאה דפטור מן המעשר ושל עניים חייב דהיינו מה שנתן בעל הבית לעני מתבואתו דחייב במעשר וקודם שיתן לעני חייב לעשר כדאשכחן לעיל (מ"ב) גבי שבולת שנתערבה : שנים שקבלו · והם עניים ועשים כבעל הבית כדאמרינן בפרק קמא דגיטין (דף יב.) להזהיר עני על שלו ודווקא על חלקו נעשה כבעל הבית ולא על של חבירו לפיכך מותרין ליתן זה לזה : שקיבלו · ממנו למחצה שזכה במחובר אבל כי אמר ליה מה שאתה קוצר אין לו חלק אלא בתלוש וחייב דלקט שכחה ופאה על בעל השדה ואע"פ ששכחת עמרים בתלוש בשעת עימור וטעינן ליה לרבי יהודה בפירקין דלעיל (מ"ו) גבי גר דאע"פ דאין לו שכחה בקמה יש לו שכחה בעומרים מ"מ פטר כאן דלא קרינא ביה קצירך הואיל ולא זכה אלא בתלוש וגר שנתגייר לאחר קצירה דחייב בשכחה נר"י (לעיל פ"ד מ"ו) היינו משום דקרינא ביה שדך מידי דהוה אמכר קמה ושייר שדה דאסור בלקט שכחה ופאה כמו שאפרשנו בסמוך מ"מ מהאי טעמא לא מחייבינן גר בלקט מאחר דעיקרו במחובר : ירושלמי (הל' ד) תני אב ובנו איש וקרובו שני אחים שני שותפין פודין זה לזה מעשר שני ונותנין זה לזה מעשר עני אמר ר' יודא תבא מארה למי שנותן פאה לאביו ומעשר עני אמרו מנין אם היו שניהם עניים פי' פודין מעשר שני זה לזה בלא חומש משום דכתיב (ויקרא כג) אם גאל יגאל איש ממעשרו חמישיתו יוסף עליו על מעשר שלו מוסיף חומש ולא על מעשר שני של חברו · אם היו שניהם עניים אב ובנו דקאמר ת"ק בשניהם עניים : ו המוכר · הוא מותר בלקט ירו' (הל' ה) מתני' בשמכר לו שדה וקמתה אבל מכר לו קמה ושייר לו שדה אצל זה אני קורא שדך ואצל זה אני קורא קצירך : על מנת שילקט בנו אחריו והא דתניא בפרק שנים אוחזין (דף י"ב·) השוכר את הפועל ילקט בנו אחריו התם בסתם אבל הכא דהתנה פוחת לו הפועל משכרו בשביל בנו שמלקט אחריו : ירושלמי (שם) בעל הבית שעשה כן הרי זה גוזל את העניים פועל שעשה כן גוזל לבעל הבית ולעניים פירוש בעה"ב מוכר חלקו של עניים שהפועל מנכה לו משכרו והפועל מוליא לבנו ד] יותר מדין לקט לפיכך קרי ליה גוזל בעה"ב ולעניים : גבול עולים · ירושל' (שם) רבי ירמיה ורב יוסף חד אמר אלו יולאי מצרים וחד אמר אלו שירדו מנכסיהם לסמיא נוחי סגי נהיר פי' עולים דרשו בלשון עליה וקרי ליה ליורד מנכסיו עולים בל' כבוד כמו שמכנים לסומא סגי נהור בלשון כבוד : ז ולא שכחו בעל הבית · וכגון דבעל הבית בשדה דקאי גביה דליזכי ביה אבל אי הוה בעל הבית בעיר הוי שכחה אע"ג דלא שכחו בעל הבית כדאיתא בפרק שנים אוחזין (דף י"א·):ירושלמי (הל' ז) עומר ששכחוהו פועלים ולא שכחו בעה"ב אינו שכחה דכתיב (דברים כד) קצירך ושכחת שכחו בעה"ב ולא שכחוהו פועלים אינו שכחה דכתיב (שם) כי תקצור ושכחת ר' שמעון בן יהודה משום ר' שמעון אומר אפי' אחרים שעברו ולאו עומר ששכחו פועלים ולא (ג) שכחו בעה"ב אינו שכחה עד שישכחוהו כל אדם הי' עומד (ד) בעיר ואמר יודע אני שהפועלי' שכחו עומרים שבמקו' פלוני ושכחוהו [אינו שכחה] הי' עומד (ה) בשדה ה] ואמר הפועלים שכחו עומרים שבמקום פלוני ושכחוהו ה"ז שכחה שנ' (שם) בשדה ושכחת ולא בעיר ושכחת פי' קצירך ושכחת משמע שבעל הקציר ישכח דהיינו בעל הבית וכי תקצור ושכחת משמע דהקוצר ישכח דהיינו פועלים עד שישכחוהו כל אדם בכל הספרים כתוב במילתיה דר' שמעון ולא שכחו בעה"ב וצריך לומר דבשלא שכחו בעל הבית אז בעי שיהא שכוח מכל אדם ולי אפשר לומר דגרסינן ושכחו בעל הבית דאי בעומד בעיר הא אמר ר' שמעון בסיפא דלא הוי שכחה ואי בעומד בשדה אפי' לא שכחו בעל הבית הויב ליה שכחה בסיפא שנאמר בשדה ושכחת ולא בעיר ושכחת וקסבר ר' שמעון דגזירת הכתוב הוא כי קושיא דמקשינן בפרק שנים אוחזין (דף יא·) ודילמא גזירת הכתוב הוא דבשדה הוי שכחה בעיר לא הוי שכחה ולית ליה דאמר רב אשי התם אמר קרא (שם) יהיה לרבות שכחת העיר : עמדו עניים בפניו או שחיפוהו בקש בספרי בפ' כי תלא זו דברי ר' יהודה וחכמים אומרים בשדך לרבות את הסמונים וברים עגלה ערופה מפרש טעמייהו במס' סוטה (דף מה·): ח המעמר לכובעות · לעשות מהם כובע לראש כדאשכחן שהיו עושים עטרות שבולים : ירו' (שם) ר' יונה אומר מן לעיל כמה דתימר וכובע נחושת על ראשו (שמואל א יז) לכומסו' מלרע כמה דתימא (דברים לב) הלא הוא כמוס עמדי לחררה גלגל לעמרים א"ר יונה כי תקצור קצירך בשדה ושכחת עומר בשדך מה קציר שאין אחריו קציר אף עומר שאין אחריו עמור פי' מן לעיל למעלה מראשו כדפרישית מן לרע למטה מן הראש שאין נראה כלל כדבר הכמוס (ד) וי"מ כובעות ראשי שבולים כומסות תחתיו של שבולים גלגל ל' גלגול עיסה והיינו דקתני חררה כמו חררה ע"ג גחלים פ"ק דשבת (דף יט:) שהיא עוגה קטנה : לעמרים · לא עמרים להגדיש אלא עמרים אחרים קטנים לעשות מהן עוד עמרים אחרים להוליכן לגדיש כדתנן בתוספתא האוגד כריכות

ג מגלגלין . ידוע : וטופח . שם מין מגיני הגרגרין קרובים בדמותם וטבעם מן השעורים והרופאים קוראין אותן בלשון ערב קורטומ"ן ואמר ר"מ שיש להשמר מזה המין שלא יקראוהו בכלל הזרע מפני שיזיק לעניים שמא יהיה הלקט הנופל מן המין ההוא וחכמים מתירין כי הם אומרים שאפשר שיהיה הלקט מן הזרע הטוב ולא מזה המין ואין הלכה כר"מ: ד כשיצטרך אדם בדרך ללקט שכחה ופאה אע"פ שיש לו ממון אינו חייב לשלם כשיחזור לביתו אלא במדת חסידות: ה כשיחליף עם העניים מה שלקט פטור מן המעשרות מפני שהיה של עניים ואין עליו חובת מעשרות ומה שבא ליד העניים יהיה אחר התרומה מפני שהיה ממון בעה"ב שהוא חייב במעשרות·ופירוש אריסות השותפות בתבואת הארץ ושם השותף בענין ההוא אריס והוא שיקח הארץ לעבוד אותה ולהתעסק בעניניה וכבר הקדמנו שהכהן והלוי כשיקנו הזרע יש להם להוציא מידיהם המעשרות אף על פי שהם שלהם ויתנו אותם לאחרים וכמו כן העניים כשיקנה עני או יהיה אריס יש לנו להוציא מתנות העניים מידו ויתנו לאחרי' לפיכך הודיענו שאם יקחו שני עניים שדה באריסו' אין לנו להוציא מתנות העניים מתחת ידם אבל יתן כל א' מהם לחברו מעשר עני מחלקו שנתחייב בו ונתבארו דברי חכמים בדברי רבי יהודה ופירושו שבזמן שקבל השדה באריסות שיקח מתבואתה חליה או שלישית' או רביעיתה או זולתו מן החלקים כל שנעשה השדה א] כולה ברשותו ובחזקתו ולפיכך אסור בלקט ובשכחה ובפאה אבל אם יאמר לו חלק ממה שאתה קוצר יהיה לך אין לו חלק אלא במה שהוא קוצר ולא נעשית השדה ברשותו ומותר לו לקט ושכחה ופאה ומחייבין אותו מעשר עני המחויב לדבר הקצור מפני שיש לו בו חלק והלכה כרבי יהודה שהוא מבאר דברי חכמים: ו ענין זה שמכר השדה כולה ותבואתה והמוכר ההוא שנשאר עני מותר בלקט שכחה ופאה והלוקח אסור בלקט שכחה ופאה ואפי' לא נתן הכסף או אפי' לוה דמיה . וכשישכור הפועל עצמו על מנת שילקט בנו עמו הוא גוזל העניים . ומה שאמר עולים ·והפסוק אמר עולם . לא יקשה בעיניך שזה על דרך דרש ומעיקרי לשון הקדש כי אותיות המשך והנוח יתחלפו קצתם עם קצתם והם טפלות מן הכתיבה להקל ור"ל בעולים עולי מצרים כלומר המצות והחוקים אשר לוה האל ליוצאי מצרים: ז חפוהו בקש. כסוהו והסתירוהו בתבן ודומה לו:ח המנהג לקצור החטה ולעשותה ערימות ערימות במקומות רבות עד שיקבצו הכל במקום אחד ומןהמקום ההוא למקום הדישה והוא נקרא גורן.וכל אשר יקבצו מן הערימות מעל הארץנקראו טבעות שהם דומים לטבע וכל מה שיקבצו בחפירה שהיא נעשית בארץ נקראו כומסות גזור ממלת הלא הוא כמוס עמדי (דברים לב) ומה שיתקבצו ממנה כעגולה דמות רחים נקראו חררה וכן ביאר הגמרא ולעמרים הוא שיוליך האלומים הקטרים לעשות מהם עמרים גדולים וזה הוא נקרא לעמרים וכל מה שיוליכם ממקום

תורה אור

ונותן לו : ג אין מגלגלין בטופח דברי ר"מ וחכמים מתירין מפני שאפשר : ד א) בעה"ב שהיה עובר ממקום למקום וצריך ליטול לקט שכחה ופאה ומעשר עני יטול וכשיחזור לביתו ישלם דברי ר"א וחכ"א (ב) אעני היה באותה שעה : ה בהמחליף עם העניים *בשלו פטור *ובשל עניים חייב גשנים שקיבלו את השדה באריסות זה נותן לזה חלקו מעשר עני וזה נותן לזה חלקו מעשר עני דהמקבל שדה לקצור אסור בלקט שכחה ופאה ומעשר עני אמר ר' יהודה אימתי הבזמן שקבל ממנו למחצה לשליש ולרביע אבל אם אמר לו שליש מה שאתה קוצר שלך מותר בלקט ובשכחה ובפאה ואסור במעשר עני : ו והמוכר את שדהו המוכר מותר והלוקח אסור זלא ישכור אדם את *הפועלים על מנת שילקט בנו אחריו חמי שאינו מניח את העניים ללקוט או שהוא מניח את אחד ואחד לא או שהוא מסייע את אחד מהן הרי זה גוזל את העניים על זה נאמר °אל תסג גבול *עולים : ז כהעומר ששכחוהו פועלים ולא שכחו בעל הבית שכחו בעל הבית ולא שכחוהו פועלים עמדו עניים בפניו או (ג) שחיפוהו בקש הרי זה אינו שכחה : ח כהמעמר לכובעות ולכומסאות לחררה ולעמרים אין לו שכחה ממנו ולגורן יש

משלי כב

פי' מהר"י בן מלכי צדק

דר' אליעזר תמן הוא אמר לא זכה לו וכה אמר הדין כשיטתן השיבן כשיטתכם שאתם אומרים ע"י חילופין היאך העני מחליף וכו' אלא בכל הגדיש בעי לזכותו אבל בשבולת אחת לא : ג אין מגלגלין בטופח וכו'. פי' אין מכניסין פועלין בשדה לקצירה כשהיא מטופחה ומרובצת ממים שהעניים אינם יכולים לבוא וחכמי' אומרים מגלגלים ואף על גב דאיכא פסידא לעניים לא חיישינן אלא שאין ההפסד לעניים ובעל הבית משלם ולמי משלם לעניי אותה העיר מה ששמין לו ב"ד : ד בעה"ב וכו'. פשוטה היא : וחכמים אומרים

פירוש הרא"ש

הגהות הגר"א

הגהות הרי"ד לנדא

ו המוכר שדהו המוכר מותר. פי' בלקט שכחה ופאה. גרסינן בירושלמי אימתי בשמכר לו שדה וקמתה אבל אם מכר לו הקמה ושייר לו הקרקע שניהן אסורין פי' הלוקח והמוכר אצל זה אני קורא שדך ואצל זה אני קורא קצירך : לא ישכור אדם את הפועל על מנת שילקט וכו'. גרסינן בעל הבית שעשה כן גוזל את העניים ופועל שעשה כן גוזל בעל הבית ועניים : גבול עולים . פליגי בה רב ירמיה ורב יוסף חד אמר אילו עולי מצרים כלומר אל תשג גבול עולים שנגבל לעולי מצרים והיא מצות התורה . והרינא אמר עולין אלו שירדו מנכסיהן וקרי להן עולין כינוי כמו דלסמיא צווחין סגי נהור : ז העומר ששכחוהו פועלין ולא שכח בעל הבית אינו שכחה. דכתיב קצירך ושכחת: שכח בעל הבית ולא שכחוהו פועלין אינו שכחה דכתיב כי תקצור ושכחת : ח המעמר לכובעות פי' כמו כובע · גרסינן בירושלמי·ר' יונה אמר מן לעיל פי' מראש כדכתיב וכובע נחשת על ראשו ולכומסות ר' אבינא אמר מלרע פי' למטה מן הראש כמו צירקיסלו כמה דאת אמר הלא הוא כמוס

ועתיד לעומרן וכן אגודי השום ואגודות השום והבצלים אין להם שכחה וכל הני דמתני' כולהו עדיין סופו לעמר לעשות משנים אחד וטעמא כדדרשינן בירושלמי (שם) דומיא דקציר שאין אחריו קציר הכא נמי בעינן עימור שלא יהא אחריו עימור אלא משם ולגורן יש לו שכחה : המעמר לגדיש · דמשעימר הכל רוצה לעשות מהם גדים יש לו שכחה אבל אם אחר כן רצה לעשות מן הגדים גורן אין לו שכחה כדקא תני זה הכלל :

א הבקר. א] כמו הפקר דאם הפקיר לעניים ולא לעשירים פטור מן המעשר:אינו הבקר· וחייב במעשר ואפילו קדם עני וזכה לא עשה כלום כדמוכח בפרק אלו מציאות (דף ל:) בעובדא דר' ישמעאל בר' יוסי בההוא גברא דהוי דרי פתכא דאופי ואפקריה רבי ישמעאל ברבי יוסי לכולי עלמא בר מההוא גברא ופריך עלה מי הוי הפקר כי האי גוונא ובירושלמי (הל' א) מפרש טעמייהו מקראי: ירושלמי (שם) ר' חייא בשם ר' יוחנן טעמייהו דב"ש (ויקרא יט) לעני ולגר מה ת"ל תעזוב אותם יש לך עזיבה אחרת כזו מה זו לעניים ולא לעשירים אף מה שנאמר במקום אחר לעניים ולא לעשירים אמר ריש לקיש טעמייהו דב"ה תשמטנה (שמות כג) מה ת"ל ונטשתה יש לך נטישה אחרת כזו מה זו לעניים ולעשירים אף מה שנאמר במקום אחר לעניים ולעשירים מה מקיימין ב"ה טעמייהו דב"ש תעזוב אותם מיעוט זה לעניים ולא לעשירים אבל מה שנאמר במקום אחר לעניים ולעשירים מה מקיימין ב"ש טעמייהו דב"ה תשמטנה ונטשתה מיעוט זה לעניים ולעשירים אבל מה שנאמר במקום אחר לעניים ולא לעשירים א"ר אבין ליסן מתני' מסייע ליה לריש לקיש עד שיבקיר לעשירים כשמטה הבקיר לבהמה ולא לאדם לנכרים ולא לישראל לעשירים ולא לעניים (זה) [ד"ה] אין הבקרו הבקר הבקיר לאדם ולא לבהמה לישראל ולא לנכרים לעניי אותה העיר ולא לעניי עיר אחרת(א)בפלוגתא דרבי יוחנן וריש לקיש על דעתיה דרבי יוחנן הבקרו הבקר על דעתיה דריש לקיש אין הבקרו הבקר אמר רבי לא בפירוש פליגי רבי יוחנן אמר הבקר ריש לקיש אמר אין הבקר פי' פאה ושמטה פטורין מן המעשר כדדרשינן בספרי ובא הלוי כי אין לו חלק ונחלה עמך יצא זה שיש לו חלק ונחלה עמך דהא לוי עני נוטל פאה ובמכילתא בפרשת ואלה המשפטים יליף שביעית מדכתיב ואכלו אביוני עמך ויתרם תאכל חית השדה הקיש אדם לחיה מה חיה אוכלת שלא מן המעושר אף אדם אוכל שלא מן המעושר וקסבר רבי יוחנן דבית שמאי ילפי מפאה וב"ה אותם מיעוטא היא ולא צריכי למילף משמטה וריש לקיש סבר דמשמטה ילפי בית הלל ומעמייהו דבית שמאי דתשמטנה מיעוטא היא ולאו משום דילפי מפאה והכי קאמר רבי אבין דליסן דמתני' מסייעא לריש לקיש דקתני כשמטה אלמא משמטה ילפא ור' יוחנן סבר דכשמטה סימנא בעלמא נקטיה : אין הבקרו הבקר ולא דמי לא לפאה ולא לשמטה על דעתיה דרבי יוחנן הבקרו הבקר ופטור מן המעשר אע"ג דלא הוי כעין שמטה דבית הלל לאו משמטה ילפי אלא מדכתיב אותם דריש דבעינא אף לעשירים והא דקאמר לעניי אותה העיר לאו דוקא אלא כלומר לבני אותה העיר ואע"פ שלכל הפקיר נקט לעניים משום דסתמא לפי שראה צורך עניים עשה לריש לקיש לא הוי הפקר לבית הלל דקסבר דבעי דומיא דשמטה והיא דפ' אלו מציאות (ל:) דמשמע מעובדא דר' ישמעאל בר' יוסי דאפי' הפקירה לכולי עלמא חוץ מחד גברא לא הוי הפקר התם רוצה לייסב דלא תיקשי לריש לקיש מילתיה דרבי ישמעאל בר' יוסי וסוגיא דהגמ' בסוף השולח (דף מז·) כריש לקיש גבי הא דקאמר רבה אין קנין לנכרי בא"י להפקיע מיד מעשר דדייק לה ממתני' דהלקט והפאה של נכרי חייבין במעשר אא"כ הפקיר ה"ד אילימא דישראל ולקטינהו נכרי הא מיפקרי וקיימי אלא דנכרי ולקטינהו ישראל וטעמא דהפקיר הא לא הפקיר לא לעולם דישראל ולקטינהו נכרי וכדקאמרת הא מפקרי וקיימי נהי דמפקרי אדעתא דישראל אדעתא דנכרי מי מפקרו ומיהו י"ל דהתם כמו הפקר בטעות הוא דלא הפקיר על דעת שיזכה בה כותי אבל אם הפקיר על דעת ישראל וזכה ישראל פטור מן המעשר אע"פ שלא הפקיר לנכרי והיא דבן בוהין פסחים (דף נז·) דנתן פאה לירק ומצאו אביו אמר להם בניי הניחו לי ואני אתן לכם כפלים במעושר ולא מפני שעיני צרה אלא מפני שאמרו חכמים אין פאה לירק והיה ירא שלא יאכלו בלא מעשר כדין פאה לב"ה ניחא שאינו פטור עד שיפקיר אף לעשירים ואפילו לב"ש הוי כמו הפקר בטעות דלא הפקיר אלא מפני ברית ג] חיוב פיאה והא דקאמר בב"ק (דף כח·) בעה"ב שהניח פאה מלד אחד ובאו עניים ונטלו מלד אחר זה וזה ג) לפטור מן המעשר כדאשכחן במפקיר כרמו ולמחר השכים ובצרו אפי' לב"ה ניחא דראשונה מיד נפטרה כשהניחה לשם פאה דמשום דחזר וזכה בה לא נתחייבה וזאת נמי שנפלו לדעתו נפלה ופטורה. בירושלמי(הל' א) מפרש טעמא דב"ש שהוא יכול לחלקו עמרים של קב קב ולעשות ממנו שורה הואיל ועומרי השדה קטנים שאין בכל אחד וא' כי אם קב וכן עומרי השדה של ב' קבין וא' של ח' קבין וב"ש לטעמייהו דאמרי בפרקין ג' לעניים וד' לבעה"ב וב"ה צ"ל רואין: ב גפה. גדר אבנים סדורות זו על זו בלא טיט : ירושלמי (שם) וקשיא לב"ש הגפה וגדיש דבר שהוא מסוייס ואינון אמרין אינו שכחה וקשיא לב"ה בקר וכלים דבר שאינו מסוייס ואינון אמרין שכחה פי' דבר שהוא מסוייס מתוך הסברא היה נראה איפכא דדבר שהוא מסוייס קשיא לב"ה אמאי הוי שכחה דכיון שהוא במקום מסוייס הרי הוא כאילו לא שכחו ודבר שאינו מסוייס קשיא לב"ש אמאי לא הוי שכחה ושמא טעות סופר יש בירושלמי:תניא בתוספתא ובירושלמי א"ר עילעא שאלתי את ר' יהושע באלו עומרים היו ב"ש וב"ה חולקין אמר בתורה הזאת על העומר סמוך לגפה ולגדיש ולבקר ולכלים ושכחו וכשבאתי ושאלתי את ר' אליעזר אמר לי מודים באלו שהן שכחה על מה נחלקו על העומר שהחזיק בו להוליכו לעיר ונתנו בצד הגפה או בצד הגדר שב"ש אומרים אינו שכחה מפני שזכה בה וב"ה אומרים שכחה וכשבאתי והרציתי דברים לפני רבי אלעזר בן עזריה אמר לי הברית הן הן הדברים שנאמרו לו למשה בחורב פי' ברית היא התורה כדכתיב ע"פ הדברים האלה כרתי אתך ברית:בירושלמי (שם) פריך אמאי לא תנינן גבי קולי בית שמאי והומרי בית הלל בעדיות הא דתנן בפ' האשה שנפלו לה נכסים משנתארסה בית שמאי אומרים תמכור ובית הלל אומרים לא תמכור (כתובות פ"ח דף עח·) ומשני לא אתיא מתניתין אלא דבר שהוא חמור מצד אחד וקל מצד אחד ופריך והתנן והעומר שהוא סמוך לגפה הרי הוא קל לבעה"ב וחומר לעניים [א"ל] שעדיין לא זכו בהן ופריך אף הכא קל הוא לאשה ואינו חומר לבעל שעדיין לא זכה בהן [א"ל] מכיון שקדשה לזכותה ולזכותו כפלו ומשניתינו לא מלאנו בעדיות אבל פלוגתא דהבקר לעניים ופלוגתא דעומר של ארבע קבין שנויים שם: ג ראשי שורות · אינו שכחה בין בתחלת שורה בין בסוף שורה: העומר שכנגדו מוכיח.לסוף שורה אילטריך כמו שאפרש : מודים· בית שמאי ובית הלל לעיל בתוספתא ואליבא דרבי יהושע ודלא כרבי אליעזר : (ב) תניא בתוספתא העומר שהחזיק בו להוליכו לעיר ונתנו ע"ג חבירו ושכח את שניהם התחתון שכחה והעליון אינו שכחה ר' שמעון אומר שניהן אינו שכחה התחתון מפני שהוא מכוסה והעליון מפני שזכה בו פי' נתנו ע"ג חבירו ע"ג עומר אחר שהיה רוצה להוליך שניהם לעיר אלא שלא החזיק בתחתון שזכה בו כשהחזיק בו ובסוטה בריש עגלה ערופה (דף מה·) גרסי' מפני שהוא צף ומפרש התם משום דכתיב בשדך דמשמע בארץ והתחתון מפני שהוא טמון ובעינן דומיא דקציר שהוא בגלוי ועוד מפרש התם טעמים ד] אחרים דמפרשי' טעמא דזכה בו: ד זה פניו לצפון וזה פניו לדרום · ונשאר עומר אחד באמצע השורה : לאחריהם · שהניחוהו זה וזה : אינו שכחה · לפי ששניהם סמכו זה על זה ושכחו ועוד בירושלמי (הל' ג) דריש מקרא דאין חשוב שכחה אלא ממקום שמתחיל ואילך דאם יש שם שורה של עומרים והתחיל לעמר בעומר השני או שלישי והניח ראש השורה שהיה בדעתו לקחת וחזר ושכח לא הוי שכחה : יחיד שהתחיל מראש השורה · כגון שיש כאן עשר שורות של עשר עשר עומרים מסודרים בשורות בין

לו שכחה (ה) המעמר לגדיש יש לו שכחה ממנו ולגורן אין לו שכחה זה הכלל כל המעמר למקום שהוא גמר מלאכה יש לו שכחה ממנו ולגורן אין לו שכחה למקום שאינו גמר מלאכה אין לו שכחה ממנו ולגורן יש לו שכחה :

פרק ששי

א א) **בית** שמאי אומרים הבקר לעניים הבקר ובית הלל אומרים *אינו *הפקר עד *שיופקר אף לעשירים כשמיטה כל עומרי השדה של קב קב ואחד של ארבעת קבין ושכחו ב"ש אומרים אינו שכחה ובית הלל ב) אומרים שכחה : **ב** ג) העומר שהוא סמוך לגפה ולגדיש לבקר ולכלים ושכחו ב"ש (א) אומרים אינו שכחה וב"ה ג) אומרים שכחה : **ג** ראשי שורות העומר שכנגדו מוכיח ד) העומר שהחזיק בו להוליכו אל העיר ושכחו מודים שאינו שכחה : **ד** ואלו הן ראשי שורות ה) שנים שהתחילו באמצע השורה זה *פניו לצפון וזה *פניו לדרום ושכחו (ג) לפניהם ולאחריהם את שלפניהם שכחה ואת שלאחריהם אינו שכחה ו) יחיד שהתחיל מראש השורה ושכח לפניו ולאחריו ג) שלפניו אינו שכחה ושל אחריו שכחה

ממקום הקצירה אל אחד המקומות האלה אם שכח כלום במקום הקצירה אינו שכחה ואם הוליך מאלה המקומות למקום הדישה ושכח דבר באחת מאלו המקומות יש לו שכחה וזה ענין מה שאמרו ממנו ולגורן יש לו שכחה. וענין המעמר לגדיש ידוע . ומה שאמרו גמר המלאכה ר"ל המקום שאין מוליכין אליו כי אם לקבץ שם העמרים בלבד ולא יקבץ אותם העמרים אחר כן לעשות מהם עמרים גדולים ואמר הכתוב כי תקצור קצירך בשדך ושכחת עומר בשדה ואמר מה קציר שאין אחריו קציר אף עומר שאין אחריו עמור ואז יתחייב בשכחה :

כבר בארנו כי ההפקר אינו מחויב במעשרות ומה שהפקיר לעניים בלבד אומרים ב"ש שהוא הפק' ואינו מחויב במעשר והביאו ראיה עליו מה שאמר הכתוב (ויקרא יט) לעני ולגר תעזוב אותם ואמרו יש לך עזיבה אחרת שהיא לעניים ולא לעשירים וב"ה אומרים אמר הכתוב בשמטה (שמות כג) תשמטנה מה ת"ל ונטשתה יש לך נטישה אחרת כזו . ואתה צריך לדעת כי לבית שמאי מי שהפקיר לאדם ולא לבהמה לישראל ולא לנכרים לעניי אותה העיר ולא לעניי עיר אחרת שכל זה הפקר ואינו מחויב במעשרות : **ב** גפה. הוא שער המגולה והוא ממלת ויניפו הדלתות (נחמיה ז) : גדיש. הוא לבור העמרים : ולבלים. כלי חרישה . וכבר בארנו בגמרא שהם לא נחלקו כנראה מן המשנה הזאת שאינו שכחה אבל נחלקו כשיקח העומר להוליכו במדינה ונתנו באחד מן המקומות הנזכרות ושכח אותו שבית שמאי אומרים אחר שלקחו זכה בו ואינו שכחה ובית הלל אומרים שכחה : **ג** מה שאומר העומר שכנגדו מוכיח סדר המשנה היה ראוי להיות כך העומר השכוח ראש שורה שכנגדו מוכיח אם שכוח הוא אם אינו שכוח ומה שאמר ומודים שאינו שכחה בשלא שכחה סמוך לגפה ולגדיש כאשר בארנו במה שהקדמנו : **ד** מה שאמר ושלפניהם שכחה . כי מה שיש לפני כל אחד ואחד מהם הוא אחורי השני ואסור לו לחזור לאחוריו ולקחת מה שיש מן העומרים לשם כמו שיתבאר : שלפניו אינו שכחה . ר"ל העומר שהניחו במקום שהתחיל ממנו לפי שהוא מחובר עמהם בעמרי' הערוכי' ממזרח למערב וכאילו התחילו השורה האחרת למזרח או למערב *וזו הצורה וזה הענין ממה שאמר מוכיח כמה שהקדים ואלו השורות הם שורות של עומרים ואני ציירתי לך נקודות במקום העומרים כדי שיתבאר לך וכזאת תהיה טרת העומרים אשר בהם זה הדין ומה שאמר בל תשוב רצה לומר שהוא עובר על דברי הכתוב

מזרח

* *
* * * * * * * * * *
* * * * * * * * * *
* * * * * * * * * *
* * * * * * * * * *
* * * * * * * * * *
* * * * * * * * * *
* * * * * * * * * *
* * * * * * * * * *
* * * * * * * * * *

צפון — דרום

מערב

נחלקו· בית שמאי ובית· הלל על העומר הסמוך וכו' שהוא שכחה ועל מה נחלקו על העומר שנטלו ונתנו בצד הגפה בצד הגדיש וכו' שבית שמאי אומרין אינו שכחה מפני שזכה בה ובית הלל אומרין שכחה וכשבאתי והרציתי הדברים לפני ר' אלעזר בן עזריה אמר לי הברית הן הן הדברים שנאמרו לו למשה בחורב . פי' נשבע לו בברית ואיכא דאמרי [ברית התורה] דכתיב כי על פי הדברים האלה כרתי אתך ברית : ג ראשי השורות וכו'. פי' אם שכחם אינן שכחה וראשי השורות מפורש לקמן : ד אילו הן ראשי השורות וכו' ושכחו לפניהן ולאחריהן לפניהן שכחה. דהוה לה סוף שורה וכיון ששכחו ובאו אל ראש השורה אמר רחמנא לא תשוב לקחתו כלומר ממקום שבאתה לא תשוב לקחתו . ולאחריהן אינו שכחה דאמרינן זה סמך על זה וזה סמך על זה : היחיד משהתחיל מראש השורה. פי' כגון שורה של י' עומרין ובשדה שורות הרבה כו'* ועימר ד' עומרין והחמישי שכח וחזר אל ראש השורה השניה ועימר עוד ה' עומרין אותו עומר החמישי ששכח בשורה ראשונה אינו שכחה מפני שיש לומר על כן הניחו כדי לקצרו עם האחרים ובראש שורה הוא וזהו פי' לפניו אבל אם כשהיה מעמר שורה הראשונה שכח החמישי ועימר הששי וכן כולם עד סוף ודאי הוי שכחה מפני שהוא בבל תשב זה הכלל וכו' : שנים שהתחילו באמצע השורה זה פנה לרוח צפון וזה פנה לרוח דרום ושכחו לפניהן ולאחריהן שלפניהן שכחה ושלאחריהם אינו שכחה מפני שהן ראשי השורות וזה צורתו* דיש לומר כל אחד ואחד סמך על חבירו ואמר חבירו יקצור נמצא שלא קצרוהו לא זה ולא זה ולא הוי שכחה . מנין לראשי השורות א"ר יונה

זה התחיל מיכן . מיכן ולמטה זה לפניו

* *

דכתיב כי תקצור ושכחת מה שאתה קוצר אתה שוכח כלומר ממקום שהתחלתה לקצור ושכחת הוי שכחה יצאו ראשי השורות שלא התחיל בהן כלל ומשום הכי לא הוי שכחה : העומר שכנגדו מוכיח . אם שכחו אינו שכחה . תניא כיצד היו לו י' שורות של י' עומרין התחיל לעמר שורה אחת מצפון לדרום
[illegible]

כל חד וחד הוי ראש לשורתו

* * * * * * * * * *
* * * * * * * * * *
* * * * * * * * * *
* * * * * * * * * *
* * * * * * * * * *
* * * * * * * * * *
* * * * * * * * * *
* * * * * * * * * *
* * * * * * * * * *

עין משפט נר מצוה

א א מיי' פ"ב מהל' נדרים הלכה טו טוש"ע חו"מ סימן רעג סעיף ס :
ב ב מיי' פ"ה מהל' מתנות עניים כ"ז:
ג ג שם הלכה ג :
ד ד מיי' פ"ה מהל' מתנות עניים ה"ג:
ה ה שם הלכה יא :
ו ו שם הלכה י :

פי' הרא"ש

(ה) המעמר לגדיש ורוצה שישארו באותו מקום יש לו שכחה אבל אם דעתו להוליכם משם ולגורן אין לו שכחה . ממנו ולגורן פירוש אם אח"כ נמלך להוליכם לגורן אין לו שכחה: פ"ו (א) ב"ש סברי כיון שמונח אצל דבר המסויים עתיד לזוכרו ולא הוי שכח': (ב) דבתוספתא הוכיח דפליגי בעומר שהחזיק בו להוליכו לעיר והניחו בצד הגפה או בצד הגדר הן הן דברי ר"א אבל רבי יהושע אומר דפליגי בלא החזיק בו אבל בהחזיק בו מודי' ור"מ תפס לו שיטה אחרת דיותר הוי שכחה כשהניחו בצד הגפה או בצד הגדר וטעם דבריו לא נתברר לי: (ג)לפניה' אחר שהתחילו לעמר דלגו עומר ושכחוהו הוי שכחה דקרינן ביה לא תשוב לקחתו: ולאחריהם כשהפכו פניהם זה לצד צפון וזה לדרום והתחילו (לקצור)[לעמר] נשאר עומר אחד ביניהם ושכחוהו אינו שכחה לפי ששניהם סמכו זה על זה ומתוך כך נשכח :

הגהות הגר"א

פ"ו (א) מ"א בר"ש לעניי אותה עיר ולא לעניי עיר אחרת. נמחק וכ"ה בתוספת' ליתא :

הגהות הרי"ל לנדא

פ"ו א] מ"א בר"ש הבקר כמו הפקר . עיין ברא"ש תולינפ' שליש סי' מ: ב] אלא מפני ברית . צ"ל תורת פאה : ג] זה וזה לפטור . צ"ל זה וזה פאה כ"ה בגמ' : מ"ב ד] ועוד מפרש התם טעמים . צ"ל טעם אחר ומפרש :

מסורת הש"ס

א) ב"מ דף ל: עדיות פ"ד מ"ג: ב) עדיות שם משנה ד: ג) ב"מ פ"א דף יא.

פי' מהר"י בן מלכי צדק

כמוס עמדי ודייק מדכתיב עמדי ולא עלי . פ"א טבעות ראשי שבולין כוסמות תחתון של שבולין. לחררה פי' לעשות ממנו חררה ורבינו נתן בעל הערוך ור"ש פירשו הנשדף מן הזרע . ותניא בתוספתא [בפ"ג] המעמר מפני הדליקה [אין לו שכחה] והיינו לחררה : ולעומרין פי' לא עומרין להגדיש אלא עומרין קטנין לעשות מהן עוד עומרין אחרים להוליכן לגדיש כדתניא החותך כריכות ועתיד לעמרן אין להן שכחה: ממנו ולגורן . פירש משם ועד הגורן יש לו שכחה : המעמר לגדיש יש לו שכחה. ומשעימר הכל לגדיש רוצה לעשות ממנו גורן שוב אין לו שכחה: זה הכלל וכו' פשוטה היא : פ"ו א בית שמאי אומרים הבקר לעניים הבקר.פי' אם הבקיר לעניים לבד הבקר ופטור מן המעשרו'(כדאמרי') [גרסי'] בירושל' מאי טעמא דבית שמאי אמר ר' חייא א"ר יוחנן לעני ולגר מה ת"ל תעזוב אותם יש לך עזיבה אחרת כזו מה זו לעניים ולא לעשירים אף מה שנאמר במקום אחר לעניים ולא לעשירים אמר ר"ל טעמייהו דב"ה תשמטנה מה ת"ל ונטשתה יש לך נטישה אחרת שהיא כזו מה זו לעניים ולעשירים אף מה שנאמר במקום אחר לעניים ולעשירים : כל עומרי השדה וכו'. כל העומרין בני קב קב פי' קב ד' לוגין והוא שתות הסאה ואחד של ד' קבין ב' שלישי סאה : ב"ש אומרים אינו שכחה . פי' כיון שהוא יכול לחלקו ולעשותו שורה רואין אותו כאילו ד' עומרין ובית הלל לית להו רואין : ב העומר שהוא סמוך לגפה ולגדיש וכו'. גפה הוא גדר בלא טיט כדכתיב יגיפו הדלתות וסתימת החבית נקראת מגופה כך סגירת השד' נקראת גפה . תניא אמר ר' אלעאי שאלתי את ר' יהושע על אלו עומרין נחלקו בית שמאי ובית הלל אמר לי בתורה הזאת על העומר הסמוך לגפה וכו' וכשבאתי [אצל] (ושאלתי את) ר' אליעזר אמר לי לא

SHEAF DOES APPLY. IF ONE PILES UP THE SHEAVES FOR THE STACK,[3] HE IS SUBJECT TO THE LAW OF THE FORGOTTEN SHEAF; IF HE AFTERWARDS REMOVES THEM THENCE TO THE THRESHING-FLOOR, THE LAW OF THE FORGOTTEN SHEAF DOES NOT APPLY.[4] THIS IS THE GENERAL PRINCIPLE: WHOEVER PILES UP THE SHEAVES AT THE PLACE WHICH MARKS THE END OF THE WORK [WHERE THEY ARE GOING TO BE THRESHED], IS SUBJECT TO THE LAW OF THE FORGOTTEN SHEAF; BUT [IF THEY ARE REMOVED] FROM THENCE TO THE THRESHING-FLOOR, THE LAW OF THE FORGOTTEN SHEAF DOES NOT APPLY. HE, HOWEVER, WHO PILES UP THE SHEAVES AT A PLACE WHICH IS NOT TO MARK THE END OF THE WORK, IS NOT SUBJECT TO THE LAW OF THE FORGOTTEN SHEAF; BUT [IF THEY ARE REMOVED] FROM THENCE TO THE THRESHING-FLOOR, THE LAW OF THE FORGOTTEN SHEAF APPLIES.

CHAPTER VI

MISHNAH 1. BETH SHAMMAI SAY THAT RENUNCIATION
a OF OWNERSHIP[1] [OF THE CROP] IN FAVOUR OF THE POOR IS VALID; BUT BETH HILLEL SAY THAT IT IS NOT 'OWNERLESS'[2] UNLESS THE RENUNCIATION IS ALSO MADE IN FAVOUR OF THE RICH, AS IN THE CASE OF THE YEAR OF RELEASE.[3] IF ALL THE SHEAVES IN A FIELD ARE A ḲAB[4] EACH IN QUANTITY, WHEREAS ONE COMPRISES FOUR ḲABS AND THAT ONE IS FORGOTTEN, BETH SHAMMAI SAY IT IS NOT DEEMED 'FORGOTTEN';[5] BUT BETH HILLEL SAY THAT IT IS DEEMED 'FORGOTTEN'.[6]

MISHNAH 2. IF A SHEAF IS LEFT NEAR A STONE FENCE[7] OR NEAR A STACK [OF CORN], OR NEAR OXEN AND [FIELD] IMPLEMENTS,[8] BETH SHAMMAI SAY IT IS NOT DEEMED 'FOR-
b GOTTEN';[1] BETH HILLEL SAY THAT IT IS DEEMED 'FORGOTTEN'.

MISHNAH 3. [WHETHER OR NOT ANY SHEAF] AT THE END OF THE ROW IS TO BE REGARDED AS 'FORGOTTEN', THE SHEAF LYING OVER AGAINST IT SERVES AS AN INDICATION.[2] IF [THE OWNER] TOOK UP A SHEAF WITH THE INTENTION OF BRINGING IT TO THE CITY AND FORGOT IT, ALL AGREE[3] THAT IT IS NOT DEEMED A 'FORGOTTEN SHEAF'.

MISHNAH 4. THESE ARE TO BE CONSIDERED ENDS OF THE ROWS:[4] IF TWO MEN BEGIN [TO GATHER] FROM THE MIDDLE OF THE ROW, ONE FACING NORTHWARDS AND THE OTHER SOUTHWARDS[5] AND THEY FORGET [SOME SHEAVES] EITHER IN FRONT OF THEM OR BEHIND THEM,[6] THEN THOSE LEFT IN FRONT OF THEM ARE TO BE DEEMED 'FORGOTTEN',[7] BUT THOSE LEFT BEHIND THEM ARE NOT DEEMED 'FORGOTTEN'.[8] IF[9] AN INDIVIDUAL BEGINS FROM THE END OF THE ROW AND HE FORGETS [SOME SHEAVES] EITHER IN FRONT OF HIM OR BEHIND HIM, THOSE IN FRONT OF HIM ARE NOT TO BE DEEMED 'FORGOTTEN',[10] WHEREAS THOSE BEHIND HIM

(3) On the understanding that they are going to be threshed there. (4) This change of mind shows that the process was not to be finished there and hence it does not conform to the general principle enunciated at the end of our Mishnah.

a (1) Heb. *Hefker* (v. Glos.). The word הבקר in our Mishnah is the Palestinian dialect for הפקר. Cf. 'Ed. IV, 3. Deemed as ownerless, the standing crop is exempt from all tithes as is the case with all the other gifts to the poor discussed in this Tractate. The Shammaites find support for their view in Lev. XIX, 10 (v. Bert.). (2) And, therefore, not exempt from tithes. (3) Deut. XV, 1–6 describes the Sabbatical year in which the soil was to rest and in which all debts were cancelled. Beth Hillel argue that no *hefker* can be exempt from tithes unless it be declared the property of rich and poor alike, as is the case with the products of the Sabbatical year which *all* could enjoy. (4) The *ḳab* was four *logs* = 24 eggs in size, and equal to a sixth of a *se'ah*. (5) Since it comprises four *ḳabs*, it is to be regarded as a sheaf from which a row of four smaller sheaves could be made; and according to Beth Shammai (*infra*, Mishnah 5) only three sheaves belonged to the poor, but not four. A similar provision would apply to a field in which all the sheaves were two ḳabs each in size and the Forgotten Sheaf of 8 *ḳabs*. (6) Beth Hillel refuse to regard the large sheaf as so many potential smaller ones and regard it only as *one* sheaf that is left. (7) Or a heap of stones piled one on top of another loosely (Bert.). (8) Including the outfit of the oxen.

b (1) The very fact that the sheaf had been left near these objects is an indication that the owner had but temporarily deposited it there. (2) If a sheaf is left at the end of the row, then the other sheaf over against it at the end of the second row indicates whether it is to be deemed 'Forgotten'. A fuller explanation of what is implied by 'the ends of a row' is given in the Mishnah following. (3) Even Beth Hillel. V. *supra* VI, 2. (4) The reference is to many rows equally arranged; for example, ten rows of ten sheaves each, all arranged side by side. (5) I.e., they stand back to back and face the two opposite ends of the fields. Each would thus recede further away from each other as they proceed. (6) In the course of their gathering a sheaf or two came to be overlooked. (7) Because Deut. XXIV, 19 can be applied to it. (8) Since the sheaf is behind both of them, each relies on the other to pick it up. (9) An illustration of the statement in the preceding Mishnah that the sheaf lying over against the ends of the row serves as an indication whether a sheaf is to be regarded as 'Forgotten' or not (Bert.). (10) His intention may have been to include it in the new row about to be formed from east to west (Bert.).

ARE DEEMED 'FORGOTTEN'; FOR THIS COMES UNDER THE CATEGORY OF 'THOU SHALT NOT GO BACK [TO FETCH
a IT].[1] THIS IS THE GENERAL RULE: ANYTHING THAT CAN BE SAID TO FALL UNDER THE LAW 'THOU SHALT NOT GO BACK' IS DEEMED 'FORGOTTEN'; BUT THAT TO WHICH THE PRINCIPLE OF 'THOU SHALT NOT GO BACK' CANNOT BE APPLIED IS NOT DEEMED 'FORGOTTEN'.[2]

MISHNAH 5. TWO SHEAVES [LEFT LYING TOGETHER] ARE DEEMED 'FORGOTTEN', BUT THREE ARE NOT DEEMED 'FORGOTTEN'.[3] TWO BUNDLES[4] OF OLIVES OR CAROBS [LEFT LYING] ARE DEEMED 'FORGOTTEN', BUT THREE ARE NOT DEEMED 'FORGOTTEN'. TWO FLAX-STALKS[5] ARE DEEMED 'FORGOTTEN', BUT THREE ARE NOT DEEMED 'FORGOTTEN'. TWO BERRIES ARE DEEMED 'GRAPE GLEANINGS',[6] BUT THREE ARE NOT DEEMED 'GRAPE GLEANINGS'. TWO EARS OF CORN ARE DEEMED 'GLEANINGS'[7] BUT THREE ARE NOT DEEMED 'GLEANINGS'. ALL THESE [RULINGS] ARE ACCORDING TO BETH HILLEL;[8] OF THEM ALL BETH SHAMMAI SAY THAT THREE [THAT ARE LEFT] BELONG TO THE POOR, AND FOUR BELONG TO THE OWNER.[9]

MISHNAH 6. IF A SHEAF OF TWO SE'AHS[10] WAS FOR-
b GOTTEN IT IS NOT DEEMED 'FORGOTTEN'.[1] IF TWO SHEAVES [BE FOUND] THAT TOGETHER COMPRISE TWO SE'AHS, RABBAN GAMALIEL SAYS THEY BELONG TO THE OWNER, BUT THE SAGES SAY THAT THEY BELONG TO THE POOR.[2] THEREUPON RABBAN GAMALIEL SAID: 'ARE THE RIGHTS OF THE OWNER STRENGTHENED OR WEAKENED ACCORDING TO THE GREATER NUMBER OF THE SHEAVES?' [TO WHICH] THEY REPLIED, 'HIS RIGHTS ARE STRENGTHENED'.[3] THEN SAID HE UNTO THEM: 'IF, THEREFORE, ONE SHEAF OF TWO SE'AHS IS NOT DEEMED "FORGOTTEN", THEN HOW MUCH MORE SHOULD BE THE CASE OF TWO SHEAVES THAT TOGETHER CONTAIN TWO SE'AHS?' THEREUPON THEY REPLIED: 'NO. IF YOU ARGUE IN THE CASE OF ONE SHEAF [TO WHICH WE AGREED], BECAUSE IT IS LARGE ENOUGH TO BE CONSIDERED A STACK, ARE YOU GOING TO ARGUE LIKEWISE IN THE CASE OF TWO SHEAVES WHICH ARE AS SMALL BUNDLES?'

MISHNAH 7. IF STANDING CORN[4] THAT CONTAINS TWO SE'AHS WAS FORGOTTEN, IT IS NOT DEEMED 'FORGOTTEN'. IF IT DOES NOT CONTAIN TWO SE'AHS NOW, BUT WAS FIT TO YIELD TWO SE'AHS,[5] EVEN IF IT WAS OF AN INFERIOR KIND OF BARLEY,[6] IT IS REGARDED AS A YIELD[7] OF BARLEY.

MISHNAH 8. STANDING CORN[8] CAN SAVE A SHEAF AND OTHER STANDING CORN[9] [FROM BEING REGARDED AS 'FOR-
c GOTTEN'].[1] THE SHEAF,[2] HOWEVER, CANNOT SAVE EITHER ANOTHER SHEAF OR STANDING CORN.[3] WHAT STANDING CORN CAN SAVE THE SHEAF?[4] THAT WHICH HAS NOT BEEN FORGOTTEN, EVEN THOUGH IT IS A SINGLE STALK.[5]

MISHNAH 9. A SE'AH OF PLUCKED CORN AND A SE'AH OF UNPLUCKED CORN[6] (AND THE SAME APPLIES TO FRUIT TREES,[7] GARLIC AND ONIONS)[8] CANNOT BE COMBINED TOGETHER FOR THE PURPOSE OF COUNTING THEM AS TWO SEAHS,[9] BUT THEY MUST BE LEFT TO THE POOR. R. JOSE

a (1) Deut. XXIV, 19. (2) For other interpretations of this difficult Mishnah v. Tosaf. Y.Ṭ. (3) The underlying principle seems to be, according to Beth Hillel, that whereas two can be deemed 'Forgotten', the number three suggests that these had been deposited there temporarily. Three is a number too large to be overlooked. (4) 'Bundles' of olives, not single ones; for there must be a completion of the process of gathering (גמר מלאכה) before the law of the 'Forgotten Sheaf' is applied. (5) These stalks must still be in the hard state, prior to being prepared for spinning and also fit for human food; otherwise the law of the 'Forgotten Sheaf' does not apply to them. (6) V. Lev. XIX, 10. (7) V. Ibid. XIX, 9. (8) They find support for their contention in the words *'for the poor and the stranger'*, Ibid. XIX, 10, one for each; hence two in all. (9) They cite Deut. XXIV, 19 instead of Lev. XIX, 10, and cite the words *'the stranger, the orphan and the widow'* as proof that even three are to be regarded as the property of the poor. (10) Twelve *kabs* are more than a man could carry, and the law regarding the 'Forgotten Sheaf' seems to stress the word *to take it* (Deut. XXIV, 19) that is, a sheaf which a man can easily carry.

b (1) Since in size and weight it is almost as a stack, it cannot come under the law of the 'Forgotten Sheaf', which refers only to the single sheaf. V. *supra* the argument of the Sages. (2) Both their views are clarified in the course of their discussion. (3) Because the law refers only to a single sheaf that is left. (4) The same law equally operates upon the standing corn as upon the sheaf. (5) I.e., in a more fruitful year. (6) 'An aquatic plant like the Colocasia' (Jast.). Maim. defines it as 'a seed similar to barley', cf. Kil. I, 1. (7) I.e., though the ears of corn have been blasted and do not contain two *se'ahs*, they are treated as if they were full (Bert.). (8) That has clearly not been overlooked. (9) Which seems to have been overlooked and that stands near to the corn that has not been so overlooked.

c (1) For when he will return to cut the corn, he will bethink himself of the sheaf and the other corn unintentionally left. According to Bert. this is based on Deut. XXIV, 19. (2) Which has obviously not been forgotten. (3) Which have been forgotten and which lie in its proximity. (4) Or the forgotten standing corn near it. (5) *Aliter:* 'Even a single ear of corn left unforgotten in the whole corn, can save'. (6) Both had evidently been left forgotten; for had he forgotten only the plucked corn and not the other, the first would have saved the other from coming under the category of the 'Forgotten Sheaf'. V. preceding Mishnah. (7) Plucked and unplucked fruit that only together combine to make two *se'ahs* that have been forgotten. Had all the fruit been plucked, they would have belonged to the owner, according to Rabban Gamaliel (*supra* VI, 6). (8) The same refers to all vegetables; two kinds cannot be combined together. (9) And thus not be regarded as liable to the law; *supra* 6, n. 10.

ממזרח למערב בין מלפון לדרום ובא היחיד והתחיל מראש השורה ראשון מלפון לדרום אם התחיל והעביר באותה השורה עומר אחד ושכחו הוי שכחה דהניחו לאחריו והוי בבל תשוב אבל אם שכח אחד או שנים בסוף השורה דהיינו לפניו דלא העבירם אלא חזר לו לשורה שניה לא הוי שכחה דכיון שלא העבירם לא קרינא ביה בל תשוב דמה שחזר לשורה שניה אין זה בל תשוב דכיון דשורותיהן יכולות להמנות ממזרח למערב והיינו דקתני לעיל העומר שכנגדו מוכיח עליו שלא ישכח דיכולות השורות ליחשב בענין אחר: ירושלמי (שם) מנין לראשי שורות א״ר יונה כתיב (דברים כד) כי תקצור קצירך [בשדך] ושכחת מה שאתה קוצר אתה שוכח עד כדון

ראשי שורות קמה סוף שורות עומרים (א) א״ר יונה לא תשוב לקחתו ממקום שבאת לא תשוב לקחתו עד כדון (דאס) [וכו'] *כילף ראשי שורות עומרים מראשי שורות קמה וסוף שורות קמה מסוף שורות עומרים פי' מה שאתה קוצר ממקום שהתחלת לקצור יש

שכחה מפני שהוא בבל תשוב זה הכלל כל שהוא בבל תשוב שכחה ושאינו בבל תשוב אינו שכחה: ה (א) אשני עומרים שכחה ושלשה אינם שכחה בשני צבורי זיתים וחרובין שכחה ושלשה אינן שכחה שני (ד) הוצני פשתן שכחה ושלשה אינן שכחה שני גרגרים פרט ושלשה אינן פרט שני שבלים לקט ושלשה אינן לקט אלו כדברי בית הלל ועל כולן בית שמאי אומרים שלשה לעניים וארבעה לבעל הבית: ו (ג) גהעומר שיש בו סאתים ושכחו אינו שכחה שני עומרים ובהם סאתים רבן גמליאל אומר לבעל הבית דוחכמים אומרים לעניים אמר רבן גמליאל וכי מרוב העמרים יופי כח של בעל הבית או הורע כחו אמרו לו יופי כחו אמר להן ומה אם בזמן שהוא עומר אחד ובו סאתים ושכחו אינו שכחה שני עמרים ובהם סאתים אינו דין שלא יהא שכחה אמרו לו לא אם אמרת בעומר אחד שהוא כגדיש תאמר בשני עמרים שהן ככריכות: ז הקמה שיש בה סאתים ושכחה אינה שכחה אין בה סאתים אבל היא ראויה לעשות סאתים אפי' היא של טופח רואים אותה כאילו היא *ענוה של שעורים: ח והקמה מצלת את העומר ואת הקמה העומר אינו מציל לא את העומר ולא את הקמה אי זו היא קמה שהיא מצלת את העומר כל שאינה שכחה אפילו קלח אחד: ט זסאה תבואה עקורה וסאה שאינה עקורה וכן באילן והשום והבצלים אינן מצטרפין לסאתים אלא של עניים הם ר' יוסי אומר אם

באת

הכתוב שאמר (דברים כד) לא תשוב לקחתו לגר ליתום ולאלמנה יהיה: ה צבורי. הם הערמות: הוצני פשתן. קני הפשתי' קודם שיכתשוהו וישרוהו כשיתלשו אותו: ופרט הוא מה שנא' ופרט כרמך לא תלקט (ויקרא יט) וב״ה מביאין ראיה ממה שאמר (שם) לעני ולגר תעזוב אותם ויש לו לעזוב שנים. וב״ש מביאין ראיה ממה שאמר (דברים כד) לגר ליתום ולאלמנה ויש לו לעזוב שלשה: ו מה שאמר רבן גמליאל וכי מרוב העמרים הוא לשון שאילה שאמר להם רוב העמרים השכוחות יש בהם תועלת לבעל הבית או יש לו בהם הפסד. והודו לו ואמרו שיש ברובם תועלת לבעל הבית ואינה שכחה כשיהיו רבים. וכאשר הודו על זה השיב עליהם מדבריהם ואמר להם איך אמרתם שרובם הפסד לבעל הבית שהרי אתם אומרים כשיהיה עומר אחד אינו שכחה ואם יהיה שנים הם שכחה השיבוהו ואמרו לו כשיהיה עומר אחד הוא כמו הגדיש והכתוב אומ' (שם) ושכחת עומר ולא גדיש וכשיהיה שני עמרים הוא כמו שאר עומרים הקטנים. ועוד אמרו (שם) לא תשוב לקחתו עומר שאתה יכול לפשוט ידך וליטלו יצא זה שאינך יכול לפשוט ידך וליטלו ואין הלכה כרבן גמליאל. ופירוש כריכות אגודות: ז דע שהשכחה היא מחויבת לקמה כמו שהיא מחויבת לעמרים לפי שאמר הכתוב (שם) ושכחת ולא תשוב: וכבר בארנו (לעיל פ״ה מ״ג) כי טופח ממיני הגרגרים הידוע קורטמאן בלשון ערב ובקעה גדולה ממנו תוליא זרע מעט וילא רובו בתבן וקש לפיכך הוא אומר שאף על כי שאחר שיודש ומרחו אותם לא תקבץ ממנו סאתים רואין אותם השבלים כאילו הם שעורים אשר גרגיריו גסים וכאילו יש בהם סאתים ולא תהיה הקמה ההיא של טופח שכחה: ח אמר

וסאה קמה של בצלים אין מצטרפין לסאתים קמה והוו שכחה אי נמי סאה שום עקור וסאה שום שאינו עקור וכן סאה בצלים עקורים וסאה בצלים שאין עקורין אין מצטרפין : רשות העני באמצע. כגון שיש לקט בין סאה לסאה ומיהו באילן לא משכחת לה דאין לקט באילן אלא שכחה ופאה אבל בכרם משכחת לה לפי שיש פרט בכרם: תניא בתוספתא רבי יוסי אומר *חנניה בן אחי רבי יהושע אומר כל שבאת רשות עני באמצע כגון תבואה והכרם אין אלו מצטרפות וכל שלא באת רשות עני באמצע כגון פירות האילן הרי אלו מצטרפות (ז) ירושלמי (הל' ו') מה עד שתבא ממש או אפי' נראית לבוא כשמעינה מן הדא תבואה והכרם כרם (א) לא על אתר הוא הדה אמרה אפי' נראית לבא פירוש מה לשון בעיא הוא הא דאמר רבי יוסי אם באת אם בשכבר באת או אפי' בראוי ופשיט ליה מברייתא דתוספתא דקתני כרם ואין דרך פרט לבא על אתר ועוד קאמר התם בירושלמי (שם) דהא דקתני מתני' דעקורה ושאינה עקורה אין מצטרפין והוו שכחה כששכח את הקמה תחלה ומסיק רבי יונה א] תפתר בקוצר שורה ומעמר וכבר שכח את הקמה עד שלא ישכח את העמרים אבל אם שכח העמרים תחילה עקורה שאינה עקורה הדא אמרה דבר שהוא ראוי להציל ושכחו הרי היא שכחה ויש ליתן טעם לדר' יונה דכיון דסאה של קמה מציל על סאה של עקורה הרי הוא כקמה שיש בה סאתים ואם שכחה אינו שכחה : י שנתנה לשחת · להאכיל לבהמתו : אלומה · לאסור בה עמרי' (ח): אגודי השום · שומין שליקטן לאגוד בהן שאר השומין : ואגודות השומין והבצלים . היא אגודה של שומין ואגודה של בצלים אם שכחה אינו שכחה דמכיון שאוגדה זכה בה ולא דמי לעמרים האגודים דשייכא בהו שכחה דאגידתן לאוספן לגדיש אבל הני להוליכן לבית ולהצניעם ומיהו לא מסתבר לפוטרן מטעם זה דמ"ש ממנו ולגורן דתנן לעיל בסוף פרק ה' (משנה ח') דלא הוי שכחה דדרך שומין ובצלים שעושין מהם אגודות קטנות וחוזרין ואוגדן כאחת כה' או כו' מן הקטנות וכן נוהגים גם עכשיו ועל אותן הקטנות קאמר דלא הוי שכחה ולכך חשיב ליה בתוספתא בהדי חותך כריכות ועתיד לעמרן כדפרשינן בסוף פרק ה' : לוף שום ובצלים הטמונים בארץ אין להם שכחה לטמונים אבל גלויים יש להם שכחה וטעמא דרבי יהודה ורבנן בסוטה (מה:) ובירו' (הל' ז) מחלפא שיטתי' דר' יהוד' תמן אמר לרבות את הטמון בפרק הכונס (דף סא:) דמחייב ר"י טמון בא"ש ובההוא אמר פרט לטמון תמן ונאכל גדיש או הקמה ממשמע שנאמר קמה איני יודע שהגדיש בכלל מה ת"ל גדיש לרבות את הטמון (ב) ורבנן תמן אומר הקמה או השדה מה שדה שבגלוי' ברם הכא שדך בגלוי פרט לטמון קצירך בגלוי פרט לטמון אין מיעוט אחר מיעוט אלא לרבות את הטמון : יא הקוצר בלילה: והמעמר · בלילה : והסומא. בין ביום ובין בלילה : ואם היה מתכוין · ליטול הגס הגס · כיון דמתכוין ליטול הגסים אפילו דקין אין להן שכחה כדמפרש בירושלמי (הל' ח) : על מנת מה שאני שוכח אני נוטל . דהמתנה על מה שכתוב בתורה תנאו בטל :

עקורה לא נאמר יצטרף זה לזה ולא יהיה שכחה וכן באילן כשיהיה קלת השיעור שלא יהיה כמוהו שכחה באילן וקלתו תלוש ועקור מן הארץ וכן השומים והבצלים כשישכח מקלתם בארץ ומקלתם תלושים והמחובר משניהם אינו שכחה ולא נאמר שיצטרפו כדי שלא יהיה שכחה ור' יוסי אומר שהם מצטרפים עד שיפרים ביניהם רשות העני ויהיה זה כשיזכה בקלת הדבר ההוא התלוש או במחובר ואחר כך שכח קלתו האחד אז לא יצטרף עמו הקלת האחר ויהיה כמו כן שכחה ואין הלכה כרבי יוסי : י כבר בארנו שחת הוא הגז הקצור לאכילת הסוסים : ולאלומה . הוא עומרים והענין ההוא שיקצרנה כולה ויחלוק אותה לאלומות ואל יקבוץ מן האלומות ההם עומרים כי האלומות כשיתקבצו נעשים עומרים : ואגודי השום · הוא השום המחובר חבור הטבע בשרשי למחיו ויהיה מהם שורש אחד כולל ראשים רבים: אגודות השום · שיחבוט אותם ביד חביטה קלה קודם שיתקבץ מהם עומרים : ופירוש טמונים בארץ ר"ל שיהיה הנאכל מהן מתחתית לארץ כגון הבצלים והשומים והלפתות : ופי' הלוף מין ממיני הבצלים בלא ספק ואין הלכה כר' יהודה : יא כבר בארנו בפרק זה שיש לקוצר שכחה כשישכח קמה וכן למעמר. והתנאי שישוב ויקח מה ששכח בטל שהעיקר בידינו כל המתנה על מה שכתוב בתורה תנאו בטל אלא בממון כמו שיתבאר במקומו :

באת רשות העני באמצע אינן מצטרפין ואם לאו הרי אלו מצטרפין : י [א]תבואה שנתנה לשחת או לאלומה וכן באגודי השום ואגודות השום והבצלים אין להם שכחה וכל הטמונים בארץ כגון הלוף והשום והבצלים ר' יהודה אומר אין להם שכחה [ב]וחכ"א יש להם שכחה : יא [ג]הקוצר בלילה והמעמר והסומא יש להם שכחה ואם היה מתכוין ליטול את הגס הגס אין לו שכחה אם אמר הרי אני קוצר על מנת מה שאני שוכח אני אטול יש לו שכחה :

פרק שביעי

א **כל** [ד]זית שיש לו שם בשדה אפילו כזית הנטופה בשעתו ושכחו אינו שכחה בד"א (א) בשמו ובמעשיו ובמקומו בשמו שהיה שפכוני או בישני במעשיו שהוא עושה הרבה במקומו שהוא עומד בצד הגת או בצד הפרצה [ה]ושאר כל הזיתים שנים שכחה ושלשה אינן שכחה ר' יוסי אומר אין שכחה לזיתים : **ב** [ו]זית שנמצא עומד בין שלש שורות של שני מלבנים ושכחו אינו שכחה [ז]זית שיש בו סאתים ושכחו אינו שכחה בד"א בזמן שלא התחיל בו אבל אם התחיל בו אפי' כזית הנטופה בשעתו ושכחו יש לו שכחה [ח]כל זמן שיש לו תחתיו יש לו בראשו רבי מאיר אומר משתלך המחבא : **ג** [ט]איזהו פרט הנושר בשעת הבצירה [י]היה בוצר עקץ את

א אמר הכתוב (דברים כד) ושכחת עומר בשדה ואמרו עומר שאתה שוכחו לעולם יצא זה שאתה זוכרו לאחר זמן וכשישכח אילן ידוע ותהיה ידיעתו מפני הגבלת מקומו או לרוב זיתיו או לרוב שמנו האילן ההוא לא יקרא שכחה כי הוא זוכרו לאחר זמן : ונטופה שם מקום ופעמים רבות מיחסים שם מיני האילנות לארצות : ושפכוני. זיתים נקראים על שם המקום שהיה מוליא שמן הרבה ועל כן פירשוהו שפכוני וענינו שפיכת שמן לרוב גזור ממלת שפך : ובישני הוא נקרא על שם המקום והזיתים ההם לא היו עושין שמן הרבה על כן נקראו בישני לקוח מבושה : ומה שאמר עושה הרבה הוא רוב הזיתים: ודברי רבי יוסי קבלה מפני שאמר אותו בזמן אנדריאנוס המלך שהיו הזיתים מעטים מאד שזה המלך החריב הארץ וכרת הזיתים ומפני מיעוטם בזמן ההוא לא היה שכחה שהיה זוכרו אחר זמן ואחר כך כשחזרו הארצות לישובן ורבו הזיתים לא היה מחלוקת שיש לו שכחה : **ב** כשיהיה ג' שורות מן האילנות שיש ביניהם ערוגות שתים ושכח אילן באמצע השורה השלישית אינה שכחה שהאילנות הסתירוהו וזו היא צורתה

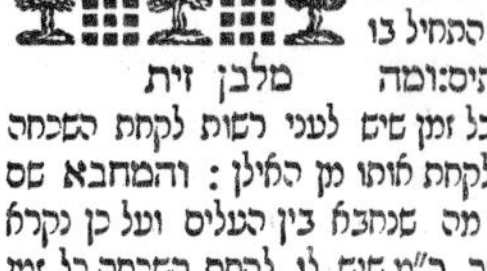
מלבן זית

וכבר בארו בגמרא ובתוספתא כי מה שאמר בד"א חוזר על ענין ראשון מן הפרק. ויהיה סדור הדברים כן כל זית שיש לו שם בשדה אפי' כזית הנטופה בשעתו ושכחו אינו שכחה בד"א בזמן שלא התחיל בו אבל התחיל בו ושכחו הרי זו שכחה עד שיהיה בו סאתים: ומה שאמר כל זמן שיש לו תחתיו · ר"ל כל זמן שיש לעני רשות לקחת השכחה מתחת האילן יש לו כמו כן רשות לקחת אותו מן האילן : והמחבא שם העץ שחובטין בו הזיתים עד שיפול מה שנחבא בין העלים ועל כן נקרא מחבא כי הוא מגלה מה שנחבא ואמר ר"מ שיש לו לקחת השכחה כל זמן שנשאר באילנות פרי ומשיכלה פרי מן האילן ויחבטו אותו ולא יפול ממנו דבר והוא מה שאמר משתלך המחבא אין לעניים אז שכחה וחכ"א עד שיכלה הפרי מתחת האילנות הוא מה שאמר כל זמן שיש לו תחתיו יש לו בראשו ואין הלכה כר"מ : **ג** כבר הקדמנו פי' הנוסר שהוא הנופל: ועוקץ הוא קנה הדבר ועשו ממנו שמוש פעל ואמרו עקץ ר"ל כרת העוקץ : ופי' הוסכך

א הנטופה. מפרש בירושלמי (הל' א) נוטף שמן: שפכוני. שהוא עושה שמן הרבה : במעשיו. שהוא עושה זיתים הרבה : בישני. אית דבעי מימר בישני ממש כלומר יבשין שאין עושין שמן אית דבעי מימר דמבעית לחבריה כלומר שמבייש שאר אילנות מרוב (ג) זיתים שהוא עושה דמכיון שעושה יותר מחבירו כמו שהוא מסויים ובעו בירושלמי (שם) עד דעביד כל שנה ושנה ומסיק מכיון שעושה רובן של שנים כמו שהוא מסויים והתם דריש מקרא אמר רבי לא כתיב ושכחת עומר בשדה עומר שאתה שוכחו לעולם יצא זה שאתה זוכרו לאחר זמן : שנים שכחה · באילן עצמו קאמר ששכח שני זיתי אילן וסתמא כב"ה בפרקין דלעיל (משנה ה) דאמרי שנים לעניים: אין לזיתים שכחה· בירושלמי (שם) אמרי' אמר רבי שמעון בר יקים (ד) לא אמר רבי יוסי אלא ברא‍שונה שלא היו זיתים מצוין שבא אנדריאנוס המלך והחריב הארץ אבל עכשיו שזיתים מצוין יש להם שכחה ומדקדק מתוך כך דהיתה כל שדה נטופה יש להן שכחה דנטופין מצוין : **ב** בין ג' שורות של שני מלבנים · שכל שורה רחוקה מחברתה שיעור ב' לבינים דהיינו ו' טפחים שכל לבינה שלשה טפחים כדאיתא בב"ב בפ"ק (דף ב·) ומלבנים לשון לבינה אי נמי כגון מלבנות תבואה ומלבנות בצלים דלעיל בפ"ג (משנה א וד) ומיירי כשאורך השורה כשיעור ב' מלבנים וידוע היה להם שיעור המלבן ולא באויר שבין שורה איירי : אינו שכחה · כיון דעומד בין השורות [והיו מקיפין אותו מג' רוחותיו כזה

זית

הוי כמו דבר מסוים] והאי דנקט בין ג' שורות לאשמעי' דאע"פ דג' השורות מקיפות ג] אותו כל סביביו וליקטן לא הוי שכחה (דדמי) [דלא דמי] לשדה שעומריה מעורבבין דתניא אין שכחה עד שיעמר כל סביביו כדפרשינן לעיל בפרקין ומהאי טעמא נמי בעי שתהא אורך השורה כשיעור שני מלבנים דאז חשיבא שורה ואינו נחשב ג] שזיתיה מעורבבין ולא מסתבר כלל לפרש טעמא לפי שהשורות מכסות את הזית והוי כחיפוהו בקש או עמדו עניים כנגדו דלעיל בפ"ה (משנה ז) : במה דברים אמורים שלא התחיל בו · כלומר שעדיין לא התחיל ללקט בו ושכחו ומשמע ממתני' דכל זית שלא התחיל ללקט בין נטופה בין שאינו נטופה אם יש בו סאתים אינו שכחה ואם התחיל ללקט בו בין נטופה בין אין נטופה בין יש בו סאתים בין אין בו סאתים הוי שכחה ומה שמחלק ברישא דמתני' בין נטופה לשאין נטופה היינו שאין בו סאתים ולא התחיל בו דנטופה לא הוי שכחה ובתוספתא לא משמע הכי דתניא כל זית שיש לו שם בשדה כזית נטופה בשעתו ושכחו אינו שכחה בד"א בזמן שלא התחיל בו אבל התחיל בו ושכחו הרי זו שכחה עד שיהא בו סאתים משמע דאם יש בו סאתים אפי' התחיל בו לא הוי שכחה בזית הנטופה ושמא הך ברייתא פליגא אמתני' ואם באנו ליישב צריך לומר דבמה דברים אמורים דמתני' לאו אזית שיש בו סאתים קאי אלא אמה שחילקנו בין נטופה לשאינה נטופה קאי דהני מילי בלא התחיל אבל התחיל שניהם שוין באין בו סאתים דהיכא דיש בו סאתים אדרבה חלוקים בהתחיל ובלא התחיל שוין : שיש לו תחתיו זיתים יש לו זיתים בראשו ולא חשיב שכחה כיון דנזכר בעוד שיש זיתים תחתיו אבל אם אין זיתים תחתיו הרי הם של עניים (ב): משתלך המחבא · מלשון אשר יחבא שם כלומר משבדק המלקט בכל מחבואי זיתים של עניים כשאין לו תחתיו: תניא בסיפרי בפ' כי תצא כי תחבוט זיתך בראשונה היו חובטין זיתיהם והיו נותנים בעין יפה (ה) מיכן אמרו הזית שהוא עומד על שלש שורות של שני מלבנים פירוש כיון שהיו נוהגים עין יפה בזיתים בפאה ובשכחה הם עליהן כגרגרים של זיתים ואמרו דזה שעומד על שלש שורות ד] אינו שכחה: **ג** איזהו פרט. אקרא קאי דכתיב (ויקרא יט) ופרט כרמך לא תלקט: עקץ. אחד מלשון עוקץ

אלפנינו תתחיל כאן הקושיא תליל עקורה שאינה עקורה עד ויש ליתן כו' ומסיק רבי יונה נ"ל רבי יונתן *) : פ"ז מ"ב בר"ש ב] דאע"פ דהג' שורות מקיפות כו'. ונ"ל ולא לקטן הוי שכחה ונ"ד לשדה שעומריה מעורבבין כדפרשינן לעיל פ"ו מ"ג וכוונתו דקמ"ל דבהתחיל בו מיסת הוי שכחה דבד"א דסיפא גם עליה קאי: שם ג] ואינו נחשב כשורה ג' כ"ד ואז : שם ד] דזה שעומד על ג' שורות. נ"ל דזית שעומד בין ג' שורות אינו שכחה ועי' בס' זית רענן מהגאון בעל מ"א מה שפי' ע"ד הספרי :

*) א"ה לפמ"ש הגאון נ"כ נכון מה שהוגה בר"ש ויש ליתן טעם לדר' יונה כו' הדא אמרה שבירושלמי מתרץ הקושיא תליל עקורה דדבר שראוי להציל ושכחו א"כ ר"ל אפי' שכח העמרים תחלה דע"כ לא אמרו הקמה מצלת אלא בלא שכחו א"כ אבל בשכחו אינו מציל ור' יונה פליג דאפי' שכחו הקמה א"כ מציל ע"ז כתב הר"ש ויש ליתן טעם לדר"י דכיון דקמה מצלת א"כ כ"ז שלא שכח הקמה העקורה ג"כ אינה שכחה ושוב כששכח הקמה הוי כשכח שניהם שיש בו סאתים ולא הוי שכחה :

עומר בשדה עומר שאת שוכחו לעולם. יצא זה שאתה זוכרו לאחר זמן בד"א וכו' פי' נטופה נוטף שמן : שפכוני. שהוא עושה שמן הרבה : במעשיו. שהוא עושה זיתים הרבה : בישני . אית דאמר בישני ממש כלומר זיתין יבשין שאין עושין שמן כדכתיב הנה יבש והיה נקודים וכן בתענית י' טובעני ולא ייבשני ואית דאמר דמבייש לחבריה כלומר מרוב הזיתין שהוא עושה מבייש שאר האילנות עד דעבד ד' כפלטין כדתנן כל עומרי השדה של קב קב ואחד של ד' קבין : **ב** זית שנמצא עומד בין ג' שורות של ב' מלבנין. פי' כל שורה רחוקה מחבירו ב' מלבנין מלבן מלשון לבינה וכדגרסינן בכתובות אריח על גבי לבנה. פ"א ב' ערוגות : **כל** זמן שיש תחתיו. פי' כל זמן שתחתיו זיתים יש לו זיתים בראשו ואכתי דבעל הבית הוא והוא מלקטו ולא קא עבר משום לא תפאר הא אם אין לו תחתיו דעניים : ר"מ אומר משתלך המחבא. פי' משבדק המלקט כל מחבואי הזית כדכתיב וראו ודעו מכל המחבואים אשר יתחבא שם או לעניים אבל אם לא בדק אכתי דבעל הבית הוא אם לא משייר את המחבואין : **ג** איזהו פרט וכו'. תנא אקרא קאי דכתיב ופרט

הגהות הגר"א

מ"מ (א) בר"ש והכרם כרם. נ"ב תבואה: שם (ב) הטמון נ"ב והכא קצירך בגלוי פרט לטמון : פרק ז (ג) מרוב. נמחק ונ"ב מגודל : (ד) אמר ר"ש בר יקים : נ"ב רבי יוסי פליג שם ואמר דלא חייב אדם שכחה לזיתים אלא ר"ע דדריש אחריך כו' : (ה) בעין יפה. נ"ב חסרון יש כאן ועמ"ש שם :

הגהות הרי"ל לנדא

מ"מ א] בר"ש ומסיק ר' יונה.

כתיב בשדה מה שדה בגלוי פרט לטמון הוי מיעוט אחר מיעוט וכו' :

יא הקוצר בלילה וכו' כן היא מתני' הקוצר בלילה והמעמר בלילה והסומא בין ביום ובין בלילה יש לו שכחה ואם היה מתכוין ליטול את הגס פי' הגסין והדקין מניח מדעתו מאחר שדרכו לבוין בגסין אפי' דקין אין להן שכחה: אם אמר הרי אני קוצר וכו'. מ"מ שהתנה על מה שכתוב בתורה וכל המתנה על מה שכתוב בתורה תנאו בטל :

פרק ז א כל זית שיש לו שם בשדה כזית הנטופה וכו'. מנהני מילי אמר ר' אילא כתיב ושכחת

SAYS: IF ANYTHING THAT BELONGS TO THE POOR[10] INTERVENES, THE TWO CANNOT BE COMBINED TOGETHER;[11] OTHERWISE, THEY MAY BE SO COMBINED.

MISHNAH 10. CORN USED FOR FODDER[12] OR [GRAIN-STALKS] USED FOR BINDING A SHEAF, (THE SAME APPLIES TO GARLIC-STALKS[13] USED FOR TYING OTHER BUNCHES, OR TIED BUNCHES[14] OF GARLIC AND ONIONS)[15] DO NOT COME
a UNDER THE LAW OF THE 'FORGOTTEN SHEAF'.[1] ANYTHING STORED IN THE GROUND LIKE THE ARUM[2] AND GARLIC AND ONIONS, R. JUDAH SAYS, THEY DO NOT COME UNDER THE CATEGORY OF THE 'FORGOTTEN SHEAF';[3] BUT THE SAGES SAY, THE LAW OF THE 'FORGOTTEN SHEAF' APPLIES TO THEM.[4]

MISHNAH 11. ONE WHO REAPS BY NIGHT AND BINDS SHEAVES [BY NIGHT] OR ONE WHO IS BLIND[5] IS SUBJECT TO THE LAW OF THE 'FORGOTTEN SHEAF'. IF HE INTENDS TO REMOVE ONLY THE LARGE LEAVES,[6] THEN THE LAW DOES NOT APPLY.[7] IF HE SAYS: 'BEHOLD, I AM REAPING ON THE CONDITION THAT I TAKE AFTERWARDS THAT WHICH I HAVE FORGOTTEN', THE LAW OF THE 'FORGOTTEN SHEAF' STILL APPLIES TO HIM.[8]

CHAPTER VII

MISHNAH 1. AN OLIVE TREE THAT HAS A DISTINGUISH-
b ING NAME[1] IN THE FIELD, LIKE[2] THE OLIVE TREE OF 'NEṬOFAH' IN ITS SEASON,[3] AND THAT HAS BEEN LEFT FORGOTTEN, IS NOT DEEMED 'FORGOTTEN'.[4] WHEN DOES THIS STIPULATION APPLY? [ONLY TO A TREE THAT IS DISTINGUISHED] BY ITS NAME, OR ITS PRODUCE, OR ITS SITUATION. 'BY ITS NAME': IF IT WERE [FOR INSTANCE] A SHIFKONI[5] OR BESHANI[6] TREE. 'ITS PRODUCE': IF IT YIELDS LARGE QUANTITIES. 'ITS SITUATION': IF IT STANDS AT THE SIDE OF THE WINEPRESS OR NEAR THE GAP IN THE FENCE.[7] AS FOR OTHER KINDS OF
c OLIVE TREES,[1] TWO [IF THEY ARE LEFT] ARE DEEMED 'FORGOTTEN', BUT THREE ARE NOT DEEMED 'FORGOTTEN'.[2] R. JOSE IS OF THE OPINION THAT THE LAW OF THE 'FORGOTTEN SHEAF' DOES NOT AT ALL APPLY TO OLIVE TREES.[3]

MISHNAH 2. IF AN OLIVE-TREE WAS FOUND STANDING BETWEEN THREE ROWS [OF OLIVE TREES] AT A DISTANCE OF TWO PLOTS[4] FROM ONE ANOTHER, AND FORGOTTEN, IT IS DEEMED, 'FORGOTTEN'.[5] IF AN OLIVE TREE CONTAINING TWO SE'AHS[6] HAS BEEN LEFT, IT IS NOT DEEMED 'FORGOTTEN'. WHEN DOES THIS APPLY?[7] ONLY WHEN HE [THE OWNER] HAD NOT YET BEGUN [TO PLUCK THE TREE]; BUT IF HE HAD BEGUN, (EVEN IF IT WERE LIKE THE OLIVE TREE NEṬOFAH IN ITS SEASON)[8] AND THEN FORGOTTEN IT, IT IS DEEMED 'FORGOTTEN'. AS LONG AS THE OWNER HAS SOME OF THE FRUIT BELONGING TO HIM LYING AT THE FOOT OF THE TREE, HE CAN CLAIM POSSESSION OF THOSE STILL ON TOP OF THE TREE.[9] R. MEIR SAYS: [THE LAW APPLIES ONLY] AFTER THOSE WITH THE BEATING-ROD[10] HAVE DEPARTED.

d *MISHNAH* 3. WHAT IS MEANT BY PEREṬ?[1] THAT WHICH FALLS DOWN DURING THE VINTAGE. IF WHILE HE WAS CUTTING [THE GRAPES], HE CUT OFF AN ENTIRE CLUSTER

(10) This refers only to the field or vineyard, where there can be 'Gleanings' or 'Grape Gleanings' between one *se'ah* and another. Unapplicable in the case of trees, where these laws do not operate. (11) To make two *se'ahs;* but they belong to the poor. (12) The Hebrew term for corn that had not yet reached a third of its full maturity. It was usually given to the cattle, cf. *supra* II, 1. (13) Others render: 'bunches of garlic on one stalk'. (14) Tosef. Pe'ah III, 8, אותרי. (15) These small bundles are afterwards re-tied into larger bundles; the 'finishing process' is not yet completed, hence the law is not yet applicable. Cf. *supra* V, 8.

a (1) They are not used for human food. (2) A species of onion whose root is exceedingly bitter. 'A plant similar to colocasia with edible leaves and root, and bearing beans' (Jast.). Like תפס in Mishnah 7 *supra*. V. Sheb. V, 2; VII, 1; Ter. IX, 6. A full discussion of the word '*arum*' will be found in Kohut's ed. of the 'Aruch s.v. חלוף. (3) R. Judah is of the opinion that the law of the 'Forgotten Sheaf' does not apply to things, though edible, that are stored in the ground. (4) V. Bert. for the exegetical basis for the respective opinions of R. Judah and the Sages. (5) Night-time or blindness cannot be grouped into the category of things that had been forgotten owing to an untoward accident. V. *supra* IV, 10. (6) The largest leaves are those that began to grow first. Cf. Sheb. IV, 1. Nid. 2*b*. (7) Since he does not gather them all but selects only the largest, the forgetfulness may be said to be due to untoward circumstances. (8) The principle throughout the Talmud is that, 'If one makes a stipulation which is contrary to what is written in the Torah, his stipulation is void'. Keth. IX, 1.

b (1) A differentiating epithet given on account of its general excellence. (2) The word 'even' in our editions is best omitted; its inclusion here is due to its occurring in the next Mishnah. (3) V. Ezra II, 22; Neh. VII, 26. In II Kings XXV, 23 it refers to a city near Bethlehem, in Judah, wherein olive trees were renowned. Others derive the word from נטף 'to flow', because it was a tree always overflowing with oil, and render: like an olive tree that yields much oil in its season. An alternative rendering: An olive tree which at one time bore a special name like the Neṭofah (olive tree). (4) The literal interpretation of the law in Deut. XXIV, 19: '*and thou shalt forget a sheaf in the field*' is of a sheaf that will always be left forgotten; but an olive tree of the kind referred to here is remembered after a time. (5) The name applied to a species of olive tree, literally pouring forth (שפך) large quantities of oil. Others take the word as a place-name, like the following 'Beshani'. (6) The general explanation of this word is that it is an abbreviation of the place-name 'Beth-Shean'. Others interpret the word figuratively, thus: 'A tree, that on account of the abundance of its fruit and oil, puts all the other trees to shame'. The two words are thus either taken as adjectives or proper names; though logically they would point to being place-names, since they are included under the rubric of 'in its name' and not 'in its produce'. But then the retort of those who treat them as adjectives would be: 'If so, then why are they not included as examples of "in its situation"?' Others again render as the 'ill-yielding'. (7) When its trunk is used to block up the gap in the fence.

c (1) Those not distinghuished by a special title. (2) Agreeing with Beth Hillel, v. *supra* VI, 5. (3) R. Jose referred to the days when owing to the Hadrianic persecutions (2nd cent. C.E.) Palestinian olive trees were rare; for the owner who left behind olives would bethink himself of them later, but at a time when the olive trees were no rarity, he would agree that the law of the 'Forgotten Sheaf' applies even to them (v. Bert.). (4) A *malben* is a small garden plot, quadrangular in shape and three handbreadths in width, cf. *supra* III, 1, 4. (5) As it is hidden from view by the other trees. V. *supra* V, 7. The reason why olive trees receive here such frequent mention, though the law applies to other trees, is that they are the most common trees of Palestine. (6) V. *supra* VI, 6. (7) This refers back to the opening Mishnah of this Chapter: 'When does the law *not* apply to the tree of a special name?' (8) It would be considered 'Forgotten' unless the fruit comprised two *se'ahs*. (9) The fruit still ungathered at his feet is an indication that the 'finishing process' of plucking the whole tree has not yet been completed. V. *supra* V, 8. (10) *Aliter:* 'The workers searching after the remaining (hidden) olives'. This searching was done with the aid of a stick, with which they used to beat the branches, so that the olives still nestling between the leaves may fall down. T.J. Pe'ah substitutes the word כרכר 'turner' for the מחבא of our Mishnah.

d (1) 'Grape Gleanings'. Lev. XIX, 10. V. *supra* VI, 5, n. 6.

BY ITS STALK AND THIS WAS INTERCEPTED BY THE FOLIAGE, AND THEN IT FELL FROM HIS HAND TO THE GROUND AND THE SINGLE BERRIES DISPERSED THEREFROM, THEY STILL BELONG TO THE OWNER.[2] HE WHO PLACES A BASKET UNDER THE VINE[3] WHEN HE IS CUTTING [THE GRAPES], IS ROBBING THE POOR;[4] OF HIM IT HAS BEEN SAID: 'REMOVE NOT THE LANDMARK OF THOSE THAT COME UP'.[5]

MISHNAH 4. WHAT CONSTITUTES A DEFECTIVE CLUSTER?[6] ANY CLUSTER[7] WHICH HAS NO SHOULDER[8] AND [OF WHICH THE TOP GRAPES] DO NOT HANG DOWN [FROM THE TRUNK].[9] IF IT HAS A SHOULDER OR ITS TOP GRAPES HANG DOWN, IT BELONGS TO THE OWNER; IF THERE IS A DOUBT, IT BELONGS TO THE POOR.[10] AS TO A DEFECTIVE CLUSTER ON THE JOINT[11] OF A VINE, IF IT[12] CAN BE NIPPED OFF WITH THE CLUSTER,[13] IT BELONGS TO THE OWNER; BUT IF IT CANNOT, IT BELONGS TO THE POOR. R. JUDAH SAYS: A SINGLE
a STALK [OF BERRIES][1] IS DEEMED AS A WHOLE CLUSTER,[2] BUT THE SAGES CONTEND THAT [THEY ARE TO BE REGARDED] AS A DEFECTIVE CLUSTER.[3]

MISHNAH 5. HE WHO IS ENGAGED IN THINNING OUT[4] VINES MAY THIN OUT THE VINES THAT BELONG TO THE POOR JUST AS HE THINS OUT WHAT BELONGS TO HIMSELF;[5] SO R. JUDAH. BUT R. MEIR SAYS: HE CAN ONLY DO SO TO THAT WHICH BELONGS TO HIM BUT NOT TO THAT WHICH IS THE PROPERTY OF THE POOR.[6]

MISHNAH 6. [AS FOR THE GRAPES OF] A VINEYARD IN ITS FOURTH YEAR,[7] BETH SHAMMAI SAY, THE LAWS OF THE ADDED FIFTH[8] AND REMOVAL[9] DO NOT APPLY TO THEM; BUT BETH HILLEL SAY, THEY DO. BETH SHAMMAI FURTHER SAY: THE LAWS OF PERET[10] AND THE DEFECTIVE CLUSTERS[11] APPLY TO THEM, AND THE POOR CAN REDEEM THE GRAPES FOR THEMSELVES;[12] BUT BETH HILLEL MAINTAIN THAT THE WHOLE MUST GO TO THE WINE-PRESS.[13]

(2) Only those grapes belong to the poor that fall to the ground in the natural course of the vintage. The case cited in the Mishnah can be construed as an accidental cause. (3) With the intention of collecting therein the single grapes that fall. (4) The reason being that single grapes (*peret*) are already prior to their reaching earth the property of the poor. (5) V. *supra* V, 6, n. 3. (6) *'Oleleth* (lit., 'grape gleaning') which, according to Lev. XIX, 10 must be given to the poor. *'Oleleth* here used for a defective cluster is connected with עולל (a small child), the defective cluster being in proportion to the full cluster as that of the child to the man. (7) That still remains on a stem. (8) Its grapes hang loose and do not rest on other stalks as if on a shoulder as is usual with fully ripe grapes. (9) Lit., 'have no pendant'. (10) Who always receive the benefit of the doubt. V. *supra* IV, 11. (11) The word usually applied to the knee-joint, or the leg from under the hip bone to the ankle; Ḥul. IV, 6. Here it refers to one branch of the vine that comes out of another branch, like so many joints, or to that part of the vine which is bent down and laid in the ground to rise at another place; cf. Kil. VII, 1. (12) Namely, the defective cluster on the joint of the vine. (13) That adjoins it.
a (1) Single grapes that are joined to the stem itself or to the rib of the cluster and not small bunches on top of one another. (2) Belonging, accordingly, to the owner. (3) And, therefore, the property of the poor. (4) המדל V. *supra* III, 3, n. 4. (5) The reason being a logical one: since the object of this thinning out process is so that the grapes, or the clusters, may grow better by being less cramped together. V. next note. (6) According to R. Meir, the poor are to be regarded only in the role of purchasers of the defective clusters, not as partners (which is the view of R. Judah) with the original owners; hence the latter have no right to touch these grapes. (7) Cf. Lev. XIX, 23–25. After the first three years during which the fruit of any tree could not be eaten (ערלה), the fruit was in the fourth year taken to Jerusalem to be enjoyed there. (8) Though the grapes required redemption if not taken to Jerusalem, yet the 'Fifth' which is prescribed for Second Tithe, need not be added; for the Torah mentions this only in the case of the Second Tithe. V. B.M. 55*b*. (9) This refers to the removal from the house of fruits in the third and sixth year of the Sabbatical period; Deut. XIV, 28; XXVI, 13; Ma'as. Sh. V, 3, 6; Sheb. VII, 1. (10) V. *supra* VII, 3. (11) V. *supra* VII, 4. (12) The poor can eat the grapes wherever they are, provided that they afterwards bring the redemption money to Jerusalem. (13) Since in their view the grapes are 'consecrated', the poor have no right to them and they are, therefore, the property of the owner to bring them to Jerusalem or redeem them, as he thinks fit. Even the 'defective clusters' are thus 'trodden' together with the other grapes and the value of the whole yield taken off to the Holy City.

◁ *For the continuation of the English translation of this page see overleaf.*

תורה אור

את האשכול הוסבך בעלים נפל [מידו] לארץ ונפרט הרי הוא של בעל הבית המניח את הכלכלה תחת הגפן בשעה שהוא בוצר הרי זה גוזל את העניים על זה נאמר אל תסג גבול עולם: ד איזהו עוללת כל שאין לה לא כתף ולא נטף אם יש לה כתף או נטף של בעל הבית אם ספק לעניים עוללת שבארכובה (ה) אם נקרצת עם האשכול הרי היא של בעה"ב ואם לאו הרי היא של עניים גרגר יחידי רבי יהודה אומר אשכול וחכ"א עוללת: ה המדל בגפנים כשם שהוא מדל בתוך שלו כן הוא מדל בשל עניים דברי רבי יהודה רבי מאיר אומר בשלו הוא רשאי ואינו רשאי בשל עניים: ו כרם רבעי ב"ש אומרים אין לו חומש ואין לו ביעור ובה"א יש לו ב"ש אומרים יש לו פרט ויש לו עוללות והעניים פודין לעצמם ובה"א כולו לגת: ז כרם שכולו עוללות ר' אליעזר אומר לבעל הבית ר"ע אומר לעניים אר"א וכי תבצור לא תעולל אם אין בציר מנין עוללות אמר לו ר"ע וכרמך לא תעולל אפילו כולו עוללות אם כן למה נאמר כי תבצור לא תעולל אין לעניים בעוללות קודם הבציר המקדיש את כרמו עד שלא נודעו בו העוללות אין העוללות לעניים משנודעו בו העוללות העוללות לעניים רבי יוסי אומר יתנו שכר גידוליו להקדש איזה היא שכחה בערים כל שאינו (ו) יכול לפשוט את ידו וליטלה וברגליות משיעבור הימנה:

פרק שמיני

א מאימתי כל אדם מותרין בלקט משילכו הנמושות בפרט

האשכלות כעולל לפני האיש ועוד יש לפרש דיש באשכול סמוך לעוקלה פסיגין גדולים ומכל פסיגה ופסיגה יוצאין כמה פסיגין והיינו פסיגין זה על גב זה וקרי ליה כתף במתניתין דדמי לכתף הטעון משאוי אבל ללשון זה לא יתכן לפרש אם ספק דלישנא קמא ניחא טפי דקרי ספק נראים כשוכבין על שתחתיהן ואין שוכבין יפה דאי אפשר לומר כגון שנמצאת עוללות בגת ולא ידיע אם ניטלו פסיגיה לאחר בצירה אי לא דספק כזה אינו כדמוכח בירושלמי (שם) דאמרי' בן לוי שנתמנה לו מעשר טבל ומצא בו עוללות עושה אותן תרומה ומעשר על מקום אחר ופריך עוללות לאו של עניים הוא ומשני רבי אבהו בשם רבנין דתמן אני אומר מן הנקרצות עם האשכולות: ולא נטף בירושלמי (שם) אמרינן יש לה כתף ולא נטף נטף ולא כתף לבעל הבית ואם ספק לעניים: שבארכובה. יחור שבזמורה שתלוין בו אשכלות הרבה והבולר קוצצה והיא נקראת רכובה ופעמים שגם עוללות תלויות בה עמהם (ד) ובירושלמי (שם) מפ' שיעור הרחקתם רבי בא בשם רבי יודא

והן שיהו כולן נוגעו' בפס ידו ופריך לא כן א"ר חייא מעשה ששקלו עוללו' שבע ליטרות בציפורי פירוש עוללות שנמצאו בגת ובשיעור מועט בפס ידו לא שכיח כולי האי א"ר חנינא שאם נתנה ע"ג טבלא והן שיהיו כולן נוגעות בטבלא כלומר טבלא קטנה מלשון טבלא ופינקס: נקרצת [פירוש נחתכת] מל' קרץ מלפון בא (ירמיה מו): גרגר יחידי · כגון אשכול שאין בו פסיגין ומלא גרגרים וגרגרים שלו מחוברין בשדרה עלמה וקסבר רבי יהודה דכיון שיש בו יותר משלשה גרגרים לא חשיב עוללות אלא אשכול כדפרשינן טעמא בירושלמי (שם) א"ר סימון טעמא דרבי יהודה ונשאר בו עוללות כנוקף זית שנים שלשה גרגרים בראש אמיר (ישעיה יז) יותר מכאן אשכול וכגון שהגרגרים זה על גב זה ועשוין כעין כתף ונטף: ה המדל בגפנים· בפרק קמא דמועד קטן (ד:) מייתי לה ובפ' ד' דשביעית (משנה ד) איזהו המדל אחד או שנים והכא נמי

...שכר גידולים שכר מה שהוליא האילן ... פגיו ונתבשלו: ועריס הוא גפן ... וגבה קומתם ונקרא בלשון ערב ... על הארץ שהרגל נוגעת בהם כמו ... רגל והלכה כרבי יוסי:

... עניי' לעני ולגר העזוב אותם (ויקר') ... בקט אותם הם מותרים לכל בני אדם ... לעופות: ונמושות · הם הזקנים ... שאילו בכאן זה השם ללוקטים אחר הלוקטים

Continuation of translation from previous page as indicated by ◁

MISHNAH 7. IF A VINEYARD CONSISTS ENTIRELY OF
b 'DEFECTIVE CLUSTERS',[1] R. ELIEZER SAYS IT BELONGS TO THE OWNER, BUT R. AKIBA SAYS, TO THE POOR. SAID R. ELIEZER: [IT IS WRITTEN,] 'WHEN THOU GATHEREST THE GRAPES OF THY VINEYARD, THOU SHALT NOT TAKE THE DEFECTIVE CLUSTERS AFTER THEE'.[2] IF THERE IS NO GRAPE GATHERING,[3] WHENCE WILL YOU HAVE 'DEFECTIVE CLUSTERS'? SAID R. AKIBA TO HIM: [IT IS WRITTEN,] 'AND FROM THY VINEYARD SHALT THOU NOT TAKE THE DEFECTIVE CLUSTERS'[4]—EVEN IF IT CONSISTS ENTIRELY OF DEFECTIVE CLUSTERS. IF THAT IS SO, WHY IS IT SAID: 'WHEN THOU GATHEREST THE GRAPES OF THY VINEYARD THOU SHALT NOT TAKE THE DEFECTIVE CLUSTERS AFTER THEE'?—[TO TEACH THAT] THE POOR HAVE NO RIGHT TO CLAIM THE DEFECTIVE CLUSTERS PRIOR TO THE VINTAGE.[5]

MISHNAH 8. IF ONE DEDICATES HIS ENTIRE VINEYARD [TO THE SANCTUARY] BEFORE EVEN THE 'DEFECTIVE CLUSTERS'[6] WERE RECOGNISABLE, THE 'DEFECTIVE CLUSTERS' DO NOT BELONG TO THE POOR; BUT [IF THE DEDICATION TOOK PLACE] AFTER THE 'DEFECTIVE CLUSTERS' WERE RECOGNI-
c SABLE,[1] THEN THEY DO BELONG TO THE POOR.[2] R. JOSE SAYS: LET [THE POOR] GIVE THE VALUE OF THEIR IMPROVED GROWTH TO THE TEMPLE.[3] WHAT CAN BE DEEMED 'FORGETFULNESS' IN THE CASE OF AN 'ESPALIER'?[4] WHEN ONE IS NO LONGER ABLE TO STRETCH FORTH HIS HAND AND TAKE THEREFROM.[5] AND IN THE CASE OF RUNNERS?[6] ONLY AFTER [THE GATHERERS] HAD PASSED BY IT.[7]

CHAPTER VIII

MISHNAH 1. FROM WHAT TIME ARE ALL MEN PERMITTED TO TAKE THE 'GLEANINGS'? AFTER THE LAST TROOP OF THE
d POOR[1] HAD GONE. AND IN THE CASE OF 'PEREṬ'[2] AND 'DEFEC-

b (1) I.e., in the entire vineyard there is not a single cluster which has either shoulder (כתף) or pendant (נטף). (2) Deut. XXIV, 21. (3) The extent of a vintage is at least three *full* clusters yielding at least one fourth of a *log* (v. Glos.). Since our Mishnah speaks of defective clusters, hardly likely to produce this required vintage the grapes therefore belong, according to R. Eliezer, to the owner. (4) Lev. XIX, 10. This verse does not mention grape gathering' at all but just '*thy vineyard*'; hence, according to R. Akiba, even a vineyard of defective clusters belongs to the poor. (5) They must wait until the owner has finished gathering his grapes. R. Eliezer would take R. Akiba's verse to debar the owner from taking possession of the defective clusters before he has finished the vintage. (6) V. *supra* VII, 4. In ordinary circumstances, these would become the share of the poor.

c (1) To be defective and not *full* clusters. (2) The generally accepted principle being that a man cannot consecrate anything which does not belong to him. (3) Unto the Temple authorities is due the value of the improvement the grapes have made since they were first dedicated. Cf. Me'il. III, 6. (4) A lattice-work on which trees or shrubs are trained. In Kil. VI, 1 the word is explained as a row of at least five vines running along a fence, or perched on any high pole. (5) When, later, he recalls the grapes thereon, he finds that he can no longer reach them. (6) These are ground-trained vines; grapes growing in a row on isolated vines, almost foot level. (7) Forgetting all about them. Each 'runner' vine is regarded as a border-bed or an outmost furrow by itself; on this account, the owner, after having forgotten to collect them once, can no longer return to them.

d (1) נמושות from מוש, 'to grope', 'search'. T.J. gives two explanations of the word. They are either so called because they are the very last searchers; or because they are the very old people, who have to grope their way painfully along (*supra* IV, 5). When these last have gone and the poor no longer seem to claim it, it becomes 'ownerless'—the property of rich and poor alike. (2) V. *supra* VII, 3.

מסורת השׁ״ס

א) מו״ק דף ד׳: ב) מעשר שני פ״ה משנה ג קדושין פ״ב דף נד: עדיות פ״ד משנה ה:ג) ב״מ פרק ב׳ דכ״ח: תענית פ״א דף ו:

פי׳ מהר״י בן מלכי צדק

כרמך לא תלקט: הוסבך האשכול בעלין תפל בארץ ונפרט וכו׳ הוסבך מלשון נאחז בסבך בקרניו:

ד איזהו עוללת. פי׳ תנא אקרא קאי דכתיב וכרמך לא תעולל כל שאין לו לא כתף ולא נטף. איזהו כתף פסיגין זה על גבי זה. איזהו נטף תלויות בשדרה ויורדות: עוללת שבארכובה. פירוש בסוף האשכול עומדת מפורשת מן האשכול: אם נקרצת. פי׳ נאחות דהיינו שנבצרת ונחתכת עם האשכול מלשון קרץ מצפון דומיא מה ששנינו לענין שבולת אם נקצרת עם הקמה: גרגר יחידי. פי׳ אם (עומד) [עומר] בראש האמיר של גפן גרגר יחידי: רבי יהודה אומר אשכול. והרי הן לבעל הבית. א״ר סימון טעמא דר׳ יהודה ונשאר בו עוללות כנוקף זית שנים שלשה גרגרים בראש אמיר הא פחות מיכן כגון גרגר יחיד אשכול הוי. וחכ״א לעניים דעוללות היא*:

ה המדל בגפני׳ וכו׳. [עיין בר״ש] כשהגפנים סמוכין זה לזה נוטל מבין ב׳ גפנים גפן ומרויחו כדי שייעבו בגפנין ויש עוללות או פאה שהן לעניים: כשם שמידל בשלו כך מידל בשל עניים. אף על גב דמפסדי עניים מפני שהן גרמו בעצמן שהיה להן לבוא: ר׳ מאיר וכו׳ מאי טעמא דר״מ מפני שאפשר להדל אחר שילקטו העניים את הפאה. גרסינן הכל מודין במוכר לחבירו י׳ אשכולות שאסור להדל הגפנין שעומדין שם האשכולות והכל מודין בשותף שכשם שמידל בשלו כך מידל בשל חבירו כי פליגי בכרם שיש בהן לעניי׳ ר׳ יהודה עביד ליה כשותף ור׳ מאיר עביד ליה כמוכר: ו כרם רבעי וכו׳. פי׳ בין נטע בין כרם שיש לה ד׳ שנים קדוש שנאמר ובשנה הרביעית יהיה כל פריו קדש הלולים לה׳. וטעון פדיון לדברי הכל דא״ר זעירא הלולים חילולים לא מתמנעי

רמ

הוסבך בעלים נסתבך בעלים: וכלכלה הוא הסל וכבר פירשנו אל תסג גבול עולם: ד כתף הוא שילאו מן האשכול שריגים דקים מלאים ענב וכן הענף כמו ההדס המזרחי אבל פי׳ נטף הוא נוזל ר״ל שהוא דבר נוטף ונזל ונוגע קלתו על קלתו עד יתכנס ויתאבק זה על זה וכל מה שהוא זולת זה הוא מה שקראו הכתוב עוללות: וארכובה הם הכרותות שיש בזמורות: נקרצת היא נחתכת ונגזרה מן קרץ מצפון (ירמיה מו) ואין הלכה כר׳ יהודה: ה המדל. התולש ועניינו כמו שהוא מותר שיכרת הזלזלים וישליכם כאשר יכרתו מן האשכולות כן הוא מותר לו לכרות מן העוללות ואין הלכה כדברי רבי מאיר: ו אמר הכתוב בכל אילן שנטע (ויקרא יט) שלש שנים יהיה לכם ערלים לא יאכל ובשנה הרביעית יהיה כל פריו קדש הלולים ודינו שיאכלו אותו בעליו בירושלים כמעשר שני ובה״א כשקרא הקב״ה תבואת השנה הרביעית קדש הלולים וקרא המעשר קדש משפטו כמשפט המעשר וכשיפדה נטע רבעי שלו לעצמו יוסיף חמישיתו על מה שהוא שוה כאשר אמר הכתוב (שם כז) במעשר אם גאל יגאל איש ממעשרו חמישיתו יוסף עליו. וביעור הוא להסירו מביתו כשישלם זמנו כמו שנבאר במסכת מעשר שני והוא מה שאמר הכתוב בערתי הקדש מן הבית וב״ש לא יחייבוהו כלום מכל זה שלא נכתב דבר בענין זה כלל כי אלו הפסוקים באו בענין המעשר ואינם מדמים כרם רבעי למעשר: ז מן העקרים שבידינו אין אדם מקדיש דבר שאינו שלו לפיכך כשנראו העוללות לא יוכל לעשותם הקדש מפני שהן ממון עניים: וענין שכר גידולים שכר מה שהוציא האילן מן הפרי בשעת הקדש עד אשר חנטו פניו ונתבשלו: ועריס הוא גפן הדרת אשר נטשו קליריה בענפי האילנות וגבה קומתם ונקרא בלשון ערב עריס: וברגליות הם הגפנים השטוחות על הארץ שהרגל נוגעת בהם כמו הכרמים שלם והוא גזור ממלת רגל והלכה כרבי יוסי:

א אומר הכתו׳ בזה החלק הנעזב לעניי׳ לעני ולגר העזוב אותם (ויקר׳ יט) וכשיפסקו העניים מלבקש אותם הם מותרים לכל בני אדם כי לא נוה הקב״ה שיעזבוה לאיבוד או לעופות: ונמושות · הם הזקנים הבאים בימים ועיקר לשונם הוא כן והשאילו בכאן זה השם ללוקטים אחר הלוקטים

תורה אור

את האשכול הוסבך בעלים נפל [מידו] לארץ ונפרט הרי הוא של בעל הבית [א]המניח את הכלכלה תחת הגפן בשעה שהוא בוצר הרי זה גוזל את העניים על זה נאמר °אל תסג גבול *עולם: ד [ב]איזהו עוללת כל שאין לה לא כתף ולא נטף אם יש לה כתף או נטף של בעל הבית אם ספק לעניים [ג]עוללת שבארכובה (ה) אם נקרצת עם האשכול הרי היא של בעה״ב ואם לאו הרי היא של עניים גרגר יחידי רבי יהודה אומר אשכול [ד]וחכ״א עוללת: ה [א] המדל בגפנים כשם שהוא מדל בתוך שלו כן הוא מדל בשל עניים דברי רבי יהודה רבי מאיר אומר בשלו הוא רשאי ואינו רשאי בשל עניים: ו [ג] כרם רבעי ב״ש אומרים אין לו חומש ואין לו ביעור [ה]ובה״א יש לו ב״ש אומרים יש לו פרט ויש לו עוללות והעניים פודין לעצמם [ו]ובה״א כולו לגת: ז כרם שכולו עוללות ר׳ אליעזר אומר לבעל הבית [ז]ר״ע אומר לעניים אר״א °וכי תבצור לא תעולל אם אין בציר מנין עוללות אמר לו ר״ע °וכרמך לא תעולל אפילו כולו עוללות אם כן למה נאמר כי תבצור לא תעולל אין לעניים בעוללות קודם הבציר [ח]המקדיש את כרמו עד שלא נודעו בו העוללות אין העוללות לעניים משנודעו בו העוללות העוללות לעניים [ט]רבי יוסי אומר יתנו שכר גידוליו להקדש [י]איזה היא שכחה בערים כל שאינו (ו) יכול לפשוט את ידו וליטלה וברגליות משיעבור הימנה:

משלי כב · ויקרא יט · דברים כד · ויקרא יט

פרק שמיני

א מאימתי ג) [כ]כל אדם מותרין בלקט משילכו הנמושות בפרט

ר״ש

עקוץ תאנה מתאנתי: הוסבך בעלים · כלומר נקשר בעלים: של בעה״ב. דאין זה דרך בצירה: גוזל את העניים · בירושלמי (הל׳ ג) דייקי הדא אמרה פרט בנשירתו קדש (ג): גבול עולם. פירשתי לעיל בפרק ה׳ (משנה ו): ד איזהו עוללת. אקרא קאי דכתיב (ויקרא יט) וכרמך לא תעולל: כתף. בירו׳ (שם) אמרי׳ איזהו כתף פסיגין זה על גב זה איזהו נטף תלויות בשדרה ויורדות ובתוספתא תני איזהו כתף פסיגין המחוברות בשדרה זו על גב זו נטף ענבים המחוברות בשדרה ויורדות פירוש שרבים האמצעי שבאשכול הוא קרוי שדרה ואשכלות קטנים הרבה מחוברים בו שבהן הגרגרים של ענבים לכן קרי ליה [שדרה דדמי] לשדרה שהצלעות מחוברות בה ולאותן אשכלות קטנים קרי פסיגים בירושלמי ובתוספתא כההיא דתנן בריש עוקצין (מ״ה) פסיגה של אשכול שריקנה טהור׳ דאין נחשב עוד יד לאשכול לקבל טומאה על ידו פסיגי מלשון נתחים דכתיב (ויקרא א) ונתח אותו לנתחיו ומתרגמינן בירושלמי ופסג יתיה לפסיגייהו שהן נתחי׳ של אשכול וכשהפסיגי׳ שוכבים זה על זה כמשאוי שעל כתפו של אדם נקרא כתף אבל מפוזרין בשדרה אין כאן כתף ונטף הן גרגרים של ענבים המחוברים בשדרה עצמה מלמטה בסופה שתלוין שם ענבים הרבה ועל שם שענביו נוטפין מלמטה קרוי נטף א״נ על שענביו נוטפין זה על זה למעוטי מפוזרות ונקרא שם אותו אשכול עולל לפי שהוא לפני שאר האשכלות כעולל לפני האיש ועוד יש לפרש דיש באשכול סמוך לעוקצה פסיגין גדולים ומכל פסיגה ופסיגה יוצאין כמה פסיגין והיינו פסיגין זה על גב זה וקרי ליה כתף במתניתין דדמי לכתף הטעון משאוי אבל ללשון זה לא יתכן לפרש אם ספק דלישנא קמא ניחא טפי דקרי ספק נראים כשוכבין על שתחתיהן ואין שוכבין יפה דאי אפשר לומר כגון שכמלאת עוללות בגת ולא ידיע אם ניטלו פסיגיה לאחר בצירה אי לא דספק כזה אינו כדמוכח בירושל׳ (שם) דאמרי׳ בן לוי שנתמנה לו מעשר טבל ומלא בו עוללות עושה אותן תרומה ומעשר על מקום אחר ופריך עוללות לאו של עניים הוא ומשני רבי אבהו בשם רבנין דתמן אני אומר מן הנקרצות עם האשכולות: ולא נטף · בירושלמי (שם) אמרינן יש לה כתף ולא נטף נטף ולא כתף לבעל הבית ואם ספק לעניים: שבארכובה. יחור שבזמורה שתלוין בו אשכלות הרבה והבולר קוללה והיא נקראת רכובה ופעמים שגם עוללות תלויות בה עמהם (ד) ובירושלמי (שם) מפ׳ שיעור הרחקתם רבי בא בשם רבי יודא

עין משפט נר מצוה

[א שם הלכה טז: ח ב שם הלכה יז: ט ג שם הלכה כ: י ד שם הלכה יט: יא ה מיי׳ פ״ט מהל׳ מעשר שני ונטע רבעי הלכה כ: יב ו שם הלכה ד טוש״ע יו״ד סי׳ רצ״ד סעיף ו: יג ז מיי׳ פ״ד מהל׳ מתנות עניים הלכה כא: יד ח ט שם הל׳ כג: טו י מיי׳ פ״ה שם הלכה כו: א כ מיי׳ פ״א שם הלכה יא:

פירוש הרא״ש

(ג) שאם לא היה קדוש עד נפלו לארץ מותר להניח כלכלה תחתיו: (ד) ורחוקי׳ קצת מן האשכול: (ה) כשחותך האשכול מן הארכובה אסנחתך העולל עם האשכול היא של בעל הבית: (ו) פי׳ אם שכחה ועבר ממנה כל כך שאם הי׳ זוכר באותו מקום לא היה יכול לפשוט ידיו משם וליטלה: (א) ומתוך שהולכי׳ כפופים ועיניהם מסתכלות למטה רואים כל מה שמוטל לפניהם בקרקע: ואינם מאחירים כלום וכשיודעים שאר עניים שהלכו מתיאשים הם:

הגהות הגר״א

מ״ז [א] בר״ש וע״ס הוא כו׳ עד שיבצור כל סביביו. נמחק:

ר״ש

ולא כן א״ר חייא מעשה שמקלו עוללו׳ שבע ליסרות בציפורי פירוש עוללות שנמצאו בגת ובשיעור מועט בפס ידו לא שכיח והן שיהו כולן נוגעו׳ בפס ידו ופריך כולי האי א״ר חנינא שאם נתנה ע״ג סבלא והן שיהיו כולן נוגעות בסבלא כלומר סבלא קטנה מלשון סבלא ופינקס: נקרצת [פירוש נחתכת] מל׳ קרץ מלפון בא (ירמיה מו): גרגר יחידי · כגון אשכול שאין בו פסיגין ומלא גרגרים וגרגרים שלו מחוברין בשדרה עצמה וקסבר רבי יהודה דכיון שיש בו יותר משלשה גרגרים לא חשיב עוללות אלא אשכול כדפרשינן טעמא בירושלמי (שם) א״ר סימון טעמא דרבי יהודה ונשאר בו עוללות כנוקף זית שנים שלשה גרגרים בראש אמיר (ישעיה יז) יותר מכאן אשכול וכגון שהגרגרים זה על גב זה ועשוין כעין כתף ונטף: ה המדל בגפנים · בפרק קמא דמועד קטן (ד:) מייתי לה ובפ׳ ד׳ דשביעית (משנה ד) איזהו המדל אחד או שנים והכא נמי כשהגפנים רצופים עוקר את האמצעים והאחרים מתקיים בכך ואע״פ שיש בהן פאה או עוללות של עניים מדל בשלהן כמו בשלו שלא היה להם לעניים לאחר מללקט ור׳ מאיר סבר דאין רשאי בשל עניים לפי שיכול להמתין עד שילקטו העניים: ירושלמי (הל׳ ה) הכל מודים במוכר לחבירו י׳ אשכלות שאסור ליגע בהן והכל מודים בשותף כשם שהוא מדל בתוך שלו כך הוא מדל בתוך של חבירו רבי יהודה עבד ליה כשותף ורבי מאיר עבד ליה כמוכר: ו כרם רבעי · בריש כילד מברכין (דף לה·) אמרינן רבי חייא ורבי שמעון ברבי חד תני כרם רבעי וחד תני נטע רבעי דאין רבעי נוהג אלא בכרם וחד תני נטע רבעי דנוהג רבעי בכל האילנות: אין לו חומש · מודו בית שמאי דטעון חילול או מעלהו לירושלים ומפרש התם טעמא קדש הלולים אחליה לקדושתיה והדר אכליה דהלולים כמו חילולים כדאמר עלה בירושלמי (שם) לא מתמנעין רבנן בין ה׳ לח׳ אלא קסברי בית שמאי דאין מוסיף חומש ולא הוי כפודה מעשר שני דמוסיף חומש: ואין לו ביעור · דאינו חייב לבערו בשנת הביעור דתנן במס׳ מעשר שני פרק ה׳ (משנה ו) ערב יו״ט ראשון של פסח ברביעית ובשביעית היה ביעור: ובית הלל אומרים יש לו ביעור. בפרק האיש מקדש (נד:) אמרינן דבית הלל ילפי קדש קדש ממעשר מה מעשר יש לו חומש ויש לו ביעור אף כרם רבעי יש לו חומש ויש לו ביעור ובית שמאי לא ילפי קדש קדש ותימה לבית הלל למה לן קדש הלולים למשמע דאחליה והדר אכליה ויש לומר דאי לאו הלולים נילף קדש קדש משביעית דלא מהני חילול ועוד יש לומר דמהכי האי הלולים באותן שנים שאין מעשר שני נוהג כגון בשנה שלישית וששית ופלוגתא דתנאי היא בירושלמי (שם) דתניא רבי אומר לא אמרו ב״ש אלא בשביעית אבל בשני שבוע בית שמאי אומרים יש לו חומש ויש לו ביעור על דעתיה דהדין תנא לא למדו נטע רבעי אלא ממעשר שני כמה דתימא אין מעשר שני בשביעית ודכוותיה אין נטע רבעי בשביעית מעתה אל יהו לו קדושה וקדושתו מאליו ולמדו קודש הלולים הרי הוא כקודש שאומר עליו הלל והדר קאמר תני רשב״ג אומר אחד שביעית ואחד שאר שני שבוע בית שמאי אומרים אין לו חומש ואין לו ביעור והשתא סוגיא דקדושין כרשב״ג והו פריך בירושל׳ אליבא דרבי שמואל בר בא בעי הא בית שמאי אמרי לא למדו נטע רבעי אלא ממעשר שני כמה דתימא אין מעשר שני בשביעית ודכוותיה [אין נטע רבעי בשביעית דכוותיה נמי] שלישית וששית הואיל ואין בהן מעשר שני [לא יהא בהן נטע רבעי אמר רבי יוסי שלישית וששית אף על גב דאין בהן מעשר שני] יש בהן מעשרות שביעית אין בהן מעשר כל עיקר: יש לו פרט ויש לו עוללות · משום דילפי ממעשר וסבירא להו כרבי מאיר דאמר מעשר שני ממון גבוה הוא כדאי׳ ב:׳ האיש מקדש (נד:): ובית הלל אומרים כולו לגת · דכחולין חשיבי ליה: ז אין העוללות לעניים. מפרש בירושלמי (הל׳ ז) כהדא דתני הנוטע כרם להקדש פטור מן הערלה ומרבעי ומעוללות וחייב בשביעית: משנודעו העוללות· שיודע מהו עוללות ומהו אשכול: העוללות לעניים. מפורש בירושלמי (שם) ובתוספתא שאין אדם מקדיש דבר שאינו שלו: יתנו שכר גידולין להקדש · מה שמשביחין בקרקע של הקדש ותנא קמא סבר דאין לריכין ליתן כיון דכבר נתחייב הכרם בעוללות: בערים· כרם הגבוה המודלית על גבי עלים מלשון אף ערשנו רעננה (שיר א): כל שאינו יכול לפשוט וליטול קרינא ביה לא תשוב לקחתו אבל רוגלית משיעבור הימנה דכל רוגלית ורוגלית חשיב אומן בפני עלמו ואסור לשוב מאומן לאומן כך הוא בירושל׳ (שם): תניא בתוספתא איזה שכחה בעריסין קנים משיעבור הימנו בדלית ובדקל משירד מהן ושאר כל האילנות משיפנה וילך לו בד״א בזמן שלא התחיל בו אבל התחיל בו ושכחו אינו שכחה עד שיבצור כל סביביו [א] וטעות סופר הוא אדרבה כל הני דרישא מיירי בהתחיל אלא איפכא גרסינן בד״א בזמן שהתחיל בו אבל אם לא התחיל בו אינו שכחה עד שיבצור כל סביביו: שכולו עוללות שאין בכרם אשכול שיהא לו כתף או נטף*: אם אין בציר. בירושלמי (הל׳ ו) אמרינן כמה הוא בציר דבי ר׳ שילא אמרי שלשה אשכלות שעושין רביע ופריך [והא ר׳ עקיבא מקיים תרי קראי] ומה דרבי אליעזר ופריק לא תעולל שלא תאמר הואיל ואין לעניים בעוללות קודם לבציר יזכה בהן בעל הבית לפיכך לריך לומר וכרמך לא תעולל:

*צ״ל ונטף וכ״ה ברע״ב ופני משה.

א עד שילכו הנמושות. דמשהלכו מתייאשין העניים וכרים אלו מליאות (כח:) מייתי לה גבי יאוש שלא מדעת ומפרש התם סבי דאזלי אתיגרא שמטעין במסה שבידם מחזיק בפלך (שמואל ב ג) תרגום בתגריו (א): ירושלמי (הלכה א) אבא שאול קורא אותן משושות אית תנויי תני נמושות [ואית תנויי תני

רבנן בין חי״ת להא אלא כי פליגי בחומש בית הלל סברי מוסיף חומש כמעשר שני דכתיב אם גאל יגאל איש ממעשרו חמישתו יוסף עליו. ותניא שתי גאולות הן אחת לנטע רבעי ואחת למעשר שני וחייב לבערן בעת הביעור. ואימתי היה הביעור תנן במעשר שני פרק ה׳ ערב יו״ט הראשון של פסח של רביעית ושל שביעית היה הביעור. ותנן התם [כנ״ע דף נ״ם] הפודה נטע רבעי שלו מוסיף חומש וסתמא כבית הלל. גרסי׳ תני ר׳ אומר לא אמרו בית שמאי אלא בשביעית מאי טעמא סבר לא למדו נטע רבעי אלא ממעשר שני כמה דאת אמר אין מעשר שני בשביעית ודכוותיה אין נטע רבעי בשביעית אבל בשאר שני שבוע יש לו חומש ויש לו ביעור אפילו לבית שמאי. ור״ש בן גמליאל אומר היא שביעית היא שאר שני שבוע אין לו חומש: ב״ש אומרים יש לו פרט ויש לו עוללות. לכרם רבעי. והעניים פודין לעצמן. כללא דמילתא בית שמאי עבדין יתיה ככרם חולין אלא שטעון פדיון אבל חומש לא מוספי: ובית הלל אומרים כולו לגת. דהקדש הוא ואין לעניים בהקדש כלל. וזו המשנה איתינה הכא ואיתינה במעשר שני וי״ל הכא תניתה משום עוללות והכא תניתה משום חומש וביעור והתם פירשנו באר היטב: ז כרם שכולו עוללות. פי׳ שאין לכל הכרם אשכול שיהיה לו או כתף או נטף וכו׳: אם אין בציר וכו׳. גרסי׳ בירושלמי כמה שיעור בציר דבית שילא אמרי ג׳ אשכולות שעושין רביע ואמרינן בשלמא ר״ע מפרש לתרוייהו קראי אלא ר׳ אליעזר הא כבר נאמר וכרמך לא תעולל דמשמע אפילו כולו עוללות ור׳ אליעזר אמר לך האי וכרמך לא תעולל להכי הוא דאתא שלא תאמר הואיל ואין לעניים בעוללות קודם לבציר יזכה בהן בעל הבית לפום כן כתיב וכרמך לא תעולל: המקדיש את כרמו עד שלא נודעו העוללות אין העוללות לעניים. מאי טעמא שהוא כרם הקדש ותניא הנוטע כרם של הקדש פטור מן הערלה ומן הרבעי ומן העוללות: ומשנודעו העוללות. פי׳ משיודע איזהו עוללת ואיזהו אשכול העוללות לעניים מ״ט דתניא שאין אדם מקדיש דבר שאינו שלו: רבי יוסי אומר וכו׳. ותנא קמא אמר לך אין צריכין לתת שכבר נתחייב הכרם לגז״ל העוללות. וכן מפרש בתוספתא: איזה היא שכחה בערים. פי׳ כרם גבוה עומד על עצים: כל שאינו יכול לפשוט וכו׳. פי׳ שמכיח שעבר מעליה זה השיעור שבמקום שנזכר אינו יכול [illegible]

פרק ח א מאימתי כל אדם מותרין בלקט [illegible]

[*הג״ה. בירושלמי [illegible] ודברי רבינו המחבר ז״ל סייעתא לדבריו]

משוטות מ״ד נמוסות מפני] שבאין בסוף מאן דאמר משוטות שכן ממשמשין ובאין עוד מפרש בירושלמי (שם) בפרט ובעוללות משילכו העניים בכרם ויבאו ולא תנינן נמוסות על ידי שהן חביבין הם באין על אתר ואית דגרסי לאלתר (ב): ובזיתים משתרד רביעה שניה · ולא תנינן נמוסות מפני שהוא לנה ואינם יוצאים אלא בחורים : שאינם מוסקין· לשון מסיקה בזיתים כמו קוצר בתבואה ובצירה בענבים : בד׳ איסרות · דהיינו ב׳ פונדיון ותנן אין פוחתין לעני העובר ממקום למקום מככר בפונדיון דהיינו מזון שתי סעודות וכיון דאינו מביא שוה ד׳ איסרות דהיינו שתי סעודות לו ושתי סעודות לאשתו אינו יוצא וכן מפרש בירושלמי (שם) שמתוך שהוא יודע שאינו מביא פרנסתו אף הוא אינו יוצא : ב נאמנים העניים לומר חטים של לקט שכחה ופאה הן ופטורין מן המעשרות כדתנן במסכת חלה (פ״א משנה ג): בשעתו· כלומר בעת הקציר נאמנין : ירושלמי (הל׳ ג) עד היכן א״ר חנינא עד מקום שדרכו לילך ולבוא בו ביום מעשה היה והאמין רבי לחמשה אחים בחמשה כורים של חטים ופריך ואפשר כן אלא מינה ליבחר ומינה ליבחר כורא סלק פירוש ליבחר מעט שקיבץ כאן מעט וכאן מעט עד שהיה לו כור : ועל מעשר עני · נאמנים העניים לומר חטים הללו של מעשר עני הם ופטורים מן המעשרות : כל שנתו · נאמן עליו דהיינו שלישית וששית שהוא מעשר עני : ובן לוי נאמן לעולם · דמעשר ראשון אין לו הפסק ונוהג בכל השנים דהוקש לנחלה שאין לה הפסק ואין לכהן אלא תרומה וכיון דאמר של מעשר הוא לא חיישינן ונאמן בן לוי לומר שנתן לכהן תרומתו דאמרינן בירושל׳ (שם) דר׳ אליעזר א״ר הושעיא כשם שלא נחשדו ישראל על תרומה גדולה כך לא נחשד בן לוי על תרומת מעשר א״ר הושעיא מתניתא אמרה כן מפרש בירושלמי (שם) [א] היכא מתניתא : אין נאמנין אלא על דבר שדרך בני אדם נותנין כן · כדקתני באידך בבא נאמנין על החטין : ג נאמנין על החטין · לומר חטים הללו מעשר עני הן שניתן לי אבל אין נאמנים לומר קמח ופת זה מעשר עני שניתן לי קמח ופת ואין להאמינו במגו דאי בעי אמר חטים ניתן לי ועשיתיו פת וקמח דמשמע בירושלמי (הל׳ ג) כי הוא נאמן דמאחר שאין לו דרך נהלקן כלל קמח ופת ...

ובעוללות משילכו העניים בכרם ויבואו ובזיתים משתרד רביעה שניה אמר ר׳ יהודה והלא יש שאינם מוסקין את זיתידהם אלא לאחר רביעה שניה אלא כדי שיהא העני יוצא ולא יהא מביא בארבע איסרות : ב [א]נאמנים על הלקט ועל השכחה ועל הפאה בשעתן ועל מעשר עני בכל שנתו [ב]ובן לוי נאמן לעולם אינן נאמנין אלא על דבר שבני אדם נוהגין כן : ג [ג]נאמנין על החטים ואין נאמנין על הקמח ולא על הפת [ד]נאמנין על השעורה של אורז ואין נאמנין עליו בין חי בין מבושל נאמנין על הפול ואין נאמנין על הגריסין לא חיין ולא מבושלין נאמנין על השמן לומר של מעשר עני הוא ואין נאמנין עליו לומר של זיתי ניקוף הוא : ד [ה]נאמנים על הירק חי ואין נאמנין על המבושל אלא אם כן היה לו דבר מועט שכן דרך בעל הבית להיות מוציא מלפסו : ה [ו]אין (א) פוחתין לעניים בגורן מחצי קב חטים וקב שעורים רבי מאיר אומר חצי קב קב וחצי כוסמין וקב גרוגרות [ז]או מנה דבלה רבי עקיבא אומר פרס [ח]חצי לוג יין רבי עקיבא אומר רביעית [ט]רביעית שמן רבי עקיבא אומר שמינית ושאר כל הפירות אמר אבא שאול כדי שימכרם ויקח בהן מזון שתי סעודות : ו מדה זו אמורה (ו) בכהנים ובלוים ובישראלים [י]היה מציל נוטל מחצה ונותן מחצה [כ]היה [ב] לו דבר מועט נותן לפניהם והן מחלקין ביניהן :

אין

הלוקטים והם המלקטים השניים והמשיל אותם לזקנים לאיחורם מפני שבושש לבא ולא ימלאו אלא מעט : ורביעה שניה · המטר השני בזמן הרביעה השניה מן השנה והשאילו כמו כן שם הרביעה לזמן הסתיו לפי שהוא מגדל הצמחים ויוליאם מבטן הארץ כמעשה הבועל בנקבה והוא גזור ממלת תרביע וכן אמרו (תענית ו:) מטרא בעלה דארעא וזמן רביעה שניה בארץ הצבי בשנה המבכרת היא בי״ז במרחשון ובשנה הבינונית בכ״ג במרחשון ובשנה המאוחרת בראש חדש כסליו ומה שירד מן הגשם קודם י״ז מרחשון הוא ממטרות החורף לא מתחלת הסתיו כל זה בארץ ישראל ועליו נאמר הדבר: ופירוש מוסקין מנפלין או חובטין הזיתים והחובט נקרא מוסק כמו שיקרא לחורש עודר ולכורת ענבים בוצר ואוסף מיני התבואה קוצר : איסרות. קיבוץ איסר ושיעור איסר ארבע׳ גרות כסף ואין הלכה כר׳ יהודה: ב כבר הקדמנו שמתנות עניים אינן חייבות במעשרות וכן הלוי אינו חייב מן המעשרות אשר ניתן לו חוץ מתרומת מעשר כמו שביארנו בפרק שביעי מברכות ואמר שיהיה העני נאמן בשעת הלקט שיאמר זה לקט ונקח אותו ממנו ולא נתחייב להוציא ממנו מעשר ושאר ההלכה מבואר על זה העיקר : ומה שאמר אינן נאמנין אלא על דבר שבני אדם נוהגין ר״ל שהם אינם ...

TIVE CLUSTERS'?[3] AFTER THE POOR HAD GONE INTO THE VINEYARD AND COME BACK AGAIN.[4] AND IN THE CASE OF THE OLIVE TREES? AFTER THE DESCENT OF THE SECOND RAINFALL.[5] SAID R. JUDAH: 'BUT ARE THERE NOT SOME WHO
b DO NOT HARVEST THEIR OLIVES BEFORE THE SECOND RAINFALL?' NO;[6] [THE TIME LIMIT FOR OLIVES IS] AFTER THE POOR MAN GOES OUT[7] AND CANNOT BRING BACK WITH HIM [MORE THAN THE VALUE OF] FOUR ISSARS.[8]

MISHNAH 2. THEY[9] ARE TO BE BELIEVED CONCERNING 'GLEANINGS', THE FORGOTTEN SHEAF AND PE'AH DURING THEIR [HARVEST] SEASON, AND CONCERNING THE POOR
a MAN'S TITHE[1] DURING THE WHOLE YEAR THEREOF. A LEVITE IS ALWAYS TO BE TRUSTED.[2] THEY MUST NOT BE TRUSTED [IN OTHER CASES] SAVE IN THOSE THINGS WHICH MEN ARE WONT TO GIVE THEM.[3]

MISHNAH 3. THEY ARE TO BE TRUSTED CONCERNING WHEAT,[4] BUT NOT CONCERNING FINE FLOUR OR BREAD;[5] CONCERNING RICE STILL IN ITS STALK,[6] BUT NOT WHEN IT IS EITHER RAW OR COOKED.[7] THEY CAN BE TRUSTED CONCERNING BEANS BUT NOT WHEN THESE ARE POUNDED, WHETHER RAW OR COOKED. THEY ARE TO BE BELIEVED WHEN THEY DECLARE THAT THEIR OIL IS FROM THE 'POOR MAN'S TITHE', BUT THEY ARE NOT BELIEVED WHEN THEY CLAIM THAT IT IS FROM THE FEW OLIVES THAT HAVE BEEN KNOCKED DOWN.[8]

MISHNAH 4. THEY ARE TO BE TRUSTED CONCERNING RAW VEGETABLES,[9] BUT NOT CONCERNING THOSE THAT ARE COOKED, UNLESS HE HAD ONLY A SMALL QUANTITY; FOR SO IT WAS THE CUSTOM OF THE HOUSEHOLDER TO TAKE OUT OF HIS STEW-POT [AND GIVE TO THE POOR].[1]

MISHNAH 5. ONE MUST NOT GIVE TO THE POOR FROM THE THRESHING-FLOOR,[2] LESS THAN A HALF ḲAB OF WHEAT OR A ḲAB OF BARLEY.[3] R. MEIR SAYS: [ONLY] HALF A ḲAB.[4] [ONE MUST GIVE] A ḲAB AND A HALF OF SPELT, A ḲAB OF DRIED FIGS OR A MINA[5] OF PRESSED FIGS; R. AKIBA SAYS: [ONLY] HALF. [ONE MUST GIVE] HALF A LOG[6] OF WINE; BUT R. AKIBA SAYS: A QUARTER.[7] [ONE MUST GIVE] A QUARTER OF OIL; BUT R. AKIBA SAYS: AN EIGHTH.[8] AS FOR OTHER KINDS OF PRODUCE, ABBA SAUL SAYS, [THE AMOUNT GIVEN MUST BE SUCH] AS TO ENABLE THE POOR MAN TO SELL THEM AND BUY WITH THE PRICE THEREOF FOOD SUFFICIENT FOR TWO MEALS.

MISHNAH 6. THIS MEASURE IS STIPULATED FOR THE PRIEST, LEVITE AND ISRAELITE ALIKE.[9] SHOULD HE DESIRE
c TO SAVE AUGHT,[1] HE CAN ONLY RETAIN A HALF[2] AND GIVE THE OTHER HALF AWAY. IF HE HAS ONLY A VERY SMALL QUANTITY,[3] THEN HE MUST PLACE IT BEFORE THEM AND THEY THEN DIVIDE IT AMONG THEMSELVES.[4]

(3) V. *supra* VII, 4. (4) A second time; v. Ta'an. 6*a*. (5) *Circa* 23rd Ḥeshwan (Ned. VIII, 5; Ta'an. I, 4). So called because this rain fructifies the soil. 'The rain is husband to the soil' (Ta'an. 6*b*). Cf. also Lev. XIX, 19. The Talmud (Ta'an. 6*b*) explains what is meant by a satisfactory second rainfall; when the soil is left fit to be used for sealing the mouth of a cask. (6) This, therefore, cannot be the stipulated time. (7) Of the vineyard. (8) An *issar* = 8 *peruṭahs* (the smallest copper coin current). This sum was calculated as sufficient for a man to buy meals—two for himself and two for his wife. Cf. *infra* 7. (9) Even the uninstructed poor (*'amme ha-areẓ*) are to be relied on when they claim that the wheat they sell is what they received as gifts and hence exempt from all tithes.

a (1) The tithe was given during the third and sixth year of the Sabbatical cycle. (2) He is to be trusted in his declaration that the wheat is the 'First Tithe'. Since this tithe to the Levite was unrestricted as to time, there is no doubt that he must afterwards give the tithe due to the priest. Just as an Israelite *'am ha-areẓ* was not suspected of retaining for himself the *terumah* due to the priest, because the penalty of eating this *terumah* was death at the hands of heaven, so the Levite is not to be suspected of having failed to give the 'tithe of the tithe' which he owes to the priest. (Num. XVIII, 26). (3) As explained in the following Mishnah. (4) To state that they receive it as Poor Man's Tithe. (5) It is not usual to give these to the poor on account of the additional trouble and expense they involve. The same reason applies to the other instances cited in our Mishnah. (6) Because in this state it was usually given to the poor. The word שערה is also explained as the kernels of the rice after the threshing and prior to the peeling of the husks. (7) That is after the rice has been threshed or peeled. (8) It is hardly likely that the oil could have been produced from the few olives left on the tree after the continual beatings (נקוף) made upon it during the harvest-time, for the olives to drop down. (Cf. Isa. XVII, 6; XXIV, 13); and since the poor only receive the few remaining olives, their statement is not credible. Cf. Ḥallah III, 9. (9) Vegetables (since they are perishable) though exempt from *Pe'ah, supra* I, 4, are subject rabbinically to the Poor Man's Tithe.

b (1) It is very likely that the owner, having forgotten to give his dues, does so afterwards direct from the stew-pot. This, however, would only be a small quantity; for as explained (*supra* 3, n. 5) it is unlikely for the owner to give the poor readily prepared food. (2) The measures quoted in the Mishnah are based on the stipulation of Deut. XXVI, 12 that the gifts to the poor must be such as to satisfy them. This refers to the Poor Man's Tithe only; for with regard to 'Gleanings' or *Pe'ah* or the 'Forgotten Sheaf', the owner could leave these dues in the field for the poor to divide among themselves (*supra* IV, 1). (3). A *ḳab* = 4 *logs* = one sixth of a *se'ah* = 24 eggs (in size). (4) The variance as to the amounts mentioned here is due to what is considered sufficient to satisfy temporarily the needs of the poor. (5) A weight measure equalling 25 *sela's* or 100 *denars*. After the figs are pressed, they are sold according to weight. (6) A *log* (v.n. 3) was 2 *liṭras*. (7) Of a *log*. This is the standard measure mentioned in connection with religious ceremonies. V.B.B. 58*b*. (8) All the measures given here apply only when the distribution takes place in the threshing-floor, amidst the scene of plenty; in his house, however, the owner can obey the dictates of his own heart, since the Rabbis have not fixed a minimum. (9) The priest and the Levite, like the Israelite, are subject to the Poor Man's Tithe of which they must give sufficient for at least two meals (Bert.). Moreover, even if the priest and Levite had already received their tithes, they are further entitled, should they be very poor, to the stipulated minimum due to the poor (R. Samson of Sens).

c (1) He is not desirous of giving away all the tithes he has at once, but would save some for his own poor relatives. (2) For this purpose, but not more. (3) After setting aside the half for his poor relative, the remainder is not sufficient with which to give each poor man the stipulated amount. (4) As long as the poor have all that is left, it does not matter even if each does not receive the stipulated amount. The onus is thus shifted from the owner to the poor.

MISHNAH 7. ONE MUST NOT GIVE THE WANDERING POOR MAN LESS THAN A LOAF WORTH A PONDION[5] AT A TIME WHEN FOUR SE'AHS [OF WHEAT COST] ONE SELA'.[6] IF HE SPENDS THE NIGHT [AT A PLACE], ONE MUST GIVE HIM THE COST OF WHAT HE NEEDS FOR A NIGHT.[7] IF HE STAYS OVER THE SABBATH HE IS GIVEN FOOD FOR THREE MEALS.[8] HE WHO HAS THE MEANS FOR TWO MEALS, MUST NOT ACCEPT ANYTHING FROM THE CHARITY DISH;[9] AND IF HE HAS FOR FOURTEEN MEALS, HE MAY NOT ACCEPT ANY SUPPORT FROM THE COMMUNAL FUND.[10] THE COMMUNAL FUND IS COLLECTED BY TWO[11] AND DISTRIBUTED BY THREE PEOPLE.[12]

a MISHNAH 8. HE WHO POSSESSES TWO HUNDRED ZUZ,[1] MAY NOT TAKE 'GLEANINGS', THE FORGOTTEN SHEAF, PE'AH OR THE POOR MAN'S TITHE. IF HE POSSESSES TWO HUNDRED MINUS ONE DENAR,[2] THEN EVEN IF A THOUSAND [MEN] EACH GIVE HIM [ONE ZUZ], HE MAY ACCEPT.[3] IF HIS PROPERTY IS MORTGAGED UNTO HIS CREDITORS OR TO THE KETHUBAH[4] OF HIS WIFE, HE MAY ACCEPT. THEY[5] CANNOT COMPEL HIM[6] TO SELL HIS HOUSE OR HIS TOOLS.[7]

MISHNAH 9. IF A MAN POSSESSES FIFTY ZUZ AND HE USES THEM FOR HIS BUSINESS, HE MUST NOT TAKE [THE POOR GIFTS].[8] WHOEVER DOES NOT NEED TO TAKE [CHARITY] AND YET TAKES, WILL NOT DEPART FROM THIS WORLD BEFORE BEING ACTUALLY IN NEED OF HIS FELLOW-MEN;[9] BUT HE WHO NEEDS TO TAKE AND DOES NOT TAKE,[10] WILL NOT DIE BEFORE HE WILL HAVE COME IN OLD AGE TO SUPPORT OTHERS FROM HIS OWN [BOUNTY]. CONCERNING HIM THE VERSE SAYS: BLESSED BE THE MAN WHO TRUSTETH IN THE LORD AND WHOSE HOPE IS THE LORD.[11] THE SAME MAY BE APPLIED TO A JUDGE WHO JUDGES IN TRUTH ACCORDING TO ITS INTEGRITY.[12] AND IF A MAN IS NOT LAME,[13] BLIND OR HALTING, AND HE FEIGNS TO BE AS ONE OF THESE, HE WILL NOT DIE IN HIS OLD AGE BEFORE HE ACTUALLY BECOMES AS ONE OF
b THESE;[1] AS IT IS SAID: HE WHO SEARCHES FOR EVIL, IT SHALL COME UNTO HIM,[2] AND ALSO AS IT IS SAID: RIGHTEOUSNESS, RIGHTEOUSNESS SHALT THOU SURELY PURSUE.[3] AND ANY JUDGE WHO ACCEPTS A BRIBE OR WHO PERVERTS JUSTICE WILL NOT DIE IN OLD AGE BEFORE HIS EYES HAVE BECOME DIM, AS IT IS SAID: AND A GIFT SHALT THOU NOT ACCEPT; FOR A GIFT BLINDETH THEM THAT HAVE SIGHT.[4]

מסכת פאה

הדרן עלך והדרך עלן

תורה אור

(5) Abridged from *dupondium*, a Roman coin equal to a half *zuz* or two *issars* (Ma'as. Sh. IV, 8). (6) The *sela'* = 4 *denars* = 24 *ma'ah* = 48 *pondions*. Four *se'ahs* would equal twenty-four *kabs*, though actually in the loaf worth one *sela'*, there would be less than this amount, since the baker would wish to profit for the expense of grinding and baking. Only when the distribution takes place in the threshing-floor is the poor to receive not less than the stipulated sum—half a *kab;* when receiving a baked loaf, this need not be more than a quarter of a *kab*, or six eggs in size. V. 'Er. VIII, 2. (7) I.e., for bed and warmth; Shab. 118*a*. (8) On the Sabbath day each Jew is enjoined to partake of three meals. (9) *Tamhui*, a dish containing victuals for distribution among the poor, each receiving at least the amount of two meals, v. B.B. 8*b*. (10) The *Kuppah* from which sustenance was disbursed among the poor every Friday, and since he has enough to eat for the whole of next week, he is not entitled to poor relief from this source. (11) All charitable collections must be undertaken by at least two accredited persons, Shek. V, 2. (12) The disbursement required the presence of three adjudicators as in a Beth din; v. B.B. 8*a*.
a (1) The sum considered by the Rabbis sufficient for food and clothing for a whole year. (2) Latin *denarius*, another name for a *zuz*. Roughly speaking, a *denar* or *zuz* may be considered the equivalent of a shilling or mark (Danby). (3) The poor man's gifts above mentioned. (4) The marriage contract, v. Glos. (5) The overseers of the poor. (6) The applicant for these gifts. (7) Or such articles of furniture used to adorn his house on the Sabbath and festivals. Cf. Keth. 68*a*. (8) Fifty *zuz* sunk in business are as good as two hundred lying idle. (9) As a penalty for robbing the poor of their due. (10) Preferring to lead a humbler, more economical life instead. (11) Jer. XVII, 7. (12) Lit., 'who judges a true judgment according to its truth', i.e., an absolutely true verdict which can be arrived at by the judge if he endeavours to find out the truth himself and does not rely on evidence alone, v. Sanh. (Sonc. ed.) 7*a* n. c 8. A judge whose hope is God is one to whom the truth is above the fear of men; cf. Shab. 10. (13) The distinction drawn between חגר and פסח is that the first describes a man lame in one foot and the second a man lame in both. (cf. II Sam. IV, 4). A few versions add also 'deaf and dumb'.
b (1) In accordance with the Rabbinic principle that God punishes 'measure for measure'. (2) Prov. XI, 27. (3) Deut. XVI, 20. (4) Ex. XXIII, 8; the verse goes on: *'and perverteth the words of the righteous'*. The judge who accepts a gift to pervert judgment is compared to the man who feigns blindness. He, therefore, courts the same punishment.

DEMAI

CHAPTER I

MISHNAH 1. THE [FOLLOWING] ARE TREATED LE-
a NIENTLY[1] IN RESPECT OF [THE RULES OF] *demai:* WILD FIGS,[2] JUJUBE FRUIT,[3] CRAB APPLES, WILD WHITE FIGS,[4] YOUNG

a (1) The rules of *demai* are not enforced in the case of these fruits when bought from an *'am ha-arez*. The list consists of fruits which are esteemed of little value, and the owners of which often leave them for general use without claiming in them their property rights. Therefore it may be assumed that they had not been grown by the *'am ha-arez* who sold them, but had been picked up by him as ownerless property, in which case they would be exempt from tithes; cf. Ma'as. I, 1. Or again, even if they had been grown by the *'am ha-arez* himself, it may be assumed that he had already tithed them, since the cost of tithing them would have been small. And on account of this double doubt they are treated leniently in respect of *demai*. (2) Cf. Ber. 40*b*. (3) Or 'lote'. (4) These grow wild once in three years.

מסורת הש"ס

א) שבת פע"ז קיח. וב"ב פ"א דף ט: ב) שם ח: ג) סוטה פרק ג דף כא: ד) כתובות פרק ו דף סח.

עין משפט נר מצוה

ט א מיי' פ"ז שם הלכה ח סמג עשין קסב טור שו"ע יו"ד סי' רנ סעיף ד: י ב מיי' פ"ט מהל' מתנות עניים הל' יג סמג עשין קסב טוש"ע יו"ד סימן רנג סעיף א ב: יא ג מיי' שם ה"ה סמג שם טוש"ע יו"ד סי' רנו סעי' ג: יב ד ה מיי' שם הל' י"ג סמג שם טוש"ע יו"ד סימן רנג סעיף א: יג ו מיי' פי"ג מהל' מתנות עניים הל' יט סמג שם טור שו"ע יו"ד סימן רנה סעיף ב: יד ז מיי' פכ"ג מהל' סנהדרין הל' ט סמג לאוין רח טור חו"מ סימן א:

תורה אור

ז [א] אין (א) פוחתין לעני העובר ממקום למקום מבכר בפונדיון מארבע סאין בסלע לן נותנין לו פרנסת לינה שבת נותנין לו מזון ג' סעודות [ב] ומי שיש לו מזון ב' סעודות לא יטול מן התמחוי מזון י"ד סעודות לא יטול מן הקופה [ג] והקופה נגבית בשנים ומתחלקת בג': ח (ג) [ד] מי שיש לו מאתים זוז לא יטול לקט שכחה ופאה ומעשר עני היו לו מאתים חסר דינר אפי' אלף נותנין לו כאחת הרי זה יטול היו ממושכנים לבעל חובו או לכתובת אשתו הרי זה יטול (ד) אין מחייבין אותו למכור את ביתו ואת כלי תשמישו: ט [ה] מי שיש לו חמשים זוז והוא נושא ונותן בהם הרי זה לא יטול וכל מי שאינו צריך ליטול ונוטל אינו נפטר מן העולם עד שיצטרך לבריות וכל מי שצריך ליטול ואינו נוטל אינו מת מן הזקנה עד שיפרנס אחרים משלו ועליו הכתוב אומר ירמי' יז ברוך הגבר אשר יבטח בה' והיה ה' מבטחו וכן (א) דיין שדן דין אמת לאמתו [ב] וכל מי שאינו לא חגר ולא סומא ולא פסח ועושה עצמו כא' מהם אינו מת מן הזקנה עד שיהיה כא' מהם שנאמר [ג] דברי' טז צדק צדק תרדוף וכל דיין שלוקח שחד ומטה את הדין אינו מת מן הזקנה עד שעיניו כהות שנא' שם ולא תקח שחד כי השחד יעור עיני חכמים וגו':

חסלת מסכת פאה

ר"מ

הקטוב ויש לו לקחת האלי ויעזוב האלי ביניהם ויחלקו אותו בשוה ואף על פי שיפול לכל אחד מהם פחות מן השיעור הקטוב ויגיע זה כאשר זכרנו: ז ככר הוא לחם אחד: ופונדיון הוא חצי זוז: וסאה הוא מדה אשר שיעורה ו' קבים וכבר זכרנו שיעור קב: וסלע הוא ד' דינרים והדינר ו' זוזים ויהיה לירוף הסלע כ"ד זוזים והארבע סאין כ"ד קבין ויהיה מכירתו קב בזוז כשיהיה החטה ארבע סאין בסלע יהיה בככר שהוא בפונדיון חצי קב וכאילו אמר אין נותנין לעני העובר ממקום למקום מן הלדקה פחות מככר לחם מחצי קב: ופרנסת לינה הוא מה שלריך אליו בלילה ממטה וכר וכסת ואם יהיה העני ההוא ידוע שתנים לו מה שיחסר. והביאו ראיה החכמים כי שלש סעודות חובה על אדם לאכול בשבת מדברי הכתוב (שמות טז) אכלוהו היום כי שבת היום לה' היום לא תמלאוהו בשדה שהוסיף לשנות מלת יום ג' פעמים: ותמחוי הוא שם הכלי שיאכלו בו העניים והיו בכל יום משוטטים על הבתים בכלי ויוליאו מכל בית תבשיל מאשר היו מבשלים ויושם בכלי ההוא ויחלקוהו על העניים וחובה להיות שלשה אנשים המתעסקין לקבץ אותו ולחלק אותו לפי שתכף שיקבצוהו יחלקוהו בזמן א'. ושם הקופה היא כמו כן כלי מן הגמי או מן הקש והוא כיוי לאשר יתקבץ מהלדקה שיקבלו מיום ששי לששי והעיקר בידינו שכל מי שלא נתן לקופה מה שנתחייב באין ולוקחין עבוטו וכן אמרו (ב"ב דף ח:) ממשכנין על הלדקה אפי' בערבי שבתות ועל כן אל יעסקו לקבץ אותה פחות משנים כי העיקר בידינו שאין עושין שררה על הלבור פחות משנים וכשיחלקוה יהיו ג' מפני שהוא דין מדיני ממונות לתת לזה הרבה כפי לרכו ורוב בניו ויתנו לזה מעט כפי הראוי לו כמו כן והעיקר בידינו דיני ממונות בשלשה: ומי שיש לו מזון שתי סעודות והוא מאכל ליום אחד לא יקח מן התמחוי שיחלקו בכל יום: ומי שיש לו מזון י"ד סעודות שהוא מזון שבוע לא יקח מן הקופה שיקבלו בכל שבוע ואולם נעשו י"ד סעודות מזון לשבוע אחד מפני שיש ג' סעודות לשבת ואחד עשר בששה ימים הנשארים ב' סעודות בכל יום אחת ביום ואחת בלילה ולפי החשבון לריך שיהא י"ב סעודות אלא שהם לא חשבו לו סעודת מולאי שבת מפני שלא ילטרך אליה בשביל שאכל במנחה יום השבת והיא השלמת ג' סעודות של שבת: ח ממושכנים ידוע ואפי' אם יש לו כלי כסף וכלי זהב כגון כוסות וקערות אינו חייב למכרם עד שיקח מתנות עניים ויכתב בכללם אז יאמרו לו מכור אותם הכלים וקנה אחרים ואל תמעיט מתנות העניים: ט חמשים זוז אשר יסחרו בהם ישוו מאתים שלא יסחרו בהם כי במה שאמר בהלכה הקודמת לזו מי שיש לו מאתים זוז לא יטול כשיהיו בטלות שאינו יודע לסחור בהם אבל כשיהיה יודע לסחור בהם אפי' לא יתעסק אלא בחמשים זוזים מהם אסור לו ליקח מתנות העניים: חסלת מסכת פאה

ר"ש

ז מבכר בפונדיון· ככר הנמכר בפונדיון כשהחטים נמכרין ד' סאין בסלע (ח) ובירושלמי (הל' ה') פריך הכא איתמר אין פוחתין לעניים בגורן וכא איתמר אין פוחתין לעני העובר ממקום למקום אמר רב הונא לא מכן שליש ליליא ולכאורה קשיא היא דאדרבה הכל שיעור אחד דלפי חשבון ארבע סאין בסלע היינו חצי קב בפונדיון דזהו שיעור בגורן אלא קשיא ליה משום דבגורן נותנין חטין לעני ואיכא יגיעה בטחינה והרקדה ואפיה וחסר ליה ב' סעודות ומשני לא מכן שליש ליליא שחנוני שמכר את הככר מוליא ונמלא דליכא חצי קב בככר שחנוני מוכר בפונדיון והכי נמי אמרי' בפרק כילד משתתפין (דף פב:) לא מכן שליש לחנוני ואמרי' נמי התם לא מכן מחלה לחנוני ולא קשיא הא דיהיב בעל הבית ליבי הא דלא יהיב בעה"ב ליבי: פרנסת לינה · בפ' כל כתבי (דף קיח·) ובפ"ק דב"ב (דף ט·) אמר רב פפא פורי' ובי סדיא ובתוספתא קתני פרנסת לינה שמן וקטנית: מזון ג' סעודות· בפרק כל כתבי (שם) [א] אפילו כרבי חידקא דאמר ד' סעודות חייב אדם לאכול בשבת: לא יטול מן התמחוי · לפי שהתמחוי מתחלק בכל יום: לא יטול מן הקופה. לפי שמתחלק מערב שבת לע"ש כדתנן בפ"ק דב"ב (שם) ותני נמי התם (ח:) תמחוי לעניי עולם קופה לעניי העיר ובפרק כל כתבי מוקי לה כר"ע דאמר עשה שבתך חול ואל תלטרך לבריות: נגבית בשנים · בפ"ק דבבא בתרא (שם) אמרינן לפי שממשכנין עליו ואין עושין שררה על הלבור פחות משנים: ומתחלקת בשלשה · לפי שהיא כדיני ממונות: ח מאתים זוז · שיערו חכמים שזהו שיעור הולאתו במזונות ובמלבושיו [לשנה] וכן במשרה אשתו ע"י שליש בפרק אע"פ (דף ס"ד:) שנותן לה ב' קבין חטין בכל שבוע והוא שליש דינר שעולה לי"ז דינרין לשנה וכלים של נ' זוז ונ' זוג מנעלים ושאר פירות ויכול לעלות לק' זוז והני מאתים זוז דהכי היינו לו ולאשתו ומיהו לא יתכן דנבי קופה ותמחוי לא כייל אשתו בהדיה: היו ממושכנין לכתובת אשתו · ואפילו נשואה כדמוכח בירושלמי (הל' ז) דאמרי' עד כאן בבעל חוב שהוא דוחק ואפי' בבעל חוב שאינו דוחק נשמעינה מן הדא היו ממושכנין לכתובת אשתו או לבעל חוב ודא אשה לאו כבעל חוב שאינו דוחק הוא: את ביתו ואת כלי תשמישו· בירושלמי (שם) אמר רבי חנינא כלי רגל וכלי שבת אין מחייבין אותו למכור ובפ' מגילת האשה (סח·) פריך אמתני' מהא דתניא היה משתמש בכלי זהב ישתמש בכלי כסף בכלי כסף ישתמש בכלי נחושת ומשני במחרישה דכספא ורב פפא משני לאחר שבא לידי גיבוי שמתפרנס מקופה של לדקה שבא לידי גבאי אז מחייבין אותו למכור אפי'. כדי ליטול לקט אבל קודם שבא לידי גיבוי שמתפרנס בלנעה ולא מיד הגבאי נוטל לקט שכחה ופאה אע"פ שהיו לו מאתים זוז אם היה מוכר כלי תשמישו ויש לשונות אחרים וכמו שפירשתי עיקר: ירושלמי (שם) היה משתמש בכלי זהב נותנין לו כלי כסף כלי כסף נותנין לו כלי נחושת כלי נחושת נותנים לו כלי זכוכית א"ר מנא כלי [א] כסף וכלי זכוכית בגופיהן והתני היה משתמש בכלי מילת נותנין לו כלי מילת כאן בגופו כאן בשאינו גופו: ט הרי זה לא יטול · בירושלמי (הלכה ח) אמרינן הכי חמשין דעבדין טבין ממאתים דלא עבדין כלומר ממאתים חסר דינר דהתם יטול והכא לא יטול: שהוא לריך ליטול ואינו נוטל · בירושלמי אמרינן ר' חייא בשם [ד] ר' כיני מתניתא כל מי שלריך ליטול ואינו נוטל הרי זה שופך דמים ואסור לרחם עליו על נפשו לא חס כל שכן על אחרים משמע דפליגי אמתניתין ויש לפרש דהסיא בשאין יכול להספיק במעשה ידיו ומספק [ומסגף] את עלמו בחיים רעים ומתניתא במספק על ידי שדוחק עלמו במלאכה [כבדה ובוטח בה'] קודם שיתפרנס מאחרים ועל זה נאמר והיה ה' מבטחו: חסלת מסכת פאה

א' לחל וא' לשבת מאי ורחצת וסכת ושמת שמלותיך. וכי ערומה היתה אלא בגדי שבתה: ט מי שיש לו חמשים זוז וכו'. הדא אמר חמשין עבדין טבין ממאתים חסר דינר ולא עבדין. תנא הסמטא עיניו המקפח שוקיו והמצבה כריסו אין נפטר מן העולם עד שיהיה לו כן מי שהוא צריך ליטול וכו': חסלת מסכת פאה

פי' מהרי"ד בן מלכי צדק

אליעזר אם רצה נותן לפניהן שליש ומציל ב' ידות לקרוביו: ז אין פוחתין לעני העובר ממקום למקום מככר שהוא שוה פונדיון שיהיו הולכין ד' סאין קמח בסלע סאה בדינר והסאה כ"ד לונין והדינר ו' מעו' והמעה ב' פונדיונות נמצא הדינר י"ב פונדיונ' נמצא הולך בפונדיון בהאי שיעור בר תרין לונין: מי שיש לו מזון ב' סעודות לא יטול מן התמחוי. פי' לפי שתמחוי בכל יום ומתחלק לבו ביום והאי אית ליה מזון היום וקופה מע"ש לע"ש תמחוי לכל אדם קופה לאנשי העיר בלבד: ח מי שיש לו מאתים זוז לא יטול לקט שכחה ופאה ומעשר עני היו לו מאתים חסר דינר וכו'. חד תלמיד לר' היו לו ר' זוזין חסר דינר והוה ר' יליף זכי עימיה חדא לתלת שנין מעשר מסכינין עבדין ביה תלמידיה עין בישא ומלון ליה. פי' ר' זוז אתא בעי מזכי עימיה אמר ליה ר' אית לי שיעורא אמר ליה זה מכות פרושין נגעו ביה רמז לתלמידוי ואעילניה לקפיליך וחסרוניה חד קרם וזכה עימיה היך כמה דהוה יליף: היו ממושכנין אילו זוזין וכו'. כלי תשמישו. גרסינן בירושל' א"ר חנינה כלי רגל וכלי שבת אין מחייבין אותו למכור. א"ר חנינה צריך אדם שיהו לו ב' עטופין

פי' הרא"ש

(ח) והוא חצי קב דסאה ו' קבים וד' סאים כ"ד קבים והם מ"ח חצאי קבים וסלע ד' דינרי' ודינר ו' מעין כסף הרי כ"ד מעות ומעה ב' פונדיון הרי מ"ח פונדיון:

הגהות הב"ח

פרק ח

מ"ט (א) וכן דיין שדן דין אמת לאמתו שנאמר צדק צדק תרדוף וכל מי שאינו לא חגר וכו' כאחד מהם וכל דיין שלוקח:

הגהות הגר"א

מ"ח [א] בר"ש כסף. וכ"ב נחושת· [ב] לאמתו. נ"ב כאן צ"ל הבבא דלמטה וכל דיין כו': [ג] שנאמר. נ"ב ודורש רעה תבואתו. ונאמר צדק צדק תרדוף כו': [ד] כיני מתניתא. במחק וכ"ב מתניתא תני:

הגהות מהרי"ד לנדא

מ"ו א] בר"ש אפילו כרי חידקא. צ"ל מוקי לה אפי' כו':

מסורת הש"ס

א) ברכות פרק ו דף מ:

עין משפט נר מצוה

א א מיי' פ"ג מהל' מעשר הלכה א:

דמאי פרק ראשון

א הקלים (א) [א] שבדמאי השיתין והרימין והעוזרדין ובנות שוח ובנות

ר"מ

א היסוד שסודה עליו זאת המסכתא הוא מה שאני אומר כי הדמאי והוא הספק שלא נודע אם הוליאו ממנו מתנות הקב"ה אם לא חובה להוליא ממנו חלק ממאה והוא מעשר מן המעשר ויתנו לכהן ויוליאו ממנו מעשר שני ויאכלוהו בעליו בירושלים כמשפט מעשר שני או יגאלנו על פי מה שיתבאר במקומו ואינו חייב להוליא ממנו לא מעשר ראשון ולא מעשר עני כי מעשר ראשון ללוי ומעשר עני לעניים והעיקר אשר בידינו בדינים המוליא מחברו עליו הראיה וזה הדבר ספק ויש לומר ללוי או לעני הבא ראיה שלא הוליאו ממנו זה שאתה מבקש וטול ולא נעשה כן במעשר מן המעשר מפני שהוא תרומה כמו שביארנו והוא חוק לכהן והאוכל טבל אשר לא הורם ממנו מתנת כהן הוא חייב מיתה בידי שמים ומדרך האיסור הוליאו ממנו חוק לכהן לא מפני שהכהן יכול

ר"ש

א הקלים שבדמאי. שהקילו חכמים על פירות הללו שלא לעשרם דמאי כגון חבר הלוקח מעם הארץ אע"ג דחשידי שלא לעשר בהנך פירות משום דלא חשיבי לא נחשדו עליה (א): ופליגי בירושלמי (הל' א') דריש לקיש אמר לא שנו אלא דמאי אבל ודאי חייב ור' יוחנן אמר לא שנייא בין ודאי בין דמאי פטורים דר' יוחנן אפי' בודאי לפי שרוב מינים הללו אין באין אלא מהפקר ודמאי דמתני' לאו דוקא כי הסיא דלקמן בפירקין (מ"ג) מכזיב ולהלן פטור מן הדמאי דמה התם לא שני בין ודאי ובין דמאי (ב) אף הכא לא שני בין דמאי בין ודאי והא דנקט במתני' דמאי מפרש ר' לא לפי שבכל מקום לא (*) חשו אלא דמאי הכא לא אתיין מתני' אלא ודאי כלומר הא דנקט דמאי לפי שכל המסכתא איירי בדמאי נקט הכא דמאי אגב אחריני אע"ג דדמאי לאו דוקא: [שיתין בפ' כילד מברכין (דף מ:) אמר רבב"ח מין תאנים] ובירושלמי (שם) אמרינן אלו הן שיתין רבי שמעון בר אמי אמר שהן יוצאין מתחת העלין: רימין· כנדי: עוזרדין · עולשין: בנות שוח. (שם) אמר רבה בר בר חנה תאני חיורתא והשתא משמע הכא שהוא פרי גרוע שלא נחשדו עליו עמי הארץ וכן משמע פרק קמא דע"ג (דף יד:) דאמרינן גבי שביעית דהוסיפו עליהן מוכססין ובנות שוח אבל מעיקרא לא נהגו בהו שביעית שלא היה חשוב בעיניהם וקשה דבפ' קמא דשבועות (דף י"ב:) משמע שהוא פרי חשוב גבי מותרות קיץ למזבח כבנות שבע לאדם (ג) והיינו בנות שוח דאמרינן בבראשית רבה גבי עץ שאכל אדם הראשון דקרי ליה בנות שוח לפי שגרמו שוחה לאדם ואיכא דקרו ליה בנות שבע שגרמו ז' ימי אבילות ובפ' ד' דנדרים (דף כז·) גבי נודר מן הכלכלה והיו בה בנות שבע ואמר אילו הייתי יודע שבנות שבע לתוכה לא הייתי נודר דמשמע נמי דפרי טוב היא ולר' יוחנן דפטר בירושלמי (הלכה א) מטעם הפקר מלינן למימר דפרי הגדל ביערים הוא שהוא מקום הפקר ופטור מן המעשר אע"פ שהוא טוב וכעין אגוזים קטנים שבמקומינו וכעין ערמונים והא דלא נהגא בהו שביעית מעיקרא לא משום גריעותא דפרי

פי' מהרי"ד בן מלכי צדק

... למפרש אלא תרומת מעשר. וכן היה עושה למעשר שני א' מי' והיה נקרא מעשר שני של דמאי. אבל תרומת דמאי לא אשכחנן לפי שמפרישין היו תרומה גדולה דתניא לפי ששלח יוחנן כהן גדול בכל גבול ארץ ישראל וכו' והע"ם בשאר פירות אבל בפירות האילך אלו הקילו חכמים עליהן ופטורין בין מדמאי בין מודאי ואף על גב דתנינן מן הדמאי לחודיה דדמיא הא דתנינן הכא למאי דתנינן לקמן מכזיב ולהלן פטור מן הדמאי ולא שאני לן בין דמאי ובין ודאי. אף הכא נמי לא שניא בין מדמאי בין מודאי ופי' דמאי דין מאי פי' שיתין מין תאנין הן מן המינין הפחותין וגרסינן בירושלמי אלו הן השיתין ר' שמעון בריה דר' אבא אמר שהן יוצאין מתחת העלין: והרימין. סורבי: והעוזרדין. פורנא. גרסינן בתוספתא בשביעית פרק ד' תני רבן שמעון בן גמליאל אומר מהרצאת העלין ועד הפגין ג' יום מפגין ועד השיתין הטבלות ג' יום מן השיתין ועד התאנין ג' יום: ובנות שוח. תנן התם בשביעית פ"ה בנות שוח שביעית שלהן שניה. וגרסינן עלה סהו בנות שוח

פי' הרא"ש

... לעצמו ויפריש מעשר שני לאכלו בירושלים ומעשר עני יפריש ויעכב לעצמו כיון דספיקא הוא לא יהיב ללוי ולעני. ולא רצו לתקן שימכור תרומת מעשר לכהן דחיישינן אי מסהי ליה ישראל גביה עד שיזדמן לו כהן שיקנה דלמא אתי בו לידי תקלה וכאלו דברים אמרו שהלוקחים מן הע"ה אינו צריך לעשר משום דלא חשיבי הנך פירות מהימני עלייהו: (ב) והחי לאו דוקא לכ"ע דרחוק הוא מארץ ישראל הלכך אין צריכין לעשר כלל: (ג) פירוש כמו שאוכלין בנות שבע בקינוח סעודה כך מביאין מן המותרות עולות אחר שהקריבו תמיד היום והמזבח בטל·

הוא אלא משום דתנן במסכת שביעית פ"ה (מ"א) בנות שוח שביעית שלהן שניה שהן עושות לג' שנים והוו סברי דלא אזלינן בהו בתר חנטה א] אלא בתר לקיטה כיון דאין נגמרין בשנה שחונטין בה אבל נר"ש לקיש בירושלמי דמחייב בודאי ופטר בדמאי לפי שלא נחשדו משום גריעותא הוא וסוגיא דגמ' כוותיה בפרק כילד מברכין (דף מ') דמאי הוא דלא בעי עשורי הא ודאי בעי עשורי ועוד קשה דהתם ובפרק קמא דע"ג (דף יד:) אמרינן תאני חיוורתא ובפרק ד' דנדרים משמע דאין זה לא תאנים שחורות ולא תאנים לבנות וצריך לומר דג' מיני תאנים הן שחורות ולבנות הן סתם תאנים ובנות שוח הן תאנים רעות כגון הנך דהכא ודפרק קמא דע"ג וקראו בנות שוח לפי שתולין הקלקלה במקולקל אבל בנות שבע דשביעית ונדרים הן הטובות שגרמו ז' ימי אכלות דמסתמא מן היפות אכל שנחמד העץ להשכיל ואית דגרסי בפ"ק דע"ג מוכססין בנות שוח בלא וא"ו דהוא פרי אחד שכך שמו כדמוכח בפ"ק דבכורות (דף ח·) דאמרינן הזאב והארי והדוב והנמר והברדלס לג' שנים וכנגדן בנות שוח נחש לז' שנים ואותו רשע לא מלינו חבר וי"א מוכססין בנות שוח וכן פי' בקונטרס דמוכססין מין של בנות שוח ולא בנות שוח ממש ועוד י"ל דמשעת נטיעת האילן של בנות שוח אינו טוען פירות עד ז' שנים והכי מייתי לה גבי נחש וכי האי גוונא אמרי' התם אפעה לע' שנה וכנגדו באילן חרוב שמשעת נטיעתו עד שעת גמר פירותיו ע' שנה אבל גבי זאב וארי דלג' שנים היינו משעת חנטתו עד גמר פריו וכדתנן בשביעית: בנות שקמה-בפ' כילד מברכין (מ:) אמ' רבה בב"ח תאני דולבי כלומ' תאנה המורכבת בערמון כדאג' בר"ה (דף כג·) ערמונים דולבי ערמון תרגום דלנוב: נובלות תמרה· (שם:) ר' אליעזר ור' זירא חד אמר בושלי כומרא כלומר מניחין אותו באילן להאמק מל' עורנו כתנור נכמרו (איכה ה) ויש מפרשין שאינמתבשלין באילן אלא תולשן ועושה אותן כומר בארץ ומתבשלין וחד אמר תמרי דזיקא דמשמע דדמאי פטור אבל ודאי בעי עשורי ולא מיפטר משום הפקר למאן דאמר תמרי דזיקא מפרש התם דהכא בדמאי עסקינן כגון שעשאן גורן דאמר רבי יצחק אמר רבי יוחנן משום רבי אליעזר בן יעקב הלקט והשכחה והפאה שעשאן גורן הוקבעו: גופנין· שילהי גופני ענבים שמניחין בגפן בסוף הבציר. שבקושי מתבשלין: נצפה פרחה [והוא נלף]: האוג. פרי אדום כדתנן בפרק קמא דמעשרות (משנה ג) האוג והכותים משיאדימו: והחומץ· משום הכי נקט חומץ שביהודה משום דתני ברים אלו עוברין (דף מב·) א"ר יהודה בראשונה הלוקח חומץ מעם הארץ פטור לעשר מפני שחזקתו לא בא אלא מן התמד כדאמר התם א"ר יצחק

ובנות שקמה ונובלות התמרה והגופנין והנצפה וביהודה האוג והחומץ שביהודה והכסבר ר' יהודה אומר א) כל השיתין פטורין חוץ משל דופרה כל הרימין פטורין חוץ מרימי שקמונה כל בנות שקמה פטורות חוץ מן המוסטפות:

ב ב) אהדמאי אין לו חומש בואין לו ביעור גנאכל לאונן ג) דונכנס לירושלים ויוצא הומאבדין את מיעוטו (ו) בדרכים ונותנו לעם הארץ ויאכל כנגדו

להוליאו בדרך מדרכי הדיכים ולא נתחייב הדמאי בתרומה גדולה שהדמאי הוא הנקנה מעמי הארץ ופירות ע"ה דמאי ואין איש מיקל בתרומה גדולה לא עם הארץ ולא זולתו אלא טלס היו מפרישין אותה וכן אמרו כי יוחנן כהן גדול אשר תקן בדמאי אלו הדינים כמו שנבאר בסוף מעשר שני שלח בכל גבול ארץ ישראל וראה שאין מפרישין אלא תרומה גדולה בלבד ולפיכך שמור זה העיקר: ופירוש הקלים שאלו הדברים הנזכרים דיניהם קלים ואינם מחויבים דבר מחויבי הדמאי לא תרומת מעשר ולא מעשר שני והטעם בזה הדבר כי אלו הנזכרים הם אילנות מדבריות ואינם נכנסים ברשות איש אחד ומעט מזער הם שנוטעים אותם ורובם הפקר וכבר באר נו שהפקר אינו מחויב במעשרות ונקבצו בהם שתי ספיקות האחד אם הם הפקר אם לאו ואם הם מן השמור אם הוליאו ממנו המתנות אם לאו והעיקר אשר בידינו תרי ספיקי להקל· ופירוש אלו המינין שיהין מין ממיני התאנים המדבריים ורימין נקרא אלגב"ק ועוזרדין פירוש אלעוזו"ר ובנות שוח מין ממיני התאנים הלבנים נותנים פריים מג' שנים לג' שנים ובנות שקמה נקרא גמיז והוא ג"כ תאנים המדבריים וכל אלה לא יהיו כי אם בהרים ובמדברות: נובלות הם התמרים הנופלים מן הדקל כשהרוח מנשבת והוא גם כן רובו הפקר: וגופנים מין מהירקות דומה לשבת: ונצפה נקרא בלשון ערב קפא"ר: והאוג נקרא סמא"ק של ארץ ישראל והם אילנות עושין אשכלות אדומות ויאכלם: וחומץ ידוע ובארו בגמרא כי זה הדין היו דנין בו בזמן ההוא לפי שהיו עושין החומץ מן התמד והיה זה התמד הפקר אבל היום שחזקתו מן היין הוא חייב בחיובי הדמאי: והכוסבר. הוא זרע גד: ודופרא. מלה מורכבת די פרי ודו בלשונס הוא

ב א מיי' פ"ה מהל' מעשר שני ונטע רבעי הלכה ד סמג עשין קלו:
ג ב מיי' פי"א שם הלכה ח סמג עשין קלח:
ד ג מיי' פ"ג שם הלכה ח סמג לאוין רסד:
ה ד מיי' פ"ב שם הלכה ט יא סמג עשין קלז:
ו ה מיי' פ"ג שם הלכה ט סמג לאוין רסד:
ז ו שם הלכה ח:

א) עירובין פ"ב דף יח: ב) ב"מ פ"ד דף נד. ג) מעשר שני פ"ג משנה ו:

פי' מהר"י בן מלכי צדק

שוח פיסידיאה בגמ' בנות שוח תאני חיורתא: ובנות שקמה. פי' תאני דולבי פי' מרכיבין התאנה בערמון ופירות היוצאין מן ההרכבה ההיא נקראין תאני דולבי ויש אומרים על השקמה מרכיבין

SYCAMORE FIGS, UNRIPE DATES,[5] LATE GRAPES AND THORNY CAPERS; IN JUDEA[6] ALSO SUMACH, JUDEAN[7] VINEGAR, AND CORIANDER. R. JUDAH SAYS: ALL WILD FIGS ARE EXEMPT, EXCEPT THOSE WHICH HAVE A CROP TWICE [A YEAR]; ALL JUJUBE FRUITS ARE EXEMPT, EXCEPT THE JUJUBE FRUITS OF SHIḲMONAH;[8] ALL YOUNG SYCAMORE FIGS ARE EXEMPT, EXCEPT THOSE THAT BURST OPEN ON THE TREE.

MISHNAH 2. THE [SECOND TITHE[9] OF] DEMAI IS NOT SUBJECT TO [THE RULES OF] THE FIFTH[10] AND OF REMOVAL;[11]
a IT MAY BE EATEN BY AN ONAN;[1] IT MAY BE BROUGHT INTO JERUSALEM AND TAKEN OUT AGAIN;[2] IF SMALL IN QUANTITY[3] IT MAY BE ALLOWED TO BE LOST ON THE ROAD;[4] ONE MAY GIVE IT TO AN 'AM HA-AREZ[5] AND CONSUME ITS EQUIVALENT

(5) Which only ripen after they had been picked. According to another explanation: dates blown from the tree by the wind. (6) Where the value of these articles is small. (7) Made from wine which had been extracted from grape-skins, and therefore of little value. Ordinary wine was much used in Judea for drink-offerings in the Temple, and could not be spared for making vinegar; cf. Pes. 42*b*; Büchler, *Der galilaeische 'Am-ha-'Areṣ*, p. 18, n. 1. (8) A place in the vicinity of Haifa. ° (9) Cf. Introduction p. 50. (10) If a man set apart Second Tithe from *demai* produce and he wished to redeem it for money (Deut. XIV, 25) he need not add a fifth of its value, as in the case of Second Tithe from produce which had been certainly untithed; cf. Lev. XXVII, 31; Ma'as. Sh. IV, 3; B.M. IV, 8. The reason is because the duty of tithing *demai* is only a Rabbinic enactment; cf. B.M. 54*a*. (11) Tithes taken from *demai* need not be removed from the house and distributed on the eve of the Passover of the fourth and seventh year of the Sabbatical cycle, as in the case of tithes from ordinary produce; cf. Deut. XIV, 28; XXVI, 13; Ma'as. Sh. V, 6; also 'Ed. IV, 5 (Sonc. ed. 6*a* n. c 12; 6*a* n. d 1).

a (1) Lit., 'one who grieves', 'a mourner': on the day of the death of a kinsman whether before or after the burial, and also Rabbinically on the day of the burial. This is forbidden in the case of Second Tithe from ordinary produce, Deut. XXVI, 14; Ma'as. Sh. V, 12. (2) In the case of Second Tithe from ordinary produce this is forbidden, Ma'as. Sh. III, 5. (3) And therefore of little value. (4) If its preservation would involve risk from robbers and the like. (5) He need not be suspected of eating it outside Jerusalem, though he may be suspected of eating it in uncleanness.

°See Corrigenda.

IN JERUSALEM. [SECOND TITHE MONEY[6] OF DEMAI] MAY BE CHANGED[7] AGAIN, SILVER [COINS] FOR [OTHER] SILVER [COINS], COPPER [COINS] FOR [OTHER] COPPER [COINS], SILVER FOR COPPER, AND COPPER [BACK] INTO FRUIT, PROVIDED[8] THAT THE FRUIT WILL AGAIN BE REDEEMED FOR MONEY; THUS R. MEIR. BUT THE SAGES SAY: THE FRUIT ITSELF MUST BE BROUGHT UP AND CONSUMED IN JERUSALEM.

MISHNAH 3. IF A MAN BOUGHT [CORN][9] FOR SEED OR FOR CATTLE, FLOUR FOR HIDES,[10] OIL FOR THE LAMP, OR OIL FOR GREASING UTENSILS, IT IS EXEMPT FROM [THE RULES OF] DEMAI. [PRODUCE GROWN] BEYOND CHEZIB[11] IS EXEMPT FROM [THE RULES OF] DEMAI. THE ḤALLAH[12] OF AN 'AM
a HA-AREẒ, PRODUCE MIXED WITH TERUMAH,[1] PRODUCE BOUGHT WITH SECOND TITHE MONEY,[2] AND THE REMAINDER OF MEAL-OFFERINGS[3] ARE EXEMPT[4] FROM [THE RULES OF] DEMAI. SPICED[5] OIL, BETH SHAMMAI DECLARE LIABLE [TO THE RULES OF DEMAI]; BUT BETH HILLEL EXEMPT[6] IT.

MISHNAH 4. DEMAI MAY BE USED FOR MAKING AN 'ERUB[7] AND FOR FORMING A PARTNERSHIP.[8] A BENEDICTION IS SAID OVER IT,[9] AND GRACE IN COMPANY IS RECITED AFTER

* (6) V. n. 9, p. 53.
(7) Lit., 'rendered common'; cf. 'Ed. I, 9 (Sonc. ed. **2b** n. a 15). (8) Other texts read: 'And the fruit may again be redeemed for money'. (9) Of *demai*. (10) For use in tanning. (11) The Biblical Achzib (Josh. XIX, 29; Judg. I, 31) north of Acre. It formed the limit of Jewish territory after the return from the Babylonian exile, and what was beyond it was therefore treated as Syria; cf. *infra* VI, 11, n. 5. (12) Lit., 'cake'; the portion of dough which had to be given to the priest; cf. Num. XV, 20; 'Ed. I, 2 (Sonc. ed. **2a** n. b 2).
a (1) Cf. Introduction p. 50. If one part of *terumah* produce was mixed up with less than a hundred parts of common produce, the whole mixture could not be eaten by a non-priest, and had to be sold to a priest at the price of less than the *terumah* in the mixture. If *terumah* was mixed with common produce a hundred times in quantity, the *terumah* is neutralized in the mixture, and it may be eaten by a non-priest; cf. Ter. IV, 7. (2) To be eaten in Jerusalem. (3) After a handful of the meal had been offered on the altar. This remainder was to be eaten by the priests only, Lev. II, 3. (4) Because owing to their great sanctity, the *'am ha-areẓ* may be presumed to have duly tithed them. (5) Cf. Büchler, op. cit. p. 15, n. 2. Others explain it as Balsam oil. (6) Because it may have been already tithed owing to its scarcity and its great value. (7) Lit., 'mixture', or 'amalgamation' of boundaries; food placed before the Sabbath at a convenient spot, making that spot a temporary abode, and enabling the owner to move freely on the Sabbath day within a distance of 2000 cubits on all sides of the spot. The *'erub* thus serves to amalgamate and extend the limits of a Sabbath day journey; cf. 'Er. III, 2. (8) I.e., שתוף, *shittuf*, partnership of a courtyard or a private alley, containing several private domiciles. The owners of the domiciles combine to place jointly before the Sabbath some food in a convenient spot in the courtyard or the alley, which thus converts the several domiciles into a joint property, and enables the various owners to move freely on the Sabbath day from one domicile into the other; cf. 'Er. VII, 6–8. (9) V. Rashi Shab. 23*a*; *Aliter:* One recites grace after it (alone).

*See Corrigenda.

אוכל פירותיו בטהרה והלה עושה לרכו במעותיו ולא יאמר כן לע"ה אלא בדמאי וכדאמרי בירושלמי שאין מוסרים ודאי לע"ה: ומחללים אותו כסף על כסף. דאם יש לו כסף של מ"ש של דמאי והוא לריך לו יכול לחללו על כסף חולין שיש לו במקום אחר של ודאי אין מחללין כדתנן במסכת מ"ש בפ"ב (מ"ו) ומייתי לה בב"מ (דף נה:) סלע של מ"ש ושל חולין שנתערבו מביא בסלע מעות ואומר כ"מ שישנה סלע של מ"ש מחוללת על המעות ובורר את היפה שבהן ומחלל עליה מפני שאמרו מחללים כסף על נחשת מדוחק אבל כסף על כסף אפי' מדוחק אין מחללין דאינו בורר מתחלה היפה ויאמר כ"מ שהיא מחוללת על זו והא

כנגדו א) ומחללים אותו כסף על כסף נחשת על נחשת כסף על נחשת ונחשת על הפירות *ובלבד שיחזור ויפדה את הפירות דברי ר"מ וחכמים ב אומרים יעלו הפירות ויאכלו בירושלים: ג ג) הלוקח לזרע ולבהמה קמח לעורות שמן לנר שמן לסוך בו את הכלים פטור מן הדמאי ד מכזיב ולהלן פטור מן הדמאי ה חלת ע"ה והמדומע והלקוח בכסף מעשר שני ושירי המנחות פטורין מן הדמאי שמן ערב ב"ש מחייבין ו וב"ה פוטרין: ד ג) ז הדמאי מערבין בו ומשתתפין בו ח ומברכין עליו ומזמנין עליו

התרנו לו להתם לע"ה ילטרך להוציא מנכסיו כפי מה שהם שוים ויאכלם בירושלים כמעות מעשר שני: ודע כי מעשר שני האמתי מותר לפדותו בזוזים של כסף ויחזרו הזוזים ההם קדש ויחזרו הפירות חולין וזהו ענין מחללין ומותר לו לחלל המעות ההם על מעות כסף שניים כמו כן ויצאו המעות הראשונות לחלין ויחזרו השניים קדש וכן יעשה בזוזים השניים אם ירלה וכן יעשה אפילו אלף פעמים ואסור לפדות פירות מעשר שני האמתי בנחשת ולא להחליף מעות מעשר שני במעות נחשת מפני שאמר הכתוב וצרת הכסף אבל במ"ש של דמאי יהיה מותר על דרך הקל ועוד אבאר לך זה החלול באר היטב במסכת מעשר שני ואין הלכה כר"מ: ג קמח לעורות. לעבד בהם העורות: וכזיב. שם מקום והוא המפריש בין א"י שהחזיקו עולי בבל ובין שהחזיקו בה עולי מצרים ואשר החזיקו בה עולי מצרים הם לענין דמאי כמו חו"ל והעיקר שיש אצלנו חזקת א"י חייב עד שיודע שהוא פטור ועל כן יתחייב בה הדמאי בדינין אשר זכרנו וחזקת חולה לארץ פטור עד שיודע לך שהוא חייב לפיכך לא נחייב פירות הבאים נחולה לארץ חיובי הדמאי ולא נאמר שמא פירות ארץ ישראל הם והוליאם חולה לארץ: והמדומע הוא דבר המעורב מחולין ותרומה ועוד אבאר דינו במס' תרומות ואולם קראוהו מדומע כי התרומה שמה דמע והוא מה שאמר הכתוב (שמות כב) מלאתך ודמעך: והלקוח בכסף מעשר. הם הפירות שלקחו בירושלים בכסף מעשר שני כמו שיתבאר במקומו: ושירי המנחות. הוא הנותר מן המנחה אחר שיקריב ממנה מלא קמצו והנותר ההוא אוכלים אותו הכהנים כמו שחייב עליהם הכתוב ואמרו בגמרא בשעה שגזרו על הדמאי לא גזרו על הדברים הללו: ושמן ערב. הוא שמן המור: ד מערבין בו. ערובי חלירות וערובי תחומין: ומשתתפין בו. הוא שתופי מבואות והוא העירוב שיעשוהו אנשי המבוי כדי שיהא מותר להם להשתמש מחלר לחלר בשבת כמו שיתבאר בעירובין: ומברכין עליו. הוא שיברכו עליו ברכת המזון: ומזמנין עליו. כשיהיו האוכלים שלשה כאשר

דמשמע בב"מ (ד' מה.) דמחללין סלעים על סלעים דהכסף כסף ריבה אפי' כסף שני כגון בסלעים דשני מלכים שיכול לחלל זה על זה אם השני חריף אבל של מלך אחד לא דלאו דרך חילול הוא ובדמאי שרי ובמסכת מ"ש פירשנו ענין אחר כסף על נחשת אפי' שלא מדוחק אבל של ודאי מדוחק אין שלא מדוחק לא (ז): ובלבד שיחזור ויפדה את הפירות. בכל הספרים גרס ובלבד משמע דלא התירו נחשת על הפירות אא"כ חוזר ופודה אותן רבנן סברי יעלו פירות ויאכלו בירושלים אם. ירלה דהקלו בדמאי ולא הזקיקוהו לחזור ולחלל וכן פי' בקונטרס בפ' הזהב וקשה דמס' מ"ש (פ"ג מ"י) משמע שזו היא קולא מה שחוזר ופודה את הפירות דבשל ודאי לא התירו אלא זקוק להעלותן כדתנן לא אם אמרת במעשר עצמו שכן נפדה טהור ברחוק מקום תאמר בלקוח שאינו נפדה טהור ברחוק מקום וכן מוכיח נמי בזבחים (דף מט:) גבי כלום מלינו ספק חמור מן העיקר ועוד תנן בפ"ק דמ"ש (מ"ה) הלוקח פירות שוגג יחזרו דמים למקומן מזיד יעלו ויאכלו במקום ואי אין מקדש ירקבו וכן תני נמי גבי בהמה אלמא העלאה עדיפא ועוד תנן התם בפ"ג (מ"ד) מעות בירושלים ופירות במדינה אומר הרי מעות הללו מחוללין על הפירות ובלבד שיעלו הפירות ויאכלו בירושלים אלמא דהכי עדיף ובהגוזל קמא (לז:) אמר דזבין בהמה ומסיק לה להתם ור"מ גופא בסוכה (דף מ:) דתניא אחד שביעית ואחד מ"ש מתחללים על בהמה חיה ועוף בין חיים בין שחוטים דברי ר"מ וחוץ לירושלים איירי כדמוכח התם וכדמוכח נמי בירושלמי בפ"ג (הל' ג) דמ"ש לכן נראה דלא גרסי' ובלבד וברוב ספרים ליתא בפרק הזהב אלא גרסי' ויפדה הפירות אם ירלה דלא הזקיקוהו להעלותן וחכ"א יעלו פירות ויאכלו בירושלים דזקוק להעלותן ומחמרי רבנן טפי מר"מ וכל עיקר קושיא דרב ששת בפרק הזהב אינו אלא מזה דר"מ מיקל טפי מחכמים כמו שפירשתי שם: ג לקח תבואה לזורעה פטור ממעשר בדמאי בין אין זרעו כלה בין זרעו כלה כדקתני בתוספתא פ"א: לבהמה. להאכיל לבהמה ובפ"ק דחולין (דף ז:) גבי עובדא דחמורו דר' פינחס א"ר יוחנן לא שנו אלא שלקחן מתחלה לבהמה אבל לקחן מתחלה לאדם ונמלך עליהן לבהמה חייב לעשר אפי' בדמאי: קמח לעבד עורות כדאמר בפרק המוליא יין (דף עט:) גבי [ג' עורות] מלה חיפה ודיפתרא: מכזיב ולהלן פטור מן הדמאי. מכאן היה מתרץ רבינו תם מה שמקשין לבפרק קמא דחולין (דף ו:) גבי ר"מ שאכל עלה של ירק בבית שאן משמע דאין מעשר נוהג בחולה לארץ וכן במס' ע"ג בפרק רבי ישמעאל (דף נח:) גבי ר"ש לקיש דאיקלע לבלרה וחזנהו דאכלי פירות דלא מעשרי ואסר להו ואמר ליה רבי יוחנן זיל הדר דבלר לאו היינו בלרה ובריש עד כמה (דף כז.) מפרש דתרומת מעשר נוהג בחולה לארץ דקאמר רבה מבסלה ברוב ואכיל לה בימי טומאתו וכן בפרק בנות כותים (דף לב.) גבי לסיכה בשמן של תרומה ואין לחלק בין מעשר דגן תירוש וילהר דבארץ דאורייתא לשאר פירות דאפי' בארץ דרבנן דהא בפ"ק דבילה (דף יב:) גבי אושפזיכניה דרבה בר חנן הוה ליה אסורייתא דחרדלא משמע קלת דמחייבי בתרומה ומעשר ובפרק כילד מברכין (דף לו.) גבי המיקל בארץ הלכה כמותו בחולה לארץ אמרי' בהדיא הני מילי גבי מעשר ללף דבארץ גופיה דרבנן ותירץ ר"ת דעובדא דר"מ דחולין ועובדא דר"ש לקיש במס' ע"ג בדמאי הוה ובחולה לארץ לא גזרו על הדמאי כדתנן הכא מכזיב ולהלן פטור מן הדמאי והא דמשמע בחולין דבעי מוקף מדפריך עלה דלמא מעשר עליה ממקום אחר ומשני לא נחשדו חבירים לתרום שלא מן המוקף ובפ"ד דחלה (מ"ו) תנן דחלת דמאי ניטלת שלא מן המוקף לא קשיא מידי כדפרש' שם אבל לפי' ר"ת קשה דעל כרחך דמאי דמתני' לאו דוקא דהוא הדין מן הודאי* כדפרשינן בריש פירקין דבין רבי יוחנן ובין ריש לקיש מודו בהך דדמאי לאו דוקא ואין לחלק בין מקומות הרחוקין מארץ ישראל כגון מכזיב ולהלן למקומות הקרובים דמחייבי אפי' בדמאי דהרי בית שאן דהיא גופא היתה מארץ ישראל בכיבוש ראשון ואפילו הכי פטור בכיבוש שני ומיהו במקומות הקרובים מלינו לחלק כדברי רבינו תם בין דמאי לודאי ומיהו קשה דלקמן בפרק שני אמרינן בירושלמי (הל' א) רבי התיר בית שאן והתיר קסרין והתיר בית גוברין והתיר כפר עמעם ומשמע דכל הנך מקומות דומיא דבית שאן שכבשו עולי מלרים ולא כבשו עולי בבל ומשמע לקמן בפ"ג דפטורין אף מן הודאי דאמרי' בירושלמי (הל' ג) אמר רשב"ג שלח לי רבי יוסי ברבי אתרוגא ואמר זה בא לידי מקסרי ולמדתי ממנו ג' דברים שהוא ודאי שפירות קיסרין ודאי שהוא ממה שמרבילין עליו מים כלומר והוי מוכשר שלא בא לידו אחר שאלו בא היה מעשר מזה על זה ופריך ויעשר ממנו עליו ומשני אין דרך בני אדם שמשלחין לחבריהן דברים חסרים ופריך ולאו מתני' היא ר' יוסי מתיר בודאי ובלבד שיודיעו מסנה היא בפ"ג (מ"ג) שר' יוסי מתיר לשלוח לחבירו שאינו מעושר ושמא היה ביד ר' יוסי אחר ומה שלא עישר לפי שהודיעו שעל כן היה אומר זה בא לידי מקיסרין ומשני אע"ג דפליג על רבנן לא עבד עובדא כוותיה ופריך ולא מפירות שמותרין בקיסרין הוא ומשני ולא ר' התיר קיסרין ורשב"ג קודם רבי הוה ש"מ דאפי' בקיסרין לא נהוג אע"פ שהיה מקום קרוב ויש לומר דלענין דשרי לשלוח לחבירו בהודעה קא פריך דאפי' רבנן לא אסרי אלא בארץ ולא בחולה לארץ ועוד יש לומר *דאתרוג דקיסרין משונה משל א"י ולא גזור בחולה לארץ אלא מפירות הדומין לארץ ישראל כדתנן בפ"ב (מ"א) אלו דברים מתעשרין דמאי בכל מקום הדבילה והתמרים והחרובין האורז והכמון כלומר בכל מקום אפי' מכזיב ולהלן דבידוע שמא"י באו *אותן של חו"ל כדמפרש בירושלמי (הל' א) חיוב המינים הללו על שאין כיולא בהן בחו"ל הוצרכו חכמים למנותן ופריך והא דבילה בבלרה ומשני שחיקה היא והא תמרים באלכסנדריא ומשני רקיקין אינון וקתני סיפא האורז שבחו"ל כל המשתמש ממנו פטור כלומר אפי' בארץ דמיכר מאותן של א"י ולא אתי לאיחלופי ואומר בירושלמי (שם) באורז של חילת ושל אנטוכיא מותר במקומן כלומר דדמי לשל א"י ולא שרי לא בארץ ולא בחו"ל דסברי מא"י הוא ובמקומם מותר דאנטוכיא מכזיב ולהלן וחשיב בירושלמי מינין האסורין בקיסרין ומינין האסורים בפניס מכל הני משמע דלא מיחייבי נדולין בחולה לארץ אלא פירות הדומין לשל א"י ואפי' הדומין נמי לא מחייבי אלא עד כזיב ואין חילוק בין דמאי לודאי כדאמרי' בריש פירקין וניחא השתא דר' מאיר דירק דבית שאן לא דמי לשל ארץ ישראל דלא חשיב ליה בהדי מינין האסורים בבית שאן והכיא דריש לקיש במינין המותרין והא דמשמע במסכת ידים (פ"ד משנה ג) דמלרים ובבל חייבין במעשרות שמא קרובים לארץ ישראל יותר מכזיב אין למדין ממעשה ינן ועוד י"ל ההיא דר' מאיר וריש לקיש בשניקחו מן הכותי ולא גזרו בשל כותי אפי' בסוריא למאן דאמר לאו שמיה כיבוש כדאיתא בסוף פרק השולח (דף מז.) ויש מכאן סמך גדול למאי שאין מפרישים תרומות ומעשרות באלו הארלות דרחוקים יותר מכזיב ובירושלמי (הל' ג) תני דכזיב עלמה פטורה עוד אמרינן בירושלמי בסוף חלה (פ"ד הל"ד) רבותינו שבחוץ לארץ היו מפרישין תרומות ומעשרות על שבאו הרובין וביטלום והא דקאמרי התם לא חשו אלא לדגן תירוש ויצהר וכולה מילתא אאוכל ואח"כ מפרים קאי ובריש מעשרות כתבנוהו: חלת ע"ה. שתיקן לו גבל חבר בטהרה ורולה ליתנה לכהן חבר פטור מלעשר: והמדומע. כגון סאה תרומה שנפלה לפחות מק' חולין של עם הארץ יתן הכל לכהן או סאה שהעלה מתוך מאה: ירושלמי (שם) אמר ר' יוחנן בשעה שגזרו על הדמאי לא גזרו על הדברים הללו אמר ר' אושעיא אימת קדשים עליו ואינו נותן לכהן דבר שאינו מתוקן [וחלת ע"ה] על דעתיה דר' אושעיא בחלת ע"ה היא מתני' אבל חבר שלקח עיסה מע"ה והפריש חלתה לא על דעתיה דר' יוחנן היא הדא היא הדא והמדומע על דעתיה דר' אושעיא בפירות ע"ה היא מתני' אבל חבר שלקח פירות מע"ה ונדמעו לא על דעתיה דר' יוחנן היא הדא היא הדא: והלקוח בכסף מעשר. שלקח דמאי בכסף מעשר שני פטור מלעשר ובירושלמי (שם) מפרש בין שלקחו בכסף מעשר של דמאי בין שלקחו בכסף מעשר של ודאי: ושירי מנחות. שהקומץ למזבח ושירים נאכלים לכהנים ולא חיישי' שמא הביא ע"ה דבר שאינו מתוקן: שמן ערב. שיש עמו בשמים כגון פלייטון דאמרינן בפרק במה אשה (דף סב:) ורלאשית שמנים ימשחו (עמוס ו) זה פלייטון ומשום דנתערב עם בשמים ואינו בעין כל כך פטרי בית הלל ודבר תימה דלא דייקינן מהכא בפ"ק דחולין (דף ו:) דלא גזרו על תערובות דמאי ושמא שאני הכא דעיקרו למשיחה ולא לאכילה דחמיר: ירושלמי (שם) תני אמר ר' יודא לא פטרו בית הלל אלא שמן של פלייטון בלבד אחרים אומרים בשם ר' נתן מחייבין היו בית הלל *וורדימן: ד מערבים בו. עירובי תחומים וחלרות: ומשתתפין בו. שיתופי מבואות ובפרק בכל מערבין (דף לא:) פריך דמאי הא לא חזי ליה ומשני מינו דאי בעי מפקר נכסיה והוי עני וחזי ליה דתנן מאכילין את העניים דמאי חזי ליה: ומברכין עליו. ברכת המזון דטעונה כוס: ומזמנין עליו. כדתנן בפ' שלשה שאכלו אכל דמאי מזמנין עליו ואע"פ שהוא עשיר ואכל בעבירה מנסרף וטעמא מפרש התם בגמ' כיון דאילו בעי מפקר נכסיה והוי עני וחזי ליה דתנן מאכילין את העניים דמאי ועוד י"ל דמברכין עליו מיירי בברכה שלפניה כגון ברכת המוליא ומזמנין עליו מיירי בברכה שלאחריה כגון ברכת המזון ולפטור אחרים כגון שנים או שלשה שאוכלין ואחד עני שאוכל דמאי מברך הוא על הדמאי בין בתחלה בין בסוף ומיפטרי אחריני ובכל דוכתא דתני מברכין ומזמנין בכי האי גוונא אמרי' כההיא בריש מי שמתו (דף יז:) ובפ' אלו מגלחין (כג) גבי מי שמתו מוטל לפניו אינו מברך ואינו מזמן ואין מברכין עליו ואין מזמנין עליו ולא כמו שפי' שם בקונטרס דמותר לאכול בלא ברכה דאם כן מאי אין מברכין עליו ועוד תני עלה בירושלמי בפרק אלו מגלחין (ה"ה) ובפ' מי שמתו (ה"א) ואם בירך אין עונין אחריו אמן אחריהם שבירכו אין עונה אחריהם אמן לכך נראה דכולה מילתא איירי לפטור אחרים דאין מברך המוליא לפטור אחרים ולא אחרים פוטרין אותו וכן בברכת המזון דהיינו זימון ותדע דבכל דוכתי קתני לשון פטור דקתני פטור מק"ש ומן התפלה ומן התפילין ומכל מלות והכא קתני אינו מברך ואינו מזמן ולא קתני פטור מלברך ומלזמן אלא משום דהכא איירי להוליא אחרים ידי חובתן לא שייך ביה לשון פטור והאי דקאמר בירושל' בריש מי שמתו (שם) תני אם רלה להחמיר על עלמו אין שומעין לו מפני כבודו של מת התם לא איירי אלא בק"ש ותפלה ותפילין וכן בגמ' שלנו בריש מי

מר דהשבינן ליה כעני ותנן מאכילין את העניים דמאי ואית דאמר משום דאמר ר"י בשעה שגזרו על דמאי לא גזרו על דברים הללו.ר' בון בר חייה בעא קומי ר' זירא עד כדון בלוקח ב...
...לו בודאי: שירי מנחות. פי' המנחות היה מביא ישראל מנחת סולת והיה הכהן קומץ ומקטיר הקומץ למזבח ושאר הסולת נקראין שירים והיה לכהנים פטור מן הדמאי דאמרינן...
...העומר ושתי הלחם ולחם הפנים ושירי המנחות ותוספת הביכורים וכו' בית הלל פוטרים: ושמן ערב. א"ר יהודה לא פטרו בית הלל אלא שמן של פלייטון בלבד שנתבסל השמן בב...
...לפי שלא נתבטלו.אחרים אומרים בשם ר' נתן מחייבין היו בית הלל בשמן וורד ווירדינן: ד הדמאי מערבין בו ומשתתפין בו. ותנן בעירובין (לא:)הכי נמי.וגרסי' עלה בגמ' דמאי ה...
...נכסיה והוי עני וחזי ליה כדתנן מאכילין את העניים דמאי השתא נמי חזי ליה. ותנן בעירובין פ"ח (דף פ"ב) כיצד משתתפין בתחומין מניח את החבית ואומר הרי זו לכל בני עירי...

פירוש הרא"ש

פי' מהר"י בן מלכי צדק

שמתו (דף יח.) דקאמר הכא אפי' חוץ לד' אמות נמי אסור בק"ש ותפלה ותפילין איירי ואפי' קאי אלברך ואלזמן ניחא דאסור לאפוקי ידי חובתן : ומפרישין אותו ערום. מהכא דייקינן בפרק במה מדליקין (כג.) דלא בעי ברכה דכי קאי ערום היכי מברך הא בעינן והיה מחניך קדוש : בין השמשות. של ע"ש כדתנן בפרק במה מדליקין (דף לד.) ספק חשיכה מעשרין את הדמאי ואין מעשרין את הודאי : ואם הקדים מ"ש לראשון אין בכך כלום. שאין מעכב את הוידוי מה שאין כן בודאי (ח) דתנן בפ' בתרא דמ"ש (משנה יא) ככל מצותך אשר צויתני הא אם הקדים מ"ש לראשון אינו יכול להתודות : שהגרדי סך שהסורק נותן בצמר מפרש

ומפרישין אותו ערום בין השמשות הא אם הקדים מעשר שני לראשון אין בכך כלום שמן שהגרדי סך באצבעותיו חייב בדמאי ושהסורק נותן בצמר פטור מן הדמאי :

פרק שני

א ואלו דברים מתעשרין דמאי בכל מקום הדבילה והתמרים והחרובים האורז והכמון האורז שבחוצה לארץ כל המשתמש ממנו פטור : **ב** (א) המקבל עליו להיות נאמן מעשר את שהוא אוכל ואת שהוא מוכר ואת שהוא לוקח ואינו מתארח אצל עם הארץ רבי יהודה אומר אף המתארח אצל ע"ה נאמן אמרו לו על עצמו אינו נאמן כיצד יהא נאמן על של אחרים : **ג** המקבל עליו להיות (ב) חבר אינו מוכר לע"ה לח ויבש ואינו לוקח (ג) ממנו לח ואינו מתארח אצל ע"ה ולא (ד) מארחו אצלו בכסותו ר"י אומר אף לא יגדל בהמה דקה ולא יהא פרוץ בנדרים ובשחוק ולא יהיה מטמא למתים ומשמש בבית המדרש אמרו לו לא באו אלו לכלל : **ד** (ה) הנחתומים לא חייבו אותם חכמים להפריש אלא כדי תרומת מעשר וחלה

IT.[10] ONE MAY SEPARATE [TITHES] FROM IT EVEN WHEN ONE IS NAKED,[11] OR WHEN IT IS TWILIGHT[12] ON THE EVE OF SABBATH. LO, IF ONE HAS TAKEN FROM IT THE SECOND TITHE
a BEFORE THE FIRST TITHE IT MATTERS NOUGHT.[1] THE OIL WITH WHICH THE WEAVER GREASES HIS FINGERS IS LIABLE[2] TO [THE RULES OF] DEMAI, BUT [THE OIL] WHICH THE WOOL-COMBER PUTS ON THE WOOL IS EXEMPT[3] FROM [THE RULES OF] DEMAI.

CHAPTER II

MISHNAH 1. THE FOLLOWING THINGS MUST BE TITHED
b AS DEMAI IN ALL PLACES:[1] PRESSED FIGS, DATES, CAROBS, RICE, AND CUMIN. AS TO RICE FROM OUTSIDE THE LAND [OF ISRAEL], WHOEVER USES IT[2] IS EXEMPT FROM TITHING IT.

MISHNAH 2. IF A MAN HAS TAKEN UPON HIMSELF TO BE TRUSTWORTHY,[3] HE MUST TITHE WHATEVER HE EATS AND WHATEVER HE SELLS[4] AND WHATEVER HE BUYS;[5] AND HE MAY NOT BE THE GUEST[6] OF AN 'AM HA-AREẒ.[7] R. JUDAH SAYS: A MAN WHO IS THE GUEST OF AN 'AM HA-AREẒ MAY STILL BE CONSIDERED TRUSTWORTHY.[8] BUT THEY SAID TO HIM: IF HE IS NOT TRUSTWORTHY IN RESPECT OF HIMSELF,[9] HOW CAN HE BE CONSIDERED TRUSTWORTHY IN RESPECT OF OTHERS?[10]

MISHNAH 3. IF A MAN HAS TAKEN UPON HIMSELF TO BECOME AN ASSOCIATE,[11] HE MAY NOT SELL TO AN 'AM HA-AREẒ EITHER MOIST OR DRY[12] [PRODUCE]; NOR MAY HE
c BUY FROM HIM MOIST[1] [PRODUCE]. HE MAY NOT BE THE GUEST OF AN 'AM HA-AREẒ,[2] NOR MAY HE RECEIVE AS GUEST AN 'AM HA-AREẒ WHO IS WEARING HIS OWN GARMENT.[3] R. JUDAH SAYS: HE MAY NOT ALSO BREED SMALL CATTLE,[4] NOR MAY HE BE ADDICTED TO MAKING VOWS[5] OR TO LAUGHTER;[6] NOR MAY HE DEFILE HIMSELF BY THE DEAD,[7] BUT HE MUST BE AN ATTENDANT AT THE HOUSE OF STUDY. BUT THEY SAID TO HIM: THESE [REQUIREMENTS] DO NOT COME WITHIN THE GENERAL RULE [OF ASSOCIATESHIP].[8]

MISHNAH 4. BAKERS[9] [WHO ARE ASSOCIATES] ARE BOUND BY THE SAGES TO SET APART [FROM DEMAI PRODUCE] NO MORE THAN SUFFICES FOR THE TERUMAH OF TITHE[10] AND FOR

(10) I.e., זמון, *zimmun*, invitation. Three or more persons eating together in the same room may be invited by one of them by a prescribed formula to join together in saying grace; cf. Ber. VII, 1, 3. But produce which is certainly untithed cannot be used for these purposes, since its consumption involves a sin. (11) Since no benediction need be said on tithing *demai* produce, as on tithing produce which is certainly untithed; cf. Ter. I, 6. (12) This is forbidden in the case of produce certainly untithed; cf. Shab. II, 7.
a (1) This is forbidden in the case of ordinary produce; cf. Ter. III, 6; Ma'as. Sh. V, 11. (2) This is like anointing the body, and anointing is equivalent to drinking, Shab. IX, 4. (3) It is like the greasing of utensils, v. *supra* 3, 9a.
b (1) Even when bought beyond Chezib (I, 3, n. 11), because they may be produce grown in the Land of Israel. (2) Even in the Land of Israel, because foreign rice is easily distinguished by its reddish colour from the white rice grown in the Land of Israel. (3) נאמן, in respect of tithes, so that the produce he sells may be considered duly tithed;* cf. Introduction, p. 51. (4) From his fields. (5) For selling to others. (6) That he may not be tempted to eat untithed produce. (7) עם הארץ. Lit., 'the people of the land', an uninstructed person who is indifferent to the tithing of produce and to the observance of clean and unclean; cf. Introduction p. 51; 'Ed. I, 14 (Sonc. ed. p. 8, n. 1). (8) If he declares that he did not eat with his host anything untithed. (9) As is proved by his eating with an *'am ha-areẓ*. (10) In respect of the produce he sells to others. (11) חבר, *ḥaber*, a member of an association of scrupulous observers of the Law, especially in matters of tithes and purity. (12) Lest it contract a defilement while in the possession of the *'am ha-areẓ*.
c (1) Moisture renders produce susceptible to defilement; cf. Lev. XI, 38; 'Ed. I, 8 (Sonc. ed. 2b n. a 12); Maksh. (2) Lest he contract a defilement while at his house. (3) The garment of an *'am ha-areẓ* is considered a 'principal' cause of defilement, because it may have been used by a menstruous woman or by a person with an issue; cf. Lev. XV, 4, 20; Ḥag. II, 7. (4) Breeding small cattle is prohibited in the Land of Israel because of the damage they cause to trees and bushes; cf. B.Ḳ. VII, 7. (5) That he may not be tempted to break a vow; cf. Eccl. V, 4. (6) Which leads to immorality; cf. Ab. III, 13 (Sonc. ed. 9b n. a 3). (7) Unnecessarily. (8) Associateship is concerned only with the observance of tithing and purity. (9) Who supply bread to shopkeepers at a low profit. (10) The heave-offering which the Levite gives to the priest from the First Tithe;* cf. Introduction p. 50.

*See Corrigenda.

ḤALLAH.[11] SHOPKEEPERS[12] MAY NOT SELL DEMAI [PRODUCE]. ALL [MERCHANTS] WHO SUPPLY IN LARGE QUANTITIES[13] MAY SELL DEMAI. [MERCHANTS] WHO SUPPLY IN LARGE QUANTITIES ARE SUCH AS WHOLESALE PROVISION DEALERS AND VENDORS OF CORN.

MISHNAH 5. R. MEIR SAYS: IF [PRODUCE] WHICH IS USUALLY MEASURED OUT [FOR SALE] IN A LARGE [QUANTITY] HAPPENED TO HAVE BEEN MEASURED OUT IN A SMALL [QUANTITY], THE SMALL QUANTITY IS TREATED AS IF IT WAS A
a LARGE[1] [QUANTITY]; IF [PRODUCE] WHICH IS USUALLY MEASURED OUT FOR SALE IN A SMALL [QUANTITY] HAPPENED TO HAVE BEEN MEASURED OUT IN A LARGE [QUANTITY], THE LARGE [QUANTITY] IS TREATED AS IF IT WAS A SMALL[2] [QUANTITY]. WHAT IS CONSIDERED A LARGE QUANTITY? THREE KABS FOR DRY [PRODUCE], AND [OF THE VALUE OF] ONE DENAR FOR LIQUID [PRODUCE]. R. JOSE SAYS: IF BASKETS OF FIGS AND BASKETS OF GRAPES AND HAMPERS OF VEGETABLES ARE SOLD IN THE LUMP, THEY ARE EXEMPT [FROM THE RULES OF DEMAI].

CHAPTER III

MISHNAH 1. ONE MAY GIVE DEMAI PRODUCE FOR FOOD
b TO THE POOR[1] AND TO PASSING TROOPS.[2] RABBAN GAMALIEL USED TO GIVE DEMAI FOR FOOD TO HIS WORKMEN.[3] AS FOR COLLECTORS OF CHARITY, BETH SHAMMAI SAY: THEY SHOULD GIVE TITHED [PRODUCE] TO PERSONS WHO DO NOT TITHE, AND UNTITHED [PRODUCE] TO PERSONS WHO DO TITHE;[4] IT WILL THUS RESULT THAT EVERY ONE WILL BE EATING [PRODUCE] THAT HAS BEEN SET RIGHT.[5] BUT THE SAGES SAY: THEY MAY COLLECT INDETERMINATELY[6] AND DISTRIBUTE INDETERMINATELY, AND WHOEVER [OF THE RECIPIENTS] WISHES TO SET RIGHT[7] [HIS PORTION] MAY DO SO.

MISHNAH 2. IF A MAN WISHED TO CUT OFF LEAVES OF VEGETABLES IN ORDER TO LIGHTEN HIS BURDEN, HE MAY NOT THROW THEM DOWN UNLESS HE HAS [FIRST] TITHED THEM.[8] IF A MAN PICKED UP VEGETABLES[9] IN THE MARKET [WITH THE INTENTION OF BUYING THEM], AND THEN DECIDED TO PUT THEM BACK, HE MAY NOT PUT THEM BACK EXCEPT HE HAD [FIRST] TITHED THEM,[10] FOR NOTHING WAS NEEDED [TO MAKE THEM HIS OWN] BUT NUMBERING[11] [THEM]. BUT IF
c HE [ONLY] STOOD [THERE], BARGAINING[1] AND THEN SAW ANOTHER LOAD OF BETTER QUALITY, HE MAY PUT THEM

(11) Cf. I, 3, n. 12. (12) Who sell to the private consumer at a big profit. (13) Whose profit is small, as they generally give a liberally heaped measure.
a (1) And is exempt from tithing as *demai*. (2) It must be tithed as *demai* by the vendor.
b (1) Even if they are associates; but they must be told that the food is *demai*. (2) Who are Israelites. The Hebrew word אכסניא (from the Greek ξένος) may also mean 'passing guests'. (3) Who were poor, though he was bound to provide their food during their working hours; cf. *infra* VII, 3, n. 2. (4) Telling them that the produce is *demai*. (5) Hebrew מתוקן; i.e., that has been duly tithed; * cf. Introduction p. 49. (6) I.e., without inquiring from the donors whether the produce they give has been tithed. (7) I.e., tithe it. (8) To prevent their being eaten untithed by an *'am ha-arez* who may happen to pick them up. (9) Which are sold at a fixed price per bundle. (10) And paying the dealer the cost of the tithe. (11) Since they are sold at a fixed price per bundle, the mere act of picking them up is sufficient to make him the owner of the vegetables, and to render him responsible for tithing them.
c (1) Without having decided to buy them.

* See Corrigenda.

והכא את אמרת נחתום מפריש ר' יונה אומר איתפלגון ר' יוחנן ור' אליעזר חד אמר כאן בעושה בטהרה כאן בעושה בטומאה וחד אמר כאן במדה דקה כאן במדה גסה פי' הלוקח מנחתום היא לקמן בפ״ה·ודבר תימה מאי קשיא ליה דמתני' בנחתום חבר והתם בחבר שלוקח מנחתום עם הארץ וצריך לומר דמשמע (א) לי' דנחתום דהתם כנחתום דהכא הכל בחבר ומסיק דר' יוחנן תירץ כאן בעושה בטהרה נחתום מפריש הואיל וראויה לכהן לאכילה אבל עושה בטומאה כגון שלקח מעם הארץ פירות שהוכשרו דנטמאו לא הטריחו למוכר להפריש כיון דלא חזיא אלא להסיק תחת תבשילו ולוקח שיאכל הוא יפריש ור' אליעזר תירץ במדה דקה וטעמא דמפריש כשמוכר במדה דקה מפרש התם אמתני' דהחנוני מפני תינוקות שלא יאכלו טבל רבי לא בשם ר' יוחנן מדה דקה הואיל והמוכר משתכר הוא מפריש

מפני שהשוטרים הממונים עליהם טונסים אותם תמיד שיתקנו משקליהם ונזרו עליהם המדה במכירתם קלב ידוע: והחנונים.

אהחנונין אינן רשאין למכור את הדמאי בכל המשפיעין במדה גסה רשאין למכור את הדמאי אלו הן המשפיעין במדה גסה כגון הסיטונות ומוכרי תבואה: ד ר״מ אומר את שדרכו להמדד בגסה ג ומדדו בדקה טפלה דקה לגסה את שדרכו להמדד בדקה ומדדו בגסה טפלה גסה לדקה איזו היא מדה גסה גביבש שלשת קבין ובלח דינר רבי יוסי אומר דסלי תאנים וסלי ענבים וקופות של ירק כל זמן שהוא מוכרן אכסרה פטור:

פרק שלישי

א א) המאכילין את העניים דמאי ואת האכסניא דמאי רבן גמליאל היה מאכיל (א) את פועליו דמאי גבאי צדקה ב״ש אומרים נותנין את המעושר לשאינו מעשר ואת שאינו מעושר למעשר נמצאו כל האדם אוכלי' מתוקן וחכ״א וגובין סתם ומחלקין סתם והרוצה לתקן יתקן: ב זהרוצה לחזום עלי ירק להקל ממשאו לא (ב) ישליך עד שיעשר חהלוקח ירק מן השוק ונמלך להחזיר לא יחזיר עד שיעשר שאינו *מחוסר אלא מנין (ה) טהיה עומד ולוקח וראה טוען אחר יפה ממנו מותר להחזיר

דמים ליבש: מוכרן אכסרה· פירוש בלא שיעור ומדה אלא כפי מה שיזדמן לו ר״ל שמוכר אכסרה יהיה כמו המוכר בגסה ואין הלכה כר' מאיר ולא כר' יוסי:

א מותר· לעניים אכילת דמאי כדי להקל עליו הצדקה: ואכסניא הם האורחין ונעשה זו לחזוק מצות האכסניא בדתינו כדי להקל על בעלי האכסניא: ומה שאמר והרוצה לתקן יתקן ר״ל מי שירצה לתקן הדבר שנתנו לו ולהוציא מתנות הדמאי ממנו יעשה ואולי יקשה עליך ותאמר אחר שהתרנו לעניים אכילת דמאי מפני מה נאמר ולוקחי הצדקה הרוצה לתקן יתקן והוא עני וזה לא יקשה עליך כי מה שהתרנו לעניים דמאי והוא כשינתן להם אכילה אחת בשביל הטעם שזכרנו אבל כשיחלקו עליהם הקופה ונפל לכל אחד מהם חלק טוב ובא ברשותו נתחייב להוציא ממנה חיובו דמאי הלא תראה שאמרו מאכילין את העניים ולא אמר אוכלין עניים והלכה כחכמים ואין הלכה כרבן גמליאל: ב לחזום. לכרות או לקצור או לארות עלי הירקות וישליכם כדי להקל משאו לא ישליכם עד שיוציא מהם מעשר כדי שלא יתן מכשול לפני אחרים: והלוקח ירק מן השוק הוא כשיקנה הירקות אגודות אגודות בדמים ידועים ונטל האגודות לקנות מהן מה שצריך לו ואח״כ נמלך והחזירם למוכר אין לו להחזיר הירקות שלקח עד שיוציא

להחזיר מפני שלא משך: ג המוצא פירות בדרך ונטלן לאוכלן ונמלך להצניע לא יצניע עד שיעשר ואם מתחלה נטלן בשביל שלא יאבדו פטור כל דבר שאין אדם רשאי למכרן דמאי לא ישלח לחבירו דמאי ר' יוסי מתיר בודאי ובלבד שיודיענו: ד המוליך חטים לטוחן כותי או לטוחן ע"ה בחזקתן למעשרות ולשביעית לטוחן נכרי דמאי המפקיד פירותיו אצל הכותי או אצל עם הארץ בחזקתן למעשרות ולשביעי' אצל הנכרי כפירותיו (ח) רבי שמעון אומר דמאי: ה הנותן לפונדקית מעשר את שהוא נותן לה ואת שהוא נוטל ממנה מפני שחשודה לחלוף אמר ר' יוסי אין אנו אחראין לרמאים אינו מעשר אלא מה שהוא נוטל ממנה בלבד: ו הנותן לחמותו מעשר את שהוא נותן לה ואת שהוא נוטל ממנה מפני שהיא חשודה לחלוף את המתקלקל א"ר יהודה רוצה היא בתקנת בתה ובושה מחתנה מודה רבי יהודה בנותן לחמותו שביעית שאינה חשודה להחליף להאכיל את בתה שביעית:

פרק רביעי

א הלוקח פירות ממי שאינו נאמן על המעשרות ושכח (ו) לעשרן ושואלו בשבת יאכל על פיו חשכה מוצאי שבת לא יאכל עד שיעשר לא מצאו אמר לו אחד שאינו נאמן על המעשרות מעושרין הן אוכל על פיו חשכה מוצאי שבת לא יאכל עד שיעשר תרומת מעשר של דמאי שחזרה למקומה ר"ש

BACK [UNTITHED], SINCE HE HAD NOT YET DRAWN THEM INTO HIS POSSESSION.[2]

MISHNAH 3. IF A MAN FOUND FRUIT ON THE ROAD AND PICKED IT UP IN ORDER TO EAT IT, AND THEN DECIDED TO HIDE IT, HE MAY NOT HIDE IT UNLESS HE HAS [FIRST] TITHED IT. BUT IF FROM THE FIRST HE HAD PICKED IT UP ONLY IN ORDER TO GUARD IT AGAINST DESTRUCTION,[3] HE IS EXEMPT [FROM TITHING IT]. ANY PRODUCE WHICH A MAN MAY NOT SELL[4] [IN THE CONDITION OF] DEMAI, HE MAY NEITHER SEND IT [AS A GIFT] TO HIS FRIEND[5] [IN THE CONDITION OF] DEMAI. R. JOSE PERMITS [TO BE SENT AS A GIFT PRODUCE] THAT IS CERTAINLY UNTITHED,[6] ON CONDITION THAT HE MAKES THE MATTER KNOWN TO THE RECIPIENT.

MISHNAH 4. IF A MAN CARRIED HIS WHEAT[7] TO A MILLER WHO WAS A CUTHEAN[8] OR TO A MILLER WHO WAS AN 'AM HA-AREẒ, [THE WHEAT WHEN GROUND CONTINUES] IN ITS FORMER CONDITION IN RESPECT OF TITHES AND THE LAW OF SEVENTH YEAR[9] PRODUCE. [BUT IF HE CARRIED IT] TO A MILLER WHO WAS A GENTILE, [THE WHEAT WHEN GROUND BECOMES] DEMAI.[10] IF A MAN LEFT HIS FRUIT IN THE KEEPING OF A CUTHEAN OR OF AN 'AM HA-AREẒ, [IT CONTINUES WHEN RETURNED] IN ITS FORMER CONDITION IN RESPECT OF TITHES AND THE LAW OF SEVENTH YEAR PRODUCE. [BUT IF HE LEFT
a IT] WITH A GENTILE,[1] [IT BECOMES] LIKE THE FRUIT OF THE GENTILE.[2] R. SIMEON SAYS: [IT BECOMES] DEMAI.[3]

MISHNAH 5. IF A MAN GAVE [PRODUCE] TO THE HOSTESS OF AN INN [TO PREPARE IT FOR FOOD], HE MUST TITHE WHAT HE GIVES TO HER[4] AND WHAT HE TAKES BACK FROM HER,[5] BECAUSE SHE MAY BE SUSPECTED OF CHANGING IT. R. JOSE SAID: WE ARE NOT RESPONSIBLE FOR IMPOSTORS.[6] NAY, HE NEED TITHE ONLY WHAT HE TAKES BACK FROM HER.

MISHNAH 6. IF A MAN GAVE [PRODUCE] TO HIS MOTHER-IN-LAW [TO PREPARE IT FOR FOOD], HE MUST TITHE WHAT HE GIVES TO HER[4] AND WHAT HE TAKES BACK FROM HER, BECAUSE SHE IS SUSPECTED OF CHANGING ANY [FOOD] WHICH IS LIABLE TO BE SPOILT. R. JUDAH SAID: [SHE MIGHT HAVE TO DO IT BECAUSE] SHE DESIRES THE WELFARE OF HER DAUGHTER AND IS BASHFUL OF HER SON-IN-LAW.[7] R. JUDAH AGREES THAT IF A MAN GAVE TO HIS MOTHER-IN-LAW SEVENTH YEAR PRODUCE,[8] SHE IS NOT SUSPECTED OF CHANGING IT[9] AND GIVING HER DAUGHTER TO EAT OF SEVENTH YEAR PRODUCE.

CHAPTER IV

MISHNAH 1. IF A MAN BOUGHT FRUIT FROM ONE WHO WAS NOT TRUSTWORTHY IN RESPECT OF TITHES, AND HE
b FORGOT TO TITHE IT,[1] HE MAY EAT OF IT AT THE VENDOR'S WORD IF HE ASKED HIM ON THE SABBATH.[2] BUT AT THE NIGHTFALL OF THE SABBATH DAY, HE MAY NOT EAT OF IT[3] UNLESS HE HAD FIRST TITHED IT. IF HE COULD NOT FIND THE VENDOR, BUT ANOTHER PERSON WHO WAS NOT TRUSTWORTHY IN RESPECT OF TITHES DECLARED TO HIM THAT IT HAD BEEN TITHED, HE MAY EAT OF IT AT HIS WORD.[4] BUT AT THE NIGHTFALL OF THE SABBATH DAY, HE MAY NOT EAT OF IT UNLESS HE HAD FIRST TITHED IT. IF TERUMAH OF THE TITHE OF DEMAI[5] HAD BECOME MIXED UP AGAIN [WITH THE FRUIT] FROM WHICH IT HAD BEEN TAKEN, R. SIMEON OF

(2) I.e., he had not performed the required *Meshikah*, v. Glos. (3) Without intending to take possession of them. (4) Such as bread by shopkeepers, or produce in a small quantity; cf. *supra* II, 5. (5) Even if his friend is an associate. (6) Even in a small quantity. (7) Which had been duly tithed. (8) A man from Cutha, a Samaritan; cf. II Kings XVII, 24. (9) The Cuthean and the *'am ha-areẓ* are not suspected of having changed the tithed wheat for untithed wheat, or for wheat of Seventh Year produce in which the laws regulating the produce of the Sabbatical Year had not been observed; cf. Lev. XXV, 4–7 and Tractate Shebi'ith. (10) The Gentile may have exchanged the wheat for wheat brought to him by another Israelite, an *'am ha-areẓ* which is *demai*.
a (1) Which is exempt from tithing. (2) Unlike the case of the miller, it is not usual for people to deposit fruit with another person. (3) The Gentile may still have exchanged it for the fruit of an Israelite *'am ha-areẓ*, who happened to deposit some with him. (4) So that if she cheats him and eats it herself, she may not eat it untithed. (5) This may not be the same produce he had given her. (6) To guard them against eating untithed produce. (7) She has a high respect for him. For these reasons she may be suspected of having exchanged the produce he had given her for produce of a better quality. (8) In which the laws of Seventh Year produce had been observed, and was therefore permitted to be eaten. (9) For Seventh Year produce in which the special laws had not been observed. She would not wish to cause her daughter to commit the sin of eating prohibited Seventh Year produce.
b (1) Before the Sabbath. Tithing is not permitted on the Sabbath; cf. *supra* I, 4, n. 12. (2) It may be presumed that the vendor, though an *'am ha-areẓ*, will not lie on the Sabbath day. (3) Although he had already eaten of it on the Sabbath, because he is now able to tithe it. (4) Even another person may be believed on the Sabbath day. (5) Lit., 'which had returned to its place'; *supra* II, 4, n. 10. The quantity of this *terumah* is one tenth of the tithe, or a hundredth part of the whole, and this had become mixed up with the remaining ninety-nine parts, which are not sufficient to neutralize the sanctity of the *terumah*; cf. I, 3, n. 1.

SHEZUR SAYS: EVEN ON A WEEK-DAY HE MAY ASK THE VENDOR AND EAT AT HIS WORD.[6]

MISHNAH 2. IF A MAN IMPOSED A VOW[7] UPON HIS FRIEND TO EAT WITH HIM, AND THE FRIEND DOES NOT TRUST HIM IN
a RESPECT OF TITHES, HE MAY EAT WITH HIM[1] ON THE FIRST SABBATH[2] THOUGH HE DOES NOT TRUST HIM IN RESPECT OF TITHES, PROVIDED THAT THE MAN HAD DECLARED TO HIM THAT THE FOOD HAD BEEN TITHED. BUT ON THE SECOND SABBATH, THOUGH THE MAN HAD BOUND HIMSELF BY A VOW NOT TO ENJOY ANY BENEFIT FROM HIM,[3] HE MAY NOT EAT WITH THE MAN EXCEPT HE HAD FIRST TITHED [THE FOOD].[4]

MISHNAH 3. R. ELIEZER SAYS: A MAN NEED NOT DESIGNATE[5] THE POORMAN'S[6] TITHE OF DEMAI. BUT THE SAGES SAY: HE MUST DESIGNATE IT, BUT HE NEED NOT SET IT APART.[7]

MISHNAH 4. IF A MAN HAD DESIGNATED[8] THE TERUMAH OF THE TITHE OF DEMAI,[9] OR THE POORMAN'S TITHE OF PRODUCE THAT HAD CERTAINLY NOT BEEN TITHED,[10] HE MAY NOT TAKE THEM ON THE SABBATH.[11] BUT IF THE PRIEST AND THE POOR MAN WERE WONT TO EAT WITH HIM, THEY MAY COME AND EAT OF THEM PROVIDED THAT HE MAKES THE
b MATTER KNOWN TO THEM.[1]

MISHNAH 5. IF A MAN SAID TO ONE WHO WAS NOT TRUSTWORTHY IN RESPECT OF TITHES: 'BUY [PRODUCE] FOR ME FROM ONE WHO IS TRUSTWORTHY OR FROM ONE WHO GIVES TITHES', [THE MESSENGER] MAY NOT BE TRUSTED.[2] BUT IF THE MAN SAID: 'BUY IT FOR ME FROM SO-AND-SO', HE IS TO BE TRUSTED.[3] IF HE WENT TO BUY IT FROM HIM [AND THEN CAME BACK] AND SAID: 'I DID NOT FIND HIM, SO I BOUGHT FOR YOU FROM ANOTHER MAN WHO IS TRUSTWORTHY', HE MAY NOT BE TRUSTED.

MISHNAH 6. IF A MAN ENTERED A CITY WHERE HE KNEW NO ONE, AND SAID: 'WHO IS HERE TRUSTWORTHY? WHO GIVES TITHES HERE?', AND SOME ONE REPLIED: 'I', HE MAY NOT BE TRUSTED. BUT IF HE REPLIED: 'SO-AND-SO IS TRUSTWORTHY', HE MAY BE BELIEVED.[4] IF THE MAN WENT TO BUY FROM SO-AND-SO, AND HE ASKED HIM: 'WHO SELLS HERE OLD PRODUCE?'[5] AND SO-AND-SO REPLIED: 'HE WHO HAD SENT YOU TO ME', THOUGH THEY APPEAR AS REPAYING EACH OTHER'S FAVOUR, THEY MAY YET BE TRUSTED.[6]

MISHNAH 7. IF ASS-DRIVERS[7] ENTERED A CITY AND ONE OF THEM DECLARED: 'MY PRODUCE IS NEW BUT MY FRIEND'S PRODUCE IS OLD', OR: 'MY PRODUCE HAS NOT BEEN SET
c RIGHT BUT MY FRIEND'S PRODUCE HAS BEEN SET RIGHT',[1] THEY MAY NOT BE TRUSTED.[2] R. JUDAH SAYS: THEY MAY BE TRUSTED.[3]

(6) If the vendor declares that the produce had been tithed from the first, and that the tithing by the buyer was unnecessary, he is believed, as otherwise the whole mixture would be rendered forbidden as *terumah*, and the buyer would suffer a great loss; v. Rashi. Men. 30*b*. (7) He said: 'May you be forbidden to derive any benefit from me if you do not eat with me'; cf. Ned. III, 1; IV. The man was celebrating his marriage to a virgin.

a (1) In order to prevent ill-feeling. (2) The Hebrew word 'Sabbath' may also mean 'week'. (3) A vow by which he binds his own person is more conducive to ill-feeling than a vow by which he binds his friend. (4) The rule that an *'am ha-arez* may be believed on the Sabbath (*supra* 1, n. 2) applies only to the statement of a vendor. (5) I.e., declare that the tithe shall be in a certain part of the produce, as *infra* V, 1, 2; VII; cf. Ter. III, 5, and Introduction p. 51. R. Eliezer holds that the *'am ha-arez* does set apart the Poorman's Tithe, but keeps it for his own use.* (6) V. Introduction p. 50. (7) He need not give it to the poor, because the burden of proof that the *demai* produce had not been tithed by the *'am ha-arez* who was its original owner, lies on the poor; cf. Introduction p. 51. (8) Before the Sabbath. (9) In the case of produce that was certainly untithed, the owner himself cannot separate the *Terumah* of the Tithe. This must be done by the Levite who receives the tithe. (10) In the case of *demai* produce there is no need to give away the Poorman's Tithe, as stated above n. 7. (11) In order to deliver them respectively to the priest and to the poor. This delivery is forbidden on the Sabbath or on the Festival; cf. Bez. 12*b*.

b (1) That they may know that they are eating their own produce. It is forbidden to discharge one's personal obligations to guests by treating them with tithes. (2) When he says that he had bought it from a trustworthy person because the vendor considered trustworthy by the messenger may not really be so. (3) When he says that he bought it from the person named by the sender. (4) The rule that a person who is not trustworthy himself may not testify about the trustworthiness of another person is relaxed in this case, in view of the difficulty the enquirer may have in obtaining food in a strange place from a trustworthy person. (5) Of last year's harvest. The new produce of the current year may not be eaten before the *'Omer*, or Sheaf-offering, has been offered on the altar on the first day of the Passover; cf. Lev. XXIII, 10–14; Men. X, 5. (6) Most *'amme ha-arez* used to observe the rules respecting the consumption of new produce. (7) Who hawk their produce for sale in different localities.

c (1) Duly tithed; III, 1, n. 5. (2) This testimony may be part of a mutual arrangement to assist one another in the sale of their produce in different localities. (3) Since most *'amme ha-arez* do tithe, the strict rule of *demai* may be relaxed in this case, in order to attract produce dealers to the city and thereby promote its economic prosperity.

*See Corrigenda.

מסורת הש"ס

א) מדיס פ"א דף סד. מכות יז: ב) בכורות פ"ב דף לו: ג) כתובות פ"ב דף כב. וכפ"ה דף ט :

עין משפט נר מצוה

ה א שם הלכה ג :
ו ב מיי' פ"ט שם הלכה ג סמג עשין קלו :
ז ג מיי' פרק כ"ג מהלכות שבת הלכה טו :
ח ד מיי' פי"ב מהלכות מעשר הלכה ו :
ט ה שם הלכה ז :
י ו שם הלכה י :

אומרים בין במקומה בין שלא במקומה מדמעת (א)] והך פלוגתא דוקא בדמאי ולא בודאי: שואלו ואוכלו על פיו · בירושלמי (הלכה א) תני בר קפרא אימת הדימוע עליו והוא אומר אמת כלו' מסקרא עליה שם תרומה ירא לשקר ובתוספתא (פ"ה) קתני כשם שאימת שבת על עם הארץ כך אימת דימוע על עם הארץ ומפרש בירושלמי (שם) כילד שואלו דבדישא מאי אמר ליה לית אנא חסד לך אלא בגין דזכנית מיקך חיטי וחמית אוכלוסא עלך ואמרית דילמא אנשיית מתקנן ברס הכא לחסידתן ותקינתן ואע"ג דקיימא לן החשוד על הדבר לא דנו ולא מעידו הכא דאימת דימוע עליו נאמן: ב המדיר את חבירו שיאכל אצלו · דאמר ליה קונס שאי אתה נהנה אם אין אתה סועד אצלי: שבת הראשונה · מפרש בירושלמי (הל' ג) ר' ינאי ברבי ישמעאל בשם ר' יוחנן בשבת של פרוטגמא התירו משום איבה לסעודות בחור שנשא בתולה קורין בלשון יון פרוטגמא בויקרא רבה פרוטגמא של לדיקים לעתיד לבא (ג): ג למעשר עני · בפרק אלו הן הלוקין (דף יז·) בעי רב יוסף למימר דמר סבר טביל ומר סביר לא טביל אמר ליה אביי אי הכי אדמיפלגי בספיקו ליפלגו בודאי אלא דכולי עלמא טביל והכא בהא קא מיפלגי מר סבר לא נחשדו עמי הארץ על מעשר עני דכיון דממונא דידי' הוא (ד) אפרושי מפריש (ה) ומר סבר נחשדו כיון דטריחא ליה מילתא לא מפריש ובירושלמי (הל' ג) מפרש *רב הונא ר' אבא בשם רב האוכל פירותיו טבולי למעשר עני חייב מיתה מאי טעמא דר"א מכיון שיודע שבעון מיתה הוא מפריש מאי טעמא דרבנן בלא כך קורא עליו שם ואינו צריך להפריש כלומר בלא כך שיפסוק לך שמפריש הא סגי בקריאת שם הלכך אין לחוש אם נחמיר עליו לקרות בספק (מעם) [שם מ"ע] והיינו כההיא שיטה דמכות דר' אליעזר סבר על מעשר ראשון ומע"ש נחשדו דלא מפרשי להו הראשון משום תרומת מעשר דאית ביה והשני משום דבעי אסוקי לירושלים אבל מעשר עני מפריש ורבנן סברי אפי' הכי חשודין הן הלכך הלוקח קורא עליו שם ואינו צריך להפריש וליתן לעני: ד לתרומת מעשר של דמאי · לא מצי למינקט של ודאי דבישראל מיירי והוא חייב ליתן מעשר ראשון ללוי והלוי יתן תרומת מעשר למי שירצה אבל בדמאי מעשרותיו שלו דהמוציא מחבירו עליו הראיה אבל תרומת מעשר מפריש ונותן לכהן כדתנן בסוטה בשילהי עגלה ערופה (דף מח·) אבל גבי מעשר עני נקט הוודאי דאילו של דמאי שלו ואם תאמר וליתני תרומה גדולה של ודאי ויש לומר דמעשר עני כשקרא שם מערב שבת יכולים לאכול הוא והעני בבת אחת בלא הפרשה אלא שיקבע מערב שבת לצפון ודרומן אבל תרומה שמדמעת את החולין צריך להפריש ובשבת אסור להפריש אע"פ שקרא שם מערב שבת כדמוכח לקמן בפרק ז' (משנה א ה) דתנן המזמין חברו לאכול אצלו והוא אינו מאמינו על המעשרות אומר מערב שבת מה שאני עתיד להפריש למחר הרי הוא מעשר וגבי היו לו תאנים של טבל קתני שאני עתיד להפריש ולא קתני למחר משום דכיון דודאי הוא אסור להפרישו בשבת אע"פ שקרא שם ומיהו אין מזה ראיה דהכי נמי בסיפא דקתני היו דמאי ולא קא תני למחר והא דקתני למחר גבי מזמן משום דאין מפריש שם אלא מה שאוכל והוא הדין נמי כמי שיש לו תאנים של טבל שיכול להפריש מה שאכל בשבת אלא לפי שירצה לתקן אף המותר הכל בבת אחת לא קתני למחר דלצורך חול אסור להפריש ובהדיא אמרי' לקמן בירושלמי פרק ז' (הל' א) רבי ינאי הוה ליה תאני ודאי שאל לר' ירמיה רבה מהו מתקנא בשבת אמר ליה למען תלמד ליראה את ה' כל הימים אפי' בשבת פי' תאני ודאי תאנים שהיה לו ודאי טבל שהתנה עליו מערב שבת מה שאני עתיד להפריש יהא מעשר אלמא בהדיא דשרי והא דלא נקט הכא תרומה גדולה של ודאי יש לפרש משום דלאו אורחיה דמילתא לשהות תרומה ורגילין להפרישה לאלתר אפי' קודם שהביאה לבית כדאמרי' בירושלמי בפ"ג דמעשרות (הל' א) אי אפשר לגורן שתיעקר אא"כ נתרמה תרומה גדולה וגם לפי שאין צריך לטרוח במדידה ואדרבה מצוה באומד וקצת תימה בשובלא דר' ינאי בהאשה רבה (דף נג·) דר' ינאי גופיה עישר מפירי דביתי' שלא מן המוקף יקרא שם ויפריש בשבת מן המוקף כדעבד בירושלמי ושמא ההוא הוה ברישא ולא ידע אכתי אי שרי אי נמי הוה צריך לכולה כנתא דפירי ועוד דאין מתנה אודאי על מה שביד חברו כמו שמפרש בירושלמי בריש פרק ז' : לא ישלם · לאו דוקא אלא כלומר לא ישלם כדי ליתן לכהן ולעני שבחלר ושבמבוי סתמא כב"ש דבילה בפ"ק (דף יב:) דאין מוליכין חלה ומתנות לכהן כדמפרש בירושלמי (הלכה ב) אבל בלימודין לאכול שרי ומיהו לאחרים ולר' יהודה דאמרי התם למודו ב"ה בתרומה שאין מוליכין משום דאינו זכאי בהרמתה אתיא אפילו כב"ה : ירושלמי (הל' ג) כיני מתני' לא יתנם בשבת דתנן ב"ש אומרים אין מוליכין חלה ומתנות לכהן בי"ט בין שהורמו מאמש בין שהורמו מהיום וב"ה מתירין הדא ילפא מההיא וההיא ילפא מהדא [הדא ילפא מההיא] היא י"ט היא שבת וההיא ילפא מהדא בלימודין אבל בשאינן לימודין לא סלק בר נש מיכול פיסתיה בביתיה דחבריה פי' פיסתיה מלשון (תהלים עב) יהי פסת בר בארץ ומהאי טעמא נמי במתני' בעי שיודיעם דאפילו למודין לאכול אצלו לא סליק על דעתיה לאכול אצל חברו בשבת אא"כ הודיעו מערב שבת ועוד דפעמים אינו טהור ואסור בתרומה ועני נמי אין צריך לסמאות סהרותיו של חברו : ה דאפי' ימלא שאינו נאמן מאי לאסתמוסי בעיני היה נאמן (ז) אבל כשאמר לו מאיש פלוני אינו רשאי ליקח מאחר ובהא נמי פליג ר' יוסי : ירושלמי (הל' ד) תניא ר' יוסי אומר אפילו אומר מפלו' אינו נאמן עד שיאמר לו קח ואני נותן מעות מאי טעמא דר' יוסי אני אומר אחד קרוב מלא ולקח ממנו דתנן (גיטין דף סו·) התקבל [לי] גטי במקום פלוני אוכלת בתרומה עד שיגיע גט לאותו מקום ר' אליעזר אוסר מיד מאי טעמא דר' אליעזר אני אומר אחר הדלת מלאו אתיא דר' אליעזר כר' יוסי ודר' יוסי כרבי אליעזר דר' יוסי רובא [מן] דר' אליעזר ולא מודה ר' אליעזר שאם אמרה לו אל תקבלהו לי אלא במקום פלוני שהיא אוכלת בתרומה עד שיגיע גם לאותו מקום וכה אפילו אמר מפלוני אינו נאמן עד שיאמר קח מפלוני ואני נותן מעות פי' דרבי יוסי רובא כלומר עדיפא מדר' אליעזר דבההיא דר' יוסי הוה שרי ר' אליעזר דטעמא דר' אליעזר משום דמראה מקום היא לו כדאיתא בפ' התקבל (דף סה·) ובפ' האיש מקדש (דף מט·) ובפ' גט פשוט (דף קסה·) והכא כשאמר לו מאיש פלוני כאילו אמר לו אל תקנה מאחר דמי משום דנאמן על המעשרות קאמר ליה ואפילו הכי חייש ר' יוסי : ו הרי זה נאמן · בירושלמי (הל' ה) פריך ועד אחד נאמן בתמיה דאף על גב דבעלמא עד אחד (ראוי) נאמן לא היה ראוי כאן להאמינו כיון דהוא עצמו חשוד א"ר יוחנן קל הקילו באכסנאי מפני חיי נפש ולהכי נקט נאמן שאין מכיר אדם אבל המכיר לא התירו כדקתני בתוספתא (פ"ה) : מוכר ישן·כההיא דחמרין (בההיא) דבסמוך דמייתי בפ' אע"פ (דף נו:) פירש שם בקונטרס האי דנקט שלי חדש משום איסור חדש קודם לעומר ולמאי דמשני התם ובפ' שני דכתובות (דף כד·) בדמאי הקילו צריך לומר דחדש כדמאי דרובא לא חשידי וקשה דלא מצינו בשום מקום דעמי הארץ חשודין על החדש כלל ורבי' שמואל מפרש דלענין איסור שביעית כגון בשנה שביעית וקאמר שלי חדש וגדל בשביעית ואסור לשהותו אחר הביעור ושל חבירו ישן וגדל אשתקד ואי אפשר לומר כן כלל דהא קתני בהדיא דלשביעית אינן נאמנין וצריך לומר דלא נקט חדש וישן משום *איסור אלא משום דפירות ישנים מעולין מחדשים כדמוכח בפרק איזהו נשך (דף עב:) חדשות מד' וישנות משלש שהחדשות נמכרות ד' סאין בסלע והיינו כגומלין דהאמר מי ששלחך אצלי מוכר יין ישן משביח על חברו (ח) : תניא בתוספתא (פ"ה) היה עומד בתוך סיעה של בני אדם ואמר מי כאן נאמן מי כאן מעשר ואמר לו אחד אני (ג) נאמן איש פלוני מעשר הוא הרי זה נאמן אמר לו פלוני מעשר הוא בפניו אינו נאמן שלא בפניו נאמן בד"א שאין מכיר אדם שם אבל מכיר אדם שם לא יטול אלא מן המומחה בד"א שלא שהה שם ל' יום אבל שהה שם ל' יום לא יטול אלא מן המעושרות בד"א בתרומה ומעשרות אבל בשביעית ובטהרות הרי זה [אינו] נאמן : ז החמרים . מביאין תבואה ממקום הזול למקום היוקר : אין נאמנים · דודאי גומלין זה את זה ולמוכרה הביאה כדמוקי לה בפ' האשה שנתארמלה (דף כד:) בשכלי אומנותו בידו

שזורי אומר אף בחול שואלו ואוכלו על פיו :

ב *המדיר את חבירו שיאכל אצלו והוא אינו מאמינו על המעשרות אוכל עמו בשבת הראשונה ואע"פ שאינו *מאמינו על המעשרות ובלבד שיאמר לו מעושרין הן ובשבת שניה אע"פ שנדר ממנו הנייה לא יאכל עד שיעשר :

ג א) רבי אליעזר אומר אין אדם צריך לקרות שם למעשר עני של דמאי וחכמים אומרים ב)קורא שם ואינו צריך להפריש :

ד ג)מי שקרא שם לתרומת מעשר של דמאי ולמעשר עני של ודאי לא יטלם בשבת ואם היו כהן או עני למודים לאכול אצלו יבואו ויאכלו ובלבד שיודיעם :

ה ג) ד(ו)האומר למי שאינו נאמן על המעשרות קח לי ממי שהוא נאמן וממי שהוא מעשר אינו נאמן מאיש פלוני הרי זה נאמן הלך ליקח ממנו ואמר לו לא מצאתיו ולקחתי לך מאחר שהוא נאמן אינו נאמן :

ו ה)הנכנס לעיר ואין מכיר אדם שם אמר מי כאן נאמן מי כאן מעשר אמר לו א' אני איני נאמן *איש פלוני נאמן הרי זה נאמן הלך ליקח ממנו אמר לו מי כאן מוכר ישן אמר לו מי ששלחך אצלי אע"פ שהן כגומלין זה את זה הרי אלו נאמנין :

ז ג) ו)החמרין שנכנסו לעיר אמר א' שלי חדש ושל חבירי ישן שלי אינו מתוקן ושל חבירי מתוקן אינן נאמנין ר' יהודה אומר נאמנין :

הלוקח

לאחר הכוכבים אבל בין השמשות במוצאי שבת אוכל על פיו מפני שלא נגמר היום ומה שאמר בכאן מעשר ר"ל תרומת מעשר ומעשר שני המחויבים לדמאי כמו שבארנו והעיקר בידינו שתרומת מעשר של דמאי אע"פ שהוא ספק כשתתערב בפירות מתוקנים כמעט ודין המדומע יתבאר לך אחר זה אמר שאם יפריש ע"ה תרומת מעשר של דמאי לפנינו ואחר כך חזרה למקומה ונתערב הכל נעשה הכל מדומע וכשנשאלנו אחר כך ואמר חזרתי והפרשתי אותו ואכלתיהו והתקנתי זה שהיה מדומע אומר ר' שמעון שזורי שהוא נאמן אפי' בחול כי הוא אומר כשם שאימת שבת על עם הארץ כך אימת מדומע עליו ולא יתיר לנפשו אכילתו אחרי אשר נתערבה בו תרומה עד שיתקנהו וחכמים אינם מודים לזה ואומרים שאינו נאמן בחול בשום פנים ואפי' במדומע והלכה כר' שמעון שזורי: ב המדיר את חבירו. ר"ל הנשבע על חבירו: בשבת ראשונה · השבת הראשונה שיקראו לאכול עמו והתירו זה מפני דרכי שלום: ומה שאמר אע"פ שנדר הימנו הנייה ר"ל אף על פי שזכר לו בכלל שבועתו שלא יהנה ממנו אם לא יאכל אצלו שצריך לו לעשות כן לחזק החברה ולהרחיק האיבה שתפול ביניהם אם לא יאכל עמו אעפ"כ אינו רשאי לאכול עמו עד שיעשר הוא בעצמו או יעשרו לפניו : ג כבר בארנו שדמאי אינו חייב להוציא ממנו מעשר עני בשנים שמפרישין מעשר עני במקום מעשר שני וזהו בשנה השלישית מן השמטה והששית כמו שיתבאר ובאלו השנים אינם מפרישין מן הדמאי אלא תרומת מעשר בלבד לפיכך אומר ר' אליעזר אחר שלא יפרישו מעשר עני לא יקרא לו שם : וחכמים אומרים יקרא לו שם . והוא שיאמר אחר שיפריש תרומת מעשר עשירית מה שנשאר הוא מעשר עני ולא יפרישהו ודעת חכמים בזה כדי שיתקיים מעשר שני המחויב לדמאי וידע שצריך על כל פנים להוציאו אחר תרומת מעשר לפי שמעשר עני הוא במקום מעשר שני כמו שיתבאר ואין הלכה כרבי אליעזר : ד ענין קרא שם שיאמר תרומת מעשר המחויבת לזה הצבור מן התאנים תהיה בזה הצד וסימן עליו אך לא הפרישה מכלל התאנים על כן אמר אע"פ שהם ידועים לא יטלם בשבת ובארו בגמרא שענין מה שאמר לא יטלם הוא לא יתנם וכאילו אמר לא יטלם לנתינה מפני שהוא אסור לתת המתנות בשבת : ופירוש למודין רגילין : ומה שאמר ובלבד שיודיעם שיאמר להם זה שאני מאכיל אתכם הוא תרומה מעשר או מעשר עני שאם לא יודיעם יחשבו שמאכילם דרך נדבה ויהיה כמי שמאכיל תרומה ומעשרות לאורחין או עשה מהן צרכיו : ה מה שאמר נאמן אינו ר"ל נאמן על המעשרות לפי שהוא המעשר אבל פי' נאמן הוא איש נאמן על טומאה וטהרה שאינו מאכיל איסור ולא טמא והטעם שהוא נאמן באמרו מפלוני קח לי כי בודאי אינו לוקח מאחר לפי שהוא מתיירא שמא ישאל האיש ההוא ויאמר לו אם בא אליך פלוני אם לא: ו והעיקר אצלנו אין אדם חוטא ולא לו ולפיכך לא ישלחנו לאיש שאינו נאמן מפני שאין לו הנאה בזה הנאה קרובה מיד וכל זה כדי להקל עליו מפני שהוא גר ואינו מכיר אנשי המדינה : ז מתוקן · ידוע ר"ל כבר הוציא ממנו המעשרות : אינו נאמן · ואע"פ שהוא מגנה לזולתו מפני

פי' מהר"י בן מלכי צדק

מעשר של דמאי א' מק' כמו תרומת מעשר ודאי והפרישה האדם שכן גזר יוחנן כהן גדול כיון שראה שתרומה גדולה היו מפרישין ושאר מעשרות לא גזר והלוקח מעם הארץ ק' סאין מפריש סאה אחת דהיינו כדי תרומת מעשר ונותנה לכהן ואותה הסאה נקראת תרומת מעשר של דמאי ואם לא הספיק ליתנה לכהן ונפלה לכרי שהורם ממנו אם אירע כן היה ר' שמעון שזורי אומר אף בחול שואלו ואוכל על פיו . ושואלו הכין בגין דחשידתן ותקינתן וחזרה תרומת מעשר שהפרשתי לשם מעושרין הן בידך ואיני חושש מן הדימוע אי לא . ומה שאומר נאמן שאימת הדימוע עליו והוא אומר אמת כלומר מתיירא שיאכל הזרי' תרומה הלכך אם לא הפריש הוא יאמר לא הפרשתי אני ומה שהפרשת אתה כדין הפרשת והשתא דחזרה לה למקומה הוה ליה דימוע ואסיר ליך : ב המדיר את חבירו שיאכל אצלו. פי' אומר קונם שאת נהנה לי אם לא תאכל עמי בשבת הראשונה . גרסי' א"ר ינאי בר' ישמעאל בשם ר' יוחנן בשבת של פרוטגמא התירו משום איבה פי' לשון יון הוא זה ופירוש שבת הראשון של שמחה [אולי צ"ל פרוטו]פירוש ראשון גמי [פירוש] שמחה וכן קורין בארץ יון לרווק שנשא בתולה הנשואין ההן קורין פרוטגמו . אבל אלמן בבתולה או בחור באלמנה אין קורין כן אלא גמי · א"ר אבין כאן התירו טבלין מפני דרכי שלום ר' חנינא אמר ר' ירמיה בעי אם מפני דרכי שלום למה לי ובלבד שיאמר לו מעושרין הן : ג רבי אליעזר אומר אין אדם צריך לקרו' שם על מעשר עני של דמאי. פי' מעשר עני במקום מעשר שני קאי כיצד שנה ראשונה של שביעית מעשר ראשון ומעשר שני וכן שנה שניה שלישית מעשר ראשון ומעשר עני. גרסינן בירושלמי מאי טעמא דר' אליעזר אמרי וכו' ומחלוקת לאפרושי אבל למיתביה לעני וכן מעשר ראשון דמאי ללוי לא יהיב אלא הן שלו שהמוציא מחבירו עליו הראיה ולא יהיב לכהן אלא תרומת מעשר של דמאי דהיינו אחד ממאה והשני של דמאי פודה ושאר מעשרות מפרישין והן שלו שהמוציא מחבירו עליו הראיה וכן מיפרשא בסוף מעשר שני בגמ': ד מי [...] מעשר ולמעשר שני של דמאי לא ישלם בשבת וכו'. גרסינן בירושלמי כיני מתני' לא יתנם בשבת דתנן [בבילה דף י"ב] בית שמאי אומרים אין מוליכין חלה ומתנות לכהן ביום טוב בין שהורמ[ו ...] ובית הלל מתירין הדא ילפא מההיא וההיא ילפא מהדא הדא ילפא מהדא היא יום טוב היא שבת וההיא ילפא מהדא בלימודין לאכול אצלו: יבואו ויאכלו. פי' כהן תרומת מעשר ועני מעשר עני: ובלב[ד ...] דכהן טמא הוא . ועני [נמי י"ל דמודר] הנאה ממעשר עני אבל בשאינו לימודין לא סלק על בר נש מיכל פיסתיה פי' מעשר עני שלו בביתא דחבריה: ה האומר למי שאינו נאמן על המעשרות. פי' [...] הא נאמן לא וכו' מאיש פלוני הרי זה נאמן מאי טעמא דאמרינן מיניה זבין דאמר בליביה היום וסחר ילך וישאלהו. נאמן ומעשר הדא מילתא היא אלא נאמן הוא בחנונין הלוקחין והמוכרין ומעשר[ין ...] המעשרין פירותיהן ואינן אוכלין טבלין; ו הנכנס לעיר ואינו מכיר אדם בעיר וכו'. פי' שהוא אכסנאי וצעק ואמר מי כאן וכו' איש פלוני הרי זה נאמן . גרסינן בירושלמי ועד אחד נאמן כלומר [...] שאמר איש פלוני בתימה ותרצי' א"ר יוחנן קל הקילו באכסנאי מפני חיי נפש : ז החמרין שנכנסו לעיר אמר אחד מהן שלי חדש וכו'.מאי טעמא דדמויי מרמי לדו . מאי טעמא דר' יהודה מפני ח[...]

פירוש הרא"ש

(ג) בשבת שניה אומר לו מעושרים הם לא יאכל דדוקא בלוקח התירו בשבת לסמוך על דבריו : (ד) דטובת הנאה שלו ואם ירלה יתן : (ה) להפקיע איסור טבל ולא מחשיב לה כגזול כיון דממונו הוא ועדיין לא זכו בו עניים: (ו) האומר וכו' לא ידענא אמאי נקט כפל מלה ממי שהוא נאמן ממי שהוא מעשר : (ז)הכי מפרש בשילהי כל המוקדשין (לו.) : (ח) בשביל שגמל עליו טובה ואמר עליו שהוא נאמן משום הכי אמר גם הוא עליו שהוא מוכר ישן והו"ל למיחש דלמא משקרי אפילו הכי נאמן הראשון שאמר שחבירו נאמן ולאו דוקא נאמנים שאינו חושש על נאמנותו דלאו לענין איסור וסיתר קאמר:

הגהות הגר"א

(א) בר"ש משנה א מדמעת . נ"ב רש"א בין במקומה בין שלא במקומה אין מדמעת : (ג) שם מ"ש אחד אני. נ"ב נ"ל אני איני :

כגון סאה ותרקב ומחק כדי למחוק ומשביח של חברו בעיר זו כדי שישביח חברו את שלו בעיר אחרת ור' יהודה לא חייש לגומלין דבדמאי הקלו משום דרוב עמי הארץ מעשרין הן ובירושלמי (שם) אמרי' מ"ט דר' יהודה מפני חייסם של בני העיר ומאי טעמא דרבנן מלויין הן להתפרנס מעיר אחרת:

א כיצד מעשר · לעיל בפ' ב' (מ"ד) פירשתי דהתם נחתום מעשר והא לוקח מעשר: אחד ממאה · היינו שיעור מעשר דמאי דממאה מפריסים י' למעשר ראשון ומאותן עשר אחת לתרומת מעשר הרי שחלה עצמה מתקנת מן המעשר ומתרומת מעשר ופריך בירו' (הל' א) והלא חייבת בדמאי בתמיה

פרק חמישי

א הלוקח [א]מן הנחתום כיצד הוא מעשר נוטל כדי תרומת מעשר וחלה ואומר אחד ממאה שיש כאן הרי *בצד זה מעשר ושאר המעשר סמוך לו זה שעשיתי מעשר עשוי תרומת מעשר עליו והשאר חלה ומעשר שני בצפונו או בדרומו ומחולל על המעות: **ב** [ב]הרוצה להפריש תרומה ותרומת מעשר כאחת נוטל אחד משלשים ושלש ושליש ואומר אחד מק' ממה שיש כאן הרי זה בצד זה חולין והשאר תרומה על הכל *ומאה חולין שיש כאן הרי זה בצד זה מעשר ושאר מעשר סמוך לו זה שעשיתי מעשר עשוי תרומת מעשר עליו והשאר חלה ומעשר שני בצפונו או בדרומו ומחולל על המעות: **ג** [א] הלוקח מן הנחתום מעשר מן החמה על הצוננת ומן (ג) הצוננת על החמה אפילו מטפוסין הרבה דברי ר"מ ר' יהודה [ג]אוסר שאני אומר חטים של אמש היו משל אחד ושל היום היו משל אחר ר' שמעון אוסר בתרומת מעשר ומתיר בחלה:

CHAPTER V

a *MISHNAH* 1. IF A MAN[1] BOUGHT BREAD FROM A BAKER[2] HOW SHOULD HE TITHE? HE SHOULD TAKE[3] SUFFICIENT FOR THE TERUMAH OF THE TITHE[4] AND FOR ḤALLAH[5] AND SAY: A HUNDREDTH PART OF WHAT IS HERE[6] SHALL BE TITHE ON THIS SIDE, AND WHAT IS NEAREST TO IT SHALL BE THE REST OF THE TITHE;[7] THAT WHICH I MADE TITHE[8] SHALL BECOME THE TERUMAH OF THE TITHE FOR THE WHOLE;[9] THE REMAINDER[10] SHALL BE ḤALLAH, AND WHAT IS TO THE NORTH OR TO THE SOUTH OF IT[11] SHALL BE SECOND TITHE WHICH SHALL BE EXCHANGED[12] FOR MONEY.[13]

b *MISHNAH* 2. IF A MAN WISHED TO SET APART[1] TERUMAH[2] AND THE TERUMAH OF THE TITHE BOTH TOGETHER, HE SHOULD TAKE THREE HUNDREDTHS[3] AND SAY: ONE HUNDREDTH PART OF WHAT IS HERE SHALL BE COMMON PRODUCE[4] ON THIS SIDE, AND THE REST[5] SHALL BE TERUMAH FOR THE WHOLE; THE HUNDREDTH PART[6] COMMON PRODUCE WHICH IS HERE SHALL BE TITHE ON THIS SIDE,[7] AND WHAT IS NEAREST TO IT SHALL BE THE REST OF THE TITHE;[8] THAT WHICH I MADE TITHE[9] SHALL BECOME THE TERUMAH OF TITHE FOR THE WHOLE;[10] THE REMAINDER SHALL BE ḤALLAH,[11] AND WHAT IS TO THE NORTH OR TO THE SOUTH OF IT SHALL BE SECOND TITHE WHICH SHALL BE EXCHANGED FOR MONEY.

MISHNAH 3. IF A MAN BOUGHT FROM A BAKER, HE MAY GIVE TITHE FROM HOT[12] BREAD FOR COLD[13] OR FROM COLD BREAD FOR HOT BREAD, EVEN WHEN THEY ARE OF VARIOUS MOULDS; THUS R. MEIR. R. JUDAH PROHIBITS IT, BECAUSE IT MAY BE ASSUMED THAT YESTERDAY'S WHEAT WAS BOUGHT FROM ONE MAN[14] AND TO-DAY'S WHEAT FROM ANOTHER
c MAN.[1] R. SIMEON PROHIBITS IT IN THE CASE OF TERUMAH OF THE TITHE, BUT PERMITS IT IN THE CASE OF ḤALLAH.[2]

MISHNAH 4. IF A MAN BOUGHT FROM A BREAD DEALER HE MUST TITHE EVERY MOULD [SEPARATELY;][3] THUS R. MEIR. R. JUDAH SAYS: HE MAY GIVE TITHES FROM ONE MOULD FOR ALL THE OTHERS.[4] BUT R. JUDAH AGREES THAT IF A MAN BOUGHT FROM A MONOPOLIST[5] HE MUST TITHE EVERY MOULD [SEPARATELY].

a (1) Who is an associate. (2) Who is an *'am ha-areẓ* and who does not observe the rule laid down in II, 4; or one who sells in large quantities and is exempt from tithing *demai* produce; II, 4. (3) By word of mouth, i.e., by designating them and without actually cutting off from the bread the various portions of the tithes. (4) One hundredth part of the whole; IV, 1, n. 5. (5) Cf. I, 3, n. 12. The legal quantity of *Ḥallah* for a private person is one twenty-fourth part of the whole, and one forty-eighth part for a baker; cf. Ḥal. II, 7. (6) Of the bread. (7) I.e., 9/100 of the whole, making together with the first hundredth, one tenth of the whole for First (Levitical) Tithe. (8) I.e., the first hundredth. (9) Of the 10/100, or the First Tithe. (10) I.e., 1/24 of the 9/10 of the loaf. (11) Of the *Terumah* of the Tithes. (12) Lit., 'rendered common'; cf. I, 2, n. 7. (13) To enable it to be eaten outside Jerusalem. He need not add the Fifth; I, 2, n. 10. This rather complicated method is enjoined because the more sacred portion must be set apart before the less sacred, (cf. Ter. III, 6–7). Hence when a person who is not a Levite wishes to set apart not only First Tithe but also the *Terumah* of the Tithe (cf. IV, 4, n. 9) he must set apart the *Terumah* of the Tithe (viz., one hundredth part) before the tithe, as more sacred than the tithe. But this hundredth part cannot become *Terumah* of the Tithe before it had first become tithe, therefore the man must set apart the tithe in two portions; first one tenth of the tithe (one hundredth of the whole), which later becomes *Terumah* of the Tithe, and then the remaining nine tenths of the tithe (nine hundredths of the whole). *Ḥallah* is indeed more sacred than the tithe (since *Ḥallah* belongs to the priest), but nevertheless it may be set apart after the tithe, from the remaining nine tenths of the whole, because *Ḥallah* need not be given from the tithe. Finally, Second Tithe must be set apart only after the First Tithe; cf. I, 4, n. 1.
b (1) From produce which had certainly not been tithed. (2) The Priest's heave-offering; cf. I, 3, n. 1. (3) Lit., 'one part in thirty-three and a third'. (4) Provisionally, to be made later into First Tithe, and finally into *Terumah* of the Tithe. (5) Of the three hundredths, i.e., two hundredths, or one fiftieth of the whole, which is the usual quantity of the *terumah*;° cf. Introd. p. 50. *Terumah*, as the most sacred of all portions, must be set apart first, to be followed by *Terumah* of the Tithe, as explained in 11*b* n. a 12. (6) I.e., the first hundredth of the three hundredths. (7) Later to become *Terumah* of the Tithe, as in the last Mishnah. (8) I.e., nine tenths of the tithe, or about nine hundredths of the whole, making together with the one hundredth, which will become *Terumah* of the Tithe, one tenth of the whole. (9) I.e., the first hundredth. (10) Of the ten hundredths. (11) I.e., one twenty-fourth of the remainder of the produce after *Terumah* and the Tithe with its *terumah* have been taken off. In this way the more sacred portions, *terumah* and *Terumah* of the Tithe are separated first. (12) I.e., freshly baked. (13) Stale. (14) Who gave tithes.
c (1) Who did not give tithes. The buyer may thus be tithing from tithed produce for untithed produce, or from produce which is exempt for produce which is liable, but this is forbidden; cf. Ter. I, 5; B.M. 56*a*. (2) Because produce does not become liable to *Ḥallah*, except when turned into dough (cf. Ḥal. II, 5); so that even if the wheat was bought from two different persons, it became liable to *Ḥallah* only after it had come into the possession of the baker. (3) The dealer may have bought the bread in the different moulds from different people. Therefore if he tithed from one mould for another, he may be tithing from produce which is exempt for produce which is liable. (4) The dealer usually buys his bread from one baker. (5) A dealer who has the sole right of selling bread to the public. He usually buys from various bakers.

°See Corrigenda.

MISHNAH 5. IF A MAN BOUGHT FROM A POOR MAN[6] (LIKEWISE IF A POOR MAN WAS GIVEN SLICES OF BREAD OR PIECES OF FIG-CAKE) HE MUST TITHE EVERY PIECE;[7] BUT IN THE CASE OF DATES AND DRIED FIGS HE MAY MIX THEM TOGETHER AND TAKE [THE TITHES FROM THE MIXTURE]. R. JUDAH SAID: HE MAY DO SO ONLY WHEN THE POOR MAN WAS GIVEN A LARGE QUANTITY; BUT WHEN THE GIFT WAS SMALL [IN QUANTITY] HE MUST TITHE EACH KIND SEPARATELY.

MISHNAH 6. IF A MAN BOUGHT FROM A WHOLESALE MERCHANT[8] ONCE AND THEN AGAIN, HE MAY NOT GIVE TITHES FROM THE ONE [PURCHASE] FOR THE OTHER, EVEN WHEN BOTH CAME FROM THE SAME HAMPER AND BOTH ARE OF THE SAME KIND. BUT THE WHOLESALE MERCHANT MAY BE TRUSTED IF HE SAYS THAT BOTH CAME FROM ONE MAN.

a *MISHNAH* 7. IF A MAN BOUGHT FROM A LANDOWNER[1] ONCE AND THEN AGAIN, HE MAY GIVE TITHES FROM THE ONE [PURCHASE] FOR THE OTHER,[2] EVEN WHEN THEY CAME FROM TWO BASKETS AND EVEN FROM TWO TOWNS. IF A LANDOWNER SOLD VEGETABLES IN THE MARKET, [HE THAT BOUGHT FROM HIM] MAY GIVE TITHES FROM ONE [LOT OF VEGETABLES] FOR ALL [THE OTHER LOTS] IF THEY WERE [ALL] BROUGHT TO THE LANDOWNER FROM HIS OWN GARDENS; BUT [IF THEY WERE BROUGHT] FROM OTHER GARDENS, THE PURCHASER MUST TITHE EACH LOT SEPARATELY.

MISHNAH 8. IF A MAN BOUGHT UNTITHED PRODUCE[3] FROM TWO PLACES HE MAY GIVE TITHES FROM ONE LOT FOR THE OTHER. ALTHOUGH THEY HAVE PERMITTED [THIS, NEVERTHELESS] ONE MAY NOT SELL UNTITHED PRODUCE[4] EXCEPT IN THE CASE OF A NECESSITY.[5]

MISHNAH 9. TITHES MAY BE GIVEN FROM PRODUCE [BOUGHT] FROM AN ISRAELITE FOR PRODUCE [BOUGHT] FROM A GENTILE,[6] FROM PRODUCE [BOUGHT] FROM A GENTILE FOR PRODUCE [BOUGHT] FROM AN ISRAELITE, FROM PRODUCE [BOUGHT] FROM AN ISRAELITE FOR PRODUCE [BOUGHT] FROM CUTHEANS,[7] AND FROM PRODUCE [BOUGHT] FROM CUTHEANS FOR PRODUCE [BOUGHT] FROM [OTHER] CUTHEANS. R. ELIEZER PROHIBITS [THE TITHING] FROM PRODUCE [BOUGHT] FROM CUTHEANS FOR PRODUCE [BOUGHT] FROM
b [OTHER] CUTHEANS.[1]

MISHNAH 10. A PERFORATED POT[2] IS CONSIDERED AS THE SOIL[3] [ITSELF]. IF A MAN GAVE TERUMAH FROM [PRODUCE GROWN IN] THE SOIL FOR [PRODUCE GROWN IN] A PERFORATED POT, OR FROM [PRODUCE GROWN IN] A PERFORATED POT FOR [PRODUCE GROWN IN] THE SOIL, THE TERUMAH IS VALID. [IF HE GAVE TERUMAH] FROM [PRODUCE GROWN IN] A POT THAT WAS NOT PERFORATED FOR [PRODUCE GROWN IN] A POT THAT WAS PERFORATED, [IT BECOMES] TERUMAH,[4]

(6) Who begs from door to door. (7) To prevent tithing from what is exempt for what is liable. (8) Who buys from different people.

a (1) Lit., 'a householder', who sells the produce of his own fields. (2) Both purchases are either tithed or untithed. (3) Lit., '*tebel*,' but not quite in its stricter sense of produce from which neither *terumah* nor tithes have been separated;* cf. Introd. p. 50. (4) Even to an associate. (5) As when some tithed produce was mixed up with *tebel* which can only be set right by finding for it *Terumah* and Tithes from another similar lot; cf. Men. 31*a*. But if the owner has not got other similar produce, he must sell the mixture to one who has. (6) According to this *halachah*, produce grown by a Gentile in the soil of the Land of Israel is liable to the duty of tithes; cf. B.M. 101*a*. (7) Cf. III, 4, n. 8. Samaritans usually tithe the produce they keep for their own use, but not the produce they keep for sale.

b (1) One Cuthean may have sold tithed produce which he had originally intended for his own use, whilst the other Cuthean sold untithed produce. In tithing from one for the other, one may be tithing the exempt for the liable. (2) A pot with holes in the bottom, filled with soil, and used for growing plants. (3) Produce grown in it is liable to the laws of *Terumah* and Tithes. (4) In name, and therefore can be eaten only by a priest; but it is not valid to discharge the produce of the other pot from the duty of *terumah*.

*See Corrigenda.

א) בבא מציעא פ"ד נו. ב) מנחות פ"י דף ע. יבמות פ"י דף פט: קדושין פ"ב דף מו.

ד פלטר · הוא הלוקח מן הנחתומין ככרות הרבה בבת אחת ומוכר בשוק ור' מאיר ור' יהודה סברתן הפוכה בפלטר מנחתום דר"מ סבר דנחתום מחד גברא זבין התבואה אע"פ שעושה דפוסין הרבה ואפילו של אמש בשל יום ור' יהודה סבר כל יומא מחד גברא זבין וגבי פלטר סבר ר"מ *דיכול לקנות מב' נחתומין וכל נחתום עושה דפוס שלו ור' יהודה סבר דרך פלטר לקנות מנחתום אחד הלכך אם יש כאן כמה דפוסין מנחתום אחד היו ובלבד שלא יהא של אמש בשל יום דאפי' בנחתום עצמו אסור והכי איתא בירושלמי (הל' ד) ר"מ אומר נחתום עושה דפוס אחד ופלטר מסתמש בכמה נחתומים כלומר שאע"פ שהנחתום עושה כמה דפוסין כדקתני מתני' מ"מ לעולם

ד א) הלוקח מן הפלטר מעשר מכל טפוס וטפוס דברי ר"מ ר' יהודה אומר אמאחת על הכל מודה רבי יהודה בלוקח מן המנפול שהוא מעשר מכל אחד ואחד: ה בהלוקח מן העני וכן העני שנתנו לו פרוסות פת או פלחי דבלה מעשר מכל אחד ואחד ובתמרים ובגרוגרות בולל (*ואוכל) ונוטל אמר רבי יהודה גאימתי בזמן שמתנה מרובה אבל בזמן שמתנה מועטת מעשר מכל אחד ואחד: ו דהלוקח מן הסיטון וחזר ולקח ממנו שניה לא יעשר מזה על זה אפילו מאותו הסוג אפילו מאותו המין נאמן הסיטון לומר משל אחד הם: ז ההלוקח מבעל הבית וחזר ולקח ממנו שניה מעשר מזה על זה אפי' מב' קופות אפי' מב' עיירות ובעה"ב שהיה מוכר ירק בשוק בזמן שמביאין לו מגנותיו מעשר מאחת על הכל ומגנות אחרות מעשר מכל אחד ואחד: ח זהלוקח טבל משני מקומות מעשר מזה על זה אע"פ שאמרו האין אדם רשאי למכור טבל אלא לצורך: ט מעשרין משל ישראל על של נכרים משל נכרים על של ישראל משל ישראל על של כותים משל כותים על של כותים ר' אליעזר אוסר משל כותים על של כותים: י טעציץ נקוב הרי זה כארץ יתרם מהארץ על עציץ נקוב מעציץ נקוב על הארץ תרומתו תרומה כ) משאינו נקוב על הנקוב תרומה

פי' מהר"י בן מלכי צדק

המוקף: ד הלוקח מן הפלטר. פי' בלבד בו ביום דהיינו חם. [פלטר] פי' בלע"ז פסטיר. ר"מ סבר נחתום עושה דפוס אחד ופלטר משתמש מכמה נחתומין אהכי מעשר מכל טפוס וטפוס. פי' טפוס פורמא כדגרסינן באתרוג לא ינדלנו בדפוס. ר' יהודה סבר נחתום עושה כמה טפוסין ופלטר

ד א שם הלכה ו: ז"ל דדרכן
ה ב ג מיי' פי"ד מהל' מעשר הלכה ח:
ו ד שם הלכה א:
ז ה שם הלכה ג:
ח ו שם הלכה ד:
ט ז מיי' פ"ו שם הלכה יא טוש"ע יו"ד סימן שלא סעיף קכ:

מזה על זה: י הרי הוא כארץ · ופירותיו טבל מדאורייתא (ה): משאינו נקוב על הנקוב · בפרק האשה רבה (דף פט·) ובפ' האיש מקדש (דף מו·) מפרש לה:

תורמין ומעשרין מזה על זה: י עציץ נקוב הרי הוא כארץ. ומעשרותיו מעשר ותרומתו מדמעת וחייבין עליה חומש: ומשאינו נקוב על הנקוב תרומה ויחזור ויתרום. א"ר בון בר חייה בשם ר' זירא עציץ שאינו נקוב עשו אותו כדמאי והנקוב כודאי. פירוש כמה דאת אמר תרם מן הדמאי על הודאי תרומה ויחזור ויתרום כן הכא משאינו נקוב על הנקוב תרומה ויחזור ויתרום מן

תרומה ויחזור ויתרום מן הנקוב על שאינו נקוב תרומה ולא תאכל עד שיוציא עליה תרומות ומעשרות: **יא** תרם (ז) מן הדמאי על הדמאי מדמאי על הודאי תרומה ויחזור ויתרום מן הודאי על הדמאי תרומה ולא תאכל עד שיוציא עליה תרומות ומעשרות:

פרק ששי

א המקבל שדה מישראל מן העובד כוכבים מן הכותי יחלק לפניהם החוכר שדה מישראל תורם ונותן לו א"ר יהודה אימתי בזמן שנתן לו מאותה השדה ומאותו המין אבל אם נתן לו משדה אחרת או ממין אחר מעשר ונותן לו: **ב** החוכר שדה מן הנכרי (ד) מעשר ונותן לו ר' (א) יהודה אומר אף המקבל שדה אבותיו מן הנכרי מעשר ונותן לו: **ג** כהן ולוי שקבלו שדה מישראל כשם שחולקין בחולין כך חולקין בתרומה ר' אליעזר אומר אף המעשרו' שלהן שע"מ כן באו: **ד** ישראל שקבל מכהן ומלוי המעשרות לבעלים ר' ישמעאל אומר הקרתני שקבל שדה מירושלמי מעשר שני של ירושלמי וחכמים אומרים יכול הוא הקרתני לעלות ולאכלו בירושלים: **ה** המקבל זיתים (ו) לשמן כשם שחולקין בחולין כך חולקין בתרומה ר' יהודה אומר ישראל שקבל מכהן ומלוי זיתים לשמן למחצית שכר המעשרות לבעלים: **ו** ב"ש אומרים לא ימכור אדם את זיתיו

BUT HE MUST GIVE TERUMAH OVER AGAIN. [IF HE GAVE TERUMAH] FROM [PRODUCE GROWN IN] A PERFORATED POT FOR [PRODUCE GROWN IN] A POT WHICH WAS NOT PERFORATED, [IT BECOMES] TERUMAH, BUT MAY NOT BE EATEN[5] EXCEPT HE FIRST GAVE AGAIN TERUMAH AND TITHES FOR IT.

MISHNAH 11. IF A MAN GAVE TERUMAH FROM [PRODUCE OF] DEMAI FOR [OTHER PRODUCE OF] DEMAI, OR FROM [PRODUCE OF] DEMAI FOR [PRODUCE] WHICH WAS CERTAINLY UNTITHED, [THIS BECOMES] TERUMAH, BUT HE MUST GIVE TERUMAH OVER AGAIN.[6] [IF HE GAVE TERUMAH] FROM [PRODUCE] WHICH WAS CERTAINLY UNTITHED FOR [PRODUCE OF] DEMAI, [THIS BECOMES] TERUMAH, BUT IT MAY NOT BE EATEN[5] EXCEPT HE FIRST GAVE AGAIN TERUMAH AND TITHES FOR IT.

CHAPTER VI

MISHNAH 1. IF A MAN RENTED A FIELD FROM AN ISRAELITE, OR FROM A GENTILE, OR FROM A CUTHEAN [FOR A
a SHARE IN THE PRODUCE],[1] HE MAY SET THE [LANDLORD'S] SHARE BEFORE HIM [UNTITHED].[2] IF A MAN HIRED A FIELD FROM AN ISRAELITE [FOR A FIXED RENTAL OUT OF THE PRODUCE],[3] HE MUST FIRST GIVE TERUMAH [FROM THE RENTAL][4] AND THEN GIVE IT TO THE LANDLORD.[5] R. JUDAH SAID: THIS APPLIES ONLY WHEN HE PAYS HIM [THE RENTAL WITH PRODUCE] OF THE SAME FIELD AND OF THE SAME KIND; BUT WHEN HE PAYS HIM WITH THE PRODUCE OF ANOTHER FIELD OR OF ANOTHER KIND, HE MUST [ALSO] TITHE [THE RENTAL FIRST] AND THEN GIVE IT TO HIM.[6]

MISHNAH 2. IF A MAN HIRED A FIELD FROM A GENTILE [FOR A FIXED RENTAL OUT OF THE PRODUCE], HE MUST [FIRST] TITHE [THE RENTAL] AND THEN GIVE IT TO HIM.[7] R. JUDAH SAYS: ALSO IF A MAN RENTED FROM A GENTILE A FIELD WHICH HAD FORMERLY BELONGED TO HIS FATHERS[8] [FOR A SHARE IN THE PRODUCE], HE MUST FIRST TITHE THE RENTAL[9] AND THEN GIVE IT TO HIM.

MISHNAH 3. IF A PRIEST OR A LEVITE RENTED A FIELD FROM AN ISRAELITE [FOR A SHARE IN THE PRODUCE], THE
b TENANTS SHARE WITH THE LANDLORD THE TERUMAH[1] JUST AS THEY SHARE THE COMMON PRODUCE. R. ELIEZER SAYS: ALSO THE TITHES[2] BELONG TO THE TENANTS, FOR THEY ENTERED THE FIELD WITH THIS EXPECTATION.

MISHNAH 4. IF AN ISRAELITE RENTED A FIELD FROM A PRIEST OR FROM A LEVITE [FOR A SHARE IN THE PRODUCE,] THE TITHES BELONG TO THE LANDLORD.[3] R. ISHMAEL SAYS: IF AN INHABITANT OF THE PROVINCES RENTED A FIELD FROM AN INHABITANT OF JERUSALEM, THE SECOND TITHE BELONGS TO THE INHABITANT OF JERUSALEM.[4] BUT THE SAGES SAY: THE INHABITANT OF THE PROVINCES IS ABLE TO GO UP HIMSELF AND EAT THE SECOND TITHE IN JERUSALEM.

MISHNAH 5. IF [AN ISRAELITE] RENTED OLIVE TREES [FROM A PRIEST OR A LEVITE] FOR THE OIL, HE AND THE LANDLORD SHARE THE TERUMAH[5] JUST AS THEY SHARE THE COMMON PRODUCE. R. JUDAH SAYS: IF AN ISRAELITE RENTED OLIVE TREES FROM A PRIEST OR A LEVITE FOR THE OIL FOR A SHARE OF HALF THE PROFIT, THE TITHES BELONG TO THE LANDLORD.[6]

MISHNAH 6. BETH SHAMMAI SAY: A MAN MAY ONLY SELL HIS OLIVES TO AN ASSOCIATE.[7] BUT BETH HILLEL SAY: ONE

(5) Even by priests, because it is still *tebel*. (6) The *terumah* he gave from *demai* is not valid to discharge the other produce from the duty of *terumah*, because the *demai* from which the *terumah* was taken may have been set right originally by its former owner, and the present owner may thus be giving *terumah* from what is exempt for what is liable.
a (1) מקבל viz., באריסות; cf. Mishnah 8. (2) But he must tell the landlord that his share is untithed. (3) חוכר. (4) Because the produce becomes liable to *terumah* while still in the threshing-floor; but not tithes, which the landlord must give himself. (5) After deducting the amount of the *terumah* from the rental. (6) In this case he is like one paying a debt with his own produce, and therefore he is bound to tithe the produce before it leaves his possession. (7) This rule is intended to make it unprofitable for a Jew to rent the field from the Gentile, originally confiscated from another Jew; and this may induce the Gentile to sell his field to the Jew rather than leave it uncultivated. (8) And which the Gentile had seized by violence. (9) In order to lead to the sale of the field by the Gentile; cf. n. 7.
b (1) Including also the tithe. The landlord may give them to any other priest or Levite he likes. (2) Including the *terumah*. (3) It must be presumed that when the landlord leased his field he reserved the tithe for himself. (4) The landlord must have reserved the Second Tithe for himself, since it can only be consumed in Jerusalem. (5) In the case of trees the *terumah*, and also the tithe, belong to both landlord and tenant according to their respective shares. (6) And also the *terumah*. R. Judah holds that trees must be treated in the same way as the field in Mishnah 4. (7) An *'am ha-areẓ* may cause them to be defiled when they are pressed.

MAY SELL THEM ALSO TO A MAN WHO ONLY GIVES TITHES.[8] HOWBEIT, THE PIOUS AMONG BETH HILLEL USED TO ACT IN ACCORDANCE WITH THE OPINION OF BETH SHAMMAI.

MISHNAH 7. IF TWO MEN GATHERED [THE FRUIT OF]
a THEIR VINEYARDS INTO ONE VAT,[1] [OF WHOM] ONE GIVES TITHES AND THE OTHER DOES NOT GIVE TITHES, HE WHO GIVES TITHES MAY TITHE HIS OWN SHARE[2] AND [TAKE] HIS SHARE WHEREVER IT MAY BE.

MISHNAH 8. IF TWO MEN RENTED A FIELD [FOR A SHARE IN THE PRODUCE], OR IF THEY INHERITED [THE FIELD] OR BECAME PARTNERS IN IT, THE ONE [WHO GIVES TITHES] MAY SAY TO THE OTHER [WHO DOES NOT GIVE TITHES]: 'YOU TAKE THE WHEAT WHICH IS IN THIS PLACE AND I WILL TAKE THE WHEAT WHICH IS IN THAT PLACE', OR: 'YOU TAKE THE WINE WHICH IS IN THIS PLACE AND I WILL TAKE THE WINE WHICH IS IN THAT PLACE';[3] BUT HE MAY NOT SAY TO HIM: 'YOU TAKE THE WHEAT AND I WILL TAKE THE BARLEY', OR: 'YOU TAKE THE WINE AND I WILL TAKE THE OIL.'[4]

MISHNAH 9. IF AN ASSOCIATE AND AN 'AM HA-AREẒ INHERITED [THE PROPERTY OF] THEIR FATHER WHO WAS AN 'AM HA-AREẒ, THE ASSOCIATE MAY SAY TO HIS BROTHER: 'YOU TAKE THE WHEAT WHICH IS IN THIS PLACE AND I WILL TAKE THE WHEAT WHICH IS IN THAT PLACE', OR: 'YOU TAKE THE WINE WHICH IS IN THIS PLACE AND I WILL TAKE THE WINE WHICH IS IN THAT PLACE'; BUT HE MAY NOT[5] SAY TO HIM: 'YOU TAKE THE WHEAT AND I WILL TAKE THE BARLEY,' OR: 'YOU TAKE THE MOIST PRODUCE AND I WILL TAKE THE
b DRY[1] PRODUCE'.

MISHNAH 10. IF A PROSELYTE AND A GENTILE INHERITED [THE PROPERTY OF] THEIR FATHER WHO WAS A GENTILE, THE PROSELYTE MAY SAY TO HIS BROTHER:[2] 'YOU TAKE THE IDOLS[3] AND I WILL TAKE THE MONEY', OR: 'YOU TAKE THE WINE[3] AND I WILL TAKE THE FRUIT': BUT IF ANY [PART OF THE INHERITANCE] HAD ALREADY COME INTO THE POSSESSION OF THE PROSELYTE, HE IS FORBIDDEN[4] [TO SAY SO].

MISHNAH 11. IF A MAN SOLD FRUIT IN SYRIA[5] AND DECLARED THAT IT WAS GROWN IN THE LAND OF ISRAEL, THE PURCHASER IS BOUND TO TITHE IT.[6] [BUT IF HE ADDED THAT] IT HAD ALREADY BEEN TITHED, HE MAY BE TRUSTED, 'BECAUSE THE EVIDENCE[7] WHICH MADE IT UNLAWFUL IS THE SAME EVIDENCE WHICH MADE IT LAWFUL'. [IF HE SAID: 'THE FRUIT IS] FROM MY OWN FIELD',[8] THE PURCHASER IS BOUND TO TITHE IT. [BUT IF HE ADDED:] 'IT HAS ALREADY BEEN TITHED', HE MAY BE TRUSTED, 'BECAUSE THE EVIDENCE WHICH MADE IT UNLAWFUL IS THE SAME EVIDENCE WHICH MADE IT LAWFUL'. IF IT WAS KNOWN THAT HE HAD ANOTHER
c FIELD IN SYRIA, THE PURCHASER IS BOUND[1] TO TITHE IT.

(8) And who does not observe the laws of purity.

a (1) To press it together; and they pressed out the wine together. (2) Which is now mixed up with the other's share. According to the Palestinian Gemara he must also give tithe out of his own share for his fellow's share, as for *demai* produce. (3) So that the one who gives tithes need only tithe his own share. (4) For this would be like exchanging or selling one kind of produce for another, in which case the one who gives tithes would have to tithe also the produce he assigns to his partner who does not give tithes. (5) For the reason given in the last note.

b (1) Which is not susceptible to uncleanness; cf. II, 3, n. 1. (2) The right of a proselyte to inherit his father's property is based only on Rabbinic law. Therefore the strict law laid down in the case of an associate and an '*am ha-areẓ* inheriting from their father is relaxed in the case of the proselyte, in order not to cause him a loss of property which might lead him to relapse back into heathenism; cf. Ḳid. 17*b*; 'A. Z. 64*a*. (3) It is prohibited to derive any benefit from idols, and also from heathen wine which may have been used for libation to the idols; cf. 'A. Z. III, 1; II, 3. (4) It has become his property, therefore such an exchange would involve deriving a benefit from the idols and their wine. (5) Syria, which was conquered by David (II Sam. VIII, 10) and not by the whole nation under Joshua, was not considered a heathen country, but it did not possess the sanctity of the Land of Israel; cf. 'A. Z. 21*a*. To the produce sold in Syria the laws of *demai* did not apply, as most of the produce sold there came from outside Palestine. (6) As *demai*. (7) Lit., 'the mouth'. If you believe his statement that the produce came from the Land of Israel, which renders the produce liable to tithes as *demai*, you must also believe his statement that the produce had already been tithed; cf. 'Ed. II, 6. (Sonc. ed. 5*a* n. a 4). (8) Situated in Syria.

c (1) The produce would be liable to tithes even without the vendor's admission, so the above argument does not apply.

אלא לחבר בה"א אף למעשר וצנועי ב"ה היו נוהגין כדברי ב"ש: ז [א]שנים שבצרו את כרמיהם לתוך גת אחת אחד מעשר וא' שאינו מעשר המעשר מעשר את שלו וחלקו בכל מקום שהוא: ח [ב]שנים שקבלו שדה באריסות או שירשו או שנשתתפו יכול הוא לומר טול אתה חטים שבמקום פלוני ואני חטים שבמקום פלוני אתה יין שבמקום פלוני ואני יין שבמקום פלוני אבל לא יאמר לו טול אתה חטים ואני שעורים טול אתה יין ואני (אטול) שמן: ט [ג]חבר (א) ועם הארץ שירשו את אביהם עם הארץ יכול הוא לומר לו טול אתה חטים שבמקום פלוני ואני חטים שבמקום פלוני אתה יין שבמקום פלוני ואני יין שבמקום פלוני אבל לא יאמר לו טול אתה חטים ואני שעורים טול אתה הלח ואני (אטול את) היבש: י [ד]גר (ב) ועכו"ם שירשו את אביהם עכו"ם יכול הוא לומר טול אתה ע"א ואני מעות אתה יין ואני פירות ואם משבאו לרשות הגר אסור: יא [ה]המוכר פירות בסוריא ואמר משל א"י הן חייב לעשר מעושרין הן נאמן שהפה שאסר הוא הפה שהתיר משלי הן חייב לעשר מעושרין הן נאמן שהפה שאסר הוא הפה שהתיר ואם ידוע שיש לו שדה אחת בסוריא חייב לעשר: יב (ג) [ו]עם הארץ

ר"ש — אלא לחבר · פרוש שעושה בטהרה: אף למעשר · שקיבל עליו לעשר אף על פי שלא קיבל עליו טהרות: צנועי בית הלל · שהשירים שמחמירין על עצמן: ירושלמי (הל' ה) אמר רבי יוחנן טעמא דבית הלל דרך בני אדם לאכול זיתיהן עטונין וכן דרך בני אדם על ידי עילה בית הלל לדעתיהון דתנן לא ימכור לו פרה החורשת בשביעית ובית הלל מתירין מפני שיכול לשחטה ואורחיה דבר נש מיכוס תורא דידיה אלא על ידי עילה פי' עטונין מלשון מעטן של זיתים כלומר בעוד שלא הוכשרו ופריך וכי דרך בני אדם לאכול כן ומשני על ידי עילה מועטת התירו וב"ה לטעמייהו דשרי במס' שביעית (פרק ה משנה ח) למכור פרה להרוש ובפ' קמא דע"א מייתי לה (דף טו:): (א) ז מעשר את שלו · אבל בשל חבירו לא מחייב דאין זה נחשב כמוכר דאסור למכור טבל: וחלקו בכל מקום שהוא · דבכל מקום שחלקו שם יהא זה תרומה ומעשר עליו כדמשמע הלשון (ה) אבל בירושלמי שיטה אחרת: ירושלמי (שם) א"ר אליעזר דר' מאיר הוא דאמר לא התירו למכור דמאי אלא לסיטון בלבד הוא פתר לה כמעשר מעשר את שלו ודאי וחלקו בכל מקום שהוא דמאי ר' יונה בעי מוכר ודאי ומתקן דמאי לית לך אלא כי הא דא"ר יוחנן דברי הכל היא המעשר מעשר את שלו ודאי וחלקו בכל מקום שהוא דמאי וחצי חלקו שביד חבירו עביד דמאי פי' ר' אליעזר משום דאין ברירה חשיב כמוכר לחבירו וחלקו בכל מקום שהוא דקתני אחלק חברו קאי דחייב המעשר לתקן חלק חבירו מדין דמאי דשמא חלקו ביד חבירו וחלק חבירו בידו והמעשרו' בידו והמעשרות שמחמת דמאי מעשרן וכן שלו דהמוציא מחבירו עליו הראיה והא דחשיב ליה כמוכר דמאי אע"פ שאם חלקו ביד חבירו ודאי הוא קודם שיעשר מכל מקום קרי ליה דמאי לפי שהוא ספק דשמא חלקו בידו הוא ואין כאן מוכר ולמאן דשרי דמאי משום ספק האי נמי שרי דספק מוכר הוא ויש לפרש דאתיא אפילו כמאן דאמר יש ברירה וכגון שכל אחד בצר כרמו המיוחד לו ושניהן לגת אחת דכי האי גוונא א"א שלא יהא לכל א' חצי חלק חבירו אלא שלא יתיישב כ"כ הא דחשיב ליה מוכר ור' *יוחנן לא בעי למימר שיהא חייב לתקן כל חלקו מטעם ודאי וחלק חבירו מטעם דמאי דלא דמי למוכר כל חלקו ודברי הכל הוא דשום תנא לא שרי למכור ודאי אלא הכי קאמר וחלקו של עם הארץ בכ"מ שהוא דמאי הלכך האי חלקו של עם הארץ שביד המעשר דמאי הוא וחייב המעשר לתקן כדין דמאי דמה שבידו נחשב כאילו חצי משלו וחצי משל חבירו דמאחר דאין ברירה יש לכל אחד חלק במה שביד חבירו ורבי יוחנן לטעמיה דאמר בריש כל הגט (דף כה.) אין ברירה (ט): ח טול אתה חטים שבמקום פלוני · למאי דאמרן לעיל היה ראוי לאסור כאן ושמא יש לחלק משום דלעיל לתוך גת אחת וכאן בב' מקומות (י) אבל בירושלמי (הל' ו) מייתי עלה תני ישראל ונכרי שקנו שדה בסוריא הרי הוא כטבל ומעשר מעורבין זה בזה דברי רבי רשב"ג אומר חלק ישראל חייב חלק נכרי פטור ומסיק עלה ר' יוחנן בשחלקו שדה בקמותיה דאמר זהו חלקו המגיעו אבל חלקו עומרים אף רשב"ג מודה לר' שכל קלח וקלח של שותפות הוא משמע מתני' דהכא נמי בכי האי גוונא איירי אע"ג דקתני חטין ויין ואפי' הכי יין ושמן אסור דנראה [כמוכרים מחלקם] זה לזה: ט שירשו את אביהן ע"ה הא כבר תנא ליה רישא או שירשו והא דתני ליה הכא משום דבעי למיתני גר ונכרי שירשו את אביהם נכרי ועוד משום דקתני הכא לא ויבש דאסור למכור לעם הארץ לח ויבש כדתנן לעיל בפרק ב' (משנה ג)(יא): י טול אתה ע"א ואני מעות אתה יין ואני פירות · בפרק בתרא דע"א (דף סד.) רוצה לדקדק מכאן שרוצה בקיומא דע"א ויין נסך שרי בחילופיהן ודחי מתני' בע"א המתחלקת לפי שבריה ויין נסך בחרס הדרייני ופריך והא רוצה בקיומן שלא יאבדו ומסיק שאני ירושת גר דאקילו ביה רבנן שמא יחזור לסורו ולפי המסקנא ניהא הא דתני בירושלמי (הל' ז) ישראל ונכרי שקנו ביתו של נכרי והיה שם יין נסך וע"א ומעות לא יאמר לו טול אתה היין ועבודת אלילים ואני מעות והתם פריך מתני' פליגא בתמיה ומשני ליה הא פליגי אם משבאו לרשות הגר אסור והכא מכיון שקנה כמו שנכנס לרשותו ולפי מה שחילקנו משום דהקלו בירושת הגר לא היה צריך לטעם הזה אלא רוצה ליישב אפי' אם ת"ל דרוצה בקיומא שרי מכ"מ אסור בחילופיהן ועד שלא באו לרשותו דשרי משום דירושת הגר דרבנן דמהכא דייק לה בפרק קמא דקידושין (דף יז:) דאמר דאי סלקא דעתא דאורייתא שלא באו לרשותו נמי כי קא שקיל חליפי ע"א שקיל אבל לעיל גבי חבר ועם הארץ שירשו אביהן עם הארץ לא מפליג בטול אתה חטין ואני שעורים בין עד שלא באו לרשותו למשבאו לרשותו כיון דירושה דאורייתא היא וכי האי גוונא תני בתוספתא (פ"ו) גבי מרחץ דגר ונכרי שירשו את אביהם (ג)(ירשו) *(מרחץ אינו רשאי לומר לו טול אתה שבת בחלקך ואני חול בחלקי (ג) ואם התנה עמו *במנת כן מותר והתם נמי טעמא משום דירושת גר מדרבנן אבל לקחו כמו שבאו לרשותו ומכאן הקשה רבינו תם) א] להא דאמרי בשילהי פ' קמא דע"א (דף כב:) ישראל ונכרי שקבלו שדה בשותפות לא יאמר לו טול אתה חלקך בשבת ואני חלקי בחול ואם התנו מתחלה מותר לדוקא גבי שדה הוא דאסריכן בלא התנו משום דחלקו של ישראל מיתקן במלאכה שהנכרי עושה בשבת אבל תנור בלא התנו נמי שרי ולא יתכן כלל דהא מרחץ נמי כתנור דמי וקאסר ליה בתוספתא: יא שהפה שאסר הוא הפה שהתיר · דנאמן לומר עישרתים מגו דאי בעי אמר של חוצה לארץ הם דבחוצה לארץ לא גזרו על הדמאי כדתנן לעיל בפרק קמא (משנה ג): שיש לו שדה בסוריא חייב לעשר · דכיון דיש לו שדה בסוריא לא מהימן לומר של חוצה לארץ הם אע"פ שרוב פירות שבסוריא מחוצה לארץ באים האי כיון דיש לו שדה סתמא משל שדהו הן וחייב לעשר דכיבוש יחיד שמיה כיבוש ואפי' לאו שמיה כיבוש בסוריא גזרו על הדמאי דלא פטרו אלא מכזיב ולהלן אם יש לו שדה. בירושלמי (הל' ח) אמר בון בר חייא ושיהו מכניסין משלו כלומר אותה שדה שבסוריא: יב עם הארץ שאמר לחבר שהיה הולך חבר לשוק ליקח לו ירק לעצמו ואמר לו עם הארץ קח גם לי אגודה של ירק ולקח חבר שתי אגודות סתם ולא פירש זו לי וזו לעם הארץ פטור אותה שנתן לעם הארץ דיש ברירה כשנתנה לעם הארץ שזו היא שלקחה מתחלה לצרכו ואין חבר מחליפה בשלו כדמוכח בפ' בכל מערבין (דף לז:) יהתם אייתי ברייתא אין צריך לעשר דברי רבי יוסי וחכמים אומרים צריך לעשר ומסיק איפוך משום דשמעינן ליה לר' יוסי דלית ליה ברירה ובירושל' (הל' ט) משמע לטעמא לאו משום ברירה *ואפי' באגודה אחת פליגי שלא קנה חבר לעצמו כלום ומייתי ברייתא דרבי יוסי פוטר ורבי יהודה אומר צריך לעשר ור' יהודה סבר לא נתכוון מוכר לזכות אלא לנוקח דרבי יוסי סבר לא נתכוון לזכות אלא לבעל המעות ופריך עלה מהא דתניא בכתובות בפרק אלמנה ניזונית (דף נח:) הוסיף לו אחת יתירה הכל נשליח דברי ר' יהודה

ר"מ — ובית הלל אומרים שמותר למכרן למי שהוא נאמן על המעשרות ואף על פי שלא יהיה נאמן על הטומאה לפי שדעת בית הלל שמותר לגרום טומאה לחולין שבארץ ישראל וזו היא משנה אחרונה שהוא מותר וכן הלכה: וצנועי ב"ה · הם הם המדקדקים במצות מחבורות הלל: ז כבר בארנו בגמ' גמר זה המשנה ואמרו המעשר מעשר את שלו ודאי וחלקו בכל מקום שהוא דמאי וענין הדבר כי כשיבצרו הענבים מוציא מעשר ודאי מחלקו ולכשידרוך אותם עם חלק חבירו שאינו מעושר ונתערב הכל ולקח חלקו מן התירוש חייב להוציא ממנו מעשר דמאי המחויב לחצי מה שלקח מן התירוש לפי שהספק אינו אלא בחצי של חבירו שאינו מעושר וזה ענין מה שאמר וחלקו בכל מקום שהוא דמאי ר"ל חלק חבירו שאינו מעושר בכל מקום שהוא ממונו ואע"פ שאינו מיוחד והוא מעורב לפיכך יוציא מעשר דמאי שנתחייב בו אותו החלק: ח אלו הדינין שהוא זוכר בכאן אין בהם דבר מענין איסור והיתר *אבל הם בדיני ממונות וזכר אותם בכאן מפני שנתגלגל הענין בשותפות הקרקעות כמו שנזכר במסכת פאה שכיב מרע שכתב כל נכסיו וכל מה שנחבר אליו מן הדינין אבל יתקיים זה הדין שזכר שיהיו שני מינין מן החטה או מן היין שוין ולא יהיה ביניהם שום חלוף ושינוי אלא מקומותיהם ואז יהיה רשות לאחד מן השותפין או מן היורשין לומר לחבירו אחר שיין זה כמו היין ההוא וזה קרוב למקומי ושלך קרוב למקומך קח אתה היין שיש שם ואני אקח זה ואל תצריכני שאקח אני הרחוק ממני ואצטרך לשאתו ולא יוכל חבירו למנוע ממנו שאין היזק אליו בדבר ההוא שהעיקר אצלנו כופין על מדת סדום ר"ל דבר שיועיל לרעך ולא יזיק לך יכריחוך עליו כי מניעת דבר זה הוא ממדת אנשי סדום אך אם יש לחבירו בקחתו היין ההוא מן המקום שאמר לו שום היזק לא יכריחהו עליו: ט מבואר הוא שכל אחד מהם יש לו החצי בכל. הגמלא מנכסי אביהם וכשיאמר לו החבר טול אתה חטים ואני שעורים נמצא מוכר לו החבר חצי חטים שירש מאביו בחצי השעורים של עם הארץ ומחליף עמו ונמצא מוכר דמאי כי אביהם שמת עם הארץ ופירותיו דמאי וכבר הקדמתי לך שאסור למכור דמאי לע"ה: י יין העכו"ם הוא נסך ועוד יתבאר לך במקומות מן המשנה שיין נסך וע"א אסורין בהנאה והתירו לגר לומר לעכו"ם טול אתה ע"א ואני מעות ולא התיר כזה במה שנזכר למעלה בענין חבר וע"ה וזה כי חבר וע"ה יורשין את אביהם מן התורה וגר אינו יורש את אביו מן התורה לפי שאין ביניהם קורבא שהדת הבדיל ביניהם אבל ירשנו בתקנת החכמים שמא ימיר ויחזור לדתו כדי שירש את אביו וע"כ התירו לו החליפין כל זמן שלא הגיע חלקו לידו אבל הגיע חלקו לידו אותו הדבר האסור לא התירו לו להחליפו באחר לפי שזכה זכות גמורה לדבר ההוא והוא אסור בהנאה ויתחייב באיבודו: יא סוריא · היא הארץ אשר נכבשה ונתחלקה במלכות דוד ואינה כמו ארץ ישראל ולא כמו חולה לארץ והיא כא"י במקצת הדינין וכמו חולה לארץ בענינים אחרים ועוד יתבאר זה במקומות מן המשנה והעיקר אצלנו שכל מה שיכבשוהו הרבים הוא כמו ארץ ישראל בכל הדינין והוא הנקרא כיבוש רבים ומה שלא נמנה ארץ סוריא להיות במעלת ארץ ישראל בכל ענין הוא מה שאמר מפני שאינו מותר להלחם על ארץ מכל הארצות עד שתהיה נכבשת כל הארץ אשר גבל הקב"ה גבולותיה בתורה והיא ארץ כנען לגבולותיה וכאשר כבש דוד הארצות ההם ארם נהרים וזולתה בטרם שישלם כיבוש הארץ המוגבלות כי היבוסי היה בירושלים עדיין לפיכך לא היתה מעלת הארצות ההם אשר כבש כמו מעלת ארץ ישראל וכן אמרו שאם תאמר מפני מה כבש דוד ארם נהרים וארם צובה ואין מצות נוהגות שם יאמרו דוד עשה שלא כהוגן התורה אמרה וכו' בסיפרי (שילהי פרשת עקב) ואלו הארצות ר"ל סוריא אין חייבין בה מעשר אלא למי שקנה שם קרקע ויהיה חייב להוציא מעשר ממה שהוציא השדה אבל מי שקנה פירות מפירות סוריא אינו חייב להוציא דמאי ואין כך בפירות ארץ ישראל אלא כל מי שיקנה מהם דבר באיזה מקום שיהיה יעשר דמאי כאשר התבאר במה שהקדמנו: וזה העיקר אשר זכר בכאן והוא שהפה שאסר הוא הפה שהתיר הוא עיקר אמת תמלאהו טוהג בכל המצות כלם האמורים והקלים וכן בממונות וכן כל מי שחייב* נפשו שום חיוב והתנה בדבריו תנאי שהוא מבטל החיוב ההוא יהיה נאמן בכל דבריו אחרי שאין עליו עד ועוד אביא לך בענין ההוא דמיונות רבים בדינין מתהנים: ומה שאמר משלי הוא.ר"ל מן השדה שלי אשר בכאן בסוריא שיתחייב במעשר כמו שבארנו: יב ההלכה הזאת מיוסדת על שלשה עיקרים האחד שהוא אסור למכור דמאי כל שכן טבל לע"ה ומותר למוכרם לתלמיד חכם מפני שהוא יפריש מהם תרומות הכתוב ולא יאכלם והעיקר השני שזה המוכר תלמיד חכם והעיקר השלישי שזה המוכר ידע השליחות שלח עם הארץ לתלמיד חכם לקנות לו ועל כן כשיאמר תלמיד חכם השליח להתלמיד חכם המוכר תן לי באלו הדמים כך וכך ולא הודיעהו אם זה הדבר הקנוי לעצמו יקנהו או לעם הארץ יקנהו אשר

מסורת הש"ס — א) חגיגה פ"ג דף כה: ב) קדושין פ"ק דף יז: ע"ז פ"ה דף סד: ג) עירובין פ"ג דף לז: ע"ש:

פי' מהר"י בן מלכי צדק — ובית הלל · אומר אף למעשר. פי' שאינו עושה מהן שמן אלא לאכילה ונרסינן א"ר יוחנן טעמא דבית הלל דרך בני אדם לאכול זיתיהן עטונקכלומר שאינן מוכשרין והקשו וכן דרך בני אדם ותירצו אין על ידי עילה ובית הלל כדעתהון דתנן לא ימכור לו פרה חורשת בשביעית ובית הלל מתירין מפני שהוא יכול לשחטה ואורחיה דבר נש מיכוס תורא דיליה אלא ע"י עילה (וכן)[ואף כאן] ע"י עילה: וצנועי בית הלל. נרסינן מהו צנועי כשירי אמר רב חסדא כאן שנינו שהכשר נקרא צנוע: ז שנים שבצרו את כרמיהן וכו' חלקו בכל מקום שהוא דאמרינן זהו חלקו המגיעו משעה ראשונה: ט חבר ועם הארץ וכו'. דאמרינן זהו חלקו המגיעו משנה ראשונה ולא מזבן ליה חבר ולא מידי: אבל לא יאמר לו וכו'.דמשתכח דקא מזבן יבש ולח ותנן המקבל עליו להיות חבר אינו מוכר לעם הארץ לח ויבש וכו': י גר ונוי שירשו את אביהן נוי וכו' ואם משבאו לרשות הגר אסור. פי' ליתן ע"ז וליקח בחילופה כלום דבר. תני ישראל ונכרי שקנו ביתו של עובד כוכבים והיה שם יין נסך וע"ז ומעות לא יאמר לו טול אתה יין וע"ז ואני מעות דכיון שקנו כמו שנכנס לרשותו: יא המוכר פירות בסוריא וכו' אם ידוע שיש לו שדה בסריא חייב לעשר. קסבר כיבוש יחיד שמיה כיבוש אמר ר' בון בר חייא ושיהא רוב מכנסו משלו פי' מאותה שדה: יב עם הארץ שאמר לחבר וכו'. בהא מילתא פליגי ר' יוסי ור' יהודה ר' יוסי פוטר ור' יהודה אומר צריך לעשר. גרסי' בירושלמי במאי עסקינן אילימא כשאמר לו צא וקח לי שלוחו הוא ומאי טעמא דר' יהודה אי דאמר לו צא וקח לך שלו הן ומאי טעמא דר' יוסי ותירצו כן אנן קימא לן באומר לו לך וקח אגודת ירק אחת והמשנה דתני לי לדברי הכל. ור' יוסי ור' יהודה בהא פליגי ר' יוסי סבר לא נתכוון המוכר לזכות אלא לבעל הבית ועל כן פטור מלעשר ור' יהודה סבר לא נתכוון מוכר לזכות אלא ללוקח ועל כן חייב לעשר ובפרק בכל מערבין אמרו מעם אחר ר' יוסי סבר אית ברירה וההיא אגודה דמטא לעם הארץ הוברר כי לשמו נקיית משעה ראשונה ובר זגיה סבר לית ברירה ואישתכח דחבר הוא דמזבין ליה השתא ואסיר ליה לזבוניה דבר שאינו מעושר ומפכי' לר' יוסי בדרבנן, ידרמנן לר' יוסי וכו': פיסקא

עין משפט נר מצוה — ו א מיי' פ"ט שם הלכה יג: ז ב מיי' פ"ו מהל' מעשר הלכה יד: ח ג מיי' פי"א שם הלכה ו: ט ד מיי' פ"ז מהל' עו"ג הלכה ס סוד וש"ע י"ד סי' קמו סעיף ד': י ה מיי' פ' י"ב מהל' מעשר הל' יא: יא ו מיי' פ"ט שם הלכה ח:

פירוש הרא"ש — (ח) ומיהו קשה לפרש כן דלמא ליה למיתני וחלקו בכ"מ שהוא דלהכן פירושא חלקו בידו הוא: (ט) כללא דמלתא מתקן החצי כל מה שגדל בכרם של שניה' וודאי החצי החלק שבידו וחצי החלק שביד חבירו וחצי האחר שבידו מתקנו דמאי דשמא כל חלקו בידו וכבר תיקן כל החצי ודאי אבל החצי שביד חבירו אין צריך לתקנו כלל דודאי [של] חבירו הוא: (י) פירוש לכאורה דמיא להא דשניםשבצרו כרמיהם דכל מה שגדלו בשדה הוא של שניהם ואפי' נטל זה חטים שבמקו' פלוני וזה חטים במקום פלוני חצי חלקו של זה ביד זה וחצי חלקו של זה ביד זה אלא שיש לחלק דלעיל נבצרו ככל לגת אח' ונתערב הכל במקום א' אבל הכא לא נתערב חלקם ובדמאי הקילו כב"כ: (יא) פי' שירשו אביהם ע"ה הא כבר תניא ברישא או שירשו ולא הוסיף כלום אלא דלעיל לא מיירי אלא בדין מעשר והכא אף בדין טהרות דהזכיר לח ויבש והא מילתא דפשיטא היא כיון דרישא מיירי באינו מעשר כל שכן דאינו נאמן על הטהרות ואגב דבעי למיתני גר ונכרי שירשו אביהם נכרי טול אתה ע"ג ואני אטול מעות תניא:

הגהות הגר"א — (א) בר"ש קודם מתני' ז' כ"ב ושין שאין מוכרין גדיש של חטים ועבים של ענבים אלא לחבר: (ב) מ"י שם ירשו מרחץ נמחק: (ג)שם חול בחלקי כ"ב ישראל ועובד כוכבים שלקחו את המרחץ אינו רשאי כו': [נ"ל בתחלה על מנת]

הגהות מהר"י לנדא — א] מ"י בר"ש ומכאן הקשה ר"ת לכא דאמרינן. נ"ל לסך דאמרי אהא דאיתא בשלהי וכו' ועי"ש בתוספות:

נ"ל דאפילו

רבי יוסי אומר חולקים מחלפא שיטתיה דר' יוסי תמן אמר לא נתכוון לזכות אלא לבעל המעות וכה אמר כן ומשני באותן (א) מעות של זה רגלים של זה (ב) כלומר שאומר למוכר אני שלוחו של פלוני ולכן פטור מלעשר: קלוסקין· כמו גלוסקין דפרק הדר (דף סד:) והם ככרות: ונתערבו חייב לעשר· דדלמא את שלו נתן לעם הארץ ולסוגיא דירושלמי נמי לא מיתוקמא הך סיפא אלא בשתי האגודות שהוכררו ואחר כן נתערבו: ירושלמי (שם) תני רשב"ג אומר אם החליף את המעות צריך לעשר א"ר יוסי הדא אמר הנותן מעות לחבירו והחליפן ואבדו חייב באחריות (יב) שמואל אמר במחלק בידיו א"ר אליעזר והוא שנטל חלקו בסוף אמר ר' יונה צורכא לכן וצורכא לכן חילק בידו ולקח חלקו בתחלה אינו מעשר (ג) אלא שלו פי' חייב באחריותן דהוה ליה שולח יד בפקדונו ובמחלק בידיו לא (ד) אנתערבו קאי אלא אשמעינן שמואל דמחלק בידיו בלא נתערבו נמי חייב לעשר את שתיקן וכדמוקי לה ר' אליעזר בשנטל חלקו בסוף דהוי כמי כמזבין ליה אבל חילק בידו שאמר זו לי וזו לחברי ונטל חלקו תחלה אינו מעשר אלא על שלו דלא מזבין לי' מידי דהך דפייש ממילא שקיל לה עם הארץ:

הארץ שאמר לחבר קח לי אגודת ירק* קח לי גלוסקין אחד לוקח סתם ופטור ואם אמר שלי זה וזה של חברי ונתערבו חייב לעשר ואפילו הן מאה:

פרק שביעי

א המזמין *את חבירו שיאכל אצלו והוא אינו מאמינו על המעשרות אומר מערב השבת מה שאני עתיד להפריש למחר הרי הוא מעשר ושאר מעשר סמוך לו וזה שעשיתי מעשר עשוי תרומת מעשר עליו ומע"ש בצפונו או בדרומו ומחולל על המעות: **ב** *מזגו לו את הכוס אומר מה שאני עתיד לשייר בשולי הכוס הרי הוא מעשר ושאר מעשר סמוך לו זה שעשיתי מעשר עשוי תרומת מעשר עליו ומעשר שני בפיו ומחולל על המעות: **ג** *פועל שאינו מאמין לבעל הבית נוטל גרוגרת אחת ואומר זו ותשע הבאות אחריה עשויות מעשר על תשעים שאני אוכל זו עשויה תרומת מעשר עליהן ומעשר שני *באחרונה ומחולל על המעות וחושך גרוגרת אחת רבן שמעון בן גמליאל אומר לא יחשוך מפני שהוא ממעט מלאכתו של בעל הבית רבי יוסי אומר *לא יחשוך מפני שהוא תנאי בית דין: **ד** הלוקח (א) יין מבין הכותים אומר שני לוגין שאני עתיד

שלחו זה הדבר הקנוי פטור שמאחר שידע הלמיד חכם המוכר כי זה הקונה בשליחות עם הארץ בא לקנות לא יתן לו אלא פירות מתוקנים כדי שלא יבא עם הארץ לידי מכשול: ואם יבא ת"ח השליח אל המוכר ויאמר לו אלו הדמים לי ואלו לחבירי ר"ל לעם הארץ ששלחהו ויתן לו בזה הכסף בפני עלמו ובזה האחר בפני עלמו יש לומר אולי מה שנתן לחבירו הוא טבל מפני שידע כי לא יאכלנו עד שיוליא תרומותיו ומה שנתן לעם הארץ חבירו הם פירות מתוקנין כפי אשר בארנו וכשיתערב נתחייב הדבר ההוא המעורב במעשר: ואלו קנה לעלמו אגודה אחת ולחבירו מאה ונתערב יתחייב הכל מעשר דמאי וכל זה כשלא ישאל למוכר אבל אם ישאל למוכר ויאמר לו מתוקנין הן יהיה נאמן וכל מה שיקנה ממנו פטור מפני שהוא תלמיד חכם: ופירוש גלוסקין לחם בתבלין מתוקן היטב:

א אסור לנו להוליא מעשרות בשבת ולא ביום טוב והעיקר אללנו כי בדמאי אדם מתנה על הדבר שאינו ברשותו וכשתסתכל מה שאמרנו בפרק ה' מזאת המסכתא בענין הלוקח מן הנחתום יתבאר לך ההלכה באור שלם וכל ההלכות הבאות אחריהם כי הענין בכלל שוה:

ב אחר שהקדים התנאי מערב שבת על דרך כלל כמו שנתבאר בהלכה ראשונה

א אומר מערב שבת צריך לקרות שם מע"ש משום דאין מעשרין את הדמאי בשבת אלא בספק חשיכה כדתנן בפ' במה מדליקין (דף לד.) והיכא דקרא שם מערב שבת שרי להפריש בשבת אומר מע"ש לעיל פ"ד (מ"ב) התירו אע"פ שאינו מאמינו הני מילי במדיר והכא בלא מדיר אי נמי התם בשבת ראשונה כגון שבת של פרוסגמא כדפרישית שם: שאני עתיד להפריש למחר· היכא דקרא שם מערב שבת יכול להפריש בשבת אבל לא קרא שם אסור כדתנן בפרק במה מדליקין ספק חשיכה מעשרין את הדמאי הא ודאי חשיכה לא: הרי הוא מעשר· תרומה גדולה אין צריך להפריש דלא נחשד עליה עם הארץ ועל אחד ממאה שמפריש למחר אומר הרי הוא מעשר ראשון: ושאר מעשר· דהיינו תשעה שהוא חייב עדיין כדי שיהו עשרה ממאה ומודד לו האחד ואחר כך אומר זה שעשיתי תחלה מעשר עשוי תרומת מעשר על תשעה הסמוכין לו: מעשר שני יהיה בצפונו או בדרומו ומחולל יהיה על המעות ונמלא למחר אין צריך לתרומת מעשר וכל השאר יאכל וישתה וכענין זה פירשתי: ירושלמי (הל' א) א"ר יוחנן מתני' בספק אמרה אפילו בודאי דתנינן תמן היו לו תאנים במדרש או בשדה אין תימר בדמאי אנן קיימין ליה

MISHNAH 12. IF AN 'AM HA-AREẒ SAID TO AN ASSOCIATE:[2] 'BUY FOR ME A BUNDLE OF VEGETABLES', OR: 'BUY FOR ME A LOAF OF BREAD', THE ASSOCIATE MAY BUY IT WITHOUT INQUIRING [WHETHER IT HAD BEEN TITHED], AND HE IS ABSOLVED[3] [FROM TITHING IT]. BUT IF THE ASSOCIATE SAID: 'THIS ONE I BUY FOR MYSELF AND THIS ONE FOR MY FRIEND', AND THE TWO PURCHASES WERE MIXED UP, HE IS BOUND TO TITHE[4] [BOTH PURCHASES], EVEN IF THE PURCHASE [FOR THE 'AM HA-AREẒ] IS A HUNDRED [TIMES MORE THAN HIS OWN].

CHAPTER VII

a *MISHNAH* 1. IF A MAN INVITED[1] HIS FRIEND TO EAT WITH HIM ON THE SABBATH, AND [HIS FRIEND] DOES NOT TRUST HIM IN RESPECT OF TITHES, [THE FRIEND] MAY SAY ON THE EVE[2] OF THE SABBATH: WHAT[3] I SHALL SET APART TO-MORROW[4] SHALL BE TITHE, AND WHAT IS NEAREST TO IT SHALL BE THE REST OF THE TITHE;[5] THAT WHICH I MADE TITHE SHALL BECOME THE TERUMAH OF THE TITHE FOR THE WHOLE,[6] AND WHAT IS TO THE NORTH OR TO THE SOUTH OF IT SHALL BE SECOND TITHE WHICH SHALL BE EXCHANGED FOR MONEY.

(2) Who was going to the market to buy for himself. (3) Because from the first the particular purchase became the property of the *'am ha-areẓ*. (4) Because what he gives to the *'am ha-areẓ* may have been his own purchase, which he is now exchanging for the purchase of the *'am ha-areẓ*; cf. *supra* 8, n. 4.

a (1) Without the conditions mentioned *supra* IV, 2, n. 7; viz., the imposition of a vow and the celebration of a marriage feast. (2) But not on the Sabbath itself; cf. IV, 1, n. 1. (3) Viz., a hundredth part of the whole, which is subsequently to become *Terumah* of the Tithe. This is set apart first for the reason given *supra*, V, 1, n. 13. (4) From my food and drink at the table of the *'am ha-areẓ*. (5) Viz., nine hundredths, completing the one tenth which is to be set apart for the First Tithe. (6) Of the First Tithe. (7) Over which the benediction for the sanctification of the Sabbath day (*Ḳiddush*; cf. Ber. VIII, 1) is pronounced at the opening of the Sabbath meal. (8) At the house of the *'am ha-areẓ*. The declaration made on the eve of the Sabbath must be repeated on the Sabbath before he drinks wine, and again before he eats food, when the wine and the food are actually before him, in order to complete thereby the process of tithing by designation (IV, 3, n. 5) begun by the declaration on the eve of the Sabbath. (9) This formula must be used in the case of wine in a cup, instead of the formula 'what is to the north or the south of it', because one cannot distinguish the sides of a round cup.

MISHNAH 2. WHEN THE CUP OF WINE[7] HAS BEEN FILLED FOR HIM [ON THE SABBATH],[8] HE MAY SAY: WHAT I SHALL LEAVE AT THE BOTTOM OF THE CUP SHALL BE TITHE, AND WHAT IS NEAREST TO IT SHALL BE THE REST OF THE TITHE; THAT WHICH I MADE TITHE SHALL BECOME THE TERUMAH OF TITHE FOR THE WHOLE, AND WHAT IS AT THE MOUTH[9] OF THE CUP SHALL BE SECOND TITHE WHICH SHALL BE
b EXCHANGED FOR MONEY.[1]

MISHNAH 3. IF A WORKMAN[2] DOES NOT TRUST HIS EMPLOYER [IN RESPECT OF TITHES], HE MAY TAKE ONE DRIED FIG[3] AND SAY: THIS ONE[4] AND THE NINE WHICH COME AFTER IT SHALL BECOME TITHE FOR THE NINETY WHICH I SHALL EAT; THIS ONE SHALL BECOME THE TERUMAH OF TITHE FOR THEM, AND THE LAST ONES SHALL BE SECOND TITHE WHICH SHALL BE EXCHANGED FOR MONEY; BUT HE MUST STINT HIMSELF OF ONE DRIED FIG.[5] RABBAN SIMEON THE SON OF GAMALIEL SAYS: HE MAY NOT STINT HIMSELF, SINCE THEREBY HE MAY REDUCE HIS WORK FOR HIS EMPLOYER.[6] R. JOSE SAYS: HE NEED NOT STINT HIMSELF, BECAUSE THIS IS A CONDITION [IMPOSED UPON THE EMPLOYER] BY THE COURT.[7]

MISHNAH 4. IF A MAN BOUGHT WINE AMONG CUTHEANS,[8] HE MAY SAY [ON THE SABBATH]:[9] TWO LOGS[10] WHICH I SHALL

b (1) What he actually has to leave is one hundredth part of what he consumes for the *Terumah* of the Tithe. (2) Whose food during his working hours must be provided by his employer; cf. III, 1, n. 3; B.M. VII, 2. (3) If, for example, his meal consists of dried figs. (4) To be made subsequently into *Terumah* of the Tithe; cf. VII, 1, n. 3. (5) He must put it aside as *Terumah* of the Tithe which can be eaten by a priest only. (6) Because he may be left hungry. Therefore he must buy a fig at his own expense, and complete his meal. (7) That the employer should provide a full meal for his workmen; therefore the employer has to provide an extra fig. (8) Samaritans, before the use of their wine was prohibited to Jews; cf. Ḥul. 6*a*. Produce sold by Samaritans is real *ṭebel* (cf. V, 9, n. 7), and the buyer must give from it *terumah* as well as First Tithe and Second Tithe, but not *Terumah* of the Tithe which devolves upon the Levite who receives the First Tithe. (9) He bought on a week-day, but was prevented from tithing it before the Sabbath. (10) Of a hundred *logs*, the usual quantity of *terumah*; cf. V, 2, n. 5. For the size of a *log* cf. 'Ed. (Sonc. ed.) 2*a* n. b 3.

SET APART[11] SHALL BE TERUMAH, TEN LOGS TITHE, AND NINE
a LOGS[1] SECOND TITHE; HE MAY THEN EXCHANGE [THE SECOND TITHE FOR MONEY][2] AND DRINK IT [THE WINE].

MISHNAH 5. IF A MAN HAD FIGS OF ṬEBEL[3] IN HIS HOUSE WHEN HE WAS IN THE HOUSE OF STUDY OR IN THE FIELD,[4] HE MAY SAY: THE TWO FIGS[5] WHICH I SHALL SET APART SHALL BE TERUMAH, TEN FIGS SHALL BE FIRST TITHE, AND NINE FIGS SECOND TITHE. IF THE FIGS WERE DEMAI, HE MAY SAY: WHATEVER I SHALL SET APART TO-MORROW SHALL BE TITHE, AND WHAT IS NEAREST TO IT SHALL BE THE REST OF THE TITHE; THAT WHICH I MADE TITHE SHALL BECOME THE TERUMAH OF TITHE FOR IT, AND WHAT IS TO THE NORTH OF IT OR TO THE SOUTH OF IT SHALL BE SECOND TITHE, WHICH SHALL BE EXCHANGED FOR MONEY.

MISHNAH 6. IF HE HAD BEFORE HIM TWO BASKETS FULL OF PRODUCE OF ṬEBEL, AND HE SAID: LET THE TITHES OF THIS [BASKET] BE IN THAT [BASKET], THE FIRST [BASKET] IS THEREBY TITHED;[6] [IF HE SAID:] LET THE TITHES OF THIS [BASKET] BE IN THAT [BASKET], AND THE TITHES OF THAT [BASKET] IN THIS [BASKET], THE FIRST [BASKET ALONE][7] IS THEREBY TITHED; [IF HE SAID:] LET THE TITHES OF BOTH BE

(11) After the Sabbath.
a (1) I.e., one tenth of the produce left after taking off First Tithe;* cf. Introduction p. 50. (2) מיחל So 'Aruch. Maim. and other authorities render 'begin'. R. Hai Gaon and others read מחל, 'mix it with water'; cf. Kohut, *Aruch Completum*, III, p. 385. (3) Cf. V, 8, n. 3. (4) Late on Friday, when he had not sufficient time to return home and set apart the *terumah* and the tithes before the coming in of the Sabbath. (5) Of every hundred. (6) And he may give Tithes from the second basket both for its own contents and for the contents of the first basket. (7) But not the second basket. For as soon as he said: 'Let the tithes of the first be in the second', the first becomes thereby tithed, but not yet the second; therefore when he added: 'Let the tithes of the second be in the first', he is tithing produce which is exempt for produce which is liable; cf. V, 3, n. 1.

*See Corrigenda.

כדי לאכלו אבל כאן הוא ודאי צריך ליתן ללוי ואפי' תימא' לומר דלוקח מן הכותי כלוקח מן הנכרי דאמרי' בפ"ק דבכורות (דף יא.) דמעשרן והן שלו משום דקאתי מכח נכרא דלא מני לאשתעויי דינא בהדיה מ"מ אסור להפריש בשבת על ידי קריאת שם דבין השמשות מאחר דבין השמשות אין מעשרין את הודאי כדתנן בפ' במה מדליקין ולהכי (נמי) לא קתני [נמי] גבי מעשר שני דהכא בצפונו (ובדרומו) [או בדרומו] כדקתני גבי דמאי א] בשום מקום בהפרשה ותנן בפ' במה מדליקין אבל מעשרין את הדמאי ומתני' בין השמשות ולהכי נמי לא קתני ומחולל על המעות כדקתני גבי דמאי אלא ומיחל ושותה דאי מחלל על המעות ושותה אם כן ליתני ומחלל על המעות כדקתני בכולהו ועוד כיון דאמר שאני עתיד להפריש סתם ולא קבע לו מקום לצפונו או לדרומו אין יכול לחללו כדתנן בתוספתא דמעשר שני זה שבחפץ זה מחולל על איסר זה ולא קבע לו מקום ר' שמעון אומר קרא שם וחכמים אומרים עד שיאמר לצפונו או לדרומו ומייתי התם עובדא דרשב"ג ור' יהודה ור' יוסי שנכנסו אצל בעל הבית לכזיב והיה מחלל כענין זה אמרו לו השכרת מעות ואיבדת נפשות ור' שמעון נמי דקאמר קרא שם לא אמר אלא דאמר בתוכו דהיינו נמי פלוגתייהו דפליגי ר' שמעון ורבנן במסכת תרומות האומר תרומת הכרי זה בתוכו ותרומת מעשר בתוכו ר' שמעון אומר קרא שם ומפרש בפ' בכל מערבין (דף לז:) דלאו דוקא שאומר בתוכו באמצעיתו דקבע לו מקום אלא דבירושל' עלה דההיא דתרומות פ"ג משמע דבתוכו לאו דוקא ואם פירשתי' ועוד דעל כרחו צריך להפרישו דהא קאמר שאני עתיד להפריש ואם היה שותה בלא הפרשה נמצא שותה טבלים למפרע כמו אם יבקע הנוד דשאני עתיד להפריש אכולהו קאי כדמוכח בתוספתא (פ"ז) דקתני עשרה הבאין אחריהן תשעה הבאין אחריהן ובשבת אין מפריש כדפרישי': עשרה מעשר ראשון תשעה מעשר שני · לאו דוקא דכשר הפריש מן המאה ב' לוגין לתרומה נמצא חסר מהנך עשרה ותשעה מעשר ב' לוגין דהיינו חומש הלוג וכן גבי תאנים ומיהו יתכן שהפריש שנים ממאה ושנים דהא זימנין דמפריש א' מס' כדתנן בתרומות פ"ד (משנה ד) תורם כדעת בע"ה א' מנ' פיחת עשרה או הוסיף עשרה תרומתו תרומה כדאמרינן בכתובות פרק אלמנה (דף ק:) דאיכא דתורם בעין יפה ואיכא דתורם בעין רעה ויש מפרשים משום דכותים שמא הפרישו תרומה והשאר לא הפרישו ולכך אין מתמעט שיעור [המעשר] ולא יתכן לומר כן בתאנים של טבל לקמן ועוד יש מפרשים משום דחטה אחת פוטרת את הכרי אינה ממעטת במעשר כשמתרבה בתרומה וגם זה לא יתכן כלל (י): תניא בתוספתא הלוקח יין מבין הכותים מע"ש ושכח ולא הפריש אומר ב' לוגין שאני עתיד להפריש תרומה עשרה הבאין אחריהן מעשר ראשון תשעה הבאין אחריהן מעשר שני ומיחל ושותה מיד (יא) דברי ר' מאיר ר' יהודה ורבי יוסי ורבי שמעון אוסרין אמרו לו אי אתה מודה שמא יבקע הנוד ונמצא שותה טבלים למפרע פי' ר"מ בפ' בכל מערבין (דף לז.) ובפ' כל הגט (דף כה:) ובמרובה (דף סט.) דטעמא דר' מאיר משום דלית ליה ברירה ותימה דבפ' יש בכור (דף מח.) משמע דמספקא ליה לר' מאיר אי יש ברירה אי לא גבי פלוגתא דר' מאיר ור' יהודה דאם לא כתנו עד שחלקו דמפרש בגמ' דסבירא להו כר' אסי דאמר האחין שחלקו מחצה יורשין ומחצה לקוחות וטעמא משום דמספקא ליה כדמוכח בפ"ק דב"ק (דף ט.) ויש לומר דשאני הכא שמברר דבריו כשאומר שאני עתיד להפריש וכן צריך לומר משום דר' יהודה דמוקי ליה רבא התם כרב אסי ובריש כל הגט (דף כ.) אמר רבא גופיה דבין ר' יהודה ור' שמעון אית להו ברירה וטעמייהו הכא משום בקיעת הנוד וכן צריך לומר דלא תיקשי דשמואל אדשמואל דבסוף ביצה (דף לז:) גבי שנים שלקחו חבית ובהמה בשותפות קאמר שמואל דאף הבית אסורה משום דאין ברירה ובפ' מי שאחזו (דף עה:) אמרינן דאתקין שמואל בגיטא דשכיב מרע אם ימות יהא גט ואם לא ימות לא יהא גט ולכי מיית הוי גיטא אלמא יש ברירה ובכי האי גונא דייק בריש כל הגט (דף כה.) אמילתיה דר' יהודה גבי מה היא באותן הימים · והטעם פי' שם בקונטרס משום דאין זה כשאר תנאים דעלמא דאדם מתנה בגט שבידו לקיימן ודעתו לקיימן כשמתנה עליהם ולכשנתקיים התנאי הוי גט למפרע בלאו טעמא דברירה אבל הכא דאין בידו דבשעת התנאי הוי ספקא והתנאי מתקיים מאליו אי לאו משום ברירה לא הוי גט והא דמשמע בפ' בכל מערבין (דף לז:) גבי הני רמונים של טבל כשאמר אם ירדו גשמים היום יהא זה תרומה על זה דהוי תרומה היינו למאן דאית ליה ברירה אי נמי חשיב טפי משום דמתנה בין ירדו בין לא ירדו ומיהו טעם זה לא יתכן דגבי אם בא חכם נמי מתנה התם בכל ענין וחשיב ליה ברירה והא דפריך במרובה (דף סט:) דר"י אדר"י בההיא דכל המתלקט מההוא דהאחים שחלקו לקוחות הן ולא מחלק בין זו לזו משום דבמתלקט מברר דבריו וסומך להתברר על ידי תנאו דניחא ליה למימר לעולם כל הנלקט כדקתני ועוד ניחא ליה לומר לעולם לא תיפוך ועוד דאפילו הוה מחלק אכתי הוה קשיא ליה מההיא דר' יוחנן בריש כל הגט אף אחרון אינו פוסל משום דאין ברירה אע"פ שמברר בדבריו כשאמר איזו שארצה אגרש בו ומיהו כי מצריך בריש כל הגט תרי מילי דר' יוחנן הוה מצי למימר הך צריכותא ועוד יש לפרש דהא דדייק דאית ליה לר' יהודה ברירה מהא דלכי מיית הוי גיטא מוקי לה בפ' מי שאחזו באומר מעת שאני בעולם דהיינו שעה אחת לפני מיתתו שלא היתה שעה מבוררת ולבסוף כשמת אמרינן הוברר הדבר שאותה שעה היתה גרושה ולפי טעם זה אין לדקדק מדשמואל ומיהו פי' הקונטרס עיקר דההיא דריש כל הגט וההיא דהריני בועליך על מנת שירצה אבא ובפ' בכל מערבין בההיא דאם בא חכם למזרח אע"ג דהוו כעין תנאי משמע דלא מהני למאן דלית ליה ברירה ר' יהודה ור' יוסי [אוסרין] ג] דר' יהודה משום דלית ליה ברירה אע"ג דקתני בהדיא משום בקיעת הנוד דכוותה אשכחן טובא שאין הגמרא חושב עיקר טעם אותו טעם המפורש במשנה בפרק התערובות (דף עז.) גבי אברי תמימה שנתערבו באברי בעלת מום ובפ"ג דשבועות (דף יט:) גבי שלא אוכל ואכל כל שהוא חייב דברי ר' עקיבא ובפרק בתרא דמכות (דף יג.) גבי כמה יאכל מן הטבל ויהא חייב ר' שמעון אומר כל שהוא ואם תאמר אי ר' יהודה ל"ל ברירה אלמא סבירא ליה כר' יוחנן דבריש כל הגט ובפ' מעשר בהמה דאמר האחין שחלקו לקוחות הן ומחזירין זה לזה ביובל א"כ היאך מלא ידיו ורגליו בבית המדרש דלא משכחת דמייתי ביכורים אלא חד בר חד עד יהושע בן נון דבפ' החובל (דף ל.) אית ליה לר' יהודה קנין פירות לאו כקנין הגוף דמי גבי דין יום או יומים וכן נמי לר' יוסי דמספקא ליה התם אי כקנין הגוף דמי אי לא והכא לית ליה ברירה וכי ה"ג דייק בסוף השולח בגיטין (דף מח.) ויש לומר דמדין יום או יומים אין ללמוד בעלמא אלא גבי מילי דעבד לחוד דהתם כתיבי קראי כספו ותחת ידו ומהאי טעמא לא מייתי לה בהשולח כי מייתי ההיא דשדה אחוזה ועוד יש לומר דדוקא ר' יוחנן הוא דאית ליה הך סברא משום דלקוחות הן מחזירין זה לזה ביובל אבל איך אמוראי הוו אמרי דאע"ג דאין ברירה אין מחזירין כדאמרי' בריש כל הגט (דף כה.) ובפ' מעשר בהמה (דף נג:) דמכר הוא דאמר רחמנא ליהדר ביובל ירושה ומתנה לא ולר' יוחנן לא קשיא מר' יהודה דהוה מפרש טעמא משום בקיעת הנוד ומיהו לא יתכן טעם זה לר' יוסי דעל כורחין לית ליה ברירה כמו שאפרש ואת"ל דהכא לית ליה לר' יוסי ברירה ובפרק מי שאחזו (דף עג:) אית ליה ברירה דתנן ר' יוסי אומר מגורשת ולכי מיית הוי גיטא ולמאן דמחלק בריש כל הגט בין תולה בדעת עצמו לתולה בדעת אחרים ניחא ורבא דלא מפליג התם מפרש טעמא משום בקיעת הנוד ורבה מפרש טעמא בבכל מערבין (דף לז:) משום דבעינן ראשית ששיריה ניכרין ומיהו אכתי קשה דבפרק בכל מערבין משמע דלרבי יוסי לית ליה ברירה גבי מעשר שיש לו בבית יהא מחולל על סלע שתעלה בידי מן הכיס ר' יוסי אומר לא חילל ויש לומר משום דבההיא דמי שאחזו · הדבר עומד להתברר דלאי שהרי או יחיה או ימות ואית לן ברירה טפי מההיא דעל סלע שתעלה בידי מן הכיס דשמא לא יתברר לעולם וכי האי גוונא נוכל לתרץ דשמואל אדשמואל :

ה היו דמאי · כל הנך בבות בין בדמאי בין בודאי בע"ש איירי כמו בקמייתא בריש פירקין וכבר פירשתים : ו מעשרות · כגון מעשר ראשון ומעשר שני או מעשר עני בשעתו (יב) ובהך קמייתא ליכא חידוש במה שהראשונה [מעושרת] (יג) ומשום סיפא נקטיה ושפיר שייך למקריה ראשונה : של זו בזו ושל זו בזו הראשונה מעושרת. אבל השניה אינה מעושרת דמיד שאמר של זו בזו נעשית ראשונה חולין מתוקנין כשחוזר ואומר שניה בראשונה הוה ליה מן החיוב על הפטור ולא אמר כלום ונוטל מן השניה מעשרותיה ומעשרות הראשונה דכל מה שבראשונה מתוקן לגמרי אבל כשאמר בבת אחת מעשרות כלכלה בחברתה קרא שם ואי אפשר להפריש מאחת על שתיהן אלא מפריש מזו על זו ומזו על זו ומדאיצטריך למיתני מעשרות כלכלה בחברתה משמע דרישא הראשונה מעושרת אע"פ שאמר תוך כדי דבור של זו בזו ושל זו בזו ומיהו בתוספתא משמע דבעי למימר שהאחת תפטור את שתיהן כשאמר מעשרות כלכלה בחברתה ובירושלמי (הל' ו) אמר ר' אלעזר דר"מ היא דאמר אין תופס אלא לשון ראשון כדאמר גבי תמורת עולה תמורת שלמים בפ' כילד מערימין (דף כה:) ובפ"ק דתמורה (דף ד:) איתמר ר' אלעזר אומר לוקה מפני שהקדים מעשר שני שבה למעשר ראשון שבחברתה דמעיקרא* של זו בזו קיימת הכלכלה לפרוש ממנה מעשר ראשון ומעשר שני והשתא מפריש ממנה מעשר ראשון ומעשר שני בשביל אידך כלכלה נמצא שקדם מעשר שני של כלכלה זו למעשר ראשון שיהיה עומד להפריש מאידך קודם לכן וקא עבר משום מלאתך ודמעך לא תאחר דכי היכי דמוזהר שלא לעכב המלאה לדימוע מוזהר נמי שלא לעכב מעשר ראשון לשני דכל שיש עליו תורת דימוע דהיינו תרומה קרי ביה ודמעך לא תאחר ובירושלמי (שם) א"ר יוסי בר' חנינא הראשונה עובר בעשה השניה עובר בעשה ול"ת הראשונה עובר בעשה שקבע שני שמות כאחת השניה בעשה ול"ת שקבע שני שמות כאחת ושהקדים שני שבראשונה לראשון שבשניה וקרי עשה מה שקובע המעשרות כאחת שהיה לו להקדים מעשר ראשון למעשר שני ולא הקדים אבל לא תאחר ליכא דלא איחר ור' יוסי בר' חנינא לא קאי אמעשרות של זו בזו ושל זו בזו דלא משכחת עשה בשניה דאין בדבריו כלום השניה אינה מתוקנת אלא אמעשרות כלכלה בחברתה קאי שקבע על שתיהן המעשרות כאחת ואיכא עשה אתרוייהו אבל קשה לא תעשה אמאי איכא כלל הרי יכול להפריש תחלה מעשר ראשון מזו ומזו ואח"כ מעשר שני מזו ומזו ושמא משמע לי' דאין מתקן לתאין אלא מתקן האחת תחלה א"כ ה"ק פעמים דהשניה עובר בל"ת כגון שהוא אם מפריש ממנה כל המעשרות חברתה ואותה שמפריש ממנה תחלה קרי לה שניה ומאי ראשונה שנתקנה ראשונה ומאי שניה שנתקנה שניה וכשמפריש מכלכלה זו תחלה לצורך חברתה נמצאת חברתה מתוקנת תחלה וההפרשה זו קא עבר בלאו והיא מתוקנת בשניה כשיפריש משניה עליה וההיא הפרשה ליכא לאו :

תניא בתוספתא (פ"ז) היו לפניו שתי כלכלות של טבל בזו מאה ובזו מאה ניטלה תרומתן* מעשרות זו בזו הראשונה מעושרת של זו בזו ושל זו בזו(ג) אין הראשונה מעושרת נוטל כ' תאנים וב' עישורין ועישורו של עישור מעשרותיהן מעשרות כלכלה בחברתה קרא שם נוטל ב' תאנים מאיזו שירצה פי' ניטלה תרומתן שניטלה תרומה גדולה ועדיין יש מאה בזו ויש מאה בזו אין הראשונה מעושרת כן כתוב בכל הספרים ובמתניתא קתני הראשונה מעושרת ושמי ברייתא מקמי מתנית' אי נמי גרסינן אין השניה מעושרת אי נמי הכי קאמר אין הראשונה מעושרת מפני עצמה אלא שתיהן מעושרות כר' יוסי דכילד מערימים (דף כה:) גבי תמורת עולה

(ג) או כצ"ל

תמורת

מתני'

להפריש הרי הן תרומה ועשרה מעשר* ותשעה מעשר שני (ט) ומיחל ושותה: ה ^א^היו לו תאנים של טבל בתוך ביתו והוא בבית המדרש או בשדה אומר (א) ג] מה שאני עתיד להפריש הרי הן תרומה ועשר מעשר ראשון ותשע מעשר שני היו דמאי אומר מה שאני עתיד להפריש למחר הרי הוא מעשר ושאר מעשר סמוך לו זה שעשיתי מעשר עשוי תרומת מעשר עליו ומעשר שני בצפונו או בדרומו ומחולל על המעות: ו (א) ^ב^היו לפניו שתי *שני כלכלות של טבל ואמר מעשרות זו בזו הראשונה מעושרת של זו בזו ושל זו בזו הראשונה מעושרת ^ג^מעשרותיהן מעשרות כלכלה

ר"מ

תרומה ועשרה מעשר · זה על דרך ההעברה אבל בענין האמת כשיהיו ב' לוגין תרומה יהיה המעשר עשרה פחות חומש ומעשר שני שמנה ושמנה עשיריות וחומש עשירית על העיקר אשר בארנו לך בברכות: וזה שאמר ומיחל ר"ל שיתחיל לשתות וזאת הלכה היא לר"מ שהוא סובר יש ברירה והדבר הנשאר כאילו הופרש מתחלה ותדע שחובת התרומה והמעשרות מן התורה והעיקר בידינו דבדאורייתא אין ברירה בדרבנן יש ברירה ומפני זה אין הלכה כר"מ שהוא לו זה הכתם אבל יוציא תרומה ומעשרות קודם שתייתו על כל פנים: ה הוצרך לזה כשיהיה ערב שבת ויהיה חושש שמא יכנס השבת ולא יהיה לו פנאי להוציא המתנות וכל זה הדבר מבואר כשתבין כל מה שהקדמנו ומאשר קדם לו גם כן תדע כי מה שנאמר בתאנים של טבל אינה הלכה לפי שהטבל חייב במתנות מדאורייתא והעיקר בדאורייתא אין ברירה ואין לו תקנה אלא אם כן הוציא אלו המתנות קודם אכילתו וזה מותר בשבת בשביל התנאי שהקדים מערב שבת: ו העיקר בזה שאין תורמין ומעשרין מן הפטור על החיוב וכשיאמר מעשרות זו בזו נעשית הראשונה מעושרת ויוציא מן השנית התרומות והמעשרות שנתחייבו בהן שתיהן וכשיאמר מעשרות זו בזו נעשית הראשונה פטורה והשניה חייבת במעשרות שתיהן כמו שביארנו ואחר כן חזר ואמר של זו בזו ר"ל המעשרות שהשניה חייבת בהן יוציאם מן הראשונה ואין זו *הלכה לפי שהראשונה נפטרה בדבורו הראשון והשניה חייבת ואין מפרישין מן הפטור על החיוב. ואם לא הקדים המאמר באחת קודם השנית אבל יאמר מעשרותיהן מעשרות כלכלה בחברתה ותיקן זה הדבר ר"ל שהמעשרות שחייבין בהן אלו שני הסלים מעשר כל אחד מהם קבוע באחר וכשיאמר כן יתחייב להוציא המעשרות שהן חייבין בהן משתיהן ואי אפשר להוציא עליהן מעשרות ממקום אחר וזה ענין שאמר קרא שם רוצה לומר קרא שם מעשרותיהן בהן :

מסורת הש"ס

א) תמורה פרק א דף ד.

פי' מהר"י בן מלכי צדק

בערב שבת בין השמשות שלא הספיק לקדש עד שקדש היום : ה היו לו תאנים של טבל וכו' היו דמאי וכו'. שמעינן מתניתין דלא משכחינן תרום' גדולה דמאי: ו היו לפניו שני כלכלות של טבל.פי' שנישלה תרומתן ולא נישלו מעשרותיהן:ואמר מעשרות זו בזו [ושל זו בזו] הראשונה מעושרת. דמחויב על חיוב קא מעשר. אבל השניה אינה מעושרת דראשונה כבר נעשית חולין ומתוקנין ולא מפרשינן מן הפטור על החיוב אלא צריך לעישורי מינה ובה נמצא שצריך להוציא מן השניה מעשרותי' ומעשרו' חברתה. וכיצד מעשר עלייהו תניא בתוספתא בפ"ח נוטל משניה ב' תאנין וב' עישורין ועישורו של עישור [ופי'] הואיל ואמר מעשרות זו בזו צריך ליקח על תשעים י' ועל תשעים אחרים י' הרי (ב) [כ] תאנין ב' כהן תרומת מעשר [על] י"ח תאנין שהן ב' עישורין וב' מהן תרומת מעשר (ועל שנים*)ב'תאנין וב' עישורין שהן עשרין עישורין שנים כהן נקראין תרומת מעשר ונקראין עישור מעישור חשבון הכל ב' תאנין וב' עישורין ועישור בעישור : מעשרותיהן מעשר [בכלכלה בחברתה]. פי' היו לפניו ב' כלכלות של טבל ואחד מעשרותיהן מעשר כלכלה בחברתה כלומר מעשרות ב' הכלכלות יהיו באחת מן הכלכלות וכיון שלא אמר זו בזו וזו בזו קרא שם כלומר מה שעשה עשוי הואיל וקרא שם נוטל (ב')**תאנין מכל איזה שירצ' וכל עשר דיסב אית בהון חדא תרומת מעשר ובלבד שיהו הכלכלות שוות פי' בזו ק' ובזו ק' :

*) אית מוכן כונתו בזה ולפענ"ד ואולי צ"ל ועל זה שנים כ' תאנים יב' עישורין שהן עשרים ב' ... ונדיין צ"ע.

**) אולי צ"ל כ'.

עין משפט נר מצוה

ד א מיי' פ"ט מהל' מעשר הלכה ח :
ה ב מיי' פ"ז שם הלכה יא :
ו ג שם הל' יב יג :

פירוש הראב"ד

(ט) כלומר מתחיל ושותה אי נמי מחל בחי"ת כמו מוהל בה"א כלומר מוזג ושותה וכגון שהחך מהול במים (ישעי' א): (י) דנהי דחטה אחת פוטרת את הכרי מכל מקום יכול להפריש לתרומה כמו שירצה רק שישייר מקצת דבעי' ראשית ששיריה נכרים וכל מה שמפריש שם תרומה עליו : (יא) ולמחר במוצאי שבת יפריש ואמרינן הוברר הדבר מה ששתה היו חולין והמופרש היא תרומה וג"כ לא חיישי' שמא יבקע הנוד ונמצא שותה טבלים למפרע : (יב) ותרומה גדולה דרך להפרישו מיד בשעת הגורן : (יג) וגם לא שייך להזכיר כאן ראשונה דלא תיקן אלא אחת :

הגהות הגר"א

(א) במ"א או בשדה אומר מה. תיבת מה נמחק וג"כ שני תאנים : (ב) מ"ב בר"ש אין הראשונה. צ"ל פי' עד שיטול ממנה מעשר של שני' וכו' ואם רוצה כו' וכ' קאי גם על עישורו של עישור :

הגהות מהר"י לנדא

פ"ז א] מ"ד בר"ש כדקתני גבי דמאי בשום מקו' בהפרשה. צ"ל דשם מקום בהפרשה : ב] שם דר"י משום דל"ל ברירה. צ"ל טעמא דר"י : ג] במשנה ה אומר מה שאני. גי' ירושלמי שני תאנים שאני כו' :

עין משפט נר מצוה

ז א מיי' פ"א מהל' מעשר הלכה ג :
ח ב שם הלכה ד :
ט ג שם הלכה ה :
י ד שם הלכה ו :

תמורת שלמים הואיל ואי אפשר לקרות שני שמות כאחת דבריו קיימים נוטל ב' תאנים מכלכלה שניה וארישא קאי ולתרומת מעשר טפלין שתחלה נוטל שני תאנים ממנה בשביל מעשר ראשון שלה ומעשר ראשון של חברתה ושני תאנים הללו הם מאותן ב' לתרומת מעשר וב' עישורין היינו מעשר ראשון ומעשר שני ועישורו של עישור כלומר מאלו ב' עישורין נוטל עישורו של אחד מהן והן ב' התאנים של תרומה טפל ב' מאיזו שירצה למעשרות כלכלה בחברתה קאי ומשמע מיכן דלא בעי למימר שתפטר זו את זו וזו את זו אלא האחת תפטור את שתיהן ולא כמו שפירשתי במשנתנו · ובירושלמי (שם) נמי קתני כילד עושה נוטל ב' מאיזו שירצה מהן לכאורה כן נראה פירושה של ברייתא זו אלא שיש הרבה גמגומין חדא דלא משמע כן אין הראשונה מעושרת ועוד קשה דנוטל ב' תאנים משמע דקאי אדסליק מיניה אשל זו בזו ושל זו בזו והלא מעשר קודם לתרומת מעשר וא"כ הכי הוי ליה למיתני נוטל ב' עישורים וב' תאנים לעישורו של עישור ועוד א"א לייתב לשון הירושלמי לפי שיטה זו וזה לשון הירושלמי ותני עליה נוטל משניה ב' תאנים וב' עישורין ועישור מעישור שמואל אמר לא מלי תניגא אין יסב חדא לעשר צריך למיסב חדא למאה אין יסב חדא למאה צריך למיסב חדא לאלף אין יסב חדא לאלף צריך למיסב חדא לעשרת אלפים אלא הכא פי' הברייתא אין הראשונה מעושרת כלו' איכה כולה מעושרת שהרי הוצרך לשייר בו כדי מעשרות כלכלה שניה כר' יוסי דתפיס לשון שניהם דכיון למעשרות של זו בזו ושל זו בזו נמצא שלא תיקן אלא פ"א תאנים בכל אחת ואחת מן הכלכלה די"ט תאנים צריך בכל אחת לצורך מעשר ראשון ושני של חברתה ועל אותן י"ט קאמר נוטל ב' תאנים (דאי) דמספקא ליה לסאי תנא אי כר"מ דתפיס לשון ראשון אי כרבי יוסי דתפיס לשון שניהן ונמצא דאותן י"ט שנטל מן הראשונה בשביל השניה משום דשמא תפוס לשון שניהן וצריך לחזור ולתקן מן השניה משום דשמא סבירא לן תפוס לשון ראשון והייט דתני נוטל מן השניה שני תאנים כלומר לצורך מעשר ראשון של א] ישראל שהפריש מן הראשונה על השניה וב' עישורין צריך ליטול מן השניה לתקן אותן י"ט דהיינו מעשר ראשון ומעשר שני דאותן ב' תאנים הן למעשר ראשון של י"ט ומשום דלא סגי בב' תאנים דעל הי"ח הפריש ב' תאנים מן השניה למעשר ראשון ונמצא מן הי"ט [א'] יתירה שלא נתקנה ואותה יתירה עתידה להיות תרומת מעשר משום הכי קאמר ועישור העישור מלבד ב' תאנים יטול עדיין מן השניה מעשר ראשון הצריך לאותה תאנה שהיא תרומת מעשר ולהכי נקט כי האי לישנא עישור של עישור דתרומת מעשר קרויה מעשר מן המעשר ועלה קאמר שמואל לא מלי תניגא דקמתמה (דאמר) שמואל על ברייתא זו למה יפריש מן השניה על הי"ט לבדן שאם יסב מן השניה חדא לעשר לתקן ב] י"א תאנים שהפריש מן הראשונה על השניה מספק והלא בראשונה צריך [לתקן] מאה תאנים וצריך למיסב מן השניה בבת אחת מעשר ראשון של המאה דשמא תפוס לשון ראשון ולמה לתנא למנות בענין זה ואם יסב חדא למאה כלומר שאותן ב' כלכלות יש אלף בזו ואלף בזו ועולה מעשר ראשון של זו בזו מאה תאנים ובא ליטול מן השניה מטעם ספק חדא לכל עשר ועשר שבמאה של המעשר ראשון שהפריש מן הראשונה על השניה מספק צריך למיסב מן השניה מעשר ראשון של אלף בבת אחת ואם יסב חדא לאלף כגון שיש י' אלפים בכל אחת ואחת ועולה המעשר ראשון אלף אם כן יסב מן השניה מעשר ראשון של י' אלפים בבת אחת ובפ"ד דמס' מעשר שני בירושלמי (הל' ה) אשכחן דקאמר שמואל כי האי גוונא אמר תני דאוכל עליו אחד עשר איסר ואחד ממאה באיסר וכל חדא וחדא מפרשינן לה בכוונה ועוד יש לפרש דהכי קאמר אם יסב חד לעשרה שעל י' תאנים יפריש עליהן תאנה אחת ממקום אחר צריך למיסב חדא למאה דלא נתקנו כל העשרה אלא התשעה שהמעשר דינו אחד מעשר ונמצא שיש שם תאנה אחת שלא ניתקנה והמעשר שלה עולה אחד ממאה שבסלו דהוא עישור של תאנה ואם יסב ממקום אחר מאה לאותו מאה עישורין כדי לתקן אותה תאנה שלא ניתקנה אכתי צריך למיסב חדא לאלף דמן המאה עישורין היה לו להפריש א' כמלא כשמפרישו ממקום אחר הרי נשתייר בו עישור של עישור שלא ניתקן ואם בא לתקן נוטל מאותן עשר עלמן חדא לאלף ואם עוד חזר והפריש ממקום אחר חדא לאלף כדי לתקנו לא ניתקן עדיין בכך עד שיחזור ויפרוש מגופייהו והעישור של א' לאלף דהוא א' לי' אלפים שבהן ומתחלה ודאי כשבא לתקן ממקום אחר על אותן י' תאנים היה יכול להפריש עליהן תאנה אחת ותשיעית של תאנה והיה הכל מתוקן וכן בכל פעם ופעם כשבא להפריש עליהן ממקום אחר יש לו למנות כל מה שבא לתקן בתשיעית : ז מאה טבל ומאה חולין · אין משנה זו מתפרשת אלא על פי משנה דמסכת חלה פ"ג (משנה ט) דזיתי מסיק שנתערבו עם זיתי ניקוף דמוכח התם דטבל שנתערב בחולין אם יש לו פרנסה ממקום אחר מפריש עליו לפי החשבון ואם לאו נעשין החולין כטבל לענין תרומה דשיעור תרומה שבטבל מפריש כמו כן מן החולין כאילו הן טבל גמור אבל מעשר ראשון לא יתן ללוי מן החולין ומעשר שני נמי לא יחלל מהן אלא לפי חשבון הטבל מחלל ונותן מטעם שפירשנו במסכת חלה (יד) והשתא סלקא מתניתין בטבל שהורמה ממנו תרומה גדולה מדקתני נוטל מאה ואחת ולא קא תני מאה ושלש והכי נמי אמרי' בירושלמי (הל' ז) רבי לווינסו בשם ר' יונה כל טבל דהכא קיימין הכא טבל לראשון ולשני כלומר ולא לתרומה גדולה והשתא מתני' באין לו פרנסה ממקום אחר ולהכי קאמר מאה טבל ומאה חולין שנתערבו נוטל מאה להפריש מהן כדין טבל מעשר ראשון ומעשר שני והלוי יפריש ממעשר שלו תרומת מעשר ואחת נוטל מן המאה דלשם חולין לתרומת מעשר כאילו היה טבל כדפרשי' דלענין תרומה דוקא נוהג בהן דין טבל שנתערב בו ונמצא השתא מפסיד אחת שמפריש מן החולין : מאה טבל ומאה מעשר · שנתערבו טפל מאה לשם טבל כדפרשי' ואחת נוטל ממאה של מעשר כאילו הן טבל לשם תרומת מעשר כשתיירו שם תשעים ותשעה ומפריש מהן תרומת מעשר לפי החשבון דהיינו עשרה פחות עישור של אחת ונמצא השתא מפסיד אחת פחות עישור שבה : מאה חולין מתוקנין ומאה מעשר. ראשון שנתערבו טפל מאה לשם מעשר ראשון ועשר טפל ממאה של חולין מתוקנין כאילו הי' *שם מעשר ראשון דעשרה מהן לתרומת מעשר ונמצא השתא מפסיד עשרה והא דלא מחמרינן הכי בשנתערב עם טבל להזקיק הטבל להפריש ממנו עשרה לתרומת מעשר *ממאה של מעשר משום דלכך הוא דין דכל דבר המתערב חוזר להיות כתחלתו הלכך המעשר חוזר להיות כטבל ואין הטבל חוזר להיות כמעשר : מאה טבל ותשעים מעשר · לפי חשבון משנה ראשונה היה ראוי לומר שהתשעים נעשין טבל וחייב להפריש מהן אחת פחות עישור שבה כאילו היו טבל שכך היה עולה תרומת מעשר שבהן ותשעים טבל ושמונים מעשר היה ראוי להפריש מן השמונים אחת פחות ב' עישורין שבה אלא סברא בעלמא הוא דכיון דאיכא בטבל י' יתריס שקיל חדא ופטר הני והוי כאילו יש לו פרנסה ממקום אחר ודוקא עשרה מרובה קאמר כדאיתא בירושלמי (הל' ז) אמר רבי יונה כיני מתני' כל זמן שהטבל מרובה על המעשר עשר(א) לא הפסיד כלום: ירושלמי (שם) מה אנן קיימין מאה טבל ותשעים(ב) מעשר נוטל תשעים ושתים חסר עישור אחד מאה טבל ושמונים(ג) מעשר נוטל שמונים ושתים חסר ב' עישורין שכך עולה תרומת מעשר שלהן אם היה הכל טבל [מיכן ואילך לפי החשבון] ואינו חושש לתרץ כלום מזה כדפרשי' דסברא בעלמא הוא והאי דקאמר נוטל תשעים נוטל שמונים היינו תשעים של מעשר להפריש מהן תשעה לתרומת מעשר ושמונים להפריש מהן שמונה לתרומת מעשר מיכן ואילך לפי החשבון והיינו מן המאה של טבל פחות שנים שהחסיר :

עשר

כלכלה בחברתה קרא שם: ז [א]מאה טבל מאה חולין נוטל מאה *ואחד [ב]מאה טבל מאה מעשר נוטל מאה *ואחד [ג]מאה חולין מתוקנין מאה מעשר נוטל מאה ועשר [ד]ק' טבל תשעים מעשר תשעים טבל ושמנים מעשר לא הפסיד כלום זה הכלל כל זמן שהטבל מרובה לא הפסיד כלום:

מי

ירושלמי ואחת

ז שמור זה העיקר והוא שהרומת מעשר עולה באחד וממאה ר"ל כשיתערב חלק מתרומת מעשר במאה חלקים אחרים ויחזור הכל מאה ואחד יטול החלק ההוא שנפל בו בלבד וזהו ענין העלה ועוד יתבאר זה באר היטב אחרי זאת והענין הראשון מזאת ההלכה הוא כשנתערב מאה חלקים טבל ומאה חלקים חולין ונעשה הכל מאתים חלקים אמר שיטול מאלו המאתים חלקים ק"א ויהיו הק"א שנטל טבל והתשעים והשעה שהגיח חולין כמו שהיו ונמצא מפסיד מקהחולין אחת אבל המאה הם מאה של טבל הראשוני' והאחת היא תרומת מעשר מאותן מאה של טבל ואם יהיה זה החלק נופל בק' חולין יטלהו ממנו כאשר ביארנו והסברא נותנת שלא יטול אלא מאה של טבל בלבד ויחשב חלק ממאה מן הטבל ההוא והוא תרומת מעשר שלו שנפל בק' של חולין ועלה באחד ומאה לפי שק הוא דין הדבר שיעלה שיהיה נוטל מה שנפל ולא יחסר מן החולין כלום אבל חסרנו בכאן מן החולין אחר שאנו חוששים שמא יחשוב כשנטל המאה בלבד שזה שנטלט הם מאה של חולין והנשארים הם מאה של טבל ואין הדבר כן לפי שהטבל הוא הניטל וזה ענין מה שנאמר בגמרא וטטל מאה ואחת וא"ר יוסי אם אתה אומר אני נוטל מאה אני אומר כל חולין עלו בידו ונמצאו אלו בטבלים : והענין השני מהלכה זו כשנתערב ק' חלקים של טבל עם אחרים שהם ממעשר ראשון יטול כמו כן ק"א ויהיו מעשר ראשון והתשעה והשעים חלקים הנותרים הם טבל כמו שהיו ונמצא שחסר חלק אחד מן הטבל אבל הק' חלקים הם מאה של מעשר הראשונים והחלק הנוסף על המאה היא תרומת מעשר המחויבת למאה של טבל ונחשב שמא נתערב עם מאה חלקים של יתעשר ודינו שיעלה כמו שביארנו ואינו מדומע ומפני זה נבארו ימאה יאחת שהוליא מעשר ראשון כמו שהיו והיתה הסברא נוהגת ג"כ בכאן להוליא מאה של מעשר בלבד מפני שתרומת מעשר של טבל שהוא חלק אחד כשנחשב החלק ההוא שנתערב במאה של מעשר יעלה באחת ומאה אבל אמר נוטל מאה ואחד מפני הטעם ההוא אשר פירוש הגמרא בענין הראשון והוא שאילו נוטל מאה חלקים בלבד הייט אומרים מאה חלקים של טבל הם אשר הוליא והמאה הנשארים הם המעשר ואין הדבר כן לפי שהמעשר הוא שיוליא ומפני זה יוליא ק"א כדי שיהיה נודע שהמעשר הוא שהוליא לפי שהמעשר כלל לעלמו חלק נוסף : והענין השלישי כשיתערבו ק' חולין מתוקנין ומאה מעשר הוא אומר שיוליא מאה ועשר ויהיה הכל מעשר ראשון והתשעים הנותרים חולין כמו שהיו אבל המאה הם מאה של מעשר הראשונים ועשרה הנוספים הם תרומת מעשר המחויבים למאה של מעשר וכאילו נפלו במאה של חולין והוליא אותן וחסרו מן החולין לפי שהעשרה חלקים שהם תרומת מעשר הם עשירית מאה של חולין ואינם חלק ממאה מהם ומפני כך (לא עלתה) [העלה] כדי שישארו החולין כמו שהיו וכמו כן לא היו העשרה חלקים של תרומת מעשר מבוררות ומיוחדות כדי שיחזרו מאה של חולין כולם מדומע מפני שהן אמלעיות בין שני הקלות ר"ל שהן לא יחזרו המאה של חולין מדומע מפני שאינן מיוחדות אלא מעורבות במעשר וכמו כן אי אפשר *לשמן אותן וישארו חולין כמו שהיו אחר שהם עשירית חולין אבל העלה תרומת מעשר באחת ומאה ונזרנו בהם מן הדימוע גזירה ביטנית ואמרנו שיחסר מן החולין כמו תרומת מעשר שיש באותו מעשר כמו שהראה ונשאר בכאן ענין אחד לשאול מפני מה נאמר בענין השלישי מאה חולין מתוקנין ולא נאמר כן בענין הראשון אבל אמר מאה טבל ומאה חולין ולא אמר מתוקנין וזאת השאלה צריכה לשאול ויש בה תועלת והוא שהטבל שיוליא ממנו תרומה גדולה והתרומת מעשר יהיה לא נקרא חולין אע"פ שלא הוליאו ממנו שאר מעשרות מפני שהקדושה ניטלה ממנו וחולין מתוקנין הוא הדבר שהוליאו ממנו כל התרומות והמעשרות ויש לך לשמר בלבך זה ההפרש בין מה שאמר חולין ובין מה שאמר חולין מתוקנין בכל המשנה ואילו יאמר בזה הענין השלישי מאה מעשר ומאה חולין סטל מאה ועשר הייט אומרים שאלו החולין לא הוליאו מהן מעשר ובשנתערב עמהם ק' מעשר נטלנו הק' מעשר שנתערב עם המעשר הנשאר באלו הק' של חולין והוא עשר חלקים ועל כן הוליאט ק"י מפני שנתחבר מעשר במעשר ולא חסר כלום ולפיכך הודיעט שאלו החולין ואפי' היו מתוקנין שלא נשאר בהם שום מהגה ואח"כ נתערב בהם מעשר יחסר מאותם חולין כמו תרומת מעשר המחויבת למעשר ההיא ויאבד לגמרי וילטרף לכלל המעשר כמו שאמר טטל ק' ועשר ונשארו הל' חולין מתוקנין כמו שהיו והיק נשאר כך עד שתהיה תרומת מעשר המחויבת למעשר ההוא שנתערב עם החולין המתוקנים חלק ממאה עם החולין המתוקנין כגון שיתערב מאה מעשר עם אלף חולין מתוקנים נאמר לו שלא יפסיד כלום אבל יפריש ק' מעשר לבדם ואם החולין יהיו פחות ממה שאמרט יחסר מהם כמו תרומת מעשר שבמעשר המעורב כמו שביארט ופירשט טעמי כל הענין ההוא : והענין הרביעי כשיתערב ק' טבל וצ' מעשר יפרישו צ' של מעשר בלבד ונשארו מאה טבל כמו שהיו ולא הפסיד כלום והדבר שגרם לט בענין הזה שלא נקרא שם לתרומת מעשר של טבל וטליא ל"א מפני שהחלק האחד מן הטבל שהוא תרומת מעשר כשנחשב בלבנו שנתערב עם צ' של מעשר חזר המעשר ההוא כולו מדומע מפני שתרומת מעשר תעלה באחד ומאה כמו שביארט עיקרו לא בצ"א ומפני זה לא יקרא שם לתרומת מעשר של טבל בענין הזה כדי שלא יפסיד המעשרות וישוב מדומע ועל זה הדרך בעלמו יתבאר לך מה שאמר צ' טבל שמונים מעשר שאילו נחשב בלבנו תרומת מעשר שבטבל ההוא שנתערב עם פ' של מעשר חזר אותו המעשר מדומע בתרומת מעשר : ומ"ש כל זמן שהטבל מרובה. ר"ל על המעשר וכן אמרו כל

שהטבל

פי' הרא"ש

(יד) ומיהו צריך להפריש כולם דא"א להפריש תרומת מעשר על הכל אם לא שיפריש תחלה המעשר על הכל ועוד אם לא היה מעשר על הכל א"כ אין פירותיו מתוקנים דכל מה שמעשר יש בהם חולין לפי חשבון ונמצא מפריש מן הפטור על החיוב אלא כל המעשרות צריך להפריש אבל אינו נותן ללוי ולעני ואינו מחלל מעשר שני אלא לפי החשבון אבל תרומה ותרומת מעשר כשמפריש על הכל נמצא חולין שבהם מדומעין ונותן הכל לכהן או מוכר לכהן העודף על הראוי לתרום :

הגהות הגר"א

(א) מ"ז בר"ש עשר. נמחק וכ"כ מעשר : (ב) שם מעשר. נמחק : (ג) שם מעשר. נמחק :

הגהות מהרי"י לנדא

מ"ז בר"ש א] לצורך של ישראל. צ"ל שניה : ב] לתקן י"א תאנים. צ"ל י"ט:

צ"ל של

צ"ל כמאה

פי' מהר"י בן מלכי צדק

ז מאה טבל מאה חולין וכו'. ירושלמי ר' ליוונסי בשם ר' יונה כל טבל דנן קיימי הכא טבל לראשון ולשני כלומר הופרש ממנו תרומה גדולה הלכך כשנתערב הטבל הזה עם החולין המתוקנין נוטל ק' וא' והחולין נעשו כטבל להפריש מהן תרומת מעשר כאשר מפריש מן הטבל אבל שאר מעשרו' אינו מוציא אלא מק' דטבל אבל מן החולין לא צריך למיפרש כדתנן בחלה זיתי מסיק שנתערבו עם זיתי ניקוף כלל לכך שנינו נוטל ק' ואחד פי' נוטל ק' והוו טבל וא' נוטל תרומת מעשר מן החולין שכיון שנתערבו נעשו כטבל לענין תרומת מעשר נמצא כי הפסיד סאה אחת מחולין: ק' טבל ק' מעשר. פי' מעשר ראשון שנתערבו נוטל ק' ואחת למה שמעשר ראשון נעשה בטבל להפריש ממנו תרומת מעשר כמו כן הטבל חד למאה הלכך נוטל ק' לשם טבל וחד לשם תרומת מעשר נשתיירו לו צ"ט סאין מעשר ראשון יהא מפריש מינייהו תרומת מעשר לפי חשבון נמצא שהפסיד סאה מן המעשר פחות עישור סאה: מאה חולין מתוקנין ומאה מעשר ראשון שנתערבו נעשו החולין נ"כ מעשר הלכך נוטל ק' ועשר והן תרומת מעשר נשארו לו צ' סאין חולין נמצא שהפסיד מחוליו י' סאין : מאה טבל ותשעים מעשר. פי' שנתערבו לא הפסיד כלום. גרסי' בירושל' ק' טבל וצ' מעשר נוטל תשעים וב' חסר עישור אחד ק' טבל ופ' בעשר נוטל פ"ב חסר ב' עישורין מיכן ואילך לפי השבון ולפי הגירסא בתשעים טבל ופ' מעשר נוטל פ"ב חסר ב' עישורין. ירושלמי א"ר יונה כיני מתני' כל זמן שהטבל מרובה על המעשר עשר לא הפסיד כלום :

SO THAT THE TITHES OF EACH BASKET BE IN THE OTHER, HE HAS THEREBY DESIGNATED[8] [THE TITHES OF BOTH BASKETS].

a *MISHNAH* 7. IF A HUNDRED [PARTS OF] ṬEBEL[1] [WERE MIXED WITH] A HUNDRED [PARTS OF] COMMON[2] PRODUCE, ONE MUST TAKE OUT A HUNDRED AND ONE[3] [PARTS]. IF A HUNDRED [PARTS OF] ṬEBEL [WERE MIXED WITH] A HUNDRED [PARTS OF FIRST] TITHE,[4] ONE MUST TAKE OUT A HUNDRED AND ONE[5] [PARTS]. IF A HUNDRED [PARTS OF] COMMON PRODUCE WHICH HAD BEEN SET RIGHT[6] [WERE MIXED WITH] A HUNDRED [PARTS OF] TITHE,[7] ONE MUST TAKE OUT A HUNDRED AND TEN[8] [PARTS]. IF A HUNDRED [PARTS OF] ṬEBEL [WERE MIXED WITH] NINETY [PARTS OF] TITHE,[9] OR NINETY [PARTS OF] ṬEBEL [WERE MIXED WITH] EIGHTY[10] [PARTS OF] TITHE, ONE LOSES NOTHING. THIS IS THE GENERAL RULE: WHENEVER THE ṬEBEL IS THE GREATER [PORTION OF THE MIXTURE] ONE LOSES NOTHING.[11]

(8) And he must give tithes for each one out of the other.

a (1) Here equivalent to untithed produce, as *supra* V, 8, n. 3. (2) Produce from which *terumah* and Terumah of the Tithe had been taken. The whole mixture becomes prohibited to non-priests like *ṭebel*, because of the *Terumah* of the Tithe contained in the *ṭebel* parts of it. (3) Hundred parts being *ṭebel* from which the usual tithes must be taken, and one extra part being *Terumah* of the Tithe to free the hundred parts common produce in the mixture. The owner thus loses one part. (4) From which *Terumah* of the Tithe had not been taken. (5) Hundred parts being *ṭebel* from which the usual tithes must be taken, and one part being *Terumah* of the Tithe for the *ṭebel*. The remaining ninety-nine parts of the mixture are First Tithe, from which he must take 99/10 parts as *Terumah* of the Tithe. The owner thus loses 9/10 of a part. (6) From which all the *terumah* and tithes had been taken; III, 1, n. 5. (7) From which the *Terumah* of the Tithe had not been taken. The common produce becomes prohibited because of the ten parts *Terumah* of the Tithe in the other constituent of the mixture. (8) Hundred parts being tithe from which *Terumah* of the Tithe must be given, and ten parts being *Terumah* of the Tithe to free the hundred parts common produce. The owner thus loses ten parts. (9) Terumah of the Tithe for hundred parts *ṭebel* is one part, and for ninety parts tithe nine parts; therefore he may take ten parts as *Terumah* of the Tithe and discharge the whole mixture. (10) *Terumah* of the Tithe for ninety parts *ṭebel* is 9/10 of a part, and of eighty parts tithe eight parts; therefore he must take 89/10 parts as *Terumah* of the Tithe and discharge the whole mixture. (11) In the case of a mixture of tithed and untithed produce, one cannot take tithe from the mixture for its untithed portion, because one may happen to pick up as tithe some of the tithed portion of the mixture, and this would be tithing produce which is exempt for produce which is liable (cf. *supra* 6, n. 7). But if the owner happens to have elsewhere other untithed produce of the same kind as the untithed produce in the mixture, he may use it for tithing the untithed produce in the mixture; cf. Ḥal. III, 9 and *supra* V, 8, n. 5. Hence when the *ṭebel* in the mixture exceeds the other portion of the mixture, this excess may be used for tithing the *ṭebel* as if the excess was elsewhere, and thus the owner loses nothing in the process of freeing the mixture from the *Terumah* of the Tithe in it. Similarly, if the owner had had *ṭebel* produce apart from the mixture and of the same kind as the *ṭebel* in the mixture, he may have used it for tithing the *ṭebel* mixture also in the cases mentioned above where the two constituents of the mixture were equal in quantity, thus obviating a loss of produce in extra *Terumah* of the Tithe.

MISHNAH 8. IF A MAN HAD TEN ROWS EACH CONTAINING
a TEN JARS OF WINE,[1] AND HE HAD SAID: ONE EXTERIOR ROW[2] SHALL BE TITHE, AND IT IS NOT KNOWN WHICH ROW[3] [HE MEANT], HE MUST TAKE TWO JARS [EACH FROM THE ENDS OF] A DIAGONAL LINE.[4] [IF HE HAD SAID:] ONE HALF OF THE EXTERIOR ROW[5] SHALL BE TITHE, AND IT IS NOT KNOWN WHICH HALF ROW [HE MEANT], HE MUST TAKE FOUR JARS FROM THE FOUR CORNERS.[6] [IF HE HAD SAID:] ONE ROW[7] SHALL BE TITHE,[8] AND IT IS NOT KNOWN WHICH ROW [HE MEANT], HE MUST TAKE ONE [WHOLE] ROW IN A DIAGONAL LINE.[9] [IF HE HAD SAID:] HALF OF ONE ROW[10] SHALL BE TITHE, AND IT IS NOT KNOWN WHICH HALF ROW [HE MEANT], HE
b MUST TAKE TWO ROWS IN A DIAGONAL LINE.[1] [IF HE HAD SAID:] ONE JAR[2] SHALL BE TITHE, AND IT IS NOT KNOWN WHICH JAR [HE MEANT], HE MUST TAKE FROM EVERY JAR.[3]

a (1) Forming a square of ten by ten. (2) I.e., ten jars of which one jar will be *Terumah* of the Tithe. (3) The problem is to secure that the one jar which has to be given to a priest as *Terumah* of the Tithe shall come from the exterior row which he had originally designated as tithe, and which may be any one of the four exterior rows. (4) So that the two jars belong together to all the four exterior rows. These two jars must be sold to a priest for the price of one jar, thus both jars will be consumed by a priest, and one of them will be a gift to him in respect of *Terumah* of the Tithe. (5) Only fifty of the hundred jars had to be tithed. Here the half jar which must go as *Terumah* of the Tithe is to be found in one of the eight exterior half-rows. (6) So that the four jars belong together to all the eight exterior half-rows. The four jars must be sold to a priest for the price of three and a half jars, so that all the four jars will be consumed by a priest and one half will be a gift to him in respect of *Terumah* of the Tithe. (7) Not necessarily an exterior row. (8) For all the hundred jars. (9) I.e., ten jars, which together belong to all the ten rows of the square. These ten jars must be sold to a priest for the price of nine jars, so that all the ten jars will be consumed by a priest and one of them will be a gift to him in respect of *Terumah* of the Tithe. (10) Only fifty of the hundred jars had to be tithed. Here the half jar of *Terumah* of the Tithe will be in one of the twenty half-rows of the square.

b (1) The two diagonal lines of the square. The twenty jars of these two lines, which together belong to all the twenty half-rows of the square, must be sold to a priest for the price of nineteen and a half, and one half as a gift in respect of *Terumah* of the Tithe. (2) Only one row had to be tithed. (3) One hundredth part of it to make up one whole jar which must be sold to a priest for nine tenths of its price, one tenth being a gift to him in respect of *Terumah* of the Tithe. The explanation of the Mishnah given here follows the commentary of R. Simson of Sens and Tifereth Ysrael. It accords well with the wording of the text, and seems to be supported by the Palestinian Gemara. R. Hai Gaon, Maimonides and Bertinoro explain the Mishnah in a more complicated manner, holding that the subject under discussion is of the designation of one jar only out of the hundred in the square as tithe for wine which was elsewhere.

CORRIGENDA

DEMAI

On page 8b note a9 for 'cf. Introduction p. 50.' read 'cf. Introduction, paragraph (3) in "TERUMAH AND TITHES,"'

On page 9a note a6 for 'V. n. 9, p. 53.' read 'V. 8b n. a9, Introduction, paragraphs (3) in "TERUMAH AND TITHES,"'

On page 9b note b3 for 'cf. Introduction, p. 51.' read 'cf. Introduction, after paragraph (3), "TERUMAH AND TITHES."'

On page 9b note b7 for 'cf. Introduction p. 51, 'Ed. I, 14 (sonc. ed. p. 8, n. 1).' read 'cf. Introduction, after paragraph (3). 'Ed. I, 14 (sonc. ed. 3a n. c1).'

On page 9b note c10 for 'cf. Introduction p. 50.' read 'cf. Introduction, paragraph (2) in "TERUMAH AND TITHES,"'

On page 10a note b5 for 'cf. Introduction p. 49.' read 'cf. Introduction, paragraph "NAME."'

On page 11a note a5 for 'Introduction p. 51.' read 'Introduction, after paragraph (3), "TERUMAH AND TITHES."'

On page 11a note a6 for 'V. Introduction p. 50' read 'V. Introduction, paragraph (3) in "TERUMAH AND TITHES."'

On page 11a note a7 for 'cf. Introduction p. 51.' read 'cf. Introduction, after paragraph (3), "TERUMAH AND TITHES."'

On page 11b note b5 for 'cf. Introduction p. 50,' read 'cf. Introduction, paragraph (1) in "TERUMAH AND TITHES."'

On page 12a note a3 for 'cf. Introduction p. 50.' read 'cf. Introduction, paragraph (1) in "TERUMAH AND TITHES."'

On page 14a note a1 for 'cf. Introduction p. 50.' read 'cf. Introduction, paragraph (2) in "TERUMAH AND TITHES."'

KIL'AYIM

CHAPTER I

a *MISHNAH* I. [1]WHEAT AND DARNEL DO NOT CONSTITUTE KIL'AYIM[2] ONE WITH THE OTHER.[3] [LIKEWISE] BARLEY AND

a (1) This Mishnah deals with grain and pulse which can be ground into flour. (2) 'Mingled seeds' within the meaning of the Biblical precept, (Lev. XIX, 19) prohibiting the sowing of such. (3) Despite such dissimilarities there is between the two of each pair.

ח עשר שורות של עשר עשר שורות חביות מסודרות על הארץ שבכל ענין שתמנה בין ממזרח למערב בין מצפון לדרום תמצא שורות של עשר עשר כאילו היה כאן קרקע מרובע עשר על עשר אמות ובכל אמה חבית מונחת והרי יש כאן מאה חביות בין הכל וכולן מתוקנין חוץ מאותן שאומר עליהן שהן מעשר דהנהו מעשר ניניהו ולא ניטלה ממנו תרומת מעשר ובהכי אתי' כולה מתני' בפשיטות והא דפתח בכד וסיים בחבית לומר לך היינו חבית היינו כד (טו) כדמשנינן בפ' המניח את הכד (דף כז.): ואמר שורה החיצונה אחת מעשר ואין ידוע איזו היא · שיש כאן ד' שורות חיצונות לד' רוחות ולא ידע אי חיצונה שבמזרח או חיצונה שבמערב או שבצפון או שבדרום נוטל ב' חביות לוכסן דהיינו חבית שבקרן דרומית מזרחית וצפונית מערבית דכל חבית שבקרן נמנית מן השורה לשני רוחות וקורא על אחת מאלו השתים תרומת מעשר ואלו שתים ספק וכל השאר מותר: חצי שורה אחת חיצונה מעשר ואין ידוע איזו היא · כמאלו חמש חביות מעשר דלא ידיע איזו שורה ובאיזו צד של שורה ואם היה יודע היה מפריש חצי חבית אחת לתרומת מעשר והשאר מותר והשתא דלא ידע נוטל ד' חביות לד' זויות דממה נפשך אחת מהן מעשר כדפרישית דכל חבית שבקרן נחשבה לשתי רוחות ומפריש מכל אחת מספק חציה לתרומת

ח "מי שהיו לו עשר שורות של עשר עשר כדי יין ואמר שורה החיצונה אחת מעשר ואין ידוע איזו היא נוטל ב' חביות לוכסן "חצי שורה החיצונה אחת מעשר ואין ידוע איזו היא נוטל ארבע חביות מארבע זויות שורה אחת מעשר ואין ידוע איזו היא נוטל שורה אחת לוכסן חצי שורה אחת מעשר ואין ידוע איזו היא נוטל ב' שורות לוכסן "חבית אחת מעשר ואין ידוע איזו היא נוטל מכל חבית וחבית:

סליקא לה מסכת דמאי

שהטבל מרובה על המעשר אבל כשיהיה מעשר מרובה על הטבל יפרש בגמרא שהוא מפריש טבל ושיעור תרומת מעשר המחויבת לטבל והמחויבת למעשר ההוא (שניהם) ויתן שתי תרומות לכהן ר"ל תרומת מעשר ותרומת טבל ונמצא חסר מן הטבל שיעור שתי התרומות ואיני רואה בזו ההלכה דבר שאינו באר היטב על כן יש לך להסתכל בה מפני שנשתבשה על כל הקדמונים לפי דעתו: ח הענין הראשון והוא שאמר שורה החיצונה אחת מעשר ר"ל שהוא נתן חבית אחת מעשר והחבית ההיא בשורה החיצונה והשורות החיצונות הם ד' ויקח שתי חביות מקצת האלכסון בשביל שכל אחת מהן משתתפת עם שתי שורות וימלא משהיקן חבית אחת והיה מעשר ואם אמר חבית אחת מחצי שורה החיצונה מעשר יקח ד' חביות מד' זויות מפני שכל אחת מהן משותפת משני מחציות של שתי שורות מן השורות החיצונות וימלא (מכל א') מהן

מהן יקח עשר חביות על האלכסון ונמצא לוקח חבית מכל שורה וימלא מכלם חבית אחת ואם אמר חבית אחת מחצי שורה אחת מעשר ולא יחד איזו חצי שורה יקח עשרים חביות י' על אלכסון אחד וי' על אלכסון אחר העובר עליו ונמצא לוקח חבית מכל חצי שורה מן השורות ואחר כן יוליא מכלם מלא חבית אחת ושמא תחשוב ותאמר היאך יוליא חבית מעשר מק' חביות והלא עשירותם עשר חביות יש לך לדעת שלא גזר זה המעשר על החביות האלו והנני מצייר לך בהם צורה כדי שיהיה הדבר מבואר לעין הרואה ואשים במקום החבית עגולים א ואכתוב אותיות ובענין הראשון מזו ההלכה הוא לוקח שתי חביות שכתוב על אחת א' ועל שניה ב' ובענין השני לוקח ד' חביות שכתוב על אחת א' ועל שניה ב' ועל שלישית ג' ועל רביעית ד' ובענין השלישי לוקח העשר חביות אשר יעבור עליהם הקו העובר מא' עד ב' ובענין הרביעי לוקח העשרים אשר יעברו עליהם שני הקוים העוברים מא' עד ב' ומג' עד ד' והגה צורתה כזה:

ד

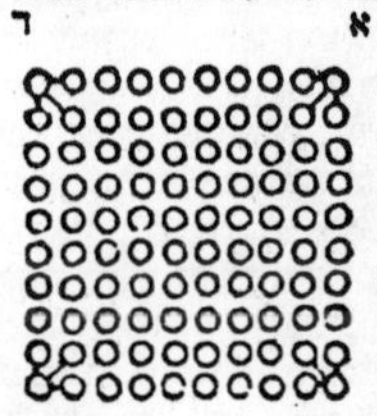

ב ג

סליקא לה מסכת דמאי

באיזו שורה נוטל שורה אחת: סליק פירקא ומסכתא

א החטין והזונין אינן כלאים. כולה מתניתין זוזי זוזי קתני כדמשמע בירושלמי (הל' א) רבי יוסי בשם רבי יוחנן כולהו זוגות זוגות מה על כל פירקא קא אמרת או על הדא הלכתא ואסיק על כל פירקא ומשמע הכא דכוסמין עם החטין כלאים ושיפון עם השעורים או עם שבולת שועל כלאים *ותימה דבמנחות פרק רבי ישמעאל (דף ע.) תנא כוסמין מין חטים שבולת שועל ושיפון מין שעורים ויש לומר דההיא לענין לצאת ידי מצה מיתניא דהא בסוף ואלו מנחות (דף עה:) תניא ליקט מכולן כזית ואכלו אם חמץ הוא ענוש כרת ואם מצה היא אדם יוצא בה ידי חובתו בפסח ומכלן הייט מכל חמשת המינים דאי מכל חמש מנחות הא קתני חמץ וכולן באות מצה ועוד שהן קדושות ולא קרינא בהו מאתכם דמשלכם בעינן דאתיא לחם לחם כדאיתא בפרק כל שעה (דף לה:) וצריך לומר דלענין חלה מיתני' והכי מייתי לה במנחות פרק רבי ישמעאל אמתני' דהתם החטין והשעורים

א זונין מין ממיני התבואה וישתנה בארץ בהבכיהו וטבעו וע"כ נקרא זונין מענין הזלילה מדרך היושר כמו לבם הזונה יחזקאל

החטין פרק ראשון

א החטין "והזונין אינן כלאים זה בזה השעורים

ושבולת שועל ושיפון הרי אלו חייבים בחלה ומצטרפין זה עם זה ולאו אכולהו קאמר שמצטרפין זה עם זה אלא *כדפרישית בברייתא בגמרא וכן פירש שם בקונטרס ומיהו בירושלמי דחלה משמע דאכולהו קאמר דמצטרפים אהדדי דמתני' דהתם שטיה כמו כן בריש מסכת חלה ותנן בפרק בתרא דחלה מין במינו חייב ושלא במינו פטור איזהו מין במינו החטים אינן מצטרפין עם הכל אלא עם הכוסמין והשעורים מצטרפין עם הכל חוץ מן החטין ובריש חלה פריך לה אהדדי בירושלמי (פ"א הל' א) ומשני רבי יוסי אמר להו פתם ורבי יונה בשם רבי יוחנן בצלין יפה ועשה מהן עיסה אחת כולן מצטרפין והעשה עיסה מכולן מין ומין בפני עצמו ואח"כ העיסות נושכות זו בזו מצטרפות בכי האי גוונא דקתני והא דקתני השעורים מצטרפין עם הכל חוץ מן החטים דמשמע דמצטרפים עם הכוסמין ובברייתא קתני כוסמין אף מין חטין ושבולת שועל ושיפון מין שעורים דוקא ואם תאמר והנך מינים שהם כלאים היאך מצטרפים הא דתנן בפרק ה' (משנה ו') דתרומות כל שהוא כלאים בחברו לא יתרום זה על זה (א) וי"ל דגבי חלה תלוי הטעם לפי שעיסותיהן דומות

ספה תרומתו תרומה חוץ מן הזונין על החטים שאינו אוכל : שבולת שועל · מפרש בפרק כל שעה (דף לה:) שבלי דישרא (ד) פול · מפרש בירושלמי (שם) פול״א [א] הספיר פייסול״א פורקדן גולביג״א טופח מילותא מרסיא

שמה שעועית שמשעת הלב* ומהלכת בני מעים כלומר המטמטמת הלב ומשלשלת מלבון ועיניו השע ועח את הבית

(הל׳ ב) אמר ר׳ יודן בר מנשה דברי חכמים אדם נוטל מטה אחת מפיסמא של קישות ונוטעה והיא נעשית אבטיח

*[ומשלשלת את כו׳ וכ״ה בירושלמי]

א) פסחים פ״ב דל״ט.

פי׳ מהר״י בן מלכי צדק

השעורים ושבולת שועל הכוסמין והשיפון הפול והספיר הפורקדן והטופח ופול הלבן והשעועים אינם כלאים זה בזה : **ב** הקשות והמלפפון אינם כלאים זה בזה ר׳ יהודה אומר כלאים חזרת א) וחזרת גלים עולשין ועולשי שדה כרישין וכרישי שדה כוסבר וכוסבר שדה חרדל וחרדל מצרי ודלעת המצרי והרמוצה ופול מצרי והחרוב אינן כלאים זה בזה : **ג** הלפת והנפוץ והכרוב והתרובתור התרדים והלעונין אינן כלאים זה בזה הוסיף רבי עקיבא השום (ז) והשומנית הבצל והבצלצול והתורמוס (ח) והפלסלוס אינן כלאים זה בזה : **ד** ובאילן האגסים והקרסתומלין והפרישים והעוזרדים אינם כלאים זה בזה התפוח (ט) והחזרד (י) הפרסקים השקדין והשיזפין והרימין אע״פ שדומין זה לזה כלאים זה בזה : **ה** הצנון והנפוץ החרדל והלפסן ודלעת יונית עם המצרית והרמוצה אע״פ שדומין זה לזה כלאים זה בזה : **ו** הזאב והכלב כלב הכופרי והשועל העזים והצבאים היעלים והרחלים הסוס והפרד הפרד והחמור החמור והערוד אע״פ שדומין זה לזה כלאים

OATS, OR SPELT AND RYE, OR BEANS AND CHICK-PEAS, OR BITTER PEAS[4] AND TOFAH,[5] OR WHITE BEANS AND KIDNEY BEANS, DO NOT CONSTITUTE KIL'AYIM ONE WITH THE OTHER.[3]

MISHNAH 2. CUCUMBERS AND CUCUMBER-MELONS[6] DO NOT CONSTITUTE KIL'AYIM ONE WITH THE OTHER. R. JUDAH SAID THEY DO CONSTITUTE KIL'AYIM. GARDEN-LETTUCE AND WILD[7] LETTUCE, OR ENDIVES AND WILD[8] ENDIVES, OR LEEK AND WILD[8] LEEK, OR CORIANDER AND WILD[8] CORIANDER, OR MUSTARD AND EGYPTIAN MUSTARD, OR THE EGYPTIAN AND THE BITTER-APPLE,[9] OR EGYPTIAN BEANS[10] AND BEANS IN CAROB-SHAPED PODS DO NOT CONSTITUTE KIL'AYIM ONE WITH THE OTHER.

MISHNAH 3. TURNIPS AND RADISHES,[11] OR CABBAGE AND CAULIFLOWER, OR BEET AND GARDEN-ORACHE DO NOT CONSTITUTE KIL'AYIM ONE WITH THE OTHER. R. AKIBA ADDED: ALSO GARLIC AND SMALL WILD GARLIC, OR ONION AND SMALL WILD ONION, OR LUPINE AND WILD LUPINE DO NOT CONSTITUTE KIL'AYIM ONE WITH THE OTHER.

MISHNAH 4. AS FOR TREES, THE PEAR AND THE CRUSTU-
a MENIAN PEAR,[1] OR THE QUINCE AND SORB-APPLE, DO NOT CONSTITUTE KIL'AYIM ONE WITH THE OTHER. THE APPLE AND THE CRAB-APPLE, OR THE PEACH AND ALMOND, OR THE JUJUBE[2] AND LOTE, EVEN THOUGH THEY ARE SIMILAR ONE TO THE OTHER, YET CONSTITUTE KIL'AYIM[3] ONE WITH THE OTHER.

MISHNAH 5. HORSE-RADISH AND RADISH,[4] OR MUSTARD AND CHARLOCK,[5] OR THE GREEK GOURD WITH THE EGYPTIAN GOURD OR [THE GREEK GOURD] WITH THE BITTER-APPLE, EVEN THOUGH THEY ARE SIMILAR ONE TO THE OTHER, ARE NEVERTHELESS,[6] KIL'AYIM ONE WITH THE OTHER.

MISHNAH 6. A WOLF AND A DOG, OR A WILD[7] DOG AND A JACKAL, OR A GOAT AND A DEER, OR A GAZELLE AND A EWE-LAMB, OR A HORSE AND A MULE, OR A MULE AND AN ASS, OR AN ASS AND A WILD-ASS, EVEN THOUGH THEY ARE SIMILAR ONE TO THE OTHER, CONSTITUTE NEVERTHELESS,

(4) פרקדן T.J. 27*a*, גולבינא which according to Jast. quoting Fleischer (in Levy *Talm. Dict.*) is *Vicia sativa, Lathyrus cicerca*. (5) Jast. An aquatic plant like the colocasia. (6) מלפפון. (7) Lit., 'mound , or 'hill'. (8) Lit., 'field'. (9) רמוצה (דלעת), a kind of gourd made edible by rolling in hot ashes. (10) Colocasia. (Jast.). (11) A species having foliage like carrots and taste like radishes.

a (1) *Crushiminum* (*pyrum*). (2) *Zizyphus*. (3) In respect of grafting only. (4) V. *supra* 3, n. 11. (5) A plant resembling the mustard plant. (6) On account of dissimilarity of flavour. (7) Lit., 'village'.

KIL'AYIM[8] ONE WITH THE OTHER.

MISHNAH 7. IT IS NOT PERMITTED TO GRAFT FROM ONE TREE TO ANOTHER,[9] OR FROM ONE HERB TO ANOTHER,[10] OR FROM A TREE TO A HERB, OR FROM A HERB TO A TREE. R. JUDAH PERMITS IT FROM A HERB TO A TREE.[11]

MISHNAH 8. IT IS NOT PERMITTED TO PLANT HERBS IN A TRUNK OF A SYCAMORE. IT IS NOT PERMITTED TO GRAFT RUE ON WHITE CASSIA, SINCE THAT IS [GRAFTING] A HERB ON A TREE. IT IS FORBIDDEN TO PLANT A YOUNG FIG-SHOOT
a IN A CISTUS SHRUB[1] FOR THE PURPOSE OF PROVIDING SHADE[2] FOR THE LATTER, OR TO INSERT A VINE-SHOOT INTO A MELON IN ORDER THAT THE LATTER MIGHT CONTRIBUTE[3] ITS MOISTURE TO THE FORMER, SINCE THAT IS [GRAFTING] A TREE ON A HERB. IT IS PROHIBITED TO PLACE GOURD SEED INTO THE JUICE OF A MALLOW FOR THE PURPOSE OF PRESERVING THE FORMER,[4] SINCE THAT CONSTITUTES [GRAFTING] A HERB ON A [HETEROGENEOUS] HERB.

MISHNAH 9. ONE WHO BURIES[5] TURNIPS OR HORSE-RADISH[6] BENEATH A VINE, WITH SOME OF THEIR LEAVES UNCOVERED,[7] NEED HAVE NO APPREHENSION AS TO TRANSGRESSING THE LAW OF KIL'AYIM,[8] OR THE LAW OF THE SEVENTH YEAR,[9] OR THAT OF TITHES;[10] THEY MAY ALSO BE PULLED UP ON THE SABBATH.[11] IF ONE SOWS A WHEAT-GRAIN AND A BARLEY-GRAIN WITH ONE THROW OF THE HAND IT
b DOES NOT CONSTITUTE KIL'AYIM.[1] R. JUDAH SAID IT IS NOT KIL'AYIM UNLESS THERE BE TWO WHEAT-GRAINS AND ONE BARLEY-GRAIN, OR ONE WHEAT-GRAIN AND TWO BARLEY-GRAINS, OR A WHEAT-GRAIN, A BARLEY-GRAIN AND A SPELT-GRAIN.[2]

(8) In respect of cross-breeding., v. Lev. XIX, 19, Deut. XXII, 10. (9) *Sc.* dissimilar to it in accordance with Mishnah 4. This prohibition applies to grafting as between one fruit tree and another dissimilar to it, between a fruit tree and a non-fruit tree, but not as between one non-fruit tree and another. (10) *Sc.* dissimilar to it in accordance with the classifications already given. 'Herb' (ירק) is the term for vegetables, garden produce planted in rows. (11) Or vice-versa, since they never coalesce to form a hybrid species, even though one may draw nourishment from the other. The original Tanna of the Mishnah held that the latter consideration is decisive, and his opinion prevails.

a (1) Used for hedging. (2) Or, cooling. (3) Lit., 'inject', 'infuse'. (4) Until it germinates in the soil (L.). (5) For keeping fresh; not 'plants'. (6) In bundles, so that it is clear that the purpose is not planting. (7) This proviso is immaterial except in respect of their being pulled out on the Sabbath. (8) Since only the sowing of 'mixed seeds' in a vineyard is prohibited (Deut. XXII, 9), not the burying. (9) Since only sowing (i.e., for purposes of reproduction), not burying (for purposes of keeping fresh) is prohibited in the Sabbatical Year. (Lev. XXV, 4). (10) Produce is subject to tithes only as harvested off the tree or ground (v. Lev. XXVII, 30). These vegetables had, it is presumed, been duly tithed already; they do not require tithing again by reason of having been buried underground to be kept fresh. (11) The prohibition of 'plucking' (תולש) on the Sabbath applies only to produce attached by roots to the ground; these vegetables had been 'plucked' already. Also the (indirect) 'handling' of the soil involved in the moving of the soil adhering to the vegetables, does not come within the prohibition of 'handling' on the Sabbath (v. Shab. 123*a*), since it is done for the purpose of what is permissible for use on the Sabbath.

b (1) Since the word *kil'ayim* is a dual, it would follow that the sowing of the minimum of two heterogeneous seeds comes under the prohibition. (2) Since Scripture says: *Thou shalt not sow* thy field *with two kinds of seed* (Lev. XIX, 19) it follows, according to R. Judah, that the sowing of two diverse seeds becomes prohibited only when it is on *'Thy field'* i.e., on ground in which at least one other seed has been, or is being, sown; the prohibition thus applies only to the sowing of a minimum of three seeds, either all three heterogeneous, or comprising two like seeds and one heterogeneous to them.

ז אין מביאין אילן באילן ירק בירק ולא אילן בירק ולא ירק באילן ר' יהודה מתיר ירק באילן: ח אין נוטעין ירקות בתוך סדן של שקמה אין מרכיבין פיגם על גבי קדה לבנה מפני שהוא ירק באילן אין נוטעין יחור של תאנה לתוך החצוב שיהא מקירו אין תוחבין זמורה של גפן לתוך האבטיח שתהא זורקת מימיה לתוכו מפני שהוא אילן בירק אין נותנין זרע דלעת לתוך החלמית שתהא משמרתו מפני שהוא ירק בירק: ט הטומן לפת וצנונות תחת הגפן אם היו מקצת עליו מגולין אינו חושש לא משום כלאים ולא משום שביעית ולא משום מעשרות ונטלין בשבת הזורע חטה ושעורה כאחת הרי זה כלאים ר' יהודה אומר אינו כלאים עד שיהו שני חטין ושעורה או חטה ושתי שעורים או חטה ושעורה וכוסמת:

המדברי: ז אין מרכיבין אילן באילן כשיטתו המינין וכן ירק בירק ואין הלכה כר' יהודה: ח פיגם נקרא בלשון ישמעאל ערב סראב ובלע"ז רודע: קדה. מין האילנות ויש לו ריח טוב הרגוס וקדה (שמו' ל) וקליעתא ואומר מור ואהלות קליעות כל בגדותיך (תהלים מה) וסדן של שקמה גוף אילן השקמה וכבר פירשתיו [בריש] מס' דמאי: והחצוב. צמח שיש לו שרשים יורדים בעומק הארץ במישור אינם נוטים לכאן ולכאן ובהם תיחם יהושע חלקי השבטים*) ועל כן נקרא חצוב**): שיהא מקירו. כדי שיקרר אותו וייסר מזג הצמח ההוא שהוא חם: אבטיח בלע"ז אלכטין א): וחלמית. מין מהירקות ולא נודע לנו פירושו וי"א שהוא העשב הנקרא קטמיה בלשון ערב ובלע"ז מליו"ן: ט משום כלאים. הוא מ"ש הכתוב (ויקרא יט) שדך לא תזרע כלאים: משום שביעית. הוא מה שאמר הכתוב (שם כה) שדך לא תזרע בשנה השביעית: ולא משום מעשרות. שלא יתחייב כשיעקור אותה מעשר שהכתוב אומר (שם כז) וכל מעשר הארץ מזרע הארץ וזה איננו צומח בארץ: ונטלים בשבת. מפני שאינם צמח מחובר בקרקע ואע"פ שינענע העפר בשעת עקירתם שהעיקר אצלנו באלו הענינים טלטול מן הצד לאו שמיה טלטול: ור' יהודה מצריך לזרוע שני מינים עם אחד משני מינים או עם מין שלישי ואז יתחייב מלקות מן התורה על הזרע ההוא והביא ראיה עליו מן כלאי הכרם שאמר הכתוב (דברים כב) לא תזרע כרמך כלאים והכלאים זולתי הכרם וכן בזרעים צריך שיהיה כלאים לבד הדבר שנזרע בו כלאים ואין הלכה כר' יהודה אבל כלאי הכרם נפסקה הלכה עליו שאינו חייב עד שיזרע חטה ושעורה וחרצן במפולת יד ואז יהיה חייב מלקות:

*) עי' בב"ב נו. **) שבו תקנו עמודי הגבול.

כיולא בהן ופרשתה הכא דאפי' בעופות הדומין זה לזה איכא איסור כלאים כגון תרנגול טווס ופסיוני כדאשכחן הכא גבי חיה ובהמה דקתני מתניתין אף על פי שדומין זה לזה כלאים זה בזה ומפרש ומתיישב בכך סוגיא דשור שנגח את הפרה דמעיקרא קאמר כאן שנה רבי תרנגול טווס ופסיוני כלאים זה בזה ופריך פשיטא ומשני אמר רבי חנינא משום דרבו בהדדי מהו דתימא חד מינה הוא והשתא אם כן [איך] הייתי דייק לה ממתני' דלמא שאני הכא דרבו בהדדי אלא על כורחי' אמתניתי' דהכא סמוך כדפרישי' ומיהו לאו קושיא היא דיש סוגיות הרבה בגמ' כיולא בו כמו שאפרש שם המרביע חיות הים כל סוגיא שנויה שם בבראשית רבה אקרא דלמינהו וכתובה שם בשיבוש ובשלהי פרק שור שנגח את הפרה (דף נה.) א"ר ירמיה המרביע שני מינים שבים לוקה ומגיה שם ר' מנחם ברבי יצחק המגיה משום ההיא דבראשית רבה דמסיק דאין הרבעה בחיות הים ועל חנם הגיה דר' ירמיה לטעמא דאמר בירושל' דשייך בהו הרבעה: ז וירק בירק. תימה בפרק ואלו טרפות (דף ס.) בעי רבי חנינא הרכיב שני מיני דשאים לרבי חנינא בר פפא מאי כיון דלא כתב בהו למינהו לא מחייב או דלמא כיון דאסכים מריה עלייהו כמאן דכתב בהו למינהו דמי תיקו מאי קא מיבעיא ליה מתני' היא דאין מביאין ירק בירק ויש לומר דמיבעיא ליה בחוצה לארץ דשרי כלאי זרעים ואסירא הרכבת האילן כדאיתא בסוף פ"ק דקדושין (דף לט.) דדרשי' שדך למעוטי זרעים שבחוצה לארץ והרכבת האילן אסור מדכתיב (ויקרא יט) בהמתך לא תרביע כלאים שדך לא תזרע כלאים מה בהמתך בהרבעה אף שדך בהרכבה ומה בהמתך בין בארץ בין בחוצה לארץ אף שדך בין בארץ בין בחוצה לארץ [ומיבעי' לי'] אי חשיבא הרכבת דשאים כהרכבת אילן משום דכתי' בהו למינהו בעשיה או לא אי נמי אפי' בארץ מיבעיא ליה לרבי יאשיה דאמר עד שיזרע חטה ושעורה וחרצן במפולת יד דלמא מתני' דהכא כרבנן אי נמי בשאר זרעים דרבנן איירי התם דאמרי' בהקומץ זוטא (דף טו.) קנבוס ולוף אסרה תורה שאר זרעים דרבנן אי נמי לבני נח מיבעיא ליה דשרי בכלאי זרעים ואסירי בהרכבת האילן כדאיתא בפרק ארבע מיתות (דף ס.) ונפקא ליה מדכתיב את חקותי תשמרו חוקים שחקקתי לך כבר [בהמתך לא תרביע כלאים שדך לא תזרע כלאים] והיינו בהרכבה דומי' דבהמה ושחקקתי לך כבר היינו בבני נח דכתיב בהו למינהו באילנות ובבהמות דלמינהו איסור כלאים משמע כדמוכח בסוף שור שנגח את הפרה (שם) דבעי ב' מינין שבים מהו מי גמרי למינהו למינהו מיבשה או לא ומיבעיא ליה בהרכבת דשאים אי מיתסרא ליה כהרכבת האילן והוי בכלל שדך אי לא ואע"ג דכתיב למינהו אצטריך את חקותי ללמד על למינהו דמשום איסור כתבי' ולמינהו נמי אצטריך דהוה אמינא חוקים שחקקתי לך כבר בתורה כדאמרינן נמי (סנהדרין דף נו:) כאשר צוך ה' אלהיך במרה: רבי יהודה מתיר ירק באילן. ירושלמי (הל' ז) מחלפא שיטתיה דרבי יהודה תמן אמר נוטל אדם מעה מפיסמא של תפוח ונותן לתוך גומא ומתאחין וכה אמר הכין תמן ע"י [שהוא נותן] זה בצד זה מתאחין ונעשים כלאים ברם הכא ירק באילן הוא פירות קשיא ליה הא דאסר ליה ר' יהודה לעיל קישות ומלפפון מהאי טעמא דעיקר מלפפון מכלאים אתו ממעה של אבטיח וממעה של תפוח דהוא אילן [וירק] שזרען יחד: ירושלמי (שם) תני מנין שאין מרכיבין עץ סרק על עץ סרק על עץ מאכל או עץ מאכל על עץ מאכל בשאינו מינו ת"ל (שם) את חקותי תשמרו משמע דעץ סרק אעץ סרק לא אסיר מדלא תני ליה ושמא ה"מ כיון דעץ סרק ניניהו אפי' מין בשאינו מינו כחד מינא חשיב ואית ספרים דגרסי שאין מרכיבין אילן סרק על עץ סרק ועל עץ מאכל (יא): ח סדן השקמה. עד שלא נקצצה נקראת בתולת השקמה משנקצצה נקראת סדן השקמה כדתנן בפ' המוכר את הבית (דף סח:): פיגם. מין ירק כדתנן בריש עוקצין שורשי המינתא והפינס וירקות שדה: קדה לבנה. מין אילן אבל סתם קדה מין ירק כדמשמע בפ' בכל מערבין (דף לד:) דאמרי' הקנים והאסדין וקידין והורבנין מין ירק: חצוב. מין ירק שבו תיחם יהושע לישראל את הארץ (יב) ומקטע רגליהון דרשיעיא בפרק אין לדין (דף כה:): מקירו. מלשון קור שתהא מקררו אי נמי לצורך עלה להיות עלין שלה כמין קירוי מלשון המקרה במים עליותיו (תהלים קד) מימיה לתוכה שהאבטיח מלאה מים ונראית הגפן שותה את המים: ירושלמי (הל' ח) רבי זכריה חתן דר' לוי בעי בלא כך אינו אסור משום זרעים תחת הגפן אמר רבי יוסי תפתר במעמיק שורש למטה מג' טפחים כהדא דתני שורשי פאה הנכנסין לתוך ד' אמות שבכרם למטה מג' טפחים מותר פי' בלא כך שהוא תוחב הגפן לתוך אבטיח אפילו נטע אילן אסור משום זרעים תחת הגפן דאפילו גפן יחיד בעי הרחקה ומשני בשהעמיק שורש הגפן והאבטיח למטה מג' טפחים ושם הכנים זה לתוך זה ובמקום שהענפים יוצאין חוץ מן הארץ רחוקין זה מזה ג' דאי משום זרעים תחת הגפן יחידי שרי ומשום אילן בירק אסור והא דנקט בירושלמי חוץ לג' לרבנן דתנן לקמן בפרק ו' (משנה א) עבודת הגפן לכל רוח ו' טפחים הוה ליה למינקט חוץ לששה ושמא סבר לה כר' עקיבא דאמר עבודת הגפן ג': וחלמית. מלשון בריר חלמות (איוב ו) מלוא בלע"ז ובלשון חכמים ארני: ט הטומן לפת. להשתמר בקרקע שכן דרך ובטומן אגודין מיירי כדתני רבי חייא בירושלמי (הל' ט) כדון אגודה של לפת ואגודה של נפון דהיינו שלא כדרך שתילתם דגלי אדעתיה [שאינו] רוצה בהשרשתם: אם היו מקצת עליו מגולין. לענין שבת נקט דוקא בכי האי גוונא דאם אין לו מקצת עלין מגולין אין לו במה לאחוז אא"כ מזיז עפר בידים ולענין כלאים ושביעית ומעשר נקטיה לרבותיה דאע"ג דמיחזי כדרך שתילה במה שמקצת העלין מגולין אפילו הכי אינו חושש כיון דאגודה טמון וגלי דעתיה דלא ניחא ליה בהשרשתן ולשון אם משמע דלדוקא נקטיה ולא לרבותא והיינו משום שבת: לא משום כלאים. בכרם דלאו כזרועין הן ואפי' הוסיף מאתים שרי אע"ג דגבי עלין בכרם הכן אם הוסיף במאתים אסור התם כדרך זריעה אבל הכא באגודה לאו כדרך זריעה (יג): ולא משום שביעית. דאם היו מששית ונכנסו לשביעית והוציאו ספיחים כדרך שעושין הבצלים בתלוש מוציאין עלין אע"ג דספיחי שביעית אסורין הני מותרין: ולא משום מעשר. דאם היה משנה שניה שדינה במעשר שני ונכנסו לשלישית והוציאו ספיחים יהביק מעשר עני לפי שאינו רוצה בהשרשתן ושלא כדרך השרשים קיימי: ונטלין בשבת. שאוחז בעלין ושומטן דכתלושין דמו ואע"ג דמזיז עפר ממקומו טלטול מן הצד הוא ובכי האי טלטול מן הצד דאינו אלא ניעור בעלמא כולי עלמא מודו דשרי כדמוכח במסכת שבת ומשנתינו איתותב שמואל בסוף במה טומנין (דף נ.) דאמר האי סכינא ביני אורבני דלה ושלפא זהדר דלה שרי ואי לא אסור ובריש פ' חלון (דף עז.) פריך מינה לרב יחיאל דאמר כפה ספל ממעט ובערוך פירוש בשם רב האי דמקצת עלין מגולין טעות הוא שאם האמהות טמונין והעלין מגולין הרי זו זריעה היא אלא דוקא אם היה מקצתן מגולין אינו חושש משום כלאים דלאו ירק באילן הוא ולא משום שביעית דלאו זריעה היא ולא משום מעשר דאי איכא התם שמנה ראשי לפתות לא מצטרפות לחייבינהו במעשר ועל חנם דחק לשבש המשנה ועוד מה שפירש דמעשר בעי צרוף לא מצינו כן בשום מקום אלא גבי מעשר בהמה דמעשר ירק פשיטא דמחייב אכל לפת ולפת: ירושלמי (הל' ט) תני פנה שסמנה בתבן וחררה שסמנה בגחלים אם מקצתן מגולין נטלין בשבת ואם לאו אין נטלין בשבת ר' אליעזר בן תדאי אומר בין כך ובין כך תוחב בשפוד או בסכין ונטלין אתיא ר' אליעזר בן תדאי כר' שמעון דתניא לא יגרור אדם את הכסא ואת המטה ואת הקתדרא בשבת משום חורץ ור"ש מתיר ר' בא בשם רבי הונא רבי חגא בשם ר' זעירא ור' יוסי בשם ר' הילא מודין חכמים לר"ש בכסא שרגליו שוקעות בטיט שמותר לטלטלו וכמה דתימא מותר לטלטלו דכוותיה מותר [להחזירו] א"ר יוסי אוף אנן תנינן נטלין בשבת אמר רבי יוסי ברבי בון רבי שמעון היא והא תנינן שביעית אית לן למימר שביעית דר' שמעון פתר לה רבי שמעון מתיר בספיחי שביעית ואת אמרת כן אע"ג דר' שמעון מתיר בספיחי שביעית אית ליה משום קדושת שביעית אוף הכא אינו חושש לא משום שביעית ולא משום קדושת שביעית פי' [דרבה] לדקדק דמתני' דלא כר' שמעון מדאצטריך למיתני ולא משום שביעית דהא אפילו ספיחי שביעית שרי ר' שמעון כדתנן במס' שביעית (פ"ט מ"א) ומייתי לה בפ' מקום שנהגו (דף נא:) ואסיק דאפי' לר' שמעון אצטריך למימר דאין בהן קדושת שביעית אע"ג דשאר ספיחים יש בהן קדושה: ירושלמי (שם) זרע שני מינין ג) בבקעה שני מינים בחורבה וחולקן גדר ר' יוחנן אמר פטור ריש לקיש אמר חייב וכו': בשתי חטין ושעורה. יש לפרש טעמא דר' יהודה משום דכתיב (ויקרא יט) שדך לא תזרע כלאים כלו' שיהא כלאים בהדי שדך והיינו נמי טעמא דר' יאשיה דלא מחייב בכלאי הכרם עד שיזרע חטה ושעורה וחרצן דבעי כלאים בהדי כרמך אע"ג דמודה דמשום כלאי זרעים מיחייב בשני מינין לר' יאשיה כמו שנפרש לקמן בפ"ח דקסבר שהקרקע בלא זרעים קרויה שדה אבל איכא כרם בלא חרצנים ורבי יהודה סבר דקרקע נמי לא מיקרי שדה בלא זרע אי נמי בקרא דלא תזרע כלאים פליגי רבנן סברי דב' מינין נמי הויא זריעה ור' יהודה לא חשיב זריעה בפחות מג' מינין וכי האי גוונא פליגי במכילתין גבי כלאי בגדים דלא חשיב ר"י חיבור בב' תכיפות עד שישלים: [מתני' פליגא על ר"י הזורע חטה ושעורה כאחת הרי זה כלאים פתר לה בנתונים בתוך ששה על ששה דאמר ר"י אינו חייב עד שיהיו ו' על ו' מוקרחים בתוך שדה תבואה או מוקפת גדר] פי' במפולת יד זרען וביציאתו מתוך ידו נתרחקו בבקעה או בחורבה או חילקן גדר ומסיק דמתני' פתר לה ר"י הכי הזורע חטה ושעורה כלאים בנותנן בתוך ששה על ששה בהדא ר"י אומר אינן כלאים [א"ר זעירא ר"י] כדעתי' דאמר בשדה ירק ספח כלומר דירק מרחיק מירק ספח לא הוי כלאים עד שיהיו ב' המין ג) ושעורה שמוכין בפחות מטפח והדר קאמר מ"ט דר"ל מכיון שהוציא מתוך ידו לזרוע חייב ומתני' פתר לה הכא הזורע חטה ושעורה כאחת כלאים אפי' בבקעה ר' יהודה אומר אינו כלאים קסבר דהוי חטה כמו ראש תור לשעורה ומותר דראש תור מותר בחורבה ופריך מעתה אפי' ב' חטין ושעורה ומשני פתר לה הטה מכאן וחטה מכאן גדר מכאן וגדר מכאן ושעורה קבוע באמצע

מסורת הש"ס
א) עירובין פ"ג דף לד: ג) שבת פ"ד ד"נ: וסט"ו דקי"ג. עירובין פ"ו דע"ז.

פי' מהר"י בן מלכי צדק
לערוד. עוף לאו הנינן אם יש בו איסור כלאים אם לאו א"ר יוחנן איתיניה כן דבר דילה דתני בר דיילה תרנגול עם הפיסיוני או עם הטווס אע"פ שדומין זה לזה כלאים זה בזה. ריש לקיש אמר משנה תמימה שנה לנו ר' בבב"ק בס"פ שור שנגח את הפרה אחד השור וכו' עד לכלאים ולשבת וכן חיה ועוף כיוצא בהן: ז אין מביאין אילן באילן. פי' כגון תפוח בחוזרד וכו' כדאמרי' ירק בירק כגון צנון בנפוס וכו': ר' יהוד' מתיר ירק באילן ירושלמי וקשיא תמן א"ר יהודה מעה של אבטיח ומעה של תפוח כלאים והכא אמר כן. ופריק תמן נותנן זה בצד זה ומתאחין ונעשין כלאים ברם הכא ירק באילן הוא ומותר. תני מנין שאין מרכיבין עץ סרק על עץ מאכל או עץ מאכל על עץ מאכל מין בשאינו מינו ת"ל את חקותי תשמרו תני אין מרכיבין זיתים ברכב של תמרה מפני שהוא אילן באילן: ח אין נוטעין ירקות בתוך סדן של שקמה. פי' שורש של שקמה: אין מרכיבין פיגם. רוטא יווני פיגא: קדה לבנה. פי' לעו קשטו ויש לו ריח טוב והוא מל' וקדה חמש מאות מפני שהפינם ירק דתנינן בריש עוקצים שורשי חמינתא והפינם וירקות שדה [והקדה] לבנה מין אילן אבל קדה סתם מין ירק כדגרסינן בפ' בכל מערבין (לד ע"ב) הקנים והקידן והאורבנין מין ירק: אין נוטעין יחור וכו' בלע"ז נובילינו: לתוך החצוב. פי' חצוב הוא שתיחם בו יהושע את הארץ והוא מין ירק וגדל ביושר ואינו נוטה לא לכאן ולא לכאן. והיינו דאמרינן חצובא מקטע רגליהון דרשיעיא. בפאה בירושלמי הצובות מפסיקין לפאה: שיהא מקירו. לשון קור. ואסור שהתאנה אילן והחצוב ירק: אין תוחבין זמורה וכו' לתוך האבטיח שתהא זורקת מימיה. פי' כי האבטיח מלאה מים ונמצאת הגפן שותה את המים ואסור שהגפן אילן והאבטיח ירק. גרסי' ר' זכריה חתן ר' לוי שאל בלא כך אינו אסור להיות האבטיח תחת הגפן ולא משום אילן בירק [אלא משום] זרעים תחת הגפן א"ר יוסי תפתר בשרשי האבטיח למטה מג' טפחים דמשום זרעים בגפן אינו אסור דתנינן שורשי פאה הנכנסין לתוך ד' אמות שבכרם למטה מג' טפחים מותרין הלכך אין האיסור אלא מפני שהוא אילן בירק: אין נותנין זרע דלעת לתוך החלמית. פי' מלשון בריר חלמות בלע"ז מלבא. ובלשון תלמא ארנא והוא מין ירק: ט הטומן לפת וצנונות תחת הגפן. תני ר' חייא כגון אגודה של לפת ואגודה של צנן ולאו דוקא לפת וצנון אלא כיון שאינו רוצה בהשרשתו שלא טמן כל אחד ואחד בפני עצמו כדרך הזריעה אלא כל האגודה טמן הלכך אפילו שאר דברים: אם היו מקצת העלין וכו'. האי אם דסיפא דקתני ונטלין בשבת דטעמא אם מגולין קצת הא לאו הכי לא ומתפרש לענין כלאים ושביעית ומעשר הכי דאף אם היו מקצת העלין מגולין אע"ג דמיחזי בדרך זריעה כיון שאגודה טמן דגלי אדעתיה שאינו רוצה בהשרשתו: אינו חושש לא משום כלאים בכרם. דלאו כזרועין הן: ולא משום שביעית. פי' אם היו מששית ונכנסו לשביעית והוציאו ספחים כדרך שעושין הבצלין (שמשרישין) [שמונחין] בעליה כיון שלא השרישו אע"ג דספיחי שביעית אסורין הני מותרין: ולא משום מעשרות. פי' אם היו משנה שניה דיהבינן מעשר שני ונכנסו לשנה ג' והוסיפו ספיחין כיון דלא אשרוש על אותן ספיחין לא יהבינן מעשר עני לפי שאינו רוצה בהשרשתן: ונטלין בשבת. פי' דכתלושין דמו: הזורע חטה ושעורה כאחת הרי זה כלאים. כסתמא דרישא דפרקין החטין והזונין וכו' ר' יהודה נמי סובר דחטה ושעורה ב' מינין. אבל בהא פליגי דתנא קמא סבר אפי' זריעת חטה אחת ושעורה אחת שמה זריעה והואיל וזריעה היא אסור דכתיב שדך לא תזרע. ור' יהודה סבר לאו שמה זריעה ולהכי פטר עד שיזרע ב' חטים ושעורה וכו' ודמי למאי דהגינן התוכף

עין משפט
נר מצוה

ח א מיי' פ"א מהל' כלאים הלכה ה טוש"ע יו"ד סי' רצה סעיף א ג:
ט ב טוש"ע שם סעיף ג:
י ג מיי' וטור שו"ע שם:
יא ד מיי' פ"ג שם הלכה יא טוש"ע שם סימן רצז סעיף י:
יב ה מיי' וטוש"ע שם סעיף יא:
יג ו מיי' פ"א מהל' שמטה ויובל הלכה טו:
יד ז מיי' פכ"ה מהל' שבת הלכה טו סמג לאוין סה טור שו"ע או"ח סי' שיא סעיף א:
טו ח מיי' פ"א מהל' כלאים הלכה ב טוש"ע יו"ד סימן רצו סעיף א:

פירוש הרא"ש
(יא) ומסתברא כגי' ראשונה דעץ סרק כיון שאינו פרי כחד מינא חשיב: (יב) והוא משריש תחתיו בעומק: (יג) כיון דבאגודה טמן אין דרך זריעה בכך:

הגהות הרי"ו לנדא
א] מ"ח בר"מ אבטיח בלע"ז אלכטין. נ"ל בערבי אלבטיך ובלע"ז מילוני ועי' תרומות פ"ח מ"ו בפירוש הרמב"ם ד"ה והאבטיחין: ב] מ"מ בר"ש ירושלמי זרע ב' מינין. הך דיבור ירושלמי עד ר"ל אמר חייב נ"ל קודם ד"ה מתני' פליגא: ג] שם עד שיהיו ב' חטין. נ"ל שני מינין. סמוכין:

פ״ד מתתיה הדה דהימא בשאין חורבה לשם אבל יש חורבה לשם מותר והשתא כי איכא גדר אסור ספי משום דלא שייך ביה ראש תור אבל בלא גדר דשייך ביה ראש תור מותר ומשמע מתוך סוגיא דירושלמי בין לרבי יוחנן בין לריש לקיש מודה רבי יהודה דחטה ושעורה לתודייהו בתוך טפח הוי כלאים:

א רובע הקב · הוא אחד מכ״ד לסאה שהסאה ששה קבין: **ימעט** · אותו מין אחר המעורב עד שיפחות מרובע ויתבטל בתוך הסאה ומותר לזרוע ולא מיתסר משום זורע כלאים: **ר' יוסי אומר יבור** · מכיון שהתחיל יסיר את הכל אבל תחלתן פחות מרובע שרי: **בין ממין אחד** · יהא אותו רובע: **בין משני מינין** · כגון חצי רובע מזה וחצי רובע מזה ימעט הואיל ובין שניהן רובע ורבי שמעון פליג קסבר דלאין שני מינין מצטרפים לרובע וחכמים אכולהו פליגי כמו שאפרש: ירושלמי (הל' א) אנן תנינן שיש...

א א ב מיי' פ״ב מהלכות כלאים הל' א טוש״ע יו״ד סימן רצז סעיף ה:

ב ג ד מיי' שם הלכה ג ה טור ש״ע שם סעיף ו:

ג ה מיי' פ״ב מהל' כלאים הלכה יג טור ש״ע יו״ד סי' רצז סעיף יג:

א) בבא בתרא פ״ה דף לג. מועד קטן פ״א דף ו.

פרק שני

א כל [א] סאה שיש בו רובע ממין אחר [א]ימעט ר' יוסי אומר יבור בין ממין אחד בין משני מינין ר״ש אומר לא אמרו אלא ממין אחד וחכמים אומרים [ב]כל שהוא כלאים בסאה מצטרף לרובע: **ב** [ג]במה דברים אמורים (ד) תבואה בתבואה וקטנית בקטנית תבואה בקטנית וקטנית בתבואה באמת אמרו זרעוני גנה שאינן נאכלין מצטרפין אחד מעשרים וארבע בנופל לבית סאה ר״ש אומר כשם שאמרו להחמיר כך אמרו להקל [ד]הפשתן בתבואה מצטרפת אחד מעשרים וארבעה בנופל לבית סאה: **ג** [ה]היתה שדהו זרועה חטים ונמלך לזרעה שעורים ימתין לה עד שתתליע ויופך ואח״כ יזרע אם צימחה לא יאמר אזרע ואח״כ אופך אלא הופך ואח״כ זורע כמה יהא חורש כתלמי

א הסאה כבר בארנו (סוף פאה מ״ז) שהיא ו' קבין ורובע היא רביעית הקב והוא אומר שבשיהיה בזרע חלק מכ״ד ממין מזרע אחר אסור לו לזרוע אותו הזרע עד שימעט זה הזרע האחר...

פי' מהר״י בן מלכי צדק

CHAPTER II

a *MISHNAH* 1. IF A SE'AH[1] CONTAINS A QUARTER [OF A KAB][2] OF A HETEROGENEOUS SPECIES, ONE SHOULD REDUCE [THE PROPORTION OF THE LATTER][3] (R. JOSE SAID ONE SHOULD PICK [IT ALL OUT]),[4] WHETHER IT [THE ADMIXTURE] CONSISTS OF ONE SPECIES OR OF TWO[5] SPECIES.[6] R. SIMEON SAID: THEY SAID THIS[7] ONLY IF IT CONSISTS OF ONE SPECIES.[8] THE SAGES SAID: [ONLY] THAT WHICH IS KIL'AYIM VIS-A-VIS THE [MAIN CONTENTS OF THE] SE'AH COUNTS IN MAKING UP THE QUARTER.[9]

MISHNAH 2. IN RESPECT OF WHAT [MIXTURES OF PRO-
b DUCE] ARE THE [ABOVE] RULES[1] STATED? IN RESPECT OF [AN ADMIXTURE OF] GRAIN [OCCURRING] IN [HETEROGENEOUS] GRAIN, OF PULSE IN [HETEROGENEOUS] PULSE, OF GRAIN IN PULSE, AND OF PULSE IN GRAIN.

IT IS AN IMMEMORIAL RULE:[2] GARDEN-SEED OF A KIND WHICH IS NOT USED AS FOOD,[3] COUNTS QUANTITATIVELY, [IN THE MATTER OF KIL'AYIM] IF [WITHIN A SE'AH OF PRODUCE] IT FORMS [AS LITTLE AS] ONE TWENTY-FOURTH OF THE QUANTITY [OF SUCH SEED] THAT CAN BE SOWN IN A BETH-SE'AH.[4] R. SIMEON SAID: EVEN AS THEY RULED[5] THUS [IN CIRCUMSTANCES WHEN THE APPLICATION OF THE RULE IS CALCULATED] TO RESULT IN A STRINGENCY,[6] EVEN SO THEY RULED THUS [IN CIRCUMSTANCES WHEN THE APPLICATION OF THE RULE IS CALCULATED] TO RESULT IN A LENIENCY.[7] [ACCORDINGLY,[8] IN THE CASE OF AN ADMIXTURE OF] LIN-
c SEED[1] IN GRAIN, THE QUANTITY [OF THE FORMER] COUNTS WHEN IT FORMS [AS MUCH AS] ONE TWENTY-FOURTH OF THE QUANTITY [OF SUCH SEED] THAT CAN BE SOWN IN A BETH-SE'AH.[2]

MISHNAH 3. IF ONE'S FIELD IS SOWN WITH WHEAT AND ON SECOND THOUGHTS HE DECIDES TO SOW IT WITH BARLEY, HE MUST WAIT UNTIL IT [THE WHEAT] ROTS,[3] THEN HE TURNS [THE SOIL],[4] AND, THEREAFTER, HE MAY SOW [THE BARLEY]. IF IT HAS ALREADY GROWN,[5] HE MUST NOT SAY: 'I SHALL [FIRST] SOW [THE BARLEY] AND, THEREAFTER TURN [THE SOIL]'[6] BUT HE MUST TURN [THE SOIL] [FIRST], AND, THEREAFTER, HE MAY SOW [THE BARLEY]. TO WHAT EXTENT SHOULD ONE [IN THE ABOVE CIRCUMSTANCES] PLOUGH? FURROWS

a (1) Of produce about to be sown. (2) Also known as a *log*. 4 *log* = 1 *kab*; 6 *kab* = 1 *se'ah*. (3) Either by adding to the main species or by taking away from the lesser admixture, so that the latter is less than one twenty-fourth of the bulk. (4) Once he has to remove the admixture he should remove the whole of it. (T.J.). Otherwise it would appear as if he is positively maintaining, or even, as if he is deliberately bringing about *kil'ayim*. (T.B., B.B. 94*b* and Rashi *ibid*). (5) Or more. (6) Even if one of them is not *kil'ayim* vis-a-vis the main species. One must in either case reduce the proportion of the total of the admixture(s) to less than one twenty-fourth of the bulk. R. Jose's view is not accepted. (7) I.e., the authorities ruled thus. (8) *Sc.* but not of two or more species, as long as these do not together amount to the greater part of the bulk; if they do, R. Simeon agrees that the proportion of the combined admixtures must be reduced. (9) E.g., a *se'ah* of grain consisting substantially of barley and partially—to the amount of the minimum of a quarter *kab*—of oats and spelt. Now whilst spelt is *kil'ayim* vis-a-vis the barley, oats are not. In such a case, the Sages said the spelt and oats do not 'combine' to form a quarter *kab* condemning the whole *se'ah* as *kil'ayim* (and there is, therefore, no need to reduce the proportion of the oats-cum-spelt); according to the anonymous original Tanna of the Mishnah they do 'combine' (and one should 'reduce'); according to R. Simeon even if both (or all) of the constituents of the quarter-*kab* of admixture are *kil'ayim* towards the main contents of the *se'ah*, they do not 'combine'.

b (1) Lit., 'words'. *Sc.* regarding the proportion of admixture to bulk, viz., 1 to 24, rendering *kil'ayim*. (2) באמת אמרו 'As a matter of (trustworthily tradited and undisputedly accepted) truth they said', a phrase which, according to R. Eleazar in T.J. to this Mishnah, introduces a rule held to have been orally communicated by God to Moses at Sinai. V. Frankel, *Darké* (ed. Warsaw 1923) p. 304, and Bacher, *Tradition*, p. 41. (3) E.g., turnip-seed or parsley-seed or any seed which, by reason of fineness or any other reason, requires extensive area for sowing. (4) A standard measure of area—to wit 2,500 square cubits—designed for sowing a *se'ah* of wheat. In relation to our problem it works out thus: Since 'garden-seed' is so much finer than wheat and its produce takes up more space, only 1½ *kab* of it can be sown in a *beth-se'ah*. A twenty-fourth of that quantity viz., one sixteenth, of a *kab* of 'garden-seed' forming part of a *se'ah* of wheat, is, accordingly, sufficient to render it *kil'ayim*. (5) Viz., that the proportion of produce which renders *kil'ayim* is one twenty-fourth of the quantity of that same produce which can be sown in a *beth-se'ah*. According to Maim. this refers to the rule in Mishnah 1 regarding an admixture consisting of one or two species. See latter part of 16*b* n. c 2. (6) Viz., necessitating the reduction of the proportion of an admixture of fine seed even when there is no more of it than one sixteenth *kab* within a *se'ah* of grain or pulse. (7) I.e., when the admixture is of a seed coarser, or which is sown more closely, and therefore requires less area than wheat. (8) Maim., however, says that what follows is not a continuation of R. Simeon's statement, but a resumption of the words of the anonymous original Tanna of the Mishnah., v. 16*b* n. c 2, latter part.

c (1) Which is sown more compactly than wheat, so that three *se'ahs* of it can be sown in a *beth-se'ah*. (2) One need not reduce the proportion of linseed in wheat unless there is as much as ¾ *kab* of the former within a *se'ah* of the latter. Maim. construes the Mishnah text thus: R. Simeon said: Even as they ruled (that two heterogeneous species do not 'combine') to effect a stringency (as implied in his statement in the preceding Mishnah., v. ibid. n. 8), even so they ruled (that two heterogeneous species do not 'combine') to effect a leniency. An instance of the latter is cited, by way of example in T.J. *ad loc*: A mixture measuring a *se'ah* (i.e., twenty-four quarter *kabs*) consists of twenty-two and a half 'quarters' of wheat, half 'quarter' of barley, and less than one 'quarter' of lentils. Now if 'combining' two or more species were permitted, then one might consider that, since the half 'quarter' of barley is too small a quantity to render the mixture (of twenty-two and a half quarter wheat plus half quarter barley) *kil'ayim*, the wheat and barley may be taken as forming a combined quantity of twenty-three quarters and since the maximum amount of lentils, viz, .9 'quarter', is less than one twenty-fourth of 23.9 (the whole of the mixture) the lentils do not render the mixture *kil'ayim*, and there would consequently be no need to 'reduce' the lentils which, of course, is a 'leniency'; but, says, R. Simeon, 'combining' is not allowed whatever the consequence, be it a stringency or a leniency. The position according to R. Simeon is that .9 'quarters' lentils got mixed with twenty-two and a half 'quarters' wheat, and .9 being more than one twenty-fourth of (22.5 plus .9), the lentils alone are sufficient to render the mixture *kil'ayim*, and the proportion of these must be reduced. (3) Or, 'until it shoots forth thin worm-like roots in the soil'. In well-watered ground this takes three days; in dry soil it takes longer. (4) With a plough; so as to destroy the first-sown crop. (5) And the wheat is already visible above ground. (6) Thinking to himself: 'I shall be able, after sowing the new grain, to see the sprouting first-sown grain to destroy it'.

a SUCH AS ARE PLOUGHED AFTER[1] THE [FIRST] RAINY SEASON.[2] ABBA SAUL SAID: [ONE SHOULD PLOUGH] SO THAT ONE DOES NOT LEAVE [UNPLOUGHED] AS MUCH [GROUND][3] AS HOLDS A QUARTER [ḲAB] TO A BETH-SE'AH.

MISHNAH 4. IF ONE'S FIELD HAS BEEN SOWN [WITH GRAIN, OR PULSE, OR 'GARDEN-SEED'], AND ON SECOND THOUGHTS HE DECIDED TO PLANT IT [WITH VINES], HE MAY NOT SAY: 'I SHALL [FIRST] PLANT [THE VINES] AND THEREAFTER TURN [THE SOIL],' BUT HE MUST [FIRST] TURN [THE SOIL] AND THEREAFTER HE MAY PLANT [THE VINES].

[IF IT WAS] 'PLANTED' [WITH VINES][4] AND ON SECOND THOUGHTS HE DECIDED TO SOW IT [WITH GRAIN ETC.], HE MAY NOT SAY: 'I SHALL SOW [THE GRAIN ETC.] AND AFTERWARDS I SHALL UPROOT [THE VINES],' BUT HE MUST [FIRST] UPROOT [THE VINES] AND THEREAFTER HE MAY SOW [THE GRAIN ETC.]. IF HE DESIRES IT, HE MAY CUT DOWN [THE VINES] TO LESS THAN A HANDBREADTH [ABOVE GROUND], WHEREAFTER HE MAY SOW [THE GRAIN ETC.] AND LATER, UPROOT [THE VINES].

MISHNAH 5. IF ONE'S FIELD IS SOWN WITH COMMON CUMIN[5] OR WITH LOF,[6] HE MUST NOT SOW[7] ON TOP OF THEM, SINCE THEY PRODUCE CROPS ONLY AFTER THREE YEARS.[8] [A FIELD OF] GRAIN AMONG WHICH SPRANG UP SOME AFTER-
b GROWTH OF ISATIS [TINCTORIA],[1] LIKEWISE THE AREA OF A THRESHING-FLOOR IN WHICH MANY SPECIES[2] SPRANG UP, LIKEWISE [A FIELD OF] FENUGREEK AMONG WHICH GREW UP A NUMBER OF SPECIES OF HERBS,[3] HE IS NOT OBLIGED TO WEED THEM OUT.[4] BUT ONCE HE HAS DONE SOME WEEDING OUT OR [EVEN ONLY] CUTTING DOWN,[5] HE IS TOLD: 'UPROOT ALL EXCEPT ONE SPECIES.'[6]

MISHNAH 6. IF ONE WISHES TO LAY OUT HIS FIELD IN

a (1) So Rash. and Bert., but Maim. (*Yad, Hilch. Kil'ayim* II, 13) 'before'. (2) I.e., wide furrows, there being no need to plough close furrows. (3) Either in one plot, or in an aggregate of more than one lesser patch. (4) So the commentators, since with regard to other trees only grafting of a tree with a heterogeneous tree, or of trees with 'herbs', is prohibited. (5) Edd. קנבוס (= hemp) which is impossible here, but read (with R. Isaac Sipponte) קרבס. (6) לוף, a plant of the bulb type. (7) *Sc.* a heterogeneous species. (8) These species stay intact in the soil for a long time without rotting. Ploughing up the soil will, therefore, not avail to destroy their productivity, so that even with 'turning the soil' a heterogeneous seed sown on top of these would constitute *kil'ayim*.

b (1) אסטים. It is injurious to grain. (2) Which spoil the threshing-floor. (3) Which are noxious to fenugreek when the latter is intended for human consumption. (4) Because (*a*) the strange species have not been deliberately sown there; (*b*) their presence there is not welcome, and, consequently (*c*) no person noticing the mixed species will even suspect the owner of intentionally sowing *kil'ayim*. Weeding out means, of course, pulling out by the roots. (5) Either of one or of some of the species springing up from the threshing-floor. This would show, or, at least, suggest, that the intention is not to clear the threshing-floor, but merely to get rid of only some of the growths and to retain the others. (6) As otherwise it would appear as if he is purposely maintaining *kil'ayim*.

◁ *For the continuation of the English translation of this page see overleaf.*

כלומר כתלמים שדרך בני אדם לחרוש אחר שתרד הרביעה שחורשים עוד תלמים גדולים : כדי שלא ישייר · קסבר אבא שאול דאין דרך לחרוש את כולה : רובע לבית סאה · יש לפרש בכל הבית סאה רובע במקום אחד ויש לפרש דכשתלטרף מה שאינו חרוש לא יעלה לרובע : ד זרועה· שהיתה שדהו זרועה תבואה ונמלך עליה לנוטעה גפנים : גומם · מלשון גוממו עם השופי דפרק גיד הנשה (דף לב:) כלומר קולץ הגפן סמוך לארץ שלא ישייר ספח: ה קנבום· אית דגרסי קנבוס והנך מינים אין להם התלעה וחרישה שעומדים בקרקע ג' שנים ואין מתליעין : איסטים · כמו סתים ניסדא בלעז שלובעין בה : מקום הגרנות · שדשין בה תבואה וקטנית : תלתן . פיטנריקו בלעז: אין מחייבין אותו לנכש.

ג "כתלמי הרביעה אבא שאול אומר כדי שלא ישייר רובע לבית סאה : ד "זרועה ונמלך לנוטעה לא יאמר אטע ואחר כך אופך אלא הופך ואח"כ נוטע "נטועה ונמלך לזורעה לא יאמר אזרע ואח"כ אשרש אלא משרש ואח"כ זורע אם רצה גומם עד פחות מטפח וזורע ואח"כ משרש: ה "היתה שדהו זרועה קנבוס או לוף לא יהא זורע ובא על גביהם שאינן עושין אלא לשלש השנים "תבואה שעלו בה ספיחי אסטים וכן מקום הגרנות שעלו בהן מינין הרבה וכן (א) תלתן שהעלה מיני צמחים אין מחייבין אותו לנכש אם נכש או כיסח אומרים לו עקור את הכל חוץ ממין אחד : ו "הרוצה לעשות שדהו משר משר מכל מין ב"ש אומרים שלשה תלמים של פתיח וב"ה אומרים מלא העול (ו) השרוני וקרובים דברי אלו להיות כדברי אלו : ז "היה (ז) ראש תור חטים נכנס בתוך של שעורים מותר מפני שהוא נראה כסוף שדהו "שלו חטים ושל חברו מין אחר מותר לסמוך לו מאותו המין "שלו חטים ושל חברו חטים מותר לסמוך לו תלם של פשתן ולא תלם של מין אחר ר' שמעון אומר אחד זרע פשתן ואחד כל המינין ר' יוסי אומר אף באמצע שדהו מותר לבדוק בתלם של פשתן : ח "אין סומכין לשדה תבואה חרדל (יא) וחריע אבל סומכים לשדה ירקות חרדל וחריע "וסומך לבור ולניר ולגפה ולדרך ולגדר שהוא גבוה עשרה טפחים ולחריץ שהוא עמוק עשרה ורחב ד' ולאילן שהוא מיסך על הארץ ולסלע שהוא גבוה עשרה ורחב ארבעה:

הרוצה

Continuation of translation from previous page as indicated by ◁

LONG BEDS EACH SOWN WITH A DIFFERENT SPECIES, BETH SHAMMAI SAY: [HE SHOULD SEPARATE THEM BY THE WIDTH OF] THREE FURROWS OF NEWLY BROKEN LAND,[7] WHILE BETH HILLEL SAY: BY THE WIDTH OF A SHARON YOKE.[8] THE DICTUM OF THE ONE IS IN EFFECT APPROXIMATE TO THE DICTUM OF THE OTHER.[9]

MISHNAH 7. IF THE POINT OF A TRIANGLE[10] OF [A] WHEAT
c [FIELD] OVERLAPS INTO[1] [A] BARLEY [FIELD],[2] IT IS PERMITTED SINCE IT IS APPARENT THAT IT IS THE END OF HIS FIELD.[3] IF ONE MAN'S FIELD IS OF WHEAT, AND THAT OF HIS NEIGHBOUR OF ANOTHER SPECIES, THE FORMER IS PERMITTED TO SOW [IN HIS OWN FIELD] CLOSE TO HIS NEIGHBOUR'S FIELD, SOME OF THE SPECIES OF THE LATTER.[4] IF ONE MAN'S FIELD IS OF WHEAT AND THAT OF HIS NEIGHBOUR LIKEWISE OF WHEAT, HE MAY SOW CLOSE THERETO A ROW OF FLAX,[5] BUT NOT A ROW OF ANY OTHER [HETEROGENEOUS] SPECIES.[6] R. SIMEON SAID: IT IS ALL THE SAME WHETHER HE SOWS FLAX OR ANY OTHER SPECIES.[7] R. JOSE SAID: EVEN IN THE MIDDLE OF ONE'S FIELD IT IS PERMITTED TO SOW, FOR EXPERIMENTAL PURPOSES, A ROW OF FLAX.[8]

d *MISHNAH* 8. IT IS FORBIDDEN TO SOW[1] MUSTARD OR SAFFRON CLOSE TO A CORN-FIELD,[2] BUT IT IS PERMITTED TO SOW MUSTARD OR BASTARD SAFFRON CLOSE TO A VEGETABLE FIELD.[3] ONE MAY SOW [HETEROGENEOUS SPECIES] CLOSE TO FALLOW LAND[4] OR TO PLOUGHED[5] LAND,[4] OR TO A LOOSE-STONE FENCE, OR TO A PATH, OR TO A FENCE TEN HANDBREADTHS HIGH, OR TO A TRENCH TEN [HANDBREADTHS] DEEP AND FOUR WIDE, OR TO A TREE FORMING A TENT OVER THE GROUND, TO A ROCK TEN [HANDBREADTHS] HIGH AND FOUR WIDE [ON EITHER SIDE OF THE INTERVENING OBJECT OR SPACE].[6]

(7) Representing a distance of two cubits. (8) A yoke, or team, as used in the plain of the Sharon, was wider than the yoke driven in the hilly districts. (9) I.e., The Hillelite standard represents also about (but rather less than) two cubits. According to T.J. it is sufficient as long as at some place between the two long beds there is this distance, even if further on the intervening space narrows down, since it is already clear that the intention, so far from sowing *kil'ayim*, was, in fact, to keep the heterogeneous species apart. (10) ראש תור. Most commentators take תור as meaning originally, a triangular feminine ornament. (v. S.S. I, 10); Others as 'ox', an 'ox-head' suggesting a triangle.

c (1) Or (as seems from the illustration within the text of Maim.'s commentary), abuts on. (2) The possibilities visualized by commentators are:—

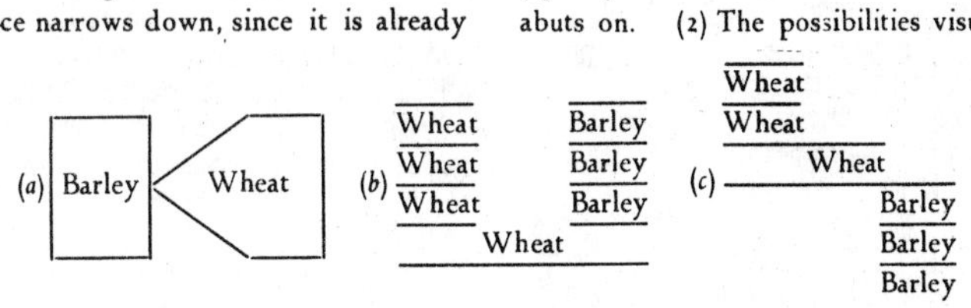

(3) The prohibition, according to Scripture, is only against sowing heterogeneous seeds with one and the same throw of the hand; otherwise the prohibition extends only to circumstances in which it would appear to strangers that *kil'ayim* had deliberately been sown. In this case it is clear to all that there was no such intention and that it is just a case of: here one field ends, and the other begins. (4) So the majority of commentators. Rash attempts an alternative rendering. The reason for permissibility here is that (*a*) in strict law it is permitted, and (*b*) there is not even a likelihood of suspicion on the part of a stranger, since anyone not acquainted with the actual facts would assume that the heterogeneous crop belonged to the other man's field, where its presence is perfectly proper. (5) No one will think that he sowed the one row of flax for its actual yield, but will assume that he did it as an experiment to test the suitability of the soil for flax. (6) Since, even if his intention is experimentation, a stranger seeing it would not, as a matter of course, assume it. (7) Either is prohibited; so Maim. and Rash. But according to T.J. *ad loc.* R. Simeon held that either is *permitted.*, v. L. to our Mishnah. (8) Because its legitimate purpose cannot be mistaken.

d (1) Where A's field adjoins B's. (2) This is forbidden, because a stranger will assume, correctly, that mustard etc. being harmful as a neighbour to corn, A would have objected to B sowing the former, and therefore, that A must have sown it himself, and, incorrectly, that it had been done with 'one and the same handthrow'. (3) Which is not harmed by the proximity of mustard etc. (4) Being in area at least a *beth-roba'* i.e., capable of being sown with a *roba'* (quarter *kab*) of wheat, viz., 104.15 square cubits; as long as there is this space somewhere between the two species, it does not matter if elsewhere the latter converge to within a narrower distance between them. (5) But unsown. (6) If the branches hang over until they reach to within three handbreadths from the ground, they are considered in law, as forming an effective partition.

כלומר כתלמים שדרך בני אדם לחרוש אחר שתרד הרביעה שחורשים עוד תלמים גדולים: כדי שלא ישייר · קסבר אבא שאול דאין דרך לחרוש את כולה: רובע לבית סאה · יש לפרש בכל הבית סאה רובע במקום אחד ויש לפרש דכשמצטרף מה שאינו חרוש לא יעלה לרובע: ד זרועה· שהיתה שדהו זרועה תבואה ונמלך עליה לנוטעה גפנים: גומם · מלשון גוממו עם השופי דפרק גיד הנשה (דף לב:) כלומר קוצץ הגפן סמוך לארץ שלא ישייר ספח: ה קנבוס· אית דגרסי קנבוס והנך מינים אין להם התלעה וחרישה שעומדים בקרקע ג' שנים ואין מתליעין: איסטים · כמו סתים גיסדא בלעז שצובעין בה: מקום הגרנות · שדשין בה תבואה וקטנית: תלתן . פינוגריקו בלעז: אין מחייבין אותו לנכש. דסופו לעוקרן בעל כורחו דקשה להו שאף למקום גרנות קאי הזרעים הגדילים שם שמחלידין את הקרקע ומלקין אותו ולא חזי תו למקום דישה ובשילהי מרובה (פא:) פריך מעשרה תנאים שהתנה יהושע דמלקטין עשבים בכל מקום חוץ משדה תלתן אלמא תלתן מעלו ליה עשבים ומשני לה התם: ואם ניכש או כיסח · אמקום גרנות קאי דכיון דניכש או כיסח אותן גלי אדעתיה דניחא ליה באותן מינין ועוקר הכל חוץ ממין אחד משום מקיים בכלאים · נוכש עוקר העשבין בידו עם השורש כיסח שחותך העלין והשורש נשאר בארץ מלשון (ויקרא כה) לא תזמור תרגום לא תכסח: ו משר משר · מלשון רב זרע לה לגינתא דבי רב משרי משרי בסוף פ"ק דקדושין (דף לט.) כלומר ערוגות ערוגות מינין הרבה כל ערוגה ממין אחד: ושלשה תלמים של פתיח · כלומר עושה המשר רחב כשיעור ג' תלמים של פתיח מלשון יפתח וישדד אדמתו (ישעיה כח) ומניח בור וזורע וכן לכל שדהו: השרוני . בקעה מל' והיה העקוב למישור (ישעי' מ): ירושלמי (הל' ד) ר' זירא בשם ר' חייא רבה עושה ב' אמות ומיצר והולך אפי' כל שהוא · פי' עושה ב' אמות על ב' אמות כל משר ומשר והמיצר שבנתים כל שהוא דלא"צ להרחיק כר"מ לקמן ושמא מלא העול הוא ב' אמות א"כ כולה בהרחקה איירי שהמשרים רחוקים זה מזה ב' אמות בראש הא' ואותן ב' אמות הולכות ומיצרות עד שכלות לראשן א' לכל שהן ושם המשר סמוך וכל שעה ושעה המשר הולך ומתקצר עד כל שהוא והא דקאמר ב' אמות על ב' אמות לא שיהו מרובעות אלא על אורך ב' אמות שכלות עד כל שהוא: ז ראש תור חטים · כגון שדה חטין אצל שדה שעורים ושורה אחרונה של חטים יוצאת ממנה ונכנסת לתוך שדה שעורין מותר מפני שאותה שורה נראה כסוף שדה חטין: מותר לסמוך לו מאותו המין · דלבעל השדה של חטים מותר לסמוך חטים אצל שדה מין אחר של חבירו ואין נראה ככלאים בשדה חבירו אלא נראה כסוף שדה חטין: (ח) ויותר נראה לפרש דמותר לסמוך אצל שדה חטים שלו מאותו המין של שדה חברו ואין נראה ככלאים בשדהו משום דנראה כסוף שדה חברו: ולא תלם של מין אחר · בירושלמי (הל' ה) פריך מה אנן קיימין אם מתכוין לבדוק (ט) אפי' באמצע שדהו מותר אם אינו מתכוין לבדוק למה לי שאר המינין אפילו זרע פשתן אסור ומשני לבדוק אנן קיימין (י) רבי יוסי לא חשש למראית העין כלומר ולפיכך שרי באמצע שדהו ורבנן חשו למראית העין: ר' שמעון אומר אחד זרע פשתן ואחד כל המינין · מפרש בירושלמי (שם) משום דרבי שמעון סבר דאין אדם מקדיש דבר שאינו שלו כלומר ומתוך דלא מיתסר משום חבירו לא מיתסר נמי משום דנפשיה ורבי יוסי נמי אף על גב דאית ליה נמי אין אדם אוסר דבר שאינו שלו בההיא דהמסכך גפנו מכל מקום אסר הכא בשלו: מותר לבדוק בתלם של פשתן · כלומר שאין מתכוין לקיים הפשתן שאינו חושש בו אלא לבדוק אם שדה זו יפה לפשתן כדי לזרוע בה פשתן בשנה אחרת: ח ירושלמי (הל' ז) כיני מתני' אין מקיפין הא לסמוך סומכין מתני' דרבי יהודה דתני עלה אין מקיפין חרדל וחריע אלא לחסיות בלבד דברי ר' מאיר רבי יהודה אומר לכל מקיפין חרדל וחריע חוץ מן התבואה רבי שמעון אומר לכל מקיפין רשב"ג אומר ערוגות קטנים [של ירק] מקיפין אותן חרדל וחריע·פי' חריע מפרש בירושלמי מוריקא חסיות בפרק הנודר מן הירק (דף נח:) תניא אלו הן חסיות כגון הלוף והשום והבצלים וטעמא דהכי תנאי לא איתפרש: סומך לבור · דאם יש בתוך שדה תבואה מקום בור בית רובע או יותר סומך שם זרע אחר: וכן ניר מקום שנחרש מלשון נירו לכם ניר (הושע י): ולדרך · אם יש לו שדה אחת כעין ב' שדות שדרך היחיד מפסיק ביניהן מותר לזרוע מין א' בזו ומין אחר בזו: ולגפה · גדר אבנים בלא טיט: מיסך על הארץ · מפרש בתוספתא שאין נופו גבוה מן הארץ ג' טפחים וכיוצא בה לענין מלמול · בפרק המוציא תפילין (דף צט:) ואם יש תחתיו זרע מותר לסמוך מבחוץ זרע אחר דכגדר דמי: ולסלע. הא ודאי דמחילה של סלע עדיפא מכולהו אלא אצטריך לאשמועינן דאפילו בסלע בעינן רוחב ד' דבפחות מכאן אין שמה מחילה להפסיק כדאשכחן בשילהי פ"ק דעירובין (דף טז)· גבי כמלאת אומר ג' מדות במחילה ורוחב ד' דקתני ברישא גבי חריץ אגפה וגדר נמי קאי ומיהו לא יתכן דאינו מענין אחד דלארבעה דגדר לאו בעובי גדר אלא ברוחב אע"פ שעוביו כל שהוא אבל ד' דחריץ אפי' ארוך כמה אמות בעי ד' טפחים משפתו לשפתו: ירושלמי (שם) גדר יש בו להקל ולהחמיר היך עבידא פחות מבית רובע מוקרח בתוך שדה תבואה אסור לזרוע בו הקיפו גדר מותר בבית רובע בבקעה מותר לזרוע בו ב' מינים הקיפו

גדר

[א]כתלמי הרביעה אבא שאול אומר כדי שלא ישייר רובע לבית סאה: ד [ב]זרועה ונמלך לנוטעה לא יאמר אטע ואחר כך אופך אלא הופך ואח"כ נוטע [ג]נטועה ונמלך לזורעה לא יאמר אזרע ואח"כ אשרש אלא משרש ואח"כ זורע אם רצה גומם עד פחות מטפח וזורע ואח"כ משרש: ה [ד]היתה שדהו זרועה קנבוס או לוף לא יהא זורע ובא על גביהם שאינן עושין אלא לשלש השנים [ה]תבואה שעלו בה ספיחי אסטים וכן מקום הגרנות שעלו בהן מינין הרבה וכן (א) תלתן שהעלה מיני צמחים אין מחייבין אותו לנכש אם נכש או כיסח אומרים לו עקור את הכל חוץ ממין אחד: ו [ו]הרוצה לעשות שדהו משר משר מכל מין ב"ש אומרים שלשה תלמים של פתיח וב"ה אומרים מלא העול (ו) השרוני וקרובים דברי אלו להיות כדברי אלו: ז [ז]היה (ז) ראש תור חטים נכנס בתוך של שעורים מותר מפני שהוא נראה כסוף שדהו [ח]שלו חטים ושל חברו מין אחר מותר לסמוך לו מאותו המין [ט]שלו חטים ושל חברו חטים מותר לסמוך לו תלם של פשתן ולא תלם של מין אחר ר' שמעון אומר אחד זרע פשתן ואחד כל המינין ר' יוסי אומר אף באמצע שדהו מותר לבדוק בתלם של פשתן: ח [י]אין סומכין לשדה תבואה חרדל (יא) וחריע אבל סומכים לשדה ירקות חרדל וחריע [כ]וסומך לבור ולניר ולגפה ולדרך ולגדר שהוא גבוה עשרה טפחים ולחריץ שהוא עמוק עשרה ורחב ד' ולאילן שהוא מיסך על הארץ ולסלע שהוא גבוה עשרה ורחב ארבעה:

הרוצה

בעוברה בארץ: ואמר אבא שאול שיהפוך אותה עד שלא ישאר ממנה מקום שאינו הפוך אלא פחות מחלק מכ"ד בשטח הארץ והוא שיעור רובע לבית סאה כמו שביארנו פעמים ואין הלכה כאבא שאול: ד זריעת הזרעונים כמו התבואה וקטניות וזרעוני גנה נקראת זריעה ומטע האילנות נקרא נטיעה ומלת אשרש ומשרש גזור ממלת שרש וענינו לכרות השרש ולעקור אותו וכבר נמצא בספרי הנבואה ושרשך מארץ חיים (תהלים נב)*: גומם עד פחות מטפח. יכרות השרשים עד שלא ישתייר מהם בארץ אלא פחות מעומק טפח ויזרע בארץ ההיא ואחר כך יעמיק לעקור את הכל עד שלא ישתייר כלום: ה קנבוס. יש אומרים שהוא הנקרא בלשון ערב כרויא: ולוף כבר פירשנוהו *שהוא מין ממיני הבצלים ואיני יודע היאך אלו עושות לשלש שנים והענין כבר ידוע שהוא למה כשיכרתו אותו וישארו שרשיו יצמחו אחר שלש שנים לפיכך אמר שאע"פ שהדבר כן אין חורשין עליו עד שיעקרו שרשיו ויש מן הצמח מה שיזרעוהו ויקצרוהו ואחר כך יצמח פעם שנית ופעם שלישית כגון העשב הנקרא ניליגה וניליגה היא אינדי בלע"ז ופספסא הוא הנקרא אספסתא בגמרא וזה הצמח שיצמח בפעם שניה נקרא ספיח ועליו נאמר את ספיח קצירך ומה שיצמח פעם שלישית נקרא שחיס ועליו אמר הכתוב (ישעיה לז) אכול השנה ספיח ובשנה השנית שחיס: ופי' אסטים הוא הניליגה והוא אינדו בלע"ז שצובעין בו תכלת: ותלתן נקרא בערבי חלבה ובלע"ז פנגריג: ונכוש הוא לנקות שרשי הצמח: וכסוח הוא כריתות קצות הענפים היוצאים מן הצמח אשר אין צורך להם כגון זמיר הכרמים ותרגום לא תזמור (ויקרא כה) לא תכסח וטעם אלה הדינים כי אותו הצמח המעורב ממינים רבים כשיודע שאין רצון בעל השדה אין מחייבין עליו לעקור ומקום הגרנות אין צורך לצמוח בהן כלום אבל צריך להיותו חלק לדוש בו וכן התלתן כשיזרענה למאכל אדם יזיקו לה העשבים ויודע שלמאכל אדם נזרעה כשיזרענה מקומות מקומות עשויין בתיקון ולא יזרענה זריעה שאינה מהודרת ואם יכרות קצת מה שצמח מאלו העשבים והניח קצת הודיע בזה שרצונו להשאיר הנשאר על כן יתחייב לעקור הכל חוץ ממין אחד: ו משר משר. מקומות מקומות והוא שיזרע מקום ארוך מן הארץ מכל המינין על הצורה הזאת

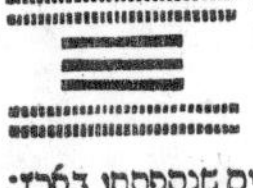

וילטרך להרויח מן ריוח הארץ בין כל מין ומין כדי שלשה תלמים של פתיח כגון זה המצויר תחת הציור האחד והארץ כשהמטר יתבקעו בה בקיעים מתרחבים ונקרא כל בקיע מהם תלם של פתיח וענינו חפירת הבקעים שנתפתחו בארץ: ומלא העול השרוני. רוחב העול שחורשין בו בשרון ר"ל שהוא רחב: ז תור שם העדי שישימו הנשים באזניהם כמו תורי זהב נעשה לך (שיר א') ותבניתו משולש כמו זה*

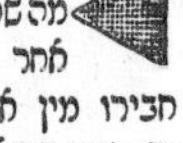

וע"כ יקרא הזוית המחודדת מכל תבנית ראש תור וענין מה שאמ' היה ראש תור הוא(א) על דמות זאת הצור'*

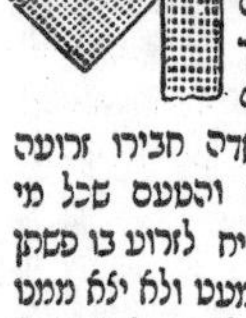

אחר כן אמר כשתהיה שדהו זרועה מחטה ושל חבירו מין אחר מותר לו לזרוע בשדהו הזרועה חטים מן המין ההוא אשר בשדה חבירו וזה ענין שאמר לסמוך לו ובלבד שיסמכהו לשדה חבירו מפני שהוא נראה סוף שדה חבירו אחר שהוא ממיט: אבל אם היתה שדהו ושדה חבירו זרועה חטים אסור לזרוע ביניהם אלא שורה של פשתן בלבד והטעם שכל מי שיראהו ידע שלא נזרע אלא להבחין בו השדה אם יצליח לזרוע בו פשתן ואם לאו שאין אדם זורע תלם אחד של פשתן מפני שהוא מעט ולא יצא ממנו שום תועלת אבל אם יזרע תלם של מין אחר יראה שהוא כלאים ונאמר שהוא לא זרעו אלא ליהנות ממנו ולא היה צריך מהמין הזה אלא לזאת השורה: ורבי שמעון אומר אחד הפשתן ואחד כל המינין אסור מפני שאפשר שיאמרו עליו שהוא לא היה צריך מן הפשתן יותר מזה השיעור: ואמר ר' יוסי שאפי' באמצע שדהו מותר לבדוק בתלם של פשתן ר"ל לבדוק ולנסות ולהבחין השדה ואינו חושש ר' יוסי למראית העין ואע"פ שהוא דומה ככלאים אמר שהוא מותר וחכמים חוששין למראית העין מפני זה אסור להבחין את השדה בתלם של פשתן אלא בסוף השדה ואין הלכה כר' יוסי ולא כרבי שמעון:

ח חריע בלשון ישמעאל עצפור ואלו שני מינין מפסידין התבואה וכבר הקדמנו שאין להזהר בענין כלאים אלא בשדה שלו וכשנראה חרדל וחריע סמוך לתבואה נדע שבעל השדה זרעו שלא היה מניח לאחר לזרוע אותו אבל היה מרחיקו ואם היה שדה ירקות יהיה מותר שאפשר לומר של אחר הן שאלו שני מינין אינן מפסידין הירקות והם סוף שדה אחר: ומה שאמר סומך לבור · ר"ל שכשיהיה בין זה החרדל והתבואה אחד מאלו המפריסים יהיה מותר: ואילן שהוא

...בתחלתו וכששורין אותו במים נמתק ואנו לועזין אותו פינוריצי ובל' יון תילי: אין מחייבין אותו לנכש. דלתלתן קשו ליה עשבין ורמינהו מלקטין עשבין בכל מקום חוץ משדה תלתן ... מעלו לה עשבים ותרצינן א"ר ירמיה לא קשיא כאן לזרע כאן לזירים פי' לעמיר מעלו לה. דכי קיימא ביני עשבים מירכבה. אביי אמר לא קשיא כאן לאדם לא בעי עשבים ... ביבא לה עשבים לבהמה מנא ידעינן אמר רב פפא עבידא מישרי משרי פי' ערוגות לאדם לא עבידא משרי משרי לבהמה. ניכש לעז מונדאו. כיסח פי' חתך לא תזמור ...סח: אומר לו עקור כל המינין. ולא תשי. אלא מין אחר: ו הרוצה לעשות שדהו משר. פי' ערוגות לזרוע בשדה מינין הרבה. בית שמאי אומרים עושה המשר בג' תלמים של פתחין הרבה כלומר רחבין מלשון יפתח וישדד אדמתו ומניח בור וזורע וכן לכל שדהו. ובית הלל אומרים מלא העול וכו' נמצא ג' תלמין של פתיח באורך עול השרוני גרסינן אמר ר' חייא רבה ב' אמות ומיצר והולך אפילו כל שהוא: שרוני. פי' בערוך פי' בקעה מן והיה העקוב למישור. בשביל ירושלים שהיא בנויה בהרים וכשתרד ממנה אל לוד וחברותיה. שמן שרון שנאמר הדר הכרמל והשרון. ואני אומר חבצלת השרון. ויש אומרים מקום ועל זה הפירוש אנו סומכין: ז היה ראש תור חטים ונכנס בתוך של שעורין אותה השורה של חטים הנכנסת בתוך של שעורים נראית כסוף שדהו של חטים *וזו צורתו: שלו חטים ושל חבירו חטים מותר לסמוך אצל שדה חבירו חטים לפי שאין [נראה שדה חבירו משל החטים שסמך לו אלא נראית כסוף שדה החטים: ח סומך לבור. פי' בתוך שדה תבואה אם יש בו מקום בור בית רובע או יותר סומך שם זרע אחר וכן ניר אלא מקום חרוש כדכתיב נירו לכם ניר ובור בקנצי: ולדרך. פי' מי שיש לו שדה כעין ב' שדות שדרך הרבים ודרך היחיד מפסיק באמצע בשביל זה הדרך מותר לזרוע מיכן מין אחד ...ר. ולגפא כבר פירשנוהו כי הוא גדר בלא טיט מלשון הגפת הדלתות: ולגדר שהוא גבוה י' טפחים [ויש בו להקל ויש בו להחמיר כיצד] פחות מבית רובע מוקרח בתוך שדה תבואה ...ר הוא הקיפו גדר מותר. וזה הדרך בגדר להקל. ולהחמיר כיצד בית רובע בבקעה מותר לזרוע בו מינין הרבה הקיפו גדר אסור. ולחריץ כמו כן: ולאילן שהוא מיסך על הארץ. פירשו בתוספתא ...

* [הגה נראה דצ"ל דדרך רוב בנ"א שאחרי רדת הרביעה חורשין עוד תלמים גדולים כצ"ל לפענ"ד וכן הוא בר"ש]

פי' מהר"י בן מלכי צדק

פירוש הרא"ש

הגהות הב"ח

גדר אסור : טו קרחת · מלשון בקרחתו (ויקרא יג) שנקרח מן השיער (יב) : כ"ד קרחות לגבי בית סאה ובכל קרחה זורע מין א' ובית סאה הוא חמשים על חמשים אמה (יג) וכשאתה עושה מהן כ"ד קרחות נמצאת כל קרחה י' אמות וב' טפחים ומהלה אורך על י' אמות רוחב כילד שאם תעשה מהם כ"ה קרחות נמלא כל קרחה י' על י' אמות קח אחת מהן ותחלקנה לכ"ד רלועות נמלא כל רלועה ב' טפחים ומהלה רוחב על אורך עשר שהאמה בת ו' טפחים נמלאו תשעה טפחים לי' אמות ותן אלה הקטנות אחת אחת על כל הגדולות : מקרחת לבית רובע . שהרי יש בסאה כ"ד רבעים של קב : כל מין שירלה · ולא בעי ר"מ הרחקה כלל : היתה בתוך שדה תבואה קרחת אחת של בית רובע או שתי קרחות זורען חרדל דאינו נראה כשדה חרדל בתוך תבואה אבל שלשה קרחות נראה כשדה חרדל בתוך שדה תבואה ואסור : והכ"א ט' קרחות מותרות · ארישא דרולה לעשות שדהו קרחת קיימי דמתנך דכ"ד אמה אין מותר לזרוע מכל מין אלא התשע כילד כשאתה מחלק חמשים על חמשים לחמש שורו' ואח"כ תחלק שורה ראשונה ושלישית וחמישי' כל אחת לחמש בית רובע זורע בכל שורה ג' בית רובע ורובע בור מפסיק ביניהן שזורע בכל א' בית רובע ומניח בית רובע ושורה כולה בורה וכן רביעית נמלא זורע תשע רביעיות שיש בית רובע בור מפסיק בין כל א' וא' ואי אפשר לזרוע השאר שלא יסמוך: י כל שהוא בתוך בית רובע · כגון נקעים מלאים מים : עולין למדת בית רובע · ליחשב הרחקה אע"ג דלא חזו לזריעה דהנהו נגאני דארעא מיקרי כדאמרי' בפ' בית כור (דף קא·) וכן גדר שאין גבוה י' כמי עולה למדת רובע כדקתני בתוספתא (פ"ב) : אבילת הגפן · מה שהגפן תופס כגון סביב הגפן כדי עבודתה ויש מפרשים גפן שיבש ולא נשאר כ"א השרש בארץ עולה למדת בית רובע להשלים י' אמות וב' טפחי' ומחלה על י' אמות דהוא שיעור בית רובע כדפרשינן לעיל : וכן הקבר כמי עולה וכן הסלע שאינו גבוה י' דאילו גבוה י' מפסיק בפני עצמו : ירושלמי (הל' ח) ר' בון בר' חייא בשם ר' זעירא לא שנו אלא אכילת הגפן ...

טו הרוצה לעשות שדהו קרחת קרחת מכל מין עושה עשרים וארבעה קרחות לבית סאה מקרחת לבית רובע וזורע בתוכה כל מין שירצה היתה קרחת אחת או שתים זורעם חרדל שלש לא יזרע חרדל מפני שהיא נראית כשדה חרדל דברי ר' מאיר וחכמים אומרים תשע קרחות מותרות עשר אסורות ראב"י אומר אפי' כל שדהו בית כור לא יעשה בתוכה חוץ מקרחת אחת : י כל שהוא בתוך רובע עולה במדת בית רובע אכילת הגפן והקבר והסלע עולין במדת בית רובע תבואה בתבואה בית רובע ירק בירק ו' טפחים תבואה בירק ירק בתבואה בית רובע ר"א אומר ירק בתבואה ו' טפחים : יא תבואה נוטה על גבי תבואה וירק על גבי ירק תבואה על גבי ירק ירק על גבי תבואה הכל מותר חוץ מדלעת יונית ר"מ אומר אף הקישות ופול המצרי ורואה אני את דבריהם מדברי :

פרק שלישי

א ערוגה [א] שהיא ששה טפחים על ששה טפחים זורעים בתוכה חמשה זרעונים ארבע בארבע רוחות הערוגה ואחת [א] באמצע

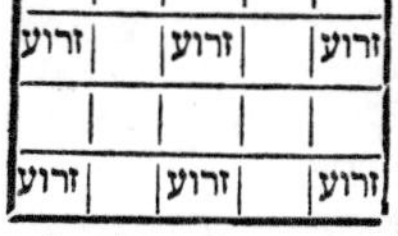

והציור הזה לפי המחבר לדעת הירושלמי

הציור הזה הוא ע"פ פי' הר"ש ז"ל

MISHNAH 9. IF ONE WISHES TO DIVIDE HIS FIELD ḲARAḤATH[7] BY ḲARAḤATH EACH TO BE SOWN WITH A DIFFERENT SPECIES, HE SHOULD DIVIDE IT INTO TWENTY-FOUR ḲARAḤATH, A ḲARAḤATH TO A BETH-ROBA',[8] AND HE MAY THEN SOW IN EACH WHATEVER SPECIES HE DESIRES.[9] IF THERE IS ONE ḲARAḤATH OR TWO,[10] HE MAY SOW THEM WITH MUSTARD, BUT IF THERE ARE THREE[10] HE MAY NOT SOW THEM WITH MUSTARD,
a SINCE IT WOULD LOOK LIKE A FIELD OF MUSTARD.[1] THIS IS THE OPINION OF R. MEIR. BUT THE SAGES SAID:[2] NINE ḲARAḤATH ARE PERMITTED,[3] TEN ARE FORBIDDEN. R. ELIEZER B. JACOB, SAID: EVEN THOUGH THE WHOLE OF ONE'S FIELD IS A BETH-KOR, HE MAY NOT MAKE WITHIN IT BEYOND ONE ḲARAḤATH.[4]

b *MISHNAH* 10. WHATEVER[1] THERE IS WITHIN A BETH-ROBA' [WHICH SEPARATES HETEROGENEOUS SPECIES] IS INCLUDED IN[2] THE AREA OF THE BETH-ROBA'. THE SPACE OCCUPIED BY VINE ROOTS,[3] LIKEWISE A GRAVE,[4] OR A ROCK,[5] IS INCLUDED. [A ḲARAḤATH SOWN WITH] GRAIN WITHIN [A FIELD OF HETEROGENEOUS] GRAIN [MUST BE SEPARATED BY] A BETH-ROBA';[6] [A ḲARAḤATH SOWN WITH] VEGETABLES WITHIN [A FIELD OF HETEROGENEOUS] VEGETABLES [BY] SIX HANDBREADTHS [SQUARE];[7] [A ḲARAḤATH SOWN WITH] VEGETABLES WITHIN [A FIELD OF] GRAIN, OR [A ḲARAḤATH

(7) Lit., 'a bald or bare patch'. A term for a piece of ground as yet unsown, forming a part of a field, and quadrilateral, approximately square in shape, and, therefore, substantial enough to sight to be readily distinguishable in its surroundings. (8) Since a *beth-se'ah* = 2,500 square cubits, a *beth-roba'* (one twenty-fourth of a *beth-se'ah* = 104.15 square cubits), i.e., an area of 10.205 cubits square. (9) Since the various species each occupy an easily distinguishable plot, nobody will mistakenly think that heterogeneous species have been sown 'with one handthrow'; there is therefore no need for any object or space to separate one species from another. (10) *Sc.* together.
a (1) Considering that it is not usual to sow large areas of mustard, three *beth-roba'* thereof constitute a field, and a field within a field of heterogeneous species is prohibited. (2) With regard to the subject of the first part of R. Meir's statement. (3) The idea is that there must be a *beth-roba'* separating heterogeneous species. A field of a *beth-se'ah* should, thus, be divided into

Diag. (*a*)

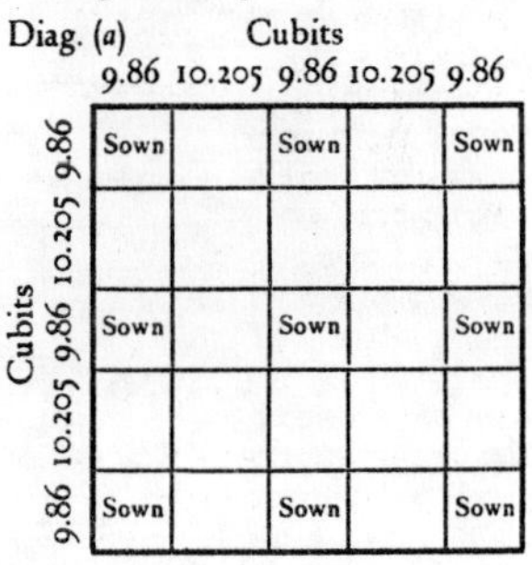

Diag. (*b*)

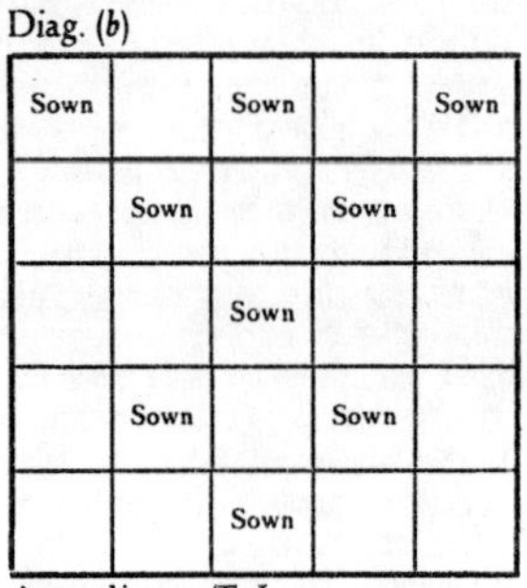

According to T. J.

twenty-five squares. Since between each *ḳaraḥath* to be sown there must be a *beth-roba'*, i.e., a square approximately 10.205 × 10.205 cubits, the former will measure 9.86 × 9.86 cubits (approx), (After Maim.), thus. V. Diag. (*a*). Rash. visualized it similarly, except that he seems content to divide the *beth-se'ah* into 25 equal squares, and to accept an intervening unsown space of 10 × 10 cubits, instead of the strict *beth-roba'* which is 10.205 × 10.205 cubits.

Diag. (*c*)

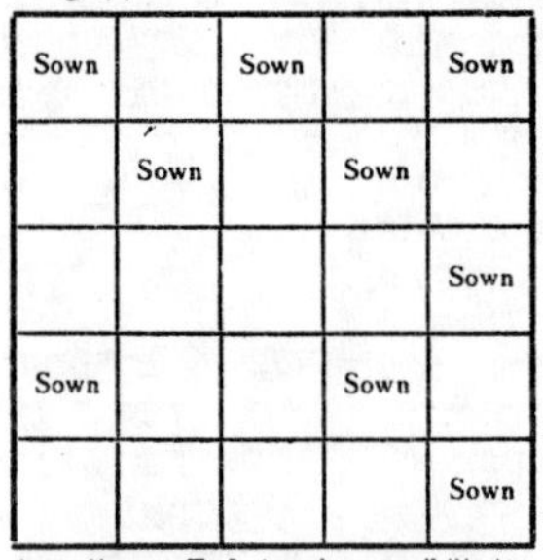

According to T. J. (another possibility)

According to T.J., however, the scheme should be either of the following. V. Diag. (*b*).

The objection to (*b*) would be that the centre square though not adjoined by another sown patch is, nevertheless, 'bound' at its four corners. It is true that this junction at corners is not forbidden as it comes under the rule at the beginning of Mishnah 7, but it might be thought that it is too much to extend such permissibility to a case where a sown patch is 'tied', at all of its four corners to heterogeneous species. Diagram (*c*) whilst fulfilling the conditions of T.J. (viz., that three patches be sown in the first line, two in the second, one in the third, two in the fourth, and one in the fifth) avoids even that possible objection. (4) What R. Eliezer b. Jacob meant was, apparently, that however large the field (one *kor* = thirty *se'ah*), it is permissible to have with it only one *ḳaraḥath* sown with a heterogeneous species.
b (1) Even if the space occupied thereby be unfit for sowing, e.g., a ditch or gutter filled with water. (2) I.e., the space occupied thereby is not deducted. (3) Calculated to be six handbreadths from the vine in all directions, within which space it is forbidden to sow anything else. (4) Which is forbidden for other use, including sowing. (5) On which it is impossible to sow. In view of the rule at the end of Mishnah 8, the reference here must be to a rock less than ten handbreadths in height and four in width. (6) Which is the minimum for a grain plantation to be termed a grain *field*. (7) The minimum for a vegetable plantation to be termed a vegetable *field*.

◁ *For the continuation of the English translation of this page see overleaf.*

יג הרוצה לעשות שדהו קרחת קרחת מכל מין עושה עשרים וארבעה קרחות לבית סאה מקרחת לבית רובע וזורע בתוכה כל מין שירצה היתה קרחת אחת או שתים זורעם חרדל שלש לא יזרע חרדל מפני שהיא נראית כשדה חרדל דברי ר' מאיר וחכמים אומרים תשע קרחות מותרות עשר אסורות ראב"י אומר אפי' כל שדהו בית כור לא יעשה בתוכה חוץ מקרחת אחת: **יד** כל שהוא בתוך רובע עולה במדת בית רובע אכילת הגפן והקבר והסלע עולין במדת בית רובע תבואה בתבואה בית רובע ירק בירק ו' טפחים תבואה בירק ירק בתבואה בית רובע ר"א אומר ירק בתבואה ו' טפחים: **יא** תבואה נוטה על גבי תבואה וירק על גבי ירק תבואה על גבי ירק ירק על גבי תבואה הכל מותר חוץ מדלעת יונית ר"מ אומר אף הקישות ופול המצרי ורואה אני את דבריהם מדברי:

פרק שלישי

א ערוגה א) שהיא ששה טפחים על ששה טפחים זורעים בתוכה חמשה זרעונים ארבע בארבע רוחות הערוגה ואחת א] באמצע

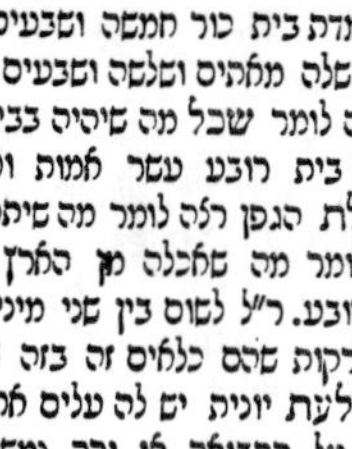
והציור הזה לפי המחבר לדעת הירושלמי

הציור הזה הוא ע"פ פי' הר"ש ז"ל
תלת קרחות זורעין כזו השורה וכן בשורה ג' וכו'

פירוש הרא"ש

הגהות הב"ח

הגהות הרי"ב לנדא

פי' מהרי"ץ בן מלכי צדק

א חמשה זרעונים

Continuation of translation from previous page as indicated by ◁

SOWN WITH] GRAIN WITHIN [A FIELD OF] VEGETABLES [BY] A BETH-ROBA'.[8] R. ELIEZER SAID: [A ḲARAḤATH SOWN WITH] VEGETABLES WITHIN [A FIELD OF] GRAIN [NEED BE SEPARATED BY] SIX HANDBREADTHS [SQUARE].[9]

MISHNAH 11. [EARS OF] CORN BENDING OVER ON TO [EARS OF HETEROGENEOUS] CORN,[10] OR VEGETABLE [LEAVES]
c ON TO [LEAVES OF A HETEROGENEOUS] VEGETABLE,[1] OR [EARS OF] CORN ON TO VEGETABLE [LEAVES],[1] OR VEGETABLE [LEAVES] ON TO [EARS OF] CORN,[1] ALL THIS IS PERMITTED,[2] EXCEPT IN THE CASE OF THE GREEK GOURD.[3] R. MEIR SAID: '[EXCEPT] ALSO IN THE CASE OF THE CUCUMBER OR EGYPTIAN BEANS;[4] BUT I RECOGNIZE THEIR[5] DICTUM AS MORE ACCEPTABLE THAN MINE'.[6]

CHAPTER III

MISHNAH 1. IN A VEGETABLE-BED MEASURING SIX HAND-
d BREADTHS BY SIX HANDBREADTHS[1] IT IS PERMITTED TO SOW FIVE [HETEROGENEOUS] VEGETABLE-SEEDS,[2] VIZ., FOUR [SPECIES], [ONE] ON [EACH OF] THE FOUR SIDES OF THE BED,

(8) I.e., when both are 'fields'; but when there is only one row of vegetables adjoining a grain field, an intervening space of six by six handbreadths is sufficient. (9) In his opinion we should not, in a case of a *ḳaraḥath* and a field, be more stringent than in a case of a row and a field. (10) *Sc.* although originally sown at the required distance from one another, and/or because, though separated by the required space at one place, the furrows or beds converge further on (cf. *supra* 8, n. 4).

c (1) V. 17*b* n. b 10. (2) Since the heterogeneous species touch, one might have thought that on account of the appearance of *kil'ayim*, this is prohibited. The Mishnah therefore makes it clear that it is permitted. (3) Whose leaves are particularly long and liable to entangle themselves with others, and thus create a very strong suggestion of *kil'ayim*. (4) Their leaves and stalks are long enough and sufficiently liable to entangling to class them for the present purpose with the Greek gourd. (5) I.e., the majority Rabbis'. (6) R. Meir felt it his duty to record the view which had been tradited to him by his teachers, but also to acknowledge that there was more justification for the view put forward by his colleagues, and which he accepted as binding.

d (1) I.e., a square cubit, the smallest area for such a bed. (2) It is possible to effect this by sowing five heterogeneous seeds set as specified *infra*.

AND ONE[3] IN THE MIDDLE.[4] IF A VEGETABLE-BED HAS A BORDER ONE HANDBREADTH HIGH,[5] ONE MAY SOW THEREIN THIRTEEN [HETEROGENEOUS SPECIES], VIZ., THREE ON EVERY BORDER, AND ONE IN THE MIDDLE. IT IS PROHIBITED TO PLANT A TURNIP-HEAD IN THE BORDER SINCE THAT WOULD FILL IT [COMPLETELY].[6]

R. JUDAH SAID: [IT IS PERMITTED TO SOW] SIX [SPECIES] IN

(3) *Sc.* single seed (Bert.). (4) For diagrams v. Shab. Sonc. ed. 84*b* . The shaded part is shown. (For another possible arrangement v. printed edition of the separate Mishnayoth). The main underlying principle is that there must be a distance of at least three handbreadths between seed and seed, allowing for each species a space of one and a half handbreadths for drawing sustenance without coming into contact with any of the roots of another species. The contact of the diverse seeds at the corners does not matter, as the very position shows that they belong to different beds, v. Shab, Sonc. ed., 84*b* n. b 5. and Feldman W.M., *Rabbinical Mathematics* pp. 45ff. (5) And of the same width, designed for a person attending to the patch to stand on, a human foot being a 'handbreadth' in width. The whole of the area of the patch is now 8 × 8 handbreadths. (6) And to appearances all the species would be mixed up.

לאו קרא הוה אמינא דאיכא ערבוב ואסורה ובהדיא מוכח בירושלמי (שם) דקרא עיקר דרשה ולאו אסמכתא מדדריש נמי מקרא טעמא דר' יהודה דאמר בסיפא ששה ועוד דאמרי' בירושלמי (הל' א). ר' יוחנן בשם רבי ינאי כולהו בתוך ששה כהנא בשם ריש לקיש כולהו חוץ לששה כלומר כולהו אותן של ד' רוחות וקסבר ריש לקיש דאפי' בא לזורען סמוך לערוגה מבחוץ אין יכול לזרוע אלא חמשה בין הכל ופריך אם כולהו חוץ לששה ניתני תשעה משמע דלמאן דאמר בתוך ששה לא קשיא מידי דאע"ג דלא ינקי אסור משום ערבוב אבל אם נזרעין מבחוץ סמוך לד' רוחות הערוגה בזה לא אסר הכתוב וכל מה שיוכל לזרוע יזרע והא דתנן

באמצע היה לה גבול גבוה טפח זורעין בתוכה שלשה עשר שלשה על כל גבול וגבול ואחד באמצע [א]לא יטע ראש הלפת בתוך הגבול מפני שהוא ממלאהו רבי יהודה אומר [ב]ששה

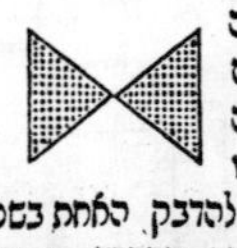

זוית זרע זה נדבקה בזוית האחר כך* ואם יהיה צלע הזרע הזה מקביל לצלע הב' כמו זאת הצורה* אסור להדבק האחת בשניה מפני שיתערב הכל ויהיה כלאים ודרך ההפרש ביניהם על אחד משלש דרכים האחד לחפור ביניהם חפירה שיהא בעמקה טפח ובארכה ו' טפחים אם שני המינים הם ירקות כמו שיתבאר בזה הפרק או ישים ביניהם גבול שיהיה רומו טפח ורחבו טפח והדרך הב' להרחיק ביניהם טפח ומחצה והוא שיעור שלא ייניק זה מזה והדרך הג' להחזיר העלים של זרע זה לזה הצד והעלים של זרע אחר לצד ב' עד שיראו מובדלות כמו שיתבאר בזה הפרק ועל כל אלו העקרים שנאמר שערוגה ו' על ו' אפשר לזרוע בה ה' מינים מן הזרעים ולא תהיה כלאים וזו צורתה* ויהיה מדה כל מה שנזרע מזו הערוגה כ"ד (א) כמו שיתבאר בגמ' וכבר יחדו זאת הערוגה בגמ' ואמרו ערוגה בחורבה שניט רצה לומר שאסור לזרוע אותם כמו שציירנו אלא אם תהיה (בחורבה) לבדה ולא תהיה סביבותיה ערוגה אחרת כדי שלא יתערבו בה הזרעים שבאחת מצדי הערוגה עם הזרעים שבערוגה הב' הסמוכה לה והקשינו שם ואמרנו מפני מה לא התרט לו לזרוע חוץ מן הערוגה כנגד הקרנות שאין בה דבר זרוע ואמרנו שהוא אסור שמא ימלא הקרנות ויהיה זריעתו לערוגה ע"ז הצורה השניה* ויהיה מה שנזרע מן הערוגה בזו הצורה שיעור מדתו כ"ז טפח וזה התכלית מה שיוכל לזרוע בערוגה שהיא ששה על ששה כשיזרע בה חמשה זרעונים בלבד על התנאי שאמרנו : היה לה גבול גבוה טפח זורעים בתוכה י"ג ג' על כל גבול וגבול כמו הצורה הזאת* ויהיה מדת הזרוע ממנה באלו השלשה עשר מינין ל' טפח כמו שנתבאר בזו הצורה למסתכל בה : ואמר רבי יהודה שאפשר שיזרע בזו הערוגה שהיא ששה על ששה ולה גבול טפח. י"ח מינין י"ב על הגבול כמו שאמר תנא קמא וששה באמצע ויהיה מדת הזרוע ממנה שלשים טפחים וירבו המינים ולא יחסר

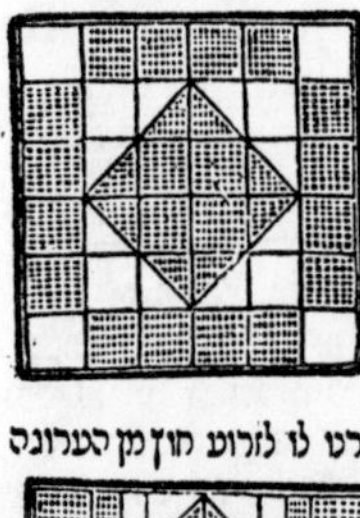

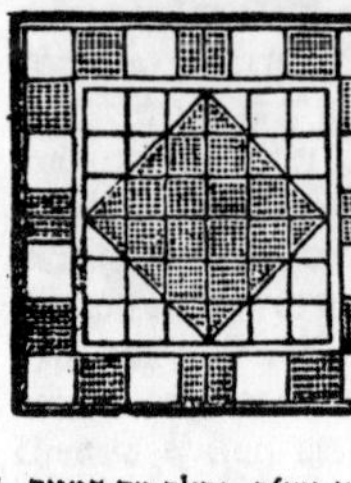

לעיל בפרק ב' (משנה י) ירק בירק ו' טפחים הני מילי בשדה גדולה שיש בה ירק הרבה אבל הכא דאין זורע מכל אחד ואחד אלא מעט לא חיישי' ודכוותיה אשכחן גבי תבואה דתנן לעיל בפרק ב' (מ"ג) תבואה בתבואה בית רובע. ואמרינן בירושל' (הל' א) מהו להקריח בית רובע ולזרוע בתוכה ה' מיני תבואה מה אם ששה על ששה שלוקין עליו דבר תורה את אמר מותר כאן שאין לוקין עליו כל שכן דבכל מקום שאין זורע מכל מין ומין אלא מעט לא חיישי' אלא שלא ייניקו המיני' זה מזה ואפי' במה שהיניקות מתערבות ויונקין ממקום אחד לא חיישינן כדאיתא בירו' (שם) אמר ר' יונה עבודה פוגעת בעבודה ואין מין פוגע בחברו לחובשו ולשון חבישה פירשתי לעיל וסדר הזריעה רגילין לפרש שזורע שורה אחת לכל רוח אלא שמניח חרב לכל קרן וקרן טפחיים וחומש מצד זה וטפחיים וחומש מצד זה דנמצאו ג' טפחים ומשהו מזרע מזרח לזרע דרום לפי חשבון כל אמתא בריבוע' אמתא ותרי חומשי באלכסונא וכן לשאר קרנות ובאמצע הערוגה נרעין אחד לבדו ולא יתכן כדפרישי' דלא בעי הרחקה אלא טפח ומחצה ועוד דבירושלמי (שם) דריש זרועיה מעוט זרעים שנים אמר רבי שמואל בר סוסרטאי משנים אתה למד ארבעה מה שנים אתה נותן בתחלת שדה ומיצר והולך אף ארבעה אתה נותן בתחלת שדה ומיצר והולך אי אפשר שלא יהא שם נקב אחד פנוי ליטע את האמצעי וסוגי' זו אי אפשר לייסב לפי אותה שיטה דמה שייך ומיצר והולך אם אין רוחב השורה אלא כמדת גרעין הנזרע אלא כך הוא הדין דאין צריך להרחיק המיני' זה מזה אלא טפח ומחצה כשיעור יניקתן ובפרק אמר ר' עקיבא פי' בקונטרס דשיעור יניקת כל ירק טפח ומחצה ואף על פי שפירש שם עם מקום הזרע לא היה צריך לפרש כן אלא לפי שיטתו פי' דמצריך להרחיק ג' טפחים זה מזה שלא יתערבו היניקות ואינו כן דלא חיישי' בעירוב היניקות אלא שלא ייניק כל א' מגופו של חברו והא דתנן בפרק לא יחפור (דף יז.) מרחיקין את הזרעין מן הכותל ג' טפחים דמשמע כך הוא שיעור יניקתן מ"מ עיקר יניקתן לא אזלא אלא טפח ומחצה ואפשר משום שהשרשים מתפשטין ג' טפחים כדאשכחן גבי אילן בפ' לא יחפור (דף כה:) דתנן מרחיקין את האילן מן הבור כ"ה אמה ואפילו הכי אין יניקתו אלא ט"ז אמה כדאיתא בשילהי לא יחפור (דף כז:) ולמאי דמסקי' נמי בפרק לא יחפור דזרעים לא משתרשי לצדדין וטעמא דהרחקה מפני שמחלידין את הקרקע ומעלין עפר תיחוח מ"מ לא ינקי כולי האי ועוד מתני' דלא יחפור דלמא בזרעים דינקי [טפי] והכא בירקות כדאיתא בפרק כל שעה (דף לט:) וכדתנן בפרקין וא"ת מה דאמר בפ' ר"ע דאמר רב ערוגה בחורבה שנינו מכ"מ גבול של ערוגה טפח ולב' ערוגות איכא ב' גבולין ונמצאו ב' טפחים בין זרע של ערוגה לזרע של חברתה וי"ל דב' ערוגות זו אצל זו גבול אחד לשתיהן דשיעור גבול כמלא רוחב פרסה להלך סביב להשקותן כדאמר התם ובחד טפח סגי והשתא כך הוא סדר הזריעה שמניח בקרנות חרב טפח וחלי חומש על טפח וחלי חומש כדי שיתרחק זרע מזרח מזרע דרום כשיעור אלכסון של טפח וחלי חומש על טפח וחלי חומש משהו יותר מטפח ומחצה ובטפח ומחצה סגי וכן לכל קרן וקרן ונמצא רוחב הזרע ד' טפחים חסר חומש בתחלת ו' ומיצר והולך מצד ימין ומצד שמאל עד שהוא כלה לרוחב טפח חסר חומש וכן לכל רוח ורוח עד שהוא מניח באמצע הערוגה ג' על ג' חרב ועושה באמצע נקב וזורע בו גרעין אחד ונמצאו כל המינין רחוקים זה מזה טפח ומחצה כזה*

והייתו דקאמר בירושלמי (שם) דזורע ד' מינין ומיצר והולך עד שמניח שם נקב אחד וזורע בו את האמצעי והא דפריך בירושל' (שם) ניתני תשעה למאן דאמר כולהו חוץ לו' פריך לפי שאף למאן דאמר כולהו בתוך ו' היה יכול לזרוע ט' אם לא משום ערבוב אבל משום יניקה לא מיתסר לפי שיכול בענין אחר שזורע באמצע כל רוח טפח על טפח ובאמצע הערוגה טפח על טפח נמצא מזרע האמצעי עד זרעוני הרוחות טפח ומחצה לכל רוח ומזרע שבאמצע הרוח עד הקרן ב' טפחים ומחצה מכאן וב' טפחים ומחצה מכאן וזורע בכל קרן וקרן טפח על טפח הרי ט' מינין שיש בכולן חרב בין זה לזה טפח ומחצה ולמאן דאמר כלהו חוץ לו' יכול לזרוע מן האמצעי של ג' על ג' ומשום הכי קשיא ליה בירושלמי (שם) ניתני ט' ומשני רב בערוגה שבערוגות ובפרק אר"ע פריך והא מיערבן אהדדי ומשני בנוטה שורה לכאן ושורה לכאן ממשיך זרע של ערוגה זו לצד צפון ושל זו לצד דרום ולפי זה ממעט זרע שבתחלת שדה כדי שיהא רחוק מערוגה שבצדה טפח ומחצה והא דקאמר בירושל' (שם) מה שנים אתה נותן בתחלת ו' ומיצר והולך היינו שאם בא לזרוע ב' מינין בערוגה של ו' זורע מצד מזרח ו' טפחים אורך על רוחב ב' טפחים ורביע ומצד מערב ו' טפחים אורך על רוחב ב' טפחים ורביע וביניהם חרב ו' טפחים אורך על רוחב טפח ומחצה ומיהו לפי שיטה זו שפירשתי אין לנו הוכחה שיהא שיעור יניקת הזרע טפח ומחצה דמה שפירש בקונטרס במסכת שבת דשיעור כל ירק טפח ומחצה על כרחו הוצרך לפרש כן לפי שיטתו שאוסר לערב היניקות דמצריך להרחיק זה מזה ג' טפחים מכלל דמדת היניקות טפח ומחצה. ומיהו לפי שיטתנו נמי אזלא יניקה מיהא טפי מטפח מדקאמר ערוגה בחורבה שנינו אע"ג דאיכא גבול טפח דמפסיק ביניהן : היה לה גבול גבוה טפח. כמין ספיו של טיט גבוה טפח סביב הערוגה דאמרי' בירושלמי (שם) רבי יסא שאל לא מסתברא בגגו של גבול טפח בתמיהה כן מוכיח שם מתוך בעיא שאחריה. ונמצאת הערוגה מבחוץ שמונה על שמונה וזורעין בתוכה י"ג זרעונין ג' על כל גבול וגבול דהיינו י"ב סביב כיצד ד' לד' קרנות וב' לכל רוח ורוח ואחד באמצע והאי דקתני מתני' ג' על כל גבול וגבול חד דקרן נמנה עם הב' ומונה קרן אחת לכל רוח ולכך קרי להו ג'. והשתא אותן י"ב שבגבול לא משכחת טפח על טפח מכל מין ומין שכל הגבול מסביב אין בו כי אם ח' טפחים אורך על רוחב טפח שהרי הערוגה עם הגבול ח' על ח' טול ממנה רצועה מצד מזרח ברוחב טפח וכן מצד מערב הרי לך ב' רצועות כל א' וא' אורכה שמונה ורחבה טפח כשאתה בא לחזור וליטול רצועה מן הדרום ורצועה מן הצפון אין בכל אחד כי אם ששה טפחים אורך שכבר נתמעטה כל אחד ואחד ב' טפחים טפח מכאן וטפח מכאן והזרעונים מרוחקין זה מזה טפח ומחצה בין כל מין ומין וי"ב. אורות לי"ב מינין שבגבול. הרי י"ב אורין לי"ב [א] טפחים ולא נשאר מקום

פי' מהר"י בן מלכי צדק

ו' על ו' טפחים וכו' בשבת בפ' ר' עקיבא גרסי' כנהגי מילי אמר רב יהודה צמחה תרי זרועיה תרי הרי ד'. תצמיח חד הרי ה' וקים להו לרבנן דה' בו' לא ינקי מהדדי. גרסינן ר' יוחנן בשם ר' ינאי כולהון בתוך ו'. פי' כיצד זורעין בה ה' כי הערוגה ממזרח למערב ו' טפחים ומצפון לדרום ששה טפחים וכל זרע תופס טפח על טפח ובין זרע לזרע טפח ומחצה עתה בפנת מזרח זרע תופס טפח על טפח באמצע זרע תופס טפח על טפח במערב תופס טפח. עתה ימצא בין זרע שבפנת מזרח לזרע אמצעי טפח ומחצה ובין זרע שבפנת מערב לזרע אמצעי טפח ומחצה וכן בין זרע שבפנת צפון לזרע אמצעי טפח ומחצה ובין זרע שבפנת דרום לזרע אמצעי טפח ומחצה ונשארו פנויין הקרנות שהוא יכול לזרוע ד' ולעשות ט'. כיצד מזרע צפון עד זרע מערב ד' טפחים הוצא טפח לזרע וג' טפחי' פנויין טפח ומחצה שיהא בין זרע הקרן לזרע צפון. וטפח ומחצה אחד בין זרע הקרן לזרע מערב וכן הדין של כל הקרנות. וקשיא אם כן ליתני ט' בערוגה ותירצו א"ר תנחום חצראה בין הערוגות היא מתנייתא פי' דאין לה מקום קרנות בפני עצמה שתלם שלה לה ולחברתה והקשו בבבלי שם א"כ באמצע הפנה לא ליזרע דהא נערבין זה עם זה ותירצו בנוטע שורה לכאן ושורה לכאן : היה לה גבול. פי' כמו גדר מטיט בלבד גבוה טפח. וכו' אמר רב נסא מסתברא הגבול רחבו טפח : ג' על כל גבול וגבול. כיצד הואיל והגבול רחב טפח נמצאת הערוגה מבחוץ ח' על ח' בכל רוח זורע ב' הרי ב' טפחים לזרע וטפח ומחצה [ריוח] הרי שלשהומחצה נמצא בין זרע מזרח לזרע צפון ד' טפחים ומחצה ויותר הוצא זרע לטפח ומחצה נמצא בין זרע הקרן לזרע מזרח טפח ומחצה מצד זה ובין זרע הקרן לזרע צפון טפח ומחצה מצד זה וכן כולן והנה אנחנו מציירין אותו כדי שיהא פתוח ומרווח להבין אותה אבל באמצע לא תוכל לזרוע אלא זרע אחד כי מבפנים אינה אלא ה' ומחצה על ה' ומחצה

ב אב מיי' פ"ד מהלכות כלאים הלכה י"ב טוש"ע יו"ד סימן [illegible] סעיף [illegible] :

הגהות הב"ח

(א) מ"א בר"מ מזו הערוגה כ"ד טפחים כמו שיתבאר:

הגהות מהר"י לנדא

א] מ"א בר"ש י"ב אורין לי"ב טפחים. צ"ל י"ח:

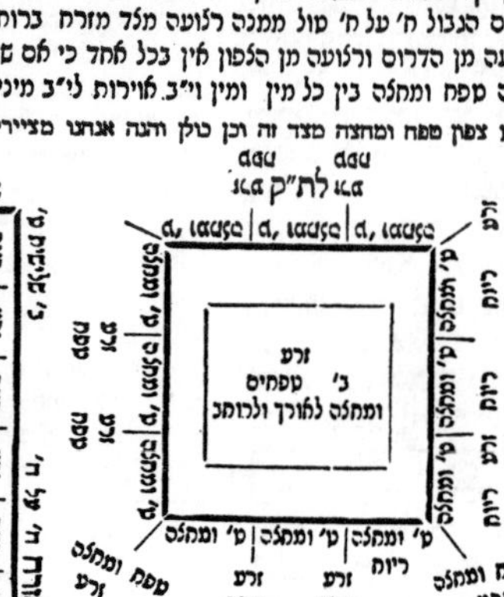

ג א מיי' שם הלכה יג וטור שו"ע שם
ד ב מיי' שם הלכה יד וטור שו"ע שם סעיף לח :
ה ג מיי' שם הל' ד' טוש"ע שם ס"ל :
ו ד מיי' פ"ג מהל' כלאים הל' יח טוש"ע י"ד סימן רל"ו סעיף כה :

הגהות הב"ח

(א) מ"א בר"מ גדר ג' ורביע והוא טפח אחד :

הגהות מהר"י לנדא

א] מ"א בר"ש גבול גבוה טפח . צ"ל רוחב : ב] מ"ב שם גמלונין גדולים ואלימי. צ"ל והקטנים אלימי וקשין :

א) פסחים דף לט ב) שבת דף פה :

לזריעת י"ב מינין כי אם י' טפחים· וכשתחלק הי' טפחים לחומשין יעלו לב' חומשין תן ד' חומשין לכל מין ומין וישתיירו ב' חומשין תחלק ב' החומשין לשתותין שתות לכל מין ומין כמלא מקום המין ד' חומשין ושתות חומש על רוחב טפח דהוא רחבו של גבול · ועוד יש למנות בדרך אחרת דכי זרעת לכל קרן טפח על טפח כמלאו ו' טפחים בין קרן לקרן לא מהן ד' טפחים ומחלה לג' אורין שביניהן לא ישארו כי אם טפח ומחלה לב' המינים הנזרעים באמצע הרוח ג' רביעי טפח לכל מין ומין וכי מצטרפת זריעת הרוחות לזריעת הקרנות כמלא י"ב מינים לי' טפחים · ובירושלמי (שם) פריך וניתני ששה טעות סופר הוא דחמש גרסי' כלומר דניתני במתני' ג' על כל גבול וגבול וה' באמצע כמו בערוגה דרישא שאין לה גבול גבוה טפח וזורעין לתוכה ה' זרעין וליהוו השתא להך דאיכא גבול י"ג [י"ז] זרעין ומשני תיפתר שהגבולין ממעטין כלו' שזרע הגבולין נכנסין לתוך הערוגה וממעטין אותה מו' על ו' טפחים וצריך לדקדק היאך ממעטין ומדוע נכנסין לתוך הערוגה דלא מסתבר כלל למימר משום דאי אפשר שלא יפול לתוך הערוגה מזרעי' שעל הגבול אלא היינו טעמא דממעט לפי שצריך להרחיק זרע הערוגה עצמה מזרע הגבולין מסביב טפח ומחצה ולא נשאר מקום פנוי לזרע אחר בערוגה כי אם ג' על ג' באמצעה לפי שצריך להרחיק טפח ומחצה מכל רוח ורוח דאמרינן בירושלמי (הל' ב) ר' יונה אמר ר' זירא ור' אסי תרויהון בשם ר' יוחנן חד אמר סומכין [לגדר ואין סומכין] לגבול · וחד אמר גבול שנתמעט פסול· ולא ידעינן מאן אמר האי ומאן אמר האי : ר' יהודה אומר ו' באמצע · בירושלמי (הל' א) מפרש טעמא דרבי יהודה דאמר ששה זרע זרעה זרעיה זרועיה · רבי חני אמר זרעיה ה' · כל הדין דאשכחן לה ו' אנא מחק ליה אשתאילת לרב הונא

באמצע: ב *כל א) מין זרעים אין זורעין בערוגה וכל מין ירקות זורעין בערוגה חרדל ואפונים השופים מין זרעים אפונים הגמלנים מין ירק ב גבול שהיה גבוה טפח ונתמעט כשר שהיה כשר מתחלתו ג התלם ואמת המים שהם עמוקים טפח זורעים לתוכן שלש זרעונין אחד מיכן ואחד מיכן ואחד באמצע: ג ד היה ג) ראש תור ירק נכנס לתוך שדה ירק אחר מותר מפני שהוא נראה כסוף שדהו היתה שדהו זרוע ירק והוא מבקש ליטע בתוכו שורה של ירק אחר רבי ישמעאל אומר עד שיהא התלם מפולש מראש השדה עד ראשו ר' עקיבא אומר

לנו ממדת הזרוע כלוס וזה צורתה*

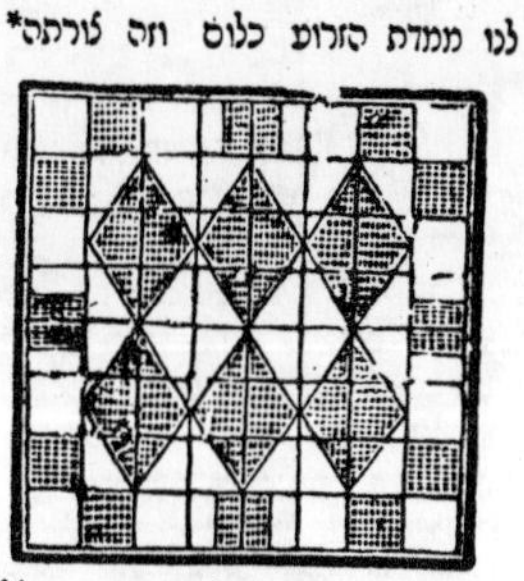

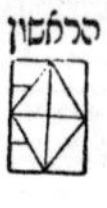

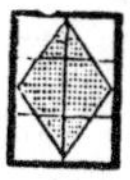

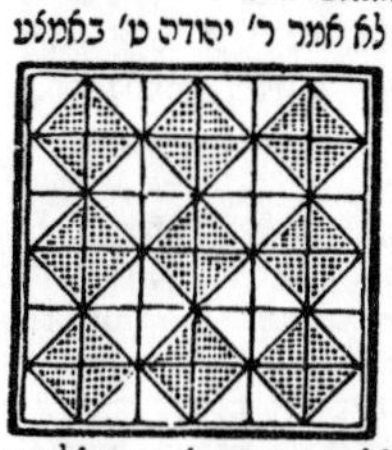

פי' מהרי"ב בן מלכי צדק

לעז ציצירי ליספידי. תניא החרדל ואפתין השופין מין זרעין אע"פ שורעו לירק

THE MIDDLE.[7]

MISHNAH 2. IT IS FORBIDDEN TO SOW HETEROGENEOUS
a SPECIES OF SEEDS[1] IN ONE BED; IT IS PERMITTED TO SOW HETEROGENEOUS SPECIES OF VEGETABLE [SEEDS][2] IN ONE BED.[3] MUSTARD AND SMALL POLISHED PEAS ARE A SPECIES OF SEED;[4] LARGE PEAS ARE A VEGETABLE SPECIES. IF A BORDER ORIGINALLY A HANDBREADTH HIGH[5] FELL IN HEIGHT, IT REMAINS VALID,[6] SINCE IT WAS VALID AT THE BEGINNING.[7]

IN A FURROW OR WATER-COURSE[8] A HANDBREADTH DEEP,[9] IT IS PERMITTED TO SOW THREE HETEROGENEOUS SPECIES OF VEGETABLE [SEEDS], ONE ON ONE SIDE, ONE ON THE OTHER SIDE, AND ONE IN THE MIDDLE.[10]

MISHNAH 3. THE HEAD OF A TRIANGLE[11] OF A VEGETABLE-FIELD OVERLAPPING INTO[11] A FIELD OF ANOTHER VEGETABLE, IS PERMITTED, SINCE IT IS APPARENT THAT IT IS THE END OF THE FORMER FIELD! IF ONE'S FIELD IS SOWN WITH A CERTAIN VEGETABLE AND HE WISHES TO PLANT THEREIN A ROW OF ANOTHER VEGETABLE,[12] R. ISHMAEL SAID: [HE MAY
b DO SO] AS LONG AS THE FURROW[1] RUNS RIGHT THROUGH FROM ONE END OF THE FIELD TO THE OTHER; R. AKIBA

(7) *Sc.* of the last bed (8 × 8 handbreadths) mentioned, (v. diagram in printed editions of the separate Mishnayoth). It is equally clear that in the first mentioned bed (6 × 6 handbreadths) also, R. Judah permitted the sowing of six species. According to Maim. R. Judah actually contested the anonymous Tanna's planning of the five species, presumably on the ground that the species on the large centre patch would predominate to such an extent as to make the whole bed look as if intended to be solely of that species and the heterogeneous species on the borders would make it appear like *kil'ayim*.

a (1) Such as grain and others which are usually sown in large quantities in fields. (2) Such as are themselves not used for human consumption, and are as a rule sown in smaller quantities in beds. (3) In the manner prescribed in the preceding Mishnah. (4) And, though used for human consumption, are not considered 'vegetable-seed', and are, consequently, not to be sown with heterogeneous varieties in the same bed. (5) The reference is to the case mentioned in the preceding Mishnah. (6) There is no need to pull up the vegetables sown on the border. (7) But before the next sowing it must be raised to the proper level. (8) When dry and fit for sowing. (9) And six handbreadths (= a cubit) wide. (10) So that there are three handbreadths between any two heterogeneous species. Rashi, followed by Bert., requires three handbreadths as the minimum in such circumstances, whereas Maim., also Rash., require only one and a half handbreadths, the radius of ground from which such a plant 'sucks'. In accordance with this it should be permitted to sow five heterogeneous vegetable seeds across a furrow etc., six handbreadths wide. (11) V. II, 7, notes. (12) According to Maim. it must be assumed that the new row is being kept at the requisite distance from the main field.

b (1) Either: (i) in which the new row is planted (Maim., Bert.) or (ii) which separates the new row from the crop already there (Rash.).

SAID: [AS LONG AS] THE LENGTH [THEREOF] IS SIX HANDBREADTHS AND THE WIDTH [THEREOF] ITS FULL ONE;[2] R. JUDAH SAID: [AS LONG AS] THE WIDTH [THEREOF] IS THE FULL WIDTH OF A FOOTSTEP.[3]

MISHNAH 4. PLANTING TWO ROWS[4] OF CUCUMBERS, TWO ROWS OF GOURDS, AND TWO ROWS OF EGYPTIAN BEANS IS PERMITTED,[5] [BUT PLANTING] ONE ROW OF CUCUMBERS, ONE ROW OF GOURDS AND ONE ROW OF EGYPTIAN BEANS IS PROHIBITED.[6] [AS FOR PLANTING] ONE ROW OF CUCUMBERS, ONE ROW OF GOURDS, ONE ROW OF EGYPTIAN BEANS AND [AGAIN] ONE ROW OF CUCUMBERS, R. ELIEZER PERMITS,[7] BUT THE SAGES FORBID.[8]

MISHNAH 5. ONE MAY PLANT A CUCUMBER AND A
a GOURD[1] IN ONE DECLIVITY[2] PROVIDED ONLY THAT ONE [SPECIES] INCLINE IN ONE DIRECTION, AND THE OTHER IN THE OPPOSITE DIRECTION,[3] OR THAT THE TIPS OF THE LEAVES OF ONE [SPECIES] INCLINE ONE WAY, AND THE OTHER THE OPPOSITE WAY,[3] SINCE ALL THE SAGES' PROHIBITIONS [IN THE MATTER OF KIL'AYIM] WERE DECREED BY THEM ON ACCOUNT OF APPEARANCES.[4]

MISHNAH 6. IF ONE'S FIELD IS SOWN WITH ONIONS,[5] AND HE WISHES TO PLANT THEREIN ROWS OF GOURDS, R. ISHMAEL SAID: HE MUST PULL UP TWO ROWS[6] [OF ONIONS], AND PLANT [IN THE CLEARED SPACE] ONE ROW [OF GOURDS],[7] LEAVE THE ONION CROP OVER A SPACE OF TWO ROWS, PULL UP TWO ROWS [OF ONIONS] AND PLANT [IN THE CLEARED
b SPACE] ONE ROW [OF GOURDS; AND SO ON].[1] R. AKIBA SAID: HE MUST PULL UP TWO ROWS [OF ONIONS], PLANT [IN THE CLEARED SPACE] TWO ROWS [OF GOURDS],[2] LEAVE THE ONION CROP OVER A SPACE OF TWO ROWS, PULL UP TWO ROWS [OF ONIONS], AND PLANT TWO ROWS [OF GOURDS; AND SO ON].[3] THE SAGES SAID: IF BETWEEN ONE ROW [OF GOURDS] AND THE NEXT THERE ARE NOT TWELVE CUBITS, ONE MAY NOT ALLOW THAT WHICH IS SOWN IN THE INTERVENING SPACE TO REMAIN.[4]

c *MISHNAH* 7. A GOURD[1] AMONG A [HETEROGENEOUS] VEGETABLE [IS TO BE SEPARATED FROM THE LATTER BY AS MUCH] AS ANY OTHER [HETEROGENEOUS] VEGETABLE.[2] [A GOURD] AMONG CORN IS TO BE GIVEN [A SEPARATING SPACE

(2) I.e., the width of a normal furrow, viz., six handbreadths. In accordance with Rash's interpretation of 'furrow' (*supra* note 1) this means that at some place between the row and the rest of the field there must be an intervening space of 6 × 6 handbreadths. Maim., however, understands the words רוחב מלואו as 'the width as its full depth' i.e., whatever the depth of the furrow (in which he plants the new row) its width must be the same. On the matter of width R. Ishmael agreed with R. Akiba, but as to length the latter held that the row itself (Maim.) or the intervening space (Rash.) need be only six handbreadths. (3) I.e., a handbreadth (v. *supra* Mishnah 1, n. 5). According to R. Judah the new row (Maim.) needs only, or the space separating the new row from the rest (Rash.) should at least, measure 6 × 1 handbreadths. (4) A normal 'row' is four cubits wide, v. *infra* 6. (5) Since two rows of each of these species present the appearance of a whole field, and as long as between the several sets of two rows there is the requisite intervening space, there is no objection to their being alongside. (6) Even if they are separated, the leaves of these species are long and intertwine one with another, and thus, present an appearance of having been sown indiscriminately with one 'handthrow'. (7) On the ground that two rows of cucumbers, though not next to one another, are yet sufficient to constitute the plot into a cucumber field, within which it is permitted, in accordance with the preceding Mishnah, to plant a row of heterogeneous vegetables. Sipponte gives as R. Eliezer's reason that these four rows are to be regarded as two separate sets of two species each, one of a row each of cucumbers and Egyptian beans and the other one of a row each of cucumbers and gourds, which, in accordance with the next Mishnah, may be planted. In T.J., R. Jannai holds that R. Eliezer's permission refers also to the case, immediately preceding, of the three rows (one of cucumbers, one of gourds, and one of Egyptian beans) in pursuance of his principle that two species combine so as to effect a permission or a leniency. According to this, in the case of the three rows, the cucumbers and gourds are (under conditions stipulated in Mishnah 5) permitted, and these two 'combine' to make the three rows together permitted; likewise in the case of the four rows. (8) Because the two rows of cucumbers, not being close to one another, do not give the appearance of a cucumber field, and the whole of the four rows look as if haphazardly sown. According to Sipponte, the Sages' prohibition is in keeping with their principle that though two species combine to effect a prohibition, they do not combine to effect a permission.

a (1) I.e., even cucumbers and gourds, although their leaves are long and liable to intertwine. (2) Without an intervening space between the two species. (3) This makes it abundantly clear that they were certainly not planted with 'one handthrow' (which is all that the Torah prohibits). (4) I.e., so as to obviate all reasonable possibility of strangers getting the impression that the Biblical prohibition had been transgressed (5) Onions are instanced merely as an example, presumably because the procedure described in this Mishnah was a common practice in onion fields (Maim.). (6) I.e., over a space of eight cubits. (7) I.e., in the middle of the cleared space of eight cubits, thus leaving two cubits unsown on either side.

b (1) Each row of gourds would thus be separated two cubits from the adjoining onions, and twelve cubits from the nearest row of gourds.

Diag. (*a*) Cubits

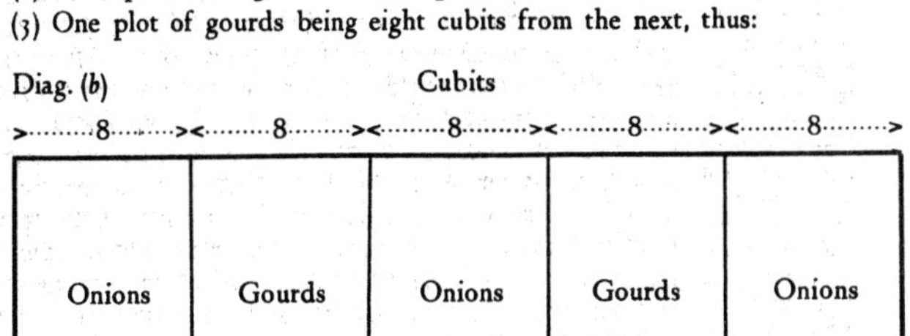

(2) One species being, of course, separated from the other by a furrow. (3) One plot of gourds being eight cubits from the next, thus:

Diag. (*b*) Cubits

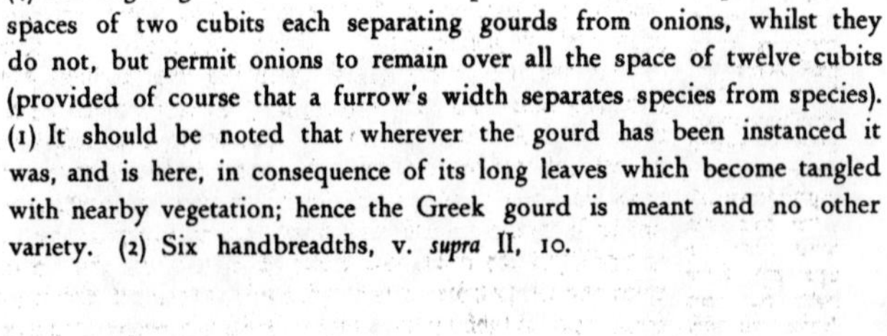

(4) The Sages agree with R. Ishmael except in so far as he requires unsown spaces of two cubits each separating gourds from onions, whilst they do not, but permit onions to remain over all the space of twelve cubits (provided of course that a furrow's width separates species from species).

c (1) It should be noted that wherever the gourd has been instanced it was, and is here, in consequence of its long leaves which become tangled with nearby vegetation; hence the Greek gourd is meant and no other variety. (2) Six handbreadths, v. *supra* II, 10.

זו כנגד זו וכאן נמי שורה מפסקת באמצע השדה מעבר לעבר: אורך ששה טפחים ורוחב מלואו · כלומר מלא התלם דהיינו ששה על ששה ולא חייש ר"ע למפולם אלא אע"פ שתלם זה מוקף ירק אחר מג' רוחות: במלא רוחב פרסה · דהיינו טפח כדאמרינן במסכת שבת בפרק אמר ר"ע (דף פה:) א"ר זירא ואיתימא ר' חנינא מאי טעמא דרבי יהודה דכתיב (דברים יא) והשקית ברגלך כגן הירק מה רגל טפח אף גבול טפח · והשתא לא פירש כאן אלא רוחב השורה הנזרעת ולשורה קרי לה תלם ובשיעור הרחקה לא איירי הכא כמה מרחיק האי זרע מן השדה ולעיל בפרק ב' (משנה י) תנינן לה ירק בירק ו' טפחים ואע"ג

[א]אורך ששה טפחים ורוחב מלואו רבי יהודה אומר (א) רוחב כמלא רוחב הפרסה: ד [ב]הנוטע שתי שורות של קשואין שתי שורות של דלועים שתי שורות של פול המצרי מותר שורה של קשואים שורה של דלועים שורה של פול המצרי אסור שורה של קשואים שורה של דלועים שורה של פול המצרי ושורה של קשואין ר"א מתיר וחכמים אוסרין: ה [ג]נוטע אדם קישות ודלעת לתוך גומא א' ובלבד שתהא זו נוטה לצד זו וזו נוטה לצד זו (ונוטה שער של זו לכאן ושער של זו לכאן שכל מה שאסרו חכמים לא גזרו אלא מפני מראית העין): ו היתה שדהו זרועה בצלים ומבקש ליטע בתוכה שורות של דלועים רבי ישמעאל אומר עוקר שתי שורות ונוטע שורה אחת ומניח קמת בצלים במקום שתי שורות ועוקר שתי שורות ונוטע שורה אחת ר"ע אומר עוקר ב' שורות ונוטע ב' שורות ומניח קמת בצלים במקום ב' שורות ועוקר ב' שורות ונוטע ב' שורות וחכ"א [ד]אם אין בין שורה לחברתה י"ב אמה לא יקיים את הזרע של בינתיים: ז [ה]דלעת בירק כירק [ו]ובתבואה

דמרחיק כדינו בעינן שיעור לאורך ורוחב של ירק אחר למר כדאית ליה ולמר כדאית ליה משום דפחות מכאן לא חשיב מילתא באנפיה נפשה ובטיל אגב שדה והוי כלאים. ותימה מילתא דר' יהודה מייתי לה לענין שיעור הרחקה בפרק אמר ר"ע ומה ענין זה אצל זה הא לא איירי כלל אלא ברוחב שורות הירק · ועוד קשה היכי מצי למימר דפחות משיעור זה לא מהניא הרחקה הא תניא בתוספתא (פ"ב) ולעיל הבאתיה בפ"ב גבי ירק בירק אפילו אין שם אלא קלח אחד נותנין לו עבודה ששה טפחים · לפיכך צריך לפרש דכולה מתני' בשיעור הרחקה דלר' ישמעאל תלם חשיב הפסק ולר' עקיבא ו' טפחים ור' יהודה פרסה ותלם לאו היינו שורה דשורה היא שורת זרע האחד ותלם הוא המפסיק ביניהן · ולא קאמר ר"ע אורך ששה ורוחב מלואו למימרא דתיסגי בהכי לשורה גדולה של ירק אחר אלא אשמעינן דאפילו בקלח אחד של ירק אחר בעינן הפסק ששה על ששה ולשולם לשורה גדולה בעינן [ששה] על פני כל השורה סביב · וכן נראה דבשיעור הפסק איירי מתני' דכוליה פרקין וכמה ברייתות כעדו בתוספתא בשיעור הרחקה: ירושלמי (הל' ג) מה אמר ר' ישמעאל ברוחב מה אין ר"ע שחושב בג' רוחות אית ליה ברוחב מלואו רבי ישמעאל שחושב בב' רוחות לא כל שכן · פירוש אין כמו [אם] · לא כל שכן דבעי רוחב מלואו דרבי ישמעאל מחמיר טפי מר"ע: ד הנוטע שתי שורות · בשדה אחת נטע ב' שורות מכל א' וא' וכיון דכן נטע אין זה ערבוב דשתי שורות חשיבן והוי שדה באנפיה נפשה והויא היכרא דכל מין ומין מילתא באנפיה נפשיה הוא ואפי' כל שדהו מותר לעשות כן כדתני בתוספתא (פ"ב) אבל שורה אחת מכל אחד הוי ערבוב ובטל את השורה: שורה של קשואין שורה של דלועין שורה של פול המצרי אסור · דלא חשיבא כל חדא שדה לנפשיה והשתים מצטרפין לאסור השלישית והיינו דאמר בפרק אמר ר"ע (דף פה:) בא ערבוב וביטל את השורה: שורה של קשואין שורה של דלועין שורה של פול המצרי ושורה של קשואין ר"א מתיר · דשני מינים מצטרפין להציל ונעשו קשואין ודלועין ב' שורות ופול המצרי וקשואין ב' שורות ולא הוו כמעורבבין אלא כנטועים שתים שתים: וחכמים אוסרין · דאין שני מינין מצטרפין להציל ומעורבבין הן · ובירושלמי (הל' ד) פליגי רב ורבי ינאי דרבי ינאי מוקי רישא כרבנן ורב מוקי לה דברי הכל [וז"ל] ירושלמי רבי ינאי אמר מחלוקת שני מינים מצטרפין להציל ואין שני מינים מצטרפין לאסור · רב אמר דברי הכל הוא כשם ששני מינים מצטרפין להציל כך מצטרפין לאסור. מתני' מסייע ליה לרבי ינאי דתני ר' אליעזר מתיר מתניתין פליגא על רב שורה של קשואין שורה של דלועין שורה של פול המצרי ושורה של קשואין עד שלא נטע הרביעי לא כבר נאסרו · תפתר שנטע ארבעתן כאחת · פירוש במחלוקת אג' שורות קאי דאתיא כרבנן דמחמרי דאין שני מינין מצטרפין להקל ולהציל אבל מצטרפין להחמיר ולאסור אבל לרבי אליעזר דמיקל להקל מצטרפין ולא לאסור · ורב סבר דלרבי אליעזר נמי מצטרפין לאסור · מתני' מסייעא לרבי ינאי דמשמע דרבי אליעזר מתיר אכולה מתני' קאי ופליגא דרב דאם בג' שורות אסר ר' אליעזר לא אתי רביעית ושריא להו כיון דכבר נאסרו · ובפרק אמר ר"ע פי' לישנא דמתני' בלשון אחר וכמו שפירשתי עיקר · ולפי שיטה זו שפירשתי כאן צריך ליישב שמעתא דהתם: ה זו נוטה לצד זו · שכל מה שאסרו חכמים לא אסרו אלא מפני מראית העין: ירושלמי (שם) תני מותר אדם לעשות בתוך שדהו גומא קטנה עמוקה טפח ולזרוע בתוכה ד' זרעונין והופכן בד' רוחותיה · ר' בא בר כהן בשם ריש לקיש בנוטין לחורבה שנו ר' מנא בעי בנוטין לחורבה ניתני שמונה ב' מכאן וב' מכאן וב' מכאן וב' מכאן · פירוש ארבע לקרנות וארבע לארבע רוחותיה: ו עוקר שתי שורות · מן הבצלים ומניחן בורות ונוטע שורה אחת של דלועין לצד חוץ שהשני שורות מפסיקות בין דלועין לקמת הבצלים: ומניח קמת בצלים · שיהיו נוטין במקום ב' שורות שעקר: ועוקר עוד מצד אחר שתי שורות של בצלים וחוזר ונוטע שורה אחת של דלועים: ונוטע ב' שורות · קסבר ר' עקיבא דאין נותנין עבודה לשורה יחידי' כדמשמע בירושלמי ואם אינו נוטע אלא שורה אחת לא היה צריך לעקור אלא שורה אחת אלא כדי עבודת בצלים אבל לשני שורות של דלועים נותנין לזה עבודתו ולזה עבודתו וצריך לעקור ב' שורות ביניהן · ולא דמי למתני' דלעיל שיכול ליטע שני שורות של קשואין וב' שורות של דלועין ושני שורות של פול המצרי דהאי שדה מב' שורות ועוד דכיון שבא לעקור חמיר טפי כדאשכחן בירושלמי בפרק ד' גבי כרם דבית שמאי מחמרי בחורבנן יותר ממטעתן: אם אין בין שורה לחברתה · כלומר בין שורה של דלועים שמצד אחד ושורה דלועים שמצד אחר לא יקיים הבצלים שבינתים והשתא לא ידעי לרבנן אי בעי ו' אמות הפסק מכאן וו' אמות הפסק מכאן או ח' אמות הפסק מכאן וד' אמות הפסק מכאן ומתוך הירושלמי ניכר הדבר · ירושלמי (הל' ה) כהנא אמר דברי ר' ישמעאל פעמים ט"ז פעמים י"ב פעמים ח' · בשעה שנותן כל עבודתה בפנים ט"ז מקצתה בפנים ומקצתה בחוץ י"ב כולה בחוץ שמונה · שמואל אמר לעולם י"ב ותני כך קולב על דברי שניהן · ר' ישמעאל אומר י"ב רבנין אמרי י"ב מה ביניהן סמיכה על דעתיה דר' ישמעאל אסור רבנן אמרי מותר · פי' פעמים ט"ז שצריך לעקור ט"ז אמות מן הבצלים כמו שמפרש בשעה שנותן כל עבודתה בפנים דהיינו כשהופך שיעור של דלועים כלפי הבצלים דאז צריך לעקור ב' שורות מכאן אחת לעבודת הדלועים ואחת לעבודת הבצלים וכן מצד אחר דהיינו ארבע שורות עקורות ורוחב השורה ד' אמות דהיינו ט"ז אמות לד' שורות פעמים י"ב כמו שמפרש כשנותן מקצת העבודה של דלועים בפנים שנוטה דלועין שמצד אחד לצד פנים ואותן שמצד אחר נוטה לצד חוץ דאותה שנוטה לצד פנים צריך שתי שורות הפסק בינן לבצלים ואותה שנוטה לצד חוץ לא בעי אלא שורה אחת הפסק · פעמים שמונה כמו שמפרש כולה בחוץ שנוטה דלועים שמכאן ומכאן לצד חוץ דלא בעי הפסק אלא שורה אחת מכאן ושורה אחת מכאן ושמואל אמר לעולם שתים עשרה ואפי' נוטה כל הדלועין לצד חוץ ותנינן כלומר תניא כ"ה שדבר קבוע על דברי שניהם דרבי ישמעאל לעולם י"ב אפי' נוטה כל הדלועין לחוץ אבל אם נוטה כולה בפנים בהא ודאי לא קאמר כדמוכח' מתניתין וקא בעי לשמואל מאי איכא בין ר' ישמעאל לרבנן ומסיק דאיכא בינייהו סמיכה דלרבי ישמעאל אסור וקרי סמיכה כשאין אלא שורה אחת מפסקת שאותה שורה לעבודת הבצלים וקאסר ר' ישמעאל לסמוך דבעי שיהא שורה ומחצה מכאן ושורה אחת ומחצה מכאן דהיינו ו' אמות מכאן וו' אמות מכאן ורבנן שרו לסמוך דלא חיישינן אלא שיהא בין דלועין לדלועין י"ב אמה אפילו ב' שורות מכאן ושורה אחת מכאן דהיינו ח' אמות מכאן וד' אמות מכאן דנמצאת השתא שורה אחת של דלועין סמוכה דאותה שורה המפסקת היא לעבודת הבצלים והבצלים נוטין בה ונמצאו דלועים סמוכין לבצלים: ז דלעת בירק

ולא יצטרך למשוך החפירה ההיא כפי אורך הזריעה. ואמר שצריך להיות רוחב החפירה ההיא כפי עומקה והוא מה שאמר מלואו ר"ל מלא התלם ואפילו יהיה עומקו אמה: ורבי יהודה אומר טפח בלבד צריך להיות רוחב החפירה והוא שאמר רוחב הפרסה ואמר רוחב הפרסה ולא אמר רוחב טפח מפני שהיא נגלה ראייתו בתוך דבריו שהוא מביא ראיה על זה השיעור מדברי הכתוב (דברים יא) והשקית ברגלך כגן הירק ויצטרך להיות בין ירק וירק מקום להנחת הרגל והוא רוחב פרסה · ומה שלא הצריכוהו בכאן להרחיק ששה טפחים כמו שהקדמנו בפרק שקודם זה באמרו ירק בירק ששה טפחים מפני שהמרחק ההוא הוא בין שדה ירק לשדה ירק אחר והלכה זו לא דבר אלא בשדה ירק כשירצה לזרוע בה שורה אחת בלבד מן ירק אחר כמו שאמר ובקש ליטע בתוכה שורה של ירק אחר ולפיכך יספיק לו התלם כמו שביארנו והלכה כר"ע: ד כשיטע שתי שורות מכל מין ונראית כאילו היא שדה של קשואין ושדה של דלועים ושדה של פול המצרי מותר ובלבד שיהא התלם בין כל שתי שורות ממין שני אבל אם היתה השורה שורה אחת מכל מין מאלו השלשה מינין הוא אסור מפני שהכל נראה כמעורב וכאילו זרע במפולת יד ולא יועיל התלם שבין שורה לשורה באלו השלשה מינין לבד מפני שהעלים שלהם מתפשטים מאד ונכנסין קצתם בקצתם ויתערבו שתי השורות וכן אמר בגמרא (שבת פה:) שאני הכא דאיכא סרכי. ואם נטע שורה של קשואים ושורה של דלועים ושורה של פול המצרי ושורה רביעית של קשואים רבי אליעזר אומר אחר שיש שם ב' שורות של קשואין נחשבים כאילו הם מחוברות כאחד והשיה מותרת ותהיה של דלועין ושל פול המצרי כאילו נזרעה בשדה קשואין ודינה שיפסיק לה התלם כמו שהקדמנו בהלכה הקודמת לזאת. וחכמים גוזרין כאן מאחר שאינן מחוברות שתי השורות של קשואין והלכה כחכמים: ה גומא היא חפירה וכבר בארנו שבכלאים יש להזהר בהן למראית עין ומפני זה כשיהיה זה נוטה לצד זה והאחר לצד אחר נראה מובדל. ויחד קישות ודלעת מפני שעליהם מתפשטים ומסתבכים כמו שבארנו ולא יספיק להם התלם ואע"פ שהם כמו שזכרנו מותר לו לאסוף אותם במקום אחד ובלבד שיפריד העלין כמו שבארנו: ו יש לך להבין ששורה של דלועין שורה ארבע אמות ומפני זה א"ר ישמעאל שיעקור שיעור שתי שורות של(א) דלועין שהם שמונה אמות ויטע מהם שורה אחת שהיא רוחב ארבע אמות ומניח מקמת בצלים שיעור שתי שורות שהם ח' אמות ויעקור כמו כן שתי שורות שהן רוחב ח' אמות ויזרע מהם שורה אחת של דלועין שהיא ארבע אמות ונמצא המרחק בין שתי שורות של דלועין לר' ישמעאל שתים עשרה אמות מפני ששתי השורות שעקר רחבם ח' אמות כמו שאמר ויזרע שורה אחת באמצע רחבה ד' אמות ונמצא בין שורה של דלועים ובין קמת בצלים שתי אמות וקמת הבצלים בעצמה שמונה אמות ומרחק השורה השנית מקמת הבצלים שתי אמות א"כ יהיה המרחק בין שתי שורות של דלועים שתים עשרה אמה וזה צורתו

ב"א ד"א ב"א ח' אמות ב"א ד"א ב"א

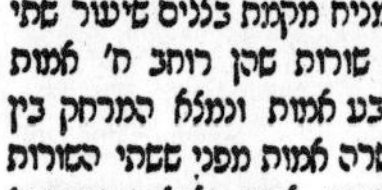

ועל סדר המרחק הזה יוסף לעשות כפי מה שירצה ועל דעת רבי עקיבא שהוא אומר נוטע שתי שורות ומניח קמת הבצלים שתי שורות ויהיה המרחק בין ב' שורות של דלועין רוחב קמת הבצלים בלבד שרחבה שמונה אמות והוא רוחב שתי שורות המחלוקת שבין חכמים ור' ישמעאל שרבי ישמעאל מצריך להיות בין שתי שורות של דלועין שתים עשרה אמה ולהיות בין כל שורה מהן ובין קמת הבצלים שתים אמות כמו שציירנו. וחכמים אומרים שלא נצטרך להרחיק בין שורה של דלועין ובין קמת הבצלים אבל יש לו להזהר שיהיה בין שתי שורות של דלועין שתים עשרה אמה כדי שלא התחבר שורה בשורה אבל תהיה כל אחת מהם שורה אחת בתוך שורה של בצלים וכדי שלא תראה כל השדה מעורבת מבצלים ודלועין וזה ענין מה שאמרו בגמרא הא ר' ישמעאל אומר שתים עשרה רבנן אמרי שתים עשרה מאי בינייהו · סמיכה · על דעתיה דר' ישמעאל אסור · ולרבנן מותר · וזה שאמר לדעת חכמים מותר לסמוך ובלבד שיהא התלם על כל פנים בין שורה של דלועין ובין קמת בצלים כמו שנתבאר בזה הפרק שחכמים הנהיגו בשורה של דלועין בתוך שדה של בצלים מנהג שאר ירקות שאינם צריכות אלא לתלם כמו שנתבאר בהלכה שלישית מפרק זה · ורבי ישמעאל מצריך מרחק שתי אמות לפי שעלי הדלועין מתפשטין כמו שבארנו · ויחד הבצלים מפני שאפשר שכן היה המנהג אצלם. והלכה כחכמים: ז דלעת בירק כירק · רוצה לומר שירחיק הירק כשיעור עבודת ירק וכבר הקדמנו שעבודת ירק ששה טפחים. ואם ירצה לטעת (שדה שורה של) דלעת [אחת בלבד] לצד שדה של תבואה ירחיק כשיעור עבודת התבואה והיא בית רובע. ואם ירצה לנטוע בשדה תבואה שורה אחת בלבד של דלועין ירחיק מן התבואה ששה

מסורת הש"ס

א) שבת דף פה:

פי' מהר"י בן מלכי צדק

הירק כלומר פרסת הרגל וכמה היא שיעור פרסה טפח: ד הנוטע שתי שורות של קשואין וב' שורות וכו' פי' בשדה אחת נוטע ב' שורות וכו': מותר שאינן מעורבין. אבל ליטע בשדה ג' שורות אחת של קשואין וכו' אסור וכו' פי' דבא עירבוב וביטל את השדה: שורה של קשואין שורה של דלועין שורה של פול המצרי שורה של קשואין ר' אליעזר מתיר. ששני מינין מצטרפין להציל ונעשה קשואין ודלועין ב' שורות ופול מצרי וקשואין ב' שורות ולא היו כמעורבבין אלא כנטועין בב': וחכמים אוסרין. דאין ב' מינין מצטרפין להציל אלא אסורין הן ורישא דתנינן שורה של קשואין שורה של דלועין שורה של פול מצרי אסור ר' ינאי אמר רבנן היא אבל ר' אליעזר מתיר דקסבר שני מינין מצטרפין להציל כדאמרינן ואין שני מינין מצטרפין לאסור פי' להיות כמעורבבין אלא כל שורה ושורה עומדת בפני עצמה ואמרינן מתניתין מסייעא לר' ינאי שורה וכו' ר' אליעזר מתיר אי אמרת בשלמא סבר ר"א אין ב' מינין מצטרפין לאסור כשהן ג' היינו דקתני מותר הא אי אמרת כשהן ג' אסור רביעית מאי הניא לן ולא כבר נאסרו אלא ש"מ אף כשהן שלשה שורות מתיר. ורב א' רישא דברי הכל היא סבר ר' אליעזר כשם שב' מינין מצטרפין להציל כך כשהן ג' שורות ותו לא מצטרפין להיות מעורבבין ואסירן. אי הכי מאי טעמא דר' אליעזר דמתיר והלא עד שלא נטע שורה הרביעית נאסרו אמר לך רב התם היינו טעמא דמתיר שנטע ארבעתן כאחת: ה נוטע אדם קישות ודלעת לתוך גומא אחת ובלבד שתהא זו נוטה לצד זו וזו נוטה לצד זו פי' שכל האיסורין לא אסרו חכמים אלא מפני מראית העין. תניא מותר אדם לעשות בתוך שדהו גומא קטנה עמוקה טפח ולזרוע בתוכה ד' זרעונין ולהפכה לד' רוחותיה ואפי' נוטא בין הערוגות דכמו דבערוגה בין הערוגות זרעין ד' זרעונין הכי נמי הכא ר' מנא בעי אם בנוטין לחורבה ניתני ח' משום קרנות ב' מיכן וב' מיכן ב' מיכן וב' מיכן: ו היתה שדהו וכו' עוקר ב' שורות. פירוש מן הבצלין ומקום שני שורות מניח בור ונוטע שורה של דלועין ומניח קמת בצלין שיהו נוטין במקום ב' שורות שעקר

עין משפט נר מצוה

ז א מיי' שם הלכה י' וטוש"ע שם סעיף י"ט:

ח ב מיי' פ"ד שם הל' א טוש"ע שם סעיף כו:

ט ג מיי' שם הלכה ה וטור שו"ע שם סעיף לא:

י ד מיי' פ"ד מהל' כלאים הלכה ב טור שו"ע יו"ד סימן רצז סעיף ט:

יא ה מיי' פ"ג מהל' כלאים הלכה י וטור שו"ע שם סעיף יז:

יב ו מיי' שם הלכה יא ופ"ד שם הלכה ג טוש"ע שם סעיף יח וסעיף כח:

הגהות הב"ח

(א) מ"ר בר"מ יש לך וכו' שיעקור שיעור שתי שורות של בצלים שהם:

פי' מהר"י בן מלכי צדק

שעקר ועוקר עוד מצד האחד מן הבצלין ב' שורות ונוטע שורה של דלועין ר' עקיבא וכו' אמר רב כהנא לדברי ר' ישמעאל פעמי' מקום העקור ממנו הבצלי' לעבוד' ט"ז פעמים י"ב פעמים ח' כיצד בשעה שתחשוב כל העקור לפנים ט"ז בשעה שתחשוב מח' אמות אחרים מקצת העקור לשבפנים ומקצת לשבחוץ ולא הכל י"ב. בשעה שתחשב שבפנים בלבד. פי' בין שורות של דלועין לשורות בצלין ח' ר' שמואל אומר לעולם לדברי ר' ישמעאל י"ב כיצד כי ב' שורות עקר קודם הן ח' אמות ונוטע הדלועין ואלמלא היה רצונו עוד ליטע שורה מרוח האחד לא היה עוקר אלא שורה דהיינו ד' אמות הרי י"ב אלא מאי טעמא עוקר ב' שורות משום שרצונו ליטע עוד שורה של דלועין השתא מב' שורות שעוקר שורה אחת חשב בשביל פנימית ושורה אחת בשביל החיצונה. תניא נמי הכי כיצד על דברי ר' ישמעאל אמר י"ב ר' עקיבא אומר ח' וחכ"א אם אין בין שורה לחברתה בין שורת בצלין לשורת בצלין י"ב לכאורה צריך לעקור ב' שורות דהיינו ח' אמות וליטע ולעקור עוד שורה הרי יבוא בין בצלין לבצלין י"ב אמות. גרסינן רבנן היינו ר' ישמעאל ותירצו סמוכה בינייהו על דעתיה דר' ישמעאל אסור אפילו לסמוך י"ב על דעתיה דרבנן מותר מדקתני לא יקיים זרע שבינתיים אם י"ב יקיים: דלעת בירק כירק וכו' פי' היתה שדהו זרועה ירק ובקש ליטע בה דלעת עושה שורה אורך ורוחב מלואו לדברי ר' עקיבא דהיינו כירק בירק. שכן שנינו לעיל היתה שדהו זרועה ירק וכו': ובתבואה פי' אם היתה שדהו זרועה תבואה ובקש ליטע בה דלעת עושה שורה אורך

כירק · עבודת ירק דהיינו ששה טפחים אבל אם בא ליטע דלעת בתבואה צריך להרחיק לו בית רובע דהיינו י' אמות
לעיל בפ"ב (מ"א): נותנין לה עבודתה ששה טפחים · בתוספתא (פ"ב) קתני ושורה של דלועין בתבואה אורך י' אמות
במתניתין רוחב תנן אורך לא תנן ומאי דשייר במתניתין פירש בברייתא וקילא שורה מדלעת יחידית דדלעת יחידית
שיעור אחר לשורה של דלועין בין שני שורות של ירק דבעינן י"ב אמה כדתנן בתוספתא (שם) ועוד מוכח בתוספתא

נותנין לה בית רובע [א]היתה שדהו זרועה תבואה ובקש ליטע לתוכה שורה של דלועין נותנין לה לעבודתה ששה טפחים ואם הגדילה יעקר מלפניה ר' יוסי אומר נותנין לה עבודתה ארבע אמות אמרו לו התחמיר זו מן הגפן אמר להן מצינו שזו חמורה מן הגפן [ב]שלגפן [א] יחידית נותנין לה עבודתה ששה טפחים ולדלעת יחידית נותנין לה בית רובע ר"מ אומר משום ר' ישמעאל כל שלשה דלועין לבית סאה לא יביא זרע לתוך בית סאה רבי יוסי בן החוטף אפרתי אמר משום ר' ישמעאל כל שלשה דלועין לבית כור לא יביא זרע לתוך בית כור:

פרק רביעי

א קרחת [ג] הכרם בש"א כ"ד אמות ובה"א י"ו אמה מחול הכרם בש"א שש עשרה אמה וב"ה אומרים שתים עשרה אמה ואיזו היא קרחת הכרם [ג]כרם שחרב מאמצעו אם אין שם שש עשרה אמה לא יביא זרע לשם היו שם שש עשרה אמה נותנין *לה עבודתה וזורע את המותר: ב איזו [ג] היא מחול הכרם [ד]בין כרם לגדר אם אין שם י"ב אמה לא יביא זרע לשם היה שם י"ב אמה נותנין לו עבודתו וזורע את המותר: ג רבי יהודה אומר אין זה (א) אלא גדר הכרם ואיזה הוא מחול הכרם בין שני הכרמים [ה]ואיזה (ג) הוא גדר שהוא גבוה עשרה טפחים וחריץ שהוא עמוק עשרה ורחב ארבעה: ד [ו]מחיצת הקנים אם אין בין קנה לחברו ג' טפחים כדי שיכנס הגדי הרי זו כמחיצה יוגדר שנפרץ עד עשרה אמות הרי הוא כפתח יתר מיכן כנגד הפרצה אסור נפרצו בו פרצות הרבה אם העומד מרובה על הפרוץ מותר ואם הפרוץ מרובה על העומד כנגד הפרצה אסור: ה הנוטע (ד) שורה של חמש גפנים ב"ש אומרים כרם וב"ה אומרים אינו כרם [ח]עד שיהו שם

כירק: התחמיר זו מן הגפן · דתנן לקמן בפ"ד (משנה ה) הנוטע שורה של ה' גפנים בית הלל אומרים אינו כרם כלומר ליתן לה עבודת כרם אפי' ד' אמות אלא ו' טפחים והכא נמי בשורה של דלועים אין להחמיר: שזו חמורה מן הגפן · כגון ביחידית כדמסיק: ירושלמי (הל' ו') מה בכל הדלועין משערים או לא כל מקום שעשית קישות ופול המצרי כדלעת יונית את עושה דלעת המצרית כדלעת יונית כאן שלא עשית קישות ופול המצרי כדלעת יונית אין את עושה דלעת מצרית כדלעת יונית · פירוש מבעיא ליה באיזו דלעת היא מתניתי' ופשטה דמתניתין בדלעת יונית מיהא דהני' רבי מונא לעיל בסוף פרק ב' גבי תבואה נוטה דאסרינן לסכך דלעת יונית על גבי התבואה שהיה רבי שונה קישות ופול המצרי ואף דלעת מצרית בכלל: ירושלמי (שם) אמר רבי יוסי בר' בון בוא וראה מה בין תחלת ר' ישמעאל לסופו שתחלתו בבית סאה וסופו בבית כור · פירוש דמה ששנה לר' מאיר בתחלת ימיו ולרבי יוסי בן החוטף בסוף ימיו · תניא בתוספתא *שדה של דלועים בירק אורך שש טפחים ורוחב מלואו אחד שורה של דלועין ואחד שורה של ירק אחר בתבואה אורך י' אמות ומחלה על רוחב ו' טפחים ושורה של ירק בירק אורך ו' טפחים ורוחב מלואו ושל תבואה בירק אחר מראש *השורה עד ראשו על רוחב ג' *טפחים של פתיח שורה של דלועים בירק בין שורה לחברתה י"ב אמות וכן *תבואה:

א קרחת הכרם בית שמאי אומרים כ"ד אמות· אם קרחתה כ"ד אמות מותר לזרוע שם ואם פחות מיכן אסור: שחרב באמצעיתו ויש גפנים כל סביבות הקרחת ס"ז אמות על ס"ז אמות וכן אם הלכה הקרחת על פני רוחב הכרם שאין גפנים אלא משתי לדי הקרחת: אם אין שם ע"ז אמה לא יביא שם זרע· אפי' באמה אמצעית דד' אמות שבלד הכרם מזה וד' אמות שבלד זה אלל הכרם הוי עבודת הכרם דעבודת הכרם ד' אמות כדתנן לקמן

OF] A BETH-ROBA'.[3] IF ONE'S FIELD IS SOWN WITH CORN, AND HE WISHES TO PLANT WITHIN IT A ROW OF GOURDS, THE LATTER IS TO BE PROVIDED WITH A SERVICE-BORDER[4] OF SIX HANDBREADTHS,[5] AND IF IT OVERGROWS [INTO THE BORDER] HE MUST PULL UP THAT WHICH IS WITHIN IT.[6] R. JOSE SAID: IT IS TO BE PROVIDED WITH A SERVICE-BORDER OF FOUR CUBITS. SAID THEY TO HIM: 'DO YOU RULE MORE STRINGENTLY WITH REGARD TO THIS THAN WITH REGARD TO A VINE'?[7]— SAID HE TO THEM: 'INDEED WE FIND THAT THIS IS TREATED MORE STRINGENTLY THAN A VINE, INASMUCH AS FOR A SINGLE VINE A SERVICE-BORDER IS PRESCRIBED OF SIX HANDBREADTHS,[8] BUT FOR A SINGLE GOURD ONE OF A BETH-ROBA'.[9] R. MEIR SAID IN THE NAME OF R. ISHMAEL: IF THERE ARE AS MANY AS THREE GOURDS IN A BETH-SE'AH, ONE MAY
a NOT BRING [HETEROGENEOUS] SEED INTO THE BETH-SE'AH.[1] R. JOSE B. HA-ḤOṬEF THE EPHRATHITE[2] SAID IN THE NAME OF R. ISHMAEL: IF THERE ARE AS MANY AS THREE GOURDS IN A BETH-KOR, ONE MAY NOT BRING [HETEROGENEOUS] SEED INTO THE BETH-KOR.[3]

CHAPTER IV

b *MISHNAH* 1. A ḲARAḤATH[1] [I.E., A BARE PATCH] WITHIN A VINEYARD, SHOULD MEASURE, BETH SHAMMAI SAY, TWENTY-FOUR CUBITS;[2] BUT BETH HILLEL SAY, SIXTEEN CUBITS.[3] A MEḤOL [I.E., AN UNSOWN BELT OF GROUND ROUND THE OUTER EDGES] OF A VINEYARD BETH SHAMMAI SAY, SHOULD MEASURE SIXTEEN CUBITS, BUT BETH HILLEL SAY, TWELVE CUBITS. NOW WHAT CONSTITUTES A ḲARAḤATH OF A VINEYARD? A PLOT WITHIN A VINEYARD WHICH HAS BEEN DENUDED[4] [OF VINES]. IF IT IS LESS THAN SIXTEEN CUBITS, THEN[5] ONE MUST NOT INTRODUCE SEED INTO IT;[6] IF IT IS SIXTEEN CUBITS, IT[7] IS GIVEN ITS SERVICE-BORDER, AND ONE MAY SOW THE REST.

MISHNAH 2. WHAT IS A MEḤOL OF A VINEYARD? [THE SPACE] BETWEEN VINEYARD [PROPER] AND FENCE. IF IT DOES NOT MEASURE TWELVE CUBITS,[8] IT IS FORBIDDEN TO INTRODUCE SEED INTO IT;[9] IF IT DOES MEASURE TWELVE CUBITS,
c IT[1] IS GIVEN ITS SERVICE-BORDER, AND ONE MAY SOW THE REST.

MISHNAH 3. R. JUDAH SAID: THE ABOVE IS BUT A VINEYARD FENCE [GADER].[2] WHAT THEN IS A MEḤOL OF A VINEYARD? [AN INTERVENING SPACE] BETWEEN TWO VINEYARDS.[3] WHAT NOW IS A [STATUTORY] VINEYARD FENCE?— ONE TEN HANDBREADTHS HIGH.[4] AND [WHAT IS] A [STATUTORY] TRENCH?— ONE TEN HANDBREADTHS DEEP AND FOUR WIDE.[4]

MISHNAH 4. [IF A VINEYARD HAS] A PARTITION OF REEDS, THEN IF BETWEEN ONE REED AND ANOTHER THERE BE LESS THAN THREE HANDBREADTHS, [THE SPACE] THROUGH WHICH A KID CAN ENTER, IT COUNTS AS A [LEGALLY EFFECTIVE] PARTITION.[5] IF A [STONE] FENCE HAS BEEN BROKEN THROUGH UP TO [THE LENGTH OF] TEN CUBITS, IT [THE BREACH] IS [REGARDED] AS A DOORWAY;[6] [IF THE BREACH IS] MORE THAN THAT, [SOWING CLOSE TO THE LINE OF THE FENCE] IMMEDIATELY OPPOSITE THE BREACH IS PROHIBITED. IN THE EVENT OF MANY BREACHES HAVING BEEN MADE THEREIN, THEN IF THAT WHICH REMAINS STANDING[7] EXCEEDS THAT WHICH IS BROKEN THROUGH,[7] IT IS PERMITTED [TO SOW CLOSE TO THE LINE OF THE FENCE OPPOSITE THE BREACHES]; BUT IF THAT WHICH IS BROKEN THROUGH EXCEEDS THAT WHICH REMAINS STANDING, IT IS FORBIDDEN [TO SOW CLOSE TO THE LINE
d OF THE FENCE] OPPOSITE THE BREACH [OR BREACHES].[1]

MISHNAH 5. WHEN A MAN HAS SOWN A LINE OF [AT LEAST] FIVE VINES, BETH SHAMMAI SAID: THESE CONSTITUTE A VINEYARD;[2] BUT BETH HILLEL SAID: THEY [VINES][3] DO NOT CONSTITUTE A VINEYARD[4] UNLESS THEY BE IN TWO ROWS.[5]

(3) V. ibid. (4) עבודה, 'service', used here as an agricultural technical term for a border along which one has access to a plantation for watering and other purposes. (5) A single gourd requires a large separating space, viz., a *beth-roba'* (approx. 10.15 cubits square), because the single gourd in the midst of a heterogeneous species would otherwise look as if haphazardly sown and constituting *kil'ayim;* a whole row of gourds, however, needs a separating space only like that for any other heterogeneous vegetable viz., of six handbreadths (= one cubit) square, since the row by itself already presents something distinctive, and makes it clear to all and sundry that it was sown separately. (6) If the gourd leaves have spread into the service-border separating the gourds from the corn, these leaves must be pulled up and the border kept clear. (7) The prohibition of *kil'ayim* in connection with vines, extending as it does to consumption and other uses, is stricter than *kil'ayim* of corn, pulse, and vegetables, applying as it does only to sowing and to deliberately suffering them to remain in one's field; here R. Jose reverses the order of stringency. (8) Cf. *infra* IV, 5. (9) As *supra* in this Mishnah.

a (1) I.e., heterogeneous species are not allowed within a third of a *beth-se'ah* of a gourd. So Maim. and Bert., but v. L. for another interpretation. (2) Mentioned here only. V. Bacher, *Tradition*, p. 91. (3) I.e., heterogeneous species are not allowed within a third of a *beth-kor* of a gourd., v. note 1.

b (1) Cf. *supra* II, 9. (2) Allowing for vineyard service-borders of four cubits each (v. *infra* VI, 1) on either side, and sixteen cubits in the middle for sowing. It should be borne in mind that Beth Shammai hold that 8 × 8 cubits is the smallest area that can be regarded as a 'field'. If therefore in our case, less than eight cubits remain, that ground is reckoned as forming a part of the vineyard, and it is forbidden to plant seeds there. As our *karaḥath* is flanked by vines on (at least) two sides there must be the minimum of eight cubits towards either side of the vineyard, i.e., a block of at least sixteen cubits in all, before it can be sown. (3) Allowing for service-borders as above, and four cubits, the minimum 'field' after Beth Hillel, towards either side, i.e., altogether eight cubits, for sowing. (4) חרב, lit., 'laid waste'. (5) *Sc.* in accordance with the Hillelite ruling. (6) Even its very centre may not be sown. (7) The vineyard. (8) The Hillelite minimum; i.e., after allowing for four cubits of service-border and after deducting the four cubits close to the fence which are not sown, there are left less than four cubits. (9) Since not being large enough to constitute a 'field' on its own, it is regarded as part of the vineyard.

c (1) V. *supra* 1, n. 7. (2) I.e., the technical term for the space 'between vineyard and fence', is not *meḥol ha-kerem*, as stated by the original anonymous Tanna, but *geder ha-kerem* ('the vineyard fence'), and it is to this *geder ha-kerem* (as long as it measures not less than six (Maim. four and a half) cubits) that the rule 'it is given its service-border, and one may sow the rest' applies. (3) And this must measure at least twelve cubits if it is in part to be sown. (4) Cf. *supra* II, 8. These are effective partitions and one may sow vines hard upon one side and seeds hard upon the other side of such partitions. (5) That a gap of less than three handbreadths does not impair the character of a partition where the law depends on the presence or absence of a partition, is 'a law (orally imparted) to Moses at Sinai', (v. 'Er. 15*a*). (6) Which is regarded *de jure* as wall or fence, and it is therefore permitted to sow immediately in front of it a vine on the side of the boundary, and seed on the other just as if the fence were actually standing between them. (7) In the aggregate.

d (1) But it is permitted to do so where the fence still stands; if, however, the standing part is less than four handbreadths and more than three (and the broken part exceeds it) it is forbidden to sow vines on one side, and seed on the other even where the fence still stands. (2) And sowing of seed within four cubits thereof is prohibited. (3) Any number of them. (4) And one may sow seed at a distance of six handbreadths. (5) Either of three vines each, vine opposite vine (v. T.J.) or of five vines altogether set out as described *infra* 6.

CONSEQUENTLY, IF ONE HAS SOWN IN THE FOUR CUBITS [OF THE SERVICE-PATH] WITHIN THE VINEYARD, BETH SHAMMAI SAID: HE HAS [THEREBY] CAUSED THE PROHIBITION [AS KIL'AYIM][6] OF ONE ROW,[7] WHEREAS BETH HILLEL SAID: HE HAS CAUSED THE PROHIBITION OF TWO ROWS.[8]

MISHNAH 6. IF ONE HAS PLANTED TWO [VINES] OPPOSITE TWO, AND ONE [OTHER VINE] FORMING A 'TAIL',[9] THIS CONSTITUTES A VINEYARD. IF ONE HAS PLANTED TWO [VINES] OPPOSITE TWO, AND ONE [OTHER VINE] IN BETWEEN,[10] OR TWO OPPOSITE TWO, AND ONE IN THE MIDDLE,[11] NEITHER OF THESE [COLLECTIONS OF VINES] CONSTITUTE A VINEYARD UNLESS THERE BE TWO OPPOSITE TWO WITH ONE [OTHER]
a PROJECTING LIKE A TAIL.[1]

MISHNAH 7. IF ONE HAS PLANTED ONE ROW[2] [OF VINES] ON HIS OWN [LAND] AND ANOTHER ROW[2] ON HIS NEIGHBOUR'S [LAND], THEN EVEN THOUGH THERE BE IN THE MIDDLE A PRIVATE ROAD,[3] OR A PUBLIC ROAD,[4] OR A FENCE LOWER THAN TEN HANDBREADTHS, THESE [TWO ROWS] COMBINE.[5] IF THERE BE A FENCE HIGHER THAN TEN HANDBREADTHS[6] THEY DO NOT COMBINE. R. JUDAH SAID: IF HE INTERTWINES THEM [THE ROWS OF VINES] ABOVE [THE FENCE, THOUGH IT BE HIGHER THAN TEN HANDBREADTHS] THEY DO COMBINE.

MISHNAH 8. IF ONE HAS PLANTED TWO ROWS [OF VINES][7] AND THERE ARE NOT EIGHT CUBITS BETWEEN THEM, HE MAY NOT INTRODUCE SEED THERE [I.E., IN THE SPACE INTERVENING BETWEEN THE TWO ROWS].[8] IF THERE BE THREE
b [ROWS],[1] THEN IF BETWEEN ONE ROW AND ITS COMPANION [ROW][2] THERE ARE NOT SIXTEEN CUBITS,[3] HE MAY NOT INTRODUCE SEED THERE. R. ELIEZER B. JACOB SAID IN THE NAME OF ḤANINA B. ḤAKINAI: IF EVEN THE MIDDLE ROW WAS LAID WASTE AND BETWEEN ONE ROW AND ITS COMPANION [ROW] THERE ARE NOT SIXTEEN CUBITS,[4] HE MAY NOT INTRODUCE SEED THERE;[5] ALTHOUGH, HAD HE AB INITIO

(6) קדש, as used in Deut. XXII, 9. (7) Since, according to them this constitutes a vineyard. (8) Which according to them form the vineyard which according to Scripture (Deut. ibid.) becomes prohibited as a result of too close a proximity of other seed. How many and which of the vines are thus affected is discussed in detail in T.J. Our Mishnah is an instance of the rare occasions on which Beth Shammai took the more lenient, and Beth Hillel the more stringent rule. Cf. 'Ed. V, 2. (Sonc. ed.) 7a-7b. (9) Thus: Rash and Bert.:

○○○
○○ ; Maim.: ○○ ○○○. (10) Maim. and Rash: 'between either pair', thus: ○○○
○ ○ ; Bert.: in the continuation of the space between the pairs, thus ○○ ○○ ○

(11) Rash. and Bert.: ○ ○○○ ○ ; Maim., Sipponte: ○ ○ ○ ○ ○.

a (1) I.e., if in addition to either of the arrangements just described there is another vine 'projecting like a tail', they constitute a vineyard. (2) One row of two vines and one row of three vines (v. preceding Mishnah). (3) Four cubits wide. (4) The standard 'public road', דרך הרבים, (referred to in *Pe'ah* II, 1) is sixteen cubits wide; this is taken by Maim. as meant here. Others, however, say that here a path less than eight cubits wide is to be understood, rather the kind designated in *Pe'ah* ibid., as שביל הרבים,' a public path' (passable in the rainy as well as in the dry season). (5) *Sc.* to constitute a vineyard so as to forbid sowing seed either between the two rows or within four cubits from either of them. Even though according to R. Jose and R. Simeon one man's vine forming a tent over another person's produce does not cause *kil'ayim* (*infra* VII, 4), here not another person's but the man's own 'seed' is concerned; moreover the second row belongs to the first man's next-door neighbour, and this might easily give rise to a notion that the two rows belong to the same man, whose sowing seed between them causes *kil'ayim*. (6) The same applies if it is only ten handbreadths high; it is on account of what follows in this Mishnah that here it is said: 'higher than ten etc.'. (7) Of two vines in each, without another one 'projecting like a tail'. (8) Because they form sufficient of a vineyard to disallow sowing in the middle of it, even though for the purposes of sowing on the outer sides they are deemed as not forming a vineyard but as just individual vines. If, however, there are eight cubits (exclusive of the ground occupied by the vines) between them, the two rows (of two vines each) are deemed as separate, unrelated rows, and one may sow even between them at a distance of six handbreadths from the vines on either side.

b (1) Of two vines each. Such three rows constitute a vineyard. (2) Some say (*a*) between the two outer rows. Others say (*b*) between one and the next. (3) The size of a *karaḥath* of a vineyard (v. *supra* 1). (4) In accordance with note 2 (*a*), this means only as long as all three rows are there, is a distance of sixteen cubits required between the two outer rows (before sowing can be done in the intervening space); but if the middle row has been razed, the character of 'vineyard' ceases and one may sow between them (six handbreadths from the vines) even if they are not sixteen cubits apart. In accordance with note 2 (*b*) it means: Three rows constitute a 'vineyard' and sowing in either inter-row space is permitted only when each of the latter measures sixteen cubits (v. 1). If the middle row is razed, the character of the vineyard ceases, etc. (5) Having once been a vineyard, it remains a vineyard even if any of the three vines, even the middle one, is razed, and a full-size *karaḥath*, i.e. of sixteen cubits, is essential, if the inter-space is to be sown.

קידש שורה אחת· דהוא שיעור כרם ולבית הלל ב' שורות ויש בדבר להקל ולהחמיר כמו שאפרש: ירושלמי (הל' ג) והוא שזרע כנגד האמצעי [זרע כנגד האמצעי] על דעתיה דבית שמאי אוסר את כל השורה אדעתיה דבית הלל אוסר שלש כנגד שלש זרע כנגד הביניים שבאמצעי אדעתיה דבית שמאי אוסר שתים מכאן ושתים מכאן · חמישי' איזו היא שאמר אם היו זרעים קרובים לאחת מהן הרי אלו אסורות ואם לאו הרי אלו מותרות · על דעתיה דבית הלל אוסר ארבע כנגד שתים · זרע כנגד הזוית על דעתיה דבית שמאי איזו שורה אסורה זו וזו · על דעתיה דבית הלל אוסר שתים כנגד שתים ואחת יוצאה זנב מכאן ואחת יוצאה זנב מכאן · זרע כנגד הביניים שבקרן זוית על דעתיה דבית שמאי אוסר כל השורה על דעתיה דבית הלל אוסר שתים כנגד שתים ואחת יוצאה זנב מכאן · שלישית איזו שלישית שבראשונה שניה שבשלישית · פי' והוא שזרע כלומר זרע כנגד אמצעי ויש ספרים שכתוב כן בהדיא ולא גרסינן והוא ומיירי הך מילתא בה' שורות של חמש חמש גפנים זו אצל זו מסודרות גפן כנגד גפן שמכל ארבע רוחות הן נראות חמש של חמש חמש ומכל ארבע רוחות אם זרע תוך ד' אמות קידש למר כדאית ליה ולמר כדאית ליה · זרע כנגד האמצעי על דעתיה דבית שמאי אוסר את כל השורה החיצונה לאותה רוח שזרע בה המשל אם רוח מזרחית זרע שורה חיצונה שבמזרח אסורה · על דעתיה דבית הלל שאוסרין ב' שורות אוסר שלשה גפנים אמצעים משורה שניה כנגד שלשה

לא ירחיק לבד ו' טפחים כמו שעשה בגפן יחידית ואמר הכתוב בכלאי הכרם (דברים כב) פן תקדש המלאה הזרע אשר תזרע ותבואת הכרם ר"ל שאסור ליהנות בשתי התבואו' · וכל מה שתמלא בזו המס' המקדש וקידש זה ענינו: וב"ש שהם אומרים שורה אחת כרם אומרים שכל מי שזורע התבואה בתוך ארבע אמות הסמוכים לכרם מבחוץ והיא עבודת הכרם הפסיד שורה אחת והיא השורה הסמוכה לזרע מפני שאמר הכתוב ותבואת הכרם ובית הלל שאומרים שלא יקרא כרם אלא עד שיהו שתי שורות אומרים קידש שתי שורות שתבואת הכרם אינה נקראת בפחות משתי שורות:

* *

שם שתי שורות לפיכך [א]הזורע [א]ד' אמות שבכרם· ב"ש אומרים קידש שורה אחת [ב]וב"ה אומרים קידש שתי שורות: ו [ג]הנוטע שתים כנגד שתים ואחת יוצא זנב ה"ז כרם שתים כנגד שתים ואחת בינתים או שתים כנגד שתים ואחת באמצע אינו כרם עד שיהו שתים נגד שתים ואחת יוצא' זנב: ז [ד]הנוטע שורה אחת בתוך שלו ושורה אחת בתוך של חבירו ודרך היחיד ודרך הרבים באמצע וגדר שהוא נמוך מי' טפחים הרי אלו מצטרפות גבוה מי' טפחים אינן מצטרפות רבי יהודה אומר אם ערסן מלמעלה הרי אלו מצטרפות: ח [ה]הנוטע שתי שורות אם אין בניהם שמונה אמות לא יביא זרע לשם היו שלש אם אין בין שורה לחבירתה ט"ז אמה לא יביא זרע לשם ראב"י אמר משום *חנינא בן חכינאי אפילו חרבה האמצעית ואין בין שורה לחבירתה ט"ז אמה לא יביא זרע לשם שאילו

ו א מיי' פ"ו שם הלכה ג וטוש"ע שם סעיף לא:
ז ב מיי' שם טור שו"ע שם סעיף כח:
ח ג מיי' פ"ז שם הלכה ו טור שו"ע שם סעיף לז:
ט ד מיי' שם הל"ה וטור שו"ע שם סעיף לה:
י ה מיי' שם הל"א וטור שו"ע שם סעיף לב:

[א] עדיות פ"ה מ"ב:

פי' מהרי"ו בן מלכי צדק
קידש ב' שורות כשיעור כרם דד' אמות לעבודת ב' שורות הוו ולבית שמאי לא קידש אלא שורה אחת

יא א מיי' פ"ז מהל' כלאים הלכה כ סמג לאוין רפ טור ש"ע יו"ד סימן רצו סעיף לד :

ב ב מיי' שם הל' ה טור שולחן ערוך שם סעיף לה :

ג ג מיי' שם הל"ט וטור ש"ע שם סעיף לט :

ד ד מיי' שם וטור שולחן ערוך שם סעיף לג :

ה ה מיי' פ"ז מהל' כלאים הלכה כ טוש"ע יו"ד סימן רצו סעיף כ :

ו ו מיי' שם הלכה כב טור ש"ע שם סעיף כב :

ח' אמות דקאמר ראב"י היינו דזורע ח' אמות מי"ו אמה : ט י"ו אמה · שכל שורה של גפנים רחוקה מחברתה י"ו אמה ואין מצריכין להיות כרם ליתן לה עבודה ד"א אפי' בכרם גדולה כדפרשי' ואין צריך להניח בה כי אם ו' ספחים דהיינו אמה סמוך לשורה כעבודת גפן יחידית ונמצא זורע י"ד אמה מהלך י"ו : הופך שיער ב' שורות · כרם גדול נטע שכל שורה רחוקה מחברתה י"ו אמה ולא היה רוצה לסכך גפנו על גבי תבואתו והיה מצרף הענפים של השורות שתים שתים ודאי הגפנים להוא השיעור של כל שתים ושתים הופך לצד אחד אלו כלפי אלו והמקום פנוי מצד זה ומצד זה וזורע אלא שמניח ו' ספחים כדפרשינן ולשנה שניה הופך לצד אחד ולא בשביל איסור אלא שדרכו היה בכך כדאמרי' באתרא דמוכרי בהגי ברים חזקת הבתים (דף כט·) שמתוך כך טוענת פירות הרבה: צלמון · שם מקום · של שמונה מותר · קסבר ר"מ ור"ש דכיון דרחוקות השורות ח' אמות הוה ליה כגפן יחידית ומניח סמוך לשורה ששה ספחים וזורע את המותר · ובירוש' (שם) פסיק רב הלכה כר"מ ור"ש וקאמר נמי משום רב מותר הזרע דיעבד אבל לכתחל' אסור לזורעו · ומיהו מסקנא דירושלמי דאפי' לכתחלה מותר :

מתחלה נטען הרי זה מותר בח' אמות :
ט הנוטע (א) את כרמו (א) י"ו אמה על י"ו אמה מותר להביא זרע לשם אמר ר' יהודה מעשה בצלמון באחד שנטע את כרמו *ט"ז אמה על ט"ז אמה והיה הופך שער שתי שורות לצד אחת וזורע את הניר ובשנה האחרת היה הופך את השער למקום *אחר וזורע את הבור ובא מעשה לפני חכמים והתירו ר"מ ור"ש אומרים (ג) אאף הנוטע את כרמו על שמונה *אמות מותר :

פרק חמישי*

א כרם בשחרב אם יש בו ללקט עשר גפנים לבית סאה ונטועות כהלכתן הרי זה נקרא כרם דל גכרם שהוא נטוע ערבוביא אם יש בו לכוין שתים נגד ג' הרי זה כרם ואם לאו אינו כרם ר"מ אומר הואיל והוא נראה כתבנית הכרמים הרי זה כרם: ב כרם (ג) שהוא נטוע על פחות מד"א ר"ש אומר אינו כרם דוחכ"א (*רואין את האמצעיות) כאילו אינן : ג החריץ שהוא עובר בכרם עמוק עשרה ורחב ד' ראב"י אומר אם היה מפולש מראש הכרם ועד סופו הרי זה נראה כבין שני כרמים וזורעים בתוכו ואם לאו הרי הוא כגת והגת שבכרם עמוקה עשרה ורחב ד' רבי אליעזר אומר זורעים בתוכה זוחכמים אוסרים חשומרה שבכרם גבוהה עשרה ורחבה ארבע זורעין בתוכה ואם היה שער כותש אסור :

א נטועות כהלכתן שתים כנגד שתים ואחת יוצאה זנב ושלא יהו רחוקות י"ו אמה ולא פחות מד' אמות : ערבוביא · שאין הגפני' מכוונות כשורה: שתים כנגד שלש · שתי שורות אחת של שתים ואחת של שלש והיינו אחת יוצאה זנב· ובירושל' (הל' א) מפרש כיצד הוא יודע אם מכוונות הן מביא חוט ומותח· ותני הכוורת מכוון והנוף אינו מכוון הרי זה כרם. הנוף מכוון והכוורת אינו מכוון אינו כרם · היו דקות ואינן מכוונות היו עבים והן מכוונות ה"ז כרם · פי' כוורת הוא הגזע : ירושלמי (שם) א"ר יוחנן היא קרחת הכרם היא כרם שחרב · אלא קרחת הכרם מקרחים אותו מאמצעי' כרם שחרב מקרחין אותו מכל לדדין רבי זירא מחוי לחבריא ס' שורין מן שבע שבע נסב שורה פרח שורה לשתי נסב שורה פרח שורה לערב נשתיירו שם כ' גפנים נסב תרתי מכאן ותרתי מכאן תרתי מכאן ותרתי מכאן חדא מכאן וחדא מכאן נשתיירו שם י' גפנים הדא הוא דתנן י' גפנים לבית סאה נמצאו ב' כנגד ב' ואחת יוצאה זנב ב' כנגד ב' ואחת יוצאה זנב ב' כנגד ב' ואחת יוצאה זנב· פי' מראה לחבריא לחבריו כיצד הוא כרם עני שחרב ס' שורין מן שבע שבע ס' שורות שיש בכ"א ז' מכוונות כנגד גפנים של חברתה שנראות השורות שתי למערב ז' גפנים והן ס' שורות ואורך השורות מלא שורות ונמצא הכרם בן ס"ג גפנים· נסב שורה פרח והחרב שורה מן השורות ההולכות לשתי והן ז' שורות

מזרח

מערב

פי' מהרי"ו בן מלכי צדק

ט הנוטע את כרמו וכו' מעשה בצלמון · פי' שם מקום ס"ז על ט"ז כ גון זה הציור

***	ט"ז שער	***
***	ניר	***
***	ט"ז שער	***

היה הופך שער ב' שורות פי' לפנים קרי להו שער והיה הופך נפני ב' שורות למ"ו אמה ומצד האחר נשארו ניר והיה זורע מטין הי"ד אמות דאמה מיכן ואמה מיכן היו עבודת הגפן ...

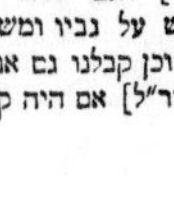

כנגד שתים ואחת יוצא זנב. ר' זירא היה מלמד זו המשנה לתלמידיו והיה עושה ס' שורין מכל שורה ז' נפנים קח שורה והנח שורה לשתי ...

PLANTED THESE [TWO ROWS], IT WOULD HAVE BEEN PERMITTED [TO SOW BETWEEN THEM] IF THEY WERE EIGHT CUBITS [APART].[6]

MISHNAH 9. IF ONE HAS PLANTED HIS VINEYARD ON [A PLAN OF] SIXTEEN CUBITS FOR EVERY INTER-SPACE,[7] IT IS PERMITTED TO INTRODUCE SEED THERE.[8] R. JUDAH SAID:
a IT HAPPENED AT ZALMON[1] THAT A MAN PLANTED HIS VINEYARD ON [A PLAN OF] SIXTEEN CUBITS TO EVERY INTER-SPACE; [ONE YEAR] HE TURNED THE TIPS OF THE VINE BRANCHES OF TWO [ADJACENT ROWS] TOWARDS ONE PLACE,[2] AND SOWED[3] THE PLOUGHED LAND, AND THE FOLLOWING YEAR HE TURNED THE TIPS OF THE VINE BRANCHES IN THE OPPOSITE DIRECTION, AND SOWED THE LAND WHICH HAD BEEN LEFT UNTILLED [THE PRECEDING YEAR]. THE MATTER CAME BEFORE THE SAGES, AND THEY DECLARED IT PERMITTED. R. MEIR AND R. SIMEON SAID: EVEN IF ONE HAS PLANTED ONE'S VINEYARD ON [A PLAN OF] EIGHT CUBITS [BETWEEN EVERY TWO ROWS], THIS IS PERMITTED.[4]

CHAPTER V

b *MISHNAH* 1. IF A VINEYARD HAS BEEN [PARTLY] RAZED,[1] THEN SHOULD IT STILL BE POSSIBLE TO PICK TEN VINES WITHIN A BETH-SE'AH,[2] AND THESE ARE PLANTED ACCORDING TO THE ESTABLISHED LAW,[3] IT CONSTITUTES A 'POOR' VINEYARD. IF A [POOR][4] VINEYARD IS PLANTED IN IRREGULAR LAY-OUT, THEN SHOULD THERE BE THEREIN AN ALIGNMENT OF [ONE LINE OF] TWO [VINES] PARALLEL AND OPPOSITE TO [A LINE OF] THREE, IT CONSTITUTES A VINEYARD;[5] BUT IF THERE IS NOT [SUCH AN ALIGNMENT] IT DOES NOT CONSTITUTE A VINEYARD. R. MEIR SAID: SINCE IT IS IN APPEARANCE LIKE VINEYARDS [IN GENERAL], IT CONSTITUTES A VINEYARD.

MISHNAH 2. IF A VINEYARD[6] HAS BEEN PLANTED ON [A PLAN OF] LESS THAN FOUR CUBITS [TO AN INTER-SPACE],[7] R. SIMEON SAID: IT DOES NOT CONSTITUTE A VINEYARD.[8] THE SAGES, ON THE OTHER HAND, SAID: IT DOES CONSTITUTE A VINEYARD, AND WE REGARD THE MIDDLE [ROWS] AS IF THEY WERE NOT [VINES].[9]

MISHNAH 3. IF A TRENCH PASSES THROUGH A VINEYARD,
c AND IS TEN [HANDBREADTHS] DEEP AND FOUR WIDE,[1] R. ELIEZER B. JACOB SAYS: IF IT RUNS RIGHT THROUGH FROM THE BEGINNING OF THE VINEYARD TO THE END THEREOF,[2] IT PRESENTS THE APPEARANCE OF TWO [SEPARATELY OWNED] VINEYARDS, AND IT IS PERMITTED TO SOW THEREIN; BUT IF IT IS NOT,[3] IT IS [DEEMED] AS [IF IT WERE] A WINE-PRESS. AND AS FOR A WINE-PRESS IN A VINEYARD THAT IS TEN [HANDBREADTHS] DEEP AND FOUR WIDE, R. ELIEZER SAYS: IT IS PERMITTED TO SOW THEREIN,[4] WHILST THE SAGES,[5] FORBID.[6] IF A WATCH-MOUND IN A VINEYARD IS TEN HANDBREADTHS HIGH AND FOUR WIDE IT IS PERMITTED TO SOW THEREIN;[7] BUT IF THE ENDS OF THE VINE-BRANCHES BECAME INTERTWINED THEREON,[8] IT IS FORBIDDEN.

(6) According to the beginning of this Mishnah. (7) Originally so, and not when there were sixteen cubits only after the elimination of one row or more. (8) At a distance from the vines of only six handbreadths. Even Beth Shammai concur that if, originally, rows of vines are planted sixteen cubits apart, it is permitted to sow there; they require twenty-four cubits (*supra* I) only when the empty space has been formed by the elimination of some vines.

a (1) A place-name. Mount Zalmon is mentioned in Judg. IX, 47-48, as near Shechem. (2) I.e., towards one another. (3) Leaving six handbreadths clear. (4) Because then they are deemed as individual vines, and one may sow seed at a distance of six handbreadths.

b (1) Not a substantial patch (*karahath*) denuded of vines within a vineyard, but a vine, or a few vines missing here and there. (2) An area of 2,500 square cubits (v. *supra* II, 9). (3) 'Two vines opposite two, with one projecting like a tail', (v. *supra* IV, 6), and not more than sixteen cubits apart (*supra* IV, 9). (4) So some versions. (5) R. Zera in T.J. (6) Of three or more rows of three vines in a row. (7) I.e., less than the minimum distance required for attendance on a vineyard (with a yoke of oxen) v. *infra* VI, 1. (8) *Sc.* but the vines are regarded as single vines, at a distance of six handbreadths (one cubit) from which it is permitted to sow other seed. (9) But intended for fuel only. Close planting of vines would seem according to this to have been practised with a view to utilizing only the best rows for their fruit, but not the inferior ones. According to the Sages the latter, if they are inner rows, are virtually eliminated (they may even be trained to hang over corn, without bringing about *kil'ayim*) and the remaining ones are sufficiently apart to constitute a vineyard. R. Simeon's view is (v. T.J.) that all the vines, including those regarded by the Sages as so negligible as if non-existent, are an essential part of the plantation (one does not plant vines with a view to pulling them out), which is therefore not a vineyard in respect of the law requiring inter-spaces of four cubits.

c (1) V. *supra* IV, 3. (2) Cf. *supra* III, 3. (3) Either ten handbreadths deep, or four wide, or it does not traverse the plantation from end to end. (4) Since, owing to its dimensions, it is deemed a separate domain. (5) As well as R. Eliezer b. Jacob. (6) Since it is within a hollow space formed by a vineyard. (7) Cf. *supra* II, 8. The Sages and R. Eliezer are agreed on this. (8) So rendered by Rash. (who insists on adding 'of their own accord and not trained by hand') and others. Maim. renders 'reach and touch'. Some render the verb used here, viz., כותש, in the sense in which it is used in the Bible, viz., 'pound', 'pulverize', and say that the point here is that if the vine branches reach the top of the mound, they will rub the soil and powder it so that the wind blows it off and the mound becomes lower than ten handbreadths and/or narrower than four. (v. Rosh. and Rash. and cf. *Pe'ah* II, 3 and commentators a.l.).

MISHNAH 4. IF A VINE IS PLANTED IN A WINE-PRESS OR IN A DEPRESSION,[9] IT IS ALLOWED ITS SERVICE-BORDER,[10] AND ONE MAY SOW IN THE REST.[11] R. JOSE SAYS: IF THERE
a ARE NOT FOUR CUBITS THERE,[1] ONE MAY NOT INTRODUCE SEED THITHER.[2] AS FOR A HOUSE THAT IS WITHIN A VINEYARD, IT IS PERMITTED TO SOW THEREIN.[3]

MISHNAH 5. IF ONE PLANTS A VEGETABLE OR SUFFERS IT TO REMAIN IN A VINEYARD, HE RENDERS PROHIBITED [AS KIL'AYIM] FORTY-FIVE VINES. WHEN? IN THE EVENT OF THEIR HAVING BEEN PLANTED ON A PLAN OF EITHER FOUR OR FIVE [CUBITS TO AN INTER-SPACE].[4] IN THE EVENT, HOWEVER, OF THEIR HAVING BEEN PLANTED ON [A PLAN OF] EITHER SIX OR SEVEN [CUBITS TO AN INTER-SPACE] HE RENDERS PROHIBITED AS KIL'AYIM [THE VINES WITHIN AN AREA OF] SIXTEEN CUBITS IN EVERY DIRECTION, IN THE FORM OF A CIRCLE,

(9) Measuring two to three cubits in length and three handbreadths in width (T.J., v. Rash. and Sipponte). (10) Of six handbreadths, like an individual vine. (11) *Sc.* of the wine-press or depression.

a (1) Either in length or in width. (2) But if there are four cubits, R. Jose agrees with the anonymous Tanna. (3) Even if the vines hang over the house; since the house has a roof over it. (4) In an area planted at intervals of four cubits (especially if it be four cubits clear, exclusive of the thickness of the vines), a circle with a radius of sixteen cubits (v. *infra* in this Mishnah) will contain forty-five vines. In an area planted, at intervals of five cubits, such a circle will actually contain only thirty-seven vines, but as the circumference passes only just four cubits (the width of a statutory service-border for a vineyard) from the outermost rows, we must visualize a virtual circle having a twenty cubit radius, which too, would contain forty-five vines. So Maim., Asheri, and Bert.

אם עירכן למעלה ודבר תימה הוא שאינה לשונו ושמא עירכן בידי אדם וכותש ממילא ויש מפרשים כאן ובפאה שער כותש שהשומרה עפר הנפרד אסור לפי שפעמים תבא הרוח ותפלנו ונמלא שומרה פחותה מארבעה ומעשרה ולכך אסור ובירושלמי (הלכה ג) גרים בגמרא דמתניתין דפאה כמה כותש כעלי במכתש או כותש על גבי גדר מן מה דתנינן שער כותש אין הגדר כותש הדא אמרת כותש ע"ג גדר משמע ומבעיא ליה כאיזה מחד מהני לישני דפרשינן האי כותש אי בגדר קאמר שהעפר תיחוח למעלה כעלי כותש במכתשת שמה שבתוכו תיחוח ודק להשיב אותו עפר כמאן דליתי' לפי שסוף הרוח לפרר העפר ולמעט הכותל מעשרה או כותש על גבי הגדר שענפי האילנות שמכאן ומכאן מסתבכין זה בזה למעלה מן הגדר ופשיט ליה מדקתני שער כותש משמע אבל אין הגדר כותש:

ד גפן שהיא נטועה בגת או א בנקע נותנין לה עבודתה וזורע את המותר ר' יוסי אומר ב אם אין שם ארבע אמות לא יביא זרע לשם ג והבית שבכרם זורעין בתוכו: **ה** ד הנוטע ירק בכרם או מקיים. הרי זה מקדש ארבעים וחמשה גפנים אימתי *שהיו נטועות על ארבע ארבע או על חמש חמש היו נטועות על ו' ו' או על ז' ז' ה הרי זה מקדש ט"ז אמה לכל רוח עגולות ולא

ר"מ: ד נקע מלשון נקעים דפ' בית כור (דף קב:) והקכעין נגומות ואמרי' בירושל' (בפרקין שם) מג' עד ד' היא מתניתין פחות מג' כסתום מג' עד ד' משלים ד' וזורע מיד והשתא לפי שיטה זו מיירי מתניתין בגת ונקע רחבין ג' ספחים וארוכין ב' וג' אמות: נותנין לה עבודתה: היינו ו' ספחים לאורך וזורע את המותר ולרוחב משלים ד' ספחים לאורך וזורע מיד בחוץ אבל אם אינם רחבין שלשה הוו להו כסתום וצריך ליתן לכל רוח ששה ספחים כדת עבודת גפן יחידית ויש ספרים שכתוב כאן נותנין לה עבודתה ד"א ושיבוש הוא: לא יביא זרע לשם · אפילו מרחיק ו"ט אבל כשיש ד"א סגי בהרחקה ששה כמו ערים דבלא גדר לרבי יוחנן בן נורי כמו שאפרש בפרק ו': והבית שבכרם · שסביבות הבית גפנים זורעין בתוכו בירושלמי (שם) דריש ליה מקרא רבי שמואל בשם ר' אבין ובבתי כלאים החבאו (ישעי' מב) בית שמחביאין בו את הכלאים: ה או מקיים · שלא נטעם אלא בא מאליו וראה אותו ולא עקרו: ד' על ד' או ה' על ה'· שיש בין גפן לגפן ד"א או ה' אז אוסר מ"ה גפנים שהרי כשיטע ז' שורות של גפנים שיש בכל שורה ושורה ז' גפנים וכל הגפנים מכוונות ד"א בין גפן לגפן תמלא מ"ט גפנים נטועין בתוך ריבוע של כ"ד אמות על כ"ד אמות דשורה של ז' גפנים יש בין הגפנים ו' אוירים של ד' ד' וכן לכל שורה ושורה וכשזרע סביב גפן אמצעית של שורה רביעית דהיא גפן האמצעית של כל גפנים הרי זה מקדש ט"ז אמה עגולות לכל רוח כדקתני סיפא היינו ל"ב על ל"ב עגולות ונמצאו כל המ"ט גפנים נטועות בתוכן חוץ מד' גפנים מד' זויות משום דכל אמתא בריבועא אמתא ותרי חומשי באלכסונא נמצא דריבוע של כ"ד אמות באלכסון עודף עליו ט' אמות וג' חומשין ונמצאו הזויות נטועות חוץ לל"ב וכן כשיש נמי ה"א בין גפן לגפן אוסר כמו כן מ"ה גפנים שהרי אורך השורה ל' אוירים ל' אמה וכשתסיר שבזויות אין אחת מהן רחוקה מן האמצעית יותר מי"ו אמה שהרי לכל זוית וזוית ה' על ה' ותמלא שאין מגפן הזרועה עד גפן הרחוקה אלא כשעור חצי האלכסון שלשים על עשרים וקל הדבר לעשות ליור ולהבין ואלכסון של שלשים על עשרים אינו מעדיף על הריבוע אפילו כעודף האלכסון של כ' על כ' [ויותר י'] תדע דאם תקשור חוט שבקרן זוית ותוליכנו באלכסון לסוף כ' ואח"כ ביושר עד למטה י' אמות נמצא אורך החוט ל"ח אמות שהעדיף ח' אמות משום אלכסון של כ' על כ' ואם באת למותחן באלכסון מקרן לקרן דבר הנראה לעינים שמתקצר הרבה ולא כרבינו שמואל שפירש בסוף המוכר פירות דאלכסון של ד' על ד' אינו מעדיף כדפרשינן ואין אדם יכול לעמוד לעשות כלל וקצבה לאלכסון של ריבוע שארכו יותר על רחבו ומתוך משנתנו יש לדקדק דאלכסון של ל' על כ' אינו מעדיף כי אם ב' אמות דהוה ליה ט"ז אמה לאמצעית ובני אדם חכמי המדות אמרו דכל מרובע ב' קוים במרובע האלכסון שמודדין מדת רחבו ועושין מרובע כמדתו ומודדין מדת ארכו ועושין ריבוע כמדתו ומודדין מדת אלכסון ועושין ריבוע כמדתו יעלה אלכסונו כשיעור אותן ב' ריבועין אחד שעשו למדת ארכו ואחד שעשו למדת רחבו תדע עשה לך ריבוע של מאה על מאה. וחלוק אותו לאמצעי שתי וערב יהיו לך ד' ריבועים שיש בכל אחד ואחד כ' על כ' חזור וחלוק אותם ריבועים לאלכסונים הנה עיניך רואות דריבוע פנימי חציו של חיצון כזה*

שהרי חילקת כל הריבועין של כ' על כ' לאלכסון והוא חציו של כל אחד ואחד ואותו ריבוע של כ' על כ' מרובע שני קוים עולה ב' פעמים כ' על כ' וכן עולה מרובע באלכסונו כאשר הראיתיך בעיניך דריבוע פנימי חציו של חיצון היינו ק' על כ' דהיינו ב' פעמים כ' על כ' עוד אבינך בדרך אחרת ב' ריבועים של כ' על כ' חלוק כל אחד לשנים באלכסון וחזור וקח אותן ד' חתיכות והפוך אלכסונן לצד חוץ ד' אלכסונין לד' רוחות תמצא לך ריבוע ארכו כרחבו מאלו ב' ריבועים של כ' על כ' שחילקת לאלכסון כזה*

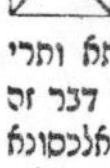

אך קשה שהרי אמרו חכמים בעירובין (דף כג:) גבי חצר המשכן שהוא ק' על כ' פול חמשים וסבב חמשים ועולה לדבר מועט שיש שבעים אמה ושירים כמו שהוכיח שם בקונטרס ולפי חשבון זה לא יעלה אותו ריבוע כי אם ע' על ע' מלומלמין דכל אמתא בריבוע אמתא ותרי חומשי באלכסונא נמצא האלכסון של כ' על כ' שבעים אמה בצמצום אבל דבר זה תלוי מה שאין כן בחשבון שכל אמתא בריבועא אמתא ותרי חומשי באלכסונא מכוון ממש כאשר תראינה עיניך באותם ב' ריבועים זה מלפנים מזה דלפי חשבון של אמתא ותרי חומשי הוי פנימי ע' על ע' ועל כרחך אלכסון של פנימי הוא מאה כמדת רוחב ריבוע החיצון ולפי חשבון של אמתא ותרי חומשי אין עולה אלכסון של שבעים כי אם צ"ח אמות ולא חשו חכמים על אותו מעט ומתקיימין דברי חכמים ודברי חכמי המדות ואע"פ שהוכחתי הדבר לריבוע שארכו כרחבו אין לו הוכחה לריבוע שארכו יותר על רחבו ועל כורחין ליתא להאי כללא דהא אלכסון של ל' על כ' אין עולה כי אם ל"ב כדמוכחא מתני' כדפרישית ואם תעשה ריבוע של ל' ושתים על ל' ושתים חסר פובא שאינו עולה ב' ריבועין אחד של ל' על ל' ואחד של כ' על כ': ירושלמי (הל' ד) רבי יוסי ברבי חנינא אמר והוא שזרע כנגד האמצעית ר' אבין בשם שמואל והוא שתהא האמצעית עגולה ירק היך עבידא שובע שורין מן שובע שובע [לא מכן] ד' גפנים לד' זויות כרם נשתיירו שם מ"ה גפנים הדא היא דתנן הרי זה מקדש מ"ה גפנים אימתי בזמן שהן נטועות ד' על ד' או ה' על ה' הדא מסייעא לרבי זירא דאמר שמנה חוץ ממקום כורתין פי' מקום כורתין הוא מקום הגזע של גפן

ר"ש: והלכה כחכמים: ד נקע. חפירה יתקבצו שם המים וכבר זכרתי לך פעמים רבות שעבוד' (הכרם) הגפן ו' שהודיעונו שאע"פ שהיה כלאים עם הגפן בחפירה אחת הוא מותר כשיהיה בין הזרעים ששה טפחים: ורבי יוסי אוסר (א) עד שיהיה בגת ד"א ואז ירחיק מן הגפן ו' טפחים וזורע את המותר על הדרך המחויב במחול הכרם וקרחת הכרם ואין הלכה כר' יוסי: ה הנוטע ירק. הוא הזורע אותם: והמקיים הוא שיראהו צומח ויניחהו: ומה שאמר הרי זה מקדש מ"ה גפנים. כפי מה שאומר והוא שהוא מקדש לעולם ששה עשר אמה לכל רוח עגולות כדי שתהיה העגולה שיתקדש כל מה שבתוכה עגולה שיש באלכסונה ל"ב אמות ומה שהצריכו לקצוב שיעור מה שנתקדש בדמיון הראשון במנין הגפנים והוא מה שאמר מ"ה גפנים ולקצוב בדמיון השני כמדת העגולה והוא מה שאמר ט"ז אמה לכל רוח עגולות מפני שהכרם כשיהיה נטוע על ד' ד' והוא שיהיה בין כל שורה ושורה ד' אמות בשורות האורך ובשורות הרוחב יהיה בין כל גפן וגפן ד"א או אם יהיה נטוע על ה' ה' שיהיה בין כל גפן וגפן ה' אמות יהיו כל הגפנים שיש בתוך העגולה מ"ה גפנים כאשר אבאר אחר שיהיה על ד' ד' או על ה' ה' אבל אם יהיה על ו' ו' או על שבעה שבעה ונעגל עגולה שיהיה באלכסונה ל"ב אמות לא יהיה מנין הגפנים המלויין בתוך העגולה כשיהיה על ו' ו' כפי מנינם כשיהיה על ז' ז' אלא ישתנה מנינם ומפני זה לקח העיקר שיכלול הכל ואמר ט"ז אמה לכל רוח ויש לך לשאול ולומר מאחר שעיקר הקידוש ט"ז אמה לכל רוח היה לו לקצר ולומר הנוטע ירק בכרם או מקיים הרי זה מקדש ט"ז אמה לכל רוח עגולות ולא מרובעות וכמו (ב) כן שלא הודיענו מנין הגפנים הנמצאים בתוך העגולה כשיהיה נטוע על ששה ועל שבעה או יותר ממנו כך לא היה צריך להודיענו מנין הגפנים הנמצאים בתוך העגולה כשיהיה נטוע על ארבע ועל ה' התשובה על זה אמת שכך היה לו לעשות לולי התועלת שהודיענו באומרו שהוא מקדש מ"ה גפנים אם יהיה נטוע על ה' שאילו עשינו הנה אלכסון העגולה ל"ב אמות כשיהיה נטוע על ה' ה' יהיה מנין הגפנים פחות ממ"ה ואשר יהיה נטוע על ה' ה' יצטרך להיות אלכסון העגולה מ' אמה ועשה זה לטעם שאבאר לך כשנצייר הצורות שאנו צריכין בזו ההלכה ואומר כשיהיה הכרם נטוע על ד' ד' והפרשנו מזה הכרם מרובע ארכו רוצה לומר ל"ב יהיה מרובע השע שורות מן הגפנים (ג) רוחב ותשע באורך וכשנעגל עגולה בתוך אותו המרובע שיהיה הקפה נוגע בשורות החיצונות כדי שיהיה חצי אלכסון העגולה ט"ז אמות ימלא בתוך העגולה מ"ה גפן וזהו צורתה* וכשתסתכל בצורה הזאת תמלא שמה שבתוך העגולה מ"ה גפנים וזהו צורתה וכשתסתכל השורות תמצאם ז' על ז' והם מ"ט גפן ויצאו מהם ד' גפנים חוץ מן העיגול והם הגפנים הארבעה שבד' הזויות אבל כשיהיה נטוע על ה' וחקקנו מרובע מ"ב על ל"ב יהיה המרובע ההוא כולל בתוכו

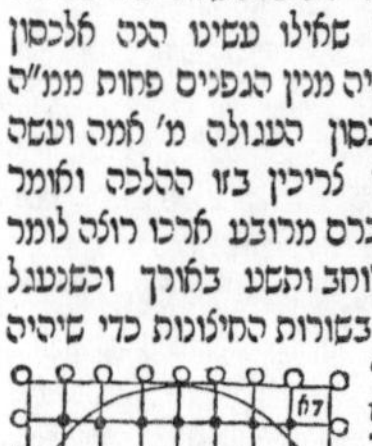

גפנים ז' על ז' שורות ויקח אמה מן השורה השמינית מכאן ואמה מן השורה השמינית מכאן מפני שהז' שורות יש ביניהן ו' מרחקים בכל מרחק ה' אמות והכל ל' אמה ואנו צריכין ל"ב אמות לפיכך יוציא צלע המרובע מן השורות השבעה ויקח אמה מכל שורה ונמלא קו העגולה שיש באלכסונה ל"ב אמה יוציא מכל שורה מן השורות החיצונות אמה אחת ונכנס במרחק שיש בין שתי השורות ויהיה מרחק קו העגולה מכל שורה מהשורות היוצאות מן העגול ארבע אמות על זו הצורה* לזה להוסיף על אלכסונה עד שיהיה נוגע הקו שלה בשורות הגפנים וכשיעשו זה נמצאו הגפנים כולם שם בז' שורות נכנסות בתוך העיגול לבד מארבע הגפנים שבד' הזויות ויהיה אז אלכסון העיגול כשנרחיב אותו כמו שאמר עד שיהיה נוגע בשורות החיצונות מ' אמה ואז יהיה זה הירק מקדש כ' אמה לכל רוח עגולות ואז נכנס בתוך העגול מ"ה גפנים וזו צורתה*

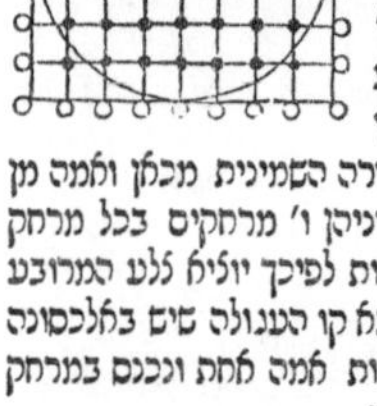

וכשתסתכל בצורה הזאת כמו כן המלאכה כמו הצורה הראשונה ותמלא שיש בתוך העגולה מרובע מז' שורות על ז' שורות ואין מהם חוץ לעגולה לבד מארבע גפנים בד' זויותיו וזה הוא אמר בגמ' על מה שאמר מקדש מ"ה גפנים [היך עבידה] ז' שורין של ז' על ז' לא מהם גפנים לארבע זויות הכרם נשתיירו שם מ"ה

גפנים ונתבאר לך זה הדבר ממה שהקדמנו בצורות באר היטב וכן נתבאר שהעגולה הכוללת מ"ה גפנים כשיהיה נטוע על ה' ה' שהאלכסונה מ' אמות שהוא א"כ כ' אמה לכל רוח וזה הענין הצריכו לומר מ"ה גפנים בנטוע

[ה]מצאו ל"ב אמות על ל"ב אמות וכן הדין שאילו נקרח באמצע קודם הזריעה [ק]רחת הכרם והיינו נותנין ד' אמות לכרם זה וד' אמות לכרם זה וח' אמות [ו]זורע ארבע אמות שנתננו לעבודה היה מקדש ב' שורות לבד וכן אם [נ]תננו לעבודת הכרם לצד אחד [נ"כ] היה מקדש שני שורות ועכשיו שזורע [עד] ט"ו אמה ולא ט"ז ממש. וכן הדין לקדש לכל סביביו שיעור כרם וכרם [מצ]רף הלכך משורה שזורעה בה הירק עד שורה הרביעית לה לכל רוח ורוח [ו]למערב כרם הוא הלכך בזמן שנטועות מד' ד' לא יקדש אלא עד שורה [ורוח] ורוח אבל בשורה הה' לא שהיא חוץ לט"ז אמה הלכך מתקדשות לה מן [illegible]

אמות והקידוש אינו מקדש אלא עד ט"ז אמות הלכך משורתה תקדש ה' נפנים לשורתה ב' שורות של ה' ה' נפנים מיכן וכן ב' שורות של ה' ה' נפנים מיכן נפנים דל מינייהו ד' נפנים של ד' זוית פשו להו ט"ז וה' נפנין של שורתה [illegible] המדה יסובב ויגיע עד שורה השלישית לה לכל רוח ורוח טפי לא. ונמצא [illegible] מה' שורות משלשה שורות האמצעיות ט"ו נפנים מכל שורה ה' ה' ומב' ש[ורות] מכל שורה ג' ג' דד' נפני הזויות שבב' שורות החיצונות אין מתקדשין [illegible] האמצעיות לנפני הזויות הוו להו ט"ז אמה והמרובע יותר על העגול רביע כל ש[כן] באלכסונא אתי ט"ז וד' חומשין בנטועות על ו' ו' ובנטועות על ז' ז' י"ז אמות וג' [illegible] אמתא בריבועא אמתא ותרי חומשא באלכסונא הוי:

עין משפט נר מצוה

ז א מיי' שם הלכה כד וטור שו"ע שם סעיף נד:
ח ב שם סעיף נה:
ט ג מיי' שם הלכה כג טור שו"ע שם סעיף נג:
י ד מיי' פ"ה מהל' כלאים הלכה ח טור שו"ע שם סעיף ד:
יא ה מיי' פ"ו שם הלכה א טוש"ע שם סעיף יע:

הגהות הב"ח

(א) מ"ד בר"מ ור' יוסי אוסר עד שיהיה ביניהם ארבע אמות כצ"ל:
(ב) מ"ה בר"מ וכמו שלא הודיענו כצ"ל ותיבת כן נמחק:
(ג) בא"ד מן הגפנים ברוחב ותשע באורך:

פי' מהר"י בן מלכי צדק

יתקשור ראש אחד בגפן הזורעה · ובראש האחר תסבב בכרם יכנסו במדה כל גפני ז' השורות לבד מד' גפנים שבזויות שמן הגפן הזורעה לזויות ימצאו ט"ז אמה ויותר שהמרובע יותר על העגול רביע. וכן בזמן שהן נטועות על הה' אמות כן יתקדשו לה דמן האמצעית לשורה הרביעית לה ט"ו אמה הוי וכן לרוח ורוח לבד מד' גפנים שבזויות ונמצא כי נתקדשו לך מ"ה גפנים. ואם תאמר מקום הגפנים יהא עולה לחשבון ובזמן שהן נטועין על [illegible]

ה"ה יהיה בין הגפן הזורעה לכשנרצה למזרח ולמערב לצפון ולדרום יותר מט"ו אמות ולא יתקדשו לך מ"ה גפנים הא לא קשיא דקיימא לן כר' זירא דאמר ח' אמות חוץ ממקום גפנים ודכותיה ט"ו אמות חוץ ממקום גפנים [ולכך] מתקדשות לך מ"ה גפנים. אבל בזמן שנטועות על ו' ו' או על ז' ז' אינו מקדש כשיעור הזה אלא כשיעור שתמצא בט"ז אמות עגולות דהיינו כ"א גפנים כיצד כשתמדוד ט"ז אמה לכל רוח עד שורה הרביעית [illegible] בזמן שנטועות על ו' ו' ובזמן שנטועות על ז' ז' תמצא כ"א

פי' מהר"י בן מלכי צדק

שומירה ואי קשיא לך גירסא דירושלמי דפאה גירסא משבשתא היא והגי' המדוקדקת מה כותש(בעלי) [כעלי] במכתש פי' כשם שהמכתש לעולם הסר והעלי כותש כן הנופות מיעשו הגדר ולכן אינו מפסיק הא בגדר [שלם] אף על פי שהנופות עליו מפסיק או די"ל כותש על גבי גדר דלא חסרוה מידי ואפילו הכי אינו מפסיק משום כתישת הנופות ופשם וכו' ועל זה הפי' אנו סומכין. ועירוס דקשיא לא קשיא מידי דעירוס מיקרי על ידי אדם כותש מעצמן: ד גפן שהיא נטועה בגת או בנקע. גרסינן בירושל' בגת ונקע רחבין [ג] ספחים או [יותר מג'] ספחים עד ד' וארוכין ב' או ג' אמות נותנין לה עבודתה. פי' ששה ספחים לאורך וזורע את המותר ולרוחב משלים ד' ספחים *) ויזרע מיד בחוץ אבל אם היה רחב פחות מג' ספחים קיימא לן [דהוי] כסתום ולכל רוח צריך ליתן כדי עבודת גפן יחידית: ר' יוסי אומר [אם] אין רוחב הנקע ד' אמות וארכה ארבע אמות לא יביא זרע לשם ואם ד' נותן כדי עבודת הכרם לכל רוח דהיינו ו' ספחים וזורע את המותר: הבית שבכרם זורעין בתוכו. פי' ואע"פ שבסביבות הבית גפנים. ובני פרקא סמכי אקרא אמר ר' אבין בשם שמואל ובבתי כלאי' החבאו בית שמביאין בו את הכלאים: ה הנוטע ירק בכרם או מקיים. פי' לא נטעו הוא אלא [שבא מאליו] בכרמו ולא תלשו הרי זה מקדש מ"ה גפנים אימתי בזמן שהן נטועות השורו' על ד' ד' אמות או על ה' ה' היך עבידא ז' שורין של [illegible] גפנים [דהיינו] מ"ט גפנים [illegible] ד' זוית הכרם [illegible] באמות עגולות ולא במרובעות [illegible] ששנינו הרי זה מקדש מ"ה גפנים וכו' ר' יוסי ב"ר חנינא אמר והוא שזורע כנגד האמצעית. ר' אבין בשם שמואל והוא שתהא האמצעית עגול הירק. פי' גפן האמצעית זרע סביבותיה ירק [illegible] המתקדשות הן ז' שורות [illegible] הזוית כיצד כי הירק מקדש [illegible]

הרואה

*) הג"ה כ"כ גם הר"ש ז"ל אבל מלשון הירושלמי משמע דקאמר דאם בנקע רוחב ד' אז זורע מיד חוץ לנקע וכן פי' ספ"מ ודו"ק:

ולא מרובעות: ו הרואה ירק בכרם ואמר כשאגיע לו אלקטנו מותר כשאחזור אלקטנו אם הוסיף במאתים אסור: ז היה עובר בכרם ונפלו ממנו זרעים או שיצאו עם הזבלים או עם המי׳ הזורע וסיערתו הרוח לאחריו מותר סיערתו הרוח לפניו רע״א אם עשבים יופך ואם אביב ינפץ ואם הביאה דגן תדלק: ח המקיים קוצים בכרם רא״א קדש וחכ״א לא קדש אלא דבר שכמוהו מקיימין הארוס והקיסום ושושנת המלך וכל מיני זרעים אינם כלאים בכרם הקנבוס ר׳ טרפון אומר אינו כלאים וחכ״א כלאים והקינרס כלאים בכרם:

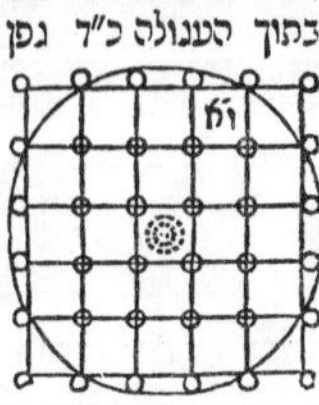

פרק ששי

א אי יזהו ערים הנוטע שורה של חמש גפנים בצד הגדר שהוא גבוה י׳ טפחים או

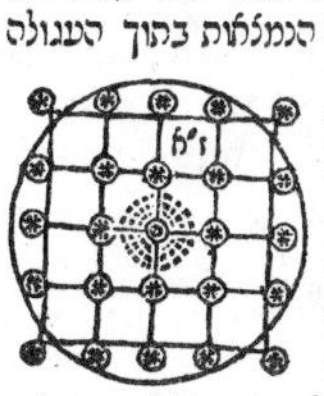

NOT OF A SQUARE.[5]

MISHNAH 6. IF ONE[6] SEES A VEGETABLE IN A VINEYARD, AND SAYS: 'WHEN I REACH IT I SHALL PLUCK IT', [ALL THAT HAS GROWN THERE] IS PERMITTED;[7] [BUT IF HE SAYS:] 'WHEN I COME BACK I SHALL PLUCK IT', THEN IF IT [THE VEGETABLE]
a HAS [IN THE MEANTIME] INCREASED BY A TWO-HUNDREDTH,[1] IT [ALL THAT HAS GROWN THERE] IS FORBIDDEN.[2]

MISHNAH 7. IF, WHEN ONE HAS PASSED THROUGH A VINEYARD, SEEDS HAVE FALLEN FROM HIM, OR [SEEDS] HAVE GONE [INTO THE FIELD] WITH MANURE OR WITH [IRRIGATION] WATER, OR IF AS HE WAS [IN A CORNFIELD] SCATTERING SEED, THE WIND BLEW SOME BEHIND HIM [INTO A VINEYARD], NO PROHIBITION APPLIES;[3] IF THE WIND BLEW THE SEED BEFORE HIM [INTO A VINEYARD][4] R. AKIBA SAID: IF[5] IT HAS PRODUCED BLADES, HE MUST TURN THE SOIL;[6] IF IT HAS REACHED THE STAGE OF GREEN EARS,[7] HE MUST BEAT THEM OUT;[8] IF IT HAS GROWN INTO CORN,[9] IT MUST BE BURNT.[10]

MISHNAH 8. IF ONE SUFFERS THORNS TO REMAIN GROWING IN A VINEYARD, R. ELIEZER SAID: [THEREBY] HE EFFECTS A STATE OF PROHIBITION,[11] BUT THE SAGES SAID: NOTHING CAUSES SUCH A STATE OF PROHIBITION EXCEPT THAT WHICH IT IS A COMMON PRACTICE [IN THE PLACE CONCERNED] TO
b PERMIT TO GROW.[1] IRIS,[2] IVY,[3] AND THE KING'S LILY,[4] LIKEWISE ALL MANNER OF SEEDS[5] [OTHER THAN THOSE ALREADY SPECIFICALLY DEALT WITH][6] ARE NOT KIL'AYIM IN A VINEYARD.[7] [AS FOR] HEMP, R. TARFON SAID: IT IS NOT KIL'AYIM, BUT THE SAGES SAY IT IS KIL'AYIM.[8] ARTICHOKES[9] ARE KIL'AYIM IN A VINEYARD.

CHAPTER VI

c MISHNAH 1. WHAT IS AN 'ARIS[1] [WHICH IS REGARDED AS A VINEYARD]?[2] IF ONE HAS PLANTED A [SINGLE] ROW CONSISTING OF FIVE VINES BESIDE A FENCE TEN HANDBREADTHS

(5) In the six-cubit plan, twenty-four, in the seven-cubit plan, twenty-one, vines become *kil'ayim*. The numbers mentioned in this and the preceding notes can be easily verified by drawing appropriate diagrams. (6) In this case, either the owner or an employee. (7) Because his evident readiness to remove the vegetable (or corn) shows that the latter is there without his knowledge or intention, whereas the Torah says: (Lev. XIX, 19) *Thy field thou shalt not sow* etc., and (Deut. XXII, 9) *Thou shalt not sow thy vineyard* etc., a prohibition, explain the Rabbis, only against such making or maintaining *kil'ayim* as is as deliberate as the act of sowing.

a (1) Since the processes of growth and withering are one the inverse of the other, it was assumed that the time taken by any species of produce to grow is the same as taken by that same species to become dried up after it had been cut or plucked, which period was of course, easily determinable by experiment. (2) Since he had knowingly allowed the 'offending' vegetable or corn to remain among the vines for a substantial period. (3) Since in each case the introduction of the seed was unintentional. If and when he notices it, he must of course remove it, as indicated in the preceding Mishnah. (4) *Sc.* and he has noticed it, then the prohibition applies, and he must retrieve the seed. (5) In the event of his having failed to retrieve the seed soon enough. (6) So as to ensure that they do not grow again. (7) I.e., before it has reached a third of its normal full growth. (8) And make no use of either grain or stalk. So R. Johanan; but in R. Hosha'ia's view only the grain is prohibited, but the stalks are permitted. (T.J.). (9) Having attained a third of its possible normal growth. (10) The rule of burning *kil'ayim* is derived from Deut. XXII, 9, which says: *Thou shalt not sow thy vineyard with* kil'ayim; *lest the fulness of the seed which thou hast sown be forfeited with the increase of the vineyard*. The Hebrew word for '*be forfeited*' viz.,תקדש, is explained as signifying 'it shall be burnt'. (11) *Sc.* of *kil'ayim;* since thorns are deliberately allowed to grow in some countries, e.g., Arabia, for camel's food, this reason, primarily local, for ruling that they produce a state of *kil'ayim* in a vineyard, is deemed, by extension, as making the ruling applicable universally.

b (1) Thus only in places where thorns are suffered gladly do they render a vineyard *kil'ayim*, but not elsewhere. (2) אירוס. (3) קיסוס. (4) שושנת המלך rendered by T.J. קירינטין which according to Kohut, is the lily flower, white in colour. Maim. renders (in Arabic) אל נעמן i.e., anemone. Danby renders 'fritillary'; there is a type called *Fritillaria imperialis*. (5) Viz., grain and vegetables. (6) Such as legumes, which also come under the term 'seeds' (*zera'im*). (7) The reason being, according to Maim., that they are 'seeds', but not vegetables (or grain) which alone constitute *kil'ayim* in a vineyard; or, according to Rabad, that even though (in his view) both 'seeds' and vegetables are prohibited in a vineyard, the specimens mentioned here are permitted because it is not the usual thing to let them grow in a vineyard. In Rabad's view, it appears, the Mishnah found it necessary to state specifically that these species do not constitute *kil'ayim,* because otherwise one might have thought that they do, on the analogy of the Sages' principle in the matter of thorns, inasmuch as both iris and ivy are, on botanical authority, eaten by cattle. The same uses probably apply to the 'king's lily'. The permissibility, however, is only as far as the purely Pentateuchal requirements are concerned. The Rabbis, however, have, some say, on the authority of a prophetic tradition, extended the prohibition to include other types of 'seeds' (Men. 15*b*). Some are of the opinion that they are prohibited also by Pentateuchal law though no penalty of stripes is prescribed for sowing these 'seeds' in a vineyard. (8) Because hemp resembles grapes. (9) קינרס, *cynara.*

c (1) עריס a plaited cradle (cf. Biblical Heb. ערש) or trellis, on which vines are trained. (2) And which forms, *infra*, a subject of dispute between the Shammaites and Hillelites.

HIGH,[3] OR BESIDE A TRENCH TEN HANDBREADTHS DEEP AND FOUR WIDE,[3] IT IS ALLOWED ITS SERVICE-BORDER OF FOUR CUBITS.[4] BETH SHAMMAI SAY: THE FOUR CUBITS ARE TO BE MEASURED FROM THE BODY OF THE VINE TO THE FIELD;[5] BUT BETH HILLEL SAY: FROM THE FENCE TO THE FIELD.[5]
a R. JOḤANAN B. NURI SAID: ALL WHO SAY SO[1] ARE MISTAKEN;[2] IN FACT [WHAT WAS SAID[3] WAS]: IF THERE BE FOUR CUBITS FROM THE BODY OF THE VINES TO THE FENCE, THE APPROPRIATE SERVICE-BORDER IS ALLOWED, AND THE REST MAY BE SOWN.[4] AND HOW MUCH IS THE SERVICE-BORDER OF A VINE? SIX HANDBREADTHS IN EVERY DIRECTION;[5] R. AKIBA SAID: THREE.[6]

MISHNAH 2. AS FOR AN 'ARIS WHICH PROJECTS FROM A TERRACE, R. ELIEZER B. JACOB SAID: IF A PERSON STANDING ON THE [LEVEL] GROUND IS ABLE TO PICK ALL OF IT, [SUCH AN 'ARIS] PROHIBITS [THE SOWING OF SEED IN] FOUR CUBITS OF THE FIELD;[7] IF [HE IS] NOT [ABLE TO DO SO], IT PROHIBITS [THE SOWING OF SEED] ONLY [IN] THE [SOIL] WHICH IS DIRECTLY OPPOSITE[8] IT.[9] R. ELIEZER SAID: LIKEWISE,[10] IF ONE HAS PLANTED ONE ON THE GROUND, AND ONE ON A TERRACE, THEN IF IT IS TEN HANDBREADTHS ABOVE THE [LEVEL] GROUND, ONE DOES NOT COMBINE WITH THE OTHER;[11] IF IT IS NOT [SO HIGH] ONE DOES COMBINE WITH THE OTHER.

MISHNAH 3. IF ONE HAS SUSPENDED VINE-BRANCHES OVER SOME OF THE LATHS [OF A TRELLIS], HE MAY NOT INTRODUCE SEED [INTO THE SOIL] BENEATH THE REMAINDER [OF THE TRELLIS]; YET IF HE DID INTRODUCE HE HAS NOT
b THEREBY BROUGHT ABOUT A PROHIBITED STATE.[1] IF, HOWEVER, NEW [TENDRILS] HAVE SPREAD [OVER THE 'REMAINDER'], THAT [WHICH HAD BEEN SOWN UNDER THE 'REMAINDER'] IS PROHIBITED.[2] EVEN SO IS IT WHEN ONE SUSPENDS VINE-BRANCHES OVER SOME PART OF A NON-FRUITBEARING[3] TREE.

(3) V. *supra* IV, 3. (4) Thus the *'aris* is regarded as a vineyard even by Beth Hillel who (*supra* IV, 5) require a minimum of two rows to form a vineyard within the meaning of the Scriptural precept. (5) Either (*a*) to a field on the same side of the fence thus:

(i) According to the Shammaites: Fence .... Vine < 4 cubits > Field

(ii) According to the Hillelites: Fence ... Vine ... Field
< 4 cubits >

or (*b*) to a field on the other side of the fence, thus:

(i) According to the Shammaites: Field .... Fence .... Vine
<......... 4 cubits ....>

(ii) According to the Hillelites: Field Fence Vine
<4 cubits>

Although interpretation (*b*) (Maim. and Bert.) is apparently borne out by T.J. there is this difficulty, that this would constitute a stringency of Beth Hillel against a leniency of Beth Shammai, which is not mentioned in the list of such instances given in 'Ed. IV, and V, (v. Rash.). L. gets over the difficulty by explaining: A field on either side of the fence.

a (1) Viz., that Beth Hillel ever, in any circumstances, recognized one row as a vineyard. (2) They did not get the correct version of the orally transmitted tradition. (3) By Beth Hillel. (4) But not if there are not four cubits between the vines and the fence, in which case it is forbidden to plant seed there altogether (cf. *supra* V, 4). (5) This is not part of R. Joḥanan b. Nuri's statement, but a consensus of opinion. (6) שלשה = three, masc. qualifying the masc. noun טפחים, 'handbreadths'. Rash. mentions a variant reading שלש = three, fem. qualifying, apparently, the fem. noun אמות, 'cubits' and referring to the distance between the vines and the fence. It is, however, clear from T.J. that the correct reading is the one accepted here. (7) I.e., four cubits in every direction outward from the edge of the plot of ground immediately beneath the *'aris*. (8) I.e., beneath. (9) R. Eliezer b. Jacob's view is accepted. L. thinks that the same rule applies when a vine planted on flat ground has its uppermost branches resting on an *'aris*. (10) In so far as the dictum following refers to a terrace. The consideration of an *'aris* does not, according to Maim. and Bert. enter into the latter case; according to Sipponte it does. V. next note. (11) Maim. and Bert. interpret: If one has planted one row of vines on the ground and another on a terrace, one row of two vines and the other of three vines, one of which projects like a tail (v. IV, 6), then if the terrace is ten handbreadths above the level, the row on the terrace does not combine with the row on the level to form a vineyard in respect of the laws of *kil'ayim*. Sipponte interprets: If one has planted one vine on the level and one on a terrace, and so on, in all five vines, three of which are on the level and two on the terrace, then if those on the terrace are ten handbreadths high, the five trees do not combine to form an *'aris* which requires that seed should not be sown within four cubits thereof. Rash. mentions both interpretations.

b (1) *Sc.* of *kil'ayim*. (2) According to Bert, this is so only if the crop of the vine increased by a two-hundredth part since the sowing under the 'remainder'. L. says, even if the increase was less. (3) סרק, v. *infra* 5. Such a tree is considered 'inconsiderable', in relation to a vine, and when the branches of the latter rest on it, the non-fruitbearing tree is deemed the same as a trellis-frame of dead wood.

◁ *For the continuation of the English translation of this page see overleaf.*

בצד חריץ שהוא עמוק י"ט ורחב ד' נותנין לו עבודתו ד"א בש"א מודדין ד"א מעיקר הגפנים לשדה ובה"א מן הגדר לשדה א"ר יוחנן בן נורי טועים כל האומרים כן אלא אם יש שם ד"א מעיקר גפנים ולגדר נותנים לו את עבודתו וזורע את המותר וכמה הוא עבודת הגפן ו"ט לכל רוח רע"א שלשה: **ב** ערים שהוא יוצא מן המדרגה ראב"י אומר אם עומד בארץ ובוצר את כולו הרי זה אוסר ד"א בשדה ואם לאו אינו אוסר אלא כנגדו ר"א אומר אף הנוטע אחת בארץ ואחת במדרגה אם גבוה מן הארץ י"ט אינה מצטרפ' עמה ואם לאו ה"ז מצטרפ' עמה: **ג** המדלה את הגפן על מקצת אפיפירות לא יביא זרע אל תחת המותר אם הביא לא קדש ואם הלך החדש אסור וכן המדלה על מקצת אילן סרק: **ד** המדלה את הגפן על מקצת אילן מאכל מותר להביא זרע אל תחת המותר ואם הלך החדש יחזירנו מעשה שהלך ר' יהושע אצל רבי ישמעאל לכפר עזיז והראהו גפן מודלה על מקצת תאנה אמר לו מה אני להביא זרע אל תחת המותר אמר לו מותר והעלהו משם לבית המגנייא והראהו גפן שהוא מודלה על מקצת הקורה וסדן של שקמה ובו קורות הרבה אמר לו תחת הקורה זה אסור והשאר מותר: **ה** איזהו אילן סרק כל שאינו עושה פירות ר' מאיר אומר הכל אילן סרק חוץ מן הזית והתאנה רבי יוסי אומר כל שאין כמוהו נוטעין שדות שלמות ה"ז אילן סרק: **ו** פסקי ערים ח' אמות ועוד וכל מדות שאמרו חכמים בכרם אין בהם ועוד חוץ מפסקי ערים אלו הן פסקי ערים ערים שחרב מאמצעו ונשתיירו בו ה' גפנים מכאן וחמש גפנים מכאן אם יש שם ח' אמות לא יביא זרע לשם ח' אמות ועוד נותנין לו כדי עבודתו וזורע את המותר: **ז** ערים שהוא יוצא מן הכותל מתוך הקרן וכלה

Continuation of translation from previous page as indicated by ◁

MISHNAH 4. IF ONE SUSPENDS [BRANCHES OF] A VINE ON PART OF [THE BRANCHES OF] A FRUIT TREE,[4] IT IS PERMITTED TO INTRODUCE SEED BENEATH THE 'REMAINDER';[5] IF A NEW [GROWTH] SPREAD [OVER THE 'REMAINDER'], HE MUST TURN IT BACK.[6] THERE WAS THE CASE OF R. JOSHUA WHO WENT TO R. ISHMAEL IN KEFAR 'AZIZ,[7] AND THE LATTER SHOWED HIM A VINE [WITH ITS BRANCHES] SUSPENDED ON PART OF [THE BRANCHES OF] A FIG-TREE. HE [R. JOSHUA] ASKED HIM [R. ISHMAEL]: 'WHAT [IS THE LAW? MAY] I INTRODUCE SEED BENEATH THE REMAINDER?' HE ANSWERED
c HIM: 'IT IS PERMITTED'.[1] HE TOOK HIM TO BETH-HAMMAGGANYAH[2] WHERE HE SHOWED HIM A VINE [WHOSE BRANCHES WERE] SUSPENDED ON PART OF A BEAM[3] BELONGING TO THE TRUNK OF A SYCAMORE,[4] WHICH HAD MANY BEAMS.[3] HE SAID TO HIM: 'BENEATH THIS BEAM IT IS PROHIBITED [TO SOW],[5] BUT BENEATH THE REMAINDER IT IS PERMITTED'.[6]

MISHNAH 5. WHAT IS A SERAK[7] TREE? ANY TREE WHICH DOES NOT YIELD FRUIT. R. MEIR SAID: ALL TREES ARE SERAK, EXCEPT OLIVE AND THE FIG TREE.[8] R. JOSE SAID: ALL SUCH TREES AS ARE NOT PLANTED IN WHOLE FIELDS, ARE SERAK TREES.

MISHNAH 6. 'ARIS-GAPS[9] MUST BE EIGHT CUBITS AND SOMEWHAT MORE.[10] [IN THE CASE OF] ALL MEASUREMENTS [BY THE CUBIT] SPOKEN OF BY THE SAGES IN CONNECTION WITH A VINEYARD,[11] THERE IS NO 'AND SOMEWHAT MORE' EXCEPT IN THAT OF 'ARIS-GAPS. THE FOLLOWING CONSTITUTES AN 'ARIS-GAP: IF AN 'ARIS WAS RAZED MIDWAY, AND FIVE VINES WERE LEFT ON ONE SIDE AND FIVE VINES ON THE
d OTHER SIDE,[1] THEN IF THE GAP[2] BE [ONLY] EIGHT CUBITS, ONE MUST NOT INTRODUCE SEED THITHER;[3] IF IT BE EIGHT CUBITS AND SOMEWHAT MORE, ONE SHOULD ALLOT THE REQUISITE SERVICE-BORDER,[4] AND HE MAY SOW THE REST.[5]

MISHNAH 7. IF AN 'ARIS TURNS AWAY FROM A WALL WHERE IT FORMS AN ANGLE, AND COMES TO AN END,[6] IT[7] IS

(4) Lit., '(human) food tree'. (5) Because such a tree retains its full individuality *vis-a-vis* the vine, and such ground beneath its branches over which vine-tendrils are not actually suspended, 'belongs' to the tree itself, and one may, therefore, sow seed there. (6) And keep it within the original bounds. (7) South of Hebron, v. Klein, S. *Beiträge* p. 52.
c (1) Because a fig-tree as a tree producing fruit for human consumption does not become subsidiary to the vine. (2) Near Hebron., v. Horowitz, I.S. *Palestine*, p. 143. (3) Apparently in view of the Tosef. (v. n. 6 *infra*) a rough beam or beams, severed from, but still resting, on the trunk. (4) Which is a kind of wild fig tree (5) Even under that part of that beam which is not itself overhung by vine-branches. (6) Maim.: since the sycamore is a fruit tree. Tosef. IV, 4, however, gives the reason: Since every single beam is like a tree by itself. This would seem to suggest that the sycamore was not universally considered an אילן מאכל, 'a tree bearing fruit for human consumption'. (7) The term has already been used at the end of Mishnah 3, where in anticipation of the accepted definition given here, it was rendered 'a non-fruitbearing tree'. (8) These alone, in R. Meir's minority view, do not become negligible *vis-a-vis* a vine in the circumstances discussed in the two preceding Mishnahs. (9) Explained *infra*. (10) Fixed in T.J. as one handbreadth, Tosef. as one sixth of a cubit (which is one handbreadth). Maim. both in Mishnah-Commentary and *Yad* (*Hil. Kil.* VIII, 6) also *Shulḥan Aruk, Yoreh De'ah* Sec. 296, sub-sec. 60, say one-sixtieth of a cubit. This is due evidently to another reading in the Tosef. (11) L. says that from T.J. it seems to him that 'in a vineyard' should be omitted.

d (1) Less than which number do not form an *'aris*. (2) Between the two short *'arisin* newly formed out of the one long one. (3) In accordance with *supra* IV, 8. (4) According to R. Joḥanan b. Nuri (Mishnah 1), six handbreadths; according to the first-quoted Tanna (ibid), four cubits. (5) R. Joḥanan b. Nuri and the original Tanna differ on the extent of this 'rest'. V. preceding note. (6) Or is completed (to the number of five vines) thus:

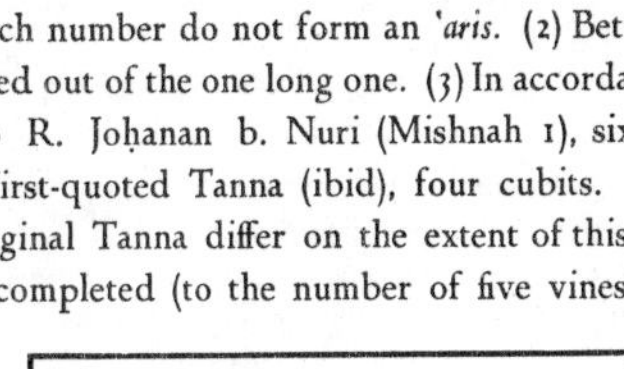

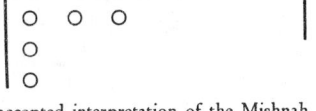

The above is the accepted interpretation of the Mishnah. Maim. interprets: If an *'aris* goes forth (i.e., commences) from the angles formed by two walls with another, and comes to a point, thus:

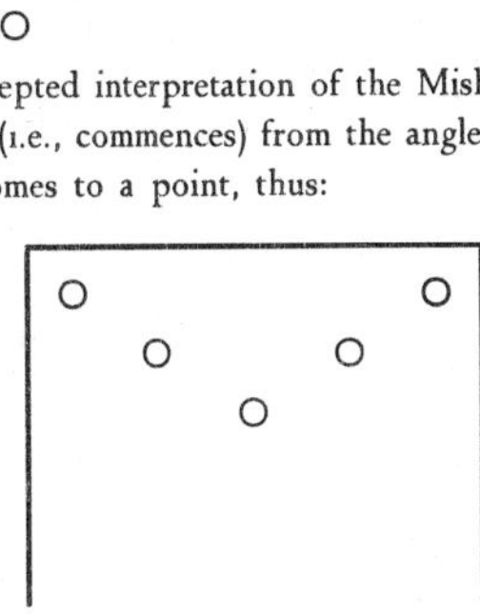

(7) I.e., each vine.

לעיל בפ"ד (משנה ה) אינו כרם עד שיהו ב' שורות : מן הגדר ולשדה · ואם הגפנים רחוקין ב' אמות מן הגדר אין מרחיק כי אם ב' אמות מן הגפנים וזורע ומיהו בירושלמי (שם) משמע דאיירי בצד אחר של גדר כגון שאם היו הגפנים נטועין למזרחה של גדר והזמורות עולין על הגדר אם בא לזרוע למערבה של גדר פליגי בית שמאי ובית הלל מהיכן מונין ד' אמות דבית שמאי אומרים מעיקר הגפנים שבמזרח ובית הלל אומרים מן הגדר דאמרי' בירושלמי (שם) היו שם ב' אמות מאן דאמר מעיקר גפנים מושחין [אינו אסור אלא שתי אמות · מ"ד מעיקר הגדר מושחין] אסור עוד ב' אמות וקשה דליתניי' בעדיות גבי קולי בית שמאי וחומרי ב"ה :

משנה

בצד חריץ שהוא עמוק י"ט ורחב ד' נותנין לו עבודתו ד"א בש"א מודדין ד"א מעיקר הגפנים לשדה ובה"א מן הגדר לשדה א"ר יוחנן בן נורי טועים כל האומרים כן אלא אם יש שם ד"א מעיקר גפנים ולגדר נותנים לו את עבודתו וזורע את המותר וכמה הוא עבודת הגפן ו"ט לכל רוח רע"א שלשה: **ב** ערים שהוא יוצא מן המדרגה ראב"י אומר אם עומד בארץ ובוצר את כולו הרי זה אוסר ד"א בשדה ואם לאו אינו אוסר אלא כנגדו ר"א אומר אף הנוטע אחת בארץ ואחת במדרגה אם גבוה מן הארץ י"ט אינה מצטרפ' עמה ואם לאו ה"ז מצטרפ' עמה: **ג** המדלה את הגפן על מקצת אפיפירות לא יביא זרע אל תחת המותר אם הביא לא קדש ואם הלך החדש אסור וכן המדלה על מקצת אילן סרק: **ד** המדלה את הגפן על מקצת אילן מאכל מותר להביא זרע אל תחת המותר ואם הלך החדש יחזירנו מעשה שהלך ר' יהושע אצל רבי ישמעאל לכפר עזיז והראהו גפן מודלה על מקצת תאנה אמר לו מה אני להביא זרע אל תחת המותר אמר לו מותר והעלהו משם לבית המגנייא והראהו גפן שהוא מודלה על מקצת הקורה וסדן של שקמה ובו קורות הרבה אמר לו תחת הקורה זה אסור והשאר מותר: **ה** איזהו אילן סרק כל שאינו עושה פירות ר' מאיר אומר הכל אילן סרק חוץ מן הזית והתאנה רבי יוסי אומר כל שאין כמוהו נוטעין שדות שלמות ה"ז אילן סרק: **ו** פסקי ערים ח' אמות ועוד וכל מדות שאמרו חכמים בכרם אין בהם ועוד חוץ מפסקי ערים אלו הן פסקי ערים שחרב מאמצעו ונשתיירו בו ה' גפנים מכאן וחמש גפנים מכאן אם יש שם ח' אמות לא יביא זרע לשם ח' אמות ועוד נותנין לו כדי עבודתו וזורע את המותר: **ז** ערים שהוא יוצא מן הכותל מתוך הקרן וכלה

ר"מ

אמות מעיקר הגפנים ואז יזרע מה שירצה מפני שעבודת הכרם ד' אמות : וב"ה אומרים * שמדות הד' אמות הוא מעיקר הגדר או החריץ אחר שריגי אותם הגפנים מתפשטים עליו וכאילו הגדרות הם עקרי אותם הגפנים ואם יהיה בין שרשי הגפנים ובין הגדרות אמה אחת ימדוד ג' אמות מעיקר הגפנים ויזרע ההבואה : ואמר ר' יוחנן בן נורי שכל זה טעות וכל ערים שיהיה על ענין זה כלומר שיהיה שורה אחת נחשבת כגפן יחידית שעבודתה ששה טפחים כמו שורה של חמש גפנים כשלא תהיה ערים שאינה כרם כמו שהקדמנו בפרק הרביעי ואע"פ שנעשית ערים לא נוסף בדינה על מה שהיה אבל נזכר ד' אמות בערים של חמש גפנים לענין אחר והוא שיהיה בין עקרי אלו הגפנים והגדרות ארבע אמות ירחיק מעקרי הגפנים שיעור עבודת הכרם והוא ו' טפחים ויזרע הנשאר שהוא שלשה אמות אבל אם יש בין העקרים והגדרות פחות מארבע אמות אסור לו לזרוע בין הגפנים לגדר על הדרך שאמרנו במחול הכרם בפרק רביעי ולענין זה בלבד אמר ר' יוחנן בן נורי שנזכר ד' אמות בזה הערים אבל מעיקרי הגפנים לשדה אין לו להרחיק אלא ששה טפחים מפני שהיא נחשבת כגפן יחידית זהו פירוש הלכה זו וענין דברי המדברים בה ועל כן התבונן בה שרבים מן המפרשים נכשלו בפירושם מכשול גדול ולא ראיתי לזכרם ולהשיב עליהם שאין זה ענין ספרנו . ואין הלכה כר' יוחנן בן נורי ולא כר' עקיבא :

ב אמר כשילא הערים ממקום גבוה ואע"פ שעקרו רחוק על הצורה הזאת אם אפשר לו לעמוד בארץ ולבצור כל הענבים התלוים מן הערים יהיה אסור בארבע אמות לכל רוח ואפי' יהיו · עקרי הגפנים במקום הערים וכנגדו ולא יהיה נקרא ערים פחות מחמשה גפנים וכבר הקדמנו זה ויש לך לשמרו בלבך תמיד ואם אי אפשר לו לבצור כל הענבים עד שיהיה אוחז בענפי הערים או שיהיה עולה על מדרגה לא יהיה אסור אלא ארבע אמות כנגדו בלבד וזה ר"ל באמרו כנגדו במקום שהוא כנגד עקרי הגפנים מסוף הערים ימוד ארבע אמות ברוח ההוא ואז יזרע : ומה שאמר אחת בארץ ואחת במדרגה . ר"ל שורה אחת בארץ ושורה אחת במדרגה ואם היתה המדרגה גבוהה על הארץ י' טפחים לא יתחברו השתי שורות ונעשה כרם והלכה כראב"י ואין הלכה כר"א : **ג** אפיפירות. הם האריגות שעשו מן הקנים והעלים כגון עריסות להשכיב עליהם שריגי הערים וענפיו כשיאריכו ואמר שהוא כשידלה ענפי הגפן על קצת הערים שעשוי לו ונשאר קצתו אסור לו שיזרע תחת המקום הריקן מן הערים העשוי אע"פ שאין עליו ענפים וכל הזורע שם לא קדש ואם האריכו הענפים הנטוים על הערים עד יסבכו על הזרע יהיה אסור אותו הזרע וזה הדין בעצמו יתחייב בכל מי שידלה ענפי הגפן על קצת ענפי אילן סרק ואילן סרק הוא אשר לא יעשה פרי כמו שיתבאר ויהיה נחשב אותו האילן סרק כמו הערים העשוי מעלים : **ד** הערים עשוי מן הקנים וזולתם וכן ענפי אילן סרק תהיה הכוונה להדלות עליו הענפים ומפני כך אסרנו כל זרע שנזרע התחיו מפני שהוא מזומן להדלות הענפים על כולו ולענין זה היתה המחשבה אבל אילן מאכל אין אדם עושה ממנו ערים ויתכוין להפסידו וכן אמר אין אדם מבטל תאנתו מפני גפנו ומפני זה התירו לו לזרוע תחת המותר ואם האריכו הענפים וסיבכו על מה שזרע יריס מענפים המתפשטים ויחזירם לצד אחר : ומה שאמר ובו קורות הרבה ר"ל בסדן של שקמה וכבר פירשנו שקמה שהוא ממין התאנים ואסור לו מה שנזרע תחת הקורה ההיא ואע"פ שהענפים על מקצתם מפני שהם אפיפירות והתיר לו לזרוע תחת שאר הקורות היוצאות מגוף השקמה מפני שהוא אילן מאכל : **ה** כבר הקדמנו לך מה בין אילן סרק לאילן מאכל לענין שהדלה עליו את הגפן ואם הוא מותר לו לזרוע תחת המותר ואם לא כפי מה שהקדמנו ואין הלכה לא כר' מאיר ולא כר' יוסי : **ו** ועוד כל שהוא באמרו בגמ' שיעור זה הנוסף שהוא חלק מששים חלק באמה והוא עשירית טפח ושיעור טפח הנזכר בכל המשנה והגמ' ובו יהיה השיעור תמיד הוא ד' אצבעות בגודל או שש באצבע אשר תחת הגודל וב' השיעורים שוין ובגמרא יתבאר כל זה ועבודתו הוא ו' טפחים לזו השורה וששה לזו שכנגדה וכבר הקדמנו לך פעמים רבות שדין השורה של ה' גפנים כדין גפן יחידית לפי שאינה כרם אבל עבודתה ששה טפחים וכן כשיהיו שתי שורות בלבד זו כנגד זו וביניהם ח' אמות מותר לו לזרוע ביניהם כמו שנתבאר בסוף פרק רביעי וזה הדין בעצמו נדון בשתי שורות אלו כשיהיו ערים אבל הוא צריך לשמונה ועוד ואז יהיה מותר לו לזרוע ביניהם לאחר שירחיק אמה מכל שורה מהם כמו שבארנו: **ז** אמר כשיתחיל הערים מקרן בין שתי קירות וילך הלוך ומתמעט עד ישוב(א)דמות התתיכה שבשפת בין הגוהר שנקרא בלשון ערבי

ר"ש

שמאי וחומרי ב"ה : טועין כל האומרים כן · דגדר לא משוי ליה כרם למתני ליה עבודה ד' אמות דסגי בו' טפחים כגפן יחידית: ד' אמות מעיקר גפנים ולגדר אבל ליכא ארבע אמות לא יביא זרע לשם אע"ג דהוא כגפן יחידית כדמפרש בירושלמי (שם) דרבי יוחנן בן נורי ורבי יוסי אמרו דבר אחד וערים בצד גדר לרבי יוחנן בן נורי כגפן שהיא נטועה בגת או בנקע אליבא דרבי יוסי בפרקין דלעיל : ר' עקיבא אומר שלשה טפחים היא עבודת גפן יחידית ואית דגרסי שלש בלא ה' וקאי אמעיקר גפנים ולגדר דאם יש שם ג' אמות נותן לו את עבודתו וזורע את המותר וליתא כדמוכח בירושלמי בריש פ' שאחר זה דבעבודת גפן פליגי דלר"ע ג' טפחים : **ב** ערים שהוא יוצא מן המדרגה · מלשון ונפלו המדרגות (יחזקאל לח) ענין מעלות כשעושין חריץ סביב המגדלים ושופכין העפר למעלה להגביה התל עושין אותו מדרגות מדרגות זו למעלה מזו ויוצאות ה' גפנים מן המדרגה אוסר ארבע אמות בשדה מאחר שעומד בארץ ובוצר את כולו רואין כל מקום שתחת הערים כאלו הוא מקום עיקרי הגפנים ואוסר ד' אמות בשדה לכל · רוח משפת הערים אבל אם אין יכול לבצור עד שיעלה במדרגה או בסולם אין אסור לזרוע אלא תחת הערים בלבד וכשהוא אוסר ד"א בשדה אינו אוסר אלא לזרוע אבל אינו מקדש אלא ו' טפחים מידי דהוה *פסקי דלקמן בפרק ז' (משנה ג) : אחת בארץ ואחת במדרגה · כל הערים נטוע כן דהוו להו ג' גפנים בארץ וב' במדרגה ואם אותן המדרגות גבוהות י' טפחים אין מצטרפות ואין צריך להרחיק מאותן שבארץ כי אם ו"ט כדי עבודת גפן יחידית ועוד י"ל אחת בארץ שורה אחת בארץ ושורה אחת במדרגה דב' שורות צריך כבית הלל ב' כנגד ב' ואחת יוצאה זנב ואם גבוה שורה שבמדרגה משורה שבארץ י' טפחים אינה מצטרפת אי נמי אם גבוה המדרגה י' אין מצטרפות: **ג** ד אפיפורות. פי' בערוך אילן העושה פירות הרבה מלשון מסעף פארה במערצה (ישעיה י) ולא יתכן כדמוכח בסיפא אלא בנין של עלים · מסודרין כמין סכך שתי וערב והדלה על מקצתן שתי וערב את הגפן אסור לזרוע תחת המותר אע"ג שאין הדלית מסכך שם : ואם זרע לא קידש וכן תנינא לקמן אלו אוסרין ולא מקדשין מותר האפיפירות : ואם הלך החדש שגדל (את) הגפן והוליא זמורות ומילא כל האפיפירות: אילן סרק · דינו כדין אפיפירות : על מקצת אילן מאכל מותר · בירושלמי (הל"ג) אמרינן מה בין אילן סרק לאילן מאכל אילן סרק אדם מבטלו על גבי גפנו אילן מאכל אינו מבטלו ויחזירנו למקום שהיה תחלה ויזרע המותר : עזיז · שם מקום : אמר לו מותר · בתוספתא (פרק ג) קתני אין אדם מבטל תאנתו מפני גפנו : המגנייא · שם מקום : תחת קורה זו אסור והשאר מותר · בתוספתא (שם) קתני שאני רואה כל קורה וקורה] כאילו בפני עצמה : **ה** חוץ מן הזית מן התאנה · קסבר ר' מאיר דשאר אילנות אדם מבטל מפני גפנו ורבי יוסי סבר דכל שכמוהו נוטעין שדות אין מבטל מפני גפנו : **ו** פסקי ערים · מפרש בסיפא : ועוד · קתני בתוספתא (שם) וכמה ועוד אחד מששה באמה ומפרש בירושלמי (הל' ד) ספח : שחרב באמצעו · כגון שנטע י"א גפנים בצד הגדר וחרב גפן האמצעית ונעשו ב' עריסין : ח' אמות ועוד נותנים לו עבודתו · לר' יוחנן בן נורי (הוא) דלא חשיב ערים כרם נותנין ו' טפחים לזה וו' טפחים לזה וזורע את המותר ולמאן דחשיב ליה כרם אין יכול לזרוע אלא ההוא ועוד *דשמעינן מינה דאפילו מאן דחשיב ליה כרם לאו לכל מילי מדלא בעי בפסקי ערים מ"ז אמה כקרחת הכרם ועוד דהזורע ארבע אמות מקדש והזורע מותר פסקי ערים מו' טפחים ואילך לא מקדש כדתנן לקמן (פ"ז משנה ג): **ז** ערים שהוא יוצא מן הכותל מתוך הקרן וכלה · כלומר ה' גפנים הנטועות בצד גדר

ספחים בנפן יחידית ואותן דמדרגה אוסרין כנגדן : **ואם** לאו. כלומר אם אינן גבוהין י' הרי זו מצטרפת עמה ועושין ערים וצריך להרחיק ד' אמות : **מדרגה** סולם מלשון בסתר המדרגה . פ"א אף הנוטע אחת בארץ וכו' פי' קיימא לן כבית הלל דאמר שני שורות כרם היכא דליכא גדר עתה אם המדרגה שנטועה בה שורה האחת גבוהה עשרה טפחים לא מצטרפת ולא הוי כרם . ואי פחות מי' מצטרפת שורה דמדרגה עם שורה הנטועה בארץ והוי כרם אף על פי שהשורה נטועה בראשה מצטרפת . פ"א ר' אליעזר אומר אף הנוטע אחת בארץ ואחת במדרגה . פי' לפני הגדר מדרגות ונטע נפן בארץ ונפן במדרגה ונפן בארץ ונפן במדרגה אם גבוהות מן המדרגות עשרה טפחים אינן מצטרפות ולית כאן ערים אף על גב דאית כאן גדר ואם אינן גבוהות מצטרפות ואית כאן ערים פי' מדרגה דבסים שבשדה ועל פירוש זה האחרון אנו סומכין : **ג** המדלה את הגפן על מקצת אפיפירות. פי' עשה עצים הרבה שתי וערב ועל מקצתם שם הגפן ומקצתם נשארו בלא גפן: לא יביא זרע אל תחת המותר . פי' לא יביא זרע אל תחת כל העצים ואפילו תחת אותן שאין הגפנים עליהן : ואם הביא תחת המותר לא קידש . וכן תנינן לקמן אילו אסורין ולא מקדשין וכו' מותר אפיפירות : ואם הלך החדש . פי' אם גדל הגפן ועשה זמורות חדשות ומילא כל אפיפירות אם הביא זרע

האמצעית נשארו ב' עריסין וזה לך צורתו: ח' אמות לא יביא זרע לשם ח' אמות ועוד טפחים לזה וו' טפחים לזה וזורע את המותר יוחנן דלא חשיב לערים כרם ברם למאן דאמר למיזרע אלא ההוא ועוד ותו לא דלכל כרם עבודתו ד' אמות ושמעת מינה דאפילו מאן דעביד ליה ככרם לאו ככרם לכל מילי דאם כן ליבעי בפיסוקי ט"ז אמה כקרחת הכרם . ותו דאילו כרם הזורע ד' אמות מקדש ואילו הזורע מותר פסקי ערים משששה טפחים ואילך אסור ולא מקדש כדתנינן לקמן מותר פסקי ערים וכו' : **ז** ערים שהוא יוצא מן הכותל מתוך קרן וכו'. כלומר אינו תופש כל הכותל אלא נשאר מן הכותל ריקן כגון זה* והואיל ובקרן [אחד] לא קיימא אלא ב' גפנים וג' מקרן האחד נותן להן עבודתו ששה טפחים מיכן ו' טפחים מיכן וזורע את שאר הכותל אע"פ שאין

גדר
גגגגגגגגגגג
זו פסקה

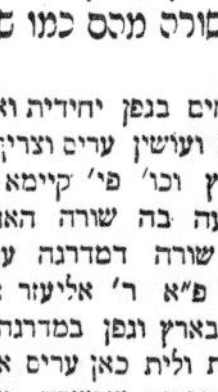

פי' מהר"י בן מלכי צדק

בצד הגדר כגון זה הציור זזזזז גרסי' בירושלמי פ"ט מ"א דבצד הגדר הא לא הוי אליבא דבית שמאי אינו כרם דהתנן הנוטע שורה של ה' גפנים בית שמאי אומר כרם ובית הלל אומר אינו כרם ותרצינן בערים מעוקם שם דבלא גדר אינו אסור משום כרם ...

... אחת בארץ ואחת במדרגה ואחת בארץ שיבואו ג' בארץ וב' במדרגה אם גבוהין אותן דמדרגה י' טפחים אינן מצטרפין להיות ערים להרחיק ד' אמו' אלא מאותן דקרקע מרחיק ו' טפחים בנפן יחידית ...

זרע תחתיהן אסור שהוא תחת הגפן. ורשינו אבל תחת הגפן ועבודת הגפן הרי אילו מקדשין. אפיפירות לעז אנברקי וכן המדלה על מקצת אילן סרק כדין המדלה על מקצת אפיפירות וכו' ...

עין משפט נר מצוה

[א] א מיי' פ"ח מהלכות כלאים הלכה ב ג טור ש"ע שם סעיף כז :
ב ב מיי' פ"ו שם הלכה ג ופ"ז הלכה א טוש"ע שם סעיף כא לא :
ג ג מיי' פ"ח שם הלכה ח טוש"ע שם סעיף סב :
ד ד מיי' פ"ז שם הלכה ו טוש"ע שם סעיף לו :
ה ה מיי' פ"ו שם הלכה יב טוש"ע שם סעיף כז :
ו ו ז שם סעיף כח :
ז ח ט שם סעיף כז :
ח י מיי' פ"ח מהל' כלאים הלכה ה טוש"ע שם סעיף ס :
ט כ מיי' פ"ח מהל' כלאים הלכה ט טור ש"ע יו"ד סימן רצו סעיף סג :

הגהות הב"ח

פ ו (א) מ"ז בר"מ דמות התתיכה שבשפת בית הנוהר וכו' :

הגהות הר"י לנדא

א] מ"ב בר"ש כל קורה וקורה כאילו · צ"ל כאילן :

י א מיי' פ"ז מהל' כלאים הלכה יד טוש"ע שם סעיף כט:

*הוי נורכא מיתני תמן :

יא ב מיי' שם טור שו"ע שם סעיף ל:

א ג מיי' שם הלכה ז טוש"ע יו"ד סי' רלה סעיף ד :

ב ד מיי' פ"ח שם הלכה י טור שו"ע יו"ד סי' רנו סעיף סד :

ג ה מיי' פ"ו מהלכות כלאים הלכה ט טוש"ע יו"ד סי' רנו סעיף כו :

ד ו מיי' פ"ה שם הלכה טז טוש"ע שם סעיף יב :

ה ז מיי' שם הלכה יט טור שו"ע שם

אין מחזיקות כל הגדר אלא שלש בראש הקרן מזה ושתים בראש הקרן השני מזה ובאמצע הכותל אין שם גפנים אלא בשתי זויות הכותל עומדות נותנין לו עבודתו ו' טפחים מכאן וו' טפחים מכאן וזורע שאר הכותל אע"פ שאין אורך הכותל ד' אמות ורבי יוסי דאסר בשאין שם ד' אמות לטעמיה דאסר בפרקין דלעיל (מ"ד) גבי גת ונקע ואמרינן בירושלמי (שם) דצריכי אלו תנינת' הכא ולא תנינת' תמן הוינן אמרי' הכא ע"י שהן הלכות ערים אתמר אסור כלומר לפי שיש כאן ה' גפנים אסרינן פחות מד' אמות תמן על ידי שאינן הלכות ערים כלומר שהיא גפן יחידית אתמר מותר*) אלו תנינת' תמן ולא תנינת' הכא הוינן אמרינן תמן על ידי שהוא מגופה*) מארבע רוחותיו כלומר דגת ונקע סתומין לכך צריך ד' אמות הוי נורכא מיתנא תמן ומיתנא הכא : ח הקנים היוצאים מן הערים · שדרך הגפנים להדלותן בקנים ויש מהן בולטין חוץ לסדר : ט הפרח היוצא

נותנין לו עבודתו וזורע את המותר ר' יוסי אומר אם אין שם ארבע אמות לא יביא זרע לשם : ח "הקנים היוצאים מן הערים וחס עליהם לפסקן כנגדן מותר עשאן כדי שיהלך עליהן החדש אסור : ט "הפרח היוצא מן הערים רואין אותו כאילו מטוטלת תלויה בו כנגדו אסור וכן בדלית המותח זמורה מאילן לאילן תחתיה אסור ספקה בחבל או בגמי תחת הספוק מותר עשאה כדי שיהלך עליו החדש אסור :

פרק שביעי

א המבריך א) ג(א) את הגפן בארץ אם אין עפר על גבה ג' טפחים לא יביא זרע עליה אפילו הבריכה בדלעת או בסילון הבריכה בסלע אע"פ שאין עפר על גבה אלא ג' אצבעות מותר להביא זרע עליה "הארכובה שבגפן ב) אין מודדין לה אלא מן העיקר השני : ב "המבריך ג) שלשה גפנים ועקריהן נראים ר' אלעזר בר' צדוק אומר אם יש ביניהם מד' אמות ועד ח' הרי אלו מצטרפות ואם לאו אינן מצטרפות "גפן שיבשה אסורה ואינה מקדשת "ר"מ אומר אף צמר גפן אסור ואינו מקדש ר"א ברבי צדוק אומר משמו אף על גבי הגפן אסור ואינו מקדש : ג אלו אוסרין ולא מקדשין "מותר חורבן הכרם "מותר מחול הכרם "מותר פסקי ערים

פירוש הרא"ש

פי' מהר"י בן מלכי צדק

הגהות הב"ח

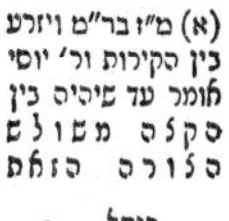

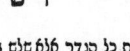

הגהות מהרי"ו לנדא

GIVEN ITS SERVICE-BORDER,[8] AND IT IS PERMITTED TO SOW THE REST.[9] R. JOSE SAID: IF THERE BE NOT FOUR CUBITS THERE,[10] ONE MAY NOT INTRODUCE SEED THITHER.[11]

MISHNAH 8. IF CANES [FORMING THE TRELLIS] PROTRUDE FROM THE 'ARIS AND ONE HAS FORBORNE FROM
a CUTTING THEM SHORT,[1] IT IS PERMITTED TO SOW DIRECTLY BENEATH[2] THEM; IF, HOWEVER, HE MADE THEM [LONG] SO THAT THE NEW [GROWTH] MIGHT SPREAD ALONG THEM, IT IS FORBIDDEN.

MISHNAH 9. IF A BLOSSOM PROTRUDED BEYOND THE 'ARIS, IT IS REGARDED AS IF A PLUMMET WERE SUSPENDED THEREFROM: DIRECTLY BENEATH IT, IT IS PROHIBITED [TO SOW].[3] IT IS LIKEWISE IN THE CASE OF A [PROTRUDING] BLOSSOM FROM A HANGING BRANCH OF A SINGLE VINE. IF ONE HAS STRETCHED A VINE-SHOOT FROM TREE TO TREE, IT IS FORBIDDEN TO SOW BENEATH IT.[4] IF HE MADE AN EXTENSION THERETO BY MEANS OF ROPE OR REED-GRASS, IT IS PERMITTED UNDER THE EXTENSION; IF HE MADE THE EXTENSION SO THAT THE NEW [GROWTH] MIGHT SPREAD ALONG IT, IT IS FORBIDDEN.[5]

CHAPTER VII

MISHNAH 1. IF ONE HAS BENT [INTO, AND CONDUCTED
b THROUGH, THE SOIL] A VINE [SHOOT][1], THEN IF THERE IS NOT SOIL OVER IT TO THE HEIGHT OF THREE HANDBREADTHS, HE MAY NOT INTRODUCE SEED ABOVE IT,[2] EVEN IF HE BENT [AND CONDUCTED IT UNDERGROUND] THROUGH A GOURD[3] OR THROUGH A PIPE.[4] IF HE BENT [AND CONDUCTED] IT THROUGH ROCKY SOIL,[5] THEN EVEN IF THERE BE NOT SOIL OVER IT TO THE HEIGHT OF THREE HANDBREADTHS, IT IS PERMITTED TO INTRODUCE SEED ABOVE IT. AS FOR A KNEE-JOINT-LIKE VINE-STEM [FORMED BY BURYING AND CONDUCTING IT UNDERGROUND],[6] ITS SERVICE-BORDER IS MEASURED FROM THE SECOND ROOT.[7]

MISHNAH 2. IF ONE HAS BENT [AND CONDUCTED UNDERGROUND] THREE VINES SO THAT THEIR [ORIGINAL] STEMS ARE VISIBLE [AS WELL AS THE CONTINUATION OF THESE EMERGING ABOVE GROUND][8], R. ELIEZER B. ZADOḲ SAID: IF
c THERE IS BETWEEN THEM FROM FOUR TO EIGHT CUBITS,[1] THEY COMBINE,[2] IF NOT, THEY DO NOT COMBINE. IF A VINE IS WITHERED, IT IS PROHIBITED [TO SOW NEAR IT],[3] BUT[4] IT DOES NOT CONDEMN [THE SEED AS KIL'AYIM]. R. MEIR SAID: THE SAME APPLIES TO A COTTON-PLANT.[5] IT IS FORBIDDEN [TO SOW NEAR IT,] BUT IT DOES NOT CONDEMN. R. ELIEZER B. ZADOḲ SAID IN HIS[6] NAME: ABOVE THE VINE[7] TOO, IT IS PROHIBITED [TO SOW], YET IT DOES NOT CONDEMN.

MISHNAH 3. IN THE FOLLOWING [SOWING] IS PROHIBITED, BUT THEY DO NOT CONDEMN [SEED ALREADY SOWN THERE]:[8] THE REMAINDER OF A [STATUTORILY INADEQUATE] ḲARAḤATH OF A VINEYARD,[9] THE REMAINDER OF A [STATUTORILY INADEQUATE] MEḤOL OF A VINEYARD,[10] THE REMAINDER OF A [STATUTORILY INADEQUATE] 'ARIS-GAP,[11] THE

(8) Of six handbreadths. (9) Even if there be less than four cubits. (10) This refers to the space between the two walls (Maim.) or to the length of the wall (Sipponte). (11) In pursuance of his (R. Jose's) view expressed *supra* V, 4.

a (1) So that the protrusion of the canes is due not to deliberation but to passivity. (2) Lit., 'opposite'. (3) I.e., even when the blossom extended beyond the six handbreadths (of the service-border) from the stem of the vine, within which space sowing is prohibited even when there is no blossom overhanging. (4) But not either side of it (as long, of course, as it is not within six handbreadths of the vine itself). (5) Since the circumstances resemble those of Mishnah 3.

b (1) And it emerges more than six handbreadths away; otherwise the question does not arise. (2) Since the roots struck by the 'seed' are then liable to penetrate into the soft vine-shoot and this would be like grafting, that is forbidden. (3) Which has been hollowed out and dried; otherwise the very putting into or passing through it of a vine-shoot would constitute *kil'ayim.* (4) Made of earthenware, which is soft enough for the roots of the 'seed' to penetrate. (5) Or through a conduit of metal or other substance impervious to penetration by the roots. (6) Emerging above the ground some distance from the root of the vine. (7) I.e., where it emerges from the ground; this applies only if the original root and stem are completely concealed underground. (8) Thus presenting six vines in two rows of three each, which constitute a statutory vineyard. In fact only two of the trees need be assumed to have been bent into the soil and conducted underground to emerge some distance away, as then the result would be five vines in two rows of two vines opposite two, and one other 'projecting like a tail'.

c (1) I.e., not less than four, and not more than eight cubits. (2) To form a statutory vineyard, and *inter alia* necessitate a service-border of four cubits. (3) On account of appearances, since people might think that the vine had cast its leaves only temporarily, which happens to all vines, as a rule in the autumn but in some instances also in the summer; this rule, therefore, applies throughout the year. (4) Once the seed has in innocence been sown. (5) צמר גפן, lit., 'vine-wool'; the cotton-plant bears resemblance to the vine. (6) R. Meir's. (7) When it is sunk underground, and there is not a depth of three handbreadths of soil over it (Maim. and Bert.). (8) As *kil'ayim.* (9) According to *supra* IV, 1, end, in a *ḳaraḥath* of the statutory measure of sixteen cubits, four cubits are allotted on each side as service-borders, and the remaining eight cubits may be sown. Here we speak of a *ḳaraḥath* less than sixteen cubits, in which case the space left for sowing is less than eight cubits. (10) V. *supra* IV, 1 and 2; a *meḥol* should be twelve cubits if any of it is to be sown, i.e., to allow for a service-border of four cubits on each side leaving four cubits for sowing. (11) V. *supra* VI, 6. An *'aris*-gap should be eight cubits and one handbreadth.

[GROUND UNDER THE] REMAINDER OF TRELLIS-LATHS.[12] BUT [THE GROUND] BENEATH A VINE,[13] AND THE SERVICE-BORDER
a OF A VINE,[1] AND THE [GROUND WITHIN] FOUR CUBITS OF A VINEYARD,[2] DO CONDEMN [SEED SOWN THERE].[3]

MISHNAH 4. IF ONE CAUSES HIS VINE TO OVERHANG THE [STANDING] CORN OF HIS NEIGHBOUR, HE RENDERS [THAT CORN] CONDEMNED [AS KIL'AYIM],[4] AND HE IS RESPONSIBLE FOR IT.[5] R. JOSE AND R. SIMEON SAID: A PERSON DOES NOT CONDEMN [AS KIL'AYIM] THAT WHICH IS NOT HIS OWN.[6]

MISHNAH 5. R. JOSE SAID: IT HAPPENED THAT A MAN SOWED [SEED IN] HIS VINEYARD IN THE SABBATICAL YEAR,[7] AND THE MATTER CAME BEFORE R. AKIBA, WHO SAID: A PERSON DOES NOT CONDEMN [AS KIL'AYIM] THAT WHICH IS NOT HIS OWN.[8]

MISHNAH 6. IF A HIGH-HANDED OCCUPIER[9] HAS SOWN SEED IN A VINEYARD,[10] AND IT LEFT HIS OCCUPATION [AND REVERTED TO THE RIGHTFUL OWNER],[11] THE LATTER SHOULD
b CUT IT DOWN,[1] EVEN IF IT BE DURING [THE MIDDLE DAYS OF] A FESTIVAL.[2] UP TO WHAT AMOUNT SHOULD HE PAY THE LABOURERS?[3] UP TO A THIRD.[4] IF [THEY DEMAND] MORE THAN THIS, HE SHOULD CUT IT IN HIS USUAL WAY EVEN IF HE HAS TO RESUME AFTER THE FESTIVAL.[5] FROM WHAT STAGE [ONWARDS] IS ONE TERMED A 'HIGH-HANDED OCCUPIER' ['ANNAS]?[6] FROM SUCH TIME AS [THE NAME OF THE ORIGINAL OWNER] HAS SUNK [INTO OBLIVION].[7]

MISHNAH 7. IF THE WIND HAS BLOWN[8] VINE-SHOOTS [SO THAT THEY] OVERHANG [STANDING] CORN, ONE SHOULD IMMEDIATELY LOP THEM OFF;[9] IF A MISHAP OCCURRED TO HIM,[10] IT [I.E., THE PRODUCE] IS PERMITTED.[11] IF CORN IS BENT [AND THE EARS REACH] BENEATH A VINE [LIKEWISE IN THE CASE OF GREENS], ONE SHOULD TURN THEM BACK, BUT [IF THIS HAS NOT BEEN DONE], IT DOES NOT CREATE A STATE OF CONDEMNATION [AS KIL'AYIM].[12] FROM WHAT STAGE IS CORN CAPABLE OF BEING CONDEMNED AS KIL'AYIM? FROM THE TIME IT HAS STRUCK ROOT.[13] AND GRAPES? FROM THE TIME THEY BECOME AS LARGE AS WHITE BEANS.[14]
c CORN WHICH HAS BECOME THROUGHLY DRY,[1] AND GRAPES

(12) As already stated in VI, 3, it is prohibited to sow beneath those laths of a trellis which are not themselves overhung with vine-shoots, but once seed has been innocently sown there; it is not condemned as *kil'ayim*. (13) I.e., beneath a vine-shoot which extends beyond the six handbreadths constituting the vine's service-border.

a (1) I.e., of an individual vine not being part of a vineyard, viz., six handbreadths. (2) I.e., its service-border. Cf. IV, 5. (3) As *kil'ayim*. (4) Just as if it were his own; especially since it was a deliberate action. (5) He must compensate his neighbour for the amount of corn which had thus become a total loss to the latter (6) Since Scripture says: *Thou shalt not sow thy vineyard with two kinds of seed* (Deut. XXII, 9); the effect of this dictum in the present case is that he has made his own vine *kil'ayim*, but not his neighbour's corn. (7) When all produce is *hefker*, i.e., ownerless, and at the disposal of any person wishing to help himself to it. (8) Applied to the case in question this would mean that, in the circumstances given, neither the seed-produce nor the grapes of the vineyard are *kil'ayim*. The vines themselves, however, are condemned as *kil'ayim*, even according to R. Akiba, since there are not *hefker* in the Sabbatical Year, (v. T.J., and L.). (9) אנס, one who has seized property illegally and by violence. (10) Since the public are under the impression that it is his own vineyard, the rule that 'a person does not condemn as *kil'ayim* that which is not his own' does not apply here. (11) Now the position is that the person who had sown the seed in the vineyard had been operating with something not his own, and that, therefore, no state of *kil'ayim* had in fact been brought about.

b (1) On account of 'appearances', i.e., in order that people might not be under the impression that this man, the rightful owner, is allowing *kil'ayim* to stay in his vineyard. (2) When, as a rule only such work may be done as is necessary to obviate deterioration or loss; here this consideration does not apply, but in order to remove suspicion through 'appearances', the work is permitted. (3) For cutting the corn. (4) Either a third more than the customary wage-rate, or a third of the value of the entire produce affected. (5) Even though by this time the produce might have increased by a two-hundredth part. (Cf. *supra* V, 6). (6) In the sense that the field is regarded as his, so that the sowing by him of seed in a vineyard results in *kil'ayim*. (7) Maim. renders: From such time as he, i.e., the original owner has sunk, i.e., disappeared, withdrawn himself, hidden, to avoid terrorization by the *'annas*. (8) Maim. 'broken'; L. adds 'but not severed'. (9) Reading יגדור Maim. Our text יגדור might mean: 'prop up (the shoots) with a fence'. (10) Preventing him from taking the measure prescribed. (11) Since it is there not with the owner's acquiescence. (12) The difference between this case and the one dealt with in Mishnah 4 is that in the latter the roots of the corn are under the foliage of the vine, and here only the top ends. (13) Reading משתשריש. Another version mentioned already in T.J. משתשליש, 'from the time it has grown a third (of its possible full size)'. Till then there is no *'fulness of the seed'*, required by the precept of *kil'ayim* (Deut. XXII, 9). (14) Till then the *'produce* (E.V. 'increase') *of the vineyard'* (ibid.) is not applicable.

c (1) After this the term *'(fulness of the) seed'* no longer applies; (it is called just wheat or barley etc. Maim.).

עריס מותר אפיפירות אבל תחת הגפן ועבודת
הגפן וארבע אמות שבכרם הרי אלו מקדשות :
ד ה המסכך א) את גפנו על גבי תבואתו של
חבירו הרי זה קדש וחייב באחריותו ורבי יוסי
ור' שמעון אומרים אין אדם מקדש דבר שאינו
שלו א"ר יוסי מעשה באחד שזרע את כרמו
בשביעית ובא מעשה לפני ר"ע ואמר אין אדם
מקדש דבר שאינו שלו : ו האנס שזרע את
הכרם ויצא מלפניו קוצרו (ח) אפילו במועד עד
כמה הוא נותן לפועלים עד שליש יתר מכאן
קוצר כדרכו והולך אפי' לאחר המועד מאימתי
הוא נקרא אנס משישקע : ז הרוח שעלעלה את
הגפנים על גבי תבואה יגדור מיד אם ארעו
אונס מותר תבואתו שהיא נוטה תחת הגפן וכן
בירק מחזיר ואינו (י) מקדש מאימתי תבואה
מתקדשת *משתשריש וענבים משיעשו כפול
הלבן תבואה שיבשה כל צרכה וענבים שבשלו
כל

ערים · דתנן לעיל בפרקין (משנה ו) אם אין א] ח' אמות לשם לא יביא זרע לשם כשתוליא ו' ספחים לכאן לעבודת הגפן ושש ספחים לכאן המותר אם זרע לא קידש והוא הדין ערים עצמו ופסקי ערים דנקט לרבותא דאפילו יש ערים מכאן ומכאן אינו מקדש המותר : ומותר אפיפירות · דתנן בפרקין דלעיל (משנה ג) המדלה את הגפן על מקצת אפיפירות לא יביא זרע לקצת המותר ואם הביא לא קידש : אבל תחת הגפן · כגון זמורה שמושכת ד' וה' אמות נותן לה ו' ספחים לעבודתה מכל צד והמותר תחתיה אסור ומקדש מן הצד מותר: ועבודת הגפן · ו' ספחים לרבנן וג' לר"ע : וד' אמות שבכרם · דתנן לעיל בפ"ד (משנה ה) דקידש ב' שורות : ירושלמי (שם) מותר מחול הכרם ד"א מותר חורבן הכרם ד' אמות מותר פסקי ערים ו' ספחים מותר אפיפירות ו' ספחים·פי' מד"א ואילך מו' ספחים ואילך ואמתני' דאפיפירות דפרקין דלעיל גרסינן בירושלמי (הל' ג) עד היכן אמר ר' אחא בשם ריש לקיש עד ו' ספחים ואם כפרש דלא נאסר המותר לזרוע אלא עד ו' ספחים אבל השאר מותר לא יתכן לפרש כן גבי אפיפירות מו' ואילך ואין לפרש דעד היכן ואם הביא לא קידש קאי דא"כ הוה משמע דו' ספחים סמוך למקצת המודלה מקדש ולרבי יעקב בר אידי עד ד' אמות ולא מסתבר כלל : ד ה וחייב באחריותו· לשלם התבואה ואפילו מאן דלא דאין דינא דגרמי דהא עביד בידים כדאמרינן בהגוזל קמא (דף ק'): אין אדם מקדש דבר שאינו שלו. אע"ג דשאר איסורין כגון בשר בחלב אוסר שאינו שלו אין לדמות איסורין התלויין בנתינת טעם לזה מיהו קשה מכלאי בגדים ורובע ונרבע דלגבוה ויש מחלקין בין איסור התלוי במחשבה לשאר איסורים דכלאים תלויין בניחותא דבעלים כדתנן לעיל בפרק ה' (משנה ו) גבי רואה ירק בכרם למחלק בין כשהגיע שם לכשאחזור וכן בין סיערתו הרוח לאחריו לסיערתו לפניו והיינו [נמי] טעמא גבי ע"ז דאינו אוסר דבר שאינו שלו בסוף פרק ב' דחולין (דף מא·) שתלוי במחשבתו שמחשבתו לע"א ולא יתכן דהרי העושה מלאכה במי חטאת ובפרת חטאת דפטור מדיני אדם וחייב בדיני שמים בפרק הניזקין (דף נג·) אלמא אוסר אע"ג דתלוי במחשבה כדאשכחן בפ' אלו מציאות (דף ל·) הכניסה לרבקה ודשה כשירה משום דלא ניחא ליה אלא כל הני היינו טעמא גבי ע"ז לאו שמיה תקרובת ע"ז כיון שאינו שלו וגבי פרה תלה הכתוב בניחותא דעושה מלאכה דכתיב גבי עגלה ערופה עבד וקרינן עובד מה עבד דניחא ליה כגון אלו מציאות ופרה ילפא מעגלה (סוטה דף מ"ו·) ומאן דלא דריש נמי ג"ש [התם] הכא מודה מסתמא כזו כן זו דילמוד סתום מן המפורש וגבי כלאים היינו טעמא דכתיב לא תזרע מה זורע דניחא ליה והא אין אדם נהנה ולא ניחא ליה של אחרים [א"נ] שאני הכא דכתיב כרמך וטעמא דתנא קמא מרבי בירושלמי (בפרקין הל' ג) מקרא דאמרינן (דברים כב) לא תזרע כרמך אין לי אלא כרמך כרם אחר מניין תלמוד לומר כלאים : ירושלמי (שם) אמר רבי יוחנן הכל מודים בענבים שאסורות

המותר וכן אם יהיה בפסקי הערים פחות מח' אמות ועוד ונתן עבודתו וזרע את המותר וכן אם הדלה על מקצת אפיפירות וזרע תחת השאר כל אלו אסורין לעשותן וענין שאמר אוסרין ר"ל שאלו הזכרים אוסרין המקום ההוא מן הארץ לזרוע בו ומקדשים הוא שישרפו כל הזרע והגפנים כפי מה שהקדמנו: ד ה חייב באחריותו לפרוע כפי מה שהפסיד ואין הלכה כר"י ולא כר' שמעון וידוע שכל הארצות בשנת השמטה הפקר הם ואין לאדם קנין גמור בהם ומפני זה נעשה כרמו בשנת השמטה כמי שאינו שלו* ואין הלכה כר"ע : ו עוד יתבאר לך במקומו שהקצירה בחולו של מועד אסורה אלא לצורך מכריח כמו שיתבאר במקומו ומותר לו לקטור הכלאים בחולו של מועד כמו שאמר: וענין עד שליש ר"ל שיוסיף להם שלישית השכר כדי למהר בעקירתו כגון אם יהי' שכרן ג' פשיטים בכל יום יתן להם ד' פשיטים ואם לא ימצא אלא בשכר גדול מזה יקצור לאטו ואפי' אם נמשכה הקצירה עד לאחר המועד ולאחר המועד יבקש פועלים בשכר הידוע ויקצרו כדרכם : ומה שאמר משישקע ר"ל משיתחבא בעל הכרם מפחד האנס הרוצה לאנוס אותו : ז עלעלה . פעל נגזר מתרגום ללע עלעא והענין הוא שהרוח שברה ענפי הגפן והפילה אותן על גבי התבואה : ופירוש יגדור שמיד יסירם מהרה : משתשריש. מעת שיתפשטו שרשיה בארץ: ופירוש בשל"ו ידוע : וענין שאמר תבואה שיבשה כל צרכה וענבים שבשלו כל צרכן אין מתקדשו'. הוא כפי מה שאומר והוא כשיטע גפן בתבואה שיבשה כל צרכה או זרע תבואה בכרם שבשלו ענביו כל צרכן אין מתקדשות וכן כשיזרע בכרם והענבים דקים מאד שהם בוסר בטרם שיהיו כפול הלבן איננה מתקדשת כמו כן והטעם בכל זה הוא מה שאמר הכתוב (דברים כב) פן תקדש המלאה(ד) הזרע וצריך שיהיה שם תבואת כרם ומלאת זרע ושתהיה כמו כן בענין גדול ותוספת ואם הגיעה לתכלית שלמותה לא יקראו אז תבואת כרם

אמר לו ר"א האוסר אינו נאסר ושאינו אוסר נאסר מה פליגין במסכך גפנו על גבי תבואתו של חברו אבל המסכך גפנו של חברו על גבי תבואתו כולי עלמא מודו שהאוסר נאסר המסכך גפנו של חברו על גבי תבואתו של חברו נשמע מן הדא א"ר יוסי מעשה באחד שזרע כרמו בשביעית ובא מעשה לפני ר"ע ואמר לו אין אדם אוסר דבר שאינו שלו הרי אין הגפן שלו ואין התבואה שלו ואיתתבת · פי' האוסר היינו זרעים שאתה אומר אוסרין הגפנים [אינו נאסר] שאינם אוסרין דהיינו גפנים דאין אוסרין זרעים אינו דין שלא יאסרו ור"א לטעמיה דאית ליה קל וחומר כי האי גוונא בריש הקומץ זוטא (דף טו·) ותמיה דמשמע התם לר"א דקנסא *הוא דעבד איסורא אפילו בשאר זרעים דרבנן כל שכן בתבואה דמדברי תורה ושמא הכא מדאורייתא פליגי ר' יוחנן ורבי אליעזר · כולי עלמא מודו שהאוסר נאסר משום דעבד מעשה בגפן חברו שזרע כרמו בשביעית שהכל הפקר ואינו חשוב כשלו ודוקא ענבים לא נאסרו אבל גפנים שהוסיפו מאתים אסורים שאין בזמורות הפקר והשתא קאמר למשמע מן הדא דפליגי במסכך גפנו של חברו על תבואתו של חברו דתבואה וענבים בשנה שביעית הכל הפקר וקא מותיב מינה רבי יוסי תיובתא לת"ק ש"מ דפליגי בה : ו קוצרו אפילו במועד · בירושלמי (הל' ד) כיני מתניתין מותר לקוצרו אפילו במועד ואע"ג דאינו אוסר דאין אדם אוסר דבר שאינו שלו : עד שליש · כדאמר רב הונא בפרק קמא דבבא קמא (דף ט:) במצוה עד שליש ופליגי הכא בירושלמי (שם) רב הונא ורב ששת חד אמר שליש לשכר וח"א שליש לדמים כלומר לשכר הראוי להם ומאן דאמר לדמים שנותן לפועלים שליש שוין של פירות שדה : קוצר כדרכו והולך אפי' לאחר המועד · ולא חיישי' משום משהה כלאים בכרם : מאימתי נקרא אנס.שנחשב כשלו לאסור : משישקע · אע"פ(א) שנאנסה כל זמן שנקראת על שם בעלים שאומר זהו שדה של פלוני אינו אוסר דבר שאינו שלו עד שישקע שם של בעלים ונקראת על שם האנס : ירושלמי (שם) א"ר אחא נשתקעו ולא נתייאשו איסורו דבר תורה נתייאשו ולא נשתקעו איסורו מדבריהן ויש קרקע נגזלת א"ר לא אעפ"כ יש יאוש לקרקע (ט) משמע לכאורה דמועיל יאוש בקרקע וא"א לומר כן דמוכח בריש לולב הגזול (דף ל·) דאמר להו רב נחמן להנהו אוונכרי כי זבניתו אסא מנכרים ליגזיז איניהו וליתבו לכו מאי טעמא סתם נכרים גזלי ארעתא דישראל וקרקע אינה נגזלת כי היכי דליהוו יאוש בידייהו דידהו ושינוי רשות בידא דידן ואי יאוש מועיל בקרקע למנ"מ במאי דאינה נגזלת אי קודם יאוש אפילו היתה נגזלת לא קני ואי לאחר יאוש הרי קונה ביאוש ועוד אמרי' בהסית שמעתא דפלוגתא דר"א ורבנן דפליגי בסוכה גזולה דמכשרי רבנן משום דקרקע אינה נגזלת והויא לה סוכה שאולה ואדם יוצא בה ידי חובתו בסוכתו של חבירו והשתא ה"ד אי לפני יאוש הא אפילו מטלטלין אין נגזלין אלא לאחר יאוש ומיהו אין משם ראיה דאם היתה סוכה מטלטלת כגון שהוציאו מסוכתו שבראש העגלה או בראש הספינה לא היה יוצא בה לא לפני יאוש ולא לאחר יאוש משום דממעטי' בפ"ק דסוכה (דף ט·) מדכתיב לך להוציא את הגזולה ולפני יאוש נמי לא חשיבא כשאולה דמטלטלין הנגזלין לאו ברשות בעלים קיימי אבל קרקע הנגזלת ברשות בעליה קיימא ויש לדקדק מהא דתניא בחזקת הבתים (דף מג:) מכר לו בית מכר לו שדה אין מעיד לו עליה מכר לו פרה מכר לו טלית מעיד לו עליה ומוקי לה בראובן שגזל שדה משמעון ומכרה ללוי ואתא יהודה וקמערער דלא ליזיל שמעון לאסהודי ללוי דניחא ליה דהדרא אבל פרה וטלית לא הדר דהוה ליה יאוש ושינוי רשות משמע בהדיא דבקרקע לא מהני יאוש וכי תימא משום דקסבר יאוש (ב) לא קני ושינוי רשות לא שייך בקרקע האי טעמא משום דיאוש לא קני משום דבאיסורא אתא לידיה כדמפרש במרובה (דף סו·) וה"נ גבי קרקע נתייאש קודם שהחזיק בה הלוקח כמו גבי פרה וטלית ולפיכך צריך לפרש הא דירושלמי הא דר' לא אמר אעפ"כ יש יאוש לקרקע דוקא לענין כלאים לאסור מדרבנן והכי קאמר נשתקעו הבעלים ולא נתייאשו איסורו דבר תורה דאם נשתקעו שם הבעלים מן השדה ונקרא על שם האנס אע"פ שלא נתייאשו הבעלים ולא אמרו ווי ליה לחסרון כיס אנן סהדי דמייאשי ואפילו עומד וצווח הוי כצווח על ספינתו שטבעה בים ואיתסרא מדאורייתא בזריעת האנס אבל נתייאשו ולא נשתקעו לא מיתסרא מדאורייתא דקרקע אינה נגזלת אבל מדרבנן אוסר ופריך ויש קרקע נגזלת כלומר אפילו מדרבנן ומשני דיש יאוש לאסור מדרבנן משום כלאים אבל מדאורייתא אין יאוש מדלא אסור מדאורייתא ומיהו הכא דנשתקעו שם הבעלים אפילו מדאורייתא יש יאוש מדהוי איסורו דבר תורה ועוד יש לפרש בענין אחר דנשתקעו הבעלים ולא נתייאשו איסורו ד"ת לא מחמת זריעת האנס קאמר אלא כשהלך לו האנס ונשאר הכרם לפני הבעלים ולא עקרו ממנו הכלאים והוסיף מאתים איסורו דבר תורה מחמת הבעלים שמקיימין כלאים בכרם דדידהו הוי כיון דלא נתייאשו אבל נתייאשו ולא נשתקעו דרבנן ואיכא פירכי טובא ללשון זה וראשון עיקר ובמסכת ערלה פרק קמא תניא בירושלמי (הל' ד) בשם ר' שמעון בן אלעזר נוטע לרבים חייב בנוטע בתוך שלו ברשות הרבים פטור בגזל קרקע ויש קרקע נגזלת א"ר אילא אע"פ שאין קרקע נגזלת יש יאוש לקרקע וכולהו מילתא תמיהא דהא מתני' דהתם קתני הגזלן שנטע חייב ותו מאי פריך בבריית' ויש קרקע נגזלת דמשמע משום דנגזלת ויש יאוש פטור מן הערלה אדרבה מכח זה יש לחייב כנוטע לתוך שלו ועוד הא [מדמה] נוטע לרשות הרבים לגזל קרקע ונטעה והיינו בלא יאוש דומיא דרשות הרבים דלא שייך בו (ג) יאוש ואם מתקנה הוא דיש יאוש צריך לאוקומא בשנשתקעו שם הבעלים : ז הרוח שעלעלה · שסיערה רוח תרגום רוח עלעולה : יגדור . יחתוך ואי גרסינן בדלי"ת הוי לשון גדר שעושה בין תבואה לגפנים : וכן בירק.אם נוטה תחת הגפן: יחזיר התבואה והירק למקומן ואינו מקדש ובירושלמי (הל"ה) תני ר"ע יחזיר בן עזאי אומר יספור כלומר גוזז במספרים כדתניא אין גוזזין את הירק בתספורת שלו : משתשליש · משתביא שליש אבל קודם לכן לא וירושלמי (שם) פליגי דרבי יוחנן תני משתשליש ורבי אושעיא אומר משתשריש : כפול הלבן . בירושלמי (שם) תני כיני מתני' אינן מתקדשין כלומר כיון דגמרו כל צורכן דשוב לא יוסיפו מאתים אבל מקדשין אחרים כגון סיכך ע"ג תבואה לחד נגמר כל צורכו וחד לא נגמר כל צורכו שהנגמר אוסר אותו שלא נגמר אם הוסיף מאתים ויש לתמוה דתבואה קודם שתשליש וענבים קודם פול הלבן נמי ליתסרו דכלאי הכרם נאסר בין עץ בין קשין כדאשכחן בפרק כל שעה (דף כו:) תנור שהסיקוהו בקליפי ערלה או בקשין של כלאי הכרם ותניא בתוספתא בפרק רביעי זמורה של גפן שהיתה מודלית אפילו היא מאה אמה כל הגפן כולה אסורה היא ופירותיה דהא דאמרי' בפ' האשה בכתובות (דף פ·) עבד רב יהודה עובדא בחבילי זמורות רב יהודה לטעמיה דאמר רב יהודה אכלה ערלה ושביעית וכלאים הרי זו חזקה התם בשהוסיף הפרי מאתים ולא הוסיף העץ שכן דרך בגפנים וקנים מיהו בזה יש לומר דלעולם קודם לכן מותר הכל [אבל] משתשליש וכפול הלבן הכל אסור אפילו זמורות וקשין אבל קשה דבפרק כל שעה* (דכ"ה·) משמע דמיתסרי אפילו בהשרשה ויש חילוק בין זרוע מעיקרו לזורע ובא כדדרש רבא בפרק כל שעה כתיב המלאה וכתיב הזרע הא כיצד זרוע מעיקרו בהשרשה זרוע ובא הוסיף אין לא הוסיף לא והשתא משמע בזרוע מעיקרו חטה ושעורה וחרצן הכל נאסר פרי עץ וקשין [וצ"ל דמתני'] דהכא בזרוע ובא כגון מעביר עציץ נקוב בכרם דכתיב המלאה ושליש בתבואה חשיב מלאה וכתיב ותבואת הכרם ובפחות מפול הלבן לא מקרי תבואת כרם והא דתניא בספרי בפרשת כי תצא המלאה הזרע מאימתי המלאה מתקדשת משתשריש וענבים משיעשו כפול הלבן התם בזורע בין הגפנים שהכרם נטוע כבר ולפיכך התבואה נאסרת בהשרשה ודריש ליה מהזרע וענבי הכרם לא מיתסרי עד שיהיו כפול הלבן דאז חשיבי פרי ותבואת הכרם איקרו ויתכן שהזמורות מיתסרי בתוספת מאתים דלדוקא בפרי הוא דכתב קרא דהא קתני התם אין לי אלא כרם שעושה פירות שאינו עושה פירות מניין ת"ל כרם מכל מקום מיהו איכא לאוקמיה לאסור את הזרעים אי נמי בזורע מעיקרו חטה ושעורה וחרצן והא דתנן לעיל בפרק ה' (משנה ז) עששים יופך אביב יגפן סביאה דגן תדלק דמשמע דאביב *בעששים לא מיתסרי עד שתביא דגן דהייט

מסורת הש"ס

א) יבמות פ"ח דף פג. ובבא קמא פ"ט דף ק.

פי' מהר"י בן מלכי צדק

שהוצאת ד' אמות לעבודת הכרם מיכן וד' אמות לעבודת הכרם מיכן נשארו ז' אמות ואמר לא יביא ואם הביא לא קידש [וכן] מותר [מחול] הכרם ז' אמות שמי"א אמות כשתקח ד' אמות לעבודה ישארו ז' אמות [ותנן דלא יביא] ואמר לך דאם הביא לא קידש : מותר אפיפירות . פירוש האפיפירות דתנן המדלה את הגפן על מקצת אפיפירות לא יביא זרע אל המותר וגרסינן עלה עד איכן א"ר אחא בשם ריש לקיש עד ששה ספחים וזה מאי דסבירא לן . אבל בירושלמי אמרינן מותר מחול הכרם ד' אמות מותר חורבן הכרם ארבע אמות מותר פיסקי ערים ששה ספחים מותר אפיפירות ו' ספחים וכסבורין אנחנו דגמ' משבשתא היא ובין ז' לד' איחלף ובין ספח לאמות איחלף. ויש לתרץ הירושלמי מותר מחול הכרם מד' אמות ואילך וכן מותר חרבן הכרם מד' אמות ואילך יקרא מותר מותר פיסקי ערים מו' ספחים ואילך [יקרא] מותר אפיפירות משששה ספחים ואילך [יקרא מותר] שד' אמות דמחול ודחורבן מיקרי עבודת הכרם ומיכן ואילך יקראו מותר ו"ס דערים ואפיפירות מיקרי עבודת הגפן ומיכן ואילך מיקרי מותר וזהו כפי' שפירשנו ולא תיזוז מינה : אבל תחת הגפן·פי' כגון שנמשכה הזמורה ח' אמות אמה אחת לעבודתה לכל רוח ותחת כל ז' האמו' נקרא תחת הגפן ואם זרע תחתיה מקדש . אבל מצדדי הזמורה מכאן ומכאן שרי : ועבודת הגפן. פי' ששה ספחים וכר' עקיבא ג'.וד' אמות שבכרם הרי אלו מקדשין הגפנין כדתנן [לעיל בפ"ד מ"ה] לפיכך הזורע ד' אמות שבכרם קידש שתי שורות : ד ה ו המסכך את נפנו על גבי תבואתו וכו' וחייב באחריותו.פי' לשלם התבואה : ז ואם אירעו אונס.פי' אבל או שהטעוהו פועלין מותר : תבואה שהיא נוטה תחת הגפן וכן בירק אם נוטה תחת הגפן מחזיר . פירוש מחזיר מתבואה והירק למקומן ואינו מקדש : מאימתי תבואה מתקדשת משתשליש . ואית תני משתשריש : וענבים משיעשו כפול הלבן . מנלן דכתיב ותבואת הכרם :

*נ"ל ועששים

עין משפט נר מצוה

ט א ב מיי' פ"ו שם הלכה יג טוש"ע שם סעיף כז :
י ג ד מיי' פ"ה מהל' כלאים הל"ח טור שו"ע שם סעיף ד :
יא ה מיי' שם הלכה יג וטור שו"ע שם סעיף ח :
יב ו מיי' פ"ה מהל' כלאים הלכה יא טוש"ע יו"ד סי' רצו סעיף ז :
יג ז מיי' פ"ה שם הלכה יא טוש"ע שם סעיף סה :
יד ח מיי' שם הלכה יג וטוש"ע שם סעיף ע :
טו ט מיי' פ"ה שם הלכה יג :

פירוש הרא"ש

(ח) אע"פ שאינו דבר האבוד דאין אדם אוסר דבר שאינו שלו מפני מראית עין התירו לקוצרה שלא יהא נראה כמקיים כלאים ונ"ל דמיירי באותו ענין שלא יוסיף מאתים במועד דאי לאו הכי הוי דבר האבוד אע"ג דאין אדם אוסר דבר שאינו שלו כיון שחוזרה לבעלים אם הוסיפה מאתים לפניו קדוש דלא גרע מלכשאחזור אלקטנו או כסערתו הרוח : (ט) נ"ל הא דקאמר רבי לא יש יאוש לקרקע לאו דוקא יאוש דאי יש יאוש לקרקע אמאי קאמר נתייאשו ולא נשתקעו אסורים מדבריהם כיון דיש יאוש לקרקע יאסור מן התורה אלא ה"ק יש שיקוע לקרקע ואפי' לא נתייאשו הבעלים שלא אמרו ווי לחסרון כיס כ"ל כצווח על ביתו שנפל ועל ספינתו שטבעה בים ה"נ כיון שנשתקע שם הבעלים ממש ונקראת על שם האנס בודאי לא תחזור עוד ואפי' מלפה הוא שתחזור לו אוסרה האנס דבר תורה אבל יאוש בלא שיקוע לא קנה וכהכי רויחן כמה שמועו' בתלמוד דמוכחי דיאוש לא מהני בקרקע בפרק לולב הגזול ובחזקת הבתים : (י) אם לא יחזור והא דאמרינן לעיל תחת הגפן אוסר ומקדש היינו כשעיקר התבואה תחת הגפן כמו המסכך גפנו ע"ג תבואות חבירו אבל הכא עיקר התבואה עומדת חוץ לגפן ונוטה תחת הגפן :

הגהות הב"ח

פ"ז (א) מ"ו ברא"ש משישקע דאע"פ וכו' א"ר לוי אע"פ וכו' וקרקע אינה נגזלת הלכך ליגזוז איניהו כי היכי דליהוו יאוש בעלים בידייהו דידהו : (ב) דקסבר יאוש כדי לא קני וכו' גבי קרקע כבר נתייאש וכו' הא דירושלמי דהא דאמר רבי לא אעפ"כ יש יאוש : (ג) דלא שייך בו יאוש ואם מסקנא היא דיש וכו' בשנשתקעו שם הבעלים הס"ד : (ד) משנה ז ברמ"ם המלאה הזרע אשר תזרע ותבואת הכרם וצריך שיהיה :

הגהות מהר"י לנדא

א] מ"ג בר"ש אם אין שם ח' אמות ועוד כצ"ל :

דהיינו שליש ובזרוע מעיקרו איירי הא איפליגו בה ר' יוחנן ור' הושעיא בירושלמי (הלכה ד) כדפרשינן שם ורבי הושעיא דשרי היכי מוקי [הא] דזרוע מעיקרו בהשרשה [וי"ל] בשנזרעו שניהן באיסור הכרם והתבואה שניהן יחד אבל אם קדש זה את זה דהוי ראשון בסיתר ושני באיסור רבי הושעיא מדמי לה לשניהן בהיתר כגון מעביר עציץ נקוב בכרם לתבואה עד שתשליש וענבים כפול הלבן ורבי יוחנן מדמי לה לשניהן באיסור ההוא דבתרא לכל הפחות מיתסרא בהשרשה הואיל ותחלתן באיסור ויתכן דזמורות וקשין לא מיתסרי אלא בזרוע מעיקרו אבל זרוע ובא לא אסר הכתוב אלא מלאה ותבואת כרם וכל שכן דניחא ספי ההיא דכתובות רב יהודה למעמיה והא דתני

בהקומץ זוטא (דף פו.) באחד שזרע כרמו של חברו סמדר ואסרו את הזרעים והתירו הגפנים לא אצטריך לאשמעינן משום זמורות אלא משום ענבים שבגפנים והא דאסרינן בכל דוכתי הוסיף מאתים אי זרוע מעיקרו דינו בהשרשה ואי בזרוע ובא הוא עד שתשליש וכפול הלבן נמצא דלא משכחת לה אלא בשהביא שליש ופול הלבן בהיתר ואחר שנעשה כלאי הכרם הוסיף מאתים: ירושלמי (שם) אית תנאי תנו משתשליש ואית תנאי תנו משתשרש מ"ד משתשרש מסייע לר' יוחנן מ"ד משהשליש מסייע ליה לר' הושעיא כתבתיה לעיל בפ"ה מ"ד משתשרש שנאסר הכל בהשרשה מסייע לר' יוחנן דאמר בפ"ה הכל אסור אף העשבים קודם שיבא בהן זרע ומאן דאמר משתשליש מסייע לרבי הושעיא דאמר בפרק ה' דלא מיתסר הכל עד שיביא שליש ומיהו לר' יוחנן נמי מיתוקמא דאפילו הוסיף מאתים לא מיתסר עד שיביא שליש: ח עציץ נקוב. המונח בכרם או בד' אמות של עבודת הכרם וזרע בתוכו מקדש כאילו זרע בארץ אבל שאינו נקוב לא ובנקוב בשורש קטן כדאמר בסוף המלניע (דף לה:) אוסרין ולא מקדשין כלומר לא יביא זרע לתוכן ואם הביא לא קידש דנקוב לר' שמעון כשאינו נקוב משוי ליה אף לענין תולש בשבת חוץ לענין הכשר זרעים כדאמרינן בסוף המלניע (שם): אם הוסיף מאתים. שיש באיסור אחד ממאתים של היתר אסור: ירושלמי (הל' ו) שמואל אמר במעביר תחת כל נפן וגפן ור' יוחנן אמר לאויר עשרה היא מתני' העביר ה' עלילין

כל צרכן אינן מתקדשות: ח עציץ נקוב מקדש בכרם ושאינו נקוב אינו מקדש ור' שמעון אומר זה וזה אוסרין ולא מקדשין המעביר ה) עציץ נקוב בכרם אם הוסיף במאתים אסור:

פרק שמיני

א כלאי הכרם אסורין מלזרוע ו) ולקיים ואסורין בהנאה כלאי זרעים אסורין מלזרוע ומלקיים ומותרין באכילה וכל שכן בהנאה כלאי בגדים מותרין בכל דבר ואינן אסורין אלא מללבוש כלאי בהמה מותרין לגדל ולקיים ואינן אסורין אלא מלהרביע כלאי בהמה אסורין זה עם זה: ב בהמה עם בהמה וחיה עם חיה בהמה עם חיה וחיה עם בהמה טמאה עם טמאה וטהורה עם טהורה טמאה עם טהורה וטהורה עם טמאה אסורין לחרוש ולמשוך ולהנהיג: ג המנהיג ג) סופג את הארבעים והיושב בקרון סופג את הארבעים ר' מאיר פוטר והשלישית שהיא קשורה לרצועות אסורה: ד אין קושרין את הסוס לא לצדדי הקרון ולא לאחר הקרון ולא את הלובדקים לגמלים ר' יהודה אומר ד) כל הנולדים מן הסוס אף על פי שאביהן חמור מותרין זה עם זה וכן הנולדים מן החמור אע"פ שאביהם סוס מותרים זה עם זה אבל הנולדים מן הסוס עם הנולדים

ומלאת זרע אלא ענבים וחטים: ח כבר הקדמנו לדבר בעציץ נקוב בפ"ה ממס' (מ"ו) דמאי ופירשנו שם דינו והקדמנו כמו כן היאך נוכל לדעת אם הוסיף חלק ממאתים בפ"ה (מ"ו) מן המסכתא הזאת ושאמר אם הוסיף במאתים אסור על תנאי חכרו אותו בגמ' והוא שאמרו ובלבד שיניחהו תחת הגפן ואין הלכה כר"ש: א אמר הכתוב בכלאי הכרם פן תקדש (דברים כב) יבא בקבלה פן תקדש תוקד אש ר"ל לשרפם ולא יהנה בהם: ופי' מלהרביע הוא להרכיב זכר על נקבה ויכנים כמכחול בשפופרת ואז ילקה: ומה שאמר כלאי בהמה אסורין זה עם זה ר"ל שאסור הרבעת הבהמות שהם מורכבות מב' מינין אלו עם אלו כגון שירכיב פרד על סוסיא כמו שיתבאר בפרק שאחר זה: ב כשאמר כלאי בהמה אין אסורין אלא מלהרביע אמר שאינו זה אלא לבהמה עם בהמה או חיה עם חיה ושאר מה שיסדר אבל בהמה טמאה עם טהורה וטהורה עם טמאה יש בה תוספת על איסור ההרבעה והוא שהם אסורין לחרוש ולמשוך ולהנהיג ולחרוש הוא שיחרוש בהם יחדיו בעול אחד ולמשוך בהם העגלה או האבן או כדומה לו ולהנהיג שיקשרם ביחד ויוליכם וזה ענין שאה"כ (שם) לא תחרוש בשור ובחמור יחדיו ואמרו

WHICH HAVE BECOME FULLY RIPE,[2] ARE NOT LIABLE TO BE CONDEMNED [AS KIL'AYIM].

MISHNAH 8. [SEED SOWN IN A] PERFORATED FLOWER-POT,[3] CREATES A STATE OF CONDEMNATION [AS KIL'AYIM] IN A VINEYARD;[4] [IN] ONE NOT PERFORATED, IT DOES NOT CREATE A STATE OF CONDEMNATION.[5] R. SIMEON, HOWEVER, SAID: [THE SOWING OF SEED IN] EITHER ONE OR THE OTHER IS PROHIBITED, BUT IT DOES NOT [IN THE EVENT] CREATE A STATE OF CONDEMNATION. IF ONE CARRIES A PERFORATED FLOWER-POT THROUGH A VINEYARD, THEN IF [THAT WHICH IS SOWN THEREIN] HAS GROWN A TWO-HUNDREDTH PART,[6] IT IS FORBIDDEN.[7]

CHAPTER VIII

MISHNAH 1. KIL'AYIM OF THE VINEYARD IT IS FORBIDDEN EITHER TO SOW OR TO SUFFER TO GROW; IT IS, MOREOVER,
a FORBIDDEN TO DERIVE USE THEREFROM.[1] KIL'AYIM OF 'SEEDS'[2] IT IS PROHIBITED EITHER TO SOW[3] OR TO SUFFER TO GROW;[3] BUT IT IS PERMITTED TO CONSUME IT, AND, SO MUCH THE MORE, TO DERIVE USE THEREFROM. KIL'AYIM OF CLOTHING MATERIALS IS PERMITTED IN ALL RESPECTS, EXCEPT THAT THE WEARING THEREOF [ALONE] IS FORBIDDEN.[4] KIL'AYIM OF CATTLE IT IS PERMITTED TO REAR AND TO KEEP,[5] THE DELIBERATE CROSS-BREEDING [PRODUCING SUCH] BEING ALONE PROHIBITED. [THE DELIBERATE MATING, OR YOKING TOGETHER OF] ONE KIND OF KIL'AYIM OF CATTLE WITH ANOTHER[6] IS PROHIBITED.[7]

MISHNAH 2. IT IS PROHIBITED TO USE A BEHEMAH[8] WITH A BEHEMAH [OF ANOTHER SPECIES], OR A ḤAYYAH[9] WITH A ḤAYYAH [OF ANOTHER SPECIES], OR A BEHEMAH WITH A ḤAYYAH, OR A ḤAYYAH WITH A BEHEMAH, OR AN UNCLEAN BEAST WITH AN UNCLEAN BEAST [OF ANOTHER SPECIES], OR A CLEAN BEAST WITH A CLEAN BEAST [OF ANOTHER SPECIES], OR AN UNCLEAN BEAST WITH A CLEAN BEAST, OR A CLEAN
b BEAST WITH AN UNCLEAN BEAST,[1] FOR PLOUGHING OR FOR TRACTION, OR TO LEAD THEM [TIED TOGETHER].[2]

MISHNAH 3. THE PERSON DRIVING[3] RECEIVES THE FORTY [LASHES],[4] AND THE PERSON SITTING IN THE WAGON RECEIVES THE FORTY [LASHES],[5] BUT R. MEIR EXEMPTS [THE LATTER].[6] [THE TYING OF] A THIRD [ANIMAL HETEROGENEOUS TO TWO ALREADY HARNESSED TO A WAGON] TO THE STRAPS [OF THOSE ANIMALS][7] IS PROHIBITED.

MISHNAH 4. IT IS PROHIBITED TO TIE A HORSE EITHER TO THE SIDES OF A WAGON [DRAWN BY OXEN] OR BEHIND THE WAGON,[8] OR [TO TIE] A LIBYAN ASS TO [THE SIDES OF, OR BEHIND, A WAGON DRAWN BY] CAMELS.[9] R. JUDAH SAID: ALL [MULES] BORN FROM MARES, NOTWITHSTANDING THAT THEIR SIRES WERE ASSES, ARE PERMITTED ONE WITH AN-
c OTHER;[1] LIKEWISE [MULES] BORN FROM SHE-ASSES, NOTWITHSTANDING THAT THEIR SIRES WERE HORSES, ARE PERMITTED ONE WITH ANOTHER;[1] BUT [MULES] BORN FROM MARES WITH

(2) After this the expression *'produce of the vineyard'* is no longer applied; (the term is just: 'grapes', Maim.). (3) The hole being sufficient to permit a thin root to go through. (4) Or within its four cubits service-border, just as if it had been sown in the soil of the vineyard itself; if the flower-pot stayed there long enough for the seed in it to grow a two-hundredth part of its normally possible full size. (5) Since the earth in the flower-pot is not exposed towards the soil of the vineyard or of its service-border. (6) Of its possible full size. For the method of calculating this, v. *supra* V, 6, notes. (7) The seed; but since the flower-pot had not been set down on the ground, the vines are not affected. Maim. understands this passage thus: Carrying a perforated flower-pot across a vineyard, if in the course of transit it could grow a two-hundredth part, is prohibited (*Yad. Hil. Kil'ayim* V, 23). It seems that according to Maim. it is prohibited *ab initio* to do this, but that in the event the seed does not thereby become forbidden.

a (1) According to *supra* V, 7, it should be burnt. (2) Including grain and vegetables. (3) Only in the Holy Land. (4) V. Lev. XIX, 19 and Deut. XXII, 11. (5) For one's use. It was necessary for the Mishnah to mention both 'rear' and 'keep'. If the former only had been mentioned one might have thought that whilst rearing was permitted, it was forbidden to use the animal. If the latter only had been mentioned one might have thought that one may use such an animal only when it had been reared by a non-Israelite. (6) E.g., the sire of one having been a horse, and of the other, an ass. (7) The prohibition applies to any two *kil'ayim* offspring of cattle which are unlike in respect of ears, tail and the sound emitted by them. (8) The word rendered in E.V. *'cattle'*; it is, however, used also for an individual piece of cattle and denotes a domestic, mostly horned, animal. (9) (One of the) animals of chase. Cf. *supra* I, 6. Scripture forbids ploughing with an ox and an ass together (Deut. XXII, 10), but on analogy with the prohibition of suffering one's animals to work on the Sabbath, this prohibition is understood as applying to any two animals of diverse species and likewise to birds.

b (1) The repetition of 'A with B, or B with A' in all these instances is for the purpose of making it clear that the prohibition applies whether animal A is the principal factor in the case and B secondary, or *vice-versa*. (2) Ploughing is expressly forbidden in Scripture, v. Deut. loc. cit.; the Rabbis extend the prohibition to all forms of traction and load-carrying, as well as to tying them together even if it be for the purpose only of leading them, without their drawing or carrying a load. T.J. discusses whether leading them together by means of the driver's call is also prohibited. According to T.B., B.M. 9a it would appear that 'drawing' (מושך) and 'leading' (מנהיג) are synonymous terms, the first being used in connection with camels and the latter with asses. (3) Lit., 'leading', *sc.* two heterogeneous animals. (4) Prescribed as the penalty for the transgression of a negative precept (v. Deut, XXV, 3). (5) Since it is on his account that the wagon is being drawn. (6) On the ground that he takes no active part in the driving. (7) I.e., even though not to the wagon itself. Maim. (in his commentary) renders: 'Sitting in a third wagon tied to the straps of a second which is attached to the first wagon'. (8) Since the horse assists in some measure in the propelling of the vehicle. (9) One would think that an ass can make no appreciable difference to the propelling of the wagon already drawn by camels, since the latter are so much the stronger. The Libyan ass, however, was of a heftier species approximately to the camel, and would, when tied even to a camel-drawn vehicle, help in pulling it.

c (1) Since their sires and dams respectively were, in each case, of the same species.

[MULES] BORN FROM SHE-ASSES ARE PROHIBITED ONE WITH ANOTHER.[2]

MISHNAH 5. MULES OF UNCERTAIN PARENTAGE[3] ARE FORBIDDEN ONE WITH ANOTHER, BUT A RAMMAK [A MULE WHOSE DAM IS KNOWN TO HAVE BEEN A MARE] IS PERMITTED [WITH ANOTHER RAMMAK].[4] WILD MAN-LIKE CREATURES[5] ARE DEEMED AS BELONGING TO THE CATEGORY OF ḤAYYAH.[6] R. JOSE SAID: [WHEN DEAD] THEY [OR PART OF THEIR CORPSES] COMMUNICATE UNCLEANNESS [TO MEN AND TO OBJECTS SUSCEPTIBLE THERETO WHICH ARE] UNDER THE SAME ROOF,[7] AS DOES [THE CORPSE OF] A HUMAN BEING.[8] THE HEDGEHOG AND THE MOLE[9] OF THE BUSHES BELONG TO THE CATEGORY OF ḤAYYAH.[10] AS FOR A MOLE, R. JOSE SAID IN THE NAME OF BETH SHAMMAI: AN OLIVE'S SIZE [OF ITS CARCASE] RENDERS A PERSON CARRYING IT UNCLEAN, AND A LENTIL'S SIZE
a THEREOF RENDERS A PERSON TOUCHING IT UNCLEAN.[1]

MISHNAH 6. THE WILD OX BELONGS TO THE CATEGORY OF BEHEMAH,[2] BUT R. JOSE SAID: TO THE CATEGORY OF ḤAYYAH.[3] THE DOG BELONGS TO THE CATEGORY OF ḤAYYAH,[4] BUT R. MEIR SAID: TO THE CATEGORY OF BEHEMAH.[4] THE SWINE BELONGS TO THE CATEGORY OF BEHEMAH; THE WILD ASS TO THAT OF ḤAYYAH,[5] THE ELEPHANT AND THE APE TO THAT OF ḤAYYAH.[4] A HUMAN BEING IS PERMITTED TO DRAW, PLOUGH, OR LEAD WITH ANY OF THEM.[6]

CHAPTER IX

MISHNAH 1. NO [CLOTHING MATERIAL] IS FORBIDDEN ON ACCOUNT OF KIL'AYIM EXCEPT [A MIXTURE OF] WOOL
b AND LINEN.[1] NO [CLOTHING MATERIAL] IS SUBJECT TO UNCLEANNESS BY LEPROSY EXCEPT [SUCH AS IS MADE OF] WOOL OR LINEN.[2] PRIESTS DON FOR SERVICE IN THE SANCTUARY, NONE BUT [GARMENTS OF] WOOL AND LINEN.[3] IF ONE HAS HACKLED TOGETHER CAMEL'S WOOL WITH SHEEP'S WOOL, IF THE GREATER PART BE CAMEL'S WOOL, IT IS PERMITTED [TO MIX LINEN THEREWITH];[4] IF THE GREATER PART BE SHEEP'S WOOL, IT IS FORBIDDEN; IF IT IS HALF AND HALF, IT IS FORBIDDEN. THE SAME APPLIES TO HEMP AND LINEN HACKLED TOGETHER.

(2) *Sc.*, for purposes of cross-breeding or use, but one is not liable to lashes. On the other hand if their respective sires were of the same species and not their dams, transgression of the prohibition is punishable by lashes. (3) In the case of these mules it is impossible, when they are young, to recognize whether its sire belonged to the horses and its dam to the asses, or *vice-versa*. (4) L., 'with other horses'. (5) אדני השדה. Perhaps a chimpanzee or gorilla. Another reading אדמי (? constr. pl. of אדם, 'man'). Some versions, אבני השדה. Cf. Rashi to Job. V, 23. T.J. renders בר נש דטורא 'man of the mountain' in connection with which Kohut suggests that the reading must be supposed to have been ארני (a fem. sing. adjective from the noun ὄρος 'mountain'). (6) And are subject to the same laws re yoking etc., together as a *ḥayyah*. Cf. *supra* 2, n. 9. (7) V. Num. XIX, 14. Cf. Oh. II, 1. (8) Which means that the creatures referred to are deemed as belonging to the human species, and not to the category of *ḥayyah*, and therefore, not subject to the laws applying to a *ḥayyah* in respect of yoking etc., together with other animals. (9) Or, weasel. (10) In respect of the laws of uncleanness.

a (1) V. B. K. 80*a*. If the mole (or weasel) חולדת הסנים is identical with חלד of Lev. XI, 23, it is a שרץ, 'a creeping thing', a lentil's-size thereof renders unclean by contact, not by carrying; if it is a *ḥayyah*, an olive's-size thereof renders a person carrying it unclean. As there is doubt as to which category the mole belongs, both disabilities attach thereto. (2) On the assumption that its origin is domestic. As a *behemah*, its *ḥeleb* (fat v. Glos.) is prohibited and when it is slaughtered its blood does not require covering with earth. (3) His assumption being that its origin is wild. As a *ḥayyah*, its *ḥeleb* is permitted, and its blood requires covering. (4) The matter is of practical importance in the event of a person entering into a contract to sell all his *ḥayyah*, or all his *behemah*. (5) And is therefore forbidden with a domestic ass. (6) I.e., a human being may pull a vehicle-drawing (or load-carrying) animal by the bridle, help to propel and guide a plough drawn by an animal, and walk beside an animal attached to him by a rope.

b (1) Termed *sha'aṭnez* cf. *infra* 8. V. Lev. XIX, 19 and, more explicitly, Deut. XXII, 11. Wool for the purpose of this prohibition, is only sheep's wool, since from II Kings III, 4 it is apparent that צמר (*zemer*) 'wool' without any qualifying description, means, sheep's wool. (2) V. Lev. XIII, 47ff. This is taken to apply only to undyed wool or linen. With regard to *kil'ayim*, however, there is no difference whether these be dyed or undyed. (3) The priestly garments were made of byssus (fine linen) and wool dyed blue-purple, red-purple and crimson. V. Ex. XXVIII, 4-8, XXXIX, 1. (4) The permission applies only when the two kinds of wool have been well mixed together e.g., by hackling or combing or crushing; but if a piece of cloth of camel's wool has one distinct thread of sheep's wool drawn through it, it is not permitted to draw a linen thread through the material.

ה פרוטיות · מין פרדות הן ואין אדם יכול לברר בהן על ידי הסימנים [האמורים בפרק] דאותו ואת בנו (דף עט.) אי זה מהן אמו חמור ואי זה מהם אמו סוס דלא מינכר בהו ולכך אסורים זה עם זה: הרמך מותר · *בכולן מין אחד דכתיב בני הרמכים (אסתר ח): מטמא באהל כאדם: ירושלמי (הל' ד') אמר רבי חמא ברבי עוקבא בשם רבי יוסי ברבי חנינא טעמא דרבי יוסי וכל אשר יגע על פני השדה (במדבר יט) בגדל מן השדה כלומר מין אדם הוא א"ר בר כה דסור הוא והוא חיי מסיבורא פסק טיבורא לא חיי ושמעתי בשם הר' מאיר ברבי קלונימוס מאספירא שהיא חיה שמה ידוע והיא ידעוני דקרא ומעלם שלה

מחמור אסורין זה עם זה: ה הפרוטיות אסורות *והרמך מותר (ג) *ואדני השדה חיה רבי יוסי אומר מטמאות באהל כאדם (ד)הקופד וחולדת הסניים חיה חולדת הסניים ר' יוסי אומר ב"ש אומרים מטמא כזית במשא וכעדשה במגע: ו ב'שור בר א) מין בהמה ור' יוסי אומר מין חיה כלב מין חיה ר' מאיר אומר מין בהמה חזיר מין בהמה ערוד מין חיה הפיל והקוף מין חיה ג) ג'ואדם מותר עם כולם למשוך ולחרוש ולהנהיג:

פרק תשיעי

א אין ד'אסור משום כלאים אלא צמר ופשתים ה'ואינו ג) מטמא בנגעים אלא צמר ופשתים ו'אין הכהנים לובשין לשמש בבית המקדש אלא צמר ופשתים ז'צמר גמלים וצמר רחלים שטרפן זה בזה אם רוב מן הגמלים מותר ואם רוב מן הרחלים אסור מחצה על מחצה אסור וכן הפשתן והקנבוס שטרפן זה בזה:

השירים

...בו דרכים שאינו שוה לא לחיה ולא לבהמה דברי הכל ולא פליגי בהו בית שמאי וב"ה אבל שאר תנאי פליגי באנדרוגינוס בפרק הערל ובכוי בפרק אותו ואת בנו: ו שור בר · מין בהמה ולרבי יוסי מין חיה וחלבו אסור ולרבי מאיר חלבו מותר ומפרש בירושלמי (שם) רבנן אמרי מכאן הוה וערק לתמן ור' יוסי אמר עיקרו מן תמן הוה ואע"ג דמפרש תמן באלו טרפות (דף נט.) אלו הן סימני חיה כל הנהו סימנים נאמרו בשור חוץ מן השור הבר: כלב מין חיה· בתוספתא קתני מה הפרש יש בין רבי מאיר לחכמים אלא שהכותב חייתו לבנו רבי מאיר אומר כתב לו כלב וחכמים אומרים לא כתב לו כלב ועוד נפקא מינה לענין מקדיש חייתו דכיולא בה אשכחן בפרק ב' דנדרים (דף יח:) גבי כוי דמקדיש חייתו ובהמתו הקדיש את הכוי ר' אליעזר אומר לא הקדיש את הכוי: ואדם מותר בכולן· בספרי דריש בפ' כי תצא אם כן למה נאמר בשור ובחמור אי אתה חורש אבל אתה חורש באדם ובהמה: תניא בתורת כהנים כל הולך על כפיו זה הקוף כל הולך להביא את הקופד וחולדת הסנאין ואדני השדה וכלב הים אין לי אלא חיה טהורה ג] חיה טמאה מנין תלמוד לומר ההולכת על ארבע לכל החיה להביא את הפיל: תניא בתוספתא (פ"א) חמשה דברים נאמרו בשור הבר אסור משום אותו ואת בנו וחלבו אסור וקרב לגבי המזבח וחייב במתנות וניקח בכסף מעשר לזבחי שלמים אבל לא לבשר תאוה ד] ר' יוסי אומר זהו תאו האמור בתורה ומותר משום אותו ואת בנו וחלבו מותר ואסור לגבי המזבח ופטור מן המתנות וניקח בכסף מעשר לבשר תאוה אבל לא לזבחי שלמים והרי הוא כחיה לכל דבר וחכ"א תאו בריה לעצמה · פי' לכל דבר לרבות כסוי הדם ולענין כותב אדם חייתו או בהמתו לבנו: ירושלמי (הל' ד) [תנא] הא שור עם שור הבר אינן כלאים דלא כרבי יוסי דאמר כלאים ומי שמתרגם [תאו] ותור ברא אמר כר' יוסי:

א ירושלמי (הל' א) כתיב (דברים כב) לא תלבש שעטנז צמר ופשתים יחדו הייתי אומר אינו אסור אלא מללבוש ת"ל (ויקרא יט) לא יעלה עליך אי לא יעלה עליך הייתי אומר לא יפשיל הקופה לאחריו ת"ל לא תלבש מה מלבוש דבר שהוא מהנה הגוף אף אין לי אלא דבר שהוא מהנה הגוף לאיזה דבר נאמר לא יעלה עליך ר' יונה בשם רבי זירא שאם היה בגד גדול מקצתו יש בו כלאים ומונח לארץ ומקצתו אין בו לא יתכסה בו מלד שני אי פשתים הייתי אומר פשתים שלם [כ"א של ים] או קנבוס ת"ל צמר מה צמר שאין לו שם לווי אף פשתן שאין לו שם לווי [מנין שאין לו שם לווי] אמר ריב"ל כתיב (מלכים ב ג) ומישע מלך מואב היה נוקד מהו נוקד רועה והשיב למלך ישראל מאה אלף כרים ומאה אלף אילים צמר אין לך קרוי צמר אלא צמר אילים: ואינו מטמא בנגעים אלא צמר ופשתים · דכתיב (ויקרא יג) בבגד צמר או בבגד פשתים יכול יהו מטמאים בנגעים בין צבועים בין שאינם צבועים ת"ל בגד צמר או בגד פשתים מה פשתים כברייתה אף צמר כברייתה אוציא הצבוע בידי אדם ולא אוציא צבוע בידי שמים ת"ל לפשתים ולצמר מה פשתים לבנה אף צמר לבנה (לשון הירושלמי שם) תניין תרתי כללי ולא דמיין דין לדין תנינן אין אסור משום כלאים אלא צמר ופשתים בין צבועין בין אינן צבועין ותנינן אינו מטמא בנגעים אלא צמר ופשתן ובלבד לבנים ר' יונה בורלאה בעי קומי ר' מונא תמן את אמר בין צבעים בין לבנים וכה את אמר ובלבד לבנים א"ל שנייה היא ששנה עליו הכתוב צמר צמר [ב' פעמים] מה (א) צמר כברייתה אף (ב) פשתים כברייתה: ואין הכהנים לובשים לשמש בבית המקדש אלא צמר ופשתים · א"ר זעירא כתיב (שם טז) בד קודש ילבש בד שעולה יחידי והרי צמר עולה יחידי פירשו בקבלה (יחזקאל מד) לא יעלה עליהם צמר בשרתם בשערי החצר הפנימית וביתה הא מבחוץ מותר להעלות עליהן ומנין שמותרין בכלאים דכתיב (שמות לט) ואת המצנפת שש ואת פארי המגבעות שש ואת מכנסי הבד שש משזר ואת האבנט שש משזר תכלת וארגמן וכתיב (יחזקאל מד) פארי פשתים יהיו על ראשם ומכנסי פשתים יהיו על מתניהם לא יחגרו ביזע את דורש שם משם שם מפארי ופארי מפארי · פי' פשתים שלם או קנבוס יש מין א' שקרוי פשתים שלם ומין אחר שנקרא פשתים קנבוס ואין נקראין פשתים סתם לעולם וממעט להו משום דיש להם שם לווי לבוע בידי שמים כגון רחלים שחורות בד שעולה יחידי קנה יחידי מכל גרגר ואין ב' קנים עולין מגרעין א' ואף האמר עולה יחידי כל נימא נימא לבדה ולהכי פריך והרי צמר עולה יחידי ובפ"ב דזבחים (דף יח:) שיגויא אחרינא את דורש (ג) שש משזר כלומר משש דאבנט מה להלן היה תכלת אף כאן תכלת ושש מפארי דידה ופארי מפארי פשתים ומיהו אי אפשר לומר כן דבהדיא מוכח בפ"ק דיומא (דף יב:) דלא הוה כלאים בד' בגדים אלא באבנט דתניא אין בין כהן גדול לכהן הדיוט אלא אבנט דברי רבי ומפרש התם דאיירי בכ"ג ביוה"כ ומשמש בבגדי לבן בפנים שכולן של בד ואית דמפרש לעולם בשאר ימות השנה ובהנך (ד) דשרו ויש לפרש דיליף שש דאבנט שהוא פשתן משש דמגבעות ושש דמגבעות מפארי שעמו ופארי דמגבעות מפארי פשתים ילבשו דכתיב בהדיא פשתים: אם רוב מן הגמלים מותר · נערב עמהם פשתן: וכן הפשתן והקנבוס שטרפן זה בזה · דאם רוב קנבוס מותר לטרוף עמהן צמר: תניא בתוספתא (ה) בזמן שהביא פשתן וטרף עמהן וטרפן זה בזה אבל העושה חלוק מצמר גמלים כולו או כולו צמר ארנבים וארג בו חוט אחד של צמר בצד זה וחוט אחד של פשתן בצד זה אסור · פי' כשבאו החוטים של צמר ושל פשתן זה אצל זה אבל אם זה

(א) פשתים כצ"ל. (ב) צמר כצ"ל. (ג) משש כצ"ל. (ד) [הגירסא לפנינו דשוין]. (ה) [(פ"ד) ואינה לפנינו כמו שהביאה הר"ש ז"ל].

בלד אחד של חלוק שכולו צמר גמלים וזה בלד אחר מותר : ב השיראין · מפרש בירושלמי (שם) מטכסא (א) : הכלך אלבין קסרי אמר רשב"ג חזרתי על כל מפרשי הים ואמרו לי כולכא שמו ובריש במה מדליקין (כח:) משמע דכלך היינו מטכסא ואית דקרי לה שירא פרנדא : אבל אסורין משום מראית העין · דלמי לצמר ופשתים ואין לאסור אותן צלאות שמשימין בסרבל של צמר שהן של משי דהיינו שיראין בעל כורחין* אותן בגדים של משי אין זה שיראין שבגמרא שהרי מצוין בינינו הרבה ושיראין אינן מצויין מדבעי למימר בריש במה מדליקין (שם) דשיראין היינו שירא פרנדא ובשילהי סוטה (מח:) אמרינן מחרב בית המקדש בטלה שירא פרנדא וזכוכית לבנה ולא בטלו לגמרי (ג) אלא שאינן מצוין כל כך : כרים וכסתות · עשוין לשכיבה ואמרי' ביומא בריש בא לו (דף סט·) לא יעלה עליך אבל אתה מותר להציעו תחתיך אבל אמרו חכמים אסור לעשות כן שמא תכרך נימא על בשרו ואפילו עשר מצעות זו על גבי זו וכלאים תחתיהן אסור לישן עליהן הכא גבי כרים וכסתות ומרדעת דלקמן בשאין בשרו נוגע לא גזור בדבר שאין דרכו בהעלאה : ירושלמי (שם) הא דאתמר מותר בריקן אבל לא במלא בכתון על גבי אסמוכות אבל לא בנתון ע"ג מטה [פי'] של חבלי' שלא א] נשקע תחתיו ונידי הכר עולים עליו אבל *לדין של עץ קשה ואין נשקע : אין עראי לכלאים · דלבישת עראי שמה לבישה ואסור ובריש התכלת (דף מא·) מייתי לה ומשמע דאיירי בטלית קטנה אע"פ שאין הגדול יוצא בה עראי : על גבי י' לבושין · ואף ע"פ שאינו נהנה ממנו : אפילו לגנוב את המכס · כדי יציאת המעבר שנוטל בו המכס שאין נותנין מכס מבגדים שלובש אדם וסבר דבר שאינו מתכוין אסור כדמוכח בריש הגוזל בתרא (דף קיג·) ופליג [אסתמא] (דאתמר) דמוכרי כסות דסיפא ובמוכס שאין לו קצבה איירי או במוכס העומד מאליו כדמוכח התם דאי בסתם מוכס בלא כלאים אסור דדינא דמלכותא דינא והא דאמר רבי יוחנן בסוף המוציא יין (דף פא:) לדבר שאינו מתכוין אסור ופריך עלה מהתם מתני' דנזיר חופף ומפספס ולא משני סתמא אחרינא אשכח מתניתא דהכא אפילו לגנוב את המכס משום דאידך דסוף פרקין עיקר דמוכ"י כסות דבתרייתא היא ומיהו איכא עוד סתמא בפרק כירה (דף מא:) מיחם שפינהו דמוקי לה אביי התם כמאן דאמר דבר שאין מתכוין אסור ועוד תנן בפרק במה בהמה (דף נד·) מכנים חבלים לתוך ידו ובלבד שלא יכרוך ומפרש בגמ' משום כלאים ופירש שם בקונטרס דסבר דבר שאין מתכוין אסור ונראה דפריך מאי אולמא דהאי סתמא מהאי סתמא ואפילו איכא סתמי טובא דאכרי הא אמרינן בפ"ב דקידושין מה לי חד סתמא מה לי תרי סתמי : ירושלמי (שם) אמר רב כל שאסור משום מראית העין אפילו בחדרי חדרים אסור מתניתא פליגא על רב פשתן שנבעה בחרת לא יעשה אותה אימרא מפורסמות ובכרים ובכסתות מותר · פי' אין דרך לצבוע פשתן אלא צמר וכשהפשתן צבוע אי אפשר לאורגו עם בגד של פשתן לבן וללבוש בפרהסיא משום דמיחזי כלאים ובכרים ובכסתות מותר אפילו מפורסמות ואע"ג דמשום כלאים גמורין נמי אין בהן כדקתני מתני' אילטריך הכא אפילו בשרו נוגע בהן ואפי' מלאים ואפילו ע"ג מטה והשתא פליגא דרב דמשמע דוקא מפורסמות הא בחדרים מותר ועוד מייתי התם טובא דפליגא דרב ומסתברא דלאו לחנם נקט אימרא אלא לפי שחוט של אימרא שעשוי לחזק הבגד שלא יקרע ודרך לשוותו גסה כעין מטוה של צמר שהוא גסה וגם מתוך שצבוע דאיכא תרתי טועין בו לומר שהוא של צמר ויש טעם משום מראית העין: ג מטפחות הידים. מפה שפורסין על השולחן דרך בני אדם מסובין כשמביאין להן פת או בשר נותנין להן במפה ובירושלמי (הל' ב') פסיק הלכה כר' אלעזר דאסר וא"ר זעירא כשהיו מביאין לר' אבינא ביעתא במפה דאית בה כלאים והוא לא מקבל על שלא יתכוונו בחמה מפני החמה כלומר שהמפה מוגעו שאינו נכוה בביצה שהיה חמה (ד) : מטפחות ספרים . הא דאסר ר' אלעזר מפרש בירושלמי (שם) ר' שמואל בר נחמני א"ר יונתן מפני שעושה אותה כמין תיק ומשימה בחיקו ונותן ספר תורה עליה ר' אבא בשם ר' חייא בשם רב מפני שמחמם בה ידיו : מטפחות הספג · כשאדם יוצא מבית המרחץ מביאין לו סדין או מטפחות ומסתפג בה : ור' אלעזר אוסר . משום דפעמים שרואה את רבו ומתעטף בה : מטפחות הספרים · ספר שמספר בני אדם פורש לפניו מפה שיפול השער עליה ויש בהן משום כלאים ואמרי' בירושלמי (שם) הדא דאיתמר במתכוין לשם מלבוש אבל אינו מתכוין לא (ה) : ד תכריכי המת . בנדה פרק האשה (דף סא:) פליגי דאמר ר' אמי ואיתימא ר' לא שנו אלא לספדו אבל לקברו אסור ור' יוחנן [אמר] אפילו לקברו דכתיב (תהלים פח) במתים חפשי כיון שמת אדם נעשה חפשי מן המצות ותימה דליתסר משום לועג לרש דאפילו ציצית אמרי' בפרק התכלת (דף מא:) דההיא שעתא ודאי רמינן ליה משום לועג לרש כל שכן שאין להלבישו כלאים משום לועג לרש ושמא שאני מצות ציצית שהיא שקולה כנגד כל המצות כדאמרינן בפרק התכלת [דף מג:] וראיתם וזכרתם אי נמי שאני כלאים דבחי דומיא דמת לא אסור דלא מיתהני כלל ואנן בעינן הנאה פורתא כדמשמע בריש יבמות (דף ד:) דבעינן העלאה דומיא דלבישה דאית בה הנאה לאפוקי מוכרי כסות (ו) והא דדייק מינה דמצות בטלות לעתיד לבא כשיחיו ואייתי סייעתא *שיעמדו בלבושיהם : ומרדעת של חמור · בנדה פרק האשה (שם) דאסרינן בגד שארג בו כלאים לעשות מרדעת שמא ישכח ויקחנו ויעשה טלאי לבגדו ומשום שמא תכרך לו נימא לא אסיר כדפרשינן גבי כרים (ז) : ירושלמי (הל' ג) תני אין מדקדקין במת ולא בכלאים בבית המדרש ר' יוסי הוה יתיב מתני והוה תמן מיתא מן דנפק ליה לא אמר כלום ר' אמי הוה יתיב מיתני אמר חד לחבריה את לביש כלאים א"ל ר' אמי שלח מאניך והב ליה · פי' אין מדקדקין במת להחמיר לענין דברי תורה שאסור לדבר לפני המת כדאמר ר' יוסי הוה מיתני ולא הודיעוהו שהיה שם מת עד שיצא ולא בכלאים בבה"מ שכעס רבי אמי על אותו שאמר לחברו את לבוש כלאים וציוהו לפשוט את בגדיו להלבישו ובפ' מי שמתו (דף יט:) משמע דאסור דאמר רב יהודה אמר שמואל המוצא כלאים בבגדו פושטו אפי' בשוק ושמא התם בכלאים דאורייתא והכא בכלאים דרבנן (ח): ה ו מוכרי כסות · שיש בהן כלאים מוכרים כדרכן לובשו להראותו בשוק (ט) : ובלבד שלא יתכוין להנאתו ומהכא דייקינן בשילהי כירה (דף מו:) דדבר שאין מתכוין מותר ואפי' במידי דכי מיכוין איכא איסורא דאורייתא ופליגא אסתמא דלעיל : והצנועין המחמירין על עצמן מפשילים במקל לאחוריהן : תופרי כסות · טעמא דהכך כטעמא דרישא : ז הברסין · מפרש בירושלמי (הל' ה) ברסין בודיא ברדיסין דולמא דלמטיקון קובלון ומעפירין מנעלות הפינון דדרסין ובערוך פירש ברסין גלופקרין שמכסין המטות וברדיסין כמו כן אלא אלו רכין ואלו עבין פינון עדילדין מן הפסולת : עד שיבדוק · שמא יש ביניהן פשתן : ממדינת הים . מפרש בירושלמי (שם) מחוף הים שבמדינת הים : אין צריכין בדיקה שחזקתן מן הקנבוס · ואמרינן בירושלמי (שם) הדא דאתמר בראשונים שלא היתה פשתן מצויה אבל עתה שמצויה הפשתן בכל מקום צריכין בדיקה ולפיכך צריך להזהר כשאדם נותן בגדי צמר לאומן שלא יתפור בחוטי פשתן לפי שהפשתן מצוי וגם במלבושיהן הניקחין מן הנכרים ויש לסמוך במקומנו להתיר לפי שהפשתן ביוקר מן הקנבוס וטוב יותר לאומן לתפור בו לפי שהוא חזק החוט בשעת תפירה אבל בארץ אנגלי"טירא ובנורמנדי"אה שאין הקנבוס מצוי להם אסור בלא בדיקה ואפילו המנעלים העשוין מבפנים בלבדין צריכין בדיקה שלא יהו תפורין בפשתן : ומנעל של זרד · ל' חימום מל' בעת יזורבו (איוב ו) כלומר מנעל העשוי לחימום הרגל ועושין מנעלים כפופין וביניהן משימין משי או פשתן ואין חוששין שמא ביניהן צמר ובערוך גריס זרד : ירושלמי (שם) מנעל של זרב אית אתרין דזרבין עמרא מלגיו כהדא דרבי זירא מפקיד לרבי אבא בר זבינא דיאמר לבר ראשון דלא יחום ליה מסאניה בכיתן אלא בצלועה ומודה רבי זירא בההן פיסקי דעמר על דכיתן דהיא שרי דהוא שכן גרמיה והיא כחתא ליה : ח שוע · לשון שעיעות תרגום חלקת צואריו שעיעות (בראשית כז) שהצמר שוי בפני עצמו ושוע בפני עצמו וכן הפשתן שוע בפני עצמו וטווי בפני עצמו ואחר כן נוז דהיינו שניהן ארוגין יחד ולא כרבינו תם דמפרש נוז משזר ואריג מדכתיב יחדו דהכא משמע בהדיא דמשעטנז נפקא לן אריג וכן בירושלמי וכן בפרק קמא דיבמות ושם הארכתי (יא) : נלוז ומליז · מרחיק את ישראל מאביהן שבשמים מ לשון אל יליזו מעיניך (משלי ד) : ט הלבדין · טורפין הצמר והפשתן זה עם זה ומחברין כעין בגד ע"י אומנות בלא טויה ואריגה : פיף של צמר ושל פשתן · אחר שמשלימין האורגין הבגד עושין בשפת הבגד ונקרא פיף ואם הבגד של פשתן

תורה אור

ב השירים (ב) והכלך אין בהם משום כלאים אבל אסורים מפני מראית העין הכרים והכסתות אין בהם משום כלאים ובלבד שלא יהיה בשרו נוגע בהם אין (א) עראי לכלאים ולא ילבש (ב) כלאי' אפי' ע"ג י' (א) אפי' לגנוב את המכס: ג מטפחות הידים מטפחות הספרים מטפחות הספג אין בהם משום כלאים ר"א אוסר ומטפחות הספרים אסורות משום כלאים: ד תכריכי המת ומרדעת של חמור אין בהם משום כלאים לא יתן המרדעת על כתיפו אפילו להוציא עליה זבל : ה מוכרי כסות (ג) מוכרין כדרכן ובלבד שלא יתכוונו בחמה מפני החמה ובגשמים מפני הגשמים והצנועים מפשילין *במקל : ו (י) תופרי כסות תופרין כדרכן ובלבד שלא יתכונו בחמה מפני החמה ובגשמים מפני הגשמים והצנועים תופרין בארץ: ז הברסין והבורדסים והדלמטיקיון ומנעלות הפינון לא (*ילבש בהן) עד שיבדוק רבי יוסי אומר הבאים מחוף הים וממדינת הים אינן צריכין בדיקה מפני שחזקתן בקנבוס ומנעל של *זרד אין בו משום כלאים : ח אין אסור משום כלאים אלא (ד) טווי וארוג שנאמר לא תלבש שעטנז דבר שהוא שוע טווי ונוז ר' שמעון בן אלעזר אומר נלוז ומליז הוא את אביו שבשמים עליו : ט לבדים אסורין מפני שהם שועים פיף של צמר בשל פשתן אסור מפני שהם

עם זה : ב שיריים והכלך מיני משי הם וידמו כאילו הם צמר ופשתים מפני שאחד מהמינים ההם חלק כמו הפשתים והשני יש בו יבשות והוא שעיר כמו הצמר : אין עראי לכלאים . ר"ל שאסור ללבשם אפי' בדרך עראי כמו שנתבאר באמרו לא ילבש כלאים אפילו על גבי שאר בגדים זה על זה ואפילו לגנוב את המכס אין לו רשות ללבשו וכן היה מנהגם: ג מטפחות הידים. הם המפות שינגבו בהם הידים ומטפחו' הספג מפות שינגבו בהם כל הגוף ומטפחות הספרים מפות מספר תורה שיאחז בהם ס"ת הקורא בשעת קריאתו : מטפחות הספרים. מפות המגלחים ישימו אותם על כתפי המתגלח והלכה כר"א שהוא אוסר אלו השלש מטפחות משום כלאים : ד תכריכי המת. הבגדים שילבישו המת שהאדם כשימות בטלו ממנו כל המצות ואינם חייבים החיים לנהוג בהם איסור ולא שום מצוה ממצות הכתוב כגון ציצית ותפילין ומזוזה ודומה לאלו: והמרדעת . הוא מרדעת החמור ונקרא בלשון ערב מרדעת: ה ר"ל שמותר להם מכירת כלים של כלאים ולהשליכם על גביהם ובלבד שלא יתכוין להתחמם בהם או לכסות גופו מן השמש : וצנועים . הם המדקדקים במצות: ומפשילין במקל. הוא שישים אותם בקצה המטה וישים המקל על כתפו כדי שלא תגע לגופו : ו כל זה מבואר : ז אלו השמות כולם לא עמדנו על פירושם אבל הענין ידוע ומובן והוא שכולם הם בגדי צמר ילבשו בהם הרגלים והשוקים כי הוא אמר שאסור ללבשם עד יחקר עליהם אם הם תפורין בפשתים וא"ר יוסי שהבאים ממדינת הים ומאיי הים אינן צריכות בדיקה שכולן יתפרו אותן בחוטי קנבוס שהפשתן אינו נמצא אצלם ודברי רבי יוסי היה אומר בשם מי שהגיד לו בזמן שלא היה נמצא פשתן בכל הארץ וכן אמרו בגמרא הדא דתימא בראשונה שלא היה הפשתן מצויה בכל מקום אבל השתא שהפשתן מצויה בכל מקום צריכה בדיקה ומנעל של זרד הוא דמות מנעל שעושים תחת כף הרגל להלוך בה על הסלעים והכסתות : ח שוע · הוא הטרוף שהוא ממחק פני הבגד ותרגומו וטח את הבית (ויקרא יד) וישוע ית ביתא : טווי . הוא לערב צמר ופשתים יחדו ויטוה מהם חוטים : ונוז . הוא שארוג משניהם האריגה והוא לשון הארמניים וענינו אצלם החבור ושיתאחה וישוב כאחד וכשיתערב הצמר בפשתים ויטוו משניהם חוטין ויעשו מן הטווי ההוא בגד ואחר כך יטרפנו וימחקנו וימרקנו כמו שיעשו בבגדי מלף הידועים אז יהיה הבגד ההוא כלאים וזה כלאים מן התורה והוא שלא יהיו כלאים עד יהיו נחברים אלו שלשה הענינים כולם* וכל מה שאינו כך הוא כלאים מד"ס וזו הלכה פסוקה באמת ואין בו ספק וכן אמרו בגמ' ואם מצאת לאחד דבר חולק על מה שאמרתי לך אל יכנס בלבך ספק שהוא שכח ההלכה ההיא האמורה בגמ' נדה (דס"א) : ונלוז ומליז . הוא נוטה מן האמת ומרחיק רחמי הקב"ה ממנו לעברו מצות שצוה הקב"ה בדבר שאין בו תאוה שהכריחהו וזה עון גדול וגזרת נלוז ומליז ממלת אל ילוזו מעיניך (משלי ג) : ט לבדים . הם יריעות הצמר שאינן ארוגות אלא טרופות ונקרא בלשון ערב לבד : ופיף של צמר בשל פשתן . עבותות

הגהות מהר"י לנדא

פרק ט א] משנה ב בר"ש שלא נשקע . צ"ל שהוא נשקע :

הגהות הב"ח

פרק ט (א) משנה ב אפילו על גבי עשרה בגדים אפילו :

MISHNAH 2. [GARMENTS MADE OF A MIXTURE OF] SILK AND FLOSS-SILK[5] DO NOT COME UNDER THE PROHIBITION OF KIL'AYIM, BUT ARE PROHIBITED ON ACCOUNT OF APPEARANCES.[6] TO MATTRESSES AND PILLOWS THE PROHIBITION OF
a KIL'AYIM DOES NOT APPLY,[1] PROVIDED ONE'S FLESH DOES NOT COME INTO [IMMEDIATE] CONTACT WITH THE MIXED MATERIAL. THERE IS NO [PERMISSIBILITY FOR THE] CASUAL [WEARING] OF KIL'AYIM,[2] NEITHER MAY ONE WEAR KIL'AYIM EVEN ON TOP OF TEN [GARMENTS], EVEN FOR THE PURPOSE OF ELUDING [UNAUTHORIZED] IMPOSTS.[3]

b *MISHNAH* 3. HAND-TOWELS, SCROLL-WRAPPINGS,[1] AND BATH-TOWELS DO NOT COME UNDER THE PROHIBITION OF KIL'AYIM.[2] R. ELIEZER DECLARED THEM SUBJECT TO THAT PROHIBITION.[3] BARBERS'-SHEETS ARE SUBJECT TO THE PROHIBITION OF KIL'AYIM.[4]

MISHNAH 4. SHROUDS FOR THE DEAD, AND THE PACK-SADDLE OF AN ASS ARE NOT SUBJECT TO THE LAW OF KIL'AYIM;[5] ONE MUST NOT [HOWEVER] PLACE A PACK-SADDLE [MADE OF KIL'AYIM] ON ONE'S SHOULDER EVEN FOR THE PURPOSE OF CARRYING DUNG OUT THEREON.

MISHNAH 5. VENDORS OF CLOTHES MAY SELL [CLOTHES MADE OF KIL'AYIM] IN ACCORDANCE WITH THEIR [TRADE] CUSTOM,[6] AS LONG AS THEY HAVE NOT THE INTENTION, IN THE SUN, [TO PROTECT THEMSELVES] FROM THE SUN, OR, IN THE RAIN, [TO PROTECT THEMSELVES THEREBY] FROM THE RAIN. THE PARTICULARLY SCRUPULOUS[7] SUSPEND [SUCH MATERIALS OR GARMENTS] ON A STICK OVER THEIR BACKS.[8]

(5) כלך. A vegetable yarn variously identified which in some respects resembles sheep's wool. (6) Since the silk resembles linen, and the floss-silk wool. Likewise silk would be forbidden with wool (and floss-silk with linen) 'on account of appearances', but since silk has become a generally known commodity, the reason 'on account of appearances' has entirely fallen away, and silk is permitted with either wool or linen. V. *Yoreh De'ah* § 298, 1, and cf. L. to our Mishnah and his בתי כלאים § 113, and *Pitheḥe Teshubah* to *Yoreh De'ah*, loc. cit.

a (1) Since Scripture says of material which is *kil'ayim*: '*it shall not come* upon *thee*' (Lev. XIX, 19) and: '*thou shalt not* wear' (Deut. XXII, 11), having it beneath a person, is not forbidden. This permission is, in practice, operative only if the bolsters or mattresses made with *kil'ayim* are hard; but if they are soft, and there is consequently the possibility of even a thread winding itself round one's body and giving some warmth, it is not permitted to lie on them even if they are under ten permitted blankets. (2) When the person's intention is that it shall serve him as a garment or covering. (3) The commentators explain: By wearing garments which, had they been carried otherwise, would have been dutiable, a device not unknown nowadays. According to the Gemara in B.Ḳ. 113*a* (Sonc. ed.) the Mishnah must have had in mind here imposts unauthorized by the proper authority, since were it otherwise, the duty of complying with the law of the land is, in Jewish teaching, beyond question; in fact the eluding of customs is denounced (*Semaḥoth* II, 9) as being as reprehensible as bloodshed, idol-worship, incest and Sabbath-desecration. In connection with an incident reported (Gen. R. LXXXII, 8) of two scholars who in time of persecution varied their garb but were, nevertheless, held up by Roman soldiers, who expressed surprise that the scholars should have attempted to save their lives by transgressing the Torah, the present writer has suggested, that since it was evidently a transgression of a *biblical* precept relating to clothing that was involved, it seems that the disguise consisted in wearing *kil'ayim* so as not to be recognized as Jews. The tax referred to in our Mishnah might thus have been the *Fiscus Judaicus* which was considered an affront to Jewish religious feelings. The editor has, as a comment on this surmise, brought to my notice an anonymous opinion cited in שאלות ותשובות מהרי"ק No. 84, to the effect that the impost referred to in our Mishnah might have been one enforced on Jews only. In B.Ḳ., loc. cit. the view is expressed that the legal principle involved is the question of דבר שאינו מתכוין i.e., the permissibility of an action which is in itself permissible, but which unavoidably, though unintentionally, results in something forbidden.

b (1) Cloth bands and 'mantles' used to tie up and cover Scrolls of the Law, or cloths spread on the desk on which the Scrolls are unrolled and read. (2) Since these are not intended for protecting or warming the human body. A table-cloth is in the same category. (3) Since when drying oneself with either towel one does warm oneself; with a bath-towel one also covers oneself as with a cloak; when one clasps the covered Torah-scroll one derives warmth therefrom. (4) Only if it has an aperture for the head; otherwise it is not an article of wear nor is it intended to protect the body, but one's clothes. (5) In the case of the shrouds the reason is that on the strength of a Rabbinic interpretation of Ps. LXXXVIII, 6, the dead are declared exempt from all precepts. The saddle-cloth is exempt because it is stiff (cf. 24*b* n. a 1). The exemption in the latter case operates only when the heterogeneous element is recognizable in the material but not otherwise, since one might in error use some of it for patching one's garments. (V. Nid. 61*b*). (6) Either by way of carrying them over their shoulder, or by way of putting them for the purpose of displaying them before prospective customers. (7) צנועים, lit., the 'modest', denoting a positive quality, probably nothing else but discretion or modesty 'Büchler' *Types* (*contra* Kohler who identifies the *Zenu'im* with the Essenes) pp. 59 ff. (8) So that the forbidden materials or garments do not touch the person carrying them.

◁ *For the continuation of the English translation of this page see overleaf*

תורה אור

ב השירים (ב) והכלך אין בהם משום כלאים אבל אסורים מפני מראית העין הכרים והכסתות אין בהם משום כלאים ובלבד שלא יהיה בשרו נוגע בהם אין עראי לכלאים ולא ילבש כלאי׳ אפי׳ ע״ג י׳ (א) אפי׳ לגנוב את המכס: ג מטפחות הידים מטפחות הספרים מטפחות הספג אין בהם משום כלאים ר״א אוסר ומטפחות הספרים אסורות משום כלאים: ד תכריכי המת ומרדעת של חמור אין בהם משום כלאים לא יתן המרדעת על כתיפו אפילו להוציא עליה זבל: ה מוכרי כסות מוכרין כדרכן ובלבד שלא יתכונו בחמה מפני החמה ובגשמים מפני הגשמים והצנועים מפשילין במקל: ו (י) תופרי כסות תופרין כדרכן ובלבד שלא יתכונו בחמה מפני החמה ובגשמים מפני הגשמים והצנועים תופרין בארץ: ז הברסין והברדסים והדלמטיקיון ומנעלות הפינון לא (ילבש בהן) עד שיבדוק רבי יוסי אומר הבאים מחוף הים וממדינת הים אינן צריכין בדיקה מפני שחזקתן בקנבוס ומנעל של זרד אין בו משום כלאים: ח אין אסור משום כלאים אלא טווי וארוג שנאמר לא תלבש שעטנז דבר שהוא שוע טווי ונוז ר׳ שמעון בן אלעזר אומר נלוז ומליז הוא את אביו שבשמים עליו: ט לבדים אסורין מפני שהם שועים פיף של צמר בשל פשתן אסור מפני שהם

הגהות מהר״י לנדא

הגהות הב״ח

פרק ט (א) משנה ב אפילו על גבי עשרה בגדים אפילו:

Continuation of translation from previous page as indicated by ◁

MISHNAH 6. TAILORS MAY SEW [MATERIALS WHICH ARE
c KIL'AYIM] IN THEIR ACCUSTOMED WAY,[1] AS LONG AS THEY HAVE NO INTENTION, IN THE SUN, [TO PROTECT THEMSELVES THEREBY] FROM THE SUN, OR, IN THE RAIN, [TO PROTECT THEMSELVES THEREBY] FROM THE RAIN. THE PARTICULARLY SCRUPULOUS SEW [SUCH MATERIALS AS THEY ARE LAID] ON THE GROUND.[2]

MISHNAH 7. THE BIRRUS BLANKET OR BRINDISIAN[3] BLANKET, OR [NETHER GARMENTS OF] DALMATIAN CLOTH, OR FELT[4] SHOES, MAY NOT BE WORN UNTIL ONE HAS EXAMINED [THEM].[5] R. JOSE SAID THAT SUCH [OF THE ABOVE] AS COME FROM THE SEA-COAST OR FROM LANDS BEYOND THE SEA, DO NOT REQUIRE EXAMINATION, SINCE THE PRESUMPTION WITH REGARD TO THEM IS [THAT THEY ARE SEWN] WITH HEMPEN THREAD.[6] TO CLOTH-LINED FOOTWEAR THE PROHIBITION OF KIL'AYIM DOES NOT APPLY.[7]

MISHNAH 8. ONLY THAT WHICH IS SPUN OR WOVEN IS
d FORBIDDEN[1] UNDER THE LAW OF KIL'AYIM, FOR IT IS SAID: THOU SHALT NOT WEAR SHA'AṬNEZ,[2] WHICH WORD IS A COMPOUND STANDING FOR SHUA',[3] TAWUI,[4] AND NUZ.[5] R. SIMEON SAID: [THE WORD SHA'AṬNEZ SUGGESTS THAT] HE [THE TRANSGRESSOR OF THE PRECEPT] IS PERVERTED[6] AND CAUSES HIS FATHER IN HEAVEN TO AVERT HIMSELF [FROM HIM].[7]

MISHNAH 9. TO FELTED MATERIALS THE PROHIBITION OF KIL'AYIM APPLIES, SINCE [THE STRANDS CONSTITUTING THEM] HAVE BEEN CARDED. IT IS PROHIBITED TO ATTACH[8] AN EDGING OF WOOL TO LINEN MATERIAL,[9] SINCE THIS

c (1) I.e., letting them lie across one's lap. (2) Placing the material on a board or table would answer the same purpose viz., avoid letting the material rest on one's body. (3) הברסין והברדסין. Our rendering is after Jast. But v. Kohut, *'Aruk* s.v. ברס for variant readings and varying renderings; he concludes that one represents a (? woven) woollen and the other a felt material. Maim., frankly admits that he is unable definitely to identify the materials mentioned here except in so far as it is apparent from T.J. that they were woollens for covering the feet and thighs, and were often sown with linen thread. (4) פינך, pile. (5) To see whether they are made with linen. (6) Since in the days of the Mishnah linen was very rare in those countries. T.J., however, says: Now that linen is common, all must be examined. Rash. (ca. 1150—1230 C.E.) says that in his own locality (Sens, district of Yonne, France) there was no need to examine because hempen thread was much cheaper there than linen and also made a stronger thread and was therefore commonly used; but, he adds, in England and Normandy (of which he was a native) where hemp is scarce, examination is essential. (7) Maim., *Yad. Hil. Kil.* X, 15 gives as the reason that the skin of the feet is very hard and that consequently in comparison with that of other parts of the body, the foot does not derive so much warmth from the cloth lining. *Kesef Mishneh* to this says that the footwear spoken of in our Mishnah was lined with linen for the summer, but additionally lined with wool for the winter. *Ikkar Tosaf. Yomtov* rightly says that the reason for this exemption is not apparent.

d (1) By the Pentateuchal law. (2) שעטנז, Deut. XXII, 11. What follows is an interpretation by the Midrashic device of *Notarikon*. (3) שוע, each thread (one of wool and the other of linen) smoothed out by the process of carding. (4) טווי, (each strand) spun. (5) נוז. Maim., and Rashi to Nid., 61*b*, 'woven', but Rashi to Lev. XIX, 19, also R. Tam (v. Tosaf. to Nid. l.c.) 'twisted'. The latter is the accepted meaning, and the Mishnah is taken to mean that according to Pentateuchal law, the prohibition of *sha'aṭnez* applies only when a strand of wool and one of linen, each carded (*shua'*), *and* spun (*tawui*), *and* twisted (*nuz*) have been joined together (יחדו in the text) by weaving or sewing or tying. According to R. Tam (also Maim.), we should understand: When each strand has been carded, *or* spun, *or* twisted etc. This is accepted as a Rabbinic extension of the Pentateuchal law. Bert., prefers a rendering which he quotes (among others) from an anonymous teacher. Viz., 'When the strands have been *shua'* (carded), and *tawui* (spun), and *nuz*, which he renders 'woven'. This authority apparently takes the word יחדו 'together' in the text as *adding* sewing and tying to the prohibition of weaving which according to him, is covered by *nuz*. (6) נלוז, *Naloz*, another play on the last syllable of the word *sha'aṭnez*. (7) So Maim., and others. An alternative rendering: 'And he perverts or subverts (the order willed by) his Father in Heaven (in that he joins together species which He ordained should be kept distinct)'. (8) Either by drawing through or interlacing, or by means of an adhesive substance (v. L.). (9) Or *vice-versa*.

RESEMBLES WEAVING.[10] R. JOSE SAID: IT IS FORBIDDEN TO USE CORDS OF RED PURPLE [WOOL] [TO TIE ROUND A LOOSE LINEN GARMENT], SINCE PRIOR TO TYING IT, ONE STITCHES IT ON. IT IS FORBIDDEN TO TIE A STRIP OF WOOLLEN MATERIAL WITH ONE OF LINEN MATERIAL FOR THE PURPOSE OF GIRDLING ONE'S LOINS THEREWITH, EVEN IF THERE IS A
a LEATHER STRAP BETWEEN THE TWO.[1]

MISHNAH 10. TO [STITCHED-ON] WEAVERS' MARKS OR LAUNDRYMEN'S MARKS THE PROHIBITION OF KIL'AYIM APPLIES. IF ONE HAS DRAWN A THREAD [THROUGH MATERIAL][2] ONCE, THIS DOES NOT [IN LAW] CONSTITUTE A CONNECTION,[3] NOR DOES [THE PROHIBITION OF] KIL'AYIM APPLY THERETO,[4] AND IF ONE HAS DRAWN IT OUT ON THE SABBATH, HE IS NOT PUNISHABLE.[5] IF ONE MADE ITS TWO ENDS COME OUT ON THE SAME SIDE [OF THE MATERIAL], THIS CONSTITUTES A CONNECTION, AND COMES UNDER THE PROHIBITION OF KIL'AYIM,[6] AND ONE WHO HAS DRAWN THIS THREAD OUT ON THE SABBATH IS LIABLE.[7] R. JUDAH SAID: [THE PROHIBITION DOES NOT APPLY] UNTIL ONE HAS MADE THREE STITCHES. A SACK AND A BASKET [ONE HAVING A STRIP OF WOOLLEN MATERIAL ATTACHED TO IT, AND THE OTHER A STRIP OF LINEN] COMBINE TO FORM KIL'AYIM.[8]

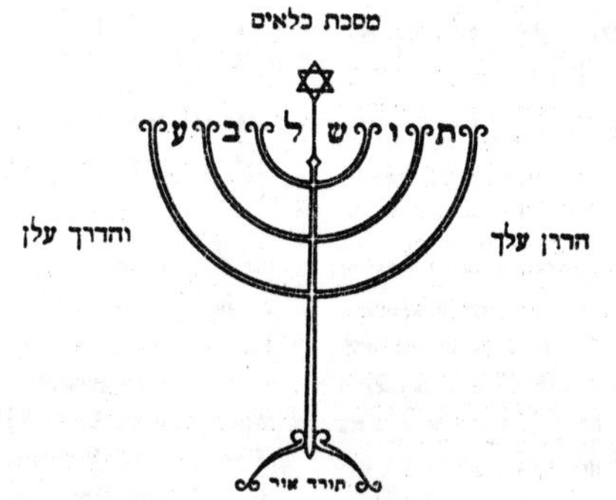

(10) Or, 'since this (i.e., the edging) is wound round (or encloses) the woven material'.

a (1) Since the woollen and linen strips will be tied together when the girdle is used. Otherwise such a combination of wool-leather-linen is not forbidden. (2) A thread of linen through woollen material, or *vice versa;* or any thread through two pieces of material one woollen and the other linen. (3) In the case of more than one piece of material, the drawing through of a thread once would not make them into one piece in respect of the laws of uncleanness, thus: If one piece becomes unclean, the other is not thereby rendered unclean; likewise if both are unclean, the ritual cleansing of the one will not restore cleanness to the other. (4) Some stipulate: As long as the ends of the thread are not tied together, (v. L.). (5) Even if he has done so in order later to sew up again, since it is 'tearing so as to sew two stitches' which is prohibited on the Sabbath (Shab. VII, 2). (6) Some say: Even if the ends of the thread are not tied together, (v. L.). (7) But only if the ends had been tied together. (8) *Sc.* when the two strips are sewn together (with at least two stitches); and we do not say that each piece of cloth, being merely an appendage to the principal article, is negligible. Maim.: A garment made of wool and linen joined together by a sack or basket. Sipponte, apparently on the basis of a variant reading in *Sifre, Deut.* § 232 (ed. Friedmann, p. 117*a*): If a sack, or a basket, contain wool and linen, the sack, or basket have the effect of combining the two species, so as to form *kil'ayim* (and it is therefore forbidden to carry such a sack or basket on one's shoulder). v. Rosh. In view of the fact that T.J. here comments: 'But tents, (covered enclosures containing wool and linen together) do not effect *kil'ayim*,' the latter interpretation seems to be the correct one.

א) שבת דף כד. מנחות דף לט. [יבמות ה:]:

פי' מהר"י בן מלכי צדק

ט משיחות של ארגמן אסורות · פי' ארגמן צמר. וכן אמר חבלים של צמר ארגמן אסורות לקשרן אם הוא לבוש פשתן מפני שהוא מולל פירוש קשר הרבה שאין עולה התגורה ולא יורדת ואח"כ קושר שזה ודאי אסור: לא יקשור סרט של צמר בשל פשתן · פי' לא יעשה חגורו' של צמר וחגורות מפשתן ויקשרם זה בזה ואפילו אם ישים ביניהן רצועה של עור אינו מותר: י התוכף תכיפה אחת. לעז פונטו: אינה חיבור · פי' לטומאה ולטהרה: ואין בה משום כלאי' פי' שאם בגד אחד צמר ובגד א' פשתי' ותכפן תכיפה אחת אינן כלאים והשומט' בשבת פטור דלא דמי למותח חוט של תפירה: עשה ב' ראשיה לצד אחת · כגון שהכניס המחט והוציאו ושייר מן החוט מאותו צד כמו טפח והכניס והוציא שנמצאין ב' ראשי החוט מצד א' וקשר חיבור: ויש בה משום כלאים והשומטה בשבת חייב ר' יהודה אומר עד שישלש · פי' ג' פעמים יכנים המחט ויוציא. גרסי' בירוש' מה ר' יהודא כר' אליעזר דתנן ר"א אומר האורג ג' חוטין בתחלה [וא' על האריג חייב] אמר עולא טעמא דר' אליעזר תמן ע"י שלישי מלאכתו מתקיימת ראשיה לצד אחד בחיבור הוא תניא תני של צמר שנתנו בפשתן מותר עשה ב' ראשים לצד אחד אסור השק והקופה מצטרפין בכלאים פי' אסור לשום בשק פשתים וצמר מטורפים להוליכן וכן בקופה וכן בסל אבל אהלים אין בהן משום כלאים פי' תחת אהל אחד מותר להיות שם פשתים וצמר זה אצל זה: **חסלת מס' כלאים**

שהם חוזרין כאריג רבי יוסי אומר [א]משיחות של ארגמן אסורות מפני שהוא מולל עד שלא קושר [ב]לא יקשור סרט של צמר בשל פשתים לחגור בו את מתניו אע"פ שהרצועה באמצע: י [ג]אותות הגרדין ואותות הכובסים אסורות משום כלאים א) התוכף תכיפה אחת אינה חיבור [ד]ואין בה משום כלאים והשומטה בשבת פטור עשה שני ראשיה לצד אחד חיבור ויש בה משום כלאים השומטה בשבת חייב רבי יהודה אומר עד שישלש [ה]השק והקופה מצטרפין לכלאים:

סליקא לה מסכת כלאים

אסור לעשות פיף מלמר : מפני שחוזרין לאריג · כלומר דומים הם לאריג וי"מ מסבבין קן את האריג ובערוך פירש פיף גלגול של למר : ירושלמי (אל' ה) ניתני שוע ולא ניתני טווי אילו תנן שוע ולא תנא טווי הוינן אמרינן טווי מותר מתני' לא אמרה כן אלא אין אסור משום כלאים אלא טווי ואריג ניתני שוע ולא ניתני נוז אילו כן אמרין נוז מותר מתני' לא אמרה כן אלא פיף של למר בשל פשתן אסור מפני שחוזרין לאריג ניתני נוז ולא ניתני שוע אילו כן הוינן אמרינן שוע מותר מתניתין לא אמרה כן אלא הלבדין אסורין מפני שהן שועין : משיחות של ארגמן · של למר לבוע ארגמן ואסורין לחגור על גבי חלוק של פשתן מפני

של למר ופשתן מפני שיתערבו חוטים אלו עם אלו כהתערב באריגה : משיחות של ארגמן · עבותות של ארגמן מנהג עושין לקבץ בהם רבות ולקשור אותם מחוטי פשתן והוא אומר שהם כלאים שהחוט ההוא יפתל אותו עם הארגמן ואז יקשור בו ובמעשה ההוא שהוא פותל יהיה טווי וזה ענין שאמר מולל עד שלא קושר : וסרט של למר בשל פשתן · הוא להדביק מחגרת או אזור או אבנט מלמר ואחד מפשתן ברלועות עור בין שניהן כדי שיקשור קלה עור באזור הלמר וקלה האחר באזור הפשתן ומכאן שאסור לתפור בגד למר בבגד פשתים ואפי' בחוטי משי או בחוטי למר גפן וכל זה כלאים מדרבנן כמו שזכרתי לך ואין הלכה כר"י : י אותות הגרדין · והכובסין הם סימני האורגין וכובסי הבגדים שהם עושים סימנים בבגדיהם כדי שלא יתערבו ואם יעשה סימן בחוטי למר על בגד פשתים או הפך הרי זה כלאים ותוכף תכיפה אחת להכנים חוט בשני בגדים כא' וכשימשכהו אדם נמשך במישור והוא אומר ששני הבגדים ההם אינן מחוברים ואם נטמא האחד לא נטמא השני וזהו ענין שאמר אינו חיבור ואם האחד מהם פשתן והשני למר אין בהם משום כלאים והמושך מהם חוט בשבת פטור ואינו קורע : עשה שני ראשיה כאחת הוא שיתחבר שני קלות החוט מלד האחד ויתחבר בגד לבגד ויהיו שתי תפירות כמו זה*  אבל תכיפה אחת הנזכרת בתחלה היא כן* 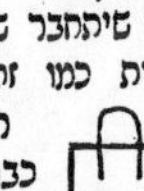 ר"י אומר שאין לנו לחשב ב' הבגדים מחוברי' כבגד אחד ולדון עליהם אלו הדינין עד שיתפור שלש תפירות ויתקיע המחט בבגד ג' תקיעות · ומה שאמר השק והקופה מלטרפין לכלאים ר"ל כשיקבון בגד למר ופשתים ויחבירם בחתיכת שק או קופה שכבר החבירם אלל השק או אל הקופה קלתם עם קלתם ויש להם קלת חיבור ונעשה כלאים ואסור ללבוש הבגד ההוא המחובר משניהם וכן אמר בספרי יחדו מ"מ ואין הלכה כרבי יהודה : סליקא לה מסכת כלאים

שהוא שולל שדרך לתופרן בחלוק או לקשרן שלא ינתק מן החלוק מלשון וכלן רשאים לשוללן למוללן לנקמן בפרק בתרא דמ"ק (דף כו:) וכמו קורע מתוך השלל מתוך המלל דהתם : עד שלא קושר · כלומר קודם שיקשור בה מתניו דרכו לחבר במלילה התגור של למר עם החלוק של פשתן ובירוש' (שם) אמרינן משיחה של ארגמן אסורות אית תניי מותרות מאן דאסר בגין אילין סורסייא דהוא מכפת מאן דמתיר דהוא שכן גרמיה והיא נחתה לה כלומר דאגד בה לבד ואינו כופתה בחלוק ועולה ויורדת : לא יקשור סרט של למר בשל פשתן · שלא יעשה אדם תגורות של למר ותגורות של פשתן ויקשרם זה בזה ואפי' ישים ביניהן רלועה של עור אסור כגון רלועה של עור שמשיחות של פשתן א) ברלשה הא' ומשיחות של למר ברלשה הב' וכשחוגר בה קושר ב' רלשיה של למר ושל פשתן ביחד דאל"ה פשיטא דשרי ופוק חזי מה עמא דבר הסרבלין שלנו של למר ויש בהן עורות של סלאים או של שפנים תפור מן הפשתן והיא דתניא בתוספתא דאסור חלוק של למר גמלים וארנבים וארג בו חוט אחד של למר בלד זה וחוט אחד של פשתן ל"ק מידי כדפרשינן לעיל והא דתנן נמי בסמוך שק וקופה מלטרפין לכלאים לא קשיא מידי כמו שאפרש : י אותות הגרדים · דרך הגרדים והכובסין לכתוב שם הבעלים על הבגד מעשה רוקם ואם הבגד של למר והאותות של פשתן אסורות משום כלאים : תכיפה אחת · תפירה אחת שתחב המחט בבגד פעם אחת אינו חיבור לטומאה ולטהרה שאם נטמא זה לא נטמא זה ואם הזה על זה לא הזה על זה : ואין בה משום כלאים · דאם חוט אחד של למר וחוט אחד של פשתן וחברן בתכיפה אחת : והשומטה בשבת פטור · ולא הוי כקורע על מנת לתפור ב' תפירות של פשתן דחייב כדתנן בפ' כלל גדול (דף עג·):שני רלשיה ללד אחד· כגון שתחב המחט והוליאו ושייר מן החוט וחזר והכנים רלש החוט הב' ונמלאו ב' הרלשין ללד האחד וקשרו כדאמר גבי התופר ב' תפירות והא לא קיימא אמר רבה בר בר חנה שקשרן (יב) : עד שישלש · שיכנים ויוליא ויחזור ויכנים ג"פ (יג): מצטרפין לכלאים · אם חתיכה של בגד למר מחובר בשק וחתיכה של בגד פשתים מחוברת בקופה ותכף החתיכות זו בזו בב' תכיפות מלטרפין אע"פ שכן ב' כלים ולא אמרי' האי לחודיה קאי והאי לחודיה קאי ואינן חבור ובסל ובקופה הוה בעי למימר בירושל' (הל' י) דשרי לפי שרגילין להחלק זה מזה יותר ומסיק דאסור ובאב ובנו מיבעיא ליה אם זה לבוש מאנין דעמר וזה מאנין דכיתן דההן בו נשוך כלומר שתכופים בב' תכיפות ודוקא היכא דנסב פיסקי דעמר ועגיל על תרווייהו כלומר שהקיף האב והבן בחגורה של למר שלא יחלקו זה מזה משמע הא לא עגיל על תרווייהו פשיטא ליה דשרי דאינן חיבור : ירושלמי (שם) מה ר' יהודה כר' אליעזר דתנן רא"א האורג ג' חוטין בתחלה ואחד על האריג חייב אמר עולא טעמא דר"א תמן ע"י שמלאכתו מתקיימת ברם הכא פחות מכאן מסתתר הוא רבי סימון בשם ריב"ל לא שנו אלא שק אבל סל לא אשכח תני הסל והקופה והשק מלטרפין בכלאים אהלים אין בהן משום כלאים רבי ירמיה בעי הוא ובנו מהו שילטרפו בכלאים והיך עבידא האב לבוש מאנין דעמר ובריה מאנין דכיתן נסב פיסקי דעמר ועגיל על תרווייהון א"ר יוסי והכן בו נשוך רבי חגי בעי הוא עלמו מהו שילטרף בכלאים היך עבידא היה לבוש ברדסין דעמר בחדא רגליה וברדסין דכיתן בחדא רגליה א"ר יוסי והכן בו נשוך (יד) עוד ירושלמי (הל' ד) אבוה דרב ספרא שאל לר' זירא מהו למיתן פריפין בגולתן ומקטרינון בחוט דכיתן ומהו למיתן פריפין לגו סדינא ומקטרינון בחוט דעמר א"ל חכים רבי לרב הונא [דר"ה אמר אסור] (לאסור) שמואל אמר מותר ר' יעקב בר אחא בשם רבי יוסי אמר מותר : סליקא לה מסכת כלאים

הס כדאיתא בפ' המוצא תפילין (דל"ז:) המוצא תכלת בשוק חוטין שזורים כשרים דמסתמא כיון שהם שזורים לשם ציצית נטוו . ואמרינן נמי בספרי פתיל תכלת טווי ושזור אין לי אלא תכלת לבן מנין וכו' וגם דרך הוא ליתן בשפת הבגד חוטים שזורים נמצא דהוי ספלית והתכלת שוע טווי ונוז וכל אחד לבד ולא תיקשי לפירושו מסכת דקתני אין אסור משום כלאים אלא טווי וארוג שנא' (דברים כב) לא תלבש שעטנז דבר שהוא שוע טווי ונוז אלמא דנוז הוי ארוג . די"ל ע"כ לאו למידרש כוליה שעטנז קאתי דא"כ אינו חייב עד שיהא שוע טווי וארוג ולא מייתי שעטנז אלא משום טווי ונוז לחודיה אבל אריג נפקא מיתהו דרשינן מיניה דאף שתי תכיפות הוי חיבור ואריג דנקט למעוטי מידי דלאו בגד כגון פיף של למר : גלוז מלשון עקום כמו (משלי ד) אל יליזו מעיניך : (יב) ומספקא לן אמאי לא הוי חיבור אם העביר החוט פעם אחת וקשר ב' ראשין על שפת הבגדים : (יג) ותמיה לי אם שלש תפירות בלא קשירה מתקיימות טפי משתי תכיפות בקשירה דא"א לקשרן דאין שני ראשי החוט מצד אחד :
(יד) כלומר שתכרס יחד מנעל של למר שברגל זה למנעל של פשתן בשתי תכיפות ומבעיא ליה אי הוי חיבור לפי שדרך הילוכו נפרדים זה מזה :

הגהות מהר"י לנדא א] משנה ט בר"ש עור שמשיחות של פשתן . צ"ל של למר ברלשה הא' ומשיחה של פשתן ברלשו הב' וכ"ה בב"י סימן ש' :

טז א טור יו"ד שם:
יז ב מיי' שם הלכה ג סמג שם וטור שו"ע שם סעיף ה:
יח ג מיי' שם הלכה כג וסמג וטור שם וש"ע סימן שא סעיף טו:
יט ד מיי' שם הל' כד וסמג שם וטור שו"ע יו"ד סימן ש סעיף ג:
כ ה מיי' שם הלכה ג וטור שו"ע שם סעיף ז:

פירוש הרא"ש

חוטא דכיתנא בגלימא ונתקי' ולא ידע אי נתקי' ספיר שרי מ"ט מדאורייתא שוע טווי ונוז בעינן וה"ל ספיקא דרבנן ולקול' וזה החוט הי' שוע טווי ונוז ונתחבר לבגד וקרי ליה דרבנן ועוד דפריך סתם ואימא או שוע או טווי או נוז ושוע בלא נוז היאך יאסר אפילו כעין לבדים אינו ועוד למה צריך לכתוב נוז בשביל ארוג הא מיהדו נפקא לן בפרק קמא דיבמו' דשתי תכיפות חייב כל שכן ארוג ופר"ת ז"ל שעטנז שוע טווי ונוז כל א' לבד ואחר כך יחדו באריגה או בשתי תכיפות ונוז היינו שזור שני חוטין יחד וכן מוכח במתניתין דקאמר ר"ש נלוז ומליז את אביו שבשמים עליו ודריש ליה מלשון נוז שהוא מעוקם הלובש כלאי' מעקם דרכי הקב"ה עליו אלמא נוז לשון שזור שמעקשים החוטים ושזורים יחד ומה שהוצרך להתיר כלאים בציצית משום דחוטי תכלת שזורים

תלמוד בבלי

מסכת

שביעית

תלמוד בבלי

מסכת

שביעית

עם פירוש רש״י ותוספות
ובצירוף תרגום ופירוש והערות באנגלית

על ידי
ישעיה מאיר לערמן ז״ל

בעריכת
יחזקאל (איזידור) אפשטין ז״ל

דפוס שונצין

שנת להחזיר העטרה ליושנה לפ״ק
לונדון

HEBREW-ENGLISH EDITION OF
THE BABYLONIAN TALMUD

SHEBI'ITH

TRANSLATED INTO ENGLISH
WITH NOTES, GLOSSARY AND INDICES BY

RABBI DR. S.M. LEHRMAN, M.A., PH.D.

UNDER THE EDITORSHIP OF

RABBI DR. I. EPSTEIN, B.A., PH.D. LITT.D.

LONDON
THE SONCINO PRESS
1989

COPYRIGHT © THE SONCINO LTD. 1989
ALL RIGHTS RESERVED INCLUDING THE RIGHT TO
REPRODUCE THIS BOOK OR PARTS THEREOF IN ANY FORM

1-871055059

PUBLISHERS' NOTE

This HEBREW-ENGLISH EDITION of THE SONCINO TALMUD is being published to facilitate the easier reference to the original text by scholars and students.

The Publishers wish to express their sincere thanks to Rabbi Dr. A. Melinek, B.A., Ph.D., for his painstaking care in examining the texts and making the necessary corrections for the preparation of these Tractates.

It has been necessary to duplicate some of the original Hebrew-Aramaic pages in this Tractate where the text has been of such length as to require more than one page of English translation.

MANUFACTURED IN THE UNITED STATES OF AMERICA

INTRODUCTION

The law of the Sabbatical year—the theme of this Tractate—is thrice
a mentioned in the Bible.[1] It is briefly this: land must lie fallow and all kinds of labour therein is forbidden; all debts must be remitted; and no trade may be carried on with seventh year produce. All the numerous restrictions and ramifications arising from this law are meticulously the subject of detailed consideration in the ten chapters and eighty-nine sections that comprise this Talmudical section.

The precise reason for this law is nowhere explicitly stated in the Bible. For an explanation we must seek Rabbinical guidance; we find it in Sanh. 39*b*. There, we are told: God said to Israel: 'Sow for six years, and let the land lie fallow for the seventh year, so that the earth may know that the land is Mine'. Thus this enforced Sabbatical rest was to impress mankind with the truth that God is the final possessor of the earth and that divisions between the landed and landless estates are but man-made, for all are equal before Him. Maimonides offers this explanation: 'The Torah was afraid lest the earth become weakened by constant labour, and its vitality impaired by constant ploughing; hence the command for it to rest to allow it to recuperate and become imbued with endowed vigour'. Similarly, he explains the law of limitation, which cancelled all debts, as a provision for the poor, that they be not always enslaved to their rich creditors.

Our Tractate is fifth in the Order of Zera'im (Seeds), and like the preceding Tractate, also deals with work prohibited in connection with tilling the soil and with forbidden produce. The Tosefta on this Tractate is divided into eight chapters, and comprises further elucidations of the laws dealt with in the Mishnah. An interesting observation from it may be cited here. In VIII, 1, we are told that it was customary in ancient times to take the extra produce of the seventh year from the owner and to store it in a granary belonging to the community, from which it was divided every Friday among all needy families.

The Palestinian Talmud which supplies our Tractate with a Gemara is especially valuable for its Haggadic material and interesting episodes in the lives of many of our noble teachers. A story that cannot be too often quoted is that of R. Abba b. Zabina who was employed in the shop of a Gentile tailor in Rome. One day he was given *ṭrefah* meat to eat and threatened with death should he refuse; but when he refused, despite the imminence of death, his Roman employer admitted that he would have killed him if he had eaten the meat. For, he argued, 'if one is a Jew, one should be a true Jew, and faithfully observe the principles of his religion'. What moral lesson could be more timely?

The following is a brief survey of the contents of this Tractate. The first nine chapters deal with the work that may and that may not be performed, not only in the seventh year itself, but thirty days before its advent, in conformance with the Rabbinic principle
b of adding the aura of holiness to mundane things.[1] The greatest restraint must be exercised with Sabbatical produce which must be treated with a modicum of holiness. Only in cases of much loss resulting were certain labours allowed; and when taxes were heaped upon Israel, work was allowed until the New Year itself, and even later. According to Josephus, Alexander the Great and Julius Caesar both remitted every seventh year their usual exactions from Jews in consideration of their enforced idleness and attendant lack of income.

Most important and far-seeing is the enactment of the *Prozbul* described in the last chapter, an instrument drawn up in a court when the loan was made, whereby a creditor secured his debts against the operation of the law of Sabbatical release. As a measure to provide for the adjustment of this law to the need of the time, it stands out as one of the most significant Rabbinical enactments ever made. Our Tractate finishes on a happy note. The Rabbis honour him who keeps his word and does not seek subterfuges to evade it. At a time when the Jewish name is besmirched, perhaps no greater defence of the principles and truths we stand for, could have been penned.

S. M. LEHRMAN

a (1) Ex. XXIII, 10–11; Lev. XXV, 2–7, 20–22; Deut. XV, 1–3.

b (1) Cf. R.H. 9*a*.

SHEBI'ITH

CHAPTER I

a *MISHNAH* 1. UNTIL WHEN MAY AN ORCHARD[1] BE PLOUGHED IN THE SIXTH YEAR?[2] BETH SHAMMAI SAY: AS LONG AS SUCH WORK WILL BENEFIT THE FRUIT;[3] BUT BETH HILLEL SAY: TILL PENTECOST.[4] [IN FACT] THE VIEWS OF ONE [SCHOOL] APPROXIMATE THE OTHER.[5]

MISHNAH 2. WHAT CONSTITUTES AN ORCHARD? ANY FIELD TO WHICH THERE ARE AT LEAST THREE TREES TO EVERY SE'AH.[6] IF EACH TREE BE CAPABLE[7] OF A YIELD OF A TALENT OF PRESSED FIGS, BEING SIXTY MANEH[8] OF THE ITALIAN [SYSTEM] IN WEIGHT, THEN THE ENTIRE AREA MAY BE PLOUGHED FOR THEIR SAKE.[9] IF LESS THAN THIS AMOUNT,[10] THEN ONLY SUCH AREA MAY BE PLOUGHED THAT IS ACTUALLY OCCUPIED BY THE GATHERER WHEN HIS BASKET[11] IS PLACED BEHIND HIM.[12]

MISHNAH 3. WHETHER THEY BE FRUIT-BEARING TREES
b OR NON-FRUIT-BEARING TREES,[1] THEY ARE TREATED AS FIG-TREES; AND IF THEY ARE ABLE TO YIELD A CAKE OF PRESSED FIGS, SIXTY MANEH OF THE ITALIAN [SYSTEM] IN WEIGHT,[2] THEN THE WHOLE AREA OF THE SE'AH MAY BE PLOUGHED ON THEIR ACCOUNT.[3] IF NOT, ONLY SUCH AREA MAY BE PLOUGHED THAT IS ESSENTIAL FOR THEM.[4]

MISHNAH 4. IF ONE TREE IS CAPABLE OF BEARING A CAKE OF DRIED FIGS, AND THE OTHER TWO UNABLE; OR, IF TWO CAN DO SO, BUT ONE CANNOT, THEN PLOUGHING IS PERMITTED ONLY WITHIN SUCH AREA ESSENTIAL FOR EACH OF THEM [THIS IS THE RULE IF THE NUMBER OF TREES IS] FROM THREE TO NINE;[5] BUT IF THERE WERE TEN TREES OR MORE, THE WHOLE AREA MAY ON THEIR ACCOUNT BE PLOUGHED, IRRESPECTIVE OF THE FACT WHETHER THEY BEAR FRUIT OR NOT.[6] BECAUSE IT SAYS: 'IN PLOUGHING-TIME AND IN HARVEST, THOU SHALT REST'.[7] NOW IT WAS UNNECESSARY TO SPEAK OF PLOUGHING AND HARVESTING IN THE SEVENTH YEAR,[8] BUT [WHAT IT MEANS IS] THE PLOUGHING OF THE YEAR PRECEDING, WHICH ENCROACHES ON THE SABBATICAL YEAR, AND THE HARVEST OF THE SEVENTH YEAR WHICH EXTENDS INTO THE YEAR AFTER. R. ISHMAEL SAYS:[9]
c JUST AS PLOUGHING IS AN OPTIONAL ACT,[1] SO HARVESTING REFERS TO SUCH AS IS OPTIONAL, THUS EXCLUDING THE

a (1) Lit., 'a field with trees'; opp. to שדה לבן, 'a field of white', 'a bright, shadeless field, sown with grain or vegetables. (2) Lit., 'on the eve of the seventh year'. Like the weekly Sabbath, the Sabbatical year also cast a foreglow of sanctity on the preceding year. This was to safeguard the inviolability of the holy day or year itself. (3) That will ripen in the sixth year; but all work must cease as soon as the fruit of the sixth year no longer needs attention. (4) All work after this period being considered as intended to benefit the crop of the seventh year. Were it a vegetable field (שדה לבן) work could only be done until Passover, v. *infra* II, 1. This is the earlier teaching; later legislation enacted for post-Temple times, however, permitted labour till the New Year itself. (5) Though Beth Hillel's view would still be the more lenient, in accordance with their usual tradition. (6) An area of 2,500 square cubits. Normally, such a space contains ten trees, each within a square of sixteen cubits. (7) Considering its size, and even if not actually bearing such a crop. Maim. and others interpret: 'If the three trees *together* are capable'. (8) A gold or silver weight equal to a hundred common, or fifty sacred, *shekels*; v. Bek. 5*a*. (9) Till Pentecost. (10) Viz., than sixty *maneh* in the Italian system. (11) In which figs picked were placed. (12) Lit., 'outside him'. More space is thus needed than if he had placed the basket in front of him; i.e., between him and the tree. Outside this area, the orchard is placed in the category of a vegetable field, to be ploughed until Passover.

b (1) Namely, the three trees above-mentioned. The phrase אילן סרק is defined in Kil. VI, 5 as fruitless trees. (2) The fruit of the fig-tree is large and abundant, hence this seemingly large criterion. (3) The stems of fruitless trees are made thicker by ploughing. (4) I.e., for the gatherer and his basket, when deposited behind him. (5) Within a *se'ah's* area. (6) Even if they do not yield the amount above stipulated. (7) Ex. XXXIV, 21. Context is Sabbath observance, but since there was no point in saying that one must not plough on the Sabbath, when all kinds of work are forbidden, the verse was applied to ploughing and harvesting of the seventh year, and even of the sixth year after periods duly prescribed. (8) Since this is specifically stated in Lev. XXV, 3ff. (9) That verse quoted applies indeed to the Sabbath.

c (1) Neither ploughing nor harvesting are found as obligatory commands, and therefore are never permitted on Sabbath.

שביעית פרק ראשון

תורה אור

א א) **עד** אימתי חורשין בשדה האילן ערב שביעית בית שמאי אומרים כל זמן שהוא יפה לפרי ובית הלל אומרים עד העצרת וקרובין דברי אלו להיות כדברי אלו: **ב** איזהו שדה האילן כל שלשה אילנות לבית סאה אם ראויין לעשות ככר דבילה של ששים מנה באיטלקי חורשים כל בית סאה בשבילן פחות מכאן אין חורשין להן אלא מלא האורה וסלו חוצה לו: **ג** אחד אילן סרק ואחד אילן מאכל רואין אותן כאילו הם תאנים אם ראוין לעשות ככר דבילה של ששים מנה באיטלקי חורשין כל בית סאה בשבילן פחות מכאן אין חורשין להם אלא לצרכן: **ד** היה אחד עושה ככר דבילה וב' אין עושין או שנים עושין אחד אינו עושה אין חורשין להם אלא לצרכן עד שיהיו משלשה ועד תשעה היו עשרה מעשרה ולמעלה בין עושין בין שאינן עושין חורשין כל בית סאה בשבילן שנאמר °בחריש ובקציר תשבות

אין ג) צ"ל חריש וקציר של שביעית אלא חריש של ערב שביעית שהוא נכנס בשביעית וקציר של שביעית שהוא יוצא למוצאי שביעית ג) רבי ישמעאל אומר מה חריש רשות אף קציר רשות

יצא

ה וחורשין כל בית סאה בשבילן · יש מפרשים עד העלרת (ב) אבל בירושלמי (הל' ד') קאמר בהדיא עד ראש השנה (ג): ביניהן· בין אילן לאילן: בקר בכליו · ב' שוורים עם העול והיינו ד' אמות כדאמרינן בפרק המוכר את הספינה (פ"ג·) אבל פחות מיכן למעקר קאי ואין חורשין: ו נטיעות· ילדות (ד) שורה שנטועה במקום אחד כחומה ואין מפוזרות אין חורשין אלא לורכן משום דכשמפוזרות נראה כחורש לצורך האילן אבל היכא דקיימן במקום אחד נראה כמתקן את הארץ לצורך שביעית ולא לצורך האילן:ומוקפות עטרה· גדר סביב:ירושלמי (הל' ס')ר' חייא בר אבא בעא קומי ר' יוחנן עכשיו למה חורשין בזקנות א"ל בשעה

יצא קציר העומר: ה א) שלשה אילנות של שלשה אנשים הרי אלו מצטרפין וחורשין כל בית סאה בשבילן וכמה יהא ביניהם רבן גמליאל אומר כדי שיהא הבקר עובר בכליו: ו ג) עשר נטיעות מפוזרות בתוך בית סאה חורשין כל בית סאה בשבילן עד ראש השנה היו עשויות שורה ומוקפות עטרה אין חורשין להם אלא לצרכן: ז הנטיעות והדלועים מצטרפין לתוך בית סאה רבן שמעון בן גמליאל אומר כל עשרה דלועים לבית סאה חורשים כל בית סאה עד ראש השנה: ח עד אימתי נקראו נטיעות רבי אליעזר בן עזריה אומר עד שיחולו רבי יהושע אומר בת שבע שנים רבי עקיבא אומר נטיעה כשמה אילן שנגמם והוציא חליפין מטפח ולמטה כנטיעה מטפח ולמעלה כאילן דברי רבי שמעון:

פרק שני

א עד ג) אימתי חורשים בשדה הלבן ערב שביעית עד שתכלה הליחה כל זמן שבני אדם חורשים ליטע במקשאות ובמדלעות א"ר שמעון נתת תורת כל א' וא' בידו אלא בשדה הלבן עד הפסח ובשדה האילן עד עצרת: ב מזבלין ומעדרין במקשאות ובמדלעות עד ראש השנה וכן בבית השלחין מיבלין מפרקין מאבקין מעשנין עד ראש השנה רבי שמעון אומר אף נוטל הוא את העלה מן האשכול בשביעית: ג מסקלין עד ראש השנה מקרסמין מזרדין מפסלין עד ראש השנה ר' יהושע אומר כזירודה וכפיסולה של חמישית כך של ששית ר' שמעון אומר כל זמן שאני רשאי בעבודת

HARVESTING OF THE OMER[2] [WHICH IS OBLIGATORY].

MISHNAH 5. IF THREE TREES BELONG TO THREE PERSONS, THEY ARE INCLUDED TOGETHER AND THE WHOLE AREA OF THE SE'AH MAY BE PLOUGHED ON THEIR ACCOUNT.[3] WHAT SPACE SHOULD THERE BE BETWEEN THEM?[4] R. GAMALIEL SAID: SUFFICIENT FOR THE DRIVER OF THE HERD[5] TO PASS THROUGH WITH HIS IMPLEMENTS.[6]

MISHNAH 6. IF TEN SAPLINGS ARE SCATTERED OVER THE ENTIRE AREA OF A SE'AH, ONE MAY PLOUGH THE WHOLE SPACE OF THE SE'AH,[7] EVEN UNTIL THE NEW YEAR;[8] BUT IF THEY WERE ARRANGED IN A ROW AND SURROUNDED BY A FENCE,[9] THEN ONLY SUCH PLOUGHING IS PERMITTED THAT IS ESSENTIAL TO THEM.[10]

MISHNAH 7. SAPLINGS AND GOURDS MAY BE INCLUDED[11] WITHIN THE SE'AH'S SPACE. R. SIMEON B. GAMALIEL SAYS: ONE MAY PLOUGH THE WHOLE SPACE UNTIL THE NEW YEAR
a WHEN THERE ARE TEN GOURDS TO THE SE'AH.[1]

MISHNAH 8. TILL WHEN ARE THEY TERMED SAPLINGS?[2] R. ELEAZAR B. AZARIAH SAYS: UNTIL THEY ARE PERMITTED FOR COMMON USE;[3] BUT R. JOSHUA SAYS: UNTIL THEY ARE SEVEN YEARS OLD. R. AKIBA SAYS: [THE WORD] SAPLING MUST BE TAKEN LITERALLY.[4] IF A TREE HAD BEEN FELLED AND PRODUCED FRESH SHOOTS OF ONE HANDBREADTH OR LESS, THEY ARE REGARDED AS SAPLINGS;[5] IF OF MORE THAN A HANDBREADTH THEY ARE REGARDED AS TREES. SO R. SIMEON.

CHAPTER II

b MISHNAH 1. UNTIL WHEN MAY A GRAIN-FIELD[1] BE PLOUGHED IN THE SIXTH YEAR? UNTIL THE MOISTURE HAS DRIED UP IN THE SOIL;[2] OR AS LONG AS MEN STILL PLOUGH IN ORDER TO PLANT CUCUMBERS AND GOURDS.[3] SAID R. SIMEON: IN THIS CASE YOU ARE PLACING THE LAW IN THE HANDS OF EACH MAN?[4] NO; [THE PRESCRIBED PERIOD] IN THE CASE OF A GRAIN-FIELD[5] IS UNTIL PASSOVER, AND IN THE CASE OF AN ORCHARD,[6] TILL PENTECOST.[7]

MISHNAH 2. BEDS OF CUCUMBERS AND GOURDS MAY BE MANURED[8] AND HOED[9] UNTIL THE NEW YEAR;[10] SO, TOO, MAY FIELDS THAT MUST BE IRRIGATED.[11] ONE MAY REMOVE PARASITIC EXCRESCENCES FROM TREES,[12] STRIP OFF LEAVES,[13]
c COVER ROOTS WITH POWDER,[1] AND FUMIGATE PLANTS.[2] R. SIMEON SAYS: ONE MAY ALSO REMOVE LEAVES[3] FROM A GRAPE CLUSTER EVEN IN THE SEVENTH YEAR ITSELF.[4]

MISHNAH 3. STONES MAY BE CLEARED AWAY UNTIL THE ADVENT OF THE NEW YEAR.[5] TREES MAY BE TRIMMED,[6] NIPPED,[7] AND THE DRY TWIGS LOPPED OFF UNTIL THE NEW YEAR. R. JOSHUA SAYS: JUST AS ONE MAY TRIM AND SNIP IN THE FIFTH YEAR [TO AID GROWTH IN THE SIXTH], SO MAY ONE PERFORM THIS WORK IN THE SIXTH YEAR [IN PREPARATION FOR THE SEVENTH];[8] BUT R. SIMEON SAYS: AS LONG AS I MAY LEGALLY

---

(2) And consequently overrides even the Sabbath; Men. X, 9; Mak. 8b. (3) As if there were only one proprietor; *supra* I, 2. (4) Between each tree. (5) Reading בֹּקֵר, *nomen agentis. Aliter:* for oxen and yoke to pass through; reading בָּקָר, 'herd'. (6) About four cubits; 'Er. III, 1. If less than this space separates each tree, it is obvious that trees are needed more for their wood than for their fruit. The more space that exists, the better will be the quality of the fruit. (7) Whereas three trees constituted an orchard (*supra* I, 2), of saplings there must be ten in this area, and each equi-distant from the other. (8) In order to safeguard the saplings that they might not wither. V. Ta'an. 3a. (9) Being thus arranged and fenced in, work done would be interpreted as intended not for the trees but for the soil, for the purpose of the Sabbatical year. (10) Namely, sufficient space for the gatherer and his basket behind him; the rest is treated as a vegetable field. (11) To complement the number of saplings required in the preceding Mishnah. The Greek gourd is meant, which is as large as a young tree. Bert. stipulates that saplings have to be in a majority of 6 : 4.

a (1) With no saplings whatsoever; regarding the gourds as tantamount to saplings. (2) So that ploughing should be allowed for the whole area until New Year. (3) In the fourth year, when they cease to be '*Orlah* (v. Glos.) Lev. XIX, 23. They are then 'redeemed', their equivalent in money plus one fifth of their value being set apart. After this, they were then fit for common use. The fruit had to be consumed in Jerusalem, wherever possible; but should distance prevent, then their money equivalent was spent there. Fruit not redeemed in the fourth year, automatically became fit for common use in the fifth year. (4) I.e., if in its first year; maintaining that after this it is called a tree. (5) Both as regards ploughing in the seventh year and also with regard to '*Orlah*.

b (1) Lit., 'field of white'; v. *supra* I, 1, n. 1. (2) After Passover, when rains cease. (3) That need much moisture in order to expedite their ripeness before the dawn of the seventh year. After this period work is forbidden. (4) For one person will claim that the moisture in his soil has dried up, and the other will claim to the contrary; not all soil being of even nature. (5) Sown after ploughing requiring more moisture. (6) Which does not need much ploughing, and all that is required is to enable the rain to descend to the soil. (7) V. *supra* I, 1, n. 4. (8) Manure is formed from the garbage of foliage that had been piled up. (9) I.e., to dig around the roots of the trees. Only such work being permitted at the approach of the Sabbatical year as is essential for the fruit of the sixth year. Work calculated to improve the tree itself is forbidden, unless it be such work that is prohibited in the seventh year by Rabbinical decree. (10) The Biblical prohibition of Sabbatical year only embraces such labour as ploughing, sowing, reaping, pruning and gleaning. According to Maim., ploughing itself is only of Rabbinical origin. (11) בית השלחין. Opp. to בית הבעל, a naturally irrigated field; v. M.Ḳ. 2a. Cucumbers must have plenty of moisture in the soil. (12) Heb. יבלת, a withered excrescence on trees, or a wart on the skin. (13) To lighten the burden of the tree.

c (1) To enhance fertility of plants. (2) So as to stay the worms gnawing around them. (3) That had withered. (4) If it would damage the cluster itself. R. Simeon is of the opinion that such work does not directly benefit the tree itself. (5) Even if the stones were piled one on top of the other to resemble some construction: loose, isolated stones could of course be removed without the slightest qualms; *infra* III, 7. (6) V. Ps. LXXX, 14. Maim. translates: Cut the ears off, leaving only the stems. (7) When shoots abound, they are clipped to accelerate and strengthen their growth. (8) Could proof be clearer that his work is intended solely for the sixth year?

TEND THE TREE ITSELF, SO LONG MAY I LOP OFF THE BRANCHES THEREOF.[9]

MISHNAH 4. SAPLINGS MAY BE BESMEARED,[10] WRAPPED ROUND,[11] AND TRIMMED,[12] AND UNTIL THE NEW YEAR ONE MAY ALSO CONSTRUCT FOR THEM SHELTERS[13] AND IRRIGATE THEM.[14] R. ELEAZAR B. ZADOK SAYS: THE FOLIAGE MAY EVEN BE WATERED IN THE SEVENTH YEAR ITSELF, BUT NOT THE
a ROOTS THEMSELVES.[1]

MISHNAH 5. UNRIPE FIGS MAY BE SMEARED WITH OIL[2] OR PIERCED[3] UNTIL THE NEW YEAR; BUT THOSE OF THE SIXTH YEAR[4] WHICH REMAIN UNPLUCKED UNTIL THE SEVENTH YEAR, OR OF THOSE OF THE SEVENTH YEAR WHICH REMAIN UNPLUCKED UNTIL THE EIGHTH, MUST NOT BE SMEARED OR PLUCKED.[5] R. JUDAH SAYS: IN PLACES WHERE IT IS THE CUSTOM TO DO SO,[6] ONE MAY NOT SMEAR [THE FIGS], SINCE THAT WOULD BE CONSIDERED WORK; BUT WHERE THIS WAS NOT DONE, THEN PERMISSION WAS GIVEN TO ONE TO DO SO. R. SIMEON PERMITTED ANY KIND OF WORK IN CONNECTION WITH THE TREE ITSELF,[7] BECAUSE ALL WORK BENEFITING THE TREE WAS LEGAL.

MISHNAH 6. ONE MAY NOT PLANT, ENGRAFT[8] TREES, NOR SINK [VINE-SHOOTS][9] IN THE SIXTH YEAR[10] WITHIN THIRTY DAYS OF THE NEW YEAR. IF HE HAS DONE SO, HE MUST UPROOT THEM ALL. R. JUDAH SAYS: ANY GRAFTING THAT HAS NOT TAKEN ROOT WITHIN THREE DAYS WILL NEVER DO SO. R. JOSE AND R. SIMEON SAY: TWO WEEKS.[11]

b *MISHNAH* 7. RICE, MILLET, PANIC[1] AND SESAME[2] THAT HAD TAKEN ROOT BEFORE THE NEW YEAR MUST BE TITHED[3]

(9) Namely, until Pentecost. (10) With rancid oil to ward off vermin. According to Jast. it means 'to cover a wound in a tree with dung and tie it up', so that the tree improves and becomes strong. (11) With rags as protection against heat and cold. (12) מקטמין Suk. 29*b*. *Aliter:* And covered with powder washes; cf. *supra* 2. (13) A booth-construction whereby to protect tender saplings from spells of heat and cold, heavy downpours or storms that might blight the fruit. Others: a fence-like arrangement, a cubit in height, filled with soil, to aid the tree's growth. (14) By pouring water on them so that their roots may receive the needed moisture. Because such work, even in the seventh year, was only due to Rabbinical prohibition, no ban was placed on it being performed in the sixth year.

a (1) For this would be to encourage work in the Sabbatical year ordinarily performed in the sixth year, and it is essential that distinction should be made. (2) To accelerate their ripeness. (3) Either to lubricate them from within, or to expedite growth by allowing rain to soak them thoroughly. (4) That usually ripen in Tishri of the seventh year. (5) Since they had not ripened in the seventh year even after oiling in the sixth, they must not be oiled in the seventh to facilitate their full growth in the eighth year. (6) To smear or pierce unripe figs in the sixth year. (7) Refers to unripe figs of the seventh year that are still on the tree in the eighth year. Though such work in the eighth year was permitted, yet fruit of the seventh year could not be eaten till the fifteenth of Shebat of the eighth year. (8) Lit., 'to form a tree'; viz., to bend a vine by driving it into the ground, and making it grow forth as an independent plant. (9) Lit., 'causing one branch to ride on another of the same kind'; another form of engrafting. (10) Even after Temple times. Laws of the Sabbatical year must not be forgotten. (11) These periods are apart from the thirty days before the New Year within which no work may be done.

b (1) Lat. *panicum;* a genus of grasses including Italian millet. According to Bert. it is a kind of pomegranate, filled with seed which can be heard rattling from within. (2) Very copious in Palestine. (3) In an ordinary year.

עין משפט
נר מצוה

ב א [מיי' שם הל' ט ופ"א הל' ה']:
ג ב מיי' פ"ג מהל' שמטה ויובל הל' ט סמג לאוין רפז :
ד ג שם הלכה י' :
ה ד ה שם הל' יא:

*) נ"א על
*) נ"א על

ו ו מיי' פ"ד שם הלכה יא ופ"א מהלכות מעשר שני ונטע רבעי הל' ח סמג לאוין רסח :

פירוש הרא"ש
(ד) ולא נהירא דהיינו מאכקין דלעיל ונראה שחותך ראשי הענפים וכו' :

הגהות הרי"י לנדא
פרק ב א] כר"ש ירושלמי מתניתא כרבנן. נ"ל מתניתין דרבי גרס כרבנן מזהמין ומתליעים :

מסירת הש"ס
א) ע"ג פ"ד דף נ':
ב) [עו"ג נ: ע"ש]:
ג) יבמות פ"ה דף פג: ור"ה פ"א דף י':
ד) [פסחים נה.]:
ה) ר"ה פ"א דף יג:

האילן רשאי אני בפיסולו : ד א) [א]מזהמין את הנטיעות וכורכין אותן וקוטמין אותן ועושין להם בתים ומשקין אותן עד ראש השנה רבי אליעזר ברבי צדוק אומר אף משקה הוא *את הנוף בשביעית אבל לא *את העיקר : ה ב) [ב]סכין את הפגים ומנקבים אותם עד ראש השנה פגי [ג]ערב שביעית שנכנסו לשביעית ושל שביעית שיצאו למוצאי שביעית לא סכין ולא מנקבין אותן ר' יהודה אומר מקום שנהגו לסוך אינן סכין מפני שהיא עבודה מקום שנהגו שלא לסוך סכין ר' שמעון מתיר באילן מפני שהוא רשאי בעבודת האילן : ו ג) [ד]אין נוטעין ואין מבריכין ואין מרכיבין ערב שביעית פחות מל' יום לפני ר"ה ואם נטע או הבריך או הרכיב יעקור ד) ר' יהודה אומר כל הרכבה שאינה קולטת [ה]לג' ימים שוב אינה קולטת ר' יוסי ור"ש אומרים לב' שבתות : ז ה) [ו]האורז והדוחן והפרגין והשומשמין שהשרישו לפני ראש השנה

רשאי בעבודת האילן רשאי אני בפיסולו עד הערלת: ד מזהמין · כשיש מכה לאילן ונשרה קצת קליפתו מדביקין שם זבל וקושרין שלא ימות ומיהו זיהום דהכא צריך לומר דמחזק את האילן ומשביחו ומשמע עד ר"ה אין בשביעית לא ובמסכת ע"ג פרק ר' ישמעאל (נ:) תניא ומתליעין ומזהמין בשביעית ומשני התם תרי זיהומי הוו חד אוקמי אילנא ושרי וחד אברויי אילנא ואסור ואע"ג דבעבודת אילן אסורה ל' יום לפני ר"ה הכא שרי שלא ימותו הנטיעות דהנך עבודות דרבנן הם כדאמרינן בריש מו"ק (ד' ג: וד' ·) אבות אסר רחמנא תולדות לא אסר רחמנא והכא לא גזור: וכורכין אותן. מפני הצנה והחמה: וקוטמין אותן · פירש בערוך אפר תרגומו קטמא(ד) ויש מפרשים שוברי' הראשים כמו נקטם ראשו : ועושין להם בתים· גדר אמה גובה סביבותיהם וממלאין אות' עפר ומיהו בירושלמי משמע בית ממש צל : על הנוף · של אילן אבל לא על העיקר שצריך לשמות ולא יעשה בשביעית כשאר השנים· ירושלמי (הל' ד') מתניתא כרבנן א] מתליעין בשביעית אבל לא במועד כאן וכאן אין מגזמין אבל נוטל הרואה רבי יוסי אמר רבי אבינא בעי מה בין המזהם לעושה בית · המזהם אינו אלא כמושיב שומר בית עושה להן צל והיא גדילה מחמתו · פירוש מתני' כרבנן · דברייתא דמייתי היינו ההיא דפ' ר"י (נ:) וקסבר בירושלמי דפלוגתא דתנאי היא ולית ליה שינויא דמשנינן תרי זיהומי הוי: עוד ירושל' (שם) תני רבי יוסי בן כיפר אומר משום ר' אלעזר בן שמוע ב"ש אומרים משקה על הנוף ויורד על העיקר וב"ה אומרים משקה בין על הנוף בין על העיקר . פירוש הך ברייתא בערב שביעית איירי עד ר"ה דקתני רישא בתוספתא (פ"א) משקין את הנטיעות עד ראש השנה והדר קתני ר' יוסי בן כיפר אומר ומסיים בה אמרו להן בית הלל לבית שמאי אם אתה מתיר להן מקצת תתיר להן את הכל ואם אין אתה מתיר להם את הכל לא תתיר להם מקצת: ה פגין· מלשון התאנה חנטה פגיה (שיר ב) וסכין אותן בשמן או בחלב כדי שימהרו להתבשל ומנקבין אותן כדי שיכנסו בהן הגשמים ויתבשלו מהרה ויש מפרשים שממלאים נקבי הפגין שמן : שנכנסו לשביעית · כלומר אם לא נתבשלו בששית ונכנסו לשביעית : ולא סכין · בשביעית ומיהו לא משמע כן דמרישא שמעת מינה עד ראש השנה אין (בששית) [בשביעית] לא ויש לפרש דאיירי בפגין שאין דרכן להתבשל עד תשרי ולכך קתני פגי ערב שביעית שנכנסו לשביעית ואפילו בששית קאמר דלא סכין ולא מנקבין מאחר דאין נגמר בישולן עד שתכנס שביעית ואפילו שנהגו שלא לסוך ור' יהודה מיקל ושרי מיהו במקום שנהגו שלא לסוך בשאר שנים דלאו עבודה היא : רבי שמעון מתיר · לסוך ולנקוב את האילן עצמו קסבר שאדם רשאי לנקוב את האילן דלא אסר רחמנא אלא עבודת קרקע ומיהו לא יתכן לומר דקאי אסיכה דאפילו רבנן מודו דאשכחן במסכת ע"ג בפ' ר' ישמעאל (דף נ:)סכין שמן לגיזום בין במועד בין בשביעית (ועוד) [אבל קשה] דלעיל אסר ר' שמעון בפיסולו של אילן ועוד הכתיב וכרמך לא תזמור אלא אתא לאשמעינן דאילן מלא פירות שביעית מותר לעשות במוצאי שביעית כל עבודות הצריכות לאילן כדתניא בתורת כהנים שבת שבתון [יהיה לארץ] כיון שיצאת שביעית אע"פ שפירותיה שמטה מותר אתה לעשות מלאכה בגופו של אילן [אבל] פירותיו אסורין עד ט"ו בשבט: ירושלמי (הל' ג') אכן תנינן סכין הפגין תני דבי רבי אלו הן פגי ערב שביעית שנכנסין לשביעית ר' אליעזר כמתני' ר' יוחנן כהדא דתני דבית רבי על דעתיה דר' אליעזר לא בא ר' יהודה אלא להקל על דעתיה דר' יוחנן לא בא רבי יהודה אלא להחמיר·פי' תנא דבי רבי לר' יוחנן קא מפרש מתני' ערב שביעית שנכנסו לשביעית ארישא קאי כלומר הא דאמרן סכין את הפגין ומנקבים אותן עד ראש השנה היינו בשל ערב שביעית שנכנסו לשביעית ושמא במתני' גופה הוה תני אלו הן והא דתני מתני' לא סכין ולא מנקבין לאו אשל ערב שביעית שנכנסו לשביעית קאי אלא אשל שביעית שיצאו למוצאי שביעית לחודייהו קאי [והשתא] רבי אליעזר הוה מפרש מתני' כפשטה בלא אלו הן וסכין ומנקבין בשל ששית שאין נכנסין לשביעית אבל בשל ששית שנכנסו לשביעית או של שביעית שיצאו למוצאי שביעית לא סכין ולא מנקבין ורבי יוחנן כדתני דבי רבי הלכך על כורחין לרבי אליעזר רבי יהודה להקל דמוכח בתוספתא דרבי יהודה אפגי ערב שביעית שנכנסו לשביעית קאי ות"ק אמר לא סכין סתם ולא מפליג בין מקום שנהגו לסוך למקום שנהגו שלא לסוך ולר' יוחנן על כורחיך להחמיר דתנא קמא שרי בכל ענין·תניא בתוספתא פגי ערב שביעית שנכנסו לשביעית ר"י אומר מקום שנהגו לסוך אין סכין מפני שהיא עבודה מקום שנהגו שלא לסוך סכין ושל שביעית שיצאו למוצאי שביעית הכל שוין שאין סכין ואין מנקבין אותן פי' הכל שוים ר"י ות"ק אבל ר"ש פליג כדפרשינן במתני':ו אין נוטעין ואין מבריכין·נטיעה שייכא באילן הברכה בגפן כדתנן (פ"ז מ"א דכלאים) המבריך את הגפן שכופף את הזמורה בארץ הרכבה שמביא ענף זית ומרכיבו בתוך זית אחר : פחות מל' יום · בפ"ק דר"ה (דף י:) אמר רב נחמן אמר רבה בר אבוה לדברי האומר ל' צריך ל' ול' לדברי האומר ג' צריך ג' ול' לדברי האומר שתי שבתות צריך שתי שבתות ול' יום שצריך שתהא נשרשת הנטיעה בארץ קודם שיבא תוספת שביעית ואי קלטה בתוספת שביעית יעקור ומיהו ר"ת מפרש דרב נחמן אמר רבה בר אבוה לאו אשביעית קאי אלא אערלה קאי משום דקשיא ליה הדא דלשון מתני' אין משמע כן ועוד מדתניא בפ"ק דראש השנה (דף ט:) אחד הנוטע ואחד המבריך ואחד המרכיב ערב שביעית ל' יום לפני ראש השנה עלתה לו שנה ומותר לקיימן בשביעית פחות מל' יום לפני ראש השנה לא עלתה לו שנה ואסור לקיימן בשביעית וקאמר התם (דף י·) לימא דלא כרבי מאיר דאמר יום אחד בשנה חשוב שנה דתניא פר האמור בתורה סתם בן כ"ד חודש ויום אחד דברי רבי מאיר ופריך אלא מאי ר"א ל' ול' בעי ומייתי מתניתין דהכא ומדרב נחמן אמר רבה בר אבוה והשתא [אי] אמתני' דהכא קאי מאי קשיא ליה אי ברייתא כר' אליעזר הא כי היכי דבמתני' דהכא קתני ל' ומוקמינן להו בקליטה בלא ל' של תוספת הכי נמי ל' דברייתא בל' של קליטה בלאו הנך דתוספת דל' ול' בעי ועוד דבסמוך גבי אורז ודוחן ופרגין ושומשמין דמחלק לענין שביעית בין השרישו לפני ר"ה להשרישו לאחר ר"ה דמשמע דלא חיישינן במה שמשרישין בתוספת שביעית דקתני שביעית דומיא דמעשר ומפרש ר"ת דהכי קאמר רב נחמן לדברי האומר ל' לקליטה בשביעית צריך ל' ול' לענין ערלה אבל לענין שביעית לא חיישינן אלא שלא תקלוט בשלשה ימים[מותר] לקיים כיון דלא נקלט בשביעית עצמה אע"פ שנטע (בשביעית) באיסור כשנטע שלשה ימים לפני ראש השנה דאסור ליטע משום תוספת שביעית מדאורייתא כמו חרישה דלא תזמור כתיב דאמרי' בריש מועד קטן (דף ג:) דזמירה בכלל זריעה ועיקר מלאכה טפי מזמירה כדמוכח בפ' כלל גדול (דף עג:) דזומר חייב משום נוטע אעפ"כ מותר לקיימם ומה שר"ת היה אומר דמותר ליטע בתוספת שביעית מידי דהויא אשאר תולדות דאמרינן בריש מועד קטן (ג·) דכתיב את ספיח קצירך לא תקצור ואת ענבי נזירך ואמרינן מכדי זריעה בכלל זמירה ובצירה בכלל קצירה [למאי הלכתא כתבינהו רחמנא] למימרא דאהני תולדות הוא דמחייב אתולדות אחריני לא מיחייב ולא גזרו בתוספת ולא יתכן כלל ואורז ודוחן ופרגין ושומשמין נמי אע"פ שזריעתן מלאכה דאורייי' דכתיב לא תזרע מ"מ לא חיישינן ובלבד שישרישו לפני ראש השנה אע"ג דבאיסור זרע והא דמייתי בסוף הערל (פג·) הא דרב נחמן גבי הלכה כר"י באנדרוגינוס ובהרכבה לאו משום דאתי רב נחמן לפרושי מתני' דשביעית דלא מייתי לה אלא למימר דאף לענין ערלה הלכה כר' יוסי : קולטת · מלשון ולא את הנמר ליורה אלא כדי שיקלוט את העין בפ"ק דשבת (דף יז:) : ז אורז ודוחן · מיני קטניות הן וקורין אותן בלע"ז מיליו : פרגין · פירש בערוך מקום בלשון כנען והוא כעין רמון מלא

אומר שהוא אסור אלא עד ערלת בלבד שהוא מותר בעבודת האילן כמו שהיתה משנה ראשונה והלכה כתנא קמא : ד זוהמא . שם לריח רע ופי' שמנהג עובדי האדמה לסוך הנטועים בשמן שיש לו ריח רע כדי שיריחו אותם התולעים אוכלי האילנות וירחקו מהם: וכורכין . הוא שיקבץ הענפים והפארות ויקשרם כדי שיעלו למעלה במישור ולא יכנו על הארץ: וקוטמין . הוא לכרות קלחם כשיצטרך לזה : ועושין להם בתים. שעושין להם צללים להסך מן הגשם והשמש שלא יזיקום : ומשקין אותן . שופכין מים על ראש האילן ויורד על גוף האילן כולו וישקהו:ואמר ר' אליעזר בר' צדוק. שבשנה שביעית עצמה מותר זה : ונוף . הוא ראש האילן ר"ל הענפים והעלין : והעיקר.הוא השרש ואין הלכה כר' אליעזר בר' צדוק : ה סכין · מושחין בשמן למהר בישולן:ומנקבין עושין בתאנים נקבים וכן מנהג התאנים בקצת מקומות אצלנו שאינן מתבשלין עד ימשחו בשמן עץ דק ונוקבין בו מקצת כל תאנה מהם והלכה כרבי יהודה ולא כר' שמעון : ו נוטעין · ידוע : מבריכין . להשכיב האילן בארץ על ארכו ולהחזיר העפר עליו ויצמחו בו אילנות רבות . ומרכיבין פירוש לנטוע בגוף האילן והתנאים כולן מסכימין שצריך שתעלה לו שנה קודם שנת השמטה ואז יהיה מותר הנטיעה ההיא ערב שביעית והם חולקין בדבר זה שדעת תנא קמא יום אחד בשנה חשוב שנה ודעת ר' יהודה ורבי יוסי ור' שמעון שלשים יום בשנה חשוב שנה וכולן מסכימין שהוא צריך שתעלה לו שנה אחר זמן קליטה ופירוש קליטה לקיחה וחטיפה והיא מגולה לחבור האילן בארץ ולהסתבכות חוטי השרש בארץ והם כמו כן חולקין בקליטה שתנא קמא אומר לשלשים יום קולטת ר' יהודה אומר לשלשה ימים ור' יוסי ור' שמעון אומרים לשתי שבתות וא"כ נתחייב ממה שיסדנו שדעת ר' יוסי ור"ש שצריך לנטוע קודם ראש השנה במ"ד יום שתי שבתות לקליטה ול' יום לאחר קליטה כדי שתעלה לו שנה ולדעת רבי יהודה צריך לנטוע קודם ראש השנה בל"ג ימים ג' לקליטה ול' יום כדי שתעלה לו שנה אחר קליטה ולדעת תנא קמא צריך לנטוע ל' יום קודם ראש השנה בלבד א"כ מסתברא שהוא צריך ל"א יום ל' לקליטה ויום אחד אחר קליטה כדי שתעלה לו שנה כמו שבארנו מדעתו שהוא אומר יום אחד בשנה חשוב שנה אבל הוא סובר יום שלשים עולה לכאן ולכאן ר"ל שהוא נמנה מימי הקליטה ונמנה עם מה שאחריו ותעלה בו שנה והלכה כר' יוסי: ז אורז . ידוע וכבר פירשנוהו: ודוחן . בערבי דכו"ן ובלע"ז מי"ל : ופרגין · בערבי שבאש : ושומשמין . סומסם ואלו ארבע מינין בלבד הוא הכוונה בהם שתשרים קודם שביעית אבל התבואה עד שתביא שליש כמו שנבארהו בעתיד והירק הולכין בו אחר זמן לקיטתו וכן אמרו ירק אחר לקיטתו למעשר ושאמר ראש השנה אין הכוונה על ראש השנה של שנה (בשנה) שביעית אבל הוא רוצה כשתשרים קודם ראש השנה יהיה דינם למעשרות דין שנה שעברה אם כן נתחייב בשנה שעברה במעשר עני יוציאו בזאת כמו כן מעשר עני ואם נתחייב בה מעשר שני יוציא מעשר שני והשנים שמוציאים בהן מעשר עני במקום מעשר שני היא הג' משנות השמטה והששית כמ"ש במה שהקדמנו (בדמאי פ"ד מ"ג) ועוד משנה אותו ונוסיף לבארו אם נזדמן להיות שנה זו שנה שביעית יהיו אלו כמו פירות ששית ומותרין בשביעית ואם לא השרישו

פי' מהר"י בן מלכי צדק

ד מזהמין את הנטיעות . פירוש מניחין צואת כלבין אצל הנטיעה כדי שלא ייבש וכנכורכין את הנטיעות בעלין כדי שלא ייבשו : וקוטמין אותן.פי' באפר כדי שלא ייבשו מלשון אפר וקטם . ויש אומרים חותכין את הנופות היבישין מן האילן : ועושין להן בתים. גרסינן [בירושלמי] מה בין המזהם לעושה לה בית מוהם אינו אלא כמושיב שומר שלא ייבש אבל אינה גדילה מחמת זיהום אבל עושה לה בית עושה לה צל והיא גדילה מחמתו : ומשקין אותה.פי' הנטיעה: ר' אלעזר ברבי צדוק אומר משקה הוא את הנוף בלעז רמו. תניא ר' יוסי בן כיפר אומר משום ר"א בר"ש בית שמאי אומרין משקה על הנוף ויורד על העיקר . ובית הלל אומרים משקה בין על הנוף בין על העיקר . אמרו בית הלל לבית שמאי אם את מתיר להן מקצת התר להן את הכל ואם אי אתה מתיר להן את הכל אל תתיר להן מקצת : ה סכין את הפגין . פי' מושחין את הבוסר מן החלב שלהן והתאנין כשהן בוסר נקראין פגין מלשון התאנה חנטה פגיה. סכין מלשון וסוך לא סכתי : ומנקבין אותן.פי' כדי שיכנסו בהן הגשמי' ויתבשלו במהרה הפגין: עד ראש השנה . פי' בפגין שאינם נכנסין לשביעית אלא בקיץ של ששית מתבשלין וכן דרכן ובזמן שרואה שמתאחר בשולן סכין אותן ומנקבין אותן . אבל פגי ערב שביעית שדרכן להתבשל בתשרי דהיינו מאחר שנכנסה השביעית לא סכין ולא מנקבין אותן אפי' בששית ואפי' שנהגו שלא לסוך ורבי יהודה מיקל דמקום שנהגו שלא לסוך מיהא סכין דבהני פליג רבי יהודה ורבנן . אבל בפני שביעית היוצאין למוצאי שביעית כולי עלמא לא פליגי דאסור דתניא בהדיא פגי ערב שביעי' שנכנסו לשביעית ר' יהודה אומר מקום שנהגו לסוך אין סכין מפני שהיא עבודה מקום שנהגו שלא לסוך סכין ושל שביעית שיצאו למוצאי שביעית הכל שוין שאין סכין ואין מנקבין אותן : פ"א סכין את הפגין ומנקבין אותן עד ראש השנה ואילו הפגין אם נכנסו לשביעית שוב לא סכין ולא מנקבין אותן בשביעית אפי' במקום שאין מנהגם לסוך התאנים בכל שני שבוע . ור' יהודה מיקל דמקום שאין מנהגן לסוך תאניהן בשאר כל השנים בשביעית סכין דלאו עבודה היא ואתי ר' יהודה לקולא : תני סכין את הפגין עד ראש השנה ואלו הן פגי ערב שביעית שנכנסו לשביעית . פי' בין במקום שנהגו לסוך בין במקום שלא נהגו לסוך ורבי יהודה מחמיר ואמר במקום שנהגו לסוך אין סכין ואתי ר' יהודה לחומרא והיינו דגרסינן בירושלמי ר' אליעזר כמתני' רבי יוחנן כהדא דתני דבי רבי פי' דתני סכין את הפגין עד ראש השנה ואילו הן פגי ערב שביעית [שנכנסו לשביעית] על דעתיה דר' אלעזר לא בא ר' יהודה אלא להקל . על דעתיה דר' יוחנן לא בא רבי יהודה אלא להחמיר : ר' שמעון מתיר באילן. פי' לסוך ולנקב את האילן עצמו עד ראש השנה מפני שהוא רשאי בעבודת האילן. פ"א ר' שמעון לאו אסיכה ונקיבה קאי אלא אתא לאשמעינן שאע"פ שהאילן מלא פירות שביעית מותר אתה לעשות כל עבודות הצריכות לאילן כגון קירסום פיסול זיבול חרישה וכדתנו רבנן שבת שבתון יהיה לארץ כיון שיצאת שביעית אע"פ שפירותיה שמטה מותר אתה לעשות מלאכה בגופו של אילן אבל פירותיו אסורין עד ט"ו בשבט : ו אין נוטעין ואין מבריכין . פי' נטיעה היא אלא שנטיעה באילן והברכה בגפן כדתנן המבריך את הגפן : ואין מרכיבין . פי' מביאין ענף זית ומביאין בתוך זית אחר זו נקראת הרכבה . והגרים עושין ענין אחר כדתניא בכלאים גוי שהרכיב אגוז על הפרסקי אע"פ שאין ישראל רשאי לעשות כן נוטל ממנו ייחור ונוטעו במקום אחר מה נפיק מינהון קדיר ופירסקא . ודתניא מזהמין ומתליעין בשביעית הא לא קשיא תרי זיהומי הוו חד אוקמי אילנות ושרי . וחד אברויי אילנא [ואסור בשביעית עצמו אבל עד ראש השנה מזהמין] : ערב שביעית פחות מל' יום . מאי טעמא דכל הני תנאי סבירא להו ל' יום לפני ראש השנה חשובין שנה מאן דאמר ל' בעי ל' ול' כיצד ל' לקליטה ול' לשנה . ומאן דאמר ג' בעי ג' ול' ג' לקליטה ול' לשנה . ומאן דבעי ב' שבתות בעי ב' שבתות לקליטה ול' לשנה . ואם נטע או הבריך או הרכיב פחות משיעורא דילהו לכל חד וחד כי טעמיה יעקור : ז האורז והדוחן וכו' . בלעז אורז ריזו דוחן מיליו: והפרגין פי' בערוך מקום בלשון כנען ובלשון ערבי כשכש . והוא ענין רמון אבל לא עגל כמוהו ומלא זרע כחרדל וכשמנענעו קורא קיש קיש וכשינקב יוצא הכל מן הנקב והוא מתוק ועושין ממנו שמן כמו השומשמין : שומשמין שהשרישו לפני ראש השנה מתעשרין לשעבר ש' שנחשבין

עין משפט נר מצוה

ז א מיי׳ פ״א מהלכות מעשר שני ונטע רבעי הלכה י ומיי׳ פ״ד מהלכות שמטה ויובל הלכה יד סמג לאוין רסח:

ח ב ג שם הלכה ח ופ״א מהלכות מעשר שני ונטע רבעי הלכה י:

ט ד מיי׳ פ״ד מהלכות שמטה ויובל הלכה יח סמג לאוין רסח:

י ה מיי׳ פ״א שם הלכה ט סמג לאוין רסז:

יא ו שם הלכה טו:

מסורת הש״ס

א) ר״ה דף יד:

מתעשרין לשעבר ומותרין בשביעית ואם לאו אסורין בשביעית ומתעשרין לשנה הבאה:

ח רבי שמעון שזורי אומר [א]פול המצרי שזרעו לזרע בתחלה כיוצא בהן ר׳ שמעון אומר אפונין הגמלונין כיוצא בהן רבי אלעזר אומר אפונין הגמלונין משתרמלו לפני ראש השנה:

ט א) [ב]הבצלים הסריסים ופול המצרי שמנע מהם מים שלשים יום לפני ראש השנה מתעשרין לשעבר ומותרין בשביעית ואם לאו אסורין בשביעית ומתעשרין לשנה הבאה ושל בעל שמנע מהם מים שתי עונות דברי רבי מאיר [ג]וחכמים אומרים שלש:

י [ד]הדלועין שקיימן לזרע אם הקשו לפני ר״ה ונפסלו מאוכל אדם מותר לקיימן בשביעית ואם לאו אסור לקיימן בשביעית התמרות שלהן אסורות בשביעית [ה]ומרביצין בעפר לבן דברי רבי שמעון רבי אליעזר בן יעקב אוסר [ו]ממרסין באורז בשביעית רבי שמעון אומר אבל אין מכסחין:

פירוש הרא״ש

(ה) ובשביעית בזמן הזה מיירי ורבי היא דאמר בפרק השולח דנוהגת מדרבנן

פי׳ מהר״י בן מלכי צדק

שנחשבין משנת ו׳ ואם לאו אסור בשביעית ובשנת מעשר מתעשרין

ACCORDING TO THE PREVIOUS YEAR,[4] AND BECOME PERMISSIBLE IN THE SEVENTH YEAR.[5] IF THEY DID NOT,[6] THEN THEY ARE FORBIDDEN IN THE SEVENTH YEAR, AND ARE TITHED ACCORDING TO THE YEAR FOLLOWING.[7]

MISHNAH 8. R. SIMEON SHEZURI[8] SAID: EGYPTIAN BEANS SOWN ORIGINALLY AS SEED ONLY,[9] FOLLOW A LIKE PROCEDURE.[10] R. SIMEON SAYS: ALSO LARGE BEANS[11] FOLLOW A LIKE PROCEDURE; BUT R. ELIEZER SAYS: [THIS IS SO] IN THE CASE OF LARGE BEANS ONLY IF THEY BEGAN TO FORM PODS[12] BEFORE THE NEW YEAR.

MISHNAH 9. SEEDLESS ONIONS[13] AND EGYPTIAN BEANS[14] FROM WHICH WATER HAS BEEN WITHHELD FOR THIRTY DAYS
a PRIOR TO NEW YEAR[1] ARE TITHED IN ACCORDANCE WITH THE
YEAR PRECEDING,[2] AND BECOME PERMITTED IN THE SEVENTH YEAR. IN OTHER CASES THEY ARE FORBIDDEN IN THE SEVENTH,[3] AND ARE TITHED IN ACCORDANCE WITH THE YEAR FOLLOWING. [A SIMILAR PROCEDURE IS FOLLOWED] SAYS R. MEIR, IN THE CASE OF A NATURALLY-WATERED FIELD[4] FROM WHICH TWO SEASONS[5] OF RAIN HAVE BEEN WITHHELD; BUT THE SAGES SAY: THREE.

MISHNAH 10. IF GOURDS HAD BEEN KEPT FOR SEED[6] AND THEY HAD HARDENED BEFORE THE NEW YEAR, THUS BECOMING UNFIT FOR HUMAN FOOD, THEY MAY BE LEFT GROWING DURING THE SEVENTH YEAR; OTHERWISE, THEY MUST NOT BE KEPT IN THE SEVENTH YEAR.[7] THEIR BUDS[8] ARE FORBIDDEN IN THE SEVENTH YEAR.[9] THE SOIL OF 'A WHITE FIELD' MAY BE IRRIGATED;[10] SO R. SIMEON; BUT R. ELEAZAR B. JACOB FORBIDS. THE SOIL OF A RICE FIELD
b MAY BE STIRRED[1] IN THE SABBATICAL YEAR [WITH WATER].
R. SIMEON SAYS: BUT [THE RICE-PLANTS] MAY NOT BE TRIMMED.[2]

(4) Thus if the previous year was the first, second, fourth or fifth of the Sabbatical cycle, the First and Second Tithe must be given; and if it was the third, then both the First Tithe and the Poor Man's Tithe must be given; R.H. 14*a*. (5) Since they took root in the sixth year, the sanctity of the seventh year does not apply to them. (6) Take root before the New Year. (7) I.e., of the year they are plucked. Should this be the seventh year itself, they are not to be tithed at all, since the sanctity of the Sabbatical year already applies to them. Tithing is due in the case of trees from their moment of blossoming, of vegetables as soon as they had been picked, and in the case of grain and olives after they had become a third ripe, but in the case of rice, etc. the time is when they have taken root. Being planted at the same time, the flowering of roots is also identical. (8) So named after his birth-place, Shezur. (9) Never intending to use them as food. (10) Described in the Mishnah preceding; i.e., when they have taken root, and not when plucked, as in the case of vegetable and edible produce. (11) Kil. III, 2 includes them with vegetables. (12) Tithing is due when beans harden, and appear encased in a kind of bag. (13) Lit., 'eunuchs'. Unlike other species of onion that are kept in the soil in order to yield seed, the shallot onion is the fruit itself, and is seedless. (14) Sown for food, and grown after irrigation. Had they been sown for seed, tithing would have been due from the time of taking root, even if they had not been watered; cf. *supra* 8.
a (1) They now become as naturally watered fields dependent on rain.
(2) Following the practice of trees and grain, and not of vegetables that are watered by hand and tithed according to the year when they are gathered. This law is derived from a comparison of phrase between 'threshing-floor' and 'wine-press' (גרן ויקב), produce of which depends on rainfalls and tithed in accordance with the preceding year. Vegetables that need hand-irrigation are regarded as naturally watered fields if water has been withheld from them. (3) Since they are still moist when the New Year dawns, it would seem as if they had been watered in the Sabbatical year. Other vegetables do not share this distinction. (4) Independent of hand-irrigation, but relying on the winter rainfalls. The term בעל is still correct among the Arab felaheen. (5) I.e., the two usual spells when rain might normally have been expected, a period longer than thirty days. (6) Left growing in the soil. (7) Even for seed. All Sabbatical year produce must be 'removed'; they may be kept only when they become unfit for human food. (8) Lit., 'palms'; the efflorescence on gourds resembles palm-leaves; Suk. 33*a*. (9) Like all other things that grow of their own accord in that year; cf. *infra* IX, 1. (10) In the sixth and seventh years, so that vegetables may ripen before the dawn of the Sabbatical year. The law was modified in the case of damage accruing to the former, so that irrigation was allowed in the seventh year to enable vegetables to ripen in the eighth year.
b (1) A rice-field requires a good soaking, so that the soil becomes well-kneaded; cf. Yoma 43*b*. (2) Calculated to benefit the growth of the rice.

CHAPTER III

MISHNAH 1. WHEN MAY MANURE BE BROUGHT OUT TO
a THE DUNG-HEAPS?[1] R. MEIR SAYS: TILL SUCH TIME WHEN THE LABOURERS HAVE CEASED;[2] BUT R. JUDAH OPINES TILL THE MANURE[3] HAS DRIED UP.[4] R. JOSE SAYS: TILL [THE DUNG DRIES] INTO KNOTTY EXCRESCENCES.[5]

MISHNAH 2. WHAT QUANTITY OF DUNG MAY BE DEPOSITED?[6] THREE DUNG-HEAPS TO EVERY SE'AH, [CONSISTING OF] TEN BASKETS [OF FOLIAGE][7] OF A LETHEK[8] EACH. YOU MAY ADD TO THE NUMBER OF BASKETS,[9] BUT NOT TO THE NUMBER OF HEAPS.[10] R. SIMEON SAYS: ALSO TO THE NUMBER OF HEAPS.[11]

MISHNAH 3. A MAN MAY DEPOSIT IN HIS FIELD THREE DUNG-HEAPS TO EVERY SE'AH-SPACE, SO R. SIMEON;[12] MORE THAN THIS,[13] HE MUST ARRANGE IN THE FORM OF A TRIPOD.[14] THE SAGES FORBID UNLESS HE DEPOSITS [THEM] THREE
b [HANDBREADTHS] BELOW OR ABOVE.[1] A MAN MAY PILE UP ALL THE MANURE INTO ONE [LARGE] STORE;[2] R. MEIR FORBIDS, UNLESS HE DEPOSITS [THEM] EITHER THREE [HANDBREADTHS] BELOW OR ABOVE [THE SOIL].[3] IF HE HAD A LITTLE PILE, HE MAY CONSTANTLY ADD TO IT.[4] R. ELEAZAR B. AZARIAH FORBIDS[5] UNLESS HE DEPOSITS [IT] THREE [HANDBREADTHS] BELOW OR ABOVE THE SOIL, OR HE DEPOSITS [IT] ON ROCKY GROUND.[6]

MISHNAH 4. HE WHO ALLOWS CATTLE TO CHANGE FOLDS WITHIN HIS FIELDS,[7] MUST MAKE AN ENCLOSURE TWO SE'AHS IN AREA.[8] HE THEN PULLS OUT THREE SIDES THEREOF,[9] AND LEAVES THE MIDDLE SIDE; HE WILL THEN POSSESS A FOLD OF FOUR SE'AHS SPACE.[10] R. SIMEON B. GAMALIEL SAYS: EVEN ONE OF EIGHT SE'AHS [MAY BE USED].[11] IF HIS ENTIRE FIELD IS ONLY FOUR SE'AHS IN AREA, HE MUST ALLOW A PORTION THEREOF TO REMAIN [UNENCLOSED] FOR APPEARANCE'S SAKE.[12] AND HE MAY TAKE THE DUNG[13] FROM THE ENCLOSURE, AND SPREAD ACROSS HIS FIELD IN THE MANNER
c OF THOSE WHO MANURE THEIR FIELDS.[1]

MISHNAH 5. A MAN MAY NOT OPEN A STONE-QUARRY WITHIN HIS FIELD FOR THE FIRST TIME,[2] UNLESS THERE BE THEREIN THREE LAYERS [OF HEWN STONES], EACH THREE [CUBITS LONG], THREE WIDE AND THREE HIGH, TOGETHER

a (1) Till what time in the seventh year may the field be manured to benefit the produce of the eighth year? Manure used to be collected in one spot during the seventh year, and when it became a huge pile was scattered across the field. (2) עובדי עבודה, work in the fields. Var. lec. עובדי עבדה, referring to those who contravene the Sabbatical laws. (3) Lit., 'sweetness', because it imparts flavour and ripeness to the fruit; *infra* IX, 6; Job XXI, 33. (4) When all work ceases, since the manure is no longer of any use to the soil. (5) Manure is said to be dried up as soon as an uppermost protuberance is noticeable. (6) Without the semblance of infringing upon the Sabbatical law. (7) Used for dung; Kel. XIX, 10. (8) Fifteen *se'ahs*, or half a *kor*. (9) To be placed on dung-hills, and add to the number of ten. (10) One may not exceed three, for this would come into the actual category of manuring. (11) Since they are all piled in one heap, it will not be interpreted as manuring. (12) Amplifying his statement in the previous Mishnah. (13) I.e., more than three heaps. (14) מחציב, an unusual word; here connected with a stand for a pitcher, triangular in shape, and not in a row, so as to avoid the appearance that he is measuring his field. Var. lec.: מותר.

b (1) Ground level; an action clearly designed to show that his purpose is not actually to manure. (2) I.e., heap. Viz., even one hundred baskets on one dung-heap; for this is not the same as placing more than three dung-heaps in a *se'ah's* space. (3) For in the event of this huge pile covering the extent of the field, the suspicion will be aroused that he is actually manuring the soil. (4) Of smaller quantity than those above mentioned; hence insufficient to take into the fields. (5) He may not procure more manure, and the little he has would give the impression of actually manuring the soil. He must then wait until he has dung below, or until it has been piled on high. (6) Unfit for sowing and hence impervious to manure. Being rocky soil it need not be raised three handbreadths. (7) By allowing his cattle to abide there, manure is collected. The case is of one who has no other place to keep his cattle; for had his intention been deliberately to gather manure, it would have been forbidden in the seventh year. (8) I.e., 100 × 50 cubits. (9) After that area has been filled with dung. (10) Having set up the three sides uprooted around the adjoining two *se'ah's* space. (11) On this device; without being suspected of manuring in the Sabbatical year. (12) Lest it appear that his primary intention was to manure his field. (13) After the enclosure had been filled.

c (1) Viz., three dung-heaps to every *se'ah's* space; *supra* III, 3. (2) In the seventh year.

פרק שלישי

א מאימתי מוציאין זבלין לאשפתות משיפסקו *עובדי עבודה דברי ר"מ ר' יהודה אומר משיבש המתוק ר' יוסי אומר [א]משיקשר[א]: **ב** [ב]עד כמה מזבלין עד שלש שלש אשפתות לבית סאה של עשר עשר משפלות של לתך לתך [ג]מוסיפין על המשפלות ואין מוסיפין על האשפתות ר"ש אומר אף על האשפתות: **ג** [ד]עושה אדם את שדהו שלש שלש אשפתות לבית סאה יתר מכן *מחציב דברי רבי שמעון וחכמים אוסרין [ה]עד שיעמיק שלשה או עד שיגביה שלשה [ו]עושה א) אדם את זבלו אוצר ר' מאיר אוסר עד שיעמיק שלשה או עד שיגביה שלשה [ז]היה לו דבר מועט מוסיף עליו והולך ר' אלעזר בן עזריה אוסר עד שיעמיק שלשה או עד שיגביה שלשה או עד שיתן על הסלע: **ד** [ח]המדייר (ג) את שדהו עושה סהר לבית סאתים עוקר שלש רוחות ומניח את האמצעית נמצא מדייר בית ארבעת סאין רבן שמעון בן גמליאל אומר בית שמונת סאין [ט]היתה כל שדהו בית ארבעת סאין משייר ממנה מקצת מפני מראית העין [י]ומוציא מן הסהר ונותן לתוך שדהו כדרך המזבלין: **ה** [כ]לא יפתח אדם מחצב בתחלה לתוך שדהו עד שיהיו בו שלש מורביות שהם שלש על שלש על רום שלש שיעורן

א בידוע שעבודת הארץ בשנה שביעית אסור ולזבל השדות נחשב מכלל עבודת הארץ ומפני זה אין מותר בשנה שביעית להוציא זבל לעשות ממנו אשפה חוץ למדינה עד זמן ידוע מהשנה ור"מ אומר שהזמן ההוא הוא כשיסתלקו עובדי הארץ מעבודתם בשנה שביעית שקודם זה יחשוב כל הרואה אותו נושא הזבל שהוא מוליכו לעבודת האדמה ושהוא מעובדי עבודה: ואמר ר' יהודה שאסור לו להוציא זבל ולעשות אשפות ממנו בשנה שביעית עד שיבש המתוק והוא הנקרא בערבי חנט"ל ובלע"ז קולק"ו ינטיד"א שבזמן ההוא אין מזבלין הארץ לעבודה: ואמר רבי יוסי מעט שיקשר המתוק ונקרא מתוק מפני שהוא מר כמו שיקראו לעור סגיא נהור והלכה כר' יוסי: **ב** המשפלות. הוא הכלי שנושאין בו הזבל ולתך חצי כור וכבר זכרנו פעמים רבות שהכור ל' סאה ובארנו שיעור הסאה בסוף פאה (מ"ז) ופירשנו כמו כן פעמים רבות שבית סאה חמשים על חמשים אמה: פירוש מוסיפין על המשפלות הוא שישימו באשפה יותר מעשר משפלות ואין מוסיפין על האשפתות הוא שלא יתן בשיעור בית סאה יותר משלש ור' שמעון מתיר להיות בבית סאה יותר משלש אשפתות ואין הלכה כר' שמעון: **ג** עד שיעמיק שלשה. ר"ל כשיהיה יותר משלש אשפתות לבית סאה אינו מותר לו עד שיעמיק מקום האשפה או יגביה כדי שיראה שאין מחשבתו וכוונתו לתיקון הארץ ועבודתה אלא לאסוף הזבל: היה לו דבר מועט. ר"ל כשיהיה לו בתוך שדהו בשביעית זבל מועט מותר לו להוסיף עליו מעט מעט עד שיעשה אשפה בזמן שיהא מותר להוציא הזבלין לאשפות ור' אלעזר בן עזריה אינו מתיר זה שמא יאמר הרואה אותו לעבודת הארץ נתכוין ר' אלעזר בן עזריה יחייבהו להוציא עשר משפלות כאחת עד שיודע לכל שהוא עושה אשפה ואין הלכה כר' מאיר ולא כר' אלעזר בן עזריה והלכה כחכמים: **ד** המדייר את שדהו. שיתן בה דיר עד שתזדבל שדהו. וסהר הוא גדרות לצאן ששם יאספו הצאן ואמר כשירצה לזבל שדהו בשנה שביעית יעשה הגדרה שיעורה כבית סאתים ויכניס בה הצאן כדי שיזבלו וכשירבה הזבל יסיר השלש קירות ויעזוב הרביעי ויחזיר השלש קירות מאחורי המקום ההוא אל הצד האחר ויהיה כמו כן סהר מבית סאתים מצד אחר נמצא מדייר בית ד' סאין ויהיה קיר אחד מארבע קירות של סהר משותף בין הסהר הראשון שיש בשיעורו בית סאתים ובין הסהר השני העשוי מצד השני והיא רוח אמצעית שזכר: ורבן שמעון בן גמליאל אומר כשיעשה סהר מבית סאתים כמו שהותר לו לעשות סהר שני מן הצד האחד כן מותר לו לעשות סהר מכל צד מצדי הסהר הראשון ויהיה בית שמונה סאין חוץ מהסהר הראשון. ותנא קמא אומר כשתהיה השדה כולה בית ד' סאין אסור לו לעשות בהם סהר של בית סאתים וסהר אחר בלדו שימלא השדה כולה דומן ונראה שנזדבלה בשביעית ויספיק לו להוציא הדומן מן הסהר ולעשות ממנו אשפה כפי מה שהתנה בעשיית האשפתות במנינם ושיעורם ואין הלכה כרשב"ג: **ה** מחצב. מקום בתוך שדהו יחצב ממנו האבנים מפני שהוא יפה לארץ כשמסיר ממנו הסלע: ג' מורביות. שלשה

א מאימתי מוציאין זבלין לאשפתות. לאחר שהוציא אשפות לרשות הרבים כדי שיהא נישוף ברגלי אדם וברגלי בהמה כונסו למקום אחד בשדה ועושה שם אשפה גדולה עד שהוא [מפזרו] בשדה לזבלה וקודם שפסקו עובדי עבודה אסור שלא יאמרו לזבל שדהו הוא מוציא ופלוגתא בירושל' (הל' א) אם מותר לעשות אשפה על פתח חצרו עד שלא פסקו עובדי עבודה ופריך בירושל' (שם) מעתה אפי' משפסקו עובדי עבודה יהא אסור מפני מראית העין שלא יהו אומרים לתוך שדה בית השלחין שלו הוא מוציא ומשני יודעין בני עירו אם יש לו בית השלחין אי לא (א) אמר רבי יוסי הדא אמרה לא חשו לעוברים ושבים: משיבש המתוק. הוא הזבל שמבשל וממתק את הפירות ובירושלמי (שם) אמרינן משיבש המתוק פקוע אמר רבי מנא ההן פקועה דבקעתא כלומר ביקוע השדות ובערוך פירש בשם הר' דניאל כמו פקועות שדה (מלכים ב ד): משיקשר. מפרש בירושל' (שם) משיעשה קשרים קשרים (ב) אמר ר' חוניא מכיון שנקשר בו קשר העליון מיד הוא יבש ותניא קרובים להיות דבריהם שוים: **ב** עד כמה מזבלין. משיבש המתוק לרבי יהודה ולר' יוסי משיקשר: משפלות. פי' בערוך קופות גדולות שמוציאין בהם זבלים ובלשון ישמעאל נקרא משפל והביא הא דאמר בויקרא רבה בפרשת זאת תהיה אמר רבי חנין דציפורי תלולית זו של עפר מה הטיפש אומר מי יכול לסייפה אבל פיקח אומר ולא אחד לגברא אף אני קוצה ב' משפלות היום ושתים למחר עד שאני מסייפה: של לתך לתך. כל משפלת מחזקת לתך דהיינו חצי כור וזהו משוי של חמור כדתנן בפרק השוכר את האומנים (דף פ.): מוסיפים על המשפלות. לעשות אשפה גדולה אפילו של ב' אשפות ויותר ואין מוסיפין על האשפות יותר משלש אשפות לבית סאה משום דמחזי כמזבל שדהו ורבי שמעון שרי דכיון דאשפה היא שהזבל צבור לא מיחזי כמזבל: **ג** יותר מיכן. כלומר אפי' יותר מג' אשפות לבית סאה מותר לעשות ור"ש לטעמיה ואף על גב ב] דהוה ליה רישא הדר תנייה הכא לפרושי מילתייהו דרבנן דאסרי עד שיעמיק או שיגביה ואז לא מיחזי כמזבל ובירושלמי (הל' ב) פריך לה ולמה תניתא תרי זמנין (אמר ר' ירמיה) כאן בפוחת מן המשפלות ברם הכא בעושה בכשיעור ותני כן על דר"ש ובלבד שלא יפחות לאשפה מג' משפלות וקצת נראה דגרס ברם התם בקמייתא בכשיעור עשר משפלות לאשפה אבל הכא בפחות מי' כדתני עלה ובלבד שלא יפחות מג' משפלות וס"ד דכיון דליכא עשר באשפה אם היה עושה יותר מג' אשפות לבית סאה היה נראה כמזבל שדהו: עושה את זבלו אוצר. דאותן ג' אשפות לבית סאה אם בא להניחן במקום א' בשדה דהייט [ל'] משפלות או אפילו ק' משפלות במקום א' מותר ולא תימא כי היכי דאסרי רבנן יותר מג' אשפות לבית סאה הכא נמי אסור במקום אחד יותר משיעור ג' אשפות קמ"ל דמותר: ורבי מאיר אוסר. משמע בירושלמי (שם) בעושה יותר מכשיעור דהיינו יותר משלשים משפלות אבל בכשיעור בג' מקומות מותר במקום אחד לא כל שכן ובפ"ק דמו"ק (דף ד: ועי"ש) פריך אהא דרבי מאיר דאמר עד שיעמיק שלשה והלא כשמעמיק נראה כעודר ומשני ר' זירא ור' אבא בר ממל חד אמר כגון שהעמיק קודם לכן וחד אמר זבלו מוכיח עליו ובירושלמי נמי משני הכי סלו ומגרפו מוכיחין עליו שעושין אשפה והא דמייתי [הך] דמועד קטן ולא מייתי מרישא וחכמים אוסרין עד שיעמיק שלשה משום דבעי לאקשויי דרבי אלעזר בן עזריה אדרבי אלעזר בן עזריה: היה לו דבר מועט מוסיף והולך. בירושל' (שם) פתר לה ב' פתרים כשהיה לו דבר מועט בתוך שדהו בשביעית ג] הרי זה מוסיף עליו והולך משיפסקו עובדי עבודה ראב"ע אוסר מאי טעמא שמא לא ימצא זבל ונמצא מזבל אותו המקום פתר ליה פתר חורין כשהיה לו דבר מועט בתוך ביתו ד] ערב שביעית ומבקש להוציאו לתוך שדהו בשביעית הרי זה מוסיף עליו והולך משפסקו עובדי עבודה ראב"ע אוסר מ"ט שמא לא ימצא זבל ונמצא מזבל אותו המקום ולא כבר מזובל הוא מערב שביעית רבי ירמיה ורבינו בשם ר' חייא משום מראית העין עד שיוציא עשר משפלות כאחת ולית להו לרבנן מפני מראית העין א"ר אידי סלו ומגרפו מוכיחין עליו שעושה אשפה: או עד שיתן על הסלע. אמרינן בירושלמי (שם) הכל מודין שאם היה לו שם אבנים או צרורות או סיד או גפסים מותר: **ד** המדייר את שדהו. בירושלמי (הל' ג) פריך תמן תנינן שדה שנתקווצה תזרע במוצאי שביעית נטייבה או נדיירה לא תזרע למוצאי שביעית ומשני א"ר יונה כיני מתני' הרוצה להעמיד צאן בתוך שדהו כלומר הא דנקט לישנא דמדייר לא שיעשה להניחה כך השדה מזובלת דלא נקט מדייר אלא בלשון העמדה בעלמא שלאחר כך מאסף כל הזבל ועושה ממנו שלש אשפתות לבית סאה כשיעור של מעלה: סהר. היקף של מחיצות סביב הצאן ואמרינן בירושל' (שם) בכל עושין סהרין [במחצלאות] ובקש ובאבנים אפי' שלשה חבלים זה למעלה מזה וזה למעלה מזה [ובלבד שיהא בין סהר לסהר כמלוא סהר אותו המקום] חולב בו וגוזז בו ומוליך ומביא הצאן דרך עליו: עוקר ג' רוחות. כשנתמלאה זבל עוקר מן הסהר שלש רוחות וזוקפו לצד אחר של אמצעית ומדייר שם כמו כן בית סאתים ועושה אשפתות בתוך שדהו כמו שאמרנו למעלה ג' ג' אשפתות לבית סאה: נמצא מדייר בית ארבעת סאין. סאתים מצד זה של אמצעית וסאתים מצד אחר והשמעינן מתני' דשרי לדייר בית ארבע סאין קודם שיעשה ממנו אשפתות בשדה אבל טפי לא שלא יאמרו לדייר שדהו מתכוין ורשב"ג שרי עד ח' סאין וכל זה בשדה גדולה שעדיין נשארה ממנו הרבה שלא נדיירה: רשב"ג אומר בית ח' סאין. בירושלמי (שם) תני רבי שמעון בן אלעזר אומר אם רצה תוקע יתד בארץ ועושה ד' סהרין [מד' רוחותיה של ח' סאין]: היתה שדה ובית ד' סאין. והא דאמרן היינו בשדה של ה' סאין אבל מכוונת של ארבע סאין משייר מקצת: מפני מראית העין שלא יהא נראה כמזבל שדהו אם היה עושה כולה סהר: כדרך המזבלין. ג' אשפתות לבית סאה: **ה** מחצב. בור שחוצבין ממנו אבנים לבניין קרוי מחצב מלשון ואבני מחצב (מ"ב יב) ופעמים שהבור מכוסה בארץ ואין ניכר על פני השדה עד שחופרין ומגלין אותו וזהו לשון פתיחה ויש שמגולה מקצתו וכשלא התחיל לפותחו מערב שביעית ובא לפותחו בתחלה בשביעית אסור לפותחו אא"כ יש בו מן הפתוח ומגולה כדי לחצוב ממנו שלש מורביות כלומ' שלש שורות של אבנים. מורביות לשון נדבכין שיש בכל אחת ואחת מן המורביות שלש אמות אורך ורוחב על רום ג' דהיינו כ"ז אבנים של אמה על אמה לכל מורביות ומורביות וכן היה דרכן לסדרן בשדה לאחר חציבתן לג' שורות של ג' ג' שהם ט' אבנים ויש כיוצא בהן ג' שורות סדורות זו על זו דהא ברום שלש קתני הרי כאן שלשה פעמים בכל אחת ולכאורה לישנא דמתני' משמע כ"ז לג' המורביות ושמא כל אבן ואבן היתה של אמה על אמה ברום ג' אמות שכן דרך לחצוב בתחלה וניחא טפי לפי שהאבנים ארוכות קוראין להן מורביות מלשון מורביות של תאנה דפרק ב' דתמיד (מ"ג) מורביות של ערבה דפ' לולב וערבה (דף מה.) וטעמא דמתני' דלא יפתח שלא יאמרו לתקן שדהו הוא מכוין להיות ראוי שדהו לזורעה בשביעית אי נמי כשחופר לגלות המחצב יאמרו עודר כדי לזרוע אבל בשיש מקום מגולה שראוי לחצוב כל כך אבנים מידע ידעי דלצורך אבני בנין עביד ואיכא דשרי בתוספתא אפילו מתכוין לעשות שדה לצורך מוצאי שביעית ולא חיישינן למיחזי כמתקן לצורך שביעית כיון דאיכא שיעור מרובה כל כך לא חשו למראית העין משום דמאן דחזי קאמר לצורך אבנים לבנין קא עביד ויש (מפרשים) ה] עוד לא יפתח אדם מחצב לכתחלה אלא אם *) יש בו כמה שחצב ממנו קודם שביעית כ"ז אבנים דאילו פחות מיכן חשיב השתא כחוצב בתחלה אבל אין לשון התוספתא משמע כן דקתני סיפא סלע שלף על גבי הארץ ואיגד יוצא ממנו אם יש בו כשיעור הזה מותר ואם לאו אסור: תניא בתוספתא (פ"ג) לא יפתח אדם מחצב בתחלה לתוך שדהו עד שיהיו בו ג' מורביות שהן ג' על ג' ברום ג' [א"ר יוסי בד"א בזמן שמתכוין לעשות שדה אבל בזמן שאין מתכוין לעשות שדה אפילו דבר מרובה מותר אמר רשב"ג] בד"א בזמן שאינו מתכוין לעשות שדה אבל בזמן שהוא מתכוין לעשות שדה אפילו כל שהוא אסור (ד) והך ברייתא קשה טובא דקאמר אפילו דבר מרובה מותר משמע שהיא רבותא ואדרבה בדבר מרובה אית לן להתיר טפי כדמוכח מתני' עד שיהא בו ושמא משום דלינו של מחצב שלא ניטול כולו כדתני סיפא דמתני' פחות מיכן מחצב

א) מ"ק פ"א דף ד:

פי' מהר"י בן מלכי צדק

פ"ג **א מאימתי** מוציאין זבלין לאשפתות משיפסקו עוברי עבירה. פי' שהיו מוציאין זבלין כדי שיהא נישוף ברגלי האדם וברגלי הבהמה והיו אומרים אנו לאשפה השלכנוהו: **רבי** יהודה אומ' משיבש המתוק. פי' הזבל שהוא ממתק ומבשל הפירות: **רבי** יוסי אומר משיקשר. פי' זה עם זה ונעשה כעפר ובלעז זבל הקשור נקרא [...]. ירושלמי אמר רבי מנא פקיעא ההן פקעתא דבקעתא פי' ביקוע השדות. וה"ר דניאל פירש פקעות השדה ממש הם המתוק ששנינו: **משיקשר** מכיון שנקשר בו קשר העליון מיד הוא יבש ומיבש המתוק לר"י ומשיקשר לר' יוסי: **ב מזבלין** עד כמה. מזבלין עד ג' ג' אשפתות לבית סאה לכל אשפה י' משפלות. בויקרא רבה תנינן א"ר חנין דציפורין תלולית זה של עפר מה הטיפש אומר מי יכול לסייפה אבל פיקח אומר ולא אחד צברה אף אני קוצה ב' משפלות היום וב' למחר עד שאני מסייפה פי' קופות שמוציאין בהן זבלין ובלשון ישמעאל משפאל ובלעז פנארי: **של** לתך לתך. פי' כל משפלת תכיל לתך דהיינו חצי כור. וכן הוא משוי של חמור דתנן בב"מ (דף פ'.) השוכר את החמור להביא לתך חטים דהיינו ט"ו סאים: **מוסיפין** על המשפלות. פי' עושין את האשפה יותר מי' משפלות ס"א עושין את המשפלות יותר מלתך אבל איני ידע כמה ומסתבר כדתנן תמן וכמה יוסיף עליהן סאה לגמל וג' קבין לחמור אבל אין עושין יותר מג' אשפתות. רבי ישמעאל אומ' אף על האשפתות מוסיפין: **ג עושה** אדם את שדהו וכו' יותר מיכן. כלומר יותר מג' אשפתות ר' שמעון כטעמיה דשרי לעיל וחכמים אוסרים ביותר מיכן עד שיעמיק ג' טפחים או עד שיגביה שלשה: **עושה** אדם את זבלו אוצר. כלומר מניחו בתוך שדהו כמו שהיה מכניסו לאוצר ולא חייש דילמא אתי לזבל שדהו וכו': **היה** לו דבר מועט. פי' היה לו מעט זבל בתוך שדהו מוסיף עליו והולך: ר' אלעזר בן עזריה אוסר. מאי טעמא שמא לא ימצא לו זבל ונמצא מזבל אותו המקום לפיכך עד שיעמיק ג' והקשו והלא כשמעמיק נראה כעודר ועודר קיי"ל דאסור מפני מראית העין. ופריק ר' אידי סלו ומגרפו מוכיחין עליו שעושה אשפה: **או** עד שיתן על הסלע. ירושלמי הכל מודין שאם היה לו שם אבנים או צרורות או סיד או גיפסים מותר בלא העמיק: **ד המדייר**. קתני המדייר למימרא דמותר לדייר והתנן נטייבה או נדיירה למימרא דאסור. א"ר יונה כיני מתני' הרוצה להעמיד צאן בתוך שדהו שהיא ד' סאין עושה סהר בית סאתים. תניא בכל עושין סהרין במחצלות ובקש ובאבנים אפילו [שלשה] חבלים זה למעלה מזה. אותו המקום. פי' היינו בית סהר חולב בו וגוזז בו ומוליך ומביא הצאן דרך עלי'. נתמלאת מן הזבל עוקר מתוך הסהר ג' רוחותיו ועושה אשפתות בתוך שדהו פי' בתוך בית סאתים כדרך המזבלין נמצא מזבל בית ד' סאין: **רבן** שמעון בן גמליאל אומר בית ח' סאין. תניא ר"ש בן אלעזר אומר אם רצה תוקע יתד בשדהו ועושה ד' סהרין בד' רוחותיה ויבוא לדייר ח' סאין: **היתה שדהו**. פי' זה שאמרו מזבל בית ד' סאין בשדהו בית ה' סאין או יותר שישאר מקום מן השדה שאינו מזובל אבל בשדה מכוונת בית ד' סאין כשמוציא הזבל מן הסהר לא יזבל כל בית סאתים אלא משייר ממנו מקצת מפני מראית העין שלא יראה כמזבל שדהו אלא כמטהר סהרו מזבלו שלא יטנפו הצאן בזבלים. תניא בתוספתא היתה כל שדהו בית סאתים לא יעשה כולה סהר אלא משייר ממנה מקצתה מפני מראית העין ומוציא מן הסהר ונותן לתוך שדהו כדרך המזבלין: **ה לא** יפתח אדם מחצב בתחלה לתוך שדהו. פי' מי שיש לו בתוך שדהו מקום של צור ורוצה לחצבו וליקח הצור ואחר כך ליזרע שם אם יש שם ג' סלעים שהן ג' אמות אורך ברוחב ג' אמות על רום ג' אמות שיבואו כ"ז אבנים כל אבן אמה על אמה ברום אמה. כיצד עושה ג' רצועות שכל רצועה רחבה אמה וארכה י' ורומה ג' וכן זו הרצועה התוך רומן והביאם בתוך אמה יבואו מן רצועה

עין משפט נר מצוה

א א ב מיי' פ"ב שם הלכה א:
ב ג שם הלכה ב:
ג ד שם הלכה ג:
ד ה שם הלכה ג:
ה ו ז שם הל' א:
ו ח שם הלכה ד:

נ"א עוברי עבירה

ז ט שם הלכה ה:
ח י שם הלכה ד:
ט כ שם הלכה ו:

נ"א מותר

פירוש הרא"ש

פרק ג (א) ולאותו שיש לו בית השלחין אסורים: (ב) כשמתחיל להתייבש מתעבה ומתקשר: (ג) מי שרוצה לקבץ זבל עושה היקף סביב שדהו ומכניס שם בהמות ואותו היקף נקרא דיר או סהר ובשביעית מותר לעשות סהר בית סאתים ק' על נ' כחצר המשכן ואחר שנתמלא זבל עוקר ג' מחיצות ומניח אחת ומעבר לאותה מחיצה שבכיה מקיף באותו עבר ג' מחיצות שעקר עוד בית סאתים: (ד) והלכה כרבנן והרמב"ם ז"ל פירש לא יפתח אדם מחצב בשביעית אלא אם כן התחיל לפסל ממנו ערב שביעית עשרים ושבע אבנים והא דנקט לשון פתיחה כי המחצב הוא שוה לארץ ומכוסה עפר על גביו וצריך לפתות הארץ קודם שיחצב תדע דבתוספתא פ"ג קתני בסיפא היה סלע שלף על גבי הארץ:

הגהות הרי"ד לנדא

פרק ג משנה א א] שדה משיקשר. עי' ר"ש מכילתין פ"ט מ"ז: ב] מ"ג בר"ש ואף על גב דהוי ליה רישא. צ"ל דתנא: ג] שם בתוך שדהו בשביעית. צ"ל ערב שביעית: ד] שם תוך ביתו ערב שביעית. צ"ל בשביעית: ה] שם ויש עוד לפרש כצ"ל:

*) [קן]

עשרים ושבעה אבנים: ו ^א^גדר שיש בו עשרה אבנים של משאוי שנים שנים הרי אלו ינטלו שיעור גדר עשרה טפחים פחות מיכן מחצב וגוממו עד פחות מהארץ טפח ^ב^בד"א מתוך שלו אבל מתוך של חברו מה שהוא רוצה יטול בד"א בזמן שלא התחיל בו מערב שביעית אבל אם התחיל בו מערב שביעית מה שהוא רוצה נוטל: ז ^ג^אבנים שזעזעתן המחרישה או שהיו מכוסות ונתגלו אם יש בהם שתים של משאוי שנים שנים הרי אלו ינטלו ^ד^המסקל את שדהו נוטל את העליונות ומניח את הנוגעות בארץ וכן גרגר של צרורות או גל של אבנים נוטל את העליונות ומניח את הנוגעות בארץ אם יש תחתיה סלע או קש הרי אלו ינטלו: ח ^ה^אין בונין מדרגות על פי הגאיות ערב שביעית משפסקו הגשמים מפני שהוא מתקנן לשביעית אבל בונה הוא בשביעית משפסקו גשמים מפני שהוא מתקנן למוצאי שביעית ולא *יסמוך בעפר אבל עושה הוא חייץ וכל אבן שהוא יכול לפשוט את ידו וליטלה הרי זו תנטל: ט ^ו^אבני כתף באות מכל מקום והקבלן מביא מכל מקום ואלו הם אבני כתף כל שאינה יכולה להינטל באחת יד דברי ר"מ רבי יוסי אומר ^ז^אבני כתף כשמן כל שהן נטלות ב' ג' על הכתף: י ^ח^הבונה גדר בינו ובין רשות הרבים מותר להעמיק עד הסלע מה יעשה בעפר צוברו ברשות הרבים ומתקנו דברי ר' יהושע ר' עקיבא אומר כדרך שאין מקלקלים ברשות הרבים כך לא יתקנו ^ט^מה יעשה בעפר צוברו בתוך שדהו כדרך המזבלין וכן החופר בור ושיח ומערה:

*) ר"א יסבך

פרק רביעי

א בראשונה ^י^היו אומרים מלקט אדם עצים ואבנים ועשבים בתוך שלו כדרך שהוא מלקט מתוך של חברו את הגס הגס משרבו עוברי עבירה התקינו שיהא זה מלקט מתוך של זה וזה מלקט מתוך של זה שלא בטובה ואין צריך לומר שיקצץ להם מזונות: ב ה) ^כ^שדה שנתקוצה תזרע במוצאי שביעית ^ל^שנטייבה או שנדיירה לא תזרע במוצאי שביעית שדה שנטייבה ב"ש אומרים אין אוכלין

*) פ"ה מ"ג ע' ח"ה ע"ב ס"ה דדרב

מחלב וגוממו עד פחות מהארץ טפח ועל זה קאמר אפי' דבר מרובה שנוטל הכל מותר וקצת משמע כן [מירושלמי] מדמייתי הך ברייתא אמתני' דגדר: ו של משוי שנים שנים. שיש באחת משוי ב' בני אדם הרי אלו ינטלו כולן ואפי' הקטנות דאילו גדולות אפי' א' ואפי' מונחת בארץ ואפי' ג' ניטלת על הכתף תנן לקמן דבאות מ"מ ולא מיחזי הכא כמפנה הגדר לעשות מקומו שדה: שיעור גדר י' טפחים. בירושלמי (הל' ד) מייתי הא דתנן בפרק י"ד דאהלות (מ"א) במה אמרו הזיז מביא את הטומאה בכל שהוא בזיז שגבוה ג' נדבכין שהן י"ב טפחים ופריך אמתני' דתנן שיעור גדר עשרה טפחים מה אנן קיימין אם כשהיו ב' נדבכין ניתני ח' טפחים אם כשהיו ג' ניתני שנים עשר טפחים אמר רבי יוסי חצי טפח לסיתות מכאן וחצי טפח לסיתות מכאן וכן לחבריה נמצאו ג' נדבכין של עשרה טפחים: פחות מיכן מחצב. ואינו נוטל כולו אלא גוממו ומניח מן הסלע בארץ טפח כדי שלא יהא ראוי לזריעה בירושלמי (שם) אמרו פחות מיכן אינו לא מחצב ולא גדר: בד"א. הא דלא יפתח מחצב והאי דגוממו: מה שהוא רוצה יטול. דלא מיחזי כמתקן שדה כיון דלאו דידיה הוא ואפילו בשלו נמי לא מיחזי כמתקן כיון דהתחיל מערב שביעית (ה): ז שזעזעתן המחרישה. אמרי' בירושל' (הל' ה') לא סוף דבר שזעזעתן אלא אפילו מחרישה עתידה לזעזעתן ובתוספתא (פ"ג) קתני אבנים התושבות כלומר שאינם מצורך השדה מלשון גר ותושב: של משוי שנים שבכל אחת משוי ב' בני אדם ינטלו כולן אגב אותן שנים דלא מיחזי כמתקן שדה: המסקל. שמעביר האבנים מן השדה מלשון סקלו מאבן (ישעיה סב). ומניח את התחתונות הנוגעות בארץ (ו) דבכי האי גוונא לא מיחזי כמתקן שדה: גרגר של צרורות גל של אבנים קטנים. מלשון שנים שלשה גרגרים בראש אמיר (שם יז): אם יש תחתיהן סלע או קש. לא מיחזי כמתקן כיון דאין כל המקום ראוי לזריעה: ח (ז) אין בונין מעלות ע"פ הגאיות. שלא יחליקו בירידתן לקחת המים שנתקבלו דנראה כמתקן להשקות בהן שדותיו בשביעית. גאיות מקום גבוה: ולא יסבוך בעפר. אם בא להיות סוכך מקום יציאת המים באבנים לא יתן עפר וטיט בין האבנים משום דמיחזי טפי שמתכוין להשקות מהן שדותיו. יסבוך מלשון נאחז בסבך בקרניו (בראשית כב): אבל עושה הוא חייץ. אבנים סדורות זו על זו כגון גדר בלא עפר וטיט ובירושל' (הל' ו) אמרי' כדכתיב והוא בונה חיץ (יחזקאל יג): כל אבן. שבשדהו אפילו קטנה אם הוא יכול לפשוט ידו וליטלה ולבנות בה גדר של אבנים כגון שסמוכין לגדר הרי זו תנטל שהגדר מוכח עליו לבנות גדר נוטלה ולא לתקן השדה לזריעה: ט באות מ"מ. אפילו מתוך שלו דמידע ידעי דלבנין בעי להו ולא לתקן השדה: והקבלן. מלשון מקבלי קיבולת שדרכו לעשות בנינים בקיבולת מביא מ"מ ואפילו פחותות מאבני כתף דאין כוונתו אלא לקבץ אבנים ואפי' מביא משדות שלו שרי דאי משדות אחרים אפי' אינו קבלן שרי כדתניא לעיל דמתוך של חברו מה שהוא רוצה נוטל ויש מפרשים קבלן שקיבל שדה באריסות דלא חשיב האי שדה כשלו ונוטל ממנו אפילו קטנות אף על פי שהוא אריס בה: י מותר להעמיק עד הסלע. ולא חיישינן דילמא מימלך וזרע ליה אי נמי לא גזרינן אטו עודר בשדה ואמר בירושלמי (הל' ז) אמר רבי יוחנן לא שנו אלא בינו לבין רשות הרבים דלא עביד איניש דזרע סמוך לרשות הרבים וליכא למיגזר טפי מידי אבל בינו לבין חברו אסור בשביעית אבל במועד אפילו בינו לבין רשות הרבים אסור ותנן נמי בפ"ק דמו"ק (דף ו: ע"ש) ומקרין את הפרצה במועד ובשביעית בונה כדרכו ומפרש בגמרא כילד מקרין צוברו לעפר ברשות הרבים ומתקנו לרשות הרבים וכן לענין סיקול נמי בשאר שני שבוע (ח) פליגי בתוספתא דגזר רבי עקיבא משום דכל מתקני דרכים מקלקלין תחלה ע"מ לתקן שמסירין העפר והטיט שנשקעין בהן העוברים או מביאים עפר ואבנים ברשות הרבים למלאות הגומות והפחתים או מאספין האבנים שנתקלין בהן בני אדם וחיישינן ליחיד הבא לתקן דלמא הדר ומימליך דתניא מסקלין דרך רשות הרבים דברי ר' יהושע רבי עקיבא אומר כדרך שאין לו רשות לקלקל כך לא יסקל ואם סיקל יוליא ליס או לנהר או למקום הטרשין מפני דרך היושר ומפני דרך הרבים ומפני העפר: מה יעשה בעפר. אליבא דר' עקיבא צוברו לתוך שדהו כדרך המזבלים דתנן לעיל ג' אשפתות לבית סאה. ואמרינן בירושלמי (שם) רבי אבינא בעי עד שלא פסקו עובדי עבודה מהו לצבור עפר בתוך שדהו כדרך המזבלין: וכן החופר בור שיח ומערה. פליגי בשאר ימות השנה דלרבי יהושע צוברו ברשות הרבים ובלבד שיתקנו ולרבי עקיבא אף על פי שדעתו לתקן אסור אלא צוברו ברשותו:

שלשה גלים מן האבנים גבוהים על הארץ וכשיתחיל לחצוב מהם קודם שביעית ופסל מהם שבעה ועשרים אבן מותר לו לפסול מהם בשביעית וכל זה אם לא נתכוין לתקן שדהו אבל אם נתכוין אסור: ו כשיהיה בגובה הגדר פחות מעשרה טפחים אסור לו להרוס אותו מעיקרו אבל נוטל ממנו האבנים ומניח ממנו פחות מטפח על פני הארץ וזה כדי שלא יתקן השדה ונוטל האבנים מעל פני שדהו וזו ההלכה כולה מבוארת: ז כבר נתבאר בגמ' בירושל' שר"ל באמרו זעזעתן המחרישה שיהיו האבני' ראויין שתזעזע אותן המחרישה אע"פ שלא נזדעזעה: גרגר של צרורות. גל מאבנים קטנים וכל זה מבואר על העיקר שיסדנו שאסור לו תיקון שדהו: ח מדרגות. ידוע וגאיות ידוע וכשיבנה מדרגה על הגאיות ההם ויישר אותם לתקן לא יסמוך בעפר ר"ל לא יחזיר העפר לגאיות ההם כדי שישוה פניהם: וחייץ הוא מחילה ר"ל להבדיל אותו הגיא מכל השדה והאבנים שיהיו קרובים ע"פ הגאיות כדי שיוכל להושיט ידו ולקחתם מותר לו לקחתם ומה שלא אפשר לקחתם עד שירד בגיא אינו מותר לו לקחת' מפני שכשנרא' אותו יורד או ישלשל עצמו לקחת אותם אמר שהוא לתקן שדהו נתכוין: ט כבר נאמר באשר הקדמנו בד"א מתוך שלו אבל מתוך של חברו מה שהוא רוצה יטול והוא אמר עתה שקבלן והוא שוכר הארץ לעבוד אותה דינה כדין מביא מתוך של חברו שהוא מביא מכל מקום ואי זה שיעור שיזדמן לו מהאבנים והלכה כר' יוסי: י מתקנו. מיישר אותו ומתקנו רבי עקיבא אוסר ליישר ולתקן רשות הרבים ולא לקלקל שכשייסר אותו ויסיר האבנים יצטרך להשליכם אל מקו' אחר ונמצא מקלקל אלא אם יהיה לוקט מהם האבנים ויסיר המקולקל וישליך מה שהסיר ויטילהו בים או באשפתות וכן הוא מבואר בגמרא והלכה כרבי עקיבא:

א הגס. הגדול. וכבר פירשנוהו פעמים *) ותיקון המשנה כך הוא בראשונה היו אומרים מלקט אדם עצים ואבנים ועשבים מתוך שלו הגס הגס כדרך שהוא מלקט משל חבירו בין דקין בין גסים ע"פ מה שהקדמנו שמתוך שהם של חברו אין עליו חובה וכאשר רבו העוברים על החוק והיו מפנין שדותיהן ואומרים הגס אנחנו מפנין מהעשבים והאבנים אסרו שלא ילקט אדם משדהו דבר לא גס ולא דק אבל מלקט משדה חברו: וענין שלא בטובה בלא הסכמה בין שניהם כגון שיאמר לחבירו הלקט אתה משדי ואני אלקט משדך או אעשה לך ענין פלוני או אגמלך עליו וכל ההולך על ענין זה וזה פירוש בטובה ויש לך לשמרו בלבבך ואל אצטרך לשנות פירושו: וא"צ לומר שיקצץ להם מזונות. כגון שיאמר לו לקוט משדי ואתן לך מזונך: ב נתקוצה. פעל נגזר מקוצים ענינו להסיר הקוצים ממנה: נטייבה. ר"ל חרשו אותה היטב והפכו אותה היטב: נדיירה. נעבדה בזבלים והוא נגזר מן דיר ודיר שם מקום יקבצו שם הצאן והבקר וילינו שם בשובם מן המרעה וכבר

א ירושלמי (הל' א) א"ר יונה היכן צורכה מיתני בראשונה היו אומרים מלקט אדם עצים ועשבים מתוך שלו [את] הגס הגס כדרך שהוא מלקט מתוך של חבירו בין דקין בין גסין נחשדו להיות מלקטין משדותיהן בין דקין בין גסין והן אומרים בגסין לקטנו התקינו שיהא זה מלקט מתוך של זה וזה מלקט מתוך של זה נחשדו להיות מלקטין בטובה והן אומרים שלא בטובה לקטנו התקינו שיהיו מביאין מן הקרוב ומן המצוי *) פי' עצים ועשבים כשמלקטין אותן מתוך השדה מיתקן לזריעה כדתנן בפ' הבונה (דף קג.) התולש עולשין והמזרד זרדין אם לאכילה כגרוגרת אם לבהמה כמלא פי גדי אם לייפות את הקרקע כל שהוא וכשמלקט הגס תליכן לצריך להן ולא לתקן את הקרקע עביד אבל דקים ודאי לצורך הקרקע כדאמר בפירקין דלעיל גבי אבנים ובשל חברו שרינן בפרקין דלעיל אפילו דקין דמידע ידעי דלא עביד לצורך הקרקע דמה חושש לתקן קרקע חברו: שלא בטובה. דודאי לא אתי-ללקט הדקין כיון דאין מחזיק לו טובה: ואין צריך לומר שיקוץ לו מזונות. דהא אפילו טובת הנאה אין מחזיקין זה לזה: ב ירושלמי (הל' ב) תמן אמרי כשניטלו קוליה (א) ורבנן דהכא אמרי משחרש על דעתין דרבנן דהכא אי זהו הטיוב כל העם חורש פעם אחד והוא חורש ב' פעמים: או שנדיירה. בדיר של בהמות שעשה סהר כדתנן בפירקין דלעיל (מ"ד) ולא עשה ממנו אשפתות שלא הניחו אלא כדי שיזדבל בו שדה: לא תזרע למוצאי שביעית. דקנסו ליה הכא טפי מנתקוצה דלמאן דאמר חורש קוצין בב' פעמים טפי מפעם אחת

*) פי' מהר"א מן ההפקר דוקא.

שביעית משפסקו גשמים. כדי שלא יכנס שם אדם לשתות המים מפני שהוא מתקנו להשקות מן המים את שדותיו בשביעית: אבל בונה הוא בשנת שביעית משפסקו גשמים. פי' מעצרת ואילך: מפני שהוא מתקנן למוצאי שביעית: ולא יסבוך בעפר. כלומר הבנין שעושה בשביעית לא יעשהו בעפר פי' לא יסתום האויר שבין אבן לאבן בעפר: אבל עושה הוא חריץ. גרסי' בירושלמי מהו חריץ חייץ ליה כמה דאת אמר והוא בונה חייץ פי' קיר אבנים בלא סיבוך עפר ובלשון ישמעאל חיים: כל אבן שהוא יכול לפשוט את ידו וליטלה הרי זו תיטול. לבנית בו מדריגתו ואכתי צריכה עיונא כל זו המשנה: ט אבני כתף באות מכל מקום. פי' ואפי' מתוך שלו: והקבלן. פי' מלשון מקבלי קיבולת כלומר המכנסן: מביאן מכל מקום. פי' ואפי' פחות מאבני כתף ואלו הן אבני כתף וכו': י הבונה גדר בינו לבין רשות הרבים. א"ר חייא בשם ר' יוחנן לא שנו אלא בינו לבין רשות הרבים הא בינו לבין חבירו אסור ובינו ובין רשות הרבים לא אמרן אלא בשביעית אבל במועד אסור. ותנן נמי במו"ק (דף ז.) מקרין את הפרצה במועד ובשביעית בונה כדרכו: צוברו לרשות הרבים ומתקנו לרשות הרבים דברי ר' יהושע וכו'. וכן לענין סיקול. תניא מסקלין רשות הרבים דברי ר' יהושע ר' עקיבא אומר כדרך שאין לו רשות לקלקל כך לא יסקל: מה יעשה בעפר. אליבא דר' עקיבא צוברו לשדהו וכו'. וכן פליגי בהחופר בור ושיח ומערה דר' יהושע סבר דצוברו לרשות הרבים ור' עקיבא סבר צוברו לתוך שדהו כלומר עפר החופר לא יצברנו ברשות הרבים ואע"פ שדעתו לתקן רשות הרבים אלא כל עפר החפירה יצברנו ברשותו וברשות הרבים כלל כלל לא:

פרק ד א בראשונה היו אומרים וכו'. א"ר יונה הכין צורכה מיתני בראשונה היו אומרים מלקט אדם עצים ועשבים מתוך שלו את הגס הגס כדרך שמלקט מתוך חבירו בין דקין בין גסין נחשדו להיות מלקטין בין דקין בין גסין והיו אומרים בגסין ליקטנו התקינו שיהא זה מלקט מתוך של זה וזה מתוך של זה שלא בטובה. דודאי לא אתו למילקט אלא בגסין שאומר הואיל ואינו מחזיק לי טובה למה אני מתקן שדהו ומלקט משום העשבים. ונחשדו שהיו מלקטין בטובה והן אומרין שלא בטובה ליקטנו התקינו שיהיו מביאין מן הקרוב ומן המצוי. נרסי' שם עוד בירושלמי ליקט הגסין מהו שיחזור וילקט מן הגסין שבדקין והשיבו אסור שאם אמר את כן אף הוא מלקט שדהו בשביעית: ואין צריך לומר שיקצץ להן מזונות. פי' הואיל ואפי' טובת הנאה אין מחזיקן זה לזה כיצד יתן זה לזה מזונות: ב שדה שנתקוצה. פי' שניטלה קוציה וירושלמי אומר שנחרשה תזרע למוצאי שביעית: שנטייבה. גרסי' בירושלמי על דעתיה דרבנן דהכא דפרשי נקווצה נחרשה. איזהו הטיוב כל העם חורשין פעם אחת והן חורשין ב' פעמים: או שנדיירה. פי' שנזבלה פעם אחת כדרך זיבול השדות ב' פעמים כמו הטיוב: שדה שנטייבה בית שמאי אומרים אין אוכלין פירות שביעית בטובה. פי' אין מהזיקין טובה

עין משפט נר מצוה

י א מיי' פ"ב מהל' שמטה ויובל הלכה ז:
יא ב שם הלכה ח:
יב ג שם הל' ט':
יג ד שם הלכה י:
יד ה שם הל' יא:
טו ו ז שם הל' יב:
טז ח ט שם הל' יד:
א י מיי' פ"א שם הלכה טו סמג לאוין רסו:
ב כ מיי' שם הלכה יד סמג לאוין רסו:
ג ל שם הל' יג:

פירוש הרא"ש

(ה) ופירוש הרמב"ם שפירשתי למעלה לא יתכן לפי המשנה זו: (ו) וכיון שאינו מסליק כולן אינו נרא' כמתקן שדהו: (ז) אין בונים וכו'. פי' גאיות הם גומות מל' כל גיא ינשא ונתמלא מים בימות הגשמים ואחר שנתמלא מים עושים מדרגות לרדת ולעלות לשאוב מים להשקות השדה מפני שמתקנו להשקות שדהו בשביעית וגם בונים הגדר סביב הגאיות שלא יכנס שם אדם לקחת המים ושבונה אותו לא יסבוך בעפר וכו': (ח) ר"ע אומר כשם שאין מקלקלין ר"ה כך לא יתקן כלומר לא מיבעיא לצבור עפרו לרשות הרבים שהוא אסור אע"פ שיסירו אח"כ דהא מקלקל הוא אלא אפילו לתקן אסור כגון אם היה עפר או אבנים מפוזרים בר"ה לא יצברם במקום אחד אלא יסלקם לגמרי מר"ה והיינו דקאמר כשם שאין מקלקלין ר"ה לצבור עפרו לר"ה לפי שעה כך לא יתקן לצבור אבנים או עפר המפוזרים בר"ה נפי שעה אלא יסלקם מיד וכיוצא בזה איתא בתוספת' (פ"ג) דתניא מסקל אדם דרך ר"ה דברי ר"י ר"ע אומר וכו' והלכה כר"ע:

[illegible]

שהוליך לזבל יותר מן השיעור כמפורש לעיל או שעשה בה סהר יותר ממה שהתירו חכמים ובדה אין שנטייבה בשביעית פליגי ב"ש וב"ה אם מותר לאכול פירותיו בשביעית:

מסורת הש"ס

א) מ"ק פ"ב דף יג: גיטין פ"ד דף מד: ובכורות פ"ס ד' לד:

פי' מהר"י בן מלכי צדק

אחת ג' רצועות שכל רצועה רחבה אמה ורומה אמה וארכה ג' הרי מן רצועה אחת ט' אבנים וכן לב' רצועות אחרות וג' פעמים ט' כ"ז. תניא בד"א במתכוין לעשות שדהו אבל אינו מתכוין לעשות שדהו אפילו דבר מרובה מותר אמר רבן שמעון בן גמליאל בד"א בזמן שאין מתכוין לעשות שדה אבל אםמתכוין לעשות שדה אפילו כל שהוא אסור. מחצב בלעז טופרא: ו גדר שיש בו י' אבנים של משוי שנים שנים. פי' שנוטל אדם מהן במשאו ב' הרי אלו ינטלו כולן: שיעור גדר י' טפחים. והן ג' נדבכין. ודתניא ג' נדבכין הוי"ב טפחים הא לא קשיא דא"ר יוסי צא חצי טפח לסיתות מיכן בלעז דולטורא וחצי טפח לסיתות מיכן וכן לחבר זה נמצאו ג' נדבכין י' טפחים בלעז לועזי מלשון נדבכין די אבנגלל תלת: פחות מיכן. ירושלמי פחות מיכן אינו לא גדר ולא מחצב ואינו נוטלו כולו אלא גוממו ומניח הסלע בארקטפח כדי שלא יהא ראוי לזריעה: בד"א. שגוממו ולעיל שאמר אינו נוטל אלא כ"ז אבנים בשדה שלו דאמרי אינשי מתקן שדהו הוא אבל מתוך של חבירו מה שהוא רוצה ליטול יטול ומתוך שלו נמי בזמן שלא התחיל בו מערב שביעית אבל אם וכו': ז אבנים שזעזעתן המחריש'. גרסינן לא סוף דבר שזעזעתן המחרישה אלא אפי' מחרישה עתידה לזעזעתן ובתוספתא תניא אבנים תושבות ומחרישה מזעזעתן: או שהיו מכוסות בעפר ונתגלו אחר תחרשה: אם יש בהן שתים. פי' ובכל אחת ואחת משוי ב' הרי אלו ינטלו: המסקל שדהו. בלעז צ'איפיירא פי' מלקט אבנים מן השדה: נוטל את העליונות ומניח את התחתונות הנוגעות בארץ וכן גרגר פי' גל של צרורות וכו' שהן כגרגרין מלשון שנים שלשה גרגרים: אם יש תחתיהן. פי' אם הן צבורין על גבי הסלע או על גבי קש ינטלו כולן: ח אין בונין מדריגות. פי' [גדר מאבנים] על גבי גאיות. פי' גיא מלשון כל גיא ינשא: ערב

MAKING TWENTY-SEVEN STONES.[3]

MISHNAH 6. A WALL OF TEN STONES, EACH A LOAD FOR TWO MEN, MAY BE REMOVED [PROVIDED] THAT THIS WALL IS [AT LEAST] TEN HANDBREADTHS HIGH;[4] LESS THAN THAT,[5] IT IS REGARDED AS A QUARRY, AND IT IS TO BE RAZED[6] WITHIN ONE HANDBREADTH OF THE GROUND.[7] THIS REFERS ONLY TO [THE REMOVAL] FROM HIS OWN FIELD;[8] BUT FROM THAT OF ANOTHER, HE MAY REMOVE WHATEVER HE WISHES.[9] THIS APPLIES ONLY TO A CASE WHERE THE REMOVAL [OF THE STONES] WAS NOT BEGUN BEFORE THE SIXTH YEAR; BUT IF HE HAD BEGUN IN THE SIXTH YEAR, HE MAY REMOVE WHATEVER HE PLEASES.[10]

MISHNAH 7. STONES WHICH THE PLOUGHSHARE HAS STIRRED UP,[11] OR WHICH HAD BEEN HIDDEN AND ARE NOW LAID BARE, MAY BE REMOVED IF THERE BE AMONG THEM AT
a LEAST TWO, [EACH] THE LOAD OF TWO MEN.[1] HE WHO REMOVES[2] STONES FROM A FIELD MAY REMOVE ONLY THE TOP LAYERS, BUT MUST LEAVE THOSE TOUCHING THE GROUND.[3] AND LIKEWISE IN THE CASE OF A HEAP OF PEBBLES, OR A PILE OF STONES; HE MAY REMOVE THE TOP LAYERS BUT MUST LEAVE THOSE TOUCHING THE GROUND. IF, HOWEVER, THERE IS BENEATH THEM ROCKY SOIL OR STUBBLE,[4] THEY MAY BE REMOVED.

MISHNAH 8. STEPS[5] LEADING TO RAVINES MUST NOT BE CONSTRUCTED IN THE SIXTH YEAR AFTER THE CESSATION OF THE RAINFALLS; FOR THIS WOULD BE [A CASE OF] IMPROVING THE FIELDS FOR THE SEVENTH YEAR. IN THE SEVENTH YEAR ITSELF, THEY MAY BE BUILT EVEN AFTER THE RAINS HAVE CEASED, SINCE SUCH AN ACT WILL BENEFIT THE FIELD IN THE EIGHTH YEAR. THEY [THE STEPS] MAY NOT BE BLOCKED WITH EARTH,[6] BUT ONLY MADE IN A LOOSE EMBANKMENT.[7] ANY STONE WHICH CAN BE TAKEN BY THE MERE STRETCHING OUT OF A HAND,[8] MAY BE REMOVED.[9]

MISHNAH 9. SHOULDER-STONES MAY BE REMOVED FROM ANY PLACE,[10] AND THEY MAY BE BROUGHT BY A CONTRACTOR[11] FROM ANYWHERE.[12] THESE ARE SHOULDER-STONES: SUCH AS
b CANNOT BE HELD WITH ONE HAND;[1] SO R. MEIR. BUT R. JOSE SAYS: THE NAME IS TO BE TAKEN LITERALLY, NAMELY, SUCH STONES AS CAN BE CARRIED ON A MAN'S SHOULDER, EITHER TWO OR THREE AT A TIME.

MISHNAH 10. IF ONE MAKES A FENCE BETWEEN HIS OWN PROPERTY AND THAT BELONGING TO THE PUBLIC DOMAIN, HE IS ALLOWED TO DIG DOWN TO ROCK LEVEL.[2] WHAT SHOULD HE DO WITH THE SOIL? HE MAY PILE IT UP IN THE PUBLIC DOMAIN,[3] AND AFTERWARDS REPAIR IT.[4] SO R. JOSHUA. R. AKIBA SAYS: JUST AS NO DAMAGE MAY BE DONE TO A PUBLIC DOMAIN, SO MAY ONE NOT RESTORE IT TO ORDER.[5] THEN WHAT SHOULD HE DO WITH THE SOIL [DUG UP]? HE HEAPS IT UP IN HIS OWN FIELD IN THE MANNER OF THOSE WHO BRING OUT DUNG [FOR MANURE].[6] IT IS LIKEWISE WHEN ONE DIGS A WELL, A TRENCH OR A CAVE.[7]

CHAPTER IV

MISHNAH 1. AT FIRST IT WAS THE PRACTICE TO ALLOW
c A MAN TO GATHER THE LARGEST[1] WOOD, STONES AND HERBS FROM HIS FIELD AS HE WAS ALLOWED TO DO FROM THE FIELD OF HIS FELLOW.[2] WHEN THE TRANSGRESSORS MULTIPLIED,[3] PERMISSION WAS ONLY GIVEN TO COLLECT THEM FROM ANOTHER'S FIELD, PROVIDED IT WAS NOT [PRE-ARRANGED] AS BESTOWING A MUTUAL FAVOUR.[4] IT GOES WITHOUT SAYING THAT NO STIPULATION COULD BE MADE THEREWITH FOR MAINTENANCE.[5]

MISHNAH 2. A FIELD FROM WHICH THORNS HAD BEEN REMOVED[6] MAY BE SOWN IN THE EIGHTH YEAR; BUT IF IT HAD BEEN IMPROVED UPON,[7] OR CATTLE HAD BEEN ALLOWED TO LIVE THEREON,[8] IT MAY NOT BE SOWN IN THE EIGHTH YEAR.[9] IF A FIELD HAD BEEN IMPROVED UPON IN THE SEVENTH YEAR, BETH SHAMMAI SAY: ITS FRUITS MAY NOT BE EATEN, BUT

(3) For a smaller quantity would excite suspicion that he is merely clearing his field in order to sow it in the Sabbatical year—an act forbidden with the advent of the seventh year; v. *supra* II, 3. Only when the quarry has sufficient stones for building purposes was the act allowed. (4) Such heavy stones are obviously for building purposes. (5) Than ten stones, each two men's burden, and ten handbreadths high. (6) Heb. גמם, 'to peel', or 'raze'; applicable to cases where no complete uprootal takes place. (7) Still regarded as unfit for sowing. Greater precaution was taken in the case of a stone quarry, whose soil was natural and lent itself to sowing. (8) Where there is the fear lest his intention be to do work forbidden on the eve of the seventh year. (9) For why should one be so eager to perform work in the field of another? (10) Even from his own field may he do so, since he had begun to clear away the stones when such action was perfectly lawful still. (11) Or loosened from the soil, so as easily to be removed.
a (1) An essential stipulation for the removal of stones. (2) Heb. מסקל. *Piel* in Heb. has the effect of the *alpha* in Greek; cf. Isa. V, 2. (3) For all to see that his intention is to build, and not to plant. (4) Unfit for sowing, even after the removal of stones. (5) To convey the water for irrigation during the rainfalls. These steps were built along mountain slopes to lead the water into the valleys. (6) To prevent the water from flowing away. Such a completed dam would be interpreted as doing work in the seventh year. (7) I.e., a pile of loose and uneven material, uncemented, forming a rough, extemporized embankment. (8) Which the builder can grasp just by the mere stretching out of a hand. (9) Otherwise, it would be deemed work. (10) Even from his own field; for such heavy stones can only be intended obviously for no other purpose than building. (11) For being a building contractor, all will divine that his purpose is for building. (12) Even from a field of his own.
b (1) Cf. *supra* III, 6; in the case of such stones which two men together could lift, we permit even the smaller stones to be removed (2) As it is unusual for one to sow on soil bordering on public property, he will not be suspected of infringing the Sabbatical laws; but if the fence demarcates his field and that of a neighbour's, digging is not allowed lest he afterwards decides to plant thereon. (3) I.e., he removes afterwards the soil from the public domain to scatter it on his own field. To do so, however, in the first instance is forbidden, lest the impression be given that he is preparing his field for sowing. (4) I.e., remove soil piled up in the public domain to fill up therewith holes in public ways. (5) For every respect must be paid to public property, lest the slightest damage accrue to it (Bert.). (6) I.e., three heaps to every *se'ah's* space; *supra* III, 2. (7) In such cases, too, the same dispute occurs between R. Joshua and R. Akiba as to what he should do with the soil dug out.
c (1) By selecting only the largest, he makes obvious his intention to use them only for building purposes. (2) From which he may collect even the smallest pieces of wood or stones, for none is keen on rendering unnecessary service in a field not his own; *supra* III, 6. (3) Who removed even the smallest stones under the pretence of clearing away only the biggest of their kind. (4) For then the fear would be instinctive that the field is being prepared for sowing. (5) To consider them as a reward for labour would to be derive benefit from work done in the Sabbatical year. (6) During the seventh year. (7) Tilled oftener than is usual; i.e., twice instead of once. Though even one ploughing was originally prohibited, yet permission was given during years of persecution when triumphant Emperors would impose a land tax on Israelitish property. (8) Thus collecting manure over the extra field; *supra* III, 4 allowed cattle-folds within a field provided a pen of two *se'ah's* space was constructed. (9) Since no such pen was erected, it seems that the field is being prepared for the seventh year.

BETH HILLEL SAY: THEY MAY BE EATEN. BETH SHAMMAI SAY: FRUITS OF THE SABBATICAL YEAR MAY NOT BE EATEN AS A
a FAVOUR,[1] BUT BETH HILLEL SAY: THEY MAY BE EATEN, WHETHER THEY BE REGARDED AS A FAVOUR OR OTHERWISE. R. JUDAH SAYS: THE STATEMENTS MUST BE REVERSED; FOR THIS IS ONE OF THE INSTANCES WHERE BETH SHAMMAI ARE THE MORE LENIENT AND BETH HILLEL THE MORE RIGOROUS.

MISHNAH 3. NEWLY-PLOUGHED LAND MAY BE HIRED FROM A GENTILE IN THE SEVENTH YEAR,[2] BUT NOT FROM AN ISRAELITE; GENTILES MAY BE ENCOURAGED DURING THE SEVENTH YEAR,[3] BUT NOT ISRAELITES. IN THE INTERESTS OF PEACEFUL RELATIONSHIPS, GREETINGS MAY BE EXCHANGED WITH THEM.[4]

MISHNAH 4. IF ONE THINS OUT HIS OLIVE-TREES [IN THE SEVENTH YEAR],[5] BETH SHAMMAI SAY: HE MAY ONLY RAZE THEM TO THE GROUND;[6] BETH HILLEL SAY: HE MAY COMPLETELY UPROOT. THEY, HOWEVER, CONCUR THAT IF ONE LEVELS HIS FIELD, HE MAY ONLY RAZE IT TO THE GROUND. WHAT IS THE PROCESS OF THINNING-OUT [MODDAL]? THE TAKING OUT OF ONE OR TWO PLANTS. AND LEVELLING?[7] THE REMOVING OF AT LEAST THREE PLANTS CLOSE TO EACH OTHER. THIS APPLIES TO HIS OWN PROPERTY ONLY, FOR FROM THE PROPERTY OF ANOTHER, EVEN HE THAT LEVELS MAY UPROOT.[8]

b *MISHNAH* 5. IF ONE CUTS DOWN AN OLIVE-TREE,[1] HE MAY NOT COVER UP [THE STUMP] WITH EARTH,[2] BUT HE MAY COVER IT WITH STONES OR STRAW.[3] IF ONE FELLS A SYCAMORE TREE,[4] HE MUST NOT COVER [THE STUMP] WITH EARTH, BUT HE MAY COVER IT WITH STONES OR STRAW. ONE MAY NOT HEW DOWN A VIRGIN SYCAMORE[5] IN THE SEVENTH YEAR, FOR THIS WOULD CONSTITUTE ACTUAL LABOUR.[6] R. JUDAH SAYS: IF [CUT DOWN] IN THE USUAL MANNER,[7] IT IS FORBIDDEN; BUT HE EITHER CUTS IT TEN HANDBREADTHS ABOVE [THE SOIL], OR HE RAZES IT TO GROUND LEVEL.[8]

MISHNAH 6. IF ONE TRIMS GRAPE-VINES,[9] OR CUTS REEDS,[10] R. JOSE THE GALILEAN SAYS: HE MUST LEAVE [UNCUT AT LEAST] ONE HANDBREADTH;[11] BUT R. AKIBA SAYS: HE MAY CUT THEM WITH THE AXE, SICKLE OR SAW IN THE USUAL MANNER, OR WITH WHATSOEVER HE PLEASES. A TREE THAT HAD SPLIT MAY BE TIED UP IN THE SEVENTH YEAR, NOT THAT IT MAY HEAL, BUT ONLY THAT IT SHOULD NOT WIDEN.

MISHNAH 7. FROM WHEN MAY ONE BEGIN TO EAT OF THE FRUIT OF THE TREES IN THE SEVENTH YEAR?[12] WITH UNRIPE FIGS AS SOON AS THEY HAD ASSUMED A ROSY APPEARANCE,[13] ONE MAY EAT THEREOF IN THE FIELD WITH HIS
c BREAD;[1] ONCE THEY HAD RIPENED, HE MAY ALSO TAKE THEM HOME. AND SIMILARLY IN THE OTHER YEARS OF THE SABBATICAL CYCLE [WHEN THIS LATTER STAGE HAS BEEN REACHED] THEY ARE SUBJECT TO TITHES.[2]

MISHNAH 8. UNRIPE GRAPES[3] AS SOON AS THEY CONTAIN JUICE,[4] MAY BE EATEN WITH BREAD IN THE FIELD; BUT AS SOON AS THEY HAVE RIPENED,[5] THEY MAY BE TAKEN HOME. AND SIMILARLY IN THE OTHER YEARS OF THE SABBATICAL CYCLE [WHEN THEY HAVE REACHED THIS LATTER STAGE] THEY ARE SUBJECT TO TITHES.[6]

MISHNAH 9. OLIVES AS SOON AS THEY PRODUCE[7] A QUARTER LOG [OF OIL] TO EACH SE'AH, MAY BE SPLIT[8] AND EATEN IN A FIELD; WHEN THEY PRODUCE A HALF-LOG,[9] THEN HE MAY CRUSH THEM IN A FIELD AND USE THEIR OIL. WHEN THEY ARE ABLE TO PRODUCE A THIRD,[10] THEY MAY BE CRUSHED IN THE FIELD[11] AND BROUGHT HOME. AND SIMILARLY IN THE OTHER YEARS OF THE SABBATICAL CYCLE [WHEN THEY HAVE REACHED THIS LATTER STAGE] THEY ARE SUBJECT TO TITHES.[12] WITH ALL OTHER FRUIT OF TREES [THE SEASON WHEN THEY BECOME DUE TO BE TITHED] IS THE SEASON WHEN THEY ARE PERMITTED IN THE SEVENTH YEAR.[13]

MISHNAH 10. FROM WHEN CAN TREES NO LONGER BE
d FELLED[1] IN THE SEVENTH YEAR?[2] BETH SHAMMAI SAY: AFTER THEY HAD PUT FORTH LEAVES.[3] BETH HILLEL SAY: CAROB-

a (1) Since all produce grown of its accord in the seventh year is declared ownerless, it is not within the prerogative of the original owner to bestow favours, or rewards; cf. 'Ed. V, 1. (2) I.e., an Israelite may hire a field in the seventh year to sow in the eighth year, though a Gentile will have ploughed it in the seventh. (3) By extending them every encouragement and greeting during their work in the seventh. (4) Irrelevant to our theme, but to emphasize the desirability of greeting them even in their pagan festivals, a reminder necessitated by Israel's care to steer clear of every association with idolatry. (5) When olives are clustered together in too close proximity, several are plucked away to afford the remainder more growing space. (6) Only as far as the roots; further would be categorized as forbidden labour. (7) A process which leaves a large portion of the soil bare of all trees, and ready for ploughing. (8) For all will gather that the plants are here wanted for fuel purposes, cf. *supra* 1, n. 2.
b (1) In the seventh year, for fuel purposes. (2) For he would thus be improving the growth of trees through work done in the seventh year. (3) To protect it from drying up. (4) For building purposes; these trunks grow again after being cut. (5) That had not known an axe before. (6) Improving the tree, which yields more abundant fruit as a result. (7) Lower than ten handbreadths from the soil, constituting work equivalent to pruning in the case of grapes. (8) Since he goes out of his way to differentiate between the usual practice; cf. *supra* I, 8. (9) I.e., clipping their ends only; not like pruning which entails an actual clipping of grapes from the top of the trees, a labour forbidden expressly in the Bible. (10) That they grow more copiously. (11) So that it does not appear as if he is working his field. (12) Fruits may not be wantonly destroyed, for the Bible emphasizes לאכלה *'for food'*; and to eat them before they are fully ripe would be a sheer waste. (13) Lit., 'to glisten', a sign of incipient ripeness.
c (1) For to take them home is forbidden. (2) Cf. Ma'as. I, 2. The criterion given above for fruit to be taken home is also the time when other fruits are liable to tithes. (3) Not yet the size of a white bean. (4) Lit., 'water'; when pressed juice comes out. (5) Lit., 'became foul'. Fruits begin to deteriorate when kernels become visible beneath their shells. (6) V. *supra* n. 2. (7) When crushed. (8) This was done to soften them and sweeten their taste prior to eating them. (9) Viz., a third of their usual quantity when fully ripe. (10) Of their full quantity. (11) This could be done even in the home; our Mishnah just cites an example at random. (12) V. *supra* n. 2. (13) Only figs, grapes and olives which were often eaten before becoming fully ripe may be eaten in the seventh year, even before they reached their season for tithes.
d (1) Since the Bible stipulates *'for eating'*, any wastage is debarred, especially since in the case of ownerless Sabbatical produce it would likewise constitute a deprivation of the poor to enjoy the fruits. (2) The Mishnah refers to fruit-trees. (3) Usually in Nisan.

אחת ובפרק השולח (דף מד:) ובפרק כל פסולי המוקדשין (דף לד:) אמרינן נקפינן הסיבה ומת בט זורעה : בטובה · שאין מחזיקין טובה לבעלים דרחמנא
אפקרינהו (ב): חילוף הדברים. דבית שמאי לקולא ובמסכת עדיות היא שנויה (פרק ה מ"א): ג חוכרין· מקבל עליו בכך וכך כורין לשנה שדה חרושה בשביעית
לזורעה למוצאי שביעית אע"פ שגורם לנכרי לחרוש בשביעית (ג) ומחזיקין ידי נכרים פליגי (ירושלמי הל' ג) ר' חייא ורבי אמי חד אמר חרוש בה טבאות ואנא
נסיב לה מינך בתר שמיטתא חרנא אמר אייסר מאן דאמר חרוש בה טבאות מהו שואלין בשלומן אייסר ומאן דאמר אייסר מהו שואלין בשלום ישראל
שלום עליך (ד) וסוגיא דהגיזקין (דף סב.)
כמאן דאמר אייסר · לא צריכה למימר להו
אחזוקי בעלמא והתם פריך השתא אחזוקי
מחזקינן להו שואלין בשלומן מיבעיא ולא

א) לקמן פ"כ מ"ט: גיטין סא: ב) ב"כ עג: נדה ה: ג) ברכות לו: מקום שנהגו נג:

פירותיה בשביעית ^א ובית הלל אומרים אוכלין
בית שמאי אומרים אין אוכלין פירות שביעית
בטובה ^ב ובית הלל אומרים אוכלין בטובה ושלא
בטובה ר' יהודה אומר חלוף הדברים זו מקולי
ב"ש ומחומרי ב"ה: ג ^ג חוכרין נירין מן הנכרים
בשביעית ^ד אבל לא מישראל א) ^ה ומחזיקין ידי
נכרים בשביעית אבל לא ידי ישראל ^ו ושואלין
בשלומם מפני דרכי שלום : ד המדל בזיתים
ב"ש אומרים יגום ^ז וב"ה אומרים ישרש ומודים
במחליק עד שיגום אי זה המדל אחד או שנים
המחליק שלשה זה בצד זה בד"א מתוך שלו
אבל מתוך של חבירו אף המחליק ישרש :
ה ^ח המבקיע בזית לא יחפהו בעפר אבל מכסה
הוא באבנים או בקש הקוצץ קורות שקמה לא
יחפהו בעפר אבל מכסה הוא באבנים או בקש
ב) ^ט אין קוצצין בתולת שקמה בשביעית מפני
שהיא עבודה ^י ר' יהודה אומר כדרכה אסור אלא
או מגביה י' טפחים או גומם מעל הארץ: ו המזנב
(ח) בגפנים והקוצץ קנים רבי יוסי הגלילי אומר
ירחיק טפח ר"ע אומר ^כ קוצץ כדרכו בקרדום או
במגל ובמגירה ובכל מה שירצה ^ל אילן שנפשח
קושרין אותו בשביעית לא שיעלה אלא שלא
יוסיף: ז ^מ מאימתי אוכלין פירות האילן בשביעית
הפגים משיזריחו אוכל בהם פתו בשדה ביחלו
כונס לתוך ביתו וכן כיוצא בהם *בשאר שני
שבוע חייב במעשרות: ח ^נ הבוסר משהביא מים
אוכל בו פתו בשדה הבאיש כונס לתוך ביתו וכן
כיוצא בו בשאר שני שבוע חייבין במעשרות:
ט ^ס זיתים משיכניסו רביעית לסאה (י) פוצע
ואוכל בשדה הכניסו חצי לוג כותש וסך בשדה
הכניסו שליש כותש בשדה וכונס לתוך ביתו
וכן כיוצא בהם ^ע *ושאר שני שבוע חייבים
במעשרות ^פ ושאר כל פירות האילן כעונתן
למעשרות כן עונתן לשביעית : ^י ג) מאימתי
אין קוצצין את האילן בשביעית ב"ש אומרים
כל האילן משיוציא ^צ ב"ה אומרים החרובין

ד א מיי' פ"ד שם הלכה א סמג לאוין רסא :
ה ב מיי' פ"ז שם הלכה טו סמג עשין קמח :
ו ג מיי' פ"ח שם הלכה ח סמג עשין קסח :

פי' מהר"י בן מלכי צדק

וכבר בארנו פי' בטובה שהוא גמילות או
שבח וכאילו עושה לו שאילתו ואין הלכה
כרבי יהודה : ג נירין. הארץ המהופכת

סעלין בימי ניסן : משישלשלו · כשיתחיל להכביד ולתלות כעין שלשלת : משיגריעו · משיגדילו הענבים קצת ונקראים גירוע ובפ' מקום שנהגו (נג·) מפרש דשיעורן כפול הלבן ובירושלמי (הל' ח) אמרי' א"ר יונה משיזחילו מים כדכתיב כי יגרע נטפי מים (איוב לו):ומשינצו משיגדל הנץ עלין והוא כעין מתחלי דפרק מקום שנהגו ודומה לו בברכות (דף לו:) הפסמא של רמון מצטרפין והנץ שלו אין מצטרף : מותר לקוצצו · דלא מפסיד כלל שכבר ראויין לאכילה ומשום קוצץ אילנות טובים ליכא כיון דמעולה בדמים כדאמר בסוף החובל (צ"א:) : וכמה יהא בזית. ולא יקוצנו משום קוצץ אילנות טובים כדכתיב (דברים כ') כי ממנו תאכל ואותו לא תכרת : רובע · הקב והאי דאמר *) האי דיקלא דטעין קבא אסור למקצייה משניקכשילהי החובל (שם) שאני זית דחשיב:

א בנות שוח · פירשתי בראש מסכת דמאי: שביעית שלהן שניה . דפירות החונטים בשביעית אין נגמר בישולן עד שנה שניה של שמטה ואז נוהג בהן דין שביעית דבתר חנטה אזלינן : פרסיות . פירש בערוך תמרי פרסייתא שהן עושין לג' שנים עוד פי' מין תאנים שעושין מב' שנים לג' שנים. ירושלמי (הל' א)מהו בנות שוח פיסריה מה בכל שנה ושנה הן עושות או אחד לג' שנים בכל שנה ושנה הן עושות אלא שאין פירותיהן נגמרים אלא לאחר ג' שנים כילד הוא יודע רבי יונה אומר תוקשר בהן חוטין תני שמואל תוחב בהן קיסמין פירוש בכל שנה ושנה הן עושות שחונטים בכל שנה ומוליאין בהן פירות גמורין בכל שנה אלא שבכולן משעת חנטה עד שעת גמר פרי ג' שנים ונמצא באילן בכל שנה ג' ממיני פירות הן של שנה זו ושל ב' שנים ושל ג' ולהכי בעי [כילד יודע] לשביעית דאע"פ שאלו נגמרו ואלו לא נגמרו זמנין דלא מיככרי כולי האי אלא במעט : **ב** הטומן את הלוף · רגילים היו להטמין בארץ כדתנן בפאה בסוף פ"ו (משנה י) כל הטמונים בארץ כגון הלוף והשום והבצלים ולא התירו הכתוב לטמון בשביעית דבר מועט משום דמיחזי כזורע עד שיטמין סאתים ולא יפזרם דצריך שיעלה גובה הכרי ג' טפחים וגובה העפר שעל גביו טפח במקום דריסת האדם כדי שלא יצמחו: ירושלמי (הל' ב)עד כדון לוף בצלים א"ר יונה הוא לוף הוא בצלים אמר ר' יוסי מסתברא בבצלים ובפחות מיכן מותר דאינון שפיין*) : **ג** לוף · של שביעית שעדיין מתקיים בארץ בשמינית ועלי הלוף יש להן ביעור ועיקרו אין לו ביעור כדתנן לקמן בפ"ז (מ"ב) ואמרינן בירושלמי (שם) דר"א סבר כרבי יהודה דאמר לקמן בפ"ח (מ"ח) עניים אוכלים אחר הביעור ולא עשירים ולכך קאמר ר"א דאם לקטו עניים עליו בשביעית לקטו ואם לאו נמצא שיש בלוף זה עלין שגדלו בשביעית מקצתן ומקצתן בשמינית גדלו וצריך לעשות חשבון עם העניים לפי שחלקו מעורב עם חלקן דמה שגדל בשביעית לעניים ומה שגדל בשמינית לבעל הבית ור' א] יהודה דאמר אין לעניים חשבון עמו סבר כר' יוסי דאמר אחד עניים ואחד עשירים אוכלין אחר הביעור וא"ת בירק אזלינן בתר לקיטה בין לענין שביעית בין לענין מעשר כדמוכח בפ"ק דר"ה (דף יג:) ובסוף הנודר מן הירק (דף נח·) כמו שמפרש לקמן בספ"ט (מ"ח) וא"כ האי לוף דלקט בשמינית אין עליו תורת שביעית ויש לומר דמתני' איירי כגון דעקרוהו עם עליו בסוף שביעית ועקרוהו במארופות כדינו והניחוהו במקומו וחזר ונשרש והוסיף גידוליו בשמינית לפיכך צריך לעשות חשבון עם העניים ועוד יש ענין דלא אזלינן בירק בתר לקיטה כמו אם נגמר גידולם כמו שאפרש לקמן בפ"ס ומיהו לוף א"ל ב] כן דלוף של שנה זו גדל בשניה כבראשונה וכן בשלישית וכן ברביעית כדמוכח בתוספתא ובירושלמי כמו שאפרש כאן ובירושלמי (שם) פריך מהא דגזרו על הספיחים ומשני שינויי טובא וזהו לשון הירושלמי (שם) אתיא דר' יודא כר' אליעזר ודרבי יוסי כרבי יהושע דתני תמן העניים אוכלין אחר הביעור [אבל לא עשירים דברי ר"י ר' יוסי אומר א' עניים וא' עשירים אוכלין אחר הביעור] ·

משישלשלו והגפנים משיגריעו והזיתים משינצו ושאר כל אילן משיוציא א וכל האילן כיון שבא לעונת המעשרות מותר לקוצצו א) ב כמה יהא בזית ולא יקוצצו רובע רבן שמעון בן גמליאל אומר הכל לפי הזית :

פירוש משיתחילו בו העלין הירוקים : משישלשלו . הוא משעה שהענפים נמשכים וגדלים : משיגריעו . משיעשו להם הגרעינין: משינינצו. משעה שיראו בהם הנלנים כיון שבא לעונת המעשרות מותר לקוצצו מפני שהוא כשר לאכילה כמו שבארנו ויקח פריו ויאכלנו ומותר לו לקצץ האילן ובלבד שיהיו דמיו יקרים לעלים ואז יהיה מותר לכרות אותו אבל אם לא יהיה לעליו מחיר גדול עד שיאמרו יותר יש לו תועלת בכריתתו מלהניחו אסור לכרות אותו מפני שהוא נושא פרי שהאילנות העושים פרי אסור מן התורה לכרות אותו בשום זמן מהזמנים אלא על זה הדרך שאמרנו והוא מ"ש הכתוב (דברים כ) לא תכרות את עלה ולזה הענין נתכוין באמרו כמה יהא בזית ולא יקוצנו רוצה לומר שאסור לכרתו בשנה מאחר השנים מפני שהוא עושה פרי : ורובע. הוא רובע קב ר"ל מנהגלגים מכל*) שאר האילנות מלבד הזיתים משעה שילך לין כשיעור קב אסור לכרתו אלא ליוקר דמי עליו כמו שאמרנו וכבר פירשנו שיעור הקב בסוף פאה ואין הלכה כרבן שמעון בן גמליאל :

*) נ"ל מן הנגלגים

פרק חמישי

א ג) **בנות** ג שוח שביעית שלהן שניה שהן עושות לג' שנים ר' יהודה אומר הפרסאות שביעית שלהן מוצאי שביעית שהן עושות לב' שנים (א) אמרו לו לא אמרו אלא בנות שוח : **ב** הטומן את הלוף בשביעית רמ"א לא יפחות מסאתים עד גובה שלשה טפחים וטפח עפר על גביו וחכמים אומרים ד לא יפחות מד' קבים עד גובה טפח וטפח עפר על גביו וטומנו במקום דריסת אדם : **ג** לוף שעברה עליו שביעית רבי אליעזר אומר אם לקטו העניים את עליו לקטו ואם לאו יעשה חשבון עם העניים רבי יהושע אומר אם לקטו העניים את עליו לקטו

א מה שאמר שביעית שלהן שניה ר"ל שאפשר להיות דינם דין פירות שביעית בשנה שניה מן השבוע וזה כשיזדמן להם שיתחילו להנץ בשנה שביעית והם עושות פרי לשלש שנים ונגמר פרים בשנה שניה מן השבוע שהיא שלישית לתחלת שנת השמטה שהתחילו להנץ בו ומפני זה מוהרים לאכול בקדושת שביעית אחר שהנצו בשמטה וכבר פירשנו שבנות שוח ממיני התאנים הלבנים· וכן הפרסיות ואין הלכה כרבי יהודה: **ב** לוף. ממיני הבצלים וכן אמרו לוף הוא הבצלים ואומר אם רוצה לטמון אותם בארץ כמו שיטמין החטה והשעורים וזולתם אינו מותר לו להטמין שיעור מועט מפני שדומה לזרע וכאילו הוא זורעו ואינו נראה שהוא טומנו אבל מותר לו לטומנו כשיעשה חפירה בארץ שיעורה מכיל סאתים והם י"ב קבים ויהיה גבוה ג' טפחים וטפח עפר על הבצלים זה דברי ר' מאיר וחכמים מתירים להטמין ארבעה קבים והוא שיהיה בגובה המקום טפח בלבד : ומה שאמר שיטמין במקום דריסת רגלי האדם כדי שלא ילמחו ואין הלכה כר' מאיר : **ג** פירוש זאת ההלכה לריכה לעקרים אחד מהן הוא שפירות שביעית נאכלין עד זמן קלוב ועוד יתבאר זה ואחר הזמן ההוא אסור לאכול מה שנשתייר מהם אלא לעניים לדעת ר"י ורבי יוסי אומר שאחר הביעור אינו מותר לאכלם לא לעניים ולא לעשירים ור"א דעתו כדעת ר' יהודה אבל ר' יהושע דעתו כדעת ר' יוסי ועוד שזה הלוף שדברו עליו בכאן הוא שזרעו קודם שנה שביעית ויגדל ממנו תחת הארץ הפרי אשר יאכל קודם שנה שביעית וכשנכנסת עליו שנה שביעית יהיו עלי הלוף נראין על הארץ ובשביל זה

ר' אמי בעי קומי רבי יוחנן מתני' עד שלא גזרו על הספיחין א"ל וכי בעלייה היית סבר ר' אמי אמר איסור ספיחין תורה אמר רבי ירמיה בעלי לוף שוטה היא מתני' אייתי רב אושעיא מתני' דבר קפרא מן דרומא ותני עלה לוף ובצלים אית לך למימר עלי בצלים השוטים מילתיה דר' ירמיה אמר דבר שיש בו ביעור שנמלא בתוך דבר שאין לו ביעור יש לו ביעור מה עבד ליה ר' ירמיה פתר ליה כששיקף בעלים ר' יוסי פתר לה מתני' לפני ר"ה בשביעית נטעו לפני ר"ה שביעית עשה בילים לפני שביעית ודיכנו בשביעית עקרו במוצאי שביעית אין תימר דדיכון כעיקור כולו לעניים אין תימר אין דיכון כעיקור אין כולו לעניים מספק יעשה חשבון עם העניים ר' חזקיה פתר מתני' ערב ר"ה שביעית נטעו ערב ר"ה שביעית ועשה בילה בתחלת שביעית ודיכנו בשביעית ועקרו בסוף בשביעית אין תימא דיכון כעיקור כולו לבעל הבית *) לפיכך אין לעניים עמו חשבון עשה בארץ ג' שנים ונתן לעניים רובע ב' שנים נותן לעניים שליש שנה אחת נותן לעניים מחצה : פירוש מתני' דשריא לאכילה עד שלא גזרו על הספיחים דתנן לקמן בפ"ט (מ"א) כל הספיחין אסורין אפילו באכילה כדמוכח בפ"ק דמנחות (דף ה:) אמר ליה וכי בעלייה היית וכי גזירה דרבנן היא ונקט עלייה לפי שהיו רגילין לעשות גזירות בעלייה. כדאמרינן בסוף בן סורר (דף עד·) בעליית בית נתזה בלוד ובפ"ק דשבת (דף יג:) בעליית חנניה בן גוריון גבי י"ח דבר ובכתובות בפרק נערה (דף נ:) מדברים טובים שנאמרו בעלייה סבר ר' אמי איסור ספיחים תורה שהבין מתוך דברי ר' יוחנן איסור ספיחים מדאורייתא אסור אמר ר' ירמיה בעלי לוף שוטה היא מתני' כלומר שלא גדלו בשביעית כי אם העלים וכבר גדל העיקר משנה ששית וכי אסרי' ספיחים היינו בהנך דתחילת גידולן בשביעית או בתבואה שלא הביאה שליש בששית כמו שמפרש לקמן בפ"ט אבל לוף שגדל בששית אלא שגדלו עליו בשביעית לית ליה דין ספיחים ליאסר באכילה והא דנקט לוף שוטה משום דלוף פיקח אפילו העיקר שלו לא היה מתקיים בארץ מן הששית עד השמינית ולא משכחת לה בלוף פיקח הנטוע משנת ששית שיוליא עלין בשביעית ובשמינית דאמרינן יעשה חשבון ומיירי דעקרו בסוף שביעית והניחו במקומו וחזר והשריש והוסיף עליו בשמינית כדמפרש במתני' ורב אושעיא ניקשי *) ליה מברייתא דבר קפרא דתני פלוגתא דר' אליעזר ור' יהושע בלוף ובצלים ולא שייך לשנויי בבצלים שוטים דאין דרך בצלים להתקיים משית לשמינית אלא גבי לוף שוטה משכחת לה דעיקרו מתקיים בארץ כדתנן לקמן בפ"ט ג] ורבי ירמיה לא חייש אהך קושיא דלית ליה הך ברייתא דבר קפרא מילתא דר' ירמיה אמרה כלומר מדבריו נוכל לדקדק דדבר שיש לו ביעור כגון עלי הלוף שוטה שנמלאו בתוך דבר שאין לו ביעור כגון עיקר הלוף שוטה יש לו ביעור ולא אמרי בטלי להו עלין אגב עיקר ולא שייך למידק הכי ממתני' דלקמן בפ"ט ד] דערלה יש לו ביעור ולעיקר אין לו ביעור דההיא פשיטא דאיכא לאוקומה כשתלש העלין לבדן [אבל] הכא עקר הכל יחד מדנתערבו בשל שמינית ומשני בששיקף בעלין שתלשן בשמינית מן העיקר קודם שיכלה לחיה מן השדה דביעור הוא בשמינית ולשון שיקוף טופל כשתולש העלין מן העיקר ר"י פתר לה מתני' לפני ר"ה של שביעית שנטען בששית ועשה בילה לפני שביעית שהביא גידולין ונקט גידולין כדי שלא יחשב ספיחי שביעית ודיכנו בשביעית מל' או דכו במדוכה (במדבר יא) שדך העלין במקום חיבורן ודכותה בסוף הנודר מן הירק (דף נח·) גבי בצלים של שביעית שלמחו בשמינית ואחר כן עקרן לגמרי דאם הדיכון כעיקור הרי נתלשו בשביעית ולעניים והשתא לא קשיא מידי מדבר שיש לו ביעור בתוך דבר שאין לו ביעור ויש לו חשבון עם העניים מפני העלין של מולאי שביעית שהגידולין מעורבין ואם אין הדיכון כעיקור הכל לבעה"ב אפילו עלין דשביעית דאזלינן בתר לקיטה ומספק נר"א יעשה חשבון עם העניים לחומרא ומני למימר השתא טעמא דר' יהושע משום דקסבר אין דיכון כעיקור ור' חזקיה פתר נמי מתני' בשנטעם בששית ועשה בילה בששית אלא דמוקי לה בשדיכנו בששית ועקרו לגמרי בשביעית דאם הדיכון כעיקור הכל לבעל הבית אפילו מה שהוסיף בשביעית דלא מארעא רבו והרי הוא כמונח בתיבה ואם אין הדיכון כעיקור הכל לעניים אפילו מה שהוליא בששית דבתר לקיטה אזלינן ומן הדין אין לעניים דין חשבון שהרי או כולו לעניים או כולו לבעל הבית אלא מדספק עביד ר"א דיכון כעיקור לגידולי ששית ושלא כעיקור לגידולי שביעית : וטעמא דר' יהושע משום

בירוק וכן לדברי האומר בירושלמי תהב בהן קיסמין ובכלים פירש בנות שוח תאנין לבנות: ר' יהודה אומר הפרסאות. פי' הן תמרי פרסייתא שהן עושין לב' שנים ויבוא מה שחונטין בשביעית נגמרין למוצאי שביעית : אמרו לו לא אמרו בנות שוח אלא תאנים אבל בשאר אילנות בשנה אחת חונטין ונגמרין תניא אמרו לו והלא עמך בטבריא ועושות לשנה אחת : **ב** הטומן את הלוף בשביעית . פי' הלוף והשום והבצלין דרכן להיטמן בארץ כדומן כדתנן בפיאה וכל הטמונין בארץ כגון הלוף והשום והבצלין והואיל וכן רשאין לטומנו בשביעית וכשיטמן לא יטמון דבר מועט אלא סאתים וגובה הכרי יהיה ג' טפחים וטפח עפר על גבן וטכן. תניא ר' מאיר אומר דרך ארץ טמנו בעציץ כדי שלא תצמיח ואע"פ שאין ראיה לדבר זכר לדבר ותתם בכלי חרש למען יעמדו ימים רבים · וחכמים אומרים לא יטמון פחות מד' קבין גובה טפח היינו כר' מאיר במד"א דר' מאיר לכל ד' קבין בעי גובה טפח כן רבנן אבל רבנן בעי לד' קבין טפח עפר על כולן · גרסי' לא שנינו הנה אלא הטומן לוף בצלין מאי א"ר יונה כדין הלוף דין הבצלין · א"ר יוסי מסתברא בבצלין אפילו בפחות מיכן מותר דאינן שפיין : **ג** לוף שעברה וכו' . ר' יוחנן פתר מתני' בלוף שנכנס בז' ונעקר במארופות כדיניה ואחר שנעקר הניחו במקומו והוציא עלין ומתני' אחר שגזרו על הספיחין ור' אליעזר כרבי יהודה הלכך העלין כולן לעניים ור' יהושע סבר כר' יוסי הלכך אם ליקטו העניים את העלין ליקטו ואם לאו אין לעניים עמו חשבון שהעלין לבעל הבית · אבל בלוף נטפיה לא פליגי דודאי מאחר שעקרו לא חל עליה קדושת שביעית ודבעל הבית ר' אימי מוקים מתני' כר' יוחנן מיהו מוקים לה מימות משה דסבר איסור ספיחין מן התורה ר' ירמיה פתר מתני' בעלי לוף שוטה שלא נצטוינו לעוקרו שלא נצטוינו לעקר אלא לוף פיקח שאין ביעור לעיקרו אפי' תלשו בשביעית אבל לעלים יש ביעור אפילו תלשן ואם לא עשה כלום מעשה בעלין אפילו רבי אליעזר מודה דאין לעניים עמו חשבון אלא כגון ששיקף בעלין פי' חתך עלי הלוף השוטה מששית ועתה בשביעית הוציא עלים אחרים ובמוצאי שביעית הלך ותלש כל הלוף בעליו ר' אליעזר סבר צריך ליתנם לעניים כר' יהודה ור' יהושע סבר אין לעניים עמו חשבון שהרי לא נתתנו בשביעית אי נמי כר' יוסי דאמר בין עניים בין עשירים ר' יוסי פתר מתני' קודם שגזרו על הספיחין ובלוף עצמו והיכי דמי כגון שנטעו בששית ועשה ביצים בששית ודיכנו בתחלת שביעית ובשמינית עקרו כולו · ר' אליעזר סבר יעשה חשבון עם העניים שאם הדיכון כעוקר כולו לבעל הבית שהרי מששית נעקר ואם אין הדיכון כעוקר אין כולו לבעל הבית אלא משו' שיהם דהנטיעה בששית ובשביעית גדל וסבר כר' יהודה דאמר לעניים הלכך יעשה חשבון סוח הלוף כמפרש בברייתא · ור' יהושע סבר אין לעניים עמו חשבון · מאי טעמא דאם דיכון כעיקר לבעל הבית הוא ואם אין דיכון כעיקר נמי לבעל הבית הוא כר' יוסי הלכך אין לעניים עמו חשבון : אם לקטו העניים עליו. לעו פרתני : ואם לאו יעשה חשבון עם העניים . דסבר כר' יהודה דאמר העניים אוכלין אחר המועד אבל לא העשירים גרסינן רבי חזקיה פתר מתני' בשנטעו ... ועשה ביצים בשנה

עין משפט נר מצוה

ב א מיי' פ"ה מהלכות שמטה ויובל הלכה יז :

רב פ"ג

כא ב מיי' פ"ד מהל' מלכים הלכה ט :

א ג מיי' פ"ד מהלכות שמטה ויובל הל' טו :

ב ד מיי' פ"ז שם הלכה טו :

פירוש הרא"ש

פרק ה (א) אמרו לו לא אמרו אלא בנות שוח. ותמה לי במאי פליגי דבר שיש למעמד עליו הא לא נאמר דבפלוגתא ר' יהודה סבר חונטין בשנה זו וגמרן בשנה שנים וחכמים סברי עיקר גדילתן בשנה ראשונה אלא שמתבשלין בתוך שנה שניה.

*) תלקון ונדחקין יחד ביותר. מכר"ל

הגהות הדר"י לנדא

פרק ה א) מ"ב בר"ש ורבי יהודה דאמר . צ"ל ורבי יהושע : ב) שם ומיהו לוף א"ל נומר כו. צ"ל א"נ אמר : ג) שם כדתנן לקמן בפ"ס. צ"ל מ"ב : ד) שם בפ"ס דערלה. צ"ל בפ"ג דערלה

*) [אין תימר אין דיכון כעיקור אין כולו לבעה"ב כצ"ל]

מקשה כצ"ל

מסורת הש"ס

א) ב"ק פ"ח נה: ב) ר"ס פ"ו :

פי' מהרי"ו בן מלכי צדק

והחוט דומה לשלשלת ואחר כך מתעבה אותו החוט ונעשה חרוב · א"ר חנינא בר פפא חרובין שלשלן היא תמן : הגפנים משיגריעו. אמר רב נחמן הוא בוסר דתנן לעיל הוא גירוע ולמה נקרא שמו גירוע מלשון כי יגרע נטפי מים כלומר שכשנוטלן ביד יזובו מים ושיעורו כפול הלבן: והזיתים משינצו. א"ר יונה משיכניסו רובע פירוש כל מקום שנאמר רובע הוא רובע הקב. נץ מלשון הנצו הרמונים: ושאר כל האילן משיוציא. אסור לקוצצו דמפסיד הוא וכל האילן כיון שבא לעונת המעשרות כגון התאנין ביחלו הזיתין הביאו שליש הענבים הבאישו מותר לקצוץ האילן דלא מפסיד ולא מידי שכבר ראוין לאכילה ומותר לכנסן לתוך ביתו : וכמה יהא בזית ולא יקצנו. פי' אפי' בשאר שני שבוע משום שאסור לנו לכרות עץ מאכל בב"ק בפ' החובל אמר רב דיקלא דטעין קבא אסור למקצייה פי' הקב ד' ריבעין הא פחות שרי מיתיבי וכמה יהא בזית ולא יקצנו רובע ופריק שאני זיתים דחשיבי:

פ"ה בנות שוח. ירושל' מהו בנות שוח פישריאה וגרסי' בנות שוח הן חרובין : שביעית שלהן שניה שהם עושות לג' שנים . כיצד מה שחונטין שנה ראשונה בשנה בוחל בשלישית מבשלות וכן מה שחונטין ברביעית בחמישית בוחל בששית מתבשלות ולפי זה החשבון מה שמוציאין בשביעית במוצאי שביעית בוחל בשנה שניה לשביעית מתבשלין עתה באילו הפירות הנלקטין לשנה ב' את נוהג בהן דין שביעית דבתר חנטה אזלינן ואילו בשביעית חנטו · ואני פירשתי כסידורן שכל שנה ושנה עושין ופירות ראשונה נגמרין בג' ופירות ב' נגמרין בד' ופירות ג' נגמרין בה' והולך כסדר הזה ושאלו ואיך ידעין כל פירות שנה ושנה ר' יונה אמר קשרין בחוט אילו בחוט לבן ואילו בחוט שחור. ובאדום

TREES AFTER THEY[4] BEGIN TO DROOP;[5] VINES AFTER THEY HAD YIELDED BERRIES; OLIVE-TREES AFTER THEY HAD BLOSSOMED, ANY OTHER TREES AFTER THEY HAD PRODUCED LEAVES.[6] ANY TREE AS SOON AS IT REACHES THE SEASON FOR TITHES MAY BE CUT DOWN.[7] WHAT QUANTITY SHALL AN OLIVE-TREE YIELD THAT IT BE NOT CUT DOWN?—A QUARTER [KAB]. R. SIMEON B. GAMALIEL SAYS: ALL DEPENDS ON THE OLIVE-TREE.[8]

CHAPTER V

MISHNAH 1. WHITE FIGS HAVE THE LAW OF THE SEVENTH
a YEAR[1] APPLIED TO THEM IN THE SECOND YEAR,[2] SINCE THEY RIPEN ONCE IN THREE YEARS. R. JUDAH SAYS: PERSIAN FIGS HAVE THE LAW OF THE SEVENTH YEAR APPLIED TO THEM IN THE YEAR FOLLOWING THE SEVENTH YEAR,[3] SINCE THEY RIPEN ONCE IN TWO YEARS. THEREUPON THEY SAID TO HIM: THIS WAS SAID ONLY OF THE SPECIES OF WHITE FIGS?[4]

MISHNAH 2. IF LOF[5] IS PLACED IN THE SOIL FOR PRESERVATION DURING THE SABBATICAL YEAR, R. MEIR SAYS: IT MUST BE NOT LESS THAN TWO SE'AHS IN QUANTITY, THREE HANDBREADTHS IN HEIGHT, AND COVERED WITH EARTH ONE HANDBREADTH DEEP.[6] THE SAGES SAY: IT MUST BE NOT LESS THAN FOUR KABS IN QUANTITY, ONE HANDBREADTH HIGH, AND COVERED WITH EARTH ONE HANDBREADTH DEEP. MOREOVER, IT SHALL BE HIDDEN IN GROUND OVER WHICH MEN MAY TREAD.[7]

MISHNAH 3. IF LOF HAS REMAINED [IN THE GROUND UNTIL] AFTER THE PASSING OF THE SEVENTH YEAR, R. ELIEZER SAYS: IF THE POOR HAD GATHERED THE LEAVES THERE-
b OF,[1] ALL IS WELL; IF NOT,[2] THEN AN ACCOUNT SHOULD BE MADE WITH THE POOR.[3] R. JOSHUA SAYS: IF THE POOR HAD

(4) Their branches. (5) The leaves become abundant, and droop from the tree like chains. *Aliter:* when carobs begin to assume a round shape. (6) When no tree may be cut down. (7) For there is no longer any wastage of fruit. A tree may not be cut if the fruit thereof be more valuable than its wood for fuel. (8) Cf. Deut. XX, 19: trees of a besieged city may not be destroyed. V. also B.K. 91*b*. T.J. refers the question to the seventh year, maintaining that if it involves loss it should not be cut down. The better the tree, the more is it forbidden to be felled; cf. Pe'ah VII, 1.

a (1) With regard to the renunciation of ownership and other regulations. (2) Of the Sabbatical cycle. Though the fruit does not actually ripen until the third year, they are already fit to be eaten in the second year. (3) I.e., the eighth year, which is the first of the new Sabbatical year. (4) And not in the case of Persian figs; for after much investigation, it was discovered that the latter ripen each year (Tosef.). Moreover, the Rabbis were mainly concerned with such fruit grown in Eretz Israel; Bez. 19*a*. (5) A plant resembling colocasia with edible leaves and root, and bearing beans. It is classified with onions and garlic (Jast.). The usual translation is 'arum'. It was placed underground for preservation. (6) To remove all semblance of sowing. (7) To avoid it burgeoning forth into fruit.

b (1) In the seventh year the leaves of the *lof* were subject to the law of Removal; v. *infra* VII, 7. (2) And the arum had increased in the eighth year. (3) The owner must give the poor the amount calculated to have grown in the seventh year. The rest he can keep for himself.

PLUCKED THE LEAVES THEREOF, ALL IS WELL; IF NOT, NO ACCOUNT IS NECESSARY.[4]

MISHNAH 4. LOF OF THE SIXTH YEAR[5] THAT REMAINS UNTIL THE SEVENTH, SIMILARLY SUMMER ONIONS[6] AND PU'AH[7] GROWN IN CHOICE SOIL, BETH SHAMMAI SAY MUST BE UPROOTED WITH WOODEN RAKES.[8] BETH HILLEL SAY: [EVEN] WITH METAL SPADES.[9] THEY[10] CONCUR IN THE CASE OF PU'AH GROWN IN STRONG SOIL[11] THAT THEY MAY BE UPROOTED WITH METAL SPADES.

MISHNAH 5. FROM WHEN MAY A MAN BUY THE LOF AFTER THE GOING OUT OF THE SEVENTH YEAR?[12] R. JUDAH SAYS: AT ONCE;[13] BUT THE SAGES SAY: [ONLY] AFTER THE NEW CROP HAS APPEARED.[14]

MISHNAH 6. THESE ARE THE IMPLEMENTS WHICH A
a CRAFTSMAN MAY NOT SELL IN THE SEVENTH YEAR:[1] A PLOUGH AND ALL ITS APPURTENANCES, A YOKE, A WINNOWING-FAN, AND A MATTOCK;[2] BUT HE MAY SELL A SICKLE USED BY HAND,[3] A SCYTHE, AND A CART WITH ALL ITS IMPLEMENTS. THIS IS THE GENERAL PRINCIPLE: ANY TOOLS DESIGNED FOR WORK INVOLVING A TRANSGRESSION IN THE SEVENTH YEAR MUST NOT BE SOLD; BUT IF IT IS USED BOTH FOR A FORBIDDEN AND A PERMISSIBLE PURPOSE, IT MAY BE [SOLD].[4]

MISHNAH 7. THE POTTER MAY SELL[5] FIVE OIL-JARS AND FIFTEEN WINE-JARS, FOR THIS IS THE USUAL AMOUNT ONE COLLECTS FROM OWNERLESS PRODUCE;[6] BUT IF HE BROUGHT MORE,[7] THIS IS STILL PERMITTED HIM.[8] HE[9] MAY ALSO SELL [MORE JARS] TO GENTILES IN PALESTINE AND TO ISRAELITES IN OTHER LANDS.[10]

MISHNAH 8. BETH SHAMMAI SAY: ONE MUST NOT SELL HIM[11] A PLOUGHING-COW IN THE SEVENTH YEAR, BUT BETH HILLEL PERMIT, SINCE HE MAY BE SLAUGHTERING IT.[12] ONE
b MAY SELL HIM FRUIT EVEN AT SOWING-TIME,[1] AND ONE MAY LEND HIM A SE'AH MEASURE THOUGH IT IS KNOWN THAT HE HAS A THRESHING-FLOOR.[2] ONE MAY GIVE HIM SMALL MONEY IN CHANGE THOUGH IT IS KNOWN THAT HE HAS LABOURERS. BUT IF ALL THESE THINGS [ARE] EXPRESSLY [KNOWN] TO BE REQUIRED FOR UNLAWFUL PURPOSES,[3] THEN THEY ARE FORBIDDEN.[4]

MISHNAH 9. A WOMAN MAY LEND TO HER NEIGHBOUR WHO IS SUSPECT OF TRANSGRESSING THE SABBATICAL LAW,[5] A WINNOW,[6] A SIEVE, A HAND-MILL, OR AN OVEN; BUT SHE MAY NOT [ACTUALLY] WINNOW OR GRIND [CORN] WITH HER.[7] THE WIFE OF A ḤABER[8] MAY LEND TO THE WIFE OF AN 'AM HA-AREẒ[9] A WINNOW AND A SIEVE[10] AND MAY EVEN WINNOW, GRIND CORN OR SIFT FLOUR WITH HER;[11] BUT ONCE SHE POURED OUT THE WATER [OVER THE FLOUR],[12] SHE SHOULD NOT TOUCH HER, FOR NO HELP MUST BE GIVEN TO THOSE WHO COMMIT TRANSGRESSION.[13] ALL THESE THINGS WERE

(4) Since he himself is also entitled to their possession after they had been liable to the law of Removal, he being of the view that after the removal, the rich too can eat of the fruit; v. *infra* VIII, 9. (5) It was perfectly ripe then; had its growth increased in the seventh, it would be forbidden to eat it as all aftergrowth; v. *infra* IX, 1. (6) Either that had been sown in summer, or had been set aside for summer use. (7) Dyer's madder (Jast.). Madder is an herbaceous climbing-plant with yellowish flowers. (8) For the usual metal implements would arouse the suspicion that he is cultivating his field in the seventh b year. (9) Since he is using spades he has averted suspicion; for this is not the usual practice. (10) Beth Shammai. (11) צלעות. Lit., 'on the ribs (sides) of the fields'. Being an unusual place for sowing, it will not appear suspicious. *Aliter:* צלעות is the same as סלעות, 'rocky'. (12) Without fear lest it is Sabbatical produce; i.e., in the case of a seller who is suspect of infringing Biblical laws. (13) Since the *lof* had to be uprooted not in the usual way, prohibited Sabbatical produce was not likely to be available in the market immediately after the termination of the seventh year; only in the case of other vegetables requiring no such differentiation was the stipulation made until such new crop could have grown (Bert.). (14) Usually from the time of Passover of the eighth year; cf. *infra* VI, 4.

a (1) To a man who is suspect only. To one who is not, this may be done, for his intentions are honourable. (2) A pronged tool. (3) Being hand-tools, only little could be cut at a time; not enough to pile up a store. One was allowed to give of it to cattle, since it was ownerless property. (4) Since the purchaser can claim that the tools are going to be used for such work as is permitted. (5) To one even suspect of disregarding Sabbatical regulations. (6) Of the seventh year. (7) I.e., the one who is suspect brought more produce for which he wants jars.. (8) The potter may sell him more jars. Perhaps he desires the other jars for legitimate uses. Wine- and oil-jars were distinctive and could not be mixed. (9) The potter. (10) To these he may sell more than the amount prescribed above and we do not fear lest the Gentile or the Israelite, if outside Palestine, will later sell them again to Israelites in Palestine suspected of illegitimate trading in the seventh year. (11) Who is suspect in regard to the Sabbatical laws. (12) Beth Shammai were of the opinion that a cow used for ploughing would not be slaughtered for food. A heifer used for ploughing was one that was barren and whose breasts had dried up. Oxen were used ordinarily.

b (1) We assume he needs it for food rather than for sowing. (2) We do not suspect him of the intention to measure therewith seventh year produce for storage purposes, but assume his intention to be for grinding purposes. (3) That his intention is deliberately to transgress the Sabbatical laws. (4) To be an accessory to the infringement of a Biblical law is indefensible. (5) Namely, eating its produce without removal after the time of its removal has been due. They may be wanted here for legal uses. (6) The holes of the נפה are smaller than those of the sieve (כברה). One may need them for sifting sand, or the mill for spices or drugs, and the oven for dry flax. (7) Actually to help a violation of the law is not to be thought of. (8) V. Glos. This statement of our Mishnah is actually more relevant to the laws of purity than to those of the Sabbatical year. (9) V. Glos. (10) The hand-mill and oven are omitted, since being large, they are not easily immersed into water for purification purposes; if they were of clay or earthenware, they had to be broken up. (11) As the majority even of the *'am ha-areẓ* give tithes. (12) Thus rendering it 'susceptible to uncleanness' (Lev. XI, 34), as was the case of all food that had received contact with liquids like water. (13) To help her rolling the dough and thus assist her in causing uncleanness to bread that becomes in the process subject to the law of *Ḥallah* (v. Glos.). Once the dough is rolled it is liable to *Ḥallah*.

דדיכון כעיקר ומילתיה דחזקיה כתובה בשיבוש בירושלמי וצריך לתקן הגירסא לפי הפתרון שפירשתי והדר מסיק בירושלמי עשה בארץ ג' שנים אחר שביעית נותן לעניים רובע שהרי שנה של שביעית לעניים ויש כאן ד' שנים א' דעניים וג' לבעל הבית וכשעקרו בסוף שביעית וחזר ונטעו בשמינית וכן כולם לפי חשבון השנים ובתוספתא (פ"ד) מיתניא בירושל' ואע"ג דאמרי' בסוף הנודר מן הירק (דף נ"ח) גידולי היתר מעלין את האיסור אפקועי ממונא שאני ואם תאמר והיכי משכחת שיחלקו עניים עם בעל הבית למחצה לשליש ולרביע הא אין עלי הלוף מתקיימין מדים להם ביעור כדתנן לקמן בפרק שביעי וי"ל דמשכחת לה כגון שעקר הלוף בחורף עם עליס וטמנו בארץ כדתנן לעיל (משנה ב') ואחר שעבר עליו זמן הקרח חזר ונטעו והוסיף גידולין על גידולין וכן בכל שנה ושנה:

לקטו ואם לאו אין לעניים עליו חשבון: **ד** לוף של ערב שביעית שנכנס לשביעית וכן בצלים הקיצונים וכן פואה של עידית ב"ש אומרים עוקרין אותן במארופות של עץ [א]וב"ה אומרים בקרדומות של מתכות ומודים בפואה של צלעות שעוקרין אותה בקרדומות של מתכות: **ה** מאימתי מותר אדם ליקח לוף במוצאי שביעית ר' יהודה אומר מיד וחכ"א [ב]משירבה החדש: **ו** [א] [ג]אלו כלים שאין האומן רשאי למכרם בשביעית מחרישה וכל כליה העול והמזרה והדקר [ד]אבל מוכר הוא מגל יד (ד) ומגל קציר ועגלה וכל כליה [ה]זה הכלל כל שמלאכתו מיוחדת לעבירה אסור לאיסור ולהיתר מותר: **ז** [ו]היוצר (ה) מוכר ה' כדי שמן וחמשה עשר כדי יין שכן דרכו להביא מן ההפקר ואם הביא יותר מכאן מותר ומוכר לנכרי בארץ ולישראל בחוצה לארץ: **ח** ב"ש אומרים [ז]לא ימכור לו פרה חורשת בשביעית וב"ה מתירין מפני שהוא יכול לשוחטה מוכר לו פירות *בשעת הזרע ומשאיל לו סאתו אע"פ שהוא יודע שיש לו גורן ופורט לו מעות אע"פ שהוא יודע שיש לו פועלים וכולן בפירוש אסורין: **ט** [ג] [ח]משאלת אשה לחברתה החשודה על השביעית נפה וכברה ורחיים ותנור אבל לא תבור ולא תטחן עמה [ט]אשת חבר משאלת לאשת עם הארץ נפה וכברה ובוררת וטוחנת ומרקדת עמה אבל משתטיל המים לא תגע אצלה שאין מחזיקין ידי עוברי עבירה

ר"ה אפילו

זה א"ר אליעזר שאם לקטו העניים את עליו בשביעית ואחר כן תלשוהו לאחר שביעית אין חייב כלום ואם לא לקטו עליו יעשה חשבון וענין החשבון כמו שאמרו והוא כשיעקר אחר השמטה לב' שנים יתן לעניים השליש ואם יעקור אחר שלש שנים יתן לעניים הרביע ועל זה הדרך יתן לעניים חלק שנה שביעית מכלל השנים שיעמוד תחת הארץ וזה על העיקר אשר יסדנו ובארנו שדעתו להתיר לעניי' ולאכול פירות שביעית אחר הביעור ורבי יהושע אומר אין לעניים עמו חשבון שדעתו כמו שאמרנו שאינו מתיר לאכול פירות שביעית אחר הביעור לאחר והלכה כר"י: ד לוף של ערב שביעית. זה הדבר כשישלים הלוף קודם שביעית ולא נשאר בו אלא לחפור עליו ולעקור הבצלים: הקיצונים. מיוחדות לזמן הקיץ וזה מפני שיבשו מאד: פואה של עידית. הוא עץ אדום צובעים בו לצבע אדום רוי"א בלע"ז ופי' של עידית הפואה הטובה: במארופות של עץ. כלים עשוין מעץ לחפור בהם כ"י שישנה ולא יחשב הרואה אותה שהוא חופר הארץ ועובד אותה: פואה של צלעות. שיש לה צלעות והיא בעומק הארץ ואי אפשר לעקור אותם בכלי עץ אלא בברזל: **ה** פירוש כל זה מבואר והלכה כחכמים: **ו** אמר הכתוב ולפני עור לא תתן מכשול (ויקרא יט) ר"ל מי שסגרה עיניו התאוה ויצר הרע אל העזור אותו להוסיף בשורנו ותוסיף להרחיקו מן היושר ומפני זה אסור לעזור עוברי עבירה ולא יתקנו להם כלים אבל ראוי לקלקל להם: ומחרישה. היא האת. והמזרה הוא שיזרו בו התבואה. והדקר הוא כלי ברזל לחפור הארץ: מגל יד. חרמש קטן שיקטף כמלא היד ומפני זה נקרא מגל יד ומגל קציר ידוע: ואמר כל שמלאכתו מיוחדת לעבירה. הם הדברים שאסור להתעסק בהם במלאכות שנעשו להם אלו הכלים בשנה שביעית כגון החרישה והקצירה שכל הכלים העשוין למלאכתם אסור למכרם בשביעית וזה אינו אסור אלא למי שהוא חשוד על השביעית אבל מי שאינו חשוד מותר למכור לו כל מה שיבקש לפי שהוא רוצה להצניעו ולהכינו למוצאי שביעית: **ז** תיקון דברי זאת המשנה מוכר לנכרים בארץ יתר מיכן ולישראל בחוצה לארץ ולא נהיה חוששין שמא ימכור הנכרי לישראל או יקנה ישראל חוצה לארץ וילך לארץ ישראל שהעיקר בידינו אחזוקי באיסורא לא מחזקינן: **ח** משאיל לו סאתו. המדה הנקראת סאה וכן פורט לו מעות כגון שיקח ממנו דינר ויתן לו מעות: וכולם בפירוש אסורין. כגון שאמר לו מכור לי זו הפרה אחרוש בה או אזרע בה זרע פלוני ותן לי הסאה אמוד בה הזרע אשר השתי ותן לי מעות בזהוב זה אתן ממנו שכירות הפעלים שנתעסקו לי בעבודת הארץ אסור לו לעזרו בדבר מכל הדברים אשר זכרנו: **ט** נפה. היא אשר יניפו בה הקמח להוציא ממנה הסובין והיא כמו כברה אבל כברה היא לתבואה ונפה לקמח וטעם התרת אלו הדברים מפני שאינן מיוחדין לעבירה שאפשר לומר בקש הנפה לתקן בו או להכין בו דבר והריחים לטחון בו רפואות והתנור לבשל בו המטוה ובשביל זה כשתבאר ותאמר שבשביל פירות שביעית היא מבקשת אותם אסור ליתן לה כלום: ומה שאמר אשת חבר משאלת לאשת עם הארץ אין בזה משום שביעית אבל משום טומאה וטהרה שעם הארץ ואשתו ובניו ובני ביתו בחזקת טומאה ומשנה ראשונה אסור לגרום טומאה לחולין שבא"י והעיקר שבידינו שהאוכלין לא יטמאו אלא אחר הכשר במים או באחד משבעה משקין כמו שיתבאר במקומן וכבר הקדמנו כל זה בפרק שני מדמאי ומפני אלו העיקרים מותר לעזור חברתה עד שתתחיל לשפוך המים

עם עליס וטמנו בארץ כדתנן לעיל (משנה ב') ואחר שעבר עליו זמן הקרח חזר ונטעו והוסיף נידולין על גידולין וכן בכל שנה ושנה: ד שנכנס לשביעית. אמרינן בירושלמי (הל' ג) ר' יוסי בשם ר' לא תפתר שעקרן עד שלא למהו דאם הוסיפו ספיחין היה אסור לעוקרן ולהפסידן: הקייצנים. מפרש בירושל' (שם) קייסנאי כלומר שנזרעין בקיץ: של עידית. משנה (ב): במארופות. מלשון מרא וחיישי ב"ש לעבודת הארץ לפיכך שעה בשל עץ וב"ה לא חיישי: צלעות. מקום אבנים ולא חשיבי שדה כדאמרינן בסוף פ' א' כלאים דמודה ריש לקיש בזורע על גבי סלעים ועל גבי טרשין שהוא פטור אי נמי צלעות לידי השדה ולא באמצע ולא מיחזי כעבודת הארץ (ג): **ה** ירושלמי מה טעמא דרבי יהודה גזרו על הלוף ולא גזרו על הירק מעתה אפילו בשבת יהא מותר בסמון אנן קיימין שלא ילך ויביא מן האיסור ואומר מן הסמון הבאתי. פי' מאי טעמא דר' יהודה כלומר מאי שנא דפליג הכא ומאי שנא גבי ירק לקמן בפ"ו (מ"ד*) דאסרי' במוצאי שביעית עד שיעשה כיוצא בו ולא פליג רבי יהודה ומשני גזרו על הלוף שלא יעקור אותו בשביעית אלא בשינוי במארופות של עץ לב"ש ובקורדום לב"ה הלכך מוצאי שביעית לא שכיח דאיסורא אבל ירק דלא גזרו לתולשן כי אורחיה שכיח נמי דאיסורא בשמינית ופריך מעתה אפילו בשבת כלומר בשביעית שנקראת שבת יהא מותר דלא תלינן ליה בשל שביעית דלא שכיח משום דלא אפשר בלא שינוי אלא אמרינן דמן הסמון בששית הוא ומשני בסמון אנן קיימין דבההוא הוא דאמרינן דאין דרך לעוקרו בשינוי כדי לסומנו עד מוצאי שביעית אבל בשביעית עצמה אם בא לקנות מע"ה חיישינן שמא יביא מן האיסור ויאמר מן הסמון הבאתי ורבנן סברי דאם כן במוצאי שביעית ניחוש משום הכי אסרי עד שירבה בחדש דהיינו מן הפסח ואילך כדתניא בירושל' (שם) א"ר יהודה מעשה שהיינו בעין כושין ואכלנו לוף ע"פ ר' טרפון במוצאי החג של מוצאי שביעית אמר לו ר' יוסי עמך הייתי ולא היה אלא במוצאי פסח: **ו** ירושלמי (הל' ג) א"ר יונה כיני מתני' אלו כלים שאין האומן רשאי למוכרן בשביעית לחשוד על השביעית מזרה שזורין בו גורן דקר קולטרא בלע"ז והוא את בלשון מקרא כדכתיב וכתתו חרבותם לאתים (ישעיה ב): **ז** יוצר. אומן שעושה כלי חרס ה' כדי שמן ט"ו כדי יין בירושלמי (שם) פריך והא יש לומר שמא החליף א"ר יונה ניכרות הן אלו של יין ואלו של שמן וא"ר עולא אדרא דהלו חכימא פי' שמא החליף לומר שקונה לצורך יין ושמן והוא קונה הכל לצורך יין או הכל לצורך שמן ומשני ניכרות הן משונות של יין משל שמן ור' עולא משני דאדרא דהלו חכימא אדרא ל' עור כמו אדרייתא דתנא דפרק ד' דנדרים (דף כה.) ופירש בערוך שהביאו עורות של בהמות מליאות תבן וסבור הנכחש שהן בהמות ובלעז והכא משל בעלמא הוא כלומר קרקע של אלו ניכר משל אלו דמאותו קרקע שעושין כדי יין אין עושין כדי שמן: ואם הביא יותר. מכשיעור זה מותר ולא חיישינן דילמא מן המשומר דשביעית: ומוכר לנכרים בארץ. אפי' סובא ולא חיישינן דילמא אתי לזבוני לישראל: ולישראל בחו"ל. ולא חיישינן שמא יוליכם בארץ. [ג]משמע שהוא רוצה לומר אע"פ שכונס בו הרבה מיין ושמן שהביא מארץ ישראל (ו): **ח** לא ימכור. לישראל החשוד פרה המלומדת לחרוש משום ולפני עור לא תתן מכשול (ויקרא יט): שיכול לשוחטה. דכל היכא דאיכא למיתלי תלינן. ולא דמי לכלים דלעיל שאין אדם מוכר דהתם ליכא למיתלי כדפרשינן בפ"ק דע"ז (דף טו:) אפילו בשעת הזרע דאיכא למיתלי לאכילה כמו לזריעה ובהא מודו ב"ש דאין דומה לפרה דאין דרך לשחוט פרה החורשת: ומשאיל לו סאתו. של מדה אע"פ שיש לומר דלגורן שואל למדוד לכנוס לאוצר משום דאיכא נמי למיתלי להיתר שאדם עשוי למדוד להוליכו לטחון: שיש עמו פועלים. דאיכא למיתלי להיתר לשאר צרכיו: וכולן בפירוש אסורין. שפירש לו פרה לחרוש פירות לזרוע סאה לגורן מעות לפועלים: **ט** החשודה על השביעית. לאכול פירות אחר הביעור בלא ביעור: נפה. מפרש בירושל' (הל' ד) אני אומר נפה לספור בה מעות כברה לכבור בה חול רחים לטחון בה סמנים תנור לסמון בו אוכין של פשתן [ג] ובתנור שמא איירי דאי בתנור טהור אין לו תקנה לטהרות [ד] דחשוד אשביעית חשוד אטהרות כדאמרי' בפרק עד כמה (דף ל.): לא תבור ולא תטחון עמה. לסייעה מפני שאסור לסייע ידי עוברי עבירה: ובוררת וטוחנת. בסוף הניזקין (דף סא.) פריך מאי שנא אשת עם הארץ מחשודה על השביעית ומשני אביי רוב עמי הארץ מעשרין הן ורבא משני סיפא בעם הארץ דרבי מאיר דמעשר פירותיו וטומאה וטהרה דרבנן וסיפא כשתטיל למים בטומאת חלה וקשה מיכן לדברי המפרש בפ"ק דחולין (דף ו:) אשת חבר טוחנת עם אשת עם הארץ איירי דהכא משמע בהדיא דאסור לרבא בסתם עם הארץ לסייע ידי עוברי עבירה דמוקי מתניתין בעם הארץ המעשר אלא שאינו אוכל חוליו בטהרה והא דלא תני במתניתין תנור וליחוס גבי עם הארץ כדקא תני גבי שביעית משום דשמעינן לה מכללא דבוררת וטוחנת עמה אי נמי כיון דתנא כולא ברישא והכא תני חדא או תרי יגיד עליו ריעו כדאמרינן בפ' לא יחפור

דף

מארופ' כל זה שלא יהנו בעליהן מן השדה ולמה בשל עץ דבית שמאי חיישי לעבודת הארץ ובית הלל לא חיישי ומודין בית שמאי בפואה של צלעות. ירושל' פיטרא. גרסינן בסוף פרק א' דכלאים מודה ריש לקיש בזורע על גבי הים על גבי פיטרא על גבי סלעים על גבי טרשים שהוא פטור הרי לענין כלאים הצלעות לא חשיבי שדה להתחייב הזורע הכי נמי לענין שביעית. ופי' צלעות מקום אבנים וגדל בהן אבנים. אי נמי [פואה הנמצאת] סביב לצלעות השדה ולא באמצע השדה והואיל וכן אינו נראה כעבודת הארץ שאין הצלעות חשיבין כשדה לפיכך (אפי') [עוקרין אותה] בקרדומות: **ה** מאימתי מותר ליקח לוף במוצאי שביעית ר' יהודה אומר מיד. מאי טעמא דר' יהודה כלומר אוסר מיבעי ליה דהאי ירק אי מלוף העקור הוא אסור משום ספיחין ואי מלוף שלא עקרו כל שכן וכל שכן דאסור. ופריק ר' יהודה סבר בשגזרו על הלוף גזרו. פי' על הלוף שלא עקרו אסור הוא וירקו אי נמי בעקרו והניח במקומו גזרו על ירקו אבל אם עקרו וטמנו בו' והוציא ירק הירק שרי הילכך מותר ליקנות ירק הלוף דסקילנן ואמרי' מיהק דלוף מטמן מייתי וא"ת אי הכי אפי' בשביעית לישתרי הא לא קשיא שאם תתיר לו הוא הולך ומביא מן האיסור ואומר מן הסמך הבאתי.ורבנן סברי א"כ אפי' במוצאי שביעית שהוא הולך ומביא מן האיסור ואומר מן הסמך הבאתי אבל משירבה החדש דהיינו מפסח ואילך ההיתר רבה על האיסור ובטלו.תניא מעשה אר"י שהיינו בעין כושין ואכלנו לוף על פי ר' טרפון במוצאי החג של מוצאי שביעית אמר לו ר' יוסי עמך הייתי ולא היה אלא במוצאי הפסח: **ו** אלו כלים שאין האומן וכו'. בירושלמי מתרצי לה הכי אילו כלים שאין האומן רשאי למוכרן למי שהוא חשוד על השביעית הא בסתם מותר: מחרישה. בלעז בומייר: וכל כליה. העול יוני: והמזרה. פי' שזורין בגורן לעז פלא ויש לה ג' ענפים. והדקר. בלעז צפא ובלשון מקרא את: מגל יד. פתישודי: מגל קציר. פלצי. העגלה וכל כליה. קרו: **ז** היוצר. לעז פוטירו והוא האומן העושה כלי חרש: מוכר ה' כדין. שישימו שם שמן וט"ו כדין שישימו שם יין וניחוש דילמא יחליף וימכור אותן של שמן ויאמר של יין הן ותירץ לא חיישינן שני כדות הן אותו של יין ואותו של שמן. א"ר עולא אדרא דאילין חכימא. פי' עפר אחד הוא לקנקני השמן ועפר אחד הוא לקנקני היין פ"א אדרא כמו אידרא לנוף הקנקן קרי עור: שכן דרכו להביא מן ההבקר. פי' שיעור ה' כדין משמן ומיין ט"ו: ואם הביא יותר מזה השיעור מותר. פי' ולא חיישינן דילמא דשביעית: מוכר לגוים בארץ. ואפי' יותר מה' וט"ו ולא חיישינן דילמא מזבנן לישראל. ולישראל בחוצה לארץ ואפי' יותר מיכן ואפי' אם היין והשמן מן הארץ: **ח** בית שמאי אומרים לא ימכור לו פרה חורשת בו'. אפילו בסתם. שאין דרך בני אדם לשחוט פרות העומדות לחרישה ותנן דבר שמלאכתה מיוחדת לעבודה אסור: ובית הלל מתירין. דדבר שמלאכתה לאיסור ולהיתר הוא לאיסור החרישה ולהיתר שהמוכרה בסתם תמצאת חורשת הוא יכול לומר לשחיטה מכרתיו לך: ומוכר לו פירות שביעית בשעת הזרע דדבר שמלאכתו לאיסור ולהיתר הוא כיצד לאיסור לזריעה ולהיתר שיכול לומר לאכלה מוכר לו: ולשאול לו סאתו. פי' כלי של מדה שהוא דבר שמלאכתו להיתר ולאיסור אסור למכור ולמכנסו לאוצר להיתר שיכול לומר לו עשוי אדם למדוד פירותיו להוליכן לטחון: ופורט לו מעות. אע"פ שיודע שיש לו פועלין דמשתכח דאולי מעותיו לשכר שביעית יש בו היתר שיכול לומר לו למאכלך נתתי המעות אבל אם בפירוש בא ואמר לו מכור לי פרה חורשת מכור לי פירות לזרע השאילני המדה למדוד בה את הגורן להכניס לאוצר פרוט לי מעות בשביל הפועלין אסור: **ט** משאלת אשה לחברתה החשודה לאכול פירות שביעית לאחר הביעור בלא ביעור. פי' נפה. מאי טעמא שאני אומר נפה לספור בה מעות כברה לכבור בה חול ריחים לטחון ביה סממנין תנור לסמן בו אתין של פשתן: אבל לא תבור ולא תטחון עמה דחיישינן להלפי דתניא אין טוחנין עם אוכלי שביעית: אשת חבר וכו' ובוררת וטוחנת ומרקדת עמה. דלא חיישינן דילמא יהיב לה טבל דאמר אביי רוב עמי הארץ מעשרין הן: אבל משתטיל את המים לא תגע אצלה. משום טומאה דעם הארץ לא עביד חלתו בטהרה. ומתני' דקתני טוחנת היכא דלא לתתה. והא דתניא אשת חבר טוחנת עם אשת עם הארץ בזמן שהיא טמאה אבל לא בזמן שהיא טהורה פי' היכא דלתתה רבי שמעון

מסורת הש"ס
א) עבודת כוכבים פרק א' דף טו: ב) משנה בגיטין פ"ה דף סא.

פי' מהר"י בן מלכי צדק

ר' ודיכנו בז' ואפ"ה הוציא עלין ועקרן במוצאי ז' היינו אחר הביעור אם תאמר דיכון כעיקר כלומר כאילו מאז עקרן תשארו לו עד מוצאי שביעית שהרי כך העמדנוה שדיכנן בז' עתה אם דיכון כעיקר הוא כולו לעניים שעניים אוכלין אחר הביעור אבל לא עשירים ואם אין דיכון כעיקר אין כולו לעניים אלא העלין ממה נפשך שהרי העלין משביעית הקחייבין בביעור ואינון לעניים הילכך יעשה חשבון עם העניים מן העלין ובתוספתא פירש אם הוא ג' שנים נותן לעניים רובע אם ב' נותן לעניים שליש ואם אחת כמו זה ששתת בז' ועקר בח' ניתן לעניים מחצה זהו טעמא של ר' אליעזר וזה הכלל תפוש בידך שנת ז' הכל אוכלין בין עניים בין עשירים מוצאי ז' לעניים אבל לא לעשירי' דר' אליעזר כר' יהודה. רבי יהושע אומר אין לעניים עמו חשבון מאי טעמא אם תאמר דיכון כעיקר כולו לבעל הבית שעניים ועשירים אוכלין אחר הביעור כלומר כל חד וחד אכיל מאי דנקיט ואם אין דיכון כעיקר נמי כולו לבעל הבית דהא במוצאי שביעית עקרו הילכך לבעל הבית דקסבר כרבי יוסי דאמר בין עניים בין עשירים אוכלין אחר הביעור לפיכך אין לעניים עמו חשבון: ד לוף של ערב שביעית שנכנס לשביעית וכו'. עוקרין. ולא מותר לעקור ולהפירש בירושלמי א"ר יוסי תיפתר עד שלא צמחו שעדיין לא הוציא ספיחין: וכן בצלים הקיצונים. פי' שורין הנזרעין בקיץ ונתלשין בקיץ וכן פתרו בירושל' קיטנא פי' קיץ תרג' קיטא איספאטיקי: וכן פואה של עידית. פי' פואה של שדה שמינה ופי' היא דימיסטיק: עוקרין אותה במארופות של עץ. מעץ חזק עשוי כמו מרה ונקרא בלשון חכמים

ג א מיי' פ"ד מהלכות שמטה ויובל הלכה יט סמג לאוין רסח:
ד ב שם הלכה ח:
ה ג מיי' פ"ח שם הלכה ג:
ו ד שם הלכה ג:
ז ה שם הלכה ב:
ח ו שם הלכה ה ופ"ח הלכה כד:
ט ז שם הלכה ו:
י ח שם הלכה ז:
יא ט מיי' פ"ח מהלכות בכורים הלכה יג:

פי' שם

פירוש הרא"ש

(ב) בגדלים בשדה שמינה: (ג) דאין דרך לזרוע שם: (ד) מגל יד ומגל קציר ועגלה מחרשה שמא הוא רוצה לעקור מן הספקר ולהביא בעגלה למחל ביתו ואין מוכר אלא לכליה הרבה ולעשות אוצר: (ה) מוכר לישראל החשוד על השביעית: (ו) דלא החמירו בו חכמים כל כך:

הגהות הרי"ל לנדא

א] מ"ד בר"ש בסוף פ"ק דכלאים כצ"ל: ב] ל"ל מ"ש שם מסתמא פלוגתא דר"י ורבנן: ג] מ"ש שם אופן של פשתן. צ"ל לכבות: ד] מ"ש שם אין לו תקנה לטהרו כצ"ל:

עין משפט
נר מצוה

יב א מיי' פ"ח מהלכות שמטה ויובל הלכה ח :
א ב מיי' פ"ד מהלכות שמטה ויובל הלכה כז :

מסורת
הש"ס

א) גיטין סב. לעיל פ"ד משנה ג :

(דף י"ס·) : ומחזיקין ידי נכרים · פי' לעיל בפ"ד (משנה ג) ולגב גררא תנייה הכא דקא חשיב מפני דרכי שלום וכל בבא זו תנינא בפרק הניזקין והכא עיקר והתם גררא : ירושלמי (שם) ר' יוסי ברבי חנינא בעי על כל פירקא את אמרת או על הדא הילכתא את אמרת רבנן דקיסרי בשם ר' יודה מן מה דלא תנינא בגיטין אלא הדא הילכתא הדא אמרה על הדא הילכתא את אמרת פירוש הא דקא תני מתניתין וכולן לא אמרו אלא מפני דרכי שלום מיבעיא ליה אי קאי אכולהו פרקין כגון שאומן מוכר ופרה חורשת ומוכר פירות ומשאיל סאתו ופורט מעות או דילמא לא קאי אלא אמשאלת אשה לחברתה לחודה ומסיק דאמשאלת לחודה קאי מדלא תני איך בגיטין בהניזקין בהדי מילי דדרכי שלום ומכל מקום צריך טעם דהכך דלעיל שרינן בלאו טעמא דדרכי שלום לפי שיש לתלות טעם להיתר ואם כן ליסרי נמי ה] בלאו טעמא דדרכי שלום וי"ל דהכא בידוע שאין לחברתה כי אם פירות שביעית וכןמוכח בירושל'(שם)דאמרי' ר' זעירא בעי קומי ר' מנא מתני' בסתם הא במפרש לא אמר לו וסתמו לאו כפירושו הוא אני אומר נפה לספור בה מעות כברה לכבור בה חול ריחים לטחון בה סממנים תנור לטמון בה אונין של פשתן ומדלא קאמר לצורך פירות שביעית משמע דאיירי אע"ג דלית ליה פירות שביעית ואפילו הכי היה רוצה ר' מנא להתיר מפני דרכי שלום דשייך בהני ספי כדאשכחן בפ' המדיר (דף עב·) גבי כדרה שלא תשאל ולא תשאיל נפה וכברה וריחים ותנור שמשיאתו שם רע בשכנותיה ור' זירא לא שרי אלא בשאלה סתם דיש לתלות ומ"מ צריך טעמא דדרכי שלום לפי שאין זו תלייה גמורה דלספור מעות ולכבור חול וא"ת הא דפריך בסוף הניזקין (דף סא·) מאי שנא רישא גבי שביעית דלא תבור ולא תטחון עמה ומאי שנא סיפא אשת עם הארץ דבוררת וטוחנת עמה הוה ליה למימר משום דזה ודאי וזה ספק למאי דפרשינן דאיירי בפירות שביעית ודאי וי"ל דרוצה לחשוב למאי כודאי לפי שחשודין עליו והעמידנו בחזקת שאינו מתוקן עוד· ירושל' (הל' ד) תמן תנינן נחתום שעושה בטומאה לא לשין ולא עורכים עמו ותני עלה לא בוררין ולא טוחנין ולא מרקדין עמו וכה אמר כן אמר רבי לא כאן בחולין כאן בתרומה והא תנן נחתום אית לך נחתום בתרומה חבריא אמרי כאן בלותת כאן בשאינו לותת פירוש מתניתין בשאינו לותת ולא יתכן תירוץ זה אליבא דרבא דאמר בשילהי הניזקין למתניתין בעם הארץ דרבי מאיר וטומאה וטהרה דרבנן וסיפא דמשתפיל למים בטומאת חלה ועל כרחו מוקי ההוא דנחתום בתרומה :

וכולן לא אמרו אלא מפני דרכי שלום א) ומחזיקין ידי נכרים בשביעית אבל לא ידי ישראל ושואלין בשלומן מפני דרכי שלום:

פרק ששי

א שלש ב ארצות לשביעית כל שהחזיקו עולי בבל מארץ ישראל ועד כזיב לא נאכל ולא נעבד וכל שהחזיקו עולי מצרים מכזיב ועד הנהר ועד אמנה נאכל אבל לא נעבד מן הנהר ומאמנה ולפנים נאכל ונעבד: ב עושין בתלוש (ב) בסוריא אבל לא במחובר דשים וזורין

ולא תבדיל ממנה שלא תקבל העיסה טומאה · ועניין שאמר וכולן לא אמרו אלא מפני דרכי שלום. ר"ל כל מה שנאמר בהלכה זו מהתרת השאלה והעזר אפילו במעט וכבר באמרנו בפ' שקודם לזה ענין שאמר מחזיקין ידי נכרים בשביעית ושואלין בשלומם :

א יש מי שקורא אמנם והוא אמנה ויש מי שקורא אמנוס. ועניין לא נאכל ולא נעבד שאסור לנו עבודת הארץ ההיא ואם תעבד ע"י אחר אסור לאכול ממה שתוציא ושאמר נאכל אבל לא נעבד ר"ל שאינו מותר עבודתה ואם נעבדה יהיה כל *הצומח בה נאכל בקדושת שביעית ושאמר נאכל ונעבד שמותרת עבודתה בשביעית והצומח בה יאכל בלא קדושת שביעית אלא כמו שיאכלו פירות כל שנה: ב כבר פירשנו בפ"ו מדמאי שסוריא הם הארצות שכבש דוד ובארנו לשם

א שלש ארצות חלוקות בדין שביעית : עולי בבל · עזרא וסיעתו ובירושלמי (הל' א) מפרש להו : לא נאכל · לאחר שביעית בלא ביעור ולא נעבד בשביעית : עולי מצרים · יהושע וסיעתו והרבה כרכים כיבשו עולי מצרים ולא כיבשו עולי בבל וקסבר קדושה ראשונה קידשה לשעתה ולא קידשה לעתיד לבא: מכזיב א] ועד נהר אמנה· מפרש בירושל' (שם) א"ר הונא כן היא מתני' מכזיב עד הנהר מכזיב עד אמנוס כלומר זה לצד מזרח וזה לצד מערב נהר הוא נהר מצרים וכן משמע קצת *) בירושל'(שם)דמייתי לה בגמ' ומייתי לה נמי (ברייתא דפ"ק) [בפ"ק]דגיטין(דף ח·)דטורי אמנון ונהר מצרים וכזיב משמע התם דלצפונה דא"י קיימא ונהרי אמנוס היינו ראש אמנה דקרא כדאי' בירושל'(שם)א"ר יוספא בר שונם לכשיגיעו הגליות לטורי אמנון הן עתידות לומר שירה שנא'(שה"ש ד) תשורי מראש אמנה והוא הר ההר דהר ההר תרגום ירושלמי טורי אמנוס וגם הוא בצפונה של א"י דכתיב (במדבר לד) וזה יהיה לכם גבול צפון מן הים הגדול תתאו לכם הר ההר ועל זה שניכן בצפונה של א"י וצריך לומר דהא דמפרש מכזיב עד הנהר ומכזיב עד אמנוס חד למזרח כזיב וחד למערבו ומיהו בפרשת אלה מסעי כשמנה גבולי א"י משמע דנחל מצרים במקצוע דרומית מערבית ומחובר לים הגדול דעומד במערב א"י וטור אמנוס דהוא הר ההר הוא לצפון א"י במקצוע צפונית מערבית נמצא דא"י בין הר ההר לנחל מצרים זה מצפונית מערבית וזה מדרומית מערבית והים במערב ויש מקום שהים נכנס לא"י בין הר ההר לנחל מצרים כדמוכח בפ"ק דגיטין(שם) ב]דעכו לצפונה של א"י וכזיב רחוק יותר דהא המהלך [מעכו] לכזיב תני מימינו למזרח אלמא פניו לצפון וכל שעה מתרחק והולך מריבוע של א"י אלא רצועה נפקא שהיא למערב הדרך ההולך מעכו לכזיב כדמשמע התם(דף ז:)ג]ועוד אמנוס לצפונה של א"י סמוך לעיקר יותר מכזיב ועוד דכי קתני מכזיב עד הנהר דאדרבה הוה ליה למימר מאמנוס עד הנהר דאמנוס בין כזיב לנהר שהרי הנהר לדרום א"י ואמנוס לצפון ועדיין כזיב רחוק יותר ושמא נהר דתנן הכא לא נחל מצרים הוא אלא נהר אחר לצפון א"י כדפרשינן דאמנוס ונהר זה למזרח כזיב וזה למערבו וכן ההוא דתנן בפ"ד דחלה (משנה ח) ואמנוס דהכא הוא הר ההר האמור בגבולין בפרשת אלה מסעי ואין זה הר ההר שמת בו אהרן דהוא בגבול ארץ אדום ודרום א"י במקצוע דרומית מזרחית של א"י שםם היתה ארץ אדום: נאכל לאחר הביעור וקסבר קדושה ראשונה לא קידשה לעתיד לבא ומ"מ לענין עבודה החמירו דלא נעבד ודוקא במחובר אבל בתלוש עושין [כמו] בסוריא דבסמוך דאי לא תימא הכי אם כן ליתני ד' ארצות לשביעית דיש לסוריא דין לעצמה (א) : מהנהר ומאמנוס ולפנים · בכל הספרים כתוב ולפנים וספי ניחא לגרוס ולחוץ ושמא קרי ליה לפנים משום דהתחלת הנהר ומתחלת אמנוס ולפנים הימנו א"ל דנהר עצמו ואמנוס עצמו א"ל ומיהו אמנוס עצמו אמרינן בפ"ק דגיטין (שם) דכל שופע מטורי אמנוס ולפנים ארץ ישראל לכך נראה דגרסינן ולחוץ כאן ובפרק בתרא דחלה (שם) : אומר נאכל ונעבד כדדרים בירושל' (שם) אלה החקים והמשפטים אשר תשמרון לעשות בארץ (דברים יב) בארץ אתם חייבין לעשות ואי אתם חייבין בח"ל עדיין אני אומר מצות התלויות בארץ אינן נוהגות אלא בארץ יכול אפילו מצות שאינן תלויות בארץ לא יהו נוהגות אלא בארץ ת"ל(שם יא)השמרו לכם פן יפתה וגו' ושמתם את דברי אלה אפילו אתם גולים ושמתם את דברי אלה מה אית לך כגון תפילין ותלמוד תורה מה תפילין ותלמוד תורה שאינן תלוין בארץ נוהגין בארץ ובחו"ל אף כל דבר שאין תלוי בארץ נוהג בארץ ובחו"ל ובפ"ק דקידושין(דף לז·) יליף לה מע"ג: ירוש' (שם) משגלו יהו פטורין כתיב (נחמיה ח) ויעשו כל הקהל השבים מן השבי סוכות וגו' כי לא עשו סוכות וגו' מימי ישוע בן נון [ולמה ישוע רבי הלל בריה דרבי שמואל בר נחמן] פגם הכתוב כבוד לדיק בקבר מפני כבוד לדיק בשעתו הקיש ביאתן בימי עזרא לביאתן בימי יהושע מה ביאתן בימי יהושע פטורים היו ונתחייבו אף ביאתן בימי עזרא פטורין היו ונתחייבו רבי יוסי בר' חנינא אמר מדבר תורה נתחייבו הדא הוא דכתיב (דברים ל)והביאך ה' אלהיך אל הארץ אשר ירשו אבותיך וירשתה הק"ש ירושתך לירושת אבותיך מה ירושת אבותיך מדבר תורה אף ירושתך מדבר תורה והיטבך והרבך מאבותיך אבותיך פטורין היו ונתחייבו ואתם פטורים הייתם ונתחייבתם אבותיכם לא היה להם עול מלכות ואתם אע"פ שעליכם עול מלכות אבותיכם לא נתחייבו עד לאחר י"ד ז' שכיבשו וז' שחילקו ואתם כיון שנכנסתם נתחייבתם אבותיכם לא נתחייבו עד דקנו כולה ואתם ראשון ראשון קנה וחייב א"ר אליעזר מאליהן קבלו עליהן את המעשרות· מ"ם ובכל זאת אנחנו כורתים אמנה וכותבים ועל החתום שרינו לוינו כהנינו (נחמיה י) מה מקיים ר' אליעזר ואת בכורי צאננו ובקרנו מכיון שקיבלו עליהן אפילו דברים שלא היו חייבים עליהם כאילו מאליהן קיבלו מה קיים ר' יוסי ובכל זאת מכיון שקיבלו עליהם בסבר פנים יפות העלה עליהם המקום כאילו מאליהם קיבלו מה מקיים רבי אליעזר מאבותיך פתר לה לעתיד לבוא דא"ר חלבו בשם ר' יוחנן אבותיך ירשו ארץ ז' אומות ואתם עתידין לירש ארץ י' אומות· פי' ובכל זאת אנחנו כורתים וכתב באותה פרשה ולהביא את בכורי אדמתנו ובכורי כל עץ שנה בשנה וכתיב בההיא פרשה חלות תרומות ומעשרות משמע דכל זאת קבלו עליהם מדעתן בברית שכרתו אבל מדאורייתא פטורין ולהכי פריך לר' אליעזר דהכי נמי כתב באותה פרשה בכורות בנינו ובהמתנו ובכורות בקרנו וצאננו דכולהו חשיב בהדייהו אע"פ שהיו מחוייבין ועומדין משמע מתוך אותה שיטה דבבית שני לא נתחייבו מדאורייתא בתרומות ומעשרות לר"א וכן משמע בירושלמי דפ"ק דתרומות (הל' ג') ובירושלמי דיבמות פרק בית שמאי (הל' ב') דפליגי רבי יהודה ורבנן בקטן שלא הביא שתי שערות דרבי יהודה אומר תרומתו תרומה וקאמר מהו שיהו חייבין על הקדשים מבחוץ כלומר דאם קטן הקדיש בהמה ובא גדול ושחטה בחוץ כהנא אמר אין חייבין על הקדשים בחוץ ר' יוחנן וריש לקיש תרווייהו אמרין חייבין על הקדשים מבחוץ וקשיא דכהנא על דר' יהודה דר' יהודה פוטר סבלו דבר תורה ואתה בן כלומר בקטן פוטר סבלו מאיסור ותרומתו תרומה לר' יהודה וא"כ הקדישו נמי יהא הקדש להתחייב עליו משום שחוטי חוץ וכעין שיטה זו בסוף יוצא דופן (מ"ז:) אלא דפלוגתא דרבי יהודה ורבי יוסי מיתניא התם איפכא ומשני בירושלמי (שם) כמאן דאמר מאליהם קבלו עליהם את המעשרות כלומר דלא אמר ר' יהודה תרומתן תרומה אלא משום דתרומה דרבנן דמאליהן קבלו וכן מוכיח בירושלמי בפרק בתרא דתרומות (הל' ד') דתני ר' חלפתא בן שאול קדירה שבישל בה תרומה מגעילה ג' פעמים בחמין ודיו א"ר בא אין למדין ממנה לענין נבלה א"ר יוסי קשייתא קומי ר' בא תרומה בעון מיתה היא ונבלה בלא תעשה ואת אמרת הכין א"ל כמאן דאמר מאליהן קיבלו עליהן את המעשרות כלומר ולכך מיקל בתרומה משום דלאו דאורייתא וכן מסוף פ"ג דדמאי(משנה ד) גבי הא דתנן אצל הנכרי כפירותיו משמע דאיכא פלוגתא דאיכא למאן דאמר מאליהן קיבלו עליהן את המעשרות וכן בפ"ק ד] דמכילתין ואמרי' אפילו למאן דאמר מעשרות דבר תורה מודה בשמיטה שהיא מדבריהן וביומי הלל איירי התם וכן בריש פ"ב דמעשרות ואמרינן במגלת רות בשם ר' יהושע בן לוי שלשה דברים גזרו בית דין של מטה והסכימו בית דין של מעלה על שאלת שלום בשם ועל מגילת אסתר ועל המעשרות ומחרם במסכת מעשרות שמעון בר בא בשם ר' יוחנן אמר בעון מעשרות ותרומות גלו וכיון שגלו נפטרו מן התרומות ומן המעשרות והן חייבו עליהן מאליהן והפרישו תרומות ומעשרות ואמרינן בבראשית רבה בפרשת ויחי ג' דברים עשו בית דין של מטה ואלו הן אחד בימי עזרא בשעה שעלו מבבל ויקם להם הקב"ה להתיר המעשרות מה עשו הלכו וגזרו על עצמן שיהיו מעשרין שנאמר ואת ראשית עריסותינו סיפא דקרא מפרש תרומות ומעשרות וכתב בפרשה דבכל זאת דמייתי בירושלמי מכל הכי משמע דלא נהגו מדאורייתא בבית שני תרומות ומעשרות ואע"ג דר' יוחנן במגילת רות אשכחן בסוף הערל (דף פב:) דאמר אנא דאמרי כרבי יוסי דסדר עולם דירושה ראשונה ושניה יש להן שלישית אין להם התם פליגי ר' יוחנן וריש לקיש אליבא דר' דמתני' דהתם דאמר אנדרוגינוס שנשא בת ישראל מאכילה בתרומה דסבר ריש לקיש דמשום דתרומה דרבנן הוא דמאכילה דקתני ר' יוסי התם בברייתא דאנדרוגינוס ספיקא הוא וברייתא דסדר עולם ר' יוסי תני ולא סבר לה כדאמרינן בפרק יוצא דופן (דף מז:) ור' יוחנן סבר דהיא דסדר עולם עיקר וליתא לברייתא דחשיב אנדרוגינוס ספקא מקמי מתני' ולא משום דר' יוחנן סבר כר' יוסי דהא בברייתא דב' קופות (יבמות דף פב·) קאמר ר' יוחנן דלא בעינן רבייה כרבנן דאמרי תרומה בזמן הזה דרבנן. ומיהו תימה הוא לומר שיאמר שום אדם דבבית שני לא נהגו מדאורייתא תרומות ומעשרות אלא ודאי מדאורייתא נהגו והא דקאמר שקיבלו מאליהן על תרומות פירות קאמר דמדאורייתא דגן תירוש ויצהר והן החמירו עליהן בבית שני לגזור אף בשאר פירות מה שלא עשו בבית ראשון ה] והכיא דב"ר ומגילת רות היינו ההיא דפרק בתרא דמכות(דף כג:)דמייתי התם קרא דכתיב ובפרוץ הדבר שהבאת מעשר עשו ב"ד של מטה ובכל פירות משתעי קרא כדמוכח בריש פרק הנודר מן הירק (דף נה·) ועוד כדאמרינן בדגן תירוש ויצהר חשיב מאליהן לפי שיהושע נלטוה לקדש כל מה שבתוך תחומין אבל בימי עזרא לא קידשו אלא מה שרצו כדאמרינן הרבה כרכים כבשו עולי מצרים ולא קידשו עולי בבל ועל זה אמרינן בבראשית רבה שביקש להתיר להם הקב"ה את המעשר שלא היה מעניקן אם היו נמנעין מלקדש והם הלכו וקידשו ונתחייבו מן התורה ולהכי קאמר רבי אליעזר דמאליהן קבלו אבל ר' יוסי אמר מדבר תורה נתחייבו שנצטוו לקדש ונפקא מינה לר' יוסי דקדושה במצות הקב"ה קיימת אפילו בזמן הזה אע"פ שחרב הבית אבל לר"א דאמר מאליהן קבלו בטלה עכשיו קדושת הארץ דסתמא לא היה בלבן אלא בזמן שהבית קיים הואיל והדבר תלוי בהם ואפי' אית ליה לר' יוחנן בטלה קדושת הארץ דתרומות ומעשרות לא קשה מידי הא דמעינן ליה בפ' השוחט והמעלה(דף קז:)דמעלה בזמן הזה דלא בטלה קדושת הארץ ואע"ג דבחורבן בית ראשון לא בטלה קדושת הבית קדושת הארץ דתרומה ומעשר בטלה דאין זה תלוי במחילות מילתא אחריתי ויתכן דנפקא לן כדדרשי' אשר לו חומה (ויקרא כה)אע"פ שאין לו עכשיו והיה לו קודם לכן א"נ מדכתיב(תהלים קלב)זאת מנוחתי עדי עד דהני קראי מוכחי דירושלים אין אחריה היתר: ב עושין בתלוש בסוריא· אפילו אצל החשודין אע"ג דבארץ תנן לא תבור ולא תטחון עמה: אבל לא במחובר· כגון חרישה וקצירה ודוקא בשמור אבל לא במופקר אפילו בארץ מותר כדתניא בארץ אצל הגוים אבל בסוריא מותר וכן אין דורכין בגתו בארץ ולא עושין זיתין בבית הבד ובסוריא מותר : אבל לא במחובר . פי' לחרוש ולקצור ולבצור בשמור לארץ מאי טעמא

פירוש הרא"ש

פרק ו (א) ואין דיוק זה
כ"ל דלא קא חשיב אלא חלוקי ארצות של ארץ ישראל וסוריא היא כיבוש יחיד ולא היתה מעולם ארץ ישראל : ומיהו לשון נעבד דקאמר משתמע עבודת קרקע וגבי סוריא תני עושים בתלוש בסוריא : (ב) סוריא הוא ארם צובה שכיבש דוד והוסיפה על ארץ ישראל וסבר האי תנא דכיבוש יחיד לא שמיה כיבוש הלכך עושים אצל ישראל החשודים :

*) בברייתא כצ"ל

הגהות הר"י לנדא

ה] בר"ש וא"כ ליסרי נמי הכא כצ"ל: פ"ו א] מ"א בר"ש כזיב בירושלמי הגי' גזיב : ב] שם דעכו לצפונה. צ"ע ועוד דעכו : ג] שם ועוד אמנוס. צ"ע ועורי אמנוס: ד] שם וכן פ"ק דמכילתין. צ"ע פרק, יו"ד דמכילתין אמרינן : ה] שם מה שלא עשו בבית א'. צ"ע כדמוכח בריש הנודר מן הירק דמייתי התם קרא דכתיב ובפרוץ הדבר וההוא דב"ר ומגילת רות היינו ההוא דפרק בתרא דמכות שהבאת מעשר וכו' משתעי קרא ועוד אומר ר"י דגם בדגן תירוש וכו' וכוון לר"י בעל תוס' יחיאל קך ע"י יבמות פ"ב מ"ב :

פי' מהר"י בן מלכי צדק

שמעון בן אלעזר אומר אף בזמן שהיא טמאה לא תטחון מפני שחברתה נותנת לה ואוכלת: ומחזיקין וכו' כדלעיל ושואלין בשלומן מפני דרכי שלום' גרסינן השתא חוזקי מחזקינן שואלין בשלומן מיבעיא · ופירק רבינא לא נצרכה ליום אידם דתניא לא יכנס אדם לביתו של נכרי ביום אידו ויתן לו שלום מצאו בשוק נותן לו בשפה רפה ובכובד ראש:

פרק ו א שלש ארצות לשביעית כל שהחזיקו עולי בבל. פי' עזרא וסיעתו מארץ ישראל עד גזיב לא נאכל. פי' לאחר שביעית בלא ביעור ולא נעבד בשביעית ופירש בירושלמי מה שכיבשו עולי בבל ואילו הן פרשת חומת מגדל שיר (ויש שנין מגדל ש־) ושינא דרור ישורא דעכו וקצריא דגלילא וכברתא ובית זניתא וקובעיא ומלתא דכור ובירייא רבתא תפנית ונפתה ומחרתה דייתיר וממציא דאבהתא וראש מנעתן ונעתין עצמה מי ספר ומרחשת ומגדל חרוב · ואילם רבתא ונקבתא דעיון ותיקרת ברכה רבה ובר סנגרא ותרנגולא עילאה דלמעלה מקיסרין ותרפתא דמתחם לבוצרה ומלח דורכאי וממרון ובית דיגלי סכלי וקנת ורפח דחגרא ודרך הגדולה ההולכת למדבר חשבקויבק ונחל זרד ויגר שהדותא ורקם רגיעא וגוניא דאשקלון. כל שהחזיקו עולי מצרי' הם יהושע וסיעתו מגזיב ועד הנהר. גרסינן רב הונא אמר כן היא מתני' מגזיב ועד הנהר מגזיב ועד אמנם ונהר משמע נחל מצרים א"ר יוסטא בר שונם לכשיגיעו הגליות לטורי אמנום עתידות לומר שירה שנא' תשורי מראש אמנה פי' נאכל אפי' לאחר הביעור אבל לא נעבד כלומר הרי היא כסוריא דתנן עושין בתלוש בסוריא אבל לא במחובר ויש לומר מדלא קתני הרי היא כסוריא שמע מינה לא נעבד דקתני בלא נעבד דכיבוש עזרא ועל זה הפיר' אנו סומכין מן הנהר ומאמנם ולחוץ הוי חוצה לארץ ונאכל ונעבד דכתיב אלה החקים והמשפטים אשר תשמרון לעשות בארץ בארץ אתם חייבין לעשות ולא בחוצה לארץ : ב עושין בתלוש בסוריא. פירוש בפירות שביעי' כגון דישה וזורה אפילו אצל החשודין ואנן תנן אבל לא תבור ולא תטחון עמה · וכן אין סוחנין פירות שביעית

a ONLY ALLOWED IN THE INTERESTS OF PEACE.[1] TO HEATHENS, ENCOURAGEMENT MAY BE OFFERED IN THE SABBATICAL YEAR,[2] BUT [ON NO ACCOUNT] TO ISRAELITES. IN THE INTERESTS OF PEACE, ONE MAY ALSO OFFER GREETINGS TO HEATHENS.[3]

CHAPTER VI

MISHNAH 1. [PALESTINE IS DIVIDED INTO] THREE COUN-
b TRIES WITH REFERENCE TO THE SABBATICAL LAW.[1] [THE FRUIT OF] THAT TERRITORY OCCUPIED BY THOSE WHO CAME UP FROM BABYLON,[2] NAMELY FROM ERETZ ISRAEL AS FAR AS CHEZIB,[3] MAY NOT BE EATEN,[4] NOR [MAY ITS SOIL] BE CULTIVATED.[5] [THE FRUIT OF] THAT TERRITORY OCCUPIED BY THOSE WHO CAME UP FROM EGYPT, NAMELY FROM CHEZIB TO THE RIVER,[6] AND UNTIL AMONAH,[7] MAY BE EATEN, BUT [ITS SOIL] NOT CULTIVATED. FROM THE RIVER TILL AMONAH AND INWARDS, [PRODUCE] MAY BE EATEN AND [THE SOIL] CULTIVATED.[8]

MISHNAH 2. IN SYRIA,[9] ONE MAY PERFORM WORK ON SUCH PRODUCE AS HAD BEEN DETACHED,[10] BUT NOT ON SUCH STILL ATTACHED [TO THE SOIL].[11] THEY MAY THRESH,[12]

a (1) Lit., 'ways of peace', cf. Prov. III, 17. (2) Even when actually working in the seventh year; cf. *supra* IV, 3. (3) And even on their pagan festivals. It must be remembered that the name of God was used in all greetings, and Jews always had an instinctive shudder at associating His name with anything pagan.

b (1) V. *infra* IX, 2. (2) Under Ezra and Nehemiah. Our Tanna is of the opinion that the land then became holy for all time. (3) The Biblical Achzib, between Acre and Tyre; Josh. XIX, 29; Judg. I, 31. North of Acre. (4) If illegally cultivated, or without the removal of the produce which grew of its own accord. (5) In the seventh year. (6) The Orontes in Northern Syria; v. Horowitz, *Palestine*, p. 20. (7) Mount Ammanon, N.W. Syria; v. Giṭ. (Sonc. ed.) 8*a* n. a 1. (8) Since its soil does not possess holiness of the Lord; and in Ex. XXIII, 10 the stress is on '*thy land*' (ארצך), thus implying that only '*thy land*' was subject to these laws. (9) Conquered by David, Mesopotamia was awarded the character of Eretz Israel in some things, and of other lands in other things. It was conquered before David had yet finally subdued the whole of the land. (10) Even with those suspect of disregarding the law; cf. *supra* V, 9. (11) Then no reaping or gleaning may be done in the Sabbatical year. The reason for this precaution was lest people, on account of the difficulties of the Sabbatical observance, forsake the cultivation of the land and settle in Mesopotamia. In the case of detached produce it was permitted, so that the poor of Eretz Israel be able to obtain extra means in Syria, which was quite near. (12) Our Mishnah defines the kinds of labour permitted when produce no longer is attached to the soil.

WINNOW, AND TREAD [THE CORN], AND EVEN BIND THEM [INTO SHEAVES], BUT THEY MAY NOT REAP [THE CROPS], NOR
a CUT THE GRAPES, NOR HARVEST THE OLIVES.[1] R. AKIBA FORMULATED THIS PRINCIPLE: THE KIND OF WORK THAT IS PERMITTED IN ERETZ ISRAEL MAY ALSO BE DONE IN SYRIA.[2]

MISHNAH 3. ONIONS[3] ON WHICH RAIN HAD DESCENDED AND WHICH HAD SPROUTED FORTH, ARE FORBIDDEN IF THEIR LEAVES HAD TURNED BLACK;[4] IF THEY HAD BECOME GREEN THEY ARE PERMITTED.[5] R. ḤANINA B. ANTIGONUS SAYS: AS LONG AS THEY CAN BE PLUCKED OUT BY THEIR LEAVES,[6] THEY ARE FORBIDDEN. IN THE YEAR AFTER THE SABBATICAL YEAR, THE LIKE OF THESE[7] ARE PERMITTED.[8]

MISHNAH 4. WHEN MAY A MAN BUY VEGETABLES AT THE OUTGOING OF THE SABBATICAL YEAR?[9] WHEN THE CROP OF THE SAME KIND BEGINS [AGAIN] TO RIPEN.[10] WHERE FRUIT RIPENS QUICKLY, EVEN THAT WHICH IS LATE IN RIPENING IS ALSO PERMISSIBLE.[11] RABBI USED TO ALLOW THE BUYING OF VEGETABLES ON THE IMMEDIATE TERMI-
b NATION OF THE SEVENTH YEAR.[1]

MISHNAH 5. ONE MAY NOT EXPORT OIL [OF TERUMAH] THAT HAD TO BE BURNT,[2] NOR PRODUCE OF THE SEVENTH YEAR,[3] FROM THE LAND [OF ISRAEL] TO OTHER COUNTRIES. R. SIMEON SAID: I HAVE HEARD IT EXPRESSLY STATED THAT THEY MAY BE EXPORTED TO SYRIA, BUT NOT TO ANY OTHER COUNTRY OUTSIDE THE LAND.

MISHNAH 6. TERUMAH MAY NOT BE IMPORTED FROM OUTSIDE THE LAND OF ERETZ ISRAEL.[4] R. SIMEON SAID: I HAVE HEARD IT EXPRESSLY STATED THAT ONE MAY BRING FROM SYRIA,[5] BUT NOT FROM OUTSIDE THE LAND.[6]

CHAPTER VII

MISHNAH 1. AN IMPORTANT GENERAL PRINCIPLE WAS LAID DOWN CONCERNING SABBATICAL YEAR PRODUCE. TO ANYTHING THAT MAY BE CONSIDERED FOOD FOR MAN OR CATTLE, OR TO A SPECIES [OF PLANTS] USED FOR DYEING, IF

a .. (1) Being work on what is still attached to the soil. (2) Work, which in Palestine could be performed provided the procedure was different from the usual (*supra* V, 4), was allowed in Syria in the ordinary way (Bert.). (3) That had remained in the soil until the Sabbatical year. (4) Not actually black, but a deep green, like all unripe onions. They are forbidden because they had benefited by the seventh year. (5) Not having benefited by the seventh year, it is as if they had been plucked before. (6) The whole onion following suit. This is evidence of their ripeness in the seventh year. When onions begin to wither, their leaves weaken. (7) Viz., onions that had been plucked in the sixth year and re-planted in the seventh, and uprooted again in the eighth year. Since they were almost ripe before the seventh year, the little improvement they received in the Sabbatical year was neutralized by their growth in the eighth year. (8) Even when pulled out by their leaves. (9) Without being suspect of trading with seventh year produce. (10) Until such time that it takes other vegetables to ripen. The quantity of vegetables permitted negative the minority prohibited. (11) Since it can be claimed that this belongs to the crop that ripened early.

b (1) Vegetables were not only imported from other lands, where they had grown legally, but could also be grown in the land in two or three days. (2) Having become unclean, it had to be burnt in Palestine. On *terumah* v. Glos. (3) The Removal of fruits of the third and sixth years of the Sabbatical period had to be done in Palestine; v. Lev. XXV, 7. (4) So that priests be not tempted to go outside the Land to fetch *terumah*, and thus be defiled by a pagan atmosphere; v. Shab. 16*b*. (5) Since its air was not held to be contaminating; moreover, it showed some of the sanctity of Palestine. (6) This Mishnah is quoted only because of the one that preceded.

בת"כ את ענבי נזירך לא תבצור מן השמור אי אתה בוצר אבל אתה בוצר מן המופקר ודייקינן בירושל' (הל' ב') מה אנן קיימין אם בפירות ששית שנכנסו לשביעית אפילו בארץ מותר אם בפירות שביעית שיצאו למוצאי שביעית לחרוש מותר ולקצור אסור אלא כי אנן קיימין בפירות שביעית בשביעית כלומר דבסוריא בתלוש מותר במחובר אסור ואמרינן בירושלמי (שם) ר' אסי בעי קומי ר' מנא מהו לטחון עם הנכרי בארץ א"ל מתני' אמרה שהוא אסור דתנן עושין בתלוש בסוריא אבל לא במחובר הא בארץ אפילו בתלוש אסור וסבר האי תנא כיבוש יחיד לאו שמיה כיבוש מדמיקל בסוריא ספי מבארץ ישראל והאי דגזור במחובר אמרינן בירושל' (שם)

א"ר אבהו שלא יהו תקועין ומשתקעין שם (ג) כלומר משום דחמיר עלייהו איסור שביעית בארץ והדר קאמר בתלוש למה הוא מותר מן גודו א] חמי רווחא קרי לא נפיק כלומר כיון שימצא לו בקרוב ריוח מועט בשביעית לא יצא מארץ ישראל להשתקע בחוצה לארץ : ג בצלים · של ששית שנכנסו בשביעית וירדו עליהן גשמים וצמחו אם הושחרו העלים בידוע שהן גדלין ומוסיפין ואתו גידולי שביעית ומבטלין העיקר אע"פ שהוא מרובה טובא אבל הוריקו העלים נ] צמחו ולא מארעא רבו : אם יכולין להתלש בעלין שלהן · דרך הבצלים כשנגמרים יוצאים מעצמן מן הארץ וכשאוחז בעלין נתלשין אם חזקים הן מעט : וכנגד כן למוצאי שביעית מותרין. לא יתכן לפרש בבצלים של שביעית דהנהו לא משתרו למוצאי שביעית כדמוכח בפרק הנודר מן הירק (דף נח·) ומה מועיל מה שעליהן שחורין ומה שיכולין ליתלש בעליהן דילמא אכתי לא רבו גידולין על עיקרו אלא סיפא נמי בבצלין של ששית איירי שעקרן בששית וחזר ונטען בשביעית ועקרן לאחר שגדלו מעט וחזר ונטען בשמינית ומתוך שכבר גדלו בששית לא הוסיפו כי אם מעט בשביעית ונאסרו וכשחזרו והוסיפו מעט בשמינית חזר אותו היתר וביטל האיסור המועט שגם של ששית מסייע לבטל אחרי שסוף גידולן בהיתר:

לשם מאי זה טעם לא נתחייבו בהם כל המלות אבל אסור לנו להתעסק בהם בדבר המחובר לארץ בשנה שביעית ואע"פ שהוא מותר לשם כדי שלא יניחו בני אדם ארץ ישראל וישכנו שם והוא מה שאמר בטעם זה כדי שלא יהיו הולכים ומשתקעין שם ודברי ר"ע אמת : ג הוריקו . נעשו ירוקין וכל זמן שהם ירוקין כאילו הם מן הפרי עצמו ומותר לאכלן ואם השחיר מה שצמח מהם יהיה כאילו צמח בארץ ויחשבו כפירות שביעית וזה ענין מה שאמר אסורין: ור' חנינא בן אנטיגנוס אומר. שאם נתלשו העלין מהם ונשארו שם ולא נעקרו עם העלין יהיה דינם כדין הצומח בארץ והן כמו פירות שביעית: וכנגד כן במוצאי שביעית מותרין. ר"ל כשיהיו בזמן שיכולין לעקור העלין וישארו הבצלים בעצמן ולא יעקרו מותר לאכול הבצל ההוא במוצאי שביעית שאינו מפירות שביעית ואין הלכה כרבי חנינא בן אנטיגנוס: ד משיעשה כיוצא בו . משילמח כמו המין ההוא : ובביר . הוא הממהר לצאת בתחלת מוצאי שביעית : ואפיל . הוא המתאחר שנשאר מפירות שנה שביעית שעברה והלכה כרבי : ה שמן שריפה . הוא שמן תרומה שנטמא ונקרא שמן שריפה שאינו ראוי אלא לשרפה ואין הלכה כר' שמעון :

ו כל זה מבואר ואין הלכה כרבי שמעון :

וזורין ודורכין ומעמרין (ד) אבל לא קוצרין ולא בוצרין ולא מוסקין כלל אמר רבי עקיבא [א]כל שכיוצא בו מותר בארץ ישראל עושין אותו בסוריא: **ג** [ה] [ב]בצלים שירדו עליהן גשמים וצמחו אם היו העלין שלהן שחורין אסורין הוריקו (ה) הרי אלו מותרין רבי חנינא בן אנטיגנוס אומר אם (אינם) יכולין להתלש בעלין שלהן אסורין וכנגד כן מוצאי שביעית מותרין : **ד** מאימתי מותר אדם ליקח ירק במוצאי שביעית משיעשה כיוצא בו עשה הבכיר הותר האפיל [ג]רבי התיר ליקח ירק במוצאי שביעית מיד : **ה** [ד]אין מוציאין שמן שרפה [ה]ופירות שביעית מהארץ לחוצה לארץ אמר רבי שמעון שמעתי בפירוש שמוציאים לסוריא ואין מוציאים לחוצה לארץ : **ו** [ו]אין מביאין תרומה מחוצה לארץ אמר ר' שמעון שמעתי בפירוש שמביאין מסוריא ואין מביאין מחוצה לארץ :

פרק שביעי

א [ג] **כלל** [ז]גדול אמרו בשביעית כל שהוא מאכל אדם ומאכל בהמה וממין הצובעים

א ענין שאמר כלל גדול כנגד הכלל הנאמר במעשרות שדין שנה שביעית חייב למאכל אדם . ופירוש ממין הטובעין . ממיני הצבעים :

ירושלמי (הל' ג') עקרן בשביעית ושתלן במוצאי שביעית ר' זעירא אמר מכיון שרבה עליו החדש מותר ר' לא ור' אמי אמרי תרויהון אסורין מתני' פליגא על רבי לא ועל ר' אמי דתני זה הכלל שהיה ר"ש אומר משום ר' יהושע כל דבר שיש לו מתירין כגון טבל ומעשר שני וחדש והקדש לא נתנו להם חכמים שיעור אלא מין במינו בכל שהוא ושלא במינו בנותן טעם וכל דבר שאין לו מתירין כגון תרומה חלה וערלה וכלאי הכרם נתנו לו חכמים שיעור בין במינו בין שלא במינו בנותן טעם התיבון הרי שביעית שאין לה היתר ולא נתנו חכמים שיעור אמר להם לא אם אמרתם בשביעית שאינה אוסרת כל שהוא אלא בביעור אבל לאכילה בנותן טעם מהו עבדן לה ר' לא ור' אמי פתרין לה בעירובין אבל בגידולין חמור הוא בגידולין דא"ר זעירא בשם ר' יוחנן *) בגל של כלאי הכרם שעקרו אפילו מוסיף כמה אסור שאין גידולי היתר מעלין האיסור מתניתין פליגא על ר"ז דתנן (תרומות פ"ט מ"ד) גידולי תרומה תרומה גידולי גידוליו חולין אבל טבל ומעשר ראשון וספיחי שביעית ותרומת חו"ל המדומע והביכורים גידוליהן חולין ותני עלה בד"א בדבר שזרעו כלה אבל בדבר שאין זרעו כלה גידולי גידולין אסורין מה עביד לה ר' זעירא פתר לה בקדושת שביעית וביעור ג] אבל באכילה כיון שרבה עלה החדש מותר · בסוף הנודר מן הירק (דף נט:) פליגא בהך מילתא נתנו לו חכמים שיעור בכל הספרים כתוב מין במינו בכל שהוא ושלא במינו בנותן טעם [כמו] ברישא וטעות סופר הוא והגירסא נכונה כמו שכתבתי ומיהו יכולים להגיה סיפא כדאיתא ולהגיה ברישא גבי דבר שיש לו מתירין בין מין במינו בין שלא במינו בכל שהוא אבל לא יתכן מלפריך הרי שביעית דלא נתנו חכמים שיעור כדתנן לקמן בפ"ז (מ"ז) השביעית אוסרת כל שהוא במינה שלא במינה בנותן טעם ש"מ דגרסינן בדבר שאין לו מתירין בין במינה בין שלא במינה בנותן טעם ומשני דהא דאמר כל שהוא במינה היינו לענין ביעור דלאו לאחר ביעור נתערב בה כל שהוא במינה חייב לבער אבל לאכילה כגון קודם הביעור אין בו קדושת שביעית אפילו במינו עד שיהא בו בנותן טעם ועוד יש לדקדק מדפריך עליה דר' לא ורבי אמי דאיירי בגידולין דהיינו מין במינו ואמרינן אסור והכא שרי באכילה בנותן טעם והא דאמרינן בסוף כילה (דף נח·) גבי אשה שאלה מים ומלח לעיסתה כו' ופריך וליבטלו מים לעיסה ומשני (דף נט·) דהוי· דבר שיש לו מתירין ואפילו באלף לא בטיל והתם מין בשאינו מינו הוא ואין דבר שיש לו מתירין בטל במינו וכן הוא טעם דתבלים ד] ושאר טעמא דהתם אמר להם לא אם אמרתם בשביעית שאינה אוסרת כל שהוא אלא בביעור · לאחר דאם לאחר הביעור נתערב כל שהוא במינה חייב לבער אבל לאכילה קודם הביעור אין בו קדושת שביעית אפי' במינו עד שיהא בו נותן טעם כן ראוי לפרש לבאורה אבל אי אפשר לומר כן כדמוכח בשילהי הנודר מן הירק (שם) דמייתי לה אההוא דרבו גידולין על עיקרן ורולה לדקדק מכאן שהגידולין מבטלין את העיקר דבתר תוספת אזלינן ולא בתר עיקר מדאוכרת בכל שהו הלכך צריך לפרש דאינה אוסרת בכל שהוא אלא בביעור

היכי שביק מתני' ושמא לכתחלה אפילו לר' שמעון בן אלעזר מודה ח] דאין מוציאין אפילו קודם הביעור ורב ספרא דאפיק גרבא דחמרא בשביעית מא"י לחוצה לארץ שוגג היה וברוב ספרים גרסי' רב ספרא נפק מא"י לחוצה לארץ הוה בהדיה גרבא דחמרא דשביעית משמע דלאו אדעתיה : ו אין מביאין תרומות · בירושלמי (שם) פריך תמן תנינן בן אנטיגנוס הביא בכורים מאספמיא וקבלו ממנו ויביא תרומתו אמר ר' אושעיא בכורים באחריות בעלים תרומה אינה באחריות בעלים אם אומר את כן אף הם מרדפין אחריה לשם כלומר ויצאו כהנים מארץ ישראל לחו"ל להביא תרומה שאין על הבעלים להביא [כמו] בכורים :

א כלל גדול · הא דתנן הכא ובפרק קמא דפאה (משנה ד) כלל אמרו בפאה ולא תנן גדול מפרש במסכת שבת בריש כלל גדול (סח·) ולדמיו

שלי' בראשונה היה הירק אסור בספרי ארץ ישראל התקינו שיהא מותר אעפ"כ היה אסור להביא ירק מחוצה לארץ לארץ התקינו שיהו מביאין אעפ"כ היה אסור ליקח ירק במוצאי שביעית ... מוצאי שביעית מיד בר מן קפלוטא מה עשו אנשי ציפורי הלבישו את הקפלוט שק ואפר והביאוהו לפני ר' אמרו לו מה חטא זה מכל ירק והתירו להן פי' שירקות חוצה לארץ רבה ...

ה אין מוציאין שמן שרפה . פי' שמן העומד לישרף ומאי ניהו שמן תרומה שנטמא ובשאר שני שבוע עסיקי'. וכן פירות שביעית אין מוציאין מארץ לחוצה לארץ. תניא פירות הארץ ... במקומן דברי ר' שמעון בן אלעזר אומר מביאין בארץ ומבערן דכתיב בארצך תהיה כל תבואתה לאכול : **ו אין** מביאין תרומה מחוצה לארץ . והקשו בירושלמי ויביא תרומה כמו ... ביא ביכורים מאספמיא וקיבלו ממנו · ותירץ ר' אושעיא ביכורין באחריות בעלין תרומה אינה באחריות בעלין אם אומר אתה כן מרדפין אחריה לשם כלומר יצאו הכהנים חוצה לא...

... תנן אין יוצאין מן הארץ לחוצה לארץ : **פ"ז א כלל** גדול אמרו בשביעית . כבר פירשנו מאי טעמא גבי שביעית תני כלל גדול : **כל** שהוא מאכל אדם ומאכ...

עין משפט נר מצוה

ב א מיי' פ"ז מהלכות שמטה ויובל הלכה ז :
ג ב שם הלכה יד :
ד ג שם הלכה טו :
ה ד מיי' פ"ו שם הלכה ב :
ו ה מיי' פ"ה מהלכות בכורות הלכה ט :
ז ו מיי' פי"ב מהלכות תרומות הלכה כא :
ח ז מיי' פ"ח מהלכות מאכלות אסורות הלכה טז סמג לאוין קלט טוש"ע י"ד סי' קיז :
ט ח מיי' פ"ו מהלכות שמטה ויובל הלכה ב :

מסורת הש"ס

א) נדה פ"ו דף נא: ב) ב"ק פ"ט דף קא: ג) נדה פ"ו דף נא:

הצובעים ואינו מתקיים בארץ יש לו שביעית ולדמיו שביעית יש לו ביעור [א]ולדמיו ביעור ואיזה זה א) עלה הלוף השוטה ועלה הדנדנה העולשין והכרישין והרגילה ונץ החלב ומאכל בהמה החוחים והדרדרים ב) וממין הצובעין ספיחי (ג) אסטים וקוצה יש להם שביעית ולדמיהן שביעית יש להם ביעור ולדמיהן ביעור:

ב [ב]ועוד כלל אחר אמרו כל *שאינו מאכל אדם ומאכל בהמה וממין הצובעין ומתקיים בארץ יש לו שביעית ולדמיו שביעית אין לו ביעור ואין לדמיו ביעור אי זהו ג) עיקר הלוף השוטה ועיקר הדנדנה והעקרבנין והחלבצין והבוכריא וממין הצובעין הפואה והרכפא יש להם שביעית ולדמיהן שביעית אין להם ביעור ולא לדמיהן ביעור ר"מ אומר דמיהן מתבערין עד ר"ה אמרו לו להן אין ביעור קל וחומר לדמיהן :

ג [ג]קליפי רמון והנץ שלו קליפי אגוזים והגלעינין יש להם שביעית ולדמיהן שביעית [ד]הצבע צובע לעצמו ולא יצבע בשכר שאין עושין סחורה בפירות שביעית [ה]ולא בבכורות [ו]ולא בתרומות [ז]ולא בנבלות ולא בטרפות ולא בשקצים ולא ברמשים [ח]ולא יהיה לוקח ירקות שדה ומוכר בשוק אבל הוא לוקט ובנו מוכר על ידו לקח לעצמו

ר"ש

ולדמיו שביעית · אם מכרן וקבל דמים יש בדמיהן קדושת שביעית : יש לו ביעור · כשכלה לחיה מן השדה ולקמן בפ"ט (משנה ח) מפרש דין ביעור : עלה הלוף שוטה הא דלא נקט לוף פיקח לוף שוטה איצטריך ליה משום דתנן בפרק בתרא דעוקצין(משנה ד) עלה לוף שוטה אין מטמאין טומאת אוכלין עד שימתקס סד"א לא ליחול עלייהו קדושת שביעית כדמפרש בירושל' (הל' א') ופריך ולא כן אמר ר' יוסי בר' חנינא עולשי חשובין הן לטמא טומאת אוכלין בשביעית כלומר ב' מיני עולשין הן כדתנן בריש כלאים (משנה ב) עולשין ועולשי שדה ובשאר שנים למטויין בשל גינה לא חשיבי דשדה לטמא טומאת אוכלין אבל בשביעית דאסור לזרוע ואין של גינה מצויין חשיבי להו דשדה ומאי איצטריך לתנא למתני' ומשני אתמר טעמא הדא אמרה עד שלא התיר ר' להביא ירק מחו"ל לארץ אבל משהתיר היא שביעית היא שאר שני שבוע ובהא לא הוי חשיבות עד שיחשב עליהם דרבי יוסי בר' חנינא קודם שהתיר רבי כדאמר בפרקין דלעיל דהתקינו שיהא מותר להביא אבל לאחר שהתיר רבי איצטריך משום דצריכות חשיבות שיש להם ירק הרבה ולא חשיבו להו קמ"ל דחשיב עלייהו ומלינו דבר בתחלה אין קדושת שביעית חלה עליו ובסוף קדושת שביעית חלה עליו ומשני התיבון הרי (מכילתין פ"ח מ"א) הספיחה האזוב והקורנים שליקטם לעצים אין קדושת שביעי' חלה עליהן חישב עליהן לאוכלים קדושת שביעית חלה עליהם א"ר חנינא שכן אם ליקטן לאוכלין קדושת שביעית חלה עליהן מיד : והכרישין · כמו שפירשנו בעולשין צריך לפרש בכרישין דים כרישי גינה וכרישי שדה כדתנן בריש כלאים (פ"א מ"ב) כרשין וכרשי שדה (א) וכן רגילה ונץ החלב כולם מאכל אדם ע"י הדחק דסתם חציר לבהמה כדכתיב מצמיח חציר (תהלים קד):רגילה· יש אומר דהן הלגלוגות (ב):ונ"ץ החלב· פירש בערוך פרחים לבנים ויש אומרים עשב כשמתחתך יוצא ממנו חלב: יש להם שביעית· להאכיל בקדושת שביעית שלא להפסידן : ולדמיהן שביעית·אם מכרן ולקח בהן דמים וקנה מהן בשר ומן הבשר דגים כדפרש:כן בע"ז בפרק ר' ישמעאל (דף נד:) כי יובל היא קודש (ויקרא כה). מה קודש תופס דמיו אף שביעית תופסת דמיה אי מה קודש תופס דמיו ויוצא לחולין אף שביעית תופסת דמיה ויוצאה לחולין ת"ל תהיה(שם)בהויתה תהא הא כיצד לקח בפירות שביעית בשר אלו ואלו מתבערין בשביעית (ד) כולה ברייתא כדאיתא התם : יש להם ביעור · כשיבוא זמן הביעור ולדמיו ביעור ויתחלק לכל אדם כדמפרש לקמן פ"ט (מ"ט) ובפרק בא סימן (דף נא:) דרשינן לה מדכתיב (שם) ולבהמתך ולחיה אשר בארצך כל זמן שחיה אוכלת מן השדה האכל לבהמתך בבית כלה לחיה בשדה כלה לבהמתך מן הבית והני כיון דאין מתקיימין כלו להן : ב עיקר לוף שוטה · מדקתני לוף שוטה ברישא ובסיפא ולא קתני לוף סתם משמע דחלוק עיקרו מלוף ובירושלמי (שם) תני תלת מילין עליו שלו יש להן שביעית ולדמיהן שביעית יש להן ביעור ולדמיהן ביעור פיקח שלו א] יש לה שביעית ולדמיה שביעית אין לה ביעור ולדמיה אין ביעור עיקר שלו אין [לו] שביעית ולא לדמיו שביעית אין לו ביעור ולדמיו אין ביעור ולא נתבררה במאי איירי אי בלוף פיקח או בשאר דברים ולכאורה בהא דאיירי בהא שמעתא ובכל ענין קשה אמאי לא תני פיקח שלו בהדי הנך דאין להן ביעור:ערקבלין· בפרק עושין פסין(דף כו:) אמר ר"ש לקיש מאי ערקבלין אצוותא דדיקלא (ה): חלביצין · מפרש בירושלמי (שם) ביצי נץ החלב והם השרשין דומין לביצים וכל הני לאוכלין ב] לאדם ולבהמה : יש להן שביעית · להאכל בתורת שביעית ולא להפסידו וכן מין הצבעין נוהג בה קדושת שביעית שלא יצבע בהן בשכר אבל צובע בהן לעצמו ואין להם ולדמיהן ביעור דהיינו [אין] חייב לבערן כשאר פירות אלא אוכל לאחר הביעור ומין הצבעין צובע לעצמו אף לאחר שביעית אבל לא לשכר ולא לסחורה ולא לאיבוד וטעמא כדאמרי' בפרק בא סימן(שם)כלה לחיה מן השדה כלה לבהמתך מן הבית והני לא כלו להו דמתקיימין בארץ: דמיהן· דכל הני כגון עיקר לוף שוטה וחבריו צריך לבערן ולאוכלן עד ראש השנה של שמינית דמשם ואילך צריך להפקירן לכל העולם (ו) : ק"ו לדמיהם · בתוספתא קתני דאהדר להו ר"מ מחמיר אני בדמים שהשמן של שביעית מדליקין בו מכרו ולקח בו שמן אחר אין מדליקין בו וטעמא משום דפרי ושמן מיכר ולא אתי לעשות בהן סחורה ובירושלמי (שם) מייתי לה ומסיק עלה ר' אמי בשם רבי יוחנן החליף שמן בשמן שניהן אסורין כלומר אסורין להדליקן וטעמא משום דמיחלפי אהדדי והיינו דאמר בתר הכי כיצד הוא [עושה] מחליף שניהן של חולין כלומר שיסברו דשניהם של חולין שהוחלף בשביעית והדר קאמר החליף יין בשמן כמה דתימא יין אין סכין בו ודכוותיה שמן אין סכין בו ואין מדליקין בו החליף עליהן בלולבין כמה דתימא עלין יש להם ביעור ודכוותיה לולבין יש להן ביעור החליף אוכלי אדם באוכלי בהמה כמה דתימא אוכלי אדם אין עושין מהן מלוגמא ודכוותה אוכלי בהמה אין עושין מהן מלוגמא והתנן מוכרים אוכלי אדם ואוכלי בהמה ליקח בהן אוכלי בהמה אוכלי בהמה אבל לא אוכלי אדם ואין צריך לומר אוכלי אדם ליקח בהן אוכלי בהמה כהדא קינסתא דירקא מסקין לה לאיגרא והיא יבשה מן גרמא כלומר אחר שיבשה דלא חזיא לאדם מותר ליקח בהן אוכלי בהמה ר' יוחנן בשם ר' שמעון בן יוצדק ביין עד הפסח ובשמן עד העצרת ובגרוגרות עד פורים ר' ביבי בשם ר' חנינא ובתמרים עד חנוכה ר' יחיאל בשם ר' יוחנן וחבורתא הוו יתבין מקשין אמרי יש להן ביעור או אין להן ביעור כלומר אמו הני דחשיב ותו לא עבר ר' ינאי אמרי הא גברא כשאלינה אתון שאלוניה אמר להון כל דבר שדרכו לישור יש לו ביעור ושאין דרכו לישור אין לו ביעור ואלו יש מהן שדרכן לישור ויש מהן שאין דרכן לישור ושרי תנייה מיניה כלומר מלשון נושר ואינו מתקיים וטובא היכא אלא שנה מקצתן ומינייהו ילפינן כל כיוצא בהן : ג קליפי רמון והנץ שלו · יש מפרשים נץ פרח שעל הפטמא ולא קאי גמר פרי ובפרק מקום שנהגו (דף נג·) גבי והזיתים משיגלו פי' בקונטרס משיגדל כן שלהן והוא כעין מתחלי ודומה לו בברכות (פ"ו דף לו:) הפיטמא של רימון מצטרף והנץ שלו אין מצטרף משמע שהוא אחר : והגלעינין · לאו אאגוזים קאי דאין להן גרעינין אלא קליפי אגוזים והגלעינים גרעיני שאר פירות כגון תמרים וזיתים ושייך בהו שביעית דקליפי אגוזים חזו לצביעה וגרעיני זיתים ותמרים חזו להסקה וחזו נמי לבהמה כדאמר בבמה מדליקין (דף כט·) רב אכל תמרי ושדא קשייתא לחיותא וגרעיני זיתים יש שמוציאין מהן שמן : צובע לעצמו · דכתיב לכם לכל צרכיכם ואין עושין סחורה וצביעה בשכר כסחורה וכתב לאכלה ולא לסחורה אפי' לצבוע בטובת הנאה אוסר בירושל' משום סחורה:ולא בבכורות ולא בתרומות·דילמא אתו בהו לידי תקלה אבל מדאורייתא שרי כדתנן בפ' כל פסולי המוקדשין (דף לא:) בבכור נאמר (במדבר י"ח) לא תפדה ונמכר הוא ובאיטלז הוא דלא מזדבן הא בביתיה מזדבן ואפי' איסור דרבנן ליכא בתחום:ולא בנבילות וטריפות ושקצים ורמשים · ואמרינן בירושלמי (הל' א) טמאים הם מה ת"ל וטמאים יהיו לכם אלא אחד איסור אכילה ואחד איסור הנאה [כל דבר שאיסורו דבר תורה אסור לעשות בו סחורה] וכל דבר שאיסורו מדבריהן מותר לעשות בו סחורה ופריך והרי חמור למלאכתו הוא גדל והרי גמל למלאכתו הוא גדל ולא אסרינן לעשות בהן סחורה אלא בדבר העומד לאכילה והדר קאמר ר' הושעיא נסיב ויהיב בהדין מורייס ר' אבין נסיב ויהיב בהדין חלתיתא דברים של נכרים באיסורא מדרבנן כדתנן בפרק אין מעמידין (דף כט:) ואע"ג דמורייס תני לה התם גבי איסור הנאה משום דרמו ביה חמרא שמא לא היה נמכר יותר בעבור היין ולא חשיב נהנה מן היין במשא ומתן דידיה אבל בשאר הנאה אסור כגון להרויח בו ועוד דיכול למוכרו חוץ מדמי יין נסך שבו:ולא יהא לוקח ירקות שדה ומוכר בשוק· היינו לוקח היינו לוקט כדתני' סיפא אבל הוא לוקט ובהדיא קתני בתוספתא(פ"ה)לא יהא לוקח ג] כשמוכר בשוק הוא עצמו [הלוקט] אסור וללקט לאכילה אמר רחמנא ולא ללקט לסחורה דהיינו מוכר הוא אבל הוא לוקט ובנו מוכר על ידו כלו' במקומו מוכרה בשוק דהוא לא ליקטן : לקח לעצמו והותיר מותר למכור אפילו הוא בעצמו בשוק כיון דליקטן לאכילה: ירושלמי (שם) תני ולא יהו חמשה מלקטין ירק ואחד מוכר אבל מוכר הוא שלו ושל חברו חמשה אחים מלקטים ואחד מוכר על ידיהן אמר ר' יוסי בר בון ובלבד שלא יעשה פלטר מהו ובלבד שלא יעשה פלטר דלא יהא מזבן בההוא אתרא בכל שנה ואית דבעי מימר דלא יהא מזבן בכל שעה · פי' כשהן ה' חברין מלקטין בשותפות וא' מהן מוכר הכל אסור אבל אם ליקט לעצמו וחברו ליקט לעצמו ומכר אותן· ב' חלקים בבת אחת מותר דהוי כעין הבלעה

ר"מ

יש לו שביעית ולדמיו שביעית . יתחייב בהן שביעית ואם נמכר יתחייבו דמיו בדינים ההם ועוד יתבאר ענין הביעור לאחר זה וכבר פירשנו שהלוף מין מהבצלים: הדנדנה נקרא נענע ובערוך נקרא מינט"א בלע"ז: ועולשין הנדבה : והכרישין . כראתי : והרגילה פ"ר קאקל"י בלע"ז נקראת רגלה : ונץ החלב מקוזנם עשב ידוע אצל הרופאין : החוחין . קבוץ חוח : והדרדרין . קבוץ דרדר ואלה מיני קוצים הם : ספיחי אסטים . הוא הצבע שצובעים בו תכלת ונקרא כן מפני שיקלרוהו וילמח והוא לעולם ספיח: וקוצה.ממיני הצבעונין ויש מי שפירש אותו אלעלפו"ר: ב עקרבנין. עשב נקרא עקרביאן והחלבלין והבוכרה עשבים לא נודעו . הפואה ידוע שוה נקראת בלשון ערב ובלע"ז רוי"א.והרכבנא נקראת בק"ם ובלע"ז ברזי"ל ושאמר בזו ההלכה וממין הצובעין אינו מפרש כל מה שנכנס בכלל ההוא אבל הוא תחלת הדבר כפי מה שהוא אומר והוא שאמר בכלל מה שהקדמנו שכל מה שהוא ממין הצובעין ואינו מתקיים בארץ יש לו שביעית וביעור וכן לדמיו ומנה בכללן ספיחי אסטים וקוצה ואחר כן אמר בכלל השני שכל מה שאינו ראוי לאלו השלשה ולא לאחד מהם לא למאכל אדם ולא לבהמה ולא לצבוע יש לו ולדמיו שביעית ואין לו ולא לדמיו ביעור וזה אם אינו מתקיים בארץ כמו כן מה שאמר בכלל מה שהקדמנו אחר כן הביא בזה הענין משלים ודמיונות וחזר והחל בדבר ואמר יש דברים ממין הצובעין שיש להם ולדמיהן שביעית אין להם ולא לדמיהן ביעור והוא הפואה והרכבנא שהם מתקיימין בארץ ולא יכנס הפסד וענין אין להם ביעור שלא ימנע מלהתעסק בהם תמיד וליהנות מהם עד שישלימו ואין לשמור בזה שעת ביעור וכן בדמיהן אם נמכרו ואין הלכה כר"מ : ג קליפי רמון ידוע והנץ שלו ידוע ונקרא גלאנר והגלעינין הם הגרעינין ואע"פ שדמי שביעית מסתפקין בהם כמו שנבאר אבל אינו מותר לאדם שיעשה ממנו סחורה אלא אם יזדמן לו אבל אם נתכוין לצבוע בשכירות מלבושי שביעית אינו מותר ואף על פי שלוקח המעות ההם ואוכל אותם בקדושת שביעית : ומה שאמר ובנו מוכר על ידו הוא

פירוש הרא"ש

(א) וכרשי שדה איצטריך לאשמעינן : (ב) ובלע"ז פורפיר: (ג) אסטים גירא וקולה גרנדא ואע"ג דעצים אין בהם משום קדושת שביעית מפרש בהגוזל קמא (קא:) שאני עצים דהנאתן וביעורם שוה משא"כ בעצי הדלקה: (ד) לקח בבשר דגים יצאו בשר ונכנסו דגים בדגים יין יצאו דגים ונכנס יין ביין שמן יצא יין ונכנס שמן הא כיצד אחרון אחרון נתפס ופרי עצמו אסור: (ה) והוא מין ירק וגדל אצל הדקל ועולה ונכרך סביב הדקל בערוך פי' בלשון ישמעאל כינגר כל אלו ראויין לאדם ולבהמה רכפא הן עיקרים שמוכרים מן הארץ ושולקים אותם ואוכלים אותם ויש לו תולעים בבטנו ימיתם : (ו) ופני הוי ניחא אי הוי תני ומתבערין לאחר ראש השנה :

הגהות הרי"ד לנדא

פרק ז א] מ"ב בר"ש פיקח שלו. צ"ל פיקה (ופי' מהר"א פיקה מה שנשתייר ממקום חיבור העליון עד עיקר הטמון בארץ] : ב] שם וכל הני לאוכלין . צ"ל לאוכלין : ג] מ"ג שם לא יהא לוקח. צ"ל לוקט :

פי' מהר"י בן מלכי צדק

ואיזה זה עלה הלוף השוטה הא עלה הלוף הפיקח לא דהדוא לא מישתכח שדינו להעקר ואפי' ספיחין שעושה אחרי כנאסרין אלא עלה לוף שוטה איצטריך ליה דסד"א כיון דמר הוא דתנן עלה לוף שוטה אין מטמאין טומאת אוכלין עד שימתקו לא ליחול עליה קדושת שביעית קמ"ל : העולשין . ציקאירי. והכרשין. פורי . פי' עולשי שדה וכרשי שדה ותרגם חציר לפי דשל גנות אינן נמצאות לפי שאסור לזרוע בז' ועולשי שדה אע"ג דלא חשיב דהא בכל השנים אינן מטמאות טומאת אוכלין אפילו הכי בשביעית חשיבי א"ר יוסי בר חנינא עולשין חשיבות הן לטמא טומאת אוכלין בשביעית וכרישין של גנות שנדילין מעצמן מיקרו ספיחין ובעור שלא גזרו על הספיחין היו מותרין הלכך כולה מתני' בירקי שדה משתעי:הרגילה. איני יודע מהו אלא בלשון יוון רפנו סיפרנא:ונץ החלב. פרח לבן ואילו כולן אין מתקיימין אילו כולן הן נאכלין לאדם אבל דוחקא שדרכן למאכל בהמה כדכתיב מצמיח חציר לבהמה: החוחים. איספיני והדרדרים. פי' וקוץ ודרדר דהני לא מיתאכלי לאדם העלין שלהן ואילו (ה) [אין] מתקיימין בארעא : ספיחי סטים וקוצה פי' קוץ ואין מתקיימין בארץ : יש להן שביעי' פי' להאכל בתורת שביעית שלא להפסידן ולדמיו שביעית כיצד מכר פירות שביעית ולקח בהן דמים ובדמים בשר יצאו דמים נתפש בשר להאכל בתורת שביעית : יש להן ביעור : פי' כשיבוא זמן ביעור וגם לדמיו ביעור ויתחלק לכל אדם ותנן בנדה כל שיש לו ביעור יש לו שביעית ופירשו כגון עלה הלוף ועלה הדנדנא הטעם כיון שאין מתקיימין בארץ כלין מן השדה וכיון דכלה לחיה מן השד' כלה לבהמתך מן הבית : ב עוד כלל אמרו כל שהוא מאכל אדם ומאכל בהמה ומתקיים בארץ . כגון עיקר הלוף השוטה ועיקר הדנדנא : הערקבלין . פי' בפ' עושין פסין גרסי' מאי ערקבלין אמר ריש לקיש אצוותא חיורתא הן ירקות שיוצאין בהן בפסח ויוצאין סביב לדקל' · ורב אשי נאקן פי' שהן צמח עבה למאד ויש בו כמעט ראשי החוחים ותחרו : והחלבצים . ירושלמי מהו חלבצים ביצי נץ חלב. פי' שרשי נץ החלב . דומין לביצים:והבוכריא . בלשון ישמעאל כנגר ואיני יודע מהו. כללא דמילתא נאכלין לבני אדם ולבהמות : וממין הצובעין ומתקיים בארץ . הפואה אע"פ שעוקרין אותה אפי' הכי מאחר שעוקרין אותה היא מוציאה הלכך התולש מפואת שביעית נוהג בה בקדושת שביעית שלא יצבע בשכר אבל צובע לעצמו ואינו חייב לבערה כשאר כל הפירות אבל צובע בה אפילו אחר שביעית אך לא בשכר ולא בסחורה ולא לאיבוד: והרכפא . בלשון ישמעאל שגר מרים הן והן עיקרין שחופרין מן הארץ וכותשין אותן וסוחטין אותן ושותין המים ומי שיש לו תולעים בבטנו ימיתם : לאילו יש להן שביעית . פי' להיאכל בתורת שביעית שלא להפסד וכן לדמיהן : אבל אין להן ביעור ולא לדמיהן ביעור . ותנן בנדה ויש שיש לו שביעית ואין לו ביעור ופירש עיקר הלוף השוטה ועיקר הדנדנא מאי טעמא דכתיב ולבהמה ולחיה אשר בארצך כל זמן שחיה אוכלת בשדה אתה מאכיל לבהמתך בבית כלה לחיה מן השדה כלה לבהמתך מן הבית כלומר בערם והני אינן כלין כל השנה ולאחר מיכן : ב רבי מאיר אומר דמיהם וכו' · דמי עיקר לוף ודמי עיקר הדנדנא וכן דמי כולן מתבערין עד ראש השנה כלומר מראש השנה ואילך צריך אתה לבערם אמרו לו חכמים להן [אין] ביעור כדאמרינן לא כל שכן לדמיהן · ובתוספתא מצאנו שהשיב להן רבי מאיר ואמר מחמיר אני בדמים מבעיקר שהשמן של שביעית מדליקין בו מכרו ולקח בו שמן אחר אין מדליקין בו ר' ינאי עבר שאלו אותו חכמים אמר להן כל דבר שדרכו לישור פי' מלשון הנושר כלומר דבר שאינו מתקיים יש לו ביעור ושאין דרכו לישור אין לו ביעור · ואילו יש מהן שדרכן לישור ויש מהן שאין דרכן לישור לפיכך שנה אותן במיניהן : ג קליפי רמון והנץ שלו · פי' נץ הוא פרח שעל פיטמא שלהן : קליפי אגוזים והגלעינים · פי' מן האגוז הקליפין ומשאר פירות כגון תמרים וזיתים הגרעינין יש להן שביעית שיש מקום שמוציאין מגרעיני זיתים שמן ועוד אוכלין אותן בני אדם ומוכרין אותן להסקה. וזהו פי' לדמיהן שביעית : הצבע צובע לעצמו · פי' מספיחי סטים וקוצה ופואה של שביעית דכתיב לכם יהיה לכם לכל צרכיכם אבל לא יצבע בשכר · ובירושלמי אסור לצבוע אפילו בטובת הנאה לפי' שאין עושין סחורה כלל דכתיב לאכלה ולא לסחורה ולא בבכורות ולא בתרומות ולא בנבילות ולא בטריפות ולא בשרצין ולא ברמשין דכתיב טמאים הם לכם מה ת"ל וטמאים יהיו לכם אלא אחד איסור אכילה ואחד איסור הנאה אילו כולן אסורין מן התורה · וכלל זה אמרו חכמים כל דבר שאסור מדבר תורה אסור לעשות בו סחורה · פירוש בקביעות וכל שאיסורו מדבריהן מותר : ולא יהא לוקח ירקות שדה ומוכרה בשוק . דהיינו סחורה : אבל הוא מלקט ובנו מוכר במקומו לקח לעצמו והותיר מותר למוכרו . פירוש הוא עצמו :

לקח

a IT IS NOT LEFT GROWING IN THE SOIL,[1] THE LAW OF THE SABBATICAL YEAR IS APPLIED BOTH TO IT[2] AND TO ITS MONEY SUBSTITUTE.[3] [SIMILARLY] THE LAW OF REMOVAL[4] APPLIES BOTH TO IT AND TO ITS MONEY SUBSTITUTE. WHICH ARE THEY?[5] THE EDIBLE LEAVES OF THE WILD ARUM,[6] OF MINT,[7] ENDIVES,[8] LEEKS,[9] PORTULACA,[10] AND ASPHODEL.[11] WHAT IS THE FOOD FOR CATTLE?[12] THORNS AND THISTLES. WHAT IS
b SPECIES OF DYEING MATTER?[1] AFTERGROWTHS OF WOAD[2] AND MADDER.[3] THE LAW OF THE SEVENTH YEAR APPLIES TO THEM AND THEIR EQUIVALENTS AND THE LAW OF REMOVAL APPLIES TO THEM AND THEIR MONEY [SUBSTITUTES].

MISHNAH 2. YET ANOTHER GENERAL PRINCIPLE WAS ENUNCIATED. EVEN SUCH THINGS NOT FIT FOR FOOD OF MAN OR BEAST, OR THOSE PLANTS NOT USED FOR DYEING PURPOSES, IF THEY HAD BEEN LEFT IN THE SOIL,[4] ARE SUBJECT TO THE SABBATICAL LAW[5] AS ARE THEIR SUBSTITUTES. BUT THE LAW OF REMOVAL DOES NOT APPLY EITHER TO THEM OR TO THEIR MONEY SUBSTITUTE. WHICH ARE THESE? THE ROOTS OF THE WILD ARUM, THE MINT, AND THE HART'S TONGUE,[6] THE ASPHODEL AND THE HAZEL-WORT.[7] WHAT IS THE SPECIES OF DYEING MATTER? DYER'S MADDER AND SOW-BREAD.[8] THE SABBATICAL LAW APPLIES TO THEM AND TO THEIR MONEY EQUIVALENT, BUT THE LAW OF REMOVAL DOES NOT APPLY EITHER TO THEM OR TO THEIR MONEY EQUIVALENT. R. MEIR SAYS: THE LAW OF REMOVAL APPLIES TO THEIR MONEY SUBSTITUTE UNTIL THE NEW YEAR.[9] THE SAGES ANSWERED: SINCE THIS LAW DOES NOT APPLY TO THE PLANTS THEMSELVES, HOW MUCH LESS DOES IT APPLY TO THEIR MONEY SUBSTITUTE![10]

MISHNAH 3. THE LAW OF THE SABBATICAL YEAR APPLIES TO HUSKS AND BLOSSOMS OF THE POMEGRANATE, TO SHELLS AND KERNELS OF NUTS, AND ALSO TO THEIR MONEY SUBSTITUTES. THE DYER MAY USE THEM[11] FOR HIMSELF, BUT NOT
c FOR PAYMENT,[1] SINCE NO TRADE MAY BE DONE WITH SEVENTH YEAR PRODUCE, OR WITH FIRSTLINGS,[2] OR WITH HEAVE-OFFERINGS, OR WITH CARRION, OR WITH ṬREFAH,[3] OR WITH REPTILES[4] OR WITH CREEPING THINGS.[5] ONE SHOULD NOT GATHER[6] WILD VEGETABLES[7] AND SELL THEM IN THE MARKET; BUT IF HE GATHERS THEM AND HIS SON SELLS THEM FOR HIM, IT IS WELL.[8] IF HE GATHERED THEM FOR HIS OWN USE,

a (1) Had it been left rooted, it would have rotted in winter. (2) Not to be sold as merchandise, but eaten free. (3) Cf. *infra* VIII, 3. Should the produce be exchanged for meat or fish, then the latter become endowed with the sanctity of the former. Should the meat or fish be in turn exchanged for other things, they too become holy. (4) Sabbatical produce could be eaten as long as similar produce grew in the country of his domicile, and was available to the beast of the field. Once the produce began to wither and was no longer available to the cattle, all similar produce that had been gathered had to be removed from one's possession; Deut. XXVI, 13 and *infra* IX, 2. (5) Plants fit for human food. (6) Though these leaves are not subject to food uncleanness ('Uḳ. III, 4), nevertheless, they have to conform to the Sabbatical rules, since they are human food. (7) Or, miltwaste. (8) Of endives there are two kinds: those grown in the orchard and those in the field. When the former abound, the latter are not regarded as human food, and hence are not subject to food uncleanness; but in the seventh year, when endives are not found in the orchard, those in the field are food and accordingly are subject to food uncleanness, and the Sabbatical laws apply to them. (9) Also of two kinds, as of endives. (10) Or purslane; 'Uḳ. III, 2. (11) A bulbous plant, Star of Bethlehem; the plants referred to by poets as 'the immortal flower in Elysium'. Some explain חלב as either referring to the colour of the plant, pure white like milk, or by the fact that when cut open, a milk juice pours forth. (12) To which the law is applied.

b (1) The Mishnah now demands details. (2) *Isatis tinctoria*, producing a deep blue dye. (3) A plant used for red dye. (4) Over the winter. (5) Since the cattle can still eat thereof. (6) Prickly creepers on palm-trees. (7) *Baccor*, an aromatic plant identified with spikenard. (8) Or round-leaved cyclamen; a tuberous rooted plant used for dyeing; a remedy for worms (Bert.). (9) Of the eighth year. (10) To which R. Meir could retort that greater rigidity was applied to substitutes than to original produce which is easily recognizable, and will not be used in the seventh year. Not so with their substitutes. (11) The plants of the seventh year.

c (1) I.e., he must not dye for others with them. (2) Ex. XIII, 2, 12. They were not to remain in his possession lest he transgress the law concerning them. When slaughtered, they could be sold, but not in market places. (3) Which could neither be eaten nor sold; Pes. 23*a*. (On *ṭrefah*, v. Glos.). Trade was forbidden with such animals as are generally used for food, but such as are specially used for work like the camel, the horse and the mule, could be sold; Lev. XXII, 8. *Ṭrefah* signified flesh of clean beasts which had been mauled, or killed by beasts of prey, and thus rendered unfit for Jewish food. (4) Lev. XI, 4ff. (5) Ibid. 29ff. (6) In the Sabbatical year. (7) Vegetables that grow of their own accord. (8) For this does not court the suspicion of trading with Sabbatical produce.

AND AUGHT REMAINS OVER, HE MAY SELL THEM.[9]

MISHNAH 4. IF ONE BUYS A FIRSTLING[10] FOR HIS SON'S [WEDDING] FEAST, OR FOR A FESTIVAL, AND THEN DECIDES THAT HE HATH NO NEED OF IT, HE MAY SELL IT.[11] HUNTERS OF WILD ANIMALS, BIRDS AND FISHES, WHO CHANCED UPON UNCLEAN SPECIES, MAY SELL THEM.[12] R. JUDAH SAYS: ALSO A MAN WHO HAPPENED TO CHANCE UPON BY ACCIDENT[13] MAY BUY OR SELL, PROVIDED THAT HE DOES NOT MAKE A REGULAR TRADE OF IT. BUT THE SAGES DO NOT ALLOW THIS.[14]

MISHNAH 5. THE LAW OF THE SABBATICAL YEAR IS
a APPLIED[1] TO THE YOUNG SPROUTS OF THE SERVICE-TREE[2] AND THE CAROBS AND THEIR MONEY EQUIVALENT; SO ALSO IS THE LAW OF REMOVAL APPLIED BOTH TO THEM AND THEIR SUBSTITUTES. THE LAW OF THE SABBATICAL YEAR IS APPLIED TO BRANCHES OF THE TEREBINTH, THE PISTACHIO TREE AND THE WHITE THORN,[3] AND TO THEIR SUBSTITUTES; BUT THEY ARE NOT LIABLE TO THE LAW OF REMOVAL, NOR IS THEIR MONEY SUBSTITUTE LIABLE TO THE LAW OF REMOVAL.[4] BUT THE LAW OF REMOVAL APPLIES TO THEIR LEAVES,[5] SINCE THEY HAD ALREADY FALLEN FROM THEIR STEM.[6]

MISHNAH 6. THE SABBATICAL LAW APPLIES TO THE ROSE, HENNA,[7] BALSAM, THE LOTUS TREE AND TO THEIR MONEY SUBSTITUTES.[8] R. SIMEON SAYS: THE SABBATICAL LAW DOES NOT APPLY TO THE BALSAM, SINCE THIS CANNOT BE REGARDED AS A FRUIT.[9]

MISHNAH 7. IF A NEW ROSE[10] HAS BEEN PRESERVED IN

(9) Namely, those left over, since his primary intention was to eat all the wild vegetables he had gathered. (10) That was blemished and could, therefore, be eaten by non-priests. (11) Only at the price he paid for it. (12) Not being forbidden to sell if accidentally acquired. (13) Lit., 'according to his way'. Even without hunting for wild game. (14) Only the professional hunter was given this concession, since he had to pay a heavy tax into the royal coffers. Where they differ from the first Tanna is that they even make the concession for a huntsman even if his deliberate intention was to catch game of the unclean species (Tosaf. Yom Ṭob).

a (1) Since they are food for cattle. (2) Whose interior is eaten as relish. (3) Which sprouts a kind of acorn. (4) Since they are there even in winter. (5) Separated from their branches. (6) Since they are now lost even to beasts of the field, they are liable to the law of Removal. (7) *Tif. Yis.* identifies it with the cypress tree. Jast. s.v. כופרא says: 'the inflorescence of palms, a spike covered with numerous flowers, and enveloped by one or more sheathing bracts called spathes'. (8) So is the law of Removal applied to them. (9) Being used as ordinary wood for fuel, to which the Sabbatical law does not apply. The Torah stresses *'for eating'*, the prohibition only of such produce as is actually food. (10) Of the seventh year.

מסורת השי"ם

א) פסחים פ"ב דף כג. ב) נדה פ"א דף ח. ג) שם דף ח:

לעצמו והותיר מותר למכרן: ד [א]לקח בכור למשתה בנו או לרגל ולא צריך לו מותר למכרו ה) [ב]ציידי חיה ועופות ודגים שנזדמנו להם מינין טמאין (ז) מותר למכרן ר"י אומר אף מי שנתמנה לו לפי דרכו לוקח ומוכר ובלבד שלא תהא אומנתו בכך [ג]וחכמים אוסרין: ה [ד]לולבי זרדים והחרובין יש להם שביעית ולדמיהן שביעית יש להן ביעור ולדמיהן ביעור לולבי האלה והבטנה והאטדין יש להן שביעית ולדמיהן שביעית אין להם ביעור ולא לדמיהן ביעור אבל לעלין יש ביעור מפני שנושרין מאביהן: ו ג) [ה]הוורד והכפר והקטף והלוטם יש להם שביעית ולדמיהן שביעית ג) ר"ש אומר [ו]אין לקטף שביעית מפני שאינו פרי: [ז]וורד חדש

הוא שאם יקח הבן ממה שאסף אביו ומכרו אין עליו חובה בזה אבל המעות ההם הם דמי שביעית ועוד נפרש דין דמי שביעית: ד הבכור הוא לכהן ואם נמצא בו מום יאכלנו בכל מקום כמש"כ (דברים טו) כי יהיה בו מום ומותר למכרו בין תמים בין בעל מום וכמו שנבאר בתחלת מסכת מעשר שני ואע"פ שמותר למכרו אסור לסחור בו ועוד נפרש דיני הבכור ומומיו במקומו במסכת בכורות: מי שנתמנה לו. הוא שיתכוין לצוד עוף טמא או חיה טמאה בכוונה או בלא כוונה שנזדמנו לו כגון שעברו עליו או יעבור הוא על קן מקיניהן והלכה כר"י: ה לולב הוא הפרח כבר אמרנו פעמים (לעיל פ"ב מ"ג) שורדים הם הענפים שיזמרו אותם מן הגפנים ויש מי שיטמין הענפים ההם כשהם לחים ויאכלו: אלה נקרא בלשון ישמעאל בלוטו. הבטנה פסתאק וקבוצ בטנים. ואטדים מין ממיני הקוצים שצומחין בו גרגרין שחורים קשים כמו אפונים ונאכלים: מפני שנושרין מאביהן. ר"ל נופלין מהענפים שהם מיוחסים אליהם כיחס האב לבן ומפני זה יהיה ביעור שלהם כשיהיו נבלות מהענפים כמו שיתבאר כשנפרש ענין ביעור: ו הוורד הם השושנים האדומים שיש להם ריח טוב ועליהם נאמר שפתותיו שושנים (שה"ש ה): והכפר נקרא בלשון ערב חנה וכן נאמר (שם א) באשכול הכופר אלחנה היא אשכלות יפות עד מאד ויש מי שיאמר שהכפר הוא גרופל"י: והקטף אילן אפרסמון הנקראת בלסם: ולוטום נקרא בערב שאה בלוט הוא קסטניאס וי"א שהוא נקרא לנובר הוא פיטלי"ש והלכה כרבי שמעון: ז וורד חדש שכבשו בשמן ישן. הוא שיטמין וורד של שביעית בשמן של ששית הרי הוא מלקט אותו מפני שלא

הבלעה כדאמר מבליע דמי אתרוג בלולב (סוכה דף לט.) אע"ג דמיירי התם לענין דמי פירות שביעית לע"ה הכא נמי לענין סחורה הוי כמבליע שלו בשל חברו. ה' אחים אע"פ שנראין כשותפין לפי שהן אחים מ"מ מוכר אחד על ידם במקומן מוכר בשוק וסוחרי שביעית דתנן בפ"ק דר"ה (כב.) ובפרק זה בורר (דף כו.) היינו בכי האי גוונא דאמרינן הכא והאי דקאמר התם בתחלה היו אומרים אוספין כשרין סוחרים פסולין משרבו ממלאי מעות לעניים ואזלי עניים ואספי ואייתו להו חזרו לומר אחד זה ואחד זה פסולין היינו אוספין כעין לוקח ובט מוכר על ידו סוחרין כגון שהלוקח עצמו [מוכר] ואפשר שהקונה מחברו בזול כדי למכור ביוקר אסור דהיינו סחורה אבל מתני' לא איירי בהכי ולענין נבילה דאסר במתני' לעשות סחורה והכתיב או מכור לנכרי אלא לקנות ולהרויח אסור והכא נזדמן נבילה הרי זה כלוקח לעצמו והותיר ובציידין שנזדמנו להם בסמוך ולא משכחת שיהיו כל הני דמתני' שוין לענין סחורה אבל לא בקונה א] למכור ולהרויח ובפ' זה בורר (שם) פירש בקונטרס אוספין כשרין דמלי למכלינהו קודם זמן ובפרק לולב הגזול (דף לט.) פי' אין מוסרין דמי פירות שביעית לעם הארץ דהתורה אמרה לאכלה ולא לסחורה שכל פירות שביעית חייבין להתבער בשביעית הן ודמיהן ולא שיעשה בהן סחורתו לאחר שביעית ודבריו תמוהים מאד דתיקשי ליה כל אותן שיש להן שביעית ואין להם ביעור שיש להם שביעית שלא לעשות בהן סחורה ושלא לאבד דכולהו מלאכלה נפקא ואכל פירות שביעית כתב לאכלה אף על אותן שאין חייב בביעור ואכל מין לבעין קתני מתני' ולא יגבע בשכר ועל חנם דחק להזכיר טעמא דסחורה דבלאו הכי איכא איסור טובא שאין עם הארץ נזהר דאסור לקנות בהן בהמה ועבדים וחלוק ואין נותנין לא לבלן ולא לספר ולא לספן דשביעית ניתנה לאכילה ולשתיה ולסיכה ולא לשאר דברים ואסור לפרוע חובו כולהו תנן לקמן בפ"ח (משנה ה ח) ודמי אוכלי אדם אסור לקנות מהן אוכלי בהמה ואסור לאכול דבר שאין דרכו לאכול כגון לכוס חטין ותרדין חיים ולבשל ירק לבהמה ואין מספר לדינין ולאיסורין שאין עם הארץ בקי ואינו נזהר בהן: ד לקח בכור בעל מום למשתה בנו או לאכול ברגל מותר למוכרו ואע"ג דמחזי כסחורה ובתוספתא (פ"ה) קתני ר' אומר אומר אני לא ימכרנו אלא לדמיו כלומר בדמים שקנאו שלא ירויח בהן כלום: ר"י אומר אף מי שנתמנה. שאינו צייד דתנא קמא נקט דוקא צייד: וחכמים אוסרין. למי שאינו צייד ומפרש טעמא בירושלמי (שם) א"ר יוסי תמן אין מלכות אונסת הכא מלכות אונסת כלומר לוקחת מס מן הציידים ובירושלמי משמע דר' יהודה קאי אפירות שביעית דמפרש היכי עביד היה יושב ועוסק במלאכתו כל שני שבוע ובשביעית התחיל לישא וליתן בפירות שביעית אם יש עמו מלאכה אחרת מותר ואם לאו אסור אבל אם היה בטל ממלאכתו כל שני שבוע ובשביעית התחיל לישא וליתן בפירות עבירה אע"פ שיש עמו מלאכה אחרת אסור והא דתנן בפרק זה בורר (דף כד:) גבי סוחרי שביעית אמר ר' יהודה אימתי בזמן שאין לו אומנות אלא הוא אבל יש לו אומנות שלא הוא הרי זה כשר מפרש הכא היך עבידא היה בטל ממלאכתו כל שני שבוע ובשביעית פשט ידו ונושא ונותן בפירות שביעית אם יש עמו מלאכה אחרת כשר ואם לאו פסול אבל אם היה עוסק במלאכה כל שני שבוע וכיון שבאת שביעית התחיל לישא וליתן בפירות עבירה אפי' אין עמו מלאכה אחרת מותר *) דאפי' איסורא ליכא וחכמים אוסרין אע"פ שיש עמו מלאכה אחרת ולענין עדות נמי פסולים: ה לולבי זרדים. אילן ששמו כך (ח) ושדים מגויים תחתיו (ט): לולבי האלה. כדכתיב (ישעיה ו) כאלה וכאלון: בטנה. לשון בטנים ושקדים (בראשית מג): אטדין. קוצים אבל עלים אין להם ב] שנושרין אבל הלולבין אין נושרין ובירושלמי (הל' ב) ברים פרקא איתמר אין אוכלין על העיקר וכה אמר אוכלין על העיקר א"ר פנחס תמן אין סופן להקשות וכה סופן להקשות ונעשו כאביהם פי' מלולבין דהכא אעלין דרים פירקין קשיא דהכא אמרינן גבי לולבין דאין להם ביעור לפי שאין נושרין מאביהן וברישא תנן גבי עלין דיש להן ביעור אע"פ שאין נושרין מאביהן ומשני דלולבין דהכא סופם להקשות נעשין כאביהן: ו וורד. שושן: כפר מין בושם (י): קטב כמו קטף והוא צרי (בראשית מג) דמתרגמינן קטף (יא): לוטם. הוא לוט דקרא (שם) דמתרגמינן ולטום דקסבר ת"ק דקטפו זהו פריו: יש להן שביעית. וצריך להפקירן ואסור לעשות בהן סחורה ולא אמרינן דהוו כעצים דאין בהן קדושת שביעית ומשום דהנאתן אחר ביעורן כדאי' בפרק לולב הגזול (דף מ.) ובנדה (פ"א דף ח:) מייתי לה וגרסינן שם בכל הספרים יש להן ביעור ולדמיהן ביעור וכאן אין כתוב בספרים ומ"מ אמת הוא דמדלא תני אין להן ביעור ש"מ דיש להם: ולדמיהן שביעית. דמה שקונה מהן אסור לאבדו ולעשות ממנו מלוגמא אלא אכילה ושתיה וסיכה ולאכול דבר שדרכו לאכול ולסוך דבר שדרכו לסוך שלא ישנה ולדמיהן ביעור דאסור לקיימן אחר ביעור אלא יפקירם בין לעשירים בין לעניים דוקא (לקמן פ"ט מ"ח) ואמרי' בפ"ק דנדה (שם) א"ר פדת מאן תנא קטפא פירא ר"א היא דתנן המעמיד בשרף הערלה אסור ור' זירא אמר בקטפא דפירא דברי הכל פירא הוא כי פליגי בקטפא דגווזא ור' פדת סבר בקטפא דפירי פליגי ור' יהושע דשמיע ליה קאמר וליה לא סבירא ליה ודוחק הוא דמנא ליה. דליה לא סבירא ליה אלא יש לפרש דא"ר יהושע גבי ערלה שמיע ליה שהמעמיד בשרף העלין והעיקרין מותר בשרף הפגין אסור מפני שהוא פרי וכתב את פריו את הטפל לפריו כגון קליפי אגוזים ורמונים והוא הדין שרף דידהו שהוא פרי אבל לענין שביעית לא והא דתניא מפני שהוא פרי לאו דוקא אלא מפני שהוא טפל לפרי ורבי זירא סבר מפני שהוא ממש קאמר וא"ת האי קטף היכי דמי אי הנאתו אחר ביעורו מאי טעמא דמאן דאסר והא לאכלה כתב דאכילתו וביעורו שוה יצאו עלים שהנאתו אחר ביעורן ואי הנאתן וביעורן שוה מ"מ דמאן דשרי ואי הוה פליגי בקטפא דגווזא אתי שפיר דמצינן למימר מאן דשרי משום דבטל אגב העץ אע"פ שהנאתו וביעורו שוה ולר' זירא דמוקי מתני' בקטפא דפירא דדברי הכל פירא צריך טעם לר' שמעון דמתני' דאמר אין לקטף שביעית וי"ל שדרך קטף לבוא באילן כפרי אילן ג] זה וזה [א] אגב אילן מאחר דקטפא לאו פירא ומיהו אכתי קשה דבירושל' (שם) משמע דלר' פדת פליגי בקטפא דגווזא דאמרי' ר' פדת ור' יוסי בשם ר' יוחנן אתיא דר' שמעון כר' יהושע דתני תמן א"ר יהושע שמעתי בפירוש שהמעמיד בשרף העלין ובשרף העיקרין מותר בשרף הפגין אסור מפני שהוא כפרי והיינו מתני' דסוף פרק קמא דערלה שמע מינה דר' פדת מוקי לה מתני' דהכא שרף העלין והעיקרין ולפירוש זה איך תתיישב סוגיא דפרק קמא דנדה (ח.) דמייתי התם מתני' דהכא דאמר ר' פדת עלה מאן תנא קטפא פירא ר' אליעזר היא אמר ליה ר' זירא חזי דמינך ומאבוך שריתו קטפא לעלמא כיון דאמרת קטפא פירא ר' אליעזר ואבוך אמר הלכה כר' אליעזר בארבע ותו לא ואמר ליה ר' ירמיה לר' זירא ואת לא תיסברא דמאן תנא קטפא פירא ר' אליעזר והתנן ר' אליעזר אומר המעמיד בשרף הערלה אסור אפילו תימא רבנן עד כאן לא פליגי רבנן עליה דר' אליעזר אלא בקטפא דגווזא אבל בקטפא דפירא מודו ליה דתנן אמר ר' יהושע שמעתי בפירוש המעמיד בשרף העלין כו' בסוף פרק קמא דערלה מיתניא פלוגתא דר' אליעזר ור' יהושע והשתא לפי שהוכחתי מכח הירושלמי דר' פדת מוקי מתני' דהכא בקטפא דגווזא [ב] מאי קאמר ליה רבי זירא משתרי קטפא כמו (כן) מר' זירא ומאבוה דר' פדת משתרי קטפא דכולהו מודו (דבכולהו) דבקטפא דגווזא פליגי ושמא היה טועה עליו לפי שסתם ר' פדת דבריו [ג] ואמר מאן תנא קטפא פירא ר' אליעזר דמשמע כל קטפא אפילו דפירא שהיה לו לפרש דבריו ולומר מאן תנא קטפא דגווזא פירא ר' אליעזר וכל זה דוחק ונראה לפרש דבין רבי פדת בין רבי זירא מודו דבקטפא דגווזא פליגי גבי ערלה אלא דר' פדת משווה שביעית לערלה להתיר לר' יהושע בקטפא דגווזא בזה כזה ור' זירא ס"ל עד כאן לא פליגי רבנן עליה דר' אלעזר גבי ערלה אלא בקטפא דגווזא אבל בקטפא דפרי מודי ליה גבי ערלה כך שוה קטפא דגווזא לגבי שביעית כקטפא דפירא לגבי ערלה משום דגבי שביעית לא בעי' פרי שהשביעית נוהגת בין במאכל אדם בין במאכל בהמה הלכך אין שרף שלו בטל לגבי העץ ול' הירושל' (שם) מוכיח כן דתני ר' פדת ור' יוסי בשם ר' יוחנן אתיא דר' שמעון כר' יהושע דאמר המעמיד בשרף העלין כו' אמר ליה ר' זירא לר' פדת כמה דתימא תמן הל' כר' יהושע וכה הלכה כר' שמעון א"ר ירמיה ודמיא היא כל דבר בטל על ידי שרפו אילין אינו בטל ע"י שרפו אוכלי בהמה קדושת שביעית הלה עליהם [ואין קדושת ערלה חלה עליהן] א"ר אבין אית לך חורי ר' יהושע אומר שמועה ור' שמעון בשם גרמיה אמרה למה שרף פרי הפגין פרי אין תימר שרף פרי עשה כן בתרומה אסור ואין תימא פגין פרי עשה כן בתרומה מותר למה שהגיית תרומה מותרת והגיית ערלה אסורה פירוש דתנינן תמן בסוף פ"ק דערלה שרף כמו שרף לפי שאת אומר דר' שמעון בשיטת ר' יהושע כמו שלפס הלכה כר' יהושע לגבי רבי אליעזר במתני' כמו כן הלכה כר' שמעון לגבי רבנן והיינו דקאמר בפ"ק דנדה (שם) האי דמינך ומאבוך שריתו קיטפא לעלמא א"ר ירמיה ודמיא היא כלומר וכי דמי אהדדי בתמיהא כל דבר בטל על ידי שרפו בההיא דערלה בטל שרף העלין והעיקרין אגב אילן ושרי ואילין כלומר והנך דשביעית אינו בטל אגב אילן כמו שמפרש שהשביעית נוהג באוכלי בהמה מה שאין בערלה אמר ר' אבין אית לך חורי עדיין יש לך ראיה אחרת דר' שמעון ור' יהושע לאו חדא ניניהו שהרי ר' יהושע אומר דבריו מפי השמועה ור' שמעון בשם גרמיה ואי איתא דחדא ניניהו אית ליה למימר נמי ר' שמעון שמעתי ומפרש למה שרף פרי בתמיהא טעמא דרבי פדת אתא לפרש וכן מוכח בירושלמי דערלה בסוף פרק קמא (הלכה ה) דגרסינן התם אמר ליה שרף פרי שהשיב רבי פדת לרבי זירא וכי השרף יש לו לחשוב פרי הפגים הוא פרי ולא השרף ויתכן דרבי פדת דחוק לומר דאפילו שרף הפגין לאו פרי והא דאסר ר' יהושע לגבי ערלה דמרבינן ליה מאת הטפל לפריו והשתא לרבי פדת גבי שביעית מאן דאסר אסר אפילו בקטפא דגווזא ומאן דשרי שרי אפילו בקטפא דפירא אין תימר כמו אם תאמר ועוד מסתבר דקסבר רבי יהושע שרי בערלה מדאורייתא אפילו בשרף הפגין אלא מדרבנן התמירו בערלה כמו שמפרש משום דהגיית הערלה אסורה אבל בשביעית ותרומה לא החמירו דהגייתן מותרת: ז רדיש. של שביעית. ישן משנה ששית:

ילקט

פי' מהר"י בן מלכי צדק

ד לקח בכור למשתה בנו. פי' בכור בעל מום או בשביל הרגל ולא צריך לו מותר למכרו ואף על גב דמיחזי כסחורה. תניא ר' אומר אני שלא ימכרנו אלא בדמיו כלומר לא ירויח בו כלום: ציידי חיה ועופות ודגים. פי' מתני' בכל שנה ושנה היא: שנזדמנו להן מינין טמאין. פי' שקצים ורמשים מותר למכרן: ר' יהודה אומר אף מי שלא היה צייד ונתמנה לו לפי דרכו לוקח ומוכר: וחכמים אוסרין. ואמרינן מאי טעמא דרבנן דבציידים שרו ובהדיוטים אסרי ותירץ ר' יוסי בר' בון תמן אין מלכות אנסת הכא מלכות אנסת. פי' לוקחת מס מן הציידין: [פ"א] ר"י אומ' אפי' שנתמנה לו לפי דרכו. פי' פירות שביעית. לוקח ומוכר ובלבד שלא תהא אומנתו בכך. פי' אלא יהיה לו אומנות אחרת וכן נמי תנן בסנהדרין א"ר יהודה אימתי בזמן שאין לו אומנות אלא היא אז פסול לעדות אבל יש לו אומנות אחרת הרי זה כשר ופירש כיצד היה יושב ובטל ממלאכתו כל שני שבוע ובשביעית התחיל מפשט ידיו ונושא ונותן בפירות עבירה אם יש לו מלאכה אחרת כשר ואם לאו פסול אבל אם היה עוסק במלאכתו כל שני שבוע וכיון שבאה שביעית התחיל לישא וליתן בפירות עבירה אפילו אין עמו מלאכה אחרת מותר ודכוותה תמן לגבי עדות אין פוסלין אותו: ה לולבי זרדים. פי' בינקני: לולבי האלה. מלשון כאלה וכאלון וכתיב כאלה נבלת. לעז צילסא: והבטנה. פירוש מל' בטנים ושקדים: והאטדין. פי' מיני קוצין הן: אבל לעלין. של אלו האילנות יש ביעור מפני שהן נובלות מאביהן אבל הלולבין אינן נושרין מאביהן ולפיכך אין להן ביעור וקשה ברישא דפירקא אמרי בעלין אע"פ שיש מהן שאינן נושרין מתבערין ולא שדינן להו בתר העיקר והכא את אמרת אכלין על העיקר ופריק רבי מנחם תמן אין סופו להקשות ברם הכא סופו להקשות ומכיון שהוקשו נעשה כאביהן: ו הוורד. פי' שושן: והכפר. כדכתיב אשכל הכופר: והקטף. תרגם צרי קטף ותנן הצרי אינו אלא שרף [הנוטף] מעצי הקטף: והלוטם. ולוט תרגם ולטום קסבר תנא קמא קטפו זה פריו בנדה פ"א [ד"ח] אייתינן לה וא"ר פדת עלה מאן תנא קטפא פירא ר' אליעזר דתנן המעמיד בשרף הערלה אסור מפני שהוא פרי קסבר ר' פדת פליגי רבנן עליה דר' אליעזר אפילו בקטף דפירי ואמרי לאו פירי הוא להכי אוקים מתני' כר' אליעזר · אמר ליה ר' זירא חזי דמינך ומאבוך שריתו קטפא לעלמא את אמרת מאן תנא קטפא פירא ר' אליעזר אבוך אמר אין הלכה כר' אליעזר בכוליה תלמודא אלא בארבע הלכות בלבד והא לאו בינהון משתכח דקא שריתו קטפא אמר ליה ר' ירמיה לר' זירא ואת לא תסברא דמאן תנא קטפא ר' אליעזר והתנן רבי אליעזר אומר המעמיד בשרף הערלה אסור אפילו תימא רבנן עד כאן לא פליגי רבנן עליה דר' אליעזר אלא בקטפא דגווזא פי' שרף היוצא מעיקר האילן או מנופו אבל בקטפא דפירא עסיק בקטף דפירא נמי מודו ליה דפירי הוא ותנינ' בקטף דפירא דפירי הוא ודברי הכל דתנן א"ר יהושע שמעתי בפירוש המעמיד בשרף העלין בשרף העיקרין מותר בשרף הפגין אסור מפני שהוא פרי ואיבעית אימא לעולם מתני' אפי' בקטף דגווזא ודברי הכל דכי פליגי רבנן עליה דר' אליעזר באילן העושה פירות תמן אמרי קטף לאו פרי אבל אילן שאינו עושה פירות מודו ליה דקטפו זהו פריו דתניא ר"ש אומר אין לקטף שביעית וחכ"א יש לקטף שביעית מפני שקטפו זהו פריו מאן חכמים לאו רבנן דפליגי עליה דר' אליעזר אמר ליה ההוא סבא הכי אמר ר' יוחנן מאן חכמים ר' אליעזר דאמר קטפא פירי אי ר' אליעזר מאי איריא אילן שאינו עושה פירות הא אפילו באילן העושה פירות אמר קטפא פירא והשיב לעולם מאן חכמים ר' אליעזר ודקא אמרת מאי איריא וכו' לדבריהן דרבנן קאמר להו לדידי אפילו אילן העושה פירות נמי קטפא פירא הוא אלא לדידכו אודו לי מיהת באילן שאינו עושה פירות דקטפו זהו פריו ורבנן אמרי ליה לא. ונדחה הפירוק השני ועמד הראשון דמתני' בקטפא דפירא ודברי הכל מיהו ר' פדת סבר אפי' בקטפא דפירי פליגי ור' יהושע מאי דשמיע ליה קאמר וליה לא סבירא ליה: ז וורד חדש. וורד של שביעית: שכבשו בשמן ישן. פי' בשמן משנת ו':

ילקט

עין משפט נר מצוה

י א מיי' פ"ה מהל' בכורות הלכה י':

יא ב ג מיי' פ"ח מהלכות מאכלות אסורות הלכה יז סמג לאוין קלב טוש"ע יו"ד סי' קיז:

יב ד מיי' פ"ז מהלכות שמטה ויובל הלכה טו:

יג ה ו שם הל' יט:

יד ז מיי' פ"ז מהלכות שמטה ויובל הלכה כא:

פירוש הרא"ש

(ז) מותר למכרן דלא אסרה תורה אלא לקונה לקיים לעשות בהם סחורה דהא כתיב גבי נבלה (דברים י"ד) או מכור לנכרי אלמא במזדמן לידו מותר: (ח) כדאיתא בפרק האשה שנפלו לה נכסים (דע"ט) אבא זרדתא: (ט) כדאמרי' בערבי פסחים (דף קי"א): (י) כדכתיב (שה"ש א) אשכול הכופר: (יא) ותניא הצרי אינו אלא שרף הנוטף מעצי הקטף:

*) נ"ל ואפילו

הגהות מהרי"ד לנדא

א] בר"ש שם אבל לא בקונה. נ"ל אם לא בקונה וכ"ה בתוס' סוכה לט: ב] ד"ה שם ועלים אין להם. נ"ל לעלים יש להם ביעור: ג] ד"ה שם כפירי אילן זה וזה נ"ל ובטל אגב אילן ומיהו וכו':

הגהות הר"ב רנשבורג

[א] מ"ע בר"ש ד"ה ולדמיהן שביעית וכו'. זה וזה בטל אגב אילן כצ"ל: [ב] שם מאי קאמר ליה ר"ז מיכך ומאבוך קשריתו קטפא הא מר"ז ומאבוה דרבי פדת נמי משתרי קטפא כצ"ל: [ג] שם תיבת ואמר נמחק:

ילקט את הוורד · ויאכלנו והשמן מותר ואין בו קדושת שביעית דוורד לא יהיב טעמא בשמן : וישן בחדש · כגון וורד של ששית בשמן של שביעית חייב לבער את הכל ופריך בירושלמי (הל' ב') הכא אתמר ילקט את הוורד (בבלי) וכה אתמר חייב בביעור רבי אבהו בשם ר' יוחנן תרין מתניין אינון אמר ר' זירא יכיל אנא פתר בתרי פתרי וורד חדש שכבשו בשרף של ששית וישן בחדש וורד שביעית בשמן שמינית כלומר רישא בוורד חדש ושמן ישן של ששית בשנה שביעית שעדיין לא הגיע זמן הביעור וילקט הוורד והשמן מותר אבל סיפא בוורד שביעית בשמן של שמינית שכבר הגיע זמן הביעור ונתחייב הוורד בביעור חייב לבער את הכל

שכבשו בשמן ישן ילקט את הוורד וישן בחדש חייב בביעור [א]חרובין חדשים שכבשן ביין ישן וישנים בחדש חייבין בביעור זה הכלל כל שהוא בנותן טעם חייב לבער מין בשאינו מינו ומין במינו כל שהוא א) שביעית אוסרת כל שהוא במינה ושלא במינה בנותן טעם :

פרק שמיני

א כלל [ב]גדול אמרו בשביעית כל המיוחד למאכל אדם אין עושין ממנו ג) מלוגמא לאדם ואין צריך לומר לבהמה וכל שאינו מיוחד למאכל אדם עושין ממנו מלוגמא לאדם אבל לא לבהמה [ג]וכל שאינו מיוחד לא למאכל אדם ולא למאכל בהמה חשב עליו למאכל אדם ולמאכל בהמה נותנין עליו חומרי אדם וחומרי בהמה חשב עליו לעצים הרי הוא כעצים כגון ג) הסיאה והאזוב והקורנים : **ב** [ד]שביעית ניתנה לאכילה ולשתיה ולסיכה [ה]לאכול דבר שדרכו לאכול [ו]ולסוך דבר שדרכו לסוך לא יסוך יין וחומץ אבל סך הוא את השמן ד) [ז]וכן בתרומה [ח]ובמעשר שני [ט]קל מהם שביעית שנתנה להדלקת הנר : **ג** [י]אין מוכרין פירות שביעית לא במדה ולא במשקל ולא במנין ולא תאנים במנין ולא ירק במשקל בית שמאי אומרים אף לא אגודות [כ]ובית הלל אומרים את שדרכו לאגוד בבית אוגדין אותו בשוק כגון הכרשין ונץ החלב : **ד** ה) [ל]האומר לפועל הא לך איסר זה ולקט לי ירק היום שכרו מותר לקט לי בו ירק היום שכרו אסור

כדקתני סיפא דמין בשאינו מינו חייב לבער בנותן טעם ודבר תימה מאי קשיא ליה אפילו איירי בחד פתרונא כגון וורד של שביעית בשמן של ששית ובוורד של ששית בשמן של שביעית מכל מקום האי חייב בביעור והאי אינו חייב בביעור דשמן נותן טעם בוורד ואין וורד נותן טעם בשמן : החרובים חדשים · הכא גבי חרובין מיירי שכנסתהו ביין עד שהגיע זמן הביעור משום הכי בכל ענין חייבים בביעור אבל בשביעית ילקט החרובין כמו בוורד ובהדיא תניא בתוספתא (פ"ה) בחרובין כדתנן הכא בוורד החרובים חדשים שכבשן ביין ישן ילקט החרובין והיין מותר ישנים בחדשים חייב בביעור : השביעית אוסרת כל שהוא במינה · כגון לאחר הביעור אבל קודם הביעור אין בו קדושת שביעית עד שיהא בו בנותן טעם : ושלא במינה · אפילו לאחר הביעור בנותן טעם וצריך עיון בסוף הנודר מן הירק *) דאיירי בגידולים וזהו תימה דשלא במינה לא יתכן בגידולים :

א מלוגמא · רפואה וממעט לה בפ' לולב הגזול (דף מ·) לפי שאינה שוה בכל אדם · ירושלי' (ה"א) בעי רבנן קומי רבי זעירא אוכלי אדם ואוכלי בהמה היו בפרשה מאי חמית מימר אוכלי אדם אין עושין מהן מלוגמא אוכלי בהמה עושין א"ל והיתה שבת הארץ לכם לאכלה (ויקרא כה) מיעט אוכלי אדם אין עושין מהן מלוגמא ומיעט אוכלי בהמה אמר ר' בון בר חייא כל מדרש שאתה דורש ושובר מדרש ראשון אין זה מדרש ר' יוסי לא אמר כן אלא והיתה שבת הארץ לכם לאכלה מיעט לך ולעבדך מיעט אין מיעוט אחר מיעוט אלא לרבות אוכלי בהמה שעושה מלוגמא לאדם וריבה אוכלי אדם כל מדרש שאתה דורש ושובר מדרש ראשון אין זה מדרש אוכלי אדם מיעטת וכשרבית אוכלי בהמה רבית עושין מהן מלוגמא הא אוכלי בהמה עושין ופריך נמי כתב לבהמתך ולחיה אשר בארצך תהיה כל

שלא יכנס כח הוורדין וטעמם בשמן שהשמן הוא ישן והוורד חדש אלא אם יניחהו זמן רב : ישן בחדש הוא להא וורד של שביעית בשמן של מוצאי שביעית וזה יכנים בו כח הוורד וטעמו מיד ומפני זה חייב לבער השמן אבל החרובין ביין יכנס בו טעם החרובין מיד ומפני זה על שני הדרכים חייב לבער היין : ושאמר מין במינו כ"ש כגון שיתערב יין של שביעית ביין של ששית ואפילו טפה אחת בכלי גדול הוא חייב לבער וזהו שאמר שביעית אוסרת כל שהוא במינה ושאמר ושלא במינה בנותן טעם כמו הוורד בשמן והחרובין ביין וכן הדין בשאר איסורין שבתורה ולשאר האיסורין כולם רמז באמרו זה הכלל כל שהוא בנותן טעם וכו' ועוד יתבאר זה בסוף ע"ז :

א אמר הכתוב (ויקרא כה) והיתה שבת הארץ לכם לאכלה · ר"ל הדבר שהיא לכם למאכל אדם בלבד יהיה לאכלה ולא למלוגמא היא מלה מורכבת מלא לוגמא ולוגמא שם לד אחד משני לדי הפה מבפנים ר"ל לעיסת מאכל שאפשר שילעוס מן החטה או התאנים לעיסה אחת לשום ע"פ מכה או שחין והענין המבורר מכל זה יתמה שאמר ולא למלוגמא הוא שלא יעשה מפירות שביעית לא התבושת ולא רטיות ולא רפואות להקיא ולא שום דבר מכל זה אלא מה שהוא מיוחד למאכל אדם כמו שבארנו : וכל שאינו מיוחד למאכל אדם עושין ממנו מלוגמא לאדם

המיוחד לכם הוא שיהיה לכם לאכלה בלבד וחולתו ...י אדם הוא שלא יעשה ממנו מלוגמא כמו שלא ...ם וחומרי בהמה הוא שיהיו כמו מאכל בהמה ...לא כל זמן שהוא נמצא אותו המין בשדה לחיות

OLD OIL,[11] THE ROSE MAY BE TAKEN OUT;[12] BUT IF AN OLD ROSE[13] WAS PRESERVED IN NEW OIL,[14] IT IS SUBJECT TO THE LAW OF REMOVAL.[15] NEW CAROBS[13] PRESERVED IN OLD WINE, OR OLD CAROBS IN NEW WINE,[16] ARE SUBJECT TO THE LAW OF REMOVAL. THIS IS THE GENERAL PRINCIPLE:[17] IF ONE KIND
a IS MIXED WITH A DIFFERENT KIND[1] AND IT HAS THE POWER TO IMPART FLAVOUR [TO THE OTHER], BOTH KINDS ARE SUBJECT TO THE LAW OF REMOVAL; BUT IF IT IS MIXED WITH THE IDENTICAL KIND, THEN [THE WHOLE IS SUBJECT TO REMOVAL] EVEN IF ONLY THE SMALLEST QUANTITY EXISTS.[2] PRODUCE OF THE SEVENTH YEAR RENDERS SIMILAR KINDS PROHIBITED[3] EVEN [IF IT EXISTS] IN THE SMALLEST QUANTITY; BUT IF THEY BE OF DIFFERENT SPECIES [PROHIBITION SETS IN] ONLY WHEN FLAVOUR IS IMPARTED.[4]

CHAPTER VIII

MISHNAH 1. AN IMPORTANT PRINCIPLE WAS LAID DOWN CONCERNING SABBATICAL YEAR PRODUCE. OF SUCH PRO-
b DUCE AS IS DESIGNATED AS FOOD FOR MAN,[1] ONE MAY NOT MAKE A POULTICE[2] FOR MAN; AND NEEDLESS TO SAY, FOR CATTLE. SUCH PRODUCE, HOWEVER, THAT IS NOT EXCLUSIVELY USED FOR HUMAN FOOD MAY BE USED AS A POULTICE FOR MAN, BUT NOT FOR CATTLE. SUCH PRODUCE NOT USUALLY DESIGNATED EITHER FOR HUMAN OR FOR CATTLE FOOD, BUT NOW INTENDED[3] AS FOOD FOR BOTH MAN AND CATTLE, HAS IMPOSED UPON IT THE STRINGENT LAWS APPLYING BOTH TO MEN[4] AND BEASTS.[5] IF HIS INTENTION[6] WAS TO USE IT [ONLY] AS FUEL, IT MUST BE ACCOUNTED ONLY AS WOOD;[7] AS, FOR EXAMPLE, SAVORY,[8] HYSSOP, OR THYME.[9]

MISHNAH 2. SABBATICAL YEAR PRODUCE MAY BE USED FOR FOOD, DRINK AND FOR ANOINTING.[10] THAT USUALLY EATEN SHOULD BE USED FOR FOOD ONLY; THAT USUALLY USED FOR ANOINTING PURPOSES IS TO BE USED AS AN UNGUENT [ONLY], AND THAT USED USUALLY FOR DRINKING IS
c TO BE USED FOR THIS PURPOSE ONLY.[1] ONE MAY NOT ANOINT WITH WINE AND VINEGAR, BUT WITH OIL ONLY.[2] SO IS THE CASE WITH HEAVE-OFFERING AND SECOND TITHE.[3] GREATER LENIENCY WAS APPLIED TO [OIL OF] THE SEVENTH YEAR, SINCE IT CAN ALSO BE USED FOR LAMP-KINDLING.[4]

MISHNAH 3. PRODUCE OF THE SEVENTH YEAR[5] MAY NOT BE SOLD BY MEASURE, WEIGHT OR NUMBER.[6] NEITHER MAY FIGS [BE SOLD] BY NUMBER, NOR VEGETABLES BY WEIGHT.[7] BETH SHAMMAI SAY: THEY MAY NOT BE SOLD, EVEN IN BUNDLES;[8] BUT BETH HILLEL SAY: PRODUCTS USUALLY TIED IN BUNDLES IN THE HOUSE[9] MAY ALSO BE TIED INTO BUNDLES FOR THE MARKET;[10] FOR EXAMPLE: LEEKS AND ASPHODEL.[11]

MISHNAH 4. IF ONE SAYS TO A LABOURER: 'TAKE THIS ISSAR[12] AND GATHER VEGETABLES FOR ME TO-DAY', HIS PAYMENT IS PERMITTED;[13] [BUT IF HE TOLD HIM THUS:] 'IN RETURN [FOR THIS ISSAR], DO THOU GATHER VEGETABLES FOR ME TO-DAY', THEN HIS PAYMENT IS FORBIDDEN.[14] IF ONE BOUGHT

(11) Of the sixth year. (12) The oil does not become subject to the law of Removal on account of the rose. (13) Of the seventh year. (14) Of the eighth year. (15) Since one flavours the other, they must be removed. (16) Of the eighth year. Since flavour is imparted, the wine cannot be drunk after the time of removal. (17) Applicable to all Sabbatical year produce.

a (1) Both the new and the old produce. (2) Even without the imparting of flavour. (3) If mixed with a similar kind allowed in the seventh year. The Mishnah refers to after the time of removal period. (4) An explanation of the opening statement of the Mishnah. This is the determining factor even after the period of removal to render the mixture forbidden.

b (1) Sabbatical produce was not to be wasted; hence if fit for human food it must not be used for healing purposes. (2) Greek μάλαγμα (Jast.); an emollient, or plaster. (3) At the time of gathering. (4) Not to make a poultice thereof. (5) Not to cook vegetables if they can be eaten raw. (6) At the time of gathering. (7) Since they were only used for burning purposes, they are not liable to the law of Removal. (8) A herb of mint, classified with hyssop, *Satureia thymbra* (Jast.). (9) A shrub with pungent aromatic leaves used in cooking. The three shrubs here specified are not usually designated for any particular purpose; hence his intention is respected. (10) Such produce as grapes and olives are borne in mind which can be used for all these three purposes.

c (1) No change was allowed in the natural purpose of the food; such food, however, that had become unfit for human consumption could be used for other purposes. (2) Wine, being used for drinking, was not to be wasted on an inferior purpose; cf. B.Ḳ. 15*b*. (3) Which can only be applied for the above-mentioned purposes. (4) Whether the oil is clean or unclean. Forbidden, however, in the case of oil of *terumah* that is clean. Oil of the Second Tithe could be burnt only when clean; but oil of the seventh year could be burnt regardless of its being clean or not. (5) Left over after having been gathered to be eaten in one's household; v. *supra* VII, 3. (6) Respect must be attached to Sabbatical produce; accordingly, different methods of sale procedure must be employed. (7) In departure from the regular procedure in order to emphasize the sanctity of seventh year products. He can only sell them by approximation. (8) To obviate the impression that they are being sold as ordinary wares. (9) For private purposes. (10) Since this is unusual it will be regarded as different produce entitled to regard. (11) Cf. *supra* VII, 1 notes. (12) Equivalent to eight *peruṭahs*. (13) The *issar* can be regarded as a gift, and the work to be done as a favour. (14) Being too much like an express wish to perform work for him in the seventh year.

a A LOAF FROM A BAKER WORTH A PONDION[1] [AND SAID:] 'WHEN I HAVE GATHERED VEGETABLES FROM THE FIELD,[2] THEN I WILL BRING THEM TO YOU', THIS IS PERMITTED.[3] IF, HOWEVER, HE BOUGHT IT OF HIM WITHOUT ANY EXPLANATION,[4] HE MAY NOT PAY HIM HIS DEBT WITH THE VALUE OF SEVENTH YEAR PRODUCE;[5] FOR NO DEBT CAN BE PAID WITH THE VALUE OF SUCH PRODUCE.

MISHNAH 5. ONE MUST NOT PAY[6] A WELL-DIGGER,[7] AN ATTENDANT AT THE PUBLIC BATH,[8] A BARBER, OR A SAILOR; BUT HE MAY GIVE THE WELL-DIGGER [THE PRODUCE] TO BUY THEREWITH TO DRINK. AS A FREE GIFT, HOWEVER, HE MAY GIVE IT TO ALL OF THEM.[9]

MISHNAH 6. SABBATICAL FIGS MAY NOT BE CUT WITH A FIG-KNIFE,[10] BUT WITH AN ORDINARY KNIFE.[11] GRAPES MAY NOT BE TRODDEN IN THE WINE-PRESS,[12] BUT THEY ARE TRODDEN IN THE KNEADING-TROUGH.[13] OLIVES MAY NOT BE PREPARED IN AN OLIVE-PRESS OR WITH AN OLIVE-CRUSHER,[14] BUT THEY MAY BE CRUSHED AND BROUGHT INTO A SMALL OLIVE-PRESS. R. SIMEON SAYS: THEY MAY EVEN BE CRUSHED IN THE [LARGER] OLIVE-PRESS, AFTERWARDS TO BE BROUGHT INTO THE SMALLER PRESS.

MISHNAH 7. SABBATICAL VEGETABLES MAY NOT BE COOKED IN OIL OF TERUMAH LEST THEY BECOME INVALI-
b DATED;[1] BUT R. SIMEON PERMITS IT.[2] THE LAST THING EXCHANGED IS ALWAYS SUBJECT TO THE SABBATICAL LAW,[3] AND THE PRODUCE ITSELF[4] ALSO REMAINS FORBIDDEN.[5]

MISHNAH 8. SLAVES, PROPERTY, OR UNCLEAN CATTLE MAY NOT BE BOUGHT WITH MONEY REALIZED BY SALE OF SEVENTH YEAR PRODUCTS; IF ONE HAS DONE SO HE MUST [BUY AND] EAT [FOOD] FOR THEIR EQUIVALENT.[6] BIRD-OFFERINGS BROUGHT BY A MAN OR WOMAN WHO SUFFERED A FLUX,[7] OR BY A WOMAN AFTER CHILDBIRTH,[8] MUST NOT BE BOUGHT WITH THE VALUE OF SABBATICAL PRODUCE; AND IF THIS HAS BEEN DONE, HE MUST [BUY AND] EAT [FOOD] FOR THEIR EQUIVALENT. VESSELS MAY NOT BE ANOINTED WITH OIL OF SEVENTH YEAR PRODUCE; WHERE THIS HAS BEEN DONE, HE MUST [BUY AND] EAT [FOOD] FOR THEIR EQUIVALENT.[9]

MISHNAH 9. A HIDE[10] SMEARED WITH OIL OF THE SEVENTH YEAR, R. ELIEZER SAYS, MUST BE BURNT; BUT THE SAGES SAY THAT HE MUST [BUY AND] EAT [PRODUCE] OF CORRESPONDING VALUE. THEY TOLD R. AKIBA THAT R. ELIEZER USED TO SAY, A HIDE THAT HAS BEEN SMEARED WITH OIL OF THE SEVENTH YEAR MUST BE BURNT. HE REPLIED: 'HOLD YOUR PEACE; FOR I WILL NOT DIVULGE TO YOU WHAT R.
c ELIEZER ACTUALLY SAID IN THIS CONNECTION'.[1]

MISHNAH 10. THEY ALSO TOLD HIM[2] THAT R. ELIEZER SAID: 'HE WHO EATS BREAD [BAKED] BY SAMARITANS[3] IS LIKE ONE WHO EATS THE FLESH OF A PIG'.[4] [TO THIS, TOO] HIS REPLY WAS: 'HOLD YOUR PEACE; FOR I WILL NOT DIVULGE TO YOU WHAT R. ELIEZER REALLY DID SAY IN THIS CONNECTION'.

MISHNAH 11. ONE MAY WASH IN A BATH HEATED WITH STRAW OR STUBBLE OF THE SEVENTH YEAR;[5] BUT IF HE IS A MAN HELD IN HONOUR, HE SHOULD NOT WASH THEREIN.[6]

CHAPTER IX

d *MISHNAH* 1. RUE,[1] GOOSEFOOT,[2] PURSLANE,[3] HILL CORI-

a (1) Equivalent to two *issars*. (2) That grow of their own accord. (3) For it is like exchanging gifts. The baker gives his loaf, he his vegetables, with no money crossing their hands. (4) I.e., on credit. (5) This would be actually a case of trading with Sabbatical produce. (6) With Sabbatical year produce. (7) Who supplies the town with water from the wells he is asked to dig. (8) Who heats the water to his liking. Though the labour of all these mentioned is for his own personal benefit, yet they must not be paid with produce of the seventh year. (9) Even though, as a consequence, no reward for labour may be demanded. (10) The one used specially for this purpose. (11) Sword-like in shape. The point emphasized is that some different procedure must be followed (שנוי). *Aliter:* These figs are not to be cut in the place usually designated for this purpose, thus taking the words מוקצה and חרבה as names of places instead of names of knives. (12) As usual. (13) To show the nature of the produce. (14) A small olive-press with a cylindrical beam with which to extract oil from olives in the press. According to Bert. it consisted of a large beam, topped by a large stone, with which oil was extracted from the olives.

b (1) Since the oil is susceptible to uncleanness, the vegetables, too, will have to be burnt, and thus wilful wastage of Sabbatical produce will accrue. *Terumah*, with its special sanctity, can suffer impurity at one further remove than ordinary food; and when invalid, must be burnt. (2) Being of the opinion that dedicated things may be brought to a state of invalidity, Pes. 98*b*. (3) The equivalent of the thing exchanged is also regarded as invested with Sabbatical sanctity, and though not all the substitutes are considered Sabbatical, yet the original produce still remains forbidden. (4) Of the seventh year. (5) V. Bert. *ad loc.* (6) Since sanctity cannot be attached to the things bought, he must eat produce of equal value. (7) Lev. XV, 14, 29; the sacrifice being two turtle-doves, or two pigeons. (8) Ibid. XII, 6, 8. These are cited here to show that though they permit the bearer to eat of holy things, nevertheless, they cannot be purchased with Sabbatical produce. (9) Only man could be anointed with Sabbatical oil. Oil preserves vessels. (10) Or any other object; a hide is cited as being the more usual object to receive such treatment.

c (1) From this it would appear that R. Eliezer held very lenient views which R. Akiba was not eager to discuss (Bert.). V. however, T. J. *ad loc.* R. Eliezer b. Hyrcanus was under a ban (v. B.M. 59*b*), and was forbidden to participate in the discussions and decisions of the court; Yad. IV, 3. (2) R. Akiba. (3) Excommunicated by Ezra for their intransigence in disturbing the construction of the Temple. (4) Not to be taken too literally. Their bread was prohibited as a punishment; v. Ḥul. 4*a*. (5) In pursuance of the policy formulated in *supra* VIII, 1 that anything not used exclusively for human food can be used for other purposes. (6) Such a man must impose upon himself added restrictions.

d (1) A perennial ever-green shrub with bitter, strong-scented leaves frequently used in medicine. (2) A kind of asparagus, says Bert. Goosefoot is so named from the shape of its leaves. (3) A low succulent herb used in salads and pickled.

שלא יאמר לו הלויני מה בין הלויני להשאילני ר' זעירא בשם ר' יוחנן מהלכות של עמעום היא פתר רבי יעקב בר אחא בשם רבי יוחנן עוד היא מהל' של עמעום כלומר הני ד' דברים היו ראויין ליאסר ועמעמו עליהן והתירום והיא דלהלן משנה היא בפ"ג דמעשר שני (מ"א) והיא דשואל משנה בשבת (דף קמח·) דטעמא דאסרינן לשון הלואה גזירה שמא יכתוב משום דהלואה אינה חוזרת בעין ואין ממהרין לפרוע רגילים לכתוב אבל שאלה דהדרא בעינה אין רגילות לכתוב ואע"ג דהכא לא הדרא בעינה מכל מקום כי אמר בלשון שאלה לא אתי למכתב ואין הטעם ברור כל כך לפיכך לא התירו אלא על ידי עמעום וכן פת שהוא מי"ח

פלוני ולפיכך כשיקח הלחם מן הנחתום ואומר לו אתן לך בו ירקות שדה כשאקבלם מותר אבל אם לקח ממנו לחם בדמים ולא פירש לו שיתן לו בהם ירקות נעשה כחוב עליו ואסור להת בחובו פירות שביעית : ואמר פונדיון ואיסר על המנהג הידוע אלא שהככר בפונדיון והירקות פחות ממה שלוקחין באיסר ואיסר רביע דרכמון ופונדיון חצי דרכמון והדרכמון ט"ז גרעיני שעורים וכבר בארנו אלו השיעורים במה שעבר (פ"ח מ"ה דפאה) : ה בייר הוא משקה המי' לבני אדם מן הבור ויקבל שכרו עליו : ובלן בעל המרחץ. וספר המגלח : וספן בעל הספינה והוא אומר שאסור לו לתת שכר אלו מדמי שביעית לפי שלא נתנה אלא לאכילה ולשתיה ולסיכה כמו שבארנו ומותר לו לתת לבעל בור המים להשקותו מפני שנתנה לשתיה כמו שנתבאר : ולכולן הוא נותן מתנת חנם ואינו עושה חשבון שכרם ואף על פי שיש בדבר ההוא דרך מדרכי גמילות חסד וכבר נתבאר לך שהוא מותר והוא מה שאמר אוכלים פירות שביעית בטובה ושלא בטובה : ו מוקצה . שם מקום ששם שוטחין עליו שטוחי התאנים והענבים : חרבה . ידוע : ובד הוא שם ליקבים שדורכין בם הזיתים ונקרא בלשון ערב בד : וקוטב הוא גת קטן לזיתים : ובודידה שם הבד והיא גת קטנה עד מאד : עריבה כלי שלשין בו העיסה והכוונה בכל זה כדי לשנות ושלא יתעסק בפירות שביעית כדרך שיתעסק בשאר השנים כמו שנא' (ויקרא כה) ואת ענבי נזירך לא תבצור וידוע באמת שאינו רוצה בפסוק זה לאסור הבצירה כלל שהרי התיר אכילתן באמרו והיתה שבת הארץ לכם לאכלה (שם) אבל ר"ל כמו ...

א לקח מן הנחתום ככר בפונדיון כשאלקוט ירקות שדה אביא לך מותר לקח ממנו סתם לא ישלם לו מדמי שביעית שאין פורעין חוב מדמי שביעית : ה ב אין נותנין לא לבייר ולא לבלן ולא לספר ולא לספן אבל נותן הוא לבייר לשתות ולכולן הוא נותן מתנת חנם : ו ג תאנים של שביעית אין קוצין אותן במוקצה אבל קוצץ אותם בחרבה אין דורכין ענבים בגת אבל דורך הוא בערבה ואין עושין זיתים בבד ובקוטב אבל כותש הוא ומכניס לבודידה ד רש"א אף טוחן הוא בבית הבד ומכניס לבודידה : ז ה אין א) מבשלין ירק של שביעית בשמן של תרומה שלא יביאנו לידי פסול ר"ש מתיר ג) ו ואחרון אחרון נתפש בשביעית והפרי עצמו אסור : ח ז אין לוקחים עבדים וקרקעות ובהמה טמאה מדמי שביעית ואם לקח יאכל כנגדן אין מביאין קיני זבים וקיני זבות וקיני יולדות מדמי שביעית ואם הביא יאכל כנגדן אין סכין כלים בשמן של שביעית ואם סך יאכל כנגדו : ט עור שסכו בשמן של שביעית רא"א ידלק וחכמים אומרים ה יאכל כנגדו אמרו לפני ר"ע אומר היה ר"א עור שסכו בשמן של שביעית ידלק אמר להם שתוקו לא אומר לכם מה ר"א אומר בו : י ועוד אמרו לפניו אומר היה ר"א האוכל פת כותים כאוכל בשר חזיר אמר להם שתוקו לא אומר לכם מה שר"א אומר בו : יא ט מרחץ שהוסקה בתבן או בקש של שביעית מותר לרחוץ בה ואם מתחשב הוא הרי זה לא ירחוץ :

פרק תשיעי

א ג) הפיגם והירבוזין השוטים והחלגלוגות

דבר ומסיק שקדהיה עמעום של פת דבמקום שאין פת ישראל מצויה בדין שתהא פת עו"ג אסורה עמעמו עליה והתירוה משום חיי נפש רבנן דקסרי בשם ר' יעקב בר חייא כדברי מי שמתיר ובלבד מן הפלטר ולא עבדין כך כלומר מחמירין על עצמן ועוד מפרש התם טעמא אחרינא [אמתני'] דקאמר התם ריש לקיש במראה לו את הירק שאינו אלא כנותן לו שכר רגליו כלומר שהוא עצמו יכול לילך וללקט (ב) רבי יוחנן אמר אפילו לא הראה כמו שהראה לו ומסיק דקל הוא שהקילו בשביעית שהוא מדבריהם וברים פ' בתרא דמסכת עו"ג (סב·) פי' בקונטרס לקט לי בו לשון מכר הוא דמשמע לקט לי שויו ירק אבל לקט לי לשון שכירות ולא לשון מכר ואין מי שיתפסש א] בקדושה : ככר בפונדיון · כלומר בשוה פונדיון ולא קצב לו דמים אלא אמר לו בשעת לקיחה כשאלקט ירקות שדה אביא מותר דעבדין דין לדין מתנת חנם לפי שירקות שדה מצויין ובירושלמי (שם) תני ר' יהודה ורבי נחמיה אוסרין לפי שאין ירקות שדה מצויין : לקח ממנו סתם · כלומר על מנת ליתן דמיה בסתם בהקפת ג] חנות : שאין פורעין מדמי שביעית·וטעמא כדאמרינן בריש פרק בתרא דמסכת עו"ג (שם) גמלא זה פורע חובו מפירות שביעית והתורה אמרה לאכלה ולא לסחורה : ה בייר · חופר בורות ואינו נותן לו מדמי שביעית שיתן לו מים לתשמישו אלא דווקא לשתות כדתני סיפא אבל [לא] לבהמתו ולמשרה ולכביסה ובירושלמי (הל' ה') משמע דר' יוסי [שרי] לכביסה דקסבר יש בה חיי נפש גבי מעיין של בני העיר בריש פ' בתרא דנדרים (דף פ:) אמר רבי יוסי כביסתן קודמת לחיי אחרים : ולא לבלן · מחמם מרחץ אפילו ר' יוסי מודי שאמר בירושלמי (שם) אדם מגלגל ברחילה ואין מגלגל בכביסה והתם בנדרים אמרינן דאלימא ...

... ולא לספר. לשכר התספורת: ולא לספן ·לשכר ... דאמרן יכול ליתן במתנה שלא לשם שכר: ו מוקצה · ... כך שמו: חרבה·סכין [לשון] חרב: עריבה· שלשין ... בערוך משימין עץ גדול וכבד על הזיתים שבבית הבד ...

ב א מיי׳ פ״ד שם הלכה כ׃
ג ב מיי׳ פ״ז מהלכות שמטה ויובל הל׳ ט סמ״ג עשין קמח׃

א) פסחים דף נא. ב) שם דף נב.

כוסבר. אלײַדרא שגדל בהרים אבל כוסבר של גינה חשוב הוא׃ כרפס של נהרות. אבל של גינה חשוב הוא יש אומרים כרפס אפי״א׃ גרגר של אפר. אורגא הגדילה באחו אבל של גינה חשוב הוא׃ פטורין במעשר בכל השנים משום דאין כיוצא בהן נשמר ומפקירים אותם והפקר פטור מן המעשר דכתיב (דברים יד) ובא הלוי כי אין לו חלק ונחלה עמך בדבר שאין לו חלק יטול מעשר יצא הפקר לקט שכחה ופאה שיש לו חלק עמך וב״ה ילפי משמטה כדפרשינן במסכת פיאה פ״ו (מ״א)׃ וניקחין מכל אדם בשביעית. ואע״ג דשביעית נוהגת בהפקר לפי שאין כיוצא בהן נשמר והוה ליה לוקח מן המופקר ואע״ג דלא ידעי׳ ביה בהאי אם הפקיר מחזקי׳ בהכי דאין דרך לשומרו לפיכך מוסרין לו דמיכן דלא חשדינן ליה שיכניס לסחורה ולא ינהוג בהם תורת שביעית ופרק לולב הגזול (דף לט:)

כוסבר שבהרים והכרפס שבנהרות והגרגר של אפר פטורין מן המעשרות ונלקחין מכל אדם בשביעית שאין כיוצא בהם נשמר רבי יהודה אומר ספיחי חרדל מותרין שלא נחשדו עליהם עוברי עבירה א) ר״ש אומר כל הספיחים מותרין חוץ מספיחי כרוב שאין כיוצא בהן בירקות שדה וחכמים אומרים א כל הספיחין אסורין׃ ב ג) ב שלש ארצות לביעור יהודה ועבר הירדן והגליל וג׳ ג׳ ארצות לכל אחת ואחת גליל העליון וגליל התחתון והעמק מכפר חנניה ולמעלן כל שאינו מגדל שקמין גליל העליון ומכפר חנניה ולמטן כל שהוא מגדל שקמין גליל התחתון ותחום טבריה העמק וביהודה ההר והשפלה

שביהודה יש הר ושפלה ועמק וכן בעבר הירדן וכן בגליל ומפרש בסיפא ולמה אמרו ג׳ ארצות שיהיו אוכלים בכל אחת ואחת עד שיכלה האחרון שבה דמפרשינן בפ׳ [illegible] מקום שנהגו (דף נג.) ולבהמתך ולחיה אשר בארצך (ויקרא כה) כל זמן שחיה אוכלת מן השדה האכל לבהמתך מן הבית וגמירי דאין חיה שביהודה גדילה על [illegible] פירות שבגליל ואין חיה שבגליל גדילה על פירות שביהודה והשתא ביהודה יש כמה עיירות דפעמים שבזו כלו ובזו לא כלו ואוכלין עד שיכלה האחרון שבה כלדתניא [illegible] אוכלין בענבים עד שיכלו לגיות *שבגבל ואם יש מאוחרות מהן אוכלים עליהן שלדך החיה כשאין מוצאה פירות כאן הולכת במקום אחר מהר להר ומשפלה לשפלה ומעמק

העמק הוא בקעת גינוסר וחברותיה.וביהודה כמו כן ג׳ ארצות הר ושפלה ועמק. ושפלת לוד כשפלת הדרום פי׳ שפלת לוד כשפלת יהודה דלשפלת יהודה קרי שפלת הדרום. וההר של שפלת לוד כהר המלך והר [illegible]

ANDER,[4] WATER-PARSLEY,[5] AND MEADOW-BERRIES, ARE EXEMPT FROM TITHES,[6] AND MAY BE PURCHASED[7] FROM ANY MAN[8] DURING THE SABBATICAL YEAR, SINCE SUCH PRODUCE IS NOT USUALLY WATCHED. R. JUDAH SAYS: AFTERGROWTHS OF MUSTARD ARE PERMITTED, SINCE TRANSGRESSORS ARE NOT SUSPECTED CONCERNING THEM.[9] R. SIMEON SAYS: ALL AFTERGROWTHS ARE PERMITTED,[10] WITH THE EXCEPTION OF THE AFTERGROWTHS OF CABBAGE,[11] SINCE SUCH CANNOT BE PLACED WITHIN THE CATEGORY OF WILD VEGETABLES. BUT THE SAGES SAY: ALL AFTERGROWTHS ARE FORBIDDEN.[12]

MISHNAH 2. THERE ARE THREE DISTINCT COUNTRIES[13] IN RESPECT OF THE LAW OF REMOVAL.[14] [THESE ARE]: JUDAH, TRANSJORDANIA, AND GALILEE, EACH OF THESE IS [IN TURN]
a DIVIDED INTO THREE TERRITORIES.[1] THUS [GALILEE[2] IS DIVIDED INTO] UPPER GALILEE, NETHER GALILEE, AND THE VALLEY; FROM KEFAR ḤANANIAH UPWARDS, [NAMELY], THE REGION WHERE SYCAMORES DO NOT GROW,[3] IS UPPER GALILEE; FROM KEFAR ḤANANIAH DOWNWARDS, WHERE THE SYCAMORES DO GROW, IS NETHER GALILEE; THE NEIGHBOURHOOD OF TIBERIAS IS THE VALLEY. THOSE OF JUDAH

(4) Annual plants with aromatic fruit used for flavouring. Kil. I, 2. (5) An umbelliferous plant. (6) Tithes are only taken from owned produce; those above-mentioned generally grow in ownerless property and are not deemed of much value. (7) For food. (8) Even from such that are suspected of trading with Sabbatical produce; for the law does not embrace ownerless produce. (9) To guard them in the seventh year. (10) Since they are usually ownerless. (11) Which are not generally ownerless and do not grow wild. (12) As a precaution against transgressors who will sow things in secret, and then claim that they are aftergrowths. Those of vegetables were permitted, according to all, since it was not usual to sow them at all. (13) Though they are all in the Land, they differ with regard to the application of this law; the reason being that produce ripens at different seasons in each of these territories. (14) Sabbatical produce stored in the house may be eaten as long as similar produce still abounds in the fields of the country of his domicile; as soon as this produce begins to wither or disappear from the fields, the time has come for him to remove that which he has stored up at home. The object of this law was to enable man and beast alike to have equal access to seventh year produce. This stipulation was based on the words in Lev. XXV, 7 (ולבהמתך ולחיה); as long only as cattle can eat thereof in the field, may man eat thereof in his house.

a (1) Though three territories, yet each is part of one country—Galilee. (2) The three partitions of Galilee are given. (3) These grow in the plain; I Kings X, 27.

ARE: THE MOUNTAIN REGION, THE SHEPHELAH,[4] AND THE VALLEY.[5] THE PLAIN OF LYDDA[6] IS LIKE THE PLAIN OF THE SOUTH, AND ITS MOUNTAIN REGION IS LIKE THE KING'S HILL-COUNTRY.[7] FROM BETH-HORON TO THE SEA IS CONSIDERED AS ONE DISTRICT.[8]

MISHNAH 3. WHY DID THEY SPEAK OF THREE COUNTRIES?[9] SO THAT THEY MAY EAT IN EACH COUNTRY UNTIL THE LAST OF THE SEVENTH YEAR PRODUCE IN THAT COUNTRY IS ENDED.[10] R. SIMEON SAID: THEY HAVE SPOKEN OF THREE COUNTRIES ONLY IN THE CASE OF JUDAH, BUT ALL OTHER
a COUNTRIES[1] ARE TO BE REGARDED AS ROYAL HILL-COUNTRY:[2] AND ALL OTHER COUNTRIES RECEIVE EQUAL TREATMENT WITH REGARD TO THE OLIVE AND DATE.[3]

MISHNAH 4. ONE MAY EAT[4] [ONLY SO LONG AS] SIMILAR PRODUCE IS STILL REGARDED AS OWNERLESS[5] [IN THE FIELDS], BUT NOT WHEN IT IS BEING WATCHED.[6] R. JOSE, HOWEVER, PERMITS IT ALSO WHEN [SIMILAR PRODUCE] IS FOUND GUARDED.[7] ONE MAY CONTINUE TO EAT[8] SO LONG AS THERE IS STILL GROWTH BETWEEN THE GRASS,[9] OR BY VIRTUE OF THE TREES THAT YIELD BI-ANNUALLY;[10] BUT ONE MUST NOT EAT BY VIRTUE OF WINTER-GRAPES.[11] R. JUDAH PERMITS [EVEN BY VIRTUE OF THE LATTER] PROVIDED THEY BEGAN TO RIPEN BEFORE THE SUMMER [OF THE SEVENTH YEAR] HAD ENDED.

b *MISHNAH* 5. IF THREE KINDS OF VEGETABLES[1] WERE PRESERVED IN ONE JAR, THEY MAY BE EATEN ONLY SO LONG AS THE FIRST STILL REMAINS;[2] SO R. ELIEZER. BUT R. JOSHUA SAYS: EVEN SO LONG AS THE LAST REMAINS.[3] RABBAN GAMALIEL SAYS: WHEN THE LIKE KIND IS NO LONGER TO BE FOUND WITHIN THE FIELD, THE CORRESPONDING KIND IN THE JAR MUST BE REMOVED.[4] AND THE HALACHAH AGREES WITH HIM. R. SIMEON SAYS: ALL VEGETABLES ARE REGARDED AS ONE [KIND] IN RESPECT OF THE LAW OF REMOVAL. PURSLANE[5] MAY BE EATEN AS LONG AS VETCHES[6] ARE STILL FOUND IN THE VALE OF BETH NETOPHA.[7]

MISHNAH 6. IF ONE GATHERED FRESH VEGETABLES,[8] HE MAY EAT THEM UNTIL THE [GROUND] MOISTURE IS DRIED UP;[9] AND IF HE GATHERED DRY [VEGETABLES] [HE MAY EAT THEM] UNTIL THE SECOND RAINFALL.[10] LEAVES OF REEDS AND OF THE VINE[11] [MAY BE EATEN] UNTIL THEY FALL FROM THE STEMS; BUT IF THEY HAVE BEEN GATHERED DRY, THEY MAY BE EATEN ONLY UNTIL THE SECOND RAINFALL. R. AKIBA SAYS: IN ALL

(4) Maritime Plain. (5) From Engedi to Jericho; Josh. X, 40. The three partitions of Transjordania seem to be inadvertently omitted; these are outlined in Josh. XV and in Tosef Shebi'ith, and also consist of hill-country, plain and valley. Machwar, Gador and the rest are the hill-country, Heshbon with its surrounding towns constitute the plain, and the valley is Beth Haran and its environs. (6) Continuing the description of Judah's territories. (7) Viz., the mountain region of Judah. In the region of Lydda, Sabbatical produce could be eaten until similar produce declines in the Judean hill-country, where, owing to its altitude, it is late in ripening. (8) As long as the cattle of that region still find food in the fields, one can continue to eat at home food stored. (9) Since each, in turn, is again partitioned into three, there are really nine in all. Why then three? (10) Viz., if produce in Judah's hilly region has ended in the field, but is still found in the plain; or if it has ceased in the fields of the plain and hill-country, but is still to be found in the valley, then the whole country of Judah may still eat. Similarly with Transjordania and Galilee. One cannot, however, eat in Judah because produce is still found in the fields of Galilee and Transjordania, for each of the three countries is perfectly autonomous with regard to the law of Removal.
a (1) I.e., Galilee and Transjordania. (2) Where there is always an abundance of fruit, even late in the year, and as long as there is produce to be found there, it may be eaten also in Galilee and Transjordania. (3) As long as they are still to be found in one place, they may be eaten in those even where they have ceased from the fields, be it Judah, Galilee, or Transjordania. (4) Stored Sabbatical produce. (5) Regardless of the fact whether it be attached or plucked from the soil. (6) Symbol of private ownership, as for example, produce from one's garden. From the words ולבהמתך ולחיה we deduce that men cannot eat from produce of which the beasts cannot avail themselves; viz., from one's garden. (7) And still attached to the soil; but once detached, and guarded, the produce is forbidden. (8) Sabbatical produce. (9) So Jast. Bert. explains it as 'a pitcher-shaped vessel, put up in walls and crevices as a bird's nest'. As long as grain is found in these pitchers, so long may one eat similar grain stored at home. *Aliter:* 'poor, stunted grain kept in soil'; also, 'the ledges placed on roofs of houses, where crumbs were scattered for birds to pick'; cf. I Kings VII, 9. (10) I.e., as long as there is on the tree fruit of the second crop. (11) Late fruits remaining on the edges of the trees till the approach of winter. I.e., one may not eat of the summer grapes by virtue of the grapes that will ripen in the winter of the eighth year.
b (1) The time of Removal of each being different. (2) In the field. I.e., as soon as one of them has ceased from the fields, the other two will then be forbidden, though their like is still in the fields. (3) Though the other two kinds similar to those in the jar have ceased from fields, those preserved can still be eaten by virtue of the one which is still in the fields with which they are intermixed. (4) And each vegetable may be eaten as long as that kind of vegetable is still found in the fields. (5) In the seventh year. (6) Of the artichoke genus, a plant of which the base of the flower and the scales thereof are edible. Those grown in the Holy Land were species of sunflower with edible tuberous roots. (7) Purslane, which after being plucked, lasts longest, owing to the moisture within, may be eaten as long as the vetches last in Beth Netopha, where on account of its fertility and plentiful supply of water, the crop remains longest in the field. Beth Netopha has been identified with the El Battof valley in Galilee, v. Klein, *Beiträge*, p. 83. (8) Of the seventh year. (9) After this drying up, those left in the field are no longer fit for food, and therefore those in the house must be removed. The word for 'moisture' (מתוק) is lit., 'sweetness', since it is this that makes them palatable. Cf. *supra* III, 1. (10) Usually the twenty-third Ḥeshwan (November) of the eighth year. Plants in the field then become unfit even for beasts in the fields. (11) Eaten as long as they were still attached to their stems.

והשפלה *והעמק ושפלת לוד כשפלת הדרום וההר שלה כהר המלך מבית חורון ועד הים מדינה אחת: ג ולמה אמרו שלש ארצות שיהו אוכלין בכל אחת ואחת עד שיכלה האחרון שבה ר"ש אומר לא אמרו שלש ארצות אלא ביהודה ושאר כל הארצות כהר המלך וכל הארצות כאחת לזיתים ולתמרים: ד אוכלין על המופקר אבל לא על השמור רבי יוסי מתיר אף על השמור אוכלין על הטפיחין ועל הדופרא אבל לא על הסתווניות רבי יהודה מתיר כל זמן שבכרו עד שלא יכלה הקיץ: ה הכובש ג' כבשים בחבית אחת רא"א אוכלין על הראשון רבי יהושע אומר אף על האחרון רבן גמליאל אומר כל שכלה מינו מן השדה יבער מינו מן החבית והלכה כדבריו רבי שמעון אומר כל ירק אחד לבעור אוכלין ברגילה עד שיכלו סגריות מבקעת בית נטופה: ו המלקט עשבים לחים עד שייבש המתוק והמגבב ביבש עד שתרד רביעה שניה עלי קנים ועלי גפנים עד שישורו מאביהן והמגבב ביבש עד שתרד רביעה שניה

רע"א

רע״א בכולן עד שתרד רביעה שניה: **ז** כיוצא בו המשכיר בית לחבירו עד הגשמים עד שתרד רביעה שניה א) המודר הנאה מחברו עד הגשמים עד שתרד רביעה שניה עד אימתי עניים נכנסים לפרדסות עד שתרד רביעה שניה ב) מאימתי נהנין ושורפין בתבן ובקש של שביעית משתרד רביעה שניה: **ח** מי שהיו לו פירות שביעית והגיע שעת הביעור מחלק מזון ג׳ סעודות לכל אחד ואחד ועניים אוכלין אחר הביעור אבל לא עשירים דברי רבי יהודה ר׳ יוסי אומר אחד עניים ואחד עשירים אוכלין אחר הביעור: **ט** מי שהיו לו פירות שביעית שנפלו לו בירושה או שנתנו לו במתנה רבי אליעזר אומר ינתנו לאוכליהן וחכמים אומרים אין החוטא נשכר אלא ימכרו לאוכליהן ודמיהן יתחלקו לכל אדם ג) האוכל מעיסת שביעית עד שלא הורמה חלתה חייב מיתה:

פרק עשירי

א שביעית ד) משמטת את המלוה בשטר ושלא בשטר הקפת החנות אינה משמטת ואם עשאה מלוה הרי זה משמט ר׳ יהודה אומר הראשון משמט שכר שכיר אינו משמט ואם עשאו מלוה ה״ז משמט רבי יוסי אומר כל מלאכה שפוסקת בשביעית משמטת ושאינה פוסקת בשביעית אינה משמטת: **ב** ה) השוחט את הפרה וחלקה בראש

a. CASES,[1] [THEY MAY BE EATEN] UNTIL THE SECOND RAINFALL.

MISHNAH 7. SIMILARLY, IF ONE HIRES TO ANOTHER A HOUSE 'UNTIL THE RAINFALL', [HE IMPLIES THEREBY] 'UNTIL THE SECOND RAINFALL'; OR IF ONE HAD VOWED NOT TO DERIVE ANY BENEFIT FROM HIS FELLOW 'UNTIL THE RAINS', [THIS LIKEWISE IMPLIES] 'UNTIL THE SECOND RAINFALL'. UNTIL WHEN MAY THE POOR ENTER THE GARDENS?[2] UNTIL THE SECOND RAINFALL.[3] AND WHEN MAY ONE BEGIN TO ENJOY OR BURN THE STRAW AND STUBBLE OF SABBATICAL PRODUCE?[4] AFTER THE SECOND RAINFALL.[5]

MISHNAH 8. IF ONE HAD SABBATICAL PRODUCE [AT HOME] AND THE TIME OF REMOVAL HAD COME,[6] HE MAY APPORTION FOOD FOR THREE MEALS TO EVERY ONE.[7] R. JUDAH SAYS: THE POOR[8] MAY EAT THEREOF, EVEN AFTER THE REMOVAL, BUT NOT THE RICH;[9] BUT R. JOSE SAYS: THE POOR AND THE RICH ALIKE MAY EAT THEREOF,[10] [EVEN AFTER THE TIME OF] THE REMOVAL.

MISHNAH 9. IF ONE HAD INHERITED SEVENTH YEAR PRODUCE,[11] OR HAD RECEIVED THEM AS A GIFT, R. ELIEZER
b SAYS: THEY MUST BE GIVEN[1] UNTO ALL WHO WISH TO EAT THEREOF.[2] BUT THE SAGES SAY: THE SINNER MUST NOT BENEFIT,[3] BUT THE PRODUCE SHOULD BE SOLD TO THOSE WHO WOULD EAT THEREOF,[4] AND ITS PRICE DIVIDED AMONG THEM ALL.[5] IF ONE EATS OF DOUGH OF THE SEVENTH YEAR [PRODUCE] BEFORE THE HALLAH[6] WAS TAKEN FROM IT, HE HAS INCURRED THEREBY THE DEATH PENALTY.[7]

CHAPTER X

MISHNAH 1. THE SABBATICAL YEAR CANCELS A CASH
c DEBT,[1] WHETHER IT IS SECURED BY BOND[2] OR NOT; BUT SHOP-DEBTS[3] IT DOES NOT CANCEL. IF, HOWEVER, IT HAD BEEN CONVERTED INTO THE FORM OF A LOAN, THEN IT IS CANCELLED. R. JUDAH SAYS: THE FORMER DEBT IS ALWAYS CANCELLED.[4] THE WAGE OF A HIRELING IS NOT CANCELLED, BUT IF IT HAD BEEN CONVERTED INTO A LOAN IT IS CANCELLED. R. JOSE SAYS: THE [PAYMENT FOR] ANY WORK THAT MUST CEASE[5] WITH THE SEVENTH YEAR, IS CANCELLED; BUT IF IT NEED NOT CEASE WITH THE SEVENTH YEAR, THEN IT IS NOT CANCELLED.[6]

MISHNAH 2. HE WHO SLAUGHTERS A COW AND DIVIDES

a (1) Of plants enumerated in the Mishnah. The *Halachah* is not in agreement with Akiba. (2) To gather gleanings, the Forgotten Sheaf and *Pe'ah* every year, and in the seventh year, the produce; Pe'ah VIII, 1. (3) But not afterwards; for they will then harm the soil that has become soft on account of the rain; B.Ḳ. 81*b*. (4) During the seventh year the produce can only be food for the cattle of the field, not for man's profit; Lev. XXV, 7. Straw and stubble were eaten by cattle, hence they must not be used for any other purpose until such time when they cease to be fit for them. (5) When nothing left in the field is fit for food, and henceforth the Sabbatical law no longer applies to things stored at home. (6) Of each species, according to its place and season; Pes. 53*a*. (7) Of his household, and friends and neighbours; the rest must be removed, after he had issued an open invitation to all to partake thereof. (8) Who had gathered ownerless produce. (9) Who had gathered from their own fields v. *Tif. Yis.* (10) Maim. reads: 'may not eat'. (11) Legally gathered, but now the period of Removal had come.

b (1) Free. (2) This is in accordance with Beth Shammai, *supra* IV, 2, who forbid the eating of Sabbatical produce when bestowed by the owner as a favour. The beneficiary consequently must share the produce he had received with others (Bert.). (3) For he has been the recipient of a forbidden gift, and if allowed to eat himself and bestow favours on others, he will be deriving benefit from forbidden gifts. (4) So that he be not the bestower of favours. (5) Perhaps by the Beth din (v., however, *Tif. Yis*). (6) Lit., 'cake'; Num. XV. 18-21. Though we deduce from לאכלה ('for eating'), ולא לשרפה ('and not for burning'), and the dough-offering if rendered unclean had to be burnt, still *Ḥallah* had to be taken from seventh year produce. (7) The 'heavenly' penalty (בידי שמים) for such an offence, no distinction being made in the dough from which *Ḥallah* had to be taken.

c (1) Deut. XV, 2. With the passing of the Sabbatical year, the creditor has no longer any claim on the debtor. (2) Though the debtor had pledged in the bond his immovable property for the recovery of the debt. (3) Goods purchased on credit. (4) When a second credit purchase is transacted, the first is always considered a loan subject to the Sabbatical law of cancellation, and the last credit purchase a trust not subject to this law. (5) Such as pruning, ploughing, sowing, etc. (6) Since it is the price of such labour as is permitted.

IT UP ON THE NEW YEAR,[7] IF THE MONTH HAD BEEN INTERCALATED,[8] [THE DEBT INCURRED BY THEN] IS REMITTED; BUT IF IT HAD NOT BEEN INTERCALATED, IT IS NOT REMITTED. [FINES FOR] OUTRAGES,[9] FOR SEDUCTION,[10] FOR DEFAMA-
a TION,[1] AND ALL OTHER OBLIGATIONS ARISING FROM LEGAL PROCEDURE,[2] ARE NOT CANCELLED. A LOAN SECURED BY A PLEDGE, AND ONE THE BONDS OF WHICH HAVE BEEN HANDED OVER TO A COURT, ARE NOT CANCELLED.[3]

MISHNAH 3. [A LOAN SECURED BY] A PROZBUL[4] IS NOT CANCELLED. THIS WAS ONE OF THE THINGS INSTITUTED BY HILLEL THE ELDER; FOR WHEN HE OBSERVED PEOPLE REFRAINING FROM LENDING TO ONE ANOTHER, AND THUS TRANSGRESSING WHAT IS WRITTEN IN THE LAW, 'BEWARE, LEST THERE BE A BASE THOUGHT IN THY HEART',[5] .... HE INSTITUTED THE PROZBUL.

MISHNAH 4. THIS IS THE FORMULA[6] OF THE PROZBUL: 'I DECLARE BEFORE YOU, SO-AND-SO,[7] JUDGES OF THAT PLACE,[7] THAT TOUCHING ANY DEBT THAT I MAY HAVE OUTSTANDING, I SHALL COLLECT IT WHENEVER I DESIRE'. AND THE JUDGES SIGN BELOW, OR THE WITNESSES.[8]

MISHNAH 5. AN ANTE-DATED PROZBUL IS LEGAL;[9] IF POST-DATED, IT IS ILLEGAL.[10] ANTE-DATED BONDS [OF LOANS]

(7) On the first of Tishri of the eighth year, he sells portions of it to purchasers. (8) I.e., Ellul, the preceding month, had been declared by the Beth din to possess thirty instead of twenty-nine days. Accordingly, the day when the cow was distributed among purchasers was the last day of the seventh year, and the debts are released. Note that debts were only released at the end of the seventh year; Deut. XV, 2. (9) Deut. XXII, 29. (10) Ex. XXII, 16. Penalty for both was fifty shekels.
a (1) Deut. XXII, 18, 19. Penalty, one hundred shekels. (2) All payments enjoined by the Beth din are regarded as if they were already claimed. (3) Being in the hands of the Beth din, the debt is considered as if it had already been paid. (4) It was a declaration made in court, to the effect that the law shall not apply to the loan transacted; cf. Pe'ah III, 6. For a full discussion v. Giṭ. 36*b* and note in Sonc. ed. a.l. (5) Deut. XV, 9. (6) Lit., 'the body of'. (7) The exact names being given. (8) The effect of this document was tantamount to the debt already having been collected before the advent of the Sabbatical year (v. *supra* 2). According to Asheri the time of writing the Prozbul was until the end of the sixth year; but Maim. is of the opinion that since the law of cancellation actually came into force at the end of the seventh year, it could be written even in the seventh year. (9) For the harm done by this is only to the lender himself; for should he lend any money after the drawing up of the Prozbul, the Prozbul will have no effect on the claim of the loan. (10) For all the debts contracted in the interval will be claimed in the seventh year, contrary to the law, which limits the operation of the Prozbul to loans made before it had been drawn up.

תורה אור

בראש השנה אם היה החדש מעובר משמט ואם לאו אינו משמט האונס והמפתה והמוציא שם רע וכל מעשה ב"ד אין משמטין המלוה (א) על המשכון והמוסר שטרותיו לב"ד אינן משמטין:

ג פרוזבול (ג) אינו משמט זה אחד מן הדברים שהתקין הלל הזקן כשראה שנמנעו העם מלהלוות זה את זה ועוברין על מה שכתוב בתורה השמר לך פן יהיה דבר עם לבבך בליעל וגו' התקין הלל פרוזבול:

ד זה (ג) גופו של פרוזבול מוסר אני לכם איש פלוני ופלוני הדיינים שבמקום פלוני שכל חוב שיש לי שאגבנו כל זמן שארצה והדיינים חותמין למטה או העדים:

ה פרוזבול המוקדם כשר והמאוחר פסול שטרי (ד) חוב המוקדמים פסולים

השמטת החוב ואין הלכה כרבי יהודה ולא כר' יוסי: ב אם היה החדש מעובר. ר"ל חדש אלול אם היה ל' יום ונעשה היום שחשב שהוא ראש השנה היום האחרון מאלול ונמצא כשמכר מכר בחוב קודס שנת השמטה שהוא לא חלק אותה אלא ב"מ שימתין בדמיה שהיום ההוא יום טוב החוב ואי אפשר למכור בו מכירה גמורה בפריעת דמים ובאה השמטה אחר זה נשמט החוב ואם נתברר שהיום ההוא יום ראש השנה לא נשמט חובו מפני שלא נעשה חובו בשנה שביעית: וכן הקנסות שחייב הכתוב לאונס ולמפתה ולמוציא שם רע אינם כשאר חובות אבל הם חיובים שהאיש נתחייב בהן והאיש ההוא לא יהיה פטור עד שיפרעם: וכל מעשה ב"ד נתבאר בגמרא שזהו פסקי הדיינים והוא שיאמר הדיין איש פלוני אתה חייב ליתן לזה כך וכך ואותו הממון לא יהיה נשמט שאחר שלוהו הדיין לתת כולו נכנס ברשות בעליו ואינו חוב והעיקר אצלנו בעל חוב קונה משכון ולפיכך כשילוה אותו על המשכון יהיה כאילו הקנהו המשכון בממון

תורה אור

והמאוחרין כשרים ‏א‏אחד לוה מחמשה כותב פרוזבול לכל א' וא' ‏ב‏חמשה לווין מאחד אינו כותב אלא פרוזבול אחד לכולם: ‏ו ‏ג‏אין א) כותבין פרוזבול אלא על הקרקע אם אין לו מזכה הוא בתוך שדהו כל שהוא ‏ד‏היתה לו שדה ממושכנת בעיר כותבין עליה פרוזבול רבי חוצפית אומר ‏ה‏כותבין לאיש על נכסי אשתו וליתומים על נכסי אפוטרופין: ‏ז כוורת ג) דבורים ר' אליעזר אומר (ה) הרי היא כקרקע ‏ו‏כותבין עליה פרוזבול ואינה מקבלת טומאה במקומה ‏ז‏והרודה ממנה בשבת חייב וחכמים אומרים אינה כקרקע ואין כותבין עליה פרוזבול ומקבלת טומאה במקומה והרודה ממנה בשבת פטור: ‏ח ‏ח‏המחזיר ג) חוב בשביעית יאמר לו משמט אני א"ל אעפ"כ יקבל ממנו שנא' °וזה דבר השמטה ‏ח‏כיוצא ד) בו רוצח שגלה לעיר מקלט ורצו אנשי העיר לכבדו יאמר להם רוצח אני אמרו לו אעפ"כ יקבל מהם שנא' °וזה דבר הרוצח: ‏ט ‏ט‏המחזיר חוב בשביעית רוח חכמים נוחה ממנו ‏י‏הלוה ה) מן הגר שנתגיירו בניו עמו לא יחזיר לבניו ואם החזיר רוח חכמים נוחה ממנו ‏כ‏כל המטלטלין נקנין במשיכה ‏ל‏וכל המקיים את דברו רוח חכמים נוחה ממנו:

סליק מסכת שביעית

a ARE NOT VALID,[1] BUT THOSE POST-DATED ARE VALID.[2] IF ONE BORROWS FROM FIVE PERSONS, A SEPARATE PROZBUL MUST BE MADE FOR EACH [CREDITOR]; BUT IF FIVE BORROW FROM THE SAME PERSON, THEN ONE PROZBUL ONLY WILL SUFFICE FOR THEM ALL.

MISHNAH 6. A PROZBUL IS WRITTEN ONLY FOR [A DEBT SECURED BY] IMMOVABLE PROPERTY; AND IF [THE DEBTOR] HAS NONE, THEN [THE CREDITOR] CAN GIVE HIM TITLE TO A SHARE, HOWEVER SMALL, OF HIS OWN FIELD.[3] IF HE[4] HAD LAND IN PLEDGE IN A CITY, A PROZBUL CAN BE WRITTEN ON [THE SECURITY THEREOF]. R. ḤUẒPETH SAYS: A PROZBUL MAY BE WRITTEN FOR A MAN ON THE SECURITY OF HIS WIFE'S PROPERTY,[5] OR FOR AN ORPHAN ON THE SECURITY OF PROPERTY BELONGING TO HIS GUARDIAN.[6]

MISHNAH 7. A BEE-HIVE, R. ELIEZER SAYS, IS CONSIDERED LANDED ESTATE;[7] A PROZBUL MAY BE DRAWN UP ON ITS SECURITY, AND IT IS NOT SUSCEPTIBLE TO UNCLEANNESS WHILE IT REMAINS IN ITS PLACE, AND HE WHO TAKES HONEY THEREFROM ON THE SABBATH DAY IS HELD CULPABLE.[8] THE SAGES, HOWEVER, SAY: IT IS NOT LIKE LANDED ESTATE, A PROZBUL MAY NOT BE DRAWN UP ON ITS SECURITY, IT DOES CONTRACT UNCLEANNESS WHILE IN ITS PLACE, AND HE WHO TAKES HONEY THEREFROM ON THE SABBATH IS EXEMPT FROM ANY PENALTY.

MISHNAH 8. IF ONE WOULD RETURN A DEBT IN THE SEVENTH YEAR, THE [CREDITOR] MUST SAY TO [THE DEBTOR]: 'I REMIT IT'; BUT SHOULD [THE LATTER] SAY: 'NONE-THE-LESS [I WILL REPAY IT]', HE MAY ACCEPT IT FROM HIM, BECAUSE IT
b SAYS: 'AND THIS IS THE WORD OF THE RELEASE'.[1] SIMILARLY, WHEN [AN INVOLUNTARY] MANSLAYER HAS ARRIVED AT HIS CITY OF REFUGE, AND THE CITIZENS THEREOF DESIRE TO DO HIM HONOUR, HE MUST SAY TO THEM: 'I AM A MURDERER'.[2] IF THEY SAY: '[NONE-THE-LESS WE WOULD HONOUR THEE]', THEN HE MAY ACCEPT [THE HONOUR] FROM THEM, BECAUSE IT SAYS: 'AND THIS IS THE WORD OF THE MANSLAYER'.[3]

MISHNAH 9. IF ONE REPAYS HIS DEBTS IN THE SEVENTH YEAR THE SAGES ARE WELL PLEASED WITH HIM. IF ONE BORROWS FROM A PROSELYTE WHOSE SONS HAD BECOME CONVERTED WITH HIM, THE DEBT NEED NOT BE REPAID TO HIS SONS;[4] BUT IF HE RETURNS IT THE SAGES ARE WELL PLEASED WITH HIM. ALL MOVABLE PROPERTY CAN BE ACQUIRED [ONLY] BY THE ACT OF DRAWING THEM;[5] BUT WHOSOEVER FULFILLS HIS [BARE] WORD, THE SAGES ARE WELL PLEASED WITH HIM.

מסכת שביעית

הדרן עלך והדרך על;

תורה אור

a (1) Because he will be illegally claiming from property which the debtor had sold before the actual transaction of the debt. (2) For the lender will then be harming only himself, as he will not be entitled to claim any property other than from such time mentioned in the bond. (3) Immovable property of little value is sufficient to secure a large debt (v. Tosaf. Yom. Tov.). (4) The debtor. (5) Even of his wife's estate of which the husband enjoys the fruit without the responsibility for loss or deterioration. (6) Where the guardian had borrowed money on behalf of the orphan. (7) All would agree with R Eliezer if it were attached to the soil with lime. On the other hand, were it suspended above ground on pegs, all would agree that it is movable property. The dispute only arose here, where the bee-hive is lying on the ground, unattached to the soil with lime; cf. 'Uk. III, 10. (8) 'Plucking' from the soil on Sabbath was classed under the category of reaping; Shab. VII, 2.

b (1) Deut. XV, 2. The emphasis is in *word*, hence by a single admission of the obligation to cancellation the law is fulfilled, and no qualms need be felt now at accepting the debt. (2) Cf. Mak. II, 8. (3) Deut. XIX, 4; having demurred but once at the honour extended to him, he may now be the recipient thereof. (4) Children of a proselyte are regarded as newly born; accordingly, they are not the legal heirs of their pagan father, and, consequently, cannot claim debts due to him. Nevertheless, if his debt is returned to them, the Rabbis are pleased with the debtor. (5) Into the possession of the purchaser; Ḳid. I, 4–5. Both parties could retract, even if money had already crossed hands, as long as the object to be acquired had not yet been drawn into the possession of the purchaser; v. Glos. s.v. *Meshikah*.

תלמוד בבלי

מסכת

תרומות

תלמוד בבלי

מסכת

תרומות

עם פירוש רש״י ותוספות
ובצירוף תרגום ופירוש והערות באנגלית

על ידי
ישעיה מאיר לערמן ז״ל

בעריכת
יחזקאל (איזידור) אפשטין ז״ל

דפוס שונצין
שנת להחזיר העטרה ליושנה לפ״ק
לונדון

HEBREW-ENGLISH EDITION OF
THE BABYLONIAN TALMUD

TERUMOTH

TRANSLATED INTO ENGLISH
WITH NOTES, GLOSSARY AND INDICES BY

RABBI DR. S.M. LEHRMAN, M.A., PH.D.

UNDER THE EDITORSHIP OF

RABBI DR. I. EPSTEIN, B.A., PH.D. LITT.D.

LONDON
THE SONCINO PRESS
1989

COPYRIGHT © THE SONCINO LTD. 1989
ALL RIGHTS RESERVED INCLUDING THE RIGHT TO
REPRODUCE THIS BOOK OR PARTS THEREOF IN ANY FORM

1-871055059

PUBLISHERS' NOTE

This HEBREW-ENGLISH EDITION of THE SONCINO TALMUD is being published to facilitate the easier reference to the original text by scholars and students.

The Soncino Press is privileged to be able to include the Novellae of Rabbi Moshe Feinstein o.b.m., on Tractate Terumoth (© Copyright 1973 Judaica Press Ltd), and we wish to thank Judaica Press Ltd. for permission to include this original material.

The Publishers wish to express their sincere thanks to Rabbi Dr. A. Melinek, B.A., Ph.D., for his painstaking care in examining the texts and making the necessary corrections for the preparation of these Tractates.

It has been necessary to duplicate some of the original Hebrew-Aramaic pages in this Tractate where the text has been of such length as to require more than one page of English translation.

MANUFACTURED IN THE UNITED STATES OF AMERICA

INTRODUCTION

The Tractate Terumoth (Heave-offering) deals in detail with the law of *terumah* (the Heave-offering) to be given to the priest, as set forth in Lev. XXII, 10–14 and Num. XVIII, 8, 11, 12, 26, 30. Though strictly confined to Palestine at first, it was early decided to include Babylon and the lands in the vicinity of Palestine. Nowadays, when most Jews live outside 'the Land', *terumah* is regarded as only of rabbinic origin, the main purpose being that the law should not be forgotten in Israel. This explains the leniency which the *halachah* so often adopts with regard to *terumah*. Before the *terumah* had been taken, the produce is *ṭebel* (untithed) and must not be eaten.

The Bible does not specify the amount to be given to the priest; the Rabbis, however, ordained that the average amount should be one-fiftieth of the produce, though the generous-minded could give one-fortieth and the mean-minded, one sixtieth. This gift of the Israelite's produce to the priest, was called *'Terumah Gedolah'* (Great Heave-offering). But there was also a heave-offering which the Levite had to give to the priest from the tithe he had received from the Israelite (Num. XVIII, 25) and known as the *'terumah* of the tithe' *(terumath ma'aser)*. Both classes of gifts come under the general term of *terumah*, which forms the theme of this Tractate.

CONTENTS OF THE TRACTATE

CHAPTER I discusses the classes of persons who may not set aside *terumah*, the different cases in which the heave-offering is considered valid, though the method by which they were selected is generally not permissible.

CHAPTER II cites other cases in which the *terumah* is valid *de facto*, though the method of procedure is not legitimate.

CHAPTER III quotes some cases where *terumah* had to be given twice and states that the owner is empowered to delegate his servant to take it for him. The order of the various dues is also given, as is the procedure to be followed on having made a slip of the tongue while taking *terumah* or making an oath.

CHAPTER IV deals with the amount of *terumah* and with the Heave-offering of tithe, which must be given according to measure.

CHAPTER V discusses admixtures of clean with unclean fruit of *terumah*.

CHAPTER VI with the compensation that must be made for deriving benefit from *terumah*.

CHAPTER VII concerns further cases of admixture and also with cases when both the value and additional Fifth had to be restored on eating *terumah*.

CHAPTER VIII introduces the subject of the wine of *terumah* that had been left uncovered and the dangers of poisoning; also that one must not wilfully defile *terumah*.

CHAPTER IX states the procedure when *terumah* has been deliberately or unwittingly sown.

CHAPTER X enumerates the cases in which the flavour of *terumah* makes other foods unlawful and the regulations regarding the cases in which lawful foods become forbidden through the flavour acquired from prohibited foods.

CHAPTER XI discusses the uses that may be made of clean and unclean heave-offerings both in solid and in liquid forms.

S. M. LEHRMAN

TERUMOTH

CHAPTER I

MISHNAH 1. FIVE MAY NOT GIVE TERUMAH, AND IF THEY
a DO SO, THEIR TERUMAH IS NOT CONSIDERED VALID:[1] THE ḤERESH [DEAF MUTE], THE IMBECILE,[2] THE MINOR,[3] AND THE ONE WHO GIVES TERUMAH FROM THAT WHICH IS NOT HIS OWN. IF A GENTILE GAVE TERUMAH FROM THAT WHICH BELONGS TO AN ISRAELITE, EVEN IF IT WAS WITH HIS FULL CONSENT, HIS TERUMAH IS NOT VALID.

MISHNAH 2. A ḤERESH, WHO SPEAKS BUT CANNOT HEAR, MAY NOT GIVE TERUMAH,[4] BUT IF HE DOES SO, HIS TERUMAH IS VALID.[5] THE ḤERESH OF WHOM THE SAGES GENERALLY SPEAK IS ONE WHO NEITHER HEARS NOR SPEAKS.

MISHNAH 3. IF A MINOR HAS NOT YET PRODUCED TWO HAIRS [OF PUBERTY] R. JUDAH SAYS: HIS TERUMAH IS VALID. R. JOSE SAYS: IF HE HAS NOT ARRIVED AT THE AGE WHEN HIS VOWS ARE VALID, HIS TERUMAH IS NOT VALID, BUT AS SOON AS HIS VOWS BECOME VALID, HIS TERUMAH BECOMES VALID.[6]

MISHNAH 4. TERUMAH SHOULD NOT BE TAKEN FROM
b OLIVES FOR OIL, OR FROM GRAPES FOR WINE.[1] IF THIS IS DONE,

a (1) And the produce remains forbidden to be eaten as *ṭebel* (v. Glos.) (2) V. Ḥag. 3*b* for some signs of idiocy, to which Maim. adds other instances. (3) A boy prior to the age of thirteen years and one day, and a girl of twelve years and one day. (4) As he cannot hear the blessing to be made when giving the *terumah;* v. Ber. II, 3; Meg. II, 4. (5) The omission of the blessing does not *de facto* affect the validity of the *terumah*, since he knows in whose honour the *terumah* is being given. (6) The age for vows is twelve years and a day for a boy, and eleven years and a day for a girl, when they already know to whom the vow is made. *Terumah* and vows all belong to the same category, since they all depend on the spoken word.

b (1) One who has olives and oil or grapes and wine subject to *terumah*, cannot take *terumah* from the olives or grapes to cover the amount of *terumah* due from both. From Num. XVIII, 27, it is inferred that *terumah* cannot be taken from produce still in the process of completion to cover also the *terumah* due from produce in a completed state. Hence olives or grapes cannot be classed together with oil or wine for purposes of *terumah*. Cf. *infra* I, 8.

אמר המעתיק [הר"מ] יוסף הקטן ב"ר יצחק נב"ת בן אלפואל חפשתי בכל המדינה על העתקת סדר זרעים ומצאתי ממנה מראש הסדר ועד סוף מסכת שביעית מהעתקת החכם הגדול הגבר הוקם על קצין על הלשונות רבי יהודה חריזי תמ"ך ומותר המסכתות לא מצאתי מאומה וכאשר היתה עלי יד אדון השלם החכם הגדול נר ישראל ר' **שלמה אדרת** ובכתב ידו זרזני וצוני על השלמת הסדר אחרי העתקת הסדר שנפל בגורלי סדר מועד ואין לשום אדם לזוז ממצותו אנה ואנה כל שכן אני הנרצה לעבודתו וזה השליח אשר הלצני אצתי רצתי למלאות מצותו ולהעתיק אלו המסכתות הנותרות ולעבוד עבודת הקדש ואמרתי לנפשי צאי לך בעקבי הרועים הגדולים אחרי הקוצרים ואלקטה בשבלים ואולי מן השמים יתנו לי שכר טרחי ועמלי כפועל בטל או כמריק מכלי אל כלי ומה יפה חבלי ומה נעים גורלי שזכיתי לעלות ולירא‍ות את פני האדון השם פה לאלם ופוקח עורים ועל כתפי אשא תרומות ומעשרות וחלה ונטע רבעי ובכורים ואולי אזכה להשלימה במפעל כמו במבטא וליהנות מסעודת לויתן ודם ענב וחלב כליות חטה ואע"פ שדחקתי עצמי ונכנסתי לפנים מן הראוי כמה פסיעות בהעתקת סדר מועד ידעתי שלא היה לי להכנס בכאן לפי שהשגיאות מצויות הנה יותר מפני מעוט ההרגל והלמוד בזה הסדר ואין מביאין קדשים לבית הפסול אבל כוונתי היתה למלאות מצות הגביר הנזכר ואפילו חרב מונחת על הכתף ומעשי לשם שמים והוא עדי וסהדי על כן אני מפיל תחנתי לפני כל רואיהן לברר מומיהן ולתקן טעיותיהן כי ידעתי שימצא שם הרבה מפני שהמסכתות אינן נהוגות כמו שזכרתי וקוצר דעתי הגובר על הכל והמתקן כפי יכלתו ישלם האל פעלו ותהי שלמה משכרתו אמן :

א ירושלמי (הל' א) ר' שמואל בר נחמן שמע לון לכולהון מן הכא דבר אל בני ישראל ויקחו לי תרומה(שמות כה) פרט לנכרי *מאת בני ישראל פרט לקטן אשר ידבנו לבו פרט לחרש שוטה דידבנו משמע דיש בו דעת לנדב כדדרשינן פ' טרף בקלפי (דף מג.)והניח מי שיש לו דעת להניח ותימה דלא ממעט קטן מידבנו לבו ויש לומר משום דכשבא לעונת נדרים יש בו דעת לנדב וזאת התרומה אשר תקחו מאתם פרט לתורם את שאינו שלו עוד דריש הת. מהאי קרא כן תרימו גם אתם אתם ולא שותפין אתם ולא אפוטרופין ופריך והא תני שותפין שתרמו זה אחר זה והוא משנה לקמן (בפ"ג מ"ב) לא פריך לר' עקיבא דאמר התם תרומת שניהן תרומה דלדידיה ניחא דלא קדשה אלא כל אחד לפי חלקו כמו שאפרש שם אבל לרבנן פריך דאמרי תרומת הראשון תרומה ומשני כאן לתרומה גדולה כאן לתרומת מעשר ופריך כלום למדו א] מתרומה גדולה אלא מתרומת מעשר אלא כאן להלכה כאן למעשר כלומר דיעבד תרומתו תרומה דשותפין לא קפדי אהדדי וחשיב כאילו מדעת חברו אבל לכתחלה לא יתרום גזירה שותף דלא קפיד אטו שותף דקפיד ותו פריך ולא אפוטרופין והתנן יתומים שסמכו אצל בעה"ב או שמינה להן אפוטרופין חייב לעשר את פירותיהן ומשני כאן באפוטרופין לעולם כאן באפוטרופין לשעה ופריך ר' יוסי אם באפוטרופין לעולם בדא תנן מוכר מטלטלין וזכן אבל לא קרקעות אלא כאן ביתום שאינו קטן ואותה משנה בפרק הניזקין (דף נב.) ומשני כאן

תרומות פרק ראשון

א חמשה א) לא א'יתרומו ואם תרמו אין תרומתן תרומה החרש והשוטה והקטן והתורם את שאינו שלו נכרי ג) שתרם את של ישראל אפילו ברשות אין תרומתו תרומה: **ב חרש** ג) ב'המדבר ואינו שומע לא יתרום ואם תרם תרומתו תרומה חרש ד) שדברו בו חכמים בכל מקום שאינו לא שומע ולא מדבר: **ג קטן** ה) שלא הביא שתי שערות ר"י אומר תרומתו תרומה רבי יוסי אומר ג'אם עד שלא בא לעונת נדרים אין תרומתו תרומה משבא לעונת נדרים תרומתו תרומה: **ד אין** תורמין זיתים על השמן ולא ענבים על היין

א **אמרם** בכל המשנה תרם ותורס ויתרום בעלי הלשון האחרונים מקפין על זה ואומרים כי השרש הרים ומרים וירים וזו אינה קושיא אמתית כיון שעיקר כל הלשון מן הלשונות הוא חוזר מה שמדברים בו בעלי אותו הלשון ומה שנשמע מהם ואלו בעלי המשנה בלא ספק עבריים היו במקומן ר"ל בארץ הצבי ונשמע מהם לשון תרם ובו נשתמשו הנה ראיה שהוא מקובל בלשון ושזו המלה לשון מלשונות העבריים, על זה הדרך תהיה התשובה לכל מי שיאמר מן האחרונים שלשון המשנה אינו לח או שהם נשתמשו במלו' שאינן כראוי בלשון וזה העיקר שזכרתי לך אמתי אצל החכמים השלמים המדברים על הדברים הכוללים כל הלשונות כלם ותרומה

לאכול כאן להניח: ירושלמי (שם) מאן תנא חרש דלא כר' יהודה דתניא א"ר יהודה מעשה בבניו של ר' יוחנן בן גודגדא שהיו חרשים והיו כל טהרות שבירושלים נעשין על גביהן ועוד תנא בפ' חרש (דף קיג.) ובריש מי שהחשיך (דף קנג.)

השמן ואינו תורם אלא לפי הזיתים כלומר כשתורם הזיתים על השמן אם ארבעה סאים זיתים מוציא סאתים שמן היה לו לתרום ד' סאין זיתים על ל"ח סאין שמן והוא לא עשה כן ולא הפריש עליהן אלא ב' סאין זיתים ופריך הגע עצמך שתרם לפי השמן ומשני כלון עבד כן וזמן חורון לא עבד כן כלומר גזירה דילמא לא עביד כן זימנא אחרינא עוד משני חברייא תמי ליה ואמר זה נתכוין לרבות (וזה)[ואני]לא מתכוין לרבות ותימה מה תירץ מ"מ קשיא מתני' דשילהי פירקי' דקתני תרומתו תרומה ולא חיישינן לגזל השבט ואין לתרץ דדוקא בזיתים ועגבים שצריך לאוצרם ויש טורח שייך גזל השבט [ולא] בשאר דברים דפלוגתא היא בירושלמי חזקיה אמר לא שנו אלא זיתים על השמן וענבים על היין הא שאר כל הדברים לא רבי יוחנן אמר לא שנייא היא זיתים על השמן וענבים על היין היא שאר כל הדברים אלמא דרבי יוחנן גופיה דמשני משום גזל השבט לא מפליג וכיוצא בזו תנן לקמן בפרקין (מ"ח) אין תורמין שמן על הזיתים הכתושים ולא יין על ענבים הנדרסות ואם תרם תרומה ויחזור ויתרום ופריך עלה בירושלמי ממתני' בסוף פרקין דקתני מדבר שנגמרה מלאכתו על דבר שלא נגמרה מלאכתו דהיינו משמן על זיתים תרומתן תרומה ולא קתני ויחזור ויתרום ומשני רבי אילא בשם רבי יוחנן מפני גדר מי חטאת שלא יהו מי חטאת בטלים והשתא מאי משני ההוא אסוף פרקין נמי נימא ויחזור ויתרום משום גדר מי חטאת והשתא קשיין הנך ג' משניות דהכא גבי זיתים על השמן וענבים על ... ולקמן גבי שמן על הזיתים ויין על הענבים קתני ... ובסוף פרקין קתני בכולהו תרומתו תרומה ול... ...ויחזור ויתרום ... תרומה ואין צריך לחזור ולתרום ואי לא ... אקמייתא דיש לחלק בין זיתים על שמן ... ירושלמי (שם) ברייתא דתני אין תורמין ... אם תרם תרומתו תרומה ואין צריך לתרום ... אומרים תורמים וב"ה אומרים אין תורמים ... הרי ברייתא זו קשה אמתני' דהכא ויש ... אין תרומתו תרומה אתורם שלא מדעת ... מן הכהן דזמנין דניחא ליה לכהן בזיתים ... אסור דיעבד תרומתו תרומה (ג) ורבי ... לפי השמן ואינו תורם אלא לפי הזיתים ... מתני' דעדיות לית כאן זיתים על השמן אלא ... נגמרה מלאכתו על דבר שנגמרה מלאכתו ... שאר פירות כגון מדבר שלא *נתרמה על

ד א מיי' פ"ה מהלכות תרומות הלכה יח סמג שם טוש"ע שם סעיף סב:

ה ב מיי' שם פ"ב הלכה ט ופ"ה הלכה יב:

ו ג מיי' שם פ"ה הלכה יג:

י ד מיי' שם הלכה יב וטוש"ע שם סעיף נח:

ח ה [מיי' שם הל' ט] שם סעיף נה:

ט ו [מיי' שם הל' יא] שם סעיף נז:

י ז [מיי' שם הל' יב] שם סעיף נח:

יא ח מיי' פ"ד שם הלכה ד טוש"ע שם סעיף לב:

א) קדושין פ"ג דף סב:

ואם תרמו ב"ש אומרים תרומת עצמן בהם ובה"א אין תרומתן תרומה: ה אין תורמין מן הלקט ומן השכחה ומן הפאה ומן ההפקר ולא ממעשר ראשון *שנטלה תרומתו ולא ממעשר שני והקדש *שנפדו ולא מן החייב על הפטור ולא מן הפטור על החייב ולא א) מן התלוש על המחובר ולא מן המחובר על התלוש ולא מן החדש על הישן ולא מן הישן על החדש ולא מפירות הארץ על פירות חו"ל ולא מפירות חו"ל על פירות הארץ ואם תרמו אין תרומתן תרומה: ו חמשה לא יתרומו ואם תרמו תרומתן תרומה האלם והשכור והערום והסומא ובעל קרי לא יתרומו ואם תרמו תרומתן תרומה:

הראויה לאותן הענבים ולאותו היין והוא חושב על מה שתרם מן הענבים שהוא תרומה על הכל בש"א כי זה שתרם מן הענבים יספיק לתרומה החייבת לענבים ונשאר עליו לתרום את היין וזהו ענין אמרו תרומת עצמן בהן: ובה"א איננה תרומה בשום פנים אלא אם יכוין שיהיו אלו הענבים תרומה על הענבים בלבד לא על הענבים ועל היין ולשון ספרי שומע אני יתרום שבלין על חטים וענבים על יין וזיתים על השמן ת"ל כדגן מן הגורן מן הגמור: ה ידוע כי הלקט והשכחה והפאה שהוא לעניים ואין לבעל השדה בהם זכות ולפיכך לא יתרום התרומה החייבת לשום דבר מנכסיו משום דבר מאלו הדברים הנזכרים שהם חוקי העניים אבל ההפקר אולי תהיה הסברא שיהיה מותר לו להוציא ממנו התרומה החייבת לממונו כיון שיש לו זכות בהפקר כי ההפקר מופקר לכל בני העולם אבל השי"ת אמר כי אין לו חלק ונחלה עמך (דברים יד) ואמר ממה שיש לך ואין לו ילא הפקר שידך וידו שוין: ואמרם ממעשר ראשון שנטלה ... מאחר שהוא חייב בתרומה בלי ספק ... ראוי לו להוציא ממנו שיעור התרומה ... לכהן באותו מעשר חק וזכות והיא ... ואח"כ יוציא ממנו התרומה החייבת ... שיתרום תרומה מפירות גמורים שכן ... מלאכתן שהן פטורין מן המעשרות ... השנה עם זרע שנה *הבאה ואין ... החייבת לשניהם וכל זה למאמר השם ... ר"ל ממנו בעינו שיוציא החק שהייב ...

פי' מהר"י בן מלכי צדק

מ"א א"ר חנינא מפני המורח של כהן לכך יתן לו שמן על שמן ויין על יין: ואם תרמו בית שמאי אומרים תרומת עצמן בהן ...

פירוש הרא"ש

(ג) ולכתחלה לא שמא פעם אחרת ...

BETH SHAMMAI SAY: THERE IS THEN TERUMAH OF [THE OLIVES OR GRAPES] THEMSELVES,[2] BUT BETH HILLEL SAY: THE [WHOLE] TERUMAH IS NOT VALID.[3]

MISHNAH 5. TERUMAH IS NOT TAKEN FROM 'GLEANINGS', FROM 'THE FORGOTTEN SHEAF', FROM PE'AH[4] OR FROM OWNERLESS PRODUCE.[5] [NEITHER IS IT TAKEN] FROM FIRST TITHE FROM WHICH ITS TERUMAH HAD ALREADY BEEN TAKEN,[6] NOR FROM SECOND TITHE AND DEDICATED PRODUCE THAT HAD NOT BEEN REDEEMED.[7] [NOR MAY IT BE TAKEN] FROM WHAT IS SUBJECT [TO TERUMAH] FOR THAT WHICH IS EXEMPT;[8] OR FROM THAT WHICH IS EXEMPT FOR THAT WHICH IS SUBJECT. ALSO, NOT FROM PRODUCE ALREADY PLUCKED [FROM THE SOIL] FOR THAT STILL ROOTED TO IT,[9] OR FROM THAT ROOTED [TO THE SOIL] FOR THAT ALREADY PLUCKED; ALSO, NOT FROM NEW PRODUCE[10] FOR OLD,[11] OR
a FROM OLD FOR NEW. ALSO NOT FROM FRUIT OF THE LAND[1] FOR FRUIT GROWN OUTSIDE THE LAND,[2] OR FROM THOSE GROWN WITHOUT THE LAND FOR THOSE GROWN IN THE LAND. [IN ALL THESE CASES] SHOULD THIS HAVE BEEN DONE, THE TERUMAH IS NOT VALID.

MISHNAH 6. FIVE MAY NOT GIVE TERUMAH, BUT IF THEY DO, THEIR TERUMAH IS VALID. HE THAT IS MUTE,[3] OR DRUNKEN,[4] OR NAKED,[5] OR BLIND,[4] OR HAS SUFFERED POLLUTION BY SEMEN;[6] THESE MAY NOT GIVE TERUMAH,[7] BUT IF THEY DO, THEIR TERUMAH IS VALID.[8]

(2) And separate *terumah* must again be given for the oil and the wine. (3) Accordingly, he must give the whole *terumah* anew, for the olives or grapes separately, and the oil and wine separately. (4) V. Pe'ah IV, 10—11, V. 7. Since they are dues belonging to the poor, they are exempt from *terumah* which can only be taken from produce of which one is the owner; but even the poor themselves cannot take *terumah* from these gifts for any other produce he may have, since these are originally exempt, v. *infra*. (5) By renouncing all ownership before the process of completion of the produce had ended, the owner renders it exempt from *terumah*. (6) I.e., the *terumah* of the tithe, even though the *terumah gedolah* had not been given. (If the Levite had obtained tithe from ears of corn, when fully grown, the produce is exempt from *terumah gedolah*). (7) Since not having been redeemed, these are not his property but the property of the Sanctuary. (8) E.g., not having yet reached a third of their full growth; cf. R.H. 13. (9) *Terumah* could only be given from detached produce. (10) Grown that year; Deut. XIV, 22. (11) That grown last year; cf. ibid. XIV, 22.
a (1) Palestine. Syria is here included. (2) The general name for the lands of the Diaspora, where fruits are exempt from *terumah*, as they do not possess the desired sanctity. (3) He can hear, but cannot speak, and his disqualification is due to his inability to recite the blessing when taking the *terumah*. (4) Being drunk or blind, he might take *terumah* from inferior produce and Num. XVIII, 29 explicitly tells us that it must be of the very best (מכל חלבו). The term DRUNKEN is applied to one who could not appear in the presence of a king (Bert.); but if the state of inebriation resembled that of Lot, his action was invalid even '*de facto*'. (5) Derived from Deut. XXIII, 15; no blessing may be recited before any nakedness. (6) Before ritual ablution, he was debarred from reciting any blessing. Lest it be asked: Why does not the Mishnah include these five classes under the one category of all those unable to recite the requisite blessing? The answer is, that if even one man combined within himself all these five disqualifications, his action would be valid. (7) The repetition to emphasize that on no account may they give *terumah* at the outset, relying on its validity after the act (Maim.). (8) Important as the blessing over the *terumah* is, the non-recital thereof does not invalidate the *terumah*. The same is true of having taken *terumah* from inferior produce (*infra* II, 6).

MISHNAH 7. TERUMAH MAY NOT BE GIVEN ACCORDING TO MEASURE,[9] OR WEIGHT, OR NUMBER, THOUGH ONE MAY
a GIVE IT FROM THAT WHICH HAS ALREADY BEEN MEASURED,[1] WEIGHED OR COUNTED. TERUMAH MAY NOT BE GIVEN IN A BASKET OR A HAMPER OF A MEASURED CAPACITY,[2] BUT IF THEY BE ONLY [ABOUT A] HALF OR A THIRD FILLED, ONE MAY GIVE TERUMAH IN THEM. TERUMAH MAY NOT BE GIVEN IN [A VESSEL] CONTAINING A SE'AH, THOUGH IT BE ONLY A HALF FULL, FOR THIS HALF CONSTITUTES A KNOWN MEASURE.[3]

MISHNAH 8. OIL MAY NOT BE GIVEN AS TERUMAH FOR OLIVES DUE TO BE CRUSHED,[4] NOR MAY WINE FOR GRAPES DUE TO BE TRODDEN; IF, HOWEVER, ONE HAS DONE SO, HIS TERUMAH IS VALID,[5] BUT HE MUST GIVE TERUMAH ANEW.[6] THE FIRST TERUMAH RENDERS [PRODUCE INTO WHICH IT HAD FALLEN] MEDUMMA'[7] AND IS SUBJECT TO THE ADDED FIFTH,[8] BUT NOT THE SECOND.[9]

MISHNAH 9. TERUMAH MAY BE GIVEN FROM OIL FOR
b OLIVES DUE FOR PICKLING[1], OR FROM WINE FOR GRAPES ABOUT TO BE MADE INTO RAISINS.[2] HE WHO GIVES TERUMAH FROM OIL FOR OLIVES INTENDED FOR EATING,[3] OR FROM [OTHER] OLIVES FOR OLIVES INTENDED FOR EATING, OR FOR WINE FOR GRAPES INTENDED FOR EATING, OF FROM [OTHER] GRAPES FOR GRAPES INTENDED FOR EATING, AND DECIDES AFTERWARDS TO PRESS THEM,[4] NEED NOT GIVE TERUMAH ANEW.[5]

MISHNAH 10. TERUMAH MAY NOT BE TAKEN FROM PRODUCE IN A FINISHED STATE[6] FOR PRODUCE IN AN UNFINISHED STATE,[7] OR FROM PRODUCE IN AN UNFINISHED STATE FOR PRODUCE IN A FINISHED STATE. NOR CAN IT BE TAKEN FROM PRODUCE IN AN UNFINISHED STATE FOR OTHER PRODUCE IN AN UNFINISHED STATE. IF, HOWEVER, TERUMAH HAD BEEN TAKEN, IT IS CONSIDERED VALID.[8]

CHAPTER II

MISHNAH 1. TERUMAH MAY NOT BE GIVEN FROM THE
c CLEAN FOR THE UNCLEAN,[1] BUT IF IT IS GIVEN, THE TERUMAH IS VALID.[2] IN TRUTH THEY HAVE SAID:[3] IF A CAKE OF PRESSED

(9) From Num. XVIII, 27 it was derived that *terumah* could only be given approximately. Since even 'the giving of one wheat exempts the whole pile', the amount given varied with the disposition of the giver and mattered not from the legal standpoint. The heave-offering of tithe had to be measured. The order followed in the Mishnah corresponds to that which was more usual. Only a minority gave it by counting.

a (1) Prior to the giving of *terumah*, the untithed produce would often be measured or weighed. (2) Though he had not measured the whole pile nor intended the basket to serve as a measure. This was to avoid the very semblance of wrong-doing. 'A thing forbidden for appearance sake, is forbidden even in the strictest privacy' (Bez. 9a). (3) Unlike a basket nor hamper, it was usual to have in a *se'ah* measure indications marking the proportional capacity of measurement at different heights in the measure; hence it was forbidden even in a *se'ah* which has no such indications. (4) For the oil to come. *Terumah* cannot be given from produce in a finished state, as oil, for oil that is still awaiting the final process—in these cases, the olives and the grapes. (5) Having fulfilled the command of the Torah, if not according to Rabbinic interpretation. (6) In order to lend strength to the ruling of the Rabbis, fresh *terumah* had to be taken after the olives and grapes had been turned into oil and wine respectively. It is not clear from our Mishnah whether even the second *terumah* (really a fine) must be given to the priest free, as his right due; or in view of his having fulfilled the Biblical command the first time, he may sell the second *terumah* to the priest; cf. *infra* V, 1. (7) מדומע. Lit., 'that which becomes *demai*,' (the priest's share of the produce, v. Ex. XXII, 28). If the *hullin* into which the *terumah* had fallen is less than 100 times the quantity of the amount that had fallen in, the whole produce becomes forbidden to non-priests and must be sold to priests with the exception of the value of the *terumah* therein, for which no money may be taken; (v. Glos.). (8) V. Lev. V. 16. (9) Since this second *terumah* was only imposed as a fine, it does not have the same sanctity as the first *terumah*, which fulfilled the injunction of the Torah. The reason why the same alternative is not given in *supra* I, 4 is because it would involve loss to the priest if *terumah* were allowed to be taken *'de facto'* from olives for oil. In our Mishnah, no such loss is entailed, hence this second giving of *terumah* makes even the first valid.

b (1) To preserve them, they were placed in salt or vinegar. Though the olives were still awaiting this final process, the Rabbis regarded them as finished products and *terumah* could, accordingly, be taken from oil on their behalf. (2) When they would no longer be deemed grapes at all. The amount of *terumah* to be given from the oil and wine must be according to the quantity yielded after the olives had been preserved and the grapes converted into raisins. (3) The best olives or grapes were eaten in their natural state. (4) Instead of his original intention of eating them; cf. Demai III, 2. (5) Having fulfilled his duty with the first giving of *terumah*, since both the grapes and olives were fit for food and were in a finished state. (6) Lit., 'a thing, the work of which is finished'. After e.g., corn had been winnowed and shaped into a pile and taken into the house for food. (7) E.g., not yet winnowed or stacked up. The priest had to be spared unnecessary trouble. From Num. XVIII, 29 it was inferred that both the produce from which *terumah* is taken and that for which it is taken must be in their finished stages; cf. Ma'as. I, 2. (8) This cannot refer to olives and grapes, concerning which *supra* I, 4 declared the *terumah* invalid even *'de facto'*; it must, therefore, refer to other kinds of fruit.

c (1) Being afraid that the unclean fruit defiles by contact the clean, he might take the *terumah* from produce that is not lying near by, contrary to the regulation; v. Hal. I, 9. (2) Being only a precautionary measure, the fear was expressed at the outset only. (3) באמת; v. Kil. II, 2.

בון חד חסיד שאל לאליהו [ערום] מהו שיקרא את שמע א"ל ולא יראה בך ערות דבר ערות דיבור ותני חזקיה בין נקרות בין נבדך : ז לא במדה. מלוה לעשות מאומד כדי שיתרום בעין יפה בירושלמי (שם) תני אבא אלעזר בן גומל אומר מנין שאין תורמין לא במדה ולא במשקל ולא במנין ת"ל (במדבר יח) ונחשב לכם תרומתכם במחשבה את תורם ואין את תורם במדה במשקל ובמנין ואם תאמר מפרק כל הגט (דף ל:) דמפרש אביי בן ישראל שאמר לבן לוי כך אמר לי אבא מעשר יש לך בידי או מעשר לאביך בידי חוששים לתרומת מעשר שבו דכיון דלא קיץ ליה לא היה מתקן ליה בעל הבית כור מעשר לאביך בידי אין חוששין לתרומת מעשר

יב א מיי' פ"ג מהלכות תרומות הלכה ד :
יג ב מיי' פ"ה שם הלכה יט :
יד ג שם הלכה יח טוש"ע י"ד סי' שלא סעיף סב :
טו ד מיי' שם הל' כ:
טז ה שם הלכה ד

ז אין תורמין לא במדה ולא במשקל ולא במנין אבל תורם הוא את המדוד ואת השקול ואת המנוי אין תורמין בסל ובקופה שהם של מדה אבל תורם הוא בהן חציין ושלישן לא יתרום בסאה חציה שחציה מדה : ח אין תורמין שמן על זיתים הנכתשים ולא יין על ענבים הנדרכות ואם תרם תרומה ויחזור ויתרום הראשונה מדמעת בפני עצמה וחייבין עליה חומש אבל לא שניה: ט ותורמין שמן על זיתים הנכבשים ויין על ענבים לעשותן צמוקין הרי שתרם שמן על זיתים לאכילה וזיתים על זיתים לאכילה ויין על ענבים לאכילה וענבים על ענבים לאכילה ונמלך לדורכן אינו צריך לתרום : י אין תורמין מדבר שנגמרה מלאכתו על דבר שלא נגמרה מלאכתו ולא מדבר שלא נגמרה מלאכתו על דבר שנגמרה מלאכתו ולא מדבר שלא נגמרה מלאכתו על דבר שלא נגמרה מלאכתו ואם תרמו תרומתן תרומה:

פרק שני

א אין תורמין מטהור על הטמא ואם תרמו תרומתן תרומה באמת אמרו העגול

ב א מיי' פ"ה מהל' תרומות הל' ח:
ג ב מיי' שם:
ד נ מיי' פכ"ג מהלכות שבת הל' ח סמג לאוין סה:
ה ד מיי' שם טוש"ע א"ח סימן שלט סעיף ד:

א) יבמות סט. פסחים לג: מנחות כה: ב) ביצה יז: ג) שם גיטין כד· ד) שבת לח· כתובות לד· גיטין נג: ב"ק ע"א· חולין טו· ה) בכורות נג: תמורה ה': ו) ברכות לט: מנחות נה.

מן הטהור על הטהור ומן הטמא על הטמא ומן הטהור על הטמא ואינה ניטלת מטמא על הטהור רבי נחמיה אומר כשם שאינה ניטלת מן הטמא על הטהור כך אינה ניטלת מן הטהור על הטמא ומודה רבי נחמיה בדמאי והך דרשה אסמכתא בעלמא ועיקר טעמא משום דבעי מוקף וגזרינן דלמא תרם שלא מן המוקף משום דמסתפי דלמא נגע טהור בטמא ותרומת מעשר ניטלת מטהור על הטמא משום דתרומת מעשר לא בעיא מוקף כדאמר בירושלמי דמלמדת ואינה למדה ותדע (א) אי מדאורייתא מה לי חד עיגול מה לי ב' עיגולין אבל למאי דפרשינן ניחא ומיהו גם מזה אין כל כך ראיה דהא אמרינן בירושלמי (שם) אעיגול ואגודה

דמתני' באמת א"ר אליעזר בכל מקום ששנו באמת הלכה למשה מסיני ומיהו לאו דוקא: העיגול של דבלה שנטמא מקצתו· אע"פ שהדבלות מדובקות זו בזו אינו חיבור לטומאה ודכוותה תנן במס' טבול יום (פ"ה) ובירושלמי פריך (שם) כיון שנטמא מקצתו אין כולו טמא ומשני במחובר במי פירות והיינו כרבי עקיבא דטבול יום פרק שלישי (מ"ד) גבי עיסה שהוכשרה ונילושה במי פירות ונגע בה טבול יום דקאמר ר' עקיבא לא פסל אלא מקום מגעו ותניא בתוספתא דעוקלין אין לך דבר שמחבר את האוכלין אלא ז' משקין בלבד ופריך בירושלמי (שם) ואין סופו ליחלק ולעשותו שנים ומשני תיפתר שקרא לה שם במחובר כלומר קודם שנחלק העגול מותר לקרות שם: וכן אגודה של ירק· מפרש בירושלמי (שם) בשנטמאת ועודה אגודה אבל נטמאת קלחין אגדלא ועביד לריכותא דאילו תנינן עגול ולא תנינן אגודה הוינן אמרין עגול שכולו גוף אחד תורם אגודה שאינו גוף א' אינו תורם (ב): ערימה·כרי (ג): ר"א אומר תורם מן הטהור על הטמא במסכת חלה (פ"ב מ"ח) תנן גבי חלה ר"א אומר ניטלת מן הטהור על הטמא· ובפרק כשם שהמים (דף ל·) מייתי לה ופירש שם בקונטרס דקשיא היא דרישא דמתניתין (שם מ"ז) כדגן מהגורן וכמלאה מן היקב זו ראיה שדינה קודם הוצאת התרומה ממנו

העגול של דבלה שנטמא מקצתו תורם מן הטהור שיש בו על הטמא שיש בו וכן אגודה של ירק וכן ערימה היו שני עגולים שני אגודות שתי ערימות אחת טמאה ואחת טהורה לא יתרום מזה על זה ר"א אומר תורמין מן הטהור על הטמא:

ב אאין) תורמין מן הטמא על הטהור ואם תרם שוגג תרומתו תרומה ומזיד לא עשה כלום וכן בן לוי שהיה לו מעשר טבל היה מפריש עליו והולך שוגג מה שעשה עשוי מזיד לא עשה כלום ר' יהודה אומר באם היה יודע בו בתחלה אע"פ שהוא שוגג לא עשה כלום: ג גהמטבילג) כלים בשבת שוגג ישתמש בהם מזיד לא ישתמש בהם דהמעשר ג) הוהמבשלד) בשבת בשוגג יאכל מזיד לא יאכל הנוטע בשבת שוגג יקיים מזיד יעקור ובשביעית בין שוגג בין מזיד יעקור:

ד זאיןה) תורמין ממין על שאינו מינו ואם תרם אין תרומתו תרומה וכל מין חטים אחד כל מין תאנים וגרוגרות ודבלה אחד ותורם מזה על זה חכלו) מקום שיש כהן תורם מן היפה וכל מקום שאין כהן תורם מן המתקיים רבי יהודה אומר

שאמר באמת הוא הלכה למשה מסיני: עגול של דבלה. הוא ככר גדול כמו רחים שעושין מהתאנים היבשים ונקראת דבלה ולפי שהיא מחוברת מחלקים רבים לא נחשב אותם כגוף אחד שיהא חבור ומקבל טומאה כולה כמו שיתבאר במקומה מן טבול יום (פ"ג משנה ו) והוא מביא לך שני דמיונים מלבד העגול כי העגול כולו גוף אחד אבל אגודה של ירק גופים מחולקים ואין שם ידוע לכלל האגודה והודיעך כי כמו שהוא מותר בעגול כמו כן מותר באגודה שהיא פחותה מן הדבלה במעלות הדבוק וגם כן בערימה שהיא יותר פחותה מן האגודה בדבוק ואין הלכה כרבי אליעזר: ב בתנאי שיהיה זה הדבר הטמא שהיתה לו שעת הכושר ואח"כ נטמא אבל אם היה נטמא קודם שתגמור מלאכתו ולא בא לעונת המעשרות אפילו בשוגג אין תרומתו תרומה: ומעשר טבל א] הוא מעשר ראשון קודם שיוציאו ממנו תרומת מעשר כי כאמר ה' ית' (במדבר יח) ונחשב לכם תרומתכם

FIGS[4] HAD BECOME PARTLY DEFILED, TERUMAH MAY BE TAKEN FROM THE CLEAN PART FOR THAT PART WHICH HAD BECOME DEFILED. THE SAME APPLIES TO A BUNCH OF VEGETABLES,[5] OR A STACK OF GRAIN.[6] IF THERE WERE TWO CAKES [OF FIGS], TWO BUNCHES, TWO STACKS OF GRAIN, AND ONE OF THEM WAS DEFILED AND THE OTHER CLEAN, TERUMAH CANNOT BE GIVEN FROM ONE FOR THE OTHER. R. ELIEZER SAYS THAT ONE CAN GIVE TERUMAH FROM THAT WHICH IS CLEAN FOR THAT WHICH IS DEFILED.[7]

MISHNAH 2. TERUMAH MAY NOT BE GIVEN FROM UNCLEAN [PRODUCE] FOR THAT WHICH IS CLEAN;[8] AND IF IT IS GIVEN UNWITTTINGLY,[9] THE TERUMAH IS VALID; IF INTEN-
a TIONALLY THE ACT IS VOID.[1] SO TOO, IF A LEVITE HAD [UNCLEAN] TITHE [FROM WHICH TERUMAH] HAD NOT BEEN GIVEN,[2] AND HE GAVE TERUMAH FROM THIS,[3] IF PERFORMED IN ERROR HIS ACTION IS VALID;[4] BUT IF INTENTIONALLY[5] HIS ACT IS OF NO EFFECT. R. JUDAH SAYS: IF HE KNEW OF IT AT THE OUTSET,[6] EVEN IF DONE IN ERROR, HIS ACTION IS OF NO EFFECT.

MISHNAH 3. HE WHO IMMERSES [UNCLEAN] VESSELS ON THE SABBATH[7] IN ERROR MAY USE THEM,[8] BUT IF DONE DELIBERATELY HE MAY NOT USE THEM.[9] HE WHO SEPARATES TITHES,[10] OR COOKS ON THE SABBATH, UNWITTINGLY, MAY EAT OF IT,[11] BUT IF INTENTIONALLY, HE MAY NOT EAT OF IT. HE WHO PLANTS ANYTHING ON THE SABBATH[12] IN ERROR CAN ALLOW IT TO REMAIN, BUT IF DELIBERATELY MUST UPROOT IT. BUT DURING THE SABBATICAL YEAR, WHETHER [IT WAS PLANTED] UNWITTINGLY OR DELIBERATELY[13] HE MUST UPROOT IT.

MISHNAH 4. TERUMAH MAY NOT BE GIVEN FROM ONE
b KIND FOR ANOTHER KIND,[1] AND IF ONE DOES SO, THE TERUMAH IS NOT VALID. ALL KINDS OF WHEAT[2] COUNT AS ONE,[3] ALL KINDS OF FRESH FIGS, DRIED FIGS AND FIG CAKES COUNT AS ONE,[4] AND TERUMAH CAN BE TAKEN FROM ONE FOR THE OTHER.[5] WHEREVER THERE IS A PRIEST, ONE MUST GIVE TERUMAH OF THE VERY BEST,[6] AND WHERE THERE BE NO PRIEST, TERUMAH MUST BE GIVEN OF THAT KIND WHICH KEEPS LONGEST.[7] R. JUDAH SAYS: AT ALL TIMES MUST IT BE

(4) Though all the figs are closely pressed together, the presence of one that is unclean does not contaminate the others, because of the absence of any of the seven liquids (dew, water, wine, oil, blood, milk, and bees' honey) that render edibles susceptible to levitical uncleanness (Maksh. VI; 4; Ṭebul Yom II, 3). The figs are connected only by their own juice, and fruit-juice does not render food susceptible to defilement; cf. Lev. XI, 34. (5) Not so tightly compressed into one mass as a cake of pressed figs. (6) Not even tied together as the vegetables. Since each of these three instances is not similar, all the three are quoted. (7) He does not fear lest he will contravene the rule mentioned in n. 1; cf. Ḥal. II, 8. (8) Since defiled *terumah* had to be burnt, he would thus be robbing the priest of his due. (9) Provided that it was at one time clean and subject to tithe, otherwise it could not be deemed *terumah*.
a (1) A fresh *terumah* is necessary, as in *supra* I, 8. According to some, even the second *terumah* is of no effect if done with intention. (2) The *terumah* of the tithe he had to give to the priest. (3) To serve as *terumah* for other untithed produce in his possession; cf. Ḥal. IV, 6. The expression היה מפריש עליו והולך means that from the very first he had set aside this tithe for this purpose, discovering only later that it had been defiled. (4) After his action, he discovered that it had been unclean. (5) Since it could not be considered *terumah* when he separated it. (6) He maintains that forgetfulness cannot be considered 'in error'. (7) When it is forbidden, being considered the equivalent of repairing and thus constituting work. (8) Even on the Sabbath day itself. (9) He must wait till the termination of the Sabbath. (10) An act considered as work since it qualifies the *ṭebel* to be eaten. (11) When Sabbath terminates. The reason why the cases of tithe and cooking are cited together is because the words 'he may eat' can be applied to them both; otherwise, the instance of tithe would have been better bracketed with the case of vessel immersion. (12) Planting is forbidden on the Sabbath. (13) Though the average Israelite would not lightly break the Sabbath, he was suspected of treating the Seventh year lightly; hence no distinction is drawn here between the unwitting and deliberate transgression.
b (1) E.g., from wheat for barley. (2) Either reddish or white in hue; B.B. V, 6. (3) For the purpose of *terumah*. (4) The black and the white species are regarded of one kind. (5) E.g., from fig cakes for fresh figs. (6) The kind best to eat, i.e., fresh figs. (7) Dried figs keep longer than fresh figs.

GIVEN ONLY FROM THE VERY BEST.[8]

MISHNAH 5. A WHOLE ONION, THOUGH SMALL, SHOULD BE GIVEN AS TERUMAH RATHER THAN HALF OF A LARGE ONION.[9] R. JUDAH SAYS: NOT SO, BUT HALF OF A LARGE ONION.[10] SO TOO, R. JUDAH SAID: TERUMAH SHOULD BE GIVEN FROM TOWN ONIONS FOR THOSE OF THE VILLAGE,[11] BUT NOT FROM VILLAGE ONIONS FOR THOSE OF THE TOWN, SINCE THESE[12] ARE THE FOOD OF ITS PRINCIPAL CITIZENS.[13]

MISHNAH 6. TERUMAH MAY BE GIVEN FROM OLIVES [TO BE USED] FOR OIL FOR THOSE DUE TO BE PRESERVED,[14] BUT NOT FROM OLIVES DUE TO BE PRESERVED FOR OLIVES [TO BE USED] FOR OIL. [IT MAY BE GIVEN] FROM UNBOILED WINE FOR BOILED WINE, BUT NOT FROM BOILED WINE FOR UNBOILED WINE. THIS IS THE GENERAL RULE: ANY TWO THINGS WHICH
a TOGETHER INFRINGE THE LAW OF DIVERSE KINDS[1] CANNOT BE USED FOR TERUMAH FROM ONE FOR THE OTHER, EVEN IF THE KIND FROM WHICH IT IS GIVEN BE SUPERIOR TO THE ONE FOR WHICH IT IS GIVEN;[2] BUT IF THEY DO NOT CONSTITUTE DIVERSE KINDS, THEN ONE MAY GIVE TERUMAH FROM THE SUPERIOR KIND FOR THAT WHICH IS INFERIOR, BUT NOT FROM THE INFERIOR KIND FOR THAT WHICH IS SUPERIOR. IF ONE DOES GIVE TERUMAH FROM THE INFERIOR KIND FOR THAT WHICH IS SUPERIOR, HIS TERUMAH IS VALID,[3] EXCEPTING WHEN TARES[4] ARE GIVEN FOR WHEAT, SINCE THESE ARE NOT FOOD. CUCUMBERS AND SWEET MELONS[5] COUNT AS ONE KIND.[6] R. JUDAH SAYS: TWO KINDS.

CHAPTER III

MISHNAH 1. IF ONE GAVE A CUCUMBER AS TERUMAH AND IT WAS FOUND TO BE BITTER, OR A MELON AND IT WAS FOUND
b TO BE ROTTEN, IT MAY BE CONSIDERED TERUMAH,[1] BUT HE MUST AGAIN GIVE TERUMAH.[2] IF ONE GAVE A JAR OF WINE AS TERUMAH AND IT WAS FOUND TO BE OF VINEGAR, IF PRIOR TO HIS ACT HE KNEW THAT IT WAS VINEGAR,[3] THE TERUMAH IS NOT VALID; BUT IF IT HAD TURNED SOUR AFTER HE HAD GIVEN IT AS TERUMAH, HIS ACTION IS VALID.[4] IN CASE OF DOUBT,[5] IT IS TERUMAH BUT HE MUST AGAIN GIVE TERUMAH.[6] THE FIRST DOES NOT OF ITSELF MAKE ANY OTHER PRODUCE[7] MEDUMMA', NOR IS IT SUBJECT TO THE LAW OF THE FIFTH.[8] THE SAME APPLIES TO THE SECOND [TERUMAH].[9]

MISHNAH 2. IF ONE OF THEM[10] FALLS INTO COMMON
c PRODUCE,[1] IT DOES NOT MAKE [THE MIXTURE] MEDUMMA'.[2] IF THE SECOND [PORTION OF TERUMAH] FALLS [THEN] INTO ANOTHER PLACE,[3] IT ALSO DOES NOT MAKE IT MEDUMMA'; BUT IF BOTH FALL INTO ONE PLACE,[4] THEY DO MAKE IT MEDUMMA', ACCORDING TO THE SIZE OF THE SMALLER OF THE TWO.[5]

MISHNAH 3. IF [TWO] PARTNERS TOOK TERUMAH, THE ONE AFTER THE OTHER,[6] R. AKIBA SAYS: THE TERUMAH OF THEM BOTH IS VALID;[7] BUT THE SAGES SAY: ONLY THE TERUMAH OF THE FIRST IS VALID.[8] R. JOSE SAYS:[9] IF THE FIRST

(8) Cf. Num. XVIII, 30. (9) Whole onions keep longest, and where there is no priest, these are to be given preference. (10) Since it is the best; v. *supra* 4. (11) Those from the town are better and healthier to eat, though wild onions of the villages keep longest; cf. Ned. 66*a*. (12) Those of the town. (13) Bert. renders: of royal courtiers. Village onions have a more pungent flavour and, being inferior, cannot be given as *terumah* for that of a superior kind. (14) Being from a superior kind for an inferior kind. (Olives which were pickled in vinegar had not oil.) The same reason applies to the case of wine.

a (1) V. Kil. I, 1—2. (2) Even '*de facto*', the *terumah* would not be valid. (3) Since they are not of two kinds. (4) Field-seed or vetch similar to wheat used as animal fodder and unfit for human food. (5) An apple-shaped melon, probably the fruit-squash (Jast); v. Kil. I, 2. (6) For *terumah* purposes.

b (1) Since it was given unintentionally; besides even a bad cucumber is used for human food in emergency. (2) A penalty for not tasting thereof prior to giving it away. Being only a Rabbinical prohibition, tasting thereof was first allowed. (3) Wine and vinegar were regarded as of two different kinds. (4) He cannot be held responsible after having discharged his obligation. (5) Whether it had turned sour before or after his act. (6) Both are given to the priest. Being a doubt concerning a Biblical prohibition, we adopt stringency and pronounce even the first portion as *terumah*. The priest, however, can have definite claim only to the second portion, which is smaller than the first, having been taken from a diminished pile, and consequently he can be asked to return the value of the first portion, on the principle that in case of doubt the claimant must bring proof of his claim. (7) Should the first portion of *terumah* fall into common produce of less than a hundred times its quantity, it does not make the whole subject to *terumah*. (8) A non-priest eating any of the two portions of terumah is not required to return its value, plus the requisite Fifth, as in the case of having eaten that which was unquestionably *terumah*; cf. Lev. V, 16. (9) For of each it can be said that the other is the real *terumah*, and this only common produce. (10) This Mishnah elaborates the one previous.

c (1) Heb. *ḥullin*, produce from which *terumah* has been taken, as opposed to untithed produce (*tebel*) (2) Since neither of them can definitely be said to be *terumah*. (3) Also common produce. (4) That is into *ḥullin* less than a hundred times the amount of both. (5) If there be a hundred times the amount of the second *terumah*, which is smaller, the *ḥullin* may be eaten after he had given to the priest the amount of the two portions that had fallen in. (6) If from a pile of fifty *se'ahs* held in joint ownership, each took one *se'ah* as *terumah*, (1/50th being the amount usually given). (7) Each of the two *se'ahs* can only be considered half *terumah* and half *ḥullin*, as each partner gave *terumah* without permission of the other. They then must give the two *se'ahs* to the priest, and the priest returns them the value of the price of one. (8) They hold that the whole *se'ah* of the first is *terumah*, and that of the second *ḥullin*. (9) Explaining the view of the sages.

א) ברכות פ"ו דף לט: ב)[תמורה ה.]: ג) יבמות פ"י דף פט. וקדושין פ"ב דף מו: ד) תמורה פ"א דף יג. [ע"ש בגמרא ובתוספות]:

ה קטן שלם מתקיים וחצי גדול יפה ממנו וטוב לאכילה (ט) ואזדו לטעמייהו בצלים מבני המדינה טובים מן הכופרים אבל אין מתקיימין : כופרים · מלשון כפר : פוליטיקין אבני מדינה קאי כלומר מאכל בני אדם חשובין ופי' בערוך פוליטיקין בני פלטין ויש אומרים מטעמת מלכים : ו זיתי כבש שכבושין בחומץ כדי להתקיים אבל זיתי שמן טובים מהן לאכילה ושאינו מבושל יפה מן המבושל אבל המבושל מתקיים יותר וכל זה מדברי רבי יהודה דתורם מן היפה ובירושלמי (הל' ה) א"ר יוחנן דמחלפא שטתיה דרבי יהודה דתנן לקמן בפרק בתרא (מ"א) אין מבשלין יין של תרומה מפני שממעיטו ר' יהודה מתיר מפני שמשביחו

לעולם הוא תורם מן היפה : ה "תורמין א) בצל קטן שלם ולא חצי בצל גדול רבי יהודה אומר לא כי אלא חצי בצל גדול וכן היה רבי יהודה אומר תורמין בצלים מבני המדינה על הכופרים אבל לא מן הכופרים על בני המדינה מפני שהוא מאכל פוליטיקין : ו ב)ותורמין זיתי שמן על זיתי כבש ולא זיתי כבש על זיתי שמן ויין שאינו מבושל על המבושל ולא מן המבושל על שאינו מבושל ג)זה הכלל כל שהוא כלאים בחברו לא יתרום מזה על זה אפילו מן היפה על הרע וכל שאינו כלאים בחברו תורם מן היפה על הרע אבל לא מן הרע על היפה ואם תרם ג) מן הרע על היפה תרומתו תרומה חוץ מן הזונין על החטים שאינן אוכל ד)והקישות והמלפפון מין אחד רבי יהודה אומר שני מינין :

פרק שלישי

א התורם ג) "קישות ונמצאת מרה אבטיח ונמצא סרוח תרומה ויחזור ויתרום התורם חבית של יין ונמצאת של חומץ אם ידוע שהיתה של חומץ עד שלא תרמה אינה תרומה אם משתרמה החמיצה הרי זו תרומה אם ספק תרומה ויחזור ויתרום הראשונה אינה מדמעת בפני עצמה ואין חייבין עליה חומש וכן השניה : ב נפלה אחת מהן לתוך החולין אינה מדמעתן נפלה שניה למקום אחר אינה מדמעתן נפלו שתיהן למקום אחד מדמעות כקטנה שבשתיהן : ג השותפין ד) שתרמו זה אחר זה רע"א תרומת שניהם תרומה וחכ"א תרומת הראשון תרומה ר'

ואין הלכה כר"י : ה בצל קטן שלם · לדעת תנא קמא שוה יותר בין במקום שיש כהן לפי שהוא אצלו יפה בין במקום שאין כהן לפי שהוא מתקיים. ובצלים בני המדינה הם בצלים גדולים : וכופרין מיוחסין לכפר ידוע והם בצלים הבאים מן הכפרים והם הקטנים ורבי יהודה סובר כי הבצל הגדול הוא יותר טוב ואמרו אבל לא מן הכפרים על בני המדינה והביא ראיה רבי יהודה כי הבצל הגדול הוא יותר טוב באמת מפני שהוא מאכל פוליטיקין והם בני אדם המעונגים והמפונקים בעלי העושר המרווחים במזונותם ואין הלכה כרבי יהודה : זיתי שמן הם הזיתים המוכנים להוציא שמן כי שמן הרבה וטוב משמן הזיתים שאינן ראוין אלא לכבישה למעוט שמנן וה' יתברך אמר (במדבר יח) בהרימכם את חלבו ממנו וחלבו הוא הטוב והיפה שבו כמו שאמר (בראשית מה) ואכלו את חלב הארץ וכבר בארנו בתחלת כלאים כי הזונין מין ממיני החטה גרוע ונפסד ולשם נתבאר דעת ר' יהודה שהוא סובר קישות ומלפפון שהם נקראין בערבי כיארוקתא שהם כלאים זה בזה ואין הלכה כר"י : א סרוח · הוא דבר נפסד ומעופש והוא שימלא הפנימי שלו שאינו ראוי לאכילה ודין אלו השתי תרומות שיתנם לכהן ויתן לו הכהן דמי הגדולה שבהם כי העיקר אצלנו המוציא מחברו עליו הראיה ואוכלן הכהן שתיהם : וענין אינה מדמעת בפני עצמה · שאם נפלה האחת בחולין לא יהיה הכל מדומע אלא שיוציאו מאותן חולין שיעור מה שנפל בהן מן התרומה בלבד: ואין חייבין עליה חומש. מי שאכלה בשוגג כמו שיתבאר וכן השניה לפי שכל א' מהן יש בו ספק אם היא תרומה אם לאו : ב התרומה כשנפל ממנה חלק במאה חלקים מחולין מוציאים מן הכל חלק אחד ויהיה תרומה ויהיה כל השאר מותר ויהיו חולין כמו שהיו ועוד יתבאר לך זה כי התרומה עולה במ' ומאה אבל אם נפל חלק מתרומה בפחות ממאה חלקים מחולין יהיה הכל מדומע וענינו דבר מעורב בדמע שהוא התרומה כמו שבארנו פעמים במה שקדם (בדמאי פ"א מ"ג ופ"ד מ"א ולעיל פ"א מ"ח) ואמר בכאן שאם היתה תרומה ראשונה שנפל בה הספק והשנית שהוציא אח"כ האחת גדולה מן האחרת ויהיה באחת על דרך הדמיון סאה ובשניה סאתים ונפלו השלש סאין בחולין צריכין אנו לדעת שיעור אותן חולין ונחשב כי סאה תרומה נפלה בהם והיא קטנה שבשתיהן ואם היתה באותן חולין מאה סאין תעלה במאה ואחד ואם הוא פחות יהיה הכל מדומע: ג נסתפקו בגמ' במה שאמר ר' יוסי כשיעור איזה שיעור ר"ל אם שיעור דאורייתא ועוד יתבאר או שיעור מה שתרם חברו ואמרו אם רצה באמרו כשיעור התורה והוא אחד מחמשים הרי הוא חולק על דברי חכמים ואם ר"ל שיעור חברו הרי הוא מפרש דברי חכמים ומסכים לדעתם והלכה

ובמתני' משמע דלרבי יהודה שאינו מבושל יפה מן המבושל א"ר אלעזר לא מחלפא תמן תנינן בכהן וכאן בבעלים כלומר שאינו מבושל יפה לשתיה אלא דלכהן התירו לבשל שמשביחו דמתקיים לו אבל בעלים צריכין לתרום מן היפה ולא חיישינן במתקיים : כלאים בחברו · כדמפרש בריש כלאים : לא יתרום · כדפרשינן לעיל דבעינן חלב לזה וחלב לזה : מן הרע על היפה · כרבי אילעא בהאשה רבה (דף פט:): זונין מין חטין ואינו מאכל אדם ומקיימין אותו ליונים כדפרשינן בריש כלאים : מין אחד· ותורמין מזה על זה רבי יהודה אומר ב' מינין ואין תורמין מזה על זה ולענין כלאים נמי פליגי וביין וחומץ פליגי רבי ורבנן (בב"ב דף פד:) :

א קישות ונמצאת מרה· בשוגג איירי כדמוכח בריש האשה רבה (דף פט·) (א) והא דמחמיר הכא טפי ממן הטמא על הטהור משום דהכא שוגג קרוב למזיד דאיבעי ליה למטעמיה ובירושל' (הל' א) פריך ניחא אבטיח ונמצא סרוח אלא קישות ונמצאת מרה ולא מעיקרא מרה היא שדרך הקישות כך והוה לן למימר אינה תרומה כלל כגון גבי יין ונמצא חומץ דגבי אבטיח ונמצא סרוח דלמא לא הוה סרוח מתחלה ניחא דמספק תרומה ויחזור ויתרום ומשני א"ר יוחנן עשו אותה כספק אוכל (ב) ולפי שיטה דיבמות משמע דלא עשו אותה כספק אוכל אלא בתורם בטעות ולא בתורם במזיד דאי במזיד הוה כתורם מטמא על הטהור דבמזיד אין תרומתו תרומה אבל בירושלמי לא משמע כן דמסיק רבי יונה בעי ולכל דבר כספק אוכל היא מטמאה טומאת אוכלין ושורפין אותה בטומאה וחייבין עליה חומש ולוקין עליה אם אכלו חוץ לחומה אם הוא מעשר שני עירב בה נעשה חמר גמל : ונמצאת של חומץ · משמע דמחומץ על יין אין תרומתו תרומה וכן משמע בריש נדה (דף ב:) בבודק את החבית להיות מפריש עליה תרומה והולך ואח"כ נמצאת חומץ והשתא ניחא לר' דאמר יין וחומץ ב' מינין הן בהמוכר את הספינה (דף פד:) אבל לרבנן דאמרי מין אחד קשה ומיהו מתני' דהכא משמע בירושלמי (שם) דאתיא כר' דאסיק רבי חייא בשם רבי יוחנן דרבי היא ובהדיא קתני בתוספתא (פ"ד) במתני' [דברי א] רבי אבל ההיא דהיה בודק משמע בתוספתא דאתא אפילו כרבנן דבתר דברי רבי קתני שר' אומר יין וחומץ שני מינים וחכ"א מין א' היה בלבו לתרום יין על יין ומה שבידו חומץ אין תרומתו תרומה מה שבידו יין היין תרום ויחזור ויתרום על החומץ היה בלבו לתרום חומץ על חומץ ומה שבידו חומץ החומץ תרום ויחזור ויתרום ומסיק לה כו' כדאיתא בריש נדה משמע בהדיא דמודו רבנן דמתכוין לתרום מיין על יין ומה שבידו חומץ [ג] שאני אלא דברישא פליגי משום דבלבו שיהא תרומה בכל ענין בין ימצא יין בין ימצא חומץ והא דתני ברייתא היין תרום ויחזור ויתרום את החומץ אין פירושה כמו תרומתו תרומה ויחזור ויתרום דבכל דוכתא דא"כ ליתני תרומה ויחזור ויתרום אלא התם מיירי כגון שיש שם כ' חביות של יין והיה בלבו על היין והפריש אחת מהן על כולן דאם מה שבידו חומץ והשאר יין אין תרומתו תרומה כלל כיון דבלבו מיין על יין אבל מה שבידו יין והשאר יש מהן חומץ ויש מהן יין היין תרום חביות שהן יין מתוקנות שתרומתן בחבית שבידו אבל הנמצאות חומץ אינו מתוקן ובכי האי גוונא אם בידו חומץ החומץ מתוקן והיין אינו מתוקן ולעיל בסוף פרק ב' (הל' ה) אמרו בירושלמי אמר רבי יהושע בן לוי מסתברא יודה רבי לדבר תורה מאי טעמא דרבי שאם אתה אומר כן שמותר לתרום מיין על חומץ אף הוא סבר מימר שמותר לתרום מחומץ על יין והוא משמע לכאורה דלא אסר רבי אלא לכתחלה אבל אי אפשר לומר כן דבהדיא תני בתוספתא במילתיה דרבי אם עד שלא תרם החמיצה אינה תרומה ויש לתמוה מאי שנא תורם מחומץ על יין לרבנן מתורם מטמא על הטהור ומאבטיח ונמצא סרוח דמשמע בהאשה רבה בשוגג תרומתו תרומה במזיד אין תרומתו תרומה והכא לרבנן איפכא דמחומץ על יין במזיד תרומתו תרומה בשוגג אין תרומתו תרומה יש לומר דלא דמי דטמא ואבטיח תקין רבנן דלא תהא תרומה במזיד משום דלא חזו לאכילה ויש כח בידם לעקור דבר מן התורה כדאמר בהאשה רבה או כמאן דאמר לא אמר כלום לתקן השירים אבל חומץ חזי לאכילה ואיכא דניחא ליה בחלא כדאמרינן בהמוכר את הספינה (דף פד:) והוי כמן הרע על היפה דלא שנא שוגג ולא שנא מזיד תרומתו תרומה חוץ מהיה בלבו דהוי כמפרש שלא יהיה תרומה : ואם ספק תרומה ויחזור ויתרום · *כדאמרינן לגבי חבית בריש נדה סוה מאי לאתויי מהך : הראשונה אינה מדמעת בפני עצמה · כדאמר באידך בבא שאחר זו : ואין חייבין עליה זר האוכלה חומש · ירושלמי (שם) כיצד עושה נותן שתיהן לכהן והכהן נותן לו דמי אחת מהן דמי גדולה או קטנה מדמתנינן מדמעות כקטנה שבשתיהן הדא אמר דמי גדולה נותן לו פי' הראשונה גדולה מן השניה שהשניה מתמעטת כפי מה שעולה תרומת הראשונה ודייקינן דיד כהן על התחתונה מ' קתני באידך בבא דאין מדמעת אלא כשיעור קטנה : ב כבר פירשתיה : ג ירושלמי (הל' ה) מה אנן קיימין אם כשאינן ממחין אף רבי עקיבא מודה אם בממחין אף רבנן מודו אלא כי אנן קיימין בסתם ר"ע סבר סתמן אינן ממחין רבנן אמרין סתמן ממחין על דעתיה דר"ע סאה של ראשון חליה טבל וחליה תרומה טבולה למעשר סאה של שני חליה תרומה וחליה טבל טבולה לכל לא צורכה דלא חלי סאה של שני מהו שתפטור חלי סאה של ראשון נשמע מן הדא אריסטון אייתי פירין ושייר גוסקא ותרם אתא עובדא קומי ר' יוסי ואמר חזקה על הכל תרם מה כשיעור תורה או כשיעור חברין אין תעבדינה כשיעור תורה לית רבי יוסי כרבנן אין תעבדינה כשיעור חברין רבי יוסי כרבנן פירוש בממחין בקיאין לתרום דניחא ליה לשותף חברו שיתרום כיון שהוא בקי אבל אם אינו בקי ודאי לא ניחא והוה ליה תורם שלא ברשות ומסיק דבסתם פליגי על דעתיה דר"ע דלאמר תרומת שניהן תרומה נמצא כשתרמו שניהן מנ' סאה זה סאה וזה סאה שלא קדשה תרומה בשל זה אלא חצי סאה ובשל זה כי אם חצי סאה כל אחד טבולה לפי חלקו טבולה למעשרות ואיפכא גרסינן. בשל ראשון טבולה לכל בשל שני טבולה למעשרות שהרי הראשון כשתרם סאה תרם על כל מה שלפניו ונמצא כל חלקו פטור מתרומה גדולה וכשבא השני חזר והפריש סאה על כל שלפניו תרם ולא על כל מה שנטל חברו ונמצא חצי סאה טבל של ראשון טבל לכל ואח"כ מסיק דחצי סאה של שני פוטר חצי סאה של ראשון דחזקה על כל חלקו תרם כדאשכחן באריסטון שהורה ר' יוסי דאף על מה ששייר בשק תרם ולמסקנא זו חצי סאה טבל של ראשון וחצי סאה טבל של שני שניהם טבולים למעשרות ולא לתרומה מה כשיעור תורה מיבעיא ליה הא דקאמר רבי יוסי אם תרם הראשון כשיעור איזה שיעור קאמר אם כשיעור דאורייתא חטה אחת פוטרת את הכרי או כשיעור חכמים אחד מנ' ור"ל דהא דאמרי רבנן תרומת הראשונה תרומה היינו בשתרם כשיעור חכמים אחד מנ' ולפי' זה על כרחך ר' יוסי בא לפרש דברי חכמים והשתא הא דאמרינן בפ' האיש מקדש (דף מא:) אתם זלא השותפים הייטו כר"ע דאמר תרומת שניהן תרומה ובריש מכילתין פריך ומשני לה כדפרשינן שם ובסוף פ"ק דתמורה (דף יג·) מייתי מתני' דהכא וכתובה שם הגירסא בענין אחר דתנן התם אין תרומה אחר תרומה ואמר בגמ' מתני' מני ר"ע היא דתנן השותפין שתרמו זה אחר זה ר"א אומר תרומת שניהן תרומה ר"ע אומר אין תרומת שניהן תרומה וחכ"א אם תרם הראשון כשיעור אין תרומת השני תרומה ואם לא תרם הראשון כשיעור תרומת השני תרומה והשתא מתני' דהתם כמאן דאמר תרומת הראשונה תרומה ותרומת שניהן תרומה היינו דכל אחת חליה תרומה וחליה חולין כדפרשינן ולא כמו שפירש שם בקונטרס

פרק ג א ב התורם חבית של יין ונמצאת אותה דתרומה חומץ אם יודע שחומץ היתה עד שלא תרמה אינה תרומה · א"ר יוחנן מתני' מני ר' היא דאמר יין וחומץ ב' מינין הן ודלא כר' ישמעאל בר' יוסי וא"ר יוחנן הלכה כר' ואקשי' ותו למה לי הא קיימא לן הלכה כרבי מחבירו ופריק איצטריך משום דתני לה ר' ישמעאל בר' יוסי משום אביו וקיימא לן הלכה כר' יוסי מחבירו משום הכי איצטריך למימר הלכה כר' : ואם משתרמה החמיצה הרי זו תרומה' דאיהו שפיר תרם ומוליה דכהן גרם: אם ספק' פי' אם ספק מקודם החמיצה ואם משתרמה החמיצה הרי זו תרומה ויחזור ויתרום פעם ב' כיצד עושה נותן לכהן והכהן נותן לו דמי גדולה והואיל וכן הראשונה אינה מדמעת בפני עצמה ובפירוש אמר לקמן נפלה אחת מהן לתוך החולין אינה מדמעת נפלה שניה למקום אחר אינה מדמעת אבל נפלו שתיהן למקום אחד מדמעות כקטנה שבשתיהן · פי' כי כשיעור הגדולה והיא הראשונה נותן ממנה דמיו וכחולין היא ושיעור הקטנה תרומה כגון שהיו לו ג' לוגין יין בראשונה ותרם לוג אחד מנ' ובשניה תרם פחות מלוג עתה אם נפלו לפחות מק' לוג פחותין מדמעת אבל אם נפלו לק' לתין פחותין עולין ואע"פ שהן ב' לוגין א"כ אין תרומה אלא שיעור לוג פחות מעט : ג השותפין שתרמו זה אחר זה וכו' · במאי עסיק' אי במומחין מאי טעמ' דר' עקיבא שפיר אמרי רבנן ואי בשותפין שאינן מומחין מאי טעמא דרבנן ופריק הכא במאי עסקינן בסתם פי' דליתנהו קמן דלישיילינהו ר' עקיבא סבר הכל אצל תרומה לאו מומחין הן לפיכך תרומת שניהן תרומה דדילמא כשיעור

פי' מהר"י בן מלכי צדק

מתקיים דאי תרים תאנן מסרחי ומתלעי ומיפסדי ר' יהודה פליג ואמר אף במקום שאין כהן תורם מן היפה דכתיב את חלבו ואי פסדא תיפסד : ה ו ותורמין זיתי שמן· פירוש דאינון יפין וזיתי כבש מתקיימין ולא יפין וכן לענין בכורין מביאין מזיתי שמן ולא מזיתי כבש פי' זיתי כבש זיתין העומדין ליכבש ולמלוח דלאו בני מיעבד מישחא · ויין שאינו מבושל שהוא יפה ואינו מתקיים והמבושל הוא רע ומתקיים וכולה מתני' רבי יהודה היא וקשיא דר' יהודה אדרבי יהודה הכא אמר המבושל רע ותנן לקמן ר' יהודה מתיר לבשל יין של תרומה מפני שהוא משביחו · אלמא מבושל יפה · רבי אלעזר אומר לעולם שאינו מבושל יפה דההיא שתו ליה כולי עלמא אבל במבושל לא שתו ליה כולי עלמא והתם דמתיר רבי יהודה בכהן עסקי' ומשביחו דמתקיים לו ולא משום דסבר דמבושל יפה דלעולם מבושל רע הוא ואהכי לא תרמינן מיניה כשבישלוהו הבעלי' דיפה בעינן ולא חיישינן למתקיים : כלאים בחברו · כגון שעורים וחטים הרוחה להן אין תורמין מזה על זה פי' דבעינן תן חלב לזה ותן חלב לזה : ואם תרם מן הרע על היפה תרומתו תרומה' כר"י אלא דא"ר אילא · תשאו עליו חטא אם אינו קדוש נשיאת חטא למה אלא בנשיאת עון את ידע מה שעשה עשוי (יבמות פ"ט.): חוץ מן הזונין פי' החטים והזונין אחד ואינן כלאים זה בזה ואם תרם מן הזונין על החטים לא עשה כלום שהזונין אינו אוכל אדם. תניא רבי ישמעאל בר' יוסי אומר משום אביו תורמין מן היין על החומץ אבל לא מן החומץ על היין ואם עבר ותרם תרומתו תרומה רבי אומר יין וחומץ ב' מינין הן : הקישות והמלפפון מין אחד והם כלאים כרביה ורבנן כרבותיהו דתנינן הקישות והמלפפון אינן כלאים זה בזה רבי יהודה אומר כלאים :

יא א מיי' שם הלכה ג:
יא ב מיי' שם הלכה יח וטוש"ע שם סעיף סג:
יב ג ד שם הל' ג:
א ה מיי' פ"ה מהלכות תרומות הלכה כב טוש"ע שם סעיף סה:
ב ו מיי' שם הל' כג:

פירוש הרא"ש

(ט) ובמקום שאין כהן מיירי: פרק ג (א) בריש האשה רבה מדקדק ומוכח מכלל בשוגג איירי: (ב) פירוש כל קישות מרה מספקא לן אם יש לה היתר אוכל או לא הלכך מספק יחזור ויתרום:

הגהות מהר"י לנדא

פרק ג א] מ"א ברא"ש דכ"י ר"י לפניו הגי' ר"י: ב] שם חומץ שאני: נ"ל שאינו תרומה:

נ"ל והא דמתכוין מתבאר בריש נדה דף ג'

א) קדושין דף נט: ב) עירובין דף לז: ג) תמורה דף ה: ד) פסחים דף סג: ה) קדושין דף מא: וגיטין דף כג: ז) קדושין דף מא:

ועל כרחך גירסא דהתם משובשת (ולפי)[דלפי]מה שפירשתי הוה ליה למימר מתני' לא כר' אליעזר ולא כר' עקיבא: ד בד"א הא דפליגי לעיל דלר' עקיבא תרומת שניהן תרומה בשלא דבר כלו' שלא נטל רשות מחברו לתרום שלא תרם מדעתו : אבל הרשה · לתרום לבן ביתו או לעבדו ושפחתו : ביטל · כגון שמינה שליח לתרום והלך לו ואח"כ ביטל שליחותו : אם עד שלא תרם ביטל· ירושלמי (שם) פריך ולית הדא פליגא על דריש לקיש דלא אין אדם מבטל שליחותו בדברים ופלוגתייהו בריש האומר ז)(דף נט·) בקדושין גבי נתנה רשות לשלוחה לקדשה וחזרה בה רבי יוחנן אמר חוזרת אתי דבור ומבטל דבור ריש לקיש אמר אינה חוזרת ולא אתי דבור ומבטל דבור ומסני תיפתר

תורה אור

יוסי אומר א)אם תרם הראשון כשיעור אין תרומת השני תרומה ואם לא תרם הראשון כשיעור תרומת השני תרומה: ד בד"א בשלא דבר אבל הרשה את בן ביתו או את עבדו או את שפחתו לתרום תרומתו תרומה ב)בטל(א) אם עד שלא תרם בטל אין תרומתו תרומה ואם משתרם בטל תרומתו תרומה ג)הפועלים אין להם רשות לתרום חוץ מן הדרוכות שהן מטמאין את הגת מיד: ה האומר ג) תרומת הכרי זה בתוכו ומעשרותיו בתוכו תרומת מעשר זה בתוכו רבי שמעון אומר קרא שם וחכמים אומרים ד)עד שיאמר בצפונו או בדרומו רבי אלעזר חסמא אומר האומר תרומת הכרי ממנו עליו קרא שם ר"א בן יעקב אומר האומר עשור מעשר זה עשוי תרומת מעשר עליו קרא שם: ו ה)המקדים ג) תרומה לבכורים מעשר ראשון לתרומה ומעשר שני לראשון אע"פ שהוא עובר בלא תעשה מה שעשה עשוי שנאמר °מלאתך ודמעך לא תאחר: ז ומנין שיקדמו הבכורים לתרומה זה קרוי תרומה וראשית וזה קרוי תרומה וראשית ו)אלא יקדמו בכורים שהן בכורים לכל ותרומה לראשון שהיא ראשית ומעשר ראשון לשני שיש בו ראשית: ח ז)המתכוין ד) לומר תרומה ואמר מעשר מעשר ואמר תרומה ח)עולה ואמר שלמים שלמים ואמר עולה שאיני נכנס לבית זה ואמר לזה שאיני נהנה לזה ואמר לזה לא אמר כלום עד שיהו פיו ולבו שוין: ט ט)הנכרי ה) והכותי תרומתן תרומה ומעשרותן מעשר והקדשן הקדש רבי יהודה אומר אין לנכרי כרם רבעי י)וחכמים אומרים יש לו תרומת ו) הנכרי מדמעת וחייבין עליה חומש ורבי שמעון פוטר:

שמות כב

פרק רביעי

א המפריש כ)מקצת תרומה ל)ומעשרות מוציא ממנו תרומה עליו אבל לא *)למקום אחר ר' מאיר אומר אף מוציא הוא

*) נ"א ממקום עי' תוי"ט שכ"ה גירסת הרמב"ם

GAVE THE PRESCRIBED AMOUNT,[10] THE TERUMAH OF THE SECOND IS NOT VALID, BUT HAD HE NOT GIVEN THE PRESCRIBED AMOUNT,[11] THE TERUMAH OF THE SECOND IS VALID.

MISHNAH 4. WHEN DO THESE WORDS APPLY?[12] ONLY IF THE ONE DID NOT CONFER WITH THE OTHER;[13] BUT IF A MAN SANCTIONS A MEMBER OF HIS HOUSEHOLD,[14] OR HIS SLAVE OR BOND-MAID TO GIVE TERUMAH FOR HIM, THIS TERUMAH IS VALID.[15] IF HE ANNULLED [THIS SANCTION],[16] THE TERUMAH IS RENDERED INVALID IF HE ANNULLED IT BEFORE THE TAKING OF THE TERUMAH, BUT IF HE ANNULLED IT AFTER THE TERUMAH HAD BEEN TAKEN, THE TERUMAH IS VALID.
a LABOURERS HAVE NO AUTHORITY TO GIVE TERUMAH,[1] SAVE THOSE WHO TREAD [GRAPES], FOR THEY[2] DEFILE THE WINEPRESS IMMEDIATELY.[3]

MISHNAH 5. IF ONE SAYS: '[LET] THE TERUMAH OF THIS PILE BE WITHIN IT', OR, 'LET ITS TITHES BE WITHIN IT', OR, 'LET THE HEAVE-OFFERING OF TITHE BE WITHIN IT', R. SIMEON SAYS: HE HAS THEREBY DESIGNATED IT;[4] BUT THE SAGES SAY: NOT UNLESS HE SAID, LET IT BE TO THE NORTH OR SOUTH OF IT.[5] R. ELEAZAR ḤISMA SAYS: HE WHO SAYS, 'LET TERUMAH BE GIVEN FROM THIS FOR THIS SAME PILE', HAS THEREBY DESIGNATED IT.[6] R. ELIEZAR B. JACOB SAYS: IF HE SAYS, 'LET THE TENTH PART OF THIS TITHE BE THE HEAVE-OFFERING OF TITHE FOR THAT PILE', HE HAS THEREBY DESIGNATED IT.[7]

MISHNAH 6. HE WHO GIVES TERUMAH BEFORE FIRST-
b FRUITS,[1] OR FIRST TITHE BEFORE TERUMAH, OR SECOND TITHE BEFORE FIRST TITHE, ALTHOUGH HE TRANSGRESSES A NEGATIVE COMMAND,[2] HIS ACTION IS VALID, FOR IT IS SAID: THOU SHALT NOT DELAY TO OFFER OF THE FULNESS OF THY HARVEST AND OF THE OUTFLOW OF THY PRESSES.[3]

MISHNAH 7. WHENCE DO WE DERIVE THAT FIRST-FRUITS MUST PRECEDE TERUMAH, SEEING THAT THE ONE IS CALLED 'TERUMAH' AND 'THE FIRST' AND THE OTHER IS CALLED 'TERUMAH' AND 'THE FIRST'?[4] FIRST-FRUITS TAKE PRECEDENCE SINCE THEY ARE THE FIRST FRUITS OF ALL PRODUCE,[5] AND TERUMAH COMES BEFORE THE FIRST TITHE ALSO, BECAUSE IT IS [CALLED] 'FIRST'. AND FIRST TITHE PRECEDES SECOND TITHE, BECAUSE IT INCLUDES THAT WHICH IS CALLED 'FIRST'.[6]

MISHNAH 8. HE WHO INTENDS SAYING 'TERUMAH' AND SAYS 'TITHE', OR 'TITHE' AND HE SAYS 'TERUMAH'; OR 'BURNT-OFFERING' AND HE SAYS 'PEACE-OFFERING', OR 'PEACE-OFFERING' AND HE SAYS 'BURNT-OFFERING'; OR '[I VOW] THAT I WILL NOT ENTER THIS HOUSE' AND SAYS INSTEAD 'THAT HOUSE', OR, 'THAT I WILL NOT DERIVE ANY BENEFIT FROM THIS [MAN]',[7] AND SAYS INSTEAD 'FROM THAT [MAN]', HE HAS SAID NOTHING UNTIL HIS HEART AND MIND ARE AT ONE.

MISHNAH 9. TERUMAH GIVEN BY A HEATHEN OR A SAMARITAN IS VALID; THEIR TITHES AND THEIR DEDICATIONS ARE
c ALSO VALID ACTS.[1] R. JUDAH SAYS: THE LAW OF THE VINEYARD IN THE FOURTH YEAR[2] IS NOT APPLICABLE TO A HEATHEN;[3] BUT THE SAGES SAY: IT IS. THE TERUMAH OF THE HEATHEN RENDERS [PRODUCE INTO WHICH IT FALLS] MEDUMMA' AND IS SUBJECT TO THE LAW OF THE FIFTH,[4] BUT R. SIMEON EXEMPTS IT.[5]

CHAPTER IV

MISHNAH 1. HE WHO SETS ASIDE ONLY PART OF TERU-
d MAH AND TITHES,[1] MAY EXTRACT FROM THAT [HEAP] THE OTHER TERUMAH DUE,[2] BUT HE MAY NOT EXTRACT THEREFROM FOR PRODUCE ELSEWHERE.[3] R. MEIR SAYS: HE CAN ALSO

(10) 1/50th of the whole produce. (11) Giving either 1/40th or 1/60th. (12) Referring to words of R. Akiba in the Mishnah preceding. (13) The partners acting independently. (14) Who has no proprietary rights in the pile. The slave here is 'a son of the Covenant' and, therefore, can act as a messenger. (15) And even if the owner himself later gives *terumah* anew, his action is void, though he gives a larger amount than the messenger; cf. *infra* IV. (16) After the departure of the messenger to perform his charge, he publicly renounces his first charge.
a (1) Though they are responsible for its growth, it is not theirs to give away. (2) The owners who are *'amme ha-arez*; v. next note. (3) The Mishnah refers to owners who are *'amme ha-arez* (v. Glos.) who defile *terumah* with their touch, and to labourers who are *ḥaberim* (associates) who, unlike their employers, were most scrupulous in observing the laws of purity and in setting apart tithes from produce. It was therefore the duty of 'associate' labourers to take *terumah* immediately they began treading, lest the owners, thinking that *terumah* had already been taken, might touch the grapes or olives and thus defile them. This is, therefore, a case where the owners tacitly give the labourers sanction to give *terumah* on their behalf in purity. Moreover, it was even allowed here to take *terumah* before the entire process was finished, contrary to the ruling of *supra* I, 8, in order to safeguard *terumah* being taken in purity, *Tif. Yis.* (4) And cannot set aside *terumah* from any other pile. (5) The designation must be more definite. Just to say 'within it' is not enough, as not sufficient distinction is made between that which is taken and that left. V. 'Er. 37*b*. (6) Agreeing with R. Simeon that it is not necessary to have a discernible distinction between the portion given as *terumah* and the remainder. (7) Differing from R. Simeon in that he insists that the tithe must be separated before the heave-offering of tithe can be taken or designated as such.

b (1) Declaring: 'Let these fruits be *terumah* as soon as they are plucked'. The fruit is not yet fully ripe. (2) V. n. 3. (3) Ex. XXII, 28. 'Fulness' and 'harvest' are respectively interpreted as referring to first fruits and to *terumah* and First Tithe. The words *'thou shalt not delay'* are also taken to enjoin against a variation of this order. Cf. Beẓ. 13*b*. (4) Deut. XII, 6 refers to first-fruits as *'the* terumah *of your hands'* (cf. Deut. XXVI, 4) and in Ex. XXIII, 19, we read *'the first of the first fruits of thy ground'*; of *terumah*, too, both terms are used (Num. XVIII, 8; Deut. XVIII, 4). (5) The word *'bikkurim'* actually implies what is brought first. (6) Since it contains the heave-offering of tithe to which applies as *terumah* the term, 'The first'. (7) Since he wrongly specifies the man or thing intended for his ban.
c (1) Only if the things tithed and dedicated are their very own. (2) Lev. XIX, 23–25. (3) In the fourth year of planting Jews could eat fruits from the vineyard of a gentile without redemption, R. Judah being of the opinion that the gentile can take 'possession' of land in Eretz Israel to exempt him from the law of the vineyard. (4) If there be not in the produce a hundred times the quantity of the *terumah* that fell in. (5) From the added Fifth, since it is not definitely *terumah;* R. Simeon, however, agrees that it does make other produce *medumma'*.
d (1) Only one *se'ah* instead of the usual two from a pile containing a hundred *se'ahs*, with the result that a part is 'tithed' and a part still untithed. (2) The other *se'ah* must be taken from that pile and we do not fear lest it be taken just from that part which is 'tithed' and thus have a case of *terumah* being taken from that which is *methukan* (v. Glos.) for that which is not. (3) If he has another pile of a hundred *se'ahs*, he may not take two *se'ahs* from the pile already partly tithed. In the case of two piles the fear is expressed lest he take *terumah* from that which is tithed for that untithed.

TAKE THEREFROM TERUMAH AND TITHES[4] FOR PRODUCE ELSEWHERE.

MISHNAH 2. IF ONE HAD HIS FRUIT IN THE STOREHOUSE,[5] AND GAVE A SE'AH TO A LEVITE,[6] AND A SE'AH TO A POOR MAN,[7] HE MAY SET ASIDE FROM THE STORE AS MANY AS EIGHT SE'AHS AND EAT THEM;[8] THIS IS THE OPINION OF R. MEIR. BUT THE SAGES SAY: HE MAY ONLY SET ASIDE AC-
a CORDING TO PROPORTION.[1]

MISHNAH 3. [THIS IS] THE AMOUNT OF TERUMAH: THE BENEVOLENT[2] [GIVES] A FORTIETH; BETH SHAMMAI SAY, ONE THIRTIETH. THE AVERAGE MAN ONE FIFTIETH[3] AND THE NIGGARDLY MAN ONE SIXTIETH.[4] IF HE GAVE TERUMAH[5] AND DISCOVERED THAT IT WAS ONLY ONE SIXTIETH, HIS TERUMAH IS VALID AND HE NEED NOT GIVE IT ANEW. IF HE ADDS TO IT,[6] THEN IT IS LIABLE TO TITHES.[7] IF HE FOUND THAT IT WAS ONLY ONE SIXTY-FIRST IT IS VALID, BUT HE MUST GIVE TERUMAH ANEW ACCORDING TO HIS ESTABLISHED PRACTICE,[8] IN MEASURE, WEIGHT OR NUMBER.[9] R. JUDAH SAYS: EVEN IF IT BE NOT FROM PRODUCE CLOSE BY.[10]

MISHNAH 4. HE WHO SAYS TO HIS MESSENGER: 'GO AND GIVE TERUMAH [FOR ME]', THEN [THE LATTER] MUST DO SO IN ACCORDANCE WITH THE MIND OF THE OWNER.[11] IF HE DOES NOT KNOW THE MIND OF THE OWNER, HE GIVES ACCORDING TO THE AMOUNT OF THE AVERAGE MAN—ONE FIFTIETH. IF HE GAVE TEN PARTS LESS OR MORE,[12] THE TERUMAH IS VALID.[13] IF, HOWEVER, HIS INTENTION WAS TO ADD EVEN ONE PART MORE, HIS TERUMAH IS NOT VALID.[14]

b *MISHNAH* 5. IF ONE WISHES TO GIVE MORE TERUMAH,[1] R. ELIEZER SAYS HE MAY GIVE UP TO A TENTH PART, AS IN

(4) R. Meir follows his principle of *bererah* (v. Glos.) 'retrospective designation'; that is, the legal effect resulting from an actual selection or disposal of things previously undefined as to their purpose; here, since part of the pile is partly untithed, we assume that it is from that part that the *terumah* for the second pile is taken. (5) Cf. Hag. II, 19. (6) As first tithe. (7) What in other years would be set apart as second tithe was, in the third and sixth years of the Sabbatical Cycle, given to the poor; v. Deut. XIV, 29. In reality, only 9/10ths of a *se'ah* is due to the poor man, as the pile had been diminished by a tenth after the Levite had received his due. (8) The case dealt with is that of an *'am ha-arez* who gives a *se'ah* each to a Levite and a poor man; should his workmen be 'associates' they may eat, on the strength of the two *se'ahs* thus set aside, eight *se'ahs*, on the assumption that the *terumah gedolah* had been set aside. For even an *'am ha-arez* was not suspected of not taking *terumah gedolah*.

a (1) I.e., the workman may eat only as much as he requires for one meal, since it is to be assumed that the owner gave tithe only in proportion of what his workman would need for one meal, and whatever he gave in excess to the Levite and poor man was to be considered a free gift. This is the interpretation of this obscure Mishnah according to the first version in Bert. (2) Lit., 'a good eye'; cf. Ex. XXV, 2. (3) Cf. Num. XXXI, 30. (4) Cf. Ezek. XLV, 13. (5) Namely, the generous or average man. Since *terumah* had to be given approximately, it was only natural to err in the amount. (6) Till it becomes his usual gift. (7) The amount added is not considered *terumah* and is subject to tithes. (8) As much as he usually gives. (9) This second *terumah* may be given by measure etc. Cf. *supra* I, 7. (10) The condition governing the first taking of *terumah*. (11) Finding out first what amount he usually gave. (12) Mistaking in each case the usual practice of the owner. (13) On the plea of the messenger that since some people do give these amounts, he had judged his sender in that light. (14) The *sine qua non* of a messenger is that he must fulfil the wishes of the one who sent him to the most minute particular, and since he knows how much his sender gave, he had no right to add to it; cf. Me'il. VI, 4.

b (1) Even more than 1/40th, the most generous measure.

עליו כל הטבל עלה בידו : ב במגורה. אוצר תבואה (ב) : ונתן סאה לבן לוי· בירושלמי (הל' ב) א"ר אליעזר בשם ר' אושעיא בר' יוסי עשו אותה כפועל שאינו מאמינו לבע"ה והשתא מיירי כגון שראה פועל את בעל הבית נותן ממגורתו *לבן לוי סתם ושאל לעני סתם ואמר ר"מ דאותו פועל יכול לאכול מן המגורה ח' סאין דסתם בתורת מעשר ראשון נתן ללוי ובתורת מעשר עני נתן לעני והרי יש כאן ח' סאין מתוקנים ומעט יותר ואע"פ שלא ראהו מפריש תרומה גדולה לא נחשדו עמי הארץ על התרומה וחכמים אומרים אינו מפריש כ"א לפי חשבון מה שהפועל אוכל מפריש כדתנן בפ' ז' דדמאי (משנה ג) גבי פועל שאין מאמין לבעל הבית וזה הלשון

*ממקום אחר תרומה ומעשרות : ב מי שהיו פירותיו במגורה ונתן סאה לבן לוי וסאה לעני מפריש עוד שמנה סאין ואוכלן דברי רבי מאיר וחכמים אומרים *אינו מפריש אלא לפי חשבון : ג [ב]שיעור א) תרומה עין יפה *אחת מארבעים ב"ש אומרים משלשים והבינונית מחמשים והרעה מששים [ג]תרם ועלה בידו אחד מששים תרומה ואינו צרי' לתרום חזר והוסיף חייב במעשרות עלה בידו משישים ואחד תרומה ויחזור ויתרום כמות שהוא למוד במדה ובמשקל ובמנין ר' יהודה אומר אף שלא מן המוקף : ד [ד]האומר ב) לשלוחו צא ותרום תורם כדעתו של בע"ה אם אינו יודע דעתו של בע"ה תורם בבינונית *אחת מנ' פיחת עשרה או הוסיף עשרה תרומתו תרומה אם נתכוון להוסיף אפי' אחת אין תרומתו תרומה : ה המרבה בתרומה רבי אליעזר אומר אחד מעשרה

ואם הפריש מקצת מעשרות יוציא ממנו המעשר שחייב לאותו קצת ואין לו להוציא על אותו קצת שהוציא תרומה ומעשרות ממקום אחר כמו שהוא מותר לעשותו בטבל כיון שזה שהוציא הוציאו לדעת שהוא מקצת תרומה ומעשרות ור"מ מתיר שיוציא עליו ממקום אחר ואין הפרש אללו בין מוציא קצת תרומה ומעשרות או שאר הטבלים ואין הלכה כרבי מאיר : ב הכוונה בזו המשנה כי כשנתן סאה לבן לוי שהוא המעשר הראוי לעשר סאין ונתן אחר כן סאה לעני והוא הראוי לעשר סאין שיכול להוציא שמונה סאין ולאכלן לפי שכבר הוציא חקם הראוי שם וכאלו היו עשר סאי' והוא הוציא מהם סאה למעשר ראשון וסאה למעשר *שני וכל זה שלא ידע אם אותה סאה שנתן ללוי ואותה סאה שנתן לעני הם כולם קיימים עד שיפרים עליהם או נאכל קצתם ונשאר קצת ואמרם סאה לעני הוא בקירוב החשבון אבל בדיוק החשבון אינו טעון לתת לעני אלא תשע עשיריות מהסאה ויפריש ג"כ אותן שמונה סאין ועשירית סאה וזה מבואר: וחכ"א אינו מפריש אלא לפי חשבון . ר"ל כשיעור מה שנשאר מן הסאה שנותן אם נשאר חציה יפריש עליו ד' סאין ואם תשאר רביעית' יוציא עליה שתי סאין ועל זה הסדר והלכה כחכמים : ג עין יפה· פי' נדבת לב ועין רעה הפך כלומר כילות וכמו מה שאמרו ב"ש עין יפה אחד משלשים כמו כן אמרו בינונית מארבעים ורעה מחמשים ואמרו התרומה תרי ממאה : ואמרו חזר והוסיף חייב במעשרות. ענינו כי התרומה אינה חייבת במעשרות ומה שנשאר אחר הוצאת התרומה הוא חייב במעשרות בלי ספק ולפיכך אם הוסיף על התרומה הראשונה יתחייב להוציא מאותו תוספת מעשרות ואז יאכלנה הכהן : ואמרם כמות שהוא למוד . ענינו שמותר לו להוציא התרומה שניה שהיא תוספת תרומה כמו שמנהגו לשער זרעו במדה או במנין או במשקל וזה אסור לעשות בתחלה כמו שאמרנו אין תורמין לא במדה ולא במשקל ולא במנין : ורבי יהודה אומר שמותר לו להוציא ממנו תוספת תרומה שלא מן המוקף ר"ל ממקום אחר וזה אסור לעשותו לכתחלה ר"ל שיוציא אדם תרומה ממקום אחד על הפירות שהם במקום אחר אבל יוציא התרומה מן המוקף רצה לומר ממה שהוא תוך הקף מקום אחד ומן הדברים שנשנו אללו פעמים לא נחשדו חברים לתרום שלא מן המוקף ואין הלכה כרבי יהודה : ד פיחת עשרה . ענינו שיוציא אחת מששים והוסיף עשרה שיוציא אחת מארבעים : אם נתכוין להוסיף אפילו אחת . ענינו שיתכוין להוציא אחת מארבעים והטעה שמחייב זה תוספת בתרומה ומתכוין לאחת מחמשים שהיא בינונית אם הוסיף בשיעור התרומה כשיעור הנזכר או פחותה] בלא כוונה מה שעשה עשוי ותרומתו תרומה ואם נתכוין להוסיף בשיעור תרומה ואפילו דבר מועט אין תרומתו תרומה ומעשיו אין להם קיום : ה כשהוציא התרומה יותר מן השיעור הנזכר אומר ר' אליעזר כי הוא אפי' הוציא מעשר הזרע תרומה שהוא מותר ודינו

אינו מיושב על פי זה דהוה ליה למימר מפריש לפי חשבון לכך נראה דמפריש דחכמים אבעל הבית קאי כמו מפריש דרבי מאיר ובהא פליגי דרבי מאיר סבר דיכול פועל לאכול כמה סעודות אצל בעל הבית עד שיכלו ח' סאין ורבנן סברי דלא הפריש בעל הבית אלא לפי חשבון סעודה זו בשביל הפועל שסועד אצלו והשאר מתנה בעלמא דיהיב ללוי ולעני ועוד יש לפרש דמיירי כגון שנתן סאה ללוי ולעני והלכו הלוי והעני ומדדום ונמצאו חסרין דרבי מאיר סבר מהמנינן ליה לבעל הבית שהפריש ב' סאין שלימין ונאבד מה שחסר או אכלוהו עכברים ורבנן סברי דלפי חשבון הנמצא מהימן ותו לא ועוד יש לפרש דמיירי כגון שהלכו להן הלוי והעני וסבר רבי מאיר דמפריש עליהן ח' סאין ואוכל בחזקת שאותן ב' סאין קיימין ורבנן אסרי ואין הירושלמי מתיישב לפי זה ומשמע דמיירי כגון דאמר בעל הבית הרי זה מעשר על מה שאוכל דגרסי' בירושלמי (הל' ב) פשיטא הדא מלתא נשרפו הפירות התרומה בטילה כלומ' נשרפו הפירות של מגורה ותרומה לאו דוקא דמתני' במעשר איירי אמעשרות קאמר שהן בטיבלן נשרפה התרומה כלומר נשרפו המעשרות לכשיאכלו הפירות קדשה התרומה למפרע *וכל זה יש ליישב ב' לשונות ראשונים שפירשתי : ג ירושלמי (הל' ג') כתיב (יחזקאל מה) ששית האיפה מחומר החטים וששיתם האיפה מחומר שעורים יכול יתרום בחטים אחד מששים ובשעורים אחד משלשים ת"ל וכל תרומה שיהו כל תרומות שוות שמואל אמר תן ששית על וששיתם ונמצאת תורם אחד מארבעים בינונים אחד מחמשים אמר רבי לוי כתיב (במדבר לא) וממחצית בני ישראל תקח אחד אחוז מן החמשים כל שאתה אוחז הרי הוא כזה מה זה אחד מחמשים אף מה שתאחוז ממקום אחר אחד מחמשים והרעה אחד מששים דכתי' (יחזקאל מה) *ששית האיפה מחומר החטים ב"ש אומרים אחד מל' וששית האיפה מחומר השעורים בינונית אחד ממ' מן הדא דשמואל והרעה אחד מנ' מן הדא דר' לוי פירוש ששית האיפה קרא ורישא דקרא זאת התרומה אשר תרימו ששית האיפה מחומר החטים וששיתם מחומר השעורים וחומר הוא כור ל' סאה ואיפה שלשה סאין נמצא דששית האיפה חצי סאה מכור של חטין דהיינו אחד מס' והיא עין רעה לב"ה ועין יפה דורש שמואל משום דכתיב וששיתם דששיתם משמע ב' ששיות וכשאתה נותן זה על זה ובאת לצרף החומרים והששיות הרי ג' ששיות מב' חומרין דהיינו סאה וחצי מס' סאין והוא אחד מארבעים לעין יפה ובינונים אחד מנ' מקרא דר' לוי וב"ש מוקמי וששיתם ב' ששיות מחומר דהיינו סאה משלשים סאין לעין יפה ובינונית אחד מארבעים ודרשה דשמואל דתן ששית על וששיתם ועין רעה אחד מנ' מקרא דרבי לוי והא דתני מתני' והבינונית מחמשים והרעה מס' לאו מדברי ב"ש אלא לתנא קמא ומעין יפה לדברי ב"ש אתה למד לדברי' עין רעה ובינונית אע"ג דלא תני ליה במתני' : ועלה בידו אחד מס'· כגון שתרם באומד ומצא באומד שלו אחד מששים והוא עין רעה : חזר והוסיף חייב במעשרות· דכבר נפטר ואין שם תרומה חל על מה שהוסיף : עלה בידו אחד מס"א· כגון שהיו בכרי ס"א סאין ועלה בידו סאה אחת אותה סאה תרומה ויחזור ויתרום כמו שהוא למוד דאם הוא רגיל לתרום אחד מחמשים נמצאו דנשארו עדיין י"א סאה שלא נתרמו : במדה במשקל· כלומר אותו מותר שהוא תורם מותר לתרום במדה במשקל במנין דלא אמרו לתרום מאומד אלא בתחלת תרומה אבל מוקף ודאי צריך ורבי יהודה סבר דאף מוקף לא צריך אלא בתחלה : ד האומר לשלוחו צא ותרום· בפ"ב דקדושין (דף מא:) נפקא לן דשלוחו של אדם כמותו מדכתיב (במדבר יח) תרימו גם אתם לרבות שלוחכם : כדעתו של בעל הבית· לפי שיש תורם בעין יפה ויש בעין רעה ויש בבינונית: פיחת עשרה· תרם מארבעים או הוסיף עשרה ותרם מששים תרומתו תרומה והא דאמרי' בריש אלו מציאות (דף כב·) כשאמר לו כלך אצל יפות אם נמצאו יפות מהן תרומתו תרומה שאני התם דגלי אדעתיה דלא ניחא ליה ומיהו פסיק ותני במתני' תרומתו תרומה אפילו אתא בעל הבית ואמר לא ניחא לי וצריך לומר דשאני הכא דלתיקון רבנן הך שיעורין כדאמר בפרק אלמנה ניזונית (דף צט:) כיון דאיכא דתורם בעין יפה ואיכא דתורם בעין רעה א"ל להכי אמדתיך אבל לענין יפות ורעות רובא דעלמא תורמין מן היפות על היפות ומן הרעות על הרעות ודוקא גבי שליח אמרינן פיחת עשרה אין תרומתו תרומה אבל בעל הבית יותר מעשרה אבל בעל הבית תניא בפ' אלמנה ניזונית (שם) תרם ועלה בידו אפי' אחד מכ' תרומתו תרומה : ואם נתכוין להוסיף· שהיה יודע דעתו של בעל הבית ובמתכוין *להוסיף אפילו אחד אין תרומתו תרומה ותימא הא דאיבעיא לן בפ' אלמנה ניזונית (צח:) זבין לי ליתכא ואזיל זבין ליה כורא מהו מוסיף על דבריו הוי וליתכא מיהא קני או מעביר על דבריו הוי וליתכא נמי לא קני תיפשוט מהכא דמעביר על דבריו הוי דאי מוסיף על דבריו הוי שיעורא מיהא ליהוי תרומה ומתני' משמע דליכא תרומה כלל ודכוות' דייק התם האומר לשלוחו תן חתיכה לאורחים כו' ודחי לה התם וי"ל דשאני הכא דאיכא פסידא לבעל הבית דאם הרבה שליח בתרומה אם תימצא לומר דכשיעור הוי תרומה נמצאו חולין מדומעין עם התרומה ואם פיחת נמצא טבלו מדומע עם החולין : ירושלמי (הל' ג) עד כדון כשאמר לו תרום לדעתי היה יודע דעתו של בעל הבית ולא אמר לו לא ותרום לדעתי נשמעינה מן הדא אם אינו יודע דעתו של בעל הבית [מפני שאינו יודע] הא אם יודע אע"פ שלא אמר לו כמי שאמר לו א"ר בון בר כהנא הפוחת אחד מי' תרומה והמוסיף אחד מי' תרומה אבל לא חולין שאין היך הפחת והתוספת שוין היך עבידא הוה יליף תריס אחד מנ' כד תרס אחד ממ' מפסיד ליה י' רבעין כל תרס אחד מס' מתגר ליה ד' רבעי' הכא אתמר תרומתו תרומה וכה אתמר אין תרומתו תרומה אמר רבי חנינא כאן במתכוין לפחות כאן במתכוין להוסיף רבי חגי בעי קומי רבי יוסי תמן תנינן (מעילה פ"ו מ"א) אמר לו תן להם חתיכה אחת והוא אומר טלו ב' והן נטלו ג' כולן מעלו וכאן אתמר הכן א"ל התם מחתיכה ראשונה נסתיימה שליחות בעל הבית ברם הכא על כל חטה וחטה נסתיימה שליחות בעל הבית מה נפק מביניהון היו לפניו ב' כריין אחד נתקן לדעתו ואחד שלא לדעתו עד כדון פי' הא מילתא פשיטא לן דמתני' מתיישבת כשאמר בעל הבית לשליח תרום לדעתי אבל הא מיבעי' לן אי מהני כשאמר לשליח תרום סתם ולא אמר לו תרום לדעתי אי תורם כדעתו של בעל הבית או בבינוני אבל אם לא אמר לו כלל לא תרום פשיטא דלא מהני כדמוכח בריש אלו מציאות (דף כב·) ומדקדק ממתני' אע"ג דלא אמר לדעתיה כמאן דא"ל דמי ובתוספ' (שרי) דקתני האומר לשלוחו לא תרום אחד מנ' פיחת י' או הוסיף עשרה תרומתו תרומה האומר לשלוחו סתם אחד מנ' יש לו לתרום הפוחת אחד מי' (או) שפיחת יותר מי' כגון שפיחת י"א ותרם אחד מל"ט או שהוסיף אחד מי' שהוסיף י"א ותרם אחד מס"א בשניהן תרומתו תרומה אבל לא לענין שיחשב כל השאר חולין מתוקנין שאין תרומתו תרומה אלא לפי חשבון דעתו של בעל הבית ונמצא כשפיחת אחד מי' טבל מעורב עם התרומה וכשמוסיף אחד מי' טבל מעורב עם החולין ואינו יודע דעתו דבעל הבית קאי ולא אמתכוין להוסיף ולפחות שאין כמו ואין כלומר פחת ותוספת אין שוין דמפסיד *בפוחת [יותר] ממה שמשתכר בתוספות דהיכא דרגיל בעל הבית לתרום אחד מנ' ותרם אחד ממ' נמצא מפסיד אחד ממ' **שנטל מי' סאין שהן ו' רביעין של קב דהיינו קב ומחצה דביו"ד סאין יש ס' קבין טול אחד ממ' הרי קב ומחצה וכשתורם אחד מס' משתכר ד' רבעי' שהרי בעל הבית שתורם אחד מנ' נמצא מגיע לס' סאין סאה וקב וחומש קב אלא דלא חשיב האי חומש בהדי ד' רבעים דמשתכר משום דאינו מגיע לרובע הכא אתמר תרומתו תרומה מתוך שינויא דר"ח דמשני כאן במתכוין לפחות כאן במתכוין להוסיף משמע דאיכא משנה או ברייתא בשום מקום מוכחא דשליח הפוחת במתכוין תרומתו תרומה משום הכי קשיא ליה דמתני' קתני גבי מוסיף דאין תרומתו תרומה וס"ד דבין מתני' בין ברייתא נקט חד והוא הדין לאידך ורבי חנינא משני דיש חילוק בין פוחת למוסיף והדבר מגומגם מאד ושמא טעות סופר בירושלמי תמן תנינן בפרק בתרא דמעילה (דף כ) וקשיא לר' חגי דהתם כולם מעלו אפי' בעל הבית אלמא מוסיף על דבריו הוי ולא מעביר והכא קתני אין תרומתו תרומה אלמא מעביר על דבריו הוא וזהו כעין קושיא שהקשיתי לעיל ומשני דגבי מעילה דמשנטלו חתיכה ראשונה נעשה שליחותו של בעל הבית אבל במתני' על כל חטה וחטה נסתיימה שליחות בעל הבית בתמיה והלא כשהוא פוחת או מוסיף ספרשתו בבת אחת עשויה והוה ליה מעביר מה נפיק מביניהן מה נוכל לדמות להיא דמעילה היו לפניו ב' כריין שנטל מן האחד כשיעור דעתו של בעל הבית ומכרי האחר הוסיף שלא לדעתו : ה אחד מעשרה· יכול להרבות תרומה גדולה אבל ריבה יותר לא קדוש בתרומה והרי היתר חולין הטבולים למעשר ומשום דלא

*) נ"ל יותר כפיחת א' **) נ"ל של י' סאין כו'

מסורת השש"ס

א) חולין פי"א דף קלז: ב) קדושין פ"ב דף מא: כתובות פרק י"א דף צט : בכורות פ"ט דף סא:

פי' מהר"י בן מלכי צדק

ואם תאמר אתי למעבדינון תרומה ולפוטרן מן המעשר לא חיישינן להא דהא המרב' בתרומ' עושה אותן תרומה ופוטרן מן המעשר אף הכא כן וצריכא עיונא : ב מי שהיו פירותיו במגורה וכו' . פירוש במקום העשוי להכניס שם הפירות שמו מגורה ובלעז למנדרו: ונתן סאה לבן לוי וסאה לעני · פי' בסתם ולא פירש כי זו מעשר ראשון וזו מעשר עני וראה הפועל בעיניו אע"פ שאינו מאמין לבעל הבית הנה יכול לאכול ח' סאין בלא כלום ספיקא דאפי' אם היו טבולין לראשון ולשני ממה נפשך ח' סאין מתוקנין ויותר דודאי מה שנתן לשם מעשר הפרישו : וחכמים אומרים אימור לשם הבקר בעלמא יהב להו ואינו יכול לאכול אם אינו מפריש לפי חשבון מה שאוכל כדתנן התם פועל שאינו מאמין לבעל הבית וכו' והכי גרסי' בירושל' א"ר אלעזר וכו' כלומר עשו המשנה הזה כפועל כלומ' בפועל אוקמוה . פ"א נתן סאה לבן לוי וסאה לעני ובן לוי מדדה ולא מצאה שלימה יש לומר שהיא סאה שהפריש ואבדה הימנו לפיכך מפריש עוד ח' סאין ואוכלן דברי רבי מאיר דנאמן בעל הבית וחכמים אומרים הואיל ואבדה מחמדה אינו נאמן לומר אני סאה נתתי לו אלא אם נמצא עתה בידו חצי סאה מפריש ח' סאין עליה ואוכלן ולא יותר וצריכא עיונא: גרסי' בירושל' א"ר אלעזר בש"ר אושעיא עשו אותה כפועל שאינו מאמין לבעל הבית פשטא מיהא נשרפו הפירות תרומה בטילה נשרפה התרומה לכשיאכלו הפירות התרומה קדשה למפרע. פ"א נתן סאה לבן לוי וכו' פי' והלכו להם לפיכך ר' מאיר סבר אע"ג דליתנהו יכול לומר מה שנתתי לפלוני יהא מעשר ומפריש עליהן ח' סאין ואוכלן ולא חיישינן שמא נאבדו או נשרפו ורבנן סברי חיישינן שמא נאבדו או שמא נשרפו הלכך מורה זו אצלו עשו אותה כפועל שאינו מאמין לבעה"ב והרי הוא כמוהו שצריך להפריש תרומת המעשר לפי חשבון אותה הסאה שנתן ואז יאכל ח' סאין וזהו פי' עשו אותה כפועל שאינו מאמין לבעה"ב ויותר נראה לנו זה הפירוש האחרון שפירשנו מב' הפירושין הראשונים : ג עלה בידו משישים ואחד . פי' כגון שהיו לו ס"א כורין ועלה בידו כור תרומה הוי ויחזור ויתרום כמות שהוא למוד.פי' אם היה למוד [אחד] *) (י') סאין פחות ב' קבין ואם היה למוד א' מס' נוטל מכור שלא לקח חצי סאה ואע"פ ששנינו אין תורמין לא במדה ולא במשקל וכו' הני מילי פעם ראשונה אבל עתה במדה במשקל ובמנין אבל מן המוקף בע ר' יהודה אומר אף לא מן המוקף . אלא נוטל ממקום שרוצה ומשלים כמו שהיה למוד:ד האומר לשלוחו וכו'.מנלן דיכלינן למנויי שליח דכתיב כן תרימו גם אתם הוה ליה לומר אתם מדקאמר גם לרבות ש יודע דעתו של בעה"ב תורם בבינונית א' מנ': פיחת י' ועשה א' מס' או הוסיף י' ועשה א' ממ' תרומתו תרומה ואינן חולין מאי טעמא שאין הפחת והתוספת שוין · כיצד היה נוהג לתרום א' מנ' כשתר א' ממ' נמצא שמפסידו י' רובעין כיצד ממ' נטל סאה וי' סאין ששים קבין ולקח מהן קב וחצי קב תרומה נמצא מפסידו ו' רובעין דקב הוי ד' רבעי וחצי קב ב' רבעים הא ו' · וכשפוחת ותרם א' מס' מר ויותר כמו שליש רובע הרי מצינו שאין הפחת והתוספת שוין הני מילי בשלא נתכוין להוסיף אבל אם ידע דעתו של בעל הבית והוסיף בכונה אפילו אחד אין תרומתן תרומה : ה המרבה בתרומה ר' אליע

*) [נ"ע דאחד מנ' מי"א בכור [שלא לקח מהם תרומה עדיין] אינו מגיע רק ששה סאין ומחצה וחצי קב ועשירית קב · ואולי נ"ל דלוקח עוד ז' סאין פחות ב' קבין ואף דמגיע פחות מעט מב' קבין מ"מ לתו

עין משפט נר מצוה

ג א מיי' פ"ז מהל' מעשר הלכה ט : [סאה]

ד ב מיי' פ"ג מהל' תרומות הלכה ב' סמג עשין קלג טוש"ע י"ד סימן שלא סעיף יט :

ה ג מיי' שם הל' ו :

ו ד מיי' פ"ד שם הלכה ז :

פירוש הרא"ש

(ב) [כדכתיב העוד הזרע במגורה חגי ב']:

הגהות מהר"י לנדא

פרק ד ה) מ"ד בר"מ או פחות י"ל או פיחות:

נ"ל ולפי

ירושלמי שלפנינו הגירסא וששיתם את האיפה מחומר השעורים :

נ"ל הוסיף

כתרומת מעשר יתר מכאן יעשנה תרומת מעשר *אבל לא למקום אחר ר' ישמעאל אומר מחצה חולין ומחצה תרומה רבי טרפון ורע"ק אומרים עד שישייר שם חולין: ו בג' פרקים משערים את הכלכלה בבכורות ובסיפות ובאמצע הקיץ המונה משובח המודד משובח ממנו והשוקל משובח משלשתן: ז ר' אליעזר אומר תרומה עולה באחד ומאה ר' יהושע אומר במאה ועוד ועוד זה אין לו שיעור רבי יוסי בן משולם אומר ועוד קב למאה סאה שתות למדמע: ח רבי יהושע אומר תאנים שחורות מעלות את הלבנות לבנות מעלות את השחורות עגולי דבלה הגדולים מעלים את הקטנים והקטנים מעלין את הגדולים העגולים מעלין את המלבנים והמלבנים מעלים את העגולים רבי אליעזר אוסר ורבי עקיבא אומר בידוע מה נפלה אין מעלות זו את זו ובשאינו ידוע מה נפלה מעלות זו את זו: ט כיצד חמשים תאנים שחורות וחמשים לבנות נפלה שחורה שחורות אסורות והלבנות מותרות נפלה לבנה לבנות אסורות ושחורות מותרות בשאינו ידוע מה נפלה מעלות זו את זו ובזו ר"א מחמיר ורבי יהושע מיקל: י ובזו ר"א מיקל ור' יהושע מחמיר בדורס ליטרא קציעות על פי הכד ואינו יודע איזוהי רבי אליעזר אומר רואין אותן כאילו הם פרודות והתחתונות מעלות את העליונות רבי יהושע אומר לא תעלה עד שיהיו שם מאה כדים: יא סאה תרומה שנפלה על פי מגורה וקפאה רבי אליעזר אומר אם יש

THE CASE OF HEAVE-OFFERING OF TITHE.[2] [IF HE GAVE] MORE THAN THIS [MEASURE] HE MUST MAKE IT TERUMAH OF TITHE FOR OTHER PRODUCE.[3] R. ISHMAEL SAYS: TILL HALF BE SECULAR AND HALF TERUMAH.[4] R. TARFON AND R. AKIBA SAY: AS LONG AS HE RETAINS A PART AS ḤULLIN.[5]

MISHNAH 6. ON THREE OCCASIONS[6] DOES ONE MEASURE THE CONTENTS OF THE BASKET:[7] AT THE FULL TIME OF THE FIRST RIPE FRUITS,[8] AND OF THE LATE SUMMER FRUITS,[9] AND IN THE MIDDLE OF THE SUMMER.[10] HE WHO COUNTS [THE FRUITS] DESERVES PRAISE,[11] HE WHO MEASURES THEM EVEN MORE PRAISE, BUT HE WHO WEIGHS THEM IS MOST MERITORIOUS.

MISHNAH 7. R. ELIEZER SAYS: TERUMAH IS NEUTRALIZED IN A HUNDRED AND ONE PARTS;[12] R. JOSHUA SAYS: IN JUST A
a LITTLE OVER A HUNDRED,[1] AND THIS 'LITTLE OVER' HAS NO DEFINITE MEASURE.[2] R. JOSE B. MESHULLAM SAYS: THIS 'LITTLE OVER' MUST BE A ḲAB TO A HUNDRED SE'AHS,[3] NAMELY A SIXTH [OF THE SE'AH][4] WHICH RENDERS THE WHOLE AS MEDUMMA'.

MISHNAH 8. R. JOSHUA SAYS: BLACK FIGS SERVE TO NEUTRALIZE WHITE ONES, AND WHITE ONES SERVE TO NEUTRALIZE BLACK ONES.[5] IN THE CASE OF CAKES OF FIGS, THE LARGE SERVE TO NEUTRALIZE THE SMALL, AND THE SMALL SERVE TO NEUTRALIZE THE LARGE.[6] ROUND CAKES OF FIGS SERVE TO NEUTRALIZE THOSE PRESSED IN SQUARE MOULDS,[7] AND THOSE PRESSED IN SQUARE MOULDS SERVE TO NEUTRALIZE THE ROUND ONES. R. ELIEZER PROHIBITS THIS. R. AKIBA SAYS: IF THE KIND WHICH FELL IN BE KNOWN,[8] THEN THE ONE KIND CANNOT NEUTRALIZE THE OTHER;[9] BUT IF THE KIND BE NOT KNOWN, THEN THE ONE KIND SERVES TO NEUTRALIZE THE OTHER.[10]

MISHNAH 9. FOR EXAMPLE?[11] IF THERE WERE FIFTY
b BLACK FIGS AND FIFTY WHITE ONES,[1] AND A BLACK ONE[2] FELL AMONG THEM, THE BLACK ONES ARE FORBIDDEN, BUT THE WHITE FIGS ARE PERMITTED; AND IF A WHITE FIG[2] FELL AMONG THEM, THE WHITE ONES ARE FORBIDDEN AND THE BLACK FIGS ARE PERMITTED. IF IT BE NOT KNOWN WHICH KIND FELL IN, THEN EACH KIND HELPS TO NEUTRALIZE THE OTHER. IN THIS CASE, R. ELIEZER IS MORE STRINGENT AND R. JOSHUA MORE LENIENT.

MISHNAH 10. BUT IN THIS INSTANCE [THAT FOLLOWS],[3] R. ELIEZER IS THE MORE LENIENT AND R. JOSHUA THE MORE STRINGENT. IF A LIṬRA[4] OF DRIED FIGS[2] WAS PRESSED INTO A JAR[5] AND IT IS NOT KNOWN INTO WHICH,[6] R. ELIEZER SAYS: THEY[7] ARE TO BE REGARDED AS IF THEY WERE SEPARATED,[8] SO THAT THOSE BELOW NEUTRALIZE THOSE ABOVE. R. JOSHUA MAINTAINS THAT NO NEUTRALIZATION CAN TAKE PLACE UNTIL THERE BE A HUNDRED JARS.[9]

MISHNAH 11. IF A SE'AH OF TERUMAH FELL ON TOP OF A PILE[10] AND HE SKIMMED IT OFF,[11] R. ELIEZER SAYS, IF THERE BE

(2) Which is also known by the name of *terumah*. (3) The surplus cannot be deemed as *terumah*, but as produce from which *terumah* has been taken but not the tithe with which *terumah* is mixed up. It can consequently be sold to a Levite who can use it only as *terumah* of tithe for other produce. (4) One may even declare half his pile *terumah*, leaving only half as *ḥullin*. (5) He may separate most of his pile as *terumah*; v. Ḥal. I, 9. (6) When the fruits vary in size. (7) In which the tithes are usually taken. *Terumah gedolah* was given approximately, yet consideration must be taken as to the size of the fruits. (8) Being large, the basket will not contain so many. (9) Of these, since they are parched and shrivelled, there will be more in the basket. (10) When the fruits are midway in quality between the first-ripe and late summer fruits. (11) With reference to tithes only. *Terumah gedolah* is to be given approximately, since the amount fixed is only a Rabbinical injunction, the Torah requiring only one grain. Tithes had to be properly measured; cf. Aboth. I, 16. (12) If into a hundred *se'ahs* of *ḥullin* there falls one of *terumah*, making a hundred and one *se'ahs* in all, one *se'ah* is taken out and given to the priest and the rest is permissible to the Israelite, though the *se'ah* of *terumah* may still be in the pile.
a (1) Even if the *se'ah* of *terumah* falls into a pile of *ḥullin* of just over ninety-nine *se'ahs*, a little more than a hundred *se'ahs* in all, the *terumah* is neutralized. (2) Even if it be the most trifling over a hundred, then *terumah* is negatived. (3) A *ḳab* equals 1/6th of a *se'ah*. The whole mixture including the *se'ah* of *terumah* must then be at least a hundred *se'ahs* plus one *ḳab*. (4) I.e., of *terumah* that fell into ninety-nine *se'ahs* and a *ḳab* of *ḥullin*. (5) If a white or black fig of *terumah* falls into a basket containing fifty of each kind so that it is impossible to discern which is *terumah* and which is *ḥullin*, the two kinds combine to neutralize the fig of *terumah*. He must, however, first give to the priest a fig of the same kind that fell in before all the figs of *ḥullin* are permitted to him. (6) Similarly, a large or small cake of figs of *terumah* falling into a pile containing fifty of each kind, is neutralized, and all the figs may be eaten after having given to the priest a cake of figs similar to the kind that fell in. (7) Cf. Pe'ah III, 1, where the word is used of a garden-bed three handbreadths in width. (8) What its colour, size or shape was. (9) Since he can only eat those figs of *ḥullin* that are of a different kind to that of the *terumah* which fell in. (10) The whole pile being in a state of doubt, one kind serves to neutralize the other. The ruling adopted is that of R. Akiba. (11) Elucidating the opinion of R. Akiba in the Mishnah preceding.
b (1) Of *ḥullin*. (2) Of *terumah*. (3) V. *infra* n. 8. (4) Latin *libra*. The figs used to be pressed into round shapes of a pound in weight. (5) Near a lot of others each containing a hundred *liṭras* of figs of *ḥullin*. (6) There is definitely a *liṭra* of *terumah* on top of one of the vessels, but of which one it is unknown. (7) The *liṭra* of dried figs that fell in. (8) And not as pressed together into one solid mass; accordingly a doubt rests on each fig of the vessel, even on those at the bottom, if it be of the *liṭra* that fell in. Hence all help to neutralize the *terumah*. But R. Eliezer will admit that this only applies when the figs in the vessel are of the same kind that fell in, but in the case of white figs that fell into black ones, or those of a different shape into those of another, no neutralization can take place, since the *terumah* is easily discernible. (9) In order to neutralize the top layer of figs in the jars. Should there be less than this number, the top layers in all the jars are prohibited, and subject to the law of *terumah*. (10) In a barn stacked with grain. (11) Together with much other grain of *ḥullin*.

IN WHAT HE SKIMMED OFF[12] A HUNDRED SE'AHS, IT BECOMES NEUTRALIZED IN ONE HUNDRED AND ONE; BUT R. JOSHUA
a SAYS THAT IT DOES NOT BECOME NEUTRALIZED.[1] [BUT WHAT SHOULD HE DO?] IF A SE'AH OF TERUMAH FELL ON TOP OF A PILE OF GRAIN, IT MUST BE SKIMMED OFF WITH THE WHOLE OF THE TOP LAYER.[2] IF THIS BE SO, WHEREFORE THEN HAVE THEY SAID THAT TERUMAH BECOMES NEUTRALIZED IN ONE HUNDRED AND ONE PARTS?[3] [ONLY] WHEN IT BE NOT KNOWN WHETHER IT HAS BECOME MIXED UP OR WHERE IT HAS FALLEN.[4]

MISHNAH 12. IF INTO TWO BASKETS OR TWO PILES[5] A SE'AH OF TERUMAH FELL, AND IT IS NOT KNOWN INTO WHICH IT HAD FALLEN, THEY SERVE TO NEUTRALIZE EACH OTHER.[6] R. SIMEON SAYS: EVEN IF THEY BE IN TWO CITIES, THEY SERVE TO NEUTRALIZE THE TERUMAH.

MISHNAH 13. R. JOSE SAID: A CASE ONCE CAME BEFORE R. AKIBA CONCERNING FIFTY BUNDLES OF VEGETABLES INTO WHICH A LIKE BUNDLE HAD FALLEN,[7] HALF OF WHICH WAS TERUMAH, AND I RULED IN HIS PRESENCE THAT IT BECAME NEUTRALIZED, NOT BECAUSE TERUMAH CAN BE NEUTRALIZED IN FIFTY AND ONE, BUT SIMPLY BECAUSE THERE WERE ONE HUNDRED AND TWO HALVES THERE.[8]

CHAPTER V

MISHNAH 1. IF A SE'AH OF UNCLEAN TERUMAH FELL
b INTO LESS THAN A HUNDRED OF ḤULLIN,[1] OR FIRST TITHE, OR SECOND TITHE, OR DEDICATED PROPERTY,[2] WHETHER THESE WERE UNCLEAN OR CLEAN, THEY MUST ALL BE LEFT TO ROT.[3] IF, HOWEVER, THAT SE'AH WAS CLEAN,[4] [THE ADMIXTURE] MUST BE SOLD TO PRIESTS AT THE PRICE OF TERUMAH,[5] EXCLUDING THE VALUE OF THAT SE'AH ITSELF.[6] IF IT FELL INTO FIRST TITHE,[7] THE WHOLE IS PRONOUNCED AS HEAVE-OFFERING OF TITHE;[8] AND IF IT FELL INTO SECOND TITHE OR DEDICATED PROPERTY, THEY MUST BE REDEEMED.[9] IF THE ḤULLIN[10] WAS UNCLEAN, IT MAY BE EATEN IN THE FORM OF DRIED CRUSTS,[11] OR PARCHED CORN,[12] OR KNEADED WITH FRUIT JUICE,[13] OR DIVIDED INTO PIECES OF DOUGH SO THAT THE CONTENTS OF ONE EGG BE NOT IN ANY ONE PLACE.[14]

(12) By skimming the entire top layer, it is clear that he does not intend including the bottom layer at all for the purpose of neutralization, for though the grain can be said to have become mixed with the whole stack, yet it is apparently only the top layer which is his concern.
a (1) On the ground that it is suspiciously like an attempt to nullify *terumah* deliberately. (V. however, Bert.) (2) This agrees with R. Joshua that no neutralization can take place, but the whole top layer must be removed. (3) Since the remedy lies in the removal of the top layer, then in which case is the principle of one hundred and one applied? (4) Either when the *terumah* is not definitely present or if he had forgotten or was unaware from the outset where it had fallen. (5) In each basket being at least fifty *se'ahs* of *ḥullin*. (6) I.e., they combine with each other to effect neutralization. This is achieved by extracting one *se'ah* from any of the two baskets, or even half a *se'ah* from each. (7) Similar in all respects to the others, but consisting half of *terumah* and half of *ḥullin*. It is immaterial whether he knew which half was *terumah* or whether he had originally just declared half of the bundle *terumah*, without precisely specifying which that half was. (8) For together with the half of the bundle that fell in, there are one hundred and one parts of *ḥullin*, and one part of *terumah*; hence the half bundle of *terumah* cannot render the whole a mixture of *terumah*.
b (1) Had there been the prescribed hundred *se'ahs*, even unclean *terumah*, though forbidden to priests, would have been neutralized. (2) For sacred Temple use, either for sacrifice purchase or for Temple repair. (3) Since even a priest cannot eat it. It must not be burnt, like other *terumah*, lest he come to eat thereof. (4) And, of course, also the *ḥullin* into which it had fallen. (5) Which is less than that of *ḥullin* since only priests can be the purchasers, and since it cannot be eaten by them when they are unclean. (6) Which must be given free to the priest, its rightful owner. (7) From which the Levite had to give heave-offering of tithe to the priest. (8) And must be sold to the priest, with the exception of the value of the *terumah* and the heave-offering of tithe therein, which already belong to the priest. (9) The redemption money to be enjoyed in Jerusalem. (10) Into which it had fallen. (11) It can only be enjoyed in these forms. Each crust must be less than half an egg in size and must be eaten without any liquid, so it be not susceptible to uncleanness. (12) If roasted in fire in its dry state, it will not be susceptible to defilement. (13) Which is not of those seven liquids that render food susceptible to uncleanness (v. Maksh. VI, 4). Once the *terumah* becomes susceptible, it can no longer be eaten by the priest. (14) The amount fixed in Ṭoh. III, 4 for foods to be susceptible to uncleanness. Unclean *terumah* cannot be eaten even in these forms.

אבל מה שלמטה אין מסייע לבטל. בירוש' (הל' ח) מחלפא שיטתיה דר' אליעזר תמן אמר התחתונות מעלות לעליונות וכה אמר אם יש בקיפוי הא ארעייתא לא ומשני רבי שמעון בר בא בשם כהנא דברי רבי אליעזר עשויה כמרבה (מיד) מזיד כלומר דגרע משום דקיפאה ואין *כקפוי דאי לא קפה ודאי מעלה ר' אסא בשם רבי יוחנן עשאוה כסאה עולה מתוך ק' כלומר הא דתני אם יש בקיפוי הייני [עם] מה שלמטה ור' אליעזר ור' יהושע למעמייהו: יקפיאנה· לכתחלה יסיר מה שלמעלה והשאר מותר: [אם כן למה אמרו] · כלומר לאיזה מקום אמרו תרומה עולה בשאין ידוע אם בלולות אם תבלבל אותה סאה בכל המגורה או אין ידוע לאין נפלה באיזה מקום במגורה :

בקפוי *מאה סאה תעלה באחד ומאה ורבי יהושע אומר *לא תעלה סאה תרומה שנפלה על פי מגורה יקפיאנה ואם כן למה אמרו תרומה עולה באחד ומאה אם אינו ידוע אם בלולות הן או לאין נפלה : יב *שתי קופות ושתי מגורות שנפלה סאה תרומה לתוך אחת מהם ואין ידוע לאיזו מהן נפלה מעלות זו את זו רבי שמעון אומר אפילו הם בשתי עיירות מעלות זו את זו : יג *אמר רבי יוסי מעשה בא לפני רבי עקיבא בחמשים אגודות של ירק שנפלה אחת מהן לתוכן חציה תרומה ואמרתי לפניו תעלה לא שהתרומה תעלה בחמשים ואחד אלא שהיו שם מאה ושני חצאים :

פרק חמישי

א *סאה* א) תרומה טמאה שנפלה לפחות ממאה חולין או למעשר ראשון או למעשר שני או להקדש בין טמאין בין טהורים ירקבו *ואם טהורה היתה אותה הסאה ימכרו לכהנים בדמי תרומה חוץ מדמי אותה סאה *ואם למעשר ראשון נפלה יקרא שם לתרומת מעשר ואם למעשר שני או להקדש נפלה הרי אלו יפדו *ואם טמאים היו אותן החולין יאכלו נקודים או קליות או ילושו במי פירות או יתחלקו לעיסות כדי שלא יהא במקום

פי המגורה ונתקבלה שם ונתעבה כגון שנפלה סאה חטים של תרומה על פי אוצר גדול מחטים שנשער פי המגורה כולה אם יש באותו עליון כדי שאם יקבץ בשטח העליון בלבד מאה סאה אז תעלה ואם לאו יהיה הכל מדומע וזה הפך מה שאמר במה שקדם שאמר התחתונות מעלות את העליונות וכן אמרו בגמרא מוחלפת שיטתיה דר' אליעזר : ואמר ר' יהושע לא תעלה · ר"ל כי אין הדין בה שתעלה במאה ואחד מן הקופה אבל דין סאה של תרומה שנפלה על פי מגורה שיקפיאנה רוצה באמרו ר' יהושע יקפיאנה שיעלה אותה בעצמו ויגרור מעל פי המגורה מה שתחתיה בלבד ר"ל מה שתחת הסאה של תרומה שנפלה וכן בארו בתוספתא כי ענין מאמר ר' יהושע יקפיאנה רואים אותה כאלו היא חטים ע"ג שעורים והקשה ואמר אם הדבר כן ונראה אותה כאלו היא חטים ע"ג שעורים ונוליא מה שנפל בלבד באיזה דבר נאמר תעלה באחד ומאה השיב ואמר כי זה הוא כשלא ידע אם נתערבה או לא נתערבה או לא ידע ג"כ באיזה מקום קפאה והלכה כר' יהושע ויהיה שיעור דבריו כן ר' יהושע אומר לא תעלה אלא סאה תרומה שנפלה על פי מגורה יקפיאנה: **יב** בארו בגמ' כי שתי קופות מלטרפות ואפי' היתה אחת בבית א' והשנית בבית אחר אבל שתי מגורות עד שיהיו בבית אחד ונתנו הטעם בזה ואמרו קופות דרכן להתפנות מגורות אין דרכן להתפנות ופי' להתפנות לטלטלן ולהעתיקן ממקום למקום וכיון שמטלטלות ונעתקות יתקבצו בשעת הטלטול הנה נתבאר לך שאין הלכה כרבי שמעון : **יג** כל זה מבואר ולמות ומה שהודיעך רבי יוסי שלא נאמר שהאגודה טלה תדמע כיון שחליה תרומה והוא מעורב ועוד יתבאר זה הענין בפרק של אחר זה (מ"ה ו) :

א **כשנפל** חלק מהתרומה בפחות ממאה חלקים מזולתה יהיה הכל מדומע וכבר בארנו זה בפרק שלפני זה ואומר בזו ההלכה שלשת הלכות מהלכות המדומע והודיענו בדיניהם האחת אם נפלה סאה תרומה טמאה בפחות ממאה חולין או מעשר שני או מעשר ראשון או הקדש בין שיהיו אותן חולין או מעשר או הקדש טמאים או טהורים דין כולם שיניחו אותם שירקבו ויפסידו· וההלכה השנית אם נפלה סאה תרומה טהורה בפחות ממאה חולין טהורים או מעשר ראשון או מעשר שני והקדש טהורים ויהיה הכל מדומע והוא טהור ואם נפלה הסאה התרומה בחולין ימכרו כל החולין לכהן חוץ מדמי תרומה ואם נפלה במעשר ראשון יקרא שם לתרומת מעשר החייבת לאותו מעשר ראשון ויצטרף לאותה התרומה גדולה שנפלה וימכר הכל לכהן חוץ מדמי תרומה שנפלו ודמי תרומת מעשר ראשון שקרא לה שם לפי שתרומת מעשר גם כן לכהן ואם נפלה בהקדש ומעשר שני פודין אותו ויהיה חולין אחר שיחזור חולין מוכרו לכהן חוץ מדמי תרומה· וההלכה השלישית היא אם נפלה סאה תרומה טהורה בפחות ממאה חולין טמאים שיהיה הכל מדומע ועיקר אצלנו כי אוכלין טמאין אין מטמאים זולתם אלא אם הם כביצה ומה שהוא פחות מכביצה ממאכלים טמאים אין מטמאין זולתם והוא ענין אמרם טומאת אוכלין בכביצה ועוד נבאר זה וטעמו באר היטב בסדר טהרות ונתגנו העיקר כי האוכלין אין מטמאין עד שיפול עליהם אחד משבעה משקין וכבר זכרנו זה פעמים ועוד יתבאר במקומו. ואם נפל עליהם מי פירות כגון מי רמונים או תותים או אגסים וזולתם אינם מטמאים לפי שלא הוכשרו לטומאה ובמסכת מכשירין נבאר כל זה ומפני אלו השני עיקרים יהי' דין זה המדומע שימכר לכהן חוץ מדמי תרומה שבו והכהן הלוקח אותו אין לו רשות ללושו במים ולא באחד מן השבעה משקין כדי שלא תכשר התרומה באותן משקין ותטמא עם החולין שהם טמאים ואסור לאכול תרומה טמאה אבל דינה שתשרף אבל נבקש דרך שיוכל לאכלה והוא שיאכלנה נקודים וקודים הוא שיעשנה ככרות קטנות תהיה כל אחת כחצי בילה וכן אמרו בגמרא ואין הכוונה שילוש אותה כולה ויעשה ממנה ככרות קטנות כחצי בילה אבל הכוונה שילוש אותה ככר אחר ככר או שיאכל הכל קלוי כדי שלא יפול עליהם משקה או שילוש אותם במי פירות שאין מכשירין כמו שאמרט או יתחלקו אותן חולין שנדמעו לעיסות כדי שלא יהא במקום אחד כבילה מאלו החולין הטמאין שנתערבו בם תרומה וכשיהיה זה כמו שאמרנו לא יטמא חלק התרומה המעורב בה לפי שהוא פחות מכבילה כמו שנתנו העיקר הנה פסק את הדין באלו הארבעה חלקים שהם לריכות והם אם נפלה תרומה טהורה לחולין טמאים או לחולין טהורין או אם נפלה התרומה טמאה לחולין טהורין או טמאים והודיעט שדיני אלו הארבעה חלקים שלשה דינים כי דין תרומה טמאה כשנפלה בטמא או בטהור הכל שוה כמו שנתבאר :

כשנפלה

אגודות דהאיכן בלולים ומשני תקנה אלא לר' יוחנן אמאי ירקבו הוה ליה למימר ידליק ומשני סבר ר' (ב) ואם למעשר שני והקדש (ג) נמי דלא בכל

כאיזה מקום במגורה : **יב** ירושלמי (שם) רבי זירא ורבי חייא בשם ר' שמעון היו לפניו ב' קופות בזו כ' סאה ובזו כ' סאה ונפלה סאה תרומה לתוך אחת מהן ואין ידוע לאיזו נפלה רלה להעלות מזה מעלה מזה מעלה מחלה מזו ומחלה מזו מעלה תניא(בתוספתא פ' ו)ב' קופות בב' עליות שתי מגורות בעליה אחת הרי אלו יעלו רבי יהודה אומר לא יעלו רבי שמעון אומר אפי' בב' עיירות מעלות זו את זו ודוקא ב' מגורות בעליה אחת אבל ב' מגורות בב' עליות לא ומפרש בירושלמי (שם) מה בין מגורות לקופות קופות דרכן להתפנות מגורות אין דרכן להתפנות ולפי טעם זה נראה דהאי דמעלות זו את זו בשים בזו ובזו כ' היינו בשמתיכן של אדם אחד שדרכן להתפנות ולהתערב אבל ב' בני אדם לא וניחא השתא הא דתני בתוספתא (שם) בזו מאה ובזו אין מאה הריני אומר לתוך ק' נפלה למאי נפקא מינה הא כיון דלא ידיע מעלות זו את זו אלא משום ב' גברי אילטריך *ואין לומר משום דב'עיירות דתני לה בתר מילתיה דרבי שמעון (ג) : **יג** אמר רבי יוסי מעשה בא· לאתויי ראיה לב' קופות אתא דרואין אותן כאילו הן מעורבות כדאשכחן באגודות דאמרינן תעלה אף על פי שאין האגודות מעורבות ובירושלמי (שם) פריך דר' יוסי אדרבי יוסי דתניא רבי יוסי אומר בלול מעלה שאינו בלול אינו מעלה והכא קתני רבי יוסי באגודות דאיכן בלולים ומשני א] רבא המקפיד על תערובתו אינו מעלה ושאין מקפיד מעלה היאך עבידא קישות טמאה שנפלה למאה קשואים טהורים כלומר שלא הוכשרו הואיל ואינמקפיד על תערובתן מעלה הוכשרו הואיל והוא מקפיד על תערובתן אין מעלה וכל זה בדבר שאינו בלול אבל בדבר בלול בין מקפיד בין שאינו מקפיד מעלה : **מאה** וב' חציין · עם התרומה יש ק' חציין ושנים :

א **לפחות** מק' תרומה טמאה נמי עולה בק"א כדיליף בסיפרי בקל וחומר : ירקבו· לפי שאי אפשר לאכול תרומה טמאה ובירושלמי (הל' א) פריך ניחא *טהורה ירקבו וטמאין ירקבו על דעתיה דחזקיה ניחא על דעתיה דר' יוחנן ידלקו בשנפלה לטהורים כיון דנפלה לפחות מק' הן נחשבו הכל תרומה והוה ליה כתרומה טמאה שנתערבה בטהורה דאסורה באכילה משום טמאה ובהדלקה משום תרומה טהורה דאסור לשרוף תרומה טהורה וטמאין נמי אליבא דחזקיה דפליג בפרק כל שעה (דף לג:) בהא דתנן מדליקין בפת ושמן תרומה שנטמאת (רבי) חזקיה אמר לא שנו אלא פת אבל חטין לא שמא יבא לידי תקלה ור' יוחנן אמר אפילו חטים והשתא לחזקיה ניחא בטמאין דירקבו דחיים לתקלה אלא לר' יוחנן אמאי ירקבו הוה ליה למימר ידליק ומשני סבר ר' יוחנן כהדא שמא ימלא בהן תקלה ואע"ג דאוקימנא לה בפ' כל שעה בשליקתא ב] דמאיסתא דלאחר שנטמאו שולקן ואח"כ זורקן לבין העלים דנמאסות וחזקיה חייש דילמא אכיל להו מקמי דליזרקינהו או מקמי שסולקן מ"מ הכא אפי' ר' יוחנן מודה דדימוע קיל להו לאינשי ואיכא למיחש טפי עוד פריך בירושלמי (שם) אנפלה להקדש אמאי ירקבו ולא כן סברינן למימר אין להקדש אלא מקומו ושעתו והיא משנה בערכין בשילהי שום היתומים זו היא שעתו דמי עלים (א) ומשני א"ר יהודה תיפתר שתרב אותו מקום ולא מלאו למוכרו אפי' בדמי עלים : ואם טהורה היתה אותו סאה · תרומה שנפלה והחולין נמי טהורין ימכרו לכהנים בדמי תרומה בזול לפי שאסור לזרים : חוץ מדמי אותה סאה · דלריך לקיים מלות נתינה : ואם למעשר ראשון · טהורה נפלה שלא נטלה ממנו תרומת מעשר יעשנו תרומת מעשר על מעשר אחר (ב) ואם למעשר שני והקדש טהורה נפלו יפדו ויאכל דמי המעשר בירושלים והדימוע ג] לכהן בדמי תרומה חוץ מדמי אותה סאה : ואם טמאין היו החולין · או מעשר ראשון שנפלה בהן התרומה טהורה לא יעשנו תרומת מעשר אלא יפריש עליו ממקום אחר וימכרו לכהנים ויאכלו הכהנים נקודים או קליות [פירוש] ביובש כמו יבש היה נקודים (יהושע ט) דאין מטמאים את התרומה בלא הכשר או קליות נמי דלא מיתכשרי ולא מיטמאי או ילוש במי פירות דלא מכשרי או יחלקו לעיסות ובכל עיסה יתן ממנו פחות מכביצה דלא מטמא ולא דמי לטמאה בחולין טהורים ירקבו משום דנעשה הכל תרומה ונחשב כתרומה טמאה וטהורה שנתערבו דהכך חולין נעשין תרומה ליאסר לזרים מכח תרומה טמאה ולכהנים נמי אסור כתרומה טמאה [אבל הכך] חולין טמאין אין נעשין תרומה אלא מכח תרומה טהורה לית לן למיסרינהו באכילה אע"ג [דלעיל מחמרינן בהו טפי מבתרומה עצמה שנתערבה בהם] דלשריפה אסור [שאני התם דהחולין טהורין נעשו תרומה וחיישינן] דלמא יאמרו תרומה טהורה נשרפת אבל הכא שהחולין טמאין נעשין תרומה לא חיישינן שמא יאמרו תרומה טמאה נאכלת [דזיל קרי בי רב הוא] וידעי דמכח תרומה טהורה אתו [שריוה באכילה כתרומה טהורה] : תניא בסיפרי בפרשת קרח מכל חלבו את מקדשו ממנו שאם נפל לתוכו הרי הוא מקדשו מכאן אמרו תרומה עולה בק"א אין לי אלא תרומה טהורה תרומה טמאה מניין אמרת קל וחומר אם יעלה איסור מן האיסור להיתר קל וחומר לאיסור מן המותר להיתר רבי אומר אינו לריך קל וחומר הוא אם יעלה איסור מן המותר להיתר קל וחומר מן המותר למותר להיתר פירוש ממנו שנפל לתוכו כגון תרומת מעשר שהוא אחד מק' דמק' נוטלין עשר למעשר ראשון ומן הי' א' לתרומת מעשר אם חזר למקום שהורם דהיינו ל"ט אוסרת ולעיל בפ' ד' (משנה ז) פליגי ר"א ור' יהושע אי בעי ק"א אי סגי בק' ד] והדר יליף

תרומה טמאה מק"ו מטבל שאסור לכל כשתוציא ממנו תרומה שאסורה לזרים הותר אותו שהיה אסור ונמצא [התרומה] שאסור לזרים כשעלה מן הטבל שהוא אסור התירו לאכילה קל וחומר לתרומה טמאה שאסורה לכהן שנפלה לק' סאין תרומה טהורה שמותרת לכהן שעולה ומתיר את המותר ומהאי קל וחומר סיתם ראויה להתבטל אחד בנ"ט כטבל שניתר כשהופרש ממנו תרומת מעשר שהוא אחד מק' ומהאי קל וחומר נמי ראיה ללמוד ממנו תרומה טהורה שעולה בלאו דרשה ממנו *ודנקיט דרך אחר ואמר אם תעלה תרומה טהורה שאסורה לזרים מן החולין המותרים לזרים קל וחומר [לתרומה טמאה] שמותרת לכהן להסיקה תחת תבשילו שתעלה מן הטהורה שמותרת לאכילה ובטלה הטמאה במיעוטה ונעשה הכל מותר ובירושלמי דערלה פ"ב (הל' א') גרסינן א"ר יונה כתיב מכל חלבו את מקדשו ממנו דבר שאתה מרים ממנו אם יפול לתוכו מקדשו וכמה הוא אחד ממאה ר' אליעזר מוסיף סאה ומעלה ר' יהושע מוסיף כל שהוא ומעלה רבי יוסי בן המשולם אומר ועוד קב למאה סאה שתות למדומע תני ר' *ישמעאל אומר תרומה עולה(בק"א) [בק' מק"ו] אם איסור עולה איסור מתוך היתר לא כ"ש

אית

אחד כביצה: ב סאה (א) תרומה טמאה שנפלה לתוך מאה חולין טהורין רבי אליעזר אומר תרום *ותשרף שאני אומר סאה שנפלה היא סאה שעלתה וחכ"א תעלה ותאכל נקודים או קליות או תלוש במי פירות או תתחלק לעיסות *כדי שלא יהא במקום אחד כביצה: ג סאה תרומה טהורה שנפלה למאה חולין טמאין תעלה ותאכל נקודים או קליות או תלוש במי פירות או תתחלק לעיסות *כדי שלא יהא במקום אחד כביצה: ד סאה תרומה טמאה שנפלה למאה סאה תרומה טהורה ב"ש אוסרים וב"ה מתירין אמרו ב"ה לב"ש הואיל וטהורה אסורה לזרים וטמאה אסורה לכהנים מה טהורה עולה אף טמאה תעלה אמרו להם ב"ש לא אם העלו החולין הקלין המותרין לזרים את הטהורה תעלה תרומה החמורה האסורה לזרים את הטמאה לאחר שהודו ר' אליעזר אומר (ו) תירום ותשרף וחכ"א אבדה במעוטה: ה סאה תרומה שנפלה למאה הגביהה ונפלה למקום אחר ר"א אומר מדמעת כתרומת ודאי וחכ"א אינה מדמעת (ז) אלא לפי חשבון: ו סאה תרומה שנפלה לפחות ממאה ונדמעו ונפל מן המדומע למקום אחר ר' אליעזר אומר מדמעת כתרומת ודאי וחכ"א אין המדומע מדמע אלא לפי חשבון ואין המחומץ מחמיץ אלא לפי חשבון ואין המים שאובים פוסלין את המקוה אלא

MISHNAH 2. If a se'ah of unclean terumah fell
a into a hundred of clean ḥullin,[1] R. Eliezer says: a se'ah must be taken out and burnt,[2] on the assumption that the se'ah taken out is the one that fell in. But the sages say: it is neutralized and eaten[3] as dried crusts, parched corn, or when kneaded with fruit-juice, or divided into pieces of dough so that the contents of one egg be not found in any one place.[4]

MISHNAH 3. If a se'ah of clean terumah fell into a hundred of unclean ḥullin, it becomes neutralized[5] and may be eaten in the form of dry crusts, or parched corn, or kneaded with fruit-juice, or divided into pieces of dough so that the contents of one egg be not found in any one place.

MISHNAH 4. If a se'ah of unclean terumah fell into one hundred se'ahs of clean terumah, Beth Shammai prohibit[6] [the whole], but Beth Hillel permit it. Said Beth Hillel to Beth Shammai: seeing that clean [terumah] is forbidden to non-priests and unclean [terumah is forbidden] to priests, then just as clean
b [terumah] becomes neutralized,[1] so should unclean [terumah] be neutralized.[2] Beth Shammai answered them: certainly not; just because ḥullin which is treated more leniently [in that it is permitted to non-priests], neutralizes clean [terumah], [shall] terumah [which is far more stringent in that it is forbidden to non-priests] also neutralize that which is unclean? After they had agreed,[3] R. Eliezer said: it should be taken out and burnt, but the sages said: it is regarded, on account of its paucity, as non-existent.[4]

MISHNAH 5. If a se'ah of terumah fell into a hundred [of ḥullin] and was lifted out and fell into [ḥullin] elsewhere, R. Eliezer says: the whole is rendered medumma'[5] as though undoubted terumah [had fallen in].[6] But the sages say: it is rendered medumma' only according to proportion.[7]

MISHNAH 6. If a se'ah of terumah fell into less than a hundred [of ḥullin], rendering the whole medumma', and part of this admixture fell after-
c wards into another place,[1] R. Eliezer says: it renders this again medumma', as though undoubted terumah [had fallen in][2]; but the sages say that the [first] mixture can affect the [second] mixture only according to the proportion.[3] [Similarly], that which is leavened [with terumah] can render other dough leavened [as with terumah], only according to the proportion;[4] and drawn water can disqualify the ritual bath also only according to the

a (1) Thus becoming neutralized. The reference is to *ḥullin* that had not been rendered susceptible by means of liquids to uncleanness. (2) As is the law regarding all *terumah* that had become defiled. Since prior to burning it had become neutralized, there is no fear lest he may eat thereof. No benefit, however, must be derived from the actual burning. (3) I.e., the whole mixture, v. Rashi. Bek. 22*b*. (4) V. notes to preceding Mishnah. One *se'ah*, however, must actually be burnt or given to a priest, since its very retention would give the appearance of 'robbing the tribe'. For other interpretations v. *Tif. Yis.* (5) Even R. Eliezer, who maintained above that the *se'ah* taken out as *terumah* must be burnt, will here admit that it may be eaten, for, when taken out, it resumes its status of clean *terumah*. Yet, despite this admission, he insists that it can be enjoyed only in the manner here prescribed, arguing that when he ruled that 'the *se'ah* which is taken out may be the one that fell in', it was meant as a stringent measure and not as a tendency to leniency. (6) Maintaining that *terumah* falling into other *terumah* is not neutralized even in one hundred and one parts.

b (1) By falling into a hundred parts of clean *ḥullin*. (2) The instance cited in our Mishnah. (3) Beth Shammai agreed to the view of Beth Hillel — said to be the only admission of such a kind. The counter-argument of Beth Hillel, omitted from the Mishnah, must have been this: If clean *terumah* (which non-priests must not eat on penalty of death) is neutralized, then surely unclean *terumah*, which the priest is debarred from eating only by a positive command, ought certainly to be neutralized! (4) The admixture pronounced clean and there is no need for even one *se'ah* to be taken out and burnt, since the whole has been neutralized. (5) V. Glos. (6) In accordance with his principle (*supra* V, 2) that the *se'ah* taken out is assumed to be the very one that fell in; hence though neutralized the first time, it is treated as *terumah* once again and requires a hundred *se'ahs* of *ḥullin* to neutralize it. (7) After it had been neutralized, only one 1/100th part thereof is actually *terumah*, and accordingly it becomes nullified in one *se'ah* of *ḥullin* the second time, and only that proportion need be separated as *terumah* to make the second admixture permissible.

c (1) Into other *ḥullin*. (2) True to his principle of *supra* V, 2. (3) Of *terumah* in the mixture that fell in. An illustration: If a *se'ah* of *terumah* fell into fifty of *ḥullin*, rendering the whole *medumma'*, and a *se'ah* of the *medumma'* afterwards fell into other *ḥullin*, it only requires two *se'ahs*, to counteract the *terumah* in the *se'ah* which fell in a second time, to neutralize it. (4) Dough leavened with *terumah* is forbidden to non-priests ('Orlah II, 4).

PROPORTION.[5]

MISHNAH 7. IF A SE'AH OF TERUMAH FELL INTO A HUNDRED [OF ḤULLIN] AND [A SE'AH] IS LIFTED OUT,[6] AND THERE FELL IN ANOTHER AND IS LIFTED OUT AND ANOTHER FELL IN,[7] THE ḤULLIN IS PERMISSIBLE AS LONG AS THE AMOUNT OF TERUMAH DOES NOT EXCEED THAT OF THE ḤULLIN.[8]

MISHNAH 8. IF A SE'AH OF TERUMAH FELL INTO A HUNDRED [OF ḤULLIN], AND BEFORE HE COULD TAKE IT OUT,
a ANOTHER FELL IN, THE WHOLE BECOMES FORBIDDEN.[1] R. SIMEON PERMITS IT.[2]

MISHNAH 9. IF A SE'AH OF TERUMAH FELL INTO A HUNDRED [OF ḤULLIN], AND THEY WERE GROUND TOGETHER AND REDUCED IN BULK, [IT IS ASSUMED THAT] JUST AS THE ḤULLIN BECAME LESS SO THE TERUMAH BECAME LESS, AND THE WHOLE IS PERMISSIBLE.[3] IF A SE'AH OF TERUMAH FELL INTO LESS THAN A HUNDRED [OF ḤULLIN] AND THEY WERE GROUND TOGETHER AND INCREASED IN BULK, [IT IS ASSUMED THAT] JUST AS THE ḤULLIN BECAME MORE, SO DID THE TERUMAH BECOME MORE,[4] AND IT IS FORBIDDEN. IF IT IS KNOWN THAT THE WHEAT OF ḤULLIN WAS BETTER THAN THE TERUMAH, IT IS PERMITTED.[5] IF A SE'AH OF TERUMAH FELL INTO LESS THAN A HUNDRED [OF ḤULLIN], AND MORE ḤULLIN FELL THEREIN LATER,[6] IF [THE OCCURRENCE WAS] ACCIDENTAL IT IS PERMISSIBLE,[7] BUT IF INTENTIONAL IT IS FORBIDDEN.[8]

CHAPTER VI

MISHNAH 1. ONE WHO EATS TERUMAH UNWITTINGLY
b MUST REPAY ITS VALUE PLUS A FIFTH,[1] WHETHER HE EATS OR DRINKS IT, OR ANOINTS HIMSELF WITH IT,[2] OR WHETHER THE TERUMAH IS CLEAN OR UNCLEAN; HE MUST PAY ITS FIFTH, AND A FIFTH OF THAT FIFTH.[3] THE REPAYMENT MUST NOT BE IN TERUMAH BUT IN ḤULLIN,[4] DULY TITHED, WHICH BECOMES TERUMAH, AND WHATEVER MAY BE REPAID IN ITS PLACE ALSO BECOMES TERUMAH.[5] IF THE PRIEST WISHES TO FOREGO

(5) A *mikweh* has to contain forty *se'ahs* of undrawn water, and if the slightest amount be lacking of this quantity and three *logs* of drawn water from a vessel were poured therein, it becomes ritually disqualified. If some water of this disqualified *mikweh* afterwards fell into another *mikweh*, likewise defective in the prescribed quantity, it only disqualifies according to the proportion of drawn water in the quantity now poured in. (6) In order to make the *ḥullin* by which it was neutralized permissible. (7) Into the same *ḥullin*, a *se'ah* of *terumah* keeps falling in and a *se'ah* is taken out. (8) As long as over fifty *se'ahs* of *terumah* have not fallen in one after another.

a (1) To a non-priest; it is as if the two had fallen in together, with no hundred to neutralize it. (2) On this principle that since it was about to be removed, we deem it as already removed. (3) And there is still the prescribed quantity in the *ḥullin* to neutralize the *terumah*. (The wheat becomes less in grinding if worms had got in and had taken out the flour). (4) Since both are ground together. (5) It being now obvious that the *ḥullin* had become more, and therefore possesses now the amount to neutralize the *terumah*. (6) Making the *ḥullin* one hundred and one *se'ahs*. (7) He must remove, however, the *se'ah* that fell in. (8) An intentional act implies a disregard of an injunction. The admixture is then treated as *medumma'*.

b (1) V. Lev. XXII, 14. This Fifth amounts to a quarter of the value of the *terumah* he ate. Thus if the *terumah* was valued at one *denar*, he must pay a *denar* and a quarter. All fifths mentioned in the Torah are computed thus. (2) Drinking wine of *terumah* is like eating *terumah*, and anointing oneself with oil of *terumah* like drinking it; cf. Shab. IX, 4. (3) If he further unwittingly eats of the Fifth he had brought, he must bring yet another fifth of this Fifth. (4) Since a debt must be repaid from one's own possessions, he cannot do so from *terumah*, which belongs to the priest. Even *terumah* which he inherits and may sell cannot be brought as compensation. (5) If he ate the *ḥullin* which he had repaid for eating *terumah*, the second repayment, too, becomes *terumah*.

מן הראשונה שיעור גדול שיהא בשאור המעורב בה כדי לחמץ אחרונה בלא צירוף חולין המדומעין ובסוף פ"ק דתמורה (דף יב.) מוקי לה כרבי אליעזר בן יעקב דתני ר"א בן יעקב אומר מקוה שיש בה כ"א סאה מי גשמים ממלא בכתף י"ט סאה ופותקן למקוה והם טהורין שהשאיבה מיטהרת ברבייה ובהמשכה והיינו לפי חשבון דאין השאובין פוסלים המקוה דרך המשכה אא"כ היו שם כ' סאין *ור"פ מפרש התם לפי חשבון כלים ויוסף בן חוני היא דתניא ג' לוגין מים שאובין שנפלו למקוה בב' וג' כלים ואפילו בד' וה' כלים פוסלין את המקוה יוסף בן חוני אומר בשנים ושלש כלים פוסלין את המקוה בארבעה וחמשה אין פוסלין את המקוה:

ז הגביהה · כדין תרומה שעולה בק"א וצריך להרים: עד שתרבה · דהיינו עד כ"א פעמים אבל מחלה על מחלה שרי והשתא לר' יוחנן דסוף הערל (דף פ"ב:) דלא בעי רבייה דרבנן ניחא אלא לריש לקיש קשה דאמר התם והוא שרבו חולין על התרומה ואין לחלק בין הך להיא דכוותה מדמי התם ברייתא למקוה דתנן נתן סאה ונפל סאה כשר ושמא הייתו טעמא דריש לקיש דעד כ' א"א שלא יהא עדיין רוב חולין דאכל סאה שהגביהה א"א שלא יעלה עמו מן התרומה ומטעם זה ניחא התם דחשיב הסיא דמקוה דרבנן אע"ג דאיירי במי פירות ומי פירות פוסלים מקוה מדאורייתא ברובה אלא לכך חשיב דרבנן דכ"א סאה נמי דרבנן א]דאכל סאה שמעלה א"א שלא יעלה מן מי הפירות לפי חשבון והרי יש כאן עדיין רוב מים:
ח עד שנפלה · סאה תרומה: הרי זו אסורה · דכמאן דנפל בבת אחת דמי ורבי שמעון סבר קמייתא בטיל בק' והיא בטילה בק"א כדפרשינן בפרק נוטל ובירושלמי (הל' ג) אמרינן ר' שמעון אומר ידיעתה מקדשתה ורבנן אמרין הרמתה מקדשתה כלומר לרבי שמעון אם לא נודע לו בראשונה עד שנפלה שניה היה הכל נאסר אבל השתא דנודע לו כיון דסופו להרים כמורם דמי כדאשכחן בעלמא דאית ליה לר"ש כל העומד ליזרק כזרוק דמי (פסחים יג:) ורבנן אזלי בתר הגבהה והכי נמי תניא [בתוספתא] (פרק ו) אמר רבי אלעזר ברבי שמעון בד"א בזמן דלא ידע בה ואח"כ נפלה אבל אם ידע בה ואח"כ נפלה אחרת מותרת שכבר היה לה לעלות וחכ"א הרמתה מקדשתה: ט וטחנן · הכל בבת אחת לא אמרינן החולין פחתו ולא התרומה ואין כאן ק"א ואסור כיון שנתבטלה שאפילו היה כך תו לא מתסרי תדע מדלא קתני בהא רישא אם ידוע שחטים של תרומה יפות כשטחן והותירו וקלא קשה למה ליה למימר פיחתה התרומה: כך הותירה התרומה · ואין כאן ק"א (י): אם ידוע שהחטין של חולין יפות משל תרומה מותר · דשל חולין הותירו ושל תרומה לא הותירו ויש כאן ק"א אע"ג דמעיקרא נאסרו חזרו והותרו בפתיחה ואמרי' בירושלמי (ה"ה) תני אף טוחן לכתחלה ומתניי' רבי יוסי דאמר אף מתכוין וילקט ויעלה במאתים ואחד א"ר זירא שכך דרך כהנים שטוחנים מדומע בבתיהן מה נפיק מביניהו (כל) כלאי הכרם על דעתיה דר' יוסי טוחן ומתיר על דעתיה דרבנן אין טוחן ומתיר: ירושלמי (שם) תני אין סנופת תרומה

לפי חשבון כלים ויוסי בן חוני היא אבל דעת החכמים שהם מצטרפין ופוסלין כמו שיתבאר במקואות והלכה כחכמים בכל:
ז עד שתרבה תרומה על החולין · הוא שיפול בק' סאה של חולין מאה ומשהו של תרומה זה אחר זה: ח נתבאר בתוספתא כי אמרם ה"ז אסורה כשלא ידע בנפילת

...

ולפיכך ג] אמרו כי מי שהרבה קנס לפי שבטל איסור ובכל מקום נתבארו בזה הפרק דיני המדומע התרומה ויהיה הנשאר מן החולין מותר כמו שבארנו:

...

קדש בשגגה ויסף חמישיתו עליו רביע מה שאכל שהוא חומש הכל מה שוה דינר ורביע דינר וכן כל וזהו ענין אמרם עד שיהא הוא עיקר שאכל ואמר השם יתעלה ולא (נדה לב.) להביא הסך והשותה מן הכתוב שאמר (דברים יד)

אלא לפי חשבון: ז [א]סאה תרומה שנפלה למאה הגביהה ונפלה אחרת *הגביהה ונפלה אחרת הרי זו מותרת עד שתרבה תרומה על החולין: ח [ב]סאה [א] תרומה שנפלה למאה ולא הספיק להגביה עד שנפלה אחרת הרי זו אסורה ר' שמעון מתיר: ט [ג]סאה תרומה שנפלה למאה וטחנם ופחתו כשם שפחתו החולין כך פחתה התרומה ומותר סאה תרומה שנפלה לפחות ממאה וטחנן והותירו כשם שהותירו החולין כך הותירה התרומה ואסור אם ידוע שהחטים של חולין יפות משל תרומה מותר [ד]סאה תרומה שנפלה לפחות ממאה ואחר כן נפלו שם חולין אם שוגג מותר ואם מזיד אסור:

פרק ששי

א האוכל ג) [ה]תרומה שוגג משלם קרן וחומש [ו]אחד האוכל אחד השותה ואחד הסך אחד תרומה טהורה ואחד תרומה טמאה משלם חומשה [ז]וחומש חומשה [ח]אינו משלם תרומה אלא חולין מתוקנים [ט]והם נעשין תרומה והתשלומין תרומה אם רצה הכהן

ז א מיי׳ פ״י מהלכ׳ תרומות הל׳ טז :

ז ב שם הלכה י :

ח ג שם הלכה כג :

ט ד שם הלכה כד :

י ה ו שם הלכ׳ יח :

א ז מיי׳ פ״י מהל׳ תרומות הל׳ ה :

ב ח שם הלכה טו :

א) כ״מ דף מד׳ ב) פסחים דף לב׳

פירוש הרא״ש

פי׳ מהרי״ן בן מלכי צדק

תורה אור

למחול אינו מוחל : ב בת ישראל שאכלה תרומה ואחר כך נשאת לכהן אם תרומה שלא זכה בה כהן אכלה משלמת קרן וחומש לעצמה אם תרומה שזכה בה כהן אכלה (ד) משלמת קרן לבעלים וחומש לעצמה מפני שאמרו האוכל תרומה שוגג משלם קרן לבעלים וחומש לכל מי שירצה : ג המאכיל את פועליו ואת אורחיו תרומה הוא (ה) משלם את הקרן והם משלמין את החומש דברי ר׳ מאיר וחכמים אומרי׳ הם משלמין קרן וחומש והוא משלם להם דמי סעודתן : ד הגונב א) תרומה ולא אכלה משלם תשלומי כפל דמי תרומה אכלה משלם ב׳ קרנים וחומש קרן וחומש מן החולין וקרן דמי תרומה גנב (ו) תרומת הקדש ואכלה משלם שני חומשים וקרן שאין בהקדש תשלומי כפל : ה אין משלמין מן הלקט ומן השכחה ומן הפאה ומן ההפקר ולא ממעשר ראשון *שנטלה תרומתו ולא ממעשר שני והקדש *שנפדו שאין הקדש פודה את הקדש דברי רבי מאיר וחכמים מתירין באלו : ו ר׳ אליעזר אומר משלמין ממין על שאינו מינו בלבד שישלם מן היפה על הרעה ור״ע אומר אין משלמין אלא ממין על מינו לפיכך אם אכל קשואין של ערב שביעית ימתין לקשואין של מוצאי שביעית וישלם מהם ממקום שרבי אליעזר מיקל משם ר׳ עקיבא מחמיר שנאמר ונתן לכהן את הקדש כל ג) שהוא ראוי להיות קדש דברי ר׳ אליעזר ור׳ עקיבא אומר ונתן לכהן את הקדש קדש שאכל :

פרק שביעי

א האוכל תרומה מזיד משלם את הקרן ואינו משלם את החומש התשלומין חולין אם רצה הכהן למחול מוחל :

בת

הגהות מהר״י לנדא

[THE FINE], HE CANNOT DO SO.[6]

MISHNAH 2. IF THE DAUGHTER OF AN ISRAELITE ATE TERUMAH[7] AND AFTERWARDS MARRIED A PRIEST,[8] IF THE TERUMAH SHE HAD EATEN HAD NOT YET BEEN ACQUIRED BY ANOTHER PRIEST SHE CAN REPAY TO HERSELF THE VALUE AND THE FIFTH;[9] BUT IF A PRIEST HAD ALREADY ACQUIRED THE TERUMAH SHE HAD EATEN, SHE MUST REPAY THE VALUE
a TO THE OWNERS,[1] BUT THE FIFTH TO HERSELF; BECAUSE IT HAD BEEN SAID THAT HE WHO EATS TERUMAH UNWITTINGLY, MUST PAY THE VALUE TO THE OWNERS AND THE FIFTH TO WHOMSOEVER[2] HE DESIRES.

MISHNAH 3. IF ONE GIVES HIS WORKMEN OR HIS GUESTS TERUMAH TO EAT HE MUST REPAY THE VALUE THEREOF,[3] WHILST THEY MUST PAY THE FIFTH;[4] SO R. MEIR. BUT THE SAGES SAY: THEY MUST PAY BOTH THE VALUE AND THE FIFTH, WHILST HE MUST PAY THEM FOR THE PRICE OF THEIR MEAL.[5]

MISHNAH 4. IF ONE STEALS TERUMAH BUT DID NOT EAT IT, HE MUST RETURN TWOFOLD AT THE PRICE OF THE TERUMAH.[6] IF HE HAD EATEN IT, HE MUST PAY TWICE THE VALUE PLUS A FIFTH: ONE VALUE AND A FIFTH FROM ḤULLIN,[7] AND THE OTHER VALUE AT THE PRICE OF TERUMAH.[8] IF ONE STEALS THE TERUMAH OF DEDICATED PROPERTY[9] AND ATE IT, HE MUST REPAY TWO FIFTHS,[10] IN ADDITION TO THE VALUE, FOR TO DEDICATED THINGS [THE LAW OF] TWOFOLD RESTITUTION DOES NOT APPLY.[11]

b *MISHNAH* 5. THIS REPAYMENT[1] CANNOT BE MADE FROM GLEANINGS, AND THE FORGOTTEN SHEAF, FROM PE'AH OR OWNERLESS PROPERTY;[2] NOR FROM FIRST TITHE FROM WHICH TERUMAH HAS BEEN TAKEN, OR FROM SECOND TITHE[3] OR DEDICATED PRODUCE[4] WHICH HAVE BEEN REDEEMED, FOR ONE DEDICATED THING CANNOT REDEEM ANOTHER WHICH HAS BEEN DEDICATED. SO R. MEIR; BUT THE SAGES PERMIT [PAYMENT] WITH THESE.[5]

MISHNAH 6. R. ELIEZER SAYS: REPAYMENT MAY BE MADE FROM ONE KIND FOR THAT OF ANOTHER,[6] PROVIDED THAT IT IS FROM A SUPERIOR FOR THAT OF AN INFERIOR KIND.[7] R. AKIBA SAYS: REPAYMENT CAN BE MADE ONLY FROM THE SAME KIND. HENCE IF A MAN ATE CUCUMBERS GROWN A YEAR BEFORE THE SEVENTH YEAR, HE MUST WAIT FOR THOSE GROWN AFTER THE TERMINATION OF THE SEVENTH YEAR AND REPAY WITH THEM.[8] THE SAME SOURCE WHICH CAUSES R. ELIEZER TO BE LENIENT CAUSES R. AKIBA TO ADOPT A STRINGENT RULING; FOR IT IS WRITTEN: AND HE SHALL GIVE UNTO THE PRIEST THE HOLY THING,[9] [IMPLYING,] WHATEVER IS LIABLE TO BECOME 'HOLY'. SO. R ELIEZER. BUT R. AKIBA SAYS: 'AND HE SHALL GIVE UNTO THE PRIEST THE HOLY THING', [MEANING] THE SAME KIND OF HOLY THING WHICH HE HAD EATEN.

CHAPTER VII

c *MISHNAH* 1. HE WHO EATS TERUMAH OF SET PURPOSE[1] MUST REPAY ITS VALUE,[2] BUT NOT THE FIFTH,[3] AND THE REPAYMENT REMAINS ḤULLIN.[4] [ACCORDINGLY,] IF THE PRIEST WISHES TO REMIT THIS, HE CAN.

(6) The priest has no power to renounce a due ordained by the Torah. (7) Before giving it to the priest, she ate of it in error. The term 'Israelite' in this connection denotes one who is not a priest. (8) Prior to bringing the required compensation of the value plus a Fifth. Being now the wife of a priest, she could eat *terumah* herself (Lev. XXII, 11). (9) For she is now like any other priest.

a (1) Here, to the priest who had already acquired the *terumah*. (2) Any priest. (3) Lit., 'the principal'. (4) As an atonement for having eaten *terumah* unwittingly, but he must pay the whole value for having 'robbed the tribe'. The case is of one who is unaware that he is giving them *terumah* to eat. The Fifth is only paid by him who actually derives benefit from the *terumah* (*supra* VI, 1), and not by him who causes it to be eaten. This is derived from Lev. XXII, 14, *'and if a man eat of the holy thing'*, which excludes one who causes damage to it. (5) He intended to give them. According to R. Meir, he has to pay them the value of the *terumah* they ate in their meal, which is cheaper in price; but according to the Sages, the full value of what they had eaten, as though it was *ḥullin*. For though they had eaten the meal, their enjoyment of it had been impaired when they learnt that they had eaten *terumah*. (6) V. Ex. XXII, 3. (7) Which becomes *terumah* automatically. (8) As the twofold restitution. (9) Which the priest had dedicated for Temple repairs. (10) One fifth for the *terumah* he ate, and the other because he had enjoyed consecrated property; Lev. V, 16. (11) Ex. XXII, 8; the word *'to his neighbour'* excludes property which has been 'dedicated'.

b (1) To the priest for eating *terumah* unwittingly. (2) These, being once exempt from all tithes and dues (*supra* I, 5), cannot become *terumah* even when now acquired by him. Cf. Pe'ah IV *passim*. (3) Being of the opinion that Second Tithe is also 'dedicated' produce. (4) Also exempt from *terumah* (*supra* I, 5), hence even after their redemption, no repayment can be made with them. (5) With tithes and dedicated produce that have been redeemed. (6) If he had eaten figs of *terumah*, he can repay with dates, but those offered must be of a superior kind to those eaten. (7) Must be of the same amount as those eaten, but of better value and more sought after by purchasers. (8) Those now left of the sixth year are no longer fit to be eaten, owing to having become hard, whilst from those grown in the Sabbatical year no benefit whatsoever may be derived (Sheb. VII, 3). Repayment, which must be of the same kind can, therefore, only be made with those grown after the Seventh year. (9) Lev. XXII, 14.

c (1) But did not receive legal warning by witnesses (התראה); for had he been so warned prior to committing the offence, he would have received flogging (מלקות) and be exempt from the monetary fine, the lesser penalty being merged in the greater offence. The wilful offender without such warning, incurred the penalty of death (heavenly) which did not, however, exempt him from repayment. (2) Having robbed a priest. (3) Which was brought as atonement only in the case of him who ate *terumah* unwittingly. (4) The repayment becomes *terumah* only when this restitution was made for an unintentional act; v. *supra* VI, 1.

MISHNAH 2. IF THE DAUGHTER OF A PRIEST MARRIED AN ISRAELITE[5] AND AFTERWARDS ATE TERUMAH, SHE MUST REPAY THE VALUE BUT NOT THE FIFTH;[6] AND HER DEATH-PENALTY [FOR ADULTERY] IS BY BURNING.[7] IF SHE MARRIED ANY OF THOSE DISQUALIFIED,[8] SHE MUST PAY BACK BOTH THE VALUE AND THE FIFTH, AND HER DEATH-PENALTY [FOR ADULTERY] IS BY STRANGLING; SO SAYS R. MEIR. BUT THE SAGES SAY: IN EITHER CASE, SHE REPAYS THE VALUE BUT NOT THE FIFTH, AND THE DEATH PENALTY IS BY BURNING.

MISHNAH 3. [AN ISRAELITE] WHO FEEDS [WITH TERUMAH] HIS SMALL SONS, OR HIS SLAVES WHETHER THEY ARE
a OF AGE OR MINORS,[1] OR WHO EATS TERUMAH FROM OUTSIDE THE LAND,[2] OR LESS THAN AN OLIVE'S BULK OF TERUMAH,[3] MUST REPAY THE VALUE THEREOF, BUT NOT THE FIFTH; AND THE REPAYMENT REMAINS ḤULLIN. [HENCE] IF THE PRIEST DESIRES TO FOREGO [THE RESTITUTION], HE MAY DO SO.

MISHNAH 4. THIS IS THE GENERAL PRINCIPLE: WHENSOEVER ONE HAS TO REPAY BOTH THE VALUE AND THE FIFTH, THE REPAYMENT BECOMES TERUMAH, AND IF THE PRIEST DESIRES TO REMIT, HE CANNOT REMIT REPAYMENT; BUT WHENSOEVER ONE HAS TO REPAY THE VALUE ONLY AND NOT THE FIFTH, THE REPAYMENT REMAINS ḤULLIN, AND IF THE PRIEST WISHES TO REMIT HE CAN REMIT.

MISHNAH 5. IF THERE WERE TWO BASKETS, ONE OF TERUMAH AND ONE OF ḤULLIN, AND A SE'AH OF TERUMAH FELL INTO ONE OF THEM, BUT IT IS NOT KNOWN INTO WHICH, I ASSUME THAT IT HAD FALLEN INTO THAT OF THE TERUMAH.[4] IF IT IS NOT KNOWN WHICH WAS OF TERUMAH AND WHICH OF ḤULLIN,[5] AND HE EATS FROM ONE OF THEM, HE IS EXEMPT,[6] AND THE SECOND BASKET IS TREATED AS TERUMAH AND SUBJECT TO THE LAW OF 'DOUGH-OFFERING', SO R. MEIR;[7] BUT R. JOSE EXEMPTS IT.[8] IF ANOTHER MAN EATS OF THE
b SECOND BASKET HE IS EXEMPT,[1] BUT IF ONE MAN ATE OF BOTH, HE MUST REPAY THE VALUE OF THE SMALLER OF THE TWO.[2]

MISHNAH 6. IF ONE OF THESE [BASKETS] FELL INTO ḤULLIN, IT DOES NOT RENDER IT MEDUMMA',[3] BUT THE SECOND IS TREATED AS TERUMAH AND SUBJECT TO THE LAW OF ḤALLAH, SO R. MEIR. R. JOSE EXEMPTS IT.[4] IF THE SECOND FALLS ELSEWHERE [INTO ḤULLIN], IT DOES NOT RENDER IT MEDUMMA'. IF BOTH OF THEM FALL INTO ONE PLACE, THEY RENDER IT MEDUMMA' ACCORDING TO [THE PROPORTION] OF THE SMALLER OF THE TWO.[5]

MISHNAH 7. IF HE USED ONE OF THESE [BASKETS] AS SEED, HE IS EXEMPT,[6] AND THE SECOND IS TREATED AS IF IT WERE TERUMAH AND SUBJECT TO THE LAW OF ḤALLAH: SO R. MEIR; BUT R. JOSE EXEMPTS IT. IF ANOTHER PERSON USES THE SECOND AS SEED, THEN HE IS EXEMPT. IF ONE MAN SOWS BOTH AS SEED, IF IT IS OF A KIND WHOSE SEED ROTS [IN THE GROUND][7] IT IS PERMISSIBLE, BUT IF IT IS OF THE KIND WHOSE SEED DOES NOT ROT,[8] IT IS PROHIBITED.

CHAPTER VIII

c MISHNAH 1. IF A WOMAN WAS EATING TERUMAH,[1] AND THEY CAME AND SAID TO HER: 'THY HUSBAND IS DEAD', OR 'HE HAS DIVORCED THEE';[2] OR, IF A SLAVE WAS EATING

(5) Thus forfeiting her right to *terumah;* Lev. XXII, 12. (6) Which was only paid by one totally alien to priesthood. Besides she may qualify again to eat *terumah* on her return to her father's household after her husband's death (Lev. XXII, 13). Since sanctity of priestly stock clings to her, she is not deemed totally a stranger to *terumah*. (7) Like all daughters of a priest, v. Lev. XXI, 9. Though irrelevant to our main issue, it is cited here *en passant*. (8) From marrying into the priesthood, e.g., a חלל, one who is profane (Lev. XXI, 7), or a Nathin, a descendant of the Gibeonites, or a ממזר, a bastard. By marrying any of these, she severs all connection with the priesthood and is deemed the daughter of an Israelite.

a (1) Not having property of their own, the owner must pay the value for them, but not the Fifth, which is only paid by him who actually eats of the *terumah*. The case here is of one who feeds them on *terumah* unintentionally. (2) Regarded as *terumah* only by an injunction of the Rabbis; cf. Yad. IV, 3. (3) The minimum standard for culpability. (4) And the basket of *ḥullin* is absolutely permissible, even if there be not therein a hundred to neutralize it. This leniency is due to the fact that *terumah* these days is only a Rabbinical injunction. (5) In this case, the above hypothetical argument cannot be applied. (6) From the value of the *terumah* and its Fifth, since he can claim that he had eaten of the *ḥullin*. (7) Doubt cannot exempt it from obligations that fall upon *ḥullin;* cf. Ḥal. I, 3. (8) From *ḥallah*, since it may contain an admixture of *terumah*.

b (1) The proviso here is that they must come independently to enquire about their own position, for we can then argue that each one had eaten of the pile of *ḥullin*, an argument hardly tenable if both come together. The exemptions refer only to the Fifth; cf. Toh. V, 5. (2) In all cases of doubt we inflict the smaller penalty on the plea that it is upon him who claims to bring proof. (3) On the plea that it might have been the *ḥullin* which fell in. (4) Each of the two instances are necessary; the first to emphasize the view of R. Jose, though the *terumah* is still actually there; and the present to emphasize the view of R. Meir who subjects the admixture to the law of *ḥallah*. (5) And if there be a hundred to neutralize this smaller of the two, the admixture is permitted. (6) I.e., what will grow therefrom will be *ḥullin* and he must not plough up the seed, as is the case where one sows undoubted *terumah;* cf. *infra* IX, 1. But where there is the slightest doubt, leniency is advised. (7) Like seed of wheat and barley. In this case it is regarded as what grows from *medumma'* and hence permissible; cf. *infra* IX, 6. (8) Like seed of garlic and onion. It is regarded as the growth of *terumah*, and hence prohibited.

c (1) The daughter of an Israelite married to a priest, unless she is divorced or widowed, may eat *terumah*. The mother of a priest's son may also eat *terumah*, v. *supra* VII, 2. (2) I.e., he had delivered the bill of divorce to your messenger at the place appointed for him to receive it (T.J.).

ב בת כהן שנשאת לישראל ואחר כך אכלה תרומה משלמת את הקרן ואינה משלמת את החומש ומיתתה בשרפה נשאת לאחד מכל הפסולין משלמת קרן וחומש ומיתתה בחנק דברי רבי מאיר וחכמים אומרים זו וזו משלמות את הקרן ואינן משלמות את החומש ומיתתן בשרפה:

ג המאכיל (א) את בניו קטנים ואת עבדיו בין גדולים בין קטנים האוכל תרומת חוצה לארץ והאוכל פחות מכזית תרומה משלם את הקרן ואינו משלם את החומש והתשלומין חולין אם רצה הכהן למחול מוחל:

ד זה הכלל כל המשלם קרן וחומש התשלומין תרומה אם רצה הכהן למחול אינו מוחל וכל המשלם את הקרן ואינו משלם את החומש התשלומין חולין אם רצה הכהן למחול מוחל:

ה שתי קופות אחת של תרומה ואחת של חולין שנפלה סאה תרומה לתוך אחת מהן ואין ידוע לאיזה מהן נפלה הרי אני אומר לתוך של תרומה נפלה אין ידוע איזו היא של תרומה ואיזו היא של חולין אכל אחת מהן פטור והשניה נוהג בה בתרומה וחייבת בחלה דברי ר"מ ר' יוסי פוטרה אכל אחר את השניה פטור אכל אחד את שתיהן משלם כקטנה שבשתיהן:

ו נפלה אחת מהם לתוך החולין אינה מדמעתן והשניה נוהג בה בתרומה וחייבת בחלה דברי ר' מאיר ור' יוסי פוטר נפלה שניה למקום אחר אינה מדמעתן נפלו שתיהם למקום אחד מדמעות כקטנה שבשתיהן:

ז זרע את אחת מהן פטור והשניה נוהג בה בתרומה וחייבת בחלה דברי רבי מאיר ורבי יוסי פוטר זרע אחר את השניה פטור זרע אחד את שתיהם בדבר שזרעו כלה (ג) מותר ובדבר שאין זרעו כלה אסור:

פרק שמיני

א האשה שהיתה אוכלת בתרומה באו ואמרו לה מת בעליך או גרשך

אליעזר שאם אמרה הבא לי גפי ממקום פלוני שאוכלת תרומה עד שמגיע גם לאותו מקום אמר ר' חנינא מכיון שאמרה לו הבא לי גפי ממקום פלוני כמו שאמרה לא יהא גם אלא אחר י' ימים ומה שאכלה ביתר אכלה: אמרו לו מת רבך · וירשו בן בתו ישראל: שהוא בן גרושה · וחלל הוא ואסור בתרומה כזר: רבי אליעזר מחייב קרן וחומש· אכולהו קאי: רבי יהושע פוטר· משום דטעה בדבר מצוה ובשילהי ארבעה אחין (דף לד·) מוקי לה בתרומה בערב הפסח דזמנה בהול: רבי יהושע מכשיר · בפ"ג דקידושין (דף סו:) בן גרושה עבודתו כשרה מדכתיב (במדבר כה) והיתה לו ולזרעו אחריו ברית כהונת בין זרע כשר בין זרע פסול אבוה דשמואל אמר מהכא (דברים לג) ברך ה'

וכן העבד שהיה אוכל בתרומה ובאו ואמרו לו מת רבך או מכרך לישראל או נתנך במתנה או עשאך בן חורין וכן א) כהן שהיה אוכל בתרומה ונודע שהוא בן גרושה או בן חלוצה ר' אליעזר מחייב קרן וחומש ור' יהושע פוטר היה ב) עומד ומקריב ע"ג המזבח ונודע שהוא בן גרושה או בן חלוצה רבי אליעזר אומר כל הקרבנות שהקריב על גבי המזבח פסולים ורבי יהושע מכשיר נודע שהוא בעל מום (ב) עבודתו פסולה: ב וכולם שהיתה תרומה בתוך פיהם רבי אליעזר אומר יבלעו ורבי יהושע אומר יפלטו אמרו לו נטמאת ונטמאת תרומה רבי אליעזר אומר יבלע ורבי יהושע אומר יפלוט טמא היית וטמאה היתה תרומה או נודע שהוא טבל ומעשר ראשון שלא נטלה תרומתו ומעשר שני והקדש שלא נפדו או שטעם ג) טעם פשפש לתוך פיו ה"ז יפלוט: ג (ד) ד) היה אוכל באשכול ונכנס מן הגנה לחצר ר' אליעזר אומר יגמור ור' יהושע אומר לא יגמור חשכה לילי שבת רבי יהושע אומר יגמור *ורבי אליעזר אומר לא יגמור: ד יין של תרומה שנתגלה ישפך ואין צריך לומר של חולין ג' משקין ה) אסורים משום גלוי המים והיין והחלב ושאר כל המשקין מותרין כמה ישהו ויהיו אסורין כדי שיצא הרחש ממקום קרוב וישתה: ה שיעור המים המגולין כדי שתאבד בהם המרה ר' יוסי אומר בכלים כל שהן ובקרקעות מ' סאה: ו נקורי תאנים וענבים וקשואין והדלועים והאבטיחים והמלפפונות אפילו הם ככר אחד גדול ואחד קטן אחד תלוש ואחד מחובר כל שיש בו ליחה אסור ונשיכת הנחש אסור מפני סכנת נפשות: ז י) המשמרת
של

TERUMAH,[3] AND THEY CAME AND SAID TO HIM: 'THY MASTER IS DEAD',[4] OR 'HE HAS SOLD THEE TO AN ISRAELITE', OR 'HE HAS GIVEN THEE AWAY AS GIFT', OR 'HE HAS EMANCIPATED THEE'; SO, TOO, IF A PRIEST WAS EATING TERUMAH AND IT BECAME KNOWN THAT HE WAS THE SON OF A DIVORCED WOMAN[5] OR OF ONE THAT HAD GIVEN ḤALIẒAH,[6] R. ELIEZER SAYS: THEY MUST REPAY BOTH THE VALUE AND THE FIFTH;[7] BUT R. JOSHUA EXEMPTS THEM.[8] IF [A PRIEST] WAS STANDING AND SACRIFICING ON THE ALTAR AND IT BECAME KNOWN THAT HE WAS THE SON OF A DIVORCED WOMAN OR OF ONE WHO HAD GIVEN ḤALIẒAH, R. ELIEZER SAYS: ALL THE SACRIFICES HE HAD OFFERED ON THE ALTAR ARE RITUALLY DISQUALIFIED; BUT R. JOSHUA PRONOUNCES THEM VALID.[9] IF IT, HOWEVER, BECAME KNOWN THAT HE POSSESSED A BLEM-
a ISH, HIS MINISTRATION IS INVALID.[1]

MISHNAH 2. IN ALL THE ABOVE CASES,[2] IF TERUMAH WAS STILL IN THEIR MOUTH,[3] R. ELIEZER SAYS: THEY MAY SWALLOW IT;[4] BUT R. JOSHUA SAYS: THEY MUST SPIT IT OUT. [IF IT WAS SAID TO HIM], 'THOU ART BECOME UNCLEAN',[5] OR THAT 'THE TERUMAH IS DEFILED', R. ELIEZER SAYS: HE MAY SWALLOW IT; BUT R. JOSHUA SAYS: HE MUST SPIT IT OUT. [IF IT WAS SAID TO HIM], 'THOU HAST BEEN UNCLEAN'[6] OR THAT 'THE TERUMAH WAS DEFILED', OR IT HAD BECOME KNOWN THAT IT WAS UNTITHED, OR THAT IT WAS FIRST TITHE FROM WHICH TERUMAH HAD NOT YET BEEN TAKEN, OR SECOND TITHE OR DEDICATED PRODUCE THAT HAD NOT BEEN REDEEMED, OR IF HE TASTED THE TASTE OF A BUG IN HIS MOUTH,[7] HE MUST SPIT IT OUT.

MISHNAH 3. IF HE WAS EATING A BUNCH OF GRAPES,[8] AND HE ENTERED FROM THE GARDEN INTO THE COURTYARD,[9] R. ELIEZER SAYS: HE MAY FINISH EATING;[10] BUT R. JOSHUA SAYS: HE MAY NOT FINISH.[11] IF DUSK SET IN AT THE EVE OF
b SABBATH,[1] R. ELIEZER SAYS: HE MAY FINISH EATING;[2] BUT R. JOSHUA SAYS: HE MAY NOT FINISH.[3]

MISHNAH 4. IF WINE OF TERUMAH HAD REMAINED UNCOVERED,[4] IT MUST BE POURED OUT;[5] AND THERE IS LESS NEED TO SAY THIS IN THE CASE OF ḤULLIN.[6] THREE KINDS OF LIQUIDS ARE FORBIDDEN ON ACCOUNT OF BEING UNCOVERED: WATER, WINE AND MILK, BUT ALL OTHER DRINKS ARE PERMITTED. HOW LONG SHOULD THEY REMAIN UNCOVERED FOR THEM TO BECOME PROHIBITED? THE TIME IT TAKES THE SERPENT[7] TO CREEP OUT FROM A PLACE NEAR BY AND DRINK.[8]

MISHNAH 5. THE AMOUNT OF WATER THAT MAY REMAIN UNCOVERED[9] MUST BE SUFFICIENT TO NEGATIVE THE POISON THEREIN. R. JOSHUA SAYS: IN VESSELS [IT IS FORBIDDEN] WHATEVER BE THE QUANTITY, BUT FOR WATER ON THE GROUND, IT MUST BE FORTY SE'AHS.[10]

MISHNAH 6. FIGS, GRAPES, CUCUMBERS, PUMPKINS, WATER-MELONS OR SWEET MELONS THAT HAVE BEEN BITTEN,[11] EVEN IF THERE IS AS MUCH AS A TALENT,[12] WHETHER THEY
c BE LARGE OR SMALL,[1] PLUCKED OR STILL ATTACHED TO THE SOIL, THEY ARE FORBIDDEN AS LONG AS THERE IS JUICE IN THEM.[2] [A BEAST] BITTEN BY A SERPENT[3] IS FORBIDDEN ON ACCOUNT OF THE DANGER TO LIFE.[4]

MISHNAH 7. A WINE-FILTER, USED AS A COVER, RENDERS

(3) Lev. XXII, 11 permits non-Hebrew slaves of priests to eat *terumah;* Hebrew slaves, not being the 'possession' of their masters, cannot eat *terumah.* (4) 'And a non-priestly relative of his has now inherited thee', such as his daughter or the son of his daughter who married an Israelite. (5) And, therefore, deprived of all the rights and privileges of the priesthood; Lev. XXI, 7 and cf. *supra* VII, 1. (6) The ceremony of taking off the levir's shoe by his childless sister-in-law on his refusing to contract with her the levitical marriage; Deut. XXV, 7–9. (7) As in all cases of an Israelite eating *terumah* unwittingly, and as if these never had connection with the priesthood. (8) On the grounds that these are cases not of mere unwitting transgression (שגגה) but of pure accident. V. Yeb. 34*a*. (9) He holds that even the work of one unfit for priesthood, owing to illegitimacy, is acceptable to God.
a (1) Even R. Joshua agrees to this. (2) Enumerated in the previous Mishnah; v. however, n. 4. (3) When word came that their right of eating *terumah* had ceased. (4) In the case of the son of a divorced woman or one who had performed *ḥaliẓah,* since he never had the right to eat *terumah,* R. Eliezer will admit that the *terumah* must be spewed out (Bert.). (5) The defilement coming after he had begun to eat the *terumah* legally. (6) Before eating the *terumah,* similar to the son of a divorced woman or *ḥaluẓah,* who never possessed the privilege of eating *terumah.* (7) In such cases, he need have no qualms for wasting *terumah* by spitting it out. In these cases, R. Eliezer agrees with R. Joshua. (8) It was permissible to take a casual snack from the produce prior to tithing. (9) Once produce enters the owner's domain, it becomes subject to tithes and even a casual meal is now disallowed; Ma'as. I, 5. (10) I.e., he returns to the garden where he may finish that which he had begun to eat legally; should he want more to eat, he must take tithe first. (11) Before he has taken tithe; even in the garden, without first tithing what he had begun to eat.
b (1) When it is forbidden to tithe (Shab. II, 7) and he had not yet finished his casual meal in the garden. The Sabbath converts even the casual meal into a fixed one. (2) After its termination (Bert.) (3) Even on the termination of the Sabbath, without first tithing it. (4) The danger being lest a serpent had drunk of it and deposited therein some of its venom, a fear more real than imaginary in Talmudic times. (5) Without the slightest qualms of wasting *terumah;* the saving of one's life being more important than a prohibition. The wine may not be given to cattle to drink, lest the poison which may not affect them may affect those who will afterwards eat of their flesh. (6) In which case no qualms exist about waste. (7) Lit., 'the creeping thing'. (8) That place may even be the vessel containing the liquid itself; namely, as long as it takes the serpent to crawl out from the crevice in the handle of the vessel, sip of its contents and creep back. (9) And be used for drinking. (10) The coldness of the ground helps to neutralize poison. (11) Lit., 'hollowed', probably by snakes. (12) Cf. R. H. 15. I.e., even though the fruit on the trees are many so that a serpent cannot be supposed to have gnawed them all, *Tif. Yis.* The phrase is obscure.
c (1) This probably refers to the holes. (2) The juice in the fruit helps to circulate the venom; if the fruit is, however, very dry, the affected part can be cut out and thrown away and the rest eaten. (3) An animal bitten by a serpent and afterwards slaughtered must not be eaten, not because it is *ṭrefah,* but because of danger to life. (4) Cf. Ḥul. 49*a*.

[THE WINE BENEATH ALSO] FORBIDDEN THROUGH BEING UNCOVERED;[5] BUT R. NEḤEMIAH PERMITS IT.[6]

MISHNAH 8. IF A DOUBT OF IMPURITY ARISES CONCERNING A JAR OF TERUMAH,[7] R. ELIEZER SAYS: IF IT HAD BEEN HITHERTO DEPOSITED IN AN EXPOSED PLACE,[8] HE MUST NOW PLACE IT IN A HIDDEN PLACE;[9] AND IF IT HAD FORMERLY BEEN UNCOVERED, IT MUST NOW BE COVERED.[10] BUT R. JOSHUA MAINTAINS THAT IF IT HAD BEEN IN A HIDDEN PLACE, HE MUST[11] NOW DEPOSIT IT IN AN EXPOSED PLACE; AND IF IT HAD FORMERLY BEEN COVERED UP, HE MUST[11] NOW UNCOVER IT.[12] R. GAMALIEL SAYS: LET HIM NOT DO ANYTHING NEW TO IT.[13]

MISHNAH 9. IF A JAR [OF TERUMAH] WAS BROKEN IN THE
a UPPER PART OF THE WINE-PRESS,[1] AND THE LOWER PART WAS UNCLEAN,[2] BOTH R. ELIEZER AND R. JOSHUA AGREE THAT IF ONE CAN SAVE AT LEAST A REBI'ITH[3] THEREOF IN CLEANNESS HE SHOULD SAVE IT;[4] BUT IF NOT,[5] R. ELIEZER SAYS: LET IT FLOW DOWN AND BECOME UNCLEAN OF ITS OWN ACCORD,[6] AND LET HIM NOT MAKE IT UNCLEAN WITH HIS OWN HANDS.[7]

MISHNAH 10. SIMILARLY, IF A JAR OF OIL [OF TERUMAH] WAS UPSET, BOTH R. ELIEZER AND R. JOSHUA AGREE THAT IF HE CAN SAVE THEREOF AT LEAST A REBI'ITH IN CLEANNESS HE SHOULD SAVE IT; BUT IF NOT, R. ELIEZER SAYS: LET IT FLOW AWAY AND BE ABSORBED [IN THE GROUND] AND LET HIM NOT GATHER IT UP WITH HIS OWN HANDS.[8]

MISHNAH 11. CONCERNING BOTH CASES,[9] R. JOSHUA SAID: 'THIS IS NOT THE KIND OF TERUMAH OVER WHICH I AM CAUTIONED LEST I DEFILE IT, BUT LEST I EAT OF IT.' OF WHICH [WAS IT CAUTIONED] 'THAT THOU MUST NOT DEFILE IT'? IF ONE WAS PASSING FROM PLACE TO PLACE WITH LOAVES OF TERUMAH IN HIS HAND AND A GENTILE SAID TO HIM: 'GIVE ME ONE OF THESE AND I WILL MAKE IT UNCLEAN; FOR IF NOT, I WILL DEFILE THEM ALL', LET HIM DEFILE THEM ALL, AND NOT GIVE HIM DELIBERATELY ONE TO DEFILE. BUT R.
b JOSHUA SAYS: HE SHOULD PLACE ONE OF THEM ON A ROCK.[1]

(5) The poison can easily percolate into the wine through the tiny holes of the strainer. (6) Maintaining that since it is the nature of poison to swim on the surface, it would be easily discernible were it in the strainer. (7) The instance is of two jars, each containing *terumah* and left in private ground, one of which had come into contact with a dead serpent, but which it was is uncertain. Being in private territory, all doubts of impurity are unclean; whereas in public grounds it would have been deemed pure; cf. Nazir 57*a*. (8) Lit., 'filth', 'dirt'. A place to which all and sundry can have access, for being an open place, uncleanness can easily come. (9) Since it is *terumah* and only a doubt has arisen as to its uncleanness, it must be further protected from uncleanness, and cannot be laid open to contamination deliberately. Even *terumah* suspected of uncleanness must be protected. (10) So that no serpent may now have access to it. (11) Or 'may' v. Rashi; Pes. 15*a*. (12) Once a doubt has arisen, it no longer requires the protection due to the sacred nature of *terumah*. When it has definitely become unclean, the wine of *terumah* may be used for aromatic sprinkling, but not when only a doubt exists concerning its nature. R. Joshua's intention is not leniency, but in order to make the wine forbidden definitely. (13) But allow it to remain in the position it was before doubt arose, not being required to guard it any more closely, or deliberately to allow it to become defiled.

a (1) The vat consisted of two parts, one above the other, so that when the grapes were trodden above, the wine flowed down below. (2) Containing wine of *ḥullin* that had become unclean and less than a hundred to neutralize the clean wine of *terumah* now about to fall in. (3) A quarter of a *log*. (4) In clean vessels; for it is more important to save the *terumah* from becoming unclean than to save the *ḥullin* below from becoming through an admixture of *terumah* forbidden both to priest and to Israelite. If it be not possible to save *terumah* in clean vessels then he must save the *ḥullin*. (5) No clean vessels being at hand. (6) With the *ḥullin* becoming forbidden as a result. (7) By saving the *terumah* in unclean vessels in order to save the *ḥullin*. (8) Lit., 'absorb it with his hands'. Had the jar been merely broken, as in the case of the wine, R. Joshua would agree with R. Eliezer that he may not save it in unclean vessels, since there would not be much loss in allowing the oil to flow down in the lower part of the vat, for the *ḥullin* oil even when containing an admixture of *terumah* that has become unclean may still be used for burning purposes. (9) In the case of *terumah* whose defilement is in doubt (*supra* 8) and in the case of the two previous Mishnahs where the *terumah* is in danger of being lost.

b (1) And on no account defile the loaves with his own hands and also not give it from hand to hand.

◁ *For the continuation of the English translation of this page see overleaf.*

של יין אסורה משום גלוי רבי נחמיה מתיר:

ח חבית של תרומה [א] שנולד בה ספק טומאה ר"א אומר אם היתה מונחת במקום תורפה יניחנה במקום המוצנע ואם היתה מגולה יכסנה ורבי יהושע אומר אם היתה מונחת במקום מוצנע יניחנה במקום תורפה ואם היתה מכוסה יגלנה רבן גמליאל אומר אל יחדש בה דבר:

ט חבית שנשברה [ב] בגת העליונה והתחתונה טמאה מודה ר"א ור' יהושע שאם יכולים להציל ממנה רביעית בטהרה יציל ואם לאו ר"א אומר תרד ותטמא ואל יטמאנה בידיו:

י וכן חבית של שמן שנשפכה מודה ר"א ור' יהושע שאם יכול להציל ממנה רביעית בטהרה יציל ואם לאו ר"א אומר תרד ותבלע ואל יבלענה בידיו:

יא על זו ועל זו א"ר יהושע לא זו היא תרומה שאני מוזהר עליה מלטמאה אלא מלאכלה ובל תטמאה כיצד היה עובר ממקום למקום וככרות של תרומה בידו אמר לו נכרי תן לי אחת מהן ואטמאנה ואם לאו הרי אני מטמא את *כולה ר"א אומר יטמא את *כולה ואל יתן לו אחת מהן ויטמא רבי יהושע אומר יניח לפניו אחת מהן על הסלע:

יב וכן נשים שאמרו להם נכרים תנו לנו אחת מכם ונטמאה ואם לאו הרי אנו מטמאין את כולכם יטמאו את כולן ואל ימסרו להם נפש אחת מישראל:

פרק תשיעי

א הזורע תרומה שוגג יופך ומזיד יקיים אם הביאה שליש בין שוגג בין מזיד יקיים ובפשתן מזיד יופך:

ב וחייבת בלקט ובשכחה ובפאה ועניי ישראל ועניי כהנים מלקטים ועניי ישראל מוכרין את שלהם לכהנים בדמי תרומה והדמים שלהם ר"ט אומר לא ילקטו אלא עניי כהנים שמא ישכחו ויתנו לתוך פיהם אמר לו ר' עקיבא אם כן לא ילקטו אלא טהורים:

ג וחייבת במעשרות ובמעשר עני ועניי ישראל ועניי כהנים נוטלים ועניי ישראל מוכרין את שלהם לכהנים בדמי תרומה והדמים שלהם החובט משובח והדש [ג] כיצד יעשה תולה כפיפות בצוארי בהמה ונותן לתוכן מאותו

Continuation of translation from previous page as indicated by ◁

MISHNAH 12. SIMILARLY,[2] IF GENTILES SAY TO WOMEN: 'GIVE US ONE OF YOU THAT WE MAY DEFILE HER,[3] AND IF NOT, WE WILL DEFILE YOU ALL', THEN LET THEM ALL BE DEFILED RATHER THAN HAND OVER TO THEM ONE SOUL FROM ISRAEL.[4]

CHAPTER IX

MISHNAH 1. HE WHO PLANTS TERUMAH, IF UNWITTINGLY, MAY UPROOT IT;[1] IF OF SET PURPOSE, HE MUST ALLOW
c IT TO REMAIN.[2] IF IT HAD ALREADY GROWN A THIRD OF ITS FULL SIZE, WHETHER HE HAD PLANTED IT UNWITTINGLY OR INTENTIONALLY, HE MUST ALLOW IT TO REMAIN;[3] BUT IN THE CASE OF FLAX, EVEN WHEN PLANTED INTENTIONALLY[4] HE MUST UPROOT IT.

MISHNAH 2. AND IT[5] IS SUBJECT TO GLEANINGS, THE FORGOTTEN SHEAF AND PE'AH.[6] POOR ISRAELITES AND POOR PRIESTS MAY GLEAN THEM, BUT THE POOR ISRAELITES MUST SELL THEIRS TO PRIESTS FOR THE PRICE OF TERUMAH[7] AND THE MONEY BECOMES THEIRS. R. TARFON SAYS: ONLY POOR PRIESTS MAY GLEAN THEM, LEST [THE OTHERS] FORGET AND PUT IT INTO THEIR MOUTHS.[8] WHEREUPON R. AKIBA SAID TO HIM: IF THAT BE SO, THEN ONLY THOSE WHO ARE CLEAN SHOULD BE ALLOWED TO GLEAN.[9]

d *MISHNAH* 3. AND IT[1] IS ALSO SUBJECT TO TITHES[2] AND POOR MAN'S TITHE. BOTH ISRAELITES AND PRIESTS THAT ARE POOR MAY ACCEPT THEM, BUT THE POOR ISRAELITES MUST SELL THAT WHICH IS THEIRS TO THE PRIEST FOR THE PRICE OF TERUMAH AND THE MONEY BELONGS TO THEM.[3] HE WHO THRESHES THE GRAIN[4] IS TO BE PRAISED;[5] BUT HE WHO TREADS IT,[6] WHAT SHOULD HE DO?[7] HE MUST SUSPEND BAGS[8] FROM THE NECK OF THE ANIMAL AND PLACE THEREIN FODDER OF THE SAME KIND, WITH THE RESULT THAT HE

(2) Irrelevant to our main theme, but indirectly connected with the preceding Mishnah. (3) By forcibly cohabiting with her. (4) The general principle is that no person may be sacrificed for the saving of others. If, however, they specify one woman in particular, then she may be given over in order to prevent the others from impurity; but if they specify any one man for slaughter, he must not be handed over unless he had been legally condemned to death as a result of some crime. But some maintain that even if he had not been condemned to death owing to some crime, he may be handed over to them if specified by name, in order to save the others (*Tif. Yis.*).

c (1) By ploughing the soil and tearing out the roots, so that the produce does not grow and be forbidden as *terumah*. (2) As a penalty, the produce will be forbidden to him. He must not plough it up, as it would appear as if he is wilfully destroying *terumah*. (3) For having attained this size, it is already fit for food and it would appear as if he is destroying *terumah* deliberately. (4) And even after it had reached a third of its full size. The reason for this additional stringency in the case of flax is lest he derive benefit from the stalks on the plea that only the seeds are forbidden as *terumah*, but not the stalks; whereas the main part about flax is just the stalks and not the seed.

(5) What grows from the *terumah* seeds. (6) Cf. *supra* VI, 5 and Pe'ah IV, 10. These Poor Man's dues are imposed since the *terumah* here is only a Rabbinic ordinance. (7) Though what grows from *terumah* is forbidden to strangers, the sanctity of the *terumah* does not descend upon the money value thereof. (8) Arguing that since they are allowed to glean the *terumah*, they may unwittingly eat of it. (9) Since a priest who had become unclean must not eat *terumah*. To this challenge, R. Tarfon's rejoinder no doubt was that a priest who is unclean is very careful not to eat *terumah*. Cf. Pes. 33*a*, 40*a*.

d (1) What grows from *terumah* seeds. (2) Including *terumah*, in the third and sixth year of the Sabbatical cycle. (3) The fear expressed by R. Tarfon in the previous Mishnah does not apply here, since not being preoccupied as at the time of gleaning, the poor Israelites will be careful not to eat the *terumah*. (4) Smiting the ears of corn with flails. (5) Because he need not muzzle the oxen in order to prevent them from eating of *terumah*, forbidden to animals not belonging to priests. (6) Employing oxen to do the threshing for him. (7) To avoid them eating *terumah*. Muzzling during threshing is forbidden in Deut. XXV, 4. (8) Containing fodder of *ḥullin* of the same kind which he is treading.

יין אע"ג דלמטה מכוסה אסורה משום עליונה שהארס עובר דרך המשמרת ור' נחמיה מתיר שהארס קף: ח שנולד בה ספק טומאה בפ"ק דפסחים (ד' י:) פירש בקונטרס כגון שנכנס בו אדם טמא ספק נגע ספק לא נגע וקשה דאי ברשות הרבים ספקו טהור ואי ברה"י ספקו טמא וי"מ כגון שרץ בפי חולדה וחולדה מהלכת על פי חבית וספק נגע ספק לא נגע כל שכן דקשה טפי דהוי דבר שאין בו דעת לישאל ואפילו ברשות היחיד ספקו טהור ואין לפרש כהסיא דתנן (פ"ה משנה ג דטהרות) גבי ב' שבילין אחד טמא ואחד טהור והלך באחד מהן ועשה טהרות והזה ושנה וטבל וחזר והלך בשני ועשה טהרות דאם הראשונות קיימות אלו ואלו

של יין אסורה משום גלוי רבי נחמיה מתיר:

ח חבית של תרומה שנולד בה ספק טומאה ר"א אומר אם היתה מונחת במקום תורפה יניחנה במקום המוצנע ואם היתה מגולה יכסנה ורבי יהושע אומר אם היתה מונחת במקום מוצנע יניחנה במקום תורפה ואם היתה מכוסה יגלנה רבן גמליאל אומר אל יחדש בה דבר:

ט חבית שנשברה בגת העליונה והתחתונה טמאה מודה ר"א ור' יהושע שאם יכולים להציל ממנה רביעית בטהרה יציל ואם לאו ר"א אומר תרד ותטמא ואל יטמאנה בידיו:

י וכן חבית של שמן שנשפכה מודה ר"א ור' יהושע שאם יכול להציל ממנה רביעית בטהרה יציל ואם לאו ר"א אומר תרד ותבלע ואל יבלענה בידיו:

יא על זו ועל זו א"ר יהושע לא זו היא תרומה שאני מוזהר עליה מלטמאה אלא מלאכלה ובל תטמאה כיצד היה עובר ממקום למקום וככרות של תרומה בידו אמר לו נכרי תן לי אחת מהן ואטמאנה ואם לאו הרי אני מטמא את *כולה ר"א אומר יטמא את *כולה ואל יתן לו אחת מהן ויטמא רבי יהושע אומר יניח לפניו אחת מהן על הסלע:

יב וכן נשים שאמרו להם נכרים תנו לנו אחת מכם ונטמאה ואם לאו הרי אנו מטמאין את כולכם יטמאו את כולן ואל ימסרו להם נפש אחת מישראל:

פרק תשיעי

א הזורע תרומה שוגג יופך ומזיד יקיים אם הביאה שליש בין שוגג בין מזיד יקיים ובפשתן מזיד יופך:

ב וחייבת בלקט ובשכחה ובפאה ועניי ישראל ועניי כהנים מלקטים ועניי ישראל מוכרין את שלהם לכהנים בדמי תרומה והדמים שלהם ר"ט אומר לא ילקטו אלא עניי כהנים שמא ישכחו ויתנו לתוך פיהם אמר לו ר' עקיבא אם כן לא ילקטו אלא טהורים:

ג וחייבת במעשרות ובמעשר עני ועניי ישראל ועניי כהנים נוטלים ועניי ישראל מוכרין את שלהם לכהנים בדמי תרומה והדמים שלהם החובט משובח והדש כיצד יעשה תולה כפיפות בצוארי בהמה ונותן לתוכן מאותו

ה א פי"א מהל' תרומות הל' כא:
ו ב שם הל' כב:
ז ג מיי' פ"ו מהל' מעשר הלכה ו סמג עשין קלה:
ח ד מיי' פ"ד מהל' שמטה ויובל הלכה ו:
ט ה מיי' פרק י"א מהלכות תרומות הלכה כב:
י ו מיי' פ"ד מהל' בכורים הל' טו:
יא ז מיי' פ"ה מהל' מעילה הל' יא:
יב ח מיי' פ"ו מהל' מ"ש ונטע רבעי הלכה טו:
יג ט מיי' פי"ג מהל' תרומות הל' יב:
יד י מיי' פ"ו מהל' מעשרות הלכה ו סמג עשין קלה
טו כ מיי' פי"א מהל' תרומות הלכה כג:
טז ל שם הלכ' כד:
א מ מיי' פט"ו

דקל כמו כפיפה מצרית (בפ"ב מ"א דסוטה): ד גידולי תרומה תרומה מדרבנן מי"ח דבר הן גזירה משום תרומה טמאה ביד כהן דלמא משהי לה (ב) ואתו בה לידי תקלה והקשה במגילת סתרים מהא דתניא [בתוספתא] בפ"ק דטהרות דגידולי תרומה חולין ודחק לתרץ דאיירי התם לענין לחייבו בלקט שכחה ופאה וחייב בתרומות ומעשרות כדתנן לעיל (משנה ב) ועל הנס דחק דהתם איירי לענין טומאה וטהרה שהגידולים כחולין ואין בהן שלישי ולעיל פרק ששי בירושלמי (הל' א) משמע כפירושו דאמר ר' זירא בשם ר' חנינא תשלומי תרומה הרי הן כתרומה לכל דבר אלא שגידוליהם חולין גידולי תרומה הרי הן כחולין לכל דבר אלא שאסורין לזרים א"ר יוסי ותנן תניגן תרויהון תשלומי תרומה הרי הן כתרומה לכל דבר דתנן אין משלמין תרומה אלא חולין מתוקנים ונעשין תרומה אלא שגידוליהן חולין דתנן גידולי תרומה תרומה הא גידולי תשלומי תרומה חולין גידולי תרומה הרי הן כחולין לכל דבר דתנן וחייבין בלקט שכחה ופאה (ג) ועניי ישראל ועניי כהנים מלקטים אלא שאסורה לזרים דתנן עניי ישראל מוכרין שלהם בדמי תרומה והדמים שלהן ומ"מ אמת הוא כדפרשינן לענין ראשון ושני מדתני בטהרות ובירוש' כמי א] לכל דבר ומה שיכול לדקדק מן המשנה מדקדק והא דתנן בפרק ב' דבכורים (משנה ב) דמעשר שני ובכורים גידוליהן אסורים לאכול בירושלים אף לזרים ולבהמה מה שאין כן בתרומה בפסחים (דף לד.) לא כיוונו יפה דאין ענינם לכאן ופירוש כמו שפירשנו במקומה: וגידולי גדולין חולין · אם חזר וזרע גידולי תרומה מה שגדל מהן חולין ובירושלמי (פרקין הל' ב) תני בד"א בדבר שזרעו כלה אבל בדבר שאין זרעו כלה גידולי גידולין אסורין: ומעשר ראשון · דלא ניטלה ממנו תרומת מעשר: ...

המין נמצא לא זומם את הבהמה ולא מאביל את התרומה: ד [א]גדולי תרומה (א) תרומה [ב]וגדולי גדולין חולין [ג]אבל הטבל ומעשר ראשון [ד]וספיחי שביעית [ה]ותרומת חוצה לארץ והמדומע [ו]והבכורים (ב) גדוליהן חולין [ז]גדולי הקדש [ח]ומעשר שני חולין ופודה אותם בזמן זרעם: ה [ט]מאה לגנה של תרומה וא' של חולין (ד) כולן מותרין בדבר שזרעו כלה אבל בדבר (ג) שאין זרעו כלה אפי' ק' של חולין ואחד של תרומה כולן אסורין: ו [י]הטבל גדוליו (ד) מותרין בדבר שזרעו כלה אבל בדבר שאין זרעו כלה גדולי גדולין אסורין איזהו דבר שאין זרעו כלה כגון הלוף והשום והבצלים ר' יהודה אומר השום כשעורים: ז המנכש עם הנכרי (ה) בחסיות אע"פ שפירותיו טבל אוכל מהם עראי [כ]שתילי תרומה שנטמאו שתלן טהרו מלטמא ואסורין מלאכול עד שיגום את האוכל רבי יהודה אומר [ל]עד שיגום וישנה:

דש שעורים יתלה בפי הבהמה כדי שתאכל מהם בעת הדישה וידוש לפי שאסור לו לקשור פי הבהמה בעת הדישה שהכתוב אומר לא תחסום שור בדישו (דברים כה) ואסור לו גם כן להכניסה בזרע התרומה לפי שהיא אוכלת ממנו אלא אם היתה בהמת כהן וזומם הוא מגזרת זממו אל תפק (תהלים קמ) וזמם שם המתג ענינו שלא ישים המתג בפיה בעת האכילה: ד כשיזרע אדם תרומה מה שילמח הוא גם כן תרומה ואם זרע אותו שלמח פעם שנית אותו הצמח הוא חולין והוא גדולי גדולין וזו הגזירה מכלל י"ח דבר שגזרו בו ביום כמו שאמר בתחלת שבת: וספיחי שביעית· הוא הדבר הצומח בשנה שביעית ונקרא ספיח לפי שהוא אינו נזרע אבל צומח הוא מן הזרע שנזרע בשנה של השתקד וכבר פירשנו זו המלה פעמים (כלאים פ"ב מ"ה ובשביעית פ"ז ופ"ט מ"א) ולא אפרשנה יותר: ה לגנה· שם למקום זרוע מן הארץ והוא אומר בכאן כי אם היתה כמו ערוגה אחת מן הארץ זרועה חולין ומאה ערוגות זרועות תרומה ...

פרק עשירי

א בצל [מ]שנתנו בתוך עדשים אם שלם מותר ואם חתכו בנותן טעם ושאר כל התבשיל בין שלם בין מחותך בנותן טעם רבי ...

WILL NEITHER MUZZLE[9] THE ANIMAL NOR CAUSE IT TO EAT TERUMAH.[10]

MISHNAH 4. WHAT GROWS FROM TERUMAH IS TERUMAH,[11] BUT THAT WHICH [FIRST] GREW OUT FROM IT IS ḤULLIN. AS FOR UNTITHED PRODUCE,[12] FIRST TITHE,[13] THE AFTERGROWTH OF THE SABBATICAL YEAR,[14] TERUMAH GROWN
a OUTSIDE THE LAND,[1] THE ADMIXTURE OF ḤULLIN WITH TERUMAH,[2] THE FIRST-FRUITS[3]—WHAT GROWS FROM THEM IS REGARDED AS ḤULLIN. WHAT GROWS FROM DEDICATED PRODUCE AND SECOND TITHE IS ḤULLIN AND IS TO BE REDEEMED [AT ITS VALUE][4] AT THE TIME WHEN IT WAS SOWN.

MISHNAH 5. IF A HUNDRED ROWS WERE PLANTED WITH TERUMAH SEEDS AND ONE WITH ḤULLIN,[5] THEY ALL ARE PERMITTED, IF THEY ARE OF A KIND WHOSE SEED PERISHES IN THE SOIL;[6] BUT IF THEY ARE OF A KIND WHOSE SEED DOES NOT PERISH IN THE SOIL, THEN EVEN IF THERE BE A HUNDRED [ROWS] OF ḤULLIN AND ONE OF TERUMAH, THEY ALL ARE PROHIBITED.

MISHNAH 6. AS FOR UNTITHED PRODUCE,[7] WHAT GROWS FROM IT IS PERMISSIBLE IF OF A KIND WHOSE SEED PERISHES [IN THE SOIL]; BUT IF OF A KIND WHOSE SEED DOES NOT PERISH, THEN EVEN WHAT GROWS FROM WHAT [LATER] GREW OUT OF IT IS FORBIDDEN. WHICH IS THE KIND WHOSE SEED DOES NOT PERISH?[8] ANYTHING LIKE ARUM,[9] GARLIC AND ONIONS. R. JUDAH SAYS: ONIONS [IN THIS RESPECT] ARE LIKE BARLEY.[10]

b *MISHNAH* 7. HE WHO WEEDS[1] LEEK-PLANTS[2] FOR A GENTILE,[3] THOUGH THE PRODUCE STILL BE UNTITHED,[4] MAY SNATCH THEREFROM A CASUAL MEAL.[5] PLANTINGS OF TERUMAH[6] WHICH HAD BECOME UNCLEAN AND WERE RE-PLANTED, BECOME CLEAN INSOFAR THAT THEY DO NOT CAUSE DEFILEMENT,[7] BUT THEY MUST NOT BE EATEN[8] UNTIL THE EDIBLE PART [OF THE STALK] HAS BEEN LOPPED OFF.[9] R. JUDAH SAYS: HE MUST [BEFORE EATING] LOP OFF A SECOND TIME THAT WHICH GREW ON THE EDIBLE PART.[10]

CHAPTER X

MISHNAH 1. IF AN ONION [OF TERUMAH] WAS PLACED
c INTO LENTILS[1] AND THE ONION WAS WHOLE, [THE LENTILS] ARE PERMISSIBLE;[2] BUT IF [THE ONION] HAD BEEN CUT UP, [IT IS FORBIDDEN[3] IF THE ONION] IMPARTS A FLAVOUR. IN THE CASE OF OTHER DISHES,[4] WHETHER THE ONION IS WHOLE OR CUT UP [IT IS FORBIDDEN] IF IT IMPARTS A FLAVOUR. R.

(9) For it still eats of the same kind which it is threshing. (10) The fodder in the bags containing *ḥullin*. (11) Being one of the eighteen decrees of the Rabbis to prevent priests in possession of *terumah* that had become unclean, from keeping it till seed-time and then sowing it in order to eat the products; Shab. 17*a*. (12) Since most of the grain is *ḥullin*, only when the seed is entirely *terumah* is what grows from it also deemed *terumah*. (13) Only a tenth being *terumah*, the rest being *ḥullin*. (14) That which falls from ears of corn at harvest time and grows again of its own accord in the Sabbatical year. This aftergrowth is dated from the sixth year. Being an infrequent occurrence, occurring once in seven years, it was not held necessary to impose this added stricture regarding what grows from it.

a (1) Eretz Israel. Since it was not so usual to import *terumah* from places outside Palestine, no additional stricture was imposed. (2) Since most of it is *ḥullin*, as in the case of untithed produce and First Tithe. (3) Brought only of the seven kinds mentioned in Deut. VIII, 8: (wheat, barley, grapes, figs, pomegranates, olives and honey dates) and they are not of such frequent occurrence to warrant the restriction upon what grows from *terumah*. (4) I.e., the value of the seeds actually sown. (5) And it be not known which this is. (6) Leniency was always followed in cases in connection with what grows from *terumah*, and thus one row of *ḥullin* makes all that grows from the hundred rows of *terumah* permitted, though no neutralization takes place in anything still attached to the soil. (7) V. *supra* Mishnah 4, which our Mishnah explains. One may partake a casual meal of what grows from *ṭebel*, as long as it does not reach the stage when it is liable to tithes. (8) So that what grows of it, even in the second grade, is forbidden. (9) V. Pe'ah VI, 10. (10) Whose seed perishes. Barley is cited because its seeds perish very quickly. Bert. explains R. Judah's statement thus: 'Only seeds of onions as large as barley do not perish, but those smaller than barley do perish'.

b (1) Removing weeds interfering with growth. (2) Species of onions whose seeds do not rot. (3) In a field belonging to a non-Jew. (4) A non-Jew cannot acquire land in Eretz Israel in order to exempt its produce from tithes. (5) During his labours. (6) שתילין. Seedlings ready for planting. (7) Because rooted to the soil, they do not receive defilement and are not yet regarded as food. (8) Being products of *terumah*, *supra* IX, 4. (9) Leaving only the root. That which grows afterwards is permitted; v. Pes. 34*a*. (10) Only that which grows a third time on the spot twice lopped off is permitted.

c (1) Of *ḥullin*, cooked but dry. Lit., 'it is permissible'. T.J., basing itself on the word in the sing., says that the case here is of an onion of *ḥullin* placed into lentils of *terumah*, and that the onion is permissible though mixed with *terumah*. (2) Even to non-priests; for a whole onion does not impart to the entire dish the pungency imparted by an onion sliced up; and similarly, if the lentils had been of *terumah* and the onion of *ḥullin*, the onion does not absorb from them or their juice any of their taste, unless they have been cooked together. (3) To non-priests. (4) Not of lentils, like garlic or leeks of *ḥullin* into which an onion of *terumah* has been placed.

JUDAH PERMITS[5] IT IN THE CASE OF PICKLED FISH,[6] BECAUSE THERE IT IS USED ONLY TO REMOVE THE UNPLEASANT FLAVOUR.

MISHNAH 2. IF AN APPLE [OF TERUMAH] WAS CHOPPED AND PLACED INTO DOUGH [OF ḤULLIN] SO THAT IT LEAVENED IT,[7] [THE DOUGH] IS FORBIDDEN.[8] IF BARLEY [OF TERUMAH] FELL INTO A CISTERN OF WATER, THOUGH [THE BARLEY] DETERIORATE IT, THE WATERS ARE PERMISSIBLE.[9]

a *MISHNAH* 3. IF ONE TAKES OFF WARM BREAD[1] FROM THE OVEN[2] AND PLACES IT OVER AN OPEN BARREL OF WINE OF TERUMAH,[3] R. MEIR SAYS: IT IS FORBIDDEN;[4] BUT R. JUDAH[5] PERMITS IT. R. JOSE PERMITS THE BREAD IF IT IS OF WHEAT BUT NOT OF BARLEY, BECAUSE BARLEY ABSORBS.[6]

MISHNAH 4. IF AN OVEN WAS HEATED WITH CUMMIN[7] OF TERUMAH AND BREAD WAS BAKED THEREIN, THE BREAD IS PERMITTED, BECAUSE IT IS THE SMELL BUT NOT THE FLAVOUR OF THE CUMMIN [THAT IS CONVEYED THEREIN].[8]

MISHNAH 5. IF FENUGREEK[9] FELL INTO A WINE-VAT AND IT WAS TERUMAH OR SECOND TITHE, AND IF THERE IS IN THE SEED ALONE WITHOUT THE STALK SUFFICIENT TO IMPART A FLAVOUR[10] [IT IS FORBIDDEN].[11] BUT IN THE CASE OF SEVENTH YEAR[12] PRODUCE, OR MIXED SEEDS IN VINEYARDS,[13] OR DEDICATED PRODUCE, [IT IS FORBIDDEN] IF IN BOTH SEED AND STALK THERE IS SUFFICIENT TO IMPART A FLAVOUR.

MISHNAH 6. IF ONE HAD BUNCHES OF FENUGREEK OF MIXED SEEDS OF THE VINEYARD, THEY MUST BE BURNT.[14] IF HE HAD BUNCHES OF FENUGREEK OF UNTITHED PRODUCE,
b HE MUST BEAT THEM AND CALCULATE[1] THE AMOUNT OF SEED WITHIN THEM AND SET ASIDE [TERUMAH] FROM THE SEED, BUT NOT FROM THE STALKS.[2] BUT IF HE DID SET ASIDE [THE TERUMAH ALSO FROM THE STALKS][3] HE MUST NOT SAY: 'I WILL BEAT OUT [THE SEED] AND TAKE THE STALKS AND GIVE ONLY THE SEED', BUT HE MUST GIVE THE STALKS TOGETHER WITH THE SEED.[4]

MISHNAH 7. IF OLIVES OF ḤULLIN WERE PICKLED TOGETHER[5] WITH OLIVES OF TERUMAH, WHETHER IT WAS A CASE WHERE CRUSHED [OLIVES] OF ḤULLIN [WERE PICKLED TOGETHER] WITH CRUSHED [OLIVES] OF TERUMAH, OR CRUSHED [OLIVES] OF ḤULLIN WITH WHOLE [OLIVES] OF TERUMAH,[6] OR WITH JUICE OF TERUMAH,[7] THEY ARE FORBIDDEN. BUT IF WHOLE [OLIVES] OF ḤULLIN WERE PICKLED WITH CRUSHED [OLIVES] OF TERUMAH, THEY ARE PERMITTED.[8]

MISHNAH 8. IF UNCLEAN FISH WAS PICKLED WITH CLEAN FISH THE BRINE THEREOF IS FORBIDDEN IF IN A BARREL OF TWO SE'AHS THE UNCLEAN FISH WEIGHS TEN ZUZ[9] IN JUDEAN MEASURE, WHICH IS FIVE SELA'S IN GALILEAN MEASURE.[10] R. JUDAH SAYS: IT NEEDS BE A QUARTER [OF A LOG] IN TWO SE'AHS;[11] R. JOSE SAYS: ONE-SIXTEENTH THEREOF.[12]

(5) The use of *terumah* in a dish of *ḥullin*. (6) Small fish pickled in brine, of unsavoury flavour. When the onion, whose sole purpose here was to absorb the unpleasant flavour of the fish, has been removed, the fish may be eaten. R. Judah will admit that if the onion had been sliced up or crushed with the fish, the dish would be forbidden. (7) With its pungent flavour; 'Orlah II, 4. (8) To all non-priests, because the dough had been flavoured with *terumah*. (9) According to the principle that any flavour which has a deteriorating effect is permissible.

a (1) Of *ḥullin*. (2) In ancient ovens, bread was stuck to the sides of the oven during baking and it required great skill to remove the bread. (3) Warm bread quickly absorbs the flavour of wine in the barrel below. (4) Because the flavour is as forbidden as the substance itself. (5) Being of the opinion that smell is of no consequence; v. Pes. 76b. (6) Its tendency is to absorb moisture of the wine. (7) An umbelliferous plant like fennel. (8) Agreeing with the opinion of R. Judah in the preceding Mishnah. (9) A leguminous plant with seeds, used in farriery. Its fruit and stalk taste alike; Kil. II, 5. (10) The flavour of *terumah* itself making the wine forbidden. Only the seed is forbidden in the case of *terumah* and second tithe, and though stalks have the same taste as seed, yet they were not considered holy enough to be counted as *terumah*. (11) If it flavours the second tithe, it must not be eaten outside Jerusalem without redemption, and in Jerusalem it must be eaten with the sanctity due to tithes. (12) When even the stalks of fenugreek are forbidden, because they have the same taste as the fruit. (13) Lev. XIX, 19; Deut. XXII, 9–11. The prohibition applies to stalks as well as to the seed. (14) Like all other products of *kil'ayim*, since even the stalks are forbidden; v. Deut. XXII, 9.

b (1) For all *terumah* had to be given approximately. (2) Though the taste of both stalk and seed is similar the stalks are not subject to *terumah*. (3) I.e., he set aside *terumah* from seed and stalk before beating them out. (4) Once *terumah* had been pronounced in regard to the stalks, they belong to the priest, and especially since they have the same taste as the seeds. (5) In salt water. (6) Once the olives of *ḥullin* are crushed they absorb the taste of those of *terumah* that are whole. (7) Water in which *terumah* olives had been pickled. (8) Because whole olives only emit flavour, but do not absorb that of the olives of *terumah*. (9) Or 1/960th of the whole contents of the barrel. A *se'ah* = 24 *logs* = 48 *litras* = 4,800 *zuzim*. If the unclean fish is less than this prescribed amount the brine is permitted. Brine, on account of its pungency, requires a greater amount than 60 to neutralize it. (10) Judean measures being double those of Galilee. (11) The brine of the unclean fish must be 1/192nd of the contents of the barrel before we declare it forbidden. (The *se'ah* = 6 *kabs* = 24 *logs*; 2 *se'ahs* = 48 *logs*, and a quarter of a *log* is, therefore, 1/192nd of two *se'ahs*). Though R. Judah is of opinion that the admixture of a prohibited matter in another of a like kind is not neutralized even in a thousand, he is more lenient in the case of brine, since it is only the perspiration of the fish and is only forbidden on Rabbinical authority. (12) Only when the brine of the unclean fish is 1/16th part of the contents of the barrel is all the brine forbidden.

מחותך : צחנה. דגים קטנים כבושים כההיא דפ׳ הנודר מן המבושל (דף נח:) הנודר מן הצחנה אסור בטרית טרופה ומותר בציר ובמוריים ואם נתן בצל תרומה
בתוך הצחנה משליך את הבצלים והדגים מותרין ובלבד שיהא הכל בצורתו שלא נתערב עם הדגים : שאין הבצל שם ליתן טעם אלא להעביר הזוהמא ואין מתייש
לפי שיטת הירושלמי דמוקי מתני׳ בבצל של חולין דכיון דהאי בתרומה סברא הוא דרישא נמי בתרומה וירושלמי (הל׳ א) מייתי הא דתנן במסכת מעשר שני
(פ״ב מ״א) דגים שנתבשלו עם הקפלוטות של מעשר שני והשביחו השבח לפי חשבון ומסיק ההיא דלא כר׳ יהודה דאמר במתני׳ גבי בצל שאינו אלא לסלק הזוהמא

וצחנה הוא הסרחות והביאוש אה״כ ועלה באשו ותעל צחנתו (יואל ב) ודרך הבצל כשמבשלים אותו עם דבר סרוח שמסיר זוהמתו ומתקן ריחו קלת התקון וא״ר יהודה כי כשנתבשל בצל של תרומה בתבשיל מוסרח שמותר לאכול אותו התבשיל לפי שהוא לא נתן הבצל לתוך התבשיל לתת בו הבצל טעם אלא נתנו שם להסיר זוהמתו ולפיכך לא נבדוק אותו בטתן טעם ואין הלכה כר׳ יהודה : ב זה התפוח הנזכר הוא של תרומה בלא ספק ופי׳ שריסקו הוא משכתשו מקלת כתישה וכבר קדם לנו כי כשהחמילה התרומה לחולין שאותן חולין תרומה ושאר המאמר מבואר : ג הסרת הפת מן התנור נקרא רודה ואומר בכאן כי כשרודה ככר אחת חמה ונתנה ע״פ חבית שיהא מזיעה ושואבת ומהלחלחת מן היין שיש באותה חבית ושואבת כמו מושכת והלכה כר׳ יוסי : ד כמון הוא הכמון והעיקר אצלנו ריחא לאו מלתא היא וזה נוהג בכל אסורים שבתורה : ה תלתן ידוע ובערבי חלבה ויודע כי תרומה ומעשר שני אין חייב בהן אלא הזרעים הנאכלים בלבד ודין ההקדש והשביעית והכלאים נוהג בזרעים ובעץ והתלתן טעם עלו כטעם זרעו קרובים זה לזה : ו ידלקו ישרפו וכבר באורנו בכלאים כי כלאי הכרם דינם שישרפו כולם ואמרם בכאן חבילי תלתן של טבל

רבי יהודה מתיר בצחנה שאינו אלא ליטול את הזוהמא : ב ^א^תפוח א) שרסקו ונתנו לתוך עיסה וחמצה הרי זו אסורה ^ב^שעורים שנפלו לתוך הבור של מים אף על פי שהבאישו (מימיו) מימיו מותרין : ג הרודה ב) פת חמה ונתנה על פי חבית של יין של תרומה רבי מאיר אוסר ורבי יהודה מתיר רבי יוסי ^ג^מתיר בשל חטים ואוסר בשל שעורים מפני שהשעורים שואבות : ד ^ד^תנור שהסיקו ג) בכמון של תרומה ואפה בו את הפת הפת מותרת שאין טעם כמון אלא ריח כמון : ה ^ה^תלתן (ג) שנפלה לתוך הבור של יין בתרומה במעשר שני אם יש בזרע כדי ליתן טעם אבל לא בעץ בשביעית ובכלאי הכרם והקדש אם יש בזרע ובעץ כדי ליתן טעם : ו ^ו^מי שהיו ד) לו חבילי תלתן בכלאי הכרם ידלקו ^ז^היו לו חבילי תלתן של טבל כותש ומחשב כמה זרע יש בהם ומפריש את הזרע ואינו צריך להפריש את העץ אם הפריש לא יאמר אכתוש ואטול את העץ ואתן את הזרע אלא נותן העץ עם הזרע : ז ^ח^זיתי חולין שכבשן עם זיתי תרומה (ז) פצועי חולין עם פצועי תרומה פצועי חולין עם שלימי תרומה או במי תרומה אסור אבל שלימי חולין עם פצועי תרומה מותר : ח ^ט^דג טמא שכבשו עם דג טהור *כל גרב שהוא מחזיק סאתים אם יש בו משקל עשרה זוז ביהודה שהן חמש סלעים בגליל ה) דג ^י^טמא צירו אסור רבי יהודה אומר רביעית בסאתים ורבי יוסי אומר אחד משׁשה עשר בו :

כדאמר בפרק גיד הנשה (דף צט:) דסאתים מאתים ואינו אלא מדרבנן וכן משמע בסוף אין מעמידין מדאורייתא דפריך אלא מעתה טעמייהו דרבנן ציר ורוטב וקיפה שלהן מדפריך ציר אחלב משמע דשרצים דריש כדמוכח בפ׳ העור והרוטב (שם) בשמעתא דהמחה החלב וגמעו דמייתי עלה דרשה דטמאים וקאמר לכתוב רחמנא בשרצים וליגמרו הנך מיניה ואע״ג דבתורת כהנים דריש גבי [דגים] שקץ לאסור ציר ורוטב וקיפה שלהן ציר אסמכתא בעלמא הוא והא דפריך בפ׳ כל הבשר (קיג:) מדג טהור שמלחו עם דג טמא מותר מהיא דאימלח ליה בשר שחוטה בהדי בשר נבילה וקאסר ליה רבא מהטמאים לאסור ציר שפיר פריך דקים ליה דלכל הפחות מדרבנן מיהא אסור בדגים כדתנן הכא ש״מ דלא בלעי כשמלחן זה עם זה וקלא קשה כיון דלריך קרא בשרצים ובבהמה טמאה דרשינן לה בתורת כהנים מדכתיב טמאים הם לכם ובדגים דליכא קרא לא אסר מדאורייתא היכי מייתי רבא התם ראיה מהטמאים לאסור ציר של (סיפס) [מריסה]:

ט חגבים [א] טמאין שנכבשו עם חגבים טהורים (י) לא פסלו את צירם *העיד ר׳ צדוק על ציר חגבים טמאים שהוא טהור: י ב׳כל הנכבשין זה עם זה מותרים (יג) אלא עם החסית חסית של חולין עם חסית של תרומה ירק של חולין עם חסית של תרומה אסור אבל חסית של חולין עם ירק של תרומה מותר: יא רבי יוסי אומר כל הנשלקים עם התרדים אסורים מפני שהן נותנין את הטעם ר׳ שמעון אומר כרוב (יד) של שקיא עם כרוב של בעל אסור (טו) מפני שהוא בולע רבי *יהודה אומר כל המתבשלין זה עם זה (טז) מותרים אלא עם הבשר ר׳ יוחנן בנורי אומר א) (יז) ג׳הכבד אוסרת ואינה נאסרת מפני שהיא פולטת ואינה בולעת: יב ד׳ביצה *שנתבלה בתבלין אסורין אפילו חלמון שלה אסור מפני שהוא בולע ה׳מי שלקות ומי כבשים של תרומה אסורים לזרים:

פרק אחד עשר

א אין ו׳נותנין דבילה וגרוגרות לתוך המוריים מפני שהוא מאבדן אבל נותנין את היין למוריים ואין מפטמין את השמן אבל עושים את היין יינומלים ז׳אין מבשלין יין של תרומה מפני שהוא ממעיטו רבי יהודה מתיר מפני שהוא משביחו: ב דבש תמרים ג) ויין תפוחים וחומץ *סתוניות ושאר כל מי פירות של תרומה ר״א מחייב קרן וחומש ח׳ורבי יהושע פוטר ור״א מטמא משום משקה אר״י לא מנו חכמים שבעה משקין כמוני פטמים אלא אמרו ט׳שבעה משקין טמאים ושאר כל המשקין טהורין: ג י׳אין עושין תמרים דבש ולא תפוחים יין ולא סתוניות חומץ ושאר כל הפירות אין משנין אותם מברייתן בתרומה כ׳ובמעשר שני אלא זיתים וענבים בלבד ל׳אין סופגין ג) ארבעים משום ערלה אלא על היוצא מן הזיתים ומן הענבים ואין

יב א מיי׳ פ״ג מהלכות מאכלות אסורות הלכה כב סמג לאוין קלב טוש״ע י״ד סי׳ פה סעיף ג:

יג ב מיי׳ פט״ו מהלכות תרומות הלכה ט:

יד ג מיי׳ פ״ו מהל׳ מאכלות אסורות הל׳ ח סמג לאוין קלז טוש״ע י״ד סי׳ פג סעיף א:

טו ד מיי׳ פט״ו מהל׳ תרומות הלכה ה:

טז ה שם הלכה יא:

א ו מיי׳ פי״א שם הלכה ג:

ב ז שם הל׳ ד:

ג ח מיי׳ פי״א מהלכות תרומות הלכה ב:

ד ט מיי׳ פ״א מה׳ טומאת אוכלין הלכה ג ד:

ה י מיי׳ פי״א מה׳

MISHNAH 9. IF UNCLEAN LOCUSTS WERE PICKLED TOGETHER WITH CLEAN ONES, THEY DO NOT MAKE THE BRINE
a FORBIDDEN.[1] R. ẒADOK TESTIFIED THAT THE BRINE OF UNCLEAN LOCUSTS[2] IS CLEAN.[3]

MISHNAH 10. WHATSOEVER [VEGETABLES] ARE PICKLED TOGETHER[4] ARE PERMITTED, SAVE [WHEN PICKLED] WITH LEEKS.[5] LEEKS OF ḤULLIN [PICKLED] WITH THOSE OF TERUMAH, OR OTHER VEGETABLES OF ḤULLIN WITH LEEKS OF TERUMAH ARE FORBIDDEN,[6] BUT LEEKS OF ḤULLIN WITH VEGETABLES OF TERUMAH ARE PERMITTED.

MISHNAH 11. R. JOSE SAYS: WHATSOEVER IS STEWED WITH BEET[7] BECOMES FORBIDDEN, BECAUSE THE LATTER IMPARTS A FLAVOUR. R. SIMEON SAYS: CABBAGE FROM A FIELD ARTIFICIALLY IRRIGATED [THAT IS STEWED] WITH CABBAGE[8] FROM A FIELD WATERED BY RAIN, IS FORBIDDEN BECAUSE IT ABSORBS.[9] R. AKIBA SAYS:[10] ALL THINGS COOKED TOGETHER[11]
b ARE PERMITTED, EXCEPT THOSE WITH MEAT.[1] R. JOḤANAN B. NURI SAYS: LIVER RENDERS OTHER THINGS FORBIDDEN,[2] BUT DOES NOT ITSELF BECOME FORBIDDEN,[3] BECAUSE IT EXUDES AND DOES NOT ABSORB.[4]

MISHNAH 12. IF AN EGG IS BOILED[5] WITH FORBIDDEN SPICES[6] EVEN ITS YOLK IS FORBIDDEN, BECAUSE IT ABSORBS.[7] THE WATER IN WHICH TERUMAH HAS BEEN STEWED OR PICKLED IS FORBIDDEN TO NON-PRIESTS.

CHAPTER XI

c MISHNAH 1. ONE MUST NOT PUT INTO FISH-BRINE[1] A CAKE OF PRESSED FIGS OR DRIED FIGS,[2] SINCE IT SPOILS THEM;[3] BUT ONE MAY PLACE WINE [OF TERUMAH] INTO FISH BRINE.[4] ONE MUST NOT PERFUME THE OIL,[5] BUT IT MAY BE MADE INTO HONIED WINE.[6] WINE OF TERUMAH MUST NOT BE BOILED, BECAUSE THAT MAKES IT DECREASE.[7] R. JUDAH PERMITS THIS, BECAUSE IT IMPROVES IT.[8]

MISHNAH 2. [IF A NON-PRIEST DRANK] HONEY OF DATES, WINE OF APPLES,[9] VINEGAR FROM WINTER GRAPES,[10] AND ALL OTHER KINDS OF FRUIT JUICE OF TERUMAH,[11] R. ELIEZER DECLARES HIM LIABLE TO REPAY THEIR VALUE AND THE FIFTH;[12] BUT R. JOSHUA EXEMPTS FROM THE FIFTH.[13] R. ELIEZER DECLARES [THESE] SUSCEPTIBLE TO UNCLEANNESS AS LIQUIDS.[14] R. JOSHUA, HOWEVER, SAYS: THE SAGES HAVE
d NOT ENUMERATED SEVEN LIQUIDS[1] AS THOSE THAT COUNT SPICES,[2] BUT HAVE EXPRESSLY STATED: SEVEN LIQUIDS MAKE THINGS SUSCEPTIBLE TO DEFILEMENT, WHEREAS ALL OTHER LIQUIDS ARE NOT SUSCEPTIBLE.[3]

MISHNAH 3. ONE MUST NOT MAKE DATES INTO HONEY,[4] APPLES INTO WINE, WINTER-GRAPES INTO VINEGAR, OR CHANGE ANY OTHER KIND OF FRUIT THAT IS TERUMAH OR SECOND TITHE FROM THEIR NATURAL STATE, WITH THE SOLE EXCEPTION OF OLIVES AND GRAPES.[5] ONE DOES NOT ADMINISTER THE FORTY LASHES[6] ON ACCOUNT OF 'ORLAH EXCEPT WITH THE PRODUCT OF OLIVES AND GRAPES.[7] LI-

a (1) This leniency is due to the fact that they have no blood, but only perspiration. (2) Forbidden in Lev. XI, 20. (3) I.e., it may be eaten; v. 'Ed. VII, 2. (4) Those of *terumah* with *ḥullin*. (5) A species of onions like leek, garlic and onions, that are very sharp in taste and pungent in smell. (6) On account of their pungency, which pervades everything. (7) Of *terumah* or *kil'ayim*. Beet, unlike other vegetables (which, in the opinion of R. Jose, as distinct from the Tanna of the preceding Mishnah, are permitted when stewed together) impart a sharp flavour. (8) Of *terumah* or *kil'ayim*. (9) The former being by nature dry and always ready for moisture, will easily absorb flavour of cabbage of *terumah*. (10) Var. lec.: R. Judah. (11) Even when one is permitted and the other is not; for one does not absorb from the other to the extent of rendering it prohibited; *Tif. Yis.*

b (1) That is when forbidden meat is cooked together with permissible meat. It is the nature of meat to exude and to absorb. (2) If it be the liver of an animal declared to be *ṭrefah*. (3) Permissible liver does not become forbidden if cooked with things forbidden; v. Ḥul. 110*a*. (4) While it is engaged in exuding its own juice, it does not absorb the juices of other flesh. (5) Var. lec.: 'that had been spiced'. (6) Of *'orlah, terumah* or *kil'ayim*. (7) The shell of the egg being thin, the yolk absorbs the spices. The white of the egg, being outside, certainly becomes forbidden.

c (1) Latin *muria* or *muries*, a kind of salted pickle, containing fish hash and occasionally wine; also salt water in which chopped fish or locusts have been pickled. (2) Of *terumah*. (3) After the brine they had absorbed is squeezed out, the figs were thrown away. (4) Wine was often put into the brine in order to deodorize it. (5) Of *terumah* with spices of *ḥullin*, since the oil of *terumah* is thus absorbed by the spices and later wasted by being thrown away. Moreover, the oil is rendered unfit for food, and used only for anointing purposes, thus causing damage to *terumah*. (6) I.e., wine of *terumah* may be mixed with water, honey and spices to make it into a sweet-honied wine; 'A.Z. 30*a*. (7) And *terumah* must not suffer damage either by reduction in quantity, or by making it fit for less people to drink, boiled wine not being agreeable to many. (8) Unboiled wine may taste better, but turns sour more quickly than boiled wine. (9) Cider. (10) Being very sour, they were usually converted into vinegar. (11) Except wine and oil. (12) As in all cases of a non-priest eating *terumah*. (13) He does not consider these as liquid of *terumah*, but simply as exudation of the fruit. (14) Lev. XI, 34, 38.

d (1) Water, dew, wine, oil, honey, milk, blood (Maksh. VI, 4). These become unclean themselves and make other foods susceptible to defilement. R. Joshua, therefore, debars those mentioned in our Mishnah, which R. Eliezer includes. (2) That are not at all precise in the enumeration of their wares. (3) Even they themselves contract no defilement. (4) Once the fruit is converted from its original state into a liquid, some loss is incurred to the *terumah* by reducing it in quantity or value. (5) Which are more usually made into oil and wine than eaten as olives and grapes; hence, it cannot be said that fruits of *terumah* have in any way been altered from their natural state. (6) In reality thirty-nine, forty being a round number. (7) The juice of any other fruit of *'orlah* not being considered as a liquid for which the penalty is administered.

QUIDS CANNOT BE BROUGHT AS FIRST FRUITS, EXCEPT THE PRODUCT OF OLIVES AND GRAPES, AND NO FRUIT JUICE IS SUSCEPTIBLE TO UNCLEANNESS AS LIQUIDS EXCEPT THE PRODUCT OF OLIVES AND GRAPES. NO FRUIT JUICE IS BROUGHT ON THE ALTAR, EXCEPT THAT WHICH PROCEEDS FROM OLIVES AND GRAPES.[8]

MISHNAH 4. THE STALKS[9] OF FRESH FIGS AND DRIED FIGS, ACORNS[10] AND CAROBS OF TERUMAH ARE FORBIDDEN TO NON-PRIESTS.[11]

a *MISHNAH* 5. KERNELS OF TERUMAH[1] ARE FORBIDDEN[2] WHEN IN THE POSSESSION OF A PRIEST, BUT PERMITTED WHEN HE CASTS THEM AWAY. SIMILARLY, THE BONES OF HOLY OFFERINGS[3] ARE FORBIDDEN WHEN [THE PRIEST HAS THEM] IN HIS POSSESSION, BUT PERMITTED WHEN HE CASTS THEM AWAY.[4] COARSE BRAN IS PERMITTED,[5] BUT FINE BRAN IS FORBIDDEN IF IT IS OF NEW WHEAT, AND PERMITTED IF IT IS OF OLD WHEAT.[6] ONE MAY ADOPT IN TERUMAH THE PRACTICE FOLLOWED IN ḤULLIN.[7] HE WHO SIFTS[8] A ḲAB OR TWO [OF FINE FLOUR] FROM A SE'AH OF WHEAT, MUST NOT ABANDON THE REST, BUT DEPOSIT IT IN SOME HIDDEN PLACE.[9]

MISHNAH 6. IF A STORE-CHAMBER WAS CLEARED OF WHEAT OF TERUMAH, ONE NEED NOT SIT DOWN AND COLLECT EACH GRAIN, BUT SWEEP IT ALL UP IN HIS USUAL MANNER[10] AND THEN DEPOSIT ḤULLIN THEREIN.

MISHNAH 7. SIMILARLY, IF A JAR OF OIL[11] IS UPSET, HE NEED NOT SIT DOWN AND SCOOP IT UP [WITH HIS FINGERS],[12] BUT DEAL WITH IT AS HE WOULD IN A CASE OF ḤULLIN.

b *MISHNAH* 8. HE WHO POURS OUT[1] FROM JAR TO JAR AND ALLOWS THREE DROPS TO DRIP,[2] MAY PLACE ḤULLIN THEREIN.[3] BUT IF HE INCLINES THE JAR [ON ITS SIDE] IN ORDER TO DRAIN IT,[4] IT IS TERUMAH. HOW MUCH TERUMAH OF TITHE OF DEM'AI[5] MUST THERE BE FOR HIM TO TAKE IT TO THE PRIEST?[6] ONE EIGHTH OF AN EIGHTH.[7]

MISHNAH 9. VETCHES[8] OF TERUMAH MAY BE GIVEN[9] TO CATTLE, BEASTS OR FOWLS.[10] IF AN ISRAELITE HIRED A COW FROM A PRIEST, HE MAY GIVE IT VETCHES OF TERUMAH[11] TO EAT, BUT IF A PRIEST HIRED A COW FROM AN ISRAELITE, THOUGH THE RESPONSIBILITY OF FEEDING IT IS HIS,[12] HE MUST NOT FEED IT WITH VETCHES OF TERUMAH. IF AN ISRAELITE UNDERTAKES THE CARE OF A COW FROM A PRIEST,[13] HE MUST NOT FEED IT WITH VETCHES OF TERUMAH[14] BUT IF A PRIEST UNDERTAKES THE CARE OF A COW FROM AN ISRAE-

(8) Oil for meal-offerings and wine for libations. (9) By which the fruit is attached to the tree. (10) כליסים. Word of dubious meaning. According to Maim.: a species of fig; Rashi; a kind of pea or bean. Others think it is the fruit of the carob-tree. (11) Being considered as part of the actual fruit.

a (1) Those that are soft and left with some sap. (2) To be eaten by a non-priest. (3) That contain marrow and can yet be enjoyed. (4) Thus showing that he has no further use for them. If the kernels and the bones cannot be enjoyed at all any more, they are permitted to non-priests even whilst still in possession of the priest. (5) Being almost useless as food. (6) When the bran is new (within thirty days of being cut), much of the flour clings to the bran even after being ground, but old wheat is dry and grinds so well that little flour is left in the bran. (7) That is, he may extract from *terumah* also the fine flour and cast away the coarse bran without scruples of wasting *terumah*. (8) A *se'ah* has six *ḳabs*, and after extracting the *ḳab* or two of fine flour, the rest was thrown away as refuse. (9) Since some of it is still edible in cases of emergency, non-priests may not eat thereof, for the name of *terumah* still adheres to it. (In other cases, food only used in cases of emergency is not deemed food at all, but being *terumah* added strictures have been imposed.) (10) That is with a broom, and even if a few grains of *terumah* are left, it matters not, since he has no intention of wilfully destroying the *terumah*. (11) Of *terumah*. (12) Cf. Shab. 143*b*.

b (1) Wine and oil of *terumah*. (2) After emptying a bottle. (3) Regardless of some drops that may still be in the first jar. (4) After the dripping of the three drops. (5) V. Glos. (6) A question somewhat irrelevant here, but cited in consequence of the reference to small grains and drops of *terumah* about which one need not bother. Note that the question only concerns doubtful *terumah*, for in a case of definite and clean *terumah*, even smallest particles must not be wasted. (7) Of a *log*, that is 1/64th of a *log*. Less than that may be wasted. (8) A species of bean rarely used as human food, serving mostly as fodder for animals, but since man eats of it in cases of emergency, *terumah* must be taken therefrom. (9) By the priest. (10) If these are his own. Of *terumah*, only that which man could not eat, was given to animals. (11) Since the cow belongs to a priest, he might just as well give the vetches to her as to any other priest. (12) Hiring not constituting a sale, the cow is still the property of the Israelite. (13) Lit., 'values'; he undertakes to tend it and to share in its increased value after he had fattened it. Thus, if the cow was now worth £20 and he improved it to be worth £30, he would share half of the £10 with the priest. (14) By this arrangement, the cow actually becomes the property of the Israelite and not of the priest: v. Lev. XXII, 11.

*ואין[א] מביאין בכורין משקין אלא (על) היוצא מן הזיתים ומן הענבים [ב]ואינו מטמא משום משקה אלא היוצא מן הזיתים ומן הענבי' ואין מקריבין על גבי המזבח אלא היוצא מן הזיתים ומן הענבים: ד [ג]עוקצי תאנים וגרוגרות הכליסים והחרובין של תרומה אסורים לזרים: ה [ד]גרעיני תרומה בזמן שהוא מכנסן אסורות ואם השליכן מותרות וכן עצמות הקדשים בזמן שהוא מכנסן אסורין ואם השליכן מותרין (ז) המורסן מותר [ה]סובין של חדשות אסורות ושל ישנות מותרות [ו]ונוהג בתרומה כדרך שהוא נוהג בחולין המסלת קב או קבים לסאה לא יאבד את השאר אלא יניחנו במקום המוצנע: ו מגורה שפנה ממנה חטי תרומה אין מחייבין אותו להיות יושב ומלקט אחת אחת אלא מכבד כדרכו ונותן לתוכה חולין: ז [ח]וכן חבית של שמן שנשפכה אין מחייבין אותו להיות יושב ומטפח אלא נוהג בה כדרך שהוא נוהג בחולין: ח [ט]המערה מכד לכד ונוטף שלש טפים *ונותן לתוך החולין הרכינה [ג] ומיצה ה"ז תרומה וכמה תהא בתרומת מעשר של דמאי ויוליכנה לכהן [י]אחד משמנה לשמינית: ט כרשיני תרומה מאכילין אותם לבהמה ולחיה ולתרנגולים [ג] [כ]ישראל ששכר פרה מכהן מאכילה כרשיני תרומה (י) וכהן ששכר פרה מישראל אע"פ שמזונותיה עליו לא יאכילנה כרשיני תרומה (יא) [ל]ישראל ששם פרה מכהן לא יאכילנה כרשיני תרומה וכהן ששם

והיא דאין מביאין בכורים מוקי בפ' העור והרוטב (דף קכ:) כר' יהושע וגבי בכורים כתיב (דברים כו) את ראשית פרי האדמה ותני *רב יוסף פרי אתה מביא ואי אתה מביא משקה הביא ענבים ודרכן מנין ת"ל תביא והא דמייתי דבכורים מקמי הכיא דערלה לשמעתא דהתם איירי בבכורים ובפ' כל שעה (כד:) משמע דאין לוקין משום ערלה על היוצא משאר פירות דזיעה בעלמא הוא ובפרק העור והרוטב משמע דטעמא מקרא דאוקי לה כר' יהושע דאמר דון מינה ואוקי באתרא וגמר לה לה [א]מבכורים ותרומה והדר מייתי לערלה פרי פרי מבכורים ועוד קשה ספי דאמר בפר' כילד מברכין (דף לח.) דמברכין על דבש תמרים שהכל ומוקי לה כרבי יהושע דזיעה בעלמא הוא ומשמע דהיינו טעמא דרבי יהושע: על גבי המזבח · שמן למנחות ויין לנסכים: ד עוקצי תאנים · אמרינן בירושלמי (הל' ג) רבי זעירא בשם רבי אליעזר אומר מתניתין במובלעים באוכל: כליסין · מיני פירות כדאמר באלו טרפות (דף סז:) יתושין שבכליסים: ה וכן עצמות קדשים · תימה במאי עסקינן אי לפני זריקה כולהו אסירי ואפילו מעילה איכא בקדשי קדשים דאין כאן שעת היתר לכהנים אי לאחר זריקה לרבה כולהו שרו ולרבי אלעזר של עולה אסורין ושל אשם וחטאת כולם מותרין כדאי' בפרק המזבח מקדש (דף פו.) וי"ל דהכא איירי בקדשים ג] הסובלין דומיא דתרומה ובעצמות דחזי קצת לאכילה ומשום נותר כדמוקי לה בירושלמי (הל' ד) אמר רבי יוחנן בגרעיני אגסין וקרוסטומלים היא מתניתין אמר ר"א ואפילו תימא בגרעיני הרוטב במחוסרות למלמץ והא תניין עצמות קדשים אית לך מימר במחוסרות למלמץ לא בראשי כנפים והסחוסין אתא רבי אבהו בשם ר' יוחנן בראשי כנפים והסחוסין היא מתניתא: המורסן · של תרומה מותר לזרים: של חדשות · אמר בירושלמי (שם) אלו הן חדשות כל זמן שהבריות רגילים לחבט ר' אחא אומר עד שלשים יום: כדרך שהוא נוהג בחולין כך ינהוג לתקן את התרומה ואין בכן משום מאבד תרומה כשמשליך את המותר: בירושלמי (שם) א"ר אבהו בשם רבי יוחנן כן הוא שיעורא והתניא מסלת בחטים כל שהוא רוצה מקנב בירק כל שהוא רוצה מסלת שמוציא מסאה קמח של תרומה קב קביים סולת מניח את השאר ואינו מאבדן: ו ז מטפח · בפסת ידו מאסף השמן בדופני החבית: ח נותן לתוכה חולין · ולא חשו חכמים לשמן תרומה הנדבק בדופני הכלי: הרכינה ומילה · בפרק המוכר את הספינה תנן הרכינה ומילה (ח) הרי היא של מוכר והתניא הרכינה ומילה הרי היא תרומה ושני משום יאוש בעלים נגעו בה (ט): תרומת מעשר של דמאי נותן לכהן · ואם ג] נשאר בידו אחד מח' שבשמינית שבלוג לא חייבוהו חכמים להחזיר לכהן ובירושלמי אמר הדא דתימא בטמא אבל בטהור אפילו כל שהוא צריך להחזיר בדמאי אבל בוודאי בין טמא בין טהור בין רב בין מעט צריך להחזיר: ירושלמי (שם) תני רבי חלפתא בן שאול קדרה שבישל בה תרומה מגעילה ג' פעמים בחמין ודיו אמר רבי בא ואין למדין ממנה לענין נבלה אמר רבי יוסי קשיתה קומי רבי בא תרומה בעון מיתה ונבילה בלאו ואת אמר' הכין אמר ליה כמ"ד *קיבלו עליהן את המעשרות רבי יוסה' בשם רבי בעא קומי רבי מנא תנן הרכינה ומילה הרי זו תרומה ואת אמר' הכין אמר ליה כאן על ידי האור הוא נגעל פירוש קדרה של חרס ואף על גב דחרס אינו יוצא מידי דופנו בתרומה הקילו לפי שמאליהן קיבלוה כמו שפירשתי בשביעית (פ"ו מ"א) סבר תרומה בזמן הזה דרבנן ופריך ממה שמחמיר במתניתין גבי הרכינה לא היה לנו להקל ומשני שהאור מגעילה ואין זו קולא ויש ללמוד ממתני' דהני גנות שדרך בהן נכרי כשבא ישראל לנגבן מכבד כדרכו ואין מחייבין אותו ללקט הרצנים שבין הגנות כדאשכחן במתני' המפנה חטים של תרומה מן המגורה ונותן לתוכה חולין ונוהג בהן מנהג חולין לאכול הזרים ושלא לשומרן בטהרה דאין זה מבטל איסור לכתחלה שלא נתכוון לבטל ומיהו כוס שפינו ממנו יין נסך לא שרי למרמי ביה חמרא אע"ג דתקן גבי חבית תרומה ולא חייבוהו לספח לא דמי דההיא לא איירי ברוצה לתת לתוכה חולין ולהאכיל לזרים אלא לענין *איסור תרומה איירי ולא חיים במה שמתייבש כוס של שמן והולך וכלה ועוד היה ראוי לפרש בנשפכה לארץ כעין סיפוה דמס' שבת בפ' חבית (דף קמג:) אי לאו משום דלא קתני הכא חבית שנשברה כדקתני התם וההיא דאמרינן בפר' אין מעמידין (דף לג.) דקנקנים של נכרים אסור למירמי בהו חמרא וכסי משכשכן במים ומיהו אין ראיה מזה לדידן דסתם יינן שבכל הגמרא אסור בהנאה ואוסר במשהו אבל עכו"ם דבזמן הזה היה אומר רבי שמואל שהן כתינוק שאינו יודע בטיב עכו"ם ומשמשיה ולא מיתסר בהנאה אלא בשתיה ואינו אוסר אלא בס' לפי מה שפסק רבינו תם דמין במינו בס': ט כרשיני תרומה · עיקרן למאכל בהמה דאי עיקרן לאדם אסור ליתנם לבהמה משום הפסד תרומה מ"מ לאדם מיהא חזו דאין תרומה ומעשר אלא במידי דחזי לאדם כדאמר בריש כלל גדול (סח.): לא יאכילנה כרשיני תרומה · אף על גב דשריא בהנאה לישראל מדתנן (פ"ג דעירובין דף כו:) מערבין לישראל בתרומה אמר ר"ת דהנאת כילוי אסירא כשנעשין בשביל ישראל כגון אכילה והדלקה וכדאסרינן להדליק במבואות האפלין שלא ברשות כהן ובפרק במה מדליקין (דף כ.) גבי אין מדליקין בטבל טמא דרשינן משמרת תרומתי (במדבר יח) בשתי תרומות הכתוב מדבר בתרומה טהורה ובתרומה טמאה מה תרומה טהורה אין לך בה אלא משעת הרמה ואילך אף תרומה טמאה נמי משעת הרמה ואילך בתרומה טהורה היינו אכילה ממש לטבל שרי בהנאה ודומיא דהכי מרבה טבל טמא כעין אכילה דהיינו הדלקה והסקה טהורה אכילתה אסורה לזרים אף טמאה אכילתה אסורה לזרים כגון הנאת הסקה אבל נאסר כההוא מעשה דר' פנחס בן יאיר בפ"ק דחולין (ד"ז) ואמרינן מעריס אדם על תבואתו ומכניסה במוץ שלה כדי שתהא בהמתו אוכלת הא לאו הכי לא והא דאמר בפ' כל שעה (דף לד.) הבא שאול גבל של בית ר' *והיו מחמין לו חמין בהסין של תרומה אומר ר"ת דהיינו לכהנים של בית ר' והא דאמר אין מדליקין בטבל טמא ה"ה בטבל טהור וגם בקונט' פי"כן כ"ש בטבל טהור והר' משה בר'אברהם דחה דהא דאין מאכיל ישראל לבהמתו כרשיני תרומה משום דכתי' (ויקרא כב) וכהן כי יקנה נפש קנין כספו ואפילו נפש בהמה במשמע כדאמר בפ"ב דבילה (דף כח:) אך אשר יאכל לכל נפש ומשמע דוקא דכהן אבל דישראל לא ובתורת כהנים דרשי' לה גבי בהמה בפרשת אמור ויליד ביתו הם יאכלו בלחמו הם אוכלים ואין בהמה אוכלת יכול לא תאכל בכרשינים ת"ל נפש ובגמרא נמי מייתי הכא בירושלמי ומיהו אמת הוא דלכלות בשביל ישראל אסור בלא אכילה כגון הדלקה כדמוכח סיפא דמתני' [דאין מדליקין במבואות האפלות אלא ברשות כהן] ובירושל' משמע דרשות כהן אחולין דוקא קאי דקא בעי מתני' על גבי חולין ברשות כהן הא קמייתא אפילו שלא ברשות כהן ש"מ דמדאורייתא כל הנאות מותרות לישראל ועוד דאמר בירושלמי בת ישראל שנכנסה להדליק מכהנת סובלת פתילה בשמן שרפה ומדלקת וצ"ל דאף למדרבנן אסור הנאת כילוי בצורך רבים לא גזור כגון בתי כנסיות ובתי

סים

למאמר השם יתברך (כל חלב דגן תירוש ויצהר) (במדבר יח) ותירוש הוא היין ויצהר הוא השמן וקראו הכתוב ראשית כמו שקרא הבכורים ראשית וחייב אותה בתרומה ולפיכך מותר להוציא מהם משקה בין שיהיו תרומה או מעשר שני וכמו כן מי שלקח פירות ערלה והוציא מהם משקה וישתה אותו המשקה אינו חייב מלקות מן התורה אלא אם הוא משקה הענבים או הזיתים כי כן מנהגם היה להוציא מהם המשקה ומה שאמרו כי הבכורים מביאין אותו יין ושמן הוא לדעת *רבי יהודה כי הוא למד הבכורים מן התרומה וכן אמר [חולין קכ:] מני ר' יהודה דאמר דון מינה ואוקי באתרא וגמר לה בכורים מן התרומה ואין הלכה *כרבי יהודה וכבר בארנו כי מכלל שבעה משקין היין והשמן ואומר כי אין בכל המשקין היוצאים מן הפירות שיקבלו טומאה משום משקה אלא היין והשמן וכן אינו קרב על גבי המזבח אלא היין והשמן והוא לשון התורה במנחות בשמן וקרבנו' ביין לנסך: ד עוקץ הוא העץ הקטן הדבק בבדי האילן ובעיקר הפרי וגרוגרות הם התאנים היבשים וכליסין מין ממיני התאנים: ה גרעינים ידועין והן אותן שבתוך הפרי ואלו הגרעינים שאמרו שהן אסורין עד שישליכם הכהן הוא על שני דרכים האחד שתהיה הגרעינה ראויה לאכילה כמו גרעיני החבושין והפריסים או שתהיה גרעינה שישאר בה לחלוחית שתהיה ראויה למלילה כגון גרעינת התמרה כשהיא לחה אבל הגרעינים האחרים מותרין באכילה לזרים כגון גרעיני החרובין אע"פ שלא השליכם הכהן וכן אלו העצמות הם העצמות הראויות לאכילה ר"ל העצמות שיש בהן לחלוחית: ומורסן הוא הגסה מן הסובין: וסובין ידוע: ואמרם ונוהג בתרומה כדרך שהוא נוהג בחולין ענינו שמותר לו שיכבור את התרומה ויפליך מן הסובין מה שאינו ראוי לאכילה כמו שהוא עושה בחולין: המסלת · נגזר מן סלת וענינו שאם לקח סאה חטה והוציא ממנה קב או קבים סלת שלא יפליך השאר לפי שהוא ראוי לאכילה ואסור לאבד התרומה אבל מניחין השאר במקום מוצנע: ו מכבד כדרכו · ר"ל שיכבד כדרך שבני אדם מכבדין האוצרות כשמפנין אותן מן הדברים שהגיעו בהם: ז מטפח · נגזר מן טפח ענינו שלא נחייב אותו לדקדק בלקיטת השמן מן הקרקע עד שלא יניח שם שום לחלוחית אלא ילקט כמו שיהיה מלקט אלו נשברה שם חבית של שמן חולין: ח אומר בכאן כי כשעירה כד שיש בו שמן של תרומה או יין של תרומה בכד שני לא נחייב אותו לקנח אותו הכד עד שלא ישאר שם לחלוחית ואז יתן שם החולין אלא מאחר שנתמלא מן הכד כל מה שהי' בתוכו ונטפו ממנו שלש טפים טפה אחר טפה כאשר יארע לכלי כשמריקין ממנו כל מה שבתוכו מותר לו לשום באותו הכד החולין ואם הניח הכד ולא נתן בו חולין אחר שעירה אותו והטהו על צדו ונתמלא ונתכנס בו שום שארית הרי זו תרומה ולא נאמר כיון שיצא ממנו כל מה שיש בו טפה אחר טפה שלש טפין כל מה שנמלא ממנו אחר כך חולין לפי שהסיח דעתו ממנו ותרגום הטי נא כדך (בראשית כד) ארכיני כען וכבר בארנו כי הדמאי אין לכהן בו אלא תרומת מעשר ושמינית הוא שמינית הלוג וכבר בארנו שיעור הלוג וכשתהיה התרומה מעשר של דמאי שמינית השמינית או יותר על זה אז יתחייב להטריח עצמו עד שיגיענה ליד כהן ואם היה פחות מזה אינו חייב להגיעו ליד כהן אבל יניחנו עד שיבא כהן ויתננו לו או עד שיפסד וזכר בכאן את זה הדין לפי שקדם לו הדבר בשיעורין הקטנים מן התרומה שאין ראוין לחוש בהם מפני מיעוטן וכמו הגרגרים שנשרו ד] באוצר והלחלוחית שנשארה בכד וג"כ זכר שיעור תרומת מעשר שאין אדם חייב לטרוח ולהוליכה לכהן מפני מיעוטו: ט תרנגולין ידוע שם טפל על הזכרים ועל הנקבות מזה המין וידוע כי כשיקנה הכהן בהמה שהוא מאכילה תרומה למאמר השם יתעלה (ויקרא כב) וכהן כי יקנה נפש קנין כספו ולפיכך כ ששכר הבהמה אינו מאכילה תרומה לפי שאינה קנין כספו: וישראל ששם פרה מכהן · ר"ל שיקנה אותה הישראלי מן הכהן בדמים ידועים ויתנה עמו שיטפל במזונותיה הישראלי עד זמן ידוע ואח"כ

א) חולין פ"ט קכ:
ב) כ"ב פ"ס פז·
ג) יבמות פ"ו סו:
ע"א פ"א דף טו·

פי' מהר"י בן מלכי צדק

משקה ערלה · השותה אלא בזמן ששותה יין ושמן דענבי' ודזיתי ערלה אבל יין תפוחי ערלה או דבש תמרי ערלה או משקה משאר פירות אם שתה אינו לוקה עליהן: ואין מביאין בכורין משקין פי' כשבצרן מתחלה לכך: ואינו מטמא משום משקה וכו' פי' יין ושמן והם מז' משקין שמנו חכמים: ד עוקצי תאנין וגרוגרות · פי' לעז פריינו כליסים מין תאנין הן: של תרומה אסורין העוקצין לזרים · א"ר זירא בש"ר אליעזר בעוקצין מובלעות באוכל אבל בעוקצין שמחוץ לאוכל מותרין לזרים: ה גרעיני תרומה בזמן שמכנסן אסורות לזרין ואם השליכן מותרין · א"ר יוחנן בגרעיני קריסטומלין *כאגסין הן: ה שכנסן ליאכל · לכן בזמן שמכנסן אסורות אבל גרעיני תמרים ואפרסקין אפילו אם מכנסן מותרין שאין דרכן ליאכל וכן עצמות הקדשין בזמן שמכנסן אסורין לזרים רבי אבהו בש"ר י' בראשי כנפים והסחוסים היא מתני' שדרכן ליאכל לכך אם מכנסן אסורין אבל שאר עצמות אפי' אם מכנסן מותרות: המורסן של תרומה · פי' מורסן קביזא: סובין של חדשות כל זמן שהבריות חובטין ר' אחא אמר עד ל' יום שדרכן ליאכל ושל ישנות מותר לזרין לאכילה דאין דרכו לאכלן ונהוג בתרומה כדרך שנוהג בחולין. פי' מסלת בחטין כל זמן שהוא רוצה מקבב בירק כל מה שהוא רוצה כמו שמקבב בירק חולין כך מקבב בירק תרומה המסלת קב פי' שמוציא מסאה דתרומה קב סולת או קביים לא יאבד את השאר אלא יניחנו במקום צנוע: ו מגורה וכו' · שהיה שם חטי תרומה ופנה משם חטי תרומה להכניס שם חולין אין מחייבין אותו להיות יושב ומלקט חטה חטה עד שיבור הכל אלא מכבד המגורה כמנהגו ונותן לתוכה חולין: ז וכן חבית של שמן שנשפכה · פי' שמן תרומה אין מחייבין אותו להיות יושב ומטפח וכו' · פי' מלקט בפסת ידו עד שיכנוס הכל אלא נוהג בה וכו': ח המערה מכד לכד · פי' כד מלאה שמן דתרומה ומערה אותה לתוך כד אחר ואחר שהערה מניחה ונטפה ג' טיפין האחרונין ואז מותר ליתן לתוכה חולין הרכינה ומיצת התמצית תרומה הוי והתם בבבא בתרא תנן הכינה ומיצות למוכר ובגמר' מקשה אהדדי ותירץ אימ' ללוקח: כמה יהא בתרומת מעשר של דמאי · פי' כגון שיש לו ק' כדין שכל אחד ספק הופרש מהן מעשר ספק לא הופרש מהן מעשר מעשר לספק לא צריך להפריש אלא אחת ונקראת תרומת מעשר דמאי וצריך ליתנה לכהן ואם לא נתנה לכהן כולה ונשאר בידו אחד משמנה לשמינית פי' לשמינית לג דהיינו אנקיאה וחצי ושמינית דשמינית משקל אחד ומשהו נמצא כשנשאר בידו משקל ומשהו שמן תרומת מעשר דמאי חייב להחזירו לכהן א"ר יודה בר אחתיה דר' יוסי בר' חנינא פחות מיכן נתנו בכרי הני מילי בדמאי אבל בודאי בין רב בין מועט חייב להחזיר: ט כרשיני תרומה מאכילין אותן וכו' · פי' אע"פ שמזונותיה עליו לא יאכילנה כרשיני תרומה דסבל

*[הגה עי' בירושלמי כאן וצ"ע קצת]:

עין משפט נר מצוה

*לפנינו הגי' ר' יוסי

ח א מיי' פ"ב מהל' בכורים הלכה ד:

ט ב מיי' פ"א מהל' טומאת אוכלין הלכה ד:

י ג מיי' פ"א מה' תרומות הלכה יג:

יא ד שם הל' יא:

יב ה שם הל' יב:

יג ו שם הלכה ה:

יד ז ח מיי' שם פ"א הלכה יד:

טו ט שם הל' טו:

טז י מיי' פ"ג שם הלכה טז:

יז כ מיי' פ"ט שם הלכה ז:

יח ל שם הלכה ח:

פירוש הרא"ש

(ז) הם הסובין הגסים מותר לזרים וכן הסובין של ישנות שהם יבשות ונעתקים היטב אבל של חדשים הם לחות ואינם נעתקים היטב ונשאר הרבה קמח מעורב עם הסובין: (ח) אחר שהטיף ג' טפין: (ט) לפי שאינם רוצים להמתין עד שיתמצה: (י) מאכילה כרשיני תרומה הואיל וגוף הבהמה (של כהן) אע"פ שמזונותיה על ישראל אין כאן משום גזל דאם היה רוצה מתן התרומה לבעל הפרה ואנן סהדי דניחא ליה לבעל הפרה שיתן לה כרשיני תרומה כדי שיאכילה בריות וה"ל כאילו זכה בה הכהן ומאכילה לבהמתו: (יא) כיון שהגוף הבהמה של ישראל: [מאליהן]

הגהות מהר"י לנדא

פי' א א] בריש ט"ג וגמר לה לה מבכורים · צ"ל וגמר לה לבכורים מתרומה והדר וכו': ב] שם מ"ה בקדשים הנאכלים · כצ"ל: ג] שם מ"ח ואם לא נשאר בידו כצ"ל: ד] בר"ם שנשרו באוצר · צ"ל שנשארו:

עין משפט נר מצוה

יט א מיי' פי"א מהל' תרומות הלכה יח:

כ ב ג שם הל' יט:

פירוש הרא"ש

(יב) ברשות כהן פירוש כשיש שם כהן דנר לאחד נר למאה:

מדרשות ומבואות האפלין ובת ישראל המדלקת מכהנת לא אתמור כלי האי לאסור לסבול הפתילה בשמן א"כ מתחלה התירו משום סכנה ושוב לא אסרו כדאמר בירושלמי (הל' ה) ר' הונא בשם ר' ינאי שעת מסלח' זאבים היתה ולא עמד ב"ד וביטל כמה דתימר תמן לא עמד ב"ד וביטל אף הכא לא עמד ב"ד וביטל פי' כדאמרינן תמן במס' שביעית בירושלמי בפר' בראשונה (הל' ג) ומהאי טעמא דפרשינן ניחא הא דאבא שאול גבל של בית רבי אפילו לצורך זרים לצורך רבים היה שרוב תלמידים סמוכין עליו ומפרנסן כדאמרינן בכילד מעברין (דף ע:) ידאון נשיא לקיסון ותימה דבמס' שביעית פ"ח בירושלמי אמר הכי אין סכין שמן שביעית במרחץ אבל סך הוא מבחוץ ונכנס ולא מדליקין בשמן שרפה לא בבתי כנסיות ובבתי מדרשות ושמא פליגא אמתני':

פרה מישראל מאכילה כרשיני תרומה:

י [א]מדליקין שמן שרפה בבתי כנסיות ובבתי מדרשות ובמבואות האפלין ועל גבי החולין ברשות כהן (יב) [ב]בת ישראל שנשאת לכהן והיא למודה אצל אביה אביה מדליק ברשותה מדליקין בבית המשתה אבל לא בבית האבל דברי רבי יהודה ורבי יוסי אומר בבית האבל אבל לא בבית המשתה רבי מאיר אוסר כאן וכאן רבי שמעון [ג]מתיר כאן וכאן:

סליקא לה מסכת תרומות

כהן ששם פרה מישראל. ביבמות בפרק אלמנה (סו:) פירש בקונטרס כששכרה הימנו מתנה עמו להחזירה בדמים הללו שאם תכחיש או תאנס יתן דמים ואי אפשר לומר כן דכי האי גוונא איכא איסור רבית כדמוכח בפרק איזהו נשך אלא צריך להעמידה בשואל: י שמן שרפה. מפרש בבמה מדליקין (דף כג:) שמן תרומה שנטמא: בבתי כנסיות ובבתי מדרשות ובמבואות אפלין. כל הני בלא כהן מותר כדאיתא בירושלמי (הלכה ה) דאמר ר"ש בר אבא בשם רבי יוחנן כיני מתני' על גבי חולין ברשות כהן הא קמייתא אפי' שלא ברשות כהן: מדליקין בבית המשתה. של ישראל דהכהנים אוכלין במשתה: אבל לא בבית אבל. ואמרינן בירושלמי (שם) מה טעם דר' יהודה בבית המשתה על ידי דמניהון נקיים לא מתעסקין ביה כלומר לא חיישינן שמא יהא ממשמשי הסעודה ויוליך הנר להדליק לעצמו בלא כהן דירא הוא בשמן הטמא שלא יטמאו כליו טהורין בבית האבל על ידי דמניהון צואין מתעסקין ביה מה טעם דרבי יוסי בית האבל על ידי דאינון כניעין לא מתעסקין ביה בית המשתה על ידי דאינון פחוזין מתעסקין ביה ור"מ בבית האבל סבר כרבי יהודה בבית המשתה כר' יוסי ר"ש בבית המשתה כרבי יהודה בבית האבל כר' יוסי ופוסק שמואל בירושלמי הלכה כר"ש ירושלמי תני בת ישראל שנכנסה להדליק מכהנת סובלת פתילה בשמן שרפה ומדלקת:

סליקא לה מסכת תרומות

ואח"כ ימררו הפרה וכל מה שירויחו על מה שהסכימו ביניהן שיחלקו אותו בשוה כמו שהוא מותר לעשותו מן הדין ועוד יתבאר בב"מ כילד הוא מותר כילד הוא אסור מלד הרבית וזהו ענין שם כי שומא בלשון חכמים כמו שיעור ואלו השנים הישראלי והכהן מעריכין דמי זאת הבהמה ויודעין כמה היא שוה עכשיו ומפטמין אותה ויודעין כמה מוסיפה דמים ולפי שזה הישראלי קנאה מכהן אע"פ שנשאר לכהן חלקו ברווח לא תאכל בתרומה לפי שאינה קנין כספו ואם הכהן קנאה מישראל על הדרך שזכרנו הרי זו אוכלת בתרומה: י שמן שרפה. הוא שמן תרומה שנטמא לפי שהוא אסור באכילה כמו שבארנו פעמי' ודינו שישרף: ואמרו ברשות כהן ענינו במאמרו ומלותו שירשה לנו זה: ורבי יהודה מתיר. להדליקו בבית המשתה לפי שכליהם נקיים ר"ל הכלים שהם אוכלים בהם ושותים בבית המשתה אין משתמשין בו בכליהם ואין אוכלין אותו ואסור להדליקו בבית האבל לפי שכליהם מלוכלכין ואינם נקיים ושמא ישתמשו בו בדבר אחר מלבד הדלקה: ורבי יוסי אומר בבית האבל. אין משתמשין בו במאכל ודומה לו מפני כי באבילותם אינם מתעסקין במאכל ולא בזולתו ובבית המשתה מפני שמחתם שמא ישתמשו בו בדבר אחר לבד ההדלקה: ור"מ אוסר. בבית המשתה מפני השמחה כדברי ר' יוסי ואוסר בבית האבל מפני טנוף הכלים כדברי רבי יהודה: ור"ש מתיר. בבית המשתה מפני נקיות הכלים שלהם ובבית האבל מפני אבלותם ודאגת נפשם שאין מתעסקין בשום דבר ואינן קרבים לשום עסק ומה שחולקים כולם בבית האבל ובבית המשתה לרוב משמוש ועסק בני אדם בחבורות הנכנסות לשם ושמא יבואו לידי פשיעה והלכה כרבי שמעון: סליקא לה מסכת תרומות

פי' מהר"י בן מלכי צדק

דמכל מקום גופה דישראל היא ולא קני לכהן גופה הלכך דומה כאילו השכירה כהן פועל עברי דאף על גב דמזונותי' עליו אינו מאכילו תרומה. ת"ר א"ר שמעון ויליד ביתו הם יאכלו הן אוכלין ואין הבהמה אוכלת יכול לא תאכל בכרשינין ת"ל וכהן כי יקנה נפש וגו' תאכל בפ' אלמנה לכהן גדול לא יאכילה בכרשיני תרומה דנהי דחייב באנטסיה בכחושה וביתורות דמרה לא מחייב הלכך לא יאכיל' ישראל ששם מכהן פרה פירוש כגון ששם לו פרה בב' זהובים קרנה ואמר לו כל מה שאפטמה אקח אני החלק והריוח נחלוק אי נמי נחלוק הריוח והקרן ואם תמות או תכחיש עלי חצי ההפסד ומישתכח דגוף דפרה דכהן הלכך מאכילה דדמיא לעבד כנעני דכהן דקני גופיה לכהן ואכיל בתרום' ומשנתנו עד שלא גזרו על הכרשינין להיות אוכל אדם. אבל משגזרו עליהן אפילו הכהן לפרתו לא יאכילם שאין מאכילין אוכלי תרומה המיוחדין לאדם לבהמה וכו': י מדליקין שמן שרפה. פי' שמן תרומה שנטמא בבתי כנסיות א"ר שמעון בר בא בשם רבי יוחנן כיני מתני' על גבי חולין ברשות כהן הא קדמיתא כגון בבתי כנסיות וכו' אפילו שלא ברשות כהן: בת ישראל שנשאת לכהן והיא למודה לבוא בבית אביה אביה מדליק בשמן שרפה ברשותה: מדליקין בשמן שרפה בבית המשתה. פי' כהנים שהולכין לאכול במשתה ישראל מדליקין שם מאי טעמא על ידי שכליהן נקיים לא מתעסקין ביה ישראל אחר שהולכין הכהנים בבתיהן למישקל מיניה. אבל כשהולכין בבית האבל על ידי שכליהן צואין מתעסקי ביה דברי רבי יהודה. רבי יוסי אומר בבית האבל מותר דעל ידי דאינון כניעין ותבירי ליבא לא מתעסקי ביה בבית המשתה על ידי דאינון פחיזין ושמחין מתעסקי ביה רבי מאיר אסר כן וכן פי' בבית המשתה כרבי יוסי ובבית האבל כרבי יהודה ורבי שמעון מתיר כן וכן בבית המשתה כרבי יהודה בבית האבל כרבי יוסי. תניא בת ישראל שנכנסה להדליק מכהנת טובלת פתילתה בשמן שרפה מדלקת בקרן של כהן שהיה מאכיל אותו אצל ישראל וכן בגד כהן שהיה נארג אצל ישראל מדליקין עליו שמן שרפה עמד והלך אעפ"כ אין מחייבין אותו לכבותו עד שיכבה מאליו. אמר רבי אבהו שנה לי יונתן בן עכמיי בת כהן שהיתה עומדת בערב שבת עם חשיכה ובידה נר עם שמן שרפה מערבת לתוכו שמן חולין ומדליק:

סליקא לה מסכת תרומות

בענין מחלוקת הפוסקים גבי חד בתרי בטל הנוגע לכמה משניות בסדר זרעים המדברים מעניני ביטול מאת הגאון המפורסם בעל עטרת ראש וז"ל:

[זה לשון התוספתא פרק ד' דתרומות ליטרא קציעות שדרסה על פי חביות ואין ידוע באיזה חביות דרסה דרסה עפ"י כוורת ואין ידוע באיזו כוורת דרסה דרסה בעיגול דבילה ואין ידוע באיזה עיגול דרסה ר"א אומר רואין את העליונות כאילו פרודות אם יש שם מאה וא' ליטרות תעלה ואם לאו לא תעלה ר"י אומר אם יש מאה פומין יעלה ואם לאו הפומין אסורין והשולים מותרים דברי רבי מאיר רבי יהודה אומר רבי אליעזר אומר אם יש שם ק' פומין תעלה ואם לאו הפומין אסורין והשולים רבי יהושע אומר אע"פ שיש שם שלש מאות פומין לא תעלה] וכתב ע"ז הגאון וז"ל:

דהנה לכאורה דברי רבי יהושע דברי תימה הן. א' למה תפס ר' יהושע מנין שלש מאות פומין. ולא אמר שני מאות או אלף פומין. ב' ק"ל לרב פפא (ביצה ג:) ובזבחים (עב: ועג.) לומר אפי' בדרבנן לא בטיל שהם דברים אך למותר. דהא תנא דתערובות חטאות ודבילה איירי בדאורייי' והוי ליה למימר סתם דאמר כל שדרכו לימנות לא בטיל. לכן נ"ל דר' יהושע אתי לאשמעינן בזה המכין דבר גדול. דהנה כ' הרא"ש בס"פ ג"ה דהא דקי"ל דחד בתרי בטיל בכל דבר שאינו חשוב ואינו דבר שבמנין. היינו דאפי' איסורא דרבנן ליכא ומותר אפי' לכתחלה לאוכלן כולן בין ביחד בין בזא"ז. ואע"פ שאוכל בוודאי לכתחלה גם את האיסור. דאין צריך להשליך א' מהן והיינו דגזירת הכתוב הוא להתיר גם את האיסור דכתיב אחרי רבים להטות ולהכי חד בתרי בטיל ונהפך האיסור עצמו להיות מותר לכתחלה היתר גמור כיון דלא ידעינן הי מנייהו ואפילו איסורא דרבנן ליכא. וזהו דעת התוספות והרשב"א והר"ן והטור בסי' ק"ט. והן מפרשין פירכת הש"ס וניבטלו ברובא. פי' חד בתרי. אך דעת רש"י והרמב"ם הוא דרק מדאורייתא הדין הוא כך דחד בתרי בטל ונעשה גם האיסור היתר גמור אבל חכמים החמירו להצריך ס' בשאר איסורים וק"א בתרומה שכ"כ רש"י בנדה דף מ"ז ז"ל דימוע תרומה. מדאורייתא חד בתרי בטיל בכל איסורין. רק מדרבנן החמירו עד ק"א עכ"ל וכ"כ הרמב"ם בפי"ג מהלכות מ"א ז"ל כל אלו הדברים דקי"ל דאפילו באלף לא בטיל. ברור הוא שאינן אסורין אלא מדרבנן דמדאורייתא חד בתרי בטיל עכ"ל וכתב הב"י בסי' ק"ט בשם הראב"ד ורש"י והרמב"ם שהם מפרשין דמאי דמקשין הש"ס וניבטלו ברובא פי' ברבים דהיינו בס' או בק"א. ונמצא שלדעתם כשנתערב תרומה בחולין עכ"פ נעשו מדאורייתא כל הג' היתר גמור ונהפך האיסור להיות היתר גמור וכל הג' אינן אסורין אלא מדרבנן שהא' של תרומה נעשה שוה להב' של חולין להיות היתר גמור: ועוד אומר אני שרבי יהושע אזיל בזה לשיטתו דס"ל בפ"ד דתרומות משנה ז' דתרומה עולה במאה ועוד. וזה ועוד אין לו שיעור. ופי' הרמב"ם שאם חלק א' של תרומה כפל בנ"ם חלקים ומשהו חולין שיהיה בין הכל רק ק' ומשהו ה"ז יעלה. והנה כמו שמה שאומר כאן ר"א שאם יש שם ק' פומין יעלה כוונתו בוודאי חוץ מאותו פוס של תרומה. שהרי ר"א ס"ל בפירוש שם בתרומות דאינו עולה עד ק"א כך ר' יהושע במה שאומר אם יש שם ש' פומין ג"כ כוונתו בוודאי חוץ מאותו פוס של תרומה דהיינו בין הכל ש"א פומין. ונמצא דלפי כל דברינו הנ"ל אותו הפוס של תרומה מדאורייתא נתבטל רק ע"י שני פומין שבלדו ואינן צריכין ליתר הרצ"ח פומין שאף בלעדם נעשין אותן הפומין הג' מדאורייתא היתר גמור. אך שחכמים החמירו שיהיו כל הג' אסורין מדרבנן. ונמצא כשנעשו כל אותן הג' פומין אסורין מדרבנן נשארו עוד רצ"ח פומין שאותן הג' פומין מעורבין בהם. והנה רצ"ז מהן הן נעשין צ"ם חלקים נגד חלק א' שהם הג' פומין שנעשו רק איסור דרבנן שג' פעמים צ"ם הן רצ"ז ונשאר עוד פוס א' מן הרצ"ח פומין שהן בין הכל ק' חלקים עם החלק א' של הג' פומין שנאסרו רק איסור דרבנן ועוד פוס א' יותר על ק' חלקים. דהא הכא א"א להיות היתרון על ק' רק משהו. דא"כ (האי) אפשר שיתערב אותו המשהו בין הפומין. ולכן ההכרח הוא שיהיה אותו היתרון פוס שלם. ולכן אי לאו הא דס"ל לר' יהושע דאפילו בדרבנן לא בטיל הוי ס"ד דעכ"פ בדרבנן בטיל ועולה התרומה דרבנן בק' ועוד דהיינו הג' פומין שנעשו רק דמוע דרבנן שיעלו ברצ"ח פומין הנשארים ואין לומר דלא שייך בתערובת אחת שני ביטולים. כי אם כשנתערב המיעוט מתערובת ראשון באחרים זהו אינו דהא דמפלגינן בין תערובת ראשון לשני היינו כשההיתר הוא מכח ספיק ספיקא דהוו תערובות ראשון ספק א' ותערובות שני ס"ס. וכמו שכתבו התוס' בד"ה ואחרות באחרות וכו' עי"ש. אבל הכא שההיתר הוא מחמת ביטול בריבוי א"כ כשנתבטל מן התורה רק בשנים שבלדו שמהם לבד בוודאי נעשה רק איסור דרבנן שאינן מתבטלין עד ק' בתרומה. שאם היה הדין לדבר שבמנין מתבטל באיסור דרבנן א"כ למה לא יהיה ס"ד לומר דאלו השלשה פומין שנעשו רק איסור דרבנן שיתבטלו ברצ"ח פומין הנותרים דהיינו בק' ועוד. ואדרבה יכול להיות דבזה הוא יותר סברא לומר להתיר כשהשני ביטולים באים כאחת. מלהתיר ע"י שני ביטולים שבאים זא"ז. שהוא דומה קצת למה שפסקו כמה פוסקים לענין ביטול ס' דכשאין בתערובת ראשונה תיכף ס' בבת אחת אמרינן חנ"נ ואין מועיל אח"כ ס' נגד האיסור כי אם נגד הכל. ולכן אתי ר' יהושע להשמיענו דאפילו בדרבנן לא בטיל כיון שהוא דבר שדרכו לימנות עכ"פ לפעמים ולכן אפי' יש שם ש' פומין או יותר הרבה אפילו אלף ורבוא אפ"ה אינו עולה. והא דקי"ל דדבר שבמנין אפי' באלף לא בטיל היינו באמר רק לפי המסקנא דקיימא לן כרבי יהושע דמוקמינן כל הני מתניתא כוותיה דלהכי תנינן דאפילו באלף לא בטיל: ונמצא דאדרבה מדאמר רבי יהושע שיעור של ש' פומין כדי להשמיענו דאפילו בדרבנן לא בטיל. מוכח דבלא"ה תרומת אילנות הם דאורייתא ולכן לא די שנסתלקה הסתירה מעל דעת הרמב"ם אלא אפילו יש כאן ראיה גדולה לדעת הרמב"ם ודו"ק:

LITE, HE MAY FEED IT ON VETCHES OF TERUMAH.[15]

MISHNAH 10. ONE MAY KINDLE OIL THAT HAS TO BE
a BURNT[1] IN SYNAGOGUES, HOUSES OF STUDY, DARK ALLEYS, AND FOR SICK PEOPLE WHEN A PRIEST IS NEAR.[2] IF THE DAUGHTER OF AN ISRAELITE MARRIED TO A PRIEST REGULARLY GOES TO HER FATHER'S HOUSE, HER FATHER MAY KINDLE [SUCH OIL] IN HER PRESENCE. IT MAY ALSO BE KINDLED AT A BANQUETING HOUSE[3] BUT NOT IN A HOUSE OF MOURNING;[4] SO R. JUDAH. R. JOSE SAYS: [IT MAY BE KINDLED] IN THE HOUSE OF MOURNING, BUT NOT IN THE BANQUETING HOUSE.[5] R. MEIR FORBIDS IT IN BOTH PLACES[6] BUT R. SIMEON PERMITS IT IN EITHER CASE.[7]

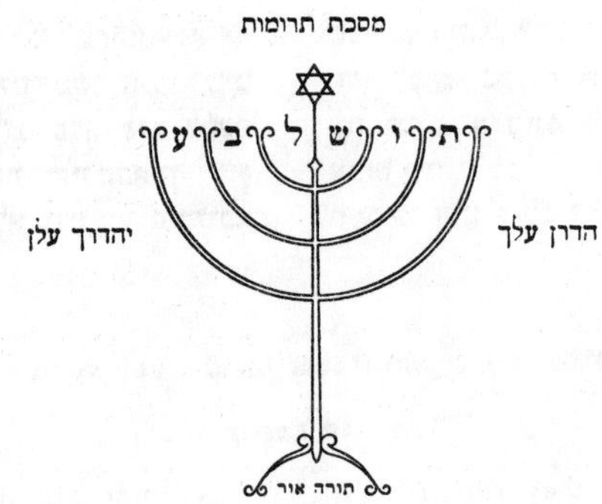

(15) Since it becomes his own possession.

a (1) Oil of *terumah* which becomes unclean must be burnt. (2) Since a priest himself may enter these places and derive benefit from the kindled oil. Only in the case of the sick should the priest be near; he is sure to enter the other places sooner or later (T.J.). (3) Since a priest may enter there; nor need one fear lest the guests will carry the lamp into a chamber where the priest is not present, for they will not risk soiling the festive garments in which they are attired. (4) In the house of mourning, where no festive garments are worn, the fear referred to in the preceding note is entertained. (5) On the contrary, argues R. Jose. In a house of mourning, all sit quietly and will not think of removing the lamp to a room where the priest is not there, but the merriment of the banqueting chamber may prompt them to do so, regardless of soiling their clothes. (6) Applying the arguments of both R. Judah and R. Jose, and adopting the stringent ruling of each. (7) Adopting the lenient ruling of both and having no fear that the lamp will be shifted to a place in which no priest is present.

חידושי הגאון מוה"ר ר' משה פיינשטיין ז"ל

תרומות

פ"ג מ"ב. נפלו שתיהן למקום אחד מדמעות כקטנה שבשתיהן פשוט לכאורה שנוטל רק כשיעור קטנה שבשתיהן ונותן לכהן דרק שיעור זה הוא, המדמע ותיקנו בשביל גזל השבט שירים משם ליתן לכהן כדנתן ברפ"ב מערלה והובא בר"ש מהירושלמי א"ר אבוה בש"ר יוחנן מפני גזל השבט, שלכן כיון שבעד הגדולה צריך הכהן לשלם כדאיתא בירושלמי ומה שצריך ליתנה לכהן הוא משום ספק איסור אכילת תרומה לזר, לכן כשנפלו למאה כשיעור הקטנה שמצד איסור אכילה נבטלו והיו מותרין לזר דלא עדיף מערלה וכלאי הכרם דכשנבטלו א"צ להרים. וההרמה הוא בשביל גזל השבט אין להצריך אלא כשיעור הקטנה וכן מפורש בשנות אליהו דמה שאמר בירושלמי כיצד הוא עושה נותן שתיהן לכהן ארישא קאי, היינו בלא נדמעו. וא"כ תמוה מש"כ הרע"ב נוטל מן החולין כשיעור שתי התרומות שנפלו בהן ונותנן לכהן וכן כתב בתפא"י שלא רק שא"צ להרים כשיעור שתיהן אלא אף כשיעור הגדולה אין צריך להרים. שוב אחר זמן נזדמן לידי משניות החדשים וראיתי שהקשה בתא"ש ורוצה לתרץ ממש"כ בתוי"ט פ"ה מ"ב בטעם שצריך להרים גם סאה תרומה טמאה שנפלאה לתוך מאה חולין טהורין לר"א שתשרף משום לא פלוג, ואינו כלום דהכא לא שייך לא פלוג משום דליכא כלל תרומה יותר מאחת שלכן לא שייך בשביל לא פלוג להצריך להרים הגדולה. ומש"כ ברא"ש שגם הר"מ בפיה"מ כתב כפירוש הרע"ב, ליכא דבר זה בפירוש הרמב"ם כלל דלא הזכיר כלל ענין ההרמה כשנדמעו וצע"ג דברי הרע"ב.

פ"ד מ"ב. וחכ"א אינו מפריש אלא לפי חשבון. פי' הר"ש בפירוש ראשון דאינו יכול הפועל לאכול אלא אותה סעודה שהיה לו לאכול אצלו והשאר מתנה בעלמא דיהיב ללוי ולעני. לכאורה תמוה וכי חשדינן לע"ה שלהכעיס לא יפריש מעשר הא רק שחשדינן שמצד תאותו לממון לא יפריש כדי שיהיה גם המעשר שלו וא"כ הכא שנתן ללוי ולעני מ"ט נחשוד שנתן למתנה בעלמא דודאי יש לנו לומר דהיה זה למעשר ולא יעבור באיסור טבל ובפרט שעל מקצת כשיעור הסעודה אמרינן שהיה לכוונת מעשר איך נימא שבדעתו היה לחלק נתינתו דעל מה שצריך הפועל לאכול הוא למעשר והשאר יהיה למתנה בעלמא דוקא, וליכא למימר דהחשש הוא דלמא היה חייב להם מה שנתן, דא"כ גם אותה סעודה תהא אסורה ואיזה חלוק אפשר לומר בין אותה סעודה לכל הח' סאין וצע"ג. ואחר זמן ראיתי בתא"ש שגם זה הקשה ותירוצו אינו כולם דא"כ גם הסעודה מ"ט מותר.

Novellae of Hagaon Rabbi Moshe Feinstein o.b.m.

Tractate Terumoth

3:2 — **But if both fall into one place, they do make it medumma, according to the size of the smaller of the two.** Apparently, he must take only according to the amount of the smaller of the two and give it to the Kohen because it is only that amount that makes the admixture medumma, and the Sages enacted that he separate it to give to the Kohen lest he rob the priestly tribe, as is stated in Orlah 2:1 and quoted by Rash from Yerushalmi: Rabbi Abahu said in the Name of R. Johanan: Because of robbing the tribe. Therefore, since the Kohen must pay for the larger amount, as is stated in Yerushalmi, and he must, nevertheless, give it to the Kohen because of the interdict of a non-Kohen to eat terumah. Therefore, when they fall into one hundred times as much as the smaller amount, which would neutralize the prohibited substance, it should be permitted to a non-Kohen, since it is no more stringent than orlah or mixed seeds in the vineyard, which, when neutralized, do not require separation, since the separation is required only to avoid robbing the tribe. Consequently, it should be necessary only to separate the amount of the smaller amount. This interpretation is stated explicitly in Shenoth Eliyahu. He construes the statement in Yerushalmi as referring to the previous mishnah, which deals with a case in which the two terumoth were not mingled with hulin. In that case, Yerushalmi states: What does he do? He gives them both to the Kohen. Accordingly, the interpretation given by R. Obadiah of Bertinoro, that he must take from the hulin the amount of the two terumoth that fell into it, and give them to the Kohen is puzzling. Indeed, Tifereth Israel states that, not only does he not have to separate the amount of both of them, but he need not even separate the larger amount. Some time later, I came across the new edition of the Mishnayoth with Tosefoth Anshei Shem, who attempts to reconcile the difficulty in accordance with Tosefoth Yom Tov to 5:2, who accounts for the ruling by R. Eliezer that a se'ah of unclean terumah that fell into one hundred se'ahs of clean hulin must be separated and burnt because the Sages did not differentiate in their enactment. He applies that same reasoning to our case, but this does not make sense, because in our case there is no more terumah than one of the two. It is, therefore, impossible to rule that, because the Rabbis did not differentiate the larger amount be given to the Kohen. Although Rosh writes that Rav's interpretation is also found in Rambam's commentary, it is, in fact, not found there. In fact, Rambam does not mention the entire matter of separating produce from the admixture. Consequently, much diligent study is necessary to understand Rav's interpretation of the mishnah.

4:2 — **But the sages say: He may only set aside according to proportion.** The first explanation of Rash is that the householder separates only in proportion to the meal he gives his worker. Therefore, the worker may eat only this meal, and we assume that the rest of the se'ah that he gave the Levite and the poor man was given merely as a gift. This is apparently puzzling, for why should we suspect the am ha'aretz of failing to separate tithes in order to provoke? We suspect him of being lax in his separation of tithes because of his greed for money, which tempts him to refrain from separating the tithes in order to keep them. Consequently, in our case, in which he gives produce to the Levite and the poor man, why should we suspect him of giving it merely as a gift? We should surely assume that he gave it for the tithes in order that he should not transgress the interdict of eating tevel, especially since we do assume that for a part in proportion to the meal he does separate tithes. How can we suspect that he divides his gift, making part of it tithes for the meal he gives his worker, and part of it a mere gift? We cannot say that perhaps he owes them what he gave them, because, if so, even that meal should be prohibited, what difference is there between that meal and the entire eight se'ahs? This requires much deliberation. Later I saw Tosefoth Anshei Shem, who poses this difficulty, but his solution is incorrect, because, according to him, even this meal should be prohibited.

חידושי הגאון מוה״ר ר׳ משה פיינשטיין ז״ל

תרומות

פ״ה מ״א או יתחלקו לעיסות. הקשה הרע״ב מ״ש מסאה תרומה טמאה שנפלה בחולין טהורים דירקבו, תמוה דלכאורה אין כאן ריח קושיא דהא התם כבר היתה התרומה טמאה ואף אם יאכל פחות מכביצה או נקודים הא יאכל תרומה טמאה שאסור ובסיפא הא לא נטמאה התרומה שלא היה הכשר וכשיתחלקו לעיסות שאז יוכשרו באופן שלא יהיה במקום אחד כביצה לא יקבלו טומאה, וכן כשיאכלו נקודים או קליות או ילושו במי פירות לא יקבלו טומאה משום שלא הוכשרו וצ״ע. ופלא שלא עמד בזה התוי״ט והתפא״י פי׳ בטוב כדכתבתי. ובר״ש משמע כהרע״ב, וצ״ע.

פ״ו מ״ה ולא ממע״ר שניטלה תרומתו. פי׳ הר״ש דכיון שקודם שניטלה תרומתו לא חזי תו לא חזי וכן פי׳ הרע״ב. טעם זה לא מובן כלל. ולכאורה הוא פשוט דר״מ לטעמיה דמע״ר אוסר לזרים ולכן הוא הקדש ואין פודה את ההקדש, וצע״ג מ״ט לא פירשו המפרשים שלכאורה הוא פירוש נכון, ולאחר זמן שנזדמן לידי משניות החדשים מצאתי שפי׳ כן במשנה ראשונה. ואולי טעמו מדנקט בהדי מע״ש והקדש שנפדו שעתה אין בהן שום קדושה ומוכרחין לומר דהוא מאחר דקודם שנפדו לא היה יכול לפטור בהם גם עתה שנפדו אינו יכול ליפטר בהם לכן משמע שגם מע״ר דנקט בהדייהו הוא מטעם זה, ומה שאסור מע״ר לזרים שלא היה בשביל זה חשיבות קדש לענין תשלומי אכילת זר תרומה מאחר דאין חייבין על מע״ר מיתה וחומש כדאיתא ביבמות דף פ״ו, שלכן אין להחשיבו בשם קדש לומר שאין הקדש פודה אחר הקדש, וגם לא מצינו שר״מ יאסור מע״ר לטמאים דלא מצינו שפליג ר״מ על מה שדרשינן בספרי ס״פ קרח בכל מקום אפילו בקבר, אף שלענין ערלות איתא ביבמות דף ע״ד שאסור לר״מ דחמור לענין מעשר ערל מטמא.

Novellae of Hagaon Rabbi Moshe Feinstein o.b.m.

Tractate Terumoth

5:1 — **or divided into pieces of dough.** R. Obadiah of Bertinoro questions the difference between this and the previous case of a se'ah of unclean terumah that fell into clean hulin, concerning which the Mishnah rules that it must all be left to rot. This question is indeed bewildering because there is apparently no difficulty, whatever, because in that case, the terumah was already unclean, and even if he eats a piece smaller than an egg's bulk or if he eats minute loaves (or dry grain), he will nevertheless eat unclean terumah, which is forbidden. In the final segment of the Mishnah, however, the terumah was not contaminated because it was not prepared to contract ritual uncleanness, since there was not an egg's bulk in one place, which is the minimum amount that can contract uncleanness. Likewise, if it is eaten dry or as parched ears or if it is kneaded with fruit juice, it does not contract uncleanness because it was not prepared for it by contact with liquid. This requires much deliberation. Surprisingly, Tosefoth Yom Tov does not call attention to this difficulty. Tifereth Israel, however, explains the Mishnah correctly, as I have written. R. Samson of Senz apparently explains the Mishnah like R. Obadiah. This requires deliberation.

6:5 — **nor from first tithe from which terumah has been taken.** R. Samson explains that, since it was unfit before its terumah was separated, it remains unfit. R. Obadiah, too, explains in this manner. This reason is apparently incomprehensible. The simple reason is that R. Meir follows his view that first tithe is prohibited for non-Levites. Therefore, the reason that dedicated produce cannot redeem dedicated produce applies to first tithe as well. It is indeed puzzling why none of the commentators explained the Mishnah in this manner. Later, when the new edition of the Mishnayoth came to my hand, I noticed this interpretation in the Mishnah Rishonah. Perhaps his (R. Samson's) reason is that since first tithe is mentioned together with second tithe and dedicated produce that were redeemed, which have no sanctity at present, and we must perforce say that, since prior to their redemption they were unfit to be used to pay for the terumah he ate, they are unfit for that purpose even after they have been redeemed, the same reasoning applies to first tithe from which the terumah was not yet separated. The reason that first tithe is forbidden for non-Levites is insufficient reason to disqualify it for payment of terumah because that does not give the tithe the stringency of dedicated produce as regards the payment of terumah eaten by a non-Kohen, since there is no payment of the principal and a fifth for eating first tithe, as in Yevamoth 86. Therefore, it cannot be considered like dedicated produce in the context of dedicated produce being unfit to redeem dedicated produce. Moreover, we do not find that R. Meir prohibits first tithe to unclean persons, because we do not find that he differs with the drash of Sifre at the end of Korah: any place, even in a grave, although concerning an uncircumcised male, we find in Yevamoth 74, that it is forbidden according to R. Meir, because one uncircumcised is more stringent than one who is ritually unclean, in the context of first tithe.

תלמוד בבלי

מסכת

מעשרות

תלמוד בבלי

מסכת

מעשרות

עם פירוש רש״י ותוספות
ובצירוף תרגום ופירוש והערות באנגלית

על ידי
פינחס כהן ז״ל

בעריכת
יחזקאל (איזידור) אפשטין ז״ל

דפוס שונצין
שנת להחזיר העטרה ליושנה לפ״ק
לונדון

HEBREW-ENGLISH EDITION OF
THE BABYLONIAN TALMUD

MA'ASEROTH

TRANSLATED INTO ENGLISH
WITH NOTES, GLOSSARY AND INDICES BY

REV. PHILLIP COHEN, B.A.

UNDER THE EDITORSHIP OF

RABBI DR. I. EPSTEIN, B.A., PH.D. LITT.D.

LONDON
THE SONCINO PRESS
1989

COPYRIGHT © THE SONCINO LTD. 1989
ALL RIGHTS RESERVED INCLUDING THE RIGHT TO
REPRODUCE THIS BOOK OR PARTS THEREOF IN ANY FORM

1-871055059

PUBLISHERS' NOTE

This HEBREW-ENGLISH EDITION of THE SONCINO TALMUD is being published to facilitate the easier reference to the original text by scholars and students.

The Publishers wish to express their sincere thanks to Rabbi Dr. A. Melinek, B.A., Ph.D., for his painstaking care in examining the texts and making the necessary corrections for the preparation of these Tractates.

It has been necessary to duplicate some of the original Hebrew-Aramaic pages in this Tractate where the text has been of such length as to require more than one page of English translation.

MANUFACTURED IN THE UNITED STATES OF AMERICA

INTRODUCTION

The Tractate Ma'aseroth ('Tithes') deals in the main with the annual tithes of agricultural produce due to the Levites (Num. XVIII, 21) commonly described as *Ma'aser Rishon* (first tithe) or, less often, as *Ma'aser Levi* (the Levite's tithe). It is necessary to define this tithe thus to distinguish it from *Ma'aser Sheni* (second tithe) taken to Jerusalem,[1] there to be consumed by the landowner and his family (Deut. XIV, 22—29); and the *Ma'aser 'Ani* (Poor Man's tithe) given every third and sixth years of the Sabbatical cycle to the poor (Deut. XIV, 28; XXVI, 12).

The Tractate is divided up into five chapters as follows:

CHAPTER I. Tithable produce was determined by the Rabbis in accordance with the following rules: it must be eatable, it must be the property of an individual, and it must be the product of the soil; fruit must be ripe enough to be eaten. There then follows a description of the respective stages at which the various fruits and vegetables are regarded as edibles, and therefore become liable to tithe.

CHAPTER II. Examples are here given of the different circumstances under which a *ḥaber* (v. Glos.) may make a meal of the produce of an *'am ha-areẓ* (v. Glos.) without fear of having transgressed the laws governing tithe. The laws governing the conditions of employment of a labourer in the gathering of produce, whereby he, the labourer, may eat of the fruit, are here mentioned.

CHAPTER III. Here, too, are designated places in which the produce renders the people who possess it liable to tithe or otherwise, and under what conditions this is the case; for example, the man in his own courtyard, produce on roofs, doorways and huts; (v. also I, 5 end).

CHAPTER IV. The stages at which produce becomes liable to tithe, when pickled, stewed or salted.

CHAPTER V. Describes the operation of the law of tithe, when the farmer transplants vegetables from one part of his domain to another, and lays down the rule, to whom and under what conditions produce may be sold once the tithing season had arrived, and also the law regarding tithe in the case of fields bought in Syria.

P. COHEN

(1) V. Ma'as. Sh.

MA'ASEROTH

CHAPTER I

MISHNAH 1. THEY HAVE LAID DOWN A GENERAL RULE
a CONCERNING TITHES:[1] WHATEVER IS [CONSIDERED] FOOD[2] AND IS GUARDED[3] AND GROWS OUT OF THE SOIL,[4] IS LIABLE TO TITHES.[5] AND THEY HAVE FURTHER LAID DOWN ANOTHER RULE [AS REGARDS TITHE]: WHATSOEVER IS CONSIDERED FOOD BOTH AT THE BEGINNING AND AT THE CONCLUSION [OF ITS GROWTH],[6] EVEN THOUGH HE WITHHOLDS IT FROM USE SO AS TO ENABLE THE QUANTITY OF FOOD TO INCREASE, IS LIABLE [TO TITHE], WHETHER [IT BE GATHERED] IN ITS EARLIER OR LATER STAGES [OF RIPENING],[7] WHEREAS WHATSOEVER IS NOT CONSIDERED FOOD IN THE EARLIER STAGES [OF ITS GROWTH] BUT ONLY IN ITS LATER STAGES,[8] IS NOT LIABLE [TO TITHE] UNTIL IT CAN BE CONSIDERED FOOD.[9]

MISHNAH 2. WHEN DO THE FRUITS BECOME LIABLE TO
b TITHE?[1] FIGS FROM THE TIME THEY ARE CALLED BOHAL,[2] GRAPES AND WILD GRAPES IN THE EARLY STAGES OF RIPENING,[3] RED BERRIES AND MULBERRIES AFTER THEY BECOME RED; [SIMILARLY] ALL RED FRUITS, AFTER THEY BECOME RED. POMEGRANATES ARE LIABLE TO TITHE AFTER THEIR CORE BECOMES PULPY,[4] DATES AFTER THEY BEGIN TO SWELL,[5] PEACHES AFTER THEY ACQUIRE [RED] VEINS,[6] WALNUTS FROM THE TIME THEY FORM DRUPES.[7] R. JUDAH SAYS: WALNUTS AND ALMONDS, AFTER THEIR KERNEL SKINS HAVE BEEN FORMED.[8]

MISHNAH 3. CAROBS [ARE SUBJECT TO] TITHES AFTER THEY FORM DARK SPOTS.[9] SIMILARLY ALL BLACK-FINISHED FRUITS[10] AFTER THEY FORM DARK SPOTS; PEARS AND CRUSTUMENIAN PEARS,[11] QUINCES,[12] AND MEDLARS[13] [ARE LIABLE TO TITHES] AFTER THEIR SURFACE BEGINS TO GROW SMOOTH.[14]
c SIMILARLY ALL WHITE FRUITS,[1] AFTER THEIR SURFACE BEGINS TO GROW SMOOTH; FENUGREEK [IS LIABLE TO TITHE, WHEN IT IS SO FAR ADVANCED] THAT THE SEEDS [CAN BE PLANTED AND] WILL GROW,[2] GRAIN AND OLIVES AFTER THEY ARE ONE-THIRD RIPE.[3]

a (1) V. Introduction. The ruling here also applies to *terumah*. (2) This excludes e.g., madder, although in times of dire necessity both are used as food. (3) In contradistinction to ownerless property, looked after by no private owner. (4) This excludes such things as mushrooms and truffles, which are not deemed to be things growing from the soil, since they are not sown. In all these cases the ruling is deduced from Deut. XIV, 22, *Thou shalt surely tithe all the produce of thy seed*, identifying *'produce'* with food; 'thy *seed*', with privately owned produce, and *'seed'* with earth-sown produce. (5) The whole of this paragraph refers to what are technically known as 'regular' meals in contradistinction to 'chance' meals, to which this ruling does not apply. (6) As for example, all herbs which become fit for consumption as soon as they begin to ripen. The owner nevertheless withholds them from being gathered until they are fully ripe, so as to enable him to accumulate the maximum quantity of produce. (7) Since they are considered as food, fit to be eaten, from the very beginning of their ripening. Lit., 'whether small or large'. (8) As for example, certain kinds of fruit which grow on trees. (9) Derived from Lev. XXVII, 30. *From the seed of the earth, from the fruit of the tree*, which is interpreted to mean that it is not to be considered food until it grows up and becomes fruit proper.

b (1) Fruit, that is to say, which in the early stages of its growth is not considered a food, and which is also eaten at regular times. (2) The commencement of the ripening is known as בוחל. Rashi: From the time their tips become white. (3) They have reached that stage of ripeness when the berries appear from inside the husks. In the case of a cluster, if one berry has reached this measure of ripeness, the whole of the cluster is liable to tithe. (4) When the eatable portion, the core, can be mashed under one's fingers. (5) Lit., 'they cast a dough'. When they rise like dough. (6) When there appears in the skin a sort of red vein. (7) Lit., 'they form a store'. When the food is actually separated from the outer shell, and gives the appearance of something laid in a store-house. (8) R. Judah refers to a thin skin nearest to the food, which does not form upon the fruit until after the completion of the ripening. (9) They begin to darken at the completion of their ripening. (10) This refers to all fruits which are black on the completion of their ripening, e.g., the berries of the myrtle and thorn. (11) Small pears resembling nuts. These have hair on them which needs smoothening. (12) V. Kil. I, 4. (13) A sort of crab-apple. (14) After the hair upon them, which covers them in the earlier stages of ripening, falls out. These fruits in their early stages are covered with small hairs, like feathers, and as they ripen they gradually become bald, so that eventually when they are completely ripe, all their hair has fallen out.

c (1) The law does not specifically apply only to those which are actually white, but it also includes those which are neither black nor red. (2) Namely when it has become so complete in its ripeness that if it were seed, it would sprout forth. The method of testing to discover when it has reached this stage is by putting the plant in water. (3) A third part of that which will eventually grow, or alternately, if he were to store them (or in the case of grain to grind them) he would be able to produce from them, at that stage, one third of the amount which will be produced when they are fully ripe.

א כל שהוא אוכל. למעוטי ספיחי סטים וקוצה : ונשמר · למעוטי הפקר : וגדוליו מן הארץ · למעוטי כמהין ופטריות ובירושלמי (הל' א) דריש להו מקראי דכתיב (דברים יד) עשר תעשר את כל תבואת זרעך דומיא דתבואה שהוא אוכל זרעך משמע דבר שנזרע ילאו כמהין ופטריות שאינן נזרעים והפקר מדכתיב (שם) ובא הלוי כי אין לו חלק ונחלה עמך ממה שיש לך ואין לו חייב אתה ליתן לו יצא הפקר שידך וידו שוין בו ולקט ושכחה ופיאה נמי פטורים מטעם זה והתם בירושלמי אמרינן אין לי אלא תבואה קטנית וכל מיני פירות מניין תרבי מכל מעשר הארץ מזרע הארץ מפרי העץ (ויקרא כז) וממעט זרעוני גינה שאינן נאכלין מדכתיב מזרע ולא כל זרע וממעט נמי חרובי שיקמי צלמונה מדכתיב מפרי העץ ולא כל פרי העץ ירקות מנייןאיסי בן *עקביא אומר המעשרות לירקות מדבריהן ולא בעי למימר שיהיו כל האחרים מן התורה דמדאורייתא לא מחייבי אלא דגן תירוש ויצהר (מדבריהן שאין להן אסמכתא מן הפסוק) דבנדרים (דף כ"ה.) משמע בהדיא דפירות אילן מדרבנן דמוקי וכפרון הדבר וגו' (דה"ב לא) לאילן מדרבנן ומדאורייתא לא מחייבה אלא אדגן תירוש ויצהר אלא מדבריהם שאין להם אסמכתא מקרא ובהדיא אמרי' בפ"ק דראש השנה (דף טו:) מעשר חרובין דרבנן ובפ' כיצד מברכין (דף ל"ו:) צלף מדרבנן ובפרק אלו עוברין (ד' מד.) תבלין דרבנן ובפרק מעשר בהמה (דף נד:) תירוש ודגן דאורייתא ב' מינין בעלמא דרבנן ובפרק העור והרוטב (דף קכ:) משקין דתירוש וזית קדשי בתרומה מידי אחרינא לא וממעט דבש *תפוחים ויין תפוחים ובריש ביצה (דף ג:) תנא דליסרא קליעות הוא דאמר כל דבר שבמנין אפי' בדרבנן לא בטיל והא דמשמע בסוף הערל (דף פא:) דעיגול אינו עולה אי תרומה בזמן הזה דאורייתא אע"ג דתרומת תאנים

מעשרות פרק ראשון

א כלל אמרו במעשרות [א] *כל שהוא אוכל ונשמר וגדוליו מן הארץ חייב במעשרו' ועוד כלל אחר אמרו [ב] כל שתחלתו אוכל וסופו אוכל אף על פי שהוא שומרו להוסיף אוכל חייב קטן וגדול [ג] וכל שאין תחלתו אוכל אבל סופו אוכל אינו חייב עד שיעשה אוכל : **ב** [ד] מאימתי הפירות חייבות במעשרות [ג] התאנים משיבחילו הענבים והאבשים משהבאישו האוג והתותים משיאדימו וכל האדומים משיאדימו הרמונים משימסו התמרים (ג) משיטילו שאור האפרסקים משיטילו גידים האגוזים משיעשו מגורה רבי יהודה אומר האגוזים והשקדים משיעשו קליפה : **ג** [ה] החרובין משינקדו וכל השחורים משינקדו (ד) האגסים והקריסטומלין והפרישין והעוזרדין משיקרחו וכל הלבנים משיקרחו [ג] התלתן משתצמח התבואה והזיתי' (ה) משיכניסו שליש :

א כל שהוא אוכל יצא הכופר והוא בערבי אלחנה והאסום והוא בלשון ערבי ניליג והקוצה הוא בל' ערבי אלעלפר ודומיהן: ונשמר. יצא המופקר: וגדוליו מן הארץ יצאו כמהין ופטריות וכל זה נסמך למה שאמר השם יתברך (דברי' יא) עשר העשר ואח"כ אמ' ואכלת לפני ה' אלהיך מעשר דגנך תירושך ויצהרך למדנו שאין חייב במעשר אלא היוצא מן השדה וראוי לאכילה ונשמר למאמר יתברך זרעך המיוחד לך לא של הפקר לפי שאין לו בעלים : ותחלתו אוכל וסופו אוכל. הם מיני ירקות לפי שהם ראויות לאכילה תכף מלמיחתן ואחר גמר גדולן ואין מניחין אותן בארץ אלא כדי שיגדילו וזה דרך רוב הירקות ולפיכך הם חייבות במעשר בשעת קטנן או גדלן לפי שהם ראויות לאכילה בין גדולות ובין קטנות ומה שאינו ראוי לאכילה בתחלת צמיחתו כמו פירות האילן אין חייבות במעשר עד שיעשו אוכל למה שאמר ה' יתברך מזרע הארץ מפרי העץ עד שיהיה פרי ואמר גם כן עשר העשר את כל תבואת זרעך עד שיעשה תבואה : **ב** כבר ביארנו שפירות האילן אין חייבות במעשר עד שיעשו פרי ולפיכך אמר התאנים משיבחילו פי' משיתחילו להתבשל וזמן זה הבשול הוא שמלקטים את התאנה מן האילן

עין משפט נר מצוה

ה א מיי' פ"ב מהל' מעשר הלכה ה :
ו ב מיי' שם ופ"א הלכה (ט) [יא] :
ו ג מיי' פ"ג מהל' מעשר הלכה א :
ז ד שם הלכ' ט :
ח ה שם הלכ' י :
ט ו שם הל' ג
י ז שם הל' יב :
יא ח שם הל' יג :
יב ט שם הלכה יד :
יג י שם הל' טו :
יד כ מיי' פ"ה שם הלכה טו :

מסורת הש"ס

א) סוכה פ"ג דף לו·
ב) חולין פ"א ד' כה:
ג) ביצה פ"א דף יג :
ב"מ פ"ז דף פח:
ד) ר"ה פ"א דף יב.
חולין פ"א דף ז.
ה) ע"ג פ"ד דף נו .
ב"מ פ"ו דף לב:
ו) שבת פ"ג דף מב:
פסחים פ"ג דף מ:

זרעך דבר שנזרע ומצמיח יצא פחות משלים שאינו נזרע ומצמיח ר' חנינא בשם רבי זיתים וענבים שלא הביאו שליש משקין היוצאין מהן אינן מכשירין : ד קשואין ואבטיחים ודלועים ומלפפונות · מין ירק וחייבין אם תלשן בקוטנן : תפוחים ואתרוגים פירות אילן ואף הן חייבין בקוטנן [ירושל' הל' ג'] · רבי שמעון יודה לרבי עקיבא ג] ור"ע לא יודה לר"ש ובפרק לולב הגזול (לו.) אמר עד כאן לא קאמר רבי עקיבא הכא אלא דבעינן הדר וליכא אבל התם כרבנן סבירא ליה ועד כאן לא קאמר ר' שמעון התם דכתיב עשר תעשר את כל תבואת זרעך כדרך שבני אדם מוציאים לזריעה אבל הכא כרבנן סבירא ליה ואתרוגים קטנים אין הנטועים צומחים אבל בתפוחים לא פליגי דאף על פי שלא בישלו כל צרכן ובקטני קטנים אפילו בתפוחים פליג הואיל וטעמא משום דמוציאין לזריעה הוא וטעמא דתנא קמא כדתני רישא כל שתחלתו אוכל וסופו אוכל : החייב בשקדים המרים תנן התם בגמרא דחולין (כה:) שקדים המרים הקטנים חייבין גדולים פטורין מתוקים גדולים חייבין קטנים פטורים רבי ישמעאל אומר משום אביו זה וזה לפטור ואמרי לה זה וזה לחיוב:
ה איזהו גרנן למעשרות· עד השתא איירינן בגודל בגידולין פירות הבאות לתורת אוכל להתחייב במעשר כשמגיעין לשיעור שאמרנו מכאן ואילך איירי לאחר שנתבשלו כל צרכן וכתלשו אימתי באו לידי דיגון וחיוב משום דכתיב דגנך דיגונך שיתמרח בכרי : משיפקסו. בפרק הפועלים (פח:) אמר רב אשי מסיכסל פקס שלהן שיער הצומח בהן כעין נוצה כשהן קטנים וכשמתגדלים הרבה נושר מאליהם וכשתולשן בינונים עדיין נוצה עליהן והמוכרן בשוק מסיר הנוצה ונקרא פקס ופעמים שנמכרין בפיקוסן משום הכי תני ואם אינו מפקס ובפ"ב דעוקצין (מ"א) קרי ליה כסות של קישות ובפרק הפועלים (פח:) פריך*הכא לר' ינאי דאמר אין הטבל מתחייב במעשר עד שיראה פני הבית ולר' יוחנן דאמר אפילו חצר קובעת והכא משיפקסו מאי לאו אפי' בשדה ומשני לא בבית והשתא כולה מתניתין דפרקין דגורנן למעשר בבית לרבי ינאי ולחצר לרבי יוחנן ואם תאמר כשיפקסו בבית להוי כמכניס התבואה במוץ שלה דפטר רבי אושעיא בפרק קמא דפסחים (דף ט·) ואפילו חזר ומירחן בבית·לא דמי כלל דהתם בעינן שיראו פני הבית בכניסתן וכל זמן שהן במוץ ליכא ראיה אבל הכא דאיירי ג] אף על פי שלא נטל פקס שלהן ד] תדע דהא קתני ואם אינו מפקס משיעמיד ערימה ומיהו קשה היכי מיתוקמא מתני' בבית הא קתני סיפא בד"א במוליך לשוק אבל במוליך לבית אוכל עראי עד שיגיע לביתו אלמא מוליך בשוק מחייב בירק משיאגד בלא ראיית פני הבית (ז) ולמאי דמסיק התם דלא אמרו אלא בזיתים וענבים ניחא : משיעמיד ערימה. כרי : משישלק · שילוק לאבטיח כפיקוס לקישואין וכירו' (הל' ד') קאמר מן די יריס פקסוסיה או די יריס שליקוקי' : מוקצה · שמנדישין אותן למכור בשוק : משיאגד. מפרש בירושלמי (שם) אגדו ליגוק גדול בשדה והיה עתיד לאוגדו ליגוק קטן לשוק נטבל : משילקט כל צרכו . אבל עד שלא ליקט כל צרכו אוכל עראי ופטור : בלבלה ליקט ירק ומכניס בכלכלה : שיחפה מנהגן לכסות יש נוהגין לכסות ויש שאין נוהגין לכסות ויש שנוהגין למלאות הכלי ה] כגון בכפר קטן שאין כלכלה מליאה נמכרת בו ביום : עד שמגיע לביתו . גבי שוק לא אמר עד שהוא מגיע לשוק ומפרש בירושלמי (שם) מה בין המוליך לשוק למוליך לביתו [בשעה שהוא מוליך לביתו] בדעתו הדבר תלוי המוליך לשוק לא בדעתו הדבר תלוי אלא בדעת לקוחות שמא ימצא לקוחות וימכנו : ן הפרד והצימוקין · רגילין ליבש בחמה תאנים וענבים ורמונים כי היכי דתאנים נקראין גרוגרות וענבים צימוקים כך רמונים נקראים פרד כדתנן בתוספת' דתרומות פרק שלישי התורם ענבים ועתיד לעשותן צמוקים תאנים ועתיד לעשותן גרוגרות רמונים ועתיד לעשותן פרד ולשון פרד מלשון נתפרדו הרמונים דסוף מסכת ערלה [illegible]

ד ״ובירק הקשואים והדלועים והאבטיחים והמלפפונות התפוחין והאתרוגין חייבים גדולים וקטנים א) רבי שמעון · פוטר את האתרוגין בקטנן ב החייב ג) בשקדים המרים פטור במתוקים החייב במתוקים פטור מן המרים: ה (ו) ג) ״איזהו גרנן למעשרות הקשואים והדלועים משיפקסו ואם אינו מפקס משיעמיד ערימה אבטיח משישלק ואם אינו משלק עד שיעשה מוקצה (ח) ד) ״ירק הנאגד משיאגד אם אינו אוגד עד שימלא את הכלי (ט) ואם אינו ממלא את הכלי עד שילקט כל צרכו ״כלכלה עד שיחפה ואם אינו מחפה עד שימלא את הכלי ואם אינו ממלא את הכלי עד שילקוט כל צרכו ׳במה דברים אמורי׳ במוליך לשוק אבל במוליך לביתו אוכל מהם עראי עד שהוא מגיע לביתו: ו ׳הפרד והצמוקין והחרובין משיעמיד ערימה הבצלים משיפקל ואם אינו מפקל משיעמיד ערימה ״התבואה משימרח ואם אינו ממרח עד שיעמיד ערימה הקטניות משיכבור ואם אינו כובר עד שימרח אע"פ שמרח נוטל מן הקוטעין ומן הצדדין וממה שבתוך התבן ואוכל: ז ״היין ה) משיקפה אע"פ שקפה קולט (י) מן הגת העליונה ומן הצנור ושותה ׳השמן משירד לעוקה אע"פ שירד נוטל מן (יא) העקל ומבית הממל ומבין הפסים י] ונותן לחמטה ולתמחוי ״אבל לא יתן לקדרה וללפס כשהם רותחין ר' י) יהודה אומר לכל הוא נותן חוץ מדבר שיש בו חומץ

המעשרות צריך שיוציאם כשיגמר בשול הפירות וטעמם : ד שיעור זה המשנה כן ובירק הקשואים והאבטיחים והדלועים והמלפפונות וכן התפוחים והאתרוגים חייבים גדולים וקטנים לפי שתחלתן אוכל וסופן אוכל וראוין הם לאכילה כשהם קטנים ואין מניחים אותן אלא להוסיף אוכל כמו שקדם וכבר בארנו פעמים מה הם הקשואים והאבטיחים והדלועין והמלפפונות התפוחים והאתרוגים: והשקדים המרים. הם ראוין לאכילה כשהם קטנים קודם בשולן לפי שאז הם ראויין לאכילה א] וכשנתבשלו נפטרו מן המעשרות לפי שאז אינם ראוים לאכילה והשקדים שמתוקים בהפך זה בתחלתן פטורים מן המעשרות לפי שאינן ראויין לאכילה וחייבין לאחר בשולן ואין הלכה כרבי שמעון : ה גרנן למעשרו' כמו מלה מושאלת והכוונה שאל התנא אימתי יהיו הפירות כמו התבואה כשהיא בגורן שאסור לאכול ממנה אכילת עראי לפי שכבר נקבעה למעשר כי קודם גרנן של מעשרות אף על פי שהגיעו לעונת המעשרות מותר לאכול מהם אכילת עראי ודרך הקשואים והדלועין שיעלה עליהם כמו שער או כמו קוץ דק מאד והוא נקרא פקס וכן יעלה על האבטיחים כמו שער ויקרא שלק ואמרם משיפקסו ומשישלקו רוצים בו מעת שיפול מהם אותו השער כשיקנחם בידו וכן אמרו בגמרא *מעת שירים שלף וקיא : עד שיעשה מוקצה . ענינו עד שישטח אותם ויסדר אותם והמקום ששוטחין בו הפירות נקרא מוקצה כי האבטיחין אין עושין מהם ערימה לפי שהם מתחברים זה עם זה : משיחפה . פי' משיכסה כמו שדרך בני אדם האוספים את הפירות שמכסין אותן בעלי האילן ודומיהן : במה דברים אמורים . שכשיגיעו לעת הזאת שקבעו למעשרות אסור לאכול מהם עראי במוליך לשוק למכור אבל במוליך לביתו אוכל עראי עד שהוא מגיע לבית וכבר קדם לך זה העיקר בפרק שמיני (מ"ג) ממסכת תרומות כי הטבל אינו מתחייב במעשרות עד שהוא רואה פני הבית שנאמר (דברים כו) בערתי הקדש מן הבית : ו פרד · הוא גרגר הרמון מפרדין אותם ומיבשין אותן ונקראו פרדים וצמוקים הענבים היבשים: משיפקל. ענינו משיכרת עלין שלו ויסיר הגללה בהם : משימרח. ענינו משיברור אותם מן התבן ברירה גמורה וכבר בארנו במסכת פאה (פ"א מ"ו) הטעם מפני מה קורין הענין הזה מריחה: משיכבור ענינו משיכבור בכברה וילא כל מה שיש בה מן התבן ומן הצרורות ושם זה הכלי כברה : קוטעין מה שהוקצה מן הגדים לאחד מן הצדדים : משיקפה. פירוש משיעלה עליו קצף ובלשון חכמים הופיא : קולט כמו חוטף : גת העליונה. גת שדורכין שם הענבים הגת התחתונה הוא המקום שהיין יורד ומתקבץ לתוכה ובלשון קודש יקב : וצנור ידוע ממנו יורד היין : עוקה . היא החפירה שמתקבץ לתוכה השמן : ועקל הוא החבל כי היו לוקחים החבלים ועושים מהם כמו [illegible]

פירוש הרא"ש

[illegible]

פי' מהר"י בן מלכי צדק

ד וביתק. פי' חיוב מעשרות שלהן אם [illegible]

הגהות מהרי"ד לנדא

[illegible]

[illegible]

MISHNAH 4. WITH REGARD TO VEGETABLES,[4] CUCUMBERS, GOURDS, WATER-MELONS, CUCUMBER-MELONS,[5] APPLES AND CITRONS ARE LIABLE [TO TITHE], WHETHER GATHERED IN THE EARLIER OR LATER STAGES OF RIPENING.[6] R. SIMEON EXEMPTS THE CITRON IN THE EARLIER STAGES.[7] THE CONDITION IN WHICH BITTER ALMONDS ARE LIABLE [TO TITHE] IS EXEMPT IN THE CASE OF SWEET ALMONDS, AND THE CONDITION IN WHICH SWEET ALMONDS ARE LIABLE [TO TITHE] IS EXEMPT IN THE CASE OF BITTER ALMONDS.[8]

MISHNAH 5. WHEN ARE THE FRUITS FIXED TO BE TITHED?[9] CUCUMBERS AND GOURDS [ARE LIABLE TO TITHE] AFTER THEIR FRINGE[10] FALLS OFF, OR IF THIS DOES NOT FALL OFF, AFTER [THE FRUIT] HAS BEEN PILED UP; MELONS SO SOON
a AS THEY BECOME SMOOTH,[1] AND IF THEY HAVE NOT BECOME SMOOTH, AFTER THEY ARE STORED AWAY;[2] VEGETABLES WHICH ARE TIED IN BUNDLES,[3] FROM THE TIME THEY ARE TIED UP IN BUNDLES; IF THEY ARE NOT TIED UP IN BUNDLES, AFTER THE VESSEL HAS BEEN FILLED WITH THEM;[4] IF THE VESSEL IS NOT TO BE FILLED WITH THEM, AFTER THERE HAS BEEN GATHERED ALL THAT HE WISHES TO GATHER. [PRODUCE WHICH IS PACKED IN] A BASKET [IS LIABLE TO TITHE] AFTER IT HAS BEEN COVERED;[5] IF IT IS NOT TO BE COVERED, AFTER A VESSEL IS FILLED; IF A VESSEL IS NOT TO BE FILLED, AFTER HE HAS GATHERED ALL HE REQUIRES. WHEN DOES THIS REGULATION APPLY?[6] WHEN A MAN BRINGS [THE PRODUCE] TO THE MARKET, BUT WHEN HE BRINGS IT TO HIS OWN HOUSE, HE MAY MAKE A CHANCE MEAL OF IT, UNTIL HE REACHES HIS HOUSE.

MISHNAH 6. DRIED SPLIT-POMEGRANATES, RAISINS AND CAROBS, ARE LIABLE [TO TITHE] AFTER THEY ARE STACKED; ONIONS, AFTER THEY ARE STRIPPED;[7] IF THEY ARE NOT STRIPPED, AFTER THEY ARE STACKED; GRAIN, AS SOON AS THE PILE HAS BEEN EVENED;[8] IF IT IS NOT EVENED, AFTER IT HAS BEEN STACKED; PULSE, AFTER IT HAS BEEN SIFTED;[9] IF IT IS NOT SIFTED, AFTER THE PILE HAS BEEN EVENED. EVEN AFTER THE PILE HAS BEEN EVENED, HE MAY [WITHOUT TITHING] TAKE OF THE TINY EARS,[10] FROM THE SIDES OF THE
b PILES, AND FROM THAT WHICH IS STILL IN THE HUSK, AND EAT.[1]

MISHNAH 7. WINE [IS LIABLE TO TITHE] AFTER IT HAS BEEN SKIMMED,[2] BUT ALTHOUGH IT HAS BEEN SKIMMED, HE MAY TAKE FROM THE UPPER WINE-PRESS,[3] OR FROM THE DUCT,[4] AND DRINK THEREOF [WITHOUT GIVING TITHE]. OIL, AFTER IT HAS DRIPPED INTO THE TROUGH,[5] BUT EVEN AFTER IT HAS DRIPPED HE MAY STILL TAKE OF THE OIL FROM THE BALE,[6] OR FROM THE PULP [UNDER THE PRESS],[7] OR FROM BETWEEN THE BOARDS OF THE PRESS,[8] [WITHOUT TITHING,] AND PUT THE OIL ON A CAKE,[9] OR PLATE,[10] BUT NOT IN A DISH OR STEWPOT, WHILE THE CONTENTS THEREOF ARE BOILING.[11] R. JUDAH SAYS: HE MAY PUT IT INTO ANYTHING[12] SAVE IN TO THAT WHICH CONTAINS VINEGAR OR BRINE.[13]

(4) The four species of vegetables enumerated here. (5) An apple-shaped melon. (6) Since both in their earlier and later stages they are considered to be food. Lit., 'whether large or small'. (7) Since he holds that they are not eaten at this stage. (8) Bitter almonds are gathered and eaten at their earlier stages, not at their later. With sweet almonds the reverse is the case. (9) To forbid even a chance meal. Lit., 'when is their threshing-floor (condition) for tithes'. In the case of corn, the tithing-season begins after the produce has been stacked on the threshing-floor. (10) In the early stages of ripening there is a woolly substance on their surface; when fully ripe this falls off.
a (1) By the loss of their woolly substance on the surface. (2) Lit., 'made into a store'. When they have been spread out to be dried. Melons are not piled up but spread out. (3) That which it is customary to sell in bundles. (4) If a man customarily fills many vessels from his field, he may eat a chance meal until the last vessel has been filled. (5) It was customary to cover the fruits with the leaf of a tree when taken to the market so that they should not wither. (6) When do the above conditions concerning the season for tithing hold good? (7) After the bad peel has been taken off. (8) After the produce has been cleansed from its chaff, it is heaped up and levelled. (9) Since it is usual to uproot the pulse with dust, it is therefore necessary to sift it in a sieve in order to cleanse it. (10) Plucked ears of corn not well threshed.
b (1) Since all these latter things are as yet not ready for tithe. (2) From the time that he removes the kernels and the husks which rise to the surface of the wine on its fermenting. (3) From the wine which has not yet gone into the press tank. (4) Formed in the mouth of the wine-press from which the wine flows into the press tank. The wine which is still in the upper wine-press or in the duct is as yet not completely ready for use. (5) The cavity into which the oil drips. (6) The meaning of this Hebrew word is obscure; Jast. translates: 'A bale of loose texture containing the olive pulp to be pressed'. Bert.: 'A vessel made of ropes in which the olives are heaped up during the time they lay the press-beam upon them'. *Tif. Yis:* A perforated basket into which the pressed-out olives are placed when they are gathered together. The oil creeps and oozes out from the holes in the basket. (7) The upper millstone with which they grind the olives (Bert.). The stone placed in the basket to press upon the olives and to squeeze them (*Tif. Yis.*). (8) The oil which comes out from between the boards. (9) A small, thin and hot cake which, when taken out of the oven, used to be smoothed with oil over its face. This last statement is made to teach us that the cake is not considered in the category of 'cooked' dishes, since generally it is forbidden to eat a chance meal from all produce, fruits and vegetables, cooked by the fire. (10) A large dish upon which there is hot cooking. (11) Even though he has removed them from the fire. (12) He may put it into all boiling pots and dishes, after he has removed it from the fire, and it is still not liable to tithe. (13) Brine-water which issues from salted fish or meat. The sharpness of these two ingredients, vinegar and brine, aids considerably in the cooking process.

MISHNAH 8. A CAKE OF PRESSED FIGS [IS LIABLE TO TITHE] FROM THE MOMENT ITS SURFACE HAS BEEN
a SMOOTHED.[1] IT MAY BE SMOOTHED WITH [THE JUICE OF] UNTITHED FIGS OR GRAPES,[2] BUT R. JUDAH FORBIDS THIS. IF IT IS SMOOTHED WITH GRAPES, IT IS NOT SUSCEPTIBLE TO [RECEIVE] LEVITICAL UNCLEANNESS;[3] R. JUDAH, HOWEVER, SAYS, IT IS SUSCEPTIBLE.[4] DRIED FIGS [ARE LIABLE TO TITHE] AFTER THEY HAVE BEEN TRODDEN,[5] AND [FIGS] STORED IN A BIN [ARE LIABLE TO TITHE] AFTER THEY HAVE BEEN PRESSED. IF ONE WAS TREADING [THE FIGS] INTO A JAR, OR PRESSING THEM IN A STORE BIN, AND THE CASK WAS BROKEN OR THE STORE BIN OPENED, IT IS NOT ALLOWED TO MAKE A CHANCE MEAL OF THEM; R. JOSE, HOWEVER, PERMITS THIS.

CHAPTER II

MISHNAH 1. IF A MAN WAS PASSING THROUGH THE
b STREET,[1] AND SAID 'TAKE YE OF MY FIGS', ONE MAY EAT AND BE EXEMPT FROM TITHE;[2] THEREFORE IF[3] THEY BROUGHT THEM INTO THEIR HOUSES,[4] THEY MUST GIVE THE PRIESTLY DUES AS IF THEY WERE CERTAINLY UNTITHED. [IF HE SAID] 'TAKE YE AND BRING INTO YOUR HOUSES',[5] THEY MAY NOT MAKE A CHANCE MEAL OF THEM.[6] THEREFORE, IF THEY BROUGHT THEM INTO THEIR HOUSES, THEY NEED TITHE THEM ONLY AS DEMAI.[7]

MISHNAH 2. IF MEN WERE SITTING IN A DOORWAY OR A SHOP, AND HE[8] SAID, 'TAKE YE OF MY FIGS',[9] THEY MAY
c EAT AND BE EXEMPT FROM TITHES,[1] BUT THE OWNER OF THE DOORWAY, OR THE OWNER OF THE SHOP, IS LIABLE [TO GIVE TITHE]. R. JUDAH, HOWEVER, EXEMPTS HIM[2] UNLESS HE TURNS HIS FACE[3] OR CHANGES THE PLACE WHERE HE WAS SITTING [AND SELLING].[4]

MISHNAH 3. IF A MAN BRINGS FRUIT FROM GALILEE TO JUDEA,[5] OR IF HE GOES UP TO JERUSALEM, HE MAY EAT OF THEM,[6] UNTIL HE ARRIVES AT THE PLACE TO WHICH HE INTENDS TO GO;[7] AND SO, ALSO, IF HE RETURNS.[8] R. MEIR, HOWEVER, SAYS: [HE MAY EAT] ONLY UNTIL HE REACHES THE PLACE WHERE HE INTENDS TO REST [ON THE SABBATH].[9] BUT PEDLARS WHO GO ABOUT THE CITIES,[10] MAY EAT,[11] UNTIL THEY REACH THE PLACE WHERE THEY INTEND STAYING OVER NIGHT.[12] R. JUDAH SAYS: 'THE FIRST HOUSE [HE REACHES] IS HIS HOUSE'.[13]

MISHNAH 4. IF ONE SET ASIDE THE TERUMAH FROM
d FRUITS BEFORE THEIR WORK WAS FINISHED,[1] R. ELIEZER SAYS: IT IS FORBIDDEN TO MAKE A CHANCE MEAL OF THEM,[2] BUT THE SAGES PERMIT IT[3] EXCEPT WHEN IT IS A BASKET OF FIGS. IF ONE SET ASIDE THE TERUMAH FROM A BASKET OF FIGS, R. SIMEON PERMITS IT,[4] BUT THE SAGES FORBID IT.[5]

MISHNAH 5. IF A MAN SAYS TO HIS FELLOW: 'HERE IS THIS ISSAR,[6] GIVE ME FIVE FIGS FOR IT', HE MAY NOT EAT OF [THEM] UNTIL HE HAS TITHED THEM;[7] SO R. MEIR. R. JUDAH SAYS: IF HE ATE THEM ONE BY ONE, HE IS EXEMPT, BUT IF SEVERAL TOGETHER,[8] HE IS LIABLE [TO TITHE.] R. JUDAH SAID: IT HAPPENED IN A ROSE-GARDEN IN JERUSALEM THAT THERE WERE FIGS BEING SOLD THREE OR FOUR FOR AN ISSAR,[9] AND NEITHER TERUMAH NOR TITHE WAS EVER GIVEN FROM IT.[10]

a (1) It is customary to smoothen its surface with juice in order to beautify it. Then, and then only, does the tithing stage begin. (2) Since juices used for smoothing purposes are considered of no consequence. R. Judah, however, holds the contrary view, and therefore, since their fruit is untithed, they are forbidden. (3) V. Lev. XI, 34, 38. This refers only to grapes and not to figs, since fig-juice does not render food susceptible to uncleanness. (4) The dispute between R. Judah and the other authorities is as to whether the juice is to be considered liquid or not. (5) The figs are dried and then are trodden with staves in a vessel, or are pressed with the hands in the store-house.

b (1) The statement speaks of an *'am ha-arez* who is suspected of not having given his tithes, and also of fruit which is not being taken to be sold. (2) Because we can say they have not been taken indoors, and therefore, the time has not yet arrived when they are liable to tithe; v. *supra* I, 5. (3) Since he uses only this phrase 'Take' in his statement, implying a chance meal. (4) The man who gave them had not tithed them, thinking they were going to eat them in the street, which does not require tithing. From the moment, however, that they are taken indoors, they are liable to tithe. In this case, they give the tithe of tithe which the Levite owes to the priest (תרומת מעשר) v. Num. XVIII, 26; the first tithe (מעשר ראשון) belonging to the Levite; the second tithe (מעשר שני) to be consumed by the owner in Jerusalem (v. Deut. XIV, 23) they may keep for themselves. (5) Thus indicating that they may be eaten, even in the house, as having been tithed, after having become liable to tithe. (6) The man is believed in so far that the produce had reached the stage when it became liable to tithe, and consequently forbidden even for a chance meal, but he is not believed that the tithe had been taken from them. (7) V. Glos. (8) The owner of the doorway or the shop, who was carrying fruit. (9) Which I have in the street; because if they were in the doorway or shop they would become liable, as if they were in the house.

c (1) Since a man's house renders produce liable to tithe only as far as he is concerned. (2) R. Judah holds that since a doorway or shop is a place where he will be ashamed to eat, it is not regarded as a courtyard or house which renders produce liable to tithe. (3) Enabling him to eat without feeling ashamed. (4) Even though his face is turned towards his buyers, by changing his position he indicates his desire to find a place where he can eat unashamed. (5) He gathered them in his field in Galilee with the intention of taking them up to Judea and selling them there. (6) A chance meal without tithing. (7) Even if he stops on the way, he is still exempt from giving tithe, because it is his intention to sell them only in Judea. (8) If before he reached Judea he decided to take them back to Galilee, he may make a chance meal of them until he reaches Galilee again. (9) That is to say until he has brought them into the house where he intends to rest on Sabbath, and as soon as he reaches his destination, and even though Sabbath has not yet arrived, he is liable to give tithe. (10) To sell spices and other perfumery of women; and they carry with them at the same time fruit which has been given to them, but which has not yet been tithed. (11) A chance meal, until they reach their destination, and then the fruit is liable to tithe. (12) He is only liable when they have been actually brought into the house. (13) As regards the law of tithes. Because as soon as the man reaches the city he will enter the first house he can find with the intention of staying there. Therefore, even although ultimately he does not settle with the owner of the house to stay in this particular house, he has, by bringing his fruit into this house, made it liable to tithe.

d (1) The season has not yet been reached when they are liable to tithe, as defined *supra* I. (2) Until all the tithes have been separated, because he holds the view that the setting aside of *terumah* fixes the liability of fruit tithes, even though they are not yet fully finished. (3) They do not accept R. Eliezer's principle. (4) Because the tithing season in this case begins only after all the fruit has been gathered or as much as is required; V. *supra* I, 5. (5) Because once the *terumah* has been set aside from the basket, it is indicative that all that is needful has been gathered. (6) V. Glos. (7) Because the sale fixes liability to tithing. (8) If the owner of the garden gives him two or more, at the same time, he is liable to tithe, because these constitute for him an immature threshing-floor. (9) Here the seller used to gather them, since he would allow no buyers to enter the garden on account of the roses. (10) Since they eat them one by one.

מסורת הש"ס

א) שבת פרק כ"ב דף קמה. ב) ביצה פרק ד דף לה. צ"ל ואסור

עין משפט נר מצוה

טו א מיי' פ"ג מהל' מעשר הלכה טו :
טז ב מיי' פ"ו שם הלכה א :
יז ג מיי' פ"ב שם הלכה טו :
א ד מיי' פ"ה שם הלכה ו :
ב ה שם הל' ח :
ג ו מיי' פרק ד שם הלכה י :
ד ז שם הל' יא :
ה ח שם הל' יב :
ו ט י מיי' פ"ג מהל' מעשר הלכה ד :
ז כ מיי' פ"ה שם הלכה ג :

משנה

וציר : ח העגול משיחליקנו מחליקין בתאנים ובענבים של טבל רבי יהודה אוסר א) המחליק בענבים לא הוכשר רבי יהודה אומר הוכשר הגרוגרות משידוש ומגורה משיעגל היה דש בחבית ומעגל במגורה נשברה החבית ונפתחה המגורה לא יאכל מהם עראי רבי יוסי מתיר :

פרק שני

א היה עובר בשוק ואמר טלו לכם תאנים (א) אוכלין ופטורין לפיכך אם הכניסו לבתיהם מתקנים ודאי טלו והכניסו לבתיכם לא יאכלו מהם עראי לפיכך אם הכניסו לבתיהם אינן מתקנין אלא דמאי : ב היו יושבין בשער או בחנות ואמר טלו לכם תאנים אוכלין ופטורין ובעל השער ובעל החנות חייבין ר' יהודה פוטר עד שיחזיר את פניו או עד שישנה מקום ישיבתו : ג המעלה פירות מן הגליל ליהודה או עולה לירושלים אוכל מהם עד שהוא מגיע למקום שהוא הולך וכן *בחזרה רבי מאיר אומר עד שהוא מגיע למקום השביתה והרוכלין המחזרין בעיירות אוכלין עד שמגיעים למקום הלינה רבי יהודה אומר הבית הראשון הוא ביתו : ד פירות שתרמן עד שלא נגמרה מלאכתן רבי אליעזר אוסר מלאכול מהם עראי וחכמים מתירים חוץ מכלכלת תאנים כלכלת תאנים שתרמה ר"ש מתיר וחכמים אוסרים : ה האומר לחברו הילך איסר זה ותן לי בו ה' תאנים לא יאכל עד שיעשר דברי ר"מ רבי יהודה אומר אוכל אחת אחת פטור ואם צרף חייב א"ר יהודה מעשה בגנת ורדים שהיתה בירושלים והיו תאנים נמכרות משלש ומארבע באיסר ולא הופרש ממנה תרומה ומעשר מעולם:

פי' הרמב"ם

ואין הלכה כרבי יהודה : ח כבר בארנו שעגול הוא כמו רחים שעושין מדבלת התאנים. ופי' משיחליקנו שספין ומחליקין אותן העגולים : ומחליקין בתאנים ובענבי' של טבל ולא נאמ' שהוא מכחיש אותן ומכין אותם להפסד מפני שכשמושחין אותן ומחליקין אותם *למהר בהם ימהר העפוש . וכשמושחין ענבים יקבלו לחלוחית ואומר ר' יהודה כי כבר הוכשר לטומא' לפי שהיין מכלל שבעה משקין המכשירין כמו שבארנו בתרומות (פי"א מ"ב) וכאילו בלל אותו ושראו במשקה הענבים: משידוש. פי' משיכתוש אותם קלתם על קלתם בכלי שהוא רוצה להכניעם בהם : והמגורה משיעגיל . ענינו כשרוצה להכניסם באוצר משיתחיל להחליקם ע"פ האוצר ולהשוותם ומעגלה שם הכלי המחליק שבו מחליקין הקרקע והגגות ואין הלכה כרבי יהודה ולא כרבי יוסי בכל זה המאמר :

א כשזה המוכר המסבב בשוקים מכריז ואומר טלו לכם תאנים מותר לאכול מהם עראי לפי שנאמר לא ראו פני הבית ולפיכך אין מכריזין עליה' אלא לאוכלן בלבד עראי והוא כנותן מתנה ואין המתנה קובעת למעשר כמו המכר ואם הביאן לביתו צריך להוציא מהם המעשרות החייבות לטבל ואם אמר טלו והכניסו לבתיכם נאמר שהם ראו פני הבית ולפיכך לא יאכל מהם עראי ואינו נאמן באומר הכניסו לבתיכם שעניינו שהן מעושרין ולפיכך יוציא מהם חקי הדמאי לפי שהוא ספק שמא אמר אמת באמרו שהן מעושרין או אמר שקר ומה שאמר לא אמר אלא כדי שיקפצו עליהם לוקחים וכל זה כשהמוכר עם הארץ כמו שבארנו במסכת דמאי : ב מבואר הוא כי בעל החנות ובעל החצר לפי שאותו מקום הוא מקום ישיבתו נקבעים במעשרות מחמתו ואין הלכה כר' יהודה: ג מקום השביתה הוא מקום שהוא שובת בו ביום השבת: הרוכלים המחזרים בעיירות . עם הבשמים ההולכים מעיר אל עיר ומכפר אל כפר ואמר בכאן שהם רשאים לאכול כל היום מה שנוהגים שם מן הפירות אע"פ שהם נכנסין בבתים עד שיגיעו למקום הלינה ואין הלכה כר' מאיר ולא כר' יהודה : ד ר"א אומר תרומה קובעת למעשר ואפי' בדבר שלא נגמרה מלאכתו . ואמרם כלכלת תאנים שתרמה ר"ש שתרמה קודם שתגמר מלאכתה ואין הלכה כר"א ולא כר' שמעון : ה והלכה כרבי יהודה

ר"ש

ח העיגול . של דבלה: משיחליקנו. שמחליק פניו מלמעלה במשקים ויקבע למעשר ואסור באכילת עראי : מחליקין בתאנים ובענבים של טבל . במשקים היוצאין מתאנים וענבים של טבל מחליקין העיגול משפשף העיגול בהן והמשקין נסחטין מהן ומחליקין אותן דמשקה של תאנים לא חשיב ושל ענבים נמי כיון דאזיל לאיבוד שרי ור' יהודה אוסר דחשיב ליה אוכל *האסור משום טבל וגבי דבש תמרים פלוגתא אי חייב במעשר אי לא כדפרשינן בפרק י"א דתרומות (משנה ב) : המחליק ענבים · משפשף ענבים בעיגול לא הוכשרו דלא חשיב משקה כיון דאזיל לאיבוד : רבי יהודה אומר הוכשר . דחשיב ליה משקה ובפרק חבית (קמה.) אמרינן דפליגי במשקה העומד לאיבוד לנלכלו: משידוש· מייבשין התאנים בחמה ואח"כ דשין אותן במקלות ומרכיבין א] אותן בידיהן ועושה אותן חבית או מגורה והמגורה הוא כלי שעושין בו העיגול ומשדש בחבית ועגול במגורה אסור לאכול מהן עראי : בירושלמי (הל' ה) מפרש משום דקסבר לא עליון צריך לתחתון ולא תחתון לעליון ור' יוסי דשרי סבר דצריך זה לזה ולא נגמרה מלאכתן עדיין ומסיק רבי אליעזר דתנא קמא רבי מאיר היא דלא תיסבר סתמא ורבי יוסי והלכה כסתמא לפום כן צריך מימר ר' מאיר היא דרבי מאיר ור' יוסי הלכה כרבי יוסי :

א אוכלין ופטורין · אע"ג דהשוכר את הפועלים (פח.) משמע דמקח קובע למעשר הכא אין מתנה כמכר ובירושלמי (הל' א) פליגי דשמואל אמר רבי מאיר היא דאמר אין מתנה כמכר ר' יוסי אומר דברי הכל היא כמאן דאמר מאליהן קבלו עליהם את המעשר כלומר בכי האי גוונא לא החמירו ומהאי טעמא נמי הקילו כדפרשינן בפ' בתרא דתרומות*: מתקנין ודאי · שהנותן אינו מעשר דסבור הוא שיאכלו בשוק ולא בעי עשורי והשתא דהכניסו לבית והוקבעו חייב : אבל אם אמר להן טלו והכניסו לבתיכם לא יאכלו מהן עראי· שהוא לא נתן אלא להכניסן לבית לפיכך כשהכניסם לבית מתקנים דמאי דשמא הנותן עישר ומטעם [דמאי] אין זקוקין להפריש אלא אחת למאה כעישור תרומת מעשר ודווקא בעם הארץ [דחבר] לא [יתן] עד שיעשר : ב ואמר טלו לכם תאנים. בעל השער אומר כן : אוכלין ופטורין . אמר בירושלמי (שם) הדא אמרה ביתו של אדם טובל לו אבל לא לאחר לפיכך בעל השער והחנות חייבין ורבי יהודה פוטר משום דשער והחנות אדם בוש לאכול בתוכו ולקמן אמר ר' נחמיה אי זו היא חצר שקובעת למעשר כל שאין אדם בוש לאכול בתוכה ואמרינן בירוש' (שם) ר' יהודה ור' נחמיה אמרו דבר אחד : עד שיחזיר פניו . מקום שיושב ומוכר הוא בוש לאכול בלא החזרת פנים אבל במקום שאינו יושב אינו בוש ואמר בירושלמי (שם) הדא אמר במקום שאינו בוש חייב : ג מן הגליל ליהודה · לוקטן בגליל כדי למוכרן ביהודה או בירושלים לא נטבלו אפילו לן בדרך עד שיגיע ליהודה או לירושלים שבמקום אחר אין דעתו למוכרן : וכן בחזרה . אם קודם שהגיע ליהודה ולירושלים נמלך להחזירן לגליל אוכל מהן עראי בדרך עד שיגיע לגליל ובירושלמי (הל' ב) תני עלה אפילו שבת כלומר אינו טובל ופריך מינה ריש לקיש לר' יוחנן דאמר דשבת טובלים אפילו לפירות שליקטם שלא לצורך שבת וכי תימא הא ר' מאיר כוותיה קאי דאמר עד שמגיע למקום השביתה רבי מאיר אפילו בחול דעל כורחן דרבנן פליגי ומשני רבי יוחנן מאי אפילו שבת ברולה לשבות תדע לך שהוא כן דתני עלה אפילו שבת בשני ויש שביתה בשני אלא ברולה לשבות אף הכא ברולה לשבות כלומר שרולה לנוח שם בתוך לילה ויום כשיעור שבת אי נמי רולה להתעכב שם עד אחר שבת אפילו הכי לא הוטבלו כל זמן שלא הגיע שבת ור' מאיר מחייב בזה דהיינו מגיע למקום השביתה לילה ויום כשיעור שביתה אי נמי רולה לנוח עד אחר שבת הוקבעו מיד והדר קאמר בירושל' הכל מודין אפילו רבי מאיר בלינה שאינה טובלת מה בין לינה מה בין שביתה אדם מגלגל בלינה ואינה מגלגל בשביתה בכל מקום אדם לן ואין אדם שובת בכל מקום כלומר כשלן על כרחו לן ולא בשביל למכור פירותיו אבל בשנה כדי שביתה שמא יקדמנו לו לקוחות ולכך נטבלו : הרוכלים המחזירים בעיירות · למכור בשמים ומוליכין עמהן פירות אוכלים מהם עראי עד שיגיעו למקום הלינה וכשמגיעין שם נטבלו ובירושלמי (שם) מייתי עובדא דרבי יהושע הוה אזיל אחר רבן יוחנן בן זכאי לברור חיל והיו בני העיירות מביאין להן פירות אמר להן ר' יהושע אם לנו כאן חייבים אנו לעשר משום דאין מאכילין אכסניא דמאי בשלנו כדפרשינן בפרק ג' דדמאי דהתם נמי (דמאי פ"ג הל' א) מייתי האי עובדא ומסיק דרבי יהושע בלווייתיה שכיחא ליה דהוא אמר הלינה טובלת ושאר כל האדם דלית לוייתה שכיחא לון אין לינה טובלת ופריך והתניא הרוכלין המחזירים בעיירות אוכלין עד שמגיעין למקום הלינה ומשני מה מקום לינה ביתו אמר ריש לקיש בשם רבי אושעיא כגון אלין דכפר חנניא דנפקין וסחרין ד' וה' קרייתא ועלין ודמכין בבתיהון : רבי יהודה אומר בית ראשון הוא ביתו · כלומר מכיון שמגיע לבית הראשון שבעיר נטבלו הפירות אף על פי שלא לן שם אלא באמצע העיר או בבית אחרון שבסוף העיר ל"ד אחר ומפרש בירושלמי (שם) למה רוצה אדם לפנה עסקיו בבית הראשון שפוגע ללון שם והא פלוגתא דירושלמי דשבת טובלת לא דמיא לשבת קובעת דבסוף המביא כדי יין (דף לה.) והתם איירי באכילת שבת : ד עד שלא נגמרה מלאכתן · משום הכי דתנן לעיל איזהו גורנן למעשרות : קודם גורנו למעשר הפריש תרומה גדולה ר"א אוסר לאכול מהן עראי עד שיפריש כל מעשר שבהן דנטבלו לפי שתרומה טובלת : וחכמים מתירין · דסברי אין תרומה טובלת אלא אם כן תרמן מתוך הכלכלה ורבי שמעון מתיר אף על פי שתרמן מתוך הכלכלה ומפרש בירושלמי (הל' ג) ר' שמעון מתיר מקל וחומר ומה בשעה שיש עליה זיקת ג' מעשרות את אומר מותר בשעה שאין עליה אלא זיקת ב' מעשרות לא כל שכן : ה לא יאכל עד שיעשר · דמקח קובע כדאמרינן בפרק הפועלים : אחת אחת . דראשונה שנותן לו אכלה וכן הכל : ואם צירף · שלקח שתים כאחת אי נמי כשיעור שקנה קיבל בבת אחת ובליקט ונתן פליגי כדאיתא בירושלמי (שם) אבל ליקט ואכל אפילו ר"מ מודי דאוכל אחת אחת ופטור וגינת וורדין דייק מינה רבי יהודה ליקט ונתן לו שלא היה מניח הכל ליכנס שלא לקלקל הוורדין ואמרי' בירושלמי (שם) חברייא בשם ר' יוחנן כך משיב ר' יהודה את ר' מאיר אין אתה מודה בלוקט ונותן לבנו שהוא פטור מה

פי' מהר"י בן מלכי צדק

דשם מתבשל בודאי והוי טבל שנגמרה מלאכתו ואסור וכי הכי דפליגי הכא הכי נמי פליגי לענין שבת בפ' כירה : ח העגול . פי' עגול של דבלה אסור לאכול ממנו עראי מכיון שהוחלק לעז דקנדלו מליפידאו מלשון ואנכי איש חלק : מחליקין העגול של דבלה . ממשקה היוצא מתאנין וענבין של טבל דנבי תאנין ליכא משקה . וגבי ענבים דאיכא משקה כיון דאזיל לאיבוד שרי וקסבר בין אוכל העומד לאיבוד בין משקה העומד לאיבוד לא חשיבי הלכך שרי : ורבי יהודה אוסר. דאוכל חשוב הוא . ומשקה חשוב הוא ואע"ג דקיימי לאיבוד וטבל דבר אסור הוא : המחליק בענבים. פי' ממשקה היוצאין מחליק העגל או הככרות וסך אותן לא הוכשרו העיגול ולא הככרות בזו הסיכה דמשקה העומד לאיבוד לאו משקה הוא.ואם נגע בהן השרץ טהורין הן: ר' יהודה אומר הוכשרו.דמשקין הן. רבנן כטעמם ור' יהודה כטעמיה . ובשבת פ' חבית אמרי' דבמשקה העומד לצחצחו פליגי רבנן סברי לא הוי משקה ור' יהודה סבר הוי משקה:הגרוגרות אסור לאכול מהן עראי משידוש אותן פי' התאנין מיבשין אותן בשמש ואח"כ דשין אותן במקלות ומרככין אותן בידיהן ועושין אותן חבילות למגורה לעשות מהן עיגולי דבלה: והמגורה. שם הכלי הוא שעושין בו העיגולין וכיון שעיגל המגורה לעז אוריםנדאו אסור לאכול מאותן הדבילות עראי עד שיעשר : היה דש הגרוגרות בחבית ומעגל במגורה ונשברה החבית ונפתחה המגורה לא יאכל מהן עראי מאי טעמא דאין עליון צריך לתחתון ולא תחתון לעליון א"ר אלעזר זו דברי רבי מאיר ומאי קמ"ל ר' אלעזר הא קמ"ל דלא תסבור לומר סתמא ורבי יוסי הלכה כסתמא לפום כן צריך לומר דרבי מאיר היא דקיימא לן רבי מאיר ורבי יוסי הלכה כרבי יוסי מאי טעמא דרבי יוסי תחתון צריך לעליון ועליון צריך לתחתון כלומר אכתי לא נגמרה מלאכתן :

פ"ב א היה עומד בשוק ואמר לבני אדם. פי' שדרכן לאכול בדרך טלו לכם מעט מאלו התאנין אוכלין ופטורין דמתנה לאו כמכר דמיא ואפי' למאן דסבר מתנה כמכר כך פטור שמאליהן קיבלו עליהן המעשרות. כלומר מעשרות לאו דבר תורה ואפו הכי לקולא אזלינן אי נמי בתנאי זה קיבלו עליהן לפיכך אוכלין ופטורין : והכניסו לבתיהם לא יאכלו מהן עראי שהוא לא נתן אלא להכניסם לבתיהן : לפיכך אם הכניסו לבתיהן אינם מתקנין אלא דמאי. ואם כן אם היו ק' תאנין יהיב מעשר עלייהו תאנה אחת. וזו המשנה מסתברא בדליתיה קמן דלישייליה. ויש אומר בדאיתיה ולא האמינוהו חכמים לומר עישרתי או לא עישרתי : ב היו יושבין בשער או בחנות ואמר בעל השער או בעל החנות טלו לכם תאנין אוכלין ופטורין מלעשר. אבל בעל השער ובעל החנות חייבין לעשר. זאת אומרת ביתו של אדם טובל לו אבל לא לאחרים : ר' יהודה פוטר · גם בעל השער גם בעל החנות ואוכלין ופטורין מלעשר מאי טעמא דחנות ושער בוש אדם חשוב לאכול שם בגלוי. ור' יהודה סבר כר' נחמיה דאמר לקמן אי זו חצר שחייבת במעשרות כל שאין אדם בוש לאכול בתוכה. ור' נחמיה ור' יהודה אמרו דבר אחד לפיכך אם החזיר פניו ואוכל חייב לעשר או אם שינה מקום ישיבתו פי' במקום שיושב ומוכר בוש אבל אם יכנס לפנים או באותו מקום עצמו שיושב אם מחזיר פניו אינו בוש וחייב. מיהא שמעינן אליבא דר' יהודה ור' נחמיה מקום שבוש פטור מקום שאינו בוש חייב : ג המעלה פירות מגליל ליהודה או מעלן לירושלים. פי' בשליקטן משעה ראשונה להוליכן לגליל או לירושלים למוכרן אבל במקום אחר לא ימכרם אלא יחזירם לביתו הואיל ובזה התנאי ליקטן אפי' לן בדרך ואפי' שבת אינן נטבלין שאנוס הוא · ותניא הביא תאנים מן השדה לאוכלן בחצרו שאינה משתמרת ושכח והכניסן לביתו או שהחזירום התינוקות הרי זה מחזירן במקומו ואוכל מהן עראי עד שהוא מגיע למקום שהוא הולך פי' אם בגליל אם בירושלים ואפי' לן בדרך ואפי' נח. אבל כיון שבא לגליל או לירושלים נטבל. ואסור לאכול מהן עראי עד שיעשר וכן בחזרה אם נמלך להחזירן בגליל אוכל מהן עראי בכל הדרך ואפי' נח ואפי' לן עד שיגיע לגליל וכיון שהגיע לגליל נטבלו ואסור לאכול מהן עראי עד שיעשר : והרוכלין המחזירין בעיירות. לילך ולמכור בשמים אוכלין עראי מן הפירות ההן שמוליכין עמהן עד שיגיעו למקום הלינה מיהא שמעינן דלינה טובלת : ר' יהודה אומר בית הראשון שפגע בעיר הוא ביתו ומאותה השעה שהגיע בבית הראשון נטבלו הפירות. פי' תני רבי חלפתא בן שאול רוצה אדם לפנות עסקיו בבית ראשון שפגע וללון שם : ד פירות שתרמן עד שלא נגמרה מלאכתן. פי' כגון תמרין ועתיד לדורסן גרוגרות ועתיד לדושן דקיימא לן עד שלא ידרום ועד שלא ידוש אוכל מהן עראי דלא נטבלו ותרמן פי' הפריש מהן תרומה רבי אליעזר אומר מכיון שהפריש מהן תרומה. נטבלו ואף על גב דלא נגמרה מלאכתן ואסור לאכול מהן עראי עד שיעשר. פי' שתרומה טובלת בפירות שלא נגמרה מלאכתן : וחכמים מתירין חוץ מכלכלת תאנין שאם תרמן נטבלו לדברי הכל ואסור לאכול מהן עראי דהני דבר שנגמרה הן בר מרבי שמעון דמתיר. ומאי טעמא דרבי שמעון דמתיר מקל וחומר ומה אם בשעה שיש עליה זיקת שלשה דברים את אומר מותר בשעה שאין עליה אלא זיקת ב' דברים לא כל שכן דמותרין : ה האומר לחבירו הילך איסר זה ולקט ותן לי בו תאנים לא יאכל עד שיעשר : ר' יהודה אומר אם אוכל וכו'. פי' ראשונה שנותן לו והוא אוכל וכן הכל פטור : ואם צירף בידו חייב לעשר אבל בלוקט ואוכל הוא עצמו אפילו רבי מאיר מודה שאוכל אחת אחת ופטור. ובליקט ונתן לו פליגי כדתני רבי יהודה גינת וורדין לסייעיה לגרמיה וגינת וורדין בלוקט ונותן לו היה שלא היה מניח אדם ליכנס שם שאם היה נכנס היה מקלקל הוורדין אמר חברייה בשם רבי יוחנן כך משיב רבי יהודה לרבי מאיר אין את מודה בלוקט ונותן לבנו שפטור מה לי נותן לבנו מה לי נותן לאחר וגינת וורדים דתנינן מימות נביאים הראשונים היתה שם דתנינן אין עושין גינות ופרדסים בירושלים חוץ מגינת וורדין שהיתה שם מימות נביאים הראשונים :

פירוש הרא"ש

פ"ב א) והוא שנתן להם דבר מועט שראוי שיאכלום בשוק אבל אם נתן להם דבר מרובה הרי כאילו אמר להם טלו והכניסו לבתיכם ואין מעשרין אלא דמאי וכן אם נתן להם דבר שאין דרכן לאכול כמו שהוא או שהוא המקבל אדם חשוב שאין דרכו לאכול בשוק הוי (גמר) כאלו אמר להם טלו והכניסו לבית :

הגהות מהרי"ר לנדא

משנה ח בר"ש א] ומרכיבין צ"ל ומרככין : ב] במשנה במסכת שבת ... חבית.

האומר

ו ×האומר לחבירו הילך איסר זה בעשר תאנים שאבור לי בורר ואוכל באשכול שאבור לי מגרגר ואוכל ברמון שאבור לי פורט ואוכל באבטיח שאבור לי *סופת ואוכל אבל אם אמר לו בעשרים תאנים אלו בשני אשכלות אלו בשני רמונים אלו בשני אבטיחים אלו אוכל כדרכו ופטור מפני שקנה במחובר לקרקע: ז א) ב השוכר את הפועל לקצות עמו בתאנים אמר לו על מנת שאוכל תאנים אוכל ופטור על מנת שאוכל אני ובני (ביתי) או שיאכל בני בשכרי הוא אוכל ופטור ובנו אוכל וחייב על מנת שאוכל בשעת הקציעה ולאחר הקציעה בשעת הקציעה אוכל ופטור ולאחר הקציעה אוכל וחייב שאינו אוכל מן התורה זה הכלל האוכל מן התורה פטור ושאינו אוכל מן התורה חייב: ח ב) ג היה עושה בלבסים לא יאכל בבנות שבע בבנות שבע לא יאכל בלבסים אבל ג) מונע הוא את עצמו עד שמגיע למקום היפות ואוכל ד) המחליף עם חברו זה לאכול וזה לאכול זה לקצות וזה לקצות זה לאכול וזה לקצות חייב רבי יהודה אומר ד המחליף לאכול חייב ולקצות פטור:

פרק שלישי

א המעביר ה) תאנים בחצרו לקצות בניו ובני ביתו אוכלים ופטורין הפועלים שעמו בזמן שאין להם עליו מזונות אוכלין ופטורין אבל אם יש להם עליו מזונות הרי אלו לא יאכלו: ב ה המוציא פועליו לשדה בזמן שאין להם עליו מזונות אוכלין ופטורים ואם יש להם עליו מזונות אוכלין אחת אחת מן התאנה אבל לא מן הסל ולא מן הקופה ולא מן המוקצה: ג ו השוכר את הפועל לעשות בזיתים אמר לו על מנת לאכול זיתים אוכל אחד אחד פטור ואם צירף חייב ז לנכש בבצלים אמר לו על מנת לאכול ירק מקרטם עלה עלה ואוכל ואם צירף חייב: ד ו) ח מצא *קציצות בדרך אפילו בצד שדה *קציצות ט וכן תאנה שהיא נוטה על

...ייחור אחד ומשני לכאן צריך שיהיו שתיהן בייחור אחד כגון שלבסים ותאנים מורכבין בייחור אחד וביר' (שם) דריש לה מדכתיב (דברים כג) כי תבא בכרם רעך ואכלת ענבים כנפשך שבעך וכי אין אנו יודעין שאין בכרם אלא ענבים מה ת"ל ואכלת ענבים אלא מכאן שאם היה עושה בתאנים לא יאכל בענבים בענבים לא יאכל בתאנים כנפשך כל דבר שיגר תאב שבעך שלא יאכל ומקיא: המחליף עם חבירו זה לאכול וזה לאכול · שזה נוטל מזה תאנים וזה מזה: וכן אם זה נוטל מזה תאנים לקצות וזה מזה לקצות היינו כמקח וחייב ואמרינן בירושלמי (שם) א"ר אלעזר רבי מאיר היא דרבי מאיר אמר מקח טובל בפירות שלא נגמרה מלאכתן א"ר אלעזר רבי מאיר ורבי אליעזר אמרו דבר אחד כמו דרבי אליעזר אמר תרומה טובלת בפירות שלא נגמרה מלאכתן כך אמר ר' מאיר מקח טובל בדבר שלא נגמרה מלאכתו ודרבי אליעזר בפירקין לעיל (מ"ד): לקצות פטור · דסבר רבי יהודה דאין מקח טובל בדבר שלא נגמרה מלאכתו:

א המעביר תאני' בחצרו לקצות · להוליכן למקום שעושי' אותם קציעות:

בני ביתו אוכלין ופטורים · דאין חצר קובעת בדבר שלא נגמר מלאכתו ובירושלמי (הל' א) בעי הוא עצמו מהו שיאכל רב אמר אסור עולא אמר מותר ומפרש טעמא דרב משום דאין אוכלין על המוקצה אלא על מקומו במקום שמקצין אותן לא בחצר משום דבמקומו ניכר שלא נגמרה מלאכתו אבל חוץ למקומו סברי דנגמרה וקאמר התם בירושלמי דרב כרבי דאמר רבי יוסי בן שאול בשם רבי אין אוכלין על המוקצה אלא על מקומו מתיב ר' יוסי בן

ואחד מהם וכבר זכרנו כי המכר קובע ... אומר כל החליפין בשטוחין כיון שהוא ... במעשר ולא נקבעו למעשר בזה המכר ...

א העיקר אללנו החלר קובעת ...

MISHNAH 6. IF A MAN SAID TO HIS FELLOW: 'HERE IS AN ISSAR FOR TEN FIGS WHICH I MAY SELECT FOR ME',[11] HE MAY SELECT AND EAT;[12] [IF HE SAID] 'FOR A CLUSTER OF GRAPES WHICH I MAY SELECT FOR ME', HE MAY PICK GRAPES
a FROM THE CLUSTER AND EAT;[1] [IF HE SAID], 'FOR A POMEGRANATE WHICH I MAY SELECT FOR ME', HE MAY SPLIT[2] [THE POMEGRANATE] AND EAT [A SLICE]; [IF HE SAID] 'FOR A WATER-MELON, WHICH I MAY SELECT FOR ME', HE MAY SLICE AND EAT;[3] IF HE, HOWEVER, SAID 'FOR THESE TWENTY FIGS', OR 'FOR THESE TWO CLUSTERS', OR 'FOR THESE TWO WATER-MELONS', HE MAY EAT THEM IN HIS USUAL WAY AND BE EXEMPT [FROM TITHE], BECAUSE HE BOUGHT THEM WHILST THEY WERE STILL ATTACHED TO THE GROUND.[4]

MISHNAH 7. IF A MAN HIRED A LABOURER TO HELP HIM HARVEST FIGS,[5] AND HE [THE LABOURER] SAID UNTO HIM, 'ON CONDITION THAT I MAY EAT THE FIGS', HE MAY EAT THEM AND BE EXEMPT [FROM TITHE].[6] IF HE, HOWEVER, SAID, 'ON CONDITION THAT I AND MY SON MAY EAT',[7] OR 'THAT MY SON MAY EAT OF THEM IN LIEU OF MY RECEIVING A WAGE',[8] HE MAY EAT AND BE EXEMPT [FROM TITHE], BUT IF HIS SON EATS HE IS LIABLE. IF HE SAID: 'ON CONDITION THAT I MAY EAT OF THEM DURING THE TIME OF THE FIG HARVEST, AND AFTER THE FIG HARVEST', DURING THE TIME OF THE FIG HARVEST HE MAY EAT AND BE EXEMPT [FROM TITHE], BUT IF HE EATS AFTER THE FIG HARVEST HE IS LIABLE, SINCE HE DOES NOT EAT OF THEM AFTER THE MANNER PRESCRIBED
b BY THE TORAH.[1] THIS IS THE GENERAL RULE: ONE WHO EATS AFTER THE MANNER PRESCRIBED BY THE TORAH IS EXEMPT [FROM TITHE], AND ONE WHO DOES NOT EAT AFTER THE MANNER PRESCRIBED BY THE TORAH IS LIABLE.[2]

MISHNAH 8. IF A MAN IS DOING [HIRED LABOUR] AMONG POOR FIGS, HE MAY NOT EAT OF GOOD FIGS,[3] AND IF HE IS DOING [HIRED LABOUR] AMONG GOOD FIGS, HE MAY NOT EAT OF THE POOR FIGS, BUT HE MAY RESTRAIN HIMSELF UNTIL HE REACHES THE PLACE WHERE THERE ARE THE BETTER FIGS,[4] AND THEN HE MAY EAT. IF A MAN EXCHANGES WITH HIS FELLOW EITHER HIS FRESH FIGS FOR HIS FRESH FIGS,[5]

(11) Which I may select and gather from the trees. (12) He may pluck them one by one, and eat without tithing. If, however, he plucked two together he is liable to give tithe.

a (1) He may gather the single berries from the cluster which he has chosen and eat. The cluster itself must be attached to the ground, otherwise even under these conditions, he is liable. (2) While the pomegranate is still attached to the ground he may eat it slice by slice. (3) He may cut off separate thin slices from the fruit whilst it is attached to the ground. (4) Since he bought that which was attached to the ground his is the same ruling as that of the owner of the garden who may eat a chance meal until he reaches his house (v. *supra* I, 5). For the sale does not fix the liability to tithe in that which is attached to the ground. (5) Either to cut them or to store them for drying. (6) The condition does not invalidate anything normally observed, since even without this stipulation he is legally entitled to eat, according to Deut. XXIII, 25: '*If thou shalt come to the vineyard of thy friend and thou shalt eat grapes*' etc., which verse refers to a workman. It is therefore not like a sale and does not therefore fix liability to tithing. (7) The eating by the son constitutes a sale and therefore fixes the liability to tithing. (8) In lieu of wages for my work, and instead of my eating.

b (1) Since his status is then not one of a workman, he eats on the basis of a condition, and hence it is like a sale. (2) V. B.M. 87*b* as to what work entitles the labourer to eat. (3) Deduced from Deut. XXIII, 25. V. *supra* 47*b* n. a 6. (4) The labourer who harvests both amongst poor and good figs restrains himself from eating whilst working amongst the poor figs, and then when he arrives at the good figs, he may eat even the amount due to him from the previous poor figs. (5) Lit., 'the one to eat, and the one to eat'. If he says, you eat my fresh figs and I yours.

◁ *For the continuation of the English translation of this page see overleaf.*

ו האומר לחבירו הילך איסר זה בעשר תאנים שאבור לי בורר ואוכל באשכול שאבור לי מגרגר ואוכל ברמון שאבור לי פורט ואוכל באבטיח שאבור לי *סופת ואוכל אבל אם אמר לו בעשרים תאנים אלו בשני אשכלות אלו בשני רמונים אלו בשני אבטיחים אלו אוכל כדרכו ופטור מפני שקנה במחובר לקרקע: ז השוכר את הפועל לקצות עמו בתאנים אמר לו על מנת שאוכל תאנים אוכל ופטור על מנת שאוכל אני ובני (ביתי) או שיאכל בני בשכרי הוא אוכל ופטור ובנו אוכל וחייב על מנת שיאכל בשעת הקציעה ולאחר הקציעה בשעת הקציעה אוכל ופטור ולאחר הקציעה אוכל וחייב שאינו אוכל מן התורה זה הכלל האוכל מן התורה פטור ושאינו אוכל מן התורה חייב: ח היה עושה בלבסים לא יאכל בבנות שבע בבנות שבע לא יאכל בלבסים אבל מונע הוא את עצמו עד שמגיע למקום היפות ואוכל המחליף עם חברו זה לאכול וזה לאכול זה לקצות וזה לקצות זה לאכול וזה לקצות חייב רבי יהודה אומר המחליף לאכול חייב ולקצות פטור:

פרק שלישי

א המעביר תאנים בחצרו לקצות בניו ובני ביתו אוכלים ופטורין הפועלים שעמו בזמן שאין להם עליו מזונות אוכלין ופטורין אבל אם יש להם עליו מזונות הרי אלו לא יאכלו: ב המוציא פועליו לשדה בזמן שאין להם עליו מזונות אוכלין ופטורים ואם יש להם עליו מזונות אוכלין אחת אחת מן התאנה אבל לא מן הסל ולא מן הקופה ולא מן המוקצה: ג השוכר את הפועל לעשות בזיתים אמר לו על מנת לאכול זיתים אוכל אחד אחד פטור ואם צירף חייב לנכש בבצלים אמר לו על מנת לאכול ירק מקרטם עלה עלה ואוכל ואם צירף חייב: ד מצא *קציצות בדרך אפילו בצד שדה *קציצות וכן תאנה שהיא נוטה על

Continuation of translation from previous page as indicated by ◁

HIS DRIED FIGS FOR HIS DRIED FIGS,[6] HIS FRESH FIGS FOR HIS DRIED FIGS, THEN HE IS LIABLE TO GIVE TITHE.[7] R. JUDAH, HOWEVER, SAYS: IF A MAN EXCHANGES [HIS FIGS] FOR [HIS FELLOW'S] FRESH FIGS HE IS LIABLE, BUT [IF FOR THE OTHER'S] DRIED FIGS HE IS EXEMPT.[8]

CHAPTER III

MISHNAH 1. If a man was taking his figs through
c his courtyard to be dried,[1] his children and the other members of his household[2] may eat [of them] and be exempt [from tithe].[3] The labourers[4] [who work] with him may eat,[5] and be exempt[6] so long as he is not obliged to maintain them;[7] if, however, he is obliged to maintain them,[8] they may not eat.[9]

MISHNAH 2. If a man brought his labourers into the field,[10] so long as he is not obliged to maintain them, they may eat and be exempt from tithes.[11] If, however, he is obliged to maintain them they may eat of the figs one at a time,[12] but not from the basket, nor from the large vessels, nor from the drying shed.[13]

MISHNAH 3. If a man hired a workman to prepare
d his olives[1] and he said to him, 'on condition that I may eat the olives',[2] he may eat of them one at a time and be exempt [from tithe]. If, however, he ate several together he is liable. [If he had been hired] to weed out onions,[3] and he said to him, 'on condition that I may eat the vegetables', he may pluck leaf by leaf,[4] and eat [without tithing]; if, however, he ate several together, he is liable [to give tithe].[5]

MISHNAH 4. If a man found cut figs[6] on the road, or even beside a field [where cut figs] have been spread [to dry] (and so, too, if a fig tree overhangs

(6) Lit., 'the one to store' etc.. A similar stipulation with regard to figs spread out to dry. (7) Since the exchange is considered equivalent to the sale. (8) R. Judah holds that a sale does not fix liability to tithe in regard to anything the work of which is unfinished, as in the case of figs stored for drying.

c (1) He was taking them through his courtyard to the place where they were to be dried. (2) His wife. (3) Because a courtyard does not fix the liability to tithing any produce the work of which is not complete. Nevertheless he himself is still forbidden to make a chance meal of them, without tithing, except in the place where they are to be dried, where it is evident that the work in connection with the figs has not been completed. (4) Whom he has hired to take the fruit through the courtyard. Then it is a work which does not entitle them to eat; v. *supra* II, 7. (5) If he offered the fruit to them. (6) A gift, unlike a sale, does not fix liability to tithing; v. *supra* II, 2. (7) Lit., 'their food is not upon him'. So long as he has not stipulated that he will maintain them. (8) He stipulated he would maintain them. (9) For this is like a sale. (10) For some other work, and not to gather fruits, and therefore, not entitled Biblically to eat. (11) If he gave unto them, because a gift does not follow the same ruling as a sale. (12) Which is a casual meal and permissible even in the case of a sale, unless the work in connection with the produce had been completed. (13) In these cases it is treated as produce taken to the market, which is in itself sufficient to fix liability to tithing; v. *supra* I, 5.

d (1) To hoe beneath the olives, but not to gather, and therefore not entitled to eat according to the Biblical law. (2) This is equivalent to a sale. (3) To weed out the bad herbs which grow beneath the onions. This also does not entitle him to eat Biblically. (4) Singly, from that which is joined to the ground. (5) The combination of several together constitutes a kind of threshing-floor and fixes liability to tithing; v. *supra* II, 5. (6) קציצות, figs partly dried. The development in the growth of figs is as follows: When they are plucked from the tree and are still juicy they are called in Hebrew תאנים; after this, when they are laid upon mats of reed grass to be dried, and their surface contracts a little when they begin to dry they are called קציעות or קציצות. Then when they are altogether dried they are called גרוגרות, and finally, when they are trodden into a round cake they are called דבילה. The vessel in which the figs are dried is called מוקצה.

THE ROAD, AND FIGS WERE FOUND BENEATH IT), THEY ARE ALLOWED [AS NOT COMING WITHIN THE LAW] OF ROBBERY,[7] AND THEY ARE EXEMPT FROM TITHE;[8] OLIVES AND CAROBS, HOWEVER, ARE LIABLE.[9] IF A MAN FOUND DRIED FIGS, THEN IF THE MAJORITY OF PEOPLE HAD ALREADY TRODDEN [THEIR
a FIGS],[1] HE IS LIABLE [TO TITHE], BUT IF NOT HE IS EXEMPT. IF A MAN FOUND SLICES OF FIG-CAKE[2] HE IS LIABLE [TO TITHE], SINCE IT IS OBVIOUS THEY COME FROM SOMETHING [THE WORK IN CONNECTION THEREWITH IS] FULLY COMPLETED. WITH CAROBS,[3] IF THEY HAD NOT YET BEEN ON THE TOP OF THE ROOF, HE MAY TAKE SOME DOWN FOR THE CATTLE[4] AND BE EXEMPT [FROM TITHE], SINCE HE MAY RETURN THAT WHICH IS LEFT OVER.[5]

MISHNAH 5. WHICH COURTYARD IS IT WHICH MAKES [THE PRODUCE] LIABLE TO TITHE.[6] R. ISHMAEL SAYS: THE TYRIAN YARD [WITH A LODGE AT THE ENTRANCE],[7] WHEREIN WATCH IS KEPT OVER THE VESSELS. R. AKIBA SAYS: ANY YARD WHICH ONE PERSON MAY OPEN AND ANOTHER MAY SHUT [AS THEY PLEASE],[8] IS EXEMPT. R. NEHEMIAH SAYS: ANY YARD IN WHICH A MAN IS NOT ASHAMED TO EAT, IS LIABLE. R. JOSE SAYS: ANY YARD INTO WHICH A PERSON[9] MAY ENTER, AND ONE DOES NOT SAY UNTO HIM, WHAT ARE YOU SEEKING? IS
b EXEMPT.[1] R. JUDAH SAYS: 'IF THERE ARE TWO YARDS ONE WITHIN THE OTHER, THE INNER ONE MAKES [THE PRODUCE] LIABLE [TO TITHE], THE OUTER ONE IS EXEMPT'.[2]

MISHNAH 6. ROOFS DO NOT RENDER [PRODUCE] LIABLE, EVEN THOUGH THEY BELONG TO A COURTYARD WHICH RENDERS IT LIABLE.[3] A GATEWAY,[4] PORTICO,[5] OR BALCONY,[6] IS CONSIDERED [IN THE SAME CATEGORY] AS THE COURTYARD [TO WHICH IT BELONGS]; IF THIS MAKES [PRODUCE] LIABLE [TO TITHE] SO DO THEY, AND IF IT DOES NOT, THEY DO NOT.

MISHNAH 7. CONE-SHAPED HUTS,[7] THE STORES IN TURRETS,[8] AND SHEDS IN THE FIELD[9] DO NOT RENDER [PRODUCE] LIABLE; THE LODGE OF GENESARETH GARDENS,[10] EVEN THOUGH IT CONTAINS HANDMILL AND POULTRY,[11] DOES NOT RENDER [PRODUCE] LIABLE. AS FOR THE POTTER'S HUT,[12] THE INNER PART RENDERS [PRODUCE] LIABLE, THE OUTER PART DOES NOT. R. JOSE SAYS: ANYTHING WHICH IS NOT BOTH A SUMMER AND WINTER DWELLING DOES NOT
c RENDER [PRODUCE] LIABLE [TO TITHES].[1] AS REGARDS THE FESTIVE BOOTHS USED ON THE FESTIVAL, R. JUDAH SAYS: THIS ALSO RENDERS [PRODUCE] LIABLE TO TITHE,[2] BUT THE SAGES SAY: IT DOES NOT.

MISHNAH 8. IF A FIG TREE STOOD IN A COURTYARD,[3] A MAN MAY EAT THE FIGS FROM IT SINGLY AND BE EXEMPT [FROM TITHE], BUT IF HE TOOK TWO OR MORE TOGETHER HE IS LIABLE. R. SIMEON SAYS: [EVEN] IF HE HAS [AT ONE AND THE SAME TIME] ONE IN HIS RIGHT HAND, ONE IN HIS LEFT HAND AND ONE IN HIS MOUTH, HE IS STILL EXEMPT.[4] IF HE ASCENDED TO THE TOP [OF IT],[5] HE MAY FILL HIS BOSOM AND EAT.[6]

MISHNAH 9. IF A VINE WAS PLANTED IN A COURTYARD,

(7) Because when a fig falls it is spoilt and the owners have therefore disclaimed ownership from it. Similarly, where the figs are found on the road, it is assumed the owner has surrendered his ownership of them. (8) As all ownerless produce. (9) It is considered robbery because the owners do not give it up; moreover its appearance proves that it fell from this tree; but when a fig falls it is spoilt, and it is not known from which tree it fell.

a (1) If the majority of the inhabitants of that city had already trodden their dried figs in their fields, we can see, therefore, that these are also from the trodden ones, and therefore have become liable to tithe, and this liability remains even when the produce becomes ownerless. (2) After the round cake has been trodden, it is divided up into many slices. (3) This does not refer to a find, but to the case where a man had carobs on his roof. Since it was his intention to bring them up on to this roof in order to dry them, therefore their work is not complete, and their liability to tithe is not fixed by the courtyard. (4) Though they are already on the roof, provided they have not been thoroughly dried, and not yet heaped up there for storing (*Tif. Yis.*). (5) To the place where he spreads them out to dry; even if he has brought down much for the cattle, he is nevertheless exempt. (6) Which like a house determines the tithe brought there. (7) In the province of Tyre there sat a watchman at the entrance to the courtyard (cf. Isa. XXIII, 8). Because all the inhabitants of Tyre were princes and dwelt in royal residences, therefore out of respect for them, there was also a lodge to their court in which sat a watchman (*Tif. Yis.*). (8) I.e., in a court in which there are two houses for two men, and where one opens the entrance of the court, the second may come in and close it; similarly where one locks it, the second may object and open it, such a court is 'not well-guarded'. (9) A stranger.

b (1) Even though he is not ashamed to eat in it. (2) Since access is gained to the inner one through the outer one, the latter is not considered 'well guarded'. (3) Even though he has brought the produce up to the roof by the way of the courtyard, it is nevertheless not liable to tithe, since at the time he brought them into the courtyard it was his intention to bring them up, and to eat them on the roof. (4) Near the entrance of the courtyard. (5) *Exedra*, a covered place in front of the house surrounded by three walls. (6) A gallery from which one descends by a ladder to the courtyard. (7) They have no roof, but the walls at the top touch one another and then gradually broaden downwards. (8) Sort of network arrangement in the field, to store therein the fruits. Often used as a station for travellers. (9) A booth erected in the summer and generally in the days of the sun as a shade. A shed for stacks in the field. (10) The district of the Sea of Galilee, where the fruits are many and good, and its inhabitants make booths in which to dwell during the entire season of the fruits, which means actually the greater part of the year. (11) Which indicates that this is their dwelling place day and night. (12) It has two booths, one within the other; in the outer one he makes dishes etc. and sells them, and in the inner one, where he lives, he keeps and stores them.

c (1) Consequently, since the potter does not live in the inner booth in the rainy season, it does not render produce liable. (2) He holds the opinion that since the booth is a regular abode it fixes liability to tithing. The law was not according to R. Judah. (3) Of a kind which renders produce liable for tithing. (4) Even three taken in this manner are not considered as taken together, and are allowed. (5) The fig-tree. (6) Only at the top of the tree. He is allowed to eat so long as he does not descend into the courtyard.

א) נדה פ"ה ד' מז: ב) [סוכה פ"א דף ח:]: ג) יומא פ"א דף י:

לא הוי יאוש : ופטורין מן המעשר כהפקר : בזיתים ובחרובין חייב . דלא מייאש ולא הוי הפקר ואסור משום גזל ומפרש באלו מציאות משום דחזותו מוכיח עליו של מי הוא אבל תאנה עם נפילתה נמאסת ולא ידיע : אם דרסו רוב בני אדם חייב . דסתמא מן הדרוסות הן (ד) ופריך בירושלמי (הל' א) ולא בבתים הן נדרסות כלומר ע"כ בשדה עסקינן (ה) ומשני א"ר בון בר חייא תיפתר שרוב דורסין על השדות רבי זעירא בעי ואינה ניכרת אם דרוסה היא אם לא בתמיהא ומשני א"ר שאול פעמים שהיא פוקעת מתחת הגלגל והיא דרוסה והיא נראית שאינה דרוסה פעמים שהרגל דורסה והיא אינה דרוסה ונראית כדרוסה : פלחי דבילה· לאחר שנדרסו בעיגול מחלקין העיגול לכמה פלחין ובפלח יש הרבה תאנים דבוקות יחד וכדתנן בפ"ה דדמאי (משנה ה) וכן עני שנתנו לו פרוסות פת או פלחי דבילה מעשר מכל אחד : מדבר גמור · למעשר שנגמרה מלאכתו: עד שלא כינס לראש הגג· דהיינו ערימה שזהו גרן של חרובין למעשר כדתנן לעיל בפרק קמא (משנה ו) : מוריד מהן לבהמה. דאוכלין על המוקצה בין במקומן בין שלא במקומן אפי' לרב כדפרשינן לעיל אבל לעולם לאו דווקא לבהמה והוא הדין לאדם והא דנקט בהמה כדמפרש בירושלמי (שם) לפי שאין דרך תלמיד חכם לאכול בשוק : שהוא מחזיר את המותר למוקצה כל היכא דמותרו חוזר לא נטבל כדאמרינן בסוף פרק המביא (דף לה) : ה שחייבת במעשרות . שקובעת תבואה למעשר דקיי"ל חצר קובעת : חצר הצורית שהכלים נשמרין בתוכה. בסוף יוצא דופן (מ"ז:) אמר רבה בר בר חנה אמר רבי יוחנן שכן בצור מעמידין שומר [על] פתח החצר : כל שאחד פותח ואחד נועל פטורה · בירושלמי (הל' ג) תניא רבי שמעון בן אליעזר משום רבי עקיבא כל שאחד פותח ואחד נועל בשני שותפין ולא בשני דיורין ופריך עלה מה בין שותף מה בין דיור כשם שהשותף ממחה כך דיור ממחה דיורין קרי ב' שוכרים ומוחה בחברו שלא ינעול ואינה משתמרת ומשני א"ר יונה בבעל הבית ודיורו היא מתני' בעל הבית ממחה ע"י דיור ואין דיור ממחה ע"י בעה"ב כלומר לא בב' דיורין דקתני היינו בבעל הבית ודיורו דמשתמרת היא : ואינו אומר מה אתה מבקש פטורים. ואע"פ שאינו בוש לאכול בתוכה : והחיצונה פטורה. לפי שהפנימית יש לה דרך על החיצונה ואין החיצונה יכולה לנעול ואמר בירושלמי (שם) רבי בון בר חייא בעי קומי רבי זעירא מה בא רבי יהודה להוסיף על דברי רבי עקיבא רבו אמר לו ולא כלום ובסוף פ' יוצא דופן (מז:) פסק הלכה כדברי כולן להחמיר ויש לתמוה דאמרינן בהשוכר את הפועלים (פח·) אמר רבי ינאי אין הטבל מתחייב במעשר עד שיראה פני הבית שנאמר בערתי הקדש מן הבית ור' יוחנן אמר אפילו חצר קובעת שנאמר ואכלו בשעריך ושבעו ורבי יוחנן הכתיב בית חצר דומיא דבית מה בית שהכלים נשמרין בתוכה ואידך הכתיב ואכלו בשעריך דמעייל להו דרך שער והשתא לרבי ינאי דפטר חצר אפילו בכלים נשמרין לתוכה תיקשי לך מתניתין דהכא ומיהו הך איכא לשנויי דאיירי לענין להכניס דרך חצר צורית לבית לאפוקי דרך חיצונה דלא והא דתני חיצונה פטור שנכנס דרך חיצונה לבתים הפתוחין לה והעביר תאנים בחצרו לקצות דריש פרקין וכן הא דתנן בפרק ח' דתרומות (מ"ג) היה אוכל באשכול ונכנס מן הגינה לחצר אע"פ שלא הזכיר בית מ"מ מיירי כשחזר והכניסן לבית אבל קשה דמתני' דתרומות משמע דדווקא התחיל בגינה אבל התחיל בחצר לדברי הכל אסור ודוחק לומר בשחזר והכניס לבית ועוד דגבי נוטה לגינה קתני (לקמן מ"י) אוכל כדרכו ועוד מדקתני בפרק הפועלים (שם) הכא בתאנה העומדת בגינה ונופה נוטה לחצר ולמאן דאמר לבית מה מועיל נופה נוטה לבית והלא דרך חצר צריך להכניס לביתו ומפרש רבינו תם דר' ינאי מדאורייתא קאמר אבל מודי דמדרבנן חצר קובעת : ו של חצר· קובעת החייבת · מפורשת לעיל ובירושלמי (שם) אמר ר"א בגג לאויר חצר היא מתניתין כלומר אע"פ שעומד באמצע חצר שמוקפת לגג מסביב וא"א להביא לגג אלא דרך חצר ופריך מכיון שהעבירם דרך חצר לא נטבלו ומשני תפתר או כרבי יוסי בר' יהודה או כר' שהיה בדעתו לעשותן מוקצה ונמלך שלא לעשותן ופלוגתא דר' יוסי בר' יהודה ורבי בתוספתא (פ"ב) דתניא המביא תאנים מן השדה לאוכלן בראש גגו שכח והכניסן לחצר חברו לא יאכל מהן עראי רבי יוסי בר"י אומר מעלן לראש גגו ואוכל ותנא קמא הוא ר' ובירושלמי (הל' א) גרסינן הביא תאנים מן השדה והעבירן בחצרו לאוכלן בראש גגו ר' מחייב ור' יוסי בר' יהודה פוטר וגירסא זו עיקר והשתא מתניתין לרבי יוסי בר' יהודה אתיא בפשיטות אבל לר' לא מתוקמא מתניתין אלא כשהיה בדעתו לעשותן מוקצה ולא נטבלו בחצר ואחר כך נמלך לאוכלן לאחר שהעלן לגגו ומסיק בירושלמי א"ר בון והוא שיהא בגג ד' אמות על ד' אמות מה הבית אינו טובל עד שיהא בו ד' אמות על ד' אמות אף הגג אינו פוטר עד שיהא בו ד' אמות על ד' אמות כלומר דלא חשיב ובטל אגב חצר חייבת דתניא בית שאין בו ד' אמות פטור מן המעקה ומן המזוזה ומן העירוב ואינו טובל למעשרות כולה הך ברייתא מייתי לה בפ"ק דסוכה (ג·) ולא קתני התם ולא טובל למעשרות ואיכא מילי התם דלא תני הכא : בית שער · לפני הבית : וכן אכסדרה. שאין לה אלא ג' דפנות כדאמרינן (ב"ב דף כה:) עולם לאכסדרה הוא דומה ורוח צפונית אינה מסובבת : מרפסת · לפני העלייה ויש עליות פתוחות לה ומחצר עולין בסולם למרפסת : ז צריפין . בית שגגו וקירותיו שוין צר מלמעלה מרחיב והולך עד הארץ בגג המשפע ורגילין לעשותן ממורביות של ערבה : בורגנין . כמין סוכבין · עשויין בשדות לאצור בהן תבואה : אלקטיות . מלשון קייטא תרגום קיץ בתים העשויין מחוץ לעיר להתקרר בהן לקיץ כדכתיב (שופטים ג) עלית המקרה תרגום בית קייטא יס כנרת תרגומו יס גינוסר (במדבר לד) ויש שם גנות ופרדסין מתוך שפירותיה מתוקין ועושין שם סוכות ואף על פי שיש שם ריחים ותרנגולים פטורה דלאו בית דירה היא ובירושלמי (שם) בעי מהו שיטבלו לבעל הבורגנין ומסיק מן מה דתני בית ספר ובית גמרא טובלין לסופר למשנה אבל לא לאחרים הדא אמרה שהן טובלין לבעל הבורגנין : סוכת היוצרין · כך היה דרך של יוצרי כלי חרס עושין להם שתי סוכות זו לפנים מזו בפנימית הוא דר ומלגיע קדרותיו א] למכור : שאינה דירת החמה ודירת הגשמים כי הך דיוצרין דאפילו פנימית אינה דירת הגשמים : רבי יהודה מחייב · כדאמר בפרק קמא דיומא (דף י:) רבי יהודה לטעמיה סוכה דירת קבע היא ומיחייבא במזוזה : ח תאנה . האילן קרי תאנה : עומדת בחצר החייבת : ר"ש אומר אחת בימינו · בכי האי גוונא שרי רבי שמעון : בירושלמי (הל' ד) רבי אליעזר ברבי שמעון שלשה בימינו ושלשה בשמאלו [ושלשה בפיו] רבי אליעזר ב"ר שמעון על ידי שהיה אכלן הוה מעשר בגרמיה : עלה לראשה · של תאנה ממלא את חיקו ואוכל שם ובלבד שלא יוריד למטה בחצר : ט בחצר החייבת : נוטל את האשכול ואוכל כדרכו ואינו צריך לגרגר וכן ברמון ואבטיח תולש אחד ואוכל כדרכו ואין צריך לפרר הרמון ולספות באבטיח ובירושלמי (שם) אמר רבי זעירא בשם רבי יוחנן רבי טרפון כרבי אליעזר דמסכת תרומות בפרק ח' (משנה ג) דתנן היה אוכל באשכול ונכנס מגינה לחצר רבי אליעזר אומר יגמור אף הכא רבי טרפון דעבד עוקצת האשכול כתחלתו דטעמא דרבי אליעזר משום שבו התחיל בהיתר וכן רבי טרפון עביד אכילה שיש בה ב' וג' אכילות באכילה ב] והדר מסיק אמר רבי נתן לא שרבי אליעזר אומר שהתחיל בו בהיתר אלא שרבי אליעזר אומר ימתין עד שתצא שבת או עד שיוציא חוץ לחצר ויגמור וכן מסקנא בסוף המביא :

מגרגר

הדרך ומצא תחתיה תאנים מותרות משום גזל ופטורות מן המעשרות ובזיתים ובחרובים חייבים [א]מצא גרוגרות אם דרסו רוב בני אדם חייב ואם לאו פטור מצא פלחי דבילה חייב שידוע שהן מדבר גמור [ב]והחרובים עד שלא כנסם לראש הגג מוריד מהם לבהמה פטור מפני שהוא מחזיר את המותר : ה [א)] איזוהי חצר שהיא חייבת במעשרות [ג]רבי ישמעאל אומר חצר הצורית שהכלים נשמרים בתוכה [ד]ר' עקיבא אומר כל שאחד פותח ואחד נועל פטורה רבי נחמיה אומר [ה]כל שאין אדם בוש מלאכול בתוכה חייבת רבי יוסי אומר [ו]כל שנכנס ואין אומר מה אתה מבקש פטורה רבי יהודה אומר [ז]שני חצרות זו לפנים מזו הפנימית חייבת והחיצונה פטורה : ו [ח]הגגות פטורין אף על פי שהם של חצר החייבת [ט]בית שער אכסדרה ומרפסת הרי אלו כחצר אם חייבת חייבין ואם פטורה פטורין : ז [י]הצריפין והבורגנין והאלקטיות פטורין סוכת גנוסר אע"פ שיש בו רחיים ותרנגולים פטורה [ג)]סוכת היוצרים הפנימית חייבת והחיצונה פטורה רבי יוסי אומר כל שאינה דירת החמה ודירת הגשמים פטורה [ג)]סוכת החג בחג רבי יהודה מחייב וחכמים [כ]פוטרין : ח [ל]תאנה שהיא עומדת בחצר אוכל אחת אחת ופטור (ו) ואם צירף חייב רבי שמעון אומר אחת בימינו ואחת בשמאלו ואחת בפיו עלה לראשה ממלא חיקו ואוכל : ט גפן שהיא נטועה בחצר נוטל את

בזיתים ובחרובים חייבים בתנאי שימצא הזיתים תחת אילן הזיתים והחרובין תחת אילן החרובין וזה מבואר כי אלו הגרגרים שנפלו מאלו האילנות נפלו ולפיכך יש בהם משום גזל וחייבין במעשרות אבל התאנים שמהלכלכין ומשהגים בלורתן כשמצא אותן תחת התאנה אינו מכיר אם מזו התאנה נפלו ונשתנו ומפני זה אינן דומים לשאר התאנים שבתאנה או אם באו ממקום אחר ואין לבעל התאנה בהם זכות ולפיכך אין בהם משום גזל ופטורים מן המעשר אבל יעשר דמאי בלבד כמו שבארנו במס' דמאי : אם דרסו כו'. ענינו אם רוב בני אדם דרסו התאנים שלהם בשדה כבר באו לגורן המעשרות ונאמר כי אלו הגרגרות הם ממה שדרסו בשדה ובאו לבית ונפלו אחר כך והוא חייב במעשרות ואם רוב בני אדם לא דרסו בשדה פטור לפי שנאמר קודם דריסה נפלו : ואמרם מפני שהוא מחזיר את המותר ענינו שהוא מחזיר אותו לגג ליבש והוא ראיה שעראי מאכיל: ה כמו שהבית קובעת למעשר כך החצר קובעת למעשר ובתנאי שלא תהיה החצר פתוחה כאילו היא הפקר שתהיה נשמרת וחלקו בזה כמו שתראה ואמרם כל שאחד פותח ואחד נועל ענינו שיהיה בחצר שני בתים לשני בני אדם ויניח זה הפתח פתוח ויבוא השני השוכן בבית האחר וינעול אותו או להפך והלכה כדברי כולם להחמיר: ו הגגות. ידוע כשהפירות לשם ולא נכנסו לבית פטורים מן המעשרו': בית שער . הוא שבוא הבית והוא נקרא פרוזדור : ואכסדרה . מקום מוקף משלש רוחותיו ובו קרוי : ומרפסת . מקום גבוה על קרקע החצר שבו הסולם קבוע שעולים בו אל העליות ועוד יתבאר זה בערובין (פ"ח מ"א) וממה שאתה צריך לידע כי הבית כשיש בו פחות מד' אמות על ד' אמות אינו קובע למעשר וכן הגג אינו פוטר למעשר אלא אם היה בו ארבע אמות על ארבע אמות או יותר : ז צריפים . הם כמו עמודים ועליהם קרוי כמין צריף והוא ידוע נקרא בערבי מכנס כזו הצורה :

והבורגנין הם כמו מגדלים עשויין לשמור הדרכים:אלקטיות. הם כמו סוכות עושים אותם בני אדם בימות החמה להיות צל על ראשם תרגום קר וחם (בראשי' ח) סיתווא וקייטא: וגנוסר מקום בארץ הצבי יש בו גנות רבות מדובר בו נכבדות ונפלאות ועושין בו אהלים לדירה כל זמן אסיפת הפירות וזה המקום הוא שקראו התורה כנרת (במדבר לד) : ויוצרים אומני כלי חרס וכבר פירשנו זה ואין הלכה כר"י והלכה כחכמים: ח ר"ש אומר שאם היתה תאנה אחת בפיו ואחת בימינו ואחת בשמאלו שאינו צירוף ואין הלכה כר"ש וזה כשהוא עומד בארץ

פי' מהר"י בן מלכי צדק

בזיתים ובחרובין אסורין*). משום גזל וחייבין דלא ידע דנתרי ולא מיאשי דיאוש שלא מדעת לא הוי יאוש כל זה פירשנו כאביי וקי"ל כוותיה אבל רבא דסבר יאוש שלא מדעת הוי יאוש בזיתין ובחרובין יהיב טעמא אחרינא דשאני זית וחרוב דחזותן מוכיח עליהו ואע"ג דנתרין (זיתיו) לא מיאש אמר לכי משכחנא להו אשקלינהו דמידע ידיען לי. אבל תאנה עם נפילתה נמאסת ולא ידיעה . א"ר יוחנן**) הא דתנן הזיתין והחרובין אסורין והוא שמצא זיתין תחת זיתין וחרובין תחת חרובין . אבל זיתין תחת חרובין וחרובין תחת זיתין לא דיש לומר מאדם אחר נפל ונתייאשו : מצא פלחי . פי' חתיכות דבילה חייב לעשר שידוע שמדבר גמור נינהו שמאחר שמעגלין אותן ונטבלו חותכין אותה במגירה כדתנן מגירה לחתוך בה את הדבילה . וכל חתיכה וחתיכה נקראת פלח דבילה: החרובין עד שלא כנסן לראש הגג . דהיינו הערימה שהן אינן נטבלין עד שיעמיד מהן ערימה : כדתנן הפרד והצימוקין והחרובין משיעמיד ערימה:מוריד מהן לבהמה ופטור מלעשר דקיימא לן אוכלין על המוקצה בין במקומו ובין שלא במקומו ואפילו רבי דאמר אין אוכלין מן המוקצה אלא במקומו . בחרובין מודה דחרובין מאכל בהמה הן : ה איזוהי חצר שחייבת במעשרות ר' ישמעאל אומר חצר הצורית שהכלים נשמרין וכו'. מאי חצר הצורית אמר רבה בר בר חנה אמר ר' יוחנן מקום שמושיבין שם שומר בחצרותיהן : רבי עקיבא א' כל שאחד פותח ואחד נועל פטורה . פי' כגון חצר דשותפין : רבי נחמיה אומר כל שאין אדם בוש לאכול בתוכה חייבת . ובוש ולא בוש מקום שבוש פטור מקום שאינו בוש חייב : רבי יהודה אומר ב' חצרות זו לפנים מזו הפנימית חייבת . דלא דרסי בני חיצונת עלה וכיון שכן הוא נועל הוא פותח : והחיצונה פטורה . פי' האיל ובני פנימית נפקי מתמן הוה ליה כחצר השותפין שהוא נועל ובני הפנימית פותחין שדרכן עליה רבי שמואל בר נחמני בשם ר' יונתן כל אלו התנאין מן הבית למדו בית טובל דבר תורה דכתיב בערתי הקדש מן הבית ובית כלים נשמרין שם ואין אדם בוש לאכול שם וכשנכנס אדם שם אומר לו מה תבקש וכו' : ו הגגות פטורין ואע"פ שהן של חצר החייבת . אמר רבי אלעזר בגג מבוצר לאויר חצר היא מתני' וקשה וכיון שכן לא באו הפירות לגג אלא דרך החצר וכיון דחצר חייבת היא נטבלו ואמאי פטורין ותירץ הא מני ר' יוסי בר' יהודה היא . דתניא הביא תאנים מן השדה והעבירן בחצרו לאוכלן בראש גגו רבי מחייב ורבי יוסי בן יהודה פוטר א"ר אבין הא דתנן גג פוטר והוא שיהא הגג ארבע אמות על ארבע אמות דומיא דבית מה בית אינו טובל עד שיהא ארבע אמות אף גג אינו פוטר עד שיהא ד' על ד' : בית שער של חצר הרי היא כחצר. פי' לחצירות איסקופות גדולות ויש להן ב' שערים זה לפנים מזה ואותו דביני ביני נקראת בית שער : אכסדרא . פי' עומדת לפני החצר ויש לה ג' רוחות ורביעית אין לה . וכך אמרו [בב"ב כ"ה] עולם לאכסדרא דומה והוא כגון זה [ב] אכסדרא ומרפסת . ובלעז קצילו ועומדת לפני החצר כל אלו אם מכנים שם פירות כמכנים לחצר אם חייבת אם פטורה פטורין : ז הצריפין . לעז פוירי : והבורגנין כמותן והן עשויין מחוץ לעיר : וכן אלקטיות . פי' בתים של קש . פ"א בתים עשויין חוץ לעיר להתקרר שם בקיץ פטורין . פ"א משעול שבין ביתו לבית חבירו כדתניא הלקט שבין שני בתים ובלעז איסטרישולא : סוכת גינוסר . פי' סוכה העשויה בגני גינוסר פי' כינרת ויש אומרים גני השרים אע"פ שיש שם רחים ותרנגולין פטורה דלאו שמה בית דירה : סוכת היוצרין . פי' סוכת יוצרי כלי חרס : הפנימית חייבת. דבית דירה היא : החיצונה פטורה. דלאו בית דירה היא:ר' יוסי אומר כל שאינה בית דירת החמה ודירת הגשמים פטורה : סוכת החג בחג . פי' סוכה בת ד' אמות ובת ד' פנות אם מכנים שם פירות בחג עצמו : רבי יהודה מחייב. דסוכת דירת קבע היא וכבית היא . וכך היה ר' יהודה מחייב בסוכת החג במזוזה: וחכמים פוטרין דדירת עראי היא : ח תאנה . פי' אילן תאנה: שעומדת בחצר. פי' בחצר חייבת אוכל אחת אחת ופטור : ואם צירף חייב . פי' שחצר טבלתן: רבי שמעון אומר . בזה הענין מותר תאנה אחת בימינו ואחת בשמאלו ואחת בפיו . תניא ר' אליעזר בר' שמעון אומר ג' בימינו וג' בשמאלו וג' בפיו רבי אליעזר בר' שמעון על ידי דרוה איניש אכלן הוה משער בגרמיה : עלה לראשה . פי' לראש התאנה : ממלא חיקו ואוכל . פי' ובלבד שלא יורידם למטה בחצר אלא שם בראש האילן יאכלם : ט גפן שהיא נטועה בחצר . פי' בחצר החייבת : נוטל את כל האשכול ואוכל כדרכו ואינו מגרגר וכן אם נטע שם אילן של רמון נוטל כדרכו ואינו

ו א מיי' פ"ג מהל' מעשר הלכה כא :
ז ב שם הלכה יח :
ח ג ד ה מיי' פ"ד שם הלכה ח :
ט ו שם :
י ז שם הלכה י :
יא ח שם הלכה ג :
יב ט שם הלכה ט :
יג י כ שם הל' ד ס :
יד ל שם הלכה טו :

פירוש הרא"ש

(ד)ונגמר' מלאכתן: (ה) דאילו מלאן בבית אסורין משום גזל וכיון שאין דרך לדרסן אלא בבית ודאי אלו לא נדרסו: (ו) ואם צירף שתים חייב וקשה דבפרק הפועלים (פח.) אמרינן גבי תאנה העומדת בגינה ונופה נוטה לחצר דלוקה חייב ובעל הבית עיניו בתאנתו ופטור והא דלוקח חייב היינו על פי שתים כדאמר התם קצן אחת אחת אוכל (שתים) ופטור ותי' התוס' בפ' הפועלים דהכא איירי בבעל הבית שאין דעתו ללקוט אלא מה שאוכל הלכך הוי לדידיה גמר בשתים והתם מיירי בבעל הבית ששכר פועל ללקוט כל התאנה הלכך עיניו בתאנתו ואינו גמר עד שילקט כל התאנה :

הגהות מהר"י לנדא

משנה ז בר"ש א] קדרותיו למכור. עי' רש"י סוכה ח. ועי' רע"ב במתניתין : שם מ"ט ב] ב' וג' אכילות כאכילה אחת. בירושלמי פ"ח דתרומות :

*) נראה דכן היה גורס במשנה אסורין וכ"ה ג"כ בב"מ כא: **) בירושלמי הגי' ר' יונה

כל האשכול וכן ברמון וכן באבטיח דברי רבי טרפון רבי עקיבא אומר ^א^מגרגר באשכול ופורט ברמון וסופת באבטיח ^ב^כסבר שהיא זרועה בחצר מקרטם עלה עלה ואוכל ואם צירף חייב ^ה)^ הסיאה והאזוב והקורנית שבחצר אם היו נשמרים חייבין : י ^ו^תאנה שהיא עומדת בחצר נוטה לגנה אוכל כדרכו ופטור עומדת בגנה ונוטה לחצר אוכל אחת אחת פטור ואם צירף חייב ^ז^עומדת בארץ ונוטה לחו"ל בחוצה לארץ ונוטה לארץ הכל הולך אחר העיקר ובבתי ערי חומה הכל הולך (ז) אחר העיקר ^ג)^ ^ח^ובערי מקלט הכל הולך אחר הנוף ^ט^ובירושלים הכל הולך אחר הנוף :

פרק רביעי

א הכובש ^א^השולק ^ב^המולח בשדה חייב ^ג^המכמן ^ג)^ באדמה פטור ^ד^המטבל בשדה פטור הפוצע זיתים שיצא מהם השרף פטור ^ה^הסוחט זיתים על בשרו פטור אם סחט ונתן לתוך ידו חייב המקפה לתבשיל פטור לקדרה חייב מפני שהוא כבור קטן : **ב** ^ג)^ ^ו^תינוקות שטמנו תאנים לשבת ושכחו לעשרן לא יאכלו למוצאי שבת עד שיעשרן ^ד)^ כלכלת שבת ב"ש פוטרין ^ז^וב"ה מחייבין ר' יהודה אומר אף הלוקט את הכלכלה לשלוח לחבירו לא יאכל עד שיעשר : **ג** ^ה)^ ^ח^הנוטל זיתים מן המעטן טובל אחד אחד במלח ואוכל אם מלח ונתן לפניו חייב ר"א אומר מן המעטן הטהור חייב ומן הטמא פטור מפני שהוא מחזיר את המותר : **ד** ^ו)^ שותין על הגת

מגרגר באשכול. גבי מקח תנן לעיל פרק ב' (משנה ו) כי האי גוונא ומודה ר' טרפון בההיא : [כוסבר· הוא] זרע גד : זרועה בחצר · בירושלמי (שם) תני בשם ר' נחמיה חצר שהיא נעדרת ונזרעת הרי היא כגינה אוכל בתוכה עראי : מקרטם · תולש : אם היו נשמרים חייבין · דאין חייב במעשר אלא אוכל ונשמר כדתנן בריש מכילתין : י בחצר החייבת : ונוטה לגינה · נוף אחד מן התאנה : אוכל כדרכו · העומד בגינה : אוכל אחת אחת · העומד בחצר : עומדת . בארץ ישראל : אחר העיקר · מקום יניקת אילן להתחייב במעשר : ובבתי ערי חומה הכל הולך אחר העיקר סתם מתניתין ר' מאיר דתנן בפרק המוכר שדהו וכו' (דף לג)· כל שהוא לפנים מן החומה הרי הוא כבתי ערי חומה חוץ מן השדות ר"מ אומר אף השדות ערי מקלט הכל הולך אחר הנוף כדאמר בפרק ואלו הן הגולין (דף יב·) אילן שהוא עומד בתוך התחום ונופו נוטה חוץ לתחום או עומד חוץ לתחום ונופו נוטה לתוך התחום הכל הולך אחר הנוף ומסיק רב אשי אף אחר הנוף דלא מיבעי עיקרו בפנים ונופו לחוץ כי היכי דבעיקרו לא מצי קטיל ליה בנופו נמי לא מצי קטיל ליה דהדי נופו בתר עיקרו אלא אפילו עיקרו בחוץ ונופו לפנים נמי כי היכי דבנופו לא מצי קטיל ליה בעיקרו נמי לא מצי קטיל ליה דהדי עיקרו בתר נופו לחומרא : וכן בירושלים הכל הולך אחר הנוף · לענין מעשר שני לחומרא דאי עיקרו בחוץ וטפו לפנים כי היכי דבנופו לא מצי פריק בעיקרו נמי לא מצי פריק ואי עיקרו בפנים ונופו לחוץ כי היכי דבנופו לא מצי אכיל ליה בלא פדייה בעיקרו נמי לא מצי אכיל ליה בלא פדייה והא דתנן במסכת מעשר שני (פ"ג מ"ז) אילן שעומד בפנים ונופו נוטה לחוץ או עומד בחוץ ונופו נוטה לפנים כנגד החומה ולפנים כלפנים כנגד החומה ולחוץ כלחוץ ההיא רבנן ומתניתין רבי יהודה ועוד יש לפרש דרב אשי דמכות *קאי לשנויי דלא תיקשי מתני' *דמעשר שני *והכי קאמר ובירושלים הלך אחר הנוף דבין נוף ובין עיקר מכנגד החומה ולפנים כלפנים ואוכלין שם מעשר שני ולא פודין מכנגד החומה ולחוץ בין נוף ובין עיקר כלחוץ ופודין מעשר שני ואין אוכלין :

א הכובש זיתים או ירקות שכבשן ביין או בשמן הכבישה קובעת וכן שליקה באור או מליחה ובירושלמי (הל' א) חשיב ו' דברים שהן טובלין אור טובל וכן מקח ומלח ושבת תרומה חצר בית שמירה טובלת אמר ר' יוחנן מקח ושבת אינן תורה רבי אמי בשם ריש לקיש המחור מכולן זו חצר בית שמירה הכונס עד שיכבוש כל צרכו השולק עד שישלוק כל צרכו נשמעיניה מן הדא מהבהב שבלין באור נטבלו בלא כן אינן מחוסרות מלאכה על ידי האור שנייא היא שהוא גמר מלאכה : מכמן באדמה · טומן הזיתים באדמה שיתחממו : מטבל · בחומץ או בציר : הפוצע בזיתים למתקן שילא המרירות שלהן : הסוחט זיתים על בשרו משום סיכה לא נטבלו בכך אא"כ סחט לתוך ידו דידו כחשבת כבור קטן וחייב : המקפה לתבשיל · אחר ששם היין בתבשיל והקפהו כמו משירד לבור ויקפה וקפוי עראי הוא לתוך התבשיל ובירושל' (שם) פריך בלא כך אין האור טובל ומשני תפתר בתבשיל צונן : לקדרה חייב · בירושלמי (שם) אמר ר' זעירא בקדרה ריקנית היא מתניתין שהניח בה היין והקפהו מתוכה והוה ליה כמקפה מתוך בור קטן וחייב : **ב** תינוקות בסוף פרק המביא (לד:) מייתי לה תינוקות רבותא אשמעינן דיש להן מחשבה ע"י מעשה המוכיח כדאמר בפ"א דחולין (דף יג·) : [שטמנו] . בשדה דאי בבית בלא שבת קובעת ובירושלמי (הל' ב) מוקי לה אביי ד] בשלקטום עם דמדומי חמה והוכיח מעשה שלהם על מחשבתן שליקטום לשבת דקסבר אין שבת קובעת אלא בשנלקט לשם שבת ופלוגתא דרבי יוחנן וריש לקיש לעיל פ"ב (הל' ג) בירושלמי דגרסינן פירות שליקטן שלא לצורך שבת וקידשה עליהן שבת רבי יוחנן אמר שבת טובלת ריש לקיש אמר אין שבת טובלת ופריך ולית הדא פליגא על ר' יוחנן דר' יוחנן אמר שבת טובלת מפני שלקטום לשבת הא אם לקטום שלא לשבת לא דרבי יוחנן אמר שבת טובלת בכל ענין ומתני' משמע דווקא שליקטום תינוקות לצורך שבת ומשני ר' יונה בשם ר' המטנא אפי' לקטום לשבת אוכל מהן עראי מערב שבת כלומר הא דנקט מתניתין שטמנו לשבת לאשמעינן דאפי' הכי לא אסרו אלא למוצאי שבת והדר קאמר אפילו על ריש לקיש לית הא פליגא ולא תינוקות איטן ואפילו ליקטום לשבת כמו שליקטום שלא לשבת. אמר רבי יוסי בשם רבי הילא תפתר בשליקטום עם דמדומי חמה דהוכיח מעשה שלהן על מחשבתן : כלכלת שבת · הכלכלה מליאה פירות שייחדה לשבת בית הלל מחייבין בדבר שאינה מיוחדת לה אין שבת טובלת כגון בפירות מוקצה אבל טובלת בכלכלה שנתייחדה לה משום דכתיב (ישעיה נח) וקראת לשבת עונג : לשלוח לחברו · נטבלה ולא יאכל עראי עד שיעשר ומפרש בירושל' (הל' ג) שהוא מקפיד עליה כמו כלכלת שבת : **ג** אחד אחד במלח. בירושל' (שם) פריך אם מלח טובל למה לי צירוף ואם צירוף ל"ל מלח אלא על ידי זה וזה : שהוא מחזיר את המותר. בסוף המביא (לה.) פריך מאי שנא רישא ומאי שנא סיפא א"ר אבהו רישא במעטן טהור וגברא טמא דלא מצי מהדר סיפא במעטן טמא וגברא טמא דמצי מהדר : **ד** שותין על הגת . כשמכנים

אבל אם עלה לראש התאנה מותר לו למלאות חיקו ולאכול מהם : ט כסבר . ידוע וכן הוא בערבי כסברה : סיאה . בערבי פונדג אזוב בערבי לעתר קורנית בערבי חסא ודרך אלו העשבים שצומחין בגנות ובבתים מבלי שזרעו אותם ואומר בכאן שאם הם נשמרים כלומר במקום שימור שחייבים במעשרות והלכה כר"ע : י הכל הולך אחר העיקר. אם יהיה עיקר האילן בחו"ל הפרי אינו חייב במעשרות אע"פ שיהי' הנוף והפרי נוטה לא"י ואם העיקר בא"י והנוף נוטה חולה לארץ חייב במעשר : ובבתי ערי חומה הכל הולך אחר העיקר . כבר ידענו דין התורה בבתי ערי חומה שיש להם גאולה עד מלאת לו שנה תמימה ואחר השנה יתקיים ביד הקונה אותו והבתים שהם חוץ לחומה אמר השם יתברך בהם על שדה הארץ יחשב וביובל יצא ועוד יתבאר בסוף ערכין כי כל שהוא לפנים מן החומה א] וטפו נוטה חוץ לחומה ב] ומכר אותו הפרי שאין דינו ודין שדה הארץ שוה : ובערי מקלט הכל הולך אחר הנוף . שיעור הגמרא זה ואמר אף אחר הנוף כגון שיהיה האילן עומד בתוך התחום ונופו נוטה חוץ לתחום כיון שהיה הרוצח תחת הנוף קלטו ואסור להרגו וכשיהיה האילן חוץ לתחום ונופו נוטה לתוך התחום לא נאמר כי הרוצח צריך להכנס בתוך התחום אבל יגלל בהגיעו לעיקר האילן *אע"פ שנופו נוטה לתוך התחום : ובירושלים הכל הולך אחר הנוף . העיקר אצלנו שמעשר שני אסור לפדותו בירושלים בשום פנים אבל חוץ לירושלים מותר ואם יהיה האילן עומד לפנים מחומות ירושלים ונופו נוטה לחוץ כיון שהגיע מעשר שני תחת הנוף אסור לפדותו אע"פ שהוא חוץ לחומה :

א אמרו בגמרא אור ומלח ומקח והתרומה ושבת וחצר ובית שמירה כולם טובלים ענינו שכל אחד מאלו קובעת למעשרות ואסור לאכול קלת מאלו עד שיעשר והכובש זה שישרה אותם במלח ומים : המכמן בעפר כמו הטומן כי כן המנהג לעשות בפירות שאינן מבושלות להטמין אותם בעפר כדי שיתרככו ויתבשלו : והמטבל . ענינו שיטבול במלח ויאכל : ואמרו פטור רוצה לומר כי זאת הטמינה בארץ אינה כמו הכבישה ולא הטבילה במלח כמו המליחה שנאמר נקבע למעשר אלא פטור מלעשר ומותר לו לאכלו עראי : שיצא השרף רוצה לומר שילא הליחה הדומה לחלב : המקפה לתבשיל . ר"ל הלוקח יין לעשות ממנו מרק לתבשיל ומקפה הוא מרק ובתנאי שיהיה אותו תבשיל צונן וכן אמרו בגמרא תפתר בתבשיל צונן אבל לבשל היין אסור כמו שאמרנו שהאש קובעת למעשר : ואמרו ולקדרה חייב ואפי' אין שם לא תבשיל ולא אש כי הטעם מה שזכרנו : ובור שם לאותה החפירה שהיין או שהשמן יורדין שם : **ב** כבר אמרנו כי שבת קובעת למעשר ומאחר שעבר עליהם שבת אסור לאכול מהם עד שיוציא מהן המעשרות : כלכלת שבת . אמרו בגמ' בתאנה המיוחדת לשבת וענינו כי כשיש לאדם אילנות מנהגו לעולם לאכול מפירותיו בשבתות ולוקט מאותו אילן כלכלה אמרו בית הלל שכיון שאותן הפירות מוכנות לשבת ושבת קובעת שנקבעו למעשר ואסור לו לאכול מהן עד שיעשר וכמו כן אמר ר' יהודה שאם לקט כלכלה לשלוח לחברו לאכול בשבת ואע"פ שלא שלחן אסור לו לאכול מהן עד שיעשר כיון שזמנן לשלחן כאילו שלחן הן חייבות במעשר ואין הלכה כרבי יהודה : **ג** מעטן . שם המקום שמקבלים שם הזיתים עד שיתרככו ויהיו ראויות להוציא שמן וכבר בארנו שהמלח קובע למעשר ולפיכך אם מלח ונתן לפניו חייב ורבי אליעזר חולק על סתם משנה ואמר מן המעטן הטהור חייב וכבר בארו בגמרא דברי ר"א ואמרו כי כוונתו באמרו מן המעטן הטהור חייב שיהיה האדם טמא והזיתים טהורים וכיון שלקח מהן נטמא מה שלקח בידו ואינו יכול להחזירו א"כ אין האכילה אכילת

הרוצח אפי' בעיקר נקלט אמאי והא בחוץ קאי אלא אי קאי בעיקרו לא נקלט והא דאמרי עיקרו כלפנים הוא דלא מצי גואל הדם למיסק מעיקרו למיקטליה כיון דנופו קאי לפנים מן התחום דלהאי מילתא משוינן העיקר כנוף ותו לא ואם העיקר בפנים ונופו לחוץ וקאי הרוצח בעיקר הא בפנים קאי ניצל . אלא כגון דקאי בנוף וכיון דנוף בחוץ לא נקלט וסליק הרוצח מעיקרו וקטיל ליה ולהכי מלתא משוינן העיקר כנוף ותו לא ורשות לגואל הדם להרגו : ובירושלים הכל הולך אחר הנוף. פי' לענין פדיון מעשר שני דאע"ג דכוליה קאי לבר ונופו לט כלפי הנוף אולינן ולא יכול למיפרקיה לא בעיקר ולא בנוף וחשוב הוא כאלו נכנס לירושלים וקיימא לן מעשר שני שנכנס לירושלים שוב אין לו פדיון ואם נופו בחוץ ועיקרו בפנים כי היכי דבנופו לא אכיל בעיקרו נמי לא אכיל מעשר שני אבל רב אשי פירש ובירושלים הלך אחר הנוף כלומר בין הנוף בין העיקר את שכנגד החומה ולפנים כלפנים ואכלינן תמן מעשר שני ולא פרקינן . שכנגד החומה ולחוץ בין נוף ובין עיקר לא אכלינן תמן מעשר שני ופרקי' ביה והיינו כמתני' דמשנת מעשר שני [פ"ג משנה ז] :

פרק ד **א הכובש**. פי' כך כובשין ב' שלישי ירק ושליש מלח : **השולק**. שלק ירקות באור : **המולח** ירקות בשדה . פי' שלא בדרך כבישה חייב לעשר עליהן מאי טעמא אור מלח כולן טובלין : **המכמר** באדמה פטור . פי' טומן הזיתין באדמה כדי שיתחממו ויתבשלו : **המטבל** בשדה . פי' טובל מלשון מטבל בחרוסת ופירושו טופת זיתים במלח ואוכל כי האי גוונא אינן נטבלין ואוכל עראי ופטור: **הפוצע** זיתין מלשון פצע כלומר מכה הזיתין כדי שיצא השרף . פי' המרירות שלהן כי האי גוונא אינן נטבלין ופטור : **הסוחט** זיתין על בשרו . פי' משום סיכה פטור דכי האי גוונא אין נטבל היוצא מהן : ואם סחט ונתן לתוך ידו חייב . פי' שידו כבור דמי : **המקפה**. פי' יין לתבשיל: **פטור** . פי' מאחר ששמו בתבשיל הקפהו שאילו הקפהו מקודם הוה מתחייב במעשר כדתנן היין משיקפה אבל הכא מאחר ששמו בתבשיל הקפהו ואפי' הכי פטור דקפיית עראי בעלמא הוא . ואקשי' בלא כך אין האור טובל ואמרי' תיפתר בתבשיל צונן : **לקדרה** חייב . פי' אע"פ שהקדרה קרה חייב מפני שהקדרה היא כבור קטן ותנן היין משיקפה לבור . ופי' נקפה כבר פירשנוהו במקומו [ועי' בפ"א משנה ז'] ויקפה ומקפה אחד הוא : **ב תינוקות** שטמנו תאנין לשבת ושכחו לעשרן למוצאי שבת לא יאכלו עד שיתעשרו מה טעם מפני שליקטום לשם שבת ואילו ליקטום מבעוד יום היו פטורין דמחשבת קטן ולא כלום הוא והוו להו כפירות שנלקטו שלא לשם שבת ועברה עליהן שבת שלא נטבלו שאין השבת קובעת אלא בדבר שנלקט לשם שבת . והכא היינו טעמא דנטבלו כגון שליקטום עם דמדומי החמה והוכיח מעשה שלהן על מחשבתן אלו כדברי ריש לקיש . אבל ר' יוחנן סבר שבת טובלת אפי' בדבר שלא נלקט בשבת דהכא במאי עסקינן שליקטום משחרית לשם שבת ומחשבת קטן ולא כלום הוא והוו להו כאלו לא נלקטו לשם שבת ואפילו הכי כי אתא שבת איטבלו להו ואשמעינן דשבת טובלת ואפי' בפירות שלא ליקטן לצורך השבת ופירוש טמנו ששמו בסתר בכלכלה כדי שלא תגע בהם יד בני אדם ועדיין בשדה הן ולא הכניסום לבית שתטבית בלא שבת טובל : **כלכלת** שבת . פי' כלכלה מלאה מפירות וייחדה לשבת בית שמאי פוטרין דלא קבעה . ובית הלל מחייבין דנהי דשבת אינה קובעת במאי דלא מיחד כגון פירות מוקצה במאי דמייחד לה מיהא כגון כלכלה זו טובלת דכתיב וקראת לשבת עונג פי' וזו המשנה היא מקולי בית שמאי ומחומרי בית הלל רבי חייא ורבי יוסי הוו יתבין עבר חד טען כלכלה דתאנין אמרו ליה ליזבן אמר להן כלכלת שבת לא מזדבנא : **רבי** יהודה אומר אף הלוקט כלכלה לשלוח לחבירו. פי' נטבלה . ולא יאכל עראי עד שיעשר · מאי טעמא משום דמקפיד עליה ככלכלת שבת : **ג הנוטל** זיתין מן המעטן טובל אחד אחד במלח ואוכל וכו'. ואקשי' אם מלח טובלת למה לי צירוף אם צירוף למה לי מלח ופריק על ידי צירוף ומלח נטבלין לפיכך אם מלח ונתן לתוכם חייב : **רבי** אליעזר אומר מן המעטן הטהור . פי' במעטן טהור וגברא טמא מאי טעמא דהואיל וגברא טמא ומעטן טהור אינו מחזיר את המותר ומן הטמא פטור פי' מן המעטן טמא וגברא טמא פטור מפני שמחזיר את המותר וכל היכא דמותרו חוזר לא קבע : **ד שותין** על הגת וכו' . פי' שיכנים ראשו ורובו

טו א שם הל' יז :
טז ב שם הל' יח :
יז ג שם הל' טז :
יח ד מיי' פ"א מה' תרומות הל' כד :
יט ה מיי' פ"ח מהלכות רוצח ושמירת נפש הל' יא :
כ ו מיי' פ"ב מהל' מ"ש ונטע רבעי הלכה טו :
א ז מיי' פ"ג מהל' מעשר הלכה ד ופ"ה הלכה יד :
ב ח מיי' פ"ה שם הלכה יח :
ג ט שם הל' טו :
ד י שם הל' יח :
ה כ מיי' פ"ג שם הלכה יט :
ו ל מיי' פ"ה שם הלכה כא :
ז מ שם הלכה כב :
ח נ שם הל' יח :

צ"ל כעי' ז"ל אמתניתין. נ"ל דהכי

פירוש הרא"ש

(ז) אף הנוף שנוטה חוץ לחומה אם לא גאלו תוך השנה נחלט ללויים :

הגהות מהר"י לנדא

מ"ש ברמ"ש א] כל שהוא לפנים מן החומה וכו' ואמר אם יהיה העיקר בתוך החומה : שם ב] ימכור : פ"ד מ"א ג] המכמן. בירושלמי איתא המכמר מלי הכתוב (דניאל יא מג) : משנה ב בר"ש ד] ובירושלמי מוקי לה אביי. הוא ט"ס כי ר"י אביי אלא בירושלמי כתוב במקום אביי ר"ז בשם רב המנונא :

א) מ"ה פ"ו דף נא :
ב) מכות פ"ב ד' יב :
ג) ביצה פ"ד דף לד :
ד) עדיות פ"ד מ"י :
ה) ביצה פ"ד ד' לה :
ו) שבת פ"א דף יא :
ערכין דף לג :

פי' מהר"י בן מלכי צדק

ואינו פורט וכן אבטיח דברי ר"ט . פי' ר"ט כר"א [כתרומות פ"ח] דאמר היה אוכל בגנה ונכנס לחצר יגמור הואיל והתחיל בהיתר. אף הכא כן ועביד תלישתם התחלה . אי נמי ר' טרפון עביד כל האשכול וכל האבטיח וכל הרמון כתאנה [אולי צ"ל כתאנה אחת] אע"ג דאית בהו כמה אכילות : ר' עקיבא אומר מגרגר וכו' . פי' משום דחצר טובלת אית למימר דסבר כר' יהושע אי נמי לא עביד כל האשכול כתאנה אחת הלכך לא יתלשם אלא יגרגרם שם במחובר ויאכלם גרגר גרגר: כסבר. פי' זרע גד שהיא זרועה בחצר : מקרטם עלה עלה ואוכל . פי' תולש. ואם צירף חייב : הסיאה והאזוב והקורנית שבחצר אם היו נשמרין שם חייבין . פי' שכל דבר שנשמר חייב במעשר . וכבר פירשנום בשביעית: י תאנה שהיא עומדת בחצר החייבת ונוטה לגנה העומדת בגנה אוכל כדרכו ופטור : עומדת בגנה ונוטה לחצר . העומד בחצר אוכל אחת אחת ופטור ואם צירף חייב : עומדת בארץ פי' בא"י ונוטה לחו"ל או בחוצה לארץ ונוטה בארץ הכל הולך אחר העיקר . פי' אם עיקר האילן בארץ והנוף נוטה בחוצה לארץ כארץ חשבינן ליה וחייב במעשרות וכו' : ובבתי ערי חומה הכל הולך אחר העיקר . פי' אם עיקרו של אילן מבפנים נידון כל האילן כבתי ערי חומה ונגאלין כל י"ב חודש . ומתניתין סני ר"מ היא דתנן [בפ"ט דערכין] כל שלפנים מן החומה הרי הוא כבתי ערי חומה חוץ מן השדות . רבי מאיר אומר אף השדות : ערי מקלט הכל הולך אחר הנוף . פי' אם עיקר האילן בחוץ ונופו לפנים בתר נופו שדינן עיקרו וכולו כלפנים. וקשה ואם עומד

A MAN MAY TAKE A WHOLE CLUSTER.[7] SIMILARLY WITH A POMEGRANATE, OR A MELON. SO R. TARFON. R. AKIBA SAYS: HE SHOULD PICK SINGLE BERRIES FROM THE CLUSTER,[8] OR SPLIT THE POMEGRANATE INTO SLICES, OR CUT SLICES OF MELON. IF CORIANDER WAS SOWN IN A COURTYARD HE MAY PLUCK LEAF BY LEAF AND EAT [WITHOUT TITHING], BUT IF HE ATE THEM TOGETHER HE IS LIABLE [TO GIVE TITHE]. SAVORY AND HYSSOP, AND THYME[9] WHICH ARE IN THE COURTYARD,[10] IF KEPT WATCH OVER, ARE LIABLE TO TITHE.[11]

MISHNAH 10. IF A FIG TREE STOOD IN A COURTYARD, AND OVERHUNG A GARDEN, A MAN MAY EAT AFTER HIS
a CUSTOMARY FASHION[1] AND BE EXEMPT [FROM TITHE]. IF, HOWEVER, IT STOOD IN THE GARDEN AND OVERHUNG THE COURTYARD, A MAN MAY EAT [THE FIGS] SINGLY[2] AND BE EXEMPT, BUT IF HE TAKES TWO OR MORE TOGETHER, HE IS LIABLE [TO TITHES]. IF IT STOOD IN THE LAND [OF ISRAEL] AND OVERHUNG [THE TERRITORY] OUTSIDE THE LAND, OR IF IT STOOD IN [THE TERRITORY] OUTSIDE THE LAND, AND OVERHUNG THE LAND, IN ALL THESE CASES [THE LAW IS] DECIDED ACCORDING TO THE POSITION OF THE ROOT.[3] AND AS REGARDS HOUSES IN WALLED CITIES, EVERYTHING IS DECIDED ACCORDING TO THE POSITION OF THE ROOT.[4] BUT AS REGARDS CITIES OF REFUGE, EVERYTHING IS DECIDED [ALSO] ACCORDING TO THE LOCATION OF THE BRANCHES.[5] AND ALSO IN WHAT CONCERNS JERUSALEM,[6] EVERYTHING IS [ALSO] DECIDED BY THE LOCATION OF THE BRANCHES.[7]

CHAPTER IV

b *MISHNAH* 1. IF A MAN PICKLED,[1] STEWED,[2] OR SALTED[3] [PRODUCE],[4] HE IS LIABLE[5] [TO GIVE TITHE]; IF HE HID [PRODUCE] IN THE GROUND,[6] HE IS EXEMPT.[7] IF HE DIPPED IT [WHILE YET] IN THE FIELD,[8] HE IS EXEMPT. IF HE BRUISED OLIVES[9] SO THAT THE ACRID SAP MAY COME OUT OF THEM, HE IS EXEMPT. IF A MAN SQUEEZED OLIVES AGAINST HIS SKIN,[10] HE IS EXEMPT; IF HOWEVER, HE SQUEEZED THEM AND PUT THEM INTO HIS HAND,[11] HE IS LIABLE. HE THAT SKIMS [WINE PUT IN] A [COLD][12] DISH[13] IS EXEMPT.[14] BUT [IF WINE IS PUT] IN AN [EMPTY] POT, HE IS LIABLE BECAUSE IT MAY BE CONSIDERED AS A SMALL VAT.[15]

MISHNAH 2. IF CHILDREN[16] HAVE HIDDEN FIGS [IN THE FIELD] FOR THE SABBATH AND THEY FORGOT TO TITHE THEM,[17] THEY MUST NOT BE EATEN[18] AFTER THE CONCLUSION
c OF THE SABBATH UNTIL THEY HAVE BEEN TITHED.[1] IN THE CASE OF A BASKET OF FRUITS FOR THE SABBATH,[2] BETH SHAMMAI EXEMPT IT FROM TITHE; BUT BETH HILLEL RENDER IT LIABLE.[3] R. JUDAH SAYS: ALSO HE WHO SELECTS A BASKETFUL OF FIGS TO SEND AS A PRESENT TO HIS FRIEND,[4] MUST NOT EAT OF THEM, UNTIL THEY HAVE BEEN TITHED.

MISHNAH 3. IF A MAN TOOK OLIVES FROM THE VAT,[5] HE MAY DIP THEM SINGLY IN SALT, AND EAT THEM;[6] IF, HOWEVER, HE SALTED THEM, AND PUT THEM IN FRONT OF HIM,[7] HE IS LIABLE [TO GIVE TITHE]. R. ELIEZER SAID: [IF AN UNCLEAN PERSON TOOK THEM OUT] FROM A CLEAN VAT HE IS LIABLE;[8] FROM AN UNCLEAN [VAT], HE IS EXEMPT BECAUSE HE IS ABLE TO RESTORE THAT WHICH IS LEFT OVER.

MISHNAH 4. ONE MAY DRINK [WINE] OUT OF THE WINE-

(7) He may eat after his customary fashion, and he need not pick single berries only nor take separate slices of pomegranate and melon. (8) Whilst it is still joined to the soil. (9) Or, origanum. (10) It is usual for these plants to grow in gardens etc., without being sown; v. Nid. 51*b*. (11) Otherwise they are ownerless property, since it is their custom to grow without being sown, and exempt from tithes.

a (1) From the branch which overhangs the garden. (2) From that branch which overhangs the courtyard. (3) This follows the principle laid down that the branches always comply with the same conditions as the root, which is the source from which the tree grows. (4) V. Lev. XXV, 29ff, and 'Ar. 31*a*ff. Whether or not the tree is included in the law depends on whether the roots are within or outside the bounds of the walled city. (5) If there is a tree the branch of which is within the area allocated to the city of refuge, and the root outside the area, as soon as the murderer reaches the root, though it is outside the area, the avenger of blood may not kill him; v. Mak. 12*a*—*b*. (6) As regards second tithe which may not be taken out of Jerusalem once it has entered the city (v. M. Sh. III, 5, 7) and the holy sacrifices which must be consumed within the wall of Jerusalem. (7) We adopt the more stringent ruling, as is done in what appertains to the cities of refuge.

b (1) Olives or vegetables in vinegar or in wine. (2) השולק. This is a more thorough preparation than mere boiling. (3) Many vegetables, olives etc. together. (4) Var. lec. add: 'while yet in the field'. (5) Any one of these acts fixed liability to tithing. (6) Fruits which have not completely ripened on the tree are hidden in the earth, where, by means of the warmth, they ripen. (7) I.e., he may take of it 'a chance meal'. (8) In salt, brine or vinegar, and eats it. (9) He crushes and pounds them so that the acrid sap should go forth from them. (10) To anoint his skin. (11) Because that which he puts into his hand can be considerd as if he had put it into a small cistern or pit into which the oil flows. (12) Boiling fixes liability to tithing, v. *supra* I, 7. (13) He removes the kernels which float above the wine after it has been put in a dish; when he skims it the work is complete, v. *supra* I, 7. (14) Liability to tithing is not fixed here by this skimming, since the wine has been already mixed before the skimming. (15) Before he puts the food into it he puts the wine into it and skims it, therefore it is as one skimming wine in a small tank, and is therefore liable. (16) Whose intention usually is of no effect. (17) On the Sabbath eve. (18) Not even a chance meal.

c (1) Sabbath fixes the liability to tithing; now since their intention to have them for the Sabbath meal has fixed the liability of them to tithing, they therefore remain forbidden for ever until they have been tithed. (2) A basket full of fruits which has been set apart for the Sabbath. (3) The dispute here is in the case of one who wishes to make a 'chance meal' of them before the Sabbath. (4) This selection fixes the liability of the fruits to tithing, and he must not make a chance meal of it until it has been tithed, even if he does not eventually send it. (5) The place where they pile up olives in order that they should become soft, and capable of exuding their oil. (6) Normally salting itself is sufficient to fix liability to tithe, provided, however, some time is allowed for the salt to penetrate and to soften the produce; if, however, it is immediately eaten as salted, salting does not fix liability to tithing. (7) That is, at least the two together. (8) Since they cannot be put back; for by so doing, the olives in the vat would be defiled; the salting fixes the liability to tithing.

PRESS,[9] WHETHER[10] [IT IS MIXED] WITH HOT OR COLD WATER, AND BE EXEMPT [FROM TITHE]; SO R. MEIR. R. ELIEZER, THE SON OF R. ZADOK, HOWEVER, RENDERS THIS LIABLE;[11] WHILST THE SAGES SAY: IF MIXED WITH HOT WATER IT IS LIABLE [TO
a TITHE], BUT WITH COLD WATER, IT IS EXEMPT.[1]

MISHNAH 5. HE WHO HUSKS BARLEY MAY HUSK EACH [GRAIN] SINGLY AND EAT[2] [WITHOUT TITHING], BUT IF HE HUSKED AND PUT THEM INTO HIS HAND, HE IS LIABLE [TO TITHE].[3] HE WHO RUBS PARCHED EARS OF WHEAT[4] MAY BLOW OUT [THE CHAFF OF THE WHEAT] FROM HAND TO HAND AND EAT,[5] BUT IF HE BLOWS AND PUTS THE GRAIN IN HIS LAP HE IS LIABLE. IF CORIANDER WAS SOWN FOR THE SAKE OF THE SEED, THE PLANT[6] IS EXEMPT [FROM TITHE], BUT IF SOWN FOR THE SAKE OF THE PLANT THEN BOTH THE SEED AND THE PLANT MUST BE TITHED. R. ELIEZER SAID: AS FOR DILL, TITHE MUST BE GIVEN FROM THE SEED AND THE PLANT, AND THE PODS. BUT THE SAGES, HOWEVER, SAY: BOTH THE SEEDS AND PLANT ARE TITHED ONLY IN THE CASE OF PEPPERWORT AND ERUCA.

MISHNAH 6. RABBAN GAMALIEL[7] SAID: SHOOTS[8] OF FENUGREEK, OF MUSTARD, AND OF WHITE BEANS ARE LIABLE [TO TITHE].[9] R. ELIEZER SAYS: AS FOR THE CAPER-TREE, TITHES MUST BE GIVEN FROM THE SHOOTS,[10] THE CAPERBERRIES AND THE CAPER FLOWER.[11] R. AKIBA SAYS: ONLY THE CAPER-BERRIES ARE TITHED SINCE THEY [ALONE] COUNT AS FRUIT.

CHAPTER V

b *MISHNAH* 1. IF ONE UPROOTS SEEDLINGS[1] OUT OF HIS OWN [PROPERTY] AND PLANTS THEM [ELSEWHERE] WITHIN HIS OWN [PROPERTY], HE IS EXEMPT FROM TITHE.[2] IF HE BOUGHT SUCH AS WERE ATTACHED TO THE GROUND,[3] HE IS EXEMPT;[4] IF HE GATHERED THEM IN ORDER TO SEND THEM TO HIS FELLOW, HE IS EXEMPT.[5] R. ELIEZER SON OF AZARIAH SAID: IF THEIR LIKE WERE BEING SOLD IN THE STREET,[6] THEY ARE LIABLE TO TITHE.

MISHNAH 2. IF A MAN UPROOTS TURNIPS AND RADISHES FROM WITHIN HIS OWN [PROPERTY] AND PLANTS [THEM ELSEWHERE] WITHIN HIS OWN [PROPERTY] FOR THE PURPOSE OF SEED,[7] HE IS LIABLE TO TITHE,[8] SINCE THIS WOULD BE [CONSIDERED] THEIR HARVEST-TIME.[9] IF ONIONS TAKE ROOT IN AN UPPER STOREY[10] THEY BECOME LEVITICALLY CLEAN FROM ANY IMPURITY;[11] IF SOME DEBRIS FELL UPON THEM AND
c THEY ARE UNCOVERED,[1] THEY ARE REGARDED AS THOUGH THEY WERE PLANTED IN THE FIELD.[2]

MISHNAH 3. NO PERSON MAY SELL HIS FRUITS[3] AFTER THE SEASON FOR TITHING HAS ARRIVED[4] TO ONE WHO IS NOT TO BE TRUSTED CONCERNING TITHES, NOR IN THE SABBATICAL YEAR [MAY ONE SELL SABBATICAL YEAR PRODUCE][5] TO ANYONE SUSPECTED OF [INFRINGING] THE SABBATICAL YEAR. IF ONLY [SOME] PRODUCE RIPENED,[6] HE TAKES THE RIPE ONES AND MAY SELL THE REMAINDER.

MISHNAH 4. A MAN MAY NOT SELL HIS STRAW,[7] NOR HIS OLIVE-PEAT,[8] NOR HIS GRAPE-POMACE[9] TO ONE WHO IS NOT TO BE TRUSTED IN [THE OBSERVANCE OF] TITHES, FOR HIM TO EXTRACT THE JUICE FROM THEM.[10] IF HE, HOWEVER, EXTRACTED THEM HE IS LIABLE TO TITHES, BUT IS EXEMPT

(9) Outside the wine-press the liability to tithing is fixed and it is forbidden to drink of the wine. (10) Whether the wine is mixed with hot or cold water. (11) This enactment has been made by R. Eliezer as a precaution lest the wine is taken outside the wine-press, and drunk there.

a (1) If mixed with hot water, the wine which is left over cannot be put back, because the wine in the press will thus be spoilt; the taking out of the wine thus fixes the liability to tithing; but if it is mixed with cold water, what is left over can be put back, hence it is exempt. (2) One barley-corn. This applies only when it is not near the threshing-floor. (3) Even if only three kernels are husked together he is liable (*T.J.*). (4) He parches ears of corn over the fire and crushes them in his hand to remove the worthless matter. (5) He shakes them from one hand to the other, and blows to separate. (6) The seed is the principal and the herb or plant secondary. The plant here means the herb or foliage. (7) Var. lec.: R. Simeon b. Gamaliel. (8) תמרות. Either the shoots or the berries. (9) Because they can be eaten. (10) Its sprouts or stalks. (11) Which protects the fruit that surrounds it.

b (1) E.g., onions or leeks which are fit to be eaten. It was customary for gardeners to uproot them and to plant them in another place, where they became thicker and broader. (2) He may make a chance meal of them, even though they have been fixed for tithe before he plants them again, since it was his intention to sow them again at the time he uprooted them, and not to eat them. (3) If one buys fruits when they were still attached. (4) Sale fixes liability to tithe only in the case of plucked produce, but not attached. (5) A gift does not fix liability to tithe (v. *supra* IV, 2) in respect of that which is attached. (6) It must be considered as though their growth was complete. (7) So that the seed should increase and multiply in the place where it was planted in the second time. (8) Before he re-plants them. (9) Their uprooting is the final work completing their harvesting (10) Where they have been stored. (11) The floor of the upper storey is treated like the natural ground that frees anything sown in it from Levitical impurity in accordance with Lev. XI, 37.

c (1) I.e., the leaves remained uncovered. (2) I.e., he who plucks of them on the Sabbath is liable, and the law of the Sabbatical year and of tithes applies to them. (3) In an unplucked condition. This ruling is laid down on the basis of the Biblical command: '*Do not put a stumbling block before the blind*', Lev. XIX, 14. (4) V. *supra* II, 2. (5) Under conditions defined Sheb. VIII, 3. (6) And thus reached the season for tithing. (7) Ears of corn which have been threshed out and sometimes some wheat grains remain. (8) The residue of the olives after they have been pressed out. (9) The residue of squeezed-out grapes. (10) From the peat and grape-pomace, and in the case of straw, to gather wheat from it.

כשמכנים שם ראשו ורובו מוקי לה בפרק קמא דשבת (יא:) (א) דלא חשיב קבע אלא אם שתה חוץ לגת: רבי אלעזר בר' צדוק מחייב. דגזר שמא יוציא: [על החמין] שמזג היין בחמין ומפרש בירושלמי (שם) א"ר יוחנן שהיא קבע: על הצונן פטור. שהוא לדבר שלא נגמרה מלאכתו ובכל הספרים גרסינן בפ"ק דשבת מפני שמחזיר את המותר ופירוש הוא א] אבל כשמוזג בחמין אם היה מחזיר לגת מתקלקל: ה המקלף שעורים. מסיר קליפתן ומקלף אחת אחת שיבולת או שעורה אחת (ב) ובפ"ק דביצה (יג:) אמר וכן לשבת: מנפח (ג) מיד ליד מפרש התם כיצד מנפח (ד): ירקה פטור הזרע לעולם חשוב אבל ירקה לא אלא אם כן החשיבו: זירין של שבת זמורות ובפ"ק דמסכת ע"ג (ז.) מוקי לה בדגנוניתא: ירוש' (הל' ה) שבת שזרעה לזרע מתעשרת זרע ואינה מתעשרת ירק זרעה לירק מתעשרת ירק וזרע ואינה מתעשרת זירין זרעה לזירין מתעשרת זרע וירק וזירין והתניא אין לך מתעשרת זרע וירק ב]: אלא שחלים וגרגיר בלבד פי' דאמרינן בפרק בכל מערבין (דף כח:) זרעו לירק מתעשרת ירק וזרע זרעו לזרע מתעשרת זרע וירק כלומר ירק וזרע הירק עיקר ואפי' בזרע אזלינן בתר לקיטה כירק זרע וירק הזרע עיקר ואזלינן בתר השרשה כפרגין ושומשמין בפרק קמא דראש השנה (דף יג:) (ה): ו תמרות של תלתן. לולבי תלתן כעין שיש לגפנים ואוכלין אותן ויש מפרשים דדרך הגבעולין כשמתחילין לצמוח ולגדל נראה מקום למיתתן כעין גרגיר ונקרא תמרה כדאמרינן גבי הדס עלתה בו תמרה: והחרדל ופול הלבן ותלתן חשובין אוכל: צלף הוא נלפא הוא פרחא כדאמרינן בפרק כיצד מברכין תמרות הן לולבין וכשהן רכין אוכלין אותן והוא עיקר העץ שגדל בו הפרי ואביונות הן עיקר הפרי שמברכין עליו בורא פרי העץ והקפרס הוא שומר לפרי שומר אביונות ונקרא כילא דפרחא ומברכין עליו נמי בורא פרי העץ ולרבי עקיבא לא חשיבי ליה אלא אביונות:

א העוקר שתלים. דרך הגננים כשזורעין בצלים וכרשין כשצומחין מעט תולשים אותן ונוטעים אותן במקום אחר ומתעבים וגדלין יותר ופטור דעדיין לא נגמרה מלאכתן ואפי' ראה פני הבית: לקח במחובר פטור. דאין מקח קובע במחובר אבל תלוש דומיא דמחובר קובע אע"פ שלא נגמרה מלאכתה וסתמא כרבי מאיר דלעיל פ' שני (מ"ה): ליקט לשלוח לחברו. בשתלין איירי ואמרינן בירושלמי (הל' א) רב אמר אסור לוכל א"ר שמואל קומי דרבי יסא בשם רבי אחא מה דאמר רב בשהכניסן לחצר בית שמירה שנסבלו כשהביאן לביתו: הרי אלו חייבים. ואותו שנשתלחו לו מעשרן (ב) כדאמר בירושל' (שם) שכן מנהג בני אדם לשלוח לחבריהן טבלים כדברים הללו: ב ג ונוטע לתוך שלו. לזרע שיבא בהן הזרע ויתבטל *במקום נטיעתן: מפני שהוא גורנן. עקירתן הוא גורן שלהן דאין להן גורן אחר להתחייב במעשר דזרען פטור ממעשר כדדרים בירושלמי (הל' א) ברים מכילתין יכול שאני מרבה זרע לוף העליון זרע כרשין זרע בצלים זרע לפת ולנונות ושאר גרעיני גנה שאינן נאכלים ת"ל מזרע הארץ ולא כל זרע: בירושל' (שם) א"ר מנא לא שנו אלא לזרע אבל לאכול פטור כלומר אין צריך לעשר בעת תלישת' שעתיד לעשרה כשיבא לאכול ורבי חייא בשם ר' יוחנן אמר לא שנא לזרע ולא שנא לאכול חייב מפני שהוא גרן בעת תלישתן באו לחיוב ומפרש רבי חנינא טעם דרבי יוחנן מפני שהוא מכניסן מן השני לעני ומן העני לשני כלומר פעמים שתולשן בשנה שניה ונוטען ועתה חוזר ותולשן בשלישית ונמצא מוציאן ממעשר שני ומביאן למעשר עני אי נמי פעמים שתולשן בשלישית ונוטען וחוזר ותולשן ברביעית משום הכי מעשר השתא: טהרו מלטמא. דכזרועין דמו ולא מקבלי טומאה כדאמר בירושלמי (שם) דריבתה תורה בטהרת זרעים על כל זרע זרוע אשר יזרע טהור הוא אבל לשאר מילי כתלושי' דמו ובחזקתן למעשר ולשביעית ודוקא השרישו בעליה אבל השרישו בקופה כתלושים דמו לכל מילי ואם היו טמאים לא עלו מידי טומאתן ואם נגע בהן שרץ טמאים: והן מגולין. עלין שלהן בדרך גדילתן: כנטועין בשדה. והתולש מהן בשבת חייב: לא ימכור אדם פירותיו. בירושלמי מפרש לא ימכור שדהו משבאו לעונת המעשרות למי שאינו נאמן (ג): ואמרינן (הל' ב) בירושלמי תני רבי שמעון מתיר שהוא אומר לו הרי מכרתי את שלי לא ותבע את שלך עבר ומכר מעשר את שהוא אוכל ואינו מעשר מה שהוא מוכר ואין אנו אחראין לרמאין והך סיפא כרבנן: ואם ביכרו. אם יש בהן בכורות שהגיעו לעונת המעשרות והשאר לא הגיעו עדיין נוטל את הבכורות ומוכר השאר: ד תבנו שנידושו ופעמים יש בהן חטין: גפתו. פסולת של זיתים: זגין. פסולת

* נ"ל ויתבטל וכ"ה בהרע"ב וכס' עץ החיים

בין על חמין בין על הצונן פטור דברי רבי מאיר רבי אליעזר בר' צדוק מחייב וחכמים אומרים [י]על החמין חייב ועל הצונן פטור: ה [א)][כ]המקלף שעורים מקלף אחת אחת ואוכל ואם קלף ונתן לתוך ידו חייב [ג)] המולל מלילות של חטים מנפח מיד ליד ואוכל ואם נפח ונתן לתוך חיקו חייב [ל]כסבר שזרעה לזרע ירקה פטור זרעה לירק מתעשרת זרע וירק [ג)] ר"א אומר השבת מתעשרת זרע וירק וזירין וחכ"א [מ]אינו מתעשר זרע וירק אלא השחלים והגרגיר בלבד: ו *רשב"ג אומר [נ]תמרות של תלתן ושל חרדל ושל פול הלבן חייבות במעשר [ד)] רבי אליעזר אומר הצלף מתעשר תמרות ואביונות וקפרס רע"א [ס]אין מתעשר אלא אביונות מפני שהן פרי:

*) גי' הירושלמי רבן גמליאל

פרק חמישי

א העוקר [ע]שתלים מתוך שלו ונטע לתוך שלו פטור [ח]לקח במחובר לקרקע פטור לקט לשלוח לחבירו פטור ר"א בן עזריה אומר (א) אם יש כיוצא בהם נמכרים בשוק הרי אלו חייבין: ב [ט]העוקר לפת וצנונות מתוך שלו ונוטע לתוך שלו לזרע חייב מפני שהוא גורנן [י]בצלים משהשרישו בעליה טהרו מלטמא נפלה עליהם מפולת והם מגולים הרי אלו כנטועים בשדה: ג [כ]לא ימכור אדם את פירותיו משבאו לעונת המעשרות למי שאינו נאמן על המעשרות ולא בשביעית למי שהוא חשוד על השביעית ואם בכרו נוטל את הבכורות ומוכר את השאר: ד [ל]לא ימכור אדם את תבנו ואת גפתו ואת זגיו למי שאינו נאמן על המעשרות להוציא מהן משקין ואם הוציא חייב במעשרות [ס]ופטור מן

ערלה והוא חייב במעשרות ומן הטומאה פטור שיהיו האדם והזיתים טמאים והוא יכול להחזיר המותר אחר אכילתו והרי היא אכילת עראי ולפיכך הוא פטור והלכה כסתם משנה: ד בין על חמין בין על הטון. ענייט בין שיהיה אותו היין שבתוך הגת מבושל או בלי מבושל דינם שוה וחכמים הלכו על העיקר כי החמין נקבעו למעשר כמו שבארנו שהאור קובעת והלכה כחכמים: ה מקלף. מסיר הקליפה העליונה: מנפח. מנער מיד ליד כמו מחליף מיד ליד אותן החטים כדי שיסור מהם הפסולת ונקראים השבלין המהובהבות באש מלילות כי המלילה בלשונם היא המעיכה והעשוי בין האצבעות וכפות הידים: מתעשרת זרע וירק. ענינו שחייב במעשר הזרע והנכרת מן העלין: השבת ג"כ נקרא בערבי אל שבת: זרע וירק וזירין. פי' הזרע והעלין והגבעולין וזירין הם הגבעולין הנעשין בראשי קלת הצמחים שבהם היה הזרע ואלו הגבעולין נראין מאד לעין בשבת והם כמו שקדים ארוכים: ושחלים נקרא בערבי חב אלשאר. וגרגיר ג"כ בערבי גרגיר ובלע"ז אירוגה ואלו השני מינין מתעשרין זרע וירק ואפי' זרע אותם סתם ולא פירש כי כוונתו על הזרע בלבד והלכה כחכמים: ו תמרות של תלתן ושל חרדל. הם פרח התלתן והחרדל: צלף הוא בערבי אל כבר יש ממנו שהוא הפרח והוא נקרא תמרות ויש ממנו פרי יבש כעץ ויש ממנו עלין והוא הנקרא קפריסין ויש ממנו פרי מבושל כל צרכו ושמו הידוע אצלנו בל' ערבי פרוס אל כבר והוא הנקרא אביונות והלכה כר"ע לבדו:

א זה המאמר שאמר שמותר לאדם לעקור שתלים ולנטעם בקרקע שלו אע"פ שיש שם פירות אין זה דעת ר"ע לבדו שנתבאר במסכת פאה שמותר אלו לזרוע הטבל קודם שתגמר מלאכתו והוא אמרו לשם נוטל אדם מן הגרן וזורע עד שימרח דברי ר"ע אבל חכמים גם כן מתירין זה בשתלים וכן אמרו מודין חכמים לר"ע בשתלים והחלוק ביניהם מה שזכרנו חטים נגמר מלאכתן שתלים לא נגמר מלאכתן כי לפי דבורו מן האילן עקרו וכבר בארנו בפ' שלפני זה כי המקח קובע למעשרות ובאר בכאן כי אין כל מקח קובע אלא כל הלוקח תלוש מן הקרקע לאכלו בלבד (לוקח) [קובע] אבל הקונה במחובר או מי שקנה תלוש לשלוח לחברו לא נקבע למעשר ויכול לאכול עראי קודם שיתעשר ור"א בן עזרי' אומר אם יש כיוצא בהן נמכרין בשוק כלומר כאותן שקנה לשלוח לחברו הרי נקבע למעשר ואין הלכה כר"א בן עזריה: ב אם לזרע חייב. ענינו שאם היתה כונתו ליקח ממנו הזרע אסור לנטעה עד שיעשר לפי שעקירתה מן הקרקע הוא גרנה שיקבע אותם למעשר ואם כונתו בנטיעת' להוסיף א] אינו חייב לפי שלא נקבעו ולא נגמרו למעשרות: בצלים שהשרישו בעליה טהרו מלטמא. לפי שאינם אוכל וכבר נפסדו: נפלה עליהם מפולת והם מגולין הרי אלו כנטועים בשדה. ענינו שהם חייבים בדיני שביעית ודיני מעשרות: ג עונת המעשרות כבר קדם זכרם ובארנו ג"כ במסכת שביעית באיזה דרך ימכרו פירות שביעית ולאיזה אדם מותר למכרם ואיך ובארנו כי אלו הדמים שהם נמכרים בהם יאכלו בשביעית והדבר הנמכר לא נסתלק ממנו דין השביעית והוא אמרם לשם האחרון נתפס בשביעית והפרי עצמו אסור וכבר בארנו זה בפרק *הרביעי מזו המסכתא וכן אמרו (פ"ד מ"ט שם) ושאר כל פירות האילן כעונתם למעשרות כן עונתם לשביעית ואם היו כל הפירות לא באו לעונת המעשרות מלקט הבכורות ומוכר את השאר שלא נתחייבו במעשרות: ד גפת. הם גרעיני הזיתים: וזג הוא קליפה הענבים הנשארים אחר דריכתן וסחיטתן והקבוץ זגי' והכונה בכאן שלא ימכור אדם הזגים והגפת למי שאינו נאמן ואמר להוציא מהם משקין מוסב על גפת וזגים והשיעור …

*) נ"ל התשיעי משנה ז' דשביעית

פי' מהר"י בן מלכי צדק

… אצבעותיו ולמעלה מחטו עלה במערבא כיון דמשנה פי' שעושה בידו ולא בקטן ולא בתמחוי מאי טעמא מקשרי אצבעותיו ותו לא אפי' בכלא ידא נמי אלא אמר ר' אלעזר מנפח בידו אחת ובכל כחו: כוסבר שזרעה משום זרע ירקה פטור מן המעשר. זרעו לירק מתעשרת זרע וירק: רבי אליעזר אומר השבת מתעשרת זרע וירק וזירין … של שבת. גרסי' לא אמר ר' אלעזר אלא בשבת דגנות אבל במידי אחריני לא. תני שבת שזרעה לזרע מתעשר זרע ולא ירק לירק מתעשר זרע וירק ואין מתעשר זירין. זרעה … זרע וירק וזירין אם כן כיצד ופריק כן היא פי' אין לך דבר שזורעו לזרע ומתעשר זרע וירק אלא שחלים וגרגיר בלבד: ו רבן גמליאל אומר תמרות של תלתן. פי' לולבי … וכו'. ויש מפרשין הגבעולין שלהן קודם שיפתחו נקראין תמרה כדאמרי' בהדס נקטם ראשו ועלתה בו תמרה ואמרי' בריש מסכתין מאי טעמא דרבן גמליאל קסבר חשובות הן לאוכל אבל אפי' רבן גמליאל לא מחייב דהא לא חשיבי לאוכל: רבי אליעזר אומר [הצלף] מתעשרת תמרות וכו'. פי' צלף הוא נצפה והוא פרחה והוא שם האילן ובלשון ישמעאל אלכפר ובלעז קפרינא פי' תמרות … וכשהן רכין נקראו שיתין ואיכלין אותן לחין והן עיקר העץ שיוצא מהן הפרי ואביונות שהן יוצאין מהן הן עיקר הפרי ובלעז טרולי: וקפרס. הוא שומר אביונות שנקרא נצא ובלעז קפריני. … הקפרס והתמרות מין אחד הן ומעשרין מזה על זה אבל לא מהן על אביונות ולא מן אביונות עליהן דהוי מדבר גמור על שאינו גמור ומדבר שאינו גמור על הגמור: רבי עקיבא אומר … פי' מן הצלף אלא האביונות מפני שהן פירות הצלף ותו לא:

פרק ה א העוקר שתלין מתוך שלו. פי' כגון בצלין קטנים וכרישין ואברוב ובלעז קנטימי וכן דרך הגננין זורעין אותן וכיון שצומחין וגדילין כמעט תולשין אותן ונוטעין אותן במקום אחר כדי שיע… ומאי טעמא פטור דאכתי לא נגמרה מלאכתן. [והלכך אף דבנוטל] חטין מן גורנו וזורע מחלוקת רבי עקיבא ורבנן בפאה [פ"א משנה ו'] ורבנן התם מחייבי [הכא מודו] מ"ט דחטין נגמרה מלא… נגמרה מלאכתן: לקח במחובר לקרקע. פי' כל דבר שמחובר לקרקע פטור דאכתי לא נגמרה מלאכתן הא תלוש דומיא דמחובר בפירות שלא נגמרה מלאכתן חייב מיהא שמעינן דמקח טובל… נגמרה מלאכתן וסתמא כר' מאיר [לעיל בסופ"ב]: ליקט שבלים לשלוח. דהיינו פירות שלא נגמר מלאכה פטור אבל הוא אסור לאכול שטבלו מפני שהביאן לביתו: רבי אלעזר בן עזריה אומר… בהן נמכרין בשוק הרי אלו חייבין דשוק טובל לחייבין במעשר לאותו שנשתלח לו תניא רבי יהודה אומר משום רבי אליעזר בן עזריה אף השולח לחבירו עטנין ושתלין וחבילי תלתן לא יאכל עד ש… בני אדם משלחין לחביריהן טבלין בדברים הללו: ב העוקר לפת וצנונות מתוך שלו ונטע לתוך שלו לזרע חייב מפני שהוא גרנו. פי' בעת שעקר [הוא] גורנו שמחייב להו במעשר הואיל וזרעו… להן גורן אחר לחיוב מעשר דזרע לפת וצנונות אין להן גורן להיות חייבין במעשר דכתיב מזרע הארץ ולא כל זרע הארץ פרט לזרע לפת וצנונות וכו': בצלין שהשרישו בעליה טהרו מלטמא. פי'… כזרועין דמו ואם יגע בהן השרץ טהורין הן ואם היו טמאין טהרו מלטמא. מאי טעמא שהתורה ריבתה בטהרת זרעין דכתיב וכי יפול מנבלתם על כל זרע זרוע אשר יזרע טהור הוא הא לשאר מילי… וכחזקתן הן למעשרות ולשביעית דלא מחייב לעשר על הנהו ספיחין ולא נאסרו משום ספיחי שביעית והוקא בעליה אבל אם השרישו בקופה לכל מילי כתלושין דמו ואפי' לענין טומאה אם היו טמאי… היו טהורין ומוכשרין תגע בהן השרץ נטמאו: נפלה עליהן מפולת והן מגולין. פי' כגון שנפלה עליהן הבית והעלין שלהן מגולין הרי הן כנטועין בשדה. פי' והתולש מהן בשבת חייב: ג לא י… פירותיו וכו': כיני מתני' לא ימכור אדם שדהו משבא לעונת המעשרות למי שאינו נאמן וכו': ואם ביכרו. פי' אם יש בשדהו אשכול שביכר כלומר לא באה כל שדהו לעונת המעשרות אלא קצת מן הפי… המעשרות שביכרו והשאר אכתי נצים וסמדר נוטל את הבכורות לעצמן שאותן אינו רשאי למכור ומוכר את השאר אפי' למי שאינו נאמן ולמי שהוא חשוד דאכתי לא באו לעונת המעשרות: ד לא ימכור אדם את תבנו למי שאינו נאמן על המעשרות להוציא מתבנו חיטין: וכן גפתו. פי' פסולת דזיתין: ואת זגיו. פי' פסולת הענבים כדכתיב מחרצנים ועד זג: ואם הוציא חייב במ…

*) [ע"ש ברש"י ותוס' דמיירי לענין יו"ט] **) [ע"ש ברש"י ותוס' דמיירי לענין שבת]

עין משפט נר מצוה

ט א שם הל' טו: י ב מיי' פ"ב מהל' מעשר הלכה יט: יא ג ד מיי' פ"ב מהלכות תרומות הלכה ה: יב ה שם הל' ד: א ו מיי' פ"א מהל' מעשר הלכה ג: ב ח מיי' פ"א שם הלכה ב: ג ט מיי' פרק ו שם הלכה ג: ד י מיי' פרק א שם הל' יא ומיי' פ"ב מהל' טומאת אוכלין הלכה יט: ה כ מיי' פ"ב מהלכות מעשר הלכה ו: ו ל מיי' שם: ז מ מיי' פ"ד מהל' תרומות הלכה כח:

פירוש הרא"ש

הגהות מהר"י לנדא

עין משפט נר מצוה

ח א מיי' פ"א שם הלכה טו :
ט ב שם הלכה טו :
י ג מיי' פ"ב מהל' מעשר הלכה ז :
יא ד מיי' פ"ג שם הלכה כג :
יב ה מיי' פ"ב מהל' תרומות הלכה יב :
יג ו מיי' פ"ח מהל' שמטה ויובל הלכה יג :
יד ז מיי' פ"ב מהלכ' תרומות הל' ג טוש"ע י"ד סי' שלא סעיף יז :
טו ח מיי' פ"ח מהל' שמטה ויובל הלכה יג :
טז ט מיי' פי"א מהל' תרומות הלכה כב :

מסורת הש"ס

א) פסחים דף מב: בבא בתרא דף לז. חולין דף כה:

התרומה שהתורם בלבו על הקוטעין ועל הצדדין ועל מה שבתוך התבן : **ה** [א]הלוקח שדה ירק בסוריא אם עד שלא בא לעונת המעשרות חייב ומשבא לעונת המעשרות פטור ולוקט כדרכו והולך רבי יהודה אומר אף ישכור פועלים וילקט אמר רשב"ג [ב]במה דברים אמורים בזמן שקנה קרקע אבל בזמן שלא קנה קרקע אם עד שלא בא לעונת המעשרות פטור רבי אומר אף לפי חשבון : **ו** א) [ג]המתמד ונתן מים במדה ומצא כדי מדתו פטור רבי יהודה מחייב מצא יתר על כדי מדתו מוציא עליו ממקום אחר לפי חשבון : **ז** [ד]חורי הנמלים שלנו בצד הערימה החייבת הרי אלו חייבים שידוע שמדבר הגמור גוררין כל הלילה : **ח** [ה]שום בעל בכי ובצל של רכפא וגריסין הקילקין והעדשין המצריות רבי מאיר אומר אף הקרקס ר' יוסי אומר אף הקוטניות פטורין מן המעשרות [ו]ונלקחים מכל אדם בשביעית [ז]זרע לוף העליון זרע כרישים זרע בצלים זרע לפת וצנונות ושאר זרעוני גנה שאינן נאכלים פטורים מן המעשרות [ח]ונלקחין מכל אדם בשביעית [ט]שאף על פי שאביהן תרומה הרי אלו יאכלו :

סליקא לה מסכת מעשרות

פסולת ענבים : שהתורם בלבו על הקוטעין . דתניא בתוספתא דתרומות (פרק ג') התורם את הגורן צריך שיכוין את לבו על מה שבקוטעין ועל מה שבצדדין ועל מה שבתבן התורם את הכור צריך שיכוין את לבו על מה שבחרצנין ועל מה שבזגין התורם את הגת צריך שיכוין את לבו על מה שבגפת ואם לא כוון תנאי ב"ד שיתרום על הכל : קוטעין . שבולת קשושות שלא נידושו : צדדין . לידי הכרי : שבתוך התבן . שאי אפשר בלא חטין : **ה** הלוקח שדה ירק בסוריא . שלקחו מן הנכרי : עד שלא בא לעונת מעשרות . לקחה חייב דבידו נשבלו : אבל לקחה משבא לעונת מעשרות פטור . שבשעת חובתה היתה פטורה שהיתה אצל הנכרי (ד) : ולוקט כדרכו והולך . ואוכל אע"פ שמוספת ברשותו אבל פועלין לא ישכור דחיישינן דילמא אתי לאיחלופי למיעבד הכי בשדה שלא בא לעונת מעשרות ור' יהודה לא גזר : בר"א. דאזלינן בתר [עונת] מעשרות : בזמן שקנה קרקע עם הפירות . אבל קנה פירות בלא קרקע אע"פ שלא בא לעונת מעשרות פטור ואמרינן בירושלמי (שם) א"ר אבין מילתא דרשב"ג כשיטת רבן גמליאל זקינו דתנינן תמן ישראל שהיו אריסין בסוריא לנכרים ר"א מחייב פירותיהן במעשרות ובשביעית רבן גמליאל פוטר : רבי אומר אף לפי חשבון . ומפרש בירושלמי (שם) דרבי אתנא קמא קאי דפטר כשבא לעונת מעשרות אע"ג שמוסיף ברשות ישראל דסבר רבי' למה שמוסיף חייב ומעשר לפי חשבון דאם הביא שליש ביד הנכרי ושני שלישי ביד ישראל שני שלישי חייב ובירושלמי (שם) תני שדה שהביאה שליש לפני הנכרי ולקחה ממנו ישראל ר"ע אומר התוספת פטור וחכמים מחייבין והשתא סתם מתני' ר"ע : **ו** המתמד . נותן מים בחרצנים או בשמרים ולכשיחמיץ תוסס נעשה יין והכא במתמד בשמרין פליגא כדאמרינן בריש אלו עוברין (דף מב:) הא בדרווקא הא בדפורצני: ומצא כדי מדתו . יהיב תלתא ואתו תלתא ופלגא פליגי כדאמרינן בפרק המוכר פירות (דף לז:) ובפ"ק דחולין (דף כה.) פליגי אמוראי דרב נחמן אמר בשהחמיץ פליגי ולאו דוקא החמיץ אלא ראוי להחמיץ כיון דאי שביק ליה הוה מחמיץ כדמוכח התם ור"א סבר בשלא החמיץ מחלוקת ועד כאן לא מחייב רבי יהודה אלא מיניה וביה אבל מעלמא לא דילמא אתי לאפרושי מן החיוב על הפטור ומן הפטור על החיוב ויש לתמוה היכי פטרי רבנן והלא כל איסורים שבתורה בנותן טעם ומבל חמור משאר איסורים כדאמר בסוף מס' ע"ז (דף עג:) דאיכא למאן דאמר כל איסורים שבתורה בנותן טעם חוץ מטבל ויין נסך דבמינן במשהו וי"ל דטעם השמרים של טבל לא חשיב טעם גמור אלא קיוהא בעלמא: ר"י מחייב. אמר בירושלמי (הל' ג) דהיינו במעשר אבל בתרומה לא כדאמר לעיל התורם בלבו על הכל: ונמצא יותר על מדתו. היינו [יותר] משיעור המפורש בפרק המוכר פירות (שם) כגון דרמא תלתא ואתו ד' : מוציא עליו ממקום אחר . כלומר לא מיבעיא דמיניה וביה יכול להפריש אלא אפי' מיין גמור יכול להפריש עליו לפי חשבון היתר לפי מדתו : **ז** **ח** שלנו . לינת לילה : לערימה החייבת . כההיא דתנן בפרק קמא (מ"ו) ואם אינו ממרח משיעמיד ערימה : שום בעל בכי . כל הני מינים וכן דרבי מאיר ורבי יוסי קיימי אפטורים מן המעשר ונלקחים מכל אדם ואף על גב דנאכלים וחשובים פטורים דהנהו לאין נאכלים חשיב לחודייהו והיינו טעמא דהכי כדאיתא בירושלמי (הל' א') בריש פרק ב' דדמאי דאמר תמן תנינן שום בעל בכי ובצל של רכפא וגריסים הקלקים ועדשים המצריות המינים הללו על ידי שיש כיוצא בהן בארץ ישראל הוצרכו חכמים ליתן להם סימן אבל האלגרין והפספקין והאסטרובלין ע"י שאין כיוצא בהן בארץ ישראל לא הוצרכו חכמים ליתן להן סימן כלומר המינים דמתני' לפי שיש שומין ובצלים וגריסין ועדשים בארץ ישראל *דהיינו כיוצא בהן הוצרכו ליתן בהן סימן בפטורין הבאים לעולם מחוצה לארץ דלא חייבו חכמים פירות חוצה לארץ במעשר אלא אותן שדוגמתן בארץ ישראל אבל אלגרין ופספקין ואסטרובלין אין גדילים בארץ ישראל לא הוצרכו למנותן וליתן סימן בהם : בבי . שם מקום כמו רכפא אי נמי כל האוכלן יורדות [עיניו] דמעה כדאמר בירושלמי (הל' ג) אי זהו שום בכי כל שאין לו אלא חור אחד מקיף את העמוד ובתוספתא (פרק ג) קתני דור אחד דשום שלנו יש לו דרא לפנים מדרא רשב"ג אומר כל שאין לו אלא קליפה אחת אי זהו בצל של רכפא כל שעוקצו נמעך לתוכו רבן שמעון בן גמליאל אומר כל שאין לו ארס אלו הן גריסי הקלקין אותן המרובעין אלו הן עדשים המצריות כל שגלגליהן חדים רשב"ג אומר כל שאין להם צרורות אלו הן הקריקס כל שעוקליהן מעוטין והלקטיהם מרובים מה דמי לה א"ר יוסי כגון אילן קונייתא : זרע העליון של לוף . מפרש בירושלמי (שם) כיני מתני' זרע הסלוין של לוף כלומר זרע לוף שוטה שכן קורין בלשון יון לשוטה סלי אבל זרע לוף סתם חייב וכל הני פטורין דריש מקרא בריש מכילתין בירושלמי (הל' א) כדפרשינן בריש פרקין : מבל אדם בשביעית . אפי' מן החשוד : שאביהן תרומה . כההיא דתנן בריש פרקין (מ"ב) העוקר לפת וצנונות מתוך שלו ונטע לתוך שלו לזרע חייב מפני שהיא גורנו ואם עשאן תרומה ונטען לזרע הזרע נאכל לזרים ובירושלמי (שם) מייתי עובדא דחדא איתתא הוה לה זרבונין דתרומה גו קופתא נפלון לגו גינתא ולמחון אתא עובדא קומי רבי יוחנן ושרא ליה א"ל רבי חייא בר בא ולא מתני' היא אע"פ שאביהן תרומה יאכלו א"ל מן דגלית לך חספא אשכחת מרגניתא ואת אמר ולא מתני' היא . זרע זרבונין הם מזרעוני גינה שאין נאכלין : סליקא לה מסכת מעשרות

פירוש הרא"ש

(ד) דכיבוש יחיד לאו שמיה כיבוש די"ש לגוי קנין להפקיע מיד מעשר :

להוציא משקים מן הגפת ומן הזגים וללקט חטים מן התבן : ואמר שהתורם בלבו על הקוטעים ועל הצדדין ענינו שהמוציא תרומה (היא) מוציא (אלא) על כל הנגלה והנסתר : **ה** כבר קדם לך בסוף פרק ששי מדמאי כי ארץ סוריא היא ארץ שכבש דוד ואינו חייב במעשר אלא למי שיש לו שם קרקע אבל מי שקנה פירות מקרקע שאינו שלו אינו חייב במעשר ובארנו לשם הטעם בזה רוצה לומר הטעם מפני מה אותן ארצות פחותו' מארץ ישראל ואמר בכאן כי מי שקנה לשם פירות במחובר לקרקע עד שלא באו לעונת המעשרות שאותן הפירות כאילו צמחו בקרקע שלו וחייב לעשר ואם קנה אחר שהגיעו לעונת המעשרות הרי הוא כאילו קנה תלוש מן הקרקע בסוריא שאינו חייב במעשר כמו שבארנו ומותר לו ללקט הוא בעצמו כדרכו אבל לא שישכור פועלים וחלק רבי יהודה על זה הסתם ואמר שמותר לו לשכור פועלים וגם כן רשב"ג חלק עליו ואמר כי אפי' קנה במחובר לקרקע עד שלא באו לעונת המעשרו' שאינו חייב במעשר בסוריא עד שיקנה הקרקע ואמר רבי שהוא חייב אע"פ שלא קנה קרקע אבל לפי חשבון והוא חולק גם כן על הסתם כילד כגון שקנה שדה ירק עד שלא באו לעונת המעשרות בחמשים סלעים והקרקע שוה מאה סלעים ובאו לעונת המעשרות ברשות הלוקח חייב ליתן מן המעשרות השליש לפי שאינו קנה קרקע עם הירקות במאה וחמשים סלעים הוא חייב בכל המעשרות והלכה כסתם בלבד : **ו** תמד . שם נופל על הזגים והחרצנים הנשארים מן הענבים אחר סחיטתן ועל השמרים היורדין לשולי הכלי: ומתמד הוא שנותנים מים על התמד ומניחין אותו עד שילא ממנו כחו במים ויהיה כמו יין גרוע ושותים אותו והוא אומר בכאן כי אם ילא ממנו אחר שהורק כמדת המים שנתן שאינו חייב מעשר לפי שאין שם יין כלל ואם מלא יותר מן המדה שנתן צריך שידע כמה הוא אותו המותר והוא שיעור היין הנשאר בתמד ומוליא עליו ממקום אחר כמה שהוא חייב באותו התוספת מן החקים וזה הוא ענין אמרם לפי חשבון ואין הלכה כר' יהודה : **ח** שום בעל בכי . הם השומין חריפין מאד ואינם ראוין לאכילה והאוכלן עיניו יורדין דמעות ולפיכך נקרא בעל בכי : בצל של רכפא . הוא בצל שאין לו אלא גלד אחד חריף מאד כשיקרב אל עין האדם מדמע דמעות רבות תרגום חשרת מים רכפת מיא (שמואל ב כב) ואולי הם מיוחסים למקום מן המקומות : וגריסין הם הפולין הטחונים ומן הפולין מין אחד שהגרגרים שלו גדולים מרובעין מיוחסים למקום והוא הידוע כגרים הקלקי : ועדשים המצריות . הם העדשים שהקלה האחד שלהם חד ואלו המינים הם מדבריות אינם נזרעות בגנות וחזקתן מן ההפקר ולפיכך פטורין מן המעשרות : וקרקס בערבי קלקאס והוא ממיני הכרוב ויש אומרים ממין הפול : וקוטנין ממיני העדשים וכבר בארנו פעמים (פ"ז מ"י דפאה ופ"ט מ"ז דתרומות) כי לוף מין ממיני הבצלים : ואמרו העליון אמרו בגמרא כי שיטת המאמר כן הזרע העליון של לוף ופירשו פעמים כרשים שהם חציר : וצנונות . ידוע : ואמרו שאע"פ שאביהן תרומה הרי אלו יאכלו רוצה לומר בזה המאמר כי כשיהיה אחד מאלו הזרעים רוצה לומר זרעוני גנה שאינם נאכלים תרומה וזרעם שהצומח ממנו חולין שאין אומרים גדולי תרומה תרומה אלא כשהזרע הזרוע ראוי לאכילה אבל אלו שאינן ראוין לאכילה מותר לאכול גדוליהן אע"פ שעיקר זרעם הוא תרומה והלכה כסתם :

פי' מהרי"ץ בן מלכי צדק

התרומה . מאי טעמא שהתורם בלבו על הקוטעין ועל הצדדין ועל מה שבתוך התבן והוא שמכר כשתרם תרם על הכל . דתניא בתרומות התורם את הגורן צריך שיכוין לבו על מה שבקוטעין ועל מה שבצדדין ועל מה שבתבן והתרומה תורמין בגורן משיעקר האלה דהיינו משיכנס ראשי השבולין הדומין לאלה תורמין את הגת משילהטו הדרוכות שתי וערב וכן בשמן אבל במעשר לא מחייבי עד שימרח בתבואה . וביין משירד לבור ויקפה ובשמן משירד לעוקה הלכך מה שבתוך התבן ומה שבזפת והזגין מתקני לענין תרומה ובטילי למעשרות אמר הכי צריך לעשר ואינו צריך לתרום : **ה** הלוקח שדה ירק בסוריא. פי' מן הגוי עד שלא בא לעונת המעשרות חייב במעשר שאצל הלוקח נשבלה : ואם משבאו לעונת המעשרות ואחר כך לקחה פטור שבשעת חובתה היתה פטורה שאצל הנכרי היתה: ולוקט כדרכו ואוכל. פי' ואע"ג דבידי גדל אבל פועלין לא ישכור דחיישינן [דילמא אתי לאחלופי] : רבי יהודה אומר אף ישכור וילקט . ולא חיישינן לאחלופי למעבד הכי בשדה שלא הביאה שליש : אמר רבן שמעון בן גמליאל. בד"א פי' דאזלי בתר עונת המעשרות בזמן שקנה קרקע אבל בזמן שלא קנה קרקע אלא פירות עד שלא בא לעונת המעשר פטור סבר לה כרבן גמליאל דתנינן תמן ישראל שהיו אריסין לנכרי בסוריא פי' וארים לית ליה קרקע . ר' אליעזר מחייב פירותיהן במעשר רבן גמליאל פוטר ר' אומר אף לפי חשבון: **ו** המתמד. פי' נותן מים בזגין וסוחטן ומה שיצא משם נקרא תמד אם מצא וכו' . פי' אחר נתן מים בשמרי יין

ואחר כך סננו אם מוצא מים כמו שנתן פטור ממעשר דכמיא חשיב : רבי יהודה מחייב . ומפריש מינייהו אבל לא למקום אחר מאי טעמא דלמא אתי למיפרש מן החיוב על הפטור ומן הפטור על החיוב (אבל) מצא יותר ממדתו לדברי הכל חייב ומוציא עליו ממקום אחר לפי חשבון כגון שנתן ק' לוגין מים ומצא ק"י לוגין י' לוגין מהן חשבינן יין ומפריש עליהן ממקום אחר מעשר לוג אחד אבל תרומה לא מאי טעמא דאמרי' שהתורם בלבו על הקוטעין וכו' : **ז** חורי הנמלין שלנו . שעשו בלילה : בצד הערימה החייבת . פי' במעשר כגון שהיתה תבואה ותנן תבואה אינו מטריח עד שיעמיד ערימה : הרי אלו חייבין. פי' אותן החטין שבחורי הנמלים חייבין במעשר אם באו לידי אדם שבידוע שבדבר גמור הן : **ח** שום בעל בכי . גרסי' בדמאי המינין הללו על ידי שכיוצא בהן בארץ ישראל צרכו חכמים למנותן כלומר שיהו פטורין שמעם מצויין הרוב מחוצה לארץ הן ועל כן הן פטורין ס"א על ידי שאין כיוצא בהן בארץ וכו' גרסי' אי זהו שום בעל בכי כל שאין לו אלא חור אחד מקיף את העמוד ובתוספתא דור אחד כלומר אינו כשום שלנו שהשום שלנו אית ליה דורא לפנים מדורא אבל שום בעל בכי אינו אלא דור אחד רשב"ג אומר כל שאין לה אלא קליפה אחת פי' בעל בכי כלומר כל האוכלו מדמע ובוכה : פ"א כולן על שם מקומן נקראו : בצל של רכפא . גרסי' איזהו בצל של רכפא כל שעוקצו נמעך בתוכו רשב"ג אומר כל שאין לו ארס : וגריסין הקליקין על שם מקומן . גרסינן בירוש' אלו גריסין הקילקין אלו המרובעין ושיעור הגרים לכל רוח ג' ערשות שהוא שיעור הגרים ס' ערשות ועדשים המצריות שגלגליהן חדין רשב"ג אומר כל שאין להן צרורות פטורין : רבי מאיר אומר אף הקריקס . אלו הן הקריקס כל שעוקציהן משטין והלקסיהן מרובין מה דמי ליה א"ר יוסי כגון אלו קנייתא פי' קנייתא הוה ידיע להן טפי מלוף : רבי יוסי אומר הקיטנין פטורין ואין אנו יודעין מה הן : זרע לוף העליון . פי' כיני מתני' זרע הסלון של לוף כלומר זרע הלוף השוטה שכן בלשון יון קורין לשוטה סלי זה פטור ולא זרע של לוף סתם . פ"א קוצי הלוף מלשון סילוא : זרע כרישין וכו' פטורין . מנא הני מילי דת"ר עשר תעשר את כל תבואת אין לי אלא תבואה קטנית מנין ת"ל וכל מעשר הארץ מזרע הארץ לרבות זרע שום ושחליים ונרגר או יכול שאני מרבה זרע הלוף העליון זרע כרישין זרע בצלים זרע לפת וצנונות ושאר זרעוני גנה שאינן נאכלין ת"ל מזרע הארץ ולא כל זרע הארץ שאע"פ שאביהן תרומה הרי אלו יאכלו . פי' אע"פ שהיו הלפת והצנונות תרומה זרען שרי לזרים חדא איתתא הוה לה זרבונין דתרו מה גו קופתא נפלו לגינה וצמחו אתא ושיילה קמיה דרבי יוחנן ושרא לזרים אמר ליה רבי חייא בר אבא ר' ולא משנתינו היא דתנן אע"פ שאביהן תרומה הרי אלו יאכלו אמר ליה בבלאה מן ד גלית לך חספא משכחתא מרגליתא את אמרת ולאו מתני' היא :

חסלת מסכת מעשרות

FROM TERUMAH; BECAUSE WHEN A MAN SEPARATES TERUMAH HE HAS IN MIND THE FRAGMENTS,[11] AND WHAT [IS] BY THE SIDES,[12] AND INSIDE THE STRAW.[13]

MISHNAH 5. IF A MAN BOUGHT A FIELD OF VEGETABLES IN SYRIA[14] BEFORE THE SEASON FOR TITHING ARRIVED, THEN HE IS LIABLE TO TITHE[15]; AFTER THE SEASON FOR TITHING HE IS EXEMPT, AND MAY GO ON GATHERING AFTER HIS USUAL
a MANNER.[1] R. JUDAH SAYS: HE MAY ALSO HIRE WORKMEN AND GATHER.[2] R. SIMEON B. GAMALIEL SAYS: THIS[3] APPLIES ONLY IF HE HAS BOUGHT THE LAND; IF, HOWEVER, HE HAS NOT BOUGHT THE LAND, THOUGH IT WAS BEFORE THE SEASON FOR TITHING ARRIVED, HE IS EXEMPT.[4] RABBI SAYS: HE MUST ALSO TITHE ACCORDING TO CALCULATION.[5]

MISHNAH 6. IF A MAN MAKES POMACE WINE,[6] PUTTING WATER ON BY MEASURE, AND HE FINDS [AFTERWARDS] THE SAME QUANTITY, HE IS EXEMPT FROM GIVING TITHE.[7] R. JUDAH RENDERS HIM LIABLE.[8] IF, HOWEVER, HE FOUND MORE THAN THE SAME QUANTITY, HE MUST GIVE [TITHE] FOR IT FROM ANOTHER PLACE, IN PROPORTION.[9]

MISHNAH 7. IF ANT-HOLES HAVE REMAINED THE WHOLE NIGHT NEAR A PILE OF CORN WHICH WAS LIABLE TO TITHE,[10] THEN THESE ARE ALSO LIABLE,[11] SINCE IT IS OBVIOUS THAT THEY [THE ANTS] HAVE BEEN DRAGGING AWAY THE WHOLE NIGHT FROM SOMETHING [OF WHICH THE WORK] HAD BEEN
b COMPLETED.[1]

MISHNAH 8. BAALBEK GARLIC,[2] RIKPA[3] ONIONS, CICILIAN BEANS AND EGYPTIANS LENTILS (R. MEIR INCLUDES ALSO COLOCASIA, AND R. JOSE SAYS: ALSO WILD LENTILS)[4] ARE EXEMPT FROM TITHES[5] AND MAY BE BOUGHT FROM ANY MAN IN THE SEVENTH YEAR.[6] THE HIGHER SEED-PODS OF THE ARUM,[7] THE SEED OF LEEKS, THE SEED OF ONIONS, THE SEED OF TURNIPS AND RADISHES, AND OTHER SEEDS OF GARDEN PRODUCE WHICH ARE NOT EATEN, ARE EXEMPT FROM TITHES, AND MAY BE BOUGHT FROM ANY MAN IN THE SEVENTH YEAR;[8] AND ALTHOUGH THE STOCK FROM WHICH THEY GREW WAS TERUMAH, THEY MAY STILL BE EATEN [BY NON-PRIESTS].[9]

מסכת מעשרות

הדרן עלך והדרך עלן

(11) The wheat fragments which have not yet been threshed. (12) The sides of the pile (store) of grain, similarly with grapes and olives; cf. *supra* I, 6. (13) Also what is in the peat, and grape-pomace. (14) V. Demai VI, 11; *supra* 13*a* n. b 5. (15) Since at the time of liability for tithing they were under the control of an Israelite.

a (1) He is exempt from tithe even as regards that which grows whilst already in his possession. But he should not hire workmen since he might do likewise in a field which he bought before the season for tithing arrives. (2) V. preceding note. (3) That he is liable if he buys before the season for tithing arrives. (4) Since he possesses nothing in the actual land. (5) This statement reverts back to the first authority. Just as he is liable, if he bought it before the tithing season, to tithe all he had acquired, so is he liable if it was after the tithing season had arrived, to tithe according to calculation that which has grown whilst in his possession; e.g., if the produce had reached only one-third of its normal growth at the time of the purchase (v. *supra* I, 3) he must tithe the two-thirds which grew after it came into his possession. (6) He puts water upon the lees of wine which is untithed so as to obtain the taste of wine from it. (7) Because it is mere water, though it has slightly absorbed the appearance and taste of wine from the husks and kernels. (8) Because its appearance and taste determine its status as wine, v. B.B. 96*b*. (9) I.e., he can even give tithe for it from other wine according to the proportion of the wine he found more than the measure of water he had put in it. (10) Cf. *supra* I, 6. (11) The produce which is found inside the holes is liable both to *terumah* and tithe.

b (1) Since it was near the pile. (2) Enbekhi, later Heliopolis, an ancient city of Syria, v. 'A.Z. 11*b*. *Aliter:* weeping garlic, i.e., the garlic is so pungent that it makes the eyes water. (3) A tuberous rooted plant used for dyeing. *Aliter:* a name of a place. (4) Kind of lentil. (5) Because they grow wild. (6) Even from one who is normally suspected of selling fruits in the Sabbatical year. (7) It is classified with onions and garlic. (8) Because all these are not considered food. (9) I.e., although the seedlings from which they grew were *terumah* (cf. *supra* 1) and the law is that what grows out of *terumah* is *terumah*, these species may be eaten even by non-priests, since they are not considered food.

תלמוד בבלי

מסכת

מעשר שני

תלמוד בבלי

מסכת

מעשר שני

עם פירוש רש״י ותוספות
ובצירוף תרגום ופירוש והערות באנגלית

על ידי
משה צבי סגל ז״ל

בעריכת
יחזקאל (איזידור) אפשטין ז״ל

דפוס שונצין
שנת להחזיר העטרה ליושנה לפ״ק
לונדון

HEBREW-ENGLISH EDITION OF
THE BABYLONIAN TALMUD

MA'ASER SHENI

TRANSLATED INTO ENGLISH
WITH NOTES, GLOSSARY AND INDICES BY

RABBI M.H. SEGAL, M.A.

UNDER THE EDITORSHIP OF

RABBI DR. I. EPSTEIN, B.A., PH.D. LITT.D.

LONDON
THE SONCINO PRESS
1989

COPYRIGHT © THE SONCINO LTD. 1989
ALL RIGHTS RESERVED INCLUDING THE RIGHT TO
REPRODUCE THIS BOOK OR PARTS THEREOF IN ANY FORM

1-871055059

PUBLISHERS' NOTE

This HEBREW-ENGLISH EDITION of THE SONCINO TALMUD is being published to facilitate the easier reference to the original text by scholars and students.

The Soncino Press is privileged to be able to include the Novellae of Rabbi Moshe Feinstein o.b.m., on Tractate Ma'aser Sheini (© Copyright 1973 Judaica Press Ltd), and we wish to thank Judaica Press Ltd. for permission to include this original material.

The Publishers wish to express their sincere thanks to Rabbi Dr. A. Melinek, B.A., Ph.D., for his painstaking care in examining the texts and making the necessary corrections for the preparation of these Tractates.

It has been necessary to duplicate some of the original Hebrew-Aramaic pages in this Tractate where the text has been of such length as to require more than one page of English translation.

MANUFACTURED IN THE UNITED STATES OF AMERICA

INTRODUCTION

SUBJECT OF THE TRACTATE

Our Tractate, as its name implies, deals with the disposal of the so-called Second Tithe with the problems arising therefrom. It is based upon the law laid down in Lev. XXVII, 30—31, and amplified in Deut. XIV, 22 ff. In Leviticus it is said: *'And all the tithe of the land, whether of the seed of the land, or of the fruit of the tree, is the Lord's; it is holy unto the Lord'*. This holy tithe is obviously not the same as the tithe ordained in Num. XVIII, 21 ff., which was to be given to the Levites in reward for their services in the Sanctuary. The Levitical tithe, which was to be eaten anywhere by the Levites and their households like the ordinary produce of the threshing-floor and the wine-press (Num. ibid., 30, 31), could not possibly be described as *'holy unto the Lord'*. Hence Jewish tradition distinguished between the secular Levitical tithe, or the First Tithe, which was an annual tax on the produce of the land, and the holy, or Second Tithe, which according to Deut. XIV, 23, was to be consumed before the Lord in the place which He would choose, viz., in Jerusalem.

Lev. XXVII, 31 further states, *'And if a man will at all redeem ought of his tithes, he shall add thereto a fifth part thereof'*, but does not indicate in what circumstances such redemption might become necessary, or what should be done with the redemption money. This omission in Leviticus is made good in Deut. XIV, 24—26 where we are told that in case the long distance of the Holy City makes it difficult for the pilgrim to carry the tithe in its original form of produce to the sanctuary, he may turn the produce into money and take up the money to the Holy City and spend it there on various kinds of provisions which must be consumed *'before the Lord thy God'*. Thus, the redemption money takes the place of the produce, and the sanctity of the Second Tithe produce is transferred to the Second Tithe money.

CONTENTS OF THE TRACTATE

CHAPTER I. Prohibition of business transactions with Second Tithe produce, or with tithe of cattle, or with first-born animals (1—2); what coins may not be used in exchanging Second Tithe produce for money; concerning purchases made with money which was derived from the exchange of Second Tithe produce (2—7).

CHAPTER II. The uses of Second Tithe produce (1—2); concerning fenugreek and vetches of Second Tithe (3—4); concerning Second Tithe money which became mixed up with secular money (5—6); on changing Second Tithe money (7—9); on exchanging a portion of the wine of a jar for Second Tithe money (10).

CHAPTER III. On payment for carrying Second Tithe to Jerusalem (1); on buying heave-offering with Second Tithe money (2); on exchanging Second Tithe money for produce (3—4); concerning produce which had entered Jerusalem (5—6); concerning a tree and olive-presses which are partly within Jerusalem and partly outside (7); concerning chambers which are partly within the precincts of the Temple and partly outside (8); on Second Tithe or the purchase with Second Tithe money which had contracted a defilement (9—10); on a wild animal bought with Second Tithe money which had died (11); concerning wine jars used for wine of Second Tithe, or heave-offering (12—13).

CHAPTER IV. Concerning the rate at which Second Tithe produce may be exchanged for money (1—3); on the duty of adding a fifth to the exchange money and how this duty may be evaded (3—5); concerning changes in the price of Second Tithe produce (6); on the need of designating Second Tithe money, or a bill of divorce and a gift of betrothal (7); concerning the consumption of produce on account of money set apart for Second Tithe (8); concerning money found or articles with inscriptions (9—12).

CHAPTER V. On the method of marking to prevent a transgression of the law (1); on a vineyard in its fourth year in the vicinity of Jerusalem (2); on the redemption of such a vineyard (3—5); on the triennial removal of dues on produce (6—8); on the designation of tithes at a distance (9); the confession accompanying the removal (10—14); the ordinances of Joḥanan the High Priest (15).

M. H. SEGAL

MA'ASER SHENI

CHAPTER I

a *MISHNAH* 1. SECOND TITHE MAY NOT BE SOLD,[1] NOR MAY IT BE PLEDGED, NOR MAY IT BE EXCHANGED,[2] NOR MAY IT BE USED AS A WEIGHT.[3] ONE MAY NOT SAY TO HIS FELLOW [EVEN] IN JERUSALEM: HERE IS WINE,[4] GIVE ME [FOR IT] OIL;[4] THIS APPLIES ALSO TO ALL OTHER PRODUCE. BUT PEOPLE MAY GIVE IT TO ONE ANOTHER AS A FREE GIFT.

MISHNAH 2. TITHE OF CATTLE[5] WHEN UNBLEMISHED MAY NOT BE SOLD[6] ALIVE,[7] AND WHEN BLEMISHED NEITHER ALIVE NOR SLAUGHTERED; NOR MAY A WIFE BE BETROTHED THEREWITH.[8] A FIRSTLING[9] WHEN UNBLEMISHED MAY BE SOLD ALIVE, AND WHEN BLEMISHED BOTH ALIVE AND SLAUGHTERED; AND A WIFE MAY BE BETROTHED THEREWITH.[10]
b SECOND[1] TITHE MAY NOT BE EXCHANGED[2] FOR UNSTAMPED COIN,[3] NOR FOR COIN WHICH IS NOT CURRENT,[4] NOR FOR MONEY WHICH IS NOT IN ONE'S POSSESSION.[5]

MISHNAH 3. IF CATTLE WAS BOUGHT[6] FOR A PEACE-OFFERING OR A WILD ANIMAL[7] FOR SECULAR MEAT,[8] THE HIDE BECOMES COMMON,[9] EVEN THOUGH THE VALUE OF THE HIDE EXCEEDS THE VALUE OF THE FLESH. IF SEALED JARS OF WINE [WERE BOUGHT] IN A LOCALITY WHERE THEY WERE USUALLY SOLD SEALED,[10] THE JARS BECOME COMMON.[9] IF WALNUTS AND ALMONDS [WERE BOUGHT], THEIR SHELLS BECOME COMMON. GRAPE-SKIN WINE[11] MAY NOT BE BOUGHT WITH SECOND TITHE MONEY BEFORE IT HAS FERMENTED,[12] BUT AFTER IT HAS FERMENTED IT MAY BE BOUGHT WITH SECOND TITHE MONEY.

MISHNAH 4. IF A WILD ANIMAL[13] WAS BOUGHT FOR A PEACE-OFFERING OR CATTLE FOR SECULAR MEAT, THE HIDE

a (1) In Jerusalem or elsewhere, even on condition that it would be taken up to Jerusalem to be consumed there as Second Tithe. But it may be sold in order that its purchase money should be taken up to Jerusalem and be spent there as Second Tithe money, just as Second Tithe can be redeemed by the owner for money; cf. *infra* IV, 6, n. 1. (2) Bartered for other produce. (3) To weigh by it other produce in the scales of a balance. Second Tithe is *'holy unto the Lord'*. (Lev. XXVII, 30), and must not be treated like secular produce. (4) Of Second Tithe. (5) Cf. Ibid. XXVII, 32–33. (6) This is deduced from the expression *'it shall not be redeemed'*. (Ibid., 33), which includes any business transaction. (7) Nor when slaughtered. The only difference between unblemished and blemished is that the unblemished has to be offered as a sacrifice and its flesh consumed by the owner in Jerusalem (cf. Zeb. V, 8), whereas the blemished may be slaughtered and eaten by the owner anywhere. The wording of the text is merely intended to bring out the difference between cattle tithes and firstlings, spoken of lower down in our Mishnah. (8) Cf. Kid. II, 8. This is also considered a business transaction. (9) Cf. Deut. XV, 19–23 etc. (10) Only when it cannot be offered as a sacrifice, viz., after the destruction of the Temple. It is then the property of the Priest.

b (1) Cf. 'Ed. III, 2. (2) Lit., render it 'non-holy' or common. (3) This cannot be called *'money'*; Deut. XIV, 25. (4) Which has become obsolete, or is of foreign origin. (5) E.g., where one has lost his money in the sea, though a diver could recover it for him. (Bert.). With such coin nothing can be bought. (Deut. ibid., 26). (6) With Second Tithe money in Jerusalem. (7) An animal of chase. (8) Lit., 'flesh of lusting'; cf. Deut. XII, 15. (9) Lit., 'non-holy'. No sanctity of Second Tithe attaches to it. (10) I.e., these jars are not sold as a rule without wine, so that the relation of the jar to the wine is that of the hide to the flesh of the animal. (11) תמד, an inferior wine made by steeping in water husks and stones of pressed grapes. (12) It is not yet wine, but mere water; cf. *infra* 5. Mik. VII, 2, nn. 8–9. (13) A wild animal may not be offered as a sacrifice.

א **אין** מוכרין אותו. אפי׳ להוליכו לירושלים כדאמר בירושלמי (הל׳ א) שלא יאמר אדם לחבירו הילך מנה זה של מעשר שני ותן לי בו ר׳ זוז של חולין שוטל ממנו פחות בשביל טורח הדרך ומפרש טעמא אין מוכרים אותו מפני שכתוב בו קודשה ואין ממשכנין אותו מפני שכתוב בו ברכה (א) ומפרש כילד אין ממשכנין אותו לא יכנס לביתו וימשכננו מעשר שני שלו (ב) ומסיק מאן תנא אין מוכרים אותו רבי מאיר ברם רבי יהודה בדין הוא שיהא מותר למוכרו קל וחומר מתרומה שאסורה לזרים ומותר למוכרה והא דתנן בכילד צולין (דף עה:) סכו בשמן של מעשר שני לא יעשו דמים על בני חבורה ההיא סתמא נמי כרבי מאיר ובקונטרס פירש שם טעם אחר : ולא מחליפין. מפרש בירושלמי (שם) לא יאמר לו הילך יין ותן לי שמן הילך שמן ותן לי יין אלא הילך יין שאין לי שמן ואנו הוה לי משח הוינא מיתן לך והלא אומר הילך וכמלאו מחליפין ולא מחליפין ומפרש דכי האי גוונא שרי כיון דאין יכול להוציא ממנו בדין : ולא שוקלין כנגדו. אם יש לו ליטרא פירות של מעשר שני לא ישקול כנגדו פירות חולין אף כנגד סלע של מעשר שני לא ישקול כסף של חולין וטעמא משום בזוי מצוה כדמוכח בפרק במה מדליקין (דף כב:) דאמרינן התם מעשר שני אין שוקלין כנגדו דינרי זהב ואפי׳ לחלל עליהן מעשר שני שמא לא יכוין משקלותיו ומפיק להו לחולין : וכן כל שאר הפירות לא יאמר הילך תאנים ותן לי תמרים : אבל נותנין זה לזה מתנת חנם. אמרינן בירושלמי (שם) מתניתין רבי מאיר היא דאמר אין מתנה כמכר א״ר יוסי דברי הכל היא כהדא דתניא אדם אומר לחבירו בירושלים מה אכלת היום והוא אומר לו קיץ והוא יודע שהוא בכור מה הקיץ נמכר בזול אף הבכור נמכר בזול היה אומר לו מן והוא יודע שהוא מעשר שני מה המן ניתן במתנה אף מעשר שני ניתן במתנה כלומר אפי׳ מאן דאמר מתנה כמכר בכי האי גוונא שמזמן את חברו שיאכל אלנו מודה דשריא ואנשי ירושלים חכמים גדולים ומבינים מתוך רמז והפירות בקיץ נמכרים בזול לפיכך כשיאכל בכור אומר לו שקיץ אכל וחברו מבין וכשיאכל מעשר שני אומר לו שאכל מן :

ב **אין** מוכרין אותו. בפרק כל פסולי המוקדשין (דף לב.) גמר גאולה גאולה מחרמים נאמר לא יגאל במעשר ונאמר לא יגאל בחרמים מה להלן מכירה עמו דכתיב בחרמים (ויקרא כז) לא ימכר ולא יגאל אף כאן מכירה עמו : לא חי ולא שחוט (ד) לאחר שחיטה מדרבנן גזירה אטו לפני שחיטה אבל מדאורייתא שרי כדאיתא התם ובמעשר בהמה של יתומים לא גזור ואפילו לגדול נמי אם שחטו מוכרו בהבלעה בעורו ובחלבו בגידו ובקרניו ואמרינן בירושל׳ (שם) תני אבל מקדשין בגידים ובעצמות ובקרנים ובטלפים א״ר אלעזר מפני שכתוב בו ברכה ויקדש בבשרו א״ר יוסי כלום למדו מעשר בהמה אלא מחרמי כהנים מה חרמי כהנים אין מקדשין בהן אשה אף מעשר בהמה אין מקדשין בו אשה : בבכור מוכרין אותו תמים חי. בפ״ק דתמורה (דף ז:) אמר ר״נ אמר

מעשר שני פרק ראשון

א מעשר א) שני [א]אין מוכרין אותו ואין ממשכנין אותו ואין מחליפין אותו [ב]ולא שוקלין כנגדו [ג]ולא יאמר אדם לחברו בירושלים הילך יין ותן לי שמן וכן שאר כל הפירות אבל נותנין זל״ז מתנת חנם : **ב** [ד]מעשר בהמה אין מוכרין אותו (ג) תמים חי ולא בעל מום חי ושחוט (ה) [ה]ואין מקדשין בו את האשה [ו]הבכור ג) מוכרין אותו תמים חי ובעל מום חי ושחוט (ו) ומקדשין בו האשה [ז]אין מחללין מעשר שני על אסימון ולא על המטבע שאינו יוצא ולא על המעות שאינן ברשותו : **ג** (ח) [ח]הלוקח בהמה לזבחי שלמים או חיה לבשר תאוה יצא העור לחולין אף על פי שהעור מרובה על הבשר [ט]כדי יין סתומות מקום שדרכן לימכר סתומות יצא קנקן לחולין [י]האגוזים והשקדים יצאו קליפיהם לחולין [כ]התמד ג) עד שלא החמיץ אינו נלקח בכסף מעשר ומשהחמיץ נלקח בכסף מעשר : **ד** [ל]הלוקח ד) חיה לזבחי שלמים בהמה לבשר

א **מעשר** שני קדש ולפיכך אסור למכרו ולמשכנו ולהחליפו לפי שהחליפין מכירה בלא ספק : ואין שוקלין בו לפי שהוא בזיון בקדשים כשהוא עושה ממנו אבני משקל ומה שפרש ואמר בירושלים לפי ששם נאכל מעשר שני :

ב מעשר בהמה דינו שאוכלין אותו בעליו בירושלים כמו מעשר שני אחר שמקריבים ממנו חלבו ודמו לפי שהוא קדש ואם נולד בו מום אוכלין אותו בעליו בכל מקום לפי שאינו ראוי לקרבן והבכור הוא לכהן יקריב ממנו חלבו ואוכלו הוא מה שאמר השם (במדבר יח) אך בכור שור או בכור כשב או בכור עז לא תפדה קדש הם את דמם תזרוק על המזבח וגו׳ ובשרם יהיה לך כחזה התנופה וגו׳ ואם נולד בו מום אוכלו הכהן בטומאה בכל מקום וימכרנו למי שירצה ואפי׳ לנכרי ואוכלו לפי שהבכור אם נפל בו מום הוא מתנה לכהן כמו שנבאר בפרק רביעי מבכורות אמר הכתוב (דברים טו) וכי יהיה בו מום פסח או עור וגו׳ בשעריך תאכלנו ואמר הש״י בבכור בהמה (במדבר יח) לא תפדה ואומר במעשר בהמה לא יחליפנו ולא ימיר אותו והיה הוא ותמורתו יהיה קדש לא יגאל (ויקרא כז) ואמרו בספרא בבכור הוא אומר לא יפדה ובמעשר א] שני אומר לא יגאל אינו נמכר לא חי ולא שחוט ולא בעל מום ולא תמים : ואסור לו לקדש אשה במעשר לפי שהוא מכר וכבר בארנו שאסור למוכרו ומותר לקדש בבכור שמותר למכרו ושמא תאמר כיון שהבכור לכהן מה התועלת לזה שקנאו הנה התועלת גלויה ומפורסמת כי אם נפל בו מום והוא אלנו יאכל אותו הקונה אותו : ואסימון הוא הסלע שאינו מפותח כלומר שאין בו צורה וזה למאמר הש״ת (דברים יד) וצרת הכסף בידך ואמר וצרת הכסף דבר שיש עליו צורה בידך פרט למעות שאין ברשותו ומה שאסר חילול מעשר שני על מטבע שאינו יוצא למה שאמר הש״י ונתתה הכסף בכל אשר תאוה נפשך וצריך שיהיה זה הכסף שיוכל להוציאו כמו שירצה מן המאכלים : ג מותר לקנות בהמה לזבחי

יג א מיי' פ"ח שם הלכה ג :
יד ב מיי' פ"ז שם הלכה יד :
טו ג שם הלכה טז ופ"ד הלכה ו :
טז ד שם הל' טז :
יז ה מיי' פ"ז מהל' מעשר שני ונ"ר הלכה יז :
א ו מיי' פ"ג שם הלכה י :
ב ז שם הל' יא :
ג ח שם הל' יג :
ד ט שם הל' יד :

א) קדושין פ"ב דף ע. ב) שם שם :

הלוקח אומן נעשה כלוקח זה בפני עצמו וזה בפני עצמו (ט) : ד לא יצא העור לחולין. במנחות בשילהי התודה (דף פג.) פליגי במתפיס מעות מעשר שני לשלמים אליבא דר"מ דאמר מעשר שני ממון גבוה דרבי אמר א] קנו שלמים ורבי יוסי ורבי אליעזר אמרי לא קנו ופריך [על] רבי אמי ממתני' דהכא למשמע דאפי' העור לא יצא מקדושת שלמים וימכר הכל ויביא בדמיו שלמים והוה מצי לשנויי רבי יהודה היא דאמר מעשר שני ממון הדיוט הוא כדמשני התם אברייתא אלא משום דסתם מתני' רבי מאיר ומשני מאי לא יצא לחולין הייני בתורת (שלמים) לצאת העור לחולין דאין חלה קדושת שלמים אחיה דאי הואי [חיילא]ממילי' הוה נפיק עור לחולין כשאר עורות שלמים ומפרש מאי טעמא לא יצא העור מקדושת מעשר דנעשה כלוקח שור לחרישה דאין דרך מקח בכך לקנות חיה לזבחי שלמים וזה תימה ובהמה לבשר תאוה יצא העור לחולין כמו בחיה לבשר תאוה דמאי שנא ויש ליתן טעם קצת משום דבשילהי התודה ילפינן ממעשר שם שם משלמים ובסיפרי מקרא דואכלת מעשר דגנך יליף שמחה שמחה הלכך בבהמה הראויה לקרבן לא יצא לחולין אלא אם כן תקדש לשלמים ובירושלמי אמר א"ר יוסי בקדמיית' הוינא אמרי' הלוקח בהמה לבשר תאוה מתפיסה לשלמים ולא הוינא אמרי' כלום מן הדא דא"ר אליעזר לא קנה מעשר ב] חזרנו בנו אדר' אליעזר ומפרש לפי שלא התירה תורה ליקח בהמה ג] טמאה בכסף מעשר אלא שלמים בלבד א"ר י גזרו על הנקבה בעלת מום מפני תקנה ד] כדמסיק דהדור אמר בשם רבי יוחנן דמדאורייתא אפי' תמימים שרו אלא גזור בהו רבנן משום דבראשונה היו לוקחין בהמה לבשר תאוה והיו מבריחין אותן מן המזבח חזרו לומר אפי' חיה אפי' עוף לא יקחו כהדא דתני אחד שביעית ואחד מעשר שני מחללין אותן על נקבה בעלת מום ועל שאר בהמה חיה ועוף בין חיים בין שחוטין דברי רבי מאיר וחכ"א אין מחללין אלא על שחוטים ומפרש טעמא שמא יגדל מהן עדרים ומסיק דלא איתמר טעמא דגזירה אלא על השביעית בסוף לולב הגזול מייתי לה (דף מ.): ולא יצא הקנקן לחולין. כיון דדרך למכור היין בלא קנקן ויאכל כנגדו : לא יצא דמי הסל לחולין דאין דרך למכור הסלים עמהם ועוד דגבי קנקן דיין מינכר אגביה כדאמרי' ברים בכל מערבין :
ה ו מים ומלח אין נקחין בכסף מעשר כדאמרי' בפ' בכל מערבין (ד' כז.) ובדגים ובעופות פליגי התם: פירות המחוברים לקרקע הרי הן כקרקע ואין כסף מתחלל עליהם כמו שאין מתחלל על הקרקע : שאין יכול להגיע לירושלים איכך מיירי אפי' לקח בירושלים אבל האי מיירי בשלקח חוץ מירושלים ואין יכולין להגיע קודם שיגישו שם [ירקבו] : פירות שוגג דלא ידע שהן מעות מעשר והוי מקח טעות משום סירחא דאורחא ולא ניחא ליה דטורח הוא בפירות ממעות ואי הוה ידע שהן של מעשר לא הוה זבין בהו והיינו טעמא דבהמה נמי : במקום. היינו ירושלים דכתיב (דברים יב) במקום אשר יבחר : ואם אין מקדש ירקבו לקוח אינו נפדה טהור ברחוק מקום כדתנן לקמן בפ' ג' (מ"י) : תעלה ותאכל במקום . ובפ' האיש מקדש (דף נו.) א"ר יהודה בד"א במתכוין ולקחה מתחלה לשם שלמים ואמזיד קאי אבל נתכוין להוציא מעות מעשר לחולין שלקחה לאכלה חוץ לירושלים בין שוגג בין מזיד יחזרו דמים למקומן שוגג לאו אמתכוין להוציא מעות לחולין קאי דאם כן לאו שוגג הוא ואמזיד קאי והכי קאמר אבל לקחה לשם חולין דמזיד דידהו מתכוין להוציא מעשר לחולין הוא בין שוגג בין במזיד יחזרו דמים למקומם שוגג דמקח טעות הוא מזיד דקנסינן ליה למוכר דלאו עכבר' גנב אלא חורא גנב ובתוספתא (פ"א) מסיים אם היתה בעלת מום בין שוגג בין מזיד יחזרו דמים למקומם אם היו פירות סמאין בין שוגג בין מזיד יחזרו דמים למקומם : על ידי עורה שנס עורה אסור : ז אין לוקחין עבדים · בסיפרי ממעט להו יכול בעבדים ושפחות וקרקעות ת"ל בבקר ובצאן : ואם לקח יאכל כנגדן בירושלים ובפ' האיש מקדש (נו.) פריך ואמאי יחזרו דמים למקומן כי התם כדאמר גבי לוקח בהמה טהורה מזיד במתכוין להוציא מעות מעשר שני לחולין ומשני אמר שמואל בבורח : אין מביאין קיני זבין · כדדרשי' כל דבר שבחובה אינו בא אלא מן החולין :

תאוה לא יצא העור לחולין *כדי יין פתוחות או סתומות מקום שדרכו לימכר פתוחות לא יצא קנקן לחולין סלי *זיתים וסלי ענבים עם הכלי לא יצא דמי הכלי לחולין : ה ג'הלוקח מים ומלח ופירות המחוברים לקרקע או פירות שאינן יכולין להגיע לירושלים לא קנה מעשר ד'הלוקח פירו' שוגג יחזרו דמים למקומן מזיד יעלו ויאכלו במקום ואם אין מקדש ירקבו : ו ד'הלוקח א) בהמה שוגג יחזרו דמיה למקומן מזיד תעלה ותאכל במקום ואם אין מקדש תקבר על ידי עורה : ז ה'אין ג) לוקחין עבדים שפחות וקרקעות ובהמה טמאה מדמי מעשר שני ואם לקח יאכל כנגדן אין מביאין קיני זבים וקיני זבות וקיני יולדות חטאות ואשמות מדמי מעשר שני ואם הביא יאכל כנגדם זה הכלל כל שהוא חוץ לאכילה ולשתיה ולסיכה מדמי מעשר שני יאכל כנגדו :

פרק שני

א מעשר 'שני ניתן לאכילה ולשתיה לסיכה 'ולאכול דבר שדרכו לאכול לסוך דבר שדרכו לסוך לא יסוך יין וחומץ אבל סך הוא את השמן אין מפטמין שמן של מעשר שני ואין לוקחין בדמי מעשר שני שמן מפוטם אבל מפטם הוא את היין *'נפל לתוכו דבש ותבלין והשביחו השבח לפי חשבון דגים שנתבשלו עם הקפלוטות של מעשר שני והשביחו השבח לפי חשבון 'עיסה של מעשר שני שאפאה *והשביחה השבח לשני זה הכלל

יוצא לחולין לפי שאינן ראוים לאכילה על הדרך שחשבו : ה אמר השם יתעלה במעות מעשר שני (דברים יד) ונתתה הכסף בכל אשר תאוה נפשך וגו' ואמרו בכל אשר תאוה כלל בבקר ובצאן וביין ובשכר פרט ובכל אשר תשאלך נפשך כלל העיקר אצלנו בזאת המדה כלל ופרט וכלל אי אתה דן אלא כעין הפרט וכמו שיבאר בפרט דבר שהוא אוכל ורבה מן הארץ כי בקר וצאן מצמח הארץ הם גדלים ואינם דבקים בארץ ואפשר להתקיים זמן כמו כן אין ט [זכות] ס) בכסף מעשר שני אלא דבר שיש בו אלו הענינין שזכרנו ולפיכך אסור ליקח ממעות מעשר שני מים ומלח לפי שאע"פ שהן נאכלים אינם גדלים מן הארץ כי המים יסוד פשוט הם ואינו גדל מן הארץ והמלח אדמה שרופה הוא ולפיכך אסור לקנות פירות מחוברים לקרקע או פירות שאינם יכולים להגיע לירושלים לפי שאנו צריכין דבר דומה לבקר וצאן ויין ושכר : ואמר לא קנה מעשר רוצה בו שאותו דבר הנקנה אינו מעשר ויצאו המעות לחולין : ואמרו יחזרו דמים למקומן ענינו שעל המוכר להחזיר דמים לבעלים ויהיו אותן הדמים מעשר כמו שהיו ויקח פירותיו שמכר לפי שהקונה הוא שוגג והוא מחשב שאין מעשר שני ולפיכך לא יצאו לחולין ולא קנה מעשר ואם קנה במזיד והוא יודע שאלו המעות מעות מעשר שני דין אותם הפירות שיאכלו בירושלים ואם אין מקדש יניחם עד שירקבו : ו תקבר על ידי עורה. ענינה שתקבר בעורה אם מתה כדי שלא יהנה אדם בעורה : ז קיני זבים וקיני זבות וקיני יולדות. הם שתי תורים או שני בני יונה שאלו הם חייבים בהם והם אחד לחטאת ואחד לעולה וכל אלו אין אוכלים אותם בעליהן אבל העולה נשרפת והכהנים אוכלין החטאת וכמו כן האשם אוכלין אותו הכהנים וכבר בארנו שאין קונין במעות מעשר שני אלא דבר הראוי לאכילה ולשתיה ר"ל שיאכלו וישתו אותו הבעלים או שיסוכו בו כמו שנתבאר בפרק שמיני (משנה ב) ממסכת שביעית : וענין יאכל כנגדו שיוציא ממנו כנגד אותן שנסתפק ממעות מעשר שני שלא לצורך אכילה ושתיה ויאכל מהם פירות בירושלים כדין מעשר שני וזה כשקנה במזיד אבל שוגג יחזרו דמיהם למקומן כמו שנתבאר בכאן :

א התורה אמרה שיהיה מעשר שני לאכול שנאמר ונתתה הכסף בכל אשר תאוה נפשך (דברים יד) אבל שיהיה מותר לסוך בו הוא דבר נסמך לאמרו ית' במעשר (שם כו) ולא נתתי ממנו למת ואמרו אם להביא לו ארון ותכריכין דבר שאסור לחי הוא לחי אסור למת לא כ"ש אלא איזה הוא דבר שמותר לחי ואסור למת זו סיכה : לאכול דבר שדרכו לאכול יש בו שני ענינים האחד שאין מטריחין אותו דבר שלקחו במעות מעשר שני אם נפסד ואינו ראוי לאכול כגון לאכול הפת המעופש או יין שנפסד טעמו והענין האחר שאין לו לאכול דבר ממעשר שני שלא כדרכו כגון האוכל ירקות בלי שלוקות או הפירות מבושלות וכיוצא בזה : ואסור לפטם ולרקוח השמן בעקרי' ומרקחות לפי שמפסידין טעמו וימעט באכילתו ולזה הטעם אסור לקנות במעות מעשר שני שמן מפוטם : קפלוטות. החציר הנעשה בארץ הצבי : והמשל באמרו השבח לפי חשבון שיהיו פירות מעשר שני שוה סלע והחולין שנתערבו עמהם או נתבשלו עמהם שוות ג' סלעים וכשיתבשל הכל או נתערב ישוה הכל ה' סלעים נמצא שהסלע הנוסף יש בו למעשר שני הרביע ולפיכך חושבין אותן הפירות בסלע ורביע סלע וחושבין ממעות מעשר שני סלע ורביע סלע יעלה ועל הדרך זה תחשוב : ואמר עיסה של מעשר שני שאפאה. ר"ל בעלים של חולין השבח לשני

א ניתן לאכילה ולשתיה· אמרינן בירושלמי (הל' א) לאכילה שכתב בו אכילה ושתיה שהיא בכלל אכילה ר' יונה שמע מן הדא (ויקרא יז) כל נפש מכם לא תאכל דם מה אנן קיימין אם בדם שקרש והתניא דם שקרש אינו לא אוכל ולא משקה אלא כמות שהוא נקרא אכילה ופריך והתניא המחה את החלב וגמעו והקפה את הדם ואכלו חייב ומה עביד ליה רבי יונה אינו אוכל לטמא טומאת אוכלין ואינו משקה לטמא טומאת משקין ולא מצי לשנויי כדמשני בהקומץ רבה (דף כא.) כאן שהקפהו באור כאן שהקפהו בחמה דהכא דם שקרש קתני שקרש מאליו וקתני סיפא חישב עליו לאכילה מטמא טומאת אוכלים למשקה בטלה דעתו והדר חזר רבי יונה ושמע מן הדא ונתתה הכסף בכל אשר תאוה וגו' מה אנן קיימין אי בטעם יין בתבשיל והלא טעם לפנם הוא והדר קאמר רבי חניא בשם רבי פנחס שמע לה מהדא שבועה שלא אוכל ואכל אוכלים שאינן ראוים לאכילה שתה משקים שאינן ראוין לשתיה פטור הא ראוין חייב ותו דריש סיכה ושתיה בכלל אכילה מדכתיב (דברים יב) לא תוכל לאכול בשעריך תירושך זה יין ויצהרך זו סיכה והתורה קראתן אכילה ורבי אליעזר דריש סיכה מדכתיב (שם כו) לא נתתי ממנו למת מה אנן קיימין אם להביא לו ארון ותכריכין לחי אסור כ"ש למת אלא איזהו דבר מותר לחי ואסור למת הוי אומר זו סיכה ובפרק בתרא דיומא (דף עו:) יליף סיכה כשתיה מקרא אחרינא : לאכול דבר שדרכו לאכול · כי האי גוונא תנן במסכת שביעית פרק ח' (מ"ב) ושם פירשתי : אין מפטמין שמן של מעשר שני . לשום בו תבלין ושרשי בשמים שבולעין את השמן ואזיל לאיבוד דשרשים לא מתאכלי : אין לוקחים בדמי מעשר שני שמן מפוטם · דבעינן דבר השוה לכל ואין זה אלא למעונגין ומפסיד הדמים שמוכרין ביוקר : אבל מפטמין את היין. לעשות קונדיטון : השבח לפי חשבון · כמה היין שוה בפני עצמו והדבש והתבלין בפני עצמו והשבח חולקין ונותן לכל אחד לפי דמיו ופודה היין ולפי שבח המגיעו וכן קפלוטות שישבחו מן הדגים ואתיא הך משנה דלא כרבי יהודה כדאמר במסכת תרומות פ"י (מ"א) וה"נ מייתי לה בירושלמי (שם): השבח לשני לעיסה של מעשר שני ואין נותנין כלל משבח הפת לעצים לפי שאין שבח עצים ניכר בפת: זה הכלל כל

פירוש הרא"ש

(ט) דווקא כשהמוכר והלוקח הדיוטים אבל אם היה אחד מהם יוצר עושה כלי חרש וכן עבדן או רצען כיון שמכירים בטוב כלי חרש ובעורות נותנים עיניהם בקנקן ובעור והוי כמוכר או כלוקח זה בפני עצמו וזה בפני עצמו ולא יצא לחולין: משהחמיץ וכגון דרמא תלתא ואתי ארבע ואף אם לא החמיץ ומשלקחו החמיץ חל עליו קדושת מעשר :

הגהות מהר"י לנדא

מ"ד בר"ש א] דרבי אמר קנו . נ"ל דר"י אמר קנו שלמים ורבי אמי ור"א אמרי לא קנו שלמים ופריך לר' אמי ממתני' מאי לא יצא העור לחולין כנ"ל: שם ב] לא קנה מעשר . פירוש חזרנו כנ"ל : ג] שם ליקח בהמה טמאה. נ"ל טהורה : שם ד] נ"ל מפני תקנת הוולד: מ"ח בר"מ ה] כמו כן אין לו ליקח כנ"ל:

פי' מהרי"י בן מלכי צדק

תאוה לא יצא העור לחולין. פי' לא קנה מעשר כלומר אינו בתורת לצאת העור לחולין לפי שלא התירה התורה ליקח בכסף מעשר שני מבהמות אלא לזבחי שלמים בלבד ולא לשום בשר תאוה דלא קריב מיניה למזבח ולא מידי ותינח תמימים בעלי מומים מאי טעמא לא זבנינן לבשר תאוה א"ר יוחנן גזרו על נקבה בעלת מום שלא תיקנה לתאוה מפני ולדה גזרו על זכר בעל מום מפני נקבה בעלת מום. הא תמימים מדאורייתא לא זבנינן להו הדור אמרו בש"ר יוחנן אפי' תמימים משום גזירה שמא יגדל מהם עדרים ותנינן וחכמים אומרים אין דמי מעשר שני ודמי שביעי' מתחללין אלא על השחוטין וקשיא דהא תנינן לקמן אין לוקחין עבדים וקרקעות ובהמה טמאה מדמי מעשר שני והוא הדין מדמי שביעית ואם לקח יאכל כנגדו אלמא הדמים נתחללו ופריק כאן דרך חילול לא נתחללו הדמים כאן דרך מכירה. [יאכל כנגדו אבל] נתחללו הדמים. ור' חייא בר יוסף אמר כאן כשהמוכר קיים כאן כשהלך לו המוכר : כדי יין פתוחות או סתומות. מקום שדרכן למכור היין בלא קנקן והוא קנה הכל לא יצא הקנקן לחולין אלא יאכל כנגדו וכן הקונה ענבים ותאנים עם הכלים לא יצא דמי הכלים לחולין אלא יאכל כנגדן פי' לפי שהתאנים והענבים אין דרכן להימכר עם הכלים : ה הלוקח מעות ממעשר שני מים ומלח. פי' בירושלים עסיק' . מתני' רבי עקיבא דדריש ריבוי ומיעוטי וקא מרבי דניקח בכסף מעשר שני כל מילי אפי' דגים ועבים וכמהין ופטריות בר סמים ומלח אבל ר' ישמעאל דדריש כללי ופרטי ממעט אפי' דגים ועבים וכמהין ופטריות דלא זבנינן מדמי מעשר שני ומתני' דקתני מים ומלח ותו לא דלא כותיה : ופירות המחוברין לקרקע או פירות תלושין שאינן יכולין להגיע לירושליםכגון ענבים ותאנין לחין :

לא קנה מעשר . פי' לא קנה המוכר המעשר אלא בטלה מקח דאתי למיכלי לוקח בכסף מעשר שני פירות. פי' שיכולין להגיע לירושלים על מנת לאכלן כי היו תלושין ונעשה בשוגג יחזרו דמים למקומן כלומר בטל המקח. א"ר תני זאת אומרת אין מחללין מעות מעשר שני על הפירות ברחוק מקום לכתחלה : מזיד יעלו הפירות ויאכלו בירושלים : ואם אין מקדש קיים ירקבו כאי טעמא קדשי הפירות : ו הלוקח בהמה ממעות מעשר שני חוץ לירושלים שוגג וכו'. כדין הפירות כן דין הבהמה תקבר על ידי עורה פי' עם עורה: תיקבר כלומר לא יפשיט העור מעל הבשר אלא זה וזה יקבר : ז אין לוקחין עבדים וקרקעות מדמי מעשר שני וכן בהמה טמאה ואם לקח יאכל בירושלים כנגד מה שנתן בעבדים ובקרקעות ובבהמה טמאה . והיינו דגרסי' רבי יוסי בן לוי אמר כי פירא כלומר כנגד מה שנתן ולא כנגד מה ששוין הקרקעות והעבדים והבהמות א"ר יוסי בשם ר' שמואל נקנה מקח . וכבר פירשנו משום דעשה דרך מכירה אי נמי איתמי יאכל כנגדן לאו משום דנקנה מקח אלא משום דליתיה המוכר קמן דניהדר : אין מביאין קיני זבין וכו'. ממה שצריך לאכול כנגדן ש"מ קדשו הקינין לשם קרבנו זה הכלל כל שהוא חוץ לאכילה ולשתיה ולסיכה ולקחן מדמי מעשר שני יאכל כנגדו בירושלים :
פרק ב א מעשר שני ניתן לאכילה . מאי טעמא דכתיב ביה אכילה. ושתיה מאי טעמא דשתיה בכלל אכילה: לאכול דבר שדרכו לאכול. כיצד אין מחייבין אותו לאכול לא פת שעיפשה ולא קיבת ירק ולא תבשיל שנתקלקלה צ ורתו. וכן הוא אם ביקש לאכול תרדין לחין או לכוס חטין חיות אין שומעין לו כיצד לשתות דבר שדרכו לשתות אין מחייבין אותו לשתות אינגרון ולא אכסגרון ולא יין בשמרין ולא לסוך דבר וכו' תניא החושש ראשו או עלו בו חטטים סך שמן אבל לא יין וחומץ : אין מפטמין שמן של מעשר שני . פי' פיטום השמן משימין תבלין ועיקרים ומתבשלין יחד עם השמן ונקרא שמן מפוטם מפני שמחסר השמן שהעיקרים בולעין: וכן אין לוקחין בדמי מעשר שני שמן מפוטם . דבעינן דבר השוה לכל: אבל מפטם הוא את היין . פי' לעשות קונדיטון : נפל לתוכו. פי' כתוך יין של מעשר שני דבש ותמרים של חולין והשביח היין אין כל השבח למעשר שני אלא לפי חשבון לשני ושאר השבח לדבש ותבלין . כיצד משערין האומנין מן הפיטום כמה היה שוה היין קודם וכמה היה שוה דבש ותבלין ומה שהשביחו חולקין אם היה היין אחד זהוב ודבש ותבלין חצי זהוב היין נוטל ב' שלישי השבח והדבש שליש תניא לוג יין שנפל לתוכו לוג דבש והרי בו ב' לוגין השבח לפי חשבון תבשיל של מעשר שני שתיבלו בתבלין של חולין השבח לפי חשבון פי' בששבח התבלין ניכרין בתבשיל : עיסה של מעשרשני שאפאה. פי' בעצי חולין : והשביחה פי' שיותר שוה עיסת אפויה מעיסת נא השבח

DOES NOT BECOME COMMON.[14] IF OPEN OR SEALED JARS OF WINE [WERE BOUGHT] IN A LOCALITY WHERE THEY ARE USUALLY SOLD OPEN, THE JARS DO NOT BECOME COMMON.[15] IF BASKETS OF OLIVES OR BASKETS OF GRAPES WERE BOUGHT TOGETHER WITH THE VESSEL, THE VALUE OF THE VESSEL DOES NOT BECOME COMMON.[16]

a *MISHNAH* 5. IF WATER OR SALT[1] WERE BOUGHT, OR PRODUCE STILL JOINED TO THE SOIL, OR PRODUCE WHICH CANNOT REACH JERUSALEM, THE PURCHASE DOES NOT BECOME SECOND TITHE. IF PRODUCE WAS BOUGHT UNWITTINGLY,[2] THE MONEY MUST BE RESTORED TO ITS FORMER PLACE;[3] BUT IF WITH FULL KNOWLEDGE, THE PRODUCE MUST BE TAKEN UP AND BE CONSUMED IN THE [HOLY] PLACE;[4] AND WHEN THERE IS NO SANCTUARY,[5] IT MUST BE LEFT TO ROT.

MISHNAH 6. IF CATTLE WAS BOUGHT UNWITTINGLY,[2] THE MONEY MUST BE RESTORED TO ITS FORMER PLACE;[3] BUT IF [IT WAS BOUGHT] WITH FULL KNOWLEDGE, THE CATTLE MUST BE TAKEN UP AND BE CONSUMED IN THE [HOLY] PLACE; AND WHEN THERE IS NO SANCTUARY, IT MUST BE BURIED TOGETHER WITH ITS HIDE.[6]

MISHNAH 7. MAN-SERVANTS OR MAID-SERVANTS, LAND OR UNCLEAN CATTLE[1] MAY NOT BE BOUGHT WITH SECOND TITHE MONEY; AND IF ANY OF THESE WERE BOUGHT, THEIR VALUE MUST BE CONSUMED [AS SECOND TITHE IN JERUSALEM].[7] BIRD-OFFERINGS OF MEN OR WOMEN WHO HAD A FLUX,[8] OR BIRD-OFFERINGS OF WOMEN AFTER CHILD-BIRTH,[9] OR SIN-OFFERINGS, OR GUILT-OFFERINGS, MAY NOT BE OFFERED OUT OF SECOND TITHE MONEY; BUT IF ANY OF THESE WERE OFFERED, THEIR VALUE MUST BE CONSUMED [AS SECOND TITHE IN JERUSALEM]. THIS IS THE GENERAL RULE: WHATEVER [IS BOUGHT] OUT OF SECOND TITHE MONEY WHICH CANNOT BE USED FOR EATING OR DRINKING OR ANOINTING, ITS VALUE MUST BE CONSUMED [AS SECOND TITHE IN JERUSALEM].

CHAPTER II

MISHNAH 1. SECOND TITHE MUST BE SET APART FOR
b EATING, FOR DRINKING[1] AND FOR ANOINTING;[2] FOR EATING WHAT IS USUALLY EATEN,[3] FOR DRINKING WHAT IS USUALLY DRUNK, AND FOR ANOINTING WHAT IS CUSTOMARILY USED FOR ANOINTING. [THUS] ONE MAY NOT ANOINT ONESELF WITH WINE OR WITH VINEGAR, BUT ONE MAY ANOINT ONESELF WITH OIL. OIL OF SECOND TITHE MAY NOT BE SPICED,[4] NOR MAY SPICED OIL BE BOUGHT WITH SECOND TITHE MONEY;[5] BUT WINE MAY BE SPICED. IF HONEY OR SPICES FELL INTO WINE[6] AND IMPROVED ITS VALUE, THE IMPROVED VALUE [IS DIVIDED] ACCORDING TO THE PROPORTION.[7] IF FISH WAS COOKED WITH LEEK OF SECOND TITHE AND IT IMPROVED IN VALUE, THE IMPROVED VALUE [IS DIVIDED] ACCORDING TO THE PROPORTION. IF DOUGH OF SECOND TITHE WAS BAKED AND IT IMPROVED IN VALUE, THE WHOLE IMPROVED VALUE BELONGS TO THE SECOND [TITHE].[8] THIS IS THE GENERAL RULE: WHENEVER THE IM-

(14) In order to encourage people to use Second Tithe money for buying peace-offerings. (15) And their value must be consumed as Second Tithe in Jerusalem. (16) Since it is unusual to sell olives and grapes without the vessel.
a (1) These do not belong to the list in Deut. XIV, 26. (2) Not knowing that the money was Second Tithe money. (3) The bargain is void. (4) In Jerusalem. Things bought with Second Tithe money cannot be redeemed. (5) After the destruction of the Temple. (6) The hide also belongs to Second Tithe; cf. III, 2. (7) I.e.. the owner must set aside an amount of money corresponding to the amount of money he had expended for them and consume it as Second Tithe. The reference is where he did it with full knowledge, otherwise the law here applies as *supra* 5 and 6. (8) Cf. Lev XV, 14, 29. (9) Lev. XII, 8.
b (1) Drinking is implied in the expression *'and for wine, or for strong drink'*. (Deut. XIV, 26). (2) Ointment is considered a drink for the bones of the human body; cf. Ps. CIX, 18. (3) But not spoilt or raw food. (4) The spices absorb oil which is thus wasted. (5) Because spiced oil is an unusual luxury. (6) Second Tithe wine. (7) If for example the wine alone was worth two *sela's* and the honey or spices which fell into it was worth one *sela'*, and the mixture was now worth six *sela's*, the wine must be assessed for redemption at four *sela's*, and two *sela's* must be assigned to the spices. (8) It must be redeemed at the price of bread without deduction for the cost of baking etc.

PROVEMENT IS RECOGNIZABLE[9] [EXTERNALLY] THE IMPROVED VALUE [IS DIVIDED] ACCORDING TO THE PROPORTION, BUT WHENEVER THE IMPROVED VALUE IS NOT RECOGNIZABLE THE IMPROVED VALUE BELONGS TO THE SECOND [TITHE].

MISHNAH 2. R. SIMEON SAYS: ONE MAY NOT ANOINT
a ONESELF WITH OIL[1] OF SECOND TITHE IN JERUSALEM. BUT THE SAGES ALLOW IT. THEY SAID TO R. SIMEON: IF A LENIENT RULING HAS BEEN ADOPTED IN THE CASE OF HEAVE-OFFERING[2] WHICH IS A GRAVE MATTER,[3] SHOULD WE NOT ALSO ADOPT A LENIENT RULING IN THE CASE OF SECOND TITHE WHICH IS A LIGHT MATTER? HE SAID TO THEM: WHY, NO; A LENIENT RULING HAS BEEN ADOPTED IN THE CASE OF HEAVE-OFFERING THOUGH IT IS A GRAVE MATTER, BECAUSE IN HEAVE-OFFERING WE HAVE ADOPTED A LENIENT RULING ALSO AS REGARDS VETCHES[4] AND FENUGREEK;[5] BUT HOW CAN WE ADOPT A LENIENT RULING IN THE CASE OF SECOND TITHE THOUGH IT IS A LIGHT MATTER, WHEN WE HAVE NOT ADOPTED A LENIENT RULING IN SECOND TITHE AS REGARDS VETCHES AND FENUGREEK?[6]

MISHNAH 3. FENUGREEK OF SECOND TITHE MAY BE EATEN [ONLY] WHEN IT IS STILL TENDER;[7] BUT AS FOR FENUGREEK OF HEAVE-OFFERING, BETH SHAMMAI SAY: WHATEVER IS DONE WITH IT MUST BE DONE IN A STATE OF PURITY,[8] EXCEPT WHEN IT IS USED FOR CLEANSING THE HEAD. BUT BETH HILLEL SAY: WHATEVER IS DONE WITH IT MAY BE DONE IN A STATE OF IMPURITY,[9] EXCEPT SOAKING IT IN WATER.[10]

MISHNAH 4. VETCHES[11] OF SECOND TITHE MAY BE EATEN ONLY WHEN STILL TENDER, AND MAY BE BROUGHT INTO
b JERUSALEM AND TAKEN OUT AGAIN.[1] IF THEY BECAME UNCLEAN, R. TARFON SAYS: THEY MUST BE DIVIDED[2] AMONG PIECES OF DOUGH. BUT THE SAGES SAY: THEY MAY BE REDEEMED.[3] [VETCHES] OF HEAVE-OFFERING, BETH SHAMMAI SAY: THEY MUST BE SOAKED AND RUBBED IN A STATE OF PURITY,[4] BUT MAY BE GIVEN AS FOOD[5] IN A STATE OF IMPURITY.[6] BETH HILLEL SAY: THEY MUST BE SOAKED [ONLY] IN A STATE OF PURITY,[7] BUT MAY BE RUBBED AND GIVEN AS FOOD IN A STATE OF IMPURITY. BETH SHAMMAI SAY: THEY MUST BE EATEN DRY[8] [ONLY]. R. AKIBA SAYS: WHATEVER IS DONE WITH THEM[9] MAY BE DONE IN A STATE OF IMPURITY.

MISHNAH 5. IF COMMON MONEY AND SECOND TITHE MONEY WERE SCATTERED TOGETHER,[10] WHATEVER IS PICKED UP [SINGLY] BELONGS TO SECOND TITHE UNTIL ITS SUM IS COMPLETED, AND THE REMAINDER BELONGS TO THE COMMON MONEY.[11] IF THEY WERE SO MIXED UP AS TO BE TAKEN UP BY THE HANDFUL, [THEY ARE DIVIDED] ACCORDING TO THE PROPORTION.[12] THIS IS THE GENERAL RULE: WHAT IS PICKED UP [SINGLY] MUST BE FIRST GIVEN TO SECOND TITHE, BUT WHAT IS PICKED UP IN A MIXED [QUANTITY MUST BE DIVIDED] ACCORDING TO THE PROPORTION.

MISHNAH 6. IF A SELA'[13] OF SECOND TITHE WAS MIXED UP WITH A SELA' OF COMMON MONEY,[1] ONE MAY BRING COPPER COINS FOR A SELA' AND SAY: LET THE SELA' OF

(9) By an increase in the weight or measure.

a (1) He holds that oil must be used for food only. (2) Oil of heave-offering may be used as an ointment; cf. Sheb. VIII, 3. (3) Heave offering is of greater sanctity than Second Tithe. (4) It may be given to animals; cf. Ter. XI, 9. (5) It may be eaten when green or dry. (6) Both these if of Second Tithe may only be eaten when green; cf. 3 and 4. (7) When it overgrows it becomes tasteless and unfit for ordinary food. But fenugreek of heave-offering may be eaten also when dry since it may be used for other purposes than eating and in an unclean state. (8) With clean hands, as mere indication that it is heave-offering, not to be eaten by non-priests. (9) With hands unclean. (10) Cf. n. 8. Because the water renders it susceptible to contract uncleanness from the touch of the unclean hands. Cf. Lev. XI, 37–38. Maksh., Introd. (11) Like fenugreek, n. 7. They are eaten by human beings only in case of great poverty.

b (1) Which is not permitted in the case of other produce; cf. III, 5. (2) In quantities less than the size of an egg, so that they may be neutralized by the dough. (3) Like other Second Tithe produce which has become unclean. (4) As in **51a** n. a 8. (5) To animals. (6) As in **51a** n. a 9. (7) As in **51a** n. a 10. (8) When it is not susceptible to uncleanness; cf. **51a** n. a 10. (9) Even soaking in water. (10) And were mixed up. (11) Stipulating to the effect that whatever coin in the remainder may belong to the Second Tithe would be exchanged for a corresponding coin in the lot first picked up. (12) If the Second Tithe money was ten and the common money twenty, a third of the money recovered belongs to the Second Tithe and two thirds to the common money. (13) סלע. It equals two silver shekels or four silver *denars*.
(1) And the owner wants to spend the common *sela'* outside Jerusalem.

כל ששבחו ניכר · בירושלמי (שם) פליגי בה רבי יוחנן וריש לקיש רבי יוחנן אומר כל שיש בו הותיר מדה השבח לפי חשבון וכל שאין בו הותיר מדה השבח לשני ריש לקיש אמר כל שטעם שבחו ניכר השבח לפי חשבון וכל שאין טעם שבחו ניכר. השבח לשני ופריך עלה דתניא א] תבלין (של תבשיל) של מעשר שני ב] שנתבשל בתבלין של חולין השבח לפי חשבון [ושל חולין] ג] שנתבשל בתבלין של מעשר שני אל יצא מעשר שני לפדיון ומשני על דעתי' דר' יוחנן והוא שהותיר מדה על דעתי' לריש לקיש והוא שיהא שבחו ניכר דמיכר שבחא טובא מה שהשביחו החולין את המעשר רובא דמיכר בעינא אי נמי ניכר בהזותא וטעמא וריחא דכיון דמיכר כולי האי אין השבח למעשר אלא לפי חשבון אבל היכא דלא מיכר שבחא דחולין במעשר כל השבח למעשר והיכא דמעשר משביח את החולין כגון תבשיל של חולין ג] שנתבשל בתבלין של מעשר אין לו תקנה לפדיון כדתני אל יצא מעשר לפדיון דלא שייך פדיון בדבר שאין בו ממש וצריך להוליכו לירושלים דכיון שהמעשר נתן טעם בחולין אסור לאוכלו בגבולין כדתני' בפרק קמא דחולין (דף ו:) הושש לשאור ותבלין שבה משום מעשר ומשום שביעית : ב אין סכין שמן של מעשר שני . דקסבר רבי שמעון דלא ניתן לסיכה : אם הקל בתרומה · דמותר לסוך כדתנן בפרק ח' דשביעית (מ"ב) וכן בתרומה וכן במעשר שני ור' שמעון לא פליג אלא אמעשר שני : שהקל בכרשינין ובתלתן של תרומה יותר משל מעשר שני כדתנן לקמן (א): ג תאכל למחוכין · כשזרע תלתן של מעשר שני וצמח (ב) ואע"ג דתנן בפ"ט דתרומות (מ"ד) גידולי מעשר שני חולין הא תני סיפא ופודה אותן בזמן זרען והכא בדלא פדה עסקינן ומפרש בירושלמי (הל' ב) כיני מתני' מותר להאכיל למחוכין ואין חוששין משום דבר שאין דרכו לאכול א"כ לא חיישינן אי אכיל ליה בטומאה דלאו אוכל הוא (ג): חוץ מחפיפתה · כהנת חופפת בה ראשה כדתניא תלתן של ד] טבל שחפפה בה בת כהן ראשה אין בת ישראל רשאי לחוף אחריה אלא מגננת שערה בשערה ולא חיישיק אי חפפה בטומאה לב"ה דכל מעשיה בטומאה דלאו אוכל חשוב הוא ואי מיטמא מיטמא אבל בשרייה מיתקן הוא ואסור לטמאותו בידים וצריך לעשותם בטהרה וכזה חמור מעשר שני דלא התרנו אלא למחוכין אבל משתגדיל כל מעשיה בטהרה : ד יאכלו למחוכין · כלומר מותרין לאוכלן : ונכנסין לירושלים ויוצאין · אמר בירושלמי (שם) מתניתין דלא כרבן שמעון בן גמליאל דתנן (בפרק ג משנה ה) מעות נכנסות לירושלים ויוצאות פירות נכנסין ואין יוצאין רבן שמעון בן גמליאל אומר אף הפירות נכנסין ויוצאים והדר מסיק דברי הכל היא הכא הקילו בכרשיני תרומות : יתחלקו לעיסות · ואינן כשאר מעשר שני שנטמא שפודין אותו אפי' בירושלים ומפרש בירושלמי דברי רבי טרפון דאין פודין את הקדשים להאכיל לבהמה ויתחלקו לעיסות של מעשר שני שחלק שבכל עיסה ועיסה יערב מאלה פחות מכביצה דלא מטמא אחרים ויאכל לאדם אגב העיסה דהשתא לא הוי פודה להאכיל לבהמה אלא לאדם ורבנן סברי דנפדה כשאר מעשר שני שנטמא : שורין · דרך להשרותן במים להכשירן לאכילה כדאמר בפ"ק דשבת (דף יז:) : ושפין · כותשין אותן להסיר קליפתן מלשון ואכות אותו תרגום ושפית (דברים ט) : בטהרה · כי היכי דלידעו שהם תרומה ולא יאכלם זר אי נמי להיכר דהוי כשאר תרומה שאין ניתנות לכהן עם הארץ וקצת משמע כן בתוספתא (פ"ב) : ומאכיל אותן בטומאה דלא חשיבי אוכל : וב"ה סברי השריי' לחודא להיכר מהם ואילך בטומאה : צריד · לשון יובש כמו צריד של מנחות בפ"ב דחולין (דף לו·) דהוא יובש מנחה שלא נבלל בה שמן בכולה כלומר מה שהתרנו להאכיל בטומאה ובלבד שיהיו ה] עושים בשעת אכילה שלא יהא ניכר שהוכשרו א"נ לאדם טמא התירו לאכול יבש שלא הוכשרו ולא לטמא במגע דאם נטמאו הן עצמן לא שרו ב"ש לאוכלן : רבי עקיבא אומר כל מעשיהם בטומאה. אפי' בשרייה תניא בתוספתא (שם) תלתן מעשר שני תאכל למחוכים ושל תרומה ב"ש אומרים כל מעשיה ו] בטומאה וב"ה אומרים כל מעשיה בטהרה חוץ מחפיפתה דברי רבי מאיר רבי יהודה אומר ב"ש אומר כל מעשיה בטהרה חוץ מחפיפתה וב"ה אומרים כל מעשיה בטומאה חוץ משרייתה כרשיני מעשר שני יאכלו למחוכין ושל תרומה בית שמאי אומר שפין ושורין בטהרה ומאכילין בטומאה וב"ה אומרים שורין בטהרה ושפין ומאכילין בטומאה דברי רבי יהודה ר' מאיר אומר בית שמאי אומרים שורין בטומאה ומאכילין בטומאה וב"ה אומרים כל מעשיה בטהרה אמר רבי יוסי זו משנת רבי עקיבא לפיכך הוא אומר ינתנו לכל וחכמים לא הודו לו והשתא סתם מתני' בין דתלתן בין דכרשינין רבי יהודה היא : ה לקט למעשר שני עד שישלים אמר בירושלמי (הל' ג) אמר ר' זעירא כדי לשכר שני שמא יאבדו השאר ויהיו אלו שבידו תפיסין על השני אמר ר' זירא וצריך להתנות ולומר אם אלו שלמטן שני יהיו אלו שבידי תפיסין עליהן אמר רבי יונה והוא שילקט מיכן ומיכן אבל אם ליקט על אומן כבולל וחופן מלשון מלא חפניו (ויקרא טז) : לפי חשבון . שאם זה מנה וזה מאתים זה טטל שני חלקים וזה טטל שליש : והנבללים . מפרש בירושלמי רבי יוסי ברבי בון בשם רבי חנינא שלקא מתניתין הנבללין והנחפנין לפי חשבון : ו שנתערבו ורוצה ליטעות בשל חולין : מביא בסלע מעות · של נחשת

כל ששבחו ניכר השבח לפי חשבון וכל שאין שבחו ניכר השבח לשני : ב רבי שמעון אומר אין סכין שמן של מעשר שני בירושלים וחכמים מתירים אמרו לו לר' שמעון אם הקל בתרומה חמורה לא נקל במעשר שני הקל אמר להם מה לא (אם) הקל בתרומה החמורה מקום שהקל בכרשינים ובתלתן נקל במעשר שני הקל מקום שלא הקל בכרשינים ובתלתן: ג תלתן של מעשר שני תאכל צמחונים ושל תרומה בית שמאי אומרים כל מעשיה בטהרה חוץ מחפיפתה ובית הלל אומרים כל מעשיה בטומאה חוץ משרייתה: ד כרשיני מעשר שני יאכלו צמחונין ונכנסין לירושלים ויוצאין נטמאו רבי טרפון אומר יתחלקו לעיסות וחכמים אומרים יפדו ושל תרומה א) בית שמאי אומרים שורין ושפין בטהרה ומאכילין בטומאה ובית הלל אומרים שורין בטהרה ושפין ומאכילין בטומאה שמאי אומר יאכלו צריד רבי עקיבא אומר כל מעשיהן בטומאה : ה מעות חולין ומעות מעשר שני שנתפזרו מה שלקט (ד) לקט למעשר שני עד שישלים והשאר חולין אם בלל וחפן לפי חשבון זה הכלל המתלקטים למעשר שני והנבללין לפי חשבון : ו סלע י) של מעשר שני ושל חולין שנתערבו מביא בסלע מעות ואומר סלע של

מעשר

רוצה בו שלא יתשוב השבח : ואמר כל ששבחו ניכר . הוא שיוסיף אותו הדבר שהשביח במשקל המעשר וכמותו לא שיראה שם החולין באיכות המעשר בלבד ולפיכך אילו רקחו תבשיל של מעשר שני בדבר שיש לו דמים יקרים ויוסיף אותו הריקוח בדמיו חושבין אותו ההוספה ממעות מעשר שני לפי שלא הוסיף בכמו' התבשיל דבר : ב רבי שמעון אינו חולק על דברי הקודם לפי שמעשר שני ניתן לסיכה כמו שסבר מי שלא הבין דברי ר' שמעון ומחלוקתו כי אין מחלוקת שמעשר שני ניתן לסיכה ולא היה רבי שמעון חולק על זה העיקר לפי שפרט ואמר בירושלים אבל היה אומר רבי שמעון אין סכין מעשר שני או היה אומר מעשר שני לא ניתן לסיכה או מה שיביא לזו הכונה ואין הדבר כן אלא שדברי ר' שמעון כמו שאגיד לך והוא שהוא אומר אסור לאדם שיאמר לחברו בירושלים שהוא מקום מיוחד להוצאת מעשר שני שימשח אותו בשמן של מעשר שני ושתמשח יד המושחו ותהיה שכרו על המשיחה שמשחו וזה אינו מותר ר"ל שישתכר אדם ממעות מעשר שני וחכמים מתירין זה כי הם אומרים שאין דמים למשיחת ידו ואין מקפידים בזה : ואמרו לרבי שמעון אם הקל בתרומה חמורה ענינו שהיא אסורה לזרים והתירו בה בזה המעשה רצה לומר שיתן הכהן לישראל שמן של תרומה וימשח אותו בו ולא נקפיד במה שידבק בידו מן השמן אינו דין שנתיר זה במעשר שני הקל שהוא מותר לזרים ועו"ד שנאמר שאנו לא נקפיד במה שידבק בידו מן השמן וכן אמרו בגמרא מה הקלו בתרומה כההיא דתניא סך כהן שמן תרומה ומביא ישראל ומעגילן על גבי מעיו ואינו חושש : ואמר להם רבי שמעון כי אם הקל בתרומה לפי שהוא מקל בתלתן ובכרשינין של תרומה ולא נקל במעשר שני לפי שהוא החמיר בו בתלתן וכרשינין והוא יבואר בהלכה שאחרי זאת ענין הכרשינין והתלתן והיאך החמירו בהם במעשר שני והלכה כחכמים : ג תאכל למחוכים . ענינו שיאכלו כשהן לחים כמו ירקות ואין מותר לו להניחם שיתייבשו כי אם נתייבשו לא יהיו ראויות לאכילה ובתרומה אסור לו להניחם עד שיגדילו : ב"ש אומרים כל מעשיה בטהרה חוץ מחפיפתה. ענינו שכל מה שמסתפקין ממאכל או שתיה וזולתו צריך להיות בטהרה כדי שלא תטמא ולא תהיה ראויה אלא לשרפה וכבר ידעת כי התרומה אסור לגרום לה טומאה כי מותר לרחוץ גופו בה בטומאה לפי שהיא כבר נפסדת ואינה ראויה לאכילה ובית הלל מתירים שיסתפק ממנו בטומאה איזה הסתפקות שירצה אע"פ שיביא אותה לשרפה לפי שאינה מאכל שנקפיד על שרפתה חוץ משרייתה ר"ל להשרותה במשקין שאסור לטמא אותה בידים לזה השיעור לפי שכשורין אותם הוכשרו לטומאה ונמצא שנטמא אותם בידים : ד הכרשינין הם נקראין בערבי כרסנא ואינם מאכל אדם וגם כן הקפיד עליהם שיאכלו למחוכים ממעות מעשר שני קודם שיתייבשו ויפסלו מאוכל אדם ומותר להוציאם מירושלים אחר שיגיעו לשם לפי שאינם פירות כי פירות מעשר שני כיון שהגיעו לירושלים אסור להוציאם כמו שיתבאר לקמן : ור"ט אומר אין פודין קדשים להאכילן לכלבים והמעשר קדש ולפיכך אומר שיתחלק לעיסות עד שיתן ממנה לכל עיסה פחות מכביצה זה השיעור שאינו מטמא טומאת אוכלין כמו שבארנו בפ' חמישי (מ"א) מתרומות : ואמרם מאכילין בטומאה ענינו שמותר להאכילו בטומאה לבהמה כיון שהוא מאכל בהמה ומותר לו שיטמא אותה בידים ואותן הידים אע"פ שאין יודעים להם טומאה הם פוסלים את התרומה כמו שיתבאר בסוף זבים (פ"ה משנה יב) וכל מה שתשמע בזה הענין יעשו או יאכלו בטומאה רוצה בו הידים שהם פוסלים את התרומה וכל מה שיחייב בכאן שיעשה בטהרה רוצה בו שיטול ידיו ואז יתעסק בהם כמו כל אוכל תרומה : שמאי אומר יאכלו צריד . ענינו שלא ישרו אותם ולא יהיו מוכנים לטומאה מאכילין אותם לבהמה בטומאה אבל דינם שיאכלו כתושים והדבר הטחון הטב נקרא צריד ואומר שמאי שכותשין אותן ואין שורין אותן ומאכילין אותן לבהמות כשהן כתושין שמא יטמאו ואין הלכה כשמאי ולא כרבי עקיבא והלכה כחכמים : ה עד שישלים . ענינו עד שישלים מנין הזהב של מעשר שני והשאר חולין ואם נאבד מהם דבר משל חולין נאבד : והנבללין לפי חשבון · כיצד כגון שיהיו מעות מעשר שני מאה סלעים ושל חולין מאתים ובלל וערב הש' סלעים ונתפזרו ונאבד מהם בדבר הדמיון שלשים סלעים נאמר שאותן שלשים סלעים שנאבדו יהיו עשרים של חולין ועשרה ממעשר שני לפי חשבון הממון ועל זה הדרך העשה הקש ופירש הנבללין המעורבים כי שם בלל ה' (בראשית יא) ובכלל זה צריך תנאי והוא שיאמר אם אלו המעות שנשארו מעות מעשר שני הרי אלו שבידי תמורתם והם מחוללין על אלו : ו הסלע הוא מכסף והמעות מנחשת משותח ואומר בכאן שכשנתערבו שני סלעים שיביא חלופי סלע אחת ממעות סלע של מעשר שני ויהיה הכל חולין ואחר כך יקח את היפה שבשני הסלעים ויחלל עליו המעות ויחזיר אותה הסלע מעשר שני ויחלו המעות לחולין :

ואמר

א) עדיות פ"א משנה ה: ב) ב"מ פ"ד דף נה :

פי' מהר"י בן מלכי צדק

השבח לשני . פי' כל השבח לעיסה מאי טעמא דעצים אין בהן ממש : ב רבי שמעון אומר אין סכין שמן של מעשר שני בירושלים . דקסבר אין ניתן לסיכה : וחכמים מתירין . אמרו לו לר' שמעון אם הקל לסוך בתרומה חמורה דמותר לסוך גרסי' מה הקל בתרומה כדתניא סך כהן שמן של תרומה ומביא בן ישראל ומעגלו על גבי מעיו ואינו חושש לא נקל לסוך במעשר שני הקל שמותר לזרים. אמר להן מה לי הקל בתרומה חמורה לסוך שהקל בכרשינין ובתלתן נקל לסוך במעשר שני שלא היקל בכרשינין ובתלתן . בתרומה הקל בכרשינין ובתלתן להיאכל ולהיעשות בטומאה מה שאין כן בתלתן וכרשיני מעשר שני כדבעינן למימר לקמן : ג תלתן של מעשר שני תאכל צמחונין . כיני מתני' מותר לאכול צמותים פי' לא חיישינן להפסד מעשר שני . ויש אומרים מותרת לטמאים עד שהוא צמותים . אבל משתגדיל כל מעשיה בטהרה : ותלתן של תרומה בית שמאי אומרים כל מעשיה בטהרה חוץ מחפיפתה שנעשית בטומאה . פי' דאי אפשר לחפיפה בלא משקה דהיינו שמשימין התלתן . בשמן וחופפת בה הכהנת ראשן וכדתניא תלתן של תרומה שחפפה בה בת כהן ראשה אין בת ישראל רשאי לחוף אחריה אלא מגננת שערה בשערה : ובית הלל אומרים כל מעשיה בטומאה. כלומר דלאו אוכל חשוב : חוץ משרייתה . פי' כששורין התלתן של תרומה במים יהו עושין בטהרה כלומר שלא יטמאה ביד אבל אין נמנעין מלעשות כל מעשיו על ידי משקה ואי מיטמא מיטמא : ד כרשיני מעשר שני מותרין להיאכל צמותים ונכנסין לירושלים ויוצאין . פי' כשישר כדי לעשות עיסה מהן חוץ לירושלים ולחזור ואפי' לרבנן דאמרי פירות מעשר שני נכנסין

ואין יוצאין בכרשינין שדו דנכנסין ויוצאין . מאי טעמא קל היקלו בכרשינין : נטמאו רבי טרפון אומר יתחלק לעיסות . כלומר לא יפדו אלא יתחלק לעיסות של כרשיני מעשר שני שלא יהא במקום אחד מהן כביצה לפי שאין פודין את הקדשים להאכילן לבהמות : וחכמים אומרים יפדו . כדין מעשר שני שנטמא שיפדה : כרשיני תרומה בית שמאי אומרים שורין ושפין . פי' כששורין אותן במים כדי להכשירן לאכול וכששפין אותן פירוש כשמסיר הקליפה מעליהן א"נ שוחקן כדמתרגמינן ואכות אותו ושפית יתיה נשמרין ועושין אותן בטהרה כי היכי דלידעו דתרומה הן ולא יתנום לכהנים עם הארץ ומאכילין אותו בטומאה אפילו לכהן . שמא דלא חשיבי אוכלין ובית הלל [אומרים] השריה בטהרה כי היכי דליתו להו לכהן חבר ושפין ומאכילין בטומאה דעתיהו דבית הלל בכרשינין כמו בתלתן : שמאי אומר יאכלו צריד . כלומר אף [דמאכילם בטומאה] מכל מקום יאכלו יבשין בלי כלום הכשר ובלא שריה : רבי עקיבא אומר כל מעשיהן של כרשינין בטומאה . פי' לא שיעשום שאין לכתחלה אלא מעשיהן על ידי משקה וקוקות לטומאה אם נגע בהן השרץ דלא אוכלין הן ולפיכך ינתנו לכל כהן : ה מעות חולין ומעות מעשר שני שנתפזרו וכו' . פי' כגון שהיו ק' זוזין חולין וק' זוזין מעשר שני ונתפזרו מה שלקט ליקט למעשר שני עד שישלים ק' זוזים והשאר חולין אמר רבי זירא צריך להתנות ולומר אם אלו שלמטה של מעשר שני יהיה אלו שבידי תפיסין עליהן אבל אם בלל המעות וחפן והיה מלקט מלא חפניו : לפי חשבון . פי' מה שליקט ליקט לשניהן : זה הכלל המתלקטין למעשר שני . פירש עד שישלים והנבללין לפי חשבון . אמר רבי יוסי בר בון בשם רב התנא מתני' הנבללין והנחפנין לפי חשבון : ו סלע של מעשר שני ושל חולין שנתערבו מביא בסלע מעות . פי' שהן נחשת ואומר סלע של מעשר שני בכל מקום שהן מחוללת על המעות האלו

ובורר

עין משפט נר מצוה

ה א שם הל' ג :
ו ב מיי' פ"ב מהל' מעשר שני הל' יד :
ז ג מיי' פי"ב מהל' תרומות הל' ז :
ח ד מיי' פ"ב מהל' מעשר שני הל' יד :
ט ה מיי' שם :
י ו מיי' פי"ב מהל' תרומות הלכה ו :
יא ז מיי' פ"ו מהל' מעשר שני הלכה ח :
יב ח שם הלכה ט :

פירוש הרא"ש

[illegible]

הגהות מהר"י לנדא

[illegible]

מעשר שני בכל מקום שהיא מחוללת על המעות האלו ובורר את היפה שבהן ומחללן עליה מפני שאמרו מחללין כסף על נחשת מדוחק ולא שיתקיים כן אלא חוזר ומחללם על הכסף: **ז** בית שמאי אומרים לא יעשה אדם את סלעיו דינרי זהב ובית הלל מתירין אמר רבי עקיבא אני עשיתי לרבן גמליאל ולרבי יהושע את כספן דינרי זהב: **ח** הפורט סלע ממעות מעשר שני ב"ש אומרים כל הסלע מעות וב"ה אומרים שקל כסף ושקל מעות ר"מ אומר אין מחללין כסף ופירות על הכסף וחכמים מתירין: **ט** הפורט סלע של מעשר שני בירושלים ב"ש אומרים כל הסלע מעות וב"ה אומרים שקל כסף ושקל מעות הדנין לפני חכמים אומרים בשלשה דינרי כסף ודינר מעות ר"ע אומר שלשה דינרים כסף וברביעית מעות ר"ט אומר ד' אספרי כסף שמאי אומר יניחנה בחנות ויאכל כנגדה: **י** מי שהיו מקצת בניו טמאין ומקצתן טהורין מניח את הסלע ואומר מה שהטהורים שותים סלע זו מחוללת על זו ונמצאו טהורים וטמאין שותין מכד אחד:

פרק שלישי

א לא יאמר אדם לחבירו העל (לי) את הפירות האלו לירושלים לחלק אלא אומר לו העלם שנאכלם ונשתם בירושלים אבל נותנין זה לזה מתנות חנם: **ב** אין לוקחין תרומה בכסף מעשר מפני שהוא ממעט באכילתו ורבי שמעון מתיר אמר להם רבי שמעון מה אם היקל בזבחי שלמים שהוא מביאן

SECOND TITHE WHEREVER IT MAY BE, BE EXCHANGED FOR THESE COPPER COINS;[2] AND THEN HE MUST SELECT THE BETTER OF THE TWO SELA'S, AND CHANGE [AGAIN] THE COPPER COINS FOR IT.[3] FOR THEY HAVE DECLARED: ONE MAY CHANGE SILVER FOR COPPER [ONLY] IN CASE OF NECESSITY, AND NOT TO LEAVE IT SO BUT TO CHANGE IT AGAIN FOR SILVER.

MISHNAH 7. BETH SHAMMAI SAY: ONE MAY NOT TURN HIS SELA'S[4] INTO GOLD DENARS.[5] BUT BETH HILLEL ALLOW IT. R. AKIBA SAID: ONCE I TURNED SILVER COINS FOR GOLD DENARS FOR RABBAN GAMALIEL AND R. JOSHUA.

MISHNAH 8. IF[6] ONE CHANGES FOR A SELA' COPPER COINS OF SECOND TITHE,[7] BETH SHAMMAI SAY: HE MAY CHANGE COPPER COINS FOR A WHOLE SELA'. BUT BETH HILLEL SAY: SILVER FOR ONE SHEKEL AND COPPER COINS FOR THE OTHER SHEKEL.[8] R. MEIR SAYS: SILVER AND PRODUCE MAY NOT BE EXCHANGED TOGETHER FOR SILVER.[9] BUT THE SAGES ALLOW IT.

MISHNAH 9. IF[10] ONE CHANGES A SELA' OF SECOND TITHE IN JERUSALEM,[11] BETH SHAMMAI SAY: HE MAY CHANGE THE WHOLE SELA' FOR COPPER COINS. BETH HILLEL SAY: SILVER FOR ONE SHEKEL AND COPPER COINS FOR THE OTHER
a SHEKEL. THE DISPUTANTS[1] BEFORE THE SAGES SAY: SILVER FOR THREE DENARS AND COPPER COINS FOR ONE DENAR. R. AKIBA SAYS: SILVER FOR THREE DENARS AND COPPER COINS FOR A FOURTH [OF THE FOURTH DENAR].[2] R. TARFON SAYS: FOUR ASPERS[3] IN SILVER. BETH SHAMMAI SAY: HE MUST LEAVE IT[4] IN A SHOP AND EAT ON THE CREDIT THEREOF.

MISHNAH 10. IF ONE HAD SOME OF HIS SONS CLEAN AND SOME UNCLEAN,[5] HE MAY LAY DOWN A SELA'[6] AND SAY: 'MAY THIS SELA' BE AN EXCHANGE FOR WHAT THE CLEAN SHALL DRINK.' THUS THE CLEAN AND THE UNCLEAN MAY DRINK FROM ONE JAR.[7]

CHAPTER III

MISHNAH 1. A MAN MAY NOT SAY TO HIS FELLOW: 'CARRY UP THIS [SECOND TITHE] PRODUCE TO JERUSALEM
b THAT YOU MAY HAVE A SHARE THEREIN';[1] BUT HE MAY SAY TO HIM: 'CARRY IT UP THAT WE MAY BOTH EAT AND DRINK OF IT IN JERUSALEM'. 'BUT[2] PEOPLE MAY GIVE IT TO ONE ANOTHER AS A FREE GIFT'.

MISHNAH 2. HEAVE-OFFERING MAY NOT BE BOUGHT WITH SECOND TITHE MONEY, BECAUSE THEREBY THE NUMBER OF THOSE WHO CAN EAT IT BECOMES REDUCED.[3] BUT R. SIMEON ALLOWS IT. R. SIMEON SAID TO THEM: WHY, IF A LENIENT RULING HAS BEEN ADOPTED IN THE CASE OF PEACE-OFFERINGS,[4] THOUGH THEY MAY BECOME UNFIT OR A REMNANT

(2) So that now both *sela's* are common. (3) Thus turning the better *sela'* back into Second Tithe. (4) Of Second Tithe money. (5) The difficulty of changing again the gold into silver may cause the owner to delay his pilgrimage to Jerusalem. (6) Cf. 'Ed. I, 9. (Sonc. Ed.). (7) He changes copper coin into silver *sela's*, in order to lighten for the journey to Jerusalem the weight of the money. (8) If pilgrims will bring to Jerusalem only silver coin, copper coin will go up in price and thus cause a loss to Second Tithe. (9) Half a silver *denar* and its value in produce may not together be changed for a silver *denar*. (10) Cf. 'Ed. I, 10. (Sonc. Ed.). (11) Silver for copper in order to buy provisions.

a (1) Young Sages who were not yet members of the Sanhedrin. For their identity cf. Sanh. 17*b*. (2) I.e., for one sixteenth of a *sela'*. So the commentaries, The text is uncertain. (3) According to Bert. it equals one fifth of a *denar*, or one twentieth of a *sela'*. (4) The whole *sela'* without changing it at all, lest when there is any surplus he may unwittingly use it as common money. (5) Unclean persons may not consume Second Tithe produce, but the father wants all the sons to drink wine out of one jug, and the drink of the clean ones should be on the account of Second Tithe. (6) Second Tithe money. (7) The wine drunk by the clean sons becomes Second Tithe, while the wine drunk by the unclean sons (without, of course, coming into contact with the jar itself) remains common.

b (1) It is the duty of the owner to carry up his Second Tithe to Jerusalem. If he employs another person to do it for him, he must not pay him out of the Second Tithe. But he may make him a gift of Second Tithe. (2) A quotation from I, 1. (3) Heave-offering may only be eaten by priests, and by them also only when they are in a state of purity. (4) Allowing it to be bought with Second Tithe money.

OR UNCLEAN,[5] SHOULD WE NOT ALSO ADOPT A LENIENT RULING IN THE CASE OF HEAVE-OFFERING?[6] BUT THEY SAID TO HIM: WHY, IF A LENIENT RULING HAS BEEN ADOPTED IN THE CASE OF PEACE-OFFERINGS, IT IS BECAUSE THEY ARE PERMITTED TO NON-PRIESTS,[7] BUT HOW CAN WE ADOPT A LENIENT RULING IN THE CASE OF HEAVE-OFFERING, SEEING THAT IT IS FORBIDDEN TO NON-PRIESTS?

MISHNAH 3. IF A MAN HAD [SECOND TITHE] MONEY IN
a JERUSALEM AND HE NEEDED [TO SPEND] IT,[1] AND HIS FELLOW HAD [COMMON] PRODUCE, HE MAY SAY TO HIS FELLOW: 'LET THIS MONEY BE EXCHANGED FOR YOUR PRODUCE'. THUS, THE ONE EATS HIS PRODUCE IN A CONDITION OF PURITY[2] AND THE OTHER MAY DO WHAT HE NEEDS WITH HIS MONEY. BUT HE MAY NOT SAY THUS TO AN 'AM HA-AREZ[3] EXCEPT WHEN [THE MONEY WAS] FROM [SECOND TITHE OF] DEMAI.[4]

MISHNAH 4. IF [ONE HAD COMMON] PRODUCE IN JERUSALEM AND [SECOND TITHE MONEY] IN THE PROVINCES,[5] HE MAY SAY: 'LO, LET THAT MONEY BE EXCHANGED FOR THIS PRODUCE'.[6] IF [HE HAD SECOND TITHE] MONEY IN JERUSALEM AND [COMMON] PRODUCE IN THE PROVINCES, HE MAY SAY: 'LO, LET THIS MONEY BE EXCHANGED FOR THAT PRODUCE', BUT ONLY ON CONDITION THAT THE PRODUCE SHALL BE CARRIED UP AND BE EATEN IN JERUSALEM.

MISHNAH 5. [SECOND TITHE] MONEY MAY BE BROUGHT INTO JERUSALEM AND BE TAKEN OUT AGAIN, BUT [SECOND TITHE] PRODUCE MAY ONLY BE BROUGHT IN, BUT MAY NOT BE TAKEN OUT AGAIN.[7] RABBAN SIMEON B. GAMALIEL SAYS: PRODUCE[8] ALSO MAY BE BROUGHT IN AND BE TAKEN OUT AGAIN.

MISHNAH 6. IF PRODUCE HAD ALL ITS WORK FINISHED[9]
b AND IT PASSED THROUGH JERUSALEM,[1] THE SECOND TITHE THEREOF MUST BE BROUGHT BACK AND EATEN IN JERUSALEM.[2] IF ALL ITS WORK HAD NOT BEEN FINISHED, [SUCH AS] BASKETS OF GRAPES [THAT WERE GOING] TO THE WINE-PRESS OR BASKETS OF FIGS [THAT WERE GOING] TO THE DRYING-PLACE, BETH SHAMMAI SAY: THE SECOND TITHE THEREOF MUST BE BROUGHT BACK AND BE EATEN IN JERUSALEM,[3] BUT BETH HILLEL SAY: IT MAY BE REDEEMED AND EATEN ANYWHERE. R. SIMEON B. JUDAH SAYS IN THE NAME OF R. JOSE: THERE WAS NO CONTROVERSY BETWEEN BETH SHAMMAI AND BETH HILLEL CONCERNING PRODUCE WHICH DID NOT HAVE ALL ITS WORK FINISHED THAT THE SECOND TITHE THEREOF MAY BE REDEEMED AND BE EATEN ANYWHERE. BUT ABOUT WHAT WAS THEIR CONTROVERSY? ABOUT PRODUCE WHICH HAD ALL ITS WORK FINISHED, OF WHICH BETH SHAMMAI SAID THAT THE SECOND TITHE THEREOF MUST BE BROUGHT BACK AND BE EATEN IN JERUSALEM, AND BETH HILLEL SAID THAT IT MIGHT BE REDEEMED AND BE EATEN ANYWHERE.[4] IN THE CASE OF DEMAI,[5] [THE SECOND TITHE THEREOF] MAY BE BROUGHT IN AND TAKEN OUT AGAIN AND BE REDEEMED.[6]

MISHNAH 7. IF A TREE STOOD WITHIN[7] AND WAS BENDING OUTWARDS, OR IF IT STOOD OUTSIDE AND WAS BENDING INWARDS, WHAT FACES THE WALL INWARDS IS DEEMED AS BEING WITHIN,[8] AND WHAT FACES THE WALL OUTWARDS IS DEEMED AS BEING OUTSIDE. OLIVE-PRESSES WHICH HAVE THEIR ENTRANCE WITHIN AND THEIR INNER SPACE OUTSIDE, OR WHICH HAVE THEIR ENTRANCE OUTSIDE AND THEIR INNER SPACE WITHIN, BETH SHAMMAI SAY: THE WHOLE IS DEEMED
c AS BEING WITHIN.[1] BUT BETH HILLEL SAY: WHAT FACES THE WALL INWARDS IS DEEMED AS BEING WITHIN, AND WHAT FACES THE WALL OUTWARDS IS DEEMED AS BEING OUTSIDE.

MISHNAH 8. IN CHAMBERS WHICH WERE BUILT ON HOLY GROUND[2] BUT WERE OPEN TOWARDS COMMON GROUND,[3] THE INTERIOR WAS DEEMED COMMON[4] AND THEIR ROOFS WERE DEEMED HOLY.[5] IN THOSE WHICH WERE BUILT ON COMMON GROUND BUT WERE OPEN TOWARDS HOLY GROUND, THE INTERIOR WAS DEEMED HOLY AND THEIR ROOFS WERE DEEMED COMMON. IN THOSE WHICH WERE BUILT BOTH ON HOLY AND ON COMMON GROUND AND WERE OPEN BOTH TOWARDS HOLY AND COMMON GROUND, [THE INTERIOR AND THE ROOFS] FACING HOLY GROUND INWARDS[6] WERE DEEMED

(5) Which restricts the consumption of peace-offerings. Cf. Lev. VII, 17, 19; Zeb. I, 2 ff. (6) And allow it to be bought with Second Tithe money. (7) Thus everybody can eat of it.

a (1) On things which cannot be bought with Second Tithe money; cf. II, 1. (2) The produce has now become Second Tithe which may be eaten only by those who are clean. (3) Who does not observe the laws of purity; cf. Demai, Introd. (4) And thus it is doubtful whether it is really Second Tithe. (5) And he needed the money for things which may not be bought with Second Tithe money. (6) The produce becomes Second Tithe and the money becomes common. For the purpose of such an exchange the produce and the money need not be both in one and the same place. (7) Once produce enters Jerusalem, it must be consumed there as Second Tithe and cannot be redeemed for money. (8) Such as wheat may be taken out of Jerusalem to be ground and baked and then be brought back to Jerusalem for consumption. (9) In connection with its harvesting, when it becomes liable for tithing; cf. Ma'as. I, 1 ff.

b (1) Before it had been tithed. (2) It may not be redeemed for money. For since the produce was already liable to tithing when it reached Jerusalem, a tenth part of it is considered as virtual Second Tithe which had entered Jerusalem; cf. 52a n. a 7. (3) Like regular Second Tithe which had once been brought into Jerusalem. (4) Since the Second Tithe had not actually been separated from the produce. (5) Even if all its work had been finished. (6) Even according to Beth Shammai. (7) Within the wall of Jerusalem. (8) And the Second Tithe of its fruit may not be redeemed, like Second Tithe which has once entered into Jerusalem, 52a n. a 7.

c (1) It all belongs to the precincts of the Holy City in respect of the consumption of sacrificial flesh (cf. Zeb. V, 6–8), of Second Tithe, etc. (2) On the Temple court. (3) Outside the Temple precincts. (4) As outside the Temple. (5) As within the Temple. (6) Lit., 'towards the holy'.

א) מכות פ"ג דף כד: ב) דמאי פ"א משנה ב: ג) מכות פ"ב דף יב. ד) פסחים פ"ז דף פו. ה) יומא פ"ב דף כה. ו) זבחים פ"ס דף ט.

שנתבשל בו אמר רבי יונה דברי הכל היא אוכלי תרומה זריזין הם התיב ר' חנינא קומי רבי מנא והתנן (פסחים פ"ט מ"ח) נתערב בבכורות רבי שמעון אומר אם חבורת כהנים יאכלו ותני עלה יאכלו כחמור שבהן א"ל אוכלי פסח בשעתו זריזין הם כאוכלי תרומה תדע לך שהיא כן דתניק (שבת פ"א מ"י) אין צולין בשר בצל וביצה אלא כדי שיצלו מבעוד יום ותנן (שם) משלשלים את הפסח לתנור עם חשיכה א] ומוכח בסוף מי שהיה טמא (דף לח:) ב] ר' שמעון לטעמיה דמביאין קדשים לבית הפסול דתנן אם שנתערב בשלמים רבי שמעון אומר ישחטו *ויאכלו כחמור שבהן : ג וצריך להם לשאר דברים שלא לאכילה ושתיה וסיכה: ולחבירו פירות והוא אוהבו שיתחלל מעותיו עליהן : אוכל פירותיו · דאין מעשר שני נאכל אלא לטבולי יום : ולא יאמר כן לעם הארץ · שאין נזהר לאוכלן בטהרה : אלא בדמאי · כלומר במעות מעשר שני של דמאי משום דבדמאי הקילו : ד פירות בירושלים · כולה מתני' בשיש לו מעות וצריך להן ולחברו פירות (ב) : ה נכנסין ואין יוצאין · משום דקלטן מחיצות: רשב"ג אומר אף הפירות · מפרש בירושלמי (הל' ג) כדי לעשות עיסה ולחזור כלומר אין יוצאין לפדות כדאמר בפרק הזהב (דף נג:) דמחילה לקלוט דרבנן אלא פעמים יש רחים ותנורים בזול ומוציאן לתקן ומחזירן לירושלים ואוכלן : ו שנגמרה מלאכתן · כדתנן בפ"ק דמעשרות (מ"ה) איזהו גורנן למעשרות : ועברו בתוך ירושלים · בעודן טבל : יחזור מעשר שני שלהן · קסבר מתנות שלא הורמו כמי שהורמו דמיין כדאשכחן ברים הזרוע (דף קל:) והרי קלטוה מחיצות : ושלא נגמרה מלאכתן · כגון סלי ענבים לגת סלי תאנים למוקצה לעשותן קציעות אבל סלי תאנים וענבים לאכילה גמר מלאכתן הן : ר' שמעון בן יהודה בשם רבי יוסי · [ס"ל] מתנות שלא הורמו לאו כמי שהורמו דמיין דמוקי פלוגתייהו בנגמר מלאכתן ואמרו ב"ה יפדה ויאכל בכל מקום ודוקא לענין מחילה לקלוט דרבנן אבל לענין שאר דברים סבר כמי שהורמו דמיין כדאיתא בפרק בתרא דמכות (דף כ:): והדמאי · כלומר טבל של דמאי נכנס ויוצא ונפדה אבל מעשר של דמאי לא ונקט הך סיפא דאפי' תנא קמא מודה. תניא בתוספתא (פ"ב) רבי שמעון בן יהודה בשם רבי יוסי כך אמרו ב"ה לב"ש אי אתם מודים בפירות שלא נגמרה מלאכתן שיפדה מעשר שני שלהן ויאכל בכל מקום אף פירות שנגמרה מלאכתן כיוצא בהן אמרו להם ב"ש לא אם אמרתם בפירות שלא נגמרה מלאכתן שיכול להפקירן להוציאן מידי תרומה ומעשרות אמרו להן בית הלל אף פירות שנגמרה מלאכתן יכול הוא לעשותם תרומה ומעשר עד שירימו פי' יכול לעשותם תרומה ומעשר על מקום אחר כגון תרומה ומעשר ראשון דלא בעו חומה והוא הדין דמצי למימר דממקום אחר יכול לעשר על אלו ונמצא אלו כולן חולין ובירושלמי יש גירסא אחרת אמרו להן ב"ה אף פירות שנגמרה מלאכתן יכול להפקירן ולפוטרן מן המעשרות וגירסא דתוספתא עיקר וטעות סופר בירושלמי דתנן בסוף פ"א דפאה (מ"ו) ונוטל משום הפקר ופטור מן המעשר עד שימרח משמע הא מירח חייב ולא מסתבר למימר דתיתי מתני' כב"ש ומיהו אין כל כך תימה דהא רישא נמי סתמא כב"ש דקתני לעיל נותן פאה ופטור מן המעשרות עד שימרח ואמרי' עלה בירושלמי (הל' ה) דב"ש היא דאמרי הפקר לעניים הפקר ושם פירשנוה במקומה ועוד יש ליישב ההוא דנוטל משום הפקר לפי גירסת ירושל' דהכא אף כב"ה ואיירי התם כשמירח בבית ולא הכניסה במוץ שלה והכא בשמירח בשדה : ז שהוא עומד לפנים· פירשנוה בסוף פ"ג דמעשרות (מ"י) (ג): כלפנים· לענין קדשים קלים ומעשר שני ושילוח מצורעים : בתי הבדים · שעושין שם השמן : ח בנויות בקודש · בתוך העזרה וגגותיהם קדש בפ' כיצד צולין (דף פו.) פריך לרב דאמר גגין ועליות לא נתקדשו ומשני רב חסדא בשגגותיהן שוין לקרקע עזרה : תוכן קודש · כולה מתני' לענין אכילת קדשי קדשים ושחיטת קדשים קלים ולהתחייב עליהן משום טומאה כדתניא בתוספתא. דתניא בתוספתא (פ"ב) לשכה בנויה בקודש ופתוחה לחול תוכה חול וגגה קודש אין אוכלין בה קדשי קדשים ואין שוחטין בה קדשים קלים ואין חייבין עליהן משום טומאה בנויה בחול ופתוחה לקדש אע"פ שאין מקיימין כן תוכה קדש וגגה חול ואוכלין בה קדשי קדשים ושוחטין בה קדשים קלים וחייבין עליה משום טומאה בנויה בקדש ופתוחה לקדש ולחול כולה קדש בנויה בחול ופתוחה לקדש ולחול כולה חול בנויה בקדש ובחול ופתוחה לקודש ולחול כגון לשכת בית המוקד תוכן וגגותיהן מכנגד הקדש ולקדש קודש מכנגד החול ולחול חול בפ' איזהו מקומן (דף נו.) מסיק בנויות בחול ופתוחות לקדש דאין שוחטין ואין חייבין והאי דאוכלים לפי שהתורה רבתה אכילות הרבה מדכתיב (ויקרא ו) בחצר אהל מועד

לידי פיגול ונותר וטמא לא נקל בתרומה א"ל מה אם היקל בזבחי שלמים שהן מותרין לזרים נקל בתרומה שהיא אסורה לזרים :

ג. מי שהיו לו מעות בירושלים וצריך *לו ולחברו פירות אומר לחברו הרי המעות האלו מחוללין על פירותיך נמצא זה אוכל פירותיו בטהרה והלה עושה צרכו במעותיו ולא יאמר כן לעם הארץ אלא בדמאי :

ד פירות בירושלים ומעות במדינה אומר הרי המעות ההם מחוללין על פירות האלו מעות בירושלים ופירות במדינה אומר הרי המעות האלו מחוללין על פירות ההם ובלבד שיעלו הפירות ויאכלו בירושלים :

ה מעות נכנסות לירושלים ויוצאות ופירות נכנסין ואינן יוצאין רבן שמעון בן גמליאל אומר אף הפירות נכנסין ויוצאין :

ו פירות שנגמרה מלאכתן ועברו בתוך ירושלים יחזור מעשר שני שלהם ויאכל בירושלים ושלא נגמרה מלאכתן סלי ענבים לגת וסלי תאנים למוקצה ב"ש אומרים *יחזור מעשר שני שלהם ויאכל בירושלים וב"ה אומרים יפדה ויאכל בכל מקום א) ר"ש בן יהודה אומר משום רבי יוסי לא נחלקו ב"ש וב"ה על פירות שלא נגמרה מלאכתן שיפדה מעשר שני שלהם ויאכל בכל מקום ועל מה נחלקו על פירות שנגמרה מלאכתן שב"ש אומרים יחזור מעשר שני שלהם ויאכל בירושלים וב"ה אומרים יפדה ויאכל בכל מקום ב) והדמאי נכנס ויוצא ונפדה :

ז ג) אילן שהוא עומד בפנים ונוטה לחוץ או עומד בחוץ ונוטה לפנים מכנגד החומה ולפנים כלפנים מכנגד החומה ולחוץ כלחוץ בתי הבדים שפתחיהן לפנים וחללן לחוץ או שפתחיהן לחוץ וחללן לפנים בש"א הכל כלפנים ובה"א מכנגד החומה ולפנים כלפנים מכנגד החומה ולחוץ כלחוץ:

ח ד) הלשכות בנויות בקודש (ד) ופתוחות לחול תוכן חול וגגותיהן קודש בנויות בחול ופתוחות לקודש תוכן קודש וגגותיהם חול בנויות בקודש ובחול ופתוחות לקודש ולחול תוכן וגגותיהן מכנגד הקודש ולקודש קודש מכנגד

ממנו (דברים טו) וגם כן אסור לאכלו אלא בירושלים כמו שנתבאר בתורה וכבר קדם לך כי מעות מעשר שני קונין בהם בהמות ומקריבין אותן זבחי שלמים והשלמים בלי ספק קדש ויפסלו כשהן פגול או נותר או טמא והסור לאכלן והתרומה אין בה לא דין פגול ולא דין נותר ועוד כי לא כל הדברים המטמאין את הקדש הם מטמאין את התרומה כמו שיתבאר בפ' שני ממס' טהרות (משנה ב) ופגול ענינו שתהיה מחשבתו בשעת הזביחה שיאכל ממנו אחר הזמן הקצוב לאכילתו הוא מה שאמר השם (ויקרא ז) ואם האכל יאכל מבשר זבח שלמיו פגול הוא לא ירצה ונותר הוא מה שאמר השם והנותר באש תשרופו (שם ח) ואמר בבשר טמא והבשר אשר יגע בכל טמא לא יאכל באש ישרף (שם ז) ועוד יתבארו דיני הפגול והנותר בפרט במסכת זבחים ואין הלכה כר' שמעון : ג אלו המעות הם מעות ממעשר שני והפירות שהם אצל חברו חולין והם גם כן בירושלים וכשחלל מעותיו על פירות חברו יצאו המעות לחולין ומותר לו למכור ולקנות בהן ואותן הפירות חוזרין פירות מעשר שני ואוכלן בטהרה כדין מעשר שני ויהנו הבעלים בדמיהן שהם מעות מעשר שני ואסור לו לעשות זה עם עם הארץ לפי שהוא חשוד על הטומאה ושמא יאכלנו בטומאה ואם היו אותן מעות של מעשר שני של דמאי הרי זה מותר לפי שזה ספק אם הוא מעשר שני ודאי או לאו ואסור לטמאים או לא וכבר בארנו כי הדמאי חייב במעשר שני בתחלת מסכת דמאי (פ"ב מ"ב) : ד מדינה נקרא כל מדינה ומדינה ממדינת ארץ ישראל לבד מירושלים והכונה כי כשיהיו הפירות או המעות חוץ לירושלים אפשר לו לחללם אבל השמיענו שאין מתנאי החילול שיהיו נמצאות הפירות והמעות במקום אחד ועוד השמיענו שחילול מעות מעשר שני מותר בירושלים אבל פדיית פירות מעשר שני בירושלים אל יעלה על דעתך כאשר יתבאר בזה הפרק ועוד נתבאר לך לקמן ההפרש שיש בין הפירות והמעות : ה ואין הלכה כר' שמעון בן גמליאל : ו כבר קדם לנו כי פירות מעשר שני כשנכנסו לירושלים אסור להוציאם אלא שנאכלות לשם וכל זמן שלא יגיעו לירושלים יכול לפדותם ויעלו המעות לירושלים ועוד אגלנו עיקר אחר ושמרהו והוא שאין פודין מע"ש בירושלים וכשנכנסו פירות שנגמרה מלאכתן בירושלים והוציאו מהן מע"ש החייב להם ונכנסו לירושלים שאין שם שום דרך שיפדה אלא יאכל בירושלים ולפיכך יחזור מעשר שני שלהם ויאכל בירושלים ושלא נגמרה מלאכתן כסלי ענבים לגת שעדיין נשאר לגמר מלאכתן הדריכה והסחיטה או סלי תאנים למוקצה שנשאר ג"כ ליבשן ב"ה אומרים יפדה ויאכל בכל מקום כדין פירות מעשר שני שלא נכנסו לירושלים : והדמאי נכנס ויוצא ונפדה . ענינו כי מעשר שני של דמאי נכנס לירושלים ויוצא ממנה ויפדה אחר יציאתו וזה אסור לעשותו במעשר שני של ודאי וכבר נתבאר לך זה בתחלת מסכת דמאי ואין הלכה כר' שמעון בן יהודה במה שפי' מחלוקת ב"ש וב"ה : ז אמרם לפנים רוצה בו לפנים מחומת ירושלים ובחוץ חוץ לחומת ירושלים ואמר מכנגד החומה ולפנים כלפנים לענין אכילת מעשר שני וזה שאם היה האילן עומד בפנים וטפו נוטה לחוץ שאסור לו לאכול המעשר תחת הנוף אלא לפנים מן החומה ואסור לו לפדותו ר"ל למע"ש כיון שנכנס תחת הנוף וכאילו נכנס בירושלים לענין שלא יפדה וזהו ענין אמרם בפ"ג מן המסכת הקודמות לזו (משנה י) בירושלים הלך אחר הגוף וכבר בארנו זה לשם אבל לענין אכילתו אסור לאכלו עד שיכנס לפנים מן החומה בירושלים וזה לחומרא מב' פנים: בתי הבדים שפתחיהן בפנים וחללן חוץ. חללן ידוע מלשון חלול וזה הוא דמיונם

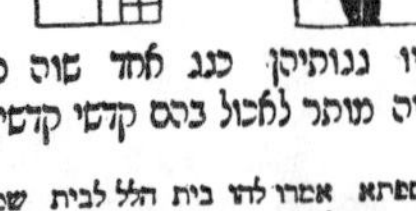

ומאמר ב"ש הכל כלפנים לחומרא וכן נתבאר בתוספתא ר"ל שלא יפדה בהם מעשר שני ולא יאכלנו וב"ה אומרים מכנגד החומה ולפנים מותר לאכול בהם המעשר והקדשים ולא יפדה בו ממעשר שני ומכנגד החומה ולחוץ כלחוץ שמותר לו לפדות בו מעשר שני ואסור לו לאכלו לשם ואמר בתי הבדים לפי שהבדים הידועים לעולם שהם על זו הצורה ר"ל בחומות המדינה הם בתי הבדים: ח לשכות · שם לדיורי העזרה: ואמר גגותיהן קודש בתנאי שיהיו גגותיהן כגג אחד שוה עם קרקע העזרה וזה אפשר כי העזרה בנויה בהר ועוד יתבאר זה במסכת מדות ותועלת היותם קודש כדי שיהיה מותר לאכול בהם קדשי קדשים ולשחוט בהם קדשים קלים ומי שנכנס טמא שם חייב קרבן כמו שיתבאר בשבועות ואלו היו חול היה דינם ודין ירושלים

רבי שמעון בן יהודה אומר משום רבי יוסי לא נחלקו בית שמאי ובית הלל וכו'. תניא בתוספתא אמרו להו בית הלל לבית שמאי אינכם מודים לנו בפירות שלא נגמרה מלאכתן שיפדה מעשר שני שלהן ויאכל בכל מקום אף פירות שנגמרה מלאכתן כך אמרו להן ב...
לא אם אמרתם בשלא נגמרה מלאכתן שיכול להפקירן ולפוטרן מן המעשר תאמר בשנגמר' מלאכתן שאינו יכול להפקירן ולפוטרן מן המעשר והואיל ואינו יכול להפקירן גם המעשר שני שלהן לא יפדה אמרו להן...
אף פירות שנגמרה מלאכתן יכול להפקירן וחולקין בפירות הטבולין למעשר שני ודאי אבל בפירות הטבולין למעשר שני דמאי נכנסין לירושלים ויוצאין ונפדין לדברי הכל : ז אילן שהוא עומד בפנים ונוטה לחו...
ונוטה בפנים מכנגד החומה ולפנים כלפנים וכו' · (גמר' מכות יב) ורמינהו אילן העומד בתוך התחום ונופו נוטה חוץ לתחום או שעומד חוץ לתחום ונופו נוטה בתוך התחום הכל הולך אחר הנוף ופרקי' ערי מקלט...
קא רמית מעשר בחומה תלה רחמנא דכתיב במקום אשר יבחר ה' אלהיך ערי מקלט בדירה תלה רחמנא בנופו מיתדר ליה בעיקרו לא מיתדר ליה ורמי מעשר אמעשר דתנן במעשרות בירושלים הלך...
ופרקי' הא מני ר' יהודה היא דאמר באילן הלך אחר הנוף אבל רבנן קא אזלי בתר חומה כדתנינן ומתני' דהכא רבנן ודמעשרות רבי יהודה . רב אשי אמר אף מתני' דמעשרות דברי הכל ואימא הלך אף...
וכבר פירשנוה במקומה פ"ג דמעשרות תבוקש משם: בתי הבדים. פי' מקום שעושין בו השמן: בית שמאי אומר הכל כלפנים. ואוכלין שם קדשים קלים ואין פודין שם מעשר שני ומצורעין נשלחין משם : ובית הל...
מכנגד החומה ולפנים כלפנים ומכנגד החומה ולחוץ כלחוץ. פי' ואין אוכלין שם קדשים קלים ואין אוכלין שם מעשר בלא פדיה לחומרא: ח הלשכות בנויות בקודש. פי' בעזרה: ופתוחות לחול תוכן חול. ואין נאכלין...
קדשים ואין שוחטין בהן קדשים קלים ואין חייבין עליה משום טומאה : וגגותיהן קודש. אוקימנא בביצד צולין (דף פו) לאו קודש ממש לאכול שם קדשי קדשים ולשחוט שם קדשים קלין . דתניא הגגות האלו אין...
קדשי קדשים ואין שוחטים שם קדשים קלים אלא למאי הלכתא קרי להו קודש לענין הבנין . היכי דמי דבכל הבניי האומנין נוטלין בקטנה ומחזירין בגדולה : בנויות בחול ופתוחות לקודש . פי' לעזרה.
לענין

טז א מיי׳ פ״ב מהל׳ מע״ש וכ״ה הלכה י כ:
יז ב מיי׳ פ״ז שם הלכה א כ:
יח מיי׳ פ״ח שם הלכה ו:
יט ד שם הלכה ס:
כ ה מיי׳ פט״ו מהלכות תרומות הלכה א:

החולולחול חול: טז מעשר שני שנכנסלירושלים ונטמא בין שנטמא באב הטומאה בין שנטמא (ה) בוולד הטומאה בין בפנים בין בחוץ ב״ש אומרים יפדה ויאכל הכל בפנים חוץ משנטמ׳ באב הטומאה בחוץ ובית הלל אומרים הכל יפדה ויאכל בחוץ חוץ משנטמ׳ בוולד הטומאה בפנים: י א) הלקוח בכסף מעשר שני שנטמא יפדה רבי יהודה אומר יקבר אמרו לו לרבי יהודה ומה אם מעשר שני עצמו שנטמא הרי הוא נפדה הלקוח בכסף מעשר שני שנטמא אינו דין שיפדה אמר להם לא אם אמרתם במעשר שני עצמו שכן הוא נפדה בטהור ברחוק מקום תאמרו בלקוח בכסף מעשר שאינו נפדה בטהור ברחוק מקום: יא צבי שלקחו בכסף מעשר ומת יקבר על ידי עורו (ה) ר״ש אומר יפדה לקחו חי ושחטו ונטמא יפדה רבי יוסי אומר יקבר לקחו שחוט ונטמא הרי הוא כפירות: יב המשאיל קנקנין למעשר שני אע״פ שגפן לא קנה מעשר זלף לתוכן סתם עד שלא גפן לא קנה מעשר משגפן קנה מעשר עד שלא גפן עולות באחד ומאה ומשגפן מקדשות בבל שהן עד שלא גפן תורם מאחת על הכל ומשגפן תורם מכל אחת ואחת: יג בש״א מפתיח

HOLY, BUT THOSE FACING COMMON GROUND OUTWARDS[7] WERE DEEMED COMMON.

MISHNAH 9. IF SECOND TITHE WAS BROUGHT INTO JERUSALEM AND IT BECAME UNCLEAN, WHETHER IT BECAME UNCLEAN BY A PRINCIPAL DEFILEMENT[8] OR BY A SECONDARY DEFILEMENT,[9] WHETHER IT BECAME UNCLEAN WITHIN [JERUSALEM] OR OUTSIDE, BETH SHAMMAI SAY: IT MUST ALL BE REDEEMED AND BE EATEN WITHIN EXCEPT WHAT BECAME UNCLEAN BY A PRINCIPAL DEFILEMENT OUTSIDE.[10] BUT BETH HILLEL SAY: IT MUST ALL BE REDEEMED AND BE EATEN OUTSIDE EXCEPT WHAT BECAME UNCLEAN BY A SECONDARY DEFILEMENT WITHIN.

MISHNAH 10. IF WHAT WAS BOUGHT WITH SECOND TITHE MONEY BECAME UNCLEAN, IT SHOULD BE REDEEMED.
a R. JUDAH SAYS: IT MUST BE BURIED.[1] THEY SAID TO R. JUDAH: WHY, IF SECOND TITHE ITSELF WHEN IT BECAME UNCLEAN MAY BE REDEEMED, SHOULD NOT ALSO WHAT IS BOUGHT WITH SECOND TITHE MONEY BE REDEEMED WHEN IT BECAME UNCLEAN? HE SAID TO THEM: NO; IF YOU SAY THUS OF SECOND TITHE ITSELF, IT IS BECAUSE IT MAY BE REDEEMED ALSO WHEN CLEAN AT A DISTANCE FROM THE [HOLY] PLACE;[2] BUT HOW CAN YOU SAY THUS OF WHAT IS BOUGHT WITH SECOND TITHE MONEY, SEEING THAT IT CANNOT BE REDEEMED WHEN CLEAN AT A DISTANCE FROM THE [HOLY] PLACE.

MISHNAH 11. IF A GAZELLE WHICH HAD BEEN BOUGHT WITH SECOND TITHE MONEY DIED, IT MUST BE BURIED TOGETHER WITH ITS HIDE. R. SIMEON SAYS: IT MAY BE REDEEMED.[3] IF IT WAS BOUGHT ALIVE AND SLAUGHTERED AND IT THEN BECAME UNCLEAN, IT MAY BE REDEEMED. R. JOSE SAYS: IT MUST BE BURIED. IF IT WAS BOUGHT SLAUGHTERED AND IT BECAME UNCLEAN, THIS IS LIKE PRODUCE.[4]

MISHNAH 12. IF JARS WERE LENT[5] FOR SECOND TITHE [WINE], EVEN IF THEY WERE CORKED,[6] THEY DO NOT ACQUIRE [THE SANCTITY OF] SECOND TITHE.[7] IF UNDEFINED WINE[8] WAS POURED INTO THEM THEY DO NOT ACQUIRE [THE SANCTITY OF] SECOND TITHE BEFORE THEY ARE CORKED,[9] BUT AFTER THEY ARE CORKED[10] THEY ACQUIRE [THE SANCTITY OF] SECOND TITHE. BEFORE THEY ARE CORKED THEY ARE NEUTRALIZED IN A HUNDRED AND ONE,[11] BUT AFTER THEY
b ARE CORKED THEY SANCTIFY ANY QUANTITY.[1] BEFORE THEY ARE CORKED HEAVE-OFFERING MAY BE TAKEN FROM ONE JAR FOR ALL THE OTHERS, BUT AFTER THEY ARE CORKED HEAVE-OFFERING MUST BE TAKEN FROM EACH JAR SEPARATELY.

MISHNAH 13. BETH SHAMMAI SAY: THE JARS MUST BE

(7) Lit., 'towards the common'. (8) By the touch of a carcase or a dead creeping thing; cf. Kelim I, 1 ff. (9) A defilement produced by the touch of a principal defilement; cf. 'Ed., (Sonc. Ed.), 3b n. a 4. (10) The rule that Second Tithe which had entered Jerusalem may not be redeemed does not apply to such unclean Second Tithe.

a (1) It may not be redeemed again. (2) From Jerusalem. (3) And given to dogs for food. (4) Viz., like the case of produce bought with Second Tithe money, which had become unclean, discussed in the last Mishnah. (5) Outside Jerusalem. (6) After being filled with Second Tithe wine. (7) And the owner need redeem the wine only. (8) Which had not been tithed. (9) If after pouring in the wine and before corking the jars he designated the wine as Second Tithe. (10) If he designated the wine as Second Tithe. (11) If such an open jar containing heave-offering wine was mixed up with 101 jars of common wine, it is neutralized and becomes common, as in the case of heave-offering becoming mixed up with ordinary common produce; cf. Ter. IV, 7.

b (1) If a corked jar of heave-offering wine was mixed with any number of jars containing common wine, all the jars become forbidden to the non-priest, and the owner must sell all the jars, but one, to a priest at the price of heave-offering wine (which is lower than the price of common wine, because its consumption is restricted to the small public of priests), and one jar he must give away to a priest as heave-offering.

OPENED AND EMPTIED INTO THE WINE-PRESS.[2] BETH HILLEL SAY: THEY MUST BE OPENED BUT NEED NOT BE EMPTIED. WHERE IS THIS THE CASE?[3] IN A PLACE WHERE THEY ARE USUALLY SOLD CLOSED;[4] BUT IN A PLACE WHERE THEY ARE USUALLY SOLD OPEN, THE JAR DOES NOT REMAIN COMMON.[5] IF, HOWEVER, THE DEALER WISHED TO IMPOSE A STRINGENCY UPON HIMSELF AND TO SELL [ONLY] BY MEASURE, THE JAR REMAINS COMMON.[6] R. SIMEON SAYS: ALSO WHEN ONE SAYS TO HIS FELLOW: 'THIS JAR [OF WINE] I SELL THEE[7] WITHOUT THE EMPTY JAR', THE JAR[8] REMAINS COMMON.

CHAPTER IV

MISHNAH 1. IF A MAN CARRIED PRODUCE OF SECOND TITHE FROM A PLACE WHERE IT WAS DEAR TO A PLACE WHERE IT WAS CHEAP, OR FROM A PLACE WHERE IT WAS CHEAP TO A PLACE WHERE IT WAS DEAR, HE MAY REDEEM IT ACCORDING TO THE MARKET PRICE OF THE PLACE [OF REDEMPTION]. IF A MAN BROUGHT PRODUCE FROM THE THRESHING-FLOOR INTO THE CITY, OR JARS OF WINE FROM THE WINE-PRESS INTO
a THE CITY, THE INCREASE IN THE PRICE[1] BELONGS TO THE SECOND TITHE AND THE EXPENSES[2] [MUST BE COVERED] FROM HIS HOUSEHOLD.

MISHNAH 2. SECOND TITHE MAY BE REDEEMED AT THE LOWER MARKET PRICE, AT THE PRICE AT WHICH THE SHOPKEEPER BUYS AND NOT AT WHICH HE SELLS, AT THE PRICE AT WHICH THE MONEY-CHANGER TAKES[3] SMALL CHANGE AND NOT AT THE PRICE AT WHICH HE GIVES[4] SMALL CHANGE. SECOND TITHE MAY NOT BE REDEEMED IN A LUMP.[5] IF ITS VALUE IS KNOWN,[6] IT MAY BE REDEEMED ACCORDING TO THE VALUATION OF ONE WITNESS;[7] BUT IF ITS VALUE IS NOT KNOWN, IT MUST BE REDEEMED ACCORDING TO THE VALUATION OF THREE, AS FOR INSTANCE IN THE CASE OF WINE WHICH HAS FORMED A FILM,[8] OR PRODUCE WHICH HAS BEGUN TO ROT, OR COINS WHICH HAVE BECOME RUSTY.

b *MISHNAH* 3. IF THE OWNER OFFERED A SELA'[1] AND A STRANGER OFFERED A SELA', THE OWNER HAS THE FIRST RIGHT, BECAUSE HE MUST ADD A FIFTH.[2] IF THE OWNER OFFERED A SELA' AND A STRANGER OFFERED A SELA' AND AN ISSAR,[3] THE ONE WHO OFFERED A SELA' AND AN ISSAR HAS THE FIRST RIGHT, BECAUSE HE ADDED TO THE PRINCIPAL.[4] IF A MAN REDEEMS HIS SECOND TITHE HE MUST ADD A FIFTH,[5] WHETHER IT IS HIS OWN OR IT WAS GIVEN HIM AS A GIFT.[6]

MISHNAH 4. ONE MAY USE AN ARTIFICE IN RESPECT OF SECOND TITHE.[7] IN WHAT MANNER? A MAN MAY SAY TO HIS GROWN-UP SON OR DAUGHTER, OR TO HIS HEBREW MAN-SERVANT OR MAID-SERVANT: 'TAKE THIS MONEY[8] AND REDEEM[9] THIS SECOND TITHE FOR THYSELF'. BUT HE MAY NOT SAY SO

(2) If he wants to give heave-offering from one corked jar for other corked jars. (3) That if he designated the wine as Second Tithe after he had corked the jars they acquire the sanctity of Second Tithe. (4) Cf. *supra* I, 3. (5) And the jar has to be redeemed together with its contents. (6) If he sold for Second Tithe money a jar full of wine by measure, whether the jar was open or closed. (7) For Second Tithe money. (8) Var. lec. 'its jar'.

a (1) In the city, as compared with the lower price at the threshing-floor or wine-press. (2) Of the transport to the city. (3) For a *sela'* in exchange for the customer's copper coin. He receives copper coin at a lower rate than its real value. (4) For the *sela'* of his customer. He charges the copper coin at a higher rate than its true value. (5) But only according to its exact measure or weight. (6) It has a more or less fixed price. (7) Who acts as valuer. (8) שקרם. Var. lec. שקסם 'which has become pungent'.

b (1) For Second Tithe produce which is to be redeemed. (2) As *infra*, n. 5. (3) The Roman *As*. Its value was 1/24 of a *denar*, or 1/96 of a *sela'*; cf. B.M. IV, 5. (4) Thus increasing the real price of the Second Tithe, although the increase is less than the fifth which the owner would have to add. (5) In accordance with the law in Lev. XXVII, 31; cf. Introd.; B.M. IV, 8. (6) I.e., the produce was given him as a gift before the Second Tithe was taken from it. Cf. *supra* I, 1. (7) To escape the duty of adding a fifth. (8) As a gift. (9) I.e., buy, and since they are not the owners, they need not add the fifth.

תקרא לה שם עד שתאפה דאמר בירושלמי (פסחים פ' ג' הל' ג) ר' ירמיה בעי ויטליננה ויפרידנה לאויר הבית ויקרא לה שם וקאמר התם גבי ב' חלאי זיתים דאויר הבית מצרף לאחד ותימה דמדכתיב ממנו דרשינן מוקף בירושלמי כדפרשי' בפ"ב דתרומות (מ"ב) ואם כן ניבעי שיהא הכל בכלי אחד כדאשכחן גבי מנחה בהקומץ רבה (דף כד) דדרשי' והרים ממנו (ויקרא ו) מן המחובר שלא יביא עשרון בב' כלים ויקמוץ ועוד משמע התם דאפילו אמה קפיזא בקבא אע"ג דעריב מעילאי כיון דפסקי מחילתה מתתאי לא חשיב מחובר וי"ל דשאני מנחה דתליא בקידוש כלי ובעינן קמיצה מכלי שרת משום הכי חשיבי כלים לאפסוקי והא דאמר בפ' הרי עלי עשרון (דף קו:) ואפשר דמייתו שיתין בחד מנא וחד בחד מנא ואגע להו קומץ ההיא כגון עריבה של תרנגולין דאע"ג דמיפסקא מחילתא חשיב מחובר משום דהוי כלי אחד כדאיתא בהקומץ רבה (שם) דהא דדרשי' ברים התודה (דף עז:) גבי תרומות לחמי תודה והקריב ממנו (ויקרא ז) מן המחובר לא כמו שפי' בקונטרס שיהיו הכל בכלי אחד מכיון דלא בעי קידוש כלי דאין מתקדשים אלא בשחיטת הזבח *אלא להצריך כלי משום מוקף מידי דהוה אתרומות דגן וחלה ומעשר דידהו יליף התם מתרומת מעשר והא דדריש התם (שם כג) ואת כל חלבו ירים ממנו מן המחובר שלא ינתח הבשר עד שיטול האימורין כל אחד נדרש לפי עניינו:

בד"א. דמשגפן קרא שם קנה מעשר במקום שדרכן לימכר סתומות דכי האי גוונא בירושלים קנקן טפל ליין כדתנן בפ' קמא (משנה ד) ויוצא לחולין הילכך בגבולין נמי קנה מעשר אבל במקום שדרכן לימכר פתוחות לא יצא קנקן לחולין בירושלים אלא [צריך] לאכול כנגדן הלכך בגבולין נמי לא קנה מעשר: ואם רצה להחמיר על עצמו למכור במדה יצא הקנקן לחולין לא בעי למימר שימכור מעשר שני במדה דאין מעשר שני נמכר כדתנן בריש מכילתין דאין מוכרין אותו ואין מחליפין אותו אלא משום דאמרי' בירושלמי (פ"ק הל' ג) כדפרשינן בפ"ק דאם היה המוכר או הלוקח אומן נעשה כלוקח יין בפני עצמו והקנקן בפני עצמו ואין יוצא הקנקן לחולין מידי דהוה אמוכר במדה והוא הדין בגבולין אם הוא אומן דמשגפן קרא שם לא קנה מעשר דכל היכא דבירושלים אין הקנקן טפל ליין בגבולין נמי אין הקנקן טפל ליין והשתא הכי קאמר אם רצה להחמיר על עצמו זה האומן שהוא כמוכר במדה שכנס היין בקנקן וגפה וקרא שם ומן הדין כיון שהוא אומן יצא הקנקן לחולין ולא קנה מעשר אלא אם רצה יכול להחמיר על עצמו: חבית זו אני מוכר לך חוץ מקנקנה. מילתא דר' שמעון לא מפרשה אלא ע"פ הירושלמי והתוספתא (פרק ג) דתניא התם אבל הפקיד לתוכה רביעית של חולין לא קנה מעשר ואמרינן בירושלמי אמר רביעית של חולין בחבית זו יצא קנקן לחולין אמר ר' חייא בשם ר' יוחנן מתני' אמרה כן ר' שמעון אומר אף האומר לחברו חבית זו אני מוכר לך חוץ מקנקנה יצא קנקן לחולין ועל זה קאי ר"ש דקאמר תנא קמא דאם משגפן קרא שם קנה מעשר ואשמעי' ר"ש דדוקא שקורא שם לכל היין [אבל] אם אמר כל היין מעשר חוץ מרביעיה אע"פ כשבא למכור לחברו אותו רביעית אומר לו חבית זו כלומר רביעית זו אני מוכר לך חוץ מן הקנקן שאני רוצה לשייר בשביל מעשר שני שבתוכה אפי' הכי לא נעשית הקנקן טפל למעשר ויצא הקנקן לחולין ולא קנה מעשר:

א בשער מקומו. כשער מקום שהוא בשעת פדיה בין להקל בין להחמיר (א): השבח לשני. בעיר דמיו יקרים והשבח למעשר שני: ויציאות מביתו. מגלט מה שהוציא להביאו בעיר: ב בשער הזול. מפרש בירושלמי (הל' א') א"ר ירמיה כמה בר נשי בעו בערובתא בפתי רמשא מנשייא קלען ומעביר עליהון ומתיין פריסין ומפריקנא פי' בערובתא בערב שבת בפתי רמשא סמוך לחשיכה מנשייא קלען מן הנשים הסורקות ראשיהן וקולעות שערן ומעביר עליהם דוחק עצמו לקנות מהן פירות דאדם הדוחק לחזר כל כך בכל המקומות הולך עד שקונה בזול: כמות שהחנוני לוקח. דרך חנוני לוקח בזול ומוכר ביוקר: כמות שהשולחני פורט. כששמין מעשר שני בפרוטות ובא לחלל הפרוטות על הסלע מונה פרוטות בסלע כמו שהשולחני מוכרם: ולא כמו שהוא מצרף. שנותן מעות ולוקח סלע שמצרף בזול ובתוספתא (פ"ג) תני הפורט דינר כסף למעשר שני כמו שהשולחני פורט ולא כמו שמוכר המצרף דינר זהב למעשר שני כמו שהשולחני פורט ולא כמו שהוא מצרף:

ושל ליר ושל דבש בין שנפן בין שלא גפן לא קנה מעשר קנקן: יג עיקר ההלכה כי כשמכר אדם יין בירושלים וקנה ממנו במעות מעשר שני בש"א שפותחין הקנקנים ומערין אותן מה שבהן לגת ומוכר לגת ואז יצאו הקנקנים לחולין אבל אם מכר היין והוא בקנקניו לא יצא קנקן לחולין ואמר ב"ה שאם היה דרכו למכור אותם הקנקנים סתומות ומוכרן פתוחות יצא קנקן לחולין ואינו צריך לערות ואז ימכור לפי שכיון שפתחם גלה דעתו שאין רצונו למכור הקנקן ואם מכר במדה ואמר מדת כך וכך בכך וכך דמים יצא קנקן לחולין אפילו היו סתומות ודברי ר"ש אמת ואין עליו חולק:

ומערה לגת "ובה"א מפתיה ואינו צריך לערות בד"א במקום שדרכן לימכר סתומות אבל במקום שדרכן לימכר פתוחות לא יצא קנקן לחולין אבל אם רצה להחמיר על עצמו למכור במדה יצא קנקן לחולין ר"ש אומר אף האומר לחברו חבית זו אני מוכרה לך חוץ מקנקניה יצא קנקן לחולין:

פרק רביעי

א **המוליך** פירות מעשר שני ממקום היוקר למקום הזול או ממקום הזול למקום היוקר פודהו כשער מקומו המביא פירות מן הגורן לעיר וכדי יין מן הגת לעיר השבח לשני ויציאות מביתו: **ב** פודין מעשר שני בשער הזול כמות שהחנוני לוקח לא כמות שהוא מוכר כמות שהשולחני פורט ולא כמות שהוא מצרף ואין פודין מעשר שני אכסרה את שדמיו ידועין יפדה ע"פ עד אחד ואת שאין דמיו ידועים יפדה על פי ג' כגון היין שקרם ופירות שהרקיבו ומעות שהחליאו: **ג** בעל הבית אומר בסלע ואחר אומר בסלע בעל הבית קודם מפני שהוא מוסיף חומש בעל הבית אומר בסלע ואחר אומר בסלע ואיסר את של סלע ואיסר קודם מפני שהוא מוסיף על הקרן הפודה מעשר שני שלו מוסיף עליו חמישית בין שהוא שלו ובין שניתן לו במתנה: **ד** מערימין על מעשר שני כיצד אומר אדם לבנו ולבתו הגדולים לעבדו ולשפחתו העברים הילך מעות אלו ופדה לך מעשר שני זה אבל לא יאמר כן

א יוקר וזול הפכים ועניינם ידוע ואמרו המוליך אם עבר והוליך אבל לכתחלה אסור אלא פודהו במקומו או מעלה אותו לירושלים: השבח לשני. עניינו כי אותו השבח שהשביחו דמיהן הם למעשר שני לפי שהפירות יותר שוות במדינה ממה שהם שוות בשדה בלי ספק שאם היו הפירות שוות בשדה על דרך הדמיון סלע אחד והכניסן למדינה והם שוין שני סלעים צריך לפדות' בשני סלעים ה] ומי שהוא חייב להוליכן עד שיגיעו למדינה אין לו לחשוב השכר על מעשר שני וזהו ענין אמרם והיציאות מביתו ויציאה כמו ההוצאה וקראו אותה כן לפי שהוא ממון יוצא מרשותו של אדם: ב אמרו בשער הזול הוא מה שפירש ואמר כמו שהחנוני לוקח ושולחני הוא המחליף: ושולחן שם להיבת השלחוני ויחסוה אליו ופורט הוא מה שלוקח השלחוני מבני אדם ומצרף מה שנותן להם אמר בכאן שאם היה השלחוני בדרך הדמיון לוקח בסלע עשרים וחמש מעות הוא נותן בו כשמחליף עשרים וארבעה מעות ומי שרצה להחליף מעות והם המעות בדרך הדמיון שהוא רוצה להחליף סלע יש לו להחליף אותו סלע בעשרים וארבעה מעות שהם חלופי סלע כשלוקח משלחני: אכסרה. כלומר באומד וכבר בארנו זה (דמאי פ"ב מ"ה) והטעם בזה כי הפדיון לא יהיה אלא בדמי הדבר הנמכר ואם פדאו בעליו יוסיף חומש למאמר השם יתברך (ויקרא כז) וחמישיתו יוסף עליו וכשיהיה מכר הנמכר שהוא רוצה לפדותו יפה יהיה ואין בו הפסד יהיה ערכו ידוע וכשהתחיל להפסד לא יודע ערכו לפי שכשיעור ההפסד ישתנה הערך ואמרם על פי שלשה צריך שיהיו סוחרים ואפי' יהיה אחד מהם נכרי או בעל הממון הרי זה מותר: היין שקרם. כלומר שהתחיל להחמיץ: ופירות שהרקיבו. כמו נתעפשו: ומעות שהחליאו. עניינו שכהו או העלו חלודה ושהגה מראיהן והוא כמו החלידו: ג כבר בארנו במה שקדם כי החומש הוא רביע עיקר הממון והוא אומרו עד שיהא הוא וחומשו חמשה שהוא נותן במה שישוה סלע סלע ודינר כי הסלע ארבעה דינרים והדינר ששה מעין והמעה ארבעה איסרים אם כן איסר חלק משמונה ותשעים מן הסלע ומה שנתנו מעלה לסלע ואיסר על סלע ודינר שאע"פ שהוא יותר לפי שהוא יכול להערים על החומש ולא יתן אותו כמו שיתבאר לקמן על כן נחוש לתוספת שתהיה בעיקר וכן נתנו הטעם בגמרא ודע כי מעשר שני ממון גבוה הוא ולפיכך לא תתקיים בו המתנה אלא בהגלאי והוא שיהגנו לו והוא טבל ר"ל קודם הולאתו והפרשתו אבל כשהוציאו אין לו רשות ליתנו במתנה בשום פנים: ד עבד עברי אין גופו קנוי אלא מעשה ידיו בלבד והוא

אכסרה. בלא מדה ובלא משקל כדתניא בתוספתא (שם) אין פודין מעשר שני אכסרה כיצד היו לו פירות מרקיבין מעות מחלידין לא יאמר כמה אדם רוצה ליתן בצבור זה וכמה אדם רוצה ליתן בכרי זה אלא אומר כמה אדם רוצה ליקח פירות בסלע וכמה אדם רוצה ליקח מעות בדינר: על פי עד אחד. על פי שומת לוקח אחד: שאין דמיו ידועין. צריך בקיאות יותר משום הכי בעי שלשה ואמרי' בפרק קמא דסנהדרין (דף יד:) בשלשה לקוחות ולא בשלשה שאינם לקוחות ואפי' אחד מהן בעלים או נכרי: שהקסים בפרק קמא דסנהדרין (שם) תני יין שהקרים והכל חד והוא כשהיין מתחיל להחמיץ קסם מלשון פריו יקוסס (יחזקאל יז): ג שמוסיף חומש. כדכתיב אם גאל יגאל איש ממעשרו (ויקרא כז) על מעשר שני שלו מוסיף חומש ולא על מעשר שני של חברו: [של סלע ואיסר קודם. מפני שמוסיף על הקרן] בפ' המקדיש שדהו (כז:) פריך ממתני' דהכא אמתני' דהתם דמשמע גבי הקדש בחומש עדיף ומשני התם לחומשא רווחא דהקדש הוא חומש עדיף הכא דהומשא רווחא דבעל הבית הוא קרנא עדיפא תיפרוק שפיר ובירושלמי (הל' ב) מסיק טעם אחר דפריך ואין חומשא מרובין על תוספתו של זה א"ר בון והוא שיכול להערים עליו ולפוטרו מחומש: בין שניתן לו במתנה. בפ' האיש מקדש (דף נב:) דייקינן מני אי רבי מאיר מי מצי יהיב ליה מתנה הא מעשר ממון גבוה הוא אלא לאו ר' יהודה היא ומסיק לעולם רבי מאיר והכא במאי עסקינן כגון דיהיב ניהליה במתנה בטיבלא וקסבר מתנות שלא הורמו לאו כמי שהורמו דמיין: ד מערימין. לפדותו בלא חומש ומפרש בירושלמי (הל' ג) למה מערימים עליו מפני שכתוב בו ברכה (ב) ולמה פודין אותו בשער הזול מפני שכתוב בו ברכה (ג): ופדה לך. כלומר פדה לעצמך כדתני בתוספתא (פ"ד) ובלבד שלא יאמר פדה לי בכן את מעשר זה אבל כשפודה לעצמו אע"פ שפודה במעות של בעל הבית אינו מוסיף חומש והכי תני בירושלמי (שם) פדה לי משלך פדה לך משלי אינו מוסיף חומש א"ר יוחנן כל מעשר שאין הוא ופדיונו משלו אינו מוסיף חומש רבי יוסי בר בון בשם רבי יונה טעמא דר' יוחנן ואם גאל יגאל איש ממעשרו חמישיתו יוסף עליו (ויקרא כז) כדי שיהא הוא ופדיונו משלו ודייק בירושלמי (שם) גבי שפחתו העבריה מה אנן קיימין אם בגדולה זכתה בה בסימנין כלומר מאי בעיא גביה ואם בקטנה קטן זוכה בתמיהא ומשני כמאן דאמר קטן תורם [ופריך אפי' למ"ד קטן תורם] וכי קטן זוכה ומשני על דעתי' דרבנן דתמן ניחא דתמן אמרי בשם רב נחמן* כל שנותנין לו אגוז ומשליכו צרור ונוטלו היא זוכה

עמוד שני ממקום היוקר למקום הזול. פודהו כשער מקומו. פי' זול. וכן ממקום הזול למקום היוקר פודהו כשער מקומו. פי' יוקר: המביא פירות מן הגורן לעיר. פי' יותר שוין הפירות בזמן שישנן בעיר משישנן בגורן וכדי יין של מעשר מן הגת לעיר פי' יותר שוה בעיר ממה ששוה בגת: השבח לשני. ומה שהוציא אינו מחייב לשני אלא מפסידם הוא: ב כמות שהשולחני פורט. פי' הרוצה לפדות על הסלע פירות של מעשר שני פודה בסלע פירות הרבה לפי חשבון שהיה פורטו השולחני כשמבקשין ממנו בני האדם סלע במעותיהן ולא כמות שמצרף השולחני שנותן מעות ולוקח סלע שכשמצרף השולחני מצרף בזול ויבוא ליקח פירות מעט: אין פודין מעשר שני אכסרה את שדמיו ידועין יפדה על פי עד אחד. פי' שואלין לוקח אחד כמה שוין כך וכך פירות וכמו שאומר אותו הלוקח כך נותן ומעשר יוצא לחולין והמעות נכנסין בקדושה: ואת שאין דמיו ידועין יפדה על פי ג' לקוחות. פי' שקונין בזול בפחות משויו: כגון יין שקסס. פי' התחיל להחמיץ: ופירות שהרקיבו ומעות שהחלידו. ופירושו החלידו מלשון חולאה: אכסרה. כן פירוש כל דבר שאינו לא מדוד ולא שקול ונמכר נקרא אכסרה: ג בעל הבית אומר בסלע. פי' בעל המעשר אמר אני אפדה זה המעשר בסלע: אבל הבעל הבית אומר בסלע ואחד אומר בסלע ואיסר האחר קודם מפני שהוסיף על הקרן. וקשיא והלא האחר אין מוסיף חומש וזה מוסיף חומש ונותן ה' דינרין מן הכל וזה אינו נותן אלא ד' דינרין ואיסר ויהא קודם בעל המעשר. ותרצי' א"ר אבין זה שמוסיף על הקרן קודם דהחומש לא הוי כלום דאי בעי מערים עליו ופוטרו מן החומש כדתנינן כיצד מערימין וכו': הפודה מעשר שני שלו מוסיף עליו חמישיתו בין שהוא שלו בין שניתן לו במתנה. ירושלמי מתני' כרבי מאיר דאמר אין מתנה כמכר רבי יונה אמר דברי הכל היא תיפתר בפירות שהן טבולים למעשר שני פי' האי דקתני שנותן לו במתנה לאו מעשר שני ממש דלא מצי למיהביה אלא כגון שנתן לו פירות הטבולין למעשר שני וקסבר מתנות שלא הורמו לאו כמי שהורמו דמיין ואיתא בקידושין בבבלי פרק האיש מקדש: ד מערימין על מעשר שני. פירוש לפוטרו מן החומש היה

עין משפט נר מצוה

הגהות מהר"י לנדא

המולא בידו כמולא באשפה אגוז וטפלו לרור ומשליכו יש גזל מפני דרכי שלום אגוז ומלניעו ומחזירו לאחר זמן גזלו גזל זוכה לעלמו ואינו זוכה לאחרים רב הונא אמר כשם שזוכה לעלמו כך זוכה לאחרים אבל מודה שאין מתנתו מתנה שנאמר (שמות כב) כי יתן איש מתנת איש מתנה ואין מתנת קטן מתנה לענין שבועה דרשי' בפ' שבועת הדיינים (דף מב.) כי יתן איש ואין נתינת קטן כלום מ"מ משמע הכא למתני' איירי בזכיה לעלמו כדפרישית וניחא מתני' לרב נחמן בר יעקב דאמר זוכה לעלמו ואין זוכה לאחרים וקשה דבפ' התקבל (דף סה:) דדייק ממתני' דזוכה בין לעלמו בין לאחרים ופריך מינה למ"ד זוכה לעלמו ואין זוכה לאחרים

וככל הספרים כתוב אל לכם מעות הללו ופדו בהן מ"ש ושמא ברייתא היא ומזכה לכם המעות והן פודין המעשר לנעש"ב ולא לעלמן ונמלא בפדייתו כזוכה לאחרים

לבנו ולבתו הקטנים לעבדו ולשפחתו הכנענים מפני שידן כידו: ה [א]היה [א)] עומד בגורן ואין בידו מעות אומר לחברו הרי הפירות האלו נתונים לך במתנה חוזר ואומר הרי אלו מחוללין על מעות שבבית: ו [ב]משך [ב)] ממנו מעשר בסלע ולא הספיק לפדותו עד שעמד בשתים נותן לו סלע ומשתכר בסלע *ומעשר שני שלו [ג]משך ממנו מעשר בשתים ולא הספיק לפדותו עד שעמד בסלע נותן לו סלע מחולין וסלע של מעשר שני שלו אם היה עם הארץ נותן לו *מדמאי: ז [ד]הפודה מעשר שני ולא קרא שם רבי יוסי אומר דיו ר' יהודה אומר צריך לפרש [ה]היה מדבר [ג)] עם האשה על עסקי גיטה וקדושיה ונתן לה גיטה וקדושיה ולא פירש רבי יוסי אומר דיו רבי יהודה אומר צריך לפרש: ח [ו]המניח איסר ואכל עליו חציו והלך למקום אחר והרי הוא יוצא בפונדיון אוכל עליו עוד איסר המניח פונדיון ואכל עליו חציו והלך למקום אחר והרי הוא יוצא באיסר אוכל עליו עוד פלג המניח איסר של מעשר שני *ואכל עליו אחד עשר באיסר ואחד ממאה באיסר ב"ש אומרים הכל עשרה [ז]ובית הלל אומרים בודאי אחד עשר ובדמאי

TO HIS SON OR DAUGHTER WHO ARE MINORS OR TO HIS CANAANITE MAN-SERVANT OR MAID-SERVANT, BECAUSE THEIR HAND IS AS HIS OWN HAND.[10]

MISHNAH 5. IF A MAN WAS STANDING IN HIS THRESHING-FLOOR AND HE HAD NO MONEY,[11] HE MAY SAY TO HIS FELLOW: 'LO, THIS PRODUCE IS GIVEN TO THEE AS A GIFT', AND THEN HE MAY SAY AGAIN: 'LO, LET THIS PRODUCE BE EXCHANGED FOR MONEY WHICH I HAVE IN THE HOUSE'.[12]

a *MISHNAH* 6. IF A MAN[1] TOOK POSSESSION[2] FROM THE OWNER OF SECOND TITHE FOR A SELA', BUT BEFORE HE HAD TIME TO REDEEM[3] IT, IT STOOD AT THE PRICE OF TWO SELA'S, HE MAY GIVE HIM ONE SELA' AND MAKE A PROFIT OF ONE SELA' AND THE SECOND TITHE REMAINS HIS.[4] IF HE TOOK POSSESSION FROM THE OWNER OF SECOND TITHE FOR TWO SELA'S, BUT BEFORE HE HAD TIME TO REDEEM[3] IT, IT STOOD AT THE PRICE OF ONE SELA',[5] HE MAY GIVE HIM ONE SELA' OUT OF COMMON [MONEY] AND ONE SELA' OUT OF HIS SECOND TITHE [MONEY].[6] IF THE OWNER WAS AN 'AM HA-AREẒ, HE MAY GIVE HIM OUT OF [SECOND TITHE OF] DEM'AI.[7]

MISHNAH 7. IF A MAN REDEEMED SECOND TITHE BUT DID NOT CALL IT BY ITS NAME,[8] R. JOSE SAYS: IT IS SUFFICIENT. BUT R. JUDAH SAYS: HE MUST NAME IT EXPLICITLY. IF A MAN WAS SPEAKING TO A WOMAN CONCERNING HER DIVORCE OR HER BETROTHAL, AND GAVE HER HER BILL OF DIVORCE OR HER GIFT OF BETROTHAL BUT DID NOT NOTIFY IT EXPLICITLY,[9] R. JOSE SAYS: IT IS SUFFICIENT. BUT R. JUDAH SAYS: HE MUST NOTIFY IT EXPLICITLY.

MISHNAH 8. IF A MAN PUT DOWN AN ISSAR[10] [FOR THE REDEMPTION OF SECOND TITHE] AND ON THE ACCOUNT THEREOF HE ATE [THE VALUE OF] HALF [AN ISSAR] AND THEN WENT TO ANOTHER PLACE WHERE THE PRODUCE WAS
b SOLD FOR A PONDION,[1] HE MAY EAT OF IT [ONLY TO THE VALUE OF] ANOTHER ISSAR.[2] IF HE PUT DOWN A PONDION [FOR THE REDEMPTION OF SECOND TITHE] AND ON THE ACCOUNT THEREOF HE ATE [TO THE VALUE OF] HALF [A PONDION] AND THEN WENT TO ANOTHER PLACE WHERE THE PRODUCE WAS SOLD FOR AN ISSAR, HE MAY EAT OF IT [ONLY TO THE VALUE OF ANOTHER] HALF [AN ISSAR].[3] IF HE PUT DOWN AN ISSAR[4] OF SECOND TITHE [MONEY] HE MAY EAT ON THE ACCOUNT THEREOF [UNTIL THERE IS LEFT] AN ELEVENTH PART[5] OF [THE VALUE OF] AN ISSAR,[6] OR [UNTIL THERE IS LEFT] A HUNDREDTH PART OF [THE VALUE OF] AN ISSAR.[7] BETH SHAMMAI SAY: IN BOTH CASES[8] [HE MAY EAT UNTIL THERE IS LEFT THE VALUE OF] ONE TENTH PART[9] [OF AN ISSAR]. BUT BETH HILLEL SAY: IN THE CASE OF CERTAIN[10] [SECOND TITHE HE MAY EAT UNTIL THERE IS LEFT THE VALUE OF] AN ELEVENTH PART[11] [OF AN ISSAR]

(10) Whatever they do possess is deemed his possession. (11) He wants to evade paying the fifth in redeeming his Second Tithe, but has no money in hand which he might give to his fellow that his fellow should redeem the Second Tithe for him. (12) It is as if he had bought back his gift from his fellow.

a (1) Who had bought Second Tithe produce in order that its purchase money might be turned by the owner. (2) Lit., 'drew into his possession'. I.e., he acquired it by means of Meshikah, v. Glos. (3) To pay its purchase money. (4) The produce became the property of the purchaser as soon as he took possession of it; cf. B.M. IV, 2. But it still retained its sanctity as Second Tithe until its price was paid. Therefore the *sela'* increase in its value becomes Second Tithe money, and the purchaser must redeem the produce at its new price of two *sela's*, one of which is Second Tithe which must be spent in Jerusalem. (5) But he must still pay the seller two *sela's*. (6) Thus redeeming the produce at its present price of one *sela'*. (7) מדמאי, the sanctity of which is not as great as of certain Second Tithe. Var. lec., מדמיו, 'of his own money'. I.e., he may pay the *sela'* with common money. (8) He had not designated the money as Second Tithe money; cf. *infra*, V. 9. (9) That what he gave her was a bill of divorce or a gift of betrothal. (10) Cf. *supra*, 3, n. 3.

b (1) Which is equal to two *issars*. (2) And not one *issar* and a half. (3) And not to the value of half a *pondion*. (4) To serve as the purchase price of produce. (5) Lit., 'eleven'. The interpretation of this passage is difficult and doubtful. The explanation given here follows Maim. and Bert. (6) In case the *issar* was the redemption money of Second Tithe of *demai*, and then the remaining eleventh becomes common produce. (7) In case the *issar* was the redemption money of certain Second Tithe, and then the remaining hundredth becomes common produce. (8) Whether the *issar* was the redemption money of *demai* Second Tithe or of certain Second Tithe. (9) Lit., 'ten'. (10) The *issar* was the redemption money of certain Second Tithe. (11) Lit., 'eleven', 'ten'.

BUT IN THE CASE OF [SECOND TITHE] OF DEMAI,[12] [HE MAY EAT UNTIL THERE IS LEFT THE VALUE OF] A TENTH PART[11] [OF AN ISSAR].

MISHNAH 9. ANY MONEY FOUND[13] IS CONSIDERED COMMON,[14] EVEN A GOLD DENAR WITH SILVER AND WITH COPPER COINS.[15] IF A POTSHERD WAS FOUND WITH THE MONEY ON WHICH WAS WRITTEN 'TITHE' THIS IS CONSIDERED SECOND TITHE [MONEY].

MISHNAH 10. IF A VESSEL WAS FOUND ON WHICH WAS
a WRITTEN 'KORBAN'[1] R. JUDAH SAYS: IF IT WAS OF EARTHENWARE, IT IS ITSELF COMMON AND WHAT IS IN IT IS KORBAN;[2] BUT IF IT WAS OF METAL IT IS ITSELF KORBAN AND WHAT IS IN IT IS COMMON. BUT THEY SAID UNTO HIM: IT IS NOT THE CUSTOM OF PEOPLE TO PUT WHAT IS COMMON INTO WHAT IS KORBAN.[3]

MISHNAH 11. IF A VESSEL WAS FOUND ON WHICH WAS WRITTEN A KOF,[4] IT IS KORBAN; IF A MEM, IT IS MA'ASER;[5] IF A DALETH, IT IS DEMAI; IF A TETH, IT IS TEBEL;[6] IF A TAW, IT IS TERUMAH,[7] FOR IN THE TIME OF DANGER[8] PEOPLE WROTE TAW FOR TERUMAH. R. JOSE SAYS: THEY MAY ALL STAND FOR THE NAMES OF MEN.[9] R. JOSE SAID: EVEN IF A JAR WAS FOUND WHICH WAS FULL OF PRODUCE AND ON IT WAS WRITTEN 'TERUMAH'[10] IT MAY YET BE CONSIDERED COMMON PRODUCE, BECAUSE I MAY ASSUME THAT LAST YEAR IT WAS FULL OF PRODUCE OF HEAVE-OFFERING AND WAS AFTERWARDS EMPTIED.[11]

MISHNAH 12. IF A MAN SAID TO HIS SON: 'THERE IS SECOND TITHE [MONEY] IN THIS CORNER', BUT THE SON FOUND [MONEY] IN ANOTHER CORNER, THIS MAY BE CONSIDERED COMMON[12] [MONEY]. [IF THE FATHER SAID] THERE WAS THERE A HUNDRED AND THE SON FOUND TWO HUNDRED, THE REMAINDER IS COMMON. [IF THE FATHER SAID THERE WERE THERE] TWO HUNDRED AND THE SON FOUND ONE HUNDRED, IT IS ALL SECOND TITHE MONEY.

CHAPTER V

b *MISHNAH* 1. A VINEYARD[1] IN ITS FOURTH YEAR[2] MUST BE MARKED[3] WITH CLODS OF EARTH, [TREES OF] 'ORLAH[4] WITH POTTER'S CLAY, AND GRAVES[5] WITH LIME WHICH IS DISSOLVED AND POURED ON.[6] RABBAN SIMEON B. GAMALIEL SAID: WHEN IS THIS DONE?[7] IN THE SEVENTH YEAR.[8] THE CONSCIENTIOUS[9] USED TO PUT DOWN MONEY AND SAY: 'ANY FRUIT GATHERED FROM THIS VINEYARD MAY BE EXCHANGED FOR THIS MONEY'.

MISHNAH 2. [THE FRUIT OF] A VINEYARD IN ITS FOURTH YEAR WAS BROUGHT UP TO JERUSALEM[10] WITHIN A DISTANCE OF ONE DAY'S JOURNEY ON EACH SIDE. AND WHAT WAS THE LIMIT THEREOF? ELATH ON THE SOUTH, AKRABAH ON THE NORTH, LYDDA ON THE WEST, AND THE JORDAN ON THE EAST.[11] WHEN FRUIT INCREASED,[12] IT WAS ORDAINED THAT IT SHOULD BE REDEEMED EVEN IF THE VINEYARD WAS CLOSE TO THE WALL;[13] BUT THIS WAS DONE ON THE CONDITION THAT WHENEVER IT WAS SO DESIRED, THE ARRANGEMENT
c WOULD BE RESTORED AS IT HAD BEEN BEFORE.[1] R. JOSE SAYS: THIS WAS THE UNDERSTANDING AFTER THE TEMPLE WAS DESTROYED, AND THE UNDERSTANDING WAS THAT WHEN THE TEMPLE SHOULD BE REBUILT THE ARRANGEMENT WOULD BE RESTORED AS IT HAD BEEN BEFORE.[1]

MISHNAH 3. A[2] VINEYARD[3] IN ITS FOURTH YEAR, BETH SHAMMAI SAY, IS NOT SUBJECT TO THE LAW OF THE FIFTH[4] NOR TO THE LAW OF REMOVAL.[5] BUT BETH HILLEL SAY: IT IS SUB-

(12) The *issar* was the redemption money of *demai* Second Tithe. (13) Except in Jerusalem during a festival or pilgrimage; cf. Shek. VII, 2. (14) It need not be suspected of being Second Tithe money. (15) Which is not usual to mix together, except in the case of Second Tithe money; cf. *supra*, II, 7 ff.

a (1) 'Offering', or gift to the Temple. (2) Holy property, because people did not make gifts to the Temple of earthenware articles and therefore the inscription was intended for the contents, and not for the vessel itself. (3) Therefore in the case of a metal vessel, both the vessel and its contents are holy. (4) This and the following are names of letters of the Hebrew alphabet. (5) 'Tithe'. (6) Produce from which heave-offering and tithes have not yet been taken. (7) Heave-offering. (8) When Jews were persecuted by the Romans for the observance of the Torah. (9) The initials of the names of the owners of the vessels. (10) The word in full. (11) And then filled again with common produce. (12) The Second Tithe money had been removed before the son came to look for it, and this is other money, which is usually common money.

b (1) The same applies also to a single vine or other fruit tree. (2) Cf. Lev. XIX, 24. The fruit of the fourth year since the tree was planted was considered like Second Tithe. It had to be consumed in Jerusalem, or redeemed and its value spent in Jerusalem. (3) As a sign that its fruit must not be picked and eaten. (4) 'Uncircumcision', Lev. XIX, 23. (5) To mark them as a place of impurity; cf. Shek I, 1; M.K. I, 2. (6) On the grave. (7) The marking of forbidden fruit. (8) The sabbatical year when all produce was ownerless and free to everybody; cf. Lev. XXV, 6. But in other years no marking was needed because strangers who were scrupulous about the observance of religious laws would not in any case eat of fruit which was private property. (9) Who were eager to prevent the commission of a religious transgression through their fruit. Lit., 'the modest', v. Kil'ayim, IX, 5. (10) The fruit itself, and not its redemption money, in order to enrich the Holy City with an abundance of fruit. (11) V. Bez. 5*a*, R.H. 31*b*. (12) And there was a superfluity of fruit in Jerusalem. (13) Of Jerusalem.

c (1) That no redemption of such fruit should be allowed within a day's journey from Jerusalem. When Jerusalem was in the hand of the enemy there was no eagerness to increase the supply of fruit in Jerusalem, and it was therefore permitted to redeem all such fruit from outside Jerusalem, even within a day's journey from the city. (2) Cf. Pe'ah. VII, 6; 'Ed. IV, 5. (3) The same applies also to a single fruit tree; cf. 54*a* n. b 1. (4) Like Second Tithe; cf. IV, 3, n. 5. (5) Like Second Tithe; cf. *infra Mishnah* 6.

Novellae of Hagaon Rabbi Moshe Feinstein o.b.m.
Tractate Ma'aser Sheni

5:1 — **The conscientious used to put down money.** Rambam explains that this refers to the Sabbatical Year as does R. Obadiah. This is very puzzling, because, if the conscientious concur with Rabban Simeon ben Gamaliel, that we do not care to benefit the sinners, [for which reason they did not exchange the produce for money during the other years of the cycle, when taking the fruit would constitute theft,] why did they not consider it sufficient [in the Sabbatical Year] to make a sign? We are, therefore, forced to conclude that they concur with the first tanna, who rules that they feared that perhaps sinners would take the produce and not care to exchange it and eat it in its prohibited state. If so, they concur with the first tanna, that we must consider for the benefit of sinners, only that the first tanna holds that a sign, which is merely bother, is all that is required to benefit the sinners. Therefore, a sign suffices both during the Sabbatical Years and the other years of the cycle. The conscientious, however, were more stringent insofar as they would even give away their money to prevent the sinners from eating the produce in its prohibited state. If so, they should have done so in other years as well as during the Sabbatical Year, because there is no reason to differentiate.

מסורת הש"ם

א) יבמות פט"ו דף קטו : ב) בבא קמא פ"ז סס פא: ג) שם סח ע"ב: ד) בילה פ"א ה ע"א ר"ה פ"ד לא ע"ב ה) קדושין פ"ב דף נד פלא פ"ז משנה ו עדיות פ"ד משנה ס :

עין משפט נר מצוה

טז א מיי' פ"ו מהל' מעשר שני ונ"ר הלכה ט :

יז ב ג שם הלכה ח :

א ד מיי' שם הל' ג:

ב ה מיי' פ"ט מהל' מ"ש ונטע רבעי הלכה ז :

ג ו מיי' פ"ח מהל' טומאות מת הלכה ט :

ד ז מיי' פ"ט מהל' מע"ש הל' ז' :

ה ח שם הלכה ה :

ובדמאי עשרה : **ט** "כל המעות הנמצאים הרי אלו חולין אפילו דינר זהב עם הכסף ועם המעות מצא בתוכן חרס וכתוב עליו מעשר הרי זה מעשר : **י** המוצא כלי וכתוב עליו קרבן רבי יהודה אומר אם היה של חרס הוא חולין ומה שבתוכו קרבן ואם היה של מתכת הוא קרבן ומה שבתוכו חולין אמרו לו "אין דרך בני אדם להיות כונסין חולין לקרבן : **יא** "המוצא כלי א) וכתוב עליו ק' קרבן מ' מעשר ד' "דמאי ט' טבל ת' תרומה שבשעת סכנה היו כותבים ת' תחת תרומה רבי יוסי אומר כולם שמות בני אדם הם אמר רבי יוסי אפילו מצא חבית והיא מלאה פירות וכתוב עליה תרומה הרי אלו חולין שאני אומר אשתקד היתה מלאה פירות תרומה ופנה: **יב** "האומר לבנו מעשר שני בזוית זו ומצא בזוית אחרת הרי אלו חולין היה שם מאה ומצא מאתים השאר חולין מאתים ומצא מנה הכל מעשר :

פרק חמישי

א כרם ג) "רבעי מציינין אותו "בקוזזות אדמה ושל ערלה בחרסית "ושל קברות בסיד וממחה ושופך א"ר שמעון בן גמליאל במה "דברים אמורים בשביעית והצנועים ג) מניחין את המעות ואומרים כל הנלקט מזה יהא מחולל על המעות האלו : **ב** "כרם ד) רבעי היה עולה לירושלים מהלך יום אחד לכל צד ואי זו היא תחומה אילת מן הדרום ועקרבה מן הצפון לוד מן המערב והירדן מן המזרח ומשרבו הפירות התקינו שיהא נפדה סמוך לחומה ותנאי היה הדבר שאימתי שירצו יחזור הדבר לכמות שהיה ר' יוסי אומר משחרב בית המקדש היה התנאי הזה ותנאי היה אימתי שיבנה בית המקדש יחזור הדבר לכמות שהיה: **ג** כרם ה) רבעי בית שמאי אומרים אין לו חומש ואין לו בעור

פי' מהר"י בן מלכי צדק

פירוש הרא"ש

הגהות מהר"י לנדא

ה א שם הלכה ד :
ו ב שם טוש"ע י"ד סימן רנ"ד סעיף ו :
ז ג ד מיי' שם הל' ו:
ח ה מיי' (פ"י מהל' מאכלות אסורות הל' יד) ופ"ט מהל' מ"ש ונ"ר הלכה ב סמג עשין קלז טוש"ע י"ד סי' רנד סעיף ו :
ט ו מיי' פי"א מהלכות מע"ש ונ"ר הלכה ג סמג עשין קלח טוש"ע י"ד סימן שלא סעיף קמד :
י ז מיי' שם הל' ח:
יא ח שם הלכה ט :
יב ט מיי' פ"ב שם ופ"י מהל' מאכלות אסורות הל' יז סמג לאוין קמד טוש"ע י"ד סימן רנ"ד סעיף ו :
יג י מיי' פי"א מהלכות מע"ש ונ"ר הלכה י סמג עשין קלח טוש"ע י"ד סימן שלא סעיף קמד :
יד כ מיי' שם הלכה יא טוש"ע שם סעיף קמה :

א) קדושין פ"ב דף נד: ב"מ פ"ד דף נה : ב) קדושין פ"א דף ט: ב"מ דף יא .

ובה"א יש לו ב"ש אומרים יש לו פרט ויש לו עוללות והעניים פודין לעצמן ובית הלל אומרים כולו לגת: **ד** כיצד פודין נטע רבעי מניח את הסל על פי ג' ואומר כמה אדם רוצה לפדות לו בסלע על מנת להוציא יציאות מביתו מניח את המעות ואומר כל הנלקט מזה מחולל על המעות האלו בכך סלים בסלע: **ה** ובשביעית (א) פודהו בשוויו ואם היה הכל מופקר אין לו אלא שכר לקיטה הפודה א) נטע רבעי שלו מוסיף עליו חמישיתו בין שהוא שלו ובין שנתן לו מתנה: **ו** ערב י"ט הראשון של פסח של רביעית ושל שביעית היה בעור כיצד *נותנין תרומה ותרומת מעשר לבעלים ומעשר ראשון לבעליו ומעשר עני לבעליו ומעשר שני והבכורים מתבערים בכל מקום רבי שמעון אומר הבכורים נתנין לכהנים כתרומה התבשיל בית שמאי אומרים צריך לבער ובית הלל אומרים הרי הוא כמבוער: **ז** מי שהיו לו פירות בזמן הזה והגיעה שעת הבעור בית שמאי אומרים צריך לחללן על הכסף ובית הלל אומרים אחד שהן כסף וא' שהן פירות: **ח** אמר רבי יהודה בראשונה היו שולחין אצל בעלי בתים שבמדינות מהרו והתקינו את פירותיכם עד שלא תגיע שעת הבעור עד שבא רבי עקיבא ולמד שכל הפירות שלא באו לעונת המעשרות פטורים מן הבעור: **ט** מי שהיו פירותיו רחוקים ממנו צריך לקרוא להם שם מעשה ג) ברבן גמליאל והזקנים שהיו באין בספינה אמר רבן גמליאל עשור שאני עתיד למוד נתון ליהושע ומקומו מושכ' לו עשור אחר שאני עתיד למוד נתון לעקיבא בן יוסף

(*משנה פ"ב היה הביעור)

של שמטה שהמעשרות מתבערים מן הבית שאסורים להשהותם יותר כדכתיב כי תכלה לעשר (דברים כו) : ובה"א אומרים יש לו · כדמפרש' בפ' האיש מקדש (דף נד:) דילפינן קדש קדש ממעשר מה מעשר יש לו חומש ויש לו ביעור אף כרם רבעי כן ומשנה זו במס' פיאה פ"ז (מ"ז) ושם פירשנוה יפה : **ד ה** על פי שלשה· הא דתנן בפ"ק דסנהדרין (דף יד:) נטע רבעי ומעשר שני שאין דמיו ידועין בג' אין דמיו ידועים לאו אנטע רבעי קאי א) (דבסל) דתניא [עלה] איזהו מעשר שני שאין דמיו ידועין פירות שהרקיבו ויין שהקרים ולא קתני בהדיא איזהו כרם רבעי [וטעמא] משום דטלהו אין דמיו ידועין דמצריך לפחות היציאה כדתנן הכא ושמא הכא בשו ב"ד חשוב אע"ג דהתם גבי מעשר שני אמרינן בג' לקוחות אפי' אחד מהן נכרי ואפי' אחד מהן בעלים : לפדות לו בסלע · כלומר ליקח לו מסלע כדאמרי' בירושלמי : על מנת להוציא יציאות מביתו . יציאת הלקיטה כלומר כמה אדם רוצה ליקח לו פירות בסלע שעדיין מחוברין ב] בעלין ויצטרך לשכור פועלים ללקט: מניח את המעות · לאחר שישומו ג' כמה סלים השומדים ללקוט ראוי ליקח בסלע : ואומר כל הנלקט מחולל על מעות הללו מכך וכך סלים בסלע · כמו ששמו הן אם ב' ב' ואם ג' ג': ובשביעית פודהו בשויו · ואין פוחת מן הרבעי יציאות הלקיטה : ואם היה נטע רבעי הפקר מבעלים אם בא א' וזכה בהן אין לו אלא שכר הלקיטה ולא אמרי' כיון דמהפקיר' קא זכי פטור מנטע רבעי ולא בעי פדייה אלא טעון הזוכה לפדותן או להעלותן לירושלים וא"ת שכר הלקיטה נמי לא יהא לו אלא יפדהו בשויו כמו בשביעית לא דמי דשביעית הואיל ודינו להיות הפקר ואין ראוי ליתן בו שכר לקיטה (את) להבעלים עצמן ופודין אותו בשויו אבל האי תחלתו היה עומד לפחות ממנו שכר לקיטה ולא פקע משום דאפקרי' וי"מ על מנת להוציא היציאות מביתו הוצאת הכרם חפירה וזמירה (מיכול) ובשביעית פודהו בשויו דכל הנך מלאכות לית ביה דאסירן בשביעית : ובין שניתן לו במתנה . בפ' האיש מקדש (נד:) אמרי' מני אילימא ר' מאיר מי מצי יהיב ליה במתנה הא גמר קדש קדש ממעשר אלא לאו ר' יהודה ומסיק לעולם ר"מ וכגון דיהיב ליה כשהוא סמדר ולא כר' יוסי דאמר סמדר אסור בערלה מפני שהוא פרי : תני' בתוספתא (פרק ה) כרם רבעי אין פודין אותן ענבים אלא יין דברי ב"ש וב"ה אומרים יין וענבים הכל מודין שאין פודין במחובר וקלא הי' נראה הטעם שאין מועיל חילול במחובר משום דילפי' קדש קדש ממעשר ואין מעשר במחובר אבל אי אפשר לומר כן דמשמע במרובה (דף סח.) דמועיל דאמר לא תימא כל הנלקט אלא אימא כל המתלקט כלומר שקודם לקיטה לנוטעין מחללין ולא לאחר לקיטה שכבר זכו בהן אחרים ולא היה כח ביד הבעלים לחלל דמכה קושיא זו חוזר בו מכל הנלקט והא דאין פודין במחובר היינו לפי שאין בקיאין בשומא בעודו מחובר מידי דהוה אענבים לב"ש והא דמחללין במחובר גבי לנוטעים התם משום תקנה עביד שלא יכשלו ומה שלא היו מחללין כל הכרם בבת אחת פעמים שרוצים להוליך [שאר הפירות] בירושלים אי נמי לפי שאין מועיל חילול למה שגדל אחרי כן וגבי לנוטעין מה שהיו יכולין לתקן מתקנים ועוד דהגדל אח"כ אע"פ שיש לו מתירין מדאורייתא בטיל ברובא* : **ו** ערב י"ט של רביעית ושל שביעית . מפרש' בירושלמי (שם) דכתיב (דברים יד) מקצה שלש שנים תוציא את כל מעשר תבואתך יכול פעם אחת בשבוע אתה חייב לבער ת"ל מקצה שלש שנים יכול כיון שהגיע בראש שנה שלישית אתה חייב לבער ת"ל מקצה אין מקצה אלא בסוף בסוף שנה את מבער ואי את מבער בראש שנה אי בסוף שנה יכול בראשה של [רביעית ושל] שביעית ת"ל וכי תכלה לעשר כשתכלה לעשר את כל הפירות יכול אף בחנוכה נאמר כאן מקצה ונאמר להלן מקץ שבע שנים במועד שנת השמטה בחג הסוכות מה מקץ שנאמר להלן במועד אף כאן במועד אי מה להלן בחג הסוכות אף כאן בחג הסוכות ת"ל כי תכלה לעשר אימתי הוא מכלה לעשר את כל הפירות בפסח של רביעית : תרומה ותרומת מעשר לבעלים · לכהנים : ומעשר ראשון לבעליו · ללוי : ומעשר עני לבעליו · לעניים ואיתא בפ"ב דביכורים (מ"ב) ומייתי לה בפ' הערל (דף עג) יש במעשר וביכורים מה שאין כן בתרומה (וקדשים) ביעור אלמא לא מיחייבי בביעור וי"ל דהכא בביעור של נתינה לכהן אבל התם בביעור שאוכלים אותו ומבערים אותו מן העולם כדתנן הכא מעשר שני והביכורים מתבערים בכל מקום שאף הכהן חייב לבערן והמעשר הי' נאכל עד זמן הוידוי שהיה במנחה בי"ט אחרון כדתנן בפרקין (מ"י) והיינו דפליג התם ר"ש גבי בכורים דקתני ור"ש פוטר כלומר דאין ביעור כביעור של מעשר שני כדקתני הכא ר"ש כדמפרש בפרק הערל משום דתרומה קרינהו רחמנא כדדרשי' ותרומת ידך אלו הביכורים דכתיב בהו ולקח הכהן הטנא מידך : התבשיל שיש בו יין ושמן של מעשר שני וחשבו ליה ב"ה כמבוער לפי שאין ממשו ניכר ובירושלמי (שם) אמרי' הכל מודין בפת ושמן שצריך לבער ביין ותבלין שהוא כמבוער מה פליגן בתבשיל ב"ש אומרים צריך לבער וב"ה אומרים א"צ לבער משמע שרוצה לומר פת ושמן שהוא בעין ויין ותבלין *שהן בעין ופליגי בתבשיל הנעשה מפירות : **ז** בזמן הזה שאין בית המקדש קיים (ב) : צריך לחלל על הכסף · ומפרש בירושלמי (שם) ומאי טעמא דב"ש וצרת הכסף בידך (דברים יד) ובלבד בידך וטעמא דב"ה מפרש בירושלמי (שם) אפי' מחללו מה מועיל אחד כסף ואחד פירות מטמין גניזה ומניח הפירות במקום המוצנע עד שירקבו : **ח** שלא באו לעונת מעשר · קודם מירוח כל אחד כמפורש בפ"ק דמעשרות ובירושלמי (הל' ד) פריך ולא סבל הוא כלומר דלאפי' הגיע לעונת מעשרות אמאי חייב בביעור כל זמן שלא הופרשו ומשני ר' זירא בשם שמואל יאות הוא אומר שטבל קרוי קודש וברא שונה היו סבורין דאפי' קודם מירוח קרוי קודש והא דאמרי' בפ"ק דסנהדרין (דף יא:) ששלח רבן גמליאל לבני גלילא עילאה ותתאה דזמן ביעורא מטא לאפרושי מעשרי מעשרי שבולייא וממעטני זיתיא דהוא קודם ר' עקיבא : **ט** רחוקים ממנו · ואין יכול ליתנן לבעליהן כאשר אמרנו צריך לקרות להם שם שיזכה אותן לבעלים כדאשכחן בשעבדא דרבן גמליאל וזקנים ולא כמו שמפרש שם בקונטרס בפ' שנים אוחזין (דף יא:) דרבן גמליאל היה ירא שלא יאכלו בני ביתו שיסמכו אחזקה על חבר דלדבריו הרי זה לא עשה כלום שלא אמר יהא מעשר אלא שקבע בעלים אלא משום ביעור עבד והשתא למ"ד מתנות שלא הורמו כמי שהורמו דמיין ניחא שהיה יכול לזכותן אבל למ"ד לאו כמי שהורמו דמיין אין יכול לזכותן כדמוכח בפרק הזרוע (דף קל:) וא"כ מה הועיל לענין ביעור ושמא מקודם לכן אמר מה שאני עתיד להפריש יהא מעושר ומה שלא הזכיר רבן גמליאל תרומה גדולה אע"ג דמיחייב' בביעור כדאמרי' לעיל שמא הפרישה קודם שילא מביתו שלא היה טורח בדבר למדוד דנטלת באומד ובמחשבה ועוד דדרך להפרישה בגורן כדאמרי' בירושלמי דמעשרות (פ"ג הל' א) דבר שיש לו גורן מפרישין אותו תרומת מעשר ואין צריך להפריש תרומה גדולה כהדא דתנן *פירות ממורחין בשדה מכונסין אסור משום גזל מפוזרין מותרים משום גזל בין כך ובין כך חייבים במעשר ופטורים מתרומה גדולה שאי אפשר לגורן שתעקר אלא אם כן נתרמה ממנו תרומה גדולה ובהאי דרבן גמליאל כבר היתה תבואה בבית דקאמר בתר הכי מעשרות מהיכן הם ניטלין מן הבית או מן השדה נישמעינה מן הדא חבר שמת כו' ר' חגיגא בר פפא שמע לה מן הכא עישור אחר שאני עתיד למוד נתון לעקיבא בן יוסף שיזכה בו לעניים הדא אמרה מן הבית ומה שהניח רבן גמליאל טבל בביתו ולא תיקן אע"ג דחזקה על חבר [כו'] קודם שילא מביתו הודיען שהוא טבל : נתון ליהושע · שהי' לוי כדאמר בערכין (דף יא:) מעשה שהלך ר' יהושע בן חנניה לסייע את ר' יוחנן בן גודגדא בהגפת דלתות אמר לו חזור בך שאתה מן המשוררין ואני מן השוערין ואף על גב דקנסינהו עזרא למאן דאמר קנסא לעניים נטל בתורת עניות דעני היה ומה שלא נתן לו מעשר עני דאמרי' הנותן מתנותיו לכהן אחד מביא רעב לעולם אי נמי היו לו מאתים זוז ואף על פי כן מעשר ראשון דלאו דאורייתא לעני היה טפל הואיל ומתפרנס בדוחק שהיה פחמי כדאמר בברכות פרק רביעי (דף כח·) ואמרי' בהוריות (דף י:) כל כך יש בידך ואתה יורד בספינה ולמאן דאמר קנסא לכהנים [סבירא ליה כרבי עקיבא דאמר בפרק יש מותרות פו: למיקמי קנסא היה ללוי דוקא] ובתר דקנסינהו הוא אף לכהן : נתון

בעוללות לפי שהוא ממון גבוה אבל דורכים אותו כולו וזהו מאמרם כולו לגת וב"ש אומרים שהוא ממון בעלים וחייב בפרט ובעוללות וכבר קדמה לשון זו ההלכה במסכת פאה (פ"ז מ"ו) : **ד** על מנת להוציא יציאות מביתו . פי' היציאות הראויות לעבודת הכרם ושמירתה מן הגנבים ועבודת האילנות ושאר הצריך בעבודה: **ה** בשויו. כלומר בערכו ולא אמר להוציא יציאות לפי שאין בשנה שביעית יציאות לפי שהארץ אינה נעבדת ואינה צריכה שמור . ואמר ואם היה הכל מופקר עניינו שאם היה אותו הכרם הפקר שהוא חייב לפדותו בשויו ולא יפחות מן הדמים אלא שכר לקיטה בלבד כילד כגון שיהיה סל בסלע ושכר לקיטתו איסר וכשלקט סל של ענבים מכרם רבעי הפקר פודה אותו בסלע פחות איסר ולא נעשה כן בשנת השמטה לפי שכל אחד מלקט לעצמו : ואמר ומוסיף עליו חומש . הוא דעת ב"ה שמחייבים לכרם רבעי חומש כאשר קדם ולא תתקיים מתנה בכרם רבעי אלא אם נתנו הפירות קודם שיבאו לעונת המעשרות לפי שכבר בארנו שהוא ממון גבוה ולא התקיים בו מתנה : **ו** כבר בארנו פעמים (פ"ד מ"ג דדמאי) במה שקדם כי בשנה השלישית והששית מן השבוע שיוליא מעשר עני במקום מעשר שני ואמר הש"י (דברים יד) מקלה שלש שנים ואמר (שם לא) מקץ שבע שנים במועד שנת השמטה בחג הסכות ואמרו מה קץ האמור להלן רגל אף קץ האמור כאן רגל יכול חג הסכות הלמוד לומר (שם טו) כי תכלה לעשר את כל מעשר תבואתך רגל שכל המעשרות כלין בו הוי אומר זה פסח לפי שלא יחול פסח מן השנה הרביעית אלא אחר שנגמרה כל מה שלמח בשנה השלישית ממה שהוא חייב מעשר עני וכמו כן כל מה שלמח בששית שהיא גם כן שנת המעשר ועניין מתבערים שיתבערו ויאבדו אותן הפירו' עד שלא ימלא מהם אלנו וברשותו כלל לפי שנאמר (שם) בערתי הקדש מן הבית ואמר ר"ש כי הבכורים אם נשאר מהם כלל שיתנסלכהן כמו שנותנין לו התרומה ואינו חייב להשליכם או לשורפם ועניין הבער בכאן שיתן מכל האמחים כל המתנות שנתחייב לתתן ושיתן כל מתנה לבעליו ומה שהוא חייב לאכלו כגון מע"ש ונטע רבעי ומאבד מה שנשאר ואם היה אלנו תבשיל ממעשר שני אומרים ב"ה הרי הוא כמבוער לפי שאם ישאר וישהה יפסיד ואין הלכ' כרבי שמעון : **ז** בזמן הזה . עניינו בזמן שאין בית המקדש קיים אומרים ב"ש ולרת הכסף בידך (דברים יד) הכסף בלבד מעלין וב"ה אומרים כי הוא כשיש שם מקום להעלות הפירות ולאכלן בו אבל בזמן הזה שאין שם מקדש הדין הוא שיבער הפירות: **ח** התקינו פירותיכם . עניינו כשיהיו עושין בהם כל הראוי כדי להגיען בירושלים בעונת המעשרות הנזכר במסכת מעשרות ושיוליאו מהם המתנות הראויות ויעשו בהם מה שזכר ודברי ר' עקיבא אמת: **ט** ר' עקיבא היה פרנס לעניים ורבי יהושע לוי היה ור"א בן עזריה כהן עשירי' לעזרא והעיקר המפורסם אצלנו קרקע נקנה בכסף ובשטר ובחזקה וכבר זכרנו זה (פ"ג מ"ו דפאה) ועוד יתבאר במקומו בקידושין (פ"א מ"ה) ועוד יש עיקר אצלנו כשם שקרקע נקנה בכסף ובשטר ובחזקה כך שכירות קרקע נקנית בכסף ובשטר ובחזקה ומכלל הכח שנקנין בו המטלטלין

פי' מהרי"ו בן מלכי צדק

לה' הרי הוא כקודש שקורא עליו את ההלל . ויהא מותר לאונן . תני קודש מלמד שאסור לאונן כקודש ומניין שטעון פדיון א"ר אבהו דכתיב קודש הלולים לא מתמנעין רבנן דרשי בין ה' לה' : ובית הלל אומר יש לו. פי' חומש דכתיב ואם גאל יגאל איש ממעשרו תנו' ב' גאולות הללו למה פי' גאל יגאל אחד בנטע רבעי ואחד למעשר שני : בית שמאי אומר יש לו פרט ויש לו עוללות פי' לכרם רבעי והעניין פודין ואוכלין כללא דמילתא בית שמאי עבדי לכרם רבעי ככרם חולין אלא שקדוש ובית הלל אומר הרי הוא כהקדש .ואין לעניים בו כלום לא פרט ולא עוללות : **ד ה** כיצד פודין נטע רבעי מניח את הסל של נטע רבעי על פי ג' בני אדם. פי' שהן בית דין : ואומר כמה אדם רוצה לפדות לו בסלע . גרסינן כן היא מתני' לוקח לו בסלע מנטע רבעי שעומד באילן : ולהוציא יציאות מביתו . פי' לשכור פועלין ללקט פירות: ומניח את המעות ואומר כל הנלקט מזה מחולל על המעות הללו וכו' וכמו ששמין לו פודה ומניח את המעות ואומר כל הנלקט מזה הכרם יהא מחולל על המעות הללו מכך וכך סלין בסלע כמו שאמרו אם ב' סלים בסלע ב' אם ג' ג' הכל כפי מה שאמרו לו : ואם היה נטע רבעי. הפקר שהפקירוה בעליו : אין לו אלא שכר לקיטה . פי' לאותו שלקט אותן דלא אמרינן מהפקירא קא זכי ויהא שלו אלא צריך לפדות הכל ויקח הוא שכר לקיטתו . רבינו ור"ש מניח את הסל על פי שלשה ששמין לבעל הכרם את הענבין שיש בו . ואומר בעל הכרם בפניהן כמה אדם רוצה ליתן לפדות לו בסלע על מנת להוציא הוצאות בכרם כגון החפירה זמורה זיבול וממה ששמין לו פודה ומוסיף חומש : ובשביעית פודהו בשויה . פי' לתת הסלע מיד ואין צריך כלום שהוא שאין מוציאין כלום הוצאות בשביעית ואליבא דבית הלל אפי' בשביעית פודה בשוויו ומוסיף חומש ואליבא דבית שמאי פודה בשויו ואינו מוסיף חומש **ח** אמר רבי יהודה בראשונה היו שולחין אצל בעלי בתים של מדינות מהרו והתקינו פירותיכם עד שלא יגיע שעת הביעור ותהיה עבירה בידכם ולא תוכלו להתודות.פי' שהיו סוברין שהמעשר בטיבלו קרוי קודש ואע"פ שלא הגיע לעונת המעשרות כגון הטיבולין וזיתין דמעטן חייבין בביעור:**ט** מי שהיו פירותיו רחוקין והגיע זמן הבעור ואינו יכול ליתנם לבעליהן כאשר אמרנו צריך לקרות להן שם פלוני יאמר תרומה לפלוני מעשר ראשון לפלוני מעשר עני לפלוני:ומקומו של מעשר מושכר

פירוש הרא"ש

פ"ה (א) שאין שכר שמירה ולא עבודת קרקע: (ב) והוא רוצה לעשות מדת חסידות לפדותו בשויו דמן הדין יכול לחללו על שוה פרוטה אע"ג דאמרינן הקדש שוה מנה שחיללו על ש"פ מחולל דיעבד אין לכתחלה לא בזמן הבית אבל בזמן הזה אפילו לכתחלה כדאמרינן גבי הכהנים בגבלה דאחרמינהו לנכסיה:

הגהות מהרי"ץ לנדא

מ"ד ברי"ש א] לאו אנטע רבעי קאי דבגי' כל' : ב] שם מחוברין בעלין. צ"ל באילן:

מלא

JECT. BETH SHAMMAI SAY: IT IS SUBJECT[6] TO THE LAW OF THE GRAPE GLEANING AND TO THE LAW OF DEFECTIVE CLUSTER, AND THE POOR MUST REDEEM THEM FOR THEMSELVES.[7] BUT BETH HILLEL SAY: ALL OF IT[8] GOES TO THE WINE-PRESS.[9]

MISHNAH 4. HOW DOES ONE REDEEM THE FRUIT OF A PLANT IN ITS FOURTH YEAR? THE OWNER PUTS DOWN A BASKET IN THE PRESENCE OF THREE [PERSONS][10] AND SAYS: 'HOW MANY SUCH BASKETS WOULD A MAN WISH TO REDEEM[11] FOR HIMSELF FOR A SELA' ON CONDITION THAT THE OUTLAY[12] SHALL BE BORNE BY THIS HOUSE?'[13] HE THEN PUTS DOWN THE MONEY[14] AND SAYS: WHATEVER SHALL BE PICKED FROM THIS PLANT MAY IT BE EXCHANGED FOR THIS MONEY AT THE PRICE OF SO MANY BASKETS FOR A SELA'.

a *MISHNAH* 5. BUT IN THE SEVENTH[1] YEAR HE MUST REDEEM IT FOR ITS FULL VALUE.[2] IF IT HAD ALL BEEN MADE OWNERLESS PROPERTY,[3] THE PERSON WHO SEIZED IT CAN ONLY CLAIM THE COST OF PICKING IT.[4] IF A MAN REDEEMED HIS FRUIT OF A PLANT IN ITS FOURTH YEAR, HE MUST ADD A FIFTH OF ITS VALUE,[5] WHETHER THE FRUIT WAS HIS OWN OR WAS GIVEN HIM AS A GIFT.

MISHNAH 6. ON THE EVE OF THE FIRST FESTIVAL-DAY OF THE PASSOVER IN THE FOURTH AND IN THE SEVENTH[6] [YEARS OF THE SABBATICAL CYCLE] THE REMOVAL[7] WAS PERFORMED. HEAVE-OFFERING AND THE HEAVE-OFFERING OF TITHE[8] WERE GIVEN TO THEIR OWNERS,[9] THE FIRST TITHE WAS GIVEN TO ITS OWNER,[10] THE TITHE OF THE POOR TO ITS OWNER,[11] AND SECOND TITHE AND FIRST-FRUITS[12] WERE REMOVED EVERYWHERE. R. SIMEON SAYS: FIRST-FRUITS WERE GIVEN TO THE PRIESTS[13] LIKE HEAVE-OFFERING. AS FOR BROTH,[14] BETH SHAMMAI SAY: IT MUST BE REMOVED. BUT BETH HILLEL SAY: LO, IT MAY BE CONSIDERED AS ALREADY REMOVED.[15]

MISHNAH 7. IF A MAN HAD PRODUCE AT THIS TIME[16] AND THE TIME OF REMOVAL ARRIVED, BETH SHAMMAI SAY: HE MUST
b EXCHANGE IT FOR MONEY.[1] BUT BETH HILLEL SAY: IT IS ALL THE SAME WHETHER IT BECOMES MONEY OR IT REMAINS FRUIT.[2]

MISHNAH 8. R. JUDAH SAID: FORMERLY THEY USED TO SEND TO HOUSEHOLDERS IN THE PROVINCES [SAYING:] 'HASTEN TO SET RIGHT YOUR PRODUCE[3] BEFORE THE TIME OF REMOVAL ARRIVES', UNTIL R. AKIBA CAME AND TAUGHT THAT ALL PRODUCE WHICH HAS NOT REACHED THE SEASON[4] OF TITHING IS EXEMPT FROM THE REMOVAL.

MISHNAH 9. IF A MAN HAD HIS PRODUCE AT A DISTANCE FROM HIM,[5] HE MUST CALL BY NAME [THE RECIPIENTS OF THE TITHE] THEREOF.[6] ONCE IT HAPPENED THAT RABBAN GAMALIEL AND THE ELDERS WERE TRAVELLING HOME BY SHIP,[7] AND RABBAN GAMALIEL SAID: 'ONE TENTH WHICH I SHALL MEASURE IS GIVEN TO JOSHUA,[8] AND THE PLACE THEREOF IS LEASED TO HIM;[9] THE OTHER TENTH WHICH I SHALL MEASURE IS GIVEN TO AKIBA B. JOSEPH[10] THAT HE MAY HOLD IT FOR THE POOR,

(6) Like common fruit; cf. Lev. XIX, 10; Pe'ah VII, 3—4. (7) If they will not take up their gleanings to Jerusalem. (8) The whole crop, including defective cluster and gleanings. (9) As the property of the owner, who must take up to Jerusalem either itself or its redemption money. (10) Who are expert valuers of fruit. (11) I.e., to buy it on the tree. (12) The cost of guarding, hoeing, picking etc. (13) Thus reducing the value of the fruit by the amount of this outlay. (14) As fixed by the valuers in reply to his inquiry.

a (1) When there is no work on the soil, nor guarding of produce in the field; Lev. XXV, 4. (2) And without having to value by experts the cost involved by the fruit on the tree until it is gathered. (3) In years other than the seventh year. (4) He must redeem it at its full value minus the cost of picking it. (5) In accordance with the opinion of Beth Hillel in Mishnah 3. (6) Cf. Deut. XIV, 28: *'At the end of every three years'*, i.e., at the end of each period of three years, viz., the fourth and the seventh years; cf. also Deut. XXVI, 12. (7) בעור, derived from the verb בערתי, Deut. XXVI, 13; cf. *infra* 10. All the dues on the produce which had not been paid in the previous three years had to be removed from the house and given to those who had a right to receive them. (8) Of the First, or Levitical, Tithe; cf. Num. XVIII, 26ff. (9) Viz., the priests. (10) The Levites; cf. Mishnah 10. (11) The poor. (12) Of the previous three years were removed and destroyed. (13) They originally belonged to the priests. (14) Containing produce subject to removal. (15) Such produce is absorbed and neutralized by the broth. (16) After the destruction of the Temple.

b (1) And destroy the money. (2) Since neither itself nor its value in money can nowadays be consumed in Jerusalem; therefore it should just be destroyed. (3) By distributing its dues in the manner prescribed by the law. (4) As laid down in Ma'as. I, 2ff. (5) When the season for removal arrived. (6) And this is considered as if the tithes were already given away. (7) At the season of removal. (8) Who was a Levite. (9) That this place may secure for him the ownership of the tithe. (10) Who was a guardian of the poor.

AND THE PLACE THEREOF IS LEASED TO HIM'. R. JOSHUA SAID: 'THE TENTH WHICH I SHALL MEASURE[11] IS GIVEN TO ELEAZAR B. AZARIAH,[12] AND THE PLACE THEREOF IS LEASED TO HIM', AND THEY EACH RECEIVED RENT[13] ONE FROM ANOTHER.

MISHNAH 10. IN THE AFTERNOON OF THE LAST FESTIVAL-DAY THE CONFESSION[14] WAS MADE. HOW WAS THE CONFESSION MADE? [HE SAID:] 'I HAVE REMOVED THE HALLOWED
a THINGS OUT OF MINE HOUSE'—THIS MEANS[1] SECOND TITHE AND THE FRUIT OF PLANTS IN THEIR FOURTH YEAR; 'I HAVE GIVEN THEM TO THE LEVITE'—THIS MEANS THE TITHE OF THE LEVITES; 'AND ALSO[2] I HAVE GIVEN THEM'—THIS MEANS HEAVE-OFFERING AND THE HEAVE-OFFERING OF TITHE; 'UNTO THE STRANGER, TO THE FATHERLESS, AND TO THE WIDOW'—THIS MEANS THE TITHE OF THE POOR, GLEANINGS, FORGOTTEN SHEAF, AND THE CORNER OF THE FIELD, ALTHOUGH THESE DO NOT DEBAR[3] [ONE FROM MAKING] THE CONFESSION; 'OUT OF MINE HOUSE'—THIS MEANS THE DOUGH-OFFERING.[4]

MISHNAH 11. 'ACCORDING TO ALL THY COMMANDMENTS WHICH THOU HAST COMMANDED ME'—LO, IF HE TOOK OFF THE SECOND TITHE BEFORE THE FIRST TITHE HE CANNOT MAKE THE CONFESSION; 'I HAVE NOT TRANSGRESSED ANY OF THY COMMANDMENTS'—I HAVE NOT SET APART [DUES] FROM ONE KIND FOR SOME OTHER KIND, NOR FROM PLUCKED [PRODUCE] FOR [PRODUCE STILL] JOINED [TO THE SOIL], NOR FROM NEW [PRODUCE] FOR OLD [PRODUCE], NOR FROM OLD [PRODUCE] FOR NEW;[5] 'NEITHER HAVE I FORGOTTEN'—I HAVE NOT FORGOTTEN TO BLESS THEE, NOR TO MAKE MENTION OF THY NAME OVER IT.[6]

MISHNAH 12. 'I HAVE NOT EATEN THEREOF IN MY MOURNING'—LO, IF HE HAD EATEN THEREOF IN HIS MOURNING,[7] HE CANNOT MAKE THE CONFESSION; 'NEITHER HAVE I REMOVED OUGHT THEREOF WHEN UNCLEAN'—LO, IF HE HAD SET IT APART IN UNCLEANNESS HE CANNOT MAKE THE CONFESSION; 'NOR GIVEN OUGHT THEREOF FOR THE DEAD'—I HAVE NOT TAKEN THEREOF FOR A COFFIN OR SHROUDS FOR THE DEAD, NOR HAVE I GIVEN THEREOF TO OTHER MOURNERS: 'I HAVE HEARKENED TO THE VOICE OF THE LORD MY
b GOD'—I HAVE BROUGHT IT TO THE CHOSEN HOUSE.[1] 'I HAVE DONE ACCORDING TO ALL THAT THOU HAST COMMANDED ME'—I HAVE REJOICED AND MADE OTHERS[2] TO REJOICE.

MISHNAH 13. 'LOOK DOWN FROM THY HOLY HABITATION, FROM HEAVEN'—WE HAVE DONE WHAT THOU HAST DECREED CONCERNING US, DO THOU ALSO WHAT THOU HAST PROMISED US; 'LOOK DOWN FROM THY HOLY HABITATION, FROM HEAVEN, AND BLESS THY PEOPLE ISRAEL'—WITH SONS AND DAUGHTERS; 'AND THE LAND WHICH THOU HAST GIVEN US'—WITH DEW AND RAIN AND WITH OFFSPRING OF CATTLE; 'AS THOU DIDST SWEAR UNTO OUR FATHERS, A LAND THAT FLOWETH WITH MILK AND HONEY'—THAT THOU MAYEST GRANT A GOOD TASTE IN THE FRUIT.

MISHNAH 14. HENCE[3] IT WAS DEDUCED THAT ISRAELITES AND BASTARDS MAY MAKE THE CONFESSION, BUT NOT PROSELYTES, NOR FREED BONDMEN, SINCE THEY HAVE NO SHARE IN THE LAND. R. MEIR SAYS: NEITHER MAY PRIESTS AND LEVITES SINCE THEY DID NOT RECEIVE A SHARE IN THE LAND. R. JOSE SAYS: THEY HAVE THE CITIES WITH SUBURBS.[4]

MISHNAH 15. JOḤANAN[5] THE HIGH PRIEST[6] SET ASIDE
c THE CONFESSION OF THE TITHES.[1] HE ALSO ABOLISHED THE 'WAKERS'[2] AND THE 'STRIKERS'.[3] UNTIL HIS DAYS THE HAMMER USED TO BEAT IN JERUSALEM.[4] AND IN HIS DAYS ONE HAD NO NEED TO ENQUIRE CONCERNING DEMAI.[5]

מסכת מעשר שני

תושלב״ע

הדרן עלך והדרך עלן

תורה אור

(11) The heave-offering of the Levitical tithe. (12) Who was a priest. (13) For the lease of the respective places. (14) The declaration as given in Deut. XXVI, 13ff.

a (1) Here follows a running commentary on the verses of the confession after the Midrashic method of exposition of the Torah. Cf. also Sifre, Deut., ad loc. (2) The particle גם, 'and also', implies something more than the explicit words of the text. (3) One may make the confession even if these had not been given to the poor. (4) Which was given from the home; cf. Num. XV, 20. (5) All of which acts would have rendered the tithing invalid; cf. Ter. I, 5; II, 4. (6) To pronounce the prescribed benediction prior to setting apart these dues. (7) אנינות, the interval between the death and the end of the day on which the deceased was buried.

b (1) The Temple. Cf. Deut. XII, 5. (2) The poor and the unprotected; cf. Deut. XXVI, 11; XII, 12. (3) From the expression *'the land which thou hast given us'*. (4) Cf. Num. XXXV, 2 ff. (5) Cf. Soṭ. IX, 10. (6) John Hyrcanus, 135—104 B.C.E. The rendering and explanation of this ancient Mishnah are uncertain. The interpretation given here follows the explanations found in Tosef Soṭ. XIII, 9—10; T.J. Ma'as Sh. ad loc., and Soṭ. l.c.; V. Soṭ. 47*b*, 48*a* and notes a.l. in Sonc. ed.

c (1) Because Ezra had enacted that the First Tithe should be given to the priests, not to the Levites, as a punishment for the refusal of the Levites to return from Babylon; cf. Ezra VIII, 15. Therefore one could not truthfully declare in confession, *'I have given it to the Levite'*. (2) The singing by the Levites in the temple of the verse *'Awake, why sleepest thou, O Lord?'* (Ps. XLIV, 24), because it sounded like blasphemy. (3) Those who used to strike the animal between its horns before slaughtering it for a sacrifice, in order to stun it. This appeared like causing a blemish in the sacrifice. (4) Workmen's hammers on the middle days of Passover and the Feast of Tabernacles. Joḥanan abolished work on these semi-sacred days. (5) Whether the original owner had tithed it. Joḥanan ordered that all *demai* produce of an *'am ha-areẓ* must be tithed by the new owners; cf. Demai, introd.

תורה אור

שיזכה בו לעניים ומקומו מושכר לו א"ר יהושע עשור שאני עתיד למוד נתון לאלעזר בן עזריה ומקומו מושכר לו ונתקבלו זה מזה שכר:

י במנחה ביום טוב האחרון היו מתודים כיצד היה הוידוי בערתי הקדש מן הבית זה מעשר שני ונטע רבעי נתתיו ללוי זה מעשר לוי וגם נתתיו זו תרומה ותרומת מעשר לגר ליתום ולאלמנה זה מעשר עני הלקט והשכחה והפאה אע"פ שאינן מעכבים את הוידוי מן הבית זו חלה:

יא ככל מצותך אשר צויתני הא אם הקדים מע"ש לראשון אינו יכול להתודות לא עברתי ממצותיך לא הפרשתי ממין על שאינו מינו ולא מן התלוש על המחובר ולא מן המחובר על התלוש ולא מן החדש על הישן ולא מן הישן על החדש ולא שכחתי לא שכחתי מלברכך ומלהזכיר שמך עליו:

יב לא (ג) אכלתי באוני ממנו הא אם אכלו באנינה אינו יכול להתודות ולא בערתי ממנו בטמא הא אם הפרישו בטומאה אינו יכול להתודות ולא נתתי ממנו למת לא לקחתי ממנו ארון ותכריכים למת ולא נתתיו לאוננים אחרים שמעתי בקול ה' אלהי הביאותיו לבית הבחירה עשיתי ככל אשר צויתני שמחתי ושימחתי בו:

יג השקיפה ממעון קדשך מן השמים עשינו מה שגזרת עלינו אף אתה עשה מה שהבטחתנו השקיפה ממעון קדשך מן השמים וברך את עמך את ישראל בבנים ובנות ואת האדמה אשר נתתה לנו בטל ובמטר ובולדות בהמה כאשר נשבעת לאבותינו ארץ זבת חלב ודבש כדי שתתן טעם בפירות:

יד מכאן אמרו ישראל וממזרים מתודים אבל לא גרים ולא עבדים משוחררים שאין להם חלק בארץ ר' מאיר אומר אף לא כהנים ולוים שלא נטלו חלק בארץ רבי יוסי אומר יש להם ערי מגרש:

טו יוחנן כהן גדול העביר הודיית המעשר אף הוא בטל את המעוררים ואת הנוקפים ועד ימיו היה פטיש מכה בירושלים ובימיו אין אדם צריך לשאול על הדמאי:

סליקא לה מסכת מעשר שני

סליקא לה מסכת מעשר שני

תלמוד בבלי

מסכת

חלה

תלמוד בבלי

מסכת

ערלה

תלמוד בבלי

מסכת

בכורים

תלמוד בבלי

עם פירוש רש״י ותוספות

ובצירוף תרגום ופירוש והערות באנגלית

מסכת

חלה

על ידי

יעקב איזריעלסטאם ז״ל

מסכת

ערלה

על ידי

יעקב איזריעלסטאם ז״ל

מסכת

בכורים

על ידי

ישעיה מאיר לערמן ז״ל

בעריכת

יחזקאל (איזידור) אפשטין ז״ל

דפוס שונצין

שנת להחזיר העטרה ליושנה לפ״ק

לונדון

HEBREW-ENGLISH EDITION OF
THE BABYLONIAN TALMUD

HALLAH

TRANSLATED INTO ENGLISH
WITH NOTES, GLOSSARY AND INDICES BY
REV. J. ISRAELSTAM, B.A.

‘ORLAH

TRANSLATED INTO ENGLISH
WITH NOTES, GLOSSARY AND INDICES BY
REV. J. ISRAELSTAM, B.A.

BIKKURIM

TRANSLATED INTO ENGLISH
WITH NOTES, GLOSSARY AND INDICES BY
RABBI DR. S.M. LEHRMAN, M.A., PH.D.

UNDER THE EDITORSHIP OF
RABBI DR. I. EPSTEIN, B.A., PH.D. LITT.D.

LONDON
THE SONCINO PRESS
1989

COPYRIGHT © THE SONCINO LTD. 1989
ALL RIGHTS RESERVED INCLUDING THE RIGHT TO
REPRODUCE THIS BOOK OR PARTS THEREOF IN ANY FORM

1-871055059

PUBLISHERS' NOTE

This HEBREW-ENGLISH EDITION of THE SONCINO TALMUD is being published to facilitate the easier reference to the original text by scholars and students.

The Publishers wish to express their sincere thanks to Rabbi Dr. A. Melinek, B.A., Ph.D., for his painstaking care in examining the texts and making the necessary corrections for the preparation of these Tractates.

It has been necessary to duplicate some of the original Hebrew-Aramaic pages in this Tractate where the text has been of such length as to require more than one page of English translation.

MANUFACTURED IN THE UNITED STATES OF AMERICA

INTRODUCTION

ḤALLAH

Tractate Ḥallah is so called because it deals with the laws relating to the Biblical precept (Num. XV, 17–21) enjoining the separation of some portion of dough *(ḥallah)* to be given to the priests as one of their twenty-four statutory dues. The practice is referred to in Ezek. XLIV, 30 and in Neh. X, 38. Mishnah Ma'aser Sheni V, 10 interprets, *I have put away the hallowed thing* from my house (Deut. XXVI, 13) as referring to the *ḥallah*-gift. Philo[1] and Josephus[2] also record the precept.

The place of the tractate in the Seder is in accordance with the chronological order in which the gift-portions were to be separated viz., *terumah, ma'aser* (tithe), *ma'aser sheni* (second tithe), *ḥallah* (so Maimonides).[3] Frankel[4] classes our tractate with the two that follow it, viz., 'Orlah and Bikkurim, as dealing with particular classes of produce (viz., Ḥallah, with the five grain-species; 'Orlah, with trees bearing fruit for human consumption, and Bikkurim, with the seven classes of produce for which, according to Deut. VIII, 8 the Land of Israel is famed), as distinguished from the preceding tractates from Pe'ah to Ma'aser Sheni, which deal with laws concerning all, or most, types of agriculture and agricultural produce. Tractate Ḥallah thus concludes a series in accordance with one grouping of tractates, and commences a division in accordance with another grouping.

CONTENTS OF THE TRACTATE

CHAPTER I. The grain species; specific legal categories of these; the varieties of dough liable to *ḥallah;* the prohibitions appertaining to the *ḥallah*-portion.

CHAPTER II. The circumstances in which grain grown out of non-Palestinian soil is liable to *ḥallah;* the state of propriety and purity of the person performing the precept; the stage at which liability to *ḥallah* is present; the minimum quantity of dough liable to, and the minimum portion thereof to be separated as, *ḥallah;* the circumstances in which a *ḥallah*-portion taken from one dough is deemed to exempt also other doughs.

CHAPTER III. The laws relating to: a person who has eaten dough whilst it is liable to *ḥallah;* dough which has acquired a status making it usable either only by priests, or for Temple purposes; a non-Israelite's dough in the hands of an Israelite; a proselyte's dough; dough made out of a species which is liable and a species which is not liable to *ḥallah;* a dough either *ab initio* not liable to or already exempt from *ḥallah* which has received an admixture of dough or leaven which is liable.

CHAPTER IV. The circumstances in which doughs smaller than the minimum liable to *ḥallah,* when belonging to more than one person, or made of varying types of grain, are 'reckoned together' to make up a quantity which is liable; the distinctions in the applicability of the law of *ḥallah* in the Land of Israel, Syria and other countries respectively.

J. ISRAELSTAM

(1) *On the Rewards of Priests,* Ch. I Yonge's Translation Vol. III, p. 205. (2) *Antiquities,* Bk. IV, Ch. IV § 4. (3) *Introduction to Seder Zera'im,* part VI. (4) *Darke ha-Mishnah* p. 272.

INTRODUCTION

ORLAH

Tractate 'Orlah (uncircumcision) is so named because it deals in detail with the law (Lev. XIX, 23–25) that the fruit of trees within three years after planting be considered *'orlah,* 'uncircumcised', and entirely forbidden. In the fourth year the fruit is in Biblical phraseology, *'holy, for giving praise unto the Lord',* and in the technical term of the Mishnah *neta' reba'i,* 'a plant in its fourth year' (v. I, 8, 60*b* n. c 7). Since the procedure enjoined with regard to the latter, viz., that it be itself consumed in Jerusalem, or redeemed and the proceeds spent on food there, is the same as that for the Second Tithe, the subject is dealt with largely in Tractate Ma'aser Sheni. Both precepts (*'orlah* and *neta' reba'i*) are
a mentioned by Philo[1] and Josephus.[2]

THE PLACE OF THE TRACTATE IN THE SEDER

Maimonides[3] says that Tractate 'Orlah should have followed Tractate Kil'ayim in accordance with the order in which these precepts occur in the Pentateuch, viz., Lev. XIX, 19 *(kil'ayim);* ibid. 23ff *('orlah),* but the editing authority thought it best to deal first with laws relating to grain, vegetable- and tree-produce, and then with those concerning purely tree-produce, the laws of *'orlah.*[4]

SYNOPSIS OF THE TRACTATE

CHAPTER I. The kind of fruit-trees that are liable to *'orlah;* the effect on permitted trees, of *'orlah* trees known to grow among them but unidentifiable (or of 'mixed seeds' of the vineyard, in similar circumstances); the constituent parts of various trees, which parts not being deemed 'fruit', are not liable to *'orlah;* the conditions governing the permissibility of planting or grafting *'orlah* shoots.

CHAPTER II. The effect on permitted matter of lesser admixtures of *terumah, demai, ḥallah,* first-ripe fruits, *'orlah,* or 'mixed seeds' of the vineyard, one of which in some instances combines with the bulk to neutralize another, or, in other instances, combines with another to form a prohibition; and, *en passant,* in what circumstances do admixtures of seasonings of the above categories, when unclean, render unclean the whole mixture. Also, the effect on non-sacred flesh of sacrificial flesh cooked together with it.

CHAPTER III. The laws regarding cloth dyed with colouring matter derived from shells or peel of *'orlah* fruit; cloth into which some thread so dyed has been woven; dishes cooked, or bread baked before the flames of *'orlah* peelings; particular fruits and vegetables, wine, etc. which are *'orlah,* etc.; such as are commonly bought and sold by *number,* and the effect of admixtures of these; the similarities and differences as between the Land of Israel, Syria and other countries, in regard to (i) 'doubtful' *'orlah,* (ii) 'new' produce, (iii) *'orlah* and (iv) mixed seeds.

J. ISRAELSTAM

a (1) *On Humanity,* Chap XXI, Yonge's Translation (ed. Bohn, Vol. III, p. 449). (2) *Antiquities,* Book IV, Chap. VIII § 19. (3) Introduction to Seder Zera'im, Part VI. (4) On Frankel's view, v. Introduction to Ḥallah.

INTRODUCTION

BIKKURIM

The Tractate *Bikkurim* (First-Fruits) is an elaborate commentary on Deut. XXVI, 1–11 discussing all the conditions governing the offering of first-fruits. The first chapter is emphatic that only legitimate owners of land and only those choice fruits enumerated in Deut. VIII, 8, for which Eretz Israel was renowned, were subject to the law of *Bikkurim*.

The second chapter develops the theme and draws distinctions between *Terumah*, the Second Tithe, and *Bikkurim*. The palm for sheer beauty of description must be awarded to the third chapter for its moving description of the procession that wended its way to the Temple Mount. The fulfilment of this command, applicable only in Temple times, was made the occasion of much joy, and served as a visible sign of the Jew's gratitude to God—the source of all his blessings. On handing over the fruits to the priest, who deposited them at the S. W. corner of the altar, the owner repeated after the priest the solemn declaration of Deut. XXVI.

Entirely irrelevant to this tractate is chapter four. Its presence is accounted merely by the reference to the hermaphrodite in I, 5 which it develops. Its text varies in many editions, and is chiefly noted for the interesting comparisons between man, woman, and the *androgenos*—a cross between male and female.

S. M. LEHRMAN

חלה פרק ראשון

א חמשה דברים חייבין בחלה א) *החטים והשעורים והכוסמים ושבולת שועל ושיפון הרי אלו חייבין בחלה ומצטרפין זה עם זה ואסורין בחדש מלפני הפסח ומלקצור לפני העומר ואם השרישו קודם לעומר העומר מתירן ואם לאו אסורין עד שיבא העומר הבא:

ב האוכל מהם כזית מצה בפסח יצא ידי חובתו כזית חמץ חייב בה כרת נתערב אחד מהם בכל המינים הרי זה עובר בפסח הנודר מן ג) הפת ומן התבואה אסור בהם דברי רבי מאיר וחכמים אומרים הנודר מן הדגן אינו אסור אלא מהן וחייבין בחלה ומעשרות:

ג אלו חייבין בחלה ופטורים מן המעשרות הלקט והשכחה והפאה וההפקר ומעשר ראשון שנטלה תרומתו ומעשר שני והקדש שנפדו ומותר העומר ותבואה שלא הביאה שליש רבי אליעזר אומר תבואה שלא הביאה שליש פטורה מן החלה:

ד אלו חייבין במעשרות ופטורין מן החלה האורז והדוחן והפרגין והשומשמין והקטניות ופחות מחמשת רבעים בתבואה הסופגנין ג) והדובשנין והאסקריטין וחלת המשרת והמדומע פטורין מן החלה:

ḤALLAH

CHAPTER I

MISHNAH 1. FIVE SPECIES [OF CEREALS] ARE SUBJECT
a TO [THE LAW OF] ḤALLAH:[1] WHEAT, BARLEY, SPELT, OATS AND RYE.[2] THESE ARE SUBJECT TO ḤALLAH, AND [SMALL QUANTITIES OF DOUGH MADE OF THE DIFFERENT SPECIES] ARE RECKONED TOGETHER ONE WITH ANOTHER [AS ONE QUANTITY],[3] AND ARE ALSO SUBJECT TO THE PROHIBITION OF [THE CONSUMPTION OF] 'NEW' [PRODUCE][4] PRIOR TO THE OMER,[5] AND TO [THE PROHIBITION OF] REAPING PRIOR TO PASSOVER.[6] IF THEY TOOK ROOT PRIOR TO THE OMER, THE
b OMER RELEASES THEM;[1] IF NOT, THEY ARE PROHIBITED UNTIL THE NEXT OMER HAS COME.

MISHNAH 2. IF ONE HAS EATEN ON THE PASSOVER AN OLIVE-SIZE[2] OF UNLEAVENED BREAD [MADE] OF THESE [CEREALS], HE HAS FULFILLED HIS OBLIGATION;[3] [IF ONE HAS EATEN ON THE PASSOVER] AN OLIVE-SIZE OF LEAVEN [MADE OF THESE CEREALS], HE HAS INCURRED THE PENALTY OF KARETH.[4] IF ONE OF THESE [CEREALS, HAVING BECOME LEAVENED,] HAS BECOME MIXED WITH ANY OTHER SPECIES, ONE TRANSGRESSES THE [LAWS OF] PASSOVER.[5] IF ONE HAS VOWED [TO ABSTAIN] FROM [CONSUMING] BREAD AND

a (1) The law relating to the portion of dough assigned to the priests in accordance with Num. XV, 17–21, ... *When ye eat the bread of the land ... of the first of your dough ye shall set apart a cake (ḥallah) for a gift .... Of the first of your dough ye shall give unto the Lord a portion for a gift throughout your generations.* (2) V. Kil. I, notes. These species are held to be subject to *Ḥallah* because the word לחם (*bread*) is used here and also in connection with Passover, *'bread of affliction'*, Deut. XVI, 3. The argument, by *gezerah shawah* (v. Glos.) is: Since, in the case of Passover, לחם obviously implies a cereal capable of becoming leavened, so too does the capacity for leavening determine the liability of produce to *ḥallah*. (3) Amounting to the minimum subject to *ḥallah*. It is only when all of these are mixed together in the flour, or if after having been kneaded separately, they are kneaded together, that this rule applies unconditionally. If, however, the doughs (each less than the minimum) were kneaded out of various species and later they stuck together (v. *infra* II, 4) their being deemed as forming one quantity liable to *ḥallah* depends on which particular species have been used (v. note ibid). (4) V. Lev. XXIII, 14. (5) *'This selfsame day'* (ibid.) refers to the day on which the Omer was brought to the Temple, viz., the second day of Passover. (6) V. ibid. v. 10ff. The expression *'The sheaf* (Omer) *of the first of your harvest'*, is taken to imply that the reaping of the Omer must be the first reaping, and that, therefore, there must be no reaping prior thereto, i.e., before Passover. The analogy between liability to *ḥallah* and liability to *Ḥadash* (the law relating to 'new' *sc.* produce) is based — by *gezerah shawah* — on the use of the term ראשית *'first'* in the case of *ḥallah* (*the first of your dough*) as well as in the case of new produce (*the first of your harvest*).

b (1) For harvesting. (2) The statutory minimum in matters of this kind. (3) Only species which are liable to leaven can, when deliberately prevented from doing so, serve for unleavened bread for Passover. (4) 'Cutting off', 'excision'; a punishment by the hand of God as distinct from one by that of man; v. Ex. XII, 19: *For whosoever eateth that which is leavened, that soul shall be cut off from the Congregation of Israel.* (5) If he keeps the mixture in his possession during the festival; v. ibid. XII, 19; XIII, 7.

◁ *For the continuation of the English translation of this page see overleaf.*

א חמשה דברים חייבין בחלה. אמרי' בירושלמי (הל' א) מי כתיב (במדבר טו) והיה באכלכם לחם הארץ הייתי אומר כל הדברים יהיו חייבין בחלה ת"ל מלחם ולא כל לחם אי מלחם ולא כל לחם אין לי אלא חטים ושעורים בלבד ת"ל ראשית עריסותיכם ריבה הכל ובשם רבי שמעון נאמר לחם בפסח ונאמר לחם בחלה מה לחם האמור בפסח דבר שהוא בא לידי חמץ ומצה אף לחם שנאמר בחלה דבר שהוא בא לידי חמץ ומצה ובדקו ומצאו שאין לך בא לידי חמץ ומצה אלא חמשת המינים בלבד ושאר כל המינים אינן באין לידי חמץ ומצה אלא לידי סרחון רבי שמעון בר נחמן שמע סלהון מן הדא (ישעיה כח) ושם חטה שורה ושעורה נסמן וכסמת גבולתו ושם חטה אלו חטים שורה זו שבולת שועל ולמה נקראת שורה שהיא עשויה כשורה שעורה אלו שעורים נסמן זה שיפון הכוסמת אלו הכוסמין גבולתו עד כאן גבולתו של לחם: ומצטרפין זה עם זה. בבלול איירי כדאמרי' בריש כלאים: אסורין בחדש. לפני העומר* במנחות בפ' א"ר ישמעאל א) [עיי' תוי"ט] אמר ר"ש לקיש אתיא לחם לחם ממצה: ומלקצור מלפני הפסח א"ר יוחנן אתיא ראשית ראשית מחלה: ואם השרישו קודם העומר. במנחות בפ' רבי ישמעאל (דף ע:) פליגי מאי קודם העומר ר' יונה אמר קודם קצירת העומר ר' יוסי בר' חנינא [אומר] קודם הבאת העומר והאי דמתיר בהשרשה מסיק התם (שם) מדכתיב (שמות כג) אשר תזרע בשדה משעת זריעה דמשמע מדכתיב בשדה: **ב** יצא ידי חובתו. בפ' כל שעה (דף לה.) דריש ליה מדכתיב (דברים טז) לא תאכל עליו חמץ שבעת ימים תאכל עליו מצות דברים הבאים לידי חימוץ אדם יוצא ידי חובתו בפסח: נתערב אחד מהן בכל המינים כגון חמץ בכותח וכל הנהו דתנן בפ' אלו עוברין (דף מג.) דמרבינן חמץ ע"י תערובת: הנודר מן הדגן. בפ' הנודר מן הירק (דף נה.) אמרי' דכל דמידגן משמע: וחייבים בחלה ובמעשר. משום דבעי למיתני אלו חייבין בחלה ופטורין מן המעשרות ואלו חייבין במעשרות ופטורין מן החלה תנא הכא וחייבין בחלה ובמעשר הכא כן שוין ולא בשאר דוכתי: **ג** הלקט השכחה והפאה וההפקר דפטורים מן המעשר נפקא בירושל' (הל' ג) מדכתיב (דברים יד) ובא הלוי כי אין לו חלק ונחלה עמך ממה שיש לך ואין לו חייב אתה ליתן לו יצאו כל אלו שיש לו עמך: מעשר ראשון שניטלה תרומתו. מפרש בירושלמי (שם) שהקדימו בשבלין פטור מתרומה גדולה כדר' אבהו בפ' כל שעה (דף לה:) וחייב בחלה: ומעשר שני והקדש שנפדו. בעיסה של מעשר שני בירושלמי (א) פלוגתא דרבי מאיר ורבי יהודה בפ' כל שעה דלר' מאיר פטורים משום דממון גבוה הוא וכתיב (במדבר טו) עריסותיכם ולר' יהודה חייבין אבל בגבולים פטורין אפי' לר' יהודה כדאמר בסוף חלק (קי"ב:) ומתני' דהכא בגבולים ואפי' כר' יהודה מפרש בירושלמי מעשר שני שהקדימו בשבלין פטור מתרומה גדולה ומן המעשרות בד"א שמירח ופדה אבל פדה ומירח חייב בכל והוא הדין לענין הקדש: ומותר העומר. שהעומר היה בא מג' סאין ותנן במנחות בפרק רבי ישמעאל דמוציאי' ממנו עשרון שהוא מנופה בי"ג נפה והשאר נפדה ונאכל לכל אדם וחייב בחלה ופטור מן המעשרות (א) ור' עקיבא מחייב בחלה ובמעשרות וטעמא מפרש התם בגמרא (ב) וסתם מתני' דהכא דלא כר' עקיבא: ותבואה שלא הביאה שליש. מפרש בירושלמי (שם) מה טעמא דרבנן נאמר בפסח לחם ונאמר בחלה לחם מה לחם האמור בפסח דבר שהוא בא לידי חמץ ומצה אף לחם שנאמר בחלה דבר הבא לידי חמץ ומצה כלומר תבואה שלא הביאה שליש נמי באה לידי חמץ ומצה ופטור מן המעשרות כדפרשי' בפ"ק דמעשרות דכתיב (דברים יד) תבואת זרעך שהוא נזרע ומצמיח וטעמא דרבי אליעזר דפטור מן החלה מפרש בירושלמי (שם) דכתיב (במדבר טו) כתרומת גורן כן תרימו אותה ותרומת גורן פטורה מתבואה שלא הביאה שליש. ירושל' רב הושעיא שאל לכהנא מנין שחייבין בחלה ופטורה מן המעשרות אמר לו לא תימא לי (תרימו) וכן תרימו חזר ואמר מי"ד מה י"ד חייבין בחלה ופטורין מן המעשרות אף אלו חייבין בחלה ופטורים מן המעשרות פירש רב הושעיא היה תמיה לכל הני דתנן אמאי לא פטירי מן החלה כמו מן המעשרות והשיב לו כהנא לא תימא לי כלומר לא תיקשי לי ממה דכתיב (שם) כתרומת גורן כן תרימו אותה [חזר ואמר] דיש ללמוד מז' שכיבשו וז' שחילקו שנתחייבו בחלה ולא נתחייבו במעשר כדאיתא בסוף יוצא דופן (דף מז.): **ד** אורז ודוחן פרגין ושומשמין. פירשתי בפ"ב (מ"ז) דשביעית: (ג) פחות מה' רבעים בתבואה. שנמדדה בעודה תבואה ומיהו אין נראה דהא בקמח מודדו כדתנן חמשת רבעים קמח אלא נקט תבואה כלומר אף בתבואה פטורה פחות מה' רבעים וברובע הקב איירי ודוקא פחות אבל מצומצמין חייבין: סופגנין כספוג עשויה א"כ רקיקין דקין מלשון רקיקי מצות (שמות כט) תרגום אספוגין: והדובשנין. מטוגנין בדבש: אסקריטין. לפיחית (שם טז) תרגום אסקריטין עיסתו רכה מאד וכולם מין לחם: וחלת המשרת. בפסחים (דף לז.) אמר ריב"ל זה חלוט של בעלי בתים איט נעשה כתיקון לחם של שאר אדם דמתוך עושרן חולטין אותן במחבת ופליגי התם דאמר ר"ל מעשה אילפס הן ופטורים דקא סבר אין לחם אלא האפוי בתנור ור' יוחנן אמר מעשה אילפס חייבין והללו שעשאן בחמה ובספרי זוטא תניא מלחם הארץ ולא כל לחם פרט למבושל וסופגנין ודובשנין ואסקריטין וחלת המשרת מחבת (ויקרא א) תרגום מסריתא: והמדומע. תרומה שנפלה לפחות מק' חולין אבל נפלה לתוך ק' חולין הכל חולין וחייבין בחלה וטעמא דמדומע משום דתרימו תרומה כתיב ולא שכבר נתרמה וקסבר האי תנא חלה בזמן הזה דרבנן כדאמר בשילהי יוצא דופן (ד) דאי מדאורייתא לא אתי דימוע דרבנן ומפקיע חלה דאורייתא ובירושל' (הל' ג) אמרי' כהנא שאל לשמואל לא מסתברא כהכן מדומע דתנינן הכא שרובו תרומה אמר ליה אוף אנא סבר כן אלא כד תיסק לארעא דישראל שאל לה כד סליק שמע רב אסי בשם ר' יוחנן אפי' סאה אחת שנפלה לתוך צ"ט חולין ומשמע שם במסקנא דמדומע פטור מן החלה היינו כשאין מן החולין ה' רבעים דאם נתערב סאה תרומה בצ"ט של חולין ולקח מהן ה' רבעים קמח ונלגן נמצא אחד מק' שבהן תרומה ולכך פטורה מן החלה אבל אם אחר שתסיר אחד מק' נשתיירו עדיין ה' רבעים לפי חשבון תרומה שנתערבה נתחייבת בחלה: ירושלמי (שם) העושה עיסה מן הטבל חלה חייבת בחלה מנין שחייבת בחלה בתרומה ותרומה חייבת בתרומה ר' יצחק בר שמואל בר מרתא בשם רב חלה

חלה פרק ראשון

א חמשה דברים חייבין בחלה א) [א]החטים והשעורים והכוסמים ושבולת שועל ושיפון הרי אלו חייבין בחלה [ב]ומצטרפין זה עם זה [ג]ואסורין בחדש מלפני הפסח ומלקצור לפני העומר [ד]ואם השרישו קודם לעומר העומר מתירן ואם לאו אסורין עד שיבא העומר הבא: **ב** [ה]האוכל מהם כזית מצה בפסח יצא ידי חובתו [ו]כזית חמץ חייב בהכרת [ז]נתערב אחד מהם בכל המינים הרי זה עובר בפסח הנודר מן ג) הפת ומן התבואה אסור בהם דברי רבי מאיר וחכמים אומרים [ח]הנודר מן הדגן אינו אסור אלא מהן וחייבין בחלה [ט]ומעשרות: **ג** [י]אלו חייבין בחלה [יא]ופטורים מן המעשרות הלקט והשכחה והפאה וההפקר ומעשר ראשון שנטלה תרומתו ומעשר שני והקדש שנפדו ומותר העומר ותבואה שלא הביאה שליש ורבי אליעזר אומר תבואה שלא הביאה שליש פטורה מן החלה: **ד** אלו חייבין במעשרות [יב]ופטורין מן החלה האורז והדוחן והפרגין והשומשמין והקטניות ופחות מחמשת רבעים בתבואה [יג]הסופגנין ג) והדובשנין והאסקריטין וחלת המשרת והמדומע פטורין מן החלה:

עיסה

א כבר בארנו בתחלת כלאים כי הכוסמים הם חטים מדבריות ושבולת שועל ושיפון מינין מן השעורים והכתוב אמר בענין חלה (במדבר טו) והיה באכלכם מלחם הארץ ואמר במצה (דברים טז) לחם עוני כמו שהלחם הנאמר בפסח איט בא אלא מחמשת מינין כמו שנבאר כמו כן הלחם הנאמר בחלה לא יהיה אלא מחמשת המינין: ומצטרפין זה עם זה. ענינו שיעור חלה כשיהיו מאלו החמשה מינין נתחייבה אותה עיסה בחלה: ואסורין בחדש מלפני הפסח הוא מאמר השי"ת ולחם וקלי וכרמל לא תאכלו (ויקרא כג) וכבר בארנו שאלו החמשה מינין נקראין לחם: ומלקצור מלפני העומר. למה שאמר השי"ת בעומר התנופה וקצרתם את קצירה והבאתם את עומר ראשית קצירכם אל הכהן (שם) ואמרו בספרא ראשית קצירכם שתהא תחלה לכל הנקצרים כן אסור לקצור דבר מחמשת המינין קודם קצירת עמרי התנופה: ומה שהיה מהן זרוע ונמשכו שרשיו בקרקע קודם קצירת העומר מותר לקצרו אחר קצירת העומר ומה שנזרע מהם ולא השריש אלא אחר קצירת העומר אסור לקצרו עד שיקצור העומר של שנה הבאה אמרו בגמרא רבי שמואל בר נחמן שמע כלהון מן הדין קרא (ישעי' כח) ושם חטה שורה ושעורה נסמן וכסמת גבולתו חטה אלו החטים שורה זו שבולת שועל ולמה נקרא שמה שורה שהיא עשויה כשורה ושעורה אלו השעורים נסמן זה שיפון וכוסמת אלו הכוסמין גבולתו עד כאן גבולו של לחם וזו היא אסמכתא כאשר תראה: **ב** אכילת מצה בליל פסח מצות עשה למה שאמר השי"ת בערב תאכלו מצות (שמות יב) ועוד אמר לא תאכל עליו חמץ שבעת ימים תאכל עליו מצות לחם עוני (דברים טז) והדבר שהוא אסור משום חמץ אדם יוצא בו ידי חובתו משום מצה ר"ל אם אכל ממנו כזית מצה בליל הפסח יצא ידי חובתו ושאר שבעת ימים רצה אוכל מצה רצה אוכל קטנית וכיוצא בהן ועוד יתבאר זה במקומו ואלו החמשה מינין הם שמתחמצים ובאין לידי חמוץ אבל השאר אינן מתחמצין אבל מתעפשים ומסריחין והוא אמרם (פסחים דף לה.) יצא אורז ודוחן ופרגין ושומשמין שאין באים לידי חמוץ אלא לידי סרחון: ואמר הרי זה עובר בפסח. ענינו כי המניחן ברשותו בפסח הוא עובר עליו בבל יראה ובבל ימצא וכשהתערב באחד מהן שום תערובת ויהיה באותו התערובת מים כמו שיתבאר בפסחים ואין מחלוקת בין החכמים שהנודר מן הפת ומן התבואה שאסור בחמשת המינים בלבד וחולק רבי מאיר לחכמים בנודר מן הדגן שחכמים אומרים אינו אסור אלא בה' המינין בלבד ור' מאיר אומר שהנודר מן הדגן אסור בכל ומותר בפירות האילן כי לדעת ר"מ דגן כולל התבואה והקטנית ולדעת החכמים דגן והתבואה שוה ועוד יתבאר זה מדעתם במסכת נדרים: ואמרם וחייבין בחלה ובמעשרות נאמר למה שעתיד לומר חייבין בחלה ופטורים מן המעשרות וחייבין במעשר ופטורים מן החלה ואין הלכה כר"מ: **ג** כבר בארנו במה שקדם כי לקט שכחה ופאה וההפקר שהן פטורין מן המעשרות: ומותר העומר הוא מה שישאר מן הנקצר להקריב ממנו העומר לפי שהיו לוקחים מן היפה שבו עומר ומניחים את המותר כמו שיתבאר במקומו: ותבואה שלא הביאה שליש עיסתה באה לידי חימוץ וכבר אמר כל מה שהוא בא לידי חימוץ חייב בחלה ורבי אליעזר מביא ראיה מן הכתוב שאומר בחלה (במדבר טו) כתרומת גרן כן תרימו אותה וכמו שתרומת גורן לא תבוא אלא מתבואה שהביאה שליש כמו שבארנו כמו כן החלה ואין הל' כר"א: **ד** כבר קדם לנו בשביעית פי' אורז ודוחן הם זרעים ידועים ופרגין הוא הנקרא בערבי כשבא"ש שומשמין גם כן ידוע ובערבי נקרא אל סמסם: ופחות מה' רבעים בתבואה הוא פחות משעור חלה: וסופגנין ודובשנין ואסקריטין וחלת המשרת הם מיני פת אלא שמתחלת לישתן עושין בהם מלאכה אחרת ומערבין בהן שמן או דבש או מתבלין אותן בתבלין ואופין אותן במינים משונים ממיני האפי' וקורין להם שמות כפי הדברים המעורבין בהם וכפי מלאכת אפייתם ג"כ תרגום רקיקי מצות (שמות כט) אספוגין פטירין ודובשנין נקראין כן לפי שהן נילושין בדבש ואסקריטין תרגום לפיחית (שם טז) ותרגום מחבת (ויקרא א) מסריתא ומזו הגזירה אמרו חלת המשרת: והמדומע הם החולין המעורבין בתרומה וכבר נתבאר זה במס' תרומות בתכלית הביאור: ואמרם בסוף זו המשנה פטורין מן החלה חוזר על סופגנין ודובשנין ואסקריטים וחלת

Continuation of translation from previous page as indicated by ◁

TEBU'AH [(CEREAL) PRODUCE],[6] HE IS PROHIBITED FROM CONSUMING THESE [FIVE SPECIES]; THIS IS THE OPINION OF R. MEIR. THE SAGES SAY: IF ONE HAS VOWED [TO ABSTAIN] FROM [CONSUMING] DAGAN [CORN], HE IS PROHIBITED FROM [CONSUMING] THESE [SPECIES] ONLY.[7] THEY ARE SUBJECT TO ḤALLAH AND TITHES.[8]

MISHNAH 3. THE FOLLOWING ARE SUBJECT TO ḤALLAH, BUT EXEMPT FROM TITHES: LEḲEṬ,[9] SHIKEḤAH,[10] PE'AH,[11]
c AND PRODUCE, OWNERSHIP OF WHICH HAS BEEN WAIVED,[1] AND THE FIRST TITHE[2] OF WHICH TERUMAH [THE PRIEST'S PORTION] HAD BEEN TAKEN OFF,[3] AND THE SECOND TITHE,[4] AND CONSECRATED [PRODUCE][5] WHICH HAVE BEEN REDEEMED, AND THAT WHICH REMAINS OVER FROM THE OMER,[6]
d AND GRAIN WHICH HAS NOT GROWN ONE-THIRD [RIPE].[1] R. ELIEZER SAID: GRAIN WHICH HAS NOT GROWN ONE-THIRD [RIPE] IS EXEMPT [ALSO] FROM ḤALLAH.[2]

MISHNAH 4. THE FOLLOWING ARE SUBJECT TO TITHES, BUT EXEMPT FROM ḤALLAH: RICE, MILLET, POPPY-SEED, SESAMUM, PULSE,[3] AND LESS THAN FIVE-FOURTHS [OF A ḲAB] OF [THE FIVE KINDS OF] GRAIN,[4] SPONGE-BISCUITS, HONEY-CAKES,[5] DUMPLINGS,[6] CAKE [COOKED] IN A PAN[7] AND MEDUMMA'[8] ARE EXEMPT FROM ḤALLAH.

(6) A term which, in the opinion of all, denotes only the five species enumerated in Mishnah 1. (7) Because they considered *Tebu'ah* and *Dagan* synonymous, whereas R. Meir—who was at one with the Sages with regard to the word *Tebu'ah*—considered *Dagan* a more comprehensive term including also all seed- and pulse-foods, and held that a man using that term in his vow debarred himself not only from the five species but also from seed- and pulse-foods. (8) There are also other species subject to tithes, but the species so far enumerated are subject to both tithes and *ḥallah*. The Mishnah proceeds to specify categories which are subject to *ḥallah* but not to tithes, and vice-versa. (9) Gleanings, v. Lev. XIX, 9. (10) The Forgotten, *sc.* Sheaf. Deut. XXIV, 19. (11) The Corner, *sc.* of the field. Lev. XIX, 9.
c (1) Such waiving of ownership is termed *hefḳer*. It is only when the owner declared the produce *hefḳer* before smoothing the pile of grain that it is exempt from tithing. The Levites were entitled to tithes from commodities belonging to Israelites, in which the former, on account of being Levites, had no share (deduced from Deut. XIV, 29, v. T.J.); but since the Levites were included among those entitled to help themselves to the produce coming under the categories named (v. Deut. ibid.), the latter were not subject to being tithed for the benefit of the Levites. (2) Assigned to the Levites. (3) The *terumah* which the Levite had to give, a tithe out of the tithe received by him from the Israelite, to the Priests. In Ter. I, 5, a marginal reading is 'of which *terumah* had *not* been taken', meaning the *terumah gedolah* due from the Israelite to the Priest. The case contemplated in our reading is, according to T.J., one in which a Levite took his tithe from an Israelite whilst the grain was still in ears, and before the ordinary *terumah* had been taken off. In that event a Levite is bound to give thereof only *his terumah* (a tithe from the tithe he received) to the priest, but he is not expected to give to the priest anything on account of the *terumah* which would have accrued to the latter from the Israelite if the Levite had not claimed his tithe so soon. It might have been thought that as the Levite's portion in such a case contained something that might be regarded as due to the priest, it would, for that reason, be exempt from *ḥallah*; the Mishnah therefore makes it clear that it *is* subject thereto. (4) Which at the end of the agricultural year was to be taken to Jerusalem and consumed there. In the event of inconvenience through distance, it was to be redeemed and the money spent in Jerusalem on food, drink and anointing oneself, in which case (v. Lev. XXVII, 31) the proceeds of the redemption were to be increased by an amount equal to one-fifth of the eventual sum total, i.e., by one-fourth of the money-value of the tithe. The Mishnah here intimates that in the event of the second tithe having been separated whilst the corn was in a state when it was not liable to *terumah* or tithes (viz., when still in ear, v. T. J. and L.) it is exempt from the (first) tithe even after redemption, cf. Terumoth I, 5. Such redeemed second tithe is, however, subject to *ḥallah*, because the latter is to be taken from the dough, and at the time of kneading the produce is already *ḥullin* (non-sacred). (5) Being Temple property, technically termed *heḳdesh*. V. Lev. XXVII, 11—27; cf. *infra* III, 3. (6) In the Omer they offered up one-tenth of an ephah taken from flour made from three *se'ah* of barley; the remainder of the flour (spoken of here) was redeemed and could thereafter be eaten by anybody, and was therefore subject to *ḥallah*. It is, on the other hand, exempt from tithes, because at the material time, i.e., 'when the pile was made even' it was Temple property and thus exempt from tithes.
d (1) T.J. deduces this exemption from Deut. XIV, 22, *Thou shalt surely tithe the produce of thy sowing*, the argument being: If the sowing has been productive it is to be tithed, if it has not been productive (and if it has resulted in a crop less than one-third ripe it cannot be said to have been productive) it does not require to be tithed. To *ḥallah*, however, it is subject because even when only one-third ripe it is capabe of leavening (v. *supra* 1, n. 2). (2) This view is based on Num. XV, 20, where with reference to *ḥallah* it is said: *As that which is set apart* (terumah) *of the threshing-floor so shall ye set it* (*i.e.*, ḥallah) *apart*, from which R. Eliezer deduces that whatever applies to *terumah* applies equally to *ḥallah* and, therefore, that just as a grain which has not grown one-third ripe is exempt from *terumah* and tithes it is likewise exempt from *ḥallah*. (3) These are liable to tithes as produce, but not being capable of leavening, are not subject to *ḥallah* (v. *supra* 1, n. 2). There are other species of produce which do not leaven, but these are particularized because they were often milled into flour and made into dough. (4) The statutory minimum amount subject to *ḥallah*, as laid down *infra* II, 6; somewhat over $3^1/_2$ lbs. V. 'Ed. I, 2 and notes (Sonc. ed.) 2a. (5) T.J. renders 'honey-milk (cake)', v. Simponte a.l. Cake made of ordinary dough cooked in honey. According to some, also if made of dough kneaded with honey, it is exempt from *ḥallah*, but v. *infra* **56b** n. d 1. (6) אסקריטין Jast. 'dumpling'. B. here and Rashi (to Pes. 37*a*) 'something made of a very soft (light) dough'. T.J. (p. 57*d*) renders *Ḥaliṭa*, 'sold in the open market'. *Ḥaliṭa*, according to Pes. 37*b* (explaining the terms of Ḥallah I, 5), is dough made by pouring boiling water on flour, but according to R. Ishmael b. Jose (T.J.) it is flour poured into hot water. Aruch identifies the term with the Latin *crustulum*, 'small cake'. For other possible etymologies v. Kohut in *Aruch Completum* s.v. (7) A cake or loaf prepared in a משרת pan (rather in a manner of frying) and not in an oven, and it is only something baked inside an oven and also styled bread (לחם) which is liable to *ḥallah*. T.J. renders *ḥaliṭa*, of water v. preceding note. Maim. emphasizes that the point about these four preparations is that from the very beginning they are kneaded with oil, or honey, or spices and are cooked in unusual ways, and are, in fact, designated not as bread but are named after the various admixtures which give them their distinctive character. (8) I.e., produce or (as here) dough to which originally no holiness attached, but which by accidentally receiving an admixture of *terumah* of a quantity more than one-hundredth part of the original amount, becomes thereby prohibited to non-priests and permitted only to priests and is, therefore, not liable to *ḥallah*. Tosaf Yom-Tob and other commentators say that here the Mishnah has in mind post-Temple days, for the following reason: In Temple times *ḥallah* is a Biblical precept, but *medumma'* is a Rabbinic institution (in purely Biblical law the admixture of *terumah* of a lesser quantity than the original amount of non-sacred produce is considered as neutralized, 'lost' and ritually of none effect, so that the whole mixed quantity would, in such a case, be non-sacred, *ḥullin*, and subject to *ḥallah*); and a remission resulting from the application of a Rabbinic ordinance cannot cancel a duty imposed by Scriptural command. In non-Temple times, however, when *ḥallah*, too, is only on Rabbinic authority, it can be, and is over-ridden by the Rabbinic regulation of *medumma'*.

MISHNAH 5. DOUGH WHICH WAS ORIGINALLY [INTENDED
a FOR] FANCY-BAKING,[1] AND FINALLY [COOKED AS] FANCY-BAKING, IS EXEMPT FROM ḤALLAH.[2] [IF IT WAS] ORIGINALLY [ORDINARY] DOUGH, BUT FINALLY [COOKED AS] FANCY-BAKING, [OR IF IT WAS] ORIGINALLY [INTENDED FOR] FANCY-BAKING, BUT FINALLY [COOKED AS ORDINARY] DOUGH, IT IS SUBJECT TO ḤALLAH; SIMILARLY ARE RUSKS[3] SUBJECT [TO ḤALLAH].[4]

MISHNAH 6. THE [FLOUR-PASTE CALLED] ME'ISAH[5] BETH SHAMMAI DECLARE EXEMPT [FROM], BUT BETH HILLEL
b DECLARE SUBJECT [TO ḤALLAH].[1] THE [FLOUR-PASTE CALLED] ḤALIṬA[2] BETH SHAMMAI DECLARE SUBJECT [TO], AND BETH HILLEL DECLARE EXEMPT [FROM ḤALLAH].[3] AS FOR THE LOAVES OF THE THANKSGIVING SACRIFICE[4] AND THE WAFERS OF A NAZIRITE,[5]—IF ONE MADE THEM FOR ONESELF, THEY ARE EXEMPT [FROM ḤALLAH],[6] [IF ONE MADE THEM] TO SELL IN THE MARKET,[7] THEY ARE SUBJECT [TO ḤALLAH].

MISHNAH 7. IF A BAKER MADE DOUGH FOR DISTRIBUTING,[8] IT IS SUBJECT TO ḤALLAH.[9] IF WOMEN GAVE [FLOUR][10]

a (1) סופגנין, the word translated 'sponge-biscuits' in Mishnah 4, but used here for all fancy-baking, various kinds of which are enumerated there. (2) This is explanatory of Mishnah 4. (3) הקנובקאות, explained by Maim. and others as brittle cakes of parched flour kneaded with oil, which after having been baked, are crushed and prepared as gruel for very young children, v. Jast. For possible etymologies v. *Aruch Completum*. (4) R. Joshua b. Levi (T.J. Ḥallah 58*a*) explains: Since these are to be crushed back into flour, it might have been thought that they are exempt from *hallah*; the Mishnah had, therefore, to make it clear that this is not the case. (5) Made by pouring hot water on flour.
b (1) Cf. 'Ed. V, 2 where this is mentioned as one of six exceptional instances in which Beth Hillel hold the stringent, and Beth Shammai the lenient view. (2) Made by pouring flour into hot water (v. Mish. 4, n. 6). (3) For the purposes of practical law the difference between *me'isah* and *haliṭa* does not matter. The relevant difference between the two statements is that whilst the first-reported Tanna held that in this instance Beth Hillel were stringent and Beth Shammai the lenient, the latter Tanna held that the reverse was the case. The final state of the law with regard to any variety of plain dough is that if cooked inside an oven (i.e., baked), it is subject to *ḥallah*, but if cooked in a pan over a flame that passes underneath it, it is exempt. (4) V. Lev. VII, 12ff. (5) Forming part of the sacrifice brought by a Nazirite when the period for which he vowed self-consecration is completed, Num. VI, 15. In fact, both loaves and wafers were required in either case. (6) Being intended for the offering the dough was thus consecrated *ab initio*. (7) But, naturally, with the intention of making ordinary use of them should there be no buyers requiring them for sacrificial purposes; thus at the material time (viz., of kneading) these loaves or wafers were not consecrated. (8) In portions every one of which is less than the minimum liable to *ḥallah*. (9) Because it is obviously his intention, in the event of there being no customers, to bake it all himself. (10) But not money, v. Yoreh De'ah, 326, 3.

◁ *For the continuation of the English translation of this page see overleaf.*

ה ״עיסה שתחלתה סופגנין וסופה סופגנין פטורה מן החלה תחלתה עיסה וסופה סופגנין תחלתה סופגנין וסופה עיסה חייבת בחלה וכן הקנובקאו׳ חייבו׳: ו המעיסה א) ב״ש פוטרין ב וב״ה מחייבין החליטה ב״ש מחייבין וב״ה פוטרין ג חלות תודה ורקיקי נזיר עשאן לעצמו פטור למכור בשוק חייב: ז ד נחתום שעשה שאור לחלק חייב בחלה ה נשים שנתנו לנחתום לעשות להם שאור אם אין בשל אחת מהן כשיעור פטורה מן החלה: ח ו עיסת ג) הכלבים בזמן שהרועים אוכלין ממנה חייבת בחלה ומערבין בה ומשתתפין בה ומברכין עליה ומזמנין עליה *ונעשית ביו״ט ז ויוצא בה אדם ידי חובתו בפסח אם אין הרועים אוכלין ממנה אינה חייבת בחלה ואין מערבין בה ואין משתתפין בה ואין מברכין עליה ואין מזמנין עליה ואינה נעשית ביו״ט ואין אדם יוצא בה ידי חובתו בפסח ס בין כך ובין כך (ח) מטמאה טומאת

המשרת והמדומע ואמרס בתחלתן חייבין במעשרות ופטורין מן החלה נופל על אורז ודוחן ופרגין ושומשמין וקטניות ופחות מה׳ רבעים קמח בתבואה: ה קנובקאות. הוא קמח קלוי נילוש בשמן ואחר לישתו ואפייתו מפרכין אותו בידים ומחזירין אותו קמח: ו כשהמים הם רותחין בתכלית הרתיחה נותנין בו קמח ולשין הכל וקורין אותו מעיסה וכשנותנים המים הרותחים על הקמח קורים אותו חליטה ואין הפרש בין מעיסה וחליטה אלא שאחד כתב מחלוקת ב״ש וב״ה במעיסה שבית שמאי פוטרין וב״ה מחייבין וכן הדין אלנו בחליטה ואחד כתב מחלוקתם בחליטה שבית שמאי מחייבין וב״ה פוטרין וכן הדין אלנו במעיסה והלכה כי מעיסה וחליטה אם נאפו בתנור שהם חייבות בחלה ואם הם מעשה אילפס הוא שמהגין אותן במרחשת ומבערין תחתיה אש עד שתאפה הם פטורין מן החלה:

Continuation of translation from previous page as indicated by ◁

TO A BAKER TO MAKE FOR THEM DOUGH,[11]—AND IF THERE IS NOT IN THAT WHICH BELONGS TO [ANY] ONE OF THEM THE [MINIMUM] MEASURE,[12] IT[13] IS EXEMPT FROM ḤALLAH.[14]

c *MISHNAH* 8. DOUGH FOR DOGS,[1] AS LONG AS [IT IS SUCH AS] SHEPHERDS PARTAKE THEREOF,[2] IS SUBJECT TO ḤALLAH;[3] AND ONE MAY MAKE AN 'ERUB[4] THEREWITH,[5] AND EFFECT A SHITTUF[6] THEREWITH;[5] AND ONE SHOULD SAY THE BLESSINGS FOR [BEFORE[7] AND AFTER[8] EATING] IT, AND ONE SHOULD SAY THE INTRODUCTORY FORMULA TO A CORPORATE RECITAL OF GRACE AFTER IT;[9] AND IT MAY BE COOKED ON A FESTI-
d VAL,[1] AND A PERSON DISCHARGES THEREWITH ONE'S OBLIGATION ON THE PASSOVER;[2] BUT IF [THE DOUGH BE SUCH AS] SHEPHERDS DO NOT PARTAKE THEREOF,[3] IT IS NOT SUBJECT TO ḤALLAH;[4] NOR MAY ONE MAKE AN 'ERUB THEREWITH, NOR EFFECT A SHITTUF THEREWITH; NOR SHOULD ONE SAY THE BLESSINGS FOR [BEFORE[5] AND AFTER][6] IT, NOR SAY THE INTRODUCTORY FORMULA TO A CORPORATE RECITAL OF GRACE AFTER IT;[7] NOR MAY IT BE COOKED ON A FESTIVAL; NOR DOES A PERSON DISCHARGE THEREWITH ONE'S OBLIGATION ON THE PASSOVER. IN EITHER CASE IT IS SUSCEPTIBLE
e TO RITUAL DEFILEMENT AFFECTING FOODSTUFFS.[1]

(11) And he, without their knowledge, kneaded all the flour together. (12) Liable to *ḥallah*, viz., 1 1/4 *kab*, v. *supra* Mish. 4. (13) I.e., the whole dough. (14) Though the dough as a whole is now large enough to be subject to *ḥallah*; for the reason that it is taken for granted that those who gave their flour to the baker were 'particular' that their several quantities of flour be kneaded separately.—The Mishnah here speaks of women, because it is, as a rule, they who attend to a matter of this kind.

c (1) I.e., for baking bread or biscuits for dogs. It consisted of flour and coarse bran (T.J.). (2) When it contains rather less bran. (3) The law of *ḥallah* is introduced (Num. XV, 19), *And it shall come to pass when ye eat of the bread* .... Since this dough (when baked) is fit for *human* food, it is liable to *ḥallah*. (4) Lit., 'a merging' of rights, interests or privileges; the legal device whereby permission is contrived for (*a*) carrying on the Sabbath from a private to a public domain, and vice-versa (v. Shabb. 6*a*), known as 'The 'Erub of Courtyards', for (*b*) walking on the Sabbath more than the Sabbath limit (2000 cubits) outside a town, known as 'The 'Erub of Boundaries', and for (*c*) cooking food on a festival for the following day, if a Sabbath, known as 'The 'Erub of Cooked Foods' (Beẓah II, 1). In (*a*), the food, contributed to by all the participants and kept in a place accessible to all of them, creates and represents a community of possession, constituting the area concerned a private domain *ad hoc;* in (*b*), the placing of food at the Sabbath boundary is presumed to constitute, for those having and deemed as having, a share in that food, a 'dwelling-place' which serves as a starting-point for a further Sabbath-limit of 2000 cubits; in (*c*), the setting aside of food cooked on the day prior to the festival, and leaving it till the end of the Sabbath is presumed to have the effect of rendering the cooking on the festival day (originally permitted in the Bible, Ex. XII, 16 for that day only) merely a continuation of the cooking in preparation for the Sabbath which had been commenced on the week-day prior to the festival. (5) For the above purposes human food is obviously essential. (6) Lit., 'a partnership'; the full form is 'a partnership in an alley or street', presumed to create 'a private domain', and conferring the right to carry on the Sabbath between a number of courtyards and an alley into which these open. '*Shittuf*' is similar in significance to '*Erub*. (7) Viz., 'Who bringest forth bread from the earth', the benediction for bread. (8) ברכת המזון. The full form of Grace after Meals said only if bread was part of the meal, v. Ber. 44*a*. (9) When *three* or more adults have partaken of a common major meal (i.e., one of which bread formed part) a special formula (termed 'summoning') is pronounced by one of them, calling on his companions to join in Grace. V. Ber. 45*a*.

d (1) The law prohibiting work on festivals is qualified thus: *No manner of work shall be done in them, save that which every man may eat* (Ex., XII, 16). The word rendered '*by you*', viz., לכם, is capable of being translated 'for yourselves', from which the Rabbis infer that only food fit for human beings is permitted to be cooked on a festival. (2) *Sc.* to eat unleavened bread on the first night of Passover. Only that which is capable of leavening is (if fit for human food) subject to *ḥallah*, and is also (if deliberately prevented from leavening) usable for unleavened bread (v. *supra* I, 1, n. 2, 2, n. 3). In the course of mixing this dough it was intended that it should be eatable by human beings; it is therefore subject to the same laws as all dough meant for human consumption. (3) On account of there being too much bran in the mixture. (4) Because *ḥallah* is due only from '*your dough*' (Num. XV, 20) i.e., dough fit for human consumption (Sifre Zutta).—According to Tosef. Ḥal. I and T.J. 58*a* this rule obtains only if the 'dog's dough' was baked in the shape of boards, i.e., quite unlike bread for human consumption, but not if baked in the shape of כברין 'round cakes' (so Tosef. ed. Wilna. Jast reads there כעכין which he renders 'prongs', also in T.J. where some texts have כעבין). V. Yoreh De'ah 310, 9. In *Pitheḥe Teshubah, ad loc.*, it is pointed out that the latter ruling can be applicable only to the Land of Israel where alone *ḥallah* is a Biblical precept (cf. *infra* IV, 8), and that, even so, the insistence on separating *ḥallah* from exclusively 'dog's dough' for no other reason than their having been baked in the shape of ordinary loaves, can be attributed only to the principle of 'appearance to the eyes', i.e., the desire to avoid even the merest semblance of wrong-doing, in conjunction with the maxim 'that which the Rabbis have decreed on account of appearances is prohibited even in the strictest privacy'. (5) I.e., not 'Who bringest forth bread from the earth'; the correct blessing in this case is 'by Whose word all things came into being', (so L. q.v.). (6) I.e., not the full grace after meals. The correct one in this case is the shorter grace after food. (7) I.e., if two of the three forming the (minimum) company at the meal have eaten bread made of 'dog's dough'. If, however, two ate real bread, and only the third had the other kind (or any which is not considered bread), then the latter man may be reckoned in the company for purposes of *zimmun*.

e (1) According to Lev. XI, 34, *All food which may be eaten, that on which water cometh, shall be unclean*, when it has come into contact with the carcase of an unclean swarming thing. The Rabbis understand '*all food that may be eaten*' by anyone, whether man or beast; as long, therefore, as any food is fit for dogs, it is susceptible to ritual uncleanness. Dough, of course, satisfies the condition: '*That on which water cometh*'.

מסורות הש"ס

א) עדיות פ"ה מ"ב פסחים דף לז. ב) ביצה פ"ב דף כח:

תרימו תרומה מחלה תרימו תרומה מנין שתרומה חייבת בחלה מן קושייה פתרון הדין קרא מאותה שכתב בה ראשית תרימו חלה פי' תרומה חייבת בחלה אף ע"ג דמדומע פטור מחלה ה"מ בשנילושה אחריכן אבל הכא שנילושה קודם שקרא עליו שם תרומה חייבת בחלה: **ה** תחלתה עיסה וסופה סופגנין. פעמים שאדם לש עיסה ונמלך ועושה אותה סופגנין: קנובקאות לא איתפרש ובירושל' (שם) משמע דרגילין להחזירה לסולתה ושמא הן כעין עוגות של יונקי שדים שמחזירין לסולתם לעשות להם חליבה: ירושל' (שם) א"ר יוחנן כל שהאור מהלך תחתיו חייב בחלה ואומר עליו המוציא ואדם יוצא בו ידי חובתו בפסח [רשב"ל אומר כל שהאור מהלך תחתיו אינו חייב בחלה ואין אומרים עליו המוציא ואין אדם יוצא בו ידי חובתו בפסח] א"ל ר"י ובלבד ע"י משקה מתני' פליגי על ר"י הסופגנין והדובשנין והאסקריטין פטורין מן החלה פתר לה בסופגנין שנעשו בחמה דתני' יוצאין בסופגנין שנעשו באור ואין יוצאין בסופגנין שנעשו בחמה וסופגנין שנעשו באור לית הדא פליגא על ר"ל פתר לה בשהי' האור מהלך מן הלד משמע בה דר"י מודה לר"ל דעל ידי האור נמי פטורין היכא דליכא משקין בהדיה ומשמע נמי דברכת המוציא תלויה בחלה וכל דבר שבלילתו קשה אפי' בישלו במשקין היינו בתחלתו עיסה וסופו סופגנין ומברך עליו המוציא וטעון נטילת ידים ובה"מ וכן תחלת בלילתו רכה וסופו על ידי האור בלא משקה עד שתהיה בלילתו רכה וסופו באור ע"י משקה ותדע דבפ' כל שעה (דף לז.) פטרי' חלוט ואשישה משום דהוית לה מלה עשירה ולאו מטעם דלא חשיב לחם וחלת המשרת דמתני' דהיינו של בעלי בתים דבלילתו רכה ומיהו נראה דעיסה גמורה נמי פטור כדמוכח בפ' כילד מברכין (דף לז:) דתני ר' חייא לחם העשוי לכותח פטור

ה
ה עיסה שתחלתה סופגנין וסופה סופגנין פטורה מן החלה תחלתה עיסה וסופה סופגנין תחלתה סופגנין וסופה עיסה חייבת בחלה וכן הקנובקאו' חייבו': **ו** המעיסה א) ב"ש פוטרין וב"ה מחייבין החליטה ב"ש מחייבין וב"ה פוטרין חלות תודה ורקיקי נזיר עשאן לעצמו פטור למכור בשוק חייב: **ז** נחתום שעשה שאור לחלק חייב בחלה נשים שנתנו לנחתום לעשות להם שאור אם אין בשל אחת מהן כשיעור פטורה מן החלה: **ח** עיסת ב) הכלבים בזמן שהרועים אוכלין ממנה חייבת בחלה ומערבין בה ומשתתפין בה ומברכין עליה ומזמנין עליה *ונעשית ביו"ט ויוצא בה אדם ידי חובתו בפסח אם אין הרועים אוכלין ממנה אינה חייבת בחלה ואין מערבין בה ואין משתתפין בה ואין מברכין עליה ואין מזמנין עליה ואינה נעשית ביו"ט ואין אדם יוצא בה ידי חובתו בפסח בין כך ובין כך (ח) מטמאה טומאת

המשרת והמדומע והמרס בתחלתן חייבין במעשרות ופטורין מן החלה נופל על אורז ודוחן ופרגין והשמשמין וקטניות ופחות מה' רבעים קמח בתבואה: **ה** קנובקאות. הוא קמח קלוי נילוש בשמן ואחר לישתו ואפייתו מפרכין אותו בידים ומחזירין אותו קמח: **ו** כשהמים הם רותחין בתכלית הרתיחה נותנין בו קמח ולשין הכל וקורין אותו מעיסה וכשנותנים המים הרותחים על הקמח קורים אותו חליטה ואין הפרש בין מעיסה וחליטה אלא שאחד כתב מחלוקת ב"ש וב"ה במעיסה שבית שמאי פוטרין וב"ה מחייבין וכן הדין אלו בחליטה ואחד כתב מחלוקתם בחליטה שבית שמאי מחייבין וב"ה פוטרין וכן הדין אלו במעיסה והלכה כי מעיסה וחליטה אם נאפו בתנור שהם חייבות בחלה ואם הם מעשה אילפס והוא שנוהגין אותן במרחשת ומבערין תחתיה אש עד שתאפה הם פטורין מהחלה: וחלות תודה ורקיקי נזיר. הם האמורים בתורה שיעורן ואיכות עשייתן אם עשאן לעצמו נתקדשו ואינן חייבות בחלה ואם עשאן למכור בשוק לא נתקדשו לפי שכוונתו אם לא יוכל למכרם שיאכלם וכן יתבאר בגמרא ומה שזכרנו ממחלוקת ב"ש וב"ה מבואר בירושלמי: **ז** שיעור זו המשנה כן וכן נשים שנתנו לנחתום לעשות להם שאור ויש בשל כל אחת מהם שיעור חלה חייב בחלה ואם אין בשל אחת מהן כשיעור פטורה מן החלה ומה שאמר כי נחתום כשלש עיסה ועשאה כולה שאור לחלקה על בני אדם בתורת מכר שהוא חייב לפי שהוא מתכוין אם לא ימצא קונה לזה השאור שיעשה ממנה עיסה ויאפה אותה כמו שקדם ממאמרם למכור בשוק חייב: **ח** עיסת הכלבים. הוא שלשין אותה במורסנה ודומה לו ומתכוין להאכילה לכלבים או זולתם ממיני החיות ושלא יאכל ממנה שום אדם: אינה חייבת בחלה. למאמר הש"י באכלכם מלחם הארץ (במדבר טו): ואין עושין בה ערובי תחומין ולא שיתופי מבואות. לפי שאלו הערובין אינן נעשין אלא מן הדברים שהכוונה בהם שיאכלום בעליהן כמו שיתבאר בערובין כי זה הוא טענת העירוב וכמו כן אין מברכין עליה ואין מזמנין עליה לפי שהן כמו הקטניות: ואינה נעשית ביום טוב למה שאמר הש"י בי"ט הוא לבדו יעשה לכם (שמות יב) ואמר לכם ולא לכלבים: ואין אדם יוצא בה ידי חובתו בפסח. לפי שאין אדם יוצא ידי חובתו אלא בדבר שחייב בחלה כמו שבארנו במה שקדם ואם חשב בעת הלישה בין על אכילת הכלבים ובין על אכילת בני אדם נתחייבה אותה עיסה במה שהיה חייבת כל עיסה ואין הפרש ביניהם: בין כך ובין כך מטמאה טומאת אוכלים. לפי שהעיקר אצלנו כי כל מה שהוא מיוחד למאכל אדם יטמא טומאת אוכלין ואין צריך מחשבה ר"ל שאינו צריך שיחשוב עליו למאכל אדם אלא כיון שהיא מיוחד מטמא עד שיפסל מלאכול הכלב כמו שיתבאר בפ' שמיני מטהרות (מ"ז) ובלי ספק כי זו העיסה היא מחמשת המינים וכל מין

מחלה ופרידותניא חייב ומשני התם כדתני טעמא רי"א מעשיה מוכיחין עליה עשאה כעבין חייבת כלמודין פטורה ופירש שם בקונטרס עשוי לכותח שנאפה בחמה כו' ועוד ערוכה ומקופסת כגלוסקאות נאות גלי אדעתי' דללחם עשויה כלימודין כנסרין בעלמא שלא הקפיד על עריכתו ודומה לו במ"ק (דף יב.) עושין לו למודין לוחות לבור של יין לכסותו אלמא אף ע"ג דמשעת גלגול קאתי חיוב חלה כיון דגלגל אדעתא לאפות בחמה מפטרה דסופו לבטל מתורת לחם מדמחלק בין למודין לכעבין משום דכעבין מחלפין בשאר עיסה שאינה עשויה לכותח אבל למודין מעשי' מוכיחין עליה ולא אתי לאיחלופי ועוד דבעשאה כעבין הוא דאיכא למיגזר שמא מימלך כדאמר בירושל' אבל לענין למודין לאו אורחי' למימלך ובעבין נמי לא מחייבי אלא היכא דשקיל מינה חררה קטנה *ואפי' לש ואכל דאסר בלא חלה דלמא מימלך אכולה עיסה אבל היכא דנעשה לכותח פטורה והכי איתא בירושלמי (הל' ז) עיסת כותח חייבת בחלה שמא תימלך לעשותה חררה לבנה ועל כורחך כדי שלא תיקשי ההיא דברכות נ"ל כדפרישית דשקלה פורתא ואפה באור דחיישי' שמא תימלך ליקח כשיעור ומתני' דתחלת' עיסה וסופה סופגנין היינו בנמלך כדפרשי' במתני' אבל תחלתה עיסה לעשות סופגנין פטורה ואמרי' נמי חדא איתתא שאלה לר' מנא כגון דאנא בעינא מיעבדה אילות איטרי [דיכסבנה תהא] פטורה מן החלה א"ל אסור שמא תימלך לעשות עיסה דאלות היא עיסה עריסותיכם תרגום אצוותיכון והיא איתתא לשה עיסתה לעשותה איטרי והוא כעין סופגנין ואסקריטין דפטורים ואיבעיא ליה באותו מקצת שרגילה לקחת לאפות שלא כדרך איטרי אי יכולה לאכלה בלא חלה דלית ביה כשיעור ואמר לה שמא תימלך על כולה או על כדי חיוב חלה ועיסה העשויה לכותח נמי אם נוטל ממנה עוגה קטנה לאפות באור היתה כולה מתחייב משום גזירה זו דשמא תימלך על כולה א"ר מנא צריכין אנן מכרזין אילין דעבדין עבילין *ואינון עבדין ליה פחות מכשיעור ואינהו סברי שהיא פטורה והיא חייבת והיא מטעם גזירה כדפרשי' ודוקא היכא דאפיה מינה קצת דגזירה משום ההיא פורתא שמא תימלך על כולה אבל אי שביק כולה פטורה ורב פליג התם דאמר עיסת טתח חייבת בחלה א"ר בון שמא תימלך לעשותה חררה לבנה משמע דאפי' לא שקלה מינה כלל חייבת גזירה שמא תימלך ובגמרא שלנו לית ליה דהב דפטרי' עיסת כותח ולא חיישי' שמא תימלך אי נמי רב איירי בעשאה כעבין דזה שייך לחייב משום גזירה שמא תימלך והא דאמרי' בירושלמי בקנובקאות דמתני' לחייבת דאצטריך שלא תאמר (וכן עיסת כותח אם לקחה ממנה פחות מכשיעור לאפות באור חייב שמא תימלך לעשות ממנה חררה כדי חיוב חלה ונתחייב עמו והא דקאמר בירושלמי (שם) בקנובקאות דמתני' חייבת אצטריך שלא תאמר) הואיל ועתיד להחזירה לסולתה תהא פטורה מן החלה הכיא לאחר גמר אפייתה רגילה להחזירה לסולתה עוד א"ר יוחנן בירושלמי (הל' ה) העושה עיסה על מנת לחלקה בצק פטורה מן החלה ומתוך הסברא כ"ש עושה עיסה על מנת לעשותה סופגנין אע"ג דלכאורה משמע בירושלמי (שם) דריש לקיש קאמר לה מעות סופר הוא כמו שאפרש ולא גזר ר' יוחנן דלמא מימלך אלא בנחתום משום דתלוי בדעת לקוחות כמו שאפרש לקמן אפילו לפי טעות על טורחין קיבלה ר' יוחנן כדאמר בירושלמי בריש פ' בתרא (הל' א) יש דברים שכן חיבור בטבול יום ואינה חבור בחלה דתניק תמן בטבול יום פרק ב' (מ"ה) בשר הקודש שקרם עליו הקיפה נגע טבול יום בקיפה חתיכות מותרות וקיפה חיבור ואין סופו *לחתכו ואין חיבור לחלה דא"ר יוחנן העושה עיסה ע"מ לחלקה בצק פטורה מן החלה ומחלות תודה יש ראיה לפי מה שאפרש בבבא שאחר זו והא דאמרי' בפ' כ"מ (דף לז:) גבי אוכל מנחות בירושלים למברך עליה המוציא לאו במנחת מחבת ומרחשת איירי דמטוגנת בשמן ונתבשלה מתורת לחם אלא בדטולת או במאפה תנור אי נמי בכל המנחות ושמן מועט ואין בו כדי לבטלו והראשון נראה דריש לקיש דפסר כל שהאור מהלך תחתיו לא איירי בכל המנחות ועוד ראיה דאין מברכין המוציא על דבר שנתבשל במשקין *דההיא דסוף פ' כל שעה דא"ר יוסי דאין יוצאין ברקיק המבושל אע"פ שלא נמחה שהבישול מבטלו מתורת לחם כדמוכח התם אע"ג דר"מ פליג עליה קיי"ל כר' יוסי וכיון דלאו לחם הוא אין מברכין עליו המוציא ותבילה דכילד מברכין שלא נתבשל והא דתניא התם הכוסס הטה מברך עליו בפה"א טחנה אפאה ובשלה בזמן שהפרוסות קיימות בתחלה מברך עליו המוציא ולבסוף מברך עליו ג' ברכות ההיא ר"מ היא דלא אתי בישול מבטל לה לאפיי' ושמואל קאמר התם שלקות מברכין עליו שהכל מוקי לה כר' יוסי (ה): **ו** המעיסה בפ' כל שעה (ד' לז:) תניא המעיסה קמח ע"ג מוגלשין החליטה מוגלשין על גבי קמח מוגלשין הם מים רותחין ואמרי' התם מאי שנא החליטה ומאי שנא המעיסה ואמרי' אמר ריב"ל כמחלוקת בזו כך מחלוקת בזו ותברא מי ששנה זו לא שנה זו כלומר מאן למחייב מחייב בתרוייהו ומאן דפטר פטר בתרוייהו: עשאן לעצמו. לתודתו ולנזירתו פטור מן החלה כדאמר במנחות בפ' ר' ישמעאל (דף סו:) דגלגול הקדש פטור דכתיב עריסותיכם ולא עיסת הקדש ואע"ג דלא קדשי אלא בשחיטת הזבח הני מילי קדושת הגוף ועוד אפי' לא קדשי כלל פטירי כיון דגלגלן לקדשן מידי דהוי אלמכור בשוק אי לאו דתלוי בדעת לקוחות: למכור בשוק. נזירות תודה וכזירות חייב מפרש בירושלמי לא בדעתו הדבר תלוי (ו) שמא ימצא לקוחות ונמבלו מיד כלומר לקוחות שיקנו ודמיא להא דאמרי' בפ' כל שעה דעשאן לעצמו אין יוצא בהן ידי חובתו [בפסח] למכור בשוק יוצא בהן דכל לשוק אימלוכי אימליך אי מזדבנא מוסב ואי לא איפוק בה אנא: **ז** שעשה שאור לחלק. כדי חיוב חלה עשה בבת אחת אלא שדעתו לחלק לכמה עיסות ואין בכל חלק וחלק כשיעור ופליגא בירושלמי (הל' ה) אי נחתום דוקא אי לא: ונשים שנתנו לנחתום לעשות להן שאור ובין כלן יש כשיעור ולא הכל בבת אחת שלא מדעתן ירושל' (שם) הממרח כריו של חברו שלא מדעתו ר' יוחנן אמר נטבל ריש לקיש אמר לא נטבל מתיב רבי יוחנן (לריש לקיש) והתנן וכן נשים שנתנו לנחתום לעשות להן שאור אם אין באחת מהן כשיעור פטור בחלה ואין בשל כולהון כשיעור בתמיה לומר לא נטבל ופעות סופר בירושלמי [ובסוף מעשרות ג"כ הוא שנוי] וקאמר ר' יוחנן בעושה עיסה על מנת לחלקה בצק פטורה מן החלה כדמשני הכא א"ל שנייא היא שכן העושה עיסה לחלקה בצק פטורה מן החלה א"ל והתנן נחתום שעשה שאור לחלק חייב בחלה א"ל לא תשיבני נחתום נחתום לא בדעתו הדבר תלוי שמא ימצא לקוחות ונמבלו מיד כלומר לא יחלק אם ימצא קונין: **ח** עיסת כלבים מפרש בירושלמי (שם) כל שעירב בה מורסן ופעמים שמתערב כל כך דלא חזיא לרועי': חייבת בחלה. דכי חזיא לרועים לחם קרינא ביה: ומערבין בה. עירובי חצירות להוציא מבתים לחצר: ומשתתפין בה. שיתופי מבוי שב' חצרות פתוחות לו וכל חצר שבגמרא לפני הבתים כן ויוצאין לדרך חצר למבוי ומן המבוי לרשות הרבים: ומברכין עליה. המוציא: ומזמנין. ברכת הזימון: ונאפת ביום טוב. משום חלק הרועים ומוקי לה בפ"ב דביצה (דף כח:) כגון דאית ליה נבילה דודאי אפשר לפייסן בנבילה הא לאו הכי אסור משום דכתיב לכם ולא לכלבים ובירושלמי (שם) מוקי לה כרבי שמעון בן אלעזר דאמר בפ' ב' דביצה (דף טז.) ממלאה אשה תנור פת (ז) מפני שהפת יפה בזמן שהתנור מלא: ואדם יוצא בהן ידי חובתו בפסח. בליל ראשון שהוא חובה דכתיב (שמות יב) בערב תאכלו מצות ושאר הימים אינו חובה לאכול מצה אלא שלא יאכל חמץ: אינה חייבת בחלה. בספרי זוטא דריש

נה

ח עיסת הכלבים וכו' איזו היא עיסה של כלבים רבי שמעון בן לקיש אמר כל שעירב בה מורסן כל זמן שהרועים אוכלים ממנה [כגון שלא עירב בה מורסן הרבה] חייבת בחלה דאוכל בני אדם היא ולחם קרינא ביה: ומערבין בה עירובי חצירות. ומשתתפין בה שיתופי מבואות ומברכין עליה המוציא לחם: ומזמנין עליה. פי' אם ישבו ג' לאכול שנים אכלו מלחם נאה והאחד אכל מזו העיסה מזמנין: ונעשית ביום טוב. כרבי שמעון בן אלעזר דאמר ממלאה אשה את התנור ביום טוב פת מפני שהפת יפה כשהתנור מלא: ויוצא בה ידי חובתו. ואם אין הרועים אוכלין ממנה. פי' שעירב בה מורסן [הרבה] אינה חייבת בחלה וכו'. אבל מטמא טומאת אוכלין דכל אוכל שלא נפסל מאכילת הכלב לענין טומאה אוכל הוא גם זו העיסה של כלבים אע"פ דלאדם לא חזיא

פי' מהר"י בן מלכי צדק

והדובשנין והאיסקריטין וחלת המשרת והמדומע פטורין מן החלה: **ה** עיסה שתחלתה סופגנין וסופה סופגנין פטורה מחלה אותה העיסה תחלתה עיסה וסופה סופגנין. פי' דרך בני אדם לשין עיסה לעשות חררה בתנור ואחר כך נמלכין לעשות סופגנין ויש דרך בני אדם עוד לשין עיסה לעשות סופגנין ואחר כך נמלכין מאותה עיסה לעשות חררה חייבת בחלה: וכן הקנובקאות חייבות. א"ר חנינא בר עיגול בשם חזקיה בן קילטא פי' ואין ידוע לנו אלא אם כן מסתבר עושים אותן מן הסולת ואופין אותן בש"ש או בתנור וכשרוצה סלת כותש אותן ועושין סולת אפי' הכי חייבת בחלה כל אלו ובלבד שיהו כשיעור חלה ובלשונינו [נ"כ] קורין לכברות העשויין בסבעות בן קלטא: **ו** המעיסה בית שמאי פוטר וכו'. תניא איזהו המעיסה ואיזהו החליטה המעיסה קמח על גבי מתלשין פי' מים רותחין. החליטה מוגלשין על גבי קמח ומ"ש המעיסה דב"ש פוטרין וב"ה מחייבין. ומ"ש בחליטה דב"ש מחייבין ובית הלל פוטרין. ואמר רב יהודה בר שמואל ואי תימא ר' יהושע בן לוי כמחלוקת בזו כך מחלוקת בזו ותרי תנאי נינהו חד תנא שנה המעיסה בית שמאי פוטרין ובית הלל מחייבין ...

עין משפט נר מצוה

יג א מיי' שם וטוש"ע שם סעיף ג:
יד ב מיי' פ"ו מהל' בכורים הלכה יב טוש"ע י"ד סימן שכט סעיף ח:
טו ג מיי' שם הל' ה:
טז ד מיי' שם הל' יט טוש"ע י"ד סימן שכו סעיף ג:
יז ה מיי' שם הלכה כ וטוש"ע שם סעיף ג:
יח ו מיי' שם הלכה ח טוש"ע י"ד סי' של סעיף ט:
יט ז מיי' פ"א מהל' יו"ט הלכה יד סמג לאוין עה טוש"ע א"ח סימן תקיב סעיף ג:
כ ח מיי' פ"ו מהל' חמץ ומצה הלכה ה טוש"ע א"ח סימן תנד סעיף ג:
כא ט מיי' פ"ב מהל' טומאת אוכלין הלכה יח:

פירוש הרא"ש

ממנו מה שהוא מרים ממנו מקדשו. אסמכתא בעלמא היא דמדרכנן הוא דבעינן ק': (ה) ור' מאיר הנהיג בביתו כשהיו לשין עיסה ע"מ לבשלה במים ולטגנה בשמן שהיו לוקחין ממנה מעט לאפותה ועי"כ נתחייבת כל העיסה בחלה קודם שיקח ממנה מעט דחיישי' שמא תימלך וגם לא היה אוכל בלא המוציא אחר שנתבשלה וגם לא היה מברך עליה המוציא אלא מברך על לחם אחר המוציא ואחר כך אוכלה: (ו) אלא בדעת הלקוחות הדבר תלוי: (ז) אע"פ שאינו צריך אלא לככר אחד: (ח) מטמאה טומאת אוכלין כיון שהיא ראויה לאדם בשעת הדחק נאכלת לאדם עד שתפסל מאכילת הכלב:

לה מדכתב עריסותיכם שלכם חייבת ושל כלב אינה חייבת: ט חייבין עליה מיתה וחומש. זר האוכלן מזיד חייב מיתה בידי שמים דכתיב בתרומה ומתו בו כי יחללוהו (ויקרא כב) וחלה איקרי תרומה: וחומש. בשוגג קרן לבעלים וחומש לכל כהן שירצה: ואסורים לזרים. בפ' ב' דבכורים (מ"ו) תנן כי הא מתני' ומייתינן לה בהערל (דף עג) והתם ניחא דאע"ג דתנא חייבין עליהן מיתה תנא ואסורה לזרים משום דבעי למיתני הרי [אלו] בתרומה ובכורים מה שאין כן במעשר דשרי לזר ואפי' איסורא ליכא אבל הכא קשה (ט) ועלה דהיא מפרש בירושל' (הל' א) מתני' מסייע לר' יוחנן דאסורה לזרים פחר לה פחות מכשיעור כלומר לר' יוחנן דאמר בפ' בתרא דיומא (דף עג:)

אוכלין: ט החלה א) והתרומה חייבין *עליה מיתה וחומש ואסורין לזרים ב) והם נכסי כהן ועולין באחד ומאה ג) וטעונין רחיצת ידים ד) והערב שמש ואין נוטלין מן הטהור על הטמא ה) אלא מן המוקף ומן הדבר הגמור ו) האומר ג) כל גרני תרומה ז) וכל עיסתי חלה לא אמר כלום עד שישייר מקצת:

פרק שני

א פירות ח) חוצה לארץ שנכנסו לארץ חייבים בחלה יצאו מכאן לשם רבי אליעזר מחייב ט) ורבי עקיבא פוטר: ב י) עפר ג) חוצה לארץ שבא בספינה לארץ חייבת במעשרות ובשביעית אמר רבי יהודה אימתי בזמן שהספינה גוששת כ) עיסה שנילושה במי פירות חייבת בחלה ונאכלת בידים מסואבות: ג ל) האשה ד) יושבת וקוצה חלתה ערומה מפני שהיא יכולה לכסות עצמה אבל לא האיש מי שאינו יכול לעשות עיסתו בטהרה יעשנה קבין

MISHNAH 9. IN THE CASE OF ḤALLAH AND TERUMAH; ONE IS LIABLE, ON ACCOUNT OF [HAVING EATEN] THEM, TO DEATH,[2] OR[3] TO [REPAY] 'ONE-FIFTH';[4] AND THEY ARE FORBIDDEN [AS FOOD] TO 'STRANGERS';[5] THEY ARE THE PROPERTY OF THE PRIEST;[6] THEY ARE VOID [IF ONE PART OF EITHER IS MIXED] WITHIN ONE-HUNDRED-AND-ONE [PARTS, THE REST BEING NON-SACRED DOUGH OR PRODUCE];[7] THEY
a REQUIRE WASHING OF ONE'S HANDS,[1] AND [WAITING UNTIL] THE SETTING OF THE SUN [PRIOR TO EATING THEM];[2] THEY MAY NOT BE TAKEN OFF A CLEAN [LOT][3] FOR [DISCHARGING THE OBLIGATION[4] IN RESPECT ALSO OF] AN UNCLEAN [LOT],[5] AND [ARE NOT TAKEN OFF ONE LOT IN RESPECT ALSO OF ANY OTHER LOT][6] EXCEPT OF SUCH [LOTS] AS ARE CLOSE TOGETHER,[7] AND FROM SUCH AS ARE [IN A] FINISHED [STATE].[8] IF ONE SAID: ALL MY THRESHING-FLOOR IS TERUMAH, OR ALL MY DOUGH IS ḤALLAH, HE HAS NOT SAID ANYTHING, UNLESS HE HAS LEFT SOME OVER.[9]

(2) *Sc.* 'by the hand of heaven', Sanh. 83*a*. This refers to a non-priest who has eaten either *ḥallah* or *terumah* wittingly, though without having been first warned. If he has eaten these after statutory warning, his punishment is 'stripes' (v. Ter. VII, 1). This is deduced from Lev. XXII, 9 in conjunction with v. 10 and v. 6, it being understood from the latter that by the '*holy things*' spoken of throughout the passage, precisely *terumah* is intended (since only for eating *terumah* need the priest who had been unclean wait, on the day of his ablution, till sunset); v. Sanh. *loc. cit. Ḥallah* is considered as *terumah* since in Num. XV, 20 the latter term is applied also to the former. (3) In case of an unwitting transgressor. (4) V. Lev. XXII, 14, And if *a man eat of the holy thing unwittingly, then he shall put the fifth part thereof unto it and shall give unto the priest the holy thing*, i.e , its cost. The added sum was to be equal to a fifth of the eventual total paid, i.e., a quarter of the assessed money-value of the consecrated produce or dough eaten. Cf *supra* 3, n. 4. The principal was to be paid to the priest whose property the *terumah* or *ḥallah* was, and the added sum to any priest. (5) I.e., non-priests, non-Aaronides. Though this prohibition is already understood from the provisions preceding it in this Mishnah, its re-statement in positive form is not superfluous—as some authorities thought it to be—but is required to establish the fact that the prohibition is against non-priests consuming even less than the minimum quantity for which they are punishable. (6) He may sell it, or acquire with it anything he wishes; if it should become unclean, he may use it as fuel over which to do cooking for himself. (7) If the non-sacred is more than a hundred times the sacred (*terumah* or *ḥallah*), the non-sacred character of the mixture is in no wise affected; if the proportion of non-sacred to sacred is less than 100 to 1, the mixture is *medumma'* and prohibited to non-priests (v. *supra* 4 n. 8).

a (1) On the part of the priest, before touching or eating them. If he does not wash his hands specially he renders *terumah* (even of fruit) or *ḥallah pasul* i.e., unfit. (2) A priest who has become unclean has to undergo ablutions and wait till after sunset before eating *terumah* (or *ḥallah*), Lev. XXII, 6–7. (3) Of produce or dough. (4) Of *terumah, ḥallah* or tithes. (5) *Terumah, ḥallah* or tithes may be separated from one lot of produce or dough in a quantity sufficient to cover the *terumah-, ḥallah-* or tithe-obligation, also for other lots, but only if all such lots are close together; should one of the lots be unclean, the owner would be afraid to let it be close enough to the others lest the unclean touches the clean and makes the latter, too, unclean. Hence this regulation. Cf. *infra* IV, 6. (6) So Maim. and other commentators. (7) V. n. 5. (8) Ma'as. I, 2ff, enumerate the stages at which various kinds of produce are considered in a 'finished' state, at which they severally become liable to have *terumah* or tithes separated from them. In the case of dough the time of separating *ḥallah* is when it has been rolled (v. *infra* III, 1). (9) *Terumah* and *ḥallah* are both to be the '*first*' of the produce or the dough respectively (Deut. XVIII, 4, Num. XV, 20), which implies that there must be some left over after they have been taken off.

◁ *For the continuation of the English translation of this page see overleaf.*

לה מדכתב עריסותיכם שלכם חייבת ושל כלב אינה חייבת: **ט** חייבין עליה מיתה וחומש · זר האוכלן מזיד חייב מיתה בידי שמים דכתיב בתרומה ומתו בו כי יחללוהו (ויקרא כב) וחלה איקרי תרומה: וחומש. בשוגג קרן לבעלים וחומש לכל כהן שירצה: ואסורים לזרים. בפ' ב' דבכורים (מ"ו) תנן כי הא מתני' ומייתינן לה בהערל (דף עג) והתם ניחא דאע"ג דתנא חייבין עליהן מיתה תנא ואסורה לזרים משום דבעי למיתני הרי [אלו] בתרומה ובכורים מה שאין כן במעשר דשרי לזר ואפי' איסורא ליכא אבל הכא קשה (ט) ועלה דהסיא מפרש בירושל' (הל' א) מתני' מסייע לר' יוחנן דאסורה לזרים פתר לה פחות מכשיעור כלומר לר' יוחנן דאמר בפ' בתרא דיומא (דף עג:)

חצי שיעור אסור מן התורה ויתכן האי מתני' דהכא (י): והן נכסי כהן · כדאמרי' בפ' הזרוע גבי ביכורים והן נכסי כהן ליקח בהן עבדים וקרקעות ובהמה טמאה: וטעונין רחיצת ידים · אפילו לאכילה דפירי כדאמרי' בסוף אין דורשין (ד' יח:) דלאכילה דנהמא אפי' מעשר נמי בעי: והערב שמש · כדדרשי' בהערל להעריב שמשו אוכל בתרומה: ואינו נוטל מן הטהור על הטמא · כדתנן בפ"ב (מ"א) דתרומות ושם פירשתי הטעם: אלא מן המוקף · עיסה בנגיעה ושאר דברים בלא נגיעה אלא שיהיו במקום אחד כדפרשי' בפ"ג דמעשר שני: מן הדבר הגמור. פירות שנגמרה מלאכתן וחלה משתגלגל העיסה: עד שישייר מקצת. דחלה ותרומה כתיב בהו ראשית ששיריה ניכרים כדאיתא בפ' ראשית הגז (דף קלו:):

א חייבין בחלה · משמע בין ר' אליעזר בין ר' עקיבא מודו ואמרי' בירושלמי (הל' א) תני זו דברי ר"מ אבל ר' יודה אומר פירות חו"ל שנכנסו לארץ ר' אליעזר פוטר ור' עקיבא מחייב מה טעם דר' אליעזר והיה באכלכם מלחם הארץ (במדבר טו) ולא מלחם חוצה לארץ מה טעם דר"ע הארץ אשר אני מביא אתכם (שם) שמה אתם חייבים בין בפירות חוצה לארץ בין בפירות הארץ התם דהשיב ר"ע לר"א אי אתה מודה לי בשעה שנכנסו לארץ ומלאו קמחין וגליקות דאינון חייבין בחלה ולאו גידולי פטור הן והוא מקבל מיניה כלומר קיבל ר"א תשובתו והא דפטר ר"ע יצאו מיכן לשם דכתיב אשר אני מביא אתכם שמה שמה אתם חייבים ואי אתם חייבים בחוצה לארץ וא"ת היאך ר"ע מחייב בבליקות שמלאו והלא נכרי פוטר אפילו לאחר שנכנסו לארץ יש לומר דלטעמיה דאמר לקמן בפרק ג' (מ"ו) הכל הולך אחר הקרימה בתנור דאין גלגול נכרי פוטר אלא קרימת תנור פוטרת ובירושלמי (שם) מתמה למה קיבל ר' אליעזר תשובתו של רבי עקיבא דאמר ר' יוסי ותמיה' אני היאך ר"ע מותיב קומי ר' אליעזר והוא מקבל מיניה תמן עד שלא נכנסו לארץ למפרע ירשו דאמר ר' דוסתי בשם ר' שמואל בר' נחמן לזרעך אתן אין כתיב כאן אלא לזרעך נתתי שכבר נתתי: ירושלמי (שם) ר' יונה בעי קומי ר' ירמיה בשעה שנכנסו ישראל לארץ ומלאו קמה לחה מהו שתהא אסורה משום חדש אמר ליה ולמה לא עד כדון לחה אפי' יבשה אמר ליה ואפי' יבשה אפי' קלורה מעתה אפי' חטין בעליה כך אני אומר לא אכלו ישראל מלה בליל פסח א"ר יונה מן דנפקית תהי בי דלא אמריכן ליה שנייה היא שמצות עשה דוחה מצות לא תעשה על דעתיה דרבי יונה דאמר מצות עשה דוחה לא תעשה אף ע"פ שאינה כתובה

ומין מהם מיוחד לאכילת אדם בלא ספק: **ט** מצינו שקרא הש"י לחלה תרומה שנאמר (במדבר טו) חלה הרימו תרומה ואמר בתרומה ומתו בו כי יחללוהו (ויקרא כב) ומי שאכלה מישראל מזיד חייב מיתה בידי שמים ואם אכלה שוגג נתחייב בתוספת חומש כמו שנתבאר במסכת תרומות: והם נכסי כהן. לפי שהוא יכול לקדש בהן אשה: ועולין באחד ומאה. כמו שנתבאר בתרומות: וטעונים רחיצת ידים. אפילו שיהיו ידיו טהורות והיא מכלל י"ח דברים שגזרו ועוד יתבאר זה במקומות רבות מסדר טהרות וכשנגעה התרומה או החלה בידו אפי' היא טהורה ולא נטלה ליגע בהן כבר פסל אותן ולפיכך חייב בנטילת ידים לאכול פירות של תרומה ואינו חייב בזה לא בחולין ולא במעשר ועוד יתבאר כל אלו הדברים במקומן: והערב שמש. לאמרו הש"י ובא השמש וטהר ואחר יאכל מן הקדשים (ויקרא כב) והעיקר אצלנו ביאת שמשו מעכבתו מלאכול בתרומה וכבר בארנו זה בתחלת ברכות: אלא מן המוקף. ענינו מן הדבר שהוא מוקף ומכונס במקום אחד ולא שיוציא מזו העיסה החלה החייבת בה והחייבת לאותה עיסה האחרת שהיא במקום אחר וכמלא שהפריש שלא מן המוקף על המוקף ושיעור המאמר כן אין נוטלין מן הטהור על הטמא ואין נוטלין אלא מן המוקף וכן תרומת הגורן כמו שזכרנו בתרומות: ומן הדבר הגמור. לפי שנקראת ראשית ואמרו ראשית דגנך אינו מפריש עד שיהא דגן ענינו עד שיגמור: עד שישייר מקצת. ענינו לא נקרא ראשית אלא אם נשאר ממנה שיור והוא אמרם מראשית ולא כל ראשית וכן פסקו ההלכה במסכת תרומות:

א אמר הש"י אשר אני מביא אתכם שמה (במדבר טו) שמה אתם חייבים ואי אתם חייבים בחוצה לארץ ור' אליעזר אומר באכלכם מלחם הארץ (שם) בין בארץ בין בחוצה לארץ ולפיכך אומר שאם יצאו מן הארץ לחוצה לארץ חייבין והלכה כרבי עקיבא: **ב** פירות חוצה לארץ אינן חייבות מן התורה במעשר ולא בדיני שמטה וכשבא עפר מחוצה לארץ לארץ ישראל בספינה וזרע בתוכו עפר שבאותו הספינה אותו הזרע חייב בכל החוקים ובתנאי שתהיה הספינה מתחככת בארץ וזהו ענין גוששת ופי' לומר דבקה בארץ וגום כמו עפר וכבר בארנו כי בכל מקום שאמר ר' יהודה אימתי

אוכלין: **ט** החלה [א] והתרומה חייבין *עליה מיתה וחומש ואסורין לזרים והם נכסי כהן ועולין באחד ומאה וטעונין רחיצת ידים והערב שמש ואין נוטלין מן הטהור על הטמא אלא מן המוקף ומן הדבר הגמור האומר [ג] כל גרני תרומה וכל עיסתי חלה לא אמר כלום עד שישייר מקצת:

פרק שני

א פירות חוצה לארץ שנכנסו לארץ חייבים בחלה יצאו מכאן לשם רבי אליעזר מחייב ורבי עקיבא פוטר: **ב** עפר [ג] חוצה לארץ שבא בספינה לארץ חייבת במעשרות ובשביעית אמר רבי יהודה אימתי בזמן שהספינה גוששת עיסה שנילושה במי פירות חייבת בחלה ונאכלת בידים מסואבות: **ג** האשה [ד] יושבת וקוצה חלתה ערומה מפני שהיא יכולה לכסות עצמה אבל לא האיש מי שאינו יכול לעשות עיסתו בטהרה יעשנה קבין

Continuation of translation from previous page as indicated by ◁

CHAPTER II

b *MISHNAH* 1. PRODUCE [GROWN] OUTSIDE THE LAND,[1] THAT CAME INTO THE LAND IS SUBJECT TO ḤALLAH;[2] [IF IT] WENT OUT FROM HERE[3] TO THERE,[4] R. ELIEZER DECLARES [IT] TO BE SUBJECT [THERETO],[5] BUT R. AKIBA DECLARES [IT] TO BE EXEMPT [THEREFROM].[6]

MISHNAH 2. IF EARTH FROM OUTSIDE THE LAND HAS COME TO THE LAND IN A BOAT,[7] [THE PRODUCE GROWN THEREIN] IS SUBJECT TO TITHES AND TO THE [LAW RELATING TO] THE SEVENTH YEAR.[8] SAID R. JUDAH: WHEN [DOES THIS APPLY]? WHEN THE BOAT TOUCHES [THE GROUND].[9] DOUGH WHICH HAS BEEN KNEADED WITH FRUIT-JUICE[10] IS SUBJECT
c TO ḤALLAH,[1] AND MAY BE EATEN WITH UNCLEAN HANDS.[2]

MISHNAH 3. A WOMAN MAY SIT AND SEPARATE HER
d ḤALLAH[1] [WHILST SHE IS] NAKED,[2] SINCE SHE CAN COVER HERSELF,[3] BUT A MAN [MAY] NOT. IF ONE IS NOT ABLE TO MAKE ONE'S DOUGH IN CLEANNESS HE SHOULD MAKE IT [IN SEPARATE] ḲABS,[4] RATHER THAN MAKE IT IN UNCLEANNESS;[5]

b **(1) *Sc.* of Israel. (2) Based on Num. XV, 18 ff. *When ye come to the land whither I bring you* .... *ye shall set apart* ḥallah ...., which implies that in Palestine dough from grain whether of native or foreign growth is subject to *ḥallah* (v. T.J.). (3) Palestine. (4) Abroad. (5) Relying on *When ye eat of the bread* (i.e., cereal produce) *of the land* (ibid 19), whether made into dough in the Land or elsewhere (T.J.). (6) Being of the opinion that the word *'There'* (in Num. XV, 18, which literally translated is *When ye come to the land which I bring you there*) has the force of making the law of *ḥallah* applicable exclusively to dough kneaded in the Land (T.J.). (7) Which has an aperture in its bottom, and (as explained by R. Judah) is aground on Palestinian soil, and thus anything grown in the soil in the boat sucks up sustenance from the soil of Palestine. (8) And to all laws applicable to Palestinian produce (v. Maim.). On the 'SEVENTH YEAR' v. Ex. XXIII, 10 and Lev. XXV, 3–7; it is the subject of Tractate Shebi'ith in this Seder. (9) V. *supra* n. 1. R. Judah explains what the first reported unnamed Tanna (R. Meir) meant. The term 'WHEN' used by R. Judah in the Mishnah introduces, as here, an explanation; in Baraitha it introduces, as a rule, a differing view (v. 'Iḳḳar Tosaf. Yom. Ṭob). (10) Apparently even without water (v. *infra* 56b n. d 1).**

c **(1) There are two considerations that might have led people to assume a contrary ruling. (*a*) The principle indicated in I, 4 and 5 that any but plain dough, and especially such as had an admixture giving it a special character, is exempt from *ḥallah*. (*b*) If a standard for liquids affecting ritual considerations regarding food were sought, it could be found in the seven liquids (viz., wine, date-honey, blood, water, oil, milk and dew) which when they moisten food render it susceptible to uncleanness (v. 56b n. a 1). It might have been thought that whichever liquids rendered the flour-paste susceptible to uncleanness, also rendered it subject to *ḥallah*, in which case it would have appeared as if only those fruit-juices which had the former effect and are numbered among the seven liquids (viz., wine, date-honey and oil) rendered dough kneaded with them subject to *ḥallah*, but that dough kneaded with other fruit-juices is exempt from *ḥallah*. Hence the need for the Mishnah to make it clear that dough kneaded with *any* fruit-juice is liable to *ḥallah*. On the other hand, however, according to I, 4 (v. 55b n. d 5)** cake dough prepared with date-honey appears to be exempt from *ḥallah*. Thus there seems to be no unexceptionable guidance on the subject of how fruit-juices affect liability to *ḥallah*. In view of these uncertainties, the dilemma could, in practice, be solved either by separating *ḥallah* in such a case, but without reciting the blessing ('who .... hast commanded us to separate *ḥallah* from the dough'), or by putting that doubtful dough close to dough that is certainly subjected to *ḥallah*, and take *ḥallah* from the latter for both (cf. *supra* I, 9). V. *Yoreh De'ah*, 329, 9 and the commentators *ad loc.* (2) This can be the case only if fruit-juices are not considered as moisture rendering food liable to uncleanness, as it is only then that unclean hands will not make the dough (or whatever is baked therefrom) unclean. Incidentally the difficulty arises again in that three of the liquids rendering food susceptible to uncleanness are fruit-juices; but even if we should decide that 'fruit-juices' in this Mishnah means 'fruit-juices except those among the seven liquids' there would still arise the following dilemma: In non-Temple days *ḥallah* is separated (and a blessing recited), but it is not given to a priest to eat because *ḥallah* must be eaten only in the levitical purity of the person, which state of purity is virtually non-existent in non-Temple times (owing to the absence of means of purification). *Eo ipso* the hand of the person separating the *ḥallah*, who too, cannot be ritually clean, renders the *ḥallah* unclean, and it is for these reasons burnt. Now if it be the case that dough kneaded with fruit-juice is altogether insusceptible to defilement and yet liable to *ḥallah*, then since one is debarred from giving the *ḥallah* to a priest, the only alternative would be to burn perfectly 'clean' *ḥallah*, and that is a thing that should not be done. To avoid this dilemma it is strongly recommended by the authorities that those who bake should be sure always to mix into the dough some water or other liquid which renders it susceptible to uncleanness; *ḥallah* is then separated (accompanied with the recital of the appropriate blessing) and being through unavoidable conditions unclean is burnt (v. *Yoreh De'ah* ibid, 10).

d (1) Pronouncing the appropriate benediction. (2) Notwithstanding the rule that in the presence of nakedness one is not permitted to utter sacred words (v. Ber. 22*b*). (3) By sitting with her feet together, so that the labia cannot be seen (Maim.). The buttocks do not constitute 'nakedness' for the purpose of preventing the uttering of a benediction (v. Ber. 24*a*). (4) Less than 1 1/4 *ḳab* being exempt from *ḥallah* (v. *infra* Mishnah 6). (5) Which would result in wittingly defiling sacred matter, viz., *ḥallah*.

BUT R. AKIBA SAYS: LET HIM MAKE IT IN UNCLEANNESS RATHER THAN MAKE IT [IN SEPARATE] ḲABS, SINCE THE SAME DESIGNATION AS HE GIVES TO THE CLEAN, HE LIKEWISE GIVES TO THE UNCLEAN; THE ONE HE DECLARES ḤALLAH TO THE NAME,[6] AND THE OTHER HE DECLARES ḤALLAH TO THE NAME[6] BUT [SEPARATE] ḲABS HAVE NO PORTION [DEVOTED] TO THE NAME.[7]

MISHNAH 4. IF ONE MAKES HIS DOUGH [IN SEPARATE] ḲABS,[8] AND THEY TOUCH ONE ANOTHER,[9] THEY ARE EXEMPT
a FROM ḤALLAH,[1] UNLESS THEY STICK TOGETHER.[2] R. ELIEZER SAYS: ALSO IF ONE SHOVELS [LOAVES FROM AN OVEN][3] AND PUTS [THEM] INTO A BASKET,[4] THE BASKET JOINS THEM TOGETHER FOR [THE PURPOSES OF] ḤALLAH.[5]

MISHNAH 5. IF ONE SEPARATES HIS ḤALLAH [IN THE STATE OF] FLOUR, IT IS NOT ḤALLAH,[6] AND IN THE HAND OF A PRIEST IT IS [AS] A THING ROBBED;[7] THE DOUGH ITSELF[8] IS STILL SUBJECT TO ḤALLAH,[9] AND THE FLOUR,[10] IF THERE BE OF IT THE STATUTORY MINIMUM QUANTITY,[11] IS [ALSO[12]] SUBJECT TO ḤALLAH;[13] AND IT IS PROHIBITED TO NON-PRIESTS:[14] [THE LATTER IS] THE OPINION OF R. JOSHUA. THEY TOLD HIM OF AN OCCURRENCE WHEN A SCHOLAR—NON-PRIEST—SEIZED IT.[15] SAID HE TO THEM: INDEED, HE DID
b SOMETHING DAMAGING TO HIMSELF,[1] BUT BENEFITING TO OTHERS.[2]

MISHNAH 6. FIVE-FOURTHS [OF A ḲAB][3] OF FLOUR[4] ARE SUBJECT TO ḤALLAH. [IF] THESE[5] INCLUDING THEIR LEAVEN[6] AND THEIR LIGHT BRAN AND THEIR COARSE BRAN [MAKE UP THE] FIVE-FOURTHS, THEY ARE SUBJECT;[7] IF THEIR COARSE BRAN HAD BEEN REMOVED FROM THEM[8] AND RETURNED TO THEM, THEY ARE EXEMPT.[9]

MISHNAH 7. THE [STATUTORY MINIMUM] MEASURE OF ḤALLAH IS ONE TWENTY-FOURTH [PART OF THE DOUGH].[10] IF ONE MAKES DOUGH FOR ONESELF, OR ONE MAKES IT FOR
c HIS SON'S BANQUET,[1] IT IS ONE TWENTY-FOURTH. IF A BAKER MAKES TO SELL IN THE MARKET, AND SO [ALSO] IF A WOMAN[2] MAKES TO SELL IN THE MARKET, IT IS ONE FORTY-EIGHTH.[3] IF DOUGH IS RENDERED UNCLEAN EITHER UNWITTINGLY OR BY FORCE,[4] IT IS ONE FORTY-EIGHTH;[5] IF IT WAS RENDERED

(6) Reading not בשם but לשם the variant mentioned in the commentators. For שם as The Name of God, v. Yoma III, 8 etc. and Marmorstein *The Old Rabbinic Doctrine of God*, p. 105. (7) R. Akiba held that as *ḥallah* is given to the priest, whether—when it is clean —to be eaten or — when it is unclean—to be burnt by him as fuel for cooking for himself, it is — in either case—an expression of the Israelite's indebtedness to God, and of use to the priest, and should therefore not be avoided by deliberately kneading one's dough in quantities less than the minimum liable to *ḥallah*. R. Akiba's view is not accepted since as 'they said before R. Akiba: One does not say to a person: "Arise and commit a transgression so that thou mayest create for thyself an opportunity for a meritorious act", or "Arise and spoil in order that thou mayest mend" ' (Tosef. Ḥal. 1, 8). (8) Every separate piece of dough being thus exempt from *ḥallah*. (9) In the course of baking (Maim.).

a (1) But not from *terumah*, with regard to which, only proximity is required. (2) Lit., 'bite [one into another]', stick together in the oven so that when pulled apart a portion of one loaf is detached by the other. Even so the effectiveness of such coalescence in rendering such loaves liable to *ḥallah*, depends on the precise species thus stuck together. V. *infra* IV, 2. (3) Singly and separately, and they had not stuck together. (4) Or any container. (5) In Pes. 48*b*, it is discussed whether a flat board having no rim is to be considered as 'joining together' small quantities of dough for purposes of *ḥallah*, but the matter is left undecided. Later authorities recommend the covering over of all pieces of dough, or loaves, with a cloth, which has the same effect as a basket. (Yoreh De'ah, 325, 1). (6) Because the commandment is definitely '*the first of your dough*'. (7) He must give it back to the Israelite, else by retaining it he would cause the latter to believe that he has duly performed the obligation of *ḥallah*, and that the dough he makes from the remaining flour is thereby exempt and permitted to be eaten, which is not the case (v. Ḳid. 46*b*). (8) Made from the remaining flour. (9) V. *supra* n. 7. (10) Erroneously separated as *ḥallah*. (11) $1^1/_4$ *ḳab*, or an *Omer*. v. *infra* Mish. 6. (12) When made into dough. (13) According to Maim. this liability is not a definite one. (14) Lit., 'strangers'. This prohibition has, according to Rash and Asheri, no positive basis and is enacted only in view of the possibility of people seeing a non-priest eating something that had already been given to a priest, and thinking that the non-priest is committing the sin of partaking of consecrated food. (15) קפישה the verb is, according to Maim. a cognate of כבש. Maim. appears to say that the word occurs often, and Emden (Glosses in Wilna Talmud) says. I know no place where it occurs except Lam. III, 16 (where the root is כפש). Maim. evidently thought of the frequent occurrence of כבש. The assumption, in T.J., is that this lay scholar not only seized the flour but also *ate* it, and thus demonstrated a view opposed to that of R. Joshua. L. assumed that the scholar, before eating the flour, had separated *ḥallah* from the flour, or that the latter was less in quantity than the statutory minimum and, of course, exempt from *ḥallah*.

b (1) Since he is punished (T.J.). (2) In that 'They eat and rely on him' (T.J.) which B. and L. and the codes apparently assume to mean that non-priests will be glad to partake of such flour and escape punishment by referring to a authoritative personal example. This interpretation was evidently felt to be, and indeed it is, strained and unsatisfactory; witness that some read the reverse (v. T.J.) viz., 'he did something that is benefiting to himself, but damaging to others' which is explained (ibid.), 'he benefited himself since—anyway— he ate it, but did a disservice to others who will think that what he has eaten is exempt from *ḥallah*, whereas it is subject. (3) $1^1/_4$ of this measure, as standardized in Sepphoris, was equivalent to an *Omer* which in the wilderness was the standard measure of food per person per day (Ex. XVI, 16); v. *supra* I, 4. (4) When made into dough. (5) Quantities of flour. (6) The leaven (yeast) put into the dough-mixture. (7) Because such flour, though coarse, is largely used for human food, particularly by the poor. (8) And less than $1^1/_4$ *ḳab* is, thus, left. (9) Because whilst it is usual, for the purposes of kneading dough, to sift flour and remove the coarse bran, it is not usual to put it back once it has been removed (T.J.); also, because coarse bran itself is not subject to *ḥallah* (Maim.). (10) The proportions here laid down are not indicated in the Torah, but are 'a tradition of the Scribes'. T.J. explains that since Scripture says of *ḥallah* '*ye shall give*', the amount handed over as *ḥallah* should be sufficiently appreciable to be handed over. From the minimum quantity of dough liable to *ḥallah*, viz., $1^1/_4$ *ḳab* (which = about $3^1/_2$ lbs), one twenty-fourth amounts to 2 to $2^1/_2$ ounces.

c (1) No distinction is made between doughs whether big or small intended for private consumption. (2) This applies equally to a man in similar circumstances, viz., who bakes in a small way at home but for sale. The Mishnah speaks here of a woman because it was as a rule women who engaged in this kind of small baking-business. Again no distinction is made between doughs, whether large or small, intended for trading purposes. (3) T.J. (as corrected according to Tosef Ḥal. I, 6) explains the reason for varying the proportions: The individual person baking for one's private use is more liberal than the professional baker who bakes to sell and make profit.—In non-Temple times when, owing to the all-prevailing ritual uncleanness (from defilement, direct and indirect, by dead bodies) all *ḥallah* is unclean, and cannot be given to priests (even in Palestine, and certainly outside Palestine even in Temple times since there *ḥallah* is separated always in deference not to a Scriptural precept, but only to a Rabbinic requirement), just a *kazayith* 'the size of an olive' of dough is taken off and burnt. (4) Of unavoidable or overpowering circumstances. (5) The smaller proportion is laid down in this case because the *ḥallah* being unclean it may not be eaten and can serve the priest only as fuel (Rash and Bert.); also, because one should not deliberately increase the amount of such holy things as are *ab initio* and inevitably rendered unclean.

אלא יעשנה עיסה של קב . שאין בה שיעור חלה : ורבי עקיבא סבר טוב שיפריש חלה בטומאה ואל יפסור עיסתו מחלה דקורא שם חלה לטמאה כמו לטהורה אבל עיסה פטורה אין לשמים חלק בה ואית ספרים דגרסי לזו קורא חלה לשם ולזו קורא חלה לשם אבל קבים אין בהם חלק לשם : ד העושה עיסתו קבים · [כל] קב בפני עצמו ושיעור חלה חמש רבעים : עד שישוכו · שדבוקות זו בזו דאם בא להפרידן נתלש מזו לזו כדתניא בתוספתא דטהרות (פ"א) איזהו הנשוך התולש ממנו משהו : אף הרודה ונותן לסל · בפ"ק דנדה (דף ח·) פסק הלכה כרבי אליעזר ומדתני אף משמע דרבי אליעזר לא בעי נשיכה ותימה

ואל יעשנה בטומאה ורבי עקיבא אומר יעשנה בטומאה ואל יעשנה קבים שכשם שהוא קורא לטהורה כך הוא קורא לטמאה לזו קורא חלה *בשם ולזו קורא חלה *בשם אבל קביים אין להם חלק *בשם : ד העושה עיסתו קבים ונגעו זה בזה פטורים מן החלה עד שישוכו רבי אליעזר א) אומר אף הרודה ונותן לסל הסל מצרפן לחלה : ה המפריש חלתו ב) קמח אינה חלה וגזל ביד כהן העיסה עצמה חייבת בחלה והקמח אם יש בו כשיעור חייבת בחלה ואסורה לזרים דברי ר' יהושע אמרו לו מעשה וקפשה זקן זר אמר להם אף הוא קלקל לעצמו ותיקן לאחרים : ו חמשת רבעים ג) קמח חייבין בחלה הם ושאורן וסובן ומורסנן חמשת רבעים חייבין ניטל מורסנן מתוכן וחזר לתוכן הרי אלו פטורין : ז שיעור החלה ד) אחד מעשרים וארבעה העושה עיסה לעצמו והעושה למשתה בנו אחד מעשרים וארבעה נחתום שהוא עושה למכור בשוק וכן האשה שהיא עושה למכור בשוק אחד מארבעים ושמנה נטמאת עיסתה שוגגת או אנוסה אחד מארבעים ושמנה

טמא ויהיה בינו ובין המים יותר מארבע מילין לפניו אין מטריחין אותו ללכת עד מקום המים ולטבול וללוש אלא ילוש בטומאה אבל לא ילוש אלא קבים שהוא פחות משיעור חלה כדי שלא יתחייב בחלה וכבר בארנו שיעור הקב וכן אין מטריחין אותו לשוב לאחריו לבקש מים אפי' היה רחוק מהם שיעור מועטת אבל אם היה בינו ובין המים ושהיו המים לפניו ארבע מילין או פחות אסור לו ללוש בטומאה ואין הלכה כרבי עקיבא : ד קבים הנזכרים בכאן בזו ההלכה יש *) בהם שיעור חלה ועוד כדבר על זה בזה הפרק ואמר ונגעו זה בזה ר"ל בעת האפיה שנגעו קצת ככרות לקצתם שאין חייבות בחלה עד שידבקו קצתם בקצתם דבוק יפה ורבי אליעזר אומר שאם לש בדרך הדמיון מאה כעבין אחת אחת ואפה אותם והוציאם כולן מן התנור אחת אחת ונתקבצו כולן בסל אחד אע"פ שאין נוגעות זו בזו חייב להוציא מהן החלה אחר האפיה וכן ביארו בגמרא ואמרו שאפי' כעבין שאין נושכות זו עם זו הסל מצרפן לחלה והלכה כרבי אליעזר : ה העיסה עצמה חייבת בחלה . עניינו שאם לש מה שנשאר מן הקמח אחר שהוציא ממנה קמח ונתכוין להיות אותו הקמח חלה שאותה עיסה חייבת בחלה ואותו הקמח אם יש בו חמשת רבעים שהוא שיעור חלה כמו שיתבאר ולש אותו שהוא חייב גם כן בחלה ואותה חלה אסורה לזרים כדין כל חלה ולא נאמר זו העיסה אינה חייבת בחלה כיון שהקמח שלה לחלה היתה בו הכונה ולא יתקיים זה אלא כשהוציא החלה מן העיסה וכאילו אותה חלה הראשונה על כל הקמח הוציאה ר"ל על כל מה שנלוש ממנה ועל הקמח שהוציאו חלה : אמרו לו מעשה וקפשה זקן זר . וקפשה כמו וכבשה וכן באה זאת המלה במקומות בענין אחר וענין אכילתו אותה ראיה שאינה בכלל חלה וכי זה הקמח שהוציאו חלה אינו חייב בחלה חיוב גמור לפי שאילו היה חייב כשאר העיסות לא היה ראוי לזר שיכבוש אותה חלה לעצמו : אמר להן אף הוא קלקל לעצמו . שאכל אותה חלה לפי שחטא ותיקן לאחרים שהם חשבו שלא חייב אותו הקמח חלה ובאמת שהוא חייב והוא אמרם בגמרא קלקל לעצמו והכלה ואיענש ותיקן לאחרים דאינון אוכלין והולין ביה והלכה כר' יהושע : ו רבע . הוא רובע הקב אבל אתה חייב לדעת כי הרבעים הנזכרים בכאן במס' חלה והקבים הנזכרים אינם הקבים שקדם לנו שיעור מדהם ואין הרובע הנזכר בזו ההלכה בשיעור חלה הוא הרובע קב הנזכר בזו המס' ועוד אין הקבים הנזכרים בזו המס' כולם שוין וכבר בארנו במסכת עדיות (פ"א) כל זה ר"ל שיעור המדות בענין שיעור חלה וכמו כן כל זה כי חמשת רבעים הנזכרים בכאן יותר מקבים האמורין למעלה באמרו יעשנה קבים ולא יעשנה בטומאה אבל הם הקבים שאמרו העושה עיסתו קבים ואלו החמשה רבעים שיעורם מן הקב הנזכר במשנה בזולת זה המקום שקדם לנו שיעורם בסוף פאה קב ושמנה עשיריות הקב וממה שזכרנו לך בסוף פאה מן המדות יתבאר לך שמדת הקב הנזכר ארבע אצבעות על ארבע אצבעות ברום עשר אצבעות ושמנה עשיריות האצבע נמצא לפי זה החשבון שהמדה שהיא חייבת בחלה צריך שתהיה מדתה עשרה אצבעות על עשרה אצבעות ברום שלשה אצבעות ועשירית אצבע ועשירית עשירית אצבע וחלק מאלפים וחמש מאות מן האצבע וכל זה בדיוק וכבר בארנו בסוף פאה כי האצבע שמשערין בו המדה הוא הגודל אם כן כל המדה שיהי' בחללה זה השיעור הנזכר יתחייב בחלה אבל אם באנו לשער מה שתכיל זאת המדה במשקל ישתנה כפי שינוי דבר המדוד לפי שאין כובד המשקל השעורים והחטים שוה ולא מיני הקמח כולם משקלם שוה אע"פ שהם ממין אחד ולא נתנו לו שיעור חלה במשקל אלא במדה כמו שתראה והנותן שיעור חלה בשיעור המשקלים טועה ומקום טעותו גלוי מאד אלא אם נתן זה בקרוב במין רמוז אליו ואמרם ושאורן ומורסנן רוצה בו כי המורסן והשאור שבקמח מצטרפין לה' רבעים קמח וכשמסירין המורסן מן הה' רבעים קמח ואח"כ מחזירין אותן לתוך הקמח פטורה לפי שהמורסן אינו חייב בחלה למה שאמר הכתוב עריסותיכם דרך עיסה : ז מה שחייבו לבע"ה אחד מכ"ד לפי שהוא לש עיסה קטנה וצריך להוציא שיעור שיהיה ראוי לתתו לכהן כמו שאמר הש"י תתנו שיהא בו כדי נתינה וע"כ אין ראוי להיות פחות מחלק מכ"ד מן השיעור המשוער לחלה שהוא חמשת רבעים אבל הנחתום שהוא לש הרבה אפי' חלק מארבעים ושמנה הוא שיעור שיש בו כדי נתינה ועוד נתנו טעם אחר מפני מה נתנו שעור לבעל הבית חלק מעשרים וארבעה לפי שענין הוצאת החלה הוא נתון לאשה והאשה עינה רעה וכשמטריחין אותה להוציא חלק מעשרים וארבעה ולוואי שהוציא חלק מארבעים ושמנה והעושה עיסה למשתה בנו אע"פ ששיעורו רב והוא דומה לנחתום חייב להוציא חלק מעשרים וארבע כדי שלא תשתנה חלת בעל הבית וכמו כן לא נתן הפרש בחלת נחתום שתהיה חלק מארבעים ושמנה ואפילו תהיה זו המוכרת אשה והלוש בביתה כמו בעל הבית. ונתן שיעור (תרומה) טמאה מעט לפי שהיא לשרפה עומדת ולא נשתדל להרבות טומאה בקדש :

דאמרי' בפ' אלו עוברין (דף מח:) אהא דרבי אליעזר לא שנו אלא ככרות של בבל שנושכות זו בזו אבל כעבין לא ואי לא הוה גרסינן אף במילתיה דרבי אליעזר ניחא דבעי רבי אליעזר תרתי צירוף סל עם נשיכה ואי גרסינן אף יש לפרש דתנא קמא בעי נשיכה בעודו עיסה לפי שראויה להתחבר ולעשות ככר אחד אבל עשה ב' ככרות ונתן בסל או בתנור אי נשכו זו בזו לא סגי בהכי לתנא קמא ולרבי אליעזר מהני ופליגא בירושלמי (שם) אית תנאי תני הסל מצרפן ואין התנור מצרף ואית תנאי תני תנור מצרף ואין הסל מצרף והיינו פלוגתא דר"א ור' יהושע דפרק אלו עוברין ומסיק נשכו כאן וכאן מצרף לא נשכו כאן וכאן אינו מצרף מתני' כגון אילו ריפתא דבבל והיינו ככרות של בע"ה ומסיק בפרק אלו עוברין אפי' כעבין ונראה אע"ג דמהני סל לצירוף להתחייב בחלה היכא דלש פחות משיעור מ"מ לענין מוקף לא מהני צירוף סל דהא ר' אליעזר הוא דאמר בסוף פירקי' ומייתי לה בפרק כשם ניטלת מן הטהור על הטמא דנוטל כדי חלה מעיסה שלא הורמה חלתה ונותן פחות מכביצה באמצע כדי ליטול מן המוקף ולמה דוחק לעשות כן יניח אותו כדי חלה בכלי שהעיסה בתוכו ולא יגע אלא ודאי בהכי לא חשיב מוקף אף על פי שמצרף להתחייב ועוד יש לפרש דאפי' להתחייב לא מצרף אלא אם כן נגע ולא אתא ר' אליעזר אלא לאפוקי דלא בעינן נשיכה ומיהו לא יתכן מדקתני סל מצרפן ולא קתני מחברן כדדייקינן בהקומץ רבה (דף כד·) גבי עשרון שחלקו והניחו בכיסא ולמאן דאמר לא שנו אלא ככרות של בעל הבית שנושכות זו בזו קשה קצת ושמא לא היה מדקדק בין מצרפן למחברן כגבי ר' חייא דמנחות והא דתנן לקמן בפ' בתרא (מ"א) שתי נשים שעשו קבים ונגעו זה בזה אפי' הן ממין אחד פטורין ובזמן שהן של אשה א' מין במינו חייב אותה נגיעה היינו נשיכה למאן דאית ליה או צירוף ס למאן דאית ליה ועוד יש לפרש דאפילו תמצא לומר דלענין מוקף מועיל צירוף סל בלא נגיעה לא היה יכול לעשות כן במתניתין דטמאה וטהורה מקפיד על תערובתו אין הכלי מצרף [כדאיתא בירושלמי (הלכה ג) דפרקין דבר שהוא מקפיד על תערובתן אין הסל מצרפו] עיסה טהורה ועיסה טמאה עשו אותה כדבר שהוא מקפיד על תערובתן בעיסה תחלה אבל בעיסה שניה אין לשני מגע אלא הטבל ובדבר שאין מקפיד על תערובתו אפילו כלי לא בעיקן כדפרשי' בפ"ג דמעשר שני ולא הזכיר כאן צירוף כלי אלא לאשמעי' דאפי' כלי אין מועיל בדבר שמקפיד על תערובתו (ב) : ה אינה חלה · דראשית עריסותיכם כתיב ואף על פי שתרומה ומעשר קדשי בשיבולין התם רבי קרא כדפרשי' בסוף פ"ק דתרומות (מ"י) : וגזל ביד כהן · שלקחה מישראל שעל מנת כן נתנה ישראל שתהא עיסתו פטורה מן החלה והרי אינה פטורה (ג) ובפרק האיש מקדש (דף מו:) מייתי לה גבי פלוגתא דרב ושמואל במקדש אחותו : העיסה עצמה· שעשה ישראל מן הקמח הנשאר ומקמח שבא ליד כהן בתורת חלה אם יש בו כשיעור ה' רבעים קמח כדתנן לקמן (מ"ו) : ואסורה לזרים · כל הקמח שבא ליד כהן חומרא בעלמא (ד) : קפשה · חטפה ואכלה : קלקל לעצמו · מפרש בירושלמי (שם) קלקל לעצמו דאכלה דאיענש ותיקן לאחרים דאינון אכלי ותלו ביה אית תנאי תנו תיקן לעצמו דמ"מ אכלה וקלקל לאחרים דאינון סברין שהיא פטורה והיא חייבת : ו ה' רבעים קמח · בסוף כלל גדול (דף עו:) גרסינן בכל הספרים ה' רבעים קמח ועוד ופלוגתא דתנאי היא בפ"ק דשבת (דף טו.) ובפ' אלו עוברין (דף מח.): הם ושאורן· ושאור שלהן: וסובן ומורסנן · מצטרפין עם הקמח לה' רבעים ובסוף כלל גדול מפרש טעמא שכן עני אוכל פתו מעיסה בלוסה: וחזר לתוכן הרי אלו פטורין· מפרש בירושל' (שם) אמר ר' יוחנן דרך עיסה שנו כאן מכיון שנטל מורסן מתוכן וחזר לתוכן אין זו דרך עיסה תנן בפ"ק דעדיות (מ"ב) ומייתינן לה בפ"ק דשבת (דף טו·) שמאי אומר מקב חלה והלל אומר מקביים וחכמים אומרים לא כדברי זה ולא כדברי זה אלא קב ומחצה חייבת בחלה משהגדילו המדות אמרו ה' רבעים קמח חייבת בחלה ר' יוסי אומר ה' פטורה ה' ועוד חייבת ואומר ר"ת דשמאי משער למדת בעל הבית ובית הלל למדת נחתום דחלה לא נתנה בו תורה שיעור ותנן בפירקין (מ"ז) דבעל הבית מפריש אחד מכ"ד והקב הוא כ"ד ביצים וכמלאת חלתו כביצה דאיכא בו כדי נתינת כהן והלל אומר מקביים למדת נחתום שנותן אחד ממ"ח דהיינו כביצה מב' קבין אבל פחות מכביצה לא חזי לנתינה וצריך לומר לפי' זה דמדאורייתא השיעור גדול יותר ואחמור רבנן בהנך שיעורין דכל זה אינו אלא סברות בעלמא ויש מפרשים דטעמא דהלל משום דעומר עשירית האיפה עישור [מלבר] ב' קבין מג' סאין שהן י"ח קבין ושמאי סבר דאחציו של עומר משערין לפי שהיה נחלק לשתי סעודות אחת שחרית ואחת בין הערבים להכי קאמר מקב חלה ורבנן דאמרי מקב ומחצה היינו ירושלמית דהוסיפו שתות שהן ז' ועוד מדבריות דקסברי עשירית האיפה מלגיו ועולה העישור של י"ח קבין ז' רבעים וביצה וחומש ביצה וכשבאו לירושלים שהוסיפו שתות נכנסו בקב ומחצה דהיינו ששה לוגין וכשבאו לציפורי חזרו והוסיפו שתות ונעשו ה' לוגין דהיינו ה' רבעים ור"י דבעי חמש ועוד קסבר דראשית עריסותיכם דהיינו עיסת מדבר בעינן שישאר שיעור עיסה מדברית לאחר שהורמה חלתה : ז ירושלמי (שם) תני אמר ר' יהודה מפני מה אמרו בעל הבית אחד מכ"ד מפני שעינו יפה בעיסתו ונחתום עינו רעה בעיסתו וחכמים אומרים לא משום זה אלא בעל הבית עיסתו מעוטה ואין בה כדי מתנה לכהן נחתום עיסתו מרובה ויש בה כדי מתנה לכהן והתנן העושה עיסה למשתה בנו אחד מכ"ד שלא לחלוק בעיסת בעל הבית והתנן וכן האשה שהיא עושה למכור בשוק ממ"ח בשעה שהיא עושה לביתה עינה יפה בעיסתה בשעה שהיא עושה למכור עינה רעה בעיסתה : שוגגת או אנוסה אחד ממ"ח · משום דחלתה לא חזיא לאכילה ואמרינן בירושלמי (שם) אמר רבי מתניה בלמודה להיות מפריש אחד מכ"ד כיון דרגילה להפריש כדינה הקילו עליה בנטמאת בשגגה אבל בלמודה להיות מפריש אחד ממ"ח מפרשת אחד מכ"ד כדי שלא יהא הוטא נשכר כיון דרגילה לעבור על

חמש רבעין מצומצמין חייב בחלה אמר רבי יוחנן דרך עיסה שנינו . פירוש ודרך העיסה להיות שם קמח ושאור ומורסן : נוטל מורסנן מתוכן וחזר לתוכן הרי אלו פטורין . פירוש מה טעם שדרך עיסה שנו וכאן מכיון שנטל מורסנן מתוכן וחזר לתוכן אין זה דרך עיסה : ז נטמאת עיסתה שוגגת או אנוסה . פי' באונס מפרשת אחד ממ"ח : נטמאת במזיד מפרשת אחד מכ"ד כדי שלא תהא חוטא נשכר . ראשית עריסותיכם כדי עיסתכם וכמה עיסתכם כדי עיסת מדבר וכמה עיסת מדבר והעומר עשירית האיפה הוא. מיכן אמרו ז' רבעין קמח ועוד חייב בחלה שהן שש לירושלמיות וחמש לציפוריות . תנו רבנן מלחם ולא כל לחם פרט

*) [לכאורה אין זה נתינת טעם למה שהוא גזל דאף אם אינו מפריש חלה מ"מ אינו אלא אוכל טבלים אבל לא שייך גזל דהא אם מפריש הלה יכול ליטול לעצמו אכן באמת כבר כתב הר"ש הטעם שעל מנת כן נתנה ישראל שתהא עיסתו פטורה מן החלה והרי אינה פטורה . אבל ד' רבינו המחבר צ"ע ומטה לייצב] :

ה א ב מיי' פ"ו מהלכות בכורים הלכה י"ז טוש"ע י"ד סי' שכ"ה סעיף א':
ו ג מיי' פ"ח שם הל' א סמג עשין קמא טוש"ע י"ד סי' שכ"ז סעי' א :
ז ד מיי' פ"ו שם הלכה טו טוש"ע י"ד סי' שכד סעי' א:
ח ה מיי' שם הלכה יח טוש"ע שם

יא מיי' שם הלכה ד:
יא ב מיי' פ"ו שם הלכה יב:
יב ג מיי' פ"ה שם הלכה יד טוש"ע י"ד סי' שכג:
א ד מיי' פ"ח שם הלכה ד סמג עשין קמא טור שו"ע י"ד סי' שכו סעיף:
ב ה מיי' שם הל' ה:
ג ו מיי' שם הל' ג טוש"ע שם סעיף ב:
ד ז ח מיי' פ"ח מהל' בכורים הלכה ו:
ה ט שם הלכה ז:
ו י מיי' פ"ג מהל' מעשר הלכה ח:
*) ומערכת כ"ל וכ"ה בתוי"ט:
ז כ מיי' פ"ג שם הלכה כה:
ח ל מיי' פ"ח מהל' בכורים הלכה ח: טוש"ע י"ד סי' ש"ל סעיף ח:

מסרת הש"ס

א) סוטה דף ל:
ב) נדה דף ו:
ג) מנחות דף סז.
ד) פאה פ"ד משנה ח:

על דברי חכמים לא הקילו עליה בנטמאת : ח נטלת מן הטהור על הטמא · ולא חיישינן שמא תגע ורבנן דאסרי משום דחיישי כדפרישי' בפ"ב דתרומות : מעיסה שלא הורמה חלתה · כדי להפריש מן החיוב על החיוב : פחות מכביצה מעיסה טהורה · דכי מקבל טומאה מן הטמאה אין חוזר ומטמא כדי חלה הטהור. דפחות מכביצה לא מטמא אחרים ובפרק כשם (סוטה ל:) פריך והתניא כבילה ואיכא התם לישני טובא דמעיקרא סברה דאיירי בעיסה ראשונה וחולין הטבולים לחלה כחלה דמו ובהא מיפלגי דמר סבר שני עושה שלישי בחולין ובחוליי הטבולים לחלה מיפלגי מר סבר כחלה דמו ומר סבר לאו כחלה דמו ואיבעי' אימא דכולי עלמא לאו כחלה דמו ואין שני עושה שלישי בחולין וקא מיפלגי במותר לגרום טומאה לחולין שבארץ ישראל ובירושלמי (שם) מוקי לה בעיסה ראשונה אבל בעיסה שניה אין לשני א"ל הטבל רבי חייא ברי בא בשם ר' יהושע אין לך מחבר כולן אלא ז' משקין בלבד :

א אוכלין ערלי מן העיסה. אמר בירושל' (הל' א) אמר ר' חגי לא שנו אלא עראי אבל קבע אסור מפני שמערים לפוטרה מן החלה (א) : עד שתתגלגל. משגלגלה נטבלה ואסור לאכול ממנה עראי: ותטמטם בשעורין · פירש בערוך דרך החטים ללוש ולגלגל יפה אבל השעורים כשילוש אותן עיסתן מתפרדת ואינו יכול לגלגלן יפה על כן מטמטמו ביד *וצוזבו : חייב מיתה · (ב) שהטבל במיתה כדדרשי' בשילהי אלו הן הנשרפין (דף פג): מגבהת חלתה . (ג) טוב היה שתמתין עד לבסוף שתגמר חלתה ותעשה כל העיסה גוש אחד ובטמאה עשין כן אלא תקנה דרבנן היא בעיסה טהורה שתמהר האשה להפריש חלתה בטהרה בתחלת הגלגול פן תארע טומאה בעיסה ותטמא חלתה כדאיתא בירושלמי פרק אלו עוברין והא דאמר רבא בירושלמי כיון שהיא נותנת את המים זו היא ראשית עריסותיכם אסמכתא בעלמא היא אי נמי אשמעינן דמכתיכת מים קריגא עריסותיכם : ובלבד שיהא שם ה' רבעים קמח . בקמח שנתערב במים וזהו שיעור חיוב ובמשנה דייקני' גרסי' ובלבד שלא יהא וקאי הקמח שלא נגע במים והכי איתא בהדיא בירושלמי (שם) למה לי ובלבד שלא יהא שם ה' רבעין קמח אמר רבי מתניה מתני' קודם [עד] שלא למדו את הכהנות דכשהיו מפרישות חלה בתחלת הלישה למדו אותן להתנות דכשתגמר הלישה תקדש לשם חלה ואם היה נשאר ה' רבעים מן הקמח שלא נגע במים לא הוה מיפטר בחלה קודם והוא הדין דהוה מתייישב הירושלמי אי הוה גרסינן שיהא התנאי מועיל בכל ענין ונקט כהנות לפי שדרכם לגבל עיסתן בטהרה מפני שרגילות בטהרה ועיסה טהורה מפרישין חלתה בתחלת לישה כדפרשי' ומפרש בירושלמי מה לימדו את הכהנות הרי זו חלה על העיסה הזאת ועל השאור המתערב עמה ועל הטבל שנתערב בה ועל הקמח שנשתייר בה ועל הקרץ שניתן תחתיה לכשתעשה כולה גוש אחת תקדש זו שבידה לשם חלה ולפירוש זה צריך ללמד לנשים שלנו המפרישות חלה לאחר גלגול קודם א] עריכת הלחם להתנות תנאי זה מפני שמערבות קמח עם המקרצות בשעה שעורכות אותן ועושות מהן ככרות שאותו קמח נעשה עיסה ואע"פ שאין מערבין בכל אחת ואחת חמש רבעים קמח כיון דבין כולן איכא ה' רבעים תנור מצרפן או

פי' מהר"י בן מלכי צדק

לעיסה קטנה איזו היא גדולה שבעת רבעים מדבריים קב וחצי ירושלמית שהן חמש רבעים שלנו. ר' יוסי אומר חמשת רבעים גדושים לחיוב. ר' אליעזר בן יעקב אומר חמשת רבעים קמח לפטור: ח רבי אליעזר אומר נטלת החלה מן הטהור על הטמא ואזדא רבי אליעזר לטעמי' כמה דאמר בתרומה תורמין מן הטהור על הטמא. אף בחלה כן: כיצד עיסה טהורה ועיסה טמאה נוטל כדי חלת שתי עיסות מעיסה הטהורה שלא הורמה חלתה ונוטל מן הטהורה פחות מכביצה כדי שלא תיטמא העיסה דפחות מכביצה מיטמא אבל לא מטמא ונמצאו העיסות מדובקות טהרה נוגעת לפחות מכביצה וכן הטמאה כדי שיראה כנוטל מן המוקף ואותו שהפריש מן הטהורה קוראו לו שם חלה עליה ועל הטמאה ומה טעם הופרש שיעור חלה מקודם דחולין הטבולין לחלה כחלה דמו ואסור לטמאותא. ירושל' בעיסה ראשונה. פי' דראשון עושה שני בחולין שם צריך לעשות כי האי גוונא בפחות מכביצה אבל בעיסה שניה אין לשני מגע אצל הטבל ויכול להפסיק כל הפעולה מאחר שמפריש כדי חלתם מן הטהורה דהוו להו שני ואין שני פוסל בחולין כלום: וחכמים אוסרין. פי' ליטול אפי' בכי האי גוונא מן הטהור על הטמא אלא נוטל מן הטהורה חלתה ומן הטמאה חלתה:

פ"ג א אוכלין עראי מן העיסה של חטין עד שתתגלגל. פי' עד שתגמר לישתה: ותטמטם בשעורין. פירוש משתיכנס כל העיסה ביחד שהשעורין אינה מתחברת במהרה: גלגלה בחטין וטימטמה בשעורין האוכל ממנה חייב מיתה. פי' שכבר נטבלה: כיון שהיא נותנת. פי' האשה: את המים מגבהת חלתה. פירש וזהו ראשית עריסותיכם: ובלבד שלא יהא בעריבה ה' רבעים קמח שלא נגע בהן המים. פי' שאם נשאר שם קמח

[א]נטמאת מזידה אחד מעשרים וארבעה כדי שלא יהא חוטא נשכר : ח רבי אליעזר אומר [א] נטלת מן הטהור על הטמא [ב]כיצד עיסה טהורה ועיסה טמאה נוטל כדי חלה מעיסה שלא הורם חלתה ונותן פחות מכביצה באמצע כדי שיטול מן המוקף [ג]וחכמים אוסרין :

פרק שלישי

א אוכלין [ד]עראי מן העיסה עד שתתגלגל בחטים ותטמטם בשעורים [ה]גלגלה בחטים וטימטמה בשעורים האוכל ממנו חייב מיתה [ו]כיון שהיא נותנת את המים מגבהת חלתה ובלבד *שיהא שם חמשה רבעי קמח : ב [ז]נדמעה עיסתה עד שלא גלגלה פטורה שהמדומע פטור (ד) ומשגלגלה חייבת נולד לה [ג]ספק טומא' עד שלא גלגלה תעשה בטומאה ומשגלגלה תעשה בטהרה : ג [ח]הקדישה עיסתה [ג] עד שלא גלגלה ופדאתה חייבת ומשגלגלה פדאתה חייבת [ט]הקדישתה עד שלא גלגלה וגלגלה הגזבר ואחר כך פדאתה פטורה שבשעת חובתה היתה פטורה : ד [י]כיוצא בו [ד] המקדיש פירותיו עד שלא באו לעונת המעשרות ופדאן חייבים ומשבאו לעונת המעשרות ופדאן חייבין [כ]הקדישן עד שלא נגמרו וגמרן הגזבר ואחר כך פדאן פטורין שבשעת חובתה היו פטורין : ה [ל]נכרי שנתן לישראל לעשות לו עיסה פטורה מן

שלא יהא חוטא נשכר . פי' שלא ירויח החוטא שטמאה ויוציא פחות ממה שהיה מוציא אלו לא עבר וטמאה : ח א"ר אליעזר . שנוטל אדם מעיסה טהורה שלא הורמה חלתה שיעור תרומה החייבת לעיסה טמאה ולעיסה טהורה ואח"כ נוטל פחות מכבילה מעיסה טמאה ומחלקה ונותן בלדה מלד אחד עיסה טהורה ובלדה מלד ב' עיסה טמאה ויהיה אותו החלק שהוא פחות מכבילה באמצע ואחר כך יניח השיעור שבו שיעור שתי חלות על אותו החלק הטמא שהוא פחות מכבילה ומוליאו לשם חלה על שתי העיסות ואז יהיה תורם מן המוקף כיון שכל אותם השיעורי' דבקים זה בלד זה ותהיה החלה טהורה והעיסה טהורה ג"כ עומדת בטהרתה לפי שכל אחת מהם לא נגעה אלא בפחות מכבילה מאוכל טמא וכבר זכרתי לך כי מה שהוא פחות מכבילה מאוכל טמא שאינו מטמא טומאת אוכלים ועוד יתבאר זה ויתברר במסכת טהרות וחכמים אוסרין אלא שיוליא מן העיסה עלמה *והלכה כחכמים וכבר קדם לך שאסור להוליא מן הטהור על הטמא :

א עד שתתגלגל . פי' עד שתתערב : ותטמטם. פי' שידבקו חלקים קלתם בקלתם עד שיהיו גוף אחד : האוכל ממנו חייב מיתה . לפי שהוא טבל והטבל במיתה : כיון שהיא נותנת המים מגבהת חלתה . ואף על פי שנשאר מן הקמח בעריבה קלת שלא נלוש ולא נתערב ובתנאי שלא יהיה באותו הקמח שלא נלוש ולא נתערב שיעור חמשה רבעים שהוא שיעור חלה וכשאמר הרי זו חלה על העיסה ועל השאור ועל הקמח שנשתייר בה לכשתעשה כלה תתקדש זו שבידו לשם חלה הרי זה מותר וכן נתבאר בגמרא : ב נדמעה. פירוש שנתערבה בה התרומה וכבר באר נו (תרומות פ"ח מ"ה ולעיל פ"א מ"ד) כי המדומע פטור מן החלה : ואמר תעשה בטהרה ענינו שתגמר כמות שהיא ולא יקפיד בספק טומאה שנולד : ג ההקדש אינו חייב בחלה למאמר הש"י תרימו תרומה ואמר בספרי את שמורם ממנו קודש והנשאר חול ולא שזה וזה קודש וזה המאמר כולו מבואר כשתבין כל מה שהקדמנו בזו הסדר : ד זו הלכה כבר קדמנו לדבר עליה בפרק רביעי מפאה

סל ואפילו התנאי אינו מועיל אם הוגלכה חלתה לאור וטמא כיון דנתבטל ברוב קודם שיחול עליו שם טבל שוב אין תנור מלרף ומיהו בתוספתא (פ"א) משמע דמלרף מ"מ דתניא כהן ששייר קמח לעיסתו וכן האשה ששיירה קמח לעיסתה והקרץ והשאור מלטרפין לחמשה רבעים קמח לאסור את העיסה וע"כ אותו קמח בשעורך בו הככרות ונעשה עיסה דקמח לאו בר חיוב חלה הוא ואע"פ שכבר נתבטל מלטרף לה' רבעין עם הקרץ ושאור שלא הופרש מהן חלה ואוסרת את העיסה וקלת תימה היאך מתנה על קמח המתגלגל אחרי כן הא לא הוי מוקף ושמא לא חיישינן מאחר דעיקר היתה מן המוקף וחשיב מוקף מה שבשעת קדושת שם היו מוקף אע"פ שבשעה שחלה הקדושה לא היה מוקף וכן פירשנו בפ"ק דנדה מכח ההיא דסוטה ומיהו בפרק בתרא דמסכת טבול יום פירשתי בענין אחר : ירושלמי בפרק אלו עוברין (הלכה ג) תני הלש ביו"ט לשה מערב יו"ט ושכח להפריש חלתה ביו"ט אסור לטלטלה וא"ל ליטול ממנה עירס לא אמר אלא לש הא עירס לא ואמר שמואל אחוי דר' ברכיה תיפתר בעיסה טמאה שאינו מפריש חלתה אלא לבסוף א"ר יוסי בר בון בדין היה עיסה טהורה שלא יפריש חלתה אלא בסוף תקנה תיקט בה שיפרישנה תחלה שלא תטמא את העיסה.. פי' עירס מלשון עריסותיכם והיכא דמעיו"ט לא גמר לישתה אלא עירס בעלמא בזה לא אמר שאסור להפריש חלתה ביו"ט וכדמסיק בעיסה טמאה דמפריש חלתה בסוף ובירושלמי אמתני' דהכא ר' יוסי בשם ריש לקיש דר"ע היא דתנינן התם הנוטל חלה מקב ר' עקיבא אומר חלה וחכ"א אינה חלה כלום אר"ע אלא לשעבר שמא מתחלה ואכן בתחלה קיימינן ר' יונה א"ר חייא בשם ריש לקיש ירדו לה בשיטת ר' עקיבא א"ר יוחנן דברי הכל היא כיון שנותנת את המים זו היא ראשית עריסותיכם · פירוש דר' עקיבא היא מילתיה דר' עקיבא לקמן באידך פירקא ונראה לי דטעות סופר דאדרבה מתניתין רבנן ולא רבי עקיבא ויש דכתבו בפרק אלו עוברין (דף מ"ו) אמתניתין דכילד מפרישין חלה בטומאה ביום טוב דקאמר בירושל' (שם) דמתני' בשנטמאת קודם גלגולה אבל אם נטמאת אחר גלגולה יעשנה קבין כלומר פחות מכשיעור ואדרבה איפכא נראה דהא אחר גלגולה מה מועיל הרי כבר נתחייבה בחלה משגלגלה : ב שהמדומע שנדמע לפחות מק' ואתי דימוע דרבנן ומפקעה חלה בזמן הזה דרבנן כדפרשינן לעיל בפ"ק (מ"ד) (ד) : נולד לה ספק טומאה . לעיסה הא דמוקי לה בפ"ק דנדה (דף ו:) אפי' בנשען כגון זב וטהור שהיו פורקין מן החמור או טוענין בזמן שמשאן ככד דהיינו סיפא דמשגלגלה דתני עלה וחלתה תלויה אבל רישא דעד שלא גלגלה לא מיתוקמא בנשען דאכתי לאו טבולין לחלה ניניהו ונשען טהור לחולין כדקתני וכולן טהורין לבני הכנסת דהיינו אוכל חוליהן בטהרה והא דקאמר התם שלא תאמר בהוכחות אחלת' תלויה קאי דאילו רישא בהוכחות דוקא שנו כגון ב' שבילין שהלך באחד מהן ועשה טהרות ובא חבירו והלך בשני ועשה טהרות דקתני עלה בתוספ' לטהרות אלו ואלו מונחות הרי אלו ואלו מוכיחות: עד שלא גלגלה תעשה בטומאה·בפ"ק דנדה (דף ו·) מייתי לה ופירש שם בקונטרס דתעשה בטומאה משום דבלאו הכי לא מלי אכיל לה כהן שהרי נולד בה ספק טומאה משמע דאם לא נולד בה ספק תעשה בטהרה [דא"ל] דהוא הדין לא נולד בה אלא משום רבותא דסיפא נקטיה דקאמרי' במסכת ע"א פרק ר' ישמעאל (דף נה:) דבולרין עם הנכרי משום דמותר לגרום טומאה לחולין שבארץ ישראל אבל אין בולרין עם ישראל העושה פירותיו בטומאה משום מסייע ידי עוברי עבירה אע"פ שעדיין לא נגמרה מלאכתן למעשר והיינו טעמא משום דמקום שסופו להפריש מהן תרומה חיישי' להפסד כהן ומיהו יש לחלק דהכא אם מפריש חלה קודם גלגול הרי הוא כמפריש מן הקמח ואין שם חלה עליה אבל התם חל שם תרומה קודם גמר מלאכה כדאשכחן מעשר ראשון שהקדימו בשיבלין וגם אסור באכילת קבע אבל יש עוד ראיה מהא דתנן בהניזקין (דף סא·) משתטיל למים לא תגע משום מסייע ידי עוברי עבירה אפי' קודם גלגול ואין לומר משום דקסבר אסור לגרום טומאה לחולין שבארץ ישראל ומשתטיל למים לא תגע לפי שהוכשרו דהאמרי' התם רישא בטומאת חולין וסיפא בטומאת חלה ואמרינן בירושלמי (הלכה ב) ר' יוסי בשם ר' הילא בדין היה שיטמא את טבלו דבר תורה דכתיב (במדבר יח) משמרת תרומתי תרומה לריכה שימור ואין הטבל לריך שימור ומה אני מקיים (שם) ונתתם ממנו את תרומת ה' לאהרן הכהן עשה שיתננו לכהן בכהונתו וכאן הואיל ואין אתה רשאי ליתן לאהרן בכהונתו רשאי אתה לטמאותו : ג ד חייבת בחלה · כיון דבשעת גלגול חולין היא דאז שעת חובתה וכן לענין מעשר אזלינן בתר עונת מעשר כלמפורש בפ"ק דמעשרות (מ"ה) איזהו גרנן למעשרות ואי בשעת גמר מלאכה הוו דחולין תו לא פקע מיניה חיובא אבל גלגול הקדש (ה) ומירוח הקדש פוטר כדדרשי' מקראי במנחות בפרק ר' ישמעאל (ו) : ה ו נכרי שנתן לישראל . קמח לעשות לו עיסה פטורה מן החלה דשל נכרי הוא אלא שישראל מגלגל לנכרי בירושלמי (הלכה ה) פריך מה בינה לעיסת ארנונא אלו לעיסת ארנונא שמא אינה חייבת בחלה ומשני תמן ברשות ישראל הוא שמא ימלך הנכרי שלא ליטלה ברם הכא לדעתו היא תלויה מכאן מוכח דגרסינן בפ"ק דפסחים (דף ו·) עיסת ארנונא חייבת בחלה אע"ג [דלא] מלי מסליק ליה בזוזי

פירוש הרא"ש

פ"ג (א) לפי שאין שם עיסה עליה קודם גלגול ואין ראוי לאסור אכילת קבע דלא דמי לתבואה קודם מירוח משום הכי צריך לטמטם דשלא יערים: (ב) דנגמר מלאכתו: (ג) לא שוו היא עיקר המצוה: (ד) משנגלגלה חייבת דכיון שנתחייבה בכבר תו לא פקע ע"י דימוע בזמן הזה דהתמא אמר (במדבר טו כ*) תרומה וגו' (ה) פוטר דדרשינן עריסותיכם ולא עיסת הקדש: (ו) דדרשינן דגנך ולא דגן הקדש: *) נ"ל כבולכם

הגהות מהר"י לנדא

פ"ג מ"א בר"ש א] לאחר גלגול קודם עריסה: נ"ל עריכה:

שעור ה' רבעים יצטרך להפריש עוד חלה אחרת שלא נפטר בחלה שהפריש [בשעת] שהיה קמח : ב נולד לה ספק טומאה אם עד שלא גלגלה נולד לה ספק טומאה תיעשה בטומאה. אתינן עלה בנדה פרק ראשון עד שלא גלגלה תיעשה בטומאה דחולין נינהו ומותר לגרום טומאה בחולין שבארץ משגלגלה תיעשה בטהרה מאי טעמא דחולין הטבולין לחלה כחלה דמו ואסור לגרום טומאה לחלה .תנא וחלתה תלויה לא אכלין ולא שורפין . פי' לא אכלין דלמא טמאה ולא שורפין דילמא טהורה. הלכך תולין עד שתטמא ודאי וישרפה ובאיזה ספק אמרו בספק חלה מאי ספק חלה אביי ורבא דאמרי תרוייהו שלא תאמר בהוכחות שנו כגון ב' שבילין דהתם חולין נמי טמא מספק וטמא הוא וזה אפי' לחולין ולא תאמר הנה כגון זה הספק דתלויה דקתני בהוכחות כלומר בתלויות דאמרינן התם הלך בראשונה ועשה טהרות והלך בשני ועשה טהרות אלו ואלו תלויות נשרפו הראשונות או שנטמאו השניות טהורות שנמצאו אלו מוכיחות על אלו . ס"א שלא תאמר בהוכחות כלומר בספק שאפשר לו להיות הוכח כגון ב' שבילין שאפשר שראה אדם ויאמר לו בזה הלכת ואפשר לעמוד לפעמים על בוריו של דבר דכגון זה אפי' לחולין טמאה אלא בספק חלה של חולין יהא טהור ומאי ניהו בטוען דתנן זב וטהור שהיו פורקין מן החמור או טוענין בזמן שמשאן כבד טמאין דדילמא הסיט אחד את חבירו או נשען מספיקא טמא הוא משאן קל טהורין אפי' לתרומה וכולן טהורין פי' וכל הספיקות ששנינו טמאין לאו לכל מילי אלא טהורין לבני הכנסת פי' דהיינו לחולין וטמאין לתרומה ובזה הספק אנו עסוקין בפורק מן החמור או טוען עם הזב במשא כבד אם אירע לו זה ובא ועשה בעיסה תיעשה בטומאה כלומר תיעשה בכלים טמאים ודיים והחלה טמאה ולשרפה אולא ומשגלגלה אם אירע

UNCLEAN DELIBERATELY, IT IS ONE TWENTY-FOURTH, IN ORDER THAT ONE WHO SINS SHALL NOT PROFIT [FROM HIS SIN].[6]

MISHNAH 8. R. ELIEZER SAID: ḤALLAH MAY BE TAKEN FROM [DOUGH] THAT IS CLEAN, [IN A QUANTITY SUFFICIENT TO DISCHARGE THE OBLIGATION] IN RESPECT ALSO OF [DOUGH] THAT IS UNCLEAN![7] HOW [MAY THIS BE DONE]? [IF ONE HAS] A CLEAN DOUGH AND AN UNCLEAN DOUGH,
a HE TAKES SUFFICIENT ḤALLAH[1] OUT OF A DOUGH, ḤALLAH WHEREOF HAD NOT YET BEEN TAKEN,[2] AND PUTS [DOUGH] LESS THAN THE SIZE OF AN EGG[3] IN THE MIDDLE,[4] IN ORDER THAT HE MAY TAKE OFF [THE ḤALLAH] FROM WHAT IS CLOSE TOGETHER;[5] BUT THE SAGES PROHIBIT.[6]

CHAPTER III

MISHNAH 1. ONE MAY EAT IN A CASUAL MANNER FROM
b DOUGH BEFORE IT IS ROLLED,[1] IN [THE CASE OF] WHEATEN [FLOUR], OR BEFORE IT IS MIXED INTO A COHESIVE BATTER, IN [THE CASE OF] BARLEY [FLOUR].[2] [ONCE] ONE HAS ROLLED IT [IN THE CASE OF] WHEATEN [FLOUR], OR ONE HAS MIXED IT INTO A COHESIVE PASTE, IN [THE CASE OF] BARLEY [FLOUR], ONE WHO EATS THEREOF,[3] IS LIABLE TO DEATH.[4] AS SOON AS SHE[5] PUTS IN THE WATER SHE SHOULD LIFT OFF HER ḤALLAH,[6] PROVIDED ONLY THAT THERE ARE NOT FIVE-FOURTHS [OF A ḲAB] OF FLOUR[7] THERE.[8]

c *MISHNAH* 2. [IF] THE DOUGH BECAME MEDUMMA'[1] BEFORE SHE HAD ROLLED IT, IT IS EXEMPT [FROM ḤALLAH],[2] [IF] AFTER SHE HAD ROLLED IT, IT IS SUBJECT [THERETO].[3] [IF] THERE OCCURRED TO HER SOME UNCERTAIN UNCLEANNESS[4] BEFORE SHE HAD ROLLED IT, IT MAY BE COMPLETED[5] IN UNCLEANNESS,[6] [IF] AFTER SHE HAD ROLLED IT, IT SHOULD BE COMPLETED IN CLEANNESS.[7]

MISHNAH 3. [IF] SHE[8] CONSECRATED[9] HER DOUGH BEFORE ROLLING IT, AND REDEEMED IT,[10] SHE IS BOUND [TO SEPARATE ḤALLAH];[11] [IF SHE CONSECRATED IT] AFTER ROLLING IT, AND REDEEMED IT, SHE IS [LIKEWISE] BOUND;[12] [BUT IF] SHE CONSECRATED IT BEFORE ROLLING IT, AND THE GIZBAR[13] ROLLED IT, AND AFTER THAT SHE REDEEMED IT, SHE IS EXEMPT, SINCE AT THE TIME OF HER OBLIGATION[14] IT WAS EXEMPT.[15]

MISHNAH 4.[16] SIMILAR THERETO[17] [IS THE FOLLOWING]: [IF] ONE CONSECRATED HIS PRODUCE BEFORE IT REACHED
d THE STAGE [WHEN IT BECOMES LIABLE] FOR TITHES,[1] AND REDEEMED IT,[2] IT IS SUBJECT [TO TITHES];[3] [IF ONE CONSECRATED IT] AFTER IT HAD REACHED THE STAGE FOR TITHES, AND REDEEMED IT, IT IS [LIKEWISE] SUBJECT;[4] [BUT IF] ONE CONSECRATED IT BEFORE IT WAS 'COMPLETED',[5] AND THE GIZBAR 'COMPLETED' IT,[6] AND AFTERWARDS [THE OWNER] REDEEMED IT, IT IS EXEMPT, SINCE AT THE TIME OF ITS OBLIGATION IT WAS EXEMPT.[7]

MISHNAH 5. [IF] A NON-ISRAELITE GAVE [FLOUR] TO AN ISRAELITE TO MAKE FOR HIM DOUGH, IT IS EXEMPT FROM

(6) I.e., so that no premium be placed on transgression by way of deliberate defilement of dough for the purpose of evading half of one's obligation in respect of *ḥallah*. (7) Even if each dough is large enough to be itself subject to *ḥallah*. The advantage of this procedure is that the full quota of *ḥallah* in respect of all the doughs concerned could be eaten by the priest.

a (1) I.e., the aggregate amount due from both doughs. (2) Because it is not permitted to reckon in dough (already) exempt from *ḥallah*. (3) 'Less than the size of an egg' is a quantity which even though it may itself become unclean, does not render other objects unclean by contact ('Orlah II, 4, end). For the principle that the standard proportion in matters of food rendered unclean by contact with or being in the same vessel as, a dead reptile, is 'the size of an egg', v. Yoma 79*b*—80*a*. (4) The commentators amplify: the portion of clean dough already taken off as *ḥallah* is placed on the small piece put in the middle—between the two doughs—and lifted off as *ḥallah* for all the doughs together. By this method (*a*) all the dough has had the *ḥallah* levy discharged for it; (*b*) all the *ḥallah* is available as food (for the priest) (*c*) the (bulk of the) clean dough remains clean. (5) V *supra* 56*b* n. b 5. (6) The Sages' ruling is due to the possibility of the two main pieces of dough coming into contact (Bert.) or the middle piece (advocated by R. Eliezer) being the size of an egg (Rashi, Sotah 30*b*). For a full examination of the possible reasons underlying the difference of opinion between R. Eliezer and the Sages on this point v. Soṭah 30*a*—*b*.

b (1) I.e., properly kneaded, when it constitutes dough in the sense of the Biblical precept relating to *ḥallah*. (2) Barley flour does not form so firm a dough as wheaten flour, and there is no point in waiting for a perfect dough which cannot be achieved. (3) Without *ḥallah* having been taken from it; in that state it is termed *Ṭebel*. (4) *Sc*. 'by the hand of Heaven', v. Lev. XXII, 9; cf., *supra* I, 9. (5) This provision applies also to a man; but the Mishnah speaks here of a woman since (*a*) it is women who are usually occupied in baking, cf. *supra* II, 7, n. 2 and (*b*) the reason for the regulation which follows is the contingency of a condition more liable to occur with a woman than with a man. (6) This a Rabbinic precautionary regulation, viz., to take off *ḥallah* at the earliest possible moment (even though the stage of liability according to Scriptural requirement has not fully been reached, v. *supra* n. 1) lest the dough become unclean before there is a chance of separating *ḥallah* from the rolled dough. In non-Temple times the point of anticipating possible defilement does not arise, and *ḥallah* should be taken off when the dough has been rolled, prior to dividing it up into loaves. (7) *Sc*. left entirely unmixed with the water, and as dry flour not yet liable to *ḥallah*, being also of an amount large enough to become (when eventually mixed with water) liable thereto. T.J. rules that in these circumstances one may take *ḥallah* for the whole of the contents of the mixing vessel by deliberately and explicitly reckoning in the as yet unmixed flour which is in it.—Another reading is 'provided only that there *are* five-fourths of flour' etc. already mixed with the water. (8) In the mixing vessel.

c (1) V. *supra* I, 4, n. 8. (2) For the reason explained ibid. (3) It had already, through having been rolled, become liable to *ḥallah*, and this being a Biblical precept, it cannot be overridden by the Rabbinic regulation of *Medumma'*. (4) V. Nid. 5*a* ff. (5) Lit., 'done'. (6) Because in any case the *ḥallah* when taken will be unfit for eating owing to the possibility of its being unclean. Further, it is permitted to cause uncleanness to *ḥullin* (Soṭ. 30*b*) v. Nid. 6*b* (bottom). (7) Because *ḥullin* which is subject to *ḥallah* is like *ḥallah*, and the latter, like all *terumah* (a term also applied to *ḥallah*) the cleanness of which is in doubt, must not be made unclean deliberately. Such '*ḥallah* in suspense' is not to be eaten, as it may be unclean, nor may it be burnt, as it may be clean; one should wait until it becomes certainly unclean and then burn it (v. Nid. 7*a*). (8) V. *supra* Mishnah 1 n. 5. (9) V. Lev. XXVII, 14 and *passim*. (10) *Also* before rolling. On 'redeeming' consecrated things, v. Lev. ibid. 15 and *passim*. (11) Since at the material time, viz., that of rolling, it was her property (again), cf. *supra* I, 3. (12) Since at the material time it was obviously her property. (13) The Temple store-keeper who received and was in charge of consecrated objects. (14) I.e , the time of rolling. (15) Because at that time the dough was not her property, but that of the Sanctuary. (16) This Mishnah occurs *verbatim* also in Pe'ah IV, 8. The reason for this repetition is discussed in T.J. Ḥal. *ad loc.* and T.J. Pe'ah *ad loc.* (17) Lit., 'as something that goes in [the same way as] it (viz., the preceding case)', a case that takes the same course, follows the same lines.

d (1) The several stages at which different kinds of produce become subject to tithes are particularized in Ma'as. I, 2—4. (2) *Also* before the tithe-stage. (3) Since at the material time it was his property (again). (4) Since at the material time it was certainly his property. (5) I.e., brought to the state at which it becomes subject to *terumah* and tithes. Such 'completed state' varies according to the produce, v. ibid. I, 5 ff. (6) By the appropriate act which brings it to the *terumah* and tithe stage. (7) Having been at the time Temple property.

ḤALLAH;[8] IF HE [THE NON-ISRAELITE] GAVE IT TO HIM AS A GIFT, BEFORE ROLLING IT, HE IS LIABLE.[9] [IF] AFTER ROLLING IT, HE IS EXEMPT.[10] [IF] ONE MAKES DOUGH TOGETHER WITH A NON-ISRAELITE, [THEN] IF THERE IS NOT IN [THE PORTION] OF THE ISRAELITE THE [MINIMUM] MEASURE SUBJECT TO ḤALLAH,[11] IT IS EXEMPT FROM ḤALLAH.[12]

MISHNAH 6. [IF] ONE BECAME A PROSELYTE AND HAD DOUGH, [THEN IF] IT WAS MADE[13] BEFORE HE BECAME A PROSELYTE, HE IS EXEMPT [FROM ḤALLAH], [BUT IF] AFTER HE BECAME A PROSELYTE, HE IS LIABLE. ALSO IF THERE IS A
a DOUBT,[1] HE IS LIABLE;[2] BUT [A NON-PRIEST WHO HAS UNWITTINGLY EATEN OF SUCH ḤALLAH] IS NOT LIABLE IN RESPECT THEREOF TO [REFUND AN ADDITIONAL] 'ONE-FIFTH'.[3] R. AKIBA SAID: IT ALL DEPENDS ON THE [TIME OF THE] FORMATION OF THE LIGHT CRUST IN THE OVEN.[4]

MISHNAH 7. [IF] ONE MAKES DOUGH FROM WHEATEN [FLOUR] AND FROM RICE [FLOUR],[5] AND IT HAS A TASTE OF CORN, IT IS SUBJECT TO ḤALLAH,[6] AND ONE FULFILS THEREWITH ONE'S OBLIGATION ON PASSOVER;[7] BUT IF IT HAS NO TASTE OF CORN, IT IS NOT SUBJECT TO ḤALLAH, NOR DOES ONE FULFIL THEREWITH ONE'S OBLIGATION ON PASSOVER.

MISHNAH 8. [IF] ONE HAS TAKEN LEAVEN[8] OUT OF DOUGH FROM WHICH ḤALLAH HAD NOT BEEN TAKEN,[9] AND PUT IT INTO DOUGH FROM WHICH ḤALLAH HAD BEEN
b TAKEN,[1] [THEN] IF HE HAS A SUPPLY FROM ANOTHER PLACE,[2] HE [RECKONS IN WITH IT THE LEAVEN],[3] [AND] TAKES OUT[4] [ḤALLAH] IN ACCORDANCE WITH THE PRECISE AMOUNT;[5] BUT IF [HE HAS] NOT,[6] HE TAKES OUT ONE [PORTION OF] ḤALLAH FOR THE WHOLE [DOUGH].[7]

MISHNAH 9. SIMILAR THERETO[8] [IS THE FOLLOWING]: IF OLIVES OF [REGULAR] PICKING[9] BECAME MIXED WITH OLIVES [LEFT OVER] FOR STRIKING-OFF[10] [BY THE NEEDY],[11] OR GRAPES OF [REGULAR] VINTAGE WITH GRAPES [LEFT

(8) Since it is not the property of an Israelite, and it is only the *'first of your dough'* which is commanded, Num. XV, 20. (9) Because at the material time (viz., of rolling) it was the Israelite's property. (10) Because at the material time, it was *not* the property of an Israelite. (11) 1 1/4 *ḳab.*, v. *supra* II, 6. (12) The converse is implied, viz., if the portion belonging to the Israelite is itself sufficienly large to be subject to *ḥallah*, the *ḥallah* must be given accordingly. (13) V. *supra* Mishnah 1, n. 1.

a (1) As to whether he was a proselyte at the material time. (2) Since, however, it is doubtful whether the priest is entitled to it, it may be sold—instead of given—to him. (3) Lev. XXII, 14 *And if a man eat of the holy thing through error, then he shall put the fifth part thereof unto it, and shall give unto the priest the holy thing*. On 'one-fifth', v. *supra* I, 9, 56*b* n. a 4. In our case, in view of the doubt, he is to separate as a compensatory quantity of dough as great as, *but not greater than*, he had eaten; because of the doubt too, he is permitted to sell it to the priest. V. preceding note. Cf. Demai I, 2. (4) R. Akiba differs from the accepted view. From T.J. *ad loc.* it would appear as if R. Akiba is here confining himself to the case under discussion. Maim., however, basing himself on Sifre to Num. XV, 21 understands R. Akiba as regarding the formation of a light crust in the oven as the statutory stage at which dough, in all cases, becomes liable to *ḥallah*. (5) Which is a species not subject to *ḥallah*, v. *supra* I, 4. (6) Even if it contains less than the minimum (1 1/4 *ḳab*) liable to *ḥallah*. L. points out that this ruling applies exclusively in the case of wheat and rice, because of the latter's resemblance to the former; if, however, a species which is subject to *ḥallah* has been kneaded with some species which is exempt, then the resultant dough is subject to *ḥallah* only if both the following conditions are present: (*a*) the taste of corn is noticeable, and (*b*) it contains at least the minimum quantity (1 1/4 *ḳab*) of corn, even though the latter be exceeded by the non-liable species present in the mixture. (7) Cf. *supra* I, 2. (8) To be used for leavening another dough; likewise, for the purpose of this Mishnah, dough. (9) Such dough, or produce, from which the priestly dues had not been separated is known as *ṭebel* and may not be eaten.

b (1) This latter dough thereby becomes prohibited for eating (v. *infra* 10, n. 4) until an appropriate portion, such as the Mishnah proceeds to define, is separated as *ḥallah*. (2) I.e., some dough from which or in respect of which no *ḥallah* had yet been taken. (3) So Tosef.; so as to make up with the leaven the minimum subject to *ḥallah*. (4) From the new supply. (5) In respect of which no *ḥallah* had yet been taken, viz., the *ṭebel* leaven put into the dough, and the dough 'from another place'. (6) *Sc.* any other such dough, or flour, to reckon in with the leaven. (7) Including the leaven and the dough into which it had got mixed. In this case he takes off as *ḥallah* the appropriate proportion (1/24th or 1/48th, v. *supra* II, 7) of the whole dough. (8) V. *supra* Mishnah 4, n. 17. (9) Which are subject to *terumah* and tithes. (10) A term suggested by the expression *'the striking-off of olives'*, Isa. XVII, 6, XXIV, 13. (11) As commanded in Deut. XXIV, 20. *When thou beatest thine olive-tree, thou shalt not go over the boughs again; it shall be for the stranger, for the fatherless, and the widow*. These olives are exempt from priestly and levitical dues; v. Pe'ah I, 6.

◁ *For the continuation of the English translation of this page see overleaf.*

בזוזי ורוב הספרים דגרסי עיסת ארנונא פטורה מן החלה והוא דלא מלי מסליק ליה ושם דקדקו בדבר: העושה עיסה עם נכרי · בשותפות וכי פסרינן בראשית הגז (דף קלה:) שותפות נכרי מן החלה באין בחלקו של ישראל כשיעור ובירושלמי (שם) אמרינן ר' בון בר חייא בעי קומי ר' זעירא ואפי' יש בשל ישראל כשיעור יעשה קב מיכן וקב מיכן וקב הנכרי באמצע א"ל ר' זעירא ואינו מעורב על ידי *נכרים: ספק חייב · בפ' הזרוע (דף קלד·) פריך ממתני' דהכא אהא דתנן התם נכרי שנתגייר והיתה לו פרה נשחטה אם עד שלא נתגייר פטור משנתגייר חייב ספק פטור שהמוציא מחבירו עליו הראיה ומשני ספק איסורא להומרא ספק ממונא לקולא א' ספיקות נאמרו בגר ד' לחיוב וד' לפטור והתם מפרש להו ובירושלמי (שם) אמרינן דמפריש ונוטל דמיו מן השבט כלומר שמוכרה [לכהן]: הקרימה . בתנור דגלגול הנכרי אינה פוטרת אבל קרימת הנכרי פוטרת ואמרי' בירושל' (שם) חברייא בשם ר' אלעזר מודה ר' עקיבא לחכמים בעיסת הדיוס שגלגלה פטורה רבי הילא בשם ר' אליעזר מודה רבי עקיבא לחכמים בעיסת הקדש שגלגלה פוטרה: ז העושה עיסה מן האורז · דלאו מין דגן הוא ופטור מן החלה: אם יש בה טעם דגן חייבת בחלה · ואע"פ שאין בחטים כשיעור ואמרי' א] מתני' דלא כרשב"ג דרשב"ג אומר לעולם אינה חייבת בחלה עד שיהא בה דגן כשיעור: ויוצא בה ידי חובתו בפסח · מהכא דייקינן בפרק כל הזבחים שנתערבו (דף עח) דנותן טעם ברוב דאורייתא: ח ט לפי חשבון דאם נטל קב מעיסה חייבת ונתנו לתוך עיסה פטורה אם יש לו פרנסה ממקום אחר שיש לו עיסה חייבת שיכול להפריש ממנה על זה הקב אחד מכ"ד בקב מפריש ואין זה כמפריש מן החיוב על הפטור דאורייתא שאין השאור בטל בעיסה עיקר דאורייתא ובתוספתא קתני דמביא קמח ממקום אחר ומצרפו לה' רבעים לחייב עליו לפי חשבון [וא"ת היאך מצטרף הרי העיסה שהורמה חלתה מפסקת האמרי' בפרק בתרא נתן מדבר שהורמה חלתו באמצע מצטרפת ועוד יכול לצרפן ע"י סל למאן דאמר הסל מצרף] ואם לאו שאין לו עיסה חייבת נעשית זאת הפטורה כאילו חייבת ומוציא על הכל אחד מכ"ד: זיתי מסיק · כמו ענבי בציר ולשון מסיקה בזיתים כבצירה בענבים וזיתי ניקוף כענבי עוללות מלשון כנוקף זית כעוללות *בציר (ישעיה כד) ושניהן לעניים ופטורין מן המעשר וכשנתערבו עמהן מסיק ובציר דחייבין במעשר ויש לו פרנסה ממקום אחר מפריש לפי חשבון כדפרשינן גבי חלה ואם לאו רואין כאילו הכל חיוב לענין תרומה ותרומת מעשר ומפריש מהן לפי כולן אבל מעשר ראשון ומעשר שני או מעשר עני אין מוציאין אלא לפי חשבון *ולא שיפריש אלא לפי חשבון דהא אי אפשר להפריש תרומת מעשר על הכל עד שיפריש תחלה מעשר ראשון על הכל ועוד דכל מעשרותיו טבולים ואם לא היה *מעשרן על הכל אם כן אין פירותיו מתוקנין דכל מה שמעשר יש בהן חולין לפי חשבון ונמצא מפריש מן הפטור על החיוב אלא ודאי כל מעשרותיו נוטל על הכל והא דאמרינן לפי חשבון היינו דאין צריך [ליתן] ללוי ולעני אלא לפי חשבון והשאר מערב עם פירותיו אבל תרומה ותרומת מעשר כשמפריש על הכל כמאלו חולין מדומעי' דאסורין לזרים ונותן הכל לכהן או מוכר לו היתרות לפי חשבון ועוד יש לפרש דבלא קריאת שם מוציא תחלה כדי תרומה ותרומת מעשר על הכל אבל שאר המעשרות אין צריך להוציא כלל אלא קורא שם לצפונו או לדרומו ותדע מדלא קתני מתני' מוציא באותו ענין דתנן בדמאי פרק ה' (מ"ב) הרוצה להפריש תרומה ותרומת מעשר כאחת ושם פירשנוה אלא דשם קורא שם לכל וכאן קורא שם לפי חשבון וחילול שני ונתינת ראשון ולעני יתן לפי חשבון וא"ת והאמר שמואל בפ"ק דראש השנה (דף יג:) דלכל אין בילה הוץ מיין ושמן ודוחק להעמידה כמאן דאמר יש בילה וי"ל דתחלה דורך ענבים וכותש זיתים ועושה מענבים יין ומזיתים שמן ואח"כ מפריש ואם תאמר היכי משכחת פרנסה ממקום אחר והא בהקומץ רבה (דף לא·) גבי ר"ש בן שזורי שנתערב טבל בחולין מסיק התם לך קח מן השוק מן הדמאי והוי מחיוב אחיוב דרבנן ועל כורחין איירי התם בטבל שהורמה ממנו תרומה גדולה כעין דמאי דלא מחייב בתרומה גדולה שלא נחשדו עליה אבל הכא בשלא הורם מהן כלל איירי מדקתני ואי לא מוציא תרומה ותרומת מעשר לכולהו ומיהו למאן דאמר יש קנין משכחת לה בלך קח מן הנכרי כדאמר התם אי נמי מוציא תחלה תרומה גדולה ואח"כ לוקח מן השוק ומעשר לפי חשבון אי נמי הכא כשהטבל רוב ובתוספתא דדמאי (פרק ה) תניא הטבל שנתערב בחולין הרי זה אוסר כל שהוא ואם יש לו פרנסה ממקום אחר מוציא לפי חשבון ואם לאו נוטל את החולין כדי תרומת מעשר שבטבל אבל תרומה גדולה לא תני כדתני הכא משום דהתם מיירי בטבל של דמאי דלא חשידי עליה ואפי' תרומת מעשר נמי לא חייבו להפריש על הכל משום דבדמאי הקילו דבדמאי איירי מדתניא במסכת דמאי והא דלא תני מעשר ומעשר [שני] כדתני הכא משום דאשמעינן דאפילו תרומה לפי חשבון כ"ש מעשר ולא איצטריך בברייתא למיתני אלא מה שהיא חלוקה ממתניתין: י מעיסת חטין · בשלא הורמה חלתה איירי: ואם לאו פטורה · דלא בעי אפרושה מינה מידי ואין הטבל אוסרת כיון דליכא טעם: אם כן למה אמרו הטבל אוסר כל שהוא . דאמרינן לעיל בשיש לו פרנסה מפריש לפי חשבון ובשאין לו פרנסה כל העיסה נאסרת ומוציא על הכל הני מילי במינו אבל שלא במינו כי האי דחטים באורז ונותן טעם וטעמא דטבל בכל שהוא אמרינן בשילהי ע"א (דף ע"ג.) משום דכהתירו דחטה אחת פוטרת את הכרי כך איסורו (ה) והא דמייתי התם תניא נמי הכי היינו מתני' דהכא: א אפילו הן ממין אחד · ואין מועיל לא נשיכה ולא צירוף סל כיון דמקפידות ואפי' לשין שני הקבין בבת אחת כיון דסופו ליחלק כדפרשי' בפ"ק (משנה ז) גבי נחתום שעשה שאור לחלק: ובזמן שהן של אשה אחת מין במינו חייב · ובלבד שישוכו או בצירוף סל למאן דאית ליה כדפרשינן לעיל בפ"ב: ירושלמי (הל' א) א"ר יוחנן סתם אשה אחת אינה מקפדת סתם שתי נשים מקפידות אחת שמקפדת עשו אותה כשתי נשים שאינן מקפידות עשו אותן כאשה אחת אם אינה מקפדת למה היא עושה אותן בב' מקומות א"ר יונה בשאין לה מקום היכן ללוש מילתיה דר' יונה אמר היה לה מקום ללוש והיא עושה אותם בב' מקומות מקפדת היא נקי וקיבר מקפדת היא: ב החטים אינן מצטרפות עם הכל . והא דתנן בריש מכילתין דכל ה' מינין מצטרפין בירושלמי בפ"ק

מפאה ולשם נשנית את באות: ה זה המאמר מבואר היטב: ו נעשית עד שלא נתגייר. רולה בו נתגלגלה בחטים ונטמטמה בשעורים: ואם נולד ספק אם קודם שנתגייר נעשית או אחר שנתגייר חייבת בחלה והאוכל אותה חלה בשוגג אינו חייב חומש לפי שהוא ספק והמוציא מחבירו עליו הראיה וכבר ביארנו כי החלה האמיתית חייבין בה חומש: ור' עקיבא אומר הכל הולך אחר הקרימה בתנור. אם נתגייר קודם שיקרמו פני הפת בתנור חייב בחלה לפי שר' עקיבא סובר כי החלה מוציאין משיקרמו פני הפת ולדעתו זה היה שעת הוצאת הלה וכן נראה מדעתו בספרי אמר לשם אין מפרישין עד שתגמר מלאכתה איזה הוא גמר מלאכתה קרימתה בתנור דברי ר' עקיבא וקרימה הוא שיקפה פני הפת ויהיה לו כמין קליפה ואין הלכה כרבי עקיבא: ז כבר קדם לנו כי החלה אינה חייבת אלא מחמשת המינין וכמו כן אין אדם יוצא ידי חובתו בפסח אלא בחמשת המינים ואין האורז מכללם: ח אם יש לו פרנסה ממקום אחר מוציא לפי חשבון. ביאור זה כאשר אגיד לך והוא שמביא אדם קמח שיעורו כשיצרפו לאותו שאור שלקח מעיסה שלא הורמה חלתה שיהיה הכל חמשה רבעים שהוא שיעור חלה ואחר כך יערב הכל ומוציא ממנו החלה החייבת לחמשה רבעים ואם אין לו מה שיצרף תהיה כל העיסה טבל ויוציא ממנה החלה החייבת לה אילו היתה כולה טבולה לחלה וזהו אמרם מוציא חלה אחת על הכל: ט זיתי מסיק. הם הזיתים שמלקטין בעלי בתים שהם בעלי הקרקעות וכבר ביארנו פעמים (פאה פרק ח מ"א) כי לקיטת הזיתים יקרא בלשון חכמים מסיקה וזיתי נקוף הם הזיתים שמלקטים העניים והעד כנוקף זית שנים שלשה גרגרים (ישעיה יז) זיתי נקוף והעוללות אינן חייבין במעשרות כמו שבארנו במסכת פאה (פ"א משנה ו) וכשנתערבו זיתי נקוף שאינן חייבות בתרומה ובמעשרות עם זיתי מסיק שהן חייבות בהם אם יש אלו זיתים אחרים מלבד אותן המעורבות יוציא מהם המעשרות והתרומה החייבות לאותן זיתי מסיק המעורבות עם זיתי נקוף הפטורות וזהו ענין אמרם לפי חשבון ואם אין אלו זיתים אחרים יוציא מן הזיתים המעורבים תרומה ותרומת מעשר החייבים לכל ונחשב הכל זיתי מסיק ומה שישאר מן הדבר המעורב יוציא ממנו מעשר ראשון ומעשר שני לפי חשבון כלומר לפי מה שיש באותו הדבר המעורב מזיתי מסיק בלבד ושיעור ההלכה כך ומפריש מן השאר מעשר ראשון ומעשר שני לפי חשבונו ומה שחייבנו שנוציא התרומה ותרומת מעשר על הכל לפי שיש בהם עון מיתה כמו שבארנו בתחלת דמאי ובלי ספק שיוכל לחזור וליקח ולקנות מן העניים זיתי נקוף או העוללות המעורבות בזיתיו או בענביו על הדרך שנזכר בפאה: י אוסר כל שהוא מין במינו · כיצד כגון שיתערב חטה בחטה ואורז באורז ושלא במינו בנותן טעם כגון שיתערב חטים באורז ויוצא בו:

א זו ההלכה על דעת בית הלל שאומרים מקביים חלה כמו שיתבאר בעדיות וכבר בארנו אנחנו במה שקדם (לעיל פ"ב מ"ו) שיעור חלה והכוונה בזו ההלכה שיהיה בשתי העיסות שיעור חלה: ב זה הצירוף אין ענינו שתתערב העיסה כולה ויהיה הכל אחד לפי שכבר קדם כי חמשת המינים מצטרפין זה עם זה אבל ענינו שיסדרו עיסה אצל עיסה אחרת ותדבק בה כמו שאמר נגעו זה בזה ורוצה באמרו שאר המינים שאר חמשת

מן החלה נתנה לו מתנה עד שלא גלגל חייב ומשגלגל פטור העושה עיסה עם הנכרי אם אין בשל ישראל כשיעור חלה פטורה מן החלה:

ו גר א) שנתגייר והיתה לו עיסה נעשית עד שלא נתגייר פטור ומשנתגייר חייב ואם ספק חייב (ז) ואין חייבין עליה חומש רבי עקיבא אומר הכל הולך אחר הקרימה בתנור:

ז העושה ב) עיסה מן החטים ומן האורז אם יש בה טעם דגן חייבת בחלה ויוצא בה אדם ידי חובתו בפסח ואם אין בה טעם דגן אינה חייבת בחלה ואין אדם יוצא בה ידי חובתו בפסח:

ח הנוטל שאור מעיסה שלא הורמה חלתה ונותן לתוך עיסה שהורמה חלתה אם יש לו פרנסה ממקום אחר מוציא לפי חשבון ואם לאו מוציא חלה אחת על הכל:

ט כיוצא בו זיתי מסיק שנתערבו עם זיתי נקוף ענבי בציר עם ענבי עוללות אם יש לו פרנסה ממקום אחר מוציא לפי חשבון ואם לאו מוציא תרומה ותרומת מעשר לכל והשאר מעשר ומעשר שני לפי חשבון:

י הנוטל שאור מעיסת חטים ונותן לתוך עיסת אורז אם יש בה טעם דגן חייבת בחלה ואם לאו פטורה אם כן למה אמרו ג) הטבל אוסר כל שהוא במינו ושלא במינו בנותן טעם:

פרק רביעי

א שתי נשים שעשו שני קבים ונגעו זה בזה אפילו הם ממין אחד פטורין ובזמן שהם של אשה אחת מין במינו חייב ושלא במינו פטור:

ב איזה הוא מין במינו החטים

פי' מהר"י בן מלכי צדק

עיסה פטורה מן החלה. נתנה לו מתנה. פי' נתן הנכרי אותה העיסה לישראל במתנה אם עד שלא גלגל נתנה לו חייב בדרשתיה דישראל נתגלגלה ואם משנתגלגל הנכרי נתנה לו פטור פי' דגלגול נכרי פוטר: העושה עיסה עם הנכרי. פירוש בשותפות אם אין בשל ישראל כשיעור חיוב חלה פטורה מן החלה אבל אם יש בשל ישראל כשיעור חיוב חלה ישראל חייב להפריש חלה מעיסתו: ו גר שנתגייר והיתה לו עיסה נעשית עד שלא נתגייר פטור ...

Continuation of translation from previous page as indicated by ◁

OVER] FOR GLEANING [BY THE NEEDY],[12] [THEN] IF HE HAS A SUPPLY FROM ANOTHER PLACE[13] HE [RECKONS IN WITH IT THE REGULAR FRUIT CONTAINED IN THE MIXTURE, AND] TAKES OUT[14] [TERUMAH AND TITHES] IN ACCORDANCE WITH THE PRECISE AMOUNT,[15] IF [HE HAS] NOT,[16] HE TAKES OUT

c TERUMAH AND TERUMAH-OF-THE-TITHE[1] FOR ALL [THE FRUIT][2], AND [AS FOR] THE REST [OF THE DUES], [HE SEPARATES] THE TITHE AND THE SECOND TITHE[3] IN ACCORDANCE WITH THE PRECISE AMOUNT.[4]

MISHNAH 10. IF ONE TAKES LEAVEN FROM A DOUGH OF WHEATEN [FLOUR][5] AND PUTS [IT] INTO DOUGH OF RICE [FLOUR],[6] [THEN] IF IT HAS THE TASTE OF CORN, IT IS SUBJECT

d TO ḤALLAH,[1] [BUT] IF [IT HAS] NOT, IT IS EXEMPT.[1] IF [THAT IS] SO, WITH REGARD TO WHAT[2] THEN DID THEY SAY:[3] '[AN ADMIXTURE OF] ṬEBEL,[4] HOWEVER LITTLE OF IT[5] THERE BE, RENDERS FOOD PROHIBITED'? [WITH REGARD TO A MIXTURE OF] A SPECIES WITH ITS OWN SPECIES,[6] BUT [WITH REGARD TO A MIXTURE OF A SPECIES] NOT WITH ITS OWN SPECIES,[7] [THE PROHIBITION APPLIES ONLY] WHEN IT [THE ṬEBEL ADMIXTURE] IMPARTS TASTE.

CHAPTER IV

e *MISHNAH* 1. IF TWO WOMEN[1] MADE [SEPARATE DOUGHS] FROM TWO [SEPARATE] ḲABS,[2] AND THESE [THE DOUGHS] TOUCHED ONE ANOTHER, [THEN] EVEN IF THEY ARE OF ONE SPECIES, THEY ARE EXEMPT [FROM ḤALLAH];[3] BUT IF THEY BELONG TO ONE WOMAN, [THEN] IF IT BE [A CASE OF] ONE SPECIES WITH ITS [LIKE] SPECIES, THEY ARE SUBJECT [TO ḤALLAH],[4] BUT WITH AN UNLIKE SPECIES, THEY ARE EXEMPT.[5]

MISHNAH 2. WHAT IS IT [THAT CONSTITUTES THE CATEGORY OF] A SPECIES WITH ITS [LIKE] SPECIES?[6] WHEAT IS

(12) As commanded Deut. ibid. v. 21: *When thou gatherest the grapes of thy vineyard, thou shalt not glean after thee; it shall be for the stranger, for the fatherless, and for the widow.* These gleanings are exempt from priestly and levitical dues; v. Pe'ah ibid. (13) I.e., other lots of regular olives and grapes in respect of which *terumah* or tithes have yet to be taken. (14) From the new supply. (15) Viz., of the regular fruit mixed with the gleanings, plus the new supply, in respect of both of which *terumah* and tithes are still outstanding. (16) I.e., no new supply.

c (1) Otherwise called the 'tithe of the tithe', Num. XVIII, 26. I.e., the tithe which a Levite is enjoined to give to the priest out of the tithe which he, the Levite himself, receives from the Israelite (ibid. vv. 21ff). Here it means the amount that *would* become due for this 'tithe of the tithe', *if* the first tithe were to be taken off the total produce (which, in fact, is not the case; v. note 4) i.e., one-hundredth part of the latter. (2) I.e., the gleanings together with the admixture of regular fruit which made the whole lot *ṭebel.* (3) The designation given by tradition to the tithe (commanded in Deut. XIV, 22ff) which was itself, or its equivalent in money, to be taken to Jerusalem and there consumed in rejoicing. (4) I.e., supposing the total that had got mixed up was 100 quarters, 50 of regular fruit (still to be tithed etc.), and 50 of gleanings (which do not require to be tithed etc.). In that case the owner is to give 2 quarters (i.e, one-fiftieth of the total) as *terumah*, and 1 quarter (one-hundredth of the total, v. note 1) as 'tithe of the tithe'. For the first tithe, however, he is to separate only 5 quarters (one-tenth of the 50 quarters which alone are liable to tithing) and deduct half a quarter in respect of the 'tithe of the tithe' (which he had already set aside), thus handing over to the Levite 4½ quarters. The 'second tithe' he is to take from that which remains over from the 50 quarters which were liable to tithing (after Simponte). L. explains the procedure thus: He separates *terumah*, tithe and second tithe from all the produce; from the first tithe he gives a tithe to the priest as the 'tithe of the tithe'; but to the Levite he gives only such part of the tithe as is due from the amount that had been originally liable to tithing. The second tithe he also gives as from the bulk amount.—The requirement, here, that *terumah* and *terumah* of the tithe be levied upon a larger amount of produce than are the other dues, is attributed to the circumstance that the penalty for infringement of the law of *terumah* of the tithe is death ('by the hand of heaven'; cf. I, 9 note 2), and so as to be certain of having fully complied with these precepts, the proportions to be set aside are computed on the maximum amount of produce so 'taxable'. (5) Which is subject to *ḥallah* and from which *ḥallah* is still due. (6) Which, as such, is not subject to *ḥallah* (v. *supra* I, 4).

d (1) In accordance with the principle established in Mishnah 7. (2) Vocalizing לָמָּה. (3) The Sages,v. 'Abodah Zara 73*b*. Halevy, *Doroth* II, p. 830 says, אמרו ('they said') introduces a quotation from the Mishnah in its original form; such passages as ours are additions made at the time of the closing of the Mishnah for the purpose of finally elucidating the point under discussion by correlating all the relevant dicta having a bearing thereon. (4) Eatables at the stage when they severally become subject to the separation of priestly and levitical dues, but before that separation has been effected, at which stage they may not be eaten. (5) I.e., of the *ṭebel.* (6) E.g., wheat which is *ṭebel*, with other wheat (or like species; v. *infra* IV, 2) which is not. (7) E.g., wheat-dough which is *ṭebel*, with dough from a grain dissimilar thereto (v. IV, 2) which is exempt (either *ab initio* or so rendered) from *ḥallah*, or with rice dough which is in no circumstances subject to *ḥallah*.

e (1) Not necessarily, but most likely to occur with women in the course of their household activities. (2) One *ḳab* is not subject to *ḥallah*, in accordance with the view of the School of Hillel ('Ed. I, 2). (3) Because as a rule each of the women not only does not contemplate her dough coming into contact with someone else's, but actually objects to it; the two *ḳabs* are, therefore, considered as separate (just as their owners deem them to be) despite the fact that by chance they touched or even stuck together. (4) In circumstances explained *supra* II, 4. (5) This exemption applies also in the event of the two doughs being of the same species but otherwise different, e.g., one of coarse and the other of fine flour (T.J.) or one seasoned with saffron and the other not (v. L.). (6) So that they might combine by contact to make up the requisite minimum (viz., 1¼ *ḳab*) to be subject to *ḥallah*. It should be noted that the considerations envisaged in this Mishnah have reference only to *ḥallah* but not to other priestly or levitical dues.

א) חולין דף קלד. מנחות דף סז: ב) זבחים ד' עח: ג) ע"ז דף עג:

בזוזי ורוב הספרים דגרסי עיסת ארטנא פטורה מן החלה והוא דלא מלי מסליק ליה ושם דקדקו בדבר : העושה עיסה עם נכרי · בשותפות וכי פטרינן בראשית הגז (דף קלה:) שותפות נכרי מן החלה בשאין בחלקו של ישראל כשיעור ובירושל' (שם) אמרינן ר' בון בר חייא בעי קומי ר' זעירא ואפי' יש בשל ישראל כשיעור יעשה קב מיכן וקב מיכן וקב הנכרי באמצע א"ל ר' זעירא ואינו מעורב על ידי *נכרים : ספק חייב · בפ' הזרוע (דף קלד·) פריך ממתני' דהכא אהא דתנן התם נכרי שנתגייר והיתה לו פרה נשחטה אם עד שלא נתגייר פטור משנתגייר חייב ספק פטור שהמוציא מחבירו עליו הראיה ומשני ספק איסורא להומרא ספק ממונא לקולא ח' ספיקות נאמרו בגר ד' לחיוב וד' לפטור והתם מפרש להו ובירושלמי (שם) אמרינן דמפריש ונוטל דמיו מן השבט כלומר שמוכרה [לכהן] : הקרימה . בתנור דגלגול הנכרי אינה פוטרת אבל קרימת הנכרי פוטרת ואמרי' בירושל' (שם) חברייא בשם ר' אלעזר מודה ר' עקיבא לחכמים בעיסת הדיוט שנגלגלה טבלה רבי הילא בשם ר' אליעזר מודה רבי עקיבא לחכמים בעיסת הקדש שנגלגלה פוטרה : ז העושה עיסה מן האורז · דלאו מין דגן הוא ופטור מן החלה : אם יש בה טעם דגן חייבת בחלה · ואע"פ שאין בחטים כשיעור ואמרי' א] מתני' דלא כרשב"ג דרשב"ג אומר לעולם אינה חייבת בחלה עד שיהא בה דגן כשיעור : ויוצא בה ידי חובתו בפסח · מהכא דייקינן בפרק כל הזבחים שנתערבו (דף עח) דנותן טעם ברוב דאורייתא : ח ט לפי חשבון דאם נטל קב מעיסה חייבת ונתנו לתוך עיסה פטורה אם יש לו פרנסה ממקום אחר שיש לו עיסה חייבת שיכול להפריש ממנה על זה הקב אחד מכ"ד בקב מפריש ואין זה כמפריש מן החיוב על הפטור דאורייתא שאין השאור בטל בעיסה עיקר דאורייתא ובתוספתא קתני דמביא קמח ממקום אחר ומצרפו לה' רבעים לחייב עליו לפי חשבון [וא"ת היאך מצטרף הרי העיסה שהורמה חלתה מפסקת האמרי' בפרק בתרא נתן מדבר שהורמה חלתו באמצע מצטרפת ועוד יכול לצרפן ע"י סל למאן דאמר הסל מצרף] ואם לאו שאין לו עיסה חייבת נעשית זאת הפטורה כאילו חייבת ומוציא על הכל אחד מכ"ד : זיתי מסיק · כמו ענבי בציר ולשון מסיקה בזיתים כבצירה בענבים וזיתי ניקוף כענבי עוללות מלשון כנוקף זית כעוללות *בציר (ישעיה כד) ושניהן לעניים ופטורין מן המעשר וכשנתערבו עמהן מסיק ובציר דחייבין במעשר ויש לו פרנסה ממקום אחר מפריש לפי חשבון כדפרשינן גבי חלה ואם לאו רואין כאילו הכל חיוב לענין תרומה ותרומת מעשר ומפריש מהן לפי כולן אבל מעשר ראשון ומעשר שני או מעשר עני אין מוציאין אלא לפי חשבון *ולא שיפריש אלא לפי חשבון דהא אי אפשר להפריש תרומת מעשר על הכל עד שיפריש תחלה מעשר ראשון על הכל ועוד דכל מעשרותיו טבולים ואם לא היה *מעשרן על הכל אם כן אין פירותיו מתוקנין דכל מה שמעשר יש בהן חולין לפי חשבון וגמלא מפריש מן הפטור על החיוב אלא ודאי כל מעשרותיו נוטל על הכל והא דאמרינן לפי חשבון היינו דאין צריך [ליתן] ללוי ולעני אלא לפי חשבון והשאר מערב עם פירותיו אבל תרומה ותרומת מעשר כשמפריש על הכל נמצאו חולין מדומעי' דאסורין לזרים ונותן הכל לכהן או מוכר לו היתרות לפי חשבון ועוד יש לפרש דבלא קריאת שם מוציא תחלה כדי תרומה ותרומת מעשר על הכל אבל שאר המעשרות אין צריך להוציא כלל אלא קורא שם לנפונו או לדרומו ותדע מדלא קתני מתני' מוציא באותו ענין דתנן בדמאי פרק ה' (מ"ב) הרוצה להפריש תרומה ותרומת מעשר כאחת ושם פירשנוה אלא דשם קורא שם לכל וכאן קורא שם לפי חשבון וחילול שני ונתינת ראשון ולעני יתן לפי חשבון וא"ת והאמר שמואל בפ"ק דראש השנה (דף יג:) דלכל אין בילה חוץ מיין ושמן ודוחק להעמידה כמאן דאמר יש בילה וי"ל דתחלה דורך ענבים וכותש זיתים ועושה מענבים יין ומזיתים שמן ואח"כ מפריש ואם תאמר היכי משכחת פרנסה ממקום אחר והא בהקומץ רבה (דף לא.) גבי ר"ש בן שזורי שנתערב טבל בחולין מסיק התם לך קח מן השוק מן הדמאי והוי מחיוב דרבנן אחיוב דרבנן ועל כורחין איירי התם בטבל שהורמה ממנו תרומה גדולה כעין דמאי דלא מחייב בתרומה גדולה שלא נחשדו עליה אבל הכא בשלא הורם מהן כלל איירי מדקתני ואי לא מוציא תרומה ותרומת מעשר לכולהו ומיהו למאן דאמר יש קנין משכחת לה בלך קח מן הנכרי כדאמר התם אי נמי מוציא תחלה תרומה גדולה ואח"כ לוקח מן השוק ומעשר לפי חשבון אי נמי הכא כשהטבל רוב ובתוספתא דדמאי (פרק ה) תניא הטבל שנתערב בחולין הרי זה אוסר כל שהוא ואם יש לו פרנסה ממקום אחר מוציא לפי חשבון ואם לאו נוטל את החולין כדי תרומת מעשר שבטבל אבל תרומה גדולה לא תני כדתני הכא משום דהתם מיירי בטבל של דמאי דלא חשידי עליה ואפי' תרומת מעשר נמי לא חייבו להפריש על הכל משום דבדמאי הקילו דבדמאי איירי מדתניא במסכת דמאי והא דלא תני מעשר ומעשר [שני] כדתני הכא משום דמתני' חלוקה תרומה ממעשר שזה לכל וזה לפי חשבון אבל דמאי כיון דאשמעינן דאפילו תרומה לפי חשבון כ"ש מעשר ולא איצטריך בברייתא למיתני אלא מה שהיא חלוקה ממתניתין : י מעיסת חטין · בשלא הורמה חלתה איירי : ואם לאו פטורה · דלא בעי אפרושה מינה מידי ואין הטבל אוסרת כיון דליכא טעם : אם כן למה אמרו הטבל אוסר כל שהוא. דאמרינן לעיל בשיש לו פרנסה מפריש לפי חשבון ובשאין לו פרנסה כל העיסה נאסרת ומוציא על הכל הני מילי במינו אבל שלא במינו כי האי דחטים באורז ונותן טעם וטעמא דטבל בכל שהוא אמרינן בשילהי ע"א (דף ע"ג.) משום דכהתירו דחטה אחת פוטרת את הכרי כך איסורו (ה) והא דמייתי התם תניא נמי הכי היינו מתני' דהכא :

א אפילו הן ממין אחד· ואין מועיל לא נשיכה ולא צירוף סל כיון דמקפידות ואפי' לשין שני הקבין בבת אחת כיון דסופו ליחלק כדפרשי' בפ"ק (משנה ז) גבי נחתום שעשה שאור לחלק : ובזמן שהן של אשה אחת מין במינו חייב · ובלבד שישוכו או בצירוף סל למאן דאית ליה כדפרשינן לעיל בפ"ב : ירושלמי (הל' א) א"ר יוחנן סתם אשה אחת אינה מקפדת שתים מקפידות אחת שמקפדת עשו אותה כשתי נשים שתי נשים שאינן מקפידות עשו אותן כאשה אחת אם אינה מקפדת למה היא עושה אותן בב' מקומות א"ר יונה בשאין לה מקום היכן ללוש מילתיה דר' יונה אמר היה לה מקום ללוש והיא עושה אותם בב' מקומות מקפדת היא נקי וקיבר מקפדת היא : ב החטים אינן מצטרפות עם הכל . והא דתנן בריש מכילתין דכל ה' מינין מצטרפין בירושלמי בפ"ק

מן החלה נתנה לו מתנה עד שלא גלגל חייב ומשגלגל פטור [א]העושה עיסה עם הנכרי אם אין בשל ישראל כשיעור חלה פטורה מן החלה : ו [ב]גר א) שנתגייר והיתה לו עיסה נעשית עד שלא נתגייר פטור ומשנתגייר חייב ואם ספק חייב (ז) ואין חייבין עליה חומש רבי עקיבא אומר הכל הולך אחר הקרימה בתנור : ז [ג]העושה ב) עיסה מן החטים ומן האורז אם יש בה טעם דגן חייבת בחלה ויוצא בה אדם ידי חובתו בפסח ואם אין בה טעם דגן אינה חייבת בחלה ואין אדם יוצא בה ידי חובתו בפסח : ח [ד]הנוטל שאור מעיסה שלא הורמה חלתה ונותן לתוך עיסה שהורמה חלתה אם יש לו פרנסה ממקום אחר מוציא לפי חשבון ואם לאו מוציא חלה אחת על הכל : ט [ה]כיוצא בו זיתי מסיק שנתערבו עם זיתי נקוף ענבי בציר עם ענבי עוללות אם יש לו פרנסה ממקום אחר מוציא לפי חשבון ואם לאו מוציא תרומה ותרומת מעשר לכל והשאר מעשר ומעשר שני לפי חשבון : י [ו]הנוטל שאור מעיסת חטים ונותן לתוך עיסת אורז אם יש בה טעם דגן חייבת בחלה ואם לאו פטורה אם כן למה אמרו ג) [ז]הטבל אוסר כל שהוא במינו ושלא במינו בנותן טעם :

פרק רביעי

א שתי [ח]נשים שעשו שני קבים ונגעו זה בזה אפילו הם ממין אחד פטורין ובזמן שהם של אשה אחת מין במינו חייב ושלא במינו פטור : ב [ט]איזה הוא מין במינו החטים

מפאה ולשם נשנית את באות : ה זה המאמר מבואר היטב : ו נעשית עד שלא נתגייר. רוצה בו נתגלגלה בחטים ונטמטמה בשעורים : ואם נולד ספק אם קודם שנתגייר נעשית או אחר שנתגייר חייבת בחלה והאוכל אותה חלה בשוגג אינו חייב חומש לפי שהוא ספק והמוציא מחבירו עליו הראיה וכבר ביארנו כי החלה האמיתית חייבין בה חומש : ור' עקיבא אומר הכל הולך אחר הקרימה בתנור . אם נתגייר קודם שיקרמו פני הפת בתנור חייב בחלה לפי שר' עקיבא סובר כי החלה מוציאין משיקרמו פני הפת ולדעתו זה היה שעת הוצאת הלה וכן נראה מדעתו בספרי אמר לשם אין מפרישין עד שתגמר מלאכתה איזה הוא גמר מלאכתה קרימתה בתנור דברי ר' עקיבא וקרימה הוא שיקפה פני הפת ויהיה לו כמין קליפה ואין הלכה כרבי עקיבא : ז כבר קדם לנו כי החלה אינה חייבת אלא מחמשת המינין וכמו כן אין אדם יוצא ידי חובתו בפסח אלא בחמשת המינים ואין האורז מכללם : ח אם יש לו פרנסה ממקום אחר מוציא לפי חשבון . ביאור זה כאשר אגיד לך והוא שמביא אדם קמח שיעורו כשיצרפו לאותו שאור שלקח מעיסה שלא הורמה חלתה שיהיה הכל חמשה רבעים שהוא שיעור חלה ואחר כך יערב הכל ומוציא ממנו החלה החייבת לחמשה רבעים ואם אין לו מה שיצרף תהיה כל העיסה טבל ויוציא ממנה החלה החייבת לה אילו היתה כולה טבולה לחלה וזהו אמרם מוציא חלה אחת על הכל : ט זיתי מסיק. הם הזיתים שמלקטין בעלי בתים שהם בעלי הקרקעות וכבר ביארנו פעמים (פאה פרק ח מ"א) כי לקיטת הזיתים יקרא בלשון חכמים מסיקה וזיתי נקוף הם הזיתים שמלקטים העניים והעד כנוקף זית שנים שלשה גרגרים (ישעיה יז) זיתי נקוף והעוללות אינן חייבין במעשרות כמו שבארנו במסכת פאה (פ"א משנה ו) וכשנתערבו זיתי נקוף שאינן חייבות בתרומה ובמעשרות עם זיתי מסיק שהן חייבות בהם אם יש אצלו זיתים אחרים מלבד אותן המעורבות יוציא מהם המעשרות והתרומה החייבות לאותן זיתי מסיק המעורבות עם זיתי נקוף הפטורות וזהו ענין אמרם לפי חשבון ואם אין אצלו זיתים אחרים יוציא מן הזיתים המעורבים תרומה ותרומת מעשר החייבים לכל ונחשב הכל זיתי מסיק ומה שישאר מן הדבר המעורב יוציא ממנו מעשר ראשון ומעשר שני לפי חשבון כלומר לפי מה שיש באותו הדבר המעורב מזיתי מסיק בלבד ושיעור ההלכה כך ומפריש מן השאר מעשר ראשון ומעשר שני לפי חשבונו ומה שחייבנו שנוציא התרומה והתרומה מעשר על הכל לפי שיש בהם עון מיתה כמו שבארנו בתחלת דמאי ובלי ספק שיוכל לחזור וליקח ולקנות מן העניים זיתי נקוף או העוללות המעורבות בזיתיו או בענביו על הדרך שנזכר בפאה : י אוסר כל שהוא מין במינו · כיצד כגון שיתערב חטה בחטה ואורז באורז ושלא במינו בנותן טעם כגון שיתערב חטים באורז וכיוצא בו :

א זה ההלכה על דעת בית הלל שאומרים מקביים חלה כמו שיתבאר בעדיות וכבר בארנו אנחנו במה שקדם (לעיל פ"ב מ"ו) שיעור חלה והכוונה בזו ההלכה שיהיה בשתי העיסות שיעור חלה : ב זה הצירוף אין ענינו שתתערב העיסה כולה ויהיה הכל אחד לפי שכבר קדם כי חמשת המינים מצטרפין זה עם זה אבל ענינו שיסדרו עיסה אצל עיסה אחרת והדבק בה כמו שאמר נגעו זה בזה ורוצה באמרו שאר המינים שאר חמשת

פי' מהר"י בן מלכי צדק

עיסה פטורה מן החלה : נתנה לו מתנה . פי' נתן הנכרי אותה העיסה לישראל במתנה אם עד שלא גלגל נתנה לו חייב דברשותיה דישראל נתגלגלה ואם משגלגל הנכרי נתנה לו פטור פי' דגלגול נכרי פוטר : העושה עיסה עם הנכרי . פירוש בשותפות אם אין בשל ישראל כשיעור חיוב חלה פטורה מן החלה אבל אם יש בשל ישראל כשיעור חיוב חלה ישראל חייב להפריש חלה מעיסתו : ו גר שנתגייר והיתה לו עיסה נעשית עד שלא נתגייר פטור . נתגלגלה עד שלא נתגייר ואחר שנתגלגלה עיסתו נתגייר פטור להפריש הלה מעיסתו : ומשנתגייר חייב. פי' ואם משנתגייר נתגלגלה חייב בחלה : ואם ספק חייב . פי' ספק עד שלא נתגלגלה נתגייר ספק משנתגלגלה נתגייר חייב להפריש אבל זר האוכל משלם קרן ואינו משלם חומש. תנן התם גר שנתגייר והיתה לו פרה נשחטת עד שלא נתגייר פטור מן המתנות אם משנתגייר חייב ספק פטור שהמוציא מחבירו עליו הראיה וקשי' הא אמר ספק חייב ותירצו מפריש ונוטל דמיה מן השבט . והקשו מתנות נמי ליפריש ולישלם דמים מן השבט ותירץ רבי יוסי הלה שהיא בעון מיתה לפיכך מפריש. אבל מתנות שאין בעון מיתה אינן מפרישין . והקשו אי הכי חלה תיפרש ולא לישקל דמים משבט ופריק אפילו הכי נוטל דמים מן השבט דמוציא מחבירו עליו הראיה : ז העושה עיסה מן החטים ומן האורז . פי' אם הערים בשני עצמן פטור מן החלה ואם עירבם מן החטים ומן האורז עושה עיסה אם יש באותה העיסה טעם דגן חייבת בחלה אע"ג דלית בדגן כשיעור חיוב חלה : ויוצא בה ידי חובתו בפסח . פי' אם היא מצה מתני' דלא כר"ש בן גמליאל דתניא אינה חייבת עד שיהא בדגן שלה כשיעור : ח הנוטל שאור מעיסה שלא הורמה חלתה . פי' כגון שנטל רבע אחד מעיסה שלא הורמה חלתה ונתנו לתוך עיסה שהורמה חלתה : אם יש לו פרנסה ממקום אחר . פי' אם יש לו במקום אחר ד' רבעין מבולין לחלה מוציא מהן חלה על אותו הרובע שנתערב ושוב אינו צריך להפריש הלה מאותה העיסה שהורמה חלתה . וזהו פי' פרנסה : ואם אין לו פרנסה ממקום אחר כאשר אמרנו : מוציא חלה על כל. פי' בשביל אותו הרובע שנתערב שם צריך להפריש חלה על כל העיסה ההיא שכבר הורמה חלתה דנעשית כולה כטבל לענין חלה ואם העיסה י"א רבעין מתוקנין ורובע שנתערב שם הרי י"ב צריך להפריש חצי רובע חלה על כל העיסה : ט כיוצא בו זיתי מסיק . פי' שחייבין במעשר : עם זיתי ניקוף . שפטורין מן המעשרות : ענבי בציר . פי' שחייבין במעשר : עם ענבי עוללות . שפטורין : אם יש לו פרנסה ממקום אחר מוציא לפי חשבון . פי' אם יש לו ענבי בציר וזיתי מסיק מפריש מהן תרומה ומעשרות על זיתי מסיק ועל ענבי בציר שנתערבו ותו לא פי' כגון שאותן שנתערבו היו אותן דחיוב נ' סאין ואותן דפטור נ' סאין עתה אם יש לו ענבי חיוב וזיתי חיוב במקום אחד תורם עלייהו סאה ומעשר ה' סאין לפי חשבון : ואם אין לו פרנסה ממקום אחר מוציא מהן תרומה מהכל . פי' בין מזיתי פטור בין מזיתי חיוב דהיינו ב' סאין תרומה וסאה תרומת מעשר שכן הדין ליטול אם תיטול מכולן ושאר מעשר ומעשר שני לפי חשבון . פי' דמעשר ראשון לא יתן ללוי אלא ד' סאין וחצי דמנ' סאין דחיוב מעשר שלהן ה' סאין חצי סאה שקל תרומת מעשר וד' וחצי נשארו ומעשר שני נמי לא ישקול מכולהו אלא ממה שנשאר מן הנ' סאין דחיוב : הנוטל שאור מעיסת חטים . פי' שכבר נתגלגלה ונטבלה לחלה : ונתנו לתוך עיסת האורז . פי' שאור וכיון דאינו חייב בחלה הרי הוא כחולין מתוקנין : אם יש בעיסה ההיא טעם דגן חייבת בחלה ואם לאו פטורה . ואותה העיסה דטבל שנתן שם אינה אוסרת אותה : ואם כן למה אמרו הטבל אוסר כל שהוא מין במינו . פי' כגון עיסת טבל דחטין בעיסה מתוקנת דחטין דחולין אז אוסר בכל שהוא . ואם יש לו פרנסה ממקום אחר מוציאין לפי חשבון ואם לאו נאסרת כל העיסה וצריך להפריש חלה על כל העיסה כאשר שנינו : ושלא במינו. כגון זו חטין באורז בנותן טעם אז נאסרת עיסה וחייב להפריש על הכל אבל אם אינו נותן בה טעם פטורה העיסה מן החלה :

פרק ד א שתי נשים שעשו ב' קבין . פי' זו קב וזו קב : ונגעו הקבין זה בזה אפילו ממין אחד . פי' אפילו שניהן חטין שניהן כוסמין פטורין מפני שהן מקפידות על עירובן כלומר רוצין לחלקן : ובזמן שהקבין של אשה אחת מין במינו חייב . פי' בזמן שלשה אשה ב' קבין בב' מקומות מפני שלא היתה יכולה ללוש שניהם במקום אחד ונגעו זה בזה . פי' ונשכו זה בזה במין אחד חייבת כדבעינן למימר לקמן אבל אם מקפדת האשה שיש לה מקום ללוש שניהן במקום אחד ולא לשין ביחד אפילו נגעו ואפילו מין אחד פטורין : ב איזהו מין במינו החטין אינן מצטרפין אלא עם הכוסמין פירוש בנשוך

ט א מיי' פ"ו הל' ט טוש"ע שם ס"ג:
ס"א גידין
י ב מיי' שם פ"ח הל' ט טוש"ע שם סעיף ד :
יא ג מיי' פ"ו שם הל' יא טוש"ע י"ד סי' שכב סעיף :
יב ד מיי' פ"ו מהל' בכורים הלכה י טוש"ע י"ד סי' שכב סעיף יא :
יג ה מיי' פ"ט מהל' מעשר הלכה ב ופ"ב מהל' תרומות הלכה יג :
יד ו מיי' פ"ו מהל' בכורים הל' יא טוש"ע י"ד סי' שכד סעיף י :
טו ז מיי' פ"ו שם הלכה יא :
א ח מיי' שם הלכה א טוש"ע י"ד סי' שכו סעיף א :
ב ט מיי' שם הל' ג טוש"ע י"ד סי' שכד סעיף ג :

פירוש הרא"ש

(ז) ואין חייבים עליה חומש אבל הקרן משלם דתשלומי תרומה כפרה נינהו הלכך מפריש תשלומין ונעשה תרומה מספק ומוכרו לכהן : (ח) ולא צריך הכי טעמא אלא מין במינו :

אם כלס

שלא יפריש

נ"ל מעשר

הגהות מהר"י לנדא

משנה ז בר"ש א) ואמרינן בירושלמי מתניתין כו' :

עין משפט נר מצוה

ב א מיי' שם הל' ג' טוש"ע י"ד סי' שכ"ד סעיף ג :
ג ב מיי' פ"ז מהל' בכורים הלכה ה סמג עשין קמא טוש"ע י"ד סי' שכד סעיף ו :
ד ג מיי' שם הלכה ד טוש"ע שם סעיף ה :
ה ד מיי' פ"ז שם הלכה טו טוש"ע י"ד סי' שכו סעי' ה:
ו ה מיי' פ"ז שם הלכה ז טוש"ע שם:
ז ו מיי' שם הל' יג :
ח ז מיי' פ"א מהל' תרומות הל' יז :
ט ח מיי' פ"ה מהל' בכורים הלכה ח סמג עשין קמא טוש"ע י"ד סי' שכב סעיף ד :

מתני'

אינן מצטרפות עם הכל אלא עם הכוסמין השעורין מצטרפות עם הכל חוץ מן החטים א ר' יוחנן בן נורי אומר שאר המינים מצטרפין זה עם זה : ג ב שני קבים וקב אורז או קב תרומה באמצע אינן מצטרפין דבר שנטלה חלתו באמצע מצטרפים שכבר נתחייב בחלה : ד קב חדש וקב ישן שנשכו זה בזה רבי ישמעאל אומר יטול מן האמצע ג וחכמים אוסרים הנוטל חלה מן הקב רבי עקיבא אומר חלה ד וחכמים אומרים אינה חלה : ה שני קבים שנטלה חלתו של זה בפני עצמו ושל זה בפני עצמו חזר ועשאו עיסה אחת ר' עקיבא פוטר ה וחכמים מחייבין נמצא חומרו קולו : ו ו נוטל אדם כדי חלה מעיסה שלא הורמה חלתה (א) לעשותה בטהרה להיות מפריש עליה והולך חלת דמאי עד שתסרח שחלת דמאי נטלת מן הטהור על הטמא ושלא מן המוקף : ז ישראל שהיו אריסין לנכרי בסוריא רבי אליעזר מחייב פירותיהם במעשרות ובשביעית ז ורבן גמליאל פוטר ח רבן גמליאל אומר שתי חלות בסוריא ורבי אליעזר אומר חלה אחת אחזו קולו של רבן גמליאל וקולו של ר"א חזרו לנהוג כדברי רבן

ר"ש

בפ"ק (הל' א) משני ר"י ההוא בבלול והכא בנשוך ובריש כלאים הארכנו : ר' יוחנן בן נורי אומר שאר המינים מצטרפין · כגון שבולת שועל ושיפון דלתנא קמא אין מצטרפין אלא הנך דקתני כדאיתא בירושלמי (הל' ב) אבל שאר מינין לא ואתא ר' יוחנן בן נורי למימר דשאר מינים נמי מצטרפין : ירושלמי (הל' א) מה שיירתה רב הונא אמר אם אומר אתה שיפון מין כוסמין מצטרף עם החטין שבולת שועל מין שעורין אין מצטרפין עם החטין ר' יוחנן בן נורי אמר שאר המינין מצטרפין זה עם זה אית תנאי תני כל המינין מצטרפין זה עם זה על דעתיה דהך תניא ברא מה בין הנשוך מה בין הבלול א"ר יודן אבוי דר' מתניה כשחלקן והוסיף עליהן נשוכין חייבין בלולין פטורים פי' כגון קב חטים וקב שעורין שנשכו וחלקן והוסיף על קב חטים רובע חטים ועל של שעורים רובע שעורים דאי נשוך חבור בהן הרי כבר נתחייבו בחלה ומה שהוסיף פטורה כדאמרינן בירושלמי דפרקין דלעיל (הל' ד) שני ישראלים שעשו ב' קבין וחלקן והוסיף זה על שלו וזה על שלו פטורין שכבר היה להן שעת חובה ונפטרו ובענין זה יש חילוק בין נשוך לבלול דכי קאמר תנא בהא דכל המינים מצטרפין אף בנשוך הייתו להחמיר אבל בלול בין להקל בין להחמיר הלכך נשוכין וחלקן והוסיף חייבין בלולים וחלקן והוסיף פטורין מיהו תימה כשהוסיף על מה שכבר נתחייב למה לא יצטרף לחייב את התוספת כמו שפירשתי בפירקין דלעיל גבי שאור שנטל מעיסה שלא הורמה חלתה ונתנו לעיסה שהורמה חלתה אם יש לו פרנסה ממקום אחר דמפרש בתוספתא שמביא קמח ממקום אחר ומצרפן לחמש רבעים לחייב עליו לפי חשבון וצריך לומר דהכא איירי כשהפריש חלתו ואח"כ הוסיף וכן ההיא בשני ישראלים שעשו שני קבין כשהפרישו החלה והיינו דקאמר שכבר היה להן שעת חובה ונפטרו ע"י הרמת חלה : ג שני קבין · של מין א' מחמשת המינין : וקב אורז או קב תרומה באמצע · ונושך בזה ובזה אפילו הכי אין שני הקבין של מין אחד מצטרפין ודוקא חולין ותרומה דלאו בני חלה נינהו אין מצטרפין אבל קב שעורים מצטרפין עם ב' קבים חטין : שכבר נתחייב בחלה · כלומר אע"ג דהשתא מיהא לאו בר חלה הוא שכבר היה בר חלה מצרף : ירושלמי (הל' ב) ניתני אורז ולא ניתני תרומה אילו תנן אורז ולא תנן תרומה הוו' אמרי' תרומה ע"י שאין נגררת אינו מצטרף כלומר אורז נגרר כדתנן לעיל (פ"ג מ"י) דאם יש בו טעם דגן חייב בחלה והדר מסיק קב אורז אינו מצרף קב תרומה אינו מצרף קב הנכרי אינו מצרף קב מין אחר מצרף קב אשה אחרת מצרף קב חדש מצרף קב דבר שניטלה תרומתו מצרף ר' בון בר חייא בעי קב חלה מהו שיצטרף תני ר' חלפתא בן שאול קב הקדש מצרף קב חלה אינו מצרף מה בין הקדש ובין חלה הקדש ראוי לפדותו ולחייבו חלה אינה ראוי לפדותה ולחייבה : ד יטול מן האמצע · מקום שנושכין זה בזה ונמצא מפריש מזה ומזה ובירושל' (שם) יאות א"ר ישמעאל כוסמים וחטין שני מינין הן על ידי שדומה לו אתמר מצטרף חדש וישן לא כל שכן א"ר הילא טעמא דרבנן כוסמין וחטין שני מינין הן ואין בני אדם טועים לומר שתורמין ומעשרין מזה על זה אבל חדש וישן מין אחד הוא אם אומר את כן אף הוא סבור לומר שתורמין ומעשרין מזה על זה כלומר אם היה נוטל מן האמצע [הלכך] צריך להפריש על כל אחת ואחת מעיסה אחרת שלא הורמה חלתה מחדש על החדש ומישן על הישן : ר"ע אומר חלה · דוקא דיעבד אבל לכתחלה לא דהא לעיל בפ"ב (מ"ג) אר"ע יעשנה בטומאה ואל יעשנה קבין ומפרש בירושלמי ר"ע מדמי לה לפירות שלא נגמרה מלאכתן עבר והפריש מהן תרומה הרי זו תרומה ורבנן מדמו לה לתבואה שלא הביאה שליש עבר והפריש ממנה חלה אינה חלה חזרו לומר אינן דומין לא לפירות שלא נגמרה מלאכתן שאלו נגמרה מלאכתן ולא לתבואה שלא הביאה שליש שאלו הביאו שליש אלא ר"ע מדמי ליה לאומר הרי זו תרומה על פירות הללו לכשיתלשו ונתלשו ורבנן מדמו לה לאומר הרי זו תרומה על פירות הללו המחוברין : ה ר"ע פוטר · משום דקסבר מן הקב אי עבד תרומה הרי כבר הורמה חלתו אבל לרבנן דאינה תרומה השתא הוא דחל עלייהו חיוב ונמצא לרבי עקיבא חומרו קולו ולרבנן קולו חומרו : ו לעשות בטהרה · כגון שנילושה בעריבה שהיא טבולת יום ונוטל כדי חלה ולאחר שהפריש כדי חלה אפי' חוזר ונוגע בעיסה וקורא שם אינו חבור בטבול יום ואפילו נשכו כדתנן בריש טבול יום ונמצא העיסה טהורה וחלה טהורה דאין לטבול יום מגע אלא בחולין : עד שתסרח · מפרש בירושלמי (הלכה ג) עד שתסרח מאוכל אדם ודייקינן עלה הלא אמרה שתורמין מן הרע על היפה כלומר בחלת דמאי : שחלת דמאי ניטלת מטהור על הטמא ושלא מן המוקף . כלומר כמו שהקלו בה הנך קולות כך הקלו בה לתרום מן הרע על היפה ותימה מה היא חלת דמאי אי בלוקח עיסה או לחם מעם הארץ דמפריש חלה משום דשמא לא הפרישה עם הארץ היכן מצינו דנחשדו עמי הארץ על החלה והלא לא נחשדו אתרומה גדולה ומאי שנא חלה דהא דנחשדו על המעשר משום דהוו סברי דלא הוי במיתה משום תרומת מעשר דלאית בה כל זמן שלא קרא עליו שם מעשר ויש לפרש דחלת דמאי היינו חלה שהורמה מתבואה של דמאי שלקח תבואה מע"ה וטחנה ואפאה והפריש ממנה חלה ואותה חלה אסורה באכילה אף לכהן עד שיפריש ממנה מעשר ותרומת מעשר כדין דמאי והא דתנן בפ"ק דדמאי (משנה ג) חלת עם הארץ והמדומע פטורים מן הדמאי הני מילי בעם הארץ מפרישה כההיא דסוף הניזקין שעושין לו בטהרה אבל ישראל שלקח התבואה מן השוק ובא להפריש צריך לתקן גם החלה מן המעשרות ור' אושעיא מחלק כן בפ"ק דדמאי כדפרשי' שם ור' יוחנן פליג התם ואמר היא הדא היא הדא ובפ"ה דדמאי מוקי מתני' בחלת עם הארץ בעושה בטהרה דכיון דטרח לעשות בטהרה א"כ תיקן חלתו כדפרשי' שם הלכך בשאר דוכתי מיחייבה חלת דמאי במעשרות והשתא באותו תיקון שמפריש עליה מעשר ותרומת מעשר כגון שהניח להיות מפריש עליה חלות שלו והולך ומפריש עד שתסרח דהקלו חכמים לתרום מן הרע על היפה ומן הטהור על הטמא ושלא מן המוקף בחלת דמאי אע"פ שלא הקלו בדמאי עצמו כדמוכח בפ"ק דחולין (דף ו:) גבי ר' מאיר דאכל עלה של ירק דמוקי לה רבינו תם בדמאי ואמרינן עלה התם דלא נחשדו חברים לתרום שלא מן המוקף וכי תימא היכי אתרמי שהפריש את החלה עד שלא עישר את הדמאי זימנין דמתרמי הכי כההיא דאמר (דמאי פ"ג משנה א) מאכילים את העניים דמאי והכהן שאוכל את החלה זקוק לעשר אם הוא עשיר : ירושל' (שם) תני תרומת מעש' של דמאי איתא חמי תרומת מעשר של ודאי ניטלת מטהור על הטמא תרומת מעשר של דמאי לא כל שכן א"ר יוסי בספק תרומה גדולה אנן קיימין ספק הפריש מהן תרומה ספק לא הפריש וכדאתמר (דמאי פרק ה משנה י"א) מן הודאי על הדמאי תרומה ולא תאכל עד שיוציא עליה תרומה ומעשר ואמר מן הדמאי על הדמאי כן אמר רבי שמעון בר בסנא כאן ברוצה לאוכלה כאן ברוצה לשורפה פירוש תני תרומת מעשר של דמאי ברייתא היא דקתני שתרומת מעשר של דמאי ניטלת מן הטהור על הטמא איתא חמי קושיא היא כלו' בוא וראה איך יתכן זה תרומת מעשר של ודאי ניטלת מן הטהור על הטמא כמו שפירשנו בריש פרק ב' דתרומות ומשני רבי יוסי דהך ברייתא דקתני תרומת מעשר של דמאי לאו דוקא אלא בספק תרומה גדולה דנסתפק על סאה אחת אם הרים ממנו תרומה גדולה או לא והפריש עליו מן הדמאי דהשתא צריך לחזור ולתקן מספק מה שהפריש ונוה שחוזר ומפריש יכול לתרום מן הטהור על הטמא דאקילו ביה רבנן משום דאוקי טבל בחזקתו וזהו כעין שפירשנו חלת דמאי דמתני' ושמא ברייתא גופה אמתניתי' קיימא לפרושי בחלת דמאי לאו דוקא ופריך ואמר מן הדמאי על הדמאי כן כלו' מאי איריא מן הודאי על הדמאי לא יאכל עד שיפריש עליו תרומה ומעשר משנה היא בסוף פרק חמישי דדמאי אפילו מדמאי על הדמאי נמי כגון שלקח משני עמי הארץ דאם עישר משל זה על של זה צריך לחזור ולעשר מה שעישר דשמא זה הפריש וזה לא הפריש ומשני כאן ברוצה לאכול אפילו מדמאי על הדמאי אבל ברוצה לשרוף כגון שמן העומד להדליק ואין חושש לאכלו לא החמירו בדמאי על הדמאי ולהוציא עליו תרומת מעשר בדמאי הקלו : עוד ירושלמי בפרק שני דערלה (הל' א) רבי יונה בעי ולמה לא תנינן חלת דמאי כגון דתנינא חלת ודאי לא ניתני חלת דמאי והתני תרומה ותרומת מעשר דמאי רבי חנינא בשם שמואל שמע מינה דמאי צריך חלה א"ל ר' חייא אינו נוטל דמים מן השבט א"ל כן אמר שמואל שנוטל דמים מן השבט ר' מנא א"ר יוסי אינו נוטל דמים מן השבט למחר הוא מביא ודאי ואומר דמאי הן כדי ליטול ממנו דמים ר' יוחנן שאל מנא נהיגין אתון מפקין חלה מן דמאי אמר לו כן אמר שמואל אחוי דר' ברכיה בשעת שגזרו על הדמאי רוב עמי הארץ היו מפרישין אותו לתוך בתיהם פירוש הסיא חלת דמאי (א) בלוקח עיסה או לחם (ב) מעם הארץ אי חשיב כחלה אי לא [וקשה א] מאי בעיין (מתני') מאי מספקת לי' לר' יוחנן מתני' היא ואי משום דהוי' פלוגתא דבית שמאי ובית הלל כדפרשינן בפ"ה דדמאי (ג) דבית הלל פוטרי' הא על כורחי' לר' יוחנן פליגי במגבל עיסתו בטהרה דהא איהו מוקי מתני' (ד) בחלת עם הארץ במגבל עיסתו בטהרה כמו שפירשתי שם : ז מחייב פירותיהן . מפרש בירושל' (הל' ד') דקנס קנסן ר' אליעזר ושמא לפי שהיו אריסין לנכרי אי נמי שלא ישתקעו בסוריא : קולו של רבן גמליאל · דפוטר מן המעשר (ב) : וקולו של ר' אליעזר . דאמר חלה אחת (ג) : והזרו לנהוג כדברי ר"ג בשתיהן · משום דאמרינן

(א) נ"ל כלומר . (ב) הניקה . (ג) נ"ל הא ב"ה פוטרין וי"ל דעל כורחי' לר"י וכו' . (ד) נ"ל דהלת .

ר"מ

מינין והם שבולת שועל וכוסמין ושיפון והלכה כר' יוחנן בן נורי : ג כבר קדם לנו כי האורז והתרומה אינן חייבין בחלה וזהו כשהן נשכין זו בזו ולא יצטרך לשנות לך ענין אמרם קביים שיעור חלה כי כבר זכרנוהו : ד וחכמים אוסרים . נאמר על העיקר שקדם במסכת תרומות (פ"א מ"ה) אין מפרישין מן החדש על הישן ומן הישן על החדש : ואמר מן הקב רוצה בו פחות משיעור חלה לדעת חכמים אבל בית שמאי אומר מקב חלה כמו שיתבאר בעדיות ונטה ר' עקיבא לדעת שמאי מעט והלכה כחכמים : ה ר' עקיבא פוטר על העיקר שקדם לך מדעתו כי מי שהוציא חלה מקב אחד נקראת חלה וחכמים מחייבין לפי שהם אומרים במי שהוציאה מקב אחד אינה חלה : נמצא חומרו קולו . חזר על דעת ר"ע לפי שחומרא שהחמיר ואמר בחלה שהוציא מקב אחד קדש ואסורה לזרים הכריחו לומר בשני קבים הנזכרים בכאן פטורה מן החלה וזו היא קולא : ו אומר בכאן שלוקח אדם שיעור מן העיסה והוא טהור ומניחו להיות חלה על עיסות אחרות שילוש מן הדמאי אפי' יהיו אותן העיסות טמאות לפי שהעיקר אצלנו מה שזכר חלת דמאי ניטלת מן הטהור על הטמא ושלא מן המוקף ואמר עד שתסרח חוזר על כדי חלה שהוציא בטהרה לפי שהוא מפריש עליה עד שתסרח והפסד ולא תהיה ראויה לאכילת אדם : ז כבר קדם לנו כי סוריא הם הארצות שכבש דוד שלא מארץ ישראל וכבר בארנו במסכת דמאי (פ"ו מי"א) שפירות סוריא אינן חייבות במעשרות אלא למי שלקט אותם פירות מקרקע שלו ואחוזתו ובארנו טעם בזה ואומר בכאן שאם היו ישראל ונכרי שותפין בקרקע מארץ סוריא ר"א מחייב אותם במעשרות כי סוריא לדעתו כמו א"י בזה הענין כיון שיש לו שותפות בקרקע ונתחייב במעשרות רבן גמליאל פוטר לפי שהיא אצלו קרוב מחוצה לארץ ואינו חייב במעשרות עד שיהיה הקרקע כולו שלו ולא יהיה לנכרי חלק בו כמו שבארנו במסכת דמאי : ומה שאמר ר"ג שתי חלות בסוריא . נמשך אחר עיקרו כי סוריא דיניה קרובים מדיני חוצה לארץ וחייב אדם להוציא בה שתי חלות מן העיסה כמו שהוא חייב בחוצה לארץ האחת תשרף מפני שהיא טמאה לפי שהיא כחוצה לארץ והשני תנתן לכהן כדי שלא תשתכח תורת חלה מישראל כמו שנתבאר לקמן ועוד יתבאר זה במקומות כי עפר חוצה לארץ שורפין עליו תרומה : ורבי אליעזר אומר חלה אחת . לפי שסוריא אצלו כמו ארץ ישראל ברוב הדינים ואינו סובר שעפרה מטמא כמו חוצה לארץ על כן אינה חייבת אלא בחלה אחת והנהיג העם זמן לקולא כשתי הדעות והוא שהיו מחייבים

פירוש הרא"ש

פ"ד (א) לעשות' בטהרה כגון עיסה שנילושה בעריבה טבולת יום נוטל ממנה כדי חלה ומניחתה על העיסה ואח"כ קורא לה שם אבל אם היה קורא לה שם קודם נטילתה מן העיסה נטמאת החלה כיון שכל העיסה גוש אחד ה"ל כאילו נגעה בחלה בעריבה אבל אחר שהפריש החלה מן העיסה אפילו הניחה על העיסה ונשכה בה לא הוי חיבור כדתנן בריש מסכת טבול יום ואם בא לתקן בחלה זו עיסות דמאי שכל עיסות שילוש שיקבע חלתן מזו העיסה יכול לעשות אותה כן עד שתסרח אותה העיסה מאוכל אדם וכו' : (ב) כדין ח"ל: (ג) כדין א"י:

הגהות מהר"י לנדא

פרק ד מ"ו בר"ש א] וקשה מאי בעיין מתני'. נ"ה מאי מספקא לר"י :

פי' מהר"י בן מלכי צדק

וכן השעורין מצטרפין עם הכל בנשוך חוץ מן החטין והני מילי בנשוך אבל בבלול כולן מצטרפין : ג שני קבין וקב אורז וכו' . פי' קב עיסת חטין מיכן וקב עיסת חטין מצד אחר וקב ארז באמצע או קב תרומה באמצע אינן מצטרפין להתחייב בחלה . ואקשינן וניתני ארוז ולא ניתני תרומה ואנא אמינא הואיל וארוז מפסיק תרומה נמי מפסקא ואמרי איצטריך דאילו תנינן ארוז ולא תנינן תרומה הוינן אמרין ארוז על ידי שאינן ממינן מפסיק אבל תרומה שהיא ממינן אימא לא קמ"ל תרומה וכו' : דבר שנטלה חלתו באמצע מצטרפין . פי' קב מיכן וקב מיכן וקב עיסה שהורמה חלתה עומד באמצע מצטרפין פי' שכבר נתחייב בחלה . פי' והן שנושכות כולן זו לזו כגון ככרים : ד קב חדש וקב ישן שנגעו זה בזה ר' ישמעאל אומר יטול מן האמצע חלה כלומר מן המוקף שכבר נצטרפו . מאי טעמא דר' ישמעאל גמר מכוסמין וחטין כוסמין וחטין הלא ב' מיני נינהו ועל שהן דומין מצטרפין חדש וישן לא כ"ש ורבנן דאסרין למעבד הכי אמרי לך לא דמי דכוסמין וחטין ב' מינין הן ואין בני אדם טועין לומר שתורמין ומעשרין מזה על זה ולכך מצטרפין לענין חלה . אבל חדש וישן מין אחד הן אם את אומר כן שיטול מן האמצע אף הוא סבור לומר שתורמין ומעשרין מזה על זה פי' וכיצד יעשה אליבא דרבנן מכל מקום נפסלו לחלה ומסתבר דמייתי חדש ומשלים על החדש כדי חיוב חלה ומייתי ישן ומשלים על הישן כדי חיוב חלה : ה נוטל אדם מעיסה שלא הורמה חלתה לעשותה בטהרה . פי' כגון שלש עיסה בעריבה שהיא טבולת יום ועתה אם קורא שם חלה בעריבה נמצא החלה טמאה דטבול יום פוסל את התרומה . מה יעשה נוטל כדי חלה . פי' מסיים כשיעור החלה כדאוקמה לעיל ריש לקיש ואינו קורא עליה שם כדי שלא לעשות החלה בטהרה שטבול יום אינו פוסל את החולין ואחר כך אותו שסיים מפריש חלה על העיסה ונמצאת החלה טהורה והעיסה טהורה : ובדמאי עד שתסרח . פירוש ובעיסת דמאי יכול ליתן מה שנטל לשם חלה עד שתסרח מאוכל אדם ולא מאוכל הכלב דאע"ג דאין תורמין מן הרע על היפה. הני מילי בודאי אבל בדמאי שרי שחלת דמאי נטלת מן הטהור על הטמא ושלא מן המוקף הואיל ואית בה האי קולא אית בה נמי האי קולא שתורמין מן הרע על היפה בדמאי לכך עד שתסרח וצריכה לפנים : ז רבן גמליאל אומר שתי חלות בסוריא וכו'. אחזו קולו של ר' אליעזר לחלה וקולו של רבן גמליאל למעשר חזרו לנהוג וכו' יש לומר על כן חזרו דתניא לעולם כבית הלל. והרוצה לעשות כבית שמאי עושה כקוליהן וכחומריהן. אבל העושה כקולי בית שמאי וכקולי בית הלל רשע כחומרי בית שמאי וכחומרי בית הלל עליו הכתוב אומר והכסיל בחשך הולך. ומעיקרא דמדנג לא שמיע להו ובתר דשמיעא להו

NOT RECKONED TOGETHER WITH ANY [SPECIES][7] OTHER THAN WITH SPELT; BARLEY IS RECKONED TOGETHER WITH ALL [SPECIES] EXCEPT WHEAT. R. JOḤANAN B. NURI SAID, THE REST OF THE SPECIES[8] ARE RECKONED TOGETHER ONE WITH ANOTHER.[9]

MISHNAH 3. [IF THERE ARE TWO DOUGHS FROM] TWO
a [SEPARATE] ḲABS,[1] AND [DOUGH FROM] A ḲAB OF RICE,[2] OR [FROM] A ḲAB OF TERUMAH[3] [LYING] BETWEEN,[4] THEY ARE NOT RECKONED TOGETHER;[5] [IF THERE WAS] A THING [VIZ., DOUGH] FROM WHICH ḤALLAH HAD BEEN TAKEN[6] [LYING] BETWEEN, THEY ARE RECKONED TOGETHER, SINCE IT[7] HAD ALREADY [ONCE] BEEN SUBJECT TO ḤALLAH.[8]

MISHNAH 4. [IF DOUGH FROM] A ḲAB OF 'NEW' [CORN],[9] AND [DOUGH FROM] A ḲAB OF 'OLD' [CORN][9] STUCK ONE WITH THE OTHER,[10] R. ISHMAEL SAID: LET HIM TAKE [ḤALLAH] FROM THE MIDDLE,[11] BUT THE SAGES PROHIBIT.[12] IF ONE HAS TAKEN ḤALLAH FROM [DOUGH MADE OUT OF] ONE ḲAB,
b R. AKIBA SAYS: IT IS ḤALLAH,[1] BUT THE SAGES SAY: IT IS NOT ḤALLAH.[2]

MISHNAH 5. [IF ONE HAS] TWO [SEPARATE] ḲABS [OF DOUGH][3] FROM ONE OF WHICH ḤALLAH HAD BEEN TAKEN SEPARATELY, AND FROM THE OTHER [TOO,] SEPARATELY, AND HE WENT BACK [TO THEM] AND MADE [OF] THEM ONE DOUGH, R. AKIBA DECLARES IT EXEMPT,[4] BUT THE SAGES

(7) Of the five kinds of grain, v. *supra* I, 1. (8) Enumerated *supra* I, 1. (9) The question as to which species combine with which to form a minimum subject to *ḥallah*, arises only when the doughs touch or stick to one another; if any two or more species (liable to *ḥallah*) have *mingled*, either in the flour or in the kneading, they are without question 'reckoned together' (T.J.).

a (1) Both of one species which is liable to *ḥallah*. (2) A species not liable to *ḥallah*. (3) Which, as a priestly perquisite, is not liable to *ḥallah*. (4) And sticking to the two on either side. (5) Because the connecting intervening piece of dough, whether it is of rice or *terumah*, is one not liable to *ḥallah*. T.J. explains the necessity for instancing both rice and *terumah*: (*a*) if rice only had been mentioned, it might have been thought that just rice is not to be 'reckoned in' for the reason that it is a species *ab initio* not subject to *ḥallah*, but that *terumah*, which is of course of grain, that is in itself liable to *ḥallah*, should be reckoned in; (*b*) if *terumah* alone had been mentioned it might have been inferred, that just *terumah* is not 'reckoned in' for the reason that an admixture of it to other dough, by making the whole *Medumma'* (v. I, 4, n. 8), renders it exempt from *ḥallah*, but that rice, an admixture of which to grain does not invariably impair the liability of the dough to *ḥallah* (v. III, 7 and 10), might be 'reckoned in'. (6) And therefore no longer liable to *ḥallah*. (7) The piece of dough in the middle. (8) Constituting in this respect a category different from the preceding cases where the dough lying in the middle had never been liable to *ḥallah*. (9) According to Ter. I, 5, it is unavailing to separate *terumah* from one year's corn an amount large enough to cover the requirements for *terumah* in respect also of either the preceding or the following year's corn. The same rule applies *mutatis mutandis* to taking *ḥallah*. (10) Lit., 'bit one with the other', cf. *supra* II, 4, n. 2. (11) Where the two doughs run into one another, thus taking some from each. (12) The prohibition of the Sages is directed against taking, in these circumstances, just one *ḥallah*-portion even if it be out of the place where both doughs coalesce. The fact that the two doughs have stuck together certainly renders them jointly subject to *ḥallah*, but since one is of 'old' and the other of 'new' corn, the statutory proportion (1/24th or 1/48th v. *supra* II, 7) must be taken separately from each dough.

b (1) I.e., if subsequently the *ḳab* was increased to $1^1/_4$ *ḳab*, whereby the portion that had erroneously been taken off is deemed as having been only prematurely separated and retroactively made into *ḥallah* with all due sanctity attaching thereto. (2) Since at the time a portion was taken off the dough was, owing to the small amount thereof, not subject to *ḥallah*, the separation of the dough portion was gratuitous and entirely without effect on its non-sacred (*ḥullin*) status. (3) I.e., neither is large enough to be subject to *ḥallah*. (4) Since in accordance with the view enunciated in his name in Mishnah 4, the dough-portions taken separately from each of the doughs and, erroneously, but in good faith—intended as *ḥallah*, have been validated as such by the subsequent addition of the other dough.

◁ *For the continuation of the English translation of this page see overleaf.*

עין משפט
נר מצוה

ב א מיי' שם הל"ג' טוש"ע י"ד סי' שכ"ד סעיף ב :

ג ב מיי' פ"ז מהל' בכורים הלכה ה סמג עשין קמא טוש"ע י"ד סי' שכד סעיף ו :

ד ג מיי' שם הלכה ד טוש"ע שם סעיף ה :

ה ד מיי' פ"ו שם הלכה טו טוש"ע י"ד סי' שכו סעי' ה:

ו ה מיי' פ"ז שם הלכה ז טוש"ע שם:

ז ו מיי' שם הל' יג :

ח ז מיי' פ"א מהל' תרומות הל' יז :

ט ח מיי' פ"ה מהל' בכורים הלכה ח סמג עשין קמא טוש"ע י"ד סי' שכב סעיף ד :

אינן מצטרפות עם הכל אלא עם הכוסמין השעורין מצטרפות עם הכל חוץ מן החטים ר' יוחנן בן נורי אומר שאר המינים מצטרפין זה עם זה: ג שני קבים וקב אורז או קב תרומה באמצע אינן מצטרפין דבר שנטלה חלתו באמצע מצטרפים שכבר נתחייב בחלה: ד קב חדש וקב ישן שנשכו זה בזה רבי ישמעאל אומר יטול מן האמצע וחכמים אוסרים הנוטל חלה מן הקב רבי עקיבא אומר חלה וחכמים אומרים אינה חלה: ה שני קבים שנטלה חלתו של זה בפני עצמו ושל זה בפני עצמו חזר ועשאו עיסה אחת ר' עקיבא פוטר וחכמים מחייבין נמצא חומרו קולו: ו נוטל אדם כדי חלה מעיסה שלא הורמה חלתה (א) לעשותה בטהרה להיות מפריש עליה והולך חלת דמאי עד שתסרח שחלת דמאי נטלת מן הטהור על הטמא ושלא מן המוקף: ז ישראל שהיו אריסין לנכרי בסוריא רבי אליעזר מחייב פירותיהם במעשרות ובשביעית ורבן גמליאל פוטר רבן גמליאל אומר שתי חלות בסוריא ורבי אליעזר אומר חלה אחת אחזו קולו של רבן גמליאל וקולו של ר"א חזרו לנהוג כדברי רבן

ר"ש

בפ"ק (הל' א) מתני ר"י ההוא בבלול והכא בנשוך וברים כלאים הארכנו : ר' יוחנן בן נורי אומר שאר המינים מצטרפין · כגון שבולת שועל ושיפון דלתנא קמא אין מצטרפין אלא הנך דקתני כדאיתא בירושלמי (הל' ב) אבל שאר מינין לא ואתא ר' יוחנן בן נורי למימר דשאר מינים נמי מצטרפין : ירושלמי (הל' א) מה שייריתה רב הונא אמר אם אומר אתה שיפון מין כוסמין מצטרף עם החטין שבולת שועל מין שעורין אין מצטרפין עם החטין ר' יוחנן בן נורי אמר שאר המינין מצטרפין זה עם זה אית תנאי תני כל המינין מצטרפין זה עם זה על דעתיה דהך תניא ברא מה בין הנשוך מה בין הבלול א"ר יודן אבוי דר' מתניה כשחלקן והוסיף עליהן נשוכין חייבין בלולין פטורים פי' כגון קב חטים וקב שעורין שנשכו וחלקן והוסיף על קב חטים רובע חטים ועל של שעורים רובע שעורים דאי נשוך חבור בהן הרי כבר נתחייבו בחלה ומה שהוסיף פטורה כדאמרינן בירושלמי דפרקין דלעיל (הל' ד) שני ישראלים שעשו ב' קבין וחלקן והוסיף זה על שלו וזה על שלו פטורין שכבר היה להן שעת חובה ונפטרו ובענין זה יש חילוק בין נשוך לבלול דכי קאמר תנא בהא דכל המינים מצטרפין אף בנשוך היינו להחמיר אבל בלול בין להקל בין להחמיר הלכך נשוכין וחלקן והוסיף חייבין בלולים וחלקן והוסיף פטורין מיהו תימה כשהוסיף על מה שכבר נתחייב למה לא יצטרף לחייב את התוספת כמו שפירשתי בפירקין דלעיל גבי שאור שנפל מעיסה שלא הורמה חלתה ונתנו לעיסה שהורמה חלתה אם יש לו פרנסה ממקום אחר דמפרש בתוספתא שמביא קמח ממקום אחר ומצרפן לחמש רבעים לחייב עליו לפי חשבון וצריך לומר דהכא איירי כשהפריש חלתו ואח"כ הוסיף וכן ההיא בשני ישראלים שעשו שני קבין כשהפרישו החלה והיינו דקאמר שכבר היה להן שעת חובה ונפטרו ע"י הרמת חלה : ג שני קבין · של מין א' מחמשת המינין : וקב אורז או קב תרומה באמצע · ונושך בזה ובזה אפילו הכי אין שני הקבין של מין אחד מצטרפין ודוקא חולין ותרומה דלאו בני חלה נינהו אין מצטרפין אבל קב שעורים מצטרפין עם ב' קבים חטין : שכבר נתחייב בחלה· כלומר אע"ג דהשתא מיהא לאו בר חלה הוא שכבר היה בר חלה מצרף : ירושלמי (הל' ב) ניתני אורז ולא ניתני תרומה אילו תנן אורז ולא תנן תרומה וכו' אמרי' תרומה ע"י שאין נגררת אינו מצטרף כלומר אורז נגרר כדתנן לעיל (פ"ג מ"י) דאם יש בו טעם דגן חייב בחלה והדר מסיק קב אורז אינו מצרף קב תרומה אינו מצרף קב הנכרי אינו מצרף קב מין אחר מצרף קב אשה אחרת מצרף קב חדש מצרף קב דבר שניטלה תרומתו מצרף ר' בון בר חייא בעי קב חלה מהו שיצטרף תני ר' חלפתא בן שאול קב הקדש מצרף קב חלה אינו מצרף מה בין הקדש ובין חלה הקדש ראוי לפדותו ולחייבו חלה אינה ראוי לפדותה ולחייבה : ד יטול מן האמצע· מקום שנושכין זה בזה ונמצא מפריש מזה ומזה ובירושל' (שם) יאות א"ר ישמעאל כוסמים וחטין שני מינין הן על ידי שדומה לו אתמר מצטרף חדש וישן לא כל שכן א"ר הילא טעמא דרבנן כוסמין וחטין שני מינין הן ואין בני אדם טועים לומר שתורמין ומעשרין מזה על זה אבל חדש וישן מין אחד הוא אם אומר את כן אף הוא סבור לומר שתורמין ומעשרין מזה על זה כלומר אם היה נוטל מן האמצע [הלכך] צריך להפריש על כל אחת ואחת מעיסה אחרת שלא הורמה חלתה מחדש על החדש ומישן על הישן : ר"ע אומר חלה · דוקא דיעבד אבל לכתחלה לא דהא לעיל בפ"ב (מ"ג) א"ר"ע יעשנה בטומאה ואל יעשנה קבין ומפרש בירושלמי ר"ע מדמי לה לפירות שלא נגמרה מלאכתן עבר והפריש מהן תרומה הרי זו תרומה ורבנן מדמו לה לתבואה שלא הביאה שליש עבר והפריש ממנה חלה אינה חלה חזרו לומר אינן דומין לא לפירות שלא נגמרה מלאכתן שאלו נגמרה מלאכתן ולא לתבואה שלא הביאה שליש שאלו הביאו שליש אלא ר"ע מדמי ליה לאומר הרי זו תרומה על פירות הללו לכשיתלשו ונתלשו ורבנן מדמו לה לאומר הרי זו תרומה על פירות הללו המחוברין : ה ר"ע פוטר · משום דקסבר מן הקב אי עבד תרומה הרי כבר הורמה חלתו אבל לרבנן דאינה תרומה השתא הוא דחל עלייהו חיוב ונמצא לרבי עקיבא חומרו קולו ולרבנן קולו חומרו : ו לעשות בטהרה · כגון שנילושה בעריבה שהיא טבולת יום ונוטל כדי חלה ולאחר שהפריש כדי חלה אפי' חוזר ונוגע בעיסה וקורא שם אינו חבור בטבול יום ואפילו נשכו כדתנן בריש טבול יום ונמצא העיסה טהורה וחלה טהורה דאין לטבול יום מגע אלא החולין : עד שתסרח · מפרש בירושלמי (הלכה ג) עד שתסרח מאוכל אדם ודייקינן עלה הדא אמרה שתורמין מן הרע על היפה כלומר בחלת דמאי : שחלת דמאי ניטלת מטהור על הטמא ושלא מן המוקף . כלומר כמו שהקלו בה הנך קולות כך הקלו בה לתרום מן הרע על היפה ותימה מה היא חלת דמאי אי בלוקח עיסה או לחם מעם הארץ דמפריש חלה משום דשמא לא הפרישה עם הארץ היכן מצינו דנחשדו עמי הארץ על החלה והלא לא נחשדו אתרומה גדולה ומאי שנא חלה דהא דנחשדו על המעשר משום דהוו סברי דלא הוי במיתה משום תרומת מעשר דאית בה כל זמן שלא קרא עליו שם מעשר ויש לפרש דחלת דמאי היינו חלה שהורמה מתבואה של דמאי שלקח תבואה מע"ה וטחנה ואפאה והפריש ממנה חלה ואותה חלה אסורה באכילה אף לכהן עד שיפריש ממנה מעשר ותרומת מעשר כדין דמאי והא דתנן בפ"ק דדמאי (משנה ג) חלת עם הארץ והמדומע פטורים מן הדמאי הני מילי בשעם הארץ מפרישה כההיא דסוף הניזקין שעושין לו בטהרה אבל ישראל שלקח תבואה מן השוק ובא להפריש צריך לתקן גם החלה מן המעשרות ור' אושעיא מחלק כן בפ"ק דדמאי כלפרשי' שם ור' יוחנן פליג התם ואמר היא הדא היא הדא ובפ"ה דדמאי מוקי מתני' בחלת עם הארץ בעושה בטהרה דכיון דטרח לעשות בטהרה א"כ תיקן חלתו כלפרשי' שם הלכך בשאר דוכתי מיחייבה חלת דמאי במעשרות והשתא באותו תיקון שמפריש עליה מעשר ותרומת מעשר כגון שהניח להיות מפריש עליה חלות שלו והולך ומפריש עד שתסרח דהקלו חכמים לתרום מן הרע על היפה ומן הטהור על הטמא ושלא מן המוקף בחלת דמאי אע"פ שלא הקלו בדמאי עצמו כדמוכח בפ"ק דחולין (דף ו:) גבי ר' מאיר דאכל עלה של ירק דמוקי לה רבינו תם בדמאי ואמרינן עלה התם דלא נחשדו חברים לתרום שלא מן המוקף וכי תימא היכי אתרמי שהפריש את החלה עד שלא עישר את הדמאי זימנין דמתרמי הכי כההיא דאמר (דמאי פ"ג משנה א) מאכילים את העניים דמאי והכהן שאוכל את החלה זקוק לעשר אם הוא עשיר : ירושל' (שם) תני תרומת מעשר של דמאי איתא חמי תרומת מעשר של ודאי ניטלת מטהור על הטמא תרומת מעשר של דמאי לא כל שכן א"ר יוסי בספק תרומה גדולה אנן קיימין ספק הפרים מהן תרומה ספק לא הפרים וכדאתמר (דמאי פרק ה משנה י"א) מן הודאי על הדמאי תרומה ולא תאכל עד שיוציא עליה תרומה ומעשר ואמר מן הדמאי על הדמאי כן אמר רבי שמעון בר בסנא כאן ברוצה לאוכלה כאן ברוצה לשורפה פירוש תני תרומת מעשר של דמאי ברייתא היא דקתני שתרומת מעשר של דמאי ניטלת מן הטהור על הטמא איתא חמי קושיא היא כלו' בוא וראה איך יתכן זה תרומת מעשר של ודאי ניטלת מן הטהור על הטמא כמו שפירשנו בריש פרק ב' דתרומות ומשני רבי יוסי דהך ברייתא דקתני תרומת מעשר של דמאי לאו דוקא אלא בספק תרומה גדולה דנסתפק על שלה אחת אם הרים ממנו תרומה גדולה או לא והפריש עליו מן הדמאי דהשתא צריך לחזור ולהתקן מספק מה שהפריש ונוה שחוזר ומפריש יכול לתרום מן הטהור על הטמא דאקילו ביה רבנן משום דאוקי טבל בחזקתו וזהו כעין שפירשנו חלת דמאי דמתני' ושמא ברייתא גופה אמתניתי' קיימא לפרושי בחלת דמאי לאו דוקא ופריך ואמר מן הדמאי על הדמאי כן כלו' מאי איריא מן הודאי על הדמאי לא יאכל עד שיפריש עליו תרומה ומעשר משנה היא בסוף פרק חמישי דדמאי אפילו מדמאי על הדמאי נמי כגון שלקח משני עמי הארץ דאם עישר משל זה על של זה צריך לחזור ולעשר מה שעישר דשמא זה הפריש וזה לא הפריש ומשני כאן ברוצה לאכול אפילו מדמאי על הדמאי אבל ברוצה לשרוף כגון שמן העומד להדליק ואין חושש לאכלו לא החמירו בדמאי על הדמאי ולהוציא עליו תרומת מעשר דבדמאי הקלו : עוד ירושלמי בפרק שני דערלה (הל' א) רבי יונה בעי ולמה לא תנינן חלת דמאי כגון דתנינא חלת ודאי לא ניתני חלת דמאי והתני תרומה ותרומת מעשר דמאי רבי חנינא בשם שמואל שמע מינה דמאי צריך הלה א"ל ר' חייה אינו נוטל דמים מן השבט א"ל כן אמר שמואל שנוטל דמים מן השבט ר' מנא א"ר יוסי אינו נוטל דמים מן השבט למחר הוא מביא ודאי ואומר דמאי הן כדי ליטול ממנו דמים ר' יוחנן שאל מנא נהיגין אתון מפקין חלה מן דמאי אמר לו כן אמר שמואל אחוי דר' ברכיה בשעת שגזרו על הדמאי רוב עמי הארץ היו מכניסין אותו לתוך בתיהם פירוש ההיא חלת דמאי (א) בלוקח עיסה או לחם (ב) מעם הארץ אי חשיב כחלה אי לא [וקשה א] מאי בעיין (מתני') מאי מספקא לי' לר' יוחנן מתני' היא ואי משום דהוי' פלוגתא דבית שמאי ובית הלל כלפרשינן בפ"ה דדמאי (ג) דבית הלל פוטרי' הא על כורחי' לר' יוחנן פליגי במגבל עיסתו בטהרה דהא איהו מוקי מתני' (ד) בחלת עם הארץ במגבל עיסתו בטהרה כמו שפירשתי שם : ז מחייב פירותיהן . מפרש בירושל' (הל' ד') דקנס קנסן ר' אליעזר ושמא לפי שהיו אריסין לנכרי אי נמי שלא ישתקעו בסוריא : קולו של רבן גמליאל · דפוטר מן המעשר (ב) : וקולו של ר' אליעזר . דאמר חלה אחת (ג) : והחזרו לנהוג כדברי ר"ג בשתיהן · משום דאמרינן

(א) צ"ל כלומר . (ב) הניקח . (ג) צ"ל הא ב"ה פוטרין וי"ל דעל כורחי' לר"י וכו' . (ד) צ"ל דחלת .

ר"מ

מינין והם שבולת שועל וכוסמין ושיפון והלכה כר' יוחנן בן נורי : ג כבר קדם לנו כי האורז והתרומה אינן חייבין בחלה וזהו כשהן טשכין זו בזו ולא יצטרך לשנות לך ענין אמרם קביים שיעור חלה כי כבר זכרנוהו : ד וחכמים אוסרים . נאמר על העיקר שקדם במסכת תרומות (פ"א מ"ה) אין מפרישין מן החדש על הישן ומן הישן על החדש : ואמר מן הקב רוצה בו פחות משיעור חלה לדעת חכמים אבל בית שמאי אומר מקב חלה כמו שיתבאר בעדיות ונטה ר' עקיבא לדעת שמאי מעט והלכה כחכמים : ה ר' עקיבא פוטר על העיקר שקדם לך מדעתו כי מי שהוציא חלה מקב אחד נקראת חלה וחכמים מחייבין לפי שהם אומרים במי שהוציאה מקב אחד אינה חלה : נמצא חומרו קולו . חזר על דעת ר"ע לפי שחומרא שהחמיר ואמר בחלה שהוציא מקב אחד קדש ואסרה לזרים הכריחו לומר בשני קבים הנזכרים בכאן פטורה מן החלה וזו היא קולא: ו אומר בכאן שלוקח אדם שיעור מן העיסה והוא טהור ומניחו להיות חלה על עיסות אחרות שילום מן הדמאי אפי' יהיו אותן העיסות טמאות לפי שהעיקר אצלנו מה שזכר חלת דמאי ניטלת מן הטהור על הטמא ושלא מן המוקף ואמר עד שתסרח חוזר על כדי חלה שהוציא בטהרה לפי שהוא מפריש עליה עד שתסרח והפסד ולא תהיה ראויה לאכילת אדם : ז כבר קדם לנו כי סוריא הם הארצות שכבש דוד שלא מארץ ישראל וכבר באר במסכת דמאי (פ"ו מי"א) שפירות סוריא אינן חייבות במעשרות אלא למי שלקט אותם פירות מקרקע שלו ואחוזתו ובארנו טעם בזה ואומר בכאן שאם היו ישראל ונכרי שותפין בקרקע מארץ סוריא ר"א מחייב אותם במעשרות כי סוריא לדעתו כמו א"י בזה הענין כיון שיש לו שותפות בקרקע ונתחייב במעשרות רבן גמליאל פוטר לפי שהיא אצלו קרוב מחוצה לארץ ואינו חייב במעשרות עד שיהיה הקרקע כולו שלו ולא יהיה לנכרי חלק בו כמו שבארנו במסכת דמאי : ומה שאמר ר"ג שתי חלות בסוריא . נמשך אחר עיקרו כי סוריא דיניה קרובים מדיני חוצה לארץ וחייב אדם להוציא בה שתי חלות מן העיסה כמו שהוא חייב בחוצה לארץ האחת תשרף מפני שהיא טמאה לפי שהיא כחוצה לארץ והשני תנתן לכהן כדי שלא תשתכח תורת חלה מישראל כמו שנתבאר לקמן ועוד יתבאר זה במקומות כי עפר חוצה לארץ שורפין עליו תרומה : ורבי אליעזר אומר חלה אחת . לפי שסוריא אצלו כמו ארץ ישראל ברוב הדינים ואינו סובר שעפרה מטמא כמו חוצה לארץ על כן אינה חייבת אלא בחלה אחת והנהיג העם זמן לקולא בשתי הדעות והוא שהיו מחייבים

פי' מהר"י בן מלכי צדק

וכן השעורין מצטרפין עם הכל בנשוך חוץ מן החטין והני מילי בנשוך אבל בבלול כולן מצטרפין : ג שני קבין וקב אורז וכו' . פי' קב עיסת חטין מיכן וקב עיסת חטין מצד אחד וקב אורז באמצע או קב תרומה באמצע אינן מצטרפין להתחייב בחלה . ואקשינן וניתני אורז ולא ניתני תרומה ואנא אמינא הואיל ואורז מפסיק תרומה נמי מפסקא ואמרי איצטריך דאילו תנינן אורז ולא תנינן תרומה הוינן אמרין אורז על ידי שאינן מטינן מפסיק אבל תרומה שהיא מטינן אימא לא קמ"ל תרומה וכו' : דבר שנטלה חלתו באמצע מצטרפין . פי' קב מיכן וקב מיכן וקב עיסה שתורמה חלתה עומד באמצע מצטרפין פי' שכבר נתחייב בחלה . פי' והן שנושכות כולן זו לזו כגון טבם : ד קב חדש וקב ישן שנגעו זה בזה ר' ישמעאל אומר יטול מן האמצע חלה כלומר מן המוקף שכבר נצטרפו. מאי טעמא דר' ישמעאל גמר מכוסמין וחטין כוסמין וחטין הלא ב' מיני נינהו ועל שהן דומין מצטרפין חדש וישן לא כ"ש ורבנן דאמרינן למעבד הכי אמרי לך לא דמי דכוסמין וחטין ב' מינין הן ואין בני אדם טועין לומר שתורמין ומעשרין מזה על זה ולכך מצטרפין לענין חלה . אבל חדש וישן מין אחד הן אם את אומר כן שיטול מן האמצע אף הוא סבור לומר שתורמין ומעשרין מזה על זה פי' וכיצד יעשה אליבא דרבנן מכל מקום נסבלו לחלה ומסתבר דמייתי חדש ומשלים על החדש כדי חיוב חלה ומייתי ישן ומשלים על הישן כדי חיוב חלה : ה נוטל אדם מעיסה שלא הורמה חלתה לעשותה בטהרה . פי' כגון שלש עיסה בעריבה שהיא טבולת יום ועתה אם קורא שם חלה בעריבה נמצא החלה טמאה דטבול יום פוסל את התרומה. מה יעשה נוטל כדי חלה . פי' מסיים כשיעור החלה כדאוקמה לעיל ריש לקיש ואינו קורא עליה שם כדי שלא לעשות החלה בטהרה שטבול יום אינו פוסל את החולין ואחר כך אותו שסיים מפריש חלה על העיסה נמצאת החלה טהורה והעיסה טהורה : ובדמאי עד שתסרח . פירוש ובעיסת דמאי יכול ליתן מה שנטל לשם חלה עד שתסרח מאוכל אדם ולא מאוכל הכלב דאע"ג דאין תורמין מן הרע על היפה בדמאי לכך עד שתסרח

פירוש הרא"ש

פ"ד (א) לעשות' בטהרה כגון עיסה שנילושה בעריבה טבולת יום נוטל ממנה כדי חלה ומניחתה על העיסה ואח"כ קורא לה שם אבל אם היה קורא לה שם קודם נטילתה מן העיסה נטמאת החלה כיון שכל העיסה גוש אחד הי"ל כאילו נגעה החלה בעריבה אבל אחר שהפריש החלה מן העיסה אפילו הניחה על העיסה ונשכה בה לא הוי חיבור כדתנן בריש מסכת טבול יום ואם בא לתקן בחלה זו עיסות דמאי שכל עיסות שילום שיקבע חלתן מזו העיסה יכול לעשות אותה כן עד שתסרח אותה העיסה מאוכל אדם וכו' : (ב) כדין ח"ל: (ג) כדין א"י:

הגהות מהר"י לנדא

פרק ד מ"ו בר"ש א] וקשה מאי בעיין מתני'.

הרע על היפה. הני מילי בודאי אבל בדמאי שרי שחלת דמאי נשלת מן הטהור על הטמא ושלא מן המוקף הואיל ואית בה האי קולא אית בה נמי האי קולא שתורמין מן הרע על היפה בדמאי לכך עד שתסרח
וצריכה לפנים. ז רבן גמליאל אומר שתי חלות בסוריא וכו'. אחזו קולו של ר' אליעזר לחלה וקולו של רבן גמליאל למעשר חזרו לנהוג וכו' יש לומר על כן חזרו דתניא לעולם כבית הלל. והרוצה לעשות כבית
שמאי עושה כקוליהן וכחומריהן. אבל העושה כקולי בית שמאי וכקולי בית הלל רשע כחומרי בית שמאי וכחומרי בית הלל עליו הכתוב אומר והכסיל בחשך הולך. ומעיקרא דנהוג לא שמיע להו ובתר דשמיעא להו

Continuation of translation from previous page as indicated by ◁

DECLARE IT LIABLE.[5] [THUS] IT IS FOUND THAT [THE VERY PROPOSITION[6] GIVING RISE TO] THE STRINGENCY OF THE ONE [RULING][7] IS [THE PROPOSITION THAT GIVES RISE TO] THE LENIENCY OF THE OTHER [RULING].[8]

MISHNAH 6. A MAN MAY TAKE THE REQUISITE AMOUNT FOR ḤALLAH OUT OF A [CLEAN] DOUGH FROM WHICH ḤALLAH HAS NOT [PREVIOUSLY] BEEN TAKEN—[HIS PURPOSE BEING] TO EFFECT IT IN CLEANNESS—BY WAY OF GOING ON SEPARATING [ḤALLAH] THEREFROM IN RESPECT OF [UN-
c CLEAN] DEMAI,[1] UNTIL IT PUTRIFIES, SINCE ḤALLAH IN RESPECT OF DEMAI MAY BE TAKEN FROM CLEAN [DOUGH] IN RESPECT OF UNCLEAN [DOUGH], AND FROM [ONE DOUGH IN RESPECT OF ANOTHER DOUGH] WHICH IS NOT CLOSE TOGETHER.

MISHNAH 7. IF ISRAELITES WERE TENANTS OF GENTILES IN SYRIA,[2] R. ELIEZER DECLARES THEIR PRODUCE SUBJECT
d TO TITHES AND TO [THE LAW OF] THE SEVENTH [YEAR],[1] BUT RABBAN GAMALIEL DECLARES [IT] EXEMPT.[2] RABBAN GAMALIEL SAYS: [ONE IS TO GIVE] TWO ḤALLAH-PORTIONS IN SYRIA,[3] BUT R. ELIEZER SAYS: [ONLY] ONE ḤALLAH-PORTION.[4] THEY[5] ADOPTED THE LENIENT RULING OF RABBAN GAMALIEL,[6] AND THE LENIENT RULING OF R. ELIEZER.[7] EVENTUALLY THEY WENT BACK [ON THIS PRACTICE][8] AND INSTITUTED THE PRACTICE IN ACCORDANCE WITH RABBAN GAMALIEL IN

(5) In accordance with their view, contrary to R. Akiba's, in Mishnah 4. (6) Viz., that of R. Akiba set out *supra* n. 1. (7) I.e., the stringency which results from the application of R. Akiba's view to the case in Mish. 4, where the owner is thereby deprived of the dough-portions which are, in that view, held to have been consecrated by him as *ḥallah*. (8) I.e., the leniency which is the effect of the application of that same view to the case in our Mishnah, inasmuch as here the owner is thereby exempted from giving away a further portion of dough as *ḥallah*.

c (1) Ordinarily *demai* denotes produce with regard to which there is suspicion, inasmuch as it has been obtained from an *'am ha-areẓ*, that it may not have been properly tithed. Here, according to Maim. it means dough with regard to which there is doubt, for the same reason as above, whether *ḥallah* had been separated. Rash and Bert. say it means dough from grain that was *demai* (in the original sense, viz., in respect of tithes). Such corn presumed to have come from an *'am ha-areẓ* was unclean and so, too, the dough made from it. L. reviews and criticizes the above interpretations and finally rejects them as untenable. His own interpretation is, that this Mishnah is concerned with dough bought from a Cuthean (Samaritan) and it is uncertain whether the latter has intended the dough for his own consumption (when, in view of known Samaritan religious scruples, he can be trusted to have separated *ḥallah*), or for sale (when one cannot assume that the Samaritan had separated *ḥallah*, inasmuch as the Samaritan code did not require *ḥallah* to be taken from dough intended for sale). Such dough is thus *demai* (in respect of *ḥallah*), and it is this kind of *demai* that is meant here. Furthermore, a Samaritan's dough is, failing certain knowledge to the contrary, unclean. The dough spoken of first in our Mishnah is also *demai*, but it is clean, either because the Samaritan had, in the presence of an Israelite, undergone ritual ablution from uncleanness immediately prior to preparing the dough, or because the flour had been mixed not with water but with fruit-juice (which does not render dough capable of contracting uncleanness; cf. *supra* II, 2, 56*b* n. d 1). The position then is this: One dough is clean, the other unclean. In ordinary circumstances it is not permitted to take *ḥallah* from clean dough in sufficient quantity to exempt also unclean dough (v. *supra* I, 9), but because in our case both doughs are *demai* in respect of *ḥallah*, it is permitted to do so, as well as to take *ḥallah* from such a dough in sufficient quantity to exempt also other similar doughs without putting them close together. (2) A geographical term denoting territories *outside* the boundaries of the Land of Israel (as delimited in Num. XXXIV) which were captured by King David before he completed the conquest of the Land of Israel proper (Jebus i.e. Zion remained in gentile possession till nearly the end of David's reign; v. II Sam. XXIV). It was agreed that these adjacent territories were of lesser sanctity than the Land proper, but there were differences of opinion as to which of the precepts enjoined for the Land of Israel were applicable also to Syria.

d (1) Since in his view Syria was like the Land of Israel in these matters. In T.J. it is suggested that the intention of R. Eliezer in imposing this obligation was to 'fine' these Israelite tenants in Syria. Rash suggests that the purpose of the proposed fine was to discourage Jews from settling permanently in Syria. The law of the 'Seventh Year' is promulgated in Ex. XXIII, 10-11, Lev. XXV, 1ff and forms the subject of tractate Shebi'ith in our Seder. (2) Because he held that Syria was like the Land of Israel in regard to tithes etc., only if the land (in Syria) on which the produce was grown was the property of Israelites (v. end of chapter) but not when, as here, the latter were merely tenants. (3) One portion to burn, because it is unclean (as everywhere outside the Land), and the other to give to a priest so as to prevent the law of *ḥallah* from being entirely forgotten (v. *infra* 9). (4) Just as in the Land of Israel (v. n. 1). (5) The Jews in Syria. (6) Exempting the produce of Israelite tenants in Syria from tithes and *Shebi'ith*. (7) Demanding from them only one *ḥallah*-portion (instead of two as R. Gamaliel). (8) Because they found that it was considered unworthy, and even wicked, to take advantage of the lenient rulings of two authorities when those rulings arose from opposing principles. The norm was that if you adopt the principle of one authority giving rise to a lenient ruling, you must consistently follow that principle wherever it applies, whether the effect of such application is a leniency or a stringency.

BOTH RESPECTS.[9]

MISHNAH 8. RABBAN GAMALIEL SAYS: THERE ARE THREE TERRITORIAL DIVISIONS[10] WITH REGARD TO [LIABILITY TO]
a ḤALLAH: FROM THE LAND OF ISRAEL TO KEZIB[1]—ONE ḤALLAH-PORTION; FROM KEZIB[2] TO AMANAH[3]—TWO ḤALLAH-PORTIONS: ONE FOR THE FIRE[4] AND ONE FOR THE PRIEST,[5] TO THE ONE FOR THE FIRE THE [RULE OF THE STATUTORY] PROPORTION APPLIES,[6] TO THE ONE FOR THE PRIEST THE [RULE OF THE STATUTORY] PROPORTION DOES NOT APPLY;[7] FROM THE RIVER[1] TO AMANAH AND [THE ZONE] INWARD, TWO ḤALLAH-PORTIONS: ONE FOR THE FIRE AND ONE FOR THE PRIEST, TO THE ONE [INTENDED] FOR THE FIRE THE [RULE OF THE STATUTORY] PROPORTION DOES NOT APPLY,[8] TO THE ONE [INTENDED] FOR THE PRIEST THE [RULE OF THE STATUTORY] PROPORTION APPLIES,[9] AND [A PRIEST] WHO HAS IMMERSED HIMSELF DURING THE DAY [AND HAS TO WAIT TILL SUNSET FOR HIS PURIFICATION TO BE COM-
b PLETE][1] MAY EAT IT.[2] R. JOSE SAYS: ONE DOES NOT REQUIRE IMMERSION.[3] IT IS FORBIDDEN [AS FOOD] TO MEN WHO HAVE AN ISSUE,[4] TO WOMEN WHO HAVE AN ISSUE, TO WOMEN DURING MENSTRUATION,[5] TO WOMEN AFTER CHILDBIRTH,[6] BUT MAY BE EATEN WITH A 'STRANGER' AT THE [SAME] TABLE,[7] AND MAY BE GIVEN TO ANY PRIEST.[8]

MISHNAH 9. THESE, TOO, MAY BE GIVEN TO ANY PRIEST:[9] DEVOTED THINGS,[10] FIRSTLINGS,[11] THE [LAMB SUBSTITUTED
c AS] RANSOM FOR THE FIRSTLING OF AN ASS,[1] THE SHOULDER, THE TWO CHEEKS AND THE MAW,[2] THE FIRST OF THE FLEECE,[3] OIL [FIT ONLY] FOR BURNING,[4] CONSECRATED FOOD [OR-

(9) Lit., 'ways'; i.e., both in the matter of tithes and *Shebi'ith* (where he is lenient) and in that of *ḥallah* (where he is stringent). (10) Lit., 'lands'.

a (1) For these geographical items v. Shebi'ith VI, 1. notes. (2) That zone was authentic Land of Israel by reason of being within the boundaries mentioned in Num. XXXIV, having been occupied in the first conquest, and also reoccupied by the returned Babylonian exiles under Zerubbabel and Ezra, and therefore indubitably subject to the precepts bound up with the sanctity of the Land. (3) A zone within the Pentateuchal boundaries of the Land of Israel and therefore originally holy; but since it had not been reoccupied by those who returned from Babylon, it did not re-assume complete holiness. (4) I.e., to be burnt by the owner, being unclean *ḥallah*. Since this zone was not restored to its original holiness, its *ḥallah* is unclean just as the *ḥallah* in any land outside the Land of Israel. (5) This is not mandatory, but instituted by the authorities to draw attention to the peculiar character of that zone with regard to sanctity. This procedure is to obviate on the one hand the likely erroneous notion that the territory is to be regarded as definitely outside the Land in respect of sanctity, and on the other hand the other mistaken notion that it is to be regarded as completely holy territory. The very contradictoriness of the procedure will stimulate enquiry which will enable people to learn of the special status of the zone. (6) Because this portion is in virtue of that zone having been originally holy and liable to *ḥallah* on Biblical authority—the direction to burn it being due solely to its being unclean, in which circumstances it would have to be burnt even in the Land of Israel proper. (7) Because this portion is only an institution of the Scribes. (8) Less than the minimum may be separated because (*a*) it is on solely Scribal authority and (*b*) because it is to be burnt. (9) This *ḥallah*-portion too is only on Scribal authority, but since it is to be eaten the full amount should be given.

b (1) V. *supra* I, 9, 56*b* n. b 2. The regulations with regard to a person in that state are detailed in the tractate of that name Ṭebul Yom in *Seder Ṭohoroth*. (2) Since this *ḥallah*-portion is on the authority only of the Scribes, the eating thereof is prohibited only to such as are in a state of actual uncleanness by reason of an issue or of menstruation (v. *infra* notes 4-6) but not to anyone unclean through any other cause, or whose cleanness is, as in the case of *ṭebul yom*, in a state of suspense until the end of the day. (3) So that, according to R. Jose, outside the Land, one who has had an issue may eat *ḥallah*. (4) V. Lev. XV, 2-15. (5) V. ibid. 19-30. (6) V. ibid. XII. (7) With consecrated food it is insisted that it should not be eaten by the priest at the same table where a non-priest is eating, lest the latter partake of the consecrated food either by accident or in error. Since the *ḥallah*-portion with which we are here concerned is not scripturally ordained this precaution is not required. (8) Maim. reproduces the T.J. interpretation of 'any priest', viz., 'be it a priest who is a *ḥaber* (i.e., a scholar) or one who is an *'am ha-areẓ* (i.e., an unlearned person)'. Evidently what is meant is: whether the priest be one who takes care to eat consecrated food in cleanness, or one who does not. V. Bert. and Tosef. Yom Tob. Bert. writes as if Maim.'s explanation is at variance with that of the Talmud, whilst Maim. does nothing but reproduce T.J. *verbatim*. (9) V. preceding Mishnah, end n. 8. (10) V. Lev. XXVII, 28. *No devoted thing, a man may devote to the Lord of all that he hath . . . shall be sold or redeemed: every devoted thing is most holy unto the Lord;* Num. XVIII, 14: *Every devoted thing in Israel shall be thine* i.e., the priest's. Since it is to be redeemed with money, the latter may obviously be given to *any* priest without references to the likelihood of his being clean or unclean. (11) V. Ex. XIII, 12: *Thou shalt set apart unto the Lord all that openeth the womb; every firstling that is a male, which thou hast coming of a beast, shall be the Lord's;* Deut. XV, 19ff: *All the firstling males of thy herd and of thy flock thou shalt sanctify unto the Lord thy God . . . thou shalt eat it before the Lord thy God . . . in the place which the Lord shall choose* (i.e., the Holy City of Jerusalem) . . . *And if there be any blemish therein, lameness, or blindness, any ill blemish whatsoever, thou shalt not sacrifice it unto the Lord thy God. Thou shalt eat it within thy gates: the unclean and the clean may eat it.* Reference to Num. XVIII, 17-18 shows that '*Thou shalt eat it*' is addressed to the priest. It is clear that our Mishnah speaks of the flesh of a *blemished* firstling, and since this may be eaten by '*the unclean and the clean*' it may, obviously, be given to any priest irrespective of his cleanness.

c (1) V. Ex. XIII, 13: *And the firstling of an ass thou shalt redeem with a lamb.* This lamb is not considered consecrated (Bert.). (2) V. Deut. XVIII, 3: *And this shall be the priests' due from the people, from them that offer a sacrifice, whether it be ox or sheep, that they shall give to the priest the shoulder, the two cheeks and the maw.* V. n. 5 *infra*. (3) V. ibid. 4 . . . *the first of thy fleece shalt thou give him.* (4) I.e., oil set aside as *terumah*, which has become unclean.

דאמרי' בפ"ק דעירובין (דף ו:) אי כב"ש כקוליהון וכחומריהון אי כב"ה כקוליהון וכחומריהון : ח מכזיב עד הנהר · אמרינן בירושלמי (שם) אמר רב הונא כיני מתני' מכזיב עד הנהר [מכזיב עד] אמנה היינו אמנה דקרא דקאמר בירושל' (שם) לכשיגיעו גליות לטורי אמנה הן עתידות לומר שירה שנא' (ש"ה ד) תשורי מראש אמנה כעין משנה זו תנן בפ"ו דשביעית (משנה א) וכמו שפירשתי שם יש לפרש כאן:ירושלמי (שם) של אור יש לה שיעור שהיא מדברי תורה (ה) ושל כהן אין לה שיעור שהיא מדבריהם ויפריש לאור ולא יפריש לכהן שלא יהו אומרים וכו' ראינו תרומה טמאה נאכלת מתוך שמפריש שם שתיהן לכשהוא בא לכאן ולכאן הוא נשאל : מן הנהר ועד אמנה ולפנים : של אור אין לה שיעור מפני שנשרפת ושל כהן יש לה שיעור מפני שנאכלת וזו וזו מדבריהן מוטב לרבות הנאכלת ולא לרבות הנשרפת ...

גמליאל בב' דרכים: ח *ר"ג אומר (ד) שלש ארצות לחלה מא"י ועד כזיב חלה אחת מכזיב ועד הנהר ועד אמנה ב' חלות אחת לאור ואחת לכהן של אור יש לה שיעור ושל כהן אין לה שיעור(ו)מן הנהר ועד אמנה ולפנים ב' חלות א' לאור ואחת לכהן של אור אין לה שיעור ושל כהן יש לה שיעור וטבול יום אוכלה ר' יוסי אומר אינו צריך טבילה ואסורה לזבים ולזבות לנדה וליולדות א) ונאכלת עם הזר על השלחן ונתנת לכל כהן : ט ואלו ניתנין לכל כהן החרמים והבכורות ופדיון הבן ופדיון פטר חמור והזרוע והלחיים והקיבה וראשית הגז ושמן שרפה וקדשי

בסוריא חלה אחת ופטרין פירות האריסים מן המעשרות ואחר כך חזרו לנהוג כדברי ר"ג והלכה כר"ג בשני המאמרים : ח שלש ארצות לחלה . עניינו כי לשלשה חלקים החלק הארץ לענין חיוב חלה ...

פירוש הרא"ש

הגהות מהר"י לנדא

עין משפט נר מצוה

טז א מיי' פ"ג מהל' מעשה הקרבנות הלכה יד :
יז ב מיי' פ"ג מהל' בכורים הל' א :
יח ג מיי' פי"ב מהל' תרומות הל' ז :
יט ד מיי' פ"ה מהל' בכורים הל' ז :
כ ה מיי' פ"ב שם הלכה ו :
כא ו מיי' פ"א מהל' בכורות הל' ד :
כב ז מיי' פ"ב מהל' בכורים הלכה ד:

ר"ע מתיר . מפרש בירושלמי (שם) ר"ע לטעמיה דאמר במסכת מעשר שני פ' שני (מ"ד) כרשינין כל מעשיהן בטומאה : וחכמים אוסרים · דהשבי להו אוכל וגזרו על הכהנים שלא יאכלו לבהמתם ואין נותנין אותן לכהן עם הארץ מידי דהוה אשאר תרומה משום דלא זהירי בטומאה ומפרש בירושל' אימתי גזרו על הכרשינין ר' יוסי בר בון אמר בימי רעבון ר' חנינא בשם ר' פנחס בימי דוד אמרינן היא הדא היא הדא כלומר דבימי דוד משום רעב דכתיב (ש"ב כא) ויהי בימי דוד רעב שלש שנים : י יא איש תקוע . מארץ ישראל היא כדתנן בפרק כל קרבנות (דף פה:) תקוע אלפא לשמן : ביתר . שם מקום מחוצה לארץ : ולא קיבלו הימנו · בירושלמי (הל' ה) תני רבי חייא גזרו עליהן והחזירום למקומם אמר רבי בא בר זבדא אי אפשר לאוכלה אין את יכול שלא יהו אומרים ראינו תרומה טמאה נאכלת . לשורפה אין את יכול שלא יאמרו תרומה טהורה נשרפת· להחזירה למקומה אין את יכול שלא יהו אומרים ראינו תרומה יוצאה מא"י לחו"ל כיצד הוא עושה מניחה עד ערב הפסח ושורפה : הביאו בכורים קודם לעצרת ולא קיבלו · דשתי הלחם איקרו בכורים ותנן במנחות בפרק ר' ישמעאל (דף סח:) העומר מתיר במדינה ושתי הלחם במקדש ובירושלמי (שם) פריך אמאי לא קבלו ממנו התנן התם אין מביאין מנחות ובכורים ומנחת בהמה קודם לעומר ואם הביא פסול קודם לשתי הלחם לא יביא ואם הביא כשר ומשני שנייה היא שהדבר מסוים שלא יקבע הדבר חובה וכמו כן קשה על בן אנטינוס אמאי לא קיבלו ממנו ולא כן תנינן בתמורה בפ' ואלו קדשים (דף כא.) ואם באו תמימים יקרבו ומשני שנייה היא שהדבר מסויים שלא יקבע הדבר חובה מפני שאנשים גדולים היו ויסמכו עליהם אי נמי משום דמינכרא מילתא טובא בסוף ואלו קדשים (שם) משני רב חסדא הא רבי ישמעאל הא רבי עקיבא : הביא בכורי יין ושמן ולא קיבלו ממנו · מפרש בירושלמי (שם) מפני שלא בצרן מתחלה לכך והא דתנן בפרק בתרא דתרומות (מ"ג) אין מביאין בכורים משקה אלא מן היוצא מזיתים וענבים והיא בשבצרן מתחלה לכך : פסח קטן · פסח שני וקסבר נשים בשני חובה : והחזירוהו · דסברי רשות ולא רצו שיקבע הדבר הוא חובה : וקיבלו ממנו . בירושלמי (שם) פריך תמן תנינן אין מביאין תרומה מחולה לארץ לארץ ויביאו הבכורים אמר רבי אושעיא בכורים באחריות בעלים תרומה אינה באחריות בעלים אם אומר את כן אף הן מרדפין אחריה לשם כלומר חיישינן שמא יצאו הכהנים שבארץ ישראל לחוץ לארץ בשביל התרומה להביאה שאין על הבעלים להביאה אלא מתלקין אותה לכהנים שבחולה לארץ אבל בכורים על כרחן מביאן לירושלים : בפרוודי ירושלים . בפילכי ירושלים . ובפ"ק דגיטין (ח·) חשיב לה בדברים ששוותה סוריא לארץ ישראל וקצת משמע מכאן :

סליקא לה מסכת חלה

תורה אור

[א]וקדשי המקדש [ב]והבכורים (יב) ר' יהודה אוסר בבכורים כרשיני תרומה [ג]רבי עקיבא מתיר וחכמים אוסרים : י [ד]נתאי איש תקוע הביא חלות מביתר ולא קבלו ממנו אנשי אלכסנדריא הביאו חלותיהם מאלכסנדריא ולא קבלו מהם [ה]אנשי הר צבועים הביאו בכוריהם קודם לעצרת ולא קבלו מהם מפני הכתוב שבתורה [ו]וחג הקציר בכורי מעשיך אשר תזרע בשדה : שמות כג
יא [ז]בן אנטינוס א) העלה בכורות מבבל ולא קבלו ממנו יוסף הכהן הביא בכורי יין ושמן ולא קבלו ממנו אף הוא העלה את בניו ובני ביתו לעשות פסח קטן בירושלים והחזירוהו שלא יקבע הדבר חובה אריסטון הביא בכוריו (יג) מאפמיא וקבלו ממנו מפני שאמרו ג) הקונה בסוריא כקונה בפרווד א] שבירושלים :

סליקא לה מסכת חלה

של מצורע ושתי הלחם ולחם הפנים ושירי מנחות ושירי העומר. ומפני זה נקראין קדשי מקדש לפי שאסור לכהנים לאכול דבר מאלו העשרה אלא בעזרה ודע כי מתנות כהונה הם כולן עשרים וארבע עשרה במקדש והם אותם שאמרתי לך וארבעה שאין הכהנים זוכים בהם אלא בירושלים בלבד והם הבכורות והבכורים ומורם מתודה ואיל נזיר ועורות הקדשים . הבכורות והביכורים כבר באתו שהם ביארו בגמ' שהם ניתנין לאנשי משמר ומורם מתודה ואיל נזיר וכמו כן עורות קדשים אינן ניתנות לכל כהן אבל לוקח אותם הכהן המקריב אותו הזבח וכן בא הכתוב בעורת קדשים (ויקרא ז) והכהן המקריב את עולת איש עור העולה אשר הקריב לכהן לו יהיה ואמר במורם מתודה לכהן הזורק את דם השלמים לו יהיה (שם) ואמר במורם מאיל נזיר והניף אותם הכהן תנופה לפני ה' קודש הוא לכהן (במדבר ו) ולמדו שהכהן המניף הוא האוכל אותה . ויש מהם עשר מתנות זוכים בהם הכהנים בכל ארץ ישראל והם אותם שאמרו בהם עשר בגבולין והם תרומה ותרומת מעשר וחלה וראשית הגז והמתנות ופדיון הבן ופדיון פטר חמור ושדה אחוזה ושדה חרמים וגזל הגר . ומלינו בזו הלכה מאלו העשר מתנות שש מתנות ואמרו שהן ניתנין לכל כהן נשארו ארבעה והם תרומה ותרומת מעשר וחלה וגזל הגר . והתרומה ותרומת מעשר וחלה אינן ניתנין לעם הארץ בשום פנים מפני שהוא חשוד על הטומאה ושמא יטמאם ויאכלם וכן גזל הגר אינו ניתן אלא לכהן המקריב איל האשם והוא אמרו ית' ואם אין לאיש גואל להשיב האשם אליו האשם המושב לה' לכהן מלבד איל הכפורים אשר יכפר בו עליו (שם ה) הורנו בזה הפסוק שלאותו כהן המקריב בעבורו איל האשם נותנין לו הדבר הגזול ופירשו זה הפסוק במי שגזל גר באמרו הש"י ואם אין לאיש גואל וזה אי אפשר אלא בגר כי לישראל לא יחסר לו יורש לעולם לאמרו ונתתם את נחלתו לשארו וגו' (שם כז) ואמרו רז"ל נחלה ממשמשת ועולה עד ראובן כמו שנבאר בב"ב : ר' יהודה אוסר בבכורים. שינתנו לאיזה כהן שיזדמן וכבר זכרנו שהם ראוין לאנשי משמר ועוד יתבאר דיניהם במסכת בכורים : וכרשיני תרומה מתיר ר"ע לתתם לכל כהן לפי שהם מאכל בהמה ואם נטמאו לא נקפיד להם וחכמים אוסרין לפי שהיו נאכלים בימי הרעב ונחוש שמא יאכלם בטומאה ולפיכך אינן ניתנין אלא לחבר כדין כל תרומה וזה הוא ענין אמרם אימתי גזרו על הכרשינין בימי רעבון *והלכה כחכמים : י העיקר אצלנו אין מביאין תרומה מחוץ לארץ לארץ ואמרו בגמרא באלו התרומות הבאות לארץ ישראל לאכלם אי אפשר שלא יהיו אומרים ראינו תרומה טמאה נאכלת לפי שהיא מחולה לארץ . לשרפה אי אתה יכול שלא יהיו אומרים ראינו תרומה טהורה נשרפת לפי שלא נטמאה בטומאה מפורסמת אלא בעפר חולה לארץ ואין כל אדם יודע בזאת הטומאה · להחזירה למקומה אי אפשר שלא יהו אומרים ראינו תרומה יוצאה מהארץ לחולה לארץ כיצד הוא עושה מניחה עד ערב הפסח ושורפה וזהו ענין המעשה שנעשה בתרומות אלכסנדריא ואמר לא קבלו מהם : יא אמרו בספרי יכול יהא אדם מעלה בכורות מחולה לארץ לארץ ת"ל (דברים יד) ואכלת לפני ה' אלהיך מעשר דגנך תירושך ויצהרך ובכורות בקרך ולאנך ממקום שאתה מביא מעשר דגן אתה מביא בכורות מחולה לארץ שאין אתה מביא מעשר דגן אין אתה מביא בכורות : ואמרם הביא בכורי יין ושמן ולא קבלו ממנו . היא הסברא האמתית ועוד יתבאר לך זה בבכורים שאין מביאין בכורים משקין והמאמר שכתבנו לך בתרומות (פי"א מ"ג) אין מביאין בכורים משקין אלא היוצא מן הזיתים ומן הענבים בלבד הוא דעת ר' יהודה לבדו שהוא למד בכורים מתרומה כאשר ביארו בגמרא וכבר זכרנו זה בתרומה : אף הוא העלה את בניו . אלו הבנים קטנים היו בלי ספק ולא היו חייבין לעלות אלא בפסח ראשון שהכל חייבין בראיה לאמרו יהעלה (שמות כג) שלש פעמים בשנה יראה כל זכורך : אפמיא . שם מקום בארץ סוריא ופרוד של ירושלים מגרשי ירושלים וכפריה תרגום מגרשה פרוודה וכבר באתו בתחלת דמאי כי מי שקנה קרקע בסוריא נתחייב במעשרות באותו הקרקע וזהו עיקר אותו המאמר : סליקא לה מסכת חלה

הלחם דעצרת : יא בן אנטינוס העלה בכורות מבבל ולא קבלו ממנו . וזו המשנה ר' עקיבא היא ודתנן בתמורה פרק ג' ואם באו תמימים יקריבו רבי שמעון היא וכן תירצום בגמרא דתמורה : אף הוא . יוסף הכהן : העלה את בניו ואת ביתו ואת בני ביתו לעשות פסח קטן והחזירוהו שלא יקבע הדבר חובה. דאינהו סברי פסחן של נשים רשות א"ר יונה ואפי' למאן דאמר חובה שנייה היא ועל כן החזירוהו שהדבר מסוים שמא יקבע הדבר חובה ואקשי' ויביאו תרומה אלמא תנן אין מביאין תרומה מחוצה לארץ לארץ ותרצי' א"ר הושעיה ביכורין באחריות בעלין תרומה אינה באחריות בעלין אם אומר את כן אף הן מרדפין אחריה לשם ואתו הכהנים לצאת בחוצה לארץ עבור התרומה ההיא וקיימא לן אסור לצאת מן הארץ לחוצה לארץ אי נמי מייתו לה לאוכלה אי אפשר שלא יהו אומר תרומה טמאה נאכלת וכו' כדין החלות של ביתר ושל אלכסנדריא . הלכך כיון דכי מייתי לה לשורפה קיימא לכי מיטמיא ודאי לא ליתו לה דלמא אתו בה לידי תקלה ותו יותר שתהא לאכילה לכהני חוצה לארץ כחלת חוצה לארץ : סליקא לה מסכת חלה

פירוש הרא"ש

(יב) רבי יהודה אוסר בבכורים אע"ג דמביאים אותם לעזרה ליתנם לכהן כיון דאין עושים בהם עבודה חייש דלמא מזכיר לא זהיר בהו : (יג) מאפמיא בערודגלות ירושלים אשר בספרד עובדיה תרגום וגלות ירושלים אשר באספמיא :

הגהות מהרי"ל לנדא

במשנה יא א] משנה כקונה בפרווד . גי' גמרא פרור :

מסורת הש"ס

א) תמורה פ"ג דף כא. ב) גיטין פ"א דף ח.

פי' מהר"י בן מלכי צדק

וקדשי המקדש . כגון הטאת ואשם וכו': והבכורים . דכיון דממקדש קא זכי מהורי מהר נפשיה : ר' יהודה אוסר בבכורין . פי' רבי יהודה כדעתיה דהוא אמר אין נותנין אותן אלא לחבר בטובה : כרשיני תרומה רבי עקיבא מתיר . פי' ליתנן לכל כהן . ר' עקיבא כדעתיה דתנן במעשרות כרשיני תרומה רבי עקיבא אומר כל מעשיהן בטומאה דלאו אוכלין נינהו ותניא בתוספ' דמעשרשני כרשינין של תרומה בית שמאי אומרים שורין בטהרה ושפין ומאכילין בטומאה ובית הלל אומרים כל מעשיהן בטומאה א"ר יוסי זו משנת רבי עקיבא לפיכך נותנן לכל כהן וחכמים לא הודו לו: וחכמים אוסרין דאוכלין חשובין הן. וכשם שאסור ליתן לכהן עם הארץ תרומה טהורה וחלת הארץ הכי נמי אסור ליתן לו כרשיני תרומה שכבר גזרו עליהן שלא יאכילום הכהנים לבהמתם : י איש תקוע וכו'. ביתר שם מקום מחוצה לארץ תני רבי חייא גזרו עליהן והחזירום למקומן א"ר בא בר זבדא אי אפשר.לאוכלהאי את יכול וכו' להחזירה למקומה אין את יכול שלא יהו אומר ראינו תרומה יוצאה מהארץ לחו"ל הא כיצד מניחה עד ערב הפסח ושורפה בערב הפסח שם בארץ ולא יהירום : הר צבועין . פי' שם מקום : שנאמר וחג הקציר . כלומר שלא יביא אדם ביכורין קודם לשתי

א א ב מיי' פ"י מה' מעשר שני ונטע רבעי הלכה ב ג סמג עשין קלז טוש"ע י"ד סי' רלד סעיף כג :
ב ג מיי' פ"י מהל' מ"ש וכ"ר הל' ט:
ג ד מיי' שם הלכ' ד טוש"ע י"ד סימן רלד סעיף כה :

א לסייג . מלשון סוגה בשושנים (שיר ז) שנטע אילנות לעשות גדר לכרם סביב כדכתיב (במדבר כב) גדר מזה וגדר מזה : ולקורות. מגדל הנטיעה לעשות ממנה קורות לבית ולא לאכול פירותיה : פטור מן הערלה · כדדריש בירושלמי (הלכה א) (ויקרא יט) ונטעתם כל עץ מאכל את שהוא למאכל חייב לסייג ולעצים ולקורות פטור תניא אמר רשב"ג בד"א שנטעה לסייג ולקורות ולעצים דבר שראוי להם אבל נטע דבר שאין ראוי להם חייב יאות אמר רשב"ג מה טעמא דרבנן בשינה סדר נטיעתן לעצים ברוצף (א) לקורות במשפה (ב) לסייג מקום הסייג מוכיח עליו : הפנימי למאכל . כגון ייחור הפנימי והחיצון ייחור חיצון ובירושלמי (שם) מפרש טעמא דרבי יוסי למד דבר מתחלתו ממשמע שנאמר שלש שנים יהיה לכם ערלים לא יאכל איני יודע שבעץ מאכל דבר הכתוב מה ת"ל כל עץ מאכל לומר לך את שהוא למאכל חייב כגון הפנימי לסייג ולקורות פטור ומשמע בירושלמי דה"ה לד התחתון לסייג והעליון למאכל ואפילו לד התחתון למאכל והעליון לסייג אע"פ שגדל *לתוך איסור ועוד אמרינן בירושלמי נטעו לסייג וחשב עליו למאכל בא במחשבה למאכל וחישב עליו לסייג לא כל הימנו (ג) :
ב ומצאו נטוע פטור · דכתיב כי תבואו ונטעתם (שם) פרט לשנטעו נכרים עד שלא באו לארץ או יכול שאני מוציא אף שנטעו נכרים משבאו ישראל לארץ תלמוד לומר כל עץ מיכן אמרו אף על פי שלא כיבשו ישראל חייב : הנוטע לרבים חייב · כגון ברשות היחיד והוא של הרבה בני אדם כגון בירושלים ובירושלמי (שם) פריך מחלפא שיטתיה דרבנן תמן אינון אמרי (נגעים פי"ב מ"ד) ירושלים וחוצה לארץ אינן מיטמאין בנגעים וכה אמרין הכא תמן אשר לו הבית פרט לירושלים שהיא לכל השבטים ברם הכא ונטעתם מ"מ מחלפא שיטתיה דרבי יהודה תמן הוא אומר אני לא שמעתי אלא בית המקדש בלבד דקסבר ירושלים נתחלקה לשבטים וכה הוא אמר הכן תמן שמועה אמר ברם הכא בשם גרמיה ושיטה אחרת בפרק כל שעה (דף כג.)

פרק ראשון ערלה

א הנוטע א) אלסייג ולקורות פטור מן הערלה ר' יוסי אומר [ב]אפילו אמר הפנימי למאכל והחיצון לסייג הפנימי חייב והחיצון פטור : ב [ג]עת שבאו אבותינו לארץ ומצאו נטוע פטור נטעו אע"פ שלא כבשו חייב ג) [ד]הנוטע

א אמר הש"י ונטעתם כל עץ מאכל וערלתם ערלתו (ויקרא יט) ולפיכך כשנתכוין בנטיעתו לאכילה אז יתחייב בערלה אבל אם נתכוין בשעת נטיעת האילן שיהיה סייג או ליקח ממנו קורות או עצים אינו חייבת בערלה ורבי יוסי אומר שאפילו אילן עצמו אם היתה כונתו שיהיה אותו הצד הנוטה ממנו לרשות הרבים סייג לצד הנוטה ממנה לגנה ויתכוין גם כן שיהיה הצד הנוטה ממנו לפנים רצונו לומר לגנה למאכל שדין זה האילן נחלק והצד הפנימית נתחייב בערלה והצד החילון פטור מן הערלה ואין הלכה כרבי יוסי : ב אע"פ שלא כבשו . ענינו הע"פ שלא כבשו כל הארץ : ואמרם הנוטע לרבים . ענינו שיהא אדם נוטע אילנות בתוך שלו ולא לעצמו אלא כונתו שיאכלוה בני אדם כולם וכאילו הפקיר אותו הפרי הצומח באותו אילן

פירוש הרא"ש

פרק א (א) שלא הרחיק זה מזה כדרך שעושין לעץ מאכל : (ב) ענפים כדי שיתעבה ויהיו גבים: (ג) ואם חשב עליהם בשנה ראשונה או שניה למאכל חייב בערלה וברבעי ומונה משעת נטיעה אבל אם חשב בסוף ג' אין בו דין רבעי דאין רבעי בלי ערלה אבל

מסורת הש"ס

א) סוטה דף מג: ב) פסחים דף כג:

פי' מהר"י בן מלכי צדק

פ"א א הנוטע לסייג או לקורות

ולעצים. ומי מוכיח א"ר זירא מנסיעתן את הואה עובדין רצופן לעצים . משופין לקורות

יסייג מקום הסייג מוכיח עליו : ר' יוסי אומר אפי' אמר הפנימי למאכל . פי' יחור האמצעי רצונו שיהא למאכל והחיצון לסייג היחד הפנימי חייב והיחור החיצון פטור מאי טעמא דר' יוסי דבר למד מתחלתו ממשמע ...אמר שלש שנים יהיה לכם ערלים לא יאכל אין אני יודע שבעץ מאכל הכתוב מדבר ומה ת"ל ונטעתם כל עץ מאכל אלא לומר לך את שהוא למאכל חייב כגון הפנימי ואת שהוא לסייג לקורות ולעצים פטור : ב עת שבאו אבותינו לארץ ומצאו נטוע פטורין . פי' מה שמצאו נטוע פטורין מן הערלה דכתיב כי תבאו אל הארץ ונטעתם פרט לשנטעו נכרים עד שלא באו ישראל לארץ : או יכול שאני מוציא את שנטעו נכרים משבאו

DAINED TO BE CONSUMED WITHIN THE PRECINCTS] OF THE SANCTUARY,[5] AND THE FIRST-RIPE FRUITS.[6] R. JUDAH PROHIBITS IN [THE CASE OF] FIRST-RIPE FRUITS.[7] [AS FOR] HORSE-BEANS [SET ASIDE] FOR TERUMAH, R. AKIBA PERMITS,[8] BUT THE SAGES PROHIBIT.[9]

MISHNAH 10. NITTAI [A MAN OF] TEḲOA[10] BROUGHT ḤALLAH-PORTIONS FROM BE-JATTIR,[11] BUT THEY DID NOT
a ACCEPT [THESE] FROM HIM.[1] THE MEN OF ALEXANDRIA BROUGHT THEIR ḤALLAH-PORTIONS FROM ALEXANDRIA, BUT THEY DID NOT ACCEPT [THESE] FROM THEM.[1] THE MEN OF MOUNT ZEBOIM[2] BROUGHT THEIR FIRST-RIPE FRUITS PRIOR TO THE FESTIVAL,[3] BUT THEY DID NOT ACCEPT [THESE] FROM THEM, ON ACCOUNT OF THAT WHICH IS WRITTEN IN THE LAW: AND THE FEAST OF THE HARVEST, THE FIRST-FRUITS OF THY LABOURS, WHICH THOU SOWEST IN THE FIELD.[4]

(5) Since these are parts of sacrifices brought into the Sanctuary where no unclean priest may enter there is, obviously, no fear that it may be eaten by a priest during his uncleanness. (It is different with *ḥallah* and *terumah*; these may be eaten outside sacred precincts where there are priests of all kinds, and care should therefore be taken that these priestly dues do not get into the hands of priests who are either unclean or possibly neglectful of their ritual cleanness.) (6) V. Num. XVIII, 13: *The first-ripe fruits of all that is in their land, which they bring unto the Lord, shall be thine; every one that is clean in thy house may eat thereof.* These were to be brought by the Israelite direct to the Sanctuary, v. n. 5. (7) R. Judah's reason is: Seeing that first-ripe fruits are not offered on the altar, ignorant priests are likely to underrate the sacredness of first-ripe fruits and to eat them prior to self-purification. (8) *Sc.* to give to any priest, since these are rarely eaten by human beings, and the likelihood of these being eaten by an unclean priest is therefore remote. (9) Seeing that they are sometimes eaten by human beings, no exception is to be made of them. (10) In South Judah v. Amos I, 1, II Sam. XIV, 2. (11) Reading with Kohut, *Aruch Completum*, s.v. ביתור, בי יתיר. יתיר (or spelt *defectivum* יתר) is mentioned Josh. XV, 48, XXI, 14, I Sam. XXX, 27, I Chron. VI, 42 in S. Judah. In T.J. *Sheb.* p. 36, it is mentioned among places on the borders of the Land of Israel in relation to the applicability of the laws of the sanctity of the Land. According to the above data it would be in the neighbourhood of Tekoa. It is this place that is probably meant by Schürer (*Geschichte des Volkes Israel* I, p. 693) when he identifies our place-name as Be-jittar. Hirschensohn, *Sheba' Ḥokmoth* s.v. בתיר thinks of Botrys on the North African coast.
a (1) For the reasons: (*a*) These *ḥallah* portions could not be eaten, since, coming from not fully sacred territory, they were unclean. (*b*) They could not accept them and burn them, because (since their place of origin was in a zone of partial but not complete sanctity) the fact that such *ḥallah* is unclean is not generally known, and people might be led to think that clean *ḥallah* was being—and permitted to be—burnt in Palestine. (*c*) Accepting these *ḥallah*-portions and sending them out of Palestine to burn them, would lead people to think, entirely erroneously, that any *ḥallah* or *terumah* may be sent out of the Land of Israel. The only possible thing to do is to let these dough-portions remain till the Eve of Passover when they should be burnt with other leaven (T.J.). (2) Probably close to the valley of that name (I Sam. XIII, 18) and the town of that name (Neh. XI, 34) in Judea. (3) *Azereth*, a Rabbinic designation for the Feast of Weeks or Pentecost, on which the first-ripe fruits were due to be brought to the Temple. Lit., 'the closing', Pentecost being considered the closing festival to Passover. (4) Ex. XXIII, 16 (cf. Lev. XXIII, 15-21, Num. XXVIII, 26). According to this verse it was the first-fruits coming from '*that which thou sowest in the field*' i.e., the 'Two Loaves' (which, too, were termed '*First-fruits*') that were the first to be brought to the Temple, before the other first-ripe produce, indeed before any of the other priestly and levitical dues. Seemingly the refusal recorded here is contrary to Mishnah Men. X, 6 which lays it down that although the first-fruits are in the first instance not to be brought before the Two Loaves, nevertheless if one had already unintentionally done so, such first-fruits are valid. (They are not accepted at the time but laid aside till after the bringing of the Two Loaves on the day of the Festival, and then they are handed to the priest and the declaration prescribed in Deut. XXVI is recited.) T.J., however, explains that the refusal of the prematurely brought first-fruits, in our case, was on the ground that acceptance would, in the circumstances, have given the impression that it was the proper thing to bring first-fruits prior to the Feast of Weeks.

◁ *For the continuation of the English translation of this page see overleaf.*

עין משפט נר מצוה

טז א מיי' פ"ג מהל' מעשה הקרבנות הלכה יד :
יז ב מיי' פ"ג מהל' בכורים הל' א :
יח ג מיי' פי"ב מהל' תרומות הל' ז :
יט ד מיי' פ"ה מהל' בכורים הל' ז :
כ ה מיי' פ"ב שם הלכה ו :
כא ו מיי' פ"א מהל' בכורות הל' ד :
כב ז מיי' פ"ב מהל' בכורים הלכה ד :

מסורת הש"ס

א) תמורה פ"ג דף כא. ב) גיטין פ"א דף ח.

ר"ע מתיר . מפרש בירושלמי (שם) ר"ע לטעמיה דאמר במסכת מעשר שני פ' שני (מ"ד) כרשינין כל מעשיהן בטומאה : וחכמים אוסרים · להשבי להו אוכל וגזרו על הכהנים שלא יאכילו לבהמתם ואין נותנין אותן לכהן עם הארץ מידי דהוה אשאר תרומה משום דלא זהירי בטומאה ומפרש בירושל' אימתי גזרו על הכרשינין ר' יוסי בר בון אמר בימי רעבון ר' חנינא בשם ר' פנחס בימי דוד אמרינן היא הדא היא הדא כלומר דבימי דוד משום רעב דכתיב (ש"ב כא) ויהי בימי דוד רעב שלש שנים : י נתאי איש תקוע . מארץ ישראל היא כדתנן בפרק כל קרבנות (דף פה:) תקוע אלפא לשמן : ביתר . שם מקום מחולה לארץ : ולא קיבלו הימנו · בירושלמי (הל' ה) תני רבי חייא גזרו עליהן והחזירום למקומם אמר רבי בא בר זבדא אי אפשר לאוכלה אין את יכול שלא יהו אומרים ראינו תרומה טמאה נאכלת . לשורפה אין את יכול שלא יאמרו תרומה טהורה נשרפת· להחזירה למקומה אין את יכול שלא יהו אומרים ראינו תרומה יוצאה מא"י לחו"ל כילד הוא עושה מניחה עד ערב הפסח ושורפה : הביאו בכורים קודם לעצרת ולא קיבלו · דשתי הלחם איקרו בכורים ותנן במנחות בפרק ר' ישמעאל (דף סח:) העומר מתיר במדינה ושתי הלחם במקדש ובירושלמי (שם) פריך אמאי לא קבלו ממנו התנן התם אין מביאין מנחות ובכורים ומנחת בהמה קודם לעומר ואם הביא פסול קודם לשתי הלחם לא יביא ואם הביא כשר ומשני שנייה היא שהדבר מסוים שלא יקבע הדבר חובה וכמו כן קשה על בן אנטינוס אמאי לא קיבלו ממנו ולא כן תנינן בתמורה בפ' ואלו קדשים (דף כא.) ואם באו תמימים יקרבו ומשני שנייה היא שהדבר מסויים שלא יקבע הדבר חובה מפני שאנשים גדולים היו ויסמכו עליהם אי נמי משום דמיכרא מילתא טובא בסוף ואלו קדשים (שם) משני רב חסדא הא רבי ישמעאל הא רבי עקיבא : הביא בכורי יין ושמן ולא קיבלו ממנו · מפרש בירושלמי (שם) מפני שלא בארן מתחלה לכך והא דתנן בפרק בתרא דתרומות (מ"ג) אין מביאין בכורים משקה אלא מן היוצא מזיתים וענבים הכיא בשבארן מתחלה לכך : פסח קטן · פסח שני וקסבר נשים בשני חובה : והחזירוהו · דסברי רשות ולא רצו שיקבע הדבר הוא חובה : וקיבלו ממנו . בירושלמי (שם) פריך תמן תנינן אין מביאין תרומה מחולה לארץ לארץ ויביאו הבכורים אמר רבי הושעיא בכורים באחריות בעלים תרומה אינה באחריות בעלים אם אומר את כן אף הן מרדפין אחריה לשם כלומר חיישינן שמא יצאו הכהנים שבארץ ישראל לחוץ לארץ בשביל התרומה להביאה שאין על הבעלים להביאה אלא מחלקין אותה לכהנים שבחולה לארץ אבל בכורים על כרחן מביאין לירושלים : בפרוודי ירושלים · בפילכי ירושלים . ובפ"ק דגיטין (ח·) השיב לה בדברים ששותה סוריא לארץ ישראל וקנת משמע מכאן :

סליקא לה מסכת חלה

תורה אור

א וקדשי המקדש ב והבכורים (יב) ר' יהודה אוסר בבכורים כרשיני תרומה ג רבי עקיבא מתיר וחכמים אוסרים : י ד נתאי איש תקוע הביא חלות מביתר ולא קבלו ממנו אנשי אלכסנדריא הביאו חלותיהם מאלכסנדריא ולא קבלו מהם ה אנשי הר צבועים הביאו בכוריהם קודם לעצרת ולא קבלו מהם מפני הכתוב שבתורה ו וחג הקציר בכורי מעשיך אשר תזרע בשדה : שמות כג
יא בן אנטינוס א) העלה בכורות מבבל ולא קבלו ממנו ז יוסף הכהן הביא בכורי יין ושמן ולא קבלו ממנו אף הוא העלה את בניו ובני ביתו לעשות פסח קטן בירושלים והחזירוהו שלא יקבע הדבר חובה אריסטון הביא בכוריו (יג) מאפמיא וקבלו ממנו מפני שאמרו ב) הקונה בסוריא כקונה בפרוור א] שבירושלים :

סליקא לה מסכת חלה

של מצורע ושתי הלחם ולחם הפנים ושירי מנחות ושירי העומר. ומפני זה נקראין קדשי מקדש לפי שאסור לכהנים לאכול דבר מאלו העשרה אלא בעזרה ודע כי מתנות כהונה הם כולן עשרים וארבע עשרה במקדש והם אותם שאמרתי לך וארבעה שאין הכהנים זוכים בהם אלא בירושלים בלבד והם הבכורות והבכורים ומורם מתודה ואיל נזיר ועורות הקדשים. הבכורות והביכורים כבר בארנו שהם ביארו בגמ' שהם ניתנין לאנשי משמר ומורם מתודה ואיל נזיר וכמו כן עורות קדשים אינן ניתנות לכל כהן אבל לוקח אותם הכהן המקריב אותו הזבח וכן בא הכתוב בעורת קדשים (ויקרא ז) והכהן המקריב את עולת איש עור העולה אשר הקריב לכהן לו יהיה ואמר במורם מתודה לכהן הזורק את דם השלמים לו יהיה (שם) ואמר במורם מאיל נזיר והניף אותם הכהן תנופה לפני ה' קודש הוא לכהן (במדבר ו) ולמדו שהכהן המניף הוא האוכל אותה. ויש מהם עשר מתנות זוכים בהם הכהנים בכל ארץ ישראל והם אותם שאמרו בהם עשר בגבולין והם התרומה ותרומת מעשר וחלה וראשית הגז והמתנות ופדיון הבן ופדיון פטר חמור ושדה אחוזה ושדה חרמים וגזל הגר. ומלינו בזו הלכה מאלו העשר מתנות שש מתנות ואמרו שהן ניתנין לכל כהן נשארו ארבעה והם תרומה ותרומת מעשר וחלה וגזל הגר. והתרומה ותרומת מעשר וחלה אינן ניתנין לעם הארץ בשום פנים מפני שהוא חשוד על הטומאה ושמא יטמאם ויאכלם וכן גזל הגר אינו ניתן אלא לכהן המקריב איל האשם והוא אמרו ית' ואם אין לאיש גואל להשיב האשם אליו האשם המושב לה' לכהן מלבד איל הכפורים אשר יכפר בו עליו (שם ה) הורו בזה הפסוק שלאותו כהן המקריב בעבורו איל האשם נותנין לו הדבר הגזול ופירשו זה הפסוק במי שגזל גר באמרו הש"י ואם אין לאיש גואל וזה אי אפשר אלא בגר כי לישראל לא יחסר לו יורש לעולם לאמרו והיתה את נחלתו לשארו וגו' (שם כז) ואמרו רז"ל נחלה ממשמשת ועולה עד ראובן כמו שנבאר בב"ב : ר' יהודה אוסר בבכורים. שיתנו לאיזה כהן שיזדמן וכבר זכרנו שהם ראוין לאנשי משמר ועוד יתבאר דיניהם במסכת בכורים : וכרשיני תרומה מתיר ר"ע להתם לכל כהן לפי שהם מאכל בהמה ואם נטמאו לא נקפיד להם וחכמים אוסרין לפי שהיו נאכלים בימי הרעב ונחוש שמא יאכלם בטומאה ולפיכך אינן ניתנין אלא לחבר כדין כל תרומה וזה הוא ענין אמרם אימתי גזרו על הכרשינין בימי רעבון *והלכה כחכמים : י העיקר אצלנו אין מביאין התרומה מחוץ לארץ לארץ ואמרו בגמרא באלו התרומות הבאות לארץ ישראל לאכלם אי אפשר שלא יהיו אומרים ראינו תרומה טמאה נאכלת לפי שהיא מחולה לארץ. לשרפה אי אתה יכול שלא יהיו אומרים ראינו תרומה טהורה נשרפת לפי שלא נטמאה בטומאה מפורסמת אלא בעפר חולה לארץ ואין כל אדם יודע בזאת הטומאה· להחזירה למקומה אי אפשר שלא יהו אומרים ראינו תרומה יוצאה מהארץ לחולה לארץ כילד הוא עושה מניחה עד ערב הפסח ושורפה וזהו ענין המעשה שנעשה בתרומות אלכסנדריא ואמר לא קבלו מהם: יא אמרו בספרי יכול יהא אדם מעלה בכורות מחולה לארץ לארץ ת"ל (דברים יד) ואכלת לפני ה' אלהיך מעשר דגנך תירושך ויצהרך ובכורות בקרך וצאנך ממקום שאתה מביא מעשר דגן אתה מביא בכורות מחולה לארץ שאין אתה מביא מעשר דגן אין אתה מביא בכורות : ואמרם הביא בכורי יין ושמן ולא קבלו ממנו . היא הסברא האמתית ועוד יתבאר לך זה בבכורים שאין מביאין בכורים משקין והמאמר שכתבנו לך בתרומות (פי"א מ"ג) אין מביאין בכורים משקין אלא היוצא מן הזיתים ומן הענבים בלבד הוא דעת ר' יהודה לבדו שהוא למד בכורים מתרומה כאשר ביארו בגמרא וכבר זכרנו זה בתרומה: אף הוא העלה את בניו . אלו הבנים קטנים היו בלי ספק ולא היו חייבין לעלות אלא בפסח ראשון שהכל חייבין בראיה לאמרו יתעלה (שמות כג) שלש פעמים בשנה יראה כל זכורך : אפמיא. שם מקום בארץ סוריא ופרוור של ירושלים מגרשי ירושלים וכפריה התרגום מגרשה פרוודה וכבר בארנו בתחלת דמאי כי מי שקנה קרקע בסוריא נתחייב במעשרות באותו הקרקע וזהו עיקר אותו המאמר: סליקא לה מסכת חלה

פירוש הרא"ש

(יב) רבי יהודה אוסר בבכורים אע"ג דמביאים אותם לעזרה ליתנם לכהן כיון דאין עושים בהם עבודה חייש דלמא מזכיר לא זהיר בהו : (יג) מאפמיא בערודוגלות ירושלים אשר בספרד עובדיה תרגום וגלות ירושלים אשר באספמיא :

הגהות מהר"י לנדא

במשנה יא א] משנה כקונה בפרוור . ג"י גמרא פרוור :

פי' מהר"י בן מלכי צדק

וקדשי המקדש. כגון הבאת ואשם וכו': והבכורים. דכיון דממקדש קא זכי טהורי מטהר נפשיה : ר' יהודה אוסר בבכורין. פי' רבי יהודה כדעתיה דהוא אמר אין נותנין אותן אלא לחבר בטובה : כרשיני תרומה רבי עקיבא מתיר. פי' ליתנן לכל כהן. ר' עקיבא כדעתיה דתנן במעשרות כרשיני תרומה רבי עקיבא אומר כל מעשיהן בטומאה דלאו אוכלין נינהו ותניא בתוספ' דמעשרשני כרשינין של תרומה בית שמאי אומרים שורין בטהרה ושפין ומאכילין בטומאה ובית הלל אומרים כל מעשיהן בטומאה א"ר יוסי זו משנת רבי עקיבא לפיכך נותנן לכל כהן וחכמים לא הודו לו: וחכמים אוסרין דאוכלין חשובין הן. וכשם שאסיר ליתן לכהן עם הארץ תרומה טהורה וחלת הארץ הכי נמי אסור ליתן לו כרשיני תרומה שכבר גזרו עליהן שלא יאכילום הכהנים לבהמתם : י איש תקוע וכו'. ביתר שם מקום מהוצה לארץ תני רבי חייא גזרו עליהן והחזירום למקומן א"ר בא בר זבדא אי אפשר לאוכלה אי את יכול וכו' להחזירה למקומה אין את יכול שלא יהו אומר ראינו תרומה יוצאה מהארץ לחו"ל הא כיצד מניחה עד ערב הפסח ושורפה בערב הפסח שם בארץ ולא יחזירום : הר צבועין. פי' שם מקום : שנאמר וחג הקציר. כלומר שלא יביא אדם ביכורין קודם לשתי הלחם דעצרת : יא בן אנטינוס העלה בכורות מבבל ולא קבלו ממנו . וזו המשנה ר' עקיבא היא ודתנן בתמורה פרק ג' ואם באו תמימים יקריבו רבי שמעון היא וכן תירצום בגמרא דתמורה: אף הוא. יוסף הכהן: העלה את בניו ואת ביתו ואת בני ביתו לעשות פסח קטן והחזירוהו שלא יקבע הדבר חובה. דאינהו סברי פסחן של נשים רשות א"ר יונה ואפי' למאן דאמר חובה שנייה היא ועל כן החזירוהו שהדבר מסוים שמא יקבע הדבר חובה ואקשי' ויביאו תרומה אלמא תנן אין מביאין תרומה מחוצה לארץ לארץ ותרצי' א"ר הושעיה ביכורין באחריות בעלין תרומה אינה באחריות בעלין אם אומר את כן אף הן כרדפין אחריה לשם ואתו הכהנים לצאת בחוצה לארץ עבור התרומה ההיא וקיימא לן אסור לצאת מן הארץ לחוצה לארץ אי נמי מייתו לה לאוכלה אי אפשר שלא יהו אומר תרומה טמאה נאכלת וכו' כדין החלות של ביתר ושל אלכסנדריא . הלכך כיון דכי מייתי לה לשריפה קיימא לכי מיטמיא ודאי לא ליתו לה דלמא אתו בה לידי תקלה ותו יותר שתהא לאבילה לכהני חוצה לארץ כחלת חוצה לארץ : סליקא לה מסכת חלה

עין משפט נר מצוה

א א ב מיי' פ"י מה' מעשר שני ונטע רבעי הלכה כ ב סמג עשין קלו טוש"ע י"ד סי' רצד סעיף כג :
ב ג מיי' פ"י מהל' מ"ש ונ"ר הל' ט:
ג ד מיי' שם הלכ' ד טוש"ע י"ד סימן רצד סעיף כה :

מסורת הש"ס

א) סוטה דף מג: ב) פסחים דף כג:

א לסייג. מלשון סוגה בשושנים (שיר ז) שנטע אילנות לעשות גדר לכרם סביב כדכתיב (במדבר כב) גדר מזה וגדר מזה : ולקורות. מגדל הנטיעה לעשות ממנה קורות לבית ולא לאכול פירותיה : פטור מן הערלה · כדדריש בירושלמי (הלכה א) (ויקרא יט) ונטעתם כל עץ מאכל את שהוא למאכל חייב לסייג ולעצים ולקורות פטור תניא אמר רשב"ג בד"א שנטעה לסייג ולקורות ולעצים דבר שראוי להם אבל נטע דבר שאין ראוי להם חייב יאות אמר רשב"ג מה טעמא דרבנן בשטיה סדר נטיעתן לעצים ברוצף (א) לקורות במשפה (ב) לסייג מקום הסייג מוכיח עליו : הפנימי למאכל . כגון ייחור הפנימי והחיצון ייחור חיצון ובירושלמי (שם) מפרש טעמא דרבי יוסי למד דבר מתחלתו ממשמע שנאמר שלש שנים יהיה לכם ערלים לא יאכל איני יודע שבעץ מאכל דבר הכתוב מה ת"ל כל עץ מאכל לומר לך את שהוא למאכל חייב כגון הפנימי לסייג ולקורות פטור ומשמע בירושלמי דה"ה לד התחתון לסייג והעליון למאכל ואפילו לד התחתון למאכל והעליון לסייג אע"פ שגדל *לתוך איסור ועוד אמרינן בירושלמי נטעו לסייג וחישב עליו למאכל בא במחשבה למאכל וחישב עליו לסייג לא כל הימנו (ג) : ב ומצאו נטוע פטור · דכתיב כי תבואו ונטעתם (שם) פרט לשנטעו נכרים עד שלא באו לארץ או יכול שאני מוציא אף שנטעו נכרים משבאו ישראל לארץ תלמוד לומר כל עץ מיכן אמרו אף על פי שלא כיבשו ישראל חייב : הנוטע לרבים חייב · כגון ברשות היחיד והוא של הרבה בני אדם כגון בירושלים ובירושלמי (שם) פריך מחלפא שיטתיה דרבנן תמן אינון אמרי (נגעים פי"ב מ"ד) ירושלים וחוצה לארץ אינן מיטמאין בנגעים וכה אמרין הכן תמן אשר לו הבית פרט לירושלים שהיא לכל השבטים ברם הכא ונטעתם מ"מ מחלפא שיטתיה דרבי יהודה תמן הוא אומר אני לא שמעתי אלא בית המקדש בלבד דקסבר ירושלים נתחלקה לשבטים וכה הוא אמר הכן תמן שמועה אמר ברם הכא בשם גרמיה ושיטה אחרת בפרק כל שעה (דף כג.)

פרק ראשון ערלה

א הנוטע א) לסייג ולקורות פטור מן הערלה ר' יוסי אומר ב אפילו אמר הפנימי למאכל והחיצון לסייג הפנימי חייב והחיצון פטור: ב ג עת שבאו אבותינו לארץ ומצאו נטוע פטור נטעו אע"פ שלא כבשו חייב ג) ד הנוטע

א אמר הש"י ונטעתם כל עץ מאכל וערלתם ערלתו (ויקרא יט) ולפיכך כשנתכוון בנטיעתו לאכילה אז יתחייב בערלה אבל אם נתכוון בשעת נטיעת האילן שיהיה סייג או ליקח ממנו קורות או עצים אינו חייבת בערלה ורבי יוסי אומר שאפילו האילן עצמו אם היתה כונתו שיהיה אותו הצד הנוטה ממנו לרשות הרבים סייג לצד הנוטה ממנה לגנה ויתכוין גם כן שיהיה הצד הנוטה ממנו לפנים רצונו לומר לגנה למאכל שדין זה האילן נחלק והצד הפנימית נתחייב בערלה והצד החיצון פטור מן הערלה ואין הלכה כרבי יוסי : ב אע"פ שלא כבשו . ענינו אע"פ שלא כבשו כל הארץ : ואמרם הנוטע לרבים . ענינו שיהא אדם נוטע אילנות בתוך שלו ולא לעצמו אלא כונתו שיאכלוה בני אדם כולם וכאילו הפקיר אותו הפרי הצומח באותו אילן

פי' מהר"י בן מלכי צדק

פ"א א הנוטע לסייג או לקורות וכו' : פי' נוטע אילנות לעשות מהן גדר לכרמו דכתיב במשעול הכרמים גדר וגו' תרג' ירושל' סייג מן הכא וסייג מן הכא : ולקורות. פי' מגדל אותה נטיעה לעשות ממנה קורות פטור מן הערלה דכתיב עץ מאכל פרט לנוטע לסייג ולקורות ולעצים. ומי מוכיח א"ר זירא מנטיעתן את רואה עומדין רצופין לעצים . משופין לקורות

פירוש הרא"ש

פרק א (א) שלא הרחיק זה מזה כדרך שעושין לעץ מאכל : (ב) ענפים כדי שיתעבה ויהיו גסים: (ג) ואם חשב עליהם בשנה ראשונה או שניה למאכל חייב בערלה וברבעי ומונה משעת נטיעה אבל אם חשב בסוף ג' אין בו דין רבעי דאין רבעי בלי ערלה אבל

לסייג מקום הסייג מוכיח עליו : ר' יוסי אומר אפי' אמר הפנימי למאכל והחיצון לסייג היחוד הפנימי חייב והיחוד החיצון פטור מאי טעמא דר' יוסי דבר למד מתחלתו ממשמע שנאמר שלש שנים יהיה לכם ערלים לא יאכל אין אני יודע שבעץ מאכל הכתוב מדבר ומה ת"ל ונטעתם כל עץ מאכל אלא לומר לך את שהוא למאכל חייב כגון הפנימי ואת שהוא לסייג לקורות ולעצים פטור : ב עת שבאו אבותינו לארץ ומצאו נטוע. פטורין . פי' כה שמצאו נטועין פטורין מן הערלה דכתיב כי תבואו אל הארץ ונטעתם פרט לשנטעו נכרים עד שלא באו ישראל לארץ : או יכול שאני מוציא את שנטעו נכרים משבאו

Continuation of translation from previous page as indicated by ◁

b *MISHNAH* 11. BEN ANTIGONUS[1] BROUGHT UP[2] FIRSTLINGS FROM BABYLON, BUT THEY DID NOT ACCEPT [THESE] FROM HIM.[3] JOSEPH THE PRIEST[4] BROUGHT FIRST-RIPE FRUITS [IN THE FORM] OF WINE AND OIL,[5] BUT THEY DID NOT ACCEPT [THESE] FROM HIM;[6] HE ALSO BROUGHT UP HIS SONS AND MEMBERS OF HIS HOUSEHOLD TO CELEBRATE THE LESSER PASSOVER[7] IN JERUSALEM, BUT THEY TURNED HIM BACK,[8] SO THAT THE THING SHOULD NOT BECOME FIRMLY FIXED AS c AN OBLIGATION. ARISTON[1] BROUGHT HIS FIRST-RIPE FRUITS FROM APAMEA[2] AND THEY ACCEPTED [THESE] FROM HIM,[3] BECAUSE THEY SAID,[4] ONE WHO OWNS [LAND] IN SYRIA IS AS ONE WHO OWNS [LAND] IN THE OUTSKIRTS OF JERUSALEM.[5]

מסכת חלה

b (1) Var. lec.: Antinos. (2) To the Temple. (3) From Deut. XIV, 23, *And thou shalt eat before the Lord thy God, in the place which He shall choose . . . the tithes of thy corn, thy wine and thine oil, and the firstlings of thy cattle and thy flocks*, a deduction is made that even as *terumah* and tithes are not to be brought to the altar from outside of sacred territory so too are firstlings not to be brought from such places. Such firstlings are to be allowed to pasture till they become unfit for sacrifice and then they are eaten by priests (v. T.J.). (4) He was evidently well-known as one who was particularly concerned to avoid circumstances defiling the sanctity attaching to a priest (v. Zeb. 10*a*, Sifra to Lev. XXI, 2, 'Er. 47*b*; 'A.Z. 13*a*). (5) The law is that first-ripe fruits may be brought in liquid form only if there was such intention at the time of the picking of the olives or grapes. (6) Because there had been no prior intention to bring them in liquid form; T.J. (7) As a rule designated 'the Second Passover'. According to Num. IX, 1-12, a person who was unclean on the Eve of the Passover and therefore unable to offer up the Paschal Lamb, was to do so exactly a month later (i.e. on the eve of the 15th Iyyar). The occasion reported here was probably in the year when his wife died on the Eve of Passover. Unwilling to miss the Paschal Sacrifice, he was, then, most reluctant to allow himself to become defiled through her dead body (v. Num. XIX, 11, 14) although the death of a wife is a case in which a man is permitted to defile himself (Lev. XXI, 2, where the phrase *'for his kin that is near unto him'* refers, according to Rabbinic interpretation, to his wife). His colleagues, however, forcibly overcame his reluctance and he did allow himself to become unclean (Sifra *loc. cit.*, Zeb. *loc. cit.* and parallels). V. Hyman, *Toledoth Tannaim* s.v. where he usually corrects an erroneous inference by Weiss (*Dor* I, p. 46, n. 2, p. 47) as to the date of the *halachah* permitting a priest to defile himself on the death of his wife. (8) According to Ex. XXIII, 17, Passover was one of the three festivals when all males were to 'appear before the Lord', but that is ordained only for the real Passover and not for the 'Second (called here Lesser) Passover'. Pilgrimage to the Temple was of course permitted throughout the year and priests—like Joseph ha-Kohen—naturally had access to the Temple. Notwithstanding this and the fact that he was attending for the purposes of carrying out the precept of the 'Second Passover', he was turned back because he brought his young sons etc. with him, lest his act lead the public—as it was most likely to do—to an erroneous conclusion that the Second Passover required just like Passover itself not only the sacrifice of the Paschal Lamb by those who had been unable to do so on the real Passover, but also the pilgrimage of all males.

c (1) Perhaps not the proper name of a man, but just a man of noble birth or standing. (2) A few places of this name are known. Probably Paneas in Syria is meant here. (3) First-ripe fruits were accepted from abroad, unlike *terumah*. The decision not to subject produce abroad to *terumah* is due to a desire to discourage priests from leaving the Holy Land as they would be tempted to do in order to collect *terumah* abroad. Owners had no need to 'bring' *terumah* to the Temple but just to distribute it among priests. Such a cause did not exist in the case of first-ripe fruits which had to be brought to the Sanctuary. (4) The phrase indicates a reference to a Mishnah in the Mishnah-collection in its earliest form. Cf. *supra* III end. (5) And the product of such Jewish owned land in Syria is accordingly subject to tithes etc. This is not the case if the land in Syria is held by Jews only on tenancy v. *supra* Mish. 7. V. Giṭ. 8*a* for a list of particulars in which Syria is treated in law like the Land of Israel. MS.M. adds the following passage (which is quoted in B. Ḳ. 110*b* and Ḥul. 133*b* as a Baraitha): Twenty-four dues were given to the priests: ten in the Temple and four in Jerusalem and ten within the borders (of the Land of Israel). These are the ten given them in the Temple: Sin-offerings, sin-offerings of birds, the unconditional and suspensive guilt-offering, the peace-offering of the congregation, the *log* of oil of the leper, the remainder of the *Omer*, the Two Loaves, the Shewbread, the residue of the meal-offerings. And these are the four given in Jerusalem: The firstlings, the first-fruits, the heave-offering from the thank-offering, and the ram of the Nazirite, and the skins of hallowed sacrifices. And these are the ten given them within the borders: *Terumah*, *terumah* of the tithe, *ḥallah*, the first of the shearing, the priestly gifts (from every beast slaughtered for food), the redemption price of the firstborn son, the redemption price of the firstling of an ass, the field of possession, the devoted field, and what was wrongly obtained of a proselyte (who died without any legal issue). No priest who is not well versed in these things may receive them as gifts.

'ORLAH

CHAPTER I

MISHNAH 1. IF ONE PLANTS [A FRUIT-TREE] TO SERVE a AS FENCING[1] OR TO PROVIDE BEAMS,[2] IT IS EXEMPT FROM [THE LAW OF] 'ORLAH.[3] R. JOSE SAYS: EVEN IF HE INTENDED[4] ONLY THE INWARD [-FACING PART OF THE TREE][5] FOR FOOD, AND THE OUTWARD [-FACING PART] FOR FENCING, THE INWARD [-FACING PART] IS SUBJECT [TO 'ORLAH], AND THE OUTWARD [-FACING PART] IS EXEMPT.[6]

MISHNAH 2. IF AT THE TIME WHEN OUR FOREFATHERS CAME INTO THE LAND[7] THEY FOUND [A TREE ALREADY] PLANTED, IT WAS EXEMPT,[8] IF THEY[9] PLANTED [A TREE], WHILST THEY HAD NOT YET CONQUERED [THE LAND],[10] IT WAS SUBJECT. IF ONE PLANTED [A TREE][11] FOR [THE USE OF]

a (1) *Sc.* to the orchard or field on the outskirts of which he plants it. (2) I.e., to be ultimately lopped or cut down for timber, either for building or for fuel. (3) In Lev. XIX, 23 it is enjoined: *And when ye shall have planted all manner of trees for food, then ye shall count the fruit thereof as forbidden* (lit., 'uncircumcised', *'orlah*); *three years shall it be as forbidden unto you.* Thus only trees grown to provide food for human consumption are subject to this law of *'orlah*. (4) Lit., 'he said'; cf. the use of the verb in, e.g., I Kings V, 19. (5) I.e., the fruit on the branches spreading towards the interior of the field or orchard. (6) Also if he intended the upper part of the tree for food and the lower for timber or vice versa, only the part meant for food is liable to *'orlah* (V. T.J.). (7) I.e., the Land of Israel, led by Joshua. (8) Because *'orlah* applies only 'when *ye* shall have planted' (Lev. *loc. cit.*). (9) 'They' in the impersonal sense. I.e., someone planted, whether Israelites or non-Israelites. (10) *Sc.* completely, but as long as they had already entered it. (11) On his private ground.

THE MANY,[12] IT IS SUBJECT. BUT R. JUDAH DECLARES IT
a EXEMPT.[1] IF ONE HAS PLANTED [A TREE] IN THE PUBLIC DOMAIN,[2] OR IF A NON-ISRAELITE HAS PLANTED,[3] OR IF A ROBBER[4] HAS PLANTED ON A BOAT,[5] OR [IT IS A TREE] THAT HAS GROWN OF ITSELF,[6] IT IS SUBJECT TO 'ORLAH.

MISHNAH 3. IF A TREE WAS UPROOTED[7] AND THE HARD SOIL[8] TOGETHER WITH IT,[9] OR IF A STREAM SWEPT IT AWAY, c AND THE HARD SOIL TOGETHER WITH IT,[9] [THEN] IF IT COULD
b HAVE LIVED[1] IT IS EXEMPT,[2] BUT IF [IT COULD] NOT, IT IS SUBJECT.[3] IF THE HARD SOIL HAS BEEN DETACHED FROM ITS SIDE,[4] OR IF A PLOUGHSHARE SHOOK IT, OR IF SOMEONE SHOOK IT,[5] AND ONE RESET IT[6] WITH EARTH,[7] [THEN] IF IT COULD HAVE LIVED,[8] IT IS EXEMPT, BUT IF NOT—IT IS SUBJECT.

MISHNAH 4. IF A TREE WAS UPROOTED[9] AND ONE ROOT THEREOF IS LEFT,[10] IT IS EXEMPT.[11] NOW HOW MUCH MUST THE [THICKNESS OF THE] ROOT BE?[12] R. SIMEON B. GAMALIEL SAID IN THE NAME OF R. ELIEZER B. JUDAH A MAN OF BERTOTHA:[13] AS [THICK AS] A PIN [USED FOR] STRETCHING.[14]

MISHNAH 5. IF A TREE WAS UPROOTED AND IT HAS A BENT-DOWN [AND ROOTED] SHOOT,[15] AND IT [THE TREE] DERIVES SUSTENANCE FROM IT [THE SHOOT], THE OLD [TREE] TURNS TO BE [CONSIDERED] LIKE THE SHOOT.[16] IF ONE BENT [AND ROOTED] A SHOOT THEREFROM[1] YEAR AFTER YEAR, AND IT BECAME DETACHED, ONE COUNTS[2] FROM THE TIME IT BECAME DETACHED.[3] THE CONNECTING SHOOT OF VINES,[4] AND A CONNECTING SHOOT [GROWING] ON ANOTHER CONNECTING SHOOT, EVEN IF ONE ROOTED THEM IN THE SOIL,[5] ARE PERMITTED [FOR CONSUMPTION].[6] R. MEIR SAID: IN AN INSTANCE[7] WHERE ITS[8] [PRODUCTIVE] CAPACITY[9] IS GOOD, IT IS PERMITTED, BUT IN AN INSTANCE WHERE ITS [PRODUCTIVE] CAPACITY IS DEFICIENT,[10] IT IS PROHIBITED. SO, TOO, IF A BENT-DOWN [AND ROOTED] SHOOT HAS BECOME DETACHED AND IT IS FULL OF FRUIT, [THEN] IF IT[11] INCREASED[12] TWO HUNDREDFOLD,[13] IT IS PROHIBITED.[14]

(12) I.e., he intends to waive his property-rights in the fruit, which is thus to become available gratis to the general public. Such a tree is subject to *'orlah* in accordance with the hermeneutical application of the wording of the text (Lev. *loc. cit.*) *'shall be forbidden* unto you' (לכם) which as a plural has an 'extending' effect (*Ribbui*) on the application of the precept, viz., to make the latter include even trees planted for unrestricted public benefit.

a (1) In his opinion, if a word or expression having the force of 'extending' is followed by another word or expression itself of similar force, then the latter is to be interpreted as having the effect of 'limiting' (Men. 89*a*). In our case the wording *'when ye shall have planted* all manner of trees *for food'* by itself might have operated as 'extending' the application of the law of *'orlah* to all trees whether the owner, at the time of planting, intends to retain his right to the fruit, or not; but the immediately following wording *'forbidden* unto you' (which, too, on its own has the force of 'extending') has now the effect of 'limiting' the application of the law to trees planted for producing fruit intended to be the owner's property. (2) But for his own benefit. (3) For an Israelite, whether the non-Israelite is paid to do it, or he does it of his own free will without pay (Maim.) on an Israelite's ground (Bert.); but L. says, whether on an Israelite's or a non-Israelite's ground, as long as it is *for* an Israelite, nor does it make any difference whether it is in the Land of Israel or outside thereof—the only difference being that in Palestine the liability to *'orlah* is directly derived from Scripture, whereas in other lands (v. *infra* III, 9) *'orlah* is an ancient tradition. (4) I.e., one who had acquired another person's ground by forcible means in face of protest; Bert. adds, only if the original owners have given up hope of recovering their property. L. says he cannot see why this should make a difference here. (5) Made of earthenware, and which touches the ground (v. Ḥal. II, 2). Earthenware permits tree-roots to strike through and absorb sap from the ground beneath it (v. T.J.). If the boat is made of wood, liability to *'orlah* would apply only if the boat has a hole or crack, since otherwise wood does not allow roots to strike through. (6) I.e., was planted unintentionally (v. Rashi to Soṭ. 43*b*). *Sc.* in a fruit cultivated area, but not if in uncultivated or forest land; in the latter kind of place such a tree is exempt from *'orlah*, unless it produces enough fruit to make worth while the trouble taken over it (*sc.* in conveying it to inhabited quarters). So T.J., v. however Rash to our Mishnah. (7) *Sc.* after the three years of *'orlah* had passed. (8) Lit., 'rock'. (9) And such tree was reset into soil.

b (1) From the soil adhering to it, without the adding of more soil. (2) Even when reset in new soil, because it derives its sustenance from and through the soil in which it was originally planted, and in respect of which it had already served the *'orlah* period. (3) Because it derives its sustenance from a new source, and is therefore accounted as a tree newly planted. (4) By wind or flood. (5) I.e., pulled it up, but not right out, and shook off the earth and replaced the tree in the same spot. (6) Lit., 'made it (up)'. (7) Reading: בעפר. I.e., the loosened soil and/or other earth. Another reading is כעפר: (by shaking etc.), he made it (viz. the hardened soil) like dust (or loose earth). (8) Without the attention mentioned. (9) V. *supra* Mish. 3, n. 7. (10) *Sc.* fast in the soil. (11) Since it continues without interruption to derive its sustenance from its original soil, in which position it has already served the *'orlah* period. (12) *Sc.* so that, through its having remained in the soil, the tree might be exempt from *'orlah*. (13) In Upper Galilee. Baer (in *Siddur Abodath Israel*, to Aboth III, 7) identifies it with Berothah (Ezek. XLVII, 16) and Berothai (II Sam. VIII, 8) which places have not been precisely located (v. BDB). (14) מיתון; var. lec., מיתוח *sc.* cloth after weaving, or thread in embroidery v. Jast. (15) בריכה, a shoot bent down and its top set into the soil (where it strikes roots) whilst this shoot remains attached to the stem. (16) *Sc.* in respect of *'orlah*. Now that the tree is uprooted, the whole tree derives the whole of its sustenance through a new channel, viz., the bent and rooted shoot, and the old tree as well as the bent shoot are liable to *'orlah*. As long as the tree stood and the shoot was attached to it, the latter, notwithstanding its top being sent in the soil, was considered as deriving most of its sustenance through the medium of the old stem (and was therefore at that time exempt from *'orlah*).

c (1) I.e., a (secondary) shoot which sprouted out of an original bent shoot. (2) *Sc.* the three years of *'orlah*. (3) As soon as the shoot is detached from the tree it begins a new life of its own, and is therefore liable to *'orlah* as if it were a newly planted tree. (4) It is usual to trail and graft a long shoot of one vine on another vine. (5 The middle of a connecting shoot is sometimes set into the soil. (6) Such connecting shoots are not subject to *'orlah* because being still attached to the old vine, they are presumed to be drawing the bulk of their sustenance from the latter. (7) Lit., 'place'. (8) I.e., that of the parent vine. (9) Lit., 'strength', vitality'. (10) Lit., 'bad'. (11) I.e., the fruit. (12) After the shoot became detached. (13) V. Kil. V, 6; cf. *infra* 6. (14) The overwhelming quantity of fruit having been produced as from a new source of sustenance, the whole of the fruit is subject to *'orlah*. This applies also to a tree with fruit on it, which was completely uprooted and then replanted.

א) סוטה פ"ד דף מג:

למשמע דבקראי פליגי דרבנן מרבה נטוע לרבים מדכתיב לכם ורבי יהודה סבר דהוי רבוי אחר רבוי ומיעט נטוע לרבים: הנוטע ברשות הרבים. בהא אפי' רבי יהודה מודה דחייב דלאו הייט נטוע לרבים ובירושלמי תניא רבי שמעון בן אלעזר אומר הנוטע לרבים חייב בערלה עלה מאליו פטור הנוטע לרבים ברשות הרבים פטור הנוטע לרבים חייב בנוטע בתוך שלו ברשות הרבים פטור כגון [שגזל] קרקע ופריך ויש קרקע נגזלת ומשני אמר רבי הילא אף על פי שאין קרקע נגזלת יש יאוש לקרקע וטובא מילתא דתמיהא דהא מתניתין תנן הגזלן שנטע חייב ועוד דמשמע דלאי [יש] יאוש פטור אדרבה כל שכן דחייב דהוי כנוטע לתוך שלו ועוד דמדמי נוטע ברשות הרבים לגזל קרקע ונוטעה והיינו בלא יאוש דומיא דרשות הרבים דלא שייך ביה יאוש דמאן מייאש ובתוספתא תניא הנוטע לרבים חייב ורבי יהודה פוטר רבי שמעון בן אלעזר אומר משמו הנוטע לרבים חייב בערלה העולה לרבים מאליו פטור מן הערלה קסבר רשב"א דמודה רבי יהודה הנוטע לרבים דחייב ולא פליג אלא בעולה מאליו לרבים: ונכרי שנטע בא"י כדדרשינן מדכתיב (ויקרא יט) כל עץ כדפרישית: והגזלן שגזל קרקע ונטעה: והנוטע בספינה. אע"פ שאינה נקובה (ד) אמרינן בירושלמי (שם) הנוטע בעציץ שאינו נקוב חייב בערלה ר' יוסי אומר מפני שהשרשים מפעפעים אותו מפני שהוא כנקוב אבל האילן דאין כלי חרס עומד בפני שרשים ומסיק דהוא הדין שחשוב כנקוב אבל זרעים (ה) והגמרא שלנו אינו סובר כן כדפרשינן בפ"ב דחלה: והעולה מאליו. לעיל אמרינן בירושלמי (שם) רבי יוסי בשם ר' שמעון בן יהולדק גפן שעלתה במקום חורשין פטור מן הערלה אמר ר' אפי' נטעה והתנינן העולה מאליו חייב בערלה תמן שנטען במקום ייסוב ברם הכא בשנטען במקום חורשין אמר ר' אליעזר הדא אמר' בשאינה עושה כדי נפילתה אבל אם היתה עושה כדי נפילתה חייבת: ג אילן שנעקר באילן זקן שעברו עליו שני ערלה (ו): אם יכול לחיות. מן הסלע שנעקר בלא שום תיקון עפר פטור ואם לאו הרי זה כאילן העולה מאליו וחייב: שזעזעתו. הניעו והרעידו: עשאו בעפר · שהרבה עליו עפר אם יכול לחיות בלא עפר שתיקן בו פטור*: ד אילן שנעקר · לגמרי אלא שנשתייר מעט מן השורש בארץ: כמחט של מתון. פי' בערוך יש ספרים שכתוב בהן מיתה ויש מיתות ויש מיתוי ויש מיתון והעיקר מיתוח כמו וימתחם כאהל לשבת (ישעיה מ) וכן מנהג האורגים יש להם עץ ארוך ברוחב היריעה ובראשו ב' מחטין שבורין וטעלין ברוחב היריעה ומכלי האורגין הן והיא דקתקינה לגר או למתוח בפ' החולץ (דף מג) הייט כהאי גוונא: ה ובו בריכה · מלשון מבריך שחופר בארץ ומבריך היחור וטומנו בעפר ומוליא ראש היחור במקום אחר ונעקר האילן והבריכה קיימת והאילן חי ממנה: חזרה הזקינה. הוא האילן שהיה זקן ועברו עליו שני ערלה להיות כבריכה ואסור משום ערלה דבריכה כל זמן שלא נפסק מן האילן זקן אין בהן איסור ערלה וכשנפסקה בין לסוף שנה בין לסוף שנתים נעשית ערלה ומונין לה משעה שנפסקה כדתני מתני' והאי אילן שנעקר כיון שאין הבריכה חיה ממנו אלא אדרבה השתא הוא חי מן הבריכה הוא תלוי בבריכה ואין הבריכה תלויה בו ומונין לו כבריכה דכשתלא הבריכה מערלה ילא גם הוא ומשנעקר מונה לשניים כמו שנפסקה עכשיו: סיפוק גפנים. סיפוק אחר סיפוק לשון סיפוק בגפנים כלשון הרכבה באילן שנטל גרופית של גפן והרכיבה בגפן *הסמוכה שעברו עליה שני ערלה: וסיפוק אחר סיפוק. הייט שבאותו גרופית חזר והרכיב גרופית אחרת ושייך לשון סיפוק בדבר הקלר כשמחבר בו דבר אחר להאריכו בדבר אחר כדתנן בפ' לולב הגזול (דף לז) סיפקו בחוט: אע"פ שהבריכה בארץ · שהבריך הסיפוק הזה בארץ וטמנו בעפר דאיכא למיחש שמא השריש בארץ קודם שנתאחז בזקינה אפי' הכי מותר דאמרינן בירושלמי (הלכה ג) רבי יסא בשם רבי אליעזר בשם רבי הונא ילדה שסיבכה בזקינה מסרה את הילדה כגון שני אילנות הסמוכין חד ילדה וחד זקינה והבקיען והכניסן זה בזה ונתאחזו א"ר חנינא בר בא מתני' אמרה כן סיפוק גפנים סיפוק על סיפוק אע"פ שהבריכה בארץ מותר והא נומר שמא השרישה הילדה עד שלא תאחוז בזקינה וכיון דקדמה השרשה לאיחוי אין הזקינה מתירתה ויש ליאסר משום ערלה אלא ודאי מותר אמר רבי חנינא בריה דרבי הלל רבי יהודה היא דרבי יהודה אמר מתאחה הוא עד שלא השריש רבי יוסי בשם רבי חנינא שרשין אין בהן ממש כלומר ואפי' תמלא לומר בעלמא דאין זקינה מתרת ילדה הנטועה מקודם שספקה אפ"ה בזקינה הכא שרי אפילו השרישה קודם דאין ממש בגרופית זה שסיפק: מקום שכחה יפה מותר · כלומר כשהזקינה כחה יפה מותר אע"פ שהרכיבה בארץ והוליאה שרשים לא אמרינן הסיפוק נעשה אילן *ולא מכח הזקינה הוא חי אבל כחה רע אסור דזקינה כמאן דליתה דמי ופריך בירושלמי (שם) מה אנן קיימין אם דבר ברי הוא שחי מכח הזקינה דברי הכל מותר ואם דבר ברי הוא שהוא חי מכח הילדה דברי הכל אסור אלא מה אנן קיימין בסתם כילד הוא יודע רבי ביבי בשם רבי חנינא אמר אם העלין הפוכים כלפי הילדה דבר ברי הוא שחי מכח הזקינה ואם היו העלין הפוכין כלפי הזקינה דבר ברי הוא שחי מכח הילדה אמר רבי יודן בר חנן סימנא דאכל מן חבריה בהית מסתכלת ביה כלומר *אמאי [פליגי] נבדוק בעלים אמר רבי יודן אבוי דר' מתניא תיפתר שנשרו העלין: בריכה שנפסקה מן הזקינה · והיו בה פירות כל מה שהגדילה עד שלא נפסקה מאביה מותר ואם לאחר שנפסקה היה תולש מיד היו מותרין אבל מה שמוסיפין אחר שנפסקה שלא נעקרה מן הארץ אסור התוספת משום ערלה: ואם הוסיף מאתים אסור · שהוסיף אחד ממאתים בהיתר ומפרש בירושלמי (שם) כילד הוא יודע לוקח אחד ומניח אחד מה שזה פוחת זה מוסיף ואמר בירושלמי אמר רבי יודן לא סוף דבר בריכה אלא אפילו אילן זקן שנעקר ויש בו פירות וחזר ונטעו עם הפירות כך דינו והא דמשמע הכא שהבריכה פטורה מן הערלה ותניא נמי בת"כ ונטעתם פרט למרכיב ולמבריך מיכן אמרו סיפוק גפנים וסיפוק סיפוקי אע"פ שהבריכן בארץ מותר ובפ"ק דר"ה (דף ט:) תניא אחד

לרבים חייב רבי יהודה פוטר *הנוטע ברשות הרבים והנכרי שנטע והגזלן שנטע והנוטע בספינה ^ג^והעולה א) מאליו חייב בערלה: ג ^ג^אילן שנעקר והסלע עמו ששטפו נהר והסלע עמו אם יכול לחיות פטור ואם לאו חייב נעקר הסלע מצדו או שזעזעתו המחרישה או שזעזעו ועשאו *כעפר אם יכול לחיות פטור ואם לאו חייב: ד ^ד^אילן שנעקר ונשתייר בו שורש (ז) פטור וכמה יהא השורש רבן שמעון בן גמליאל אומר משם רבי אלעזר בן יהודה איש ברתותא כמחט של מיתון: ה ^ה^אילן שנעקר ובו בריכה והוא חי ממנה חזרה הזקינה להיות כבריכה הבריכה שנה אחר שנה ונפסקה מונה משעה שנפסקה סיפוק הגפנים וסיפוק ע"ג סיפוק אע"פ שהבריכן בארץ מותר רמ"א מקום שכחה יפה מותר ומקום שכחה רע אסור (וכן) ^ו^בריכה שנפסקה והיא מלאה פירות אם הוסיף במאתים

שנטע ורבי יהודה אומר כי מה שאמר הש"י ונטעתם משמע בין ליחיד בין לרבים שאילו אמר ונטעתם כל עץ מאכל ולא אמר דבר אחר היינו אומרים כי הנוטע לרבים חייב אבל כשאמר יהיה לכם ערלים משמע שאינו חייב אלא הנוטע לעלמו ולפי שהוא אמר ונטעתם משמע בין ליחיד בין לרבים לכם בין ליחיד בין לרבים והוא רבוי אחר רבוי ואין רבוי אחר רבוי אלא למעט א"כ הוא למעט הנוטע לרבים וחכמים אומרים כי אמר לכם הוא אזהרה ואין כוונתו בזה החבור לפרש סדרי הסקש והסברא ודרכיו כדי שהתלה נפסך בהבנת רבוי אחר רבוי ומיעוט אחר מיעוט וזולתם אבל אזכור מה שאזכור מזה המין בזה החבור זכירה פשוטה בלבד בלי ראיה אחרת: והעולה מאליו. הוא האילן הצומח מאליו שלא נטעו שום אדם ובתנאי שיהיה לומח ברשות היחיד אבל עולה מאליו *לרשות הרבים אינו חייב בערלה ועל זה אמרו בספרא ונטעתם פרט לעולה מאליו וכן אמרו בפירוש בתוספתא העולה מאליו לרבים פטור מן הערלה: ואמרו נכרי שנטע. ענינו שנטע לישראל בשכירות או בחנם שרלה לטרוח בשבילו מעצמו אבל אם נטע הנכרי לעצמו וקנה ממנו הישראל אחר כן אינו חייב בערלה ואין הלכה כרבי יהודה: ג העפר המתעבה על עיקר האילן קורין אותו סלע והם קראו זה השם לפי שהעפר הקשה היולא אחר שמעמיק אדם לחפור נקרא סלע אצלם וממנהג האילנות שימשכו שרשיהם בארץ הרבה ויתעבה עליהם העפר עד שיהיה סביב האילן כמו האבן אפילו אחר עקירתו אומר בכאן שאם נעקר האילן באותו העפר הנקרא סלע ועמד במקום אחר אם יש באותו עפר כדי שיוכל לחיות בו שאינו חייב בערלה לפי שלא נחשב זה נטיעה שניה אבל נחשוב אותו כאלו לא נעקר: שזעזעתו המחרישה. כלומר אם נענע אותו הברזל שחורשין בו: זעזעו ועשאו בעפר · פי' שינענע האילן עצמו ויעלה אותו ממקומו אבל לא יפרישנו מן הארץ ואחר כן יתן העפר סביביו כדי שירחיב מקום האילן עצמו ויעלה אם הוא בענין שיוכל לחיות ולא יפסיד אפי' לא נתן עליו עפר אינו חייב בערלה: ד אצל האורגים קנה או עץ בשתי קצותיו שני ברזלים ארוכים ויש לכל אחד מהם כמו שנים דקים כמחט ומותחין בו רוחב הבגד כשאורגין אותו נקרא כל שן מאותם השנים שהם כמו מחטין מחט של מיתון ויש שגורסין מיתוח והוא לשון לא יותר ונאות לענין וענין מיתוח הוא מגזרת וימתחם כאהל לשבת (ישעיה מ) ויש לי בפירוש זו המלה פירוש אחר עוד אבארהו בפרק שלשה עשר מכלים ומאמר רשב"ג אין שום חולק עליו: ה כשלוקחין ענפי האילן ומותחין אותם בקרקע וטומנין אותן בעפר אותם הענפים מוליאים פרי בלי ספק ויש להם שרשים בארץ ועקרם דבקים באילן הראשון אותם הענפים שהשרישו בארץ נקראין בריכה והאילן הראשון נקרא זקנה ואמרו בכאן שאם נעקר האילן והוא גדל ומושך לחלוחית מאותם הענפים היולאים ממנה הטמונים בארץ נמלא שחזר האילן עלמו כאילו הוא בריכה וחזרו הענפים שהיו בריכה כאילו הם האילן העקרי וזהו אמרם חזרה זקנה להיות כבריכה והוא יגיד ויאמר במאמר השני דין הבריכה עם הזקנה איך הוא ואמרו הבריכה שנה אחר שנה ונפסקה ענינו שאם טמן מענפי האילן בארץ בזו השנה ולמחה ולשנה השניה לקח אלו הענפים שלמחו בשנה ראשונה וטמנם בארץ ועשה כן שנה אחר שנה כל מה שילמחו באותן הענפים כלם הדבקים קלתם בקלתם אין חייבין בערלה לפי שעקרם דבקים באילן הזקן ואם נפסקו הענפים וכרתו עקריהם מן האילן הזקן מונה משעה שנפסקו וכל אילו הבריסות חייבות בערלה: ספוק גפנים וספק על גבי ספוק. הוא שיקח אדם ענף מזו הגפן וימתח אותו עד שיגיע בגפן אחרת וירכיב קלתו בה אפילו הטמינו בארץ ר"ל אפי' לקח הענף וטמנו בארץ וספק על גבי ספוק הוא שירכיב קלת ענף זה האילן בזה האילן האחר וקלת ענף זה האילן בזה האילן וכל זה הענין פטור מן הערלה ואמר בספרי ונטעתם פרט למבריך ולמרכיב ולעולה מאליו מכאן אמר ספק הגפנים ספוק על גבי ספוק אף על פי שהבריכן בארץ מותר וזו ההברכה וההרכבה שזכר בסיפרא שאין חייבים בערלה היא אותה שהמשיל בו והוא שיבריך האילן עקרו קיים עומד בארץ לא נעקר או ימתח ענף מאילן זה ויטע קלתו באילן אחר ועקרו קיים באילן הראשון אבל אם פסק ענף והרכיבו באילן או הטמינו בארץ הרי זה חייב בערלה וזו ההרכבה וההברכה הם שרמז להם באמרם אחד הנוטע ואחד המבריך ואחד המרכיב ואתה שמור אלו העקרים ולא תשתבש בהם' ותחשוב שהם זה הפך זה כשתראה לשם שנטע ומרכיב ומבריך חייבים בערלה ובסיפרא ביארו כי מבריך ומרכיב אינו חייב בערלה והם שני מינין מן ההרכבה ושני מינין מן ההברכות כמו שבארתי לך: ואמר ר' מאיר. כי זה הענף שהרכיבו קלתו אם יש בו לחלוחית הרבה והרכיבו באילן אחר ולא נתחזקה כחה הרבה לפי א] שאותו האילן (ממנה היה הענף שהרכיב) היה כחו רע וחלוש ואותו אילן שהרכיב בו יפה וחזק שהיא חייבת בערלה *ואין הלכה כרבי מאיר: ואמרו וכן בריכה שנפסקה. חוזר על מאמרם בתחלת ההלכה מונה משעה שנפסקה וכבר בארנו שהפירות שהם בבריכה אין חייבות בערלה כל זמן שעקרי הענפים דבוקים באילן הראשון ר"ל הזקנה ואם יש בהם פירות ונפסקו עקרי הענפים מן הזקנה שיהיו חייבים בדיני הערלה בזמן העתיד כמו שאמר מונה משעה שנפסקה ויהיה מותר לאכול אותם פירות לאחר לפי שהם גדלו בהיתר ואם הניח הפירות כדי שיגדילו אחר שנפסקה כשיעור אחד ממאתים שהוא שיעור איסור הערלה כמו שיתבאר

פי' מהר"י בן מלכי צדק

ישראל לארץ ת"ל כל עץ מיכן אמרו נטעו נוים עד שלא כבשו ישראל עדיין חייב: הנוטע ברשות הרבים. דכתיב ונטעתם: ונכרי שנטע. פי' בארץ ישראל חייב כדכתיב כל עץ: והגזלן שנטע חייב. פי' כגון שגזל קרקע ונטעה: והנוטע בספינה חייב. דכתי' ונטעתם מכ"מ: והעולה מאליו חייב בערלה. דכתיב כל עץ: ג אילן שנעקר וסלע עמו. אילן ישן שכבר עברו עליו שני ערלה שנעקר עם כל הגוש שלו אם יכול לחיות בלא כלום חידוש אלא יניק מגושיה ולא צריך לינק מעפר אחר הרי הוא כאשר היה. אבל אם צריך הוא לעפר אחר דבגושו בלבד היה מתייבש אע"פ שהוא ישן חייב בערלה דהוה ליה עולה מאליו וחייב: ד אילן שנעקר ונשתייר שם שורש. פי' האילן נעקר לגמרי אלא עדיין נשאר שורשו בארץ ומוציא חליפין הרי הוא כמות שהיה ופטור: וכמה יהא בשורש. פי' שיהא כמו שהיה: רשב"ג אומר משום רבי אלעזר בן יהודה איש ברתותא כמחט של מיתון. ויש שנוין של מיתה ויש שנוין של מיתוי ויש שונין של מיתוח והוא העיקר מלשון וימתחם כאהל לשבת וכך מנהגם האורגים יש להן עץ ארוך ברוחב היריעה ובראשו שני מחטים שבורים ונועצין ברוחב היריעה מיכן ומיכן כדי למשכה ומכלי אורגין היא ומאי טעמא פטור דא"ר יוחנן בש"ר ינאי מכיון שיש בו כמחט של מיתוח דבר ברי הוא שיש לו ג' שנים: ה אילן זקן שנעקר לגמרי ובו בריכה שלא נעקרה והוא חי ממנה. פי' הבריך האילן וקיימא לן דאין ערלה להברכה אלא אם כן נפסק מאביו ועתה הזקן נעקר וההברך נשאר והזקן חי ממנה חזר הזקן להיות אסור משום ערלה כבריכה: הבריכה שנה אחר שנה ונפסקה. פי' נפסקה הבריכה מן האילן והיא בפני עצמה נאסרה משום ערלה ונותן לה ג' שני ערלה משעה שנפסקה. אבל קודם שתיפסק הרי היא בחזקת היתר כזקינה: סיפוק על סיפוק. פי' ועל אותו סיפוק החדש סיפק יותר ואע"פ שהבריכן לארץ. פי' אע"פ שהבריך הגפנים שסיפק לגפן הישנה בארץ דיש לומר מרעא קא רבי תמיה באנפי נפשה היא. והסיפוק השני והסיפוק השלישי חי מן הסיפוק הסמוך לזקינה ולא מזקינה הכל מותר לא שנא הסיפוק הקרוב לה ולא שנא הסיפוקין הרחוקין ממנה מה שעם מותר כי מן הגפן: הזקינה הן חיין: ר' מאיר אומר מקום שכחה יפה מותר. פי' מקום שהגפן הזקינה בריאה וכחה יפה מותר דוודאי ממנה חי הסיפוק מקום שכחה רע אסור דלא מינה קא רבו: בריכה שנפסקה. פי' מן הזקינה ולא נעקרה והיא מלאה פירות אם הוסיף במאתים אסור. פי' אנו שנינו שמכיון שנפסקה הבריכה מן הזקינה כל הפירות שעושה מיכן ואילך אסורין משום ערלה עד ג' שנים. אבל הפירות שהוציאה עד ש"א נפסקה מאביה מותרין אם ליקטן מיד אבל אם הניחם שם משנפסקה עד שהוסיפה הפירות אחד מר' ממה שהיו אסור פי' כגון שבעת שנפסקה היה שיעור הפרי כמאתים חרדלים והוסיפו ונעשה כמאתים ואחד

ד א מיי' שם הל' ס טוש"ע שם סעי' כו:
ה ב מיי' שם הלכה יב טוש"ע שם סעיף כו:
ו ג מיי' שם הל' יד טוש"ע שם סעיף יט:
ז ד מיי' שם וטוש"ע שם סעיף כ:
ח ה מיי' שם וטוש"ע שם סעיף טז:
ט ו שם סעיף כב:

פירוש הרא"ש

אם נטעו למאס ללולב או לאתרוג חייב: (ד) אם היא של חרס: (ה) אבל של עץ בעי נקיבה: (ו) ועקרו הרוח או שטפו נהר והוליכו למקום אחר ומן העפר שסביב השרשין עמו והוסיף עליו עפר שם ונשרש בארץ אומדים אותו עובדי אדמה אם היה יכול לאיות מן העפר שבא עמו בלא תוספת עפר אחר הרי הוא כנטוע במקומו ופטור מן הערלה: (ז) אז ידוע שיכול לחיות במקומו ופטור אף אם הוסיף בו עפר:

עי' תוי"ט

הגהות מהר"י לנדא

פ"א א] מ"ה בר"מ לפי שאותו האילן ממנה היה. נ"ל שממנו היה הענף שהרכיבה היה כחו יפה מותר שאם כו':

נ"ל בשאר
נ"ל הזקינה
נ"ל אלא
נ"ל חייב נבדוק
עי' בכרע"ג

הנוטע וא' המבריך וא' המרכיב לפני ר"ה ל' יום עלתה לו שנה ומותר לקיימן בשביעית דמשמע דיש ערלה בהברכה ההיא כשנפסקה מאביה אבל כל זמן שלא נפסקה מותר כדמוכח מתני' וגבי הרכבה לא משכחת אלא ילדה בילדה וצריך לדקדק אי הוה שייך לשנויי הכי בפרק משוח מלחמה (דף מג:) גבי חוזר מן המלחמה משום מבריך דמשני כאן בהרכבת היתר ותימה דבמנחות בפ' רבי ישמעאל (דף סט:) דבעי רבי שמעון בן פזי סבולת שהביאה שליש קודם לעומר ועקרה ושתלה אחר העומר והוסיפה מהו בתר עיקר אזלינן ושריא העומר או בתר התוספת אזלינן ועד שיבא עומר הבא תיפשוט מהא

דאמר רבי אבהו אמר ר' יוחנן ילדה שסיככה בזקינה ובה פירות אפי' הוסיפו במאתים אסורים ומסיק דהיא גופא מיבעיא ליה מיפשט פשיטא ליה לרבי יוחנן דבתר עיקר אזלינן לא שנא לקולא ול"ש לחומרא או דילמא ספוקי מספקא ליה

שיתבאר נאסרו כל אותם הפירות ונעשו ערלה וידיעת שיעור תוספת אלו הפירות כמו שבארנו בפרק חמישי מכלאים (מ"ו):
ד עוד יתבאר לך בפרק של אחר זה כי הערלה וכלאי הכרם עולין באחד ומאתים

אסור: ו א) נטיעה של ערלה ושל כלאי הכרם שנתערבו בנטיעות הרי זה לא ילקוט ואם לקט יעלה באחד ומאתים ובלבד שלא יתכוין ללקוט ר' יוסי אומר א אף יתכוין ללקוט ויעלה באחד ומאתים: ז ב העלים והלולבים ומי גפנים וסמדר מותרות בערלה וברבעי ג ובנזיר ד ואסורים באשרה ב) רבי יוסי אומר הסמדר אסור מפני שהוא פרי ג) ר' אליעזר אומר המעמיד בשרף הערלה אסור אמר רבי ד) יהושע שמעתי בפירוש ה שהמעמיד בשרף העלים בשרף העקרים מותר בשרף הפגים אסור מפני שהם פרי: ח ו ענקוקלות והחרצנים והזגים והתמד שלהם ה) קליפי רמון והנץ שלו קליפי אגוזים והגרעינים אסורים בערלה ובאשרה ז ובנזיר ח ומותרין ברבעי והנובלות כולם אסורות: ט ו) ר' יוסי אומר ט נוטעין יחור של ערלה ואין נוטעין אגוז של ערלה מפני שהוא פרי י ואין מרכיבין בכפניות של ערלה:

פרק שני

א התרומה ז) כ ותרומת מעשר *של דמאי החלה והבכורים עולים באחד ומאה ומצטרפין זה עם זה

MISHNAH 6. IF A SHOOT OF 'ORLAH OR OF THE 'MIXTURE OF THE VINEYARD'[15] BECAME MIXED UP WITH [OTHER] SHOOTS,[16] IN SUCH AN EVENT ONE MAY NOT GATHER [THE FRUIT]; BUT IF ONE HAS GATHERED [IT], IT IS NEUTRALIZED
a IN TWO HUNDRED-AND-ONE,[1] PROVIDED ONLY THAT [IN GATHERING THE FRUIT] HE DID NOT ACT DELIBERATELY.[2] R. JOSE SAID: EVEN IF HE ACTED DELIBERATELY, IT BECOMES NEUTRALIZED IN TWO HUNDRED-AND-ONE.[3]

MISHNAH 7. LEAVES, SPROUTS, SAP OF VINES,[4] AND VINE-BUDS[5] ARE PERMITTED IN RESPECT OF 'ORLAH[6] AND REBA'I,[7] ALSO TO A NAZIRITE,[8] BUT ARE PROHIBITED IN [THE EVENT OF THEIR COMING FROM] AN ASHERAH.[9] R. JOSE SAID: VINE-BUDS ARE PROHIBITED BECAUSE THEY
b ARE FRUIT.[1] R. ELIEZER SAID: IF ONE CURDLES [MILK] WITH THE RESINOUS SUBSTANCES OF [A TREE LIABLE TO] 'ORLAH, IT IS PROHIBITED.[2] R. JOSHUA SAID: I HAVE RECEIVED AN EXPLICIT TRADITION[3] THAT IF ONE CURDLES [MILK] WITH THE RESINOUS SUBSTANCE OF THE LEAVES, OR WITH THE RESINOUS SUBSTANCE OF THE ROOTS, IT IS PERMITTED,[4] BUT WITH THE RESINOUS SUBSTANCE OF THE UNRIPE BERRIES, IT IS PROHIBITED, BECAUSE THESE ARE FRUIT.[5]

(15) This is prohibited in Deut. XXII, 9, v. Kil. VIII, 1. In the case of a vineyard a whole bed, and not merely one shoot, must be understood here. (16) And one cannot definitely distinguish the prohibited from the permitted.

a (1) I.e., if the permitted trees are two hundred times as many as the prohibited, the latter, if not identifiable, are considered as neutralized in the total, and all the trees are permitted. (2) The provision whereby the prohibition attaching to any prohibited commodity is neutralized through the latter being indistinguishably mixed with a given multiple of like permitted commodity, is valid only when such a state of affairs is an unintentional *fait accompli;* but not if deliberately contrived. (3) It should be noted that he does not dispute the principle on which the first-stated opinion is based (v. note 2), but he rules to the contrary on the ground that no Rabbinic precautionary prohibition is enacted for unlikely contingencies—and it is unlikely that one should plant a new tree among other, older trees without some distinguishing mark (v. Rashi to Giṭ. 54*b*). In the case of a vineyard, it may be that he is aware of having accidentally made one of his vines *kil'ayim*, but he does not know which vine (v. T.J.). (4) Which oozes out when a vine is cut during the month of Nisan (about April). (5) Incipient grape berries. (6) Since those parts of the tree are not looked upon as 'fruit' to which alone the law of *'orlah* applies, according to Lev. XIX, 23, '*ye shall declare the* fruit *thereof forbidden* ('orlah)', v. Sifra *ad. loc.* (7) Lit., 'the fourth', *sc.* year in age. Lev. XIX, 24 says of the tree the fruit of which had been prohibited as '*orlah*' for three years, *And in the fourth year all the fruit thereof shall be holy, for giving praise unto the Lord.* The technical term for this fruit is *neta'* (the plantation of) *reba'i.* The fruit of the fourth year could not be eaten without having been first redeemed in the same manner as the Second Tithe. (8) According to Num. VI, 1-4, a man who takes the vow to be a Nazirite, *shall abstain from wine and strong drink: he shall drink no vinegar of wine, or vinegar of strong drink, neither shall he drink any liquor of grapes, nor eat fresh grapes or dried. All the days of his Naziriteship shall he eat nothing that is made of the grape-vine, from the pressed grapes even to the grape-stone.* As Scripture says: '*he shall not drink . . . nor eat*' the prohibition applies only to such portions of the vine which it is usual to consume either as food or drink, and not to those other parts of the vine enumerated in the Mishnah. (9) A tree (or grove) which is itself an object of worship, or under which an idol has been placed. Not only is the planting or the appointing of an Asherah prohibited (Deut. XVI, 21) and its destruction, in the Land of Israel, commanded (ibid. XII, 2-3), but according to the general rule (ibid. XIII, 18) *and there shall cleave nought of the thing devoted* (*sc.* to idolatry) *to thy hand*, no benefit whatsoever may be enjoyed from even the most insignificant portion of an Asherah or of any other idolatrous object.

b (1) I.e., ultimately. (2) Since, in R. Eliezer's view, the resinous substance is considered as 'fruit'. (3) Lit., 'I have heard in explicit form'. Halevy (*Doroth* II, p. 265 ff) says the traditions (שמועים) cited by the Tannaim were from two main sources: (*a*) Teachers who transmitted early Mishnayoth, or decisions arrived at in the schools, literally as heard by them, but without elucidation. Such teachers are designated in T.J. רבה דמתניתא, and in T.B. רבו שלמדו מקרא ומשנה (v. B.M. 33 and Rashi ad. loc.). (*b*) Teachers who explained the reasons for the main laws, and taught in what circumstances and how these were to be varied. Sometimes a scholar had not managed to get such elucidation from the latter kind of teacher, so he brought the matter before the Assembly of Scholars where it was clarified and amplified by one of the scholars (called in T.J. רבה דאולפנא and in T.B. רבו שלמדו חכמה). In our case both R. Eliezer and R. Joshua had learnt the general rule that the resinous substance of a tree which is *'orlah* was prohibited, but R. Joshua had, in addition, (from his רבו דאולפנא) detailed instruction as to its application and was able to supply it to his colleagues in Jamnia, when the main rule was stated by R. Eliezer. (4) Because this resinous substance is from parts of trees which are definitely not considered as 'fruit'. (5) Which can be and—in certain circumstances—are consumed. R. Joshua's amplified form of the rule is the accepted law.

◁ *For the continuation of the English translation of this page see overleaf.*

הנוטע וא' המבריך וא' המרכיב לפני ר"ה ל' יום עלתה לו שנה ומותר לקיימן בשביעית דמשמע דיש ערלה בהברכה היא כשנפסקה מאביה אבל כל זמן שלא נפסקה מותר כדמוכח מתני' וגבי הרכבה לא מסכת' אלא ילדה בילדה וצריך לדקדק אי הוה שייך לשנויי הכי בפרק משוח מלחמה (דף מג:) גבי חוזר מן המלחמה משום מבריך דמשני כאן בהרכבת איסור כאן בהרכבת היתר ותימה דבמנחות בפ' רבי ישמעאל (דף סט:) דבעי רבי שמעון בן פזי שבולת שהביאה שליש קודם לעומר ועקרה ושתלה אחר העומר והוסיפה מהו בתר עיקר אזלינן ושריא העומר או בתר התוספת אזלינן ועד שיבא עומר הבא תיפשוט מהא דאמר רבי אבהו אמר ר' יוחנן ילדה שסיבכה בזקינה ובה פירות אפי' הוסיפו במאתים אסורים ומסיק דהיא גופא מיבעיא ליה מיפשט פשיטא ליה לרבי יוחנן דבתר עיקר אזלינן לא שנא לקולא ול"ש להומרא או דילמא ספוקי מספקא ליה להומרא אמרינן לקולא לא אמרינן ועלתה בתיקו והשתא תיפשוט ממתני' דהכא לקולא לא אזלינן בתר עיקר דקתני בריכה שנפסקה והיא מליאה פירות אם הוסיף במאתים אסורה ועוד תימה תיפשוט מהא דתנית המעביר עציץ נקוב בכרם אם הוסיף מאתים אסור אלמא לא אזלינן בתר עיקר אלא בתר תוספת ומיהו הכא יש לומר דשאני התם כדדרשינן בפ' כל שעה (דף כה:) כתיב המלאה וכתיב הזרע הא כיצד זרוע מעיקרו בהשרשה זרוע ובא הוסיף אין לא הוסיף לא ושמא מהתם נמי ילפינן ערלה הואיל ואיסורן שוה כי היכי דבכלאים אזלינן בתר תוספת להחמיר הוא הדין בערלה והא דמבעיא ליה אי אזיל רבי יוחנן בתר עיקר בין לקולא בין לחומרא לא בערלה ולא בכלאי הכרם קאמר אלא לשאר דברים כגון גבי חדש וגבי תרומה ושביעית דלהכי מייתי לה בנדרים בפ' הנודר מן הירק ואם תאמר דהתם במנחות משמע דרבי יוחנן סבר כרבי יונתן דאמר התם בצל ששתלו בכרם ונעקר הכרם אפי' הוסיף מאתים אסור דמתרוייהו בעי למיפשט דאזלינן בתר עיקר וכן משמע בפ' הנודר מן הירק (דף נז:) גבי בצל שעקרו בשביעית ונטעו בשמינית ורבו גידולים על עיקרו דמיבעיא לן אי גידולי היתר מעלין את האיסור אי לא ופשטה רבי ינאי מהא דאמר רבי ינאי בצל של תרומה שנטעו ורבו גידוליו על עיקרו מותר אמר ליה רבי ירמיה שביק מר תרתין דאמר רבי אבהו א"ר יוחנן ומייתי התם ילדה שסיבכה בזקינה והיא דרבי יונתן דבצל ששתלו משמע דתרוייהו אית להו להדדי ופליגי אדאמר רבי [ינאי] וקשיא דרבי יוחנן אדר"י דבההיא שמעתא גופא דמנחות ונדרים קאמר ר' יוחנן ליטרא בצל שתיקנו וזרעו מתעשר לפי כולו דאזיל בתר תוספת ובההיא דבצל של תרומה דפליג רבי יוחנן על רבי ינאי וקסבר דאפילו רבו גידוליו על עיקרו אסור אלמא אזיל בתר עיקר אם כן תיפשוט בעיא דמנחות דכי אזיל רבי יוחנן דווקא להחמיר ולא להקל דאי להקל אזיל בתר עיקר אמאי מתעשר הגדל והלא תיקנו: ו שנתערבו בנטיעות של ערלה ניחא דאיכא חדא דערלה ולא ידיעא אבל דכלאי הכרם פריך בירושלמי וכי כל הנטיעות אינן כלאים ומשני כשהעביר עציץ נקוב תחת הגפן והשתא לא ידיעה הי מינייהו: לא ילקוט מפני המעורב ר' יוסי אומר אף יתכוון ללקוט אמרינן בירושלמי (הל' ד) מה טעם דרבי יוסי שכן דרך בני אדם להיות מידל בגפנים כלומר הרואה אומר מידל הוא ובפרק הניזקין אמרי' טעמא דרבי יוסי חזקה אין אדם אוסר כרמו בנטיעה אחת ולא חיישינן דילמא אתי לאיערומי לערב הנטיעה בתחלה (ח): ז מותרות בערלה. דערלתו את פריו כתיב וכל הני לאו פריו נינהו: וברבעי נמי כתיב יהיה כל פריו: ובנזיר. אמרינן בירושלמי (הל' ה) דלא כרבי אליעזר דתנן בפרק ג' מינין מכל אשר יעשה מגפן היין אפי' עלין ולולבין במשמע: ואסורין באשרה. דכתיב ולא ידבק בידך מאומה מן החרם: ר' יוסי אומר סמדר אסור. ויש מי ששונה בירושל' דאנזיר קאי ופריך עליה דאם פרי הוא יהא אסור בכל: המעמיד הלב לעשות גבינה בשרף הערלה אסור בפ"ק דנדה אמרינן דרבי אליעזר אסר בין בקטפא דפירא בין בקטפא דגווזא בין באילן העושה פירות בין באילן שאינו עושה פירות: ח ענקוקלות. מפרש בירושל' ר' זעירא וחד מן רבנן בשם רב ענבים שלקו עד שלא הביאו שליש אמר ר' יוסי בר בון אפי' לקו משהביאו שליש אמר רבי חייא בר יעקב לשון נוטריקון הוא ענבים דלקו תליתייהו: הרצנים. בפ' ג' מינים (דף לד:) תנן חרצנים אלו החיצונים זגים אלו הפנימים דברי רבי יהודה רבי יוסי אומר כדי שלא תטעה כזוג של בהמה החיצון זוג הפנימי עינבל: תמד שלהן. שעשו מהן תמד: והנץ שלו. פרח שעל הפטמא: והגלעינין. גרעיני' של שאר פירות (ט): ומותרין ברבעי. כדתניא פרי אתה פודה ואי אתה פודה לא בוסר ולא פגים: והנובלות. בפרק כילד מברכין (דף מ:) בנובלות סתמא כולי עלמא לא פליגי דבושלי כומרא כי ... בזקינה דילמא אתי נמיכל כפניות שלו ואמרי' לעיל בירושל' מתניתין דרבי לאגור סמדר אסור מפני שהוא פרי רבי ינחק שאל מאן *אין מרכיבין כפניות של ערלה רבי יוסי:

אסור: ו א) נטיעה של ערלה ושל כלאי הכרם שנתערבו בנטיעות הרי זה לא ילקוט ואם לקט יעלה באחד ומאתים ובלבד שלא יתכוין ללקוט ר' יוסי אומר א) אף יתכוין ללקוט ויעלה באחד ומאתים: ז ב) העלים והלולבים ומי גפנים וסמדר מותרות בערלה וברבעי ג) ובנזיר ד) ואסורים באשרה ג) רבי יוסי אומר הסמדר אסור מפני שהוא פרי ג) ר' אליעזר אומר המעמיד בשרף הערלה אסור אמר רבי ד) יהושע שמעתי בפירוש ה) שהמעמיד בשרף העלים בשרף העקרים מותר בשרף הפגים אסור מפני שהם פרי: ח ו) ענקוקלות והחרצנים והזגים והתמד שלהם ה) קליפי רמון והנץ שלו קליפי אגוזים והגרעינים אסורים בערלה ובאשרה ו) ובנזיר ז) ומותרין ברבעי והנובלות כולם אסורות: ט י) ר' יוסי אומר ח) נוטעין יחור של ערלה ואין נוטעין אגוז של ערלה מפני שהוא פרי ט) ואין מרכיבין בכפניות של ערלה:

פרק שני

א התרומה י) ותרומת מעשר *של דמאי החלה והבכורים עולים באחד ומאה ומצטרפין זה עם זה

שיתבאר נאסרו כל אותם הפירות ונעשו ערלה וידיעת שיעור תוספת אלו הפירות כמו שבארנו בפרק חמישי מכלאים (מ"ו): ו עוד יתבאר לך בפרק של אחר זה כי הערלה וכלאי הכרם עולין באחד ומאתים וזהו כי כשנפל מאחד מהם חלק במאתים חלקים שמותר לאכול הכל כמו שיתבאר ואם נפל חלק מהם בפחות ממאתים חלקים נאסר הכל על כן כשיתערב זו הנטיעה האסורה בכלל נטיעות כשרות אפילו היו אלף אסור ללקוט מהם שום דבר לכתחלה לפי שאינו יודע אם מן הפרי המותר לקט אם מן האיסורים ואם לקט דבר מאותן הנטיעות דין אותו הפרי הנלקט מהן אם נתערב ממנו חלק באחד ומאתים חלקים מפירות אחרות מותרות הכל מותר לאכילה ואמר בכלאי הכרם נטיעה בגמרא תקנו ערוגה וכאילו אמר נטיעה של ערלה שנתערבה בנטיעות וערוגה של כלאי הכרם שנתערבה בערוגות לפי שכלאי הכרם הם ירק או מיני תבואה או מיני זרעים שנזרעו בכרם אבל אילן לא *ואין הלכה כרבי יוסי: ז לולבים הם הענפים הרכים היוצאים בראשי הבדים הקשים והם רכים מאד ומי גפנים המים היוצאים מן הגפנים כשפולעין וחותכין הגפן או הזמורות בימי ניסן וסמדר הוא הפרח שממנו יהיה הפרי אבל בבוסר אין חולק שהוא אסור והש"י אמר וערלתם ערלתו את פריו (ויקרא יט) ואמר בספרא פריו פרט לעלים ולולבים ולמי גפנים וסמדר: ואמר וברבעי רוצה בו שמותר לאכול כל אלו הדברים מנטע רבעי בלא פדיון לפי שהשם אמר בו יהיה כל פריו קדש הלולים לה' (שם) ואלו אינם פרי: ואמרו ובנזיר ענינו שמותר לנזיר לאכלם מן הגפן לפי שהש"י אמר (במדבר ו) מכל אשר יעשה מגפן היין מחרצנים ועד זג לא יאכל ואלו אינם מאכל: וכולם הם אסורות בהנאה כשהם מאשרה והאשרה הוא אילן נעבד כמו שנבאר בע"ז למאמר ה' (דברים יג) ולא ידבק בידך מאומה מן החרם וגו': שרף הערלה הוא השרף היוצא מן האילנות ועוקץ ערלה וכבר פירשנו פעמים בזה הסדר (שביעית פ"ד מ"ה ופ"ז מ"ז) כי פגים הם הפרי שאינו מבושל והרבה בני אדם מעמידין החלב בדבר לבן כמו חלב שיוצא שותת ויולא מעוקצי הפגים קודם בישולם ועליו אמר שרף הפגים ומעמיד פירושו שמקפיא החלב ועושה ממנו גבינה כמו וכגבינה תקפיאני (איוב י) והלכה כר' יהושע ואין הלכה כר' יוסי: ח ענקוקלות. פירשו זה בגמ' שהם הענבים שלא הבשילו כל צרכן והפסיד אותם הרוח המפסיד האילנות והוא אמרם ענבים דלקו תלתיהון: וחרצנים הם הגרעינים וזגים הקליפות שהם על גרגירי הענבים: והתמד שלהם. ענינו השריית החרצנים והזגים במים וכבר בארנו זה (פ"ה מ"ז) (בתרומות) [במעשרות]: וקליפי רמון. קליפתו החיצונים: והנץ שלו. הפרח: וגרעינין וגלעינין שוה והם הגרעינין שבתוך הפרי מכל דבר שיש לו גרעינים כגון תמרים והזיתים והאפרסקין ודומיהן וטעם איסור כל אלו הדברים באשרה כבר אמרנו הראיה והוא אמרו יתעלה ולא ידבק בידך מאומה מן החרם ואסור ענקוקלות וחרצנים והזגין והתמד בנזיר מן הכתוב שאמר הש"י מחרצנים ועד זג לא יאכל ואמר חומץ יין וחומץ שכר וכל משרת ענבים וגו': ואסר בערלה קליפי רמון והנץ שלו לא מפני שהם פרי אלא לפי שהם ראוים לצבוע ואסור לצבוע בערלה ואמר בספרי לא יאכל אין לי אלא שלא יאכל מנין שלא יצבע ולא ידליק ת"ל וערלתם ערלתו ערלים לרבות את כולם והוצרו כולם בנטע רבעי לפי שנטע רבעי אינו אסור בהנאה אבל הוא כמו מעשר שני נאכל לבעליו כמו שבארנו במסכת מעשר שני (פ"ה מ"ח) ולא יתקדש בו אלא פרי הראוי לאכילה:

... וזכרנו כי זה סמכו חכמים למה שאמר הש"י במעשר מן המעשר שהוא א' ממאה את מקדשו ממנו (במדבר יח) ואמרו דבר שאתה מרים

א התרומה ותרומת מעשר של דלאי ותרומת מעשר של דמאי · אבל תרומה גדולה לא בעי אפרושי מדמאי דלא נחשדו עליה (א) עולין בק"א סאה אחת מאלו שנפלה למאה סאין מעלהו והשאר מותר והא דעולה בא' ומאה דריש לה בסיפרי בפרשת קרח מדכתיב גבי תרומת מעשר (במדבר יח) מכל חלבו את מקדשו ממנו [מה שהורם ממנו] שאם נפל להוכו הרי הוא מקדשו דהיינו אחד במאה דק' סאין של טבל שיעור תרומת מעשר שבו הייט סאה ואם חזר ונפל לנ"ט אסר הכל אבל נפלה למאה מותר וכלאי הכרם ילין התם בגזירה שוה מלאה מלאה דיש לו ביטול ומקום שכפל את האיסור כפל את המלאה ולכך בעו מאתים: ומצטרפין זה עם זה · לאסור ואם בין כולן יש יותר מסאה שנפל לק' נדמע הכל אע"פ שבאחד מהן אין סאה ומודה ר' שמעון בהני דכולהו איקרו תרומה ושם אחד להם ולא דמי לערלה וכלאי הכרם שהן ב' שמות וחלה נמי איקרי תרומה דכתיב (שם טו) חלה תרימו תרומה וכן בכורים כדדרשינן

... לה אסורה והגיית תרומה מותרת ואגן ארוחנן בלישנא דנירסא דירושל' קטיעא טובא: ח הענקוקלות. פי' [בירושלמי] מה ענקוקלות אמר רב ענבין שלקו עד שלא הביא שליש א"ר יוסי ... דתנא בר אדא לשון נוטריקון הוא ענבין דלקין תרתיהון פי' ואת שמע מינה בין שמועת רב בין שמועת ר' יוסי פ"א לגרוס תלתיהון. פי' [היינו] ענבים. קוק דלקיין. לוה תלתיהון. הרי כאן ... שלישיתן: והתמד שלהן. פי' התמד שנעשה מן הענקוקלות ומן החרצנין ומן הזגין. כדתנינן התמד עד שלא החמיץ דכיון דאינהו אסירי התמד שלהן נמי אסור: קליפי רמון ... של רמון: קליפי אגוזין והגרעינין. פי' משל שאר פירות אסור בערלה ובאשירה ובנזיר כולן ענבים וזגים והחרצנים שלהן ותמד שלהן ומותרין ברבעי. תניא פרי אתה פודה לא בוסר ולא ... נקראין נבלות] בכולן אסורות אפי' ברבעי דפרי אינון: ט ר' יוסי אומר נוטעין יחור של ערלה מפני שמכל מקום לסוף ג' שנים ניתור היא וכשנוטע השתא סוף סוף עד ג' שנים ... היכי דמי כגון דשקל יחור של אילן בר ב' שנים ואילן שבקיה והוה משתרי בתר שתא השתא דנטעיה לא משתרי עד שישלים ג' שנים ואין נוטעין אגוז של ערלה מפני שהוא ... ערלה אסור לעולם ועתה שנוטעו לסוף ג' שנים אתי לידי היתר ואין מרכיבין בכפניות של ערלה:

פרק ב א ומצטרפין זה עם זה. פי' חצי סאה דתרומה וחצי סאה דתרומת מעשר שנפלו לפחות ממאה סאין הולין נדמעו שנצטרפו תרומה ותרומת מעשר תעשו סאה ואסרין הכרי ואפי' ... ערלה וכלאי הכרם אינן מצטרפין מודה הכא דמצטרפי' שכל אילו הדברים שם אחד הן שכולן נקראין תרומה גם החלה דכתיב תרימו תרומה גם הבכורין דכתיב ותרומת ידך אלו הבכורים

Continuation of translation from previous page as indicated by ◁

MISHNAH 8. GRAPES LESS THAN A THIRD GROWN,[6] AND
c GRAPE-STONES,[1] AND GRAPE-HUSKS,[2] AND THE TAMAD[3] MADE OF THESE, THE SKIN OF A POMEGRANATE AND ITS SPROUTINGS,[4] THE SHELLS OF NUTS, AND FRUIT-STONES,[5] ARE PROHIBITED IN RESPECT OF 'ORLAH, ASHERAH AND A NAZIRITE,[6] BUT PERMITTED IN RESPECT OF REBA'I.[7] UNDER-RIPE FRUIT[8] IS PROHIBITED [IN RESPECT OF] ALL OF THEM.[9]

MISHNAH 9. R. JOSE SAID: ONE MAY PLANT A SHOOT[10] OF [A TREE WHICH IS] 'ORLAH,[11] BUT ONE MAY NOT PLANT A NUT OF [A TREE WHICH IS] 'ORLAH, BECAUSE IT IS FRUIT;[12] AND ONE MAY NOT GRAFT [PALM BRANCHES BEARING] EARLY DATE BERRIES[13] BELONGING TO [A TREE WHICH IS] 'ORLAH.[14]

CHAPTER II

d *MISHNAH* 1. TERUMAH, TERUMAH-OF-THE-TITHE OF DEMAI,[1] OR HALLAH[2] OR FIRST-RIPE FRUITS,[3] BECOME NEUTRALIZED IN A HUNDRED-AND-ONE,[4] AND LESSER QUANTITIES OF THESE ARE RECKONED TOGETHER [AS

(6) Which have fallen off a vine (L.). For the term ענקוקלות, meaning 'undeveloped grapes', v. Dictionaries.
c (1) חרצנים. (2) זגים cf. Num. VI, 4. Our translation follows Targum Jonathan and R. Judah in Nazir 34*b* (so also Maim.); but R. Jose (Nazir *loc. cit.*) reverses the identifications as does also Targum Orkelos, v. Ibn Ezra to Num. *loc. cit.* (3) תמד a drink made by allowing grape-stones or husks or lees to steep in water (for a continuous period, a derivative of תמיד; v. Ma'as. V. 6. (4) The flower-like leaves on top of the pomegranate. These sproutings and the peel are prohibited in respect of *'orlah*, not because they are considered fruit, but because they can be used for dyeing, and it is prohibited to dye with *'orlah* (v. *infra* III, 1). (5) E.g., of dates, olives or peaches. (6) In the Nazirite's case the Mishnah thinks of grape-husks and stones; cf. *supra* Mishnah 7, n. 8. (7) *Reba'i*, like the Second Tithe, is subject to a prohibition of *eating* (outside Jerusalem) *only* (but not of otherwise enjoying benefit therefrom), so that the prohibition applies only (*a*) to fruit ripe enough to be eaten (and not e.g., to grapes only a third grown), and (*b*) to such parts of the fruit as are normally eaten (and therefore not to skin, nut-shells, fruit-stones, etc.). (8) Fruit which has fallen off the tree when it had grown more than a third of the normal full size of that particular fruit, i.e., when in a more developed condition than ענקוקלות (undeveloped grapes). (9) Viz., *'orlah, Asherah,* Naziriteship, or (since such fruit can be eaten) even *reba'i*. (10) *Sc.* on which there is no fruit. (11) Because it is only the fruit, but neither the stem nor the branch, that is prohibited in respect of *'orlah*. (12) He agrees, however, that in the event of one having already (planted) fruit of *'orlah* (without having known the law), or having already bent down and rooted, or grafted a branch of *'orlah* bearing fruit-buds, the fruit grown from these is permitted (after the three years of *'orlah*), in conformity with the principle referred to *infra* II, 10, n. 6; v. 'A.Z. 48*b* and commentaries. (13) According to M. Sh. I, 14 these are considered as fruit in all respect except that of tithes. (14) As this Mishnah reads, this statement may be either anonymous, or yet another statement by R. Jose, but in T.J. it is established that it is by R. Jose.
d (1) V. Dem. I, 1, Hal. IV, 6, n. 1. The law stated here applies of course, and with greater force, to *terumah* and *terumah*-of-the-tithe of *waddai* (i.e., certainly untithed produce). Rash's reading was: '*Terumah* and *terumah*-of-the-tithe of *waddai*, and *terumah*-of-the-tithe of *demai*'. (2) Which, too, is spoken of as '*terumah*. 'Num. XV, 20; cf. Hallah I, 3, n. 11. (3) *Bikkurim*. The word *terumah* in '*the* terumah *of thy hand*' (Deut. XII, 17) is interpreted as referring to *Bikkurim* (Sifre *ad loc.*). This is arrived at by a *gezerah shawah*, thus: Deut. XII, 17 speaks of '*the* terumah of thy hand', and of the first-ripe fruits it is said, '*And the priest shall take the basket out of* thy hand' (Deut. XXVI, 4). (4) When quantities of such consecrated produce (which is prohibited to non-priests) become mixed with a greater amount of *hullin* (i.e. non-sacred produce). If the prohibited is more than one to a hundred of the permitted, the whole becomes consecrated, and thus prohibited to non-priests (v. Ter. IV, 7). This rule is derived as follows: Num. XVIII, 29 says, *Ye shall set apart the terumah of the Lord . . . even the hallowed part thereof out of it.* By noting the words, '*the hallowed part thereof*' signifying 'that which halloweth it', the sense is obtained that if anything that had been separated unto the Lord falls into non-sacred produce etc., the former hallows the latter with its own sanctity and renders it similarly prohibited. Further, since this passage deals in particular with the tithe-of-the-tithe, the proportion for the purpose of our rule is fixed as one part of the sacred (and prohibited) to a hundred parts of the non-sacred (and permitted), i.e., a proportion of forbidden admixture greater than one per cent of the permitted renders the mixture prohibited (Sifre *ad loc.*).

FORMING THE STATUTORY MINIMUM[5]], AND IT IS NECESSARY TO TAKE OFF [FROM THE MIXTURE AN AMOUNT EQUAL TO THAT OF THE CONSECRATED PRODUCE CONTAINED
a THEREIN][1] 'ORLAH AND 'MIXED-SEEDS' OF THE VINEYARD[2] BECOME NEUTRALIZED IN TWO-HUNDRED-AND-ONE,[3] AND [LESSER QUANTITIES OF THESE] ARE RECKONED TOGETHER [AS FORMING THE STATUTORY MINIMUM], AND IT IS NOT NECESSARY TO TAKE OFF [FROM THE MIXTURE AN AMOUNT EQUAL TO THAT OF THE CONSECRATED PRODUCE CONTAINED THEREIN].[4] R. SIMEON SAID: [LESSER QUANTITIES OF THESE[5]] ARE NOT RECKONED TOGETHER [AS FORMING A STATUTORY MINIMUM].[6] R. ELIEZER SAID: THEY ARE RECKONED TOGETHER IN [INSTANCES IN WHICH THERE IS INVOLVED THE PRINCIPLE OF A 'QUANTITY] IMPARTING FLAVOUR',[7] BUT NOT FOR IMPOSING A PROHIBITION [IN OTHER CIR-
b CUMSTANCES].[1]

MISHNAH 2. TERUMAH GOES TOWARDS NEUTRALIZING 'ORLAH, AND 'ORLAH[2] TERUMAH. IN WHAT [DEFINED] MANNER? [FOR INSTANCE] IF A SE'AH OF TERUMAH HAS FALLEN INTO A HUNDRED [SE'AHS],[3] AND AFTERWARDS THREE ḲABS[4] OF 'ORLAH, OR THREE ḲABS OF 'MIXED-SEEDS' OF THE VINEYARD [FELL IN]. THIS IS [AN INSTANCE] WHEREIN TERUMAH GOES TOWARDS NEUTRALIZING 'ORLAH, AND 'ORLAH TERUMAH.

MISHNAH 3. 'ORLAH GOES TOWARDS NEUTRALIZING 'MIXED-SEEDS', AND 'MIXED-SEEDS' 'ORLAH, AND 'ORLAH
c 'ORLAH.[1] IN WHAT [DEFINED] MANNER? [FOR INSTANCE] IF A SE'AH OF 'ORLAH HAS FALLEN INTO TWO HUNDRED [SE'AHS] AND AFTERWARDS THERE FELL IN A SE'AH AND OVER OF 'ORLAH, OR A SE'AH AND OVER[2] OF 'MIXED-SEEDS' OF THE VINEYARD. THIS IS [AN INSTANCE] WHEREIN 'ORLAH GOES TOWARDS NEUTRALIZING 'MIXED-SEEDS', AND 'MIXED-SEEDS' 'ORLAH, AND 'ORLAH 'ORLAH.[1]

MISHNAH 4. WHATEVER ONE CAUSES TO FERMENT,[3] OR SEASONS,[4] OR MAKES MEDUMMA'[5] WITH TERUMAH OR 'ORLAH OR WITH 'MIXED-SEEDS' OF THE VINEYARD,[6] IS PROHIBITED; BETH SHAMMAI SAY: IT ALSO BECOMES UNCLEAN,[7] BUT BETH HILLEL SAY: IN ANY CIRCUMSTANCES NOTHING RENDERS UNCLEAN UNLESS THERE BE OF IT [A QUANTITY IN SIZE] 'LIKE AN EGG'.[8]

d *MISHNAH* 5. DOSETHAI [A MAN OF] KEFAR YATHMAH[1] WAS ONE OF THE DISCIPLES OF THE SCHOOL OF SHAMMAI, AND HE SAID: I RECEIVED A TRADITION[2] FROM SHAMMAI HA-ZAḲEN[3] WHO SAID: NEVER DOES ANYTHING RENDER

(5) For the purpose of the law here concerned—a quantity a hundredth part of the non-sacred; v. preceding note.

a (1) And give it to the priests, even though the consecrated matter has become void, so as to avoid 'robbing the tribe' *sc.* of Levi, i.e., depriving the priests and Levites of their perquisites. (2) Cf. *supra* I, 6, n. 15. (3) That 'mixed-seeds' of the vineyard also, like *terumah*, becomes neutralized in a given larger quantity of permitted produce is derived by *gezerah shawah* as follows: In Ex. XXII, 28 'the fulness *of thy harvest*' is taken to refer to *terumah*, and in Deut. XXII, 9 the same term, viz., 'the fulness *of the seed*', refers expressly to 'mixed seeds' of the vineyard.—'*Orlah* is placed for this purpose in the same category as 'mixed-seeds', because, like the latter, it is prohibited not only for consumption but also for deriving any benefit whatsoever.— The proportion of '*orlah* and 'mixed-seeds' of the vineyard becoming neutralized, viz., 1 to 200, is arrived at *a fortiori* from *terumah* as follows: Since in the case of the latter which is prohibited only for consumption the cancelling proportion is 100 of permitted to 1 of forbidden, it follows that in the case of '*orlah* and 'mixed-seeds' of the vineyard which are doubly prohibited (viz., both for consumption and deriving any benefit) the cancelling proportion should correspondingly be doubled viz., 200 of permitted to 1 of prohibited (T.J.). (4) Because (*a*) the prohibited matter has become neutralized, and (*b*) the reason for 'taking off' when the admixture was *terumah*, viz., avoiding 'robbing of the tribe' (v. note 1) does not exist here, inasmuch as priests and Levites are prohibited from consuming or deriving benefit from '*orlah* and 'mixed-seeds' just as much as any Israelite. (5) Viz., '*orlah* and 'mixed-seeds' of the vineyard. (6) Whether dry or liquid forms of produce are concerned, because '*orlah* and 'mixed-seeds' are two distinct prohibited categories, and it is R. Simeon's view (*infra* Mish. 10) that lesser quantities are 'reckoned together' only when they are of the same 'name' i.e., they belong to the same prohibited category and are, too, of a like species. (Cf. T.J.). (7) Where, in the case of liquids and cooked dishes, the prohibited admixture is of a species unlike the bulk, the question as to whether the whole mixture is rendered as forbidden depends on whether the forbidden admixture imparts its flavour to the mixture. It is computed that a prohibited component imparts flavour to a mixture and renders it prohibited, when the former is more than a sixtieth of the permitted portion (v. Ḥul. 68*b* for an explanation how this proportion is arrived at). It is the view of R. Eliezer that if such a prohibited flavour-imparting quantity is made up of '*orlah* and 'mixed-seeds' of the vineyard, then though either of these by itself be too little to impart flavour without the other, still the composite admixture renders the whole mixture prohibited.

b (1) I.e., where 'imparting flavour' is not involved, viz., with dry produce. If in such a case the two prohibited lesser amounts, each not more than a two-hundredth part of the bulk, have fallen in separately, and are of two unlike species, but one is of a like species with the bulk, then the latter being less than the statutory minimum becomes merged and neutralized in the bulk and is not 'reckoned together with' the other of the lesser prohibited amounts which is of an unlike species. The latter, now on its own less than the statutory minimum, becomes neutralized in the rest of the mixture, the whole of which thus remains permitted. (2) Or 'mixed-seeds' of the vineyard, as is evident from the rest of the Mishnah. (3) I.e., the non-sacred produce together with the terumah-admixture making a hundred *se'ahs*. One must assume that this is meant, since if there were a hundred *se'ahs* clear of permitted produce, that itself, without reckoning in the *terumah*, would suffice to make void the three *ḳabs* of '*orlah*. (4) I.e., half a *se'ah*. When this half-a-*se'ah* of '*orlah* falls into the produce which already contains an admixture of *terumah*, the latter is reckoned in with the original non-sacred produce to make void the '*orlah* which now is one part of a total quantity of 201 (v. *supra* **Introduction** n. a 3).

c (1) This must be assumed to mean: 'Orlah goes towards neutralizing *neta reba'i* fruit (v. *supra* I, 7, n. 7) and vice-versa (Asheri) Since all are agreed that two lesser quantities of the same prohibited category are reckoned together, "*orlah* .... '*orlah*' cannot be taken literally. The interchangeability here of the terms '*orlah* and *neta' reba'i* is no doubt due to the fact that the state of *neta' reba'i* is an inevitable and automatic continuation of that of '*orlah*. L. suggests the "*orlah* '*orlah*' can be taken literally by assuming the Mishnah to mean that the first admixture of '*orlah* fell into full 200 parts of *ḥullin* and became neutralized, in which case the mixture is permitted and neutralizes the second admixture of '*orlah*. In this way the first admixture of '*orlah* may be said to help to neutralize the second admixture of '*orlah*. (2) Tosef. Yom Ṭob says that 'and over' is added to intimate that a 'little over' can also be considered as becoming neutralized. See L. for a discussion of the various views on this point. (3) E.g., by means of an apple (of '*orlah*) falling into dough (T.J. cf. Terumoth X, 2). (4) Fermentation, like seasoning, of course imparts flavour (v. *supra* 1). (5) V. Ḥal. I, 4, n. 7. (6) This passage is to be understood as: '.... causes to ferment, or seasons with *terumah* or '*orlah* or 'mixed-seeds' .... or makes *medumma'* with *terumah*' (7) This is qualified in the next Mishnah. (8) *Sc.* even if it is big enough to cause prohibition in respect of *medumma'* (to priests) or of '*orlah* or 'mixed-seeds' (to all Israelites). On the fixing of the 'size of an egg' as a norm in the matter of uncleanness of comestibles, v. Yoma 79*b*—80*a*. Cf. Ḥal. II, 8, n. 3.

d (1) Perhaps Jetma, in the district of Samaria, so Jast. who refers to Neubauer. *Geographie*, p. 268. In *Kaftor wa-Feraḥ* the reading is Kefar Jama. (2) Lit., 'I heard'. Another reading has 'I asked'. (3) I.e., the Elder, or the Sage. The same designation was accorded also to Shammai's contemporary and controversialist, Hillel.

כדדרשי' בהערל (דף עג:) ותרומת ידך אלו בכורים דכתיב בהו (דברים כו) ולקח הכהן הטנא מידך ואמרינן בירושלמי (הל' א) מאן תנא תרומת מעשר של דמאי ר' מאיר דר' מאיר מחמיר בדבריהם כדברי תורה דתנינן תמן הרואה כתם הרי זו מקולקלת וחוששין משום זוב דברי ר' מאיר בפ' בא סימן (דף נג:) והיינו נמי דאמרינן בפ"ק דנדה ר"מ דמחמיר בכתמים: וצריך להרים. כשנפלה סאה למאה מרים מהן סאה ופריך בירושלמי (שם) הכא אתמר צריך והכא את אמר אין צריך להרים גבי ערלה וכלאי הכרם לחטורין מן התרומה א"ר אבהו בשם ר' יוחנן מפני גזל השבט (ב): עולין בא' ומאתים. מפרש בירושלמי (שם) מנין שהם שולים אתיא מלאה מלאה בכלאי הכרם כתיב המלאה ובבכורים כתיב מלאתך ודמעך מה מלאתך שנאמר להלן עולה אף כאן עולה אי מה כאן ק' אף כאן ק' לפי שכפל הכתוב איסורו כלומר שאסור בהנאה שינו חכמים חיובו עד כדון כלאי הכרם ערלה מנין מה זו אסורה בהנאה אף זו אסורה בהנאה ומה זו עולה אף זו עולה: ומצטרפין זה עם זה. בין לאיסור בין ליתן טעם מדפליג ר' אליעזר דאמר בנותן טעם אבל לא לאסור ולאסור היינו כדקאמר בירושלמי (שם) דאמר רבי אבהו בשם ר' יוחנן בשם ר' מאיר כל האיסורים מצטרפין ללקות עליהם בכזית משום לא תאכל כל תועבה ובפרק בתרא דע"א (דף סו.) מייתי לה אי נמי לאסור כגון ענבים דערלה וכלאי הכרם שנפלו בענבים דהיתר לפחות ממאתים ולחד מינייהו איכא מאתים ובנותן טעם כגון יין של ערלה וכלאי הכרם שנפל לתבשיל ומצטרפין לאסור בנותן טעם אע"פ שיש בו לעלות באחד ור': ר"ש אומר אין מצטרפין. (ג) מפני שהן שתי שמות במעילה (ספ"ד) משנה זו ופריך בגמ' (ד' יח:) ומי צריך ר"ש לצרופי והא תניא ר"ש אומר כל שהוא למכות תני אין צריכין ...

ממנו מקדשו אם נפל בתוכו ולפיכך כשנפל חלק בתשעים והשע חלקים יהיה הכל מדומע ואם נפל במאה יעלה כמו שבארנו שם וכן הדין בתרומת מעשר לפי שבא בה הכתוב ואין הפרש אצלנו בכל הדינים בין תרומת מעשר של דמאי או של ודאי וכבר נתבאר זה והחלה ג"כ נקראת תרומה כמו שבארנו והבכורים ג"כ נקראים תרומה כמו שאמר ותרומת ידך אלו הבכורים וכבר בארנו זה בפרק הג' מתרומות (מ"ז) ולפי שכל אלו יאסרו במאה והיא אסורה באכילה ר"ל לזרים ומותרת בהנאה נתנו הערלה והכלאים שהן אסורין באכילה ובהנאה כמו שבארנו יאסרו במאתים ולפיכך אמר בערלה ובכלאי הכרם עולין באחד ובמאתים ואיני זוכר עתה לחכמים אסמכתא שסמכו עליו זה הדין ורוצים באמרם צריך להרים שיוציא חלק שנפל ויותר השאר כמו שבארנו בתרומות: ואינו צריך להרים. ענינו שמותר לאכול הכל ואינו חייב להוציא את החלק הנופל ומה שחייב באותם להוציא את החלק הנופל לפי שהוא ...

וצריך להרים ׳הערלה וכלאי א) הכרם עולים באחד ומאתים ומצטרפין זה עם זה ואין צריך להרים רש"א אינן מצטרפין ר"א אומר מצטרפין בנותן טעם אבל לא לאסור: **ב** ׳התרומה מעלה את הערלה והערלה את התרומה כיצד סאה תרומה שנפלה למאה ואחר כך נפלו שלשה קבין ערלה ושלשה קבין כלאי הכרם זו היא שהתרומה מעלה את הערלה והערלה את התרומה: **ג** ׳הערלה מעלה את הכלאים והכלאים את הערלה והערלה את הערלה כיצד סאה ערלה שנפלה למאתים ואחר כך נפלה סאה ועוד ערלה או סאה ועוד של כלאי הכרם זו היא שהערלה מעלה את הכלאים והכלאים את הערלה והערלה את הערלה: **ד** ׳כל המחמץ והמתבל והמדמע בתרומה ובערלה וכלאי הכרם אסור ובית שמאי אומרים אף מטמא וב"ה אומרים ׳לעולם אינו מטמא עד שיהא בו כביצה: **ה** דוסתאי איש כפר יתמה היה מתלמידי בית שמאי ואמר שמעתי משמאי הזקן שאמר לעולם אינו מטמא

ז א מיי' פט"ז מהל' מאכלות אסורות הלכה ג:
ח ב מיי' פט"ו שם ומיי' פי"ג מהל' תרומות הלכה ג:
ט ג מיי' פט"ו מהל' מאכלות אסורות הלכה טו:
י ד שם הל' יד טו:

א) חולין דף לט. [ב]חולין שם] ב)ע"ז דף סח. ג)שבת פ"ט דף פט: ע"ז פ"ה דף סו: ד) פסחים פ"ב דף כו: וע"ז פ"ג דף מט. וע"ג: תמורה פ"ק דף יב:

עד שיהא בו כביצה: ו ולמה אמרו א) כל המחמץ והמתבל והמדמע להחמיר מין במינו להקל ולהחמיר מין בשאינו מינו כיצד שאור של חטים שנפל תוך עיסה של חטים ויש בו כדי לחמץ בין שיש בו לעלות באחד ומאה ובין שאין בו לעלות באחד ומאה אסור אין בו לעלות במאה ואחד בין שיש בו כדי לחמץ בין שאין בו כדי לחמץ אסור: ז ב להקל [ג] ולהחמיר מין בשאינו מינו כיצד כגון גריסין שנתבשלו עם עדשים ויש בהם בנותן טעם בין שיש בהם לעלות באחד ומאה ובין שאין בהם לעלות באחד ומאה אסור אין בהם בנותן טעם בין שיש בהם לעלות באחד ומאה ובין שאין בהם לעלות באחד ומאה מותר: ח שאור של חולין שנפל לתוך עיסה ויש בו כדי לחמץ ואח"כ נפל שאור של תרומה או שאור של כלאי הכרם ויש בו כדי לחמץ אסור: ט ג שאור ג) של חולין שנפל לתוך עיסה וחמצה ואח"כ נפל שאור של תרומה או שאור של כלאי הכרם ויש בו כדי לחמץ אסור ר"ש מתיר: י ד תבלין ג) ב' וג' שמות ממין אחד או *ממין ג' אסור ומצטרפין ר"ש אומר ב' וג' שמות ממין אחד או ב' מינין משם א' אינן מצטרפין: יא שאור ד) של חולין ושל תרומה שנפלו לתוך עיסה לא בזה כדי לחמץ ולא בזה כדי לחמץ נצטרפו וחמצו רבי אליעזר אומר אחר האחרון אני בא וחכ"א בין שנפל *שאור בתחלה בין בסוף לעולם אינו אוסר עד שיהא בו כדי לחמץ: יב יועזר איש הבירה היה מתלמידי בית שמאי ואמר שאלתי את רבן גמליאל הזקן עומד בשער המזרח ואמר לעולם אינו אוסר עד שיהא בו כדי

פירוש הרא"ש

פי' מהר"י בן מלכי צדק

מטמא עד שיהא בו כביצה דטומאת אוכלין בכביצה: ו ז ולמה אמרו

הגהות מהר"י לנדא

UNCLEAN[4] UNLESS THERE BE OF IT [A QUANTITY IN SIZE] 'LIKE AN EGG'.[5]

MISHNAH 6. NOW IN REFERENCE TO WHAT [CASES] DID THEY SAY[6] 'WHEN ANYTHING CAUSES FERMENTATION OR SEASONS[7] OR MAKES MEDUMMA' [IT IS PROPER] TO RULE STRINGENTLY'? [IN THE CASE OF] A SPECIES [MIXED] WITH ITS [LIKE] SPECIES; 'TO RULE [SOMETIMES] LENIENTLY, AND [SOMETIMES] STRINGENTLY'? [IN THE CASE OF] A SPECIES [MIXED] WITH [SOMETHING] NOT ITS [LIKE] SPECIES. IN WHAT [DEFINED] MANNER [OF A MIXTURE OF SPECIES, SHOULD ONE RULE STRINGENTLY]? IF LEAVEN OF WHEAT FELL INTO DOUGH OF WHEAT[8] AND THERE BE OF IT [THE ADMIXTURE] A QUANTITY SUFFICIENTLY [LARGE] TO CAUSE FERMENTATION, [THEN] WHETHER THERE BE OF IT A QUANTITY SUFFICIENTLY [SMALL] TO BECOME NEUTRALIZED IN ONE-HUNDRED-AND-ONE, OR THERE BE OF IT [A QUANTITY] NOT SUFFICIENTLY [SMALL] TO BECOME NEUTRALIZED IN ONE-HUNDRED-AND-ONE, IT [THE MIXTURE] IS PROHIBITED;[9] [ALSO] IF THERE BE OF IT [THE ADMIXTURE] A QUANTITY NOT SUFFICIENTLY [SMALL] TO BECOME NEUTRALIZED IN ONE-HUNDRED-AND-ONE, [THEN] WHETHER THERE BE OF IT [A QUANTITY] SUFFICIENTLY [LARGE] TO CAUSE FERMENTATION, OR THERE BE OF IT [A QUANTITY] NOT SUFFICIENTLY [LARGE] TO CAUSE FERMENTATION, [THE MIXTURE] IS [LIKE-
a WISE] PROHIBITED.[1]

MISHNAH 7. [THEY SAID 'IT IS PROPER] TO RULE [SOMETIMES] LENIENTLY AND [SOMETIMES] STRINGENTLY' IN [REFERENCE TO] A SPECIES [MIXED] WITH NOT ITS [LIKE] SPECIES. IN WHAT [DEFINED] MANNER? [FOR INSTANCE] IF POUNDED BEANS[2] WERE BOILED TOGETHER WITH LENTILS,[3] AND THERE IS OF THEM [THE FORMER] [A QUANTITY] SUCH AS IMPARTS FLAVOUR, [THEN] WHETHER THERE BE OF THEM [A QUANTITY] SUFFICIENTLY [SMALL] TO BECOME NEUTRALIZED IN ONE-HUNDRED-AND-ONE, OR THERE BE OF THEM [A QUANTITY NOT SUFFICIENTLY SMALL] TO BECOME NEUTRALIZED IN ONE-HUNDRED-AND-ONE, IT [THE MIXTURE] IS PROHIBITED;[4] [BUT] IF THERE BE NOT OF THEM [A QUANTITY] SUCH AS IMPARTS FLAVOUR, [THEN] WHETHER THERE BE OF THEM [A QUANTITY SUFFICIENTLY SMALL] TO BECOME NEUTRALIZED IN ONE-HUNDRED-AND-ONE, OR THERE BE NOT OF THEM [A QUANTITY SUFFICIENTLY SMALL] TO BECOME NEUTRALIZED
b IN ONE-HUNDRED-AND-ONE, IT [THE MIXTURE] IS PERMITTED.[1]

(4) *Sc.* as far as comestibles are concerned. (5) Thus the School of Shammai agrees on this point with the School of Hillel (Mish. 4). This is an instance of how in the Tannaitic Schools, the original *halachoth* before them—when indefinite—were amplified and defined with the aid of traditions received by one or other of those present; v. Halevy, *Doroth*, p. 846. (6) Quoted also in Ḥul. 99*a*. (7) V. *supra* 4, n. 4. (8) Likewise if leaven of barley has fallen into dough of barley, i.e., where both the bulk and the admixture are of the same species. (9) Because in the case of a mixture of a species with its like (as here, wheat with wheat) for the permitted bulk to neutralize the prohibited admixture two conditions are essential: the prohibited portion must be (*a*) not more than one within 101 of the whole, and (*b*) incapable of imparting flavour to the mixture. Here even if the former condition is present, the latter is lacking.
a (1) Because condition (*a*) referred to in the preceding note, is lacking here, even if condition (*b*) exists. (2) *Sc.* of *terumah*. The rules given in this Mishnah apply also when the admixture is of *'orlah* or 'mixed-seeds' of the vineyard, with the substitution of 201 where our Mishnah has 101. (3) This is an example of 'a species with not its species', which would cover an instance of, say, leaven of barley in wheaten dough. Pounded beans are cited as an example probably to show that though pounded beans as such have a decided flavour, yet if (as in the second contingency) the flavour cannot be distinctly felt in the mixture, the whole dish is permitted. In addition, this instance is an intimation that beans and lentils are not deemed like species, notwithstanding the fact that both are legumens. (4) In conformity with the principle that an admixture of prohibited matter of an unlike species renders the whole prohibited when the former (being in a proportion of more than one in sixty) imparts its flavour; v. *supra* 1, n. 7.
b (1) Because the circumstance of imparting flavour is absent; v. preceding note.

◁ *For the continuation of the English translation of this page see overleaf.*

עד שיהא בו כביצה: ז ולמה אמרו א) כל המחמץ והמתבל והמדמע להחמיר מין במינו להקל ולהחמיר מין בשאינו מינו *כיצד שאור של חטים שנפל תוך עיסה של חטים ויש בו כדי לחמץ בין שיש בו לעלות באחד ומאה ובין שאין בו לעלות באחד ומאה אסור אין בו לעלות במאה ואחד בין שיש בו כדי לחמץ בין שאין בו כדי לחמץ אסור: ז ב להקל [ג] ולהחמיר מין בשאינו מינו כיצד כגון גריסין שנתבשלו עם עדשים ויש בהם בנותן טעם בין שיש בהם לעלות באחד ומאה ובין שאין בהם לעלות באחד ומאה אסור אין בהם בנותן טעם בין שיש בהם לעלות באחד ומאה ובין שאין בהם לעלות באחד ומאה מותר: ח שאור של חולין שנפל לתוך עיסה ויש בו כדי לחמץ ואח"כ נפל שאור של תרומה או שאור של כלאי הכרם ויש בו כדי לחמץ אסור: ט ג שאור ב) של חולין שנפל לתוך עיסה וחמצה ואח"כ נפל שאור של תרומה או שאור של כלאי הכרם ויש בו כדי לחמץ אסור ר"ש מתיר: י ד תבלין ג) ב' וג' שמות ממין אחד או *ממין ג' אסור ומצטרפין ר"ש אומר ב' וג' שמות ממין אחד או ב' מינין משם א' אינן מצטרפין: יא שאור ד) של חולין ושל תרומה שנפלו לתוך עיסה לא בזה כדי לחמץ ולא בזה כדי לחמץ נצטרפו וחמצו רבי אליעזר אומר אחר האחרון אני בא וחכ"א בין שנפל *שאור בתחלה בין בסוף לעולם אינו אוסר עד שיהא בו כדי לחמץ: יב יועזר איש הבירה היה מתלמידי בית שמאי ואמר שאלתי את רבן גמליאל הזקן עומד בשער המזרח ואמר לעולם אינו אוסר עד שיהא בו כדי

Continuation of translation from previous page as indicated by ◁

MISHNAH 8. IF LEAVEN OF ḤULLIN HAS FALLEN INTO DOUGH, AND THERE WAS OF IT SUFFICIENT TO CAUSE FERMENTATION, AND AFTER THAT[2] THERE FELL IN LEAVEN OF TERUMAH OR LEAVEN OF 'MIXED-SEEDS' OF THE VINEYARD, OF WHICH [TOO] THERE WAS SUFFICIENT TO CAUSE FERMENTATION, IT [THE DOUGH] IS PROHIBITED.[3]

MISHNAH 9. IF LEAVEN OF ḤULLIN HAS FALLEN INTO DOUGH AND CAUSED IT TO FERMENT, AND AFTER THAT THERE FELL IN LEAVEN OF TERUMAH OR OF 'MIXED-SEEDS' OF THE VINEYARD, OF WHICH THERE WAS SUFFICIENT TO CAUSE FERMENTATION, IT [THE DOUGH] IS PROHIBITED;[4] BUT R. SIMEON DECLARES [IT] PERMITTED.[5]

MISHNAH 10. [THE ADMIXTURE OF] SEASONINGS[6] [CONSISTING] OF TWO OR THREE CATEGORIES[1] OF ONE SPECIES,[2] OR [CONSISTING] OF THREE SPECIES [OF ONE CATEGORY][3], [RENDER THE MIXTURE] PROHIBITED,[4] AND THEY ARE 'RECKONED TOGETHER'.[5] R. SIMEON SAID: [ADMIXTURES OF SEASONINGS CONSISTING OF] TWO OR THREE CATEGORIES OF ONE SPECIES, OR [CONSISTING OF] TWO SPECIES OF ONE CATEGORY, ARE NOT 'RECKONED TOGETHER'.[6]

MISHNAH 11. IF LEAVEN OF ḤULLIN AND OF TERUMAH HAVE FALLEN INTO DOUGH, AND NEITHER OF THE ONE WAS THERE SUFFICIENT TO CAUSE FERMENTATION, NOR OF THE OTHER WAS THERE SUFFICIENT TO CAUSE FERMENTATION, BUT TOGETHER THEY CAUSED [THE DOUGH] TO FERMENT, [THEN] R. ELIEZER SAYS: I GO AFTER THE LAST;[1] BUT THE SAGES SAY: WHETHER THE PROHIBITED QUANTITY FELL IN FIRST OR LAST, NEVER DOES IT [THE DOUGH] BECOME PROHIBITED UNLESS THERE BE OF IT [OF THE PROHIBITED ADMIXTURE BY ITSELF] SUFFICIENT TO CAUSE FERMENTATION.

MISHNAH 12. JO'EZER, MASTER OF THE TEMPLE,[2] [WHO] WAS ONE OF THE DISCIPLES OF THE SCHOOL OF SHAMMAI, SAID: I ASKED RABBAN GAMALIEL HA-ZAḲEN[3] AS HE WAS STANDING AT THE EASTERN GATE,[4] AND HE SAID: NEVER DOES ANY [ADMIXTURE OF PROHIBITED LEAVEN] RENDER [DOUGH] PROHIBITED UNLESS THERE BE OF IT SUFFICIENT

(2) I.e., after the non-sacred (*hullin*) dough had fallen in, but before it had time to ferment the dough. (3) One might have argued that since the dough would have fermented from the permitted leaven alone, the second admixture of leaven can be deemed as of no material effect, and that, therefore, the dough is permitted. We do not argue thus, because the second—prohibited—admixture certainly accelerated the fermentation. (4) In spite of the fact that the second admixture of leaven overferments the dough and spoils it, and the rule, which thus becomes applicable, that a prohibited admixture which imparts a *deteriorating* flavour (נותן טעם לפגם) does not render the mixture prohibited; the dough though now unfit for consumption by itself, can be used as leavening for a number of other doughs. (5) On the ground that since the dough had already become fermented before the prohibited leaven came in, the latter is deemed as of no effect. In the case stated in the preceding Mishnah, R. Simeon does not dispute the prohibition, since there, at the time the prohibited leaven fell in, the permitted leaven had not yet caused any fermentation, and the prohibited leaven, though it came in later, played an equal part with the permitted leaven in the process of fermentation. (6) Maim. points out that the term 'seasonings' (תבלין) includes not only spices but onions, garlic, wine, vinegar, oil—in fact everything used for the purpose of giving the dish a special flavour.

c (1) *Sc.* of prohibitions; lit., 'names' (שמות). So explained by Rabbenu Jacob Tam quoted in Tosaf. Shab. 89*b* in opposition to Rashi (ibid.) whose interpretation is: 'names' denoting several varieties of one species, (so also Maim. to our Mishnah). (2) E.g., (*a*) pepper of '*orlah*, of Asherah and of the city condemned for apostacy (Deut. XIII, 13 ff), or (*b*) of *terumah* of the Second Tithe, and of the Seventh-Year produce (Ex. XXIII, 10–11, Lev. XXV, 2–7), or (*c*); cummin of 'mixed-seeds' of the vineyard, of *terumah*, and of the Second Tithe; so Rash. following R. Tam in Tosaf. *(loc. cit.)*, against Rashi whose example is long (-grain) pepper, white pepper and black pepper (so also Maim. and Siponto). R. Tam points with justification to the beginning of T.J. to Mishnah 1 as conclusively bearing out his interpretation. V. Rash. to our Mishnah for a review of this point. (3) E.g., pepper and ginger and cummin of '*orlah*, or of terumah. (4) V. Rash. who favours reading איסרין rather than אסור. (5) Bert., following Maim., takes 'prohibited' and 'reckoned together' as one rule meaning that the two (or three) are reckoned together as forming the statutory proportion rendering a dish thus seasoned prohibited in-so-far as the seasonings impart taste (v. L.'s note 36). Rash. after Tosaf. (*loc. cit.*), gives also an alternative interpretation, viz., 'render prohibited' in the case of liquid food or cooked dishes (where 'imparting flavour is a factor), and 'are reckoned together' in the case of dry produce (where the principle of neutralization in 101 or in 201, operates), v. L. Another alternative explanation is: they are 'reckoned together' as forming a *kazayyith* (a quantity equal to the size of an olive) of a consecrated comestible which, when consumed by a person to whom it is prohibited, renders the consumer liable to punishment by stripes, v. Rash. (6) R. Simeon's view, as that of an individual against that of a majority, is rejected.—The general term for the principle involved in this dispute is זה וזה גורם i.e., the status (whether permitted or forbidden) of something brought into being by two contributing causes, one of which is prohibited and the other permitted, or both of which are prohibited but each subject to a different prohibition.

d (1) I.e., if the leaven of terumah was the last to fall in the dough becomes *medumma*'; if the non-sacred leaven fell in last the dough remains permitted, but only if the prohibited leaven was removed before the permitted fell in. In such a case R. Eliezer would overlook as inconsiderable the slight contribution towards the ultimate fermentation made by the prohibited leaven whilst it was with the dough. (2) איש הבירה. This Jo'ezer was apparently the senior officer of the Temple. W. Jawitz identifies this office with 'The Master of the Temple Mount', cf. Mid. I, 2. The office שר הבירה is already mentioned in Neh. VII, 2. As some Amoraim are also so designated Bacher (*Ag. Pal. Am.* I) concludes that it became eventually an honorary title of the descendants of priests who had held the post. V. Klein, S. מחקרים ארצי ישראלים II, p. 76. (3) I.e., the Sage or the Elder, the first Tanna of that name, the grandson of Hillel. Tosaf. Yom Ṭob points out that the Shammaites did not abstain from seeking knowledge from the Hillelites. Bacher, *Tradition und Tradentem* (p. 88), points out that this is the earliest instance of a legal 'tradition' recorded as having been passed on in this manner. (4) *Sc.* of the Temple.

TO CAUSE FERMENTATION.[5]

a *MISHNAH* 13. IF ONE OILED ARTICLES[1] WITH UNCLEAN OIL, AND [LATER] HE RETURNED [TO THE ARTICLES][2] AND OILED THEM WITH CLEAN OIL; OR HE [FIRST] OILED THEM WITH CLEAN OIL, AND [LATER] HE RETURNED [TO THEM] AND OILED THEM WITH UNCLEAN OIL, R. ELIEZER SAYS: 'I GO AFTER THE FIRST',[3] AND THE SAGES SAY: 'AFTER THE LAST'.[4]

MISHNAH 14. IF LEAVEN OF TERUMAH AND OF 'MIXED-SEEDS' OF THE VINEYARD HAVE FALLEN INTO DOUGH, AND NEITHER OF THE ONE IS THERE SUFFICIENT TO CAUSE FERMENTATION, NOR IS THERE OF THE OTHER SUFFICIENT TO CAUSE FERMENTATION, BUT TOGETHER THEY CAUSED FERMENTATION, IT [THE DOUGH] IS PROHIBITED TO NON-PPIESTS[5] AND PERMITTED TO PRIESTS.[6] R. SIMEON DECLARES IT PERMITTED BOTH TO NON-PRIESTS AND TO PRIESTS.[7]

MISHNAH 15. IF SEASONINGS OF TERUMAH AND OF 'MIXED-SEEDS' OF THE VINEYARD HAVE FALLEN INTO A DISH, AND THERE IS NOT OF THE ONE SUFFICIENT TO SEASON, NOR IS THERE OF THE OTHER SUFFICIENT TO SEASON, BUT TOGETHER THEY SEASONED, IT [THE DISH] IS PROHIBITED
b TO NON-PRIESTS BUT PERMITTED TO PRIESTS.[1] R. SIMEON DECLARES IT PERMITTED TO NON-PRIESTS AND TO PRIESTS.[1]

(5) The purpose of this Mishnah is purely the corroboration of the view of the Sages against that of R. Eliezer as stated in the preceding Mishnah (Maim.).

a (1) Skin or leather articles, such as sandals, oiled for the purpose of softening. (2) After the (unclean) oil had become fully absorbed in the material, and after the articles had been immersed for ritual cleansing. (3) When the oil is thoroughly absorbed and dried into the material, the article, after ritual immersion, is clean. Use of the articles expels the oil which then, as a liquid —if itself unclean— renders unclean whatever is in contact with it. R. Eliezer holds that the first oil is expelled (as well as the second oil) so that in whatever order the oils were applied, the article is rendered unclean, since one of the oils is unclean. R. Eliezer's dictum is to be understood as 'I go *even* after the first' if that was unclean. (4) Their point is that the article already saturated with oil does not readily or thoroughly absorb any more oil, so that the liquid oil (expelled by use) on the article, must be presumed to be of the oil applied last; therefore the cleanness or otherwise of the article depends on the cleanness or otherwise of the oil applied last.—The purpose of this Mishnah in the present context is apparently to give an example involving the principle of going after the first (or the last)' referred to in Mishnah 11. (5) Since to them both parts of the admixture are prohibited, and the Sages hold that admixtures of two or three prohibited categories *are* 'reckoned together' (*supra* 10). (6) Since to them the *terumah* leaven is permitted, and the leaven of 'mixed-seeds' which is prohibited to them is of a quantity insufficient by itself to cause fermentation (Bert.). Since they hold that something which results from a combination of something prohibited and something permitted, is permitted, cf. *supra* 10, n. 5 (L). (7) In conformity with his view that admixtures of two or more prohibited categories are not 'reckoned together', (v. Mish. 10).

b (1) By the same reasoning as Mishnah 14 notes 5, 6, 7. The virtual repetition of these views of R. Eliezer and of the Sages in this and the preceding Mishnahs give definite examples of the application of the principles as laid down by the disputants in Mishnah 10. Thus according to the Sages different prohibited categories of one species (the subject of this Mishnah), as well as different species subject to the same prohibition (dealt with in Mishnah 14), are 'reckoned together', whilst R. Eliezer differs from the Sages in both instances. In addition, our Mishnah establishes beyond a peradventure the application of the principles of Mishnah 10 to mixtures with cooked dishes and liquids (as well as to instances of mixtures where both the bulk and the admixture are dry).

◁ *For the continuation of the English translation of this page see overleaf.*

א) ב"ק פרק ט דף קא: ב) תמורה פ"ז דף לד. ג) פסחים פ"ב דף כו: וכז. ד) ביצה פ"א דף ג: יבמות פ"ה דף פא. זבחים פ"ח דף עב.

יג כלים שסכן בשמן טמא. כגון מנעלים ושאר כלים של עור שסכין אותן בשמן לרככן ולאחר שיבשו מן הראשון חוזר וסכן בשמן שני דאי בעודו טופח על הכלים אם כן הטמא מטמא הטהור והכלי ממה נפשך טמא דמשקה מטמא כלי ומיירי מתני' בהטבילו לאחר שסכו בשמן טמא ונגב אחר טבילה סכו בשמן טהור וכשחוזר ופולט את השמן פליגי רבי אליעזר ורבנן הי מינייהו פלים אם הראשון או אחרון והיינו דקאמר בירושלמי (הל' ז) מאי טעמא דרבי אליעזר הראשון מוציא את האחרון ומתני' מיתניא בתוספתא דתרומה [פ"ח] ומסיים בה שהיה ר' אליעזר אומר לא יהא אדם סך כלים שמן טמא וחוזר וסכן שמן טהור שכשהן מוציאין אינם מוציאין אלא מן הראשון וחכמים אומרים לא יהא אדם סך כליו שמן טהור וחוזר וסכן שמן טמא שכשהם מוציאין אין מוציאין אלא מן האחרון כלים שסכן שמן טמא ונגבו משתמש בהן בטהרה חזרו ויצאו מהן משקין טמאים: יד טו אסורין לזרים. רבנן לטעמייהו דאמרי לעיל תבלין ב' וג' מצטרפין ור' שמעון לטעמיה דאמר לעיל (מ"י) אין שני שמות מצטרפין ומותר לכהנים כדאמרן לעולם אינו אוסר עד שיהא בו כדי לחמץ: טז עם החתיכות. של חולין ויש בהן כדי לבטל של קדשי קדשים בפני עצמה ושל פיגול ונותר בפ"ע ורבנן לטעמייהו ור"ש לטעמיה: יז בשר קדשי קדשים. אסור לזרים ואפילו לטהורים וקדשים קלים מותר לזרים טהורים ואסור לטמאין וכשנתבשלו [עם בשר תאוה] דהיינו בשר חולין דשרי אף לטמאין ויש בה כדי לבטל כל אחד ואחד בפני עצמו מ"מ מצטרפין [לאסור] לטמאין אפילו לר"ש דקדשי קדשים וקדשים קלין שם אחד הן דכולם שם קדשים עליהן כדאמרן לעיל גבי תרומה ותרומת מעשר וחלה ובכורים ומותר אף לזרים טהורים אפילו לרבנן דקדשים קלים שרו לזרים וקדשי קדשים אין בהן כדי לאסור כדאמרן לעיל עד שיהא בו כדי לחמץ:

יג אחר האחרון נחשוב אותו השמן שעליהם טמא אם היה האחרון טמא או טהור אם היה האחרון טהור לפי שנאמר הראשון נבלע בעצם הכלים ונשאר האחרון ור"א חושש לראשון ולשני אומר שלפעמים שיקנח השני וישאר הראשון שנבלע בכלים והוא אותו שילא ע"ג הכלים אחר שיבש השני וכל זה כשהכלים אין מקבלים טומאה כגון כלי אבנים וכלי גללים וכלי אדמה או פשוטי כלי עץ ופשוטי כלי חרס כמו שיתבאר במסכת כלים אבל אם היו אלו הכלים מקבלין טומאה כשסכן בשמן טמא נטמאו ובזה יש חלוק והוא שאם סכן מבפנים נטמאו כלם ואם סכן מבחוץ נטמאו אחורי הכלים בלבד וכשנגעו משקים טהורים באלו הכלים שנטמאו בזה השמן הטמא הם גם כן מטמאין ויהיו תחלה כמו שבארנו אלו העקרים כלם במסכתות רבות מסדר טהרות ומשם תמלא ספקך מאלו העקרים והלכה כחכמים: יד אסור לזרים. לפי שאיסור תרומה עליהם וכמו כן שאור של כלאי הכרם וכבר נגמר החמוץ מדבר האסור עליהם אבל לכהנים הוא להם כמו שאור של חולין ושל תרומה שנפלו לתוך עיסה של ישראל שאמר בהם אינו אסור עד שיהא בו כדי להחמיץ ורבי שמעון דן דין שאור של תרומה ושל כלאי הכרם כדין מה שקדם זכרו באמרו התרומה מעלה את הערלה ואף על פי שאין דומין זה לזה דמיון גמור ואין הלכה כרבי שמעון: טו הדבר כלו מבואר אבל השמיענו כי מחלוקתם עם ר' שמעון בשני המאמרים ר"ל בשאור ותבלין שאלו השמיענו כי מחלוקתם בשאור היינו אומרים בשאור בלבד אומרים חכמים אסור לזרים כמו שאמרנו בהלכה הקודמת מפני ששאור של תרומה ושאור של כלאי הכרם שם אחד אבל תבלין של תרומה ותבלין של כלאי הכרם שהם שמות הרבה מודים לרבי שמעון שהוא מותר לזרים השמיענו בזו ההלכה שהם חולקים עליו אפי' בתבלין ותבלין ואילו השמיענו ג"כ בזו ההלכה מחלוקתם הייתי אומרים בתבלין ותבלין שהם שמות הרבה מתיר ר' שמעון לזרים אבל בשאור ושאור מודה לחכמים על כן השמיענו מחלוקתם בהלכה הקודמת ואין הלכה כר' שמעון: טז קדשי קדשים אין אוכלין אותם אלא זכרי כהונה כמו שבאר הכתוב (ויקרא ז) כל זכר בכהנים יאכל אותה אבל נותר ופגול הוא אסור על הכהנים ועל ישראל ודינו שישרף אבל אסורו על ישראל יותר חמור לפי שלא היה מותר לישראל לעולם וכשאכלו ישראל נתחייב קרבן מעילה כמו שיתבאר במסכת כריתות אבל לכהנים היתה לו שעת הכושר קודם שהיה פגול או נותר ועוד יתבאר דיני הפיגול והנותר במסכת זבחים ואמר כי כשנתבשלו אלו השלשה חתיכות עם חתיכת חולין והוליאום אחר כן ונשאר בשר הבשר שהוא אסור לזרים מפני בשר הקדשים שנתבשל עמהם ומותר לכהנים אע"פ שיש בו הנותר והפגול כיון שאין אסורו על הכהנים חמור הרבה ור' שמעון אומר כשם שמותר לכהנים כך מותר לזרים כיון שהפגול והנותר אסור על הכל וזהו מה שאמר בכאן שמותר לכהנים בין טהורים בין טמאין לפי שהכל נטמא בנותר ובפגול כמו שיתבאר במקומו וכל זה כשהם החתיכות א' מס' והם מין במינו דליכא למיקם עליה או אם לא נתנו החתיכות טעם אם הן מין בשאינו מינו כאשר נתבאר במסכת חולין אבל כשהיו פחות מששים או נתן הפגול והנותר טעם בשאר התבשיל אם היה מין בשאינו מינו או נתערבו החתיכות ואינן נכרות אע"פ שהוליאום אע"פ שהיתה אחד באלף דאיתיה לאיסורא בעיניה אין מחלוקת באחד מאלו השלשה פנים שהכל אסור בין לכהנים בין לזרים לפי שכל אלו עקרים עליהם הסיבוב ואין בהם מחלוקת ודע זה ואין הלכה כר' שמעון: יז אם היה בשר קדשי קדשים הוא זה שנתבשל עם בשר תאוה אוכלין הכל טהורי הכהנים כמו שבארנו ואם יהיה בשר קדשים קלים שנתבשל עם בשר תאוה אוכלין הכל טהורי זרים ולא נחוש בזה הענין ודומה לו לאחד מששים כיון שהכל מותר ואין שם דבר יאסר אכילתו:

יג כלים שסכן בשמן טמא וחזר וסכן בשמן טהור או שסכן בשמן טהור וחזר וסכן בשמן טמא ר' אליעזר אומר אחר הראשון אני בא וחכמים אומרים אחר האחרון: יד [א]שאור של תרומה ושל כלאי הכרם שנפלו לתוך עיסה לא בזה כדי לחמץ ולא בזה כדי לחמץ ונצטרפו וחמצו אסור לזרים ומותר לכהנים ר"ש מתיר לזרים ולכהנים: טו [ב]תבלין של תרומה ושל כלאי הכרם שנפלו בקדרה לא באלו כדי לתבל ולא באלו כדי לתבל ונצטרפו ותבלו אסור לזרים ומותר לכהנים ר"ש מתיר לכהנים ולזרים: טז [ג]חתיכה של קדשי קדשים של פגול ושל נותר שנתבשלו עם החתיכות אסור לזרים ומותר לכהנים ר' שמעון מתיר לזרים ולכהנים: יז [ד]בשר קדשי קדשים ובשר קדשים קלים שנתבשלו עם בשר התאוה אסור לטמאים ומותר לטהורים:

פרק שלישי

א א) [ה]בגד שצבעו בקליפי ערלה ידלק נתערב באחרים כולם ידלקו דברי ר"מ [ו]וחכ"א יעלה באחד ומאתים: ב הצובע מלא הסיט בקליפי ערלה וארגו בבגד ואין ידוע איזה הוא ר' מאיר אומר ידלק הבגד וחכ"א [ז]יעלה באחד ומאתים: ג ג) [ח]האורג מלא הסיט מצמר הבכור בבגד ידלק הבגד ומשער הנזיר ומפטר חמור בשק ידלק השק ובמוקדשין מקדשין כל שהן: ד [ט]תבשיל שבשלו בקליפי ערלה ידלק נתערב באחרים יעלה באחד ומאתים: ה ג) [י]תנור שהסיקו בקליפי ערלה ואפה בו את הפת תדלק הפת נתערבה באחרות תעלה באחד ומאתים: ו ד) מי שהיו לו חבילי תלתן של כלאי הכרם ידלקו נתערבו

א ידלק. בהגוזל קמא ובפ' כל שעה (דף כב:) דרשינן מנין שלא יהנה ממנו ולא יצבע בו ולא ידליק בו את הנר תלמוד לומר (ויקרא יט) וערלתם ערלתו את פריו ערלים וקליפין מרבינן [ברכות לו:] מדכתיב את פריו (א) ואמרינן בירושלמי (הל' א) אית תני בטפל את פריו ואית תני בסמוך לפריו: כולן ידלקו. לרבי מאיר י' דברים מקדשין ובגד אחד מהן ולרבנן אין מקדשין אלא ו' דברים כדלקמן (מ"ז): ב סיט הוא הפסק שבין אצבע *לאצבע במה שאדם יכול להרחיבו וחוט ארוך כשיעור זה צבעו וארגו בבגד ואין ידוע אי זהו: ר' מאיר אומר ידלק כל הבגד שזה אחד מעשרה המקדשים לרבי מאיר: ג מלא הסיט מצמר בכור. גבי בכור בעי מלא הסיט וגבי מוקדשין תני כל שהוא וצריך טעם מאי שנא אמו בכור לאו מוקדשין ושמא חד בתם וחד בבעל מום ואע"ג דתרווייהו דרבנן דסלהו סוגיא דשילהי הלוקח בהמה (דף כו:) מוכחא דגיזי פסולי המוקדשין שריא מדאורייתא ואפילו בעולה תמימה כדמוכח התם גבי תולש למר מעולה תמימה דהא דדרשינן תזבח ולא גיזה היינו שלא תגוז אבל אם גזז לא מיתסרא והא דקתני התם בעלי מומין אוסרין בכל שהן ומוקמי לה בגיזי בכור בעל מום שנתערבו בגיזי חולין ואע"ג דקתני כל שהן מ"מ מלא הסיט בעי ומיהו צריך לדקדק דמלא הסיט דהכא לא אסר אלא בליפרתא כדאמרינן בסוף תמורה (דף לד.) ובגיזה לא שייכא ליפרתא אלא באריגה: ידלק הבגד. ר' מאיר תני לה דאמר עשרה דברים מקדשים כדאיתא בירושלמי ברס כרבנן הוא סיט הוא פחות מסים גבי למר נקט בגד וגבי שער נקט שק כי אורחא דמילתא: שער נזיר אסור בהנאה כדדרשינן בפ' האיש מקדש (דף נז:) קדוש יהיה גדל פרע גידולו קדוש: פטר חמור מחייס שרי רבי שמעון בהנאה בפ"ק דבכורות (דף יב) אבל לאחר עריפה מודה דגמר עריפה עריפה מעגלה ערופה כדאמרי' התם: ידלק השק. בסוף תמורה (דף לד) פריך ממתני' דהכא אהא דתנן התם ואלו הן הנקברין שער נזיר ופטר חמור ומשני כאן בנזיר טמא כאן בנזיר טהור דנזיר טהור שריפה כתיב ביה ונתן על האש אשר תחת זבח השלמים (במדבר ו) אבל בשער נזיר טמא לא כתיב שריפה ובפטר חמור משני כאן בשק כאן בשער. שק אי אמרת יקבר אתי איניש ומיתהני ביה הואיל ואינו כלה עד לאחר זמן ובירושלמי קאמר שהשק מצוי לחשם אחריו ולא השער והתם פריך וליבטיל ברובה ומשני בליפרתא שעשה מן האיסור לורות לפור דחשיב דמייפה לכולה שק וכגון דלאי אפשר לשנופינהו דאיכא ליפרתא טובא דהתירה ולא ידיע הי מינייהו דאיסורא ודבר תימה אי בעי תרתי מלא הסיט וליפרתא: ד ה ידלק כדאמר בפ' כל שעה (דף כו:) דיש שבח עצים בפת וכן בתבשיל יעלה באחד ומאתים אפי' לר' מאיר דאין זה מי' דברים: ו ז ח חבילי תלתן. מפרש בירושל' (הל' ד) כמה היא חבילה כ"ה זירין: נתערבו באחרים. בפרק כל הזבחים שנתערבו (דף עח) ובפ"ק דביצה (דף ג) מייתי לה ויש ספרים שכתוב בהם ואחרים באחרים ולא גרים לה ר"ת בכל הני דמתני' ולא בסוף פ' כל הצלמים מדפריך בפרק התערובות (דף עד) על שמואל דאסר בספק ספיקא בע"א מברייתא שאוסר ולא משכחת דקאי כשמואל אלא ר' יהודה דברייתא שאוסר אפי' בשאר איסורין ספק ספיקא כגון רמוני בדן ושמואל סבר לה כוותיה בחדא ופליג עליה בחדא ולא מייתי מכל הנך משניות ותדע מדלא תני במתני' גבי אורג מלא הסיט בבגד נתערבו באחרים כדתני במתני' באחריני והיינו טעמא דאם נתערב בשאר בגדים יכול להסיר מכל אחד מלא הסיט ומשתרו מטעם ספק ספקא (ב) ומיהו איכא חדא ברייתא בריש ביצה (דף ג:) דאסר ספק ספקא דקתני וספקא אסורה ומוקי לה בספק טריפה שנתערבה באלף כולן אסורות ואין לחוש כיון דברייתא היא ועוד אומר ר"ת דהא דקתני התם נתערבה באלף כולן אסורות לא

א כבר בארנו כי הערלה אסורה בהנאה ואסור לצבוע בה ולא לעשות בה דבר אחר: ויעלה באחד ומאתים עניינו שיערבו אותו הבגד במאתים ויהיה הכל מותר כמו שבארנו בפרק שלפני זה והלכה כחכמים: ב הסיט (זו המלה) הוא שתות הזרת וראיתי בזו המלה פירושים הרבה וזכרתי מהם פחות שבעשרים לאומרא ונתחזק אצלי זה הפירוש מפני שהוא פירוש הקדמונים והקדמון הוא יותר חכם בלשון מן האחרון והשמיענו בהלכה הקודמת קולא לחכמים אפילו בבגד שנצבע כולו יעלה ובזו ההלכה השמיענו חומרא לר' מאיר שאמר אפילו חוט אחד כשנצבע בבגד ישרף כולו והלכה כחכמים: ג צמר הבכור טוה הש"י שלא לגזוז הבכור שנאמר (דברים טו) לא תגוז בכור צאנך ושער הנזיר טוה לשרפו שנאמר (במדבר ו) ולקח את שער ראש נזרו ונתן על האש ופטר חמור כשנערף יקבר וכל אלו מכלל איסורי הנאה כמו שנתבארו ראיותיהם בזולת זה המקום ושק נקרא הבגד הארוג מן השער ולא נאמר בזו תעלה לפי שלא נתן בהם הכתוב שיעור בשום פנים: ואמרם ובמוקדשין כל שהן ענינו כי כשיהיה אותו הצמר מוקדשים אפילו יהיה פחות מרוחב הסיט שאחר אותו הבגד כולו קודש ואסור לו ליהנות בו עד שיפדנו כמו שיתבאר במקומו: ד זה מבואר לפי ששבח ערלה בתבשיל: ה גם זה מבואר: ו פירוש כל

פי' מהר"י בן מלכי צדק

יג כלים שסכן בשמן טמא וחזר וסכן בשמן טהור או שסכן בשמן טהור ואחר כך סכן בשמן טמא רבי אליעזר אומר אחר הראשון אני בא. גרסי' בירושלמי מאי טעמיה דר' אליעזר כלומר העור שניסך טמא לדברי הכל דמשקה מטמא כלי מדרבנן. הראשון מוציא את האחרון כלומר כשסכן בשמן טהור וחזר וסכן בשמן טמא כי פלטי מן הראשון פלטי והוי משקה טהור ואינו מטמא דברים אחרים: וחכמים אומרים אחר האחרון. וכי פלטי מן האחרון פלטי ואם האחרון היה טמא משקה היוצא מהן טמא. ואם האחרון היה טהור משקה היוצא מהן טהור דלעולם האחרון פולט: יד טו שאור של תרומה ושל כלאי הכרם וכו' אסור לזרים רבנן לטעמיהו דתרומה וכלאי הכרם מצטרפי ומותר לכהנים רבנן לטעמיהו דאמרי לעולם אינו אסור לזרים עד שיהא בשאור דאיסור כדי לחמץ אף כאן לעולם אינו אסור לכהנים עד שיהא בשאור דכלאי הכרם כדי לחמץ: ור' שמעון מתיר לזרים ולכהנים. ר' שמעון לטעמיה דאמר אין מצטרפין תבלין של תרומה ושל כלאי הכרם וטולה מתורצת על פי משנה שלפניה: יז ומותר לזרים הטהורין אפי' לרבנן רבנן לטעמיהו דאמרי לעולם אינו אסור עד שיהא בו וכו'. וכי אין בקדשי קדשים כדי לאסור שהרי יש בבשר התאוה כדי להעלותן:

פרק ג א ב בגד שצבעו בקליפי ערלה ידלק מ"ט שהקליפין אסורין משום ערלה דכתיב וערלתם ערלתו את פריו בסמוך לפריו ואיזה זה הקליפין: נתערב באחרים. פי' זה הבגד כולן ידלקו: ג ומשער הנזיר ומפטר חמור בשק ידלק השק. פי' אם ארג מוק מלא חוט בשק ידלק השק ואפי' רבנן מודו: ובמוקדשין מקדשין כל שהן פי' אינן צריכין סים: ד תבשיל שבישלו בקליפי ערלה ידלק אותו תבשיל: נתערב באחר יעלה באחד ומאתים. פי' לדברי הכל דאפי' לרבי מאיר י' דברים מקדשיקוהו אין אחד מוק. ועוד אין דרכו לימנות: ה תנור שהסיקו בקליפי ערלה ואפה בו את הפת הפת אסורה משום דיש שבח עצים בפת: נתערבה באחרות תעלה באחד ומאתים דלאו מי' דברים נינהו: ו נתערבו באחרין. פי' בחבילות אחרות של היתר' כולן ידלקו דברי ר' מאיר פי' רבי מאיר לטעמיה דאמר י' דברים מקדשין והנך לא שהיה ר' מאיר אומר את שדרכו לימנות מקדש כגון אילו ד' דאמרינן ר' דבעינן למימר: חביות

עין משפט נר מצוה

יא א ב מיי' פט"ז מהלכות מאכלות אסורות הלכה יג:
יב ג מיי' פ"ז מהלכות מעשה קרבנות הלכה יג:
יג ד מיי' פ"י מהל' מעשה קרבנות הלכה יג:
א ה ו מיי' פט"ז מהלכות מאכלות אסורות הלכה כ:
ב ז שם הלכה כא:
ג ח מיי' פי"ט מה' פסולי המוקדשין הל' יב ופ"ג מהלכות בכורות הלכה יג:
ד ט מיי' פט"ז מהלכות מאכלות אסורות הלכה כ:
ה י שם הל' כב:

פירוש הרא"ש

פ"ג (א) את לרבות הטפל לפריו: (ב) דשמא אין זה הבגד שנארג בו ואם הוא זה שמא הסירו ממנו חוט האיסור:

צ"ל לאמה

Continuation of translation from previous page as indicated by ◁

MISHNAH 2. IF ONE DYED A THREAD THE WHOLE [LENGTH] OF A SIT[5] WITH SHELLS OF 'ORLAH, AND WOVE IT INTO A GARMENT, AND IT IS NOT KNOWN WHICH [THREAD] IT IS, R. MEIR SAYS: THE GARMENT SHALL BE BURNT;[6] BUT THE SAGES SAY: IT [THE THREAD] BECOMES NEUTRALIZED IN TWO-HUNDRED-AND-ONE.[7]

MISHNAH 3. IF ONE WOVE THE WHOLE OF A SIT'S LENGTH
f OF THE WOOL OF A FIRSTLING[1] INTO A GARMENT, THE GARMENT SHALL BE BURNT;[2] AND [IF ONE WOVE A SIT] OF THE HAIR OF A NAZIRITE[3] OR OF THE FIRST-BORN OF AN ASS[4] INTO SACK-CLOTH, THE SACK-CLOTH SHALL BE BURNT;[5] AND [IF ONE HAS WOVEN] WITH [SOME WOOL OR HAIR OF] CONSECRATED [ANIMALS],[6] THESE [KINDS OF WOOL OR HAIR] HAVE THE EFFECT OF RENDERING [THE WOVEN ARTICLE] CONSECRATED, WHATEVER [SMALL AMOUNT] OF THEM[7] THERE BE.[8]

g MISHNAH 4. A DISH WHICH ONE COOKED WITH SHELLS[1] OF 'ORLAH[2] SHALL BE BURNT;[3] IF IT [SUCH COOKED FOOD] BECAME MIXED UP WITH OTHER [COOKED FOODS], IT BECOMES NEUTRALIZED IN TWO-HUNDRED-AND-ONE.[4]

MISHNAH 5. IF ONE FIRED AN OVEN WITH SHELLS OF 'ORLAH, AND BAKED THEREIN BREAD, THE BREAD SHALL BE BURNT. IF IT BECAME MIXED UP WITH OTHER [LOAVES] IT BECOMES NEUTRALIZED IN TWO-HUNDRED-AND-ONE.[5]

MISHNAH 6. IF ONE HAS BUNDLES OF TREFOIL[6] OF 'MIXED-SEEDS' OF THE VINEYARD, THEY SHALL BE BURNT;

(5) A measure of length. Definitions vary; viz., (*a*) the distance between the tips of the forefinger and middle finger when fully stretched apart (the distance between the tips of the forefinger and the thumb when fully stretched apart being a 'double *sit*'), v. Rashi to Shab. 105*b*—106*a*; (*b*) a handbreadth (i.e. the width, across the knuckles, of the four fingers held together, plus the thumb when held close to them; (*c*) = a sixth of a span (*zereth*), (Maim.). (6) But he permits the material as long as the length of the '*orlah*-dyed thread is less than a *sit*. (7) Even if the length of the prohibited thread is less than a *sit*, the Sages require two hundred times of permitted thread to neutralize the prohibited.
f (1) The use of such wool is forbidden, as the whole animal is consecrated and its shearing is forbidden. Deut. XV, 19, *All the firstling males that are born of thy herd and of thy flock thou shalt sanctify unto the Lord thy God .... thou shalt not shear the firstling of thy flock*. (2) However overwhelming the amount of permitted thread it contains. (3) In Num. VI, 5, *He shall be holy, he shall let the locks of the hair of his head grow long*; the words קדש יהיה are interpreted '*it* shall be holy' and taken to refer to the hair; so that a Nazirite's hair is deemed consecrated and prohibited for use, v. Josephus *Ant*. VI, 4. (4) *Sc*. which has not been redeemed and is to have its neck broken. Ex. XIII, 13, *And every firstling of an ass thou shalt redeem .... and if thou wilt not redeem it, then thou shalt break its neck*. By analogy with Deut. XXI, 4, ... *and shall break the heifer's neck*, the rule is derived that (at any rate after the breaking of its neck) the firstling of an ass is subject to the same prohibitions of use as are prescribed, or inferred, with regard to the heifer whose neck is broken. That the use of the latter's hair is forbidden is inferred, by analogy, from the 'red heifer'. Of the firstling ass it is said (Deut. XXI, 2), *which hath not drawn in the yoke*, and of the 'red heifer' it is said (Num. XIX, 3), *upon which never came a yoke*. This common factor is interpreted to render both subject to the same prohibitions of use, and since in the case of the 'red heifer', the injunction to burn it whole deliberately mentions the skin, it is clear that its skin and hair are deemed consecrated and their use prohibited, and likewise, by analogy, the hair of the heifer-whose-neck-is-broken; by extension of the analogy, also the hair of the firstling of an ass (that has not been redeemed) is forbidden. (5) However large the proportion of permitted wool or hair. Sack-cloth is instanced in regard to hair, and a garment in regard to wool, because such were the uses to which hair and wool respectively were commonly put. (6) I.e., only such as one may redeem, e.g., קדשי מזבח, animals voluntarily designated for sacrifice which became unfit, through blemish, for the altar, and קדשי בדק הבית, such animals (or objects) devoted for purposes of the upkeep of the Temple. (7) I.e., of the prohibited hair or wool. (8) This stringent ruling applies only, as already stated, to such (consecrated) objects as can be made permitted by redemption, to which applies the principle that 'whatever may be rendered permitted is not annulled even in a thousand'. Where, however, Scripture has precluded the alternative redemption (v. note 6), the law is more lenient, viz., only if the prohibited admixture is of a given minimum measure (in our case a *sit* of consecrated wool or hair) has it the effect of rendering the rest consecrated, prohibited for use and condemned to destruction (T.J.).
g (1) V. *supra* Mish. 1, n. 2. (2) Or stubble of 'mixed-seeds' of the vineyard, used as fuel; the dish being open to the flame (v. Pes. 26*b* and Rashi *ad loc*.). (3) The dish having become prohibited by absorbing, as it were, the 'goodness' of the prohibited fuel. (4) Even R. Meir agrees with this, and does not insist, as he does in the instances cited earlier in the Chapter, that the slightest amount of matter affected by '*orlah*, should render other matter mixed therewith similarly prohibited. The reason for leniency here, is that the prohibited element in the dish is from shells etc., a material not significant enough that its flame should impose not only a *prohibition*, but also a completely *prohibitory* character on a dish cooked in front of it. (5) V. notes to Mishnah 4. (6) תלתן, from the Aramaic תלת = three, a three-leaved leguminous plant, particularly fenugreek (v. Jast.). A bundle of this consists of twenty-five stalks (T.J.).

כדי לחמץ: יג כלים שסכן בשמן טמא וחזר וסכן בשמן טהור או שסכן בשמן טהור וחזר וסכן בשמן טמא ר' אליעזר אומר אחר הראשון אני בא וחכמים אומרים אחר האחרון: יד שאור של תרומה ושל כלאי הכרם שנפלו לתוך עיסה לא בזה כדי לחמץ ולא בזה כדי לחמץ ונצטרפו וחמצו אסור לזרים ומותר לכהנים ר"ש מתיר לזרים ולכהנים: טו תבלין של תרומה ושל כלאי הכרם שנפלו בקדרה לא באלו כדי לתבל ולא באלו כדי לתבל ונצטרפו ותבלו אסור לזרים ומותר לכהנים ר"ש מתיר לכהנים ולזרים: טז חתיכה של קדשי קדשים של פגול ושל נותר שנתבשלו עם החתיכות אסור לזרים ומותר לכהנים ר' שמעון מתיר לזרים ולכהנים: יז בשר קדשי קדשים ובשר קדשים קלים שנתבשלו עם בשר התאוה אסור לטמאים ומותר לטהורים:

פרק שלישי

א הבגד שצבעו בקליפי ערלה ידלק נתערב באחרים כולם ידלקו דברי ר"מ וחכ"א יעלה באחד ומאתים: ב הצובע מלא הסיט בקליפי ערלה וארגו בבגד ואין ידוע איזה הוא ר' מאיר אומר ידלק הבגד וחכ"א יעלה באחד ומאתים: ג האורג מלא הסיט מצמר הבכור בבגד ידלק הבגד ומשער הנזיר ומפטר חמור בשק ידלק השק ובמוקדשין מקדשין כל שהן: ד תבשיל שבשלו בקליפי ערלה ידלק נתערב באחרים יעלה באחד ומאתים: ה תנור שהסיקוהו בקליפי ערלה ואפה בו את הפת תדלק הפת נתערבה באחרות תעלה באחד ומאתים: ו מי שהיו לו חבילי תלתן של כלאי הכרם ידלקו נתערבו

באחרים כולם ידלקו דברי ר״מ *וחכ״א יעלו באחד ומאתים: ז שהיה רבי מאיר אומר את שדרכו למנות מקדש וחכמים אומרים אינו מקדש אלא ששה דברים בלבד ורבי עקיבא אומר ב) שבעה ואלו הם אגוזי פרך רמוני בדן וחביות סתומות וחולפות תרדין *וקולסי כרוב ודלעת יונית ר׳ עקיבא אומר אף ככרות של בעל הבית א) הראוי לערלה ערלה לכלאי הכרם כלאי הכרם: ח *כיצד ג) נתפצעו האגוזים נתפרדו הרמונים נתפתחו החביות נתחתכו הדלועים נתפרסו הככרות יעלו באחד ומאתים: ט ג) ד) ספק הערלה (ד) בארץ ישראל אסור (ה) ובסוריא מותר ובחוצה לארץ יורד ולוקח ובלבד שלא יראנו לוקט ה) כרם ג) נטוע ירק וירק נמכר חוצה לו בא״י אסור ובסוריא מותר ובחוצה לארץ יורד ולוקט ובלבד שלא ילקוט ביד ו) החדש ד) אסור מן

ירושלמי

לא קאי אספיקא אלא אודאי תדע דאפי׳ רבי יהודה דאסר בזבחים (דף עד) ספק ספיקא דוקא ברמוני בדן דבהדיא קתני ר׳ יהודה אומר רמוני בדן דמשמע דוקא [רמוני] בדן שהם את שדרכו למנות דהוי א׳ מו׳ דברים בהנהו אסר ר׳ יהודה ספק ספיקא ור׳ יהודה כל שדרכו אית ליה כדמוכח ברייתא דליסרא קליעות בזבחים ובבילה ומאי טעמא נקט רמוני בדן אלא ודאי משום דבשאר מילי לא אסר ספק ספיקא ומיהו קשה אי נקט דוקא רמוני בדן אם כן קשיא דר׳ יהודה אדר׳ יהודה דתנן בפ׳ י״ז (משנה ה) דכלים הרמון שאמרו לא גדול ולא קטן אלא בינוני ולמה הוזכרו רמוני בדן שיהיו מקדשין כל שהן דברי ר״מ ר׳ יוחנן בן נורי אומר לשער בהן את הכלים ר״ע אומר לכך ולכך הוזכרו לשער בהן את הכלים ושיהו מקדשין כל שהן אמר ר׳ יהודה לא הוזכרו רמוני בדן ונאגרי גבע אלא שיהו מתעשרין ודאי בכל מקום לפי שסתמן באים מבין הנכרים משמע בהדיא לר׳ יהודה דאין חלוקין משאר רמונים לשום דבר אלא להיא מילתא וצריך לומר דהא דנקט בזבחים רמוני בדן משום ר״ש דפליג עליה ברמוני בדן ושרי ספק ספיקא וכן צריך לפרש באידך ברייתא דקתני התם כוס של ע״ז שנפלה לאוצר מלא כוסות כולן אסורים פירוש א׳ מהן לרבוא ומרבוא לרבוא מותרים ומאי נקט מרבוא לרבוא הא אפי׳ ברבוא קמא שרי אלא נקטיה לאשמעינן דמאן דאסר אסר אפי׳ בכמה ספיקות ומתוך ההיא משנה דכלים צריך לפרש דסתם רמונים לא חשיב כל שדרכו לרבי מאיר נר״ל דאמר התם בזבחים (דף עב) ובריש בילה (דף ג) ובפ׳ הערל (דף פא) כל שדרכו שנינו דהא לרבי מאיר לא מקדש אלא רמוני בדן ולר״מ חשיבי כל שדרכו ויש מפרשים דאפי׳ גרסינן ואחרות באחרות ניחא דלא הוי ספק ספיקא דמיירי שכל האחרות נתערבו באחרות ואצטריך ליה לאשמעינן כהאי גוונא אע״ג דאיכא תרי רובי ודכוותה אמרינן בסוף פ״ק דכתובות (דף טו) הולכין אחר רוב העיר והוא דאיכא רוב סיעה בהדיה ואפי׳ עיר קטנה ואין הולכין אחר רוב העיר גרידת׳ ואפי׳ גדולה כאנטוכיא : כולן ידלקו. לא משתמים בכל הנך איסורי דלימא יוליך הנאה ליס המלח אלא לענין ע״ז לרבי אלעזר בסוף כל הצלמים (דף מט:) ודכוותיה פסקינן התם ושמא משום דע״ז תופסת דמיה אע״פ שאינה ניתרת בכך מכל מקום מיחזי טפי כמוליך האיסור ליס המלח ולפי טעם זה בהגוזל עצים (דף קא:) גבי בגד שצבעו בקליפי שביעית אם נתערב באחרים כיון דשביעית תופסת דמיה הוה אמרינן יוליך הנאה ליס המלח וטבעות וכוסות דפ׳ התערובות (דף עד) סגיא במוליך הנאה ליס המלח ועוד יש לחלק דהתם בכל הצלמים תנור שהסיקו בעצי ע״ז ואפה בו את הפת ונפל ממנה ככרכר וארג בה את הבגד שרינן בהולכת הנאה כשנתערב׳ לפי שאין ממשות האיסור בעין וההוא גברא דאיערב ליה חביתא דחמרא כיון דאי אפשר להיות בהולכת הנאה אלא היתר [הנאה] כגון למכור לנכרי או למכור לפועלים ולא שיהנה ממש מגוף הדבר דהא אסור בשתייה שרי ע״י ד׳ זוזי והא דלא אמרי׳ בכל הכי דמתניתין ימכר כולו לנכרי חוץ מדמי איסור שבו כדאמר רשב״ג בפ׳ בתרא דע״ז (ד׳ עד.) גבי יין נסך מפרש בירושלמי דחיישי׳ בכולהו דילמא הדר נכרי ומזבין ליה לישראל אבל ביין נסך ליכא למיחש ותבית׳ דההוא חמרא דפ׳ כל הצלמים אם היה הפץ למכור כל יינו יחד הוה משתרי למכור חוץ מדמי איסור שבו: יעלו בא׳ ומאתים. בריש ביצה פירש בקונטרס אם נתערב אחד מהן במאתים יעלה אחד מהן והשאר מותרין ועל סמך פירושו נהגו במין במינו כשמתבשל ברוב נהגו להסיר ממנו כשיעור האיסור והשאר מותר וא״א לומר כן דבהדי׳ תנן לעיל בריש פ״ב (מ״ב) ערלה וכלאי הכרם עולים בא׳ ור׳ וא״צ להרים ותרומה דוקא משום גזל השבט והא דתרומה שיעורא בק׳ וערלה בר׳ בסיפרי דריש לה מקרא כדפרשינן לעיל בפ״ב (מ״א): שהיה רבי מאיר אומר את שדרכו למנות מקדש. שאין אדם מוכרו בלא מנין מתוך חשיבותו ובריש התערובות ובילה והערל פליגי דר׳ יוחנן אמר את שדרכו לימנות שנינו ור״ל אמר כל שדרכו לימנות שנינו אף על פי שאין כל שעה מונין אותו אלא זימנין דמזבנינן ליה במנין מתוך חשיבות וא״ת לר״ל [דאמר] כל שדרכו לימנות הא שמעינן לרבי מאיר בפ״ק דבילה (דף ד) דאמר ליסרא קליעות ערלה והיא עולה והיא כל שדרכו מדאסר ר׳ יהודה התם וי״ל דבסוף הערל (דף פא) דייק מינה ר״ש לקיש דתרומה בזמן הזה דרבנן שאני שונה עיגול בעיגולים עולה וא״ת למעמי׳ לא יקדש כל שדרכו בכלאי הכרם דאינהו נמי דרבנן כיון דבטלה קדושת הארץ וי״ל דהתם איכא תרי דרבנן חדא, דתרומת תאנים דרבנן ועוד דבטלה קדושת הארץ א״נ הכי פירושו שהיה ר״מ אומר כל שדרכו לימנות מקדש בדאורייתא וא״כ בכלאי הכרם דין הוא שיקדשו תב״ני תלתן שהם את שדרכו א״כ בכלאי הכרם לאסירי בהנאה חמירי שיקדש בהן כל שדרכו אע״פ שהן דרבנן ואמרי׳ בירושלמי (שם) ר׳ יוחנן ור״ש לקיש איתפלגון חד אמר י׳ דברים מקדשין דברי ר״מ פי׳ י׳ דברים השנוים במשנתינו שכולן את שדרכו וחד אמר כל הדברים מקדשין דברי ר״מ כלומר כל שדרכו לימנות ומסתברא דאותן י׳ דברים היינו הנך ו׳ דברים ותבילי תלתן הרי ז׳ ובגד שנתערב וסים שנתערב דבתרוייהו תנן לעיל דברי ר״מ ובגד וסים תרי מילי ניהו הרי ט׳ ובאורג מלא הסים מאמר בכור ובמוקדשין כל שהן אמרינן בירושל׳ עלה דאית תנא תני בשם ר״מ ואית דלא תני לה בשם ר״מ מאן דתני לה בשם ר״מ אית ליה עשרה דברים מקדשין ומאן דלא תני לה בשם ר״מ מנין אית ליה לר״מ י׳ דברים מקדשין ר״מ כרבי עקיבא דאמר אף ככרות של בע״ה ויש תימה הא איכא טובא טבעות וכוסות של ע״ז דפרק התערובות (דף עד) וגיזי נמר בכור בעל מום שנתערבו בגיזי חולין למשמע בסוף פ״ג דבכורות (דף כה:) דאוסרין בכל שהן וחתיכה הראויה להתכבד בה בפ׳ גיד הנשה (דף ק) חתיכה של חטאת בחולין בסוף הערל (דף פא:) ועוד כל הני דשילהי ע״ז (דף עד) יין נסך ועורות לבובים וצפורי מצורע ושער נזיר ופטר חמור ובשר בחלב ושור הנסקל ועגלה ערופה וחולין שנשחטו בעזרה ומפרש התם בגמ׳ דהאי תנא תרתי אית ליה דבר שבמנין ואיסור הנאה ועל כרחיה חשיבי טפי מאת שדרכו מדפריך התם ליתני אגוזי פרך ורמוני בדן וככרות ולא פריך מחבילי תלתן ש״מ דחשיבי בו׳ דברים ונראה דהא דחשיב עשרה דברים היינו משנתנו אבל אכתי איכא טובא ואם תאמר יין נסך דחשיב בע״ז היינו חביות סתומות דהא אתיא אפי׳ כרבנן כדפרישי׳ ועוד דפתוחות אפילו לר״מ לא מקדשין דהא סתומות אחד מי׳ דברים ואם כן אמאי חשיב להו התם הא תנא להו הכא גבי ערלה וכלאי הכרם דמהאי טעמא קאמר התם דלא חשיב ככרות של בעל הבית לענין חמץ בפסח משום דתני להו הכא גבי כלאי הכרם ויש לומר דאיצטריך שלא תקל ביין נסך משום דמקרא מדברי קבלה נפקא בפ׳ אין מעמידין אי נמי לאפוקי מדרבי אליעזר דשרי בפדיון בשילהי כל הצלמים (דף מט) אי נמי למעוטי סתם יינן ואם סתם יינן נמי אוסר כל שכן דאיצטריך משום סתם יינן ועוד אפשר דיין נסך אפי׳ בפתוחות אוסר בכל שהו ומפרש בירושלמי (הל׳ יב) יין נסך וע״ז ושרות לבובין על שם ולא ידבק בידך מאומה מן החרם (דברים יג) משמע שזה גורם להם להחשב לאסור בשיעור מועט כמו לענין שבת בפרק ר׳ עקיבא (ד׳ ל) דמשמשי ע״ז בכל שהן ומיהו שמא לא מיתוקמא אלא משום דמיניה נפקא לן איסור הנאה כדמייתי נמי התם קרא אכל חד וחד וע״ז דלא חשיב לעובדיהם וכן בשורות לבובין שעשה ממנו כלי חשוב כששה דברים למאי דפרישית א) דהתם אפי׳ כרבנן וציפורי מצורע חשובים כחתיכה הראויה להתכבד ובפ׳ התערובות דפריך ליבטלו ברובא ומוקי לה רב פפא כתנא דליסרא קליעות השתא פריך ב) דחתיכות קטנות לא חשיבי כעוף ולא חזי להתכבד ולפי זה מתני׳ דמסכת קינין דאסורות בכל שהן כטולי עלמא אי נמי בצפורי מצורע בשחוטין הראויין להתכבד כחתיכה אי נמי שחוטה חשובה בהדיא דאיתקש לעוף שמא דדרשי׳ בפ׳ ב׳ דקידושין (דף נז) וזה אשר לא תאכלו לרבות השחוטה ושער נזיר לאו כשארג ממנו מלא הסים דאם כן הא תנא ליה הכא במתני׳ אבל כשעשה ממנו כלי נאה וחשוב כגון נפה וכברה וכיולא בהן אי נמי חשוב בעיניה משום דחזי לפיאה נכרית ופטר חמור ושור הנסקל ועגלה ערופה בהמות גסות וחשובות ובריש התערובות עביד צריכותא בהא דתניא שור הנסקל התם ובקדשים ובשר בחלב וחולין שנשחטו בעזרה בחתיכות הראויות להתכבד ואע״ג דתני חתיכה גבי נבילה בפ׳ גיד הנשה קתני לה התם משום הדבר שבמנין ואיסורי הנאה ובירושלמי (ע״ז שם) מוקי שור הנסקל בחתיכה ולפי סברתן בשר בחלב ושור הנסקל ועגלה ערופה וחולין שנשחטו בעזרה כולהו מיתוקמי בחתיכה ותננהו לאשמעי׳ דאסירי בהנאה כשור הנסקל משום דאיכא למאן דאמר בשר בחלב שרי בהנאה וחולין שנשחטו בעזרה לאו דאורייתא אי נמי לאשמעי׳ אע״ג דלאו דאורייתא חשיבי לאסור ותנא עגלה ערופה לאשמעינן דלא משתריא במה שנעשית מצותה ומיהו מתוך צריכות׳ בפ׳ התערובות משמע דאיירי בשור הנסקל חי כי התם והא דלא תני חתיכה של חטאת ושל לחם הפנים שנתערבה בחולין דאוסרת בכל שהן כדאיתא בסוף הערל ואי דבר שבמנין ואיסורי הנאה דילמא בקדשי׳ לא מיירי וקצת קשה הא דפריך אי דבר שבמנין חשיב ליתני נמי חתיכה של נבילה ליתני הא תנא ליה בפ׳ גיד הנשה ויש לומר דהכי פריך דאי משום דתניא בפ׳ גיד הנשה שבקה אם כן בשר בחלב לא ליתני דאיירי בחתיכה: אגוזי פרך. על שם שנפרכין כדאמר בפסיקתא בפרשה דיהודה וישראל רבים אחר פ׳ כי תשא על אל גינת אגוז (ש״ה ו) דדריש שנמשלו ישראל לאגוז שיש בו ג׳ מינים של פרך שנפרך מעצמו ויש מפרשין דפרך ובדן מקומות הם: חולפי תרדין. פי׳ בערוך עלעות של תרדין הן: קולסי כרוב. כרובים גדולים הן ועלין שלהן: אף ככרות של בע״ה. אבל של נחתום לא שהן קטנות (ג) והא דמשמע בסוף הערל בחתיכה של לחם הפנים בשל חולין לא בטלה שאני לחם הפנים דחמירא טפי וראוי להתכבד כחתיכה ואפה בו את הפת דפ׳ כל הצלמים (דף מט:) צריך לאוקמי בככרות של בע״ה דקתני התם נתערב באחרים כולן אסורות בהנאה ולא אי כפת דלעיל דתנור שהסיקו בקליפי ערלה ואפה בו את הפת דההוא לאו בשל בעל הבית דקתני תעלה בא׳ ור׳ : הראוי לערלה ערלה. כגון אגוז ורמון וחביות : הראוי לכלאי הכרם. כגון חולפות תרדין וקולסי כרוב ודלעת וככרות בירושל׳ (הל׳ ה) דייק אמאי לא תני הראוי לתרומה דתרומה נמי כיון דחשיבה לא בטלי בק״א ומשני דכולן ראויין לתרומה ולא שייך למיתני האי לישנא ועל תגס דייק דהאי ידלקו באחד ומאתים לא שייכי בתרומה ועוד דדילמא לא חשיב הכא אלא דבר שבמנין ואיסורי הנאה כדמשני בשלהי ע״ז : ח נתפצעו האגוזים. בכל אחד שונה לשון הנופל בו דאיצטריך לאשמעינן דלא תימא הא דמקדשים בכל שהוא אפילו שבורים קמ״ל דאין מקדשין אלא שלמין : ט ספק ערלה. כגון נכרי שיש לו נטיעה של ערלה בגינתו ובידו פירות ולא ידיע אם משל ערלה או משל זקינה: בארץ ישראל אסור. לחומרא: יורד ולוקח. יורד בתוך הגינה וקונה מן הנכרי מאותה שכבר נלקטו ובלבד שלא יראנו לוקט וכן לענין כלאים כדפרישית והא דקתני גבי כלאים בחוצה לארץ יורד ולוקט אמרינן בירושלמי א״ר הונא כן הוא מתני׳ יורד ולוקח ובלבד שלא יראנו לוקט כדקמייתא ובפ״ק דקידושין (דף לח) פליגי בה אמוראי: החדש אסור

קודש

כל זה מטאר והלכה כחכמים: ז את שדרכו למנות מקדש. ענינו שלא נאמר יעלה באחד ומאתים אלא כשנתערבו מה שאין דרכו להמנות כגון שנתערבו חטים של כלאי הכרם בחטים של חולין או יין של ערלה ביין של חולין אבל מה שדרכו להמנות כגון חבילי תלתן אפילו נתערבה חבילה אחת באלף ישרף הכל וזהו ענין תקדש שנאמר (דברים כב) פן תקדש המלאה וענינו השרפה כמו שבארנו וחכ״א כי ששה דברים הם בלבד שנאמר בהם תקדש ולא תעלה באחד ומאתים והוסיף ר׳ עקיבא השביעי והוא ימנה אותן לקמן ואין הל׳ כר״מ: פרך ובדן שמות מקומות ידועות: וחולפות תרדין. ר״ל מה שמחליפות וצומחות: וקולסי כרוב. עיקר הכרוב ר״ל הגדל מהם: ודלעת יונית. גם כן ידוע כי כל אלו הם אללם ידועות ומנויות כל אחד ואחד בפני עצמו והיו מיוחדות בשבח על כל שאר הפירות והירקות שהיו מאותו המין ולפיכך לא היו נמכרים אלא בחשבון וכל אדם היה מקפיד עליהם חולתם ממינם היו נמכרים באומד ולא היו נמכרים א׳ א׳ אלא הרבה ביחד: הראוי לערלה ערלה והם אגוזי פרך רמוני בדן וחביות סתומות והראוי לכלאי הכרם הארבע הנשארות וחביות סתומות לפי שהערלה אינו טהג אלא באילן בלבד *ואין הלכה כר״ע : ח אמרם כיצד. רוצה בו על איזה דרך יהיו אלו מקדשות כל שהן השיב ואמר כי זה לא יהיה אלא כשהיו שלמות כמות שהיו אבל נתפלעו או נתפתחו או נתגלו פי החביות הרי אלו יעלו באחד ומאתים ובאר הגמרא שזה הסתם הוא לר׳ עקיבא שהוא מונה ככרות של בעל הבית כמו שקדם: ט ספק הערלה. באורו שהוא כשיהיה כרם הערלה ידוע וענבים נמכרים חוצה לו ולא נודע שהענבים מזה הכרם או מזולתו. ואמרם ובלבד שלא ילקט ביד ענינו שזה האוכל לא ילקוט הוא בעצמו ויאכל אבל ילקט לו זולתו: והחדש אסור מן התורה בכל מקום לאמרו הש״י (ויקרא כג) ולחם וקלי וכרמל לא תאכלו ולא נתן זה תלוי בארץ אבל ערלה וכלאי הכרם אינן אסורים מן התורה אלא בארץ ישראל

ו א שם הלכה ח :
ז ב מיי׳ שם הל׳ ז טוש״ע י״ד סימן קו סעיף א :
ח ג מיי׳ שם הלכה יא טוש״ע י״ד סימן קא סעיף ו :
ט ד מיי׳ פ״י מהל׳ מאכלות אסורות הלכה יא סמג לאוין קמא טוש״ע י״ד סי׳ רצד סעיף ט :
י ה מיי׳ שם ופ״ח מהלכות כלאים הל׳ יג טוש״ע י״ד סימן רצה סעיף סט :
יא ו מיי׳ פ״י מהלכות מאכלות אסורות הלכה ב :

פירוש הרא״ש

(ג) ודרכו למכרם ביחד : (ד) דהוי ספיקא דאורייתא : (ה) ובסוריא מותר דכיבוש יחיד לא שמיה כיבוש והחמירו בו קצת :

הגהות מהר״י לנדא

א) בר״ש מ״ג ד״ה למאי דפרישית דלאתיא מתני׳ כרבנן כצ״ל : ב) שם השתא פריך דחתיכות קטנות דלא חשיבי כצ״ל :

א) עו״ג ס״ה דף עד. ב) קידושין פ״א דף לח: ברכות דף ס״י לו: ג) קידושין לח: ד) שם :

פי׳ מהרי״ בן מלכי צדק

וחביות סתומות. פי׳ נטפות וחולפות תרדין. פי׳ הן העלין הצלעות של תרדין וקולסי כרוב לעז קרשטו ודלעת יונית אילו ששה דברים מקדשין ואינן עולין. פי׳ אם היו תרומה אע״פ שהתרומה עולה באחד ומאה אילו אינן עולין שהן חשובין וכן אם הן תרומת מעשר כדתנן במעשר שני עד שלא נפתחו החביות עולות באחד ומאה ומשנפ׳ מקדשות כל שהן ואינן עולות. ואם הן דכלאים כגון חולפות תרדים וקולסי כרוב ודלעת יונית הראוין להיות כלאים מקדשין ואינן עולים באחד ומאתים. ואם הן דערלה כגון אגוזי פרך ורימוני בדן וחביות סתומות הראוין להיות ערלה מקדשין ואינן עולין: רבי עקיבא אומר ז׳ ומוסיף ככרות של בעל הבית משום דחשיבי ולא בשלי דלעת יונית אמר ר׳ קריספה בשם ר׳ יוחנן כל אילן קריא קרוצא דאנן אכלין דלעת יונית אינן: ח כיצד נתפצעו האגוזים וכו׳ מלשון משנה את למד פציעה באגוזין פרידה ברימונין חיתוך בדלועין פרישה בככרות דכתיב הלא פרוס לרעב לחמך : נתפרסו הככרות. מתני׳ כר׳ עקיבא דאמר אף ככרות של בעל הבית:

ט החדש אסור מן התורה בכל מקום. פי׳ הא׳ מינין אסורין מן התורה לאכול עד י״ו בניסן ורבן יוחנן [בן זכאי] אמר דגם יום י״ו כולו אסור לאכול חדש כדתנן גזר שיהא יום הנף כולו אסור:

IF THEY BECAME MIXED UP WITH OTHERS,[7] ALL OF THEM SHALL BE BURNT. THIS IS THE OPINION OF R. MEIR; BUT THE SAGES SAY THEY BECOME NEUTRALIZED IN TWO-HUNDRED-AND-ONE.[8]

MISHNAH 7. BECAUSE R. MEIR USED TO SAY: [THE ADMIXTURE OF] ANYTHING WHATSOEVER ONE IS WONT TO
a COUNT [WHEN SELLING],[1] CONDEMNS TO FORFEITURE;[2] BUT THE SAGES SAY ONLY SIX THINGS CONDEMN TO FORFEITURE, AND R. AKIBA SAYS SEVEN [THINGS], AND THESE ARE THEY: NUTS WITH BRITTLE SHELLS,[3] AND POMEGRANATES OF BADAN,[4] AND STOPPED-UP CASKS,[5] AND SHOOTS OF BEET, AND CABBAGE-HEADS, AND GREEK PUMPKINS. R. AKIBA[6] SAYS: ALSO LOAVES OF A HOUSEHOLDER.[7] SUCH [OF THESE] AS ARE LIABLE TO 'ORLAH[8] [CONDEMN THE MIXTURE TO FORFEITURE] AS 'ORLAH, [SUCH OF THESE AS ARE LIABLE TO THE LAW OF] 'MIXED-SEEDS' OF THE VINEYARD[9] [CONDEMN THE MIXTURE TO FORFEITURE AS] 'MIXED-SEEDS' OF THE VINEYARD.

MISHNAH 8. IN WHAT [DEFINED] MANNER[10] [MAY THE ABOVE BECOME NEUTRALIZED]? IF THE NUTS CRACKED, OR IF THE POMEGRANATES BURST OPEN, OR THE CASKS BECAME UNSTOPPED, OR THE PUMPKINS WERE CUT, OR THE LOAVES WERE BROKEN UP, THEY BECOME NEUTRALIZED IN TWO-HUNDRED-AND-ONE.[11]

MISHNAH 9. [WHATEVER IS UNDER DOUBT] AS TO
b [WHETHER IT IS] 'ORLAH[1] IS, IN THE LAND OF ISRAEL, PROHIBITED,[2] AND IN SYRIA—PERMITTED;[3] [AND] OUTSIDE THE LAND[4] ONE MAY GO DOWN AND PURCHASE [FROM A NON-ISRAELITE],[5] PROVIDED ONLY THAT ONE HAS NOT SEEN HIM GATHERING IT.[6] IF [THERE IS] A VINEYARD PLANTED WITH GREENS, AND GREENS ARE SOLD OUTSIDE THEREOF,[7] THESE ARE, IN THE LAND OF ISRAEL, PROHIBITED,[8] AND IN SYRIA—
c PERMITTED;[1] OUTSIDE THE LAND[2] ONE MAY [PURCHASE THEM FROM A NON-ISRAELITE WHOM ONE HAS SEEN] GO DOWN AND GATHER ['MIXED-SEEDS' OF THE VINEYARD], PROVIDED ONLY THAT ONE DOES NOT GATHER [THEM] WITH [ONE'S OWN] HAND.[3] 'NEW [PRODUCE]'[4] IS PROHIBITED BY THE

(7) In the quotation of this Mishnah in Beẓ. 3*b* 'and (these) others with others' is added. Tosaf. there, in the name of R. Tam, rejects the addition. In Zeb. 72*a*—*b* the added words are enclosed in brackets. In Yeb. 81*a*—*b* the text is as in our Mishnah. (8) For reasons stated by him in the next Mishnah.
a (1) I.e., sold and bought by number (so R. Joḥanan Beẓ. 3*b*). This would include bundles of fenugreek, which are spoken of in Mishnah 6. (2) By way of disposal in a manner whereby no benefit whatsoever is derived. The term used here, viz., מקדש is based on the use of the verb in Deut. XXII, 9, *Thou shalt not sow thy vineyard with two kinds of seeds, lest the fulness of the seed which thou hast sown be forfeited* (תקדש) *together with the increase of the vineyard.* (3) פרך but Maim. and Bert. (also Rashi to Beẓ. *loc. cit.*) take it as a place known for its nuts, just as בדן mentioned immediately afterwards as a place famous for pomegranates. B., however, already mentions the alternative adopted in our translation. (4) A place N.E. of Shechem. (5) I.e., stopped-up casks of forbidden wine mixed up with stopped-up casks of permitted wine (v. T.J.); cf. M. Sh. III, 13. (6) Not R. Simeon, as in one text. (7) These are usually larger, and more distinctive than bakers' loaves. (8) I.e., such of the enumerated items as are tree-produce, viz., nuts, pomegranates and wine. (9) I.e., such of the enumerated items as are vegetable-produce or grain, viz., shoots of beet, cabbage-heads, Greek pumpkins, also loaves. (10) כיצד. The text of the Mishnah in T.J. omits the word, which, indeed, appears superfluous, though Maim. tries to justify its retention. (11) When these things are no longer whole, their significance is impaired, and they have a prohibitory effect only if there be of any of them the minimum of one part to two hundred parts of the permitted.
b (1) E.g., produce which is being sold outside a vineyard which is '*orlah*, but with regard to which fruit it is not known whether it is from that vineyard or another permitted one (T.J.); or, the fruit of an orchard of a non-Israelite (Rash, Bert.) or of an Israelite suspected of neglecting the law of '*orlah* (Rashi to Ber. 36*a*, q.v.), but it is not known whether the fruit he is selling is from an old tree or from a young tree still subject to '*orlah*; or, simply, from a tree of unknown age (Rashi to Ḳid. 38*b*, q.v.). (2) On the principle that wherever there exists a doubt, however slight, as to whether a *Scriptural* prohibition applies, the ruling is stringent, i.e., the prohibition is, the doubt notwithstanding, enforced. (3) Syria was conquered not by the Israelites coming up from Egypt but later by King David, and therefore, as the conquest of an individual, has not the full sanctity of the Land of Israel proper. This inferiority of status accounts for the difference of the treatment of 'doubtful' '*orlah* (or 'doubtful' 'mixed-seeds' of the vineyard). In the Land of Israel it is prohibited (just as is 'certain' '*orlah* or 'mixed-seeds' of the vineyard); in Syria it is permitted, but only when the presumption against its being '*orlah* (or 'mixed-seeds' of the vineyard) is a formidable one.—Tosef. has 'in Syria and outside the Land it is permitted'. (4) There '*orlah*, though not forbidden by the Torah, is nevertheless forbidden by a rule orally given to Moses at Sinai (v. later in this Mishnah). Ordinarily when there is a doubt whether anything is subject to such a prohibition, the prohibition is yet maintained (just as in the case of a doubt in connection with a Scriptural prohibition, v. *supra* n. 2), but in this case it is held that the 'Rule given to Moses at Sinai' explicitly stated that whilst 'certain' '*orlah* was forbidden, outside Palestine 'doubtful' '*orlah* was permitted (Ḳid. 39*a*). (5) Or from an Israelite suspected of neglecting '*orlah* (v. *supra* n. 1). (6) This example shows that 'doubtful' '*orlah* outside the Land of Israel is permitted even when the presumption against its being '*orlah* is a very slender one. In Syria the permission is applied in rather stricter fashion (v. *supra* n. 3). (7) These greens are thus 'doubtful' 'mixed-seeds' of the vineyard. (8) V *supra* n. 2.
c (1) V. 62*b* n. b 3. (2) Where 'mixed-seeds' of the vineyard are not prohibited by the Torah, but by Rabbinic enactment (v. later in the Mishnah and n. 7). (3) Ordinarily, where there is a doubt as to whether anything is subject to a Rabbinic (as distinct from a direct Scriptural) prohibition, the prohibition is not maintained but here in the case of 'mixed-seeds' of the vineyard outside the Land, it is maintained to a rather minor degree, viz., only forbidding an Israelite to pick such doubtful 'mixed-seed's *with his own hand*, for the purpose of impressing on the mind of the Israelite that the sowing of 'mixed-seeds' of the vineyard is something forbidden (v. L.). (4) V. Lev. XXIII, 14.

TORAH IN ALL PLACES;[5] AND 'ORLAH IS A HALACHAH;[6] AND 'MIXED-SEEDS'[7] IS ONE OF THE ENACTMENTS OF THE SCRIBES.[8]

מסכת ערלה

הדרן עלך והדרך עלן

תורה אור

(5) Outside as well as in the Land of Israel. Cf. Ḳid. I, 9, where according to the Gemara (p. 37*a*) the extension of the application of the law to countries outside the Land of Israel is in accordance with (Lev. ibid.) '*in all your dwelling places*', viz., whether in the Land or elsewhere. (6) 'Rule'. According to to T.J. *ad loc.* and Ḳid. 38*b* it means here הלכה למשה מסיני 'A Rule given to Moses at Sinai'. This is the view of R. Joḥanan, accepted against that of Samuel who thought it meant הלכתא מדינה i.e., a rule voluntarily adopted by Jews outside the Land of Israel as binding upon themselves. Cf. Bacher *Tradition und Tradenter*, p. 39; v. 62*b* n. b 4. (7) *Sc.* of the vineyard; these alone are to be understood here. As for other kinds of mixed seeds, since they are prohibited in the Land of Israel only for eating, the Rabbis made no prohibition at all regarding them outside the Land (v. Ḳid. 39*a*). Other kinds of *kil'ayim* (mixture of species) e.g., of animals or of garments (cloth) (Lev. XIX, 19) which have no connection with land, and come under the category of 'obligation of the person', are incumbent equally inside and outside the Land of Israel. (8) *Soferim*, a designation of the teachers of the period, from Ezra (cf. Ezra VII, 6, 10–11) to the beginning of the Tannaitic age. But דברי סופרים—says Bacher, *Tradition* p. 163—means the same as דברי חכמים 'the words of the Wise', which means words, or enactments of the oral tradition (v. *op. cit.* p. 160).

BIKKURIM

CHAPTER I

a *MISHNAH* 1. SOME THERE ARE WHO BRING BIKKURIM[1] AND RECITE [THE DECLARATION];[2] OTHERS WHO MAY ONLY BRING THEM, BUT DO NOT MAKE RECITAL; AND SOME THERE ARE WHO MAY NOT EVEN BRING THEM AT ALL. THESE MAY NOT BRING THEM: HE WHO PLANTS [A TREE] ON HIS OWN SOIL, BUT SINKS[3] [A SHOOT] SO THAT [IT] GROWS IN THE TERRITORY BELONGING TO AN INDIVIDUAL[4] OR TO THE PUBLIC; AND LIKEWISE IF ONE SINKS [A SHOOT] IN ANOTHER'S PRIVATE PROPERTY OR IN PUBLIC PROPERTY, SO THAT IT GROWS ON HIS OWN PROPERTY;[4] OR, IF ONE PLANTS [A TREE] ON HIS OWN [PROPERTY] AND SINKS IT SO THAT IT STILL GROWS ON HIS OWN PROPERTY, BUT THERE IS A PRIVATE OR PUBLIC ROAD BETWEEN, SUCH A ONE MAY NOT BRING BIKKURIM.[5] R. JUDAH SAYS, SUCH A ONE HAS TO BRING BIKKURIM.[6]

MISHNAH 2. FOR WHAT REASON MAY HE NOT BRING THEM? BECAUSE IT IS SAID, 'THE FIRST-FRUITS OF THY LAND', MEANING THAT THOU MAYEST NOT BRING THEM UNLESS ALL
b THE PRODUCE [COMES] FROM THY LAND. TENANTS,[1] LESSEES,[2] OR OCCUPIERS OF CONFISCATED PROPERTY,[3] OR A ROBBER MAY NOT BRING THEM FOR THE SAME REASON, BECAUSE IT SAYS, 'THE FIRST-FRUITS OF THY LAND'.

MISHNAH 3. BIKKURIM ARE BROUGHT ONLY FROM SEVEN KINDS,[4] BUT NONE [MAY BE BROUGHT] FROM DATES GROWN ON HILLS, OR FROM VALLEY-FRUITS,[5] OR FROM OLIVES THAT ARE NOT OF THE CHOICE KIND. BIKKURIM ARE NOT TO BE BROUGHT BEFORE PENTECOST.[6] THE MEN OF MT. ZEBOIM[7] BROUGHT THEIR BIKKURIM BEFORE PENTECOST,[8] BUT THEY WERE NOT ACCEPTED BECAUSE OF WHAT IS WRITTEN IN THE TORAH: 'AND THE FEAST OF HARVEST, THE FIRST-FRUITS OF THY LABOURS, WHICH THOU SOWEST IN THE FIELD'.[9]

MISHNAH 4. THESE BRING [BIKKURIM] BUT DO NOT MAKE THE RECITAL: THE PROSELYTE, SINCE HE CANNOT SAY: 'WHICH THE LORD HATH SWORN TO OUR FATHERS, TO GIVE UNTO US'.[10] IF HIS MOTHER WAS AN ISRAELITE, THEN HE BOTH
c BRINGS BIKKURIM AND RECITES THE DECLARATION.[1] WHEN HE PRAYS PRIVATELY, HE SHALL SAY: 'O GOD OF THE FATHERS OF ISRAEL'; BUT WHEN HE IS IN THE SYNAGOGUE, HE SHOULD SAY: 'THE GOD OF YOUR FATHERS'. BUT IF HIS MOTHER WAS AN ISRAELITE WOMAN, HE SAYS: 'THE GOD OF OUR FATHERS'.[1]

MISHNAH 5. R. ELIEZER B. JACOB SAYS: A WOMAN WHO IS A DAUGHTER OF A PROSELYTE MAY NOT MARRY A PRIEST UNLESS HER MOTHER WAS HERSELF AN ISRAELITE WOMAN.

a (1) Deut. XXVI, 1–11. (2) Ibid. 5–11. (3) By bending the shoot into the ground so that it springs forth as an independent plant. (4) The *sine qua non* of *bikkurim* is that the fruit had to be grown in soil indisputably that of the owner, v. next Mishnah. (5) The reason being that some of the fruit of both his fields derive their nurture from soil belonging to another. (6) Agreeing with the view of B.B. 60*a*, which permits a cavity to be dug under public property provided that the surface still remains firm enough to bear a waggon loaded with stones traversing across it. Accordingly, the fruit grown in such wise is still sufficiently his own to warrant *bikkurim*. R. Judah, however, only claims his view in the case of a public foot-path, and even then no recital is to be made. In the case of a private foot-path, he concurs that the products cannot be deemed his own.

b (1) Heb. אריסין, labourers who receive a certain share of the produce in lieu of their work for the owner. (2) Heb חכורות, labourers who, irrespective of the yield of the crops, pay the landlord a certain rent in kind. (3) Heb. סקריקין, probably of Greek origin. Lat. *sicarius*. The allusion is no doubt to the Hadrianic persecutions following the Bar Cochba wars (132–135 C.E.) when the Romans confiscated the property of the Jews killed or taken captive in the wars. The produce of such confiscated property, afterwards re-acquired by other Jews, was exempt from the law of *Bikkurim*, v. Giṭ. (Sonc. ed.) 55*b* n. b 2. (4) For which Palestine was renowned, namely wheat, barley, grapes, figs, pomegranates, olive-oil and date-honey; cf. Deut. VIII, 8. (5) Fruit grown in valleys (except dates) were not of the choice kind. (6) *Azereth*, the closing festival, Pentecost. Shabuoth being the closing festival to Passover, on this festival two wheaten loaves of new corn were offered in the Temple, and these sanctioned the use of new produce in the Temple. Lev. XXIII, 17. (7) Neh. XI, 34. (8) V. Ḥal. IV, 10. (9) Ex. XXIII, 16. (10) Deut. XXVI, 3. Proselytes did not receive any portion in the division of the land under Joshua. Maim. contends contrary to this Mishnah, that since Eretz Israel was given to Abraham, who was also the father of proselytes (Gen. XVII, 4), even the latter can conscientiously declare '*to our fathers*' in the recital, and in his prayers 'God of *our* fathers'.

c (1) In Jewish Law the child always assumes the religious status of the mother.

א) קדושין דף לח:

יב א מיי' שם הלכה י וביו"ד סי' רצד סעיף ח : יג ב שם הלכה ח וביו"ד סי' רצ"ז ס"א :

קודם לעומר בכל מקום אפי' בחוצה לארץ ובירושלמי (בפרקין הל' ז) קאמר דמתני' כר"א דסוף פ"ק דקדושין (דף לז:): הערלה הלכה בפ"ק דקדושין (דף לח:) אמרינן מאי הלכה אמר רב יהודה א"ש הלכות מדינה עולא אמר הלכה למ"מ ופריך לרב יהודה ממתניתין דכיון דערלה וכלאים שניהן דרבנן ניתני או זה וזה יורד ולוקח או זה וזה יורד ולוקח (ו) והתם פריך למאן דאמר הלכה למשה מסיני אמאי ספיקה מותר ומשני כך נאמר [הלכה] ספק מותר ודאי אסור : והכלאים מדברי סופרים· בגמ' פ"ק דקדושין (דף לט·) אמרינן דהיינו כלאי הכרם דכיון דבארץ אסירי בהנאה בחוצה לארץ גזרו בהו רבנן אבל כלאי זרעים דבארץ לא אסירי בהנאה בחו"ל לא גזרו בהו רבנן

מן התורה בכל מקום א) והערלה הלכה ב והכלאים מדברי סופרים :

סליקא לה מסכת ערלה

פי' מהר"י בן מלכי צדק

והכלאים מדברי סופרים . פי' בכלאי זרעים ובכלאי הכרם בחוצה לארץ מדברי סופרים אבל כלאי בגדים וכלאי בהמה אסורין בכל מקום מן התורה דכתיב לא תרביע כלאים ולא תלבש שעטנז . ואינן חובת קרקע אלא חובת הגוף וקיי"ל כל מצוה שהיא חובת הגוף נוהגת בארץ ובחו"ל:

סליק

לפי שהן תלויות בארץ אמר הש"י בערלה (ויקרא יט) כי תבאו אל הארץ ונטעתם וערלתם ובכלאי הכרם אמר (דברים כב) לא תזרע כרמך כלאים וזה הכנוי שב על מה שיש לאדם בארץ ישראל ודומה לו אמרו בכתוב אחר שדך לא תזרע וכרמך לא תזמור וזהו נוהג בארץ ישראל אבל איסור הערלה בחוצה לארץ הלכה למשה מסיני והוא ענין אמרם הלכה ואיסור זריעת כלאי הכרם והוא שיזרע חטה ושעורה וחרצן במפולת יד בחוצה לארץ מדרבנן ומפני שהן אסורים בהנאה בא"י גזרו בהו רבנן בחוצה לארץ שלא יהיו זורעין אותם כמו שאמרנו וזהו ענין אמרם והכלאים מדברי סופרים אבל כלאי זרעים ,וזריעת התבואה ,ונותם בכרם בלי הרחקת הריחוק הנזכר במסכת כלאים הוא מותר לכתחלה בחוצה לארץ אבל כלאי בהמה לוקין עליהם בחוצה לארץ מן התורה וכן הרכבת אילן היא מדאורייתא בין בארץ בין בחוצה לארץ ולוקין עליה בכל מקום ולוקין על כלאי זרעים בארץ ישראל מן התורה : סליקא לה מסכת ערלה

לא אסירי בהנאה בחו"ל לא גזרו בהו רבנן והרכבת האילן אמרי' התם שהיא מדאורייתא דכתיב (ויקרא יט) בהמתך לא תרביע כלאים שדך לא תזרע כלאים מה בהמתך בהרבעה אף שדך בהרכבה ומה בהמתך בין בארץ בין בחוצה לארץ אף שדך בין בארץ בין בחוצה לארץ וכולה מתניתין מוכחא דערלה נוהגת בשל נכרים ובכרם רבעי פליגי רבי יהודה ורבנן בפרק ג' דתרומות (מ"ט) דתנן רבי יהודה אומר אין לנכרי כרם רבעי אבל מודה ר"י דיש לנכרי ערלה והדיא תנן בפ"ק (מ"ב) נכרי שנטע חייב בערלה :

סליקא לה מסכת ערלה

פירוש הרא"ש

(ו) ומשני הא אמר ליה שמואל תני או זה וזה יורד ולוקח או זה וזה יורד ולוקח :

א) פסחים פ"ד דף נג: מנחות פ"ט דף פד: ב) חלה פ"ד מ"י (ברכות לה). ג) יבמות מז. קדושין דף עו.

א והבריך לתוך של יחיד או לתוך של רבים שחפר בארץ והבריך יחור אחד מן האילן וטמנו בעפר והוציא ראש היחור לרשות חברו או לרשות הרבים : וכן המבריך מתוך של יחיד או מתוך של רבים לתוך שלו · שהאילן נטוע ברשות חברו או ברשות הרבים והרכבה א] יוצאה לתוך שלו בהני תרתי אינו מביא לפי שהזקינה רבייה מן הבריכה והבריכה מן הזקינה וכתיב אדמתך דבעינן כל גידוליו מאדמתך כדקתני סיפא מאיזה טעם אינו מביא:וכשהנטיעה והבריכה שניהן לתוך שלו ודרך היחיד או הרבים מפסיק כגון שיש ב' גנות משני לדי דרך הרבים והבריך מזה לזה בהא פליגי רבי יהודה ורבנן דרבנן אפי' בהא פטרי דמכל מקום מרשות הרבים ינקי ואין כל הגידולין מאדמתו ורבי יהודה מחייב משום דיש לו רשות לעשות כן כיון דלא מפסדי רבים מידי כדאמר בירושלמי :
ב אריסי' מקבל את השדה למחצה לשליש ולרביע חכירות מקבל השדה בכך וכך כורין לשנה דבר קצוב בין עבדא בין לא עבדא : סקריקון ממונה להרוג נפשות וכשבא להורגו אומר לו שא קרקעי והניחני ולשון נוטריקון הוא ואע"ג דיהיב ליה אין מביא ממנה בכורים דלאו אחולי אחיל כדאמר בהניזקין (דף נה:) דאמר האי ליסקול למחר תבענא ליה בדינא: ירושל' (הל' א) א"ר אמי אתיא דר' יהודה כר"א דתני תמן [ב"ב ס:] אין עושים חלל תחת ר"ה בור שיח ומערה ור"א מתיר כדי שתהא עגלה טעונה אבנים מהלכת כמה דר"א תמן תחת רשות הרבים שלו כן ר' יהודה אמר הכא תחת ר"ה שלו רבי שמואל בר יצחק בעי אי כר' אליעזר יביא ויקרא א"ר יוסי מסתברא סבר רבי שמואל בר יצחק שר' אליעזר מתיר לעשות כן והן שלו לעולם אלא רבי אליעזר מתיר לעשות כן וכל הקודם בהן זכה פירוש אי כרבי אליעזר יביא ויקרא דקסבר והן שלו לעולם ומתני' קתני ר' יהודה אומר כזה מביא משמע מביא ואינו קורא ומסיק דאינו שלו לעולם ואם בא אחר להשתמש באותו חלל שתחת רשות הרבים כל הקודם זכה הלכך מביא ואינו קורא ולרבנן אינו מביא דלית להו דרבי אליעזר וקשה הא דאמר עולא בסוף לא יחפור (דף כז:) אילן הסמוך למיצר בתוך י"ו אמה גזלן הוא ואין מביא ממנו בכורים אמאי הא ברשות נוטע בתוך שלו ואפילו לרבנן יביא אף על גב דנמשכ' יניקתו עד י"ו אמה : ג חוץ משבעת המינין . חטה ושעורה ותאנה ורמון וזיתים ודבש היינו תמרים וכולהו דריש בירושלמי (הלכה ג) אילו נאמר ולקחת ראשית כל פרי האדמה הייתי אומר כל הדברים חייבין בבכורים תלמוד לומר מראשית ולא כל ראשית אי מראשית אין לך אלא חטין בלבד תלמוד לומר כל פרי האדמה ריבה וריבה את הכל נאמר כאן ארצך ונאמר להלן חטה ושעורה וגו' מה ארץ האמור להלן בז' המינים הכתוב מדבר אף כאן בשבעת המינין הכתוב מדבר זית שמן זה אגורי רבי אמי בשם רבי יוחנן אמר למה נקרא שמו אגורי שאוגר שמנו לתוכו וכל הזיתים מאבדן שמנן [בתמיה] א"ר חנינא כל הזיתים הגשמים יורדין עליהם והן פולטן שמנן וזה הגשמים יורדין עליו והוא אוגר שמנו לתוכו ודבש אלו התמרים [תמרים] שבהרים ופירות שבעמקים גרועין הן ופליגי בפ' כל הקרבנות (דף פד:) היכא דהביא אם קידש או לא קידש : ולא קבלו מהם · בסוף חלה היא שנויי' ושם פירשנו : ד הגר מביא ואינו קורא . בתוספתא (פ"א) תניא כל הגרים מביאין ולא קורין ובני קיני חותן משה מביאין וקורים דכתיב (במדבר י) לכה אתנו והטבנו לך ויכולים לומר אשר נשבעת לאבו תינו שהרי נדר לו ליתרו ובירושלמי (הל' ד) קאמר רבי יונה ור' יוסי תרויהון בשם ר' שמואל בר יצחק בבני קיני חותן משה היא מתני' ופריך עלה ובני קיני חותן משה מביאין וקורין דכתיב לכה אתנו והטבנו לך : אם היתה אמו מישראל מביא וקורא · בירושל' (שם) פריך כלום נשבע לנקבות ולא משני מידי ושמא לא חש לשנויי דלאו פירכא היא והדר קאמר תני בשם רבי יהודה גר עצמו מביא וקורא מה טעם כי אב המון גוים נתתיך לשעבר היית אב לארם מיכן ואילך אב לכל הגוים רבי יהושע בן לוי אמר הלכה כרבי יהודה אתא עובדא קומי רבי אבהו והורה כרבי יהודה כלומר לא שהיו בכורים בימיו אלא לענין מתפלל בינו לבין עצמו שאומר אלהי אבותינו אלהי אבות ישראל גרים ובני גרים אלהי אבותינו ופריך והתנינן היתה אמו מישראל אומר אלהי אבותינו אבל גרים בני גרים לא ושני בנכרי הבא על בת ישראל בעבירה ולא שנשאת לנכרי ופריך כלום הדא מתכוין אלא לאברהם ליצחק וליעקב וכי אברהם ויצחק ויעקב אבותיו היו כלומר ואפילו בבן גרים היא מתניתין ומיהו אין הלכה כן כדפרשינן דהלכה כרבי יהודה : ה בת גרים לא תנשא לכהונה · מילתיה דרבי אליעזר שנויה בפ' עשרה יוחסין (דף ע·) ופליגי תנאי ואמר רבי יוחנן וכולם מקרא אחד דרשו :

* [בירושלמי גרסי' גם הנוטע בתוך של יחיד או בתוך של רבים] והשלית

תורה אור

פרק ראשון בכורים

א יש מביאין בכורים וקוראין מביאין ולא קורין ויש שאינן מביאין אלו שאינן מביאין א*הנוטע לתוך שלו והבריך לתוך של יחיד או לתוך של רבים וכן המבריך מתוך של יחיד או מתוך של רבים לתוך שלו הנוטע לתוך שלו והבריך לתוך שלו ודרך היחיד ודרך הרבים באמצע הרי זה אינו מביא רבי יהודה אומר כזה מביא :
ב בּמאיזה טעם אינו מביא משום שנא' °ראשית בכורי אדמתך עד שיהיו כל הגדולין מאדמתך האריסין והחכורות והסקריקון והגזלן אינם מביאין מאותו הטעם משום שנאמר ראשית בכורי אדמתך : ג דאין א) מביאין בכורים חוץ משבעת המינים הלא מתמרים שבהרים ולא מפירות שבעמקים ולא מזיתי שמן שאינו מן המובחר ואין מביאין בכורים קודם לעצרת ג) אנשי הר צבועים הביאו בכוריהם קודם לעצרת ולא קבלו מהם מפני הכתוב שבתורה °וחג הקציר בכורי מעשיך אשר תזרע בשדה : ד אלו מביאין ולא קורין הגר מביא ואינו קורא (א) שאינו יכול לומר °אשר נשבע ה' לאבותינו לתת לנו ואם היתה אמו מישראל מביא וקורא וכשהוא מתפלל בינו לבין עצמו אומר אלהי אבות ישראל וכשהוא בבית הכנסת אומר אלהי אבותיכם ואם היתה אמו מישראל אומר אלהי אבותינו : ה ר"א ג) בן יעקב אומר אשה בת גרים לא תנשא לכהונה עד שתהא אמה מישראל

שם | שמות כג | דברים כו

פי' מהר"י בן מלכי צדק

א הדבר שהיו קורין הוא הכתוב בפרשת והיה כי תבוא הוא אמרו וענית ואמרת לפני ה' אלהיך עד סוף הפרשה וכבר בארנו שהמבריך הוא מי שמותח ענפי האילן בארץ וטומנם שם ועוד יתבאר לקמן מאיזה טעם אינו מביא ואין הלכה כרבי יהודה : ב אריסין הם השותפין בעבודת הקרקע בלבד והחכורות הם עובדי האדמה למחצה ולשליש ולרביע כפי מה שיסכים עם בעל הקרקע וכבר בארנו זה פעמים (דמאי פרק ו מא"ב ושביעית פ"ד מ"ג) וסקריקון הם האנשים גוזלי הקרקעות ואוכלי פירותיהם שלא ברצון בעליהן ועוד יתבאר זה במסכת גיטין (דף נה:) : ג אמר השם יתברך בבכורים ולקחת מראשית כל פרי האדמה (דברים כו) ואמרו חכמים מראשית ולא כל ראשית אין אתה מביא אלא משבעת המינים האמורים בשבח הארץ והם המנוים בפסוק (שם ח) ארץ חטה ושעורה וגו' ורצה באמרו ודבש דבש של תמרים ואינו מביא מן הזיתים אלא מן הטוב והמשובח לאומרו זית שמן ולא אמר ארץ זית ודבש : ד כל זה מבואר אלא שפסק הלכה מביא הגר עצמו בכורים וקורא וסמכו זה למה שאמר הש"י לאברהם (בראשית יז) כי אב המון גוים נתתיך אמרו לשעבר היית אב לארם עכשיו אתה אב לכל העולם כולו ומפני זה יכול כל גר לומר אשר נשבע לאבותינו לפי שאברהם היה אב לכל העולם לפי שהוא למדם אמונה : ה האשה בת גרים . ענינו שיהיו אביה ואמה גרים או מזרע גרים אפי' היו להם אבות רבות בישראל כיון שלא נתערב בהם זרע ישראל בשום פנים הרי זו לדעת רבי אליעזר בן יעקב פסולה לכהונה וכשנשאה הכהן בת גרים או בת עבדים משוחררים לא תתגרש מפני זה ממנו והבנים היוצאים ממנה כהנים בכהונם אבל לכתחלה אין מתירין לישא אותה כרבי אליעזר בן יעקב עד שיהא לה אב

וקורא והרצי' אימור דאמר ר' אליעזר דמותר לעשות אבל הן שלו מי קאמר אלא מותר לעשות כן וכל הקודם בזה קנה אהכי אינו קורא : ב מאיזה טעם אינו מביא . פי' הדר לרישא דקאמר אלו שאינן מביאין מאיזה טעם אינו מביא משום שנא' במצות ביכורין ראשית בכורי אדמתך וגו' : ג לא מתמרים שבהרים מנין [דהתמרים חייב בבכורים] דכתיב ארץ זית שמן ודבש דבש אלו תמרין ומ"מ אין מביאין לא מתמרים שבהרים וכו' מהטעם שאינו מן המובחר תניא רשב"ג אומר אין מביאין תמרין אלא מיריחו ואין קורין אלא על הטתבת ר' שמעון בן אלעזר אומר רמוני עמקים מביאין וקורין : ד אלו מביאין ולא קורין הגר וכו' ואם היתה אמו מישראל מביא וקורא . ושיילוה לר' זעירא כלום מתכוון לומר אלא לאברהם יצחק ויעקב וכי אברהם יצחק ויעקב אבותיו היו כלום נשבע הקב"ה אלא לאברהם.ומה טעם אם היתה אמו מישראל מביא וקורא ונתקיימה המשנה בבני קיני חותן משה:ה ר' אליעזר בן יעקב אומר האשה בת גרים לא תנשא לכהונה . אפילו עד עשרה דורות עד שתהא אמה מישראל וכן שפחה משוחררת לא תנשא לכהונה אפילו עד עשרה דורות עד שתהא אמה מישראל ובדבר הזה נחלקו ר' תנאין ר' יהודה אומר בת גר זכר כבת חלל זכר

ולא מני אמר לא פסיקא ליה דגרים לא נטלו חלק בארץ ולא מני למימר לתת לנו ותלמודא לא חש למיקט אלא ריבא דקרא ואסיפא קסמיך וכה"ג אשכחן בפ' אין מעמידין דפריך בטתיהם דאורייתא ניניהו דכתיב ולא תתחתן בם ולא פריך [אלא] מסיפא דקרא בתך לא תתן לבנו ובתו לא תקח לבנך דלא שייך לא תתחתן בבת נכרי דאמר ביבמות בפרק הערל בעודן נכרים לית להו תחנות כי מגיירי אית להו תחנות והא דקאמר (רבי יהושע) [רבי יהודה] דגר מביא וקורא היינו בבני קיני חותן משה שנטלו חלק בארץ כדתניא בתוספתא (פ"א רבי יהודה אומר כל הגרים מביאים ולא קורין ובני קיני חותן משה מביאים וקורין שנאמר (במדבר י) והיה הטוב ההוא אשר ייטיב ה' עמנו והטבנו לך שנתנו לו דובשה של יריחו כדאיתא בסיפרי ור"ת הקשה על (הקרא) דירושל' היכי קרא ארמי אובד אבי דהיינו יעקב וכה"ג [לרת] (לתרץ) דמשנתא היא והכיא דתוספתא מוקי ר"ת באמו מישראל וה"ק כל הגרים אפילו

והשליה. אמרינן בירושל' (הל' ה) שלח ר' יוסי בשם ר"ל בשם ר' הושעיא בשליקטן לשלחן ביד אחר אבל אם ליקטן להביא הוא לא ישלחם ביד אחר שכל הבכורים שנראו להיותן בקריאה אין ניתרין אלא בקריאה ובפ' המוכר את הספינה (דף פא:) ובסוף השולח (דף מז:) א"ר יוסי בר חנינא בלרן ושגרן ביד שליח ומת שליח בדרך מביא ואינו קורא דכתיב ולקחת והבאת עד שתהא לקיחה והבאה באחד פירש שם רבינו שמואל דאם עשה השליח הכל נהי דאין השליח קורא כדתנא הכא הבעלים מיהא קורין ואומר הנה הבאתי דשלוחו של אדם כמותו והשתא קשה דמדנקט ומת שליח בדרך משמע דלקיחה מתוך הבית היינו לקיחה שעשה השליח והבעלים עשו הבאה לעזרה ולא נקט בלרן אלא לפי שדרך הבעלים משלחין מה שרולין וא"כ מה לי ליקטן והביאן הוא מה לי ליקטן *ושלחן ביד אחר תרוייהו חזו לקריאה ניניהו ואין ניתרין אלא בקריאה ואין לפרש דהאי ומת שליח כמו או מת דאם כן הוה ליה למימר או שבלרן שליח ומת בדרך ומיהו יש לפרש דבצירה היא הלקיחה [ורבותא] נקט אע"פ שגם הם גמרו ההבאה לאחר [שמת] שליח בדרך אפילו הכי לא קרינא ביה לקיחה והבאה בא' מאחר ששליח עשה מקצתה מ"מ צ"ל דהיא בשבלרו לשלחן ביד אחר כדמוקי בירושל' (שם) מתני' דאם בלרן להביאן הוא כיון דנראו לקריאה נדחו בששיגרן ביד שליח הו"ל למימר ירקבו וה"נ אמרי' בפ' ואלו הן הלוקין (ד' יח:) הפריש בכורים קודם לחג ועבר עליהם החג ירקבו משום דנראו ונדחו וגריעי מהפרים אחר החג דמביא והפרים ומכר שדהו נמי דבסמוך מוקי לה בירושלמי בשנתן דעתו למכור מתחלה ויבש המעין ונקלץ האילן כשיבש משעה ראשונה והא דא"ר אבהו בשם ר' יוחנן היורש מביא ואינו קורא מדקדק עליה בירושל' מה אנן קיימין בחיי אביו שלוחו הוא ואם לאחר מיתת אביו שלו הן אלא כן אנן קיימין בשהיה אביו חולה או מסוכן : והאשה מביאה ואינה קוראה אבל בעלה מביא וקורא כדתנן בסוף השולח (שם) ולביתך מלמד שאדם מביא בכורים מנכסי אשתו וקורא ומסיק התם מתוך ברייתא אחרת דלא איירי בחיי אשתו לריש לקיש אלא לאחר מיתה ואילטריך קרא להיה מביא ושמע שמתה וכן בירושלמי שאינה יכולה לומר אשר נתתה לי· דבין למאן דאמר ב"ב (דף קיז·) ליוצאי מצרים נתחלקה הארץ בין למאן דאמר לבאי הארץ לא היו נקבות בכלל: ירושלמי (שם) כתיב ושמחת בכל הטוב אשר נתן לך ה' אלהיך ולביתך (דברים כו) מלמד שאדם מביא ביכורין מנכסי אשתו וקורא ריש לקיש אמר לאחר מיתה הא בחייה לא רבי יוחנן אמר לא שנייה היא מחיים היא לאחר מיתה : ך מביא ואינו קורא· בפ' המוכר את הספינה (דף פא:) מפרש דמספקא להו לרבנן אי קנה קרקע אי לא לפיכך מביא דשמא קנה קרקע ואינו קורא דשמא לא קנה קרקע ור' מאיר פשיטא ליה דקנה קרקע לפיכך מביא וקורא ואם תאמר והא לא קנה אלא תחתיהן וביניהן וחוצה להן כמלא אורה וסלו וקשיא מיכן לעולא דסוף לא יחפור (דף כז·) דבעי י"ו אמה וי"ל דהכא כשהענפים יוצאים חוץ לי"ו אמה ואם תאמר כי לא קנה קרקע נמי מביא וקורא כמו מוכר שדהו לפירות לרבי יוחנן דאמר בסוף השולח קנין פירות כקנין הגוף דמי וי"ל דהכי מילי כשהקרקע קני לפירות ולכל מה שירלה אפי' לאוקומי בה חיותא ולמישטח ביה פרי אבל כאן פירות האילן קנה : יבש המעין. שאילן חי ממנו וכשיבש או נקלץ קודם שהפרים דאי בשיבש או נקלץ אח"כ הרי נראו לקריאה ונדחו וירקבו : ר' יהודה אומר מביא וקורא· דלא חיישׁ באילן כיון שהקרקע קיים : מן החג ועד חנוכה מביא ואינו קורא· כדדרשינן בפ' כל שעה (דף לו:) מאי ושמחת זמן שמחה וכן בסיפרי דריש יכול שאתה קורא כל זמן שאתה מביא ת"ל ואמרת ושמחת אין קריאה אלא בשעת שמחה כשתמלא לומר מעלרת עד החג מביא וקורא כלומר דשעת שמחה הוא כל זמן שאדם מלקט פירותיו ומכניס לבית דהיינו עד החג האסיף אבל מהחג עד חנוכה מביא ואינו קורא דדרשינן בסיפרי אשר תביא מארלך כל זמן שמלויים מארלך ועד חנוכה מלויין ואיכן כלין לחיה מן השדה : ך והשני· אותו שקנה מאותו המין שהביא הראשון אינו מביא ומפרש בירושל' (הל' ז) מה טעמייהו דרבנן דכתיב הגדתי היום פעם אחד הוא מגיד ולא שתי פעמים ופריך ולית ליה לרבי יהודה כן דאמר אף מאותו המין מביא וקורא ומשני אית ליה באדם אחד אבל בשני בני אדם מגיד וחוזר ומגיד: ח ט נבזזו· לשון ביזה שאונסין ממנו : נימוקו· נרקבו : אין חייבין עליהן חומש· בירושלמי (שם) אמר רבי יוחנן משום יחידי אני שונה אותה (ג) ותני כן רבי שמעון בן יהודה משם רבי שמעון והשניים אין חייבים עליהם חומש : נטמאו בעזרה נופץ ואינו קורא. כלומר מפזרן בעזרה [ירושלמי] (שם) רבי עוקבא בשם רבי יוסי בר חנינא נטמאו הביכורין הסלים ניתנין לכהן דכתיב (דברים כו) ולקח הכהן הטנא מידך (ה) : והביא ממין אחר הרי זה אינו קורא. אמרינן בירושלמי (שם) למי נלרכה לרבי יהודה דאמר מגיד וחוזר ומגיד ואמריכן בירושלמי א"ר יונתן תני רבי שמעון בר יוסי ואמרת ושמחת הוי אומר על השמחה כלומר שיש שמחה במין הראשון אי נמי קאי אנימטא בעזרה דאינו קורא דכיון דנטמאו ליכא שמחה : י מעבר הירדן הוא דמביאין מכל הני אבל משאר מקומות לא כדתנן ברים פרקין (משנה ג) שאינו מן המובחר אבל מעבר לירדן מעלו : ארץ זבת חלב ודבש· בירושל' (הל' ח) תני אשר נתתה לי ולא שנטלתי מעלמי מה דביניהון א"ר בון חצי שבט מנשה ביניהון מאן דאמר אשר נתתה לי ולא שנטלתי מעלמי חצי שבט מנשה לא לקחו מעלמן מאן דאמר ארץ זבת חלב ודבש אפילו כן אינה ארץ זבת חלב ודבש : יא הקונה ג' אילנות· בסתם קנה קרקע לפיכך מביא וקורא ואפי' רבנן דפליגי עליה לעיל (מ"ו) בשנים בשלשה מודו דקנה קרקע שקנה י"ו אמה לעולא כדאמר בפרק לא יחפור (דף כז·): בעלי אריסות וחכורות· בירושלמי (הל' ט) א"ר חייא בחכירי בתי אבות היא מתני' (ו) תני חכירי בתי אבות אין מביאין רבי יהודה אומר כן עלמן מביאין וקורין :

תורה אור

אחד גרים ואחד עבדים משוחררים ואפילו עד עשרה דורות עד שתהא אמן מישראל *האפוטרופוס והשליח והעבד והאשה וטומטום ואנדרוגינוס מביאין ולא קורין שאינן יכולין לומר °אשר נתתה לי ה': ן ב'הקונה א) שתי אילנות בתוך של חברו מביא ואינו קורא ר' מאיר אומר מביא וקורא ג) ג'יבש המעין נקצץ האילן מביא ואינו קורא ר' יהודה אומר מביא וקורא ג) ד'מעצרת ועד החג מביא וקורא מן החג ועד חנוכה מביא ואינו קורא רבי יהודה בן בתירא אומר מביא וקורא: ז (ב) ה'הפריש בכוריו ומכר שדהו מביא ואינו קורא והשני מאותו המין אינו מביא ממין אחר מביא וקורא ר' יהודה אומר אף מאותו המין מביא וקורא: ח ו'הפריש בכוריו נבזזו נמקו נגנבו אבדו או שנטמאו מביא אחרים תחתיהם ז'ואינו קורא והשניים אינם חייבים עלידן חומש ח'נטמאו בעזרה (ד) נופץ ואינו קורא: ט ט'ומנין שהוא חייב באחריותם עד שיביאם להר הבית שנא' °ראשית בכורי אדמתך תביא בית ה' אלהיך מלמד שחייב באחריותם עד שיביאם להר הבית י'הרי שהביא ממין אחד וקרא וחזר והביא ממין אחר אינו קורא: י ואלו מביאין וקורין כ'מן העצרת ועד החג ל'משבעת המינים מ'מפירות שבהרים מתמרות שבעמקים נ'ומזיתי שמן מעבר הירדן ר' יוסי הגלילי אומר אין מביאין בכורים מעבר הירדן שאינה ארץ זבת חלב ודבש: יא ס'הקונה שלשה אילנות בתוך של חברו מביא וקורא רבי מאיר אומר אפילו שנים ד) ע'קנה אילן וקרקעו מביא וקורא ר' יהודה אומר אף בעלי אריסות וחכורות מביאין וקורין:

פרק שני

א התרומה ה) פ'והבכורים חייבין עלידם מיתה וחומש ואסורין לזרים והם נכסי כהן ועולין באחד ומאה וטעונין רחיצת ידים והערב השמש הרי אלו בתרומה

או אם או זקן או זקנה מישראל ואפי' למעל' הרבה ולא תנשא לכהונה כר' אליעזר בן יעקב לכתחלה : והאפוטרופין. הממונים שממנים על היתומים בין שמנה אותם אבי היתומים או בית דין : וטומטום ידוע אינו ניכר אם זכר או נקבה : ואנדרוגינוס. מי שיש לו אברי הזרע הידועים לזכר ולנקבה והערבים קורין אותו בנתי והוא מסופק ואמרו שאינם יכולין לומר אשר נתתה לי לפי שארץ ישראל לא נתחלקה אלא לזכרים המיוחסין הוא אשר אמר הש"י (במדבר כו) לשמות מטות אבותם ינחלו וכתיב (שם) איש לפי פקודיו עד שיהיה ודאי בלי ספק: ך רבי מאיר אומר כי הקונה שני אילנות קונה קרקע ולפיכך מביא וקורא ודבריו דחוי אבל העיקר אצלנו קנה שלשה אילנות קנה קרקע קנה שני אילנות לא קנה קרקע אבל לענין בכורים מביא מספק מפני שחכמים מסופקין אם קנה קרקע או לא ולענין מקח וממכר נאמר לא קנה ולענין בכורים נחייב אותו להביא מספק אבל אינו קורא לפי שאינם בכורים אמיתיים : וכשיבש מעין המים שממנו היה משקה שדהו או נקללו האילנות שמהם היה מביא הבכורים אינו קורא כלל לפי שאינו יכול לומר אשר נתתה לי לפי שכבר נפסד וכאילו אין לו קרקע ור"י אומר קורא כיון שיש לו קרקע ודברו דחוי ואמר הש"י בפ' בכורים ושמחת בכל הטוב אשר נתן לך ה' אלהיך (שם) ואמרו בספרי אין קריאה אלא בשעת שמחה כשתמלא לומר מעלרת ועד החג מביא וקורא מחג ועד חנוכה מביא ואינו קורא לפי ששמחת אותה השנה כבר נגמרה בסוף חג הסוכות שאמר השם יתברך ושמחתם לפני ה' אלהיכם ור"י בן בתירא אינו תולה הקריאה בשמחה ואין הלכה : ך השני הוא אותו שקנה הקרקע ואינו מביא מאותו המין שהביא הראשון *) וקורא ואמר השם יתברך בפרשת בכורים הגדתי היום לה' ואמרו פעם אחת אתה מגיד ולא שתי פעמים ורבי יהודה אומר הני מילי באדם אחד אבל בשני בני אדם מגיד וחוזר ומגיד ואינה הלכה : ח נמקו. כמו נמסו המק בשרו (זכריה יד) אתם ימקו (ויקרא כו) ואחרים רבים : נבזזו ג"כ ידוע מגזרת לבוז בז (ישעיה י) : ואינו קורא. לפי שאי אפשר לומר הבאתי את ראשית פרי האדמה מפני שאינו ראשית ועוד יתבאר לך שהבכורים האמיתיים חייבים עליהם חומש: ופי' נופץ כמו טער או מריק מגזרת נעור וריק: ט כבר בארנו אמרם פעם אחת אתה מגיד ולא פעם שני ולפיכך כיון שקרא פעם אחת לא יחזור ויקרא פעם שניה : י פירות שבהרים יותר טובים מפירות העמקים ויותר מוטעמים והתמרים במישור ובעמק יש בהם יותר דבש ואנחנו רלוננו מן התמרים רוב הדבש לפי שהכתוב קראם דבש כמו שזכרנו ועבר לירדן אע"פ שאינה זבת חלב ודבש הש"י נתנה לנו ואפשר לנו לומר אשר נתתה לי ואין הלכה כר' יוסי הגלילי : יא כבר בארנו שר' מאיר סובר שהקונה שני אילנות סתם קנה קרקע ור' יהודה סובר שאריס וחוכר יש לו קנין בארץ *כגון שיש לו בה חלק וזכות מן הזכיות ואין הלכה כר' מאיר ולא כר' יהודה וכבר בארנו זה :

א כבר בארנו שהבכורים נקראים תרומה וכבר בארנו בפרק ג' (מ"ז) ממסכת תרומה שהראיה מן הכתוב שאמר והבאתם שמה עולותיכם ואמר ותרומת ידך אלו בכורים על כן נתחייבו הבכורים בכל דיני תרומה כמו שבארנו בערלה (פ"ב מ"א) וענין אמרם הן נכסי כהן שהוא

א חייבין עליהן מיתה וחומש. בסוף פ"ק דחלה (מ"ט) קתני כי האי גוונא גבי חלה ותרומה ודין ביכורים כדין תרומה לאיתקוש דדרשינן ותרומת ידך אלו ביכורים בהערל (דף עג:) ואם תאמר דבתוספתא (פ"א) תניא חומר בתרומה מה שאין כן במעשר שני וביכורים שהתרומה אינה ניטלת אלא מן המוקף ואינה ניטלת אלא מן הגמור ואינה ניטלת מן הטהור על הטמא ומדמעת וחייבין עליה חומש ונוהג בכל הפירות מה שאין כן ביכורים ונוהגת בכל השנים מה שאין כן במעשר שני פירוש ביכורים לא מוקף בעי ולא נגמרה מלאכתו בעי דאפילו במחובר קורא שם ואם ליקט מקצת פירות ונטמאו מפריש מן הטהורה ותרומה אינה ניטלת כדתנן בפרק שני דתרומות וביכורים אינן נוהגין בכל הפירות אלא בשבעת המינים קתני מיהת דהתרומה מדמעת וחייבים עליה חומש מה שאין כן בביכורים ויש לומר דהתם איירי בקריאה שם בעלמא קודם שהביאן לעזרה ומתניתין דהכא דחייבין עליהן מיתה וחומש לאחר שבאו לעזרה ואפילו קודם

אבל מעשר שני שרי. פ"א נכלל לפרש והחייבין עליהן מיתה שהאוכלן במובאת הגוף חייב מיתה מה שאין כן במעשר שהאוכלו בטומאה וכו': והן נכסי כהן. אמר רבי בא בר' חייא בשם ר' יוחנן לך נתתים למשחה לגדולה להדלקה בין טמאין ובין טהורין. ובסוף מסכת תנן ולמה אמרו הביכורין נכסי כהן וכו' ואילו במעשר שני תי' אין לוקחין ממנו עבדים וקרקעות ובהמה טמאה. וגם שנינו הכנס לבית חבירו למשכנו לא ימשכן מעשר שני שלו אלמא לאו נכסי כהן נינהו : ועולין וכו' באחד ומאה וכו'. כלומר סאה של תרומה בטלה במאה חולין כמפורש בתרומות וקרא כתיב מכל חלבו את מקדשו ממנו מה ממנו אם נפל לתוכו מקדשו ותרומת מעשר ממאה סאין דחולק שבולין למעשר תרומה מעשר דידהו חדא סאה: וטעונין רחיצת ידים. פירוש דשרו על הידים ואפילו בנגיעה פוסלין את התרומה הטעם משום דידים עסקניות הן : והערב שמש. פי' כהן הטומא בכל טמאות המפורשות בתורה לא מצי למיכל תרומה עד דטביל ומעריב שמשו וקרא כתיבי ומפורש ביבמות פרק הערל :

[THIS LAW APPLIES EQUALLY TO THE OFFSPRING] WHETHER OF PROSELYTES OR FREED SLAVES, EVEN TO TEN GENERATIONS, UNLESS THEIR MOTHER IS AN ISRAELITE. A GUARDIAN,[2] AN AGENT, A SLAVE, A WOMAN,[3] ONE OF DOUBTFUL SEX, OR A HERMAPHRODITE[4] BRING THE BIKKURIM, BUT DO NOT RECITE, SINCE THEY CANNOT SAY: 'WHICH THOU, O GOD, HAST GIVEN UNTO ME'.[5]

MISHNAH 6. HE WHO BUYS TWO TREES [THAT HAD GROWN] IN PROPERTY BELONGING TO HIS FELLOW BRINGS BIKKURIM BUT IS NOT TO MAKE THE RECITAL.[6] R. MEIR SAYS: HE ALSO MAKES THE RECITAL.[7] IF THE WELL DRIED UP,[8] OR THE TREE WAS CUT DOWN,[9] HE BRINGS BUT DOES NOT RECITE. R. JUDAH SAYS: HE BRINGS AND RECITES.[10] FROM PENTECOST
a TILL SUKKOTH[1] ONE MAY BRING [BIKKURIM] AND MAKE THE RECITAL; FROM SUKKOTH TILL ḤANUKAH,[2] ONE MAY BRING, BUT DOES NOT MAKE THE RECITAL. R. JUDAH B. BATHYRA SAYS: ONE MAY BRING AND ALSO MAKE THE RECITAL.

MISHNAH 7. IF A MAN SET ASIDE HIS BIKKURIM AND SOLD [AFTERWARDS] HIS FIELD, HE BRINGS THEM BUT DOES NOT MAKE THE RECITAL;[3] WHEREAS THE OTHER [WHO BOUGHT THE FIELD] MAY NOT BRING [BIKKURIM] OF THE SAME SPECIES,[4] BUT HE BRINGS THEM OF ANOTHER KIND AND MAKES THE RECITAL. R. JUDAH SAYS: HE MAY ALSO BRING FIRST-FRUITS OF THE SAME KIND AND MAKE THE RECITAL.

MISHNAH 8. IF ONE SET ASIDE [HIS BIKKURIM] AND THEY WERE PLUNDERED, OR ROTTED, WERE STOLEN OR LOST, OR CONTRACTED UNCLEANNESS, HE MUST BRING OTHERS IN THEIR STEAD,[5] BUT DOES NOT MAKE THE RECITAL. THESE OTHERS ARE NOT SUBJECT TO THE LAW OF THE [ADDED] FIFTH.[6] IF THEY CONTRACTED UNCLEANNESS WHILE IN THE TEMPLE COURT, HE MUST SCATTER THEM[7] AND DOES NOT MAKE THE RECITAL.

MISHNAH 9. WHENCE DO WE INFER THAT A MAN IS RESPONSIBLE FOR THEM UNTIL HE BRINGS THEM INTO THE TEMPLE MOUNT? BECAUSE IT SAYS: 'THE FIRST OF THE FIRST-FRUITS OF THY LAND SHALT THOU BRING INTO THE HOUSE OF THE LORD THY GOD';[8] THIS TEACHES THAT HE IS RESPONSIBLE UNTIL HE BRINGS THEM INTO THE TEMPLE MOUNT. IF HE BROUGHT [BIKKURIM] OF ONE KIND AND MADE THE RECITAL AND THEN BROUGHT OF ANOTHER KIND, HE MAKES
b NO [SECOND] RECITAL.[1]

MISHNAH 10. THESE BRING AND MAKE THE RECITAL: [ONE WHO BRINGS BIKKURIM] FROM PENTECOST TO SUKKOTH, FRUITS OF THE SEVEN SPECIES, AND THOSE GROWN ON THE MOUNTAINS,[2] OR DATES GROWN IN THE VALLEYS,[3] OIL-OLIVES[4] [AND PRODUCE] FROM TRANSJORDANIA.[5] R. JOSE THE GALILEAN SAYS: ONE MAY NOT BRING [BIKKURIM] FROM TRANSJORDANIA, SINCE THAT IS NOT 'A LAND FLOWING WITH MILK AND HONEY'.

MISHNAH 11. IF ONE BOUGHT THREE TREES IN THE FIELD OF HIS FELLOW, HE BRINGS [BIKKURIM] AND MAKES THE RECITAL.[6] R. MEIR SAYS: EVEN [IF HE BOUGHT] ONLY TWO.[7] IF HE BOUGHT ONE TREE WITH ITS SOIL, HE BRINGS [BIKKURIM] AND MAKES THE RECITAL. R. JUDAH SAYS, ALSO TENANTS AND LESSEES[8] BRING AND RECITE.[9]

CHAPTER II

MISHNAH 1. FOR TERUMAH AND BIKKURIM ONE IS LIABLE
c TO DEATH[1] AND THE [ADDITIONAL] FIFTH;[2] AND THEY ARE FORBIDDEN TO NON-PRIESTS[3] AND ACCOUNTED AS THE PROPERTY OF THE PRIEST;[4] THEY ARE NEUTRALIZED IN A HUNDRED AND ONE PARTS,[5] REQUIRE THE WASHING OF HANDS,[6] AND [AWAITING] TILL SUNSET.[7] THESE [LAWS]

(2) An administrator of the property of orphans appointed either by the Beth din or the family of the orphan during his minority. (3) But if she has a husband, he may bring and recite for her. (4) A person of double sex. (5) Because the Land was not divided among women. Num. XXVI, 54 implies that only 'men', i.e., such whose sex was not the subject of doubt, were the inheritors. (6) Since it is doubtful whether in such a case the purchaser also acquires the soil beneath the trees, whereas the avowal is conditional on the fact that the soil that had borne the fruits was his own. Two trees are stressed, because had the number been more, the declaration could be made; for with such a purchase, the purchaser acquires the soil under the trees too. (7) Contending that even in the case of two trees, the soil beneath them becomes also the property of the purchaser. (8) From which the tree receives its vitality. (9) Prior to the offering of the first-fruits. (10) Since the soil is still there.

a (1) Lit., 'the festival', *par excellence*. (2) This is the Maccabean festival commemmorating the victory of Judas Maccabeus over the Greco-Syrians on Kislev 25th, 165 B.C.E. (I Macc. IV, 45 ff). (3) Since the land is no longer his. (4) Since the first-fruits of this field had already been set aside. (5) For only the choicest fruits could be brought; cf. Mal. I, 8. (6) V. Lev. XXII, 14. (7) The fruit is thrown out and the basket given to the officiating priest, v. *infra* III, 8. The fruit need not be substituted, as responsibility for their safety ceases with their entry into Temple precincts.

(8) Ex. XXIII, 19.

b (1) Even R. Judah (v. *supra* 7) concurs that two recitals cannot be made by the same man even over two kinds of produce. (2) These are choicer than those grown in the valley. (3) Such dates are of superior brand and contain more honey than those grown on the mountains. (4) Being the choicest of this kind. (5) So Bert. Cf. the view of R. Jose the Galilean. (6) Because in this case the soil beneath them and round about them also passes into the hands of the purchaser. V. B.B. 82*a* and *b*. (7) V. previous note. (8) Cf. *supra* I, 2. (9) The reference is such as descend from a family that have for long had this particular field farmed out to them; cf. I, 2.

c (1) If eaten by *'a stranger'*; Lev. XXII, 9. First-fruits are also designated as heave-offering. (2) V. Lev. XXII, 14. (3) This is implied in the previous ruling, but is mentioned here to contrast it with tithes. (4) In that he can employ them as *ḳiddushin* (v. Glos.) for betrothing a woman. (5) If one *se'ah* of *terumah* or *bikkurim* fell into one hundred *se'ahs* of ordinary produce, numbering one hundred and one in all, any one *se'ah* may be taken out and given to the priest; the rest is free for common use. V. Ter. I, 7. (6) He who wishes to eat them must first wash his hands, as according to the laws of levitical purity, unwashed hands which are of second degree uncleanness, cause in *terumah* uncleanness in the third grade. (7) According to Lev. XXII, 6ff, a priest who had become unclean had to immerse himself and await sunset before he could eat ***terumah***.

APPLY ONLY TO TERUMAH AND BIKKURIM, WHICH IS NOT SO IN THE CASE OF TITHE.[8]

MISHNAH 2. THERE ARE [LAWS] WHICH APPLY TO SECOND TITHE AND BIKKURIM BUT NOT TO TERUMAH: FOR [SECOND] TITHE AND BIKKURIM REQUIRE TO BE BROUGHT TO [THE APPOINTED] PLACE;[9] THEY REQUIRE CONFESSION;[10] AND ARE FORBIDDEN TO AN ONAN[11] (BUT R. SIMEON PERMITS
a [BIKKURIM TO AN ONAN]);[1] AND THEY ARE SUBJECT TO [THE LAW OF] REMOVAL[2] (BUT R. SIMEON EXEMPTS [BIKKURIM FROM REMOVAL]),[3] AND THE SLIGHTEST ADMIXTURE OF THEM [WITH COMMON PRODUCE OF A LIKE KIND] RENDERS IT FORBIDDEN TO BE CONSUMED [AS COMMON FOOD] IN JERUSALEM;[4] AND SO IS WHAT GROWS FROM THEM FORBIDDEN TO BE CONSUMED IN JERUSALEM EVEN BY NON-PRIESTS OR BY CATTLE,[5] BUT R. SIMEON PERMITS THEM.[6] THESE ARE [THE LAWS] WHICH APPLY TO [SECOND] TITHE AND BIKKURIM, WHICH IS NOT THE CASE WITH TERUMAH.

MISHNAH 3. THERE ARE [LAWS] WHICH APPLY TO TERUMAH AND TITHE BUT NOT TO BIKKURIM; TERUMAH AND THE [SECOND] TITHE RENDER FORBIDDEN [THE CONTENTS

(8) The reference is to Second Tithe. It may be eaten by non-priests; it cannot be used for *kiddushin* (v. Kid. 52*b*); it is neutralized in a *majority;* it may be eaten with unwashed hands; it can be eaten after immersion even before sunset. (9) Jerusalem; v. Deut. XIV, 22ff and XXVI, 2ff. (10) V. Deut. XXVI, 10 (*bikkurim*); ibid. 13 (tithe). (11) V. Glos. Cf. Deut. XXVI, 14.

a (1) Since *bikkurim* are designated *terumah*, which is permitted to an *onan*. (2) V. Deut. XXVI, 12ff and M. Sh. V, 6. (3) He compares *bikkurim* to *terumah* which is not removed but given to the priests; v. M. Sh. ibid. (4) I.e., if the admixture occurred after they had been brought into Jerusalem, since the whole mixture can be eaten without any extra trouble in Jerusalem respectively as second tithe or *bikkurim;* if, however, the admixture took place before they had been brought to Jerusalem, it is neutralized in one hundred and one parts, since otherwise it would mean taking up the whole of the mixture to Jerusalem. (5) I.e., the character of the *bikkurim* and second tithe is extended alike to the whole mixture referred to as well as to what grows from them, not only in that these must not be consumed outside Jerusalem but also in that that they are forbidden even in Jerusalem to non-priests and cattle. (6) With reference to what grows from them.

מסורת הש"ס

א) [יבמות עג.] :
ב) [שם פסחים לו:]

קודם קריאה ותנופה לא מעכבי : מה שאין כן במעשר שני · דשרי לזרים ואינן נכסי בעלים דאסור לקנות מהן בהמה ועבדים כדתנן בסוף פ"ק דמעשר שני (מ"ז) והוא הדין כל דבר דאסור כדפרש' בסוף מעשר שני דלא ניתן אלא לאכילה ושתיה וסיכה ובגל ברוב דאינו צריך ק"א כדדרשינן בהזהב (דף נג.)[ואין] טעונין רחיצת ידים כדאיתא בשילהי אין דורשין (דף יח:) ואין צריך הערב שמש כדדרשינן בהערל (דף עג:) דטבול יום אוכל במעשר ויש לתמוה דהא בסיפא דקתני ואסור לאונן ומפרש בהערל (שם) משום דאיתקוש בכורים למעשר וא"כ מעשר נמי נילף מבכורים לחייב מיתה האוכלו בטומאת הגוף ולענין זרות ניחא דבהדיא שרי רחמנא לזר ויש לומר דמיתה

משנה

בתרומה ובכורים מה שאין כן במעשר : ב יש במעשר א) ובכורים משא"כ בתרומה שהמעשר והבכורים טעונים הבאת מקום ומעונים ודוי ואסורין ג) לאונן ור"ש מתיר וחייבין בביעור ור"ש פוטר ואסורים בכל שהן מלאכול בירושלים וגדוליהן אסורים מלאכול בירושלים אף לזרים ולבהמה ר"ש מתיר הרי אלו במעשר ובכורים משא"כ בתרומה: ג יש בתרומה ומעשר משא"כ בבכורים כי התרומה והמעשר אוסרין את הגורן

פי' מהר"י בן מלכי צדק

מה שאין כן במעשר שני דמעשר שני אין חייבין עליו מיתה וחומש . אם אכלו קודם שיפדה מיהו הגואלו צריך להוסיף חומש דכתיב ואם גאל יגאל וגו' ואינו אסור לזרים דכל עצמן לבעלין נאכל ואין מדליקין בו כשהוא טמא דא"ר זעירא בש"ר אלעזר מנין לקונה בכסף מעשר שני שנטמא ...

ר"מ

מקדש אשה בהן : ואמר מה שאין כן במעשר. מבואר לפי שטבול יום אוכל במעשר כפי העקרים שיש בידינו והוא אמרם (נגעים פי"ד מ"ג) טבל אוכל במעשר העריב שמשו אוכל בתרומה הביא כפרתו אוכל בקדשים וכבר זכרנו זה בתחלת ברכות וכן פירות מעשר אינו חייב בנטילת ידים לאכילתם ופירות תרומה צריך ליטול ידיו קודם שיאכל אותם כמו שיתבאר במסכת חגיגה אבל הפת בין שיהיה תרומה או מעשר או חולין לא יאכלנו עד שיטול ידיו כמו שהוא העיקר בתורתנו וזה המעשר שנתן חלוק בינו ובין התרומה הוא מעשר שני : ב נאמר בתורה במעשר שני ובכורים שהם טעונים הבאת מקום ואמר במעשר שני (דברים יד) ואכלת לפני ה' אלהיך מעשר דגנך תירושך ויצהרך וגו' ואמר בבכורים (שם כו) ושמת בטנא והלכת אל המקום אשר יבחר ה' ואמרו בשניהם טעונים ודוי משא"כ בתרומה וכבר קדם לך במסכת מע"ש שהוא צריך להתודות על התרומה והוא אמרו ית' וגם נתתיו ללוי זה תרומה ותרומת מעשר ותירצו זו הקושיא בגמרא ואמרו שענין זה הדבר שלא היה אלא אלא הבכורים בלבד או מעשר שני בלבד והוא חייב בודוי ושלא היה לו אלא התרומה אינו חייב בודוי וכבר בארנו לשם איסור מעשר שני על האונן לאמרו (שם) לא אכלתי באוני ממנו ולפי שהבכורים נאמר בהם (שם) ושמחת בכל הטוב נאסרו גם כן לאונן : רבי שמעון מתיר. בכורים לאונן מפני שלא נאמר בהם זה הדבר : וחייבין בביעור. לפי שדינו ודין המעשר שוה לפי שפרשת בכורים סמוכה לפרשת ודוי שנאמר בה (שם) בערתי הקדש מן הבית : ורבי שמעון אומר תנתן לכהן כמו התרומה. כבר בארנו דעת ר"ש בפ' אחרון ממעשר שני : ואמרו ואסורין כל שהן מלאכול בירושלים. זה המאמר צריך הקדמה ואז יתבאר והוא כשנתערב דבר אסור בדבר מותר לא יהיה דרך להתיר אותו הדבר האסור לעולם כמו תערובת הערלה או כלאי הכרם או התרומה בחולין דיניהם כמו שקדם והוא שיעלה בשיעורו או יאסור בנותן טעם כמו שנתבאר בפרק שני מערלה וכשיהיה בשום דרך מן הדרכים להתיר אותו דבר האסור בשום זמן מן הזמנים יאסר אותו התערובת כולו ואפי' נתערב חלק אחד באלף חלקים עד שיהיה מותר הכל על דרך היתרו לפי שיש לנו דרך להתיר הכל כילד כגון שנפלה בילה שנולדה ביום טוב שהיא אסורה ביום טוב ונתערבה בכמה בילים כולם הם אסורין לאוכלם ולא תבטל אותה הבילה במעוטה כיון שלמחרת יהיו הכל מותרין וזהו אמרם דבר שיש

ר"ש

דבהדיא שרי רחמנא לזר ויש לומר דמיתה ממעטה דכתיב בתרומה (ויקרא כב) ומתו בו כי יחללוהו בו ולא במעשר [כדדרשינן בים מוהרות (דף פו.) בו ולא במעשר] ראשון דאפילו לרבי מאיר דאסר לזרים לענין מיתה מודה דפטור וגם במעילה כמי פטרי' ממיתה בפרק הנשרפין (דף פד.) מדכתיב בו בתרומה ולא במעילה והא דלא ילפינן מעשר מבכורים לענין ק"א משום דיש לו מתירין אפילו באלף לא בטיל והא דבטל ברוב בשאין לו מתירין כדאיתא בפרק הזהב משום דא' ומאה דרבנן היא והא דדרשינן ליה בסיפרי מאת מקדשו ממנו אסמכתא בעלמא כדמוכח בפרק יוצא דופן(ד' מז.)דדימוע דרבנן ובסוף הערל(דף פג.) (אמר)גבי שאני אומר חולין נפלו לתוך חולין נפלו וכן ערלה וכלאי הכרם דדריש בסיפר' דבטלין במאתים אמרינן בהניזקין(דף כד:)גבי נפלו ונתפלגו דמדאורייתא בטיל ונכסי כהן א] דלא ילפי ביכורים ממעשר לחומרא מקשינן [ולא לתרומה לקולא] משום דבפרשת קרח כתיב בכורי כל אשר בארצך אשר יביאו לה' לך נתתים ויש לדרוש מדכתיב לך שלך הוא לקדש את האשה כדדריש גבי גזל הגר בפ' ב"ש בזבחים (דף מד:) ובהגוזל קמא (דף קט:) : ב הבאת מקום . דכתיב (דברים יב) והבאתם שמה עולותיכם וזבחיכם ואת מעשרותיכם ותרומת ידכם והיינו בכורים כדאמרינן בהערל (דף עג:) גבי ותרומת ידך : ומעונין ודוי · (א) דכתיב גבי מעשר בערתי הקדש מן הבית : ואסורין לאונן · דכתיב במעשר (דברים כו) לא אכלתי באוני ואיתקוש בכורים למעשר : ורבי שמעון מתיר. דתרומה קרנהו רחמנא כמפורש בהערל (שם) : וחייבין בביעור. מפרש בירושלמי (הל' ב) בכורים מנין א"ר יעקב בר אחא בשם רבי אליעזר בערתי הקדש העליון במשמע : ור' שמעון פוטר · כטעמיה דתרומה קרנהו רחמנא והא דמשמע בפ' בתרא דמעשר שני (מ"י) דתרומה חייבת בביעור לא קשיא.מידי (ב) כמו שפירשתי שם : ואסורים בכל שהן מלאכול בירושלים. האי אסורין כמו אוסרין כדמפרש בירושלמי כלומר לענין שלא לאכול [אלא] בירושלים הם אוסרין בכל שהן דאפילו באלף לא בטיל משום דהוי דבר שיש לו מתירין דאפשר להעלותו לירושלים והא דתנן לעיל דבכורים עולין באחד ומאה כשנתערבו בחולין דלענין זרים לאו דבר שיש לו מתירין הוא והכא בבכורים שנתערבו בתרומה דליכא אלא איסור מחיצות ויש לאסור דיש לו מתירין לירושלים וכן הגידולין אסורין מלאכול [חוץ מירושלים] אלא יעלם ויאכלם בירושלים (ג) והמעשר אם לא ירצה להעלותו יפדה אותו בזמן זרעו כדתנן בפ' ס' (מ"ד) דתרומות : אף לזרים ולבהמה. אדרבי שמעון דבתריה קאי אף לזרים ולבהמה רבי שמעון מתיר ואין זה מדברי חכמים דהכי אמרינן בירושלמי (שם) כיני מתני' ואסורין כל שהן מלאכול בירושלים ורבי שמעון מתיר וגדוליהן אסורים מלאכול בירושלים ורבי שמעון מתיר ואף לזרים ...

למעשר ונמלא שכבר נאסר הגורן אלא דסובלת לאסור באכילה עד שיפרישנה כתרומה גדולה מה שאין כן בביכורים ובכי האי גוונא היה יכול לפרש כאן: יש להן שיעור דתרומה תרי ממאה ונוהגין בכל הפירות וביכורים בז' המינין: סיקריקון וגזלן תרומתן תרומה כדאמרינן בתרומות גבי גנב וגזלן: ד במחובר לקרקע. כדתנן לקמן אדם יורד לתוך שדהו ונפקא לן בירושלמי (שם) מדכתיב (במדבר יח) בכורי כל אשר בארצם: כל שדהו בכורים. דכתיב (יחזקאל מד) *כל בכורי כל: וחייב באחריותם. דכתיב (שמות כג) בכורי אדמתך תביא בית ה': וטעונין קרבן. נאמר כאן שמחה ונאמר להלן שמחה מה להלן שלמים אף כאן שלמים: ושיר. נאמר כאן טוב ונאמר להלן (יחזקאל לג) יפה קול ומטיב נגן: ותנופה. דכתיב (דברים כו) ולקח הכהן הטנא מידך והניחו לרבות הבכורים שיטענו תנופה כרבי אליעזר בן יעקב (סוכה דף מז:) ובפ' כל המנחות באות מצה (דף סא.) גמר יד יד משלמים: ולינה. ופנית בבוקר והלכת לאהליך כל פנות שאתה פונה לא יהו אלא בבוקר א"ר יונתן הדה דתימא בשאין עמהן קרבן אבל יש עמהן קרבן בלא כך טעונים לינה מחמת הקרבן כדדרשינן בסיפרי והארכנו בפרק לולב וערבה ובפ' קמא דר"ה (דף ה) וכל הני ליתנהו בתרומה דאין תרומה ומעשר אלא בתלוש ואין עושה כל גרנו תרומה דבעינן ראשית ששיריה ניכרין כדאמרינן בראשית הגז (דף קלו:):

[בכל ספרי הש"ס נחסר פי' הר"ש מכאן עד סוף המסכת וכן מפ' אנדרוגינוס ומלאו הסרונו בפי' ר"י בר מלכי צדק ואנחנו השבנו את האבדה מפי' ר"ש ההוא למקומה. והדפסנוהו בזה ע"פ העתקת כ"י מעקד הספרים בפארים. ואת פי' מהר"י בר מ"צ הדפסנו מתוך הכ"י המדוקדק יותר מהנדפס בספרי הש"ס]:

ה מן הטהור על הטמא. פירוש מטא"כ בתרומה גדולה והטעם פירשתי בריש פ' שני דתרומות: ושלא מן המוקף. דאמרי' בירושל' בריש פרק שני דתרומות (הל' א) מכל חלבו את מקדשו ממנו תרומת מעשר לימדה על תרומה גדולה שניטלת מן המוקף והיא נטלת שלא מן המוקף ומנין שלא מן המוקף מכל מעשרותיכם תרימו אפילו אחד ביהודה ואחד בגליל. ותימה דבסוף פרק כל הגט (דף ל:) משמע דתרומת מעשר בעי מוקף דפריך עלה וכי נחשדו חברים לתרום שלא מן המוקף ואומר ר"ת דמדרבנן בעי מוקף ותימה אי מדרבנן בעי מוקף בתרומה* כי היכי דתני יש לה שיעור כתרומה דהא דיש לה שיעור כתרומה גדולה היינו מדרבנן דמדאורייתא *(האה) אחת חוטה את הכרי. וי"ל דמיירי למטה דיש שיעור לתרומה גדולה למטה דאין אדם עושה כל גרנו תרומה משום דבעינן ראשית ששיריה ניכרין כדאי' בפ' ראשית הגז (דף קל.). אבל אדם עושה כל שדהו בכורים (כמו שפירשנו בריש מס' בכורים) והא דאמרינן בב"מ בפ' הזהב (דף מט.) ישראל שאמר לבן לוי כור מעשר יש לך בידי ראאי בן לוי לעשותו תרומת מעשר על מקום אחר משום דלא מלי הדר ביה היינו מן המוקף אי נמי שלא מן המוקף ובשבתות וימים טובים כעובדא דר' ינאי דהאשה רבה או כעובדא דפרק בכל מערבין (דף לב.) שלא יאכלו עמי הארץ טבלים ובפ' כל הגט פי' רבינו שלמה דאין חברים תורמין שלא מן המוקף דשמא אינה בעין באותה שעה ולפירושו יש לומר לפי דמוקף דהתם לאו כמוקף דהכא ואם זה וזה לפניו שם ואפילו איסורו דרבנן ליכא דלא הויא כשאר דברים דבעי מוקף אפילו בשתיהן לפניו כדמוכח בסוף פרק ג' דמעשר שני וגבי חלה בפ"ק דנדה ובסוטה בפרק כשם והתם מוקף לאו משום חששא אלא דאורייתא גזירת הכתוב כדדריש בירושלמי כדפרשתי. וילפי חלה מתרומה גדולה אבל מוקף דכל הגט משום חששא ובשניהם לפניו שרי. אבל קשה לפירוש רבינו שלמה מהא דתנן בפ' כל הגט (לא.) המניח פירות להיות מפריש עליה' תרומות ומעשרות מפריש עליהם בחזקת שהן קיימין אלמה לא חיישינן שמא אינן בעין ולפי' ר"ת איכא לאוקמא בשבתות וימים טובים או דלא ליעבד עם הארץ איסורא רבה אבל לפי' רבינו שלמה לא יתכן לומר כן דמשמע כי כולה מתני' דהתם דחשיב מילי טובא דבחזקת [שהן] קיימין ולא משום כבוד השבת ולא משום תקלה ושמא בדבר שביד אחרים איכא למיחש טפי ולפי' ר"ת קשה דבתוספתא דטבול יום משמע דתרומת מעשר לא בעי מוקף אפילו מדרבנן ובסוף טבול יום פירשנוהו: ו ובשביעית. פירוש ובשביעית ירק נמי אית ביה שביעית אלא מפרש בירושלמי (הל' ג) כגון אתרוג בת ששית הנכנסת לשביעית הכי היא לבעלים כאילן בתר חנטה ופטור ממעשר כירק דבתר לקיטה והא דלא קתני תנא שוה לאילן לענין כלאים דלא הוי כלאים בכרם מה שאין כן בירק ולענין ראש השנה שלו שוה לאילן דאע"ג דאחר לקיטתו עישורו כירק מכל מקום ראש השנה שלו שבט כאילן כדאמרינן בפ"ק דראש השנה משום דלא תנא הכא אלא מידי דבהאי אזלינן בתר חנטה ובהאי אזלינן בתר לקיטה לכל דבר בריש קדושין (דף ג.) מפרש מ"ט תני תנא קמא בלשון דרך ור' אליעזר בלשון דבר: ז דם מהלכי שתים וכו' אין חייבין עליו. פירוש דם מהלכי שתים היינו דם האדם דמכשיר כגון דם חללים כדאמרינן בפ' שני דחולין (לה:) וכן דם שחיטה דבהמה נמי מכשיר כדאמרי' התם ודם השרץ כלומר ושוה לדם השרץ לענין זה דאין חייבין עליו משום דם כדדרשינן בפ' דם שחיטה (כא:) ואפי' מצות פרוש אין בו בדם מהלכי שתים כדאמרינן בפ' אע"פ (ס.) והוא דקאמר דאין חייבין על דם השרץ היינו בהתרו בו משום דם אבל התרו בו משום טמא חייב: ח ט כוי וכו'. פירוש טי בפרק אותו ואת בנו (פ.) כוי זה איל הבר ויש אומר זה הבא מן התיש ומן הצביה ר' יוסי אומר כוי בריה בפני עצמה ולא(הכירו) [הכריעו] בו חכמים אי מין חיה הוא או מין בהמה הוא ושל בית דושאי היו מגדלין מהן עדרים טעון כסוי לחומרא כדאמרי' בפרק אותו ואת בנו : ואין שוחטין אותו ביום טוב. לפי שאסור לכסות את דמו כדקתני ומטעמא דאין מכסין אמרינן בפ"ק דביצה (דף ח.) משום דאפר כירה מוכן לודאי ואין מוכן לספק דדעתו לודאי ואין דעתו לספק: בטומאת נבלה כחיה. דחלב נבלת בהמה טהור כדדרשינן בפ' כל שעה (כג.) מדכתיב יעשה לכל מלאכה ובשל בהמה איירי דכתיב ואכל לא תאכלוהו כדדרשינן בפ' שני דחולין (כג.) יבוא איסור נבלה ויחול על איסור חלב ואין פודין בו פטר חמור דספק חיה הוא ותנן בפ"ק

משנה

הגורן ויש להם שיעור ונוהגין בכל הפירות בפני הבית ושלא בפני הבית ובאריסין ובחכורות ובסקריקון ובגזלן הרי אלו בתרומה ובמעשר מה שאין כן בבכורים: ד ויש בבכורים מה שאין בתרומה ובמעשר שהבכורים נקנין במחובר לקרקע ועושה אדם כל שדהו בכורים וחייב באחריותם וטעונים קרבן ושיר ותנופה ולינה: ה תרומת מעשר שוה לבכורים בשתי דרכים ולתרומה בשתי דרכים נטלת מן הטהור על הטמא ושלא מן המוקף כבכורים ואוסרת את הגורן ויש לה שיעור כתרומה: ו (ו) אתרוג שוה לאילן בשלשה דרכים ולירק בדרך אחד שוה לאילן בערלה וברבעי ובשביעית ולירק בדרך אחד שבשעת לקיטתו עשורו דברי רבן גמליאל רבי אלעזר אומר שוה לאילן בכל דבר: ז דם מהלכי שתים שוה לדם בהמה להכשיר את הזרעים (ז) ודם השרץ אין חייבין עליו: ח כוי יש בו דרכים שוה לחיה ויש בו דרכים שוה לבהמה ויש בו דרכים שוה לבהמה ולחיה ויש בו דרכים שאינו שוה לא לבהמה ולא לחיה: ט כיצד שוה לחיה דמו טעון כיסוי כדם חיה ואין שוחטין אותו ביום טוב ואם שחטו אין מכסים את דמו וחלבו מטמא בטומאת נבלה כחיה וטומאתו בספק ואין פודין

והמעשר לפי שהוא טבל ואינו כן בבכורים וכבר קדם לנו בתחלת פאה שהבכורים אין להם שיעור ונתבאר בפרק שלפני זה שאין חייבים בבכורים אלא שבעת המינים ואינם חייבים אלא למי שיש לו קרקע שלו מן הדין ומה שאמרנו שאינם נוהגים בכורים אלא בפני הבית בלבד פסוק מלא בתורה (דברים כו) ולקח הכהן הטנא מידך והניחו לפני מזבח ה' אלהיך עד שיהא שם מזבח ואז יתחייב בהם ואין בתרומה ומעשר שום דבר מזה וכבר קדמו דינים במקומותם: ד נקנין במחובר לקרקע. הוא שהכהן זוכה בהם מן הדין והן מחוברות לקרקע ואפשר לאדם לעשות כל פירותיו בכורים ולהיות אלו השני דינים מה שאמר השם יתברך (במדבר יח) בכורי כל אשר בארצם זה הכתוב מורה שהן נקנין במחובר לקרקע ושהוא עושה כל שדהו בכורים: וחייב באחריותם. כמו שנתבאר שם שאם נגנבו או אבדו שחייב להוליא פעם שניה עד שיגיעם למקדש: וטעונים קרבן. לאמרו הש"י בפרשת בכורים (דברים כו) ושמחת בכל הטוב ואמר (שם טז) ושמחת בחגך ואמרו חכמים מה שמחה האמורה כאן קרבן שלמים אף שמחה האמורה להלן קרבן שלמים כי ושמחת בחגך אי אפשר בלא קרבן שלמים כאשר נבאר במס' חגיגה: ושיר. כמו שיתבאר בפרק שלאחר זה: תנופה. לאמרו יתברך ולקח הכהן הטנא מידך ואמרו חכמים ז"ל (סוכה דף מז:) לרבות הבכורים שטעונים הנפה: ולינה. ענינו שחייב ללון בירושלים ואחר כן ישוב לעירו ממחרת יום בואו והוא אומרו בקרבן פסח ופנית בבקר והלכת לאהליך ואמרו חכמים (ספרי פ' ראה) כל פנות שאתה פונה לא יהיו אלא בבקר: ה מבואר הוא כי מאחר שהוא מפריש הבכורים ממקצת אילנות מספיק לו על שאר האילנות וזהו ענין שלא מן המוקף כמו שבארנו במה שקדם ואפשר בבכורים להפריש מן הטהור על הטמא אחר לקיטתן לפי שהפירות אינם מקבלות טומאה בעודם מחוברים לקרקע ושאר המאמר מבואר: ו דבר ברור הוא שהוא כאילן לערלה ולרבעי ואמרם לשביעית כמו שאגיד לך והוא שאם נגמרה פרי האתרוג בשנה שביעית ונכנסה השמינית ועדיין האתרוג באילן אותו האתרוג הפקר ככל פירות שנה שביעית כיון שנגמרה בשנה השביעית אע"פ שנלקט בשנה השמינית: ואמרם בשעת לקיטתו עשורו ענינו שאם נלקטו בשנה השלישית או הששית שיוליא ממנו מעשר עני אף על פי שאותו אתרוג נגמר בשנה השנית או החמישית וכן אם נלקט בשנה הרביעית יוליא ממנו מע"ש אע"פ שנגמר בישולו בשנה השלישית ופסק ההלכה כמו שזכרו רז"ל חזרו ונמנו אתרוג *אחר לקיטתו עשורו למעשר ולשביעית: ז דם מהלכי שתים. הוא דם האדם וכבר קדם לך פעמים בזה הסדר כי ז' משקין מכשירין ומכלל הדם והשוה בכאן דם האדם לדם בהמה וכבר ידעת כי שם שרץ נופל על ח' שרצים מב"ח והוא אמרם הש"י (ויקרא יא) וזה לכם הטמא בשרץ השורץ על הארץ החולד והעכבר: ואמרו אין חייבין עליו. רלה בו כי מי שאכל דם אלו השרצים אינו חייב כרת כאשר יתחייב אוכל הדם כי העיקר אצלנו דם השרץ כבשרו והוא אמרם רבותינו ז"ל בספרא וזה לכם הטמא לרבות דם השרץ שיהיה כבשרו ועוד יתבארו התולדות היוצאות מזה הענין ומדיני הטומאה במקום אחר: ח הכוי. הוא מין מורכב מן העז ומן הצבי וכן אמרו כוי בריה בפני עצמה היא ולא הכריעו בה חכמים אם מין בהמה או חיה היא ונתנו עליו חומרי בהמה וחומרי חיה כמו שיתבאר לקמן: ט לפי שאנו חייבים בכיסוי הדם נמנע לשוחטו ביום טוב מפני שהוא ספק. כמו שהודעתיך אם הוא חייב בכיסוי הדם או לא ואסור לאדם לטלטל האפר בי"ט לדבר ספק: וחלבו מטמא טומאת נבלה. העיקר אצלנו שחלב בהמה טהורה אינו מטמא ועוד נתבאר זה העיקר והראיה עליו במס' עוקלין (פ"ג מ"ט) ושם נבאר עוד שחלב חיה ובשרה שוה וכן בהמה טמאה חלבה ובשרה שוין ולפיכך יטמא טומאת נבילות וזה הכוי לפי שהוא ספק ודנוהו לכל הפנים להחמיר אמרו בחלבו שהוא מטמא אם הוא נבלה כמו חלב החיה שהוא מטמא כבשרה אבל טומאתו בספק והמטמא בו אם נכנס למקדש אינו חייב כרת ולא קרבן אלא קרבן מספק. והש"י אמר (שמות לד) ופטר

OF] THE THRESHING-FLOOR,[7] AND HAVE THEIR QUANTITY [PRESCRIBED],[8] AND APPLY TO ALL PRODUCE BOTH DURING AND AFTER TEMPLE TIMES,[9] AND [TO PRODUCE GROWN] BY TENANTS, LESSEES, HOLDERS OF CONFISCATED PROPERTY AND ROBBERS.[10] THESE ARE [THE LAWS] WHICH APPLY TO TERUMAH AND TITHE, WHICH IS NOT THE CASE WITH BIK-
a KURIM.[1]

MISHNAH 4. AND THERE ARE [LAWS] APPLYING TO BIKKURIM WHICH DO NOT [APPLY] TO TERUMAH AND TITHE; FOR BIKKURIM CAN BECOME ACQUIRED WHILE STILL ATTACHED [TO THE SOIL],[2] AND A MAN MAY MAKE HIS ENTIRE FIELD AS BIKKURIM; HE IS RESPONSIBLE FOR THEM,[3] AND THEY REQUIRE AN OFFERING,[4] SINGING,[5] WAVING AND THE PASSING OF THE NIGHT IN JERUSALEM.[6]

MISHNAH 5. THE TERUMAH OF THE TITHE IS LIKE TO BIKKURIM IN TWO INSTANCES, AND LIKE TO TERUMAH IN TWO OTHERS. IT MAY BE TAKEN FROM CLEAN PRODUCE FOR THAT WHICH IS UNCLEAN,[7] AND FROM SUCH PRODUCE THAT IS NOT IN CLOSE PROXIMITY LIKE BIKKURIM.[8] AND IT RENDERS THE CONTENTS OF THE THRESHING-FLOOR FORBIDDEN,[9] AND HAS A PRESCRIBED AMOUNT LIKE TERUMAH.[10]

MISHNAH 6. THE ETHROG[11] IS IN THREE THINGS LIKE TO AN [ORDINARY] TREE, AND IN ONE THING LIKE TO A VEGETABLE.[12] IT IS LIKE TO A TREE IN RESPECT OF 'ORLAH,[13] FOURTH YEAR PLANTINGS,[14] AND [THE LAW OF] THE SEVENTH YEAR;[15] AND LIKE TO A VEGETABLE IN ONE THING IN THAT ITS TITHING
b SEASON COMMENCES WITH THE SEASON OF ITS GATHERING.[1] SO R. GAMALIEL; BUT R. ELIEZER SAYS, [THE CITRON] IS LIKE A TREE IN ALL THINGS.

MISHNAH 7. THE BLOOD OF A HUMAN BEING[2] IS LIKE TO THE BLOOD OF ANIMALS IN THAT IT RENDERS SEEDS SUSCEPTIBLE [TO LEVITICAL IMPURITY];[3] AND [LIKE TO] THE BLOOD OF A REPTILE, NO CULPABILITY IS INCURRED ON ACCOUNT THEREOF.[4]

MISHNAH 8. A KOY[5] IS IN SOME WAYS LIKE TO A BEAST OF CHASE; IN SOME WAYS IT IS MORE LIKE TO CATTLE; AND AGAIN IN SOME WAYS IT IS LIKE TO BOTH A BEAST OF CHASE AND CATTLE, AND IN SOME THINGS IS NEITHER LIKE TO A BEAST OF CHASE NOR CATTLE.

MISNAH 9. WHEREIN IS IT LIKE TO A BEAST OF CHASE? ITS BLOOD MUST BE COVERED LIKE THE BLOOD OF A BEAST OF CHASE.[6] IT MAY NOT BE SLAUGHTERED ON A FESTIVAL; IF IT IS SLAUGHTERED, ITS BLOOD IS NOT TO BE COVERED.[7] ITS FAT CONVEYS CARRION UNCLEANNESS[8] LIKE A BEAST OF CHASE, BUT ITS UNCLEANNESS IS ALSO A MATTER OF DOUBT.

(7) Whereas fruit may be eaten even before the *bikkurim* were delivered in the Temple Mount, the produce of the threshing-floor could not be eaten prior to the actual taking of *terumah* and tithes; cf. Ma'as. I, 5. (8) Whereas no quantity was fixed for first-fruits, that for *terumah* has been fixed for the ordinary man as one-fiftieth of his produce. The generous man could bring one-fortieth, and the niggardly even one-sixtieth. (9) First-fruits were brought only during Temple times, being conditional on the existence of an altar; v. Deut. XXVI, 4. Hence no altar, no offering. (10) V. *supra* I, 2 notes.

a (1) V. 64*a* n. a 10. (2) They can be designated as such while still unplucked. V. *infra* III, 1. (3) Until they are brought to the Mount. If lost on the way, *bikkurim* had to be replaced; cf. *supra* I, 9. (4) The peace-offering had to be brought on all joyous occasions; v. *infra* III, 3. (5) V. *infra* III, 4. (6) Derived from Deut. XVI, 7. (7) Not permissible in the case of *terumah*. (8) Since *terumah* required proximity it was not permissible to have clean and unclean together, lest the latter defile the former. V. Ter. II, 1. (9) Prior to the separation of the *terumah* of the tithe. (10) One-tenth of what the Levite receives from the Israelite. (11) The citron used with the festive wreath in Tabernacles; Lev. XXIII, 40. (12) Because both grow by means of artificial irrigation as well as rain. (13) V. Glos. (14) V. 'Orlah I, 7. (15) Lev. XXV, 2-7, 20. In respect of these three things the citron is assimilated to trees in that the years are determined by the time of the formation of the fruit, unlike vegetables, where they are determined by the time of their gathering.

b (1) Unlike lotus where it is determined by the time of the formation of the fruits or leaves. (2) Lit., 'a two-legged creature'. (3) V. Lev. XI, 34-38; Maksh. VI, 4. Blood is likened to water in Deut. XII, 16. (4) The blood of animals is forbidden in Lev. VII, 26, but no prohibitions as blood attaches to the blood of a reptile. (5) A kind of bearded deer or antelope. The Talmud is undecided whether it belongs to the genus of cattle or beasts of chase. (6) Lev. XVII, 13. (7) Since a doubt exists regarding a *koy* whether it is in the category of a beast of chase the blood of which is to be covered, or in the category of cattle the blood of which is exempt, it may not be slaughtered perchance it is a cattle and the covering of the blood would involve handling earth unnecessarily on the festival, and if it is slaughtered the blood is not covered up, v. Beẓ. 8*a*. (8) Lev. VII, 24. Only the fat of a clean animal that died of itself was deemed clean; that of a beast of chase was regarded as carrion.

NOR CAN ONE REDEEM WITH IT THE FIRST-BORN OF AN ASS.[9]

MISHNAH 10. AND WHEREIN DOES IT RESEMBLE CATTLE?
a ITS FAT IS PROHIBITED LIKE THE FAT OF CATTLE,[1] BUT ONE DOES NOT INCUR ON ACCOUNT THEREOF THE PENALTY OF KARETH;[2] IT MAY NOT BE BOUGHT WITH THE REDEMPTION MONEY OF THE SECOND TITHE[3] TO BE EATEN IN JERUSALEM; IT IS SUBJECT TO [THE PRIEST'S DUE OF] THE SHOULDER, THE TWO CHEEKS AND THE MAW.[4] R. ELIEZER EXEMPTS IT [FROM THESE DUES] BECAUSE UPON HIM WHO WISHES TO EXACT AUGHT OF HIS NEIGHBOUR IT DEVOLVES TO BRING PROOF [OF HIS CLAIM].[5]

MISHNAH 11. AND WHEREIN IS IT NEITHER LIKE TO CATTLE NOR TO BEAST OF CHASE? IT IS FORBIDDEN ON ACCOUNT OF [THE LAW OF] KIL'AYIM[6] [TO YOKE IT] WITH EITHER A BEAST OF CHASE OR CATTLE, AND IF ONE ASSIGNED TO HIS SON HIS BEAST OF CHASE AND[7] HIS CATTLE HE HAS NOT [THEREBY] ASSIGNED THE KOY. IF ONE SAYS, 'I WILL BECOME A NAZIRITE IF THIS IS A BEAST OF CHASE' OR ['IF THIS IS] A CATTLE', HE BECOMES A NAZIRITE.[8] IN ALL OTHER WAYS IT IS LIKE BOTH ANIMALS OF CHASE AND CATTLE: IT REQUIRES SLAUGHTERING LIKE THEM BOTH,[9] IT CAN CONVEY CARRION UNCLEANNESS,[10] AND TO IT APPLIES THE LAW RELATING TO A LIMB OF A LIVING BEING—LIKE TO THEM BOTH.[11]

CHAPTER III

MISHNAH 1. HOW WERE THE BIKKURIM SET ASIDE? A MAN GOES DOWN INTO HIS FIELD, HE SEES A FIG THAT
b RIPENED,[1] OR A CLUSTER OF GRAPES THAT RIPENED, OR A POMEGRANATE THAT RIPENED, HE TIES A REED-ROPE AROUND IT AND SAYS: 'LET THESE BE BIKKURIM'.[2] R. SIMEON SAYS: NOTWITHSTANDING THIS HE MUST AGAIN DESIGNATE THEM AS BIKKURIM AFTER THEY HAVE BEEN PLUCKED FROM THE SOIL.

MISHNAH 2. HOW WERE THE BIKKURIM TAKEN UP [TO JERUSALEM]? ALL [THE INHABITANTS OF] THE CITIES THAT CONSTITUTED THE MA'AMAD[3] ASSEMBLED IN THE CITY OF THE MA'AMAD,[4] AND SPENT THE NIGHT IN THE OPEN PLACE THEREOF WITHOUT ENTERING ANY OF THE HOUSES.[5] EARLY IN THE MORNING THE OFFICER[6] SAID: 'LET US ARISE AND GO UP TO ZION, INTO THE HOUSE OF THE LORD OUR GOD'.[7]

c *MISHNAH* 3. THOSE WHO LIVED NEAR[1] BROUGHT FRESH FIGS AND GRAPES, BUT THOSE FROM A DISTANCE BROUGHT DRIED FIGS AND RAISINS.[2] AN OX WITH HORNS BEDECKED WITH GOLD AND WITH AN OLIVE-CROWN ON ITS HEAD[3] LED THE WAY.[4] THE FLUTE WAS PLAYED BEFORE THEM[5] UNTIL THEY WERE NIGH TO JERUSALEM; AND WHEN THEY ARRIVED CLOSE TO JERUSALEM THEY SENT MESSENGERS IN ADVANCE,[6] AND ORNAMENTALLY ARRAYED THEIR BIKKURIM.[7] THE GOVERNORS AND CHIEFS AND TREASURERS [OF THE TEMPLE][8] WENT OUT TO MEET THEM. ACCORDING TO THE RANK OF THE ENTRANTS[9] USED THEY TO GO FORTH. ALL THE SKILLED ARTISANS OF JERUSALEM WOULD STAND UP BEFORE THEM AND GREET THEM:[10] 'BRETHREN, MEN OF SUCH AND SUCH A PLACE, WE ARE DELIGHTED TO WELCOME YOU'.[11]

MISHNAH 4. THE FLUTE WAS PLAYING BEFORE THEM TILL THEY REACHED THE TEMPLE MOUNT; AND WHEN THEY REACHED THE TEMPLE MOUNT EVEN KING AGRIPPA WOULD TAKE THE BASKET AND PLACE IT ON HIS SHOULDER[12] AND WALK AS FAR AS THE TEMPLE COURT. AT THE APPROACH TO THE COURT, THE LEVITES WOULD SING THE SONG: 'I WILL EXTOL THEE, O LORD, FOR THOU HAST RAISED ME UP, AND HAST NOT SUFFERED MINE ENEMIES TO REJOICE OVER ME'.[13]

d *MISHNAH* 5. THE TURTLE-DOVES [TIED TO] THE BASKET[1] WERE [OFFERED UP AS] BURNT-OFFERINGS, BUT THAT WHICH

(9) Ex. XXXIV, 20. Only a lamb could be used for the purpose.

a (1) The *heleb* (v. Glos.) of the ox, lamb or goat was prohibited, v. Lev. VII, 23. (2) V. Glos. Since it may be in the category of a beast of chase. (3) As a peace-offering on account of its dubious origin. A wild beast was barred from the category of sacrifices. (4) The portions due to the priest from the slaughtered ox or sheep; Deut. XVIII, 3. (5) Since the owner of the *koy* could retort to the priest: 'Cite evidence that it is of the cattle genus and the dues are yours'. (6) Lev. XIX, 19; Deut. XXII, 10. (7) *Aliter:* 'or'. (8) The rigidity of this law is evidenced by the fact that the vow becomes valid even in the case of doubt regarding its efficacy. (9) To render it permissible for food. (10) V. Lev. XI, 8. (11) Cf. Ḥul. 101*b*.

b (1) Though the vine is enumerated first in Deut. VIII, 8, yet the fig is the first to ripen; cf. Cant. II, 13. The fruits had to be fully ripe when they were brought (Deut. XXVI, 10) but not necessarily at the time of their designation. (2) This exempts him from further specification at the time of cutting. (3) Lit., 'place of standing'. The name of a group of Israelite representatives from outlying districts, corresponding to the twenty-four courses of priests (*Mishmaroth*), each *ma'amad* serving a week in turn. Some would go to the Temple to witness the sacrificial offerings, whilst others would assemble in their home town to conduct prayers during the day corresponding to the fixed time when the sacrifices were brought in the Temple. V. Ta'an. 26*a*. (4) Where the leader resided; the idea being to form one united and impressive procession. The principle governing Jewish ceremonial being that majesty resides with a throng of worshippers. (5) Lest impurity be contracted through contact with the dead. (6) The head of the *Ma'amad*. (7) Jer. XXXI, 6. They also recited various Psalms as they wended their way to the Temple Mount (Bert.). According to the *T.Y.* the fifteen Songs of Degrees (Pss. CXX—CXXXIV) were recited.

c (1) Jerusalem. (2) For fresh fruit would rot on the way. (3) The olive-tree supplies the richest leaves, and served as a token of the kinds of fruit brought as *Bikkurim*. (4) This ox afterwards served as the peace-offering. (5) Lit., 'was struck', referring to the tapping of the tips of the fingers on the little openings of the flute. (6) To herald their coming. (7) Fresh figs would be placed as the top layer of a basket containing dried ones, and raisins would be covered by fresh grapes; whilst the choicest of the fruit would be placed on top of a basket containing only fresh fruits. (8) Cf. Sheḳ. V, 1. The 'governors' were the heads of the priests, and the 'chiefs' were the leaders of the Levites. (9) The size of the welcoming delegation would vary with the size of the procession. (10) A craftsman at his work was exempt from the command of rising before a scholar, but in order to manifest his love for the precept, he was to rise before the *Bikkurim* procession. (11) Lit., 'you have come in peace'. (12) For the priest had to receive it from his hand; Deut. XXVI, 4. (13) Ps. XXX, 2.

d (1) They were suspended from the sides of the basket so as not to soil the fruit.

דבכורות אין פודין בחיה: י כחלב בהמה · פירוש כחלב בהמה לחומרא דספק בהמה היא אבל אין חייבין עליו כרת דספק חיה היא: ואינו נלקח בכסף מעשר מלאכול בירושלים · שאין לוקחין אותו בירושלים בכסף מעשר דספק בהמה היא ואין לוקחין בהמה לבשר תאוה אלא לזבחי שלמים כדתנן בפרק קמא דמעשר שני ואם לקח בהמה לבשר תאוה לא יצא העור לחולין ולזבחי שלמים אי אפשר דספק חיה היא ובירושלמי (הל' ו) קאמר דאפי' בשעת שהיו לוקחין בהמה לבשר תאוה אינו נלקח בכסף מעשר לאכול בירושלים: וחייב בזרוע ובלחיים ובקבה · בפרק הזרוע מוקי לה בנכוי הבא על התיישה

א) דוגמא בנדרים פ"ב דף יח: ב) נזיר פ"ה דף לד. ג) קדושין דף לג. חולין דף נד: ד) מנחות ד"נח.

כו א מיי' פ"א מהלכות מאכלות אסורות הל' יג סמג לאוין קלח טוש"ע י"ד סי' סד סעיף א:
כז ב מיי' פ"ט מהלכות בכורים הלכה ה סמג עשין קמב טוש"ע י"ד סי' סא סעיף יז:
כח ג מיי' פ"ט מהלכות כלאים הלכה ה סמג לאוין רפח טוש"ע י"ד סי' רצז סעיף ג:
כט ד מיי' פ"ב מהלכות נזירות הלכה י:
א ה מיי' פ"ב מהלכות בכורים הלכה יט:
ב ו מיי' פ"ד שם הלכה טז:
ג ז מיי' פ"ג שם הלכה ה:
ד ח מיי' פ"ד שם הלכה טז:
ה ט שם הל' יז (ופי' הל' י"ג):
ו כ מיי' פ"ב שם הלכה ט:

תורה אור

פודין בו פטר חמור: י כיצד שוה לבהמה חלבו אסור כחלב בהמה ואין חייבים עליו כרת ואינו נלקח בכסף מעשר לאכול בירושלים וחייב בזרוע ולחיים וקבה ר"א פוטר שהמוציא מחבירו עליו הראיה: יא כיצד אינו שוה לא לחיה ולא לבהמה אסור משום כלאים עם החיה ועם הבהמה א) הכותב חיתו ובהמתו לבנו לא כתב לו את הכוי ואם אמר ב) הריני נזיר שזה חיה או בהמה הרי הוא נזיר ושאר כל דרכיו שוים לחיה ולבהמה וטעון שחיטה כזה וכזה ומטמא משום נבלה ומשום אבר מן החי כזה וכזה:

פרק שלישי

א כיצד מפרישין הבכורים יורד אדם בתוך שדהו ורואה תאנה שבכרה אשכול שביכר רמון שביכר קושרו בגמי ואומר הרי אלו בכורים ור"ש אומר אעפ"כ חוזר וקורא אותם בכורים מאחר שיתלשו מן הקרקע: ב כיצד מעלין את הבכורים כל העיירות שבמעמד מתכנסות לעיר של מעמד ולנין ברחובה של עיר ולא היו נכנסין לבתים ולמשכים היה הממונה אומר קומו ונעלה ציון אל בית ה' אלהינו: ג הקרובים מביאים התאנים והענבים והרחוקים מביאין גרוגרות וצמוקים והשור הולך לפניהם וקרניו מצופות זהב ועטרה של זית בראשו החליל מכה לפניהם עד שמגיעים קרוב לירושלים הגיעו קרוב לירושלים שלחו לפניהם ועטרו את בכוריהם הפחות הסגנים והגזברים יוצאים לקראתם לפי כבוד הנכנסין היו יוצאין וכל ג) בעלי אומניות שבירושלים עומדים לפניהם ושואלין בשלומם אחינו אנשי המקום פלוני באתם לשלום: ד החליל מכה לפניהם עד שמגיעין להר הבית הגיעו להר הבית אפילו אגריפס המלך נוטל הסל על כתפו ונכנס עד שמגיע לעזרה הגיע לעזרה ודברו הלוים בשיר ארוממך ה' כי דליתני ולא שמחת אויבי לי: ה הגוזלות ד) שעל גבי הסלים היו עולות

כיצד פרק שלישי בכורים

עין משפט נר מצוה

ז א שם הל' יג :
ח ב מיי' פ"ג מהל' בכורים הל' יא :
ט ג שם הלכה ח :
י ד ה ו מיי' פ"ב שם הלכה יח :
יא ז מיי' פ"ד שם הלכה יד :
יב ח מיי' פ"ג שם הלכה א :

מסורת הש"ס

א) בבא קמא דף לב.
ב) חולין דף קלא.

תורה אור

ומה שבידם ניתנין לכהנים : ו עודהו הסל על כתפו קורא מהגדתי היום לה' אלהיך עד שגומר כל הפרשה רבי יהודה אומר עד ארמי אובד אבי הגיע לארמי אובד אבי מוריד הסל מעל כתפו (ז) ואוחזו בשפתותיו וכהן מניח ידו תחתיו ומניפו וקורא מארמי אובד אבי עד שהוא גומר כל הפרשה ומניחו בצד המזבח (ח) והשתחוה ויצא : ז בראשונה כל מי שיודע לקרות קורא וכל מי שאינו יודע לקרות מקרין אותו (ט) נמנעו מלהביא התקינו שיהיו מקרין את מי שיודע ואת מי שאינו יודע : ח העשירים מביאים א) בכוריהם בקלתות של כסף ושל זהב והעניים מביאין אותם בסלי נצרים של ערבה קלופה והסלים והבכורים ניתנין לכהנים : ט רבי שמעון בן ננס אומר מעטרין את הבכורים חוץ משבעת המינים רבי עקיבא אומר אין מעטרין את הבכורים אלא משבעת המינים : י רבי שמעון אומר שלש מדות בבכורים הבכורים ותוספת הבכורים ועיטור הבכורים תוספות הבכורים מין במינו ועיטור הבכורים מין בשאינו מינו תוספת הבכורים נאכלת בטהרה ופטורה מן הדמאי ועטור הבכורים חייב בדמאי : יא אימתי אמרו תוספת הבכורים כבכורים בזמן שהיא באה מן הארץ ואם אינה באה מן הארץ אינה כבכורים : יב למה ב) אמרו הבכורים כנכסי כהן שהוא קונה מהם עבדים וקרקעות ובהמה טמאה ובעל חוב נוטלן בחובו ואשה (י) בכתובתה כספר תורה ורבי יהודה אומר אין נותנין אותם אלא לחבר בטובה וחכמים אומרים נותנין אותם לאנשי משמר והם מחלקין ביניהם כקדשי המקדש :

פירוש הרא"ש

פי' מהר"י בן מלכי צדק

THEY HELD IN THEIR HANDS[2] THEY PRESENTED TO THE PRIESTS.

MISHNAH 6. WHILE THE BASKET WAS YET ON HIS SHOULDER HE WOULD RECITE FROM: 'I PROFESS THIS DAY UNTO THE LORD THY GOD',[3] UNTIL THE COMPLETION OF THE PASSAGE.[4] R. JUDAH SAID: TILL [HE HAD REACHED] 'A WANDERING ARAMEAN WAS MY FATHER'.[5] HAVING REACHED THESE WORDS, HE TOOK THE BASKET OFF HIS SHOULDER AND HELD IT BY ITS EDGE;[6] AND THE PRIEST PLACED HIS HAND BENEATH IT AND WAVED IT; HE[7] THEN RECITED FROM 'A WANDERING ARAMEAN WAS MY FATHER' UNTIL HE COMPLETED THE ENTIRE PASSAGE. HE WOULD THEN DEPOSIT THE BASKET BY THE SIDE OF THE ALTAR,[8] PROSTRATE HIMSELF, AND DEPART.

MISHNAH 7. ORIGINALLY ALL WHO KNEW HOW TO RECITE WOULD RECITE, WHILST THOSE UNABLE TO DO SO WOULD REPEAT IT;[9] BUT WHEN THEY REFRAINED FROM BRINGING,[10] IT WAS DECIDED THAT BOTH THOSE WHO COULD AND THOSE WHO COULD NOT [RECITE] SHOULD REPEAT THE WORDS.

MISHNAH 8. THE RICH BROUGHT THEIR BIKKURIM IN BASKETS OVERLAID WITH SILVER OR GOLD, WHILST THE POOR USED WICKER-BASKETS OF PEELED WILLOW-BRANCHES, AND THEY[11] USED TO GIVE BOTH THE BASKETS AND THE BIKKURIM TO THE PRIEST.

MISHNAH 9. R. SIMEON B. NANOS SAID: THE BIKKURIM MAY BE BEDECKED [WITH PRODUCE] OTHER THAN THE SEVEN
a SPECIES,[1] BUT R. AKIBA SAYS: THEY COULD ONLY BE BEDECKED WITH PRODUCE OF THE SEVEN KINDS.[2]

MISHNAH 10: R. SIMEON SAYS: THERE ARE THREE ELEMENTS IN BIKKURIM: THE BIKKURIM,[3] THE ADDITIONS[4] TO THE BIKKURIM, AND THE ORNAMENTATIONS OF THE BIKKURIM.[5] THE ADDITIONS TO THE BIKKURIM HAD TO BE OF A LIKE KIND, BUT THE ORNAMENTAL FRUIT OF THE BIKKURIM COULD ALSO BE OF ANOTHER KIND.[6] THE ADDITIONS TO THE BIKKURIM COULD ONLY BE EATEN IN LEVITICAL PURITY, AND WERE EXEMPT FROM [THE LAW OF] DEMAI,[7] BUT THE FRUITS USED FOR ORNAMENTATIONS OF THE BIKKURIM WERE SUBJECT TO [THE LAW OF] DEMAI.

MISHNAH 11. WHEN DID [THE SAGES] DEEM THE ADDITIONS TO THE BIKKURIM IN THE SAME RANK AS THE BIKKURIM [THEMSELVES]? WHEN THEY COME FROM THE LAND [OF ISRAEL]; BUT IF THEY DO NOT COME FROM THE LAND,[8] THEY WERE NOT TO BE REGARDED AS THE BIKKURIM [THEMSELVES].

MISHNAH 12. IN WHAT RESPECT DID THEY RULE THAT THE BIKKURIM WERE THE [EXCLUSIVE] PROPERTY OF THE PRIEST? IN THAT HE CAN PURCHASE THEREWITH SLAVES AND IMMOVABLE PROPERTY AND UNCLEAN CATTLE, AND A CREDITOR [OF HIS] MAY TAKE THEM FOR HIS DEBT, AND HIS WIFE
b FOR HER KETHUBAH[1]—AS MAY BE DONE ALSO WITH A SCROLL OF THE LAW.[2] R. JUDAH SAYS: THE BIKKURIM MAY BE GIVEN ONLY TO [A PRIEST THAT IS] AN ASSOCIATE[3] AND AS A FAVOUR;[4] AND THE SAGES SAY: THEY ARE GIVEN TO THE MEN OF THE MISHMAR,[5] AND THEY DIVIDE THEM AMONG THEMSELVES AS [THEY DO] WITH ALL OTHER CONSECRATED OBJECTS.[6]

(2) I.e., the *bikkurim*. Maim. refers them to pigeons. (3) Deut. XXVI, 3. (4) Ibid. 10. (5) Ibid. 5. (6) Whilst the priest officiated (Bert.). (7) The Israelite. (8) In the S.W. corner. (9) After the priest. The declaration had to be made in Hebrew; v. Soṭ. VII, 3. (10) Abashed at this public avowal of their ignorance in reading Hebrew. (11) I.e., the poor; the rich retained their valuable baskets (Bert.). This gave rise to the saying, 'poverty drags after the poor' (v. B.Ḳ. 92a). Though the poor would thereby be abashed, yet it was considered prudent to encourage the rich to bring valuable baskets out of respect for God's house.

a (1) Deut. VIII, 8. R. Simeon maintained that they could be ornamented with citrons and quinces, or fruits imported from abroad. (2) That grew in Palestine. (3) The actual first-fruits. (4) The fruit added at the time of plucking to the first ripened figs or cluster of grapes. (5) The choice fruit placed on top and around the basket. (6) Even such fruit not enumerated in Deut. VIII, 8 could be used. (7) V. Glos. If the priest accepts them from the hands of an *'am ha-areẓ*. (8) From Transjordania. Cf. *supra* I, 10 where we learn that produce from Transjordania could be offered up as *Bikkurim*.

b (1) Marriage settlement, v. Glos. (2) Others explain: One may also buy with the *Bikkurim* a Scroll of the Law. (3) One who undertook to be conscientious in observing the laws appertaining especially to cleanness and impurity. V. Glos. s.v. *ḥaber*. (4) The priest must not sell it. *T.Y.* refers it to owners who are at liberty to give it to any *ḥaber*. (5) The men on duty in the Temple be they associates or not. V. Glos. (6) Including things dedicated to the Temple for various uses; since they are brought to the Temple, the priests will take care not to eat them in impurity.

a # CHAPTER IV[1]

MISHNAH 1. THE HERMAPHRODITE IS IN SOME THINGS LIKE TO MEN, AND IN OTHER THINGS LIKE TO WOMEN. IN OTHER THINGS AGAIN HE IS LIKE TO MEN AND TO WOMEN, AND IN OTHERS HE IS LIKE NEITHER MEN NOR WOMEN.

MISHNAH 2. WHEREIN IS HE LIKE TO MEN? HE CONTAMINATES WITH THE SEMINAL FLUX[2] LIKE MEN, AND HE DRESSES LIKE MEN;[3] HE CAN TAKE A WIFE BUT NOT BE TAKEN AS A WIFE LIKE MEN.[4] AT HIS BIRTH HIS MOTHER MUST COUNT THE BLOOD OF PURIFICATION LIKE MEN,[5] AND HE MUST NOT BE ALONE IN THE COMPANY OF WOMEN LIKE MEN.[6] HE IS NOT MAINTAINED WITH THE DAUGHTERS LIKE MEN,[7] AND MAY NOT TRANSGRESS THE LAW OF: 'YE SHALL NOT ROUND',[8] AND 'THOU SHALT NOT DEFILE FOR THE DEAD'[9] LIKE MEN; AND HE MUST PERFORM ALL THE COMMANDS OF THE TORAH[10] LIKE MEN.

MISHNAH 3. AND WHEREIN IS HE LIKE WOMEN? IN THAT HE CONTAMINATES WITH HIS MENSTRUAL FLOW LIKE WOMEN;[11] AND HE MUST NOT BE ALONE IN THE COMPANY OF MEN LIKE WOMEN; AND DOES NOT SHARE [THE INHERITANCE] WITH
b THE SONS LIKE WOMEN;[1] AND CANNOT EAT OF MOST HOLY SACRIFICES LIKE WOMEN.[2] AT HIS BIRTH HIS MOTHER REMAINS UNCLEAN ON ACCOUNT OF THE BLOOD OF HER IMPURITY;[3] AND LIKE WOMEN, TOO, HE IS DISQUALIFIED FROM ACTING AS A WITNESS. IF HE HAD BECOME THE VICTIM OF ILLICIT INTERCOURSE, HE IS DISQUALIFIED FROM THE PARTAKING OF TERUMAH LIKE WOMEN.[4]

MISHNAH 4. WHEREIN IS HE COMPARED TO BOTH MEN AND WOMEN? GUILT IS INCURRED FOR SMITING OR CURSING HIM[5] AS IN THE CASE OF MEN AND WOMEN, AND HE WHO UNWITTINGLY SLAYS HIM MUST GO INTO EXILE;[6] AND IF OF SET PURPOSE, THEN [THE SLAYER] RECEIVES THE DEATH PENALTY.[7] HIS MOTHER MUST [AT HIS BIRTH] BRING AN OFFERING AS FOR MEN AND WOMEN, AND LIKE MEN AND WOMEN HE MAY PARTAKE OF THE SACRED GIFTS[8] OF THE BORDER,[9] AND MAY INHERIT ANY INHERITANCE[10] LIKE MEN AND WOMEN.

MISHNAH 5. AND WHEREIN IS HE LIKENED NEITHER TO MEN NOR WOMEN? BECAUSE OF HIS UNCLEAN ISSUE[11] TERUMAH IS NOT TO BE BURNT, NEITHER IS ANY PENALTY INCURRED BY HIM ON ENTERING THE TEMPLE IN AN UNCLEAN STATE.[12] HE
c MUST NOT BE SOLD AS A HEBREW SLAVE, UNLIKE MEN OR WOMEN,[1] AND HE CANNOT BE EVALUATED, UNLIKE MEN OR WOMEN.[2] IF ONE SAYS: 'I WILL BECOME A NAZIRITE, IF HE IS NEITHER A MAN NOR A WOMAN', THEN HE BECOMES A NAZIRITE. R. JOSE SAYS: THE HERMAPHRODITE IS A CREATURE BY ITSELF, AND THE SAGES COULD NOT DECIDE ABOUT HIM. BUT THIS IS NOT SO WITH ONE OF DOUBTFUL SEX, FOR SUCH A ONE IS, AT TIMES, A MAN AND AT OTHERS, A WOMAN.

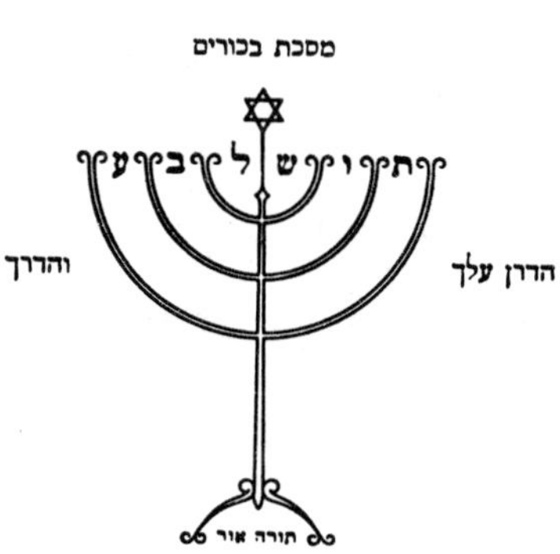

a (1) Entirely irrelevant to this tractate, yet included in all printed editions. Derived from the Tosef. of *Bikkurim* and develops the subject of the hermaphrodite; *supra* I, 5. The text is in disorder and receives various expansions in different editions. The text adopted here is of the Stettin edition 1862. (2) Lit., 'the white'; Lev. XV, 2; Zab. II, 1. (3) He must not don woman's dress, lest he be a man. (4) This would be regarded as sodomy. (5) Lev. XII, 1 ff. (6) Cf. Ḳid. IV, 12. (7) In the event of little property having been left, the hermaphrodite is thrust by the daughters among the males, who must seek maintenance elsewhere; B.B. IX, 1–2. (8) Lev. XIX, 27. (9) V. Lev. XXI, 1. (10) Even those occasioned by time from which women are exempt. (11) Lit., 'the red'; Lev. XV, 19ff

b (1) When much property was left the sons inherited and the daughters received maintenance; B.B. IX, 1. (2) I.e., of sin- and meal-offerings; for of these the Bible says (Lev. VI, 22) that only those who are definitely males may eat. (3) For two weeks, Lev. XII, 5. (4) A male, in such circumstances, would not have been disqualified, but the hermaphrodite is here treated as a woman; Bek. VII, 7. (5) Ex. XXI, 15, 17. (6) Ibid. 13. (7) Ibid. 14. (8) I.e., holy food that could be eaten, e.g., *terumah*. (9) Even outside 'the border', Jerusalem. Keth. 24*b*; Sheḳ. VII, 3. (10) If there be no other heir. We do not allow the argument lest he be a creature apart from all others to interfere with his rights of inheritance. (11) Cf. Zab. II, 1; Nid. 28*b*. (12) Because the penalty was only imposed upon those whose sex was not a matter of doubt.

c (1) V. Ex. XXI, 2, 7. (2) V. Lev. XXVII, 2ff.

פרק רביעי

א *) אנדרוגינוס יש בו דרכים שוה לאנשים ויש בו דרכים שוה לנשים ויש בו דרכים שוה לאנשים ונשים ויש בו דרכים אינו שוה לא לאנשים ולא לנשים : **ב** כיצד שוה לאנשים מטמא בלובן כאנשים וזוקק [א] ליבום כאנשים ומתעטף ומסתפר כאנשים ונושא אבל לא נישא כאנשים וחייב בכל מצות האמורות בתורה כאנשים : **ג** כיצד שוה לנשים מטמא באודם כנשים ואינו מתייחד עם האנשים כנשים ואינו עובר על בל תקיף ולא על בל תשחית ולא על בל תטמא למתים כנשים ופסול מן העדות כנשים ואינו נבעל בעבירה כנשים ונפסל מן הכהונה כנשים : **ד** כיצד שוה לאנשים ולנשים חייבים על מכתו ועל קללתו כאנשים וכנשים וההורגו שוגג גולה ומזיד נהרג כאנשים ונשים ויושבת עליו דם טמא ודם טהור כאנשים וכנשים וחולק בקדשי קדשים כאנשים וכנשים ונוחל לכל הנחלות כאנשים וכנשים ואם אמר הריני נזיר שזה איש ואשה הרי זה נזיר : **ה** כיצד אינו שוה לא לאנשים ולא לנשים אין [א] חייבים לא על מכתו ולא על קללתו לא כאנשים ולא כנשים ואינו נערך לא כאנשים ולא כנשים ואם אמר הריני נזיר שזה לא איש ולא אשה אינו נזיר ר"מ [ג] אומר אנדרוגינוס בריה בפני עצמה הוא ולא יכלו חכמים להכריע עליו אם הוא איש או אשה אבל טומטום אינו כן פעמים [ג] שהוא איש פעמים שהוא אשה :

*) **הגהת הגרי"ב** במשנה שבמשניות ליתא לכל הפרק הזה ואם אמנם בסוף הסמ"ג מונה בכורים לד' פרקים וכתב פרק הרביעי מתחיל אנדרוגינוס אכן מדכתב ג"כ מס' אבות ששה פרקים ופ"ו הוא שנו חכמים ונתן סימן שכל הפרקים תקכ"ד במנין ע"ל הר קדש"ך ולפיכך ע"כ טעות נפל שם דבכורים ליתא אלא ג' או באבות ליתא אלא חמשה דאל"כ כשהמנה שם פרטן תמצא תקכ"ה וכן בהקדמת הרמב"ם לסדר זרעים לא חשיב אלא תקכ"ג פרקים וקושטא קאי דהרמב"ם חשיב בכורים לג' פרקים ואבות לחמשה פרקים ובחיבורי י"ס למשנה בהקדמתי הארכתי בס"ד והוי יודע כי רובו ממש ככולו פרק הזה שנוי בתוספתא פרק ב' דבכורים על נכון בכמה דברים ובביאור כל צרכו תן עיניך שם :

סליק מסכת בכורים

כרחה דדווקא קאמר דאין חולקין לענין שיהא שלו לקדש בו את האשה דמהכא מייתי לה פרק שני דקדושין אי נמי לא ממעטינן הכא אלא דאין חולקין שתי מנחות זו כנגד זו אבל מנחה אחת חולקין לכמה חלקים וכן זבח אחד והא דפריך בפרק האיש מקדש מהא דתניא גבי לחם הפנים הצנועין מושכין את ידיהם והגרגרים היו חולקין ולא משני מנחה אחת שאני משום דהתם לאו מלשון חולקין גרידא דייקא מדלא מייתי דהכא ודפרק טבול יום אלא כדפירש התם רבינו שלמה דסלקא דעתין דהאי חולקין לא ניטול חלקו המגיע קאמר דלאחר שמת שמעון הצדיק נשתלחה מארה בלחם הפנים ולא היה מגיע לכהן אלא כפול וכפול למאי חזי אלא חולקין דרך עילוי שמניח חלקו לחברו ונוטל כנגדו במקום אחר אלמא אית בהו דין חלוקה ומשני דחלקו המגיע קאמר וכשאינה שוה לו חוטף חלק חבירו ואכלו והא דתנן במס' סוכה פ' בתרא הנכנסין חולקין בצפון חלקו המגיע קאמר ובעוד שהיתה בו ברכה . ירושלמי (הל' ו') תני המוכר ספר תורה של אביו אינו רואה סימן ברכה לעולם וכל המקיים ספר תורה בתוך ביתו עליו הכתוב אומר (תהלים קיב) הון ועושר בביתו וצדקתו עומדת לעד:

ב מטמא בלובן כאנשים . פי' דספק איש הוא ואיש מטמא בלובן כדאמרי' בפרק בנות כותים דזוב דומה למי בצק של שעורים ולובן בילה המוזרת : ונושא אבל לא נישא כאנשים . האי תנא סבר אנדרוגינוס ספק הוא כדמוכחא כולה מתניתא והשתא לענין מה קתני נושא אבל לא נישא אי לענין שאם קידש אשה צריכה גט ואם נתקדש לא בעי גט הא ספק אשה הוא אלא לענין תרומה איירי כדאמרינן ביבמות סוף פרק הערל גרים נקיש דתנן התם ר' יוסי ור"ש אומרים אנדרוגינוס כהן שנשא בת ישראל אוכלת בתרומה ובגמרא אמר ר"ל מאכילה בתרומה ואינה מאכילה בחזה ושוק ומפרש התם ואין מאכילה בתרומה בזמן הזה ושוק דקסבר ר"ל אנדרוגינוס לר' יוסי ספקא הוא ומאכילה בתרומה בזמן הזה דרבנן אבל לא בזמן חזה ושוק דאורייתא ופריך עלה מהא דתנן אנדרוגינוס נושא אבל לא נישא מדקתני נושא דחשיב ליה זכר וודאי ומשני תני אם נשא דיעבד ואפילו הכי אבל לא נישא דיעבד דאם נישא לכהן אין מאכילו בתרומה דרבנן והיינו טעמא דהחמירו עליו אם נישא משום דאם הוא זכר חייבין עליו סקילה כזכר לכל הפחות ממקום אחד ואיכא למאן דאמר דמחייב התם משני מקומות ולמאי דמותיב מינה התם לר"ל נשוי דתקשי ליה ברייתא דהכא דקסבר ספקא הוא וקתני נושא ושמא לא שמיעא ליה : ואינו מתייחד עם הנשים . משום ספק איש דייחוד אסור כדאיתא בפרק בתרא דקדושין. ואינו ניזון עם הבנות בנכסים מועטים כדאיתא בריש מי שמת שהנקבות דוחות אותו אצל הזכרים : ואינו נעטף ומספר כאנשים . כלומר אינו נעטף כאנשים ומספר כאנשים וכללם לפי שטעם אחד לשניהם דדרך אשה לעטוף את ראשה ולכסותו בצעיף ואין דרך איש כן דרך איש לספר ואין דרך אשה לספר אלא מגדלת שער כלילית ובענין שינהיג בעצמו בתספורת ומלבושים כעין איש שלא יבא לינשא אם יתנהג כאשה וחשו לינשא יותר מלישא כדפרישית אבל אין לפרש דתנא מספר כאיש משום פיאות דהא תנא ליה סיפא : ואינו מטמא למתים . אם הוא כהן: בל תקיף . הקפת הראש: בל תשחית . פאת זקן וכולהו ילפינן בפ"ק דקדושין דאנשים חייבין ונשים פטורות : וחייב בכל מצות . אפילו במ"ע שהזמן גרמא כגון לולב וסוכה ושופר : באודם . אשה מיטמאה באודם כדילפינן בפ"ב דנדה : ואין זקוק ליבום כנשים . כך כתוב בכל הספרים משמע דאיירי בשנתקדש לאחד מן האחים ומת דפטור מן החליצה ומן היבום מידי דהוה אאיילונית ודרשינן בפ"ק דיבמות אשר תלד פרט לאיילונית שאינה יולדת אבל א"א לפרש כן דא"כ מאי כנשים אדרבה נשים זקוקות הן אלא הכי גרסינן ואין זקוק ליבם כנשים דאם אין יבם אחר אלא הוא היבמה מותרת לינשא לשוק ופטורה מן החליצה ומן היבום אפילו הוא איש מידי דהוה אסריס דתני' בפרק הערל דבין לר' אליעזר ובין לר' עקיבא הוי אין לו רפואה ולא היתה לו שעת הכושר והיינו דקתני כנשים דאין אשה זוקקת אשת אחיה : ואין חולק עם הבנים בנכסים מרובים . שהזכרים דוחים אותו אצל נקבות כדאיתא בריש מי שמת : ואינו חולק בקדשי המקדש . דאשה אינה חולקת אפילו בחזה ושוק . דלכל בני אהרן תהיה כתיב ולא בנות אהרן ולענין חלוקה כתיב כדדרשינן בפרק האיש מקדש אי נמי כדדריש התם איש למעוטי קטן והוא הדין איש ולא אשה : ופסול לכל עדות . דאשה פסולה לעדות כדדרשינן בפרק שבועת העדות: ואינו נבעל בעבירה כנשים . כגון כל איסורי עריות בתו ובת בתו ובת בנו וכיוצא בהן הרבה ובלאו הכי אסור לבעול משום זכר למאן דמחייב משני מקומות בסוף הערל אלא פלוגתא הוא ואצטריך הכא למאן דלית ליה : ופסול מן הכהונה . דאם נבעל בעבירה נפסל מן התרומה אם הוא כהן כבת כהן שנבעלה לפסול לה פסלה כדאמרינן ביבמות בפרק אלמנה : חייב על הנזקין . כדתנן בפ"ק דב"ק והנשים בכלל הנזק ויליף לה מקרא בגמרא : ואמו יושבת עליו דם טוהר כאנשים . ארבעים יום וכנשים ימי טומאה שבועיים הכא לחומרא והכא לחומרא ומקולקלת למנינה אם תראה יום שבעים וארבעה ותחזור ותראה יום שמונים ואחד: ונוחל בקדשי הגבול . כגון תרומה ותרומת מעשר וחלה אם הוא כהן ומעשר ראשון אם הוא לוי ותנא נוחל ולא תנא חולק לפי שאין חולקין לו תרומה בגרנות אלא משגרן לביתו כדתניא בסוף נושאין על האנוסה: הריני נזיר שזה איש ואשה . כלומר שזה איש או אשה : אין חייבים על טומאתו . על ביאת מקדש אפילו ראה לובן ואודם כאחת ואין שורפין כדאיתא בפרק המפלת : ואינו נערך . לא בערך איש ולא בערך אשה כדדרשינן בפרק המפלת : ואינו נמכר לעבד עברי . משום דקטן אינו נמכר לעבד עברי וגדולה אינה נמכרת לאמה העבריה הלכך לא אפשר : שאין זה איש ואשה . כלומר שאין זה איש או שאין זה אשה : ר' יוסי אומר אנדרוגינוס בריה בפני עצמו הוא ולא יכלו החכמים להכריע אם איש הוא או אשה היא . וביבמות בסוף הערל מייתי לה אהא דתנן התם ר' יוסי ור"ש [אומרים] אנדרוגינוס כהן שנשא בת ישראל מאכילה בתרומה וקאמר רב בגמרא ליתא למתניתין דחשיב ליה ר' יוסי זכר מקמי ברייתא דחשיב ליה ספקא ותימה אם כן ר' יוסי דהכא היינו ת"ק ועוד מאי אבל טומטום אינו כן אלא או ספק איש או ספק אשה אנדרוגינוס נמי כן הוא ודוחק לומר דנקיט אינו כן משום דטומטום ספק שלו יכול להתברר אם נקרע דאם נמצא זכר הוא זכר ודאי ואם נמצא נקבה הוה נקבה ודאית משא"כ באנדרוגינוס דלעולם עומד בספק דאין הלשון משמע כן כלל אלא יש לפרש דאנדרוגינוס לרבי יוסי שלשה ספיקות יש בו ספק בריה ספק איש ספק אשה ונפקא מיניה דאמו יושבת עליו לזכר ולנקבה ולנדה והכי נמי שמעינן ליה לר' יוסי גבי כוי בפרק אותו ואת בנו דתניא ר' יוסי אומר כוי בריה בפני עצמה הוא ולא הכירו בו חכמים אם מין חיה הוא או מין בהמה דיש בו שלשה ספקות ספק בריה ספק חיה ספק בהמה וכ"מ אם אמר הריני נזיר שאין זה לא חיה ולא בהמה[ה"ז נזיר]וכן באנדרוגינוס נמי כ"מ להכי אם אמר הריני נזיר שאין זה לא איש ולא אשה הרי זה נזיר והכי נמי אשכחן ביומא בפרק בתרא תנא דאית ליה כוי בריה בפני עצמה היא לא חיה ולא בהמה וכן ההיא דבכורות בסוף [פרק] על אלו מומין דממעט מהזכר אנדרוגינוס דבריה הוא ומיהו יש ליישבו אפילו לאו בריה הוא ואע"ג דעשר בהמות מנה הכתוב ולא מנה כוי אין לחוש בכך דלא מנה הכתוב אלא בהמות וחיות והא דחשיב רב בפ' אנדרוגינוס ספקא דכי ראה לובן ואודם כאחת שורפין עליו את התרומה אלמא לא חשיב ליה בריה דלמא לא סבר לה לא כר' יוסי דמתני' ולא כר' יוסי דברייתא דהא ביבמות בסוף הערל פליגי אמוראי אליבא דרב בקידוש איכא למאן דאמר הלכה כר' יוסי ואיכא למאן דאמר אין הלכה כר' יוסי וכי היכי דאיכא אמוראי דפליגי אליבא דרב בקידוש איכא נמי אמוראי דפליגי אליבא דרב באנדרוגינוס והא דאמרינן בסוף הערל אמר רב הונא אמר רב אנדרוגינוס חייבין עליו סקילה משני מקומות שאני התם דרבי קראי ואפי' יהא נקבה כדדרשינן את זכר משכבי אשה איזהו זכר שיש בו שני משכבות ודותיה בסוף ר' אליעזר דמילה מרבינן ליה למילה מדכתיב (בראשית יז) המול לכם כל זכר :

סליק מסכת בכורים

ואינו מתייחד עם האנשים כנשים ואינו זקוק לייבום כנשים ואין חולק עם הבנים כנשים ואינו חולק בקדשי המקדש כנשים ופסול לכל עדות שבתורה כנשים ואינו נבעל בעבירה כנשים ופסול מן הכהונה כנשים : דרכים ששוה בהן לאנשים ולנשים חייב על הנזקין בין איש ובין אשה וההורגו במזיד נהרג בשוגג גולה לעיר מקלט ואמו יושבת עליו דם טוהר כאנשים וכנשים ומביאה עליו קרבן כאנשים וכנשים ונוחל בכל הנחלות כאנשים וכנשים והאומר הריני נזיר שזה איש ואשה הרי זה נזיר . דרכים שלא שוה בהן לא לאנשים ולא לנשים אין חייבין על טמאתו ואין שורפין על טמאתו ואינו נערך לא כאנשים ולא כנשים ואם אמר הריני נזיר שאין זה איש ואשה הרי זה נזיר . ר' יוסי אומר אנדרוגינוס בריה בפני עצמו הוא ולא יכלו חכמים להכריע עליו אם איש הוא או אשה היא אבל טומטום אינו כן אלא ספק איש או ספק אשה :

סליק מסכת בכורים

ואינו זוקק ליבום כנשים ואינו חולק עם הבנים כנשים ואין אוכל בקדשי המקדש כנשים ואמו יושבת עליו בדם טמא כנשים ופסול מן העדות כנשים ואם נבעל בעבירה נפסל מן התרומה כנשים : ג כיצד שוה לאנשים ונשים חייבים על מכתו וקללתו כאנשים ונשים וההורגו שוגג גולה ומזיד נהרג כאנשים ונשים ואמו מביאה עליו קרבן כאנשים ונשים ואוכל בקדשי הגבול כאנשים וכנשים ונוחל לכל הנחלות כאנשים וכנשים : ד כיצד אינו שוה לאנשים ונשים אין שורפין תרומה על טומאת זיבתו ואין חייבין עליו על ביאת מקדש לא כאנשים ונשים ואין נמכר בעבד עברי לא כאנשים ולא כנשים ואינו נערך לא כאנשים ולא כנשים ואם אמר הריני נזיר שזה לא איש ולא אשה נזיר רבי יוסי אומר אנדרוגינוס בריה בפני עצמה הוא ולא יכלו חכמים להכריע עליו אם איש או אשה אבל טומטום אינו כן פעמים שהוא איש פעמים שהוא אשה :

סליק מסכת בכורים

NOTES

GLOSSARY

AGGADAH (Lit. 'tale', 'lesson'); the name given to those sections of Rabbinic literature which contain homiletic expositions of the Bible, stories, legends, folk-lore, anecdotes or maxims. Opposed to *halachah*, q.v.

'AM HA-AREẒ pl. *'amme ha-areẓ*, (lit., 'people of the land', 'country people'); the name given in Rabbinic literature to (*a*) a person who through ignorance was careless in the observance of the laws of Levitical purity and of those relating to the priestly and Levitical gifts. In this sense opposed to *ḥaber*, q.v.; (*b*) an illiterate or uncultured man, as opposed to *talmid ḥakam*, q.v.

BERERAH (Lit., 'choice'); the selection retrospectively of one object rather than another as having been designated by a term equally applicable to both.

BETH AB (*Beth* 'house' and *Ab* 'father') 'family', one of the six family divisions into which each of the eight major divisions of the priests and Levites (*mishmar*, q.v.) was subdivided for the purpose of the Temple service.

BETH DIN (Lit., 'house of law or judgment'); a gathering of three or more learned men acting as a Jewish court of law.

BETH HAMIDRASH. House of study; the college or academy where the study of the Torah was carried on under the guidance of a Rabbinical authority.

DEMAI (Lit., 'dubious', 'suspicious'); produce concerning which there is a doubt as to whether the rules relating to the priestly and Levitical dues and ritual cleanness and uncleanness were strictly observed. Any produce bought from *'am ha-areẓ* (q.v.), unless the contrary is known, is treated as *demai;* and *terumah gedolah* and *terumah* (q.v.) of the tithe must be separated from it.

DENAR *Denarius*, a silver or gold coin, the former being worth one twenty-fourth (according to others one twenty-fifth) of the latter.

'ERUB (Lit., 'mixture'); a quantity of food, enough for two meals, placed (*a*) 2000 cubits from the town boundary, so as to extend the Sabbath limit by that distance; (*b*) in a room or in a court-yard to enable all the residents to carry to and fro in the court-yard on Sabbath.

GEMARA (Lit., 'completion' or 'learning'). The traditions, discussions and rulings of the Amoras, based mainly on the Mishnah and forming (*a*) the Babylonian Talmud and (*b*) the Palestinian Talmud.

GEZERAH SHAWAH (Lit., 'equal cut'); the application to one subject of a rule already known to apply to another, on the strength of a common expression used in connection with both in the Scriptures.

ḤABER. 'Fellow', 'associate', opp. to *'am ha-areẓ* (q.v.); one scrupulous in the observance of the law, particularly in relation to ritual cleanness and the separation of the priestly and Levitical dues.

HALACHAH (Lit., 'step', 'guidance'), (*a*) the final decision of the Rabbis, whether based on tradition or argument, on disputed rules of conduct; (*b*) those sections of Rabbinic literature which deal with legal questions, as opposed to the *Aggadah*.

ḤALLAH. The portion of the dough which belongs to the priest (v. Num. XV, 20f); in the Diaspora this is not given to the priest but burnt.

HEFḲER. Property which has no owner: a renunciation of ownership in favour of all and sundry. When used in reference to a court of law, it denotes an act of transfer of property from one person to another, in virtue of the power of the court to declare property ownerless, after which it can assign it to another.

HEḲDESH. Any object consecrated to the Sanctuary.

ḤELEB. The portion of the fat of a permitted domestic animal which may not be eaten; in sacrifices that fat was burnt upon the altar.

HIN. Measure of capacity equal to three *kabs* or twelve *logs*.

ISSAR. A small Roman coin.

ḲAB. Measure of capacity equal to four *logs* or one sixth of a *se'ah*.

KARETH. 'Cutting off'; divine punishment for a number of sins for which no human penalty is specified. Sudden death is described as '*kareth* of days', premature death at sixty as '*kareth* of years'.

KETHUBAH (Lit., 'a written [document]'); (*a*) a wife's marriage settlement which she is entitled to recover on her being divorced or on the death of her husband. The minimum settlement for a virgin is two hundred *zuz*, and for a widow remarrying one hundred *zuz;* (*b*) the marriage contract specifiying the mutual obligations between husband and wife and containing the amount of the endowment and any other special financial obligations assumed by the husband.

ḲIDDUSHIN (Lit., 'sanctification'); (*a*) the act of affiancing or betrothal; (*b*) the money or article given to effect the betrothal.

KOR. A measure of capacity = thirty *se'ahs* (q.v.).

LITRA. (*a*) a measure of capacity equal to half a *log*, q.v.; (*b*) the weight of one pound, the Roman *libra*.

LOG. A liquid measure equal to a quarter of a *ḳab* (q.v.), or the space occupied by six eggs, c. 549 cubic centimetres.

MESHIKAH (Lit., 'pulling'); one of the legal modes of acquiring a movable object which the buyer performs by drawing the object into his—though not exclusive—possession.

MISHMAR (rt. SHaMaR, 'to keep'), a guard of priests and Levites representing one of the eight divisions which carried on the Temple services in rotation. The *mishmar* again was subdivided into smaller groups each being designated *beth ab*, q.v.

MISHNAH (rt. SHaNaH, 'to learn', 'to repeat'), (*a*) the collection of the statements, discussions and Biblical interpretations of the Tannaim in the form edited by R. Judah the Patriarch c. 200; (*b*) similar minor collections by previous editors; (*c*) a single clause or paragraph the author of which was a Tanna.

ONAN. A mourner while his dead relative is awaiting burial; opposite to *abel*, a mourner from the time of burial for a period of seven or thirty days.

'ORLAH ('uncircumcised'); applied to newly-planted trees for a period of three years during which their fruits must not be eaten (v. Lev. XIX, 23ff).

SANHEDRIN (συνέδριον); the council of state and supreme tribunal of the Jewish people during the century or more preceding the fall of the Second Temple. It consisted of seventy-one members, and was presided over by the High Priest. A minor court (for judicial purposes only) consisting of twenty-three members was known as the 'Small Sanhedrin'.

SE'AH. Measure of capacity, equal to six *ḳabs*.

TALMID ḤAKAM (Lit., 'disciple of the wise'); scholar, student of the Torah.

TALMUD (Lit., 'teaching', 'learning') applies (*a*) to the Gemara (q.v.) or (*b*) generally to the Mishnah and Gemara combined.

TANNA (Lit., 'one who repeats' or 'teaches'); (*a*) a Rabbi quoted in the Mishnah or Baraitha (q.v.); (*b*) in the Amoraic period, a scholar whose special task was to memorize and recite Baraithas in the presence of expounding teachers.

ṬEBEL. Produce, already at the stage of liability to the levitical and priestly dues (v. *Terumah*), before these have been separated.

TERUMAH. 'That which is lifted or separated'; the heave-offering given from the yields of the yearly harvests, from certain sacrifices, and from the *shekels* collected in a special chamber in the Temple (*terumath ha-lishkah*). *Terumah gedolah* (great offering): the first levy on the produce of the year given to the priest, (v. Num. XVIII, 8ff). Its quantity varied according to the generosity of the owner, who could give one-fortieth, one-fiftieth, or one-sixtieth of his harvest. *Terumath ma'aser* (heave-offering of the tithe): the heave-offering given to the priest by the Levite from the tithes he receives (v. Num. XVIII, 25ff).

TORAH (Lit., 'teaching', 'learning', 'instruction'); (*a*) the Pentateuch (Written Law); (*b*) the Mishnah (Oral Law); (*c*) the whole body of Jewish religious literature.

ṬREFA or ṬEREFA (Lit., 'torn'); (*a*) an animal torn by a wild beast; (*b*) any animal suffering from a serious organic disease, whose meat is forbidden even if it has been ritually slaughtered.

ZUZ. A coin of the value of a *denarius*, six *ma'ah*, or twelve *dupondia*.

ABBREVIATIONS

Alfasi	R. Isaac b. Jacob Alfasi (1013-1103).
Aruk	Talmudic Dictionary by R. Nathan b. Jeḥiel of Rome (d. 1106).
Asheri	R. Asher b. Jeḥiel (1250-1327).
A.Z.	'Abodah Zarah.
b.	ben, bar: son of.
B.B.	Baba Bathra.
BaḤ.	Bayith Ḥadash, Glosses by R. Joel b. Samuel Sirkes (1561-1640).
Beḳ.	Beḳoroth.
Ber.	Berakoth.
B.Ḳ.	Baba Ḳamma.
B.M.	Baba Meẓi'a.
Cur. ed(d).	Current edition(s).
D.S.	*Diḳduḳe Soferim* by R. Rabbinowicz.
'Ed.	'Edduyyoth.
E.J.	*Encyclopaedia Judaica.*
'Er.	'Erubin.
E. V.	English Version.
Giṭ.	Giṭṭin.
Glos.	Glossary.
Ḥag.	Ḥagigah.
Hor.	Horayoth.
Ḥul.	Ḥullin.
J.E.	*Jewish Encyclopedia.*
J.T.	*Jerusalem Talmud.*
Jast.	M. Jastrow's Dictionary of the Targumim, the Talmud Bible and Yerushalmi, and the Midrashic Literature.
Keth.	Kethuboth.
Ḳid.	Ḳiddushin.
Ma'as.	Ma'asroth.
Mak.	Makkoth.
Meg.	Megillah.
Men.	Menaḥoth.
MGWJ.	*Monatsschrift für Geschichte und Wissenschaft des Judentums.*
M.Sh.	Ma'aser Sheni.
MS.M.	Munich Codex of the Talmud.
Naz.	Nazir.
Ned.	Nedarim.
Nid.	Niddah.
Obermeyer	Obermeyer J., *Die Landschaft Babylonien.*
P.B.	*The authorized Daily Prayer Book*, S. Singer.
Pes.	Pesaḥim.
R.	Rab, Rabban, Rabbenu, Rabbi.
Rashal	Notes and Glosses on the Talmud by R. Solomon Luria (d. 1573).
Rashi	Commentary of R. Isaac Yiẓḥaḳi (d. 1105).
R.H.	Rosh Hashannah.
R.V.	Revised version of the Bible.
Sanh.	Sanhedrin.
Shab.	Shabbath.
Sheḳ.	Sheḳalim.
Sonc. ed.	English Translation of the Babylonian Talmud, Soncino Press, London.
Soṭ.	Soṭah.
Suk.	Sukkah.
TA.	*Talmudische Archäologie*, by S. Krauss.
Ta'an.	Ta'anith.
Ter.	Terumoth.
Tosaf.	Tosafoth.
Tosef.	Tosefta.
Wilna Gaon	Notes by Elijah of Wilna (1720-1797) in the Wilna editions of the Talmud.
Yeb.	Yebamoth.
Zeb	Zebaḥim.

TRANSLITERATION OF HEBREW LETTERS

א (in middle of word)	= '
ב	= b
ו	= w
ח	= ḥ
ט	= ṭ
כ	= k
ע	= '
פ	= f
צ	= ẓ
ק	= ḳ
ת	= th

Full particulars regarding the method and scope of the translation are given in the Editor's Introduction.

NOTES

NOTES

NOTES

NOTES

NOTES

NOTES

NOTES

NOTES